Visual Guides to Nine Essential Upgrades

Dynamic visual layouts of nine essential upgrades guide you through upgrading your computer step by step, including installing video cards, adding computer memory, installing DVD drives, and installing hard drives.

Building the Ultimate Computer

Create the perfect computer for *you*. Learn what's possible and the important steps to building your own PC *from scratch*.

This Old Computer

Don't throw out your old Pentium! Learn what you need to know to rejuvenate *your legacy computers and hardware* and keep them working for you.

Hardware Management via Software Solutions

Make your computer the best it can be. Uncover the secrets of configuring your computer's hardware through the Control Panel and improving your PC's performance through software solutions.

Buyer's Guide

Learn what you need to know before you buy. "A Buyer's Guide to PCs" shows you how to get more computer for your money.

Extensive Glossary

The glossary keeps you current with the latest computer terminology and jargon.

Portable Computing

Laptops and notebook computers are the fastest growing segment of computer system purchases. Learn the important things you need to know about traveling with your PC, including connecting to networks, installing PCMCIA cards, and performing preventive maintenance for screens, cases, and batteries. The new chapter on flash memory shows you everything you need to know about all of your devices' memory cards.

Internet Resources

Put the Web to work for you. Learn how the *Internet can be an invaluable tool* in upgrading your computer.

The Complete PC Upgrade & Maintenance Guide

Praise for the Book...

A must-have for all technicians. If you only own one book as a PC technician, Mark Minasi's book is the one you should own. It is a highly recommended read (cover to cover) for anyone taking their A+ exams. The writing is clear, entertaining, easy to understand, and informative. In other words, this one won't put you to sleep like most other computer books and won't give you only half the story like the "For Dummies..." books. I only wish more books were written like this. I have owned an earlier edition of this book for two years now, and it is the only reference manual that I still use and recommend to all technicians, beginners and experts alike.

Dan D, Michigan *(courtesy of Amazon.com)*

Outstanding guide to PC hardware and its maintenance and upgrade. This instruction is lucid, erudite, and all-encompassing.... If you can afford only one guide, this would be it!

Computer Book Review

Maybe you've seen Mark Minasi on CNN, talking computers. Or maybe you've taken his legendary course on PC maintenance or heard him speak at Comdex. Or perhaps you took our advice... and purchased his dynamite *Expert Guide to Windows 98*. Regardless of how you first encounter Minasi's work, you're likely to become a fan pretty quick. So when it comes time to troubleshoot those miserable computer problems that seem as inevitable as death and taxes, who better to call?... The coverage is soup-to-nuts, with detailed chapters on topics that other troubleshooting books either skip altogether or surf over lightly. Notebook computers. CD-ROM drives. Laser printers. Scanners. Modems. Sound boards, video capture cards, and other PC devices notorious for devouring both your IRQs and your patience... whether you're out to fix everyone else's computer problems or you'd be thrilled to simply fix a few of your own, no other book delivers this much authoritative, practical, easy-to-understand help—period!

Cyberian Express, Barnes & Noble

Minasi is the man!!!!!!!!! I thought I was very knowledgeable in PC repair and maintenance—that is, until I read this book. I was amazed at the total amount of information packed into the 1500-plus-page book. Minasi's ability and knowledge are evident right from the first page. Minasi is able to simplify the technical talk while giving you a detailed breakdown of the subject. The read was easy and yet info-packed. The book is for all skill levels, from novice to expert. Everyone has something to learn from this book.

Michael Woznicki, Holland, MA, A+, Net+, and MCT certified technical trainer and freelance hardware reviewer *(courtesy of Amazon.com)*

I am the Technical Committee Chair for the Computer Maintenance Technology contest. This contest essentially follows the A+ Certification standard, and your book is a key reference. If it's not on the A+ test or in your book, it's not in the contest.

John Oliphant, Technical Committee Chair, Vocational–Industrial Clubs of America (VICA)

It solved my PC problem—what more can you ask? My CD-ROM drive had been gradually failing and now it wasn't reading CDs at all. The PC maker's support site talked about reinstalling drivers and checking the configuration files. Minasi said, "Clean the drive." So I bought a CD-ROM cleaning disk and a can of compressed air for about $25, used them, and in just minutes my drive was working fine. Thanks!

Edward E. Rigdon, Associate Professor, Marketing Department, Georgia State University *(courtesy of Amazon.com)*

The Complete PC Upgrade & Maintenance Guide

More Praise for the Book...

The chapters on hardware installation and introduction to networks are the best-written and most authoritative material I've used to learn the subtle aspects of TCP/IP, Ethernet, and token/bus ring topologies. Also, the chapters on computer upgrading and "building a dream computer from scratch" are well laid-out and detailed for avid geeks like me who like to destroy and build machines from scrap piles. I guess the best thing to say about this book is that it fostered an even deeper interest in computers than I had before reading.

JJ Kim *(courtesy of Amazon.com)*

Finally, a PC maintenance book that won't end up in storage after the first two chapters! Minasi has a gift for turning dry technical concepts and jargon into something the undergrad can understand. Fantastic book!

Troy *(courtesy of Amazon.com)*

Thanks again for writing such a wonderful book. Before I read the chapter on printers, I got a 40 percent on the pretest; after reading the two chapters on printers, I was scoring between 90–100 percent on the pretest for laser printers! I passed the A+ Certification with a 93 percent overall on the hardware and 91 percent on DOS and Windows 3.11. The teacher said that 93 percent was the highest anyone has ever scored on hardware at that school! :-) Thank you for helping me start my new career and getting me back into corporate life.

Kent Harris, Certified A+ Technician

I bought your book... this past Christmas as a present to myself. It was the best money I spent.... I now treat your book like the Bible; it is a source of useful information that I can depend on.... I'm a complete dummy as far as computers go, but your book has helped me tremendously. I can now partition my hard drive correctly without too much trouble because it is easy to understand the way you have it laid out and explained. Because of your book, I don't get that sick sinking feeling every time my computer crashes.

B. Wilson, Missisauga, Ontario, Canada

I read the first chapter and couldn't put it down! I read it from cover to cover. I now own three computers (two PCs and one laptop). One of the PCs (a 486), I bought ($20) from a friend that told me it was totally fried. He had taken it to the local PC shop and they told him it was useless. I took it apart, cleaned it up, and put it back together step by step with your book. When I turned on the power switch, it booted right up! It's still going with no problems today.... I now have fixed several of my friends' computers (Plug and Play my FOOT!!!) and believe that there is nothing that I can't fix on a computer.... Thanks for... taking the fear out of my favorite hobby.

Sergeant Derrick Ball, Loadmaster on the C-130 aircraft in the U.S. Marine Corps

The Complete PC Upgrade & Maintenance Guide was chosen by Heathkit Educational Systems as part of their PC Servicing and A+ Certification Preparation courses. Quite frankly, we use it because it is the best book on the subject available today.

Douglas M. Bonham, Heathkit Educational Systems

It is witty, easy reading, and very informative. I find most books boring and tedious..., but this book was actually fascinating to me. I read it for hours at a time and the amazing thing is it's a technical book.... I now use it as my PC bible.

Brett Havener, Computer Tech, Proprietor, Q-Point

THE COMPLETE

PC

UPGRADE &
MAINTENANCE
GUIDE

2003 Edition

MARK MINASI

San Francisco   London   SYBEX

Associate Publisher: Neil Edde
Acquisitions and Developmental Editor: Chris Denny
Editors: Anamary Ehlen, Liz Welch
Production Editor: Kylie Johnston
Technical Editor: James Kelly
Interior Designer and Compositor: Maureen Forys, Happenstance Type-O-Rama
Graphic Illustrators: Tony Jonick, Jerry Williams!
Proofreaders: Nelson Kim, Dave Nash, Laurie O'Connell, Yariv Rabinovitch, Nancy Riddiough
Indexer: Ted Laux
CD Technician: Keith McNeil
CD Coordinator: Dan Mummert
Cover Designer: John Nedwidek, emdesign

To the people who have helped me and continue to help me over the years, the people who gave me a chance or gave me a hand: Ludwig Braun, Andy Kydes, Nancy Denkhe, Pete Moulton, John, Doug, Julie, and the other Data-Tech folks, Maureen Quinn, all of the thousands of students who've read this book and helped make it better, Fred Langa, Steve Levy, Wayne Rash, the Sybex gang (Dianne, Rudy, Rodnay, Gary, Neil, Ellen, Guy, Barbara, and many others), Donna Cook, Stan Altman, and everyone else I've overlooked. Thank you all very much!

Acknowledgments

SINCE THIS BOOK'S FIRST INCARNATION in 1986, I've had help from many people. I can't thank them all here, but let me mention a few. My apologies to anyone I miss.

Michael Miller, Dave Huss, and Denise Tyler did a fantastic job in bringing this edition completely up-to-date. Their efforts are greatly appreciated. They have proven to be very resourceful and knowledgeable for both this and the twelfth editions.

A hearty thanks to Faithe Wempen, Kate Chase, and Kitty Niles for their hard work on the eleventh edition. Thanks also to Fred Jones, Bob Correll, and Rima and Tyler Regas.

Big thanks for the tenth edition updates to John Heilborn.

Thanks to Joe Jorden, Bruce Jones, and David Groth for their able contributions to the ninth edition.

Thanks to Glenn Hartwig for updating this book for the eighth edition. He provided a much needed new chapter on laptop and notebook computers (Chapter 31) as well as several new and revised topics.

Thanks to Christa Anderson for updating this book for the seventh edition. Her work was tireless, and I appreciate it.

Our artist-in-residence (even though she's no longer in residence), Elizabeth Creegan, and one of our long-time Troubleshooting instructors, Terry Keaton, did the original versions of many of the illustrations. They both excel in a world in which I've never exceeded apprentice status—the visual arts—and they've always been patient with my sometimes muddy requests. Thanks to them both, and (how could I forget?) thanks also to Doug Zimmer, instructor emeritus, for the original versions of the SCSI cable diagrams.

My associate, Paula Longhi, wrote the initial draft of the CD-ROM chapter, and I thank her for that.

Over the years, I've gotten plenty of editorial assistance and suggestions from Sheila Walsh, the biggest, baddest Tae Kwon Do black belt to ever open up a PC; Pete Moulton, my old partner and good buddy; and Rob Oreglia and Scott Foerster, more instructors emeriti. I continue to get good feedback from the staff of Tech Teach International: Kris Ashton, Peter Brondos, Shawn Caison, Patrick Campbell, David Costow, Eric Christiansen, Bob Deyo, Ceen Dowell, Brandi Dunnegan, Paul Eve, Scot Hull, Lisa Justice, Andrew McGoff, Ellen O'Day, Nicole Price, Holliday Ridge, David Sheridan, Marc Spedden, Frederick Thornton, and Steven Wright. And you, too, can give me feedback at help@minasi.com on the Internet.

And speaking of my e-mail address, thanks to all of you who have taken a few minutes to tell me how much you liked the book.

These books don't get into your hands unless some publisher who thinks they're worth it puts them there. The first such person was Stephen Levy, the publisher of the first version of this book, and my thanks go to him. Dianne King at Sybex arranged for Sybex to start publishing this; Dianne's goofing off somewhere, but we miss her. Gary Masters, the Maxwell Perkins of the computer press, remains this book's guardian angel. Thanks also to this and the previous edition's Acquisitions and Developmental Editors, Chris Denny, Ellen Dendy, Brenda Frink, and Neil Edde. Thanks go also to past and present Editors Liz Welch, Anamary Ehlen, Sharon Wilkey, Linda Stephenson, Sally Engelfried, Linda Lambeth Orlando, Doug Robert, Peter Weverka, and Vivian Perry; Technical Editors Jim Kelly, Rima Regas, Mike Hanna, Aaron Kushner, Maryann Brown, and Kim Ringer; all the

Project Editors and Production Coordinators for all the editions, because a book like this is a monster on the production side: Project Editors Ben Tomkins, Linda Good, Lee Ann Pickrell, Emily Smith, Malcolm Faulds, and Dann McDorman; Electronic Publishing Specialists Maureen Forys, Mark Ong, Susie Hendrickson, Cyndy Johnsen, Tony Jonick, and Bill Gibson; Production Editors Kylie Johnston and Leslie Higbee; Production Coordinators Shannon Murphy, Theresa Gonzalez, Kimberley Askew, Dave Nash, and Blythe Woolston; Publishing Interns Jason Holt and Chad Mack; CD Technicians Keith McNeil, Kara Schwartz, and Ginger Warner; Beta and Licensing Specialist Heather O'Connor; Graphic Illustrators Duane Bibby, Susie Hendrickson, Tony Jonick, and Jerry Williams; Proofreaders Dave Nash, Amey Garber, Emily Hsuan, Nelson Kim, Laurie O'Connell, Yariv Rabinovitch, Nancy Riddiough, Andrea Fox, Catherine Morris, Sachi Guzman, Eryn Osterhaus, and Duncan Watson; and, of course, Indexer Ted Laux.

Thanks also to the folks at Adaptec and Creative Labs, Inc., who graciously allowed us to excerpt their documentation for this book. Kudos also to Dale Palovich and his team, who put together the new videos for the tenth edition.

Contents at a Glance

Introduction . . . . *xxxv*

Visual Upgrade 1

Chapter 1 • Five Easy Pieces: PC Hardware in a Nutshell 21

Chapter 2 • Disassembling the PC 37

Chapter 3 • Inside the PC: Pieces of the Picture 75

Chapter 4 • Avoiding Service: Preventive Maintenance 185

Chapter 5 • Troubleshooting PC Problems 211

Chapter 6 • Installing New Circuit Boards (Without Creating New Problems) 239

Chapter 7 • Repairs with Circuit Boards and Chips 283

Chapter 8 • Semiconductor Memory. 309

Chapter 9 • Power Supplies and Power Protection 327

Chapter 10 • Hard Disk Drive Overview and Terminology. 349

Chapter 11 • Installing an IDE Hard Drive. 387

Chapter 12 • Understanding and Installing SCSI Devices. 399

Chapter 13 • Partitioning and Formatting IDE and SCSI Drives 431

Chapter 14 • How Hard Drives Organize Data 447

Chapter 15 • An Overview of Viruses. 463

Chapter 16 • Care and Feeding of Hard Drives 477

Chapter 17 • Understanding, Installing, and Repairing Floppy Drives. 517

Chapter 18 • Troubleshooting Printers 531

Chapter 19 • Troubleshooting Inkjet Printers 547

Chapter 20 • Troubleshooting Laser Printers. 563

Chapter 21 • Troubleshooting Scanners. 599

Chapter 22 • Modems and Other Communications Devices. 613

Chapter 23 • Keyboards and Mice 645

Chapter 24 • Video Adapters and Displays. 659

Chapter 25 • Play It Loud: Sound Cards 683

Chapter 26 • You Oughta Be in Pictures: Video Capture 709

Chapter 27 • An Overview of CD-ROM and DVD-ROM Drives 747

Chapter 28 • Flash Memory. 771

Chapter 29 • Networking Concepts and Hardware 785

Chapter 30 • A Buyer's Guide to PCs 847

Chapter 31 • Notebook/Laptop Computers 869

Chapter 32 • Using the Internet for Hardware Support 895

Chapter 33 • This Old Computer 927

Chapter 34 • Building the Ultimate Computer 945

Chapter 35 • Hardware Management via Software Solutions 985

Appendix A • A Short Overview on Reading Hexadecimal. 1047

Appendix B • Sample A+ Core Module Exam Questions. 1053

Glossary 1075

Index 1147

Contents

Introduction . . . . *xxxv*

Visual Upgrade 1

Chapter 1 • Five Easy Pieces: PC Hardware in a Nutshell 21
Introduction 22
CPUs, Peripherals, and Controllers 23
Buses and Interfaces 25
Actually, There's a Sixth Piece 27
Typical PC Components and Issues 28

Chapter 2 • Disassembling the PC 37
Introduction 38
QuickSteps: Disassembling the PC 39
Choose Your Weapons: PC Repair Tools 42
    Screwdrivers 42
    Antistatic Wrist Straps 44
    Retrieving Tools 45
    Hemostats 46
    Pliers and Diagonal Cutters 46
    Chip Extractors (PLCC and PGA) 46
    Lights and Mirrors 47
Tools to Avoid 47
General PC Disassembly Advice 48
    Be Sure That Disassembly Is Necessary 49
    Make Sure You Have Adequate Workspace 49
    Keep the Small Parts Organized 49
    Back Up the Configuration 50
    Turn the PC and Associated Peripherals Off 52
    Take the Monitor off the PC and Set It Aside 52
    Unplug the Computer and Remove the Cover 52
    Diagram! 55
    Remove the Boards Correctly 59
    Remove the Drives 60
    Remove the Power Supply 63
    Remove the CPU 66
    Remove the Motherboard 66
Reassembly Hints 68
    Connecting Cables and Edge Connectors: The Pin 1 Rule 69
    Avoiding Common Reassembly Mistakes 70
Troubleshooting Tips 72

Chapter 3 • Inside the PC: Pieces of the Picture **75**

Introduction. 76
QuickSteps: Installing a CPU 78
The System Board/Motherboard. 79
Central Processing Unit (CPU). 82
   CPU Speeds (Megahertz/Gigahertz) 83
   Megahertz Revisited: Hot Chips, Clock Doublers, Triplers, Quintuplers,
      and In-Between. 84
   Microcode Efficiency and Pipelines 89
   Word Size 90
   Data Path. 91
   Internal Cache Memory 92
   Numeric Coprocessors 96
   Superscalar and Instruction Pipelines. 98
   Memory Addressable by a CPU. 100
   Slots and Sockets 101
   Details on CPU Chips 102
PC Memory. 118
   How Memory Is Packaged: DIPs, SIMMs, and DIMMs 118
   Solving the Memory Speed Problem: DRAM, Fast Page, EDO, Burst
      EDO, SDRAM, RDRAM, and DDR SDRAM 119
   Managing Memory 125
PC Expansion Buses 141
   What Is a Bus? 141
   The First "PC" Bus 142
   The AT (ISA) Bus 144
   ISA's Not Enough: Mesozoic Local Bus 147
   The PS/2 Bus: Micro Channel Architecture (MCA). 148
   EISA (Extended Industry Standard Architecture) 149
   Local Bus. 150
   VESA Local Bus. 151
   PCI: Today's Bus. 151
   Accelerated Graphics Port (AGP): Local Bus Returns 154
   PC Card (PCMCIA): The Portable Bus 155
   Mini PCI (Portable PCI) 157
   CardBus 158
   FireWire/IEEE 1394 159
System Clock 160
Power Supply 160
Keyboard 161
Mouse 161
Controllers in Your Computer 161
   What's a Controller? 161
   Controllers Aren't Always Separate Boards 163
   Video Adapter 163
   SCSI Host Adapter. 165
   Floppy Disk Controller and Disk Drives 165

CD-ROM Drives 166
DVD Drives. 166
Hard Disks and Hard Disk Interfaces 166
Tape Drives and Other Backup Devices 167
Parallel (Centronics) Interfaces/IEEE 1284 167
Modems and Communication Ports. 168
    The Universal Serial Bus (USB). 169
System Clock/Calendar and Configuration (CMOS) Chip 171
Local Area Network (LAN) Adapters 172
Sound Boards. 172
Other Common Boards. 173
Finding Your Way around inside Your PC. 173
    Finding the Easy Stuff 174
    Locating Things on the Motherboard. 174
    CMOS Battery 177
    Identifying Circuit Boards 178
    Boards and Connectors 181

Chapter 4 • Avoiding Service: Preventive Maintenance **185**
Introduction. 186
QuickSteps: Checking the Environment 187
QuickSteps: Preventive Maintenance 188
Heat and Thermal Shock 190
    Removing Heat with a Fan 190
    Removing Heat with a Heat Sink 191
    Understanding Good and Bad Box Designs 191
    Living with Dead Fans 192
    Using Heat Sensor Devices 192
    Keeping Temperature Ranges Safe for PCs 194
Dealing with Dust 196
Magnetism 197
Stray Electromagnetism. 198
    Electromagnetic Interference 198
    Power Noise. 201
    Electrostatic Discharge 204
Avoiding Water and Other Liquids 208
    Corrosion. 208
Troubleshooting Tips 209

Chapter 5 • Troubleshooting PC Problems **211**
Introduction. 212
QuickSteps: Troubleshooting PC Problems 213
General Troubleshooting Rules 214
    Remember: "Don't Panic" and "I Will Win" 214
    Wait… and Repeat. 214
    Write Everything Down 215

Do the Easy Stuff First. 215
Reboot and Try Again. 215
Simplify, Simplify, Simplify! 216
Draw a Picture, Separate into Components, and Test 216
Never Assume. 217
Trust No One: The Documentation Sometimes Lies. 217
Observe Like Sherlock Holmes 217
Six Steps to Troubleshooting Success 218
Check for Operator Error. 219
Make Sure Everything Is Plugged In—Correctly 221
Check the Software. 222
Check External Signs 226
Run a Diagnostic Utility. 226
Look Under the Hood 230
When All Else Fails. 231
Common Problems—and Solutions. 232
Your Computer Won't Start. 232
Your Computer Locks Up. 233
A New Piece of Hardware Won't Work—or Messes Up Your System 234
Your Hard Disk Crashes 234
Your Monitor Doesn't Display Properly. 235
Your Modem Won't Connect. 236
Your Printer Won't Print. 236
Troubleshooting Tips for an Emergency. 237

Chapter 6 • Installing New Circuit Boards
           (Without Creating New Problems) **239**
Introduction. 240
QuickSteps:: Installing a New Circuit Board. 241
But I Have Plug and Play, So I Don't Have to Worry About This, Right? 242
Configuring New Circuit Boards 243
Solving Real-Life Configuration Conflicts 243
Resolving Device Conflicts 246
On Newer Systems: PnP 246
On Older Systems 247
A Word about DIP Switches 247
Software Switch Setup Advice 248
Understanding I/O Addresses, DMA, IRQs, RAM, and ROM Addresses 248
I/O Addresses 249
DMA (Direct Memory Access) Channels. 256
IRQ (Interrupt Request) Levels. 260
ROM Addresses and RAM Buffers 267
Resolving Installation Conflicts: An Example. 270
Where Do You Find Diagnostic Programs? 272
Making Plug and Play Work 272
Booting on PnP Systems 273

Configuring ATs and Beyond: Software Setup 274
Adjustable Bus Speeds 276
Replacing the Configuration Battery 277
Parallel Port Configuration Anomalies 278
Troubleshooting Tips 280

Chapter 7 • Repairs with Circuit Boards and Chips 283

Introduction 284
QuickSteps: Diagnosing and Solving Circuit Board Problems 285
How Do You Find the Bad Board? 287
Night of the Living Data: Making a Dead Machine "Undead" 288
What Makes Boards Fail? 292
Other Problems and Solutions 293
Fix or Replace Boards? 294
Maintenance Considerations for Integrated Motherboards 294
Understanding the PC Boot Process 295
Step One: PC Power 295
Step Two: Check the Hardware 296
The DBR Loads and Executes 301
Finding and Replacing Bad Chips 302
Chip "Recall" 303
Software Chip Testing 303
Temperature Chip Testing 303
Identifying Chips 304
Soldering and Desoldering 305
Chip Sockets and Chip Insertion/Removal 305
Troubleshooting Tips 307

Chapter 8 • Semiconductor Memory 309

Introduction 310
QuickSteps: Installing RAM 311
Introducing Memory Sizes, Speeds, and Shapes 313
Memory Modules 314
Motherboard Chipsets 315
Dynamic RAM 315
SDRAM 317
Matching System Memory to Cache Memory 320
Better Programs 320
Better Processors 320
Causes of False Memory Errors 320
Power Drops and Surges 321
Mismatched Chip Speeds and Manufacturers 321
Memory Tests 322
Walking Bit Test 322
Mountain/Valley and Checkerboard Tests 322
Tips on Installing Memory Chips 323
Troubleshooting Tips 324

Chapter 9 • Power Supplies and Power Protection **327**

Introduction. 328
QuickSteps: Replacing a Power Supply. 329
Components of the Power Supply 330
Power Supply Form Factors. 330
    Form Factor Connectors 331
Maintaining and Upgrading the Power Supply 335
Determining If You Need a New Power Supply 337
    The Power Supply Troubleshooting Trail 337
    Replacing a Power Supply 337
Protecting the PC from the AC. 337
    Do You Have Power Problems? 338
    Check Outlet Wiring. 338
    Check What Else Is on the Line 339
    Ensure Common Ground among Devices. 339
    Protect against Power Noise 340
    Solutions to Power Problems. 340
    Devices to Remedy Electrical Problems 341
So What Should I Buy?. 345
    The Granddaddy of Power Problems: Lightning. 345
Troubleshooting Tips 347

Chapter 10 • Hard Disk Drive Overview and Terminology **349**

Introduction. 350
Disk Types and the Future 351
Hard Drives and Interfaces 351
Disk Geometry: Heads, Tracks, Cylinders, and Sectors 355
    Disk Heads 357
    Disk Tracks 357
    Disk Cylinders 358
    Disk Sectors. 359
    Zone Bit Recording 360
    Physical and Logical Geometry 361
    Sector Translation and Logical Block Addressing 361
    Voice Coil and Stepper Head-Positioning Mechanisms. 364
Disk Performance Characteristics. 365
    Seeks and Latency. 365
    Data Transfer Rates, Interleave Factors, and Skewing. 368
    Error-Correction Code (ECC). 373
Getting Good Data Transfer Rates on Modern Systems 374
    External Transfer Rate Dependencies. 375
    Caches in Drive Subsystems. 375
BIOS and Operating System Capacity Barriers 376
    BIOS and Interface Limitations. 376
    Operating System Limitations 380
PIO and DMA Protocol Transfer Mechanisms. 381
    PIO Modes 381
    DMA Modes 382

Modern ATA Standards 382
   ATA Specifications 383
   EIDE and Fast ATA-2 383
Installing an IEEE-1394 Hard Disk Drive 384

Chapter 11 • Installing an IDE Hard Drive **387**
Introduction 388
QuickSteps: Installing an IDE/ATA Hard Drive 389
Warnings and Apologia 391
The IDE Mishmash 391
Steps in Hard Drive Installation 392
   Assemble Compatible Hardware 392
   Jumper, Cable, and Install the Drive 393
   Configure the System's CMOS 396

Chapter 12 • Understanding and Installing SCSI Devices **399**
Introduction 400
QuickSteps: Installing a SCSI Card 401
SCSI Overview 403
   SCSI Benefits 403
   Some Basic SCSI Concepts 404
SCSI Underview 405
   SCSI-1: The Beginning of a Good Idea 405
   Asynchronous and Synchronous SCSI 406
   SCSI-2 Improves on a Good Thing 406
   SCSI-3, or Ultra SCSI 407
   Comparing SCSI-1, SCSI-2, SCSI-3 408
   Fibre Channel 410
   Fibre Channel Storage Area Networks 410
Defining a SCSI Configuration 410
   SCSI Host Adapters 411
   SCSI-Compatible Peripherals 411
   SCSI Cabling 411
   SCSI Termination 412
   SCSI Drivers 412
   SCSI Installation 412
SCSI Physical Installation 412
   Choosing a SCSI Host Adapter 412
   Installing the SCSI Host Adapter 413
   Assigning a SCSI ID to the Peripheral 414
   Targets, Initiators, LUNs, and LSUNs 415
   SCSI Daisy Chaining 416
   Terminating the SCSI Chain 420
   Sample SCSI Setup: One Internal Drive 423
   Sample SCSI Setup: Two Internal Devices 423
   Sample SCSI Setup: One External Device 424
   Sample SCSI Setup: Two External Devices 424
   Sample SCSI Setup: Internal and External Devices 425

SCSI Software Installation. 426
   With Bootable Hard Disks, You Don't Need SCSI Software 427
   The ASPI Standards 428
   SCSI without Drivers: Onboard BIOS Support. 428
Troubleshooting SCSI. 428
   Installation Troubleshooting. 429

Chapter 13 • Partitioning and Formatting IDE and SCSI Drives **431**

Introduction. 432
QuickSteps: Partitioning and Formatting a Hard Disk 433
Low-Level Formatting. 434
   IDE Drives. 434
   SCSI Drives 434
Partitioning 434
   Partitioning Options 435
   Efficient Partitions: Clusters and Disks 436
   How to Partition a Drive 438
   How DOS Names Partitions. 442
   Partitioning Large Drives with Device Drivers 442
   Backing Up Partition Information 443
Formatting. 444
   A Note about Bad Areas. 444
Third-Party Partitioning and Formatting Tools. 445
Troubleshooting Tips 445

Chapter 14 • How Hard Drives Organize Data **447**

Introduction. 448
The Basics 449
How DOS Organizes Disk Areas: Overview. 449
   Absolute Sectors and DOS Sectors 450
   Clusters 452
   DOS Boot Record 454
The FAT and the Directory. 454
Subdirectories. 457
Logical Drive Structure. 458
FAT32. 460
NTFS 461
Preventive Tip: Backing Up Your Master Boot Record. 462

Chapter 15 • An Overview of Viruses **463**

Introduction. 464
Types of Viruses. 465
   File Infectors and Boot-Sector Viruses 465
   Macro Viruses: Melissa Isn't the Girl Next Door 466
   Worms Wiggle Their Way through E-mail 468
   Real-Time Messaging Viruses 468
   Web Applet Viruses 469

Techniques of Attack 470
   Polymorphic Viruses 470
   Multipartite Viruses 470
   Stealth Viruses 470
   Trojan Horses 470
   Time Bombs and Logic Bombs 471
   An Example of a Virus at Work 471
Virus Hoaxes 471
Tips for Protecting Your PC against Viruses 472
Antivirus Software 474
Resources: Stay Informed 474
Virus Hoax Lists 474
Viral Symptoms 475
Troubleshooting Tips 475

Chapter 16 • Care and Feeding of Hard Drives **477**
Introduction 478
Protecting Your Hard Drive 479
   Data Protection 479
Backing Up Your Hard Drive 480
Backing Up and Restoring Your MBR with DEBUG 480
Backing Up System Files 483
   16-Bit Applications 483
   Registry-Oriented Operating Systems (Windows 95 and Beyond) 484
   Rebuilding the Operating System 485
Backing Up User Data 485
   Backup Options 485
   What Software Do You Need? 487
   Backup Strategies 488
Preparing Boot Floppies 489
Performing Media Tests Routinely 490
   Pattern Testing Methods 492
File Defragmenters 492
Recovering Data and Fixing Hard Disks 494
   What Happens When a File Is Deleted 495
   Basic Unerasing 496
   Unerasing Partially Overwritten Files 497
   Recovering Accidentally Formatted Hard Disks 499
   Fixing Lost Clusters 499
   Invalid Subdirectory Errors 502
   Allocation Error Message 503
   File Has Invalid Cluster Message 504
   Cross-Linked Clusters 504
Understanding and Repairing Media Errors 506
   Data Recovery: A Case Study and Some Tips 506
Resurrecting Dead Hard Disk Drives 508
   Remember Your Priorities 509
   Tracing a Disk Failure 509

Recovery Step 1: Boot from a Floppy. 509
Recovery Step 2: Try to Read the MBR 509
Verifying Modern Drives. 513
Recovery Step 3: Is the Partition Table Blank? 513
The Final Step: Send Your Drive to the Mayo Clinic 514
Troubleshooting Recap 515

Chapter 17 • Understanding, Installing, and Repairing Floppy Drives. 517
Introduction. 518
QuickSteps: Replacing a Floppy Drive 519
Floppies: Past, Present, and Future. 520
In the Days before Floppies. 520
The Post-Floppy Era. 520
Floppies Nowadays. 521
The Future of Floppies. 521
The Floppy Subsystem 521
Part 1: The Floppy Disk 522
Part 2: The Floppy Drive 523
Part 3: The Disk Controller 523
Part 4: The Cable 524
Simple Preventive Maintenance for Floppies. 524
To Clean Heads or Not to Clean Heads?. 524
Defending Disks. 525
Removing, Configuring, and Installing Floppy Drives 526
Removing Floppy Drives. 526
Installing Floppy Drives 526
Troubleshooting Tips 526
A Disk Cannot Be Read 526
The Drive Refuses to Function 527
The Drive Shows Phantom Directories. 528
Floppy Troubleshooting Recap. 530

Chapter 18 • Troubleshooting Printers 531
Introduction. 532
QuickSteps: Connecting and Testing a Parallel Printer. 533
Printer Maintenance 534
Dot-Matrix Printers 534
Inkjet Printers. 535
All-in-One Combos 536
Thermal-Transfer Printers. 536
Laser Printers 537
Printer Interfaces 537
Parallel Ports 537
USB Ports 539
Serial Ports. 541
Infrared Ports. 541
Network Printing 542

Common Problems and Solutions 542
    Isolate the Problem 542
    Check Cable Lengths 543
    Set Emulation Options Correctly 543
    Check Ports, Their Settings, and Connections 544
    Consider the Weather 545
Troubleshooting Tips 545
    Printer Won't Print at All 546
    Printout Has Quality Problems 546

Chapter 19 • Troubleshooting Inkjet Printers **547**
Introduction 548
Parts of an Inkjet Printer 549
    The Case 549
    The Paper-Feed Mechanism 550
    Ink Cartridges 550
    The Ink Cartridge Carrier 551
    The Exit Tray 551
How an Inkjet Printer Works 551
Common Problems and Possible Solutions 552
    Printer Appears to Work but Nothing Prints 552
    Color Is Wrong 554
    Printer Doesn't Print at All 555
    Printing Is Slow or Intermittent 555
    Quality Is Poor 556
    Output Is Garbled or Formatted Incorrectly 558
    Paper Is Stuck or Not Moving 558
Common Error Messages 559
    Ink Low 559
    Out of Memory 559
    Out of Paper 559
    Paper Jam 560
    Print Head Failure 560
Preventive Maintenance 560
    Clean the Print Heads 560
    Align the Print Heads 560
Refilling Ink Cartridges 560
Troubleshooting Tips 561

Chapter 20 • Troubleshooting Laser Printers **563**
Introduction 564
Parts of a Laser Printer 565
    Interface Controller 565
    Input Interface 565
    Printer RAM 566
    Printing Mechanisms 568
How a Laser Printer Prints 568

Data Input 569
Drum Preparation. 569
The Paper Feed 572
Image Development. 573
Image Transfer 574
Fusing the Image to the Paper 574
Printer Disassembly Dependencies 576
Common Symptoms and Solutions 577
Vertical White Streaks on the Page 577
Smearing on the Page 578
Horizontal Streaks on the Page 578
Cloudy, Faded Output. 578
Black Line Down the Side of the Page. 579
Memory Overflow Error 579
55 Error on Startup 579
Fonts Do Not Appear on Page 580
Printer Picks Up Multiple Sheets. 580
Paper Jams 581
Basic Testing. 581
Printer Power 581
Resetting the Printer. 581
The Cable and Ports. 582
Parallel Cable Type 582
Environmental Considerations 583
Paper and Media Issues. 584
Advanced Testing 586
Voltage Tests. 586
Location of DC Voltage Test Points. 586
Testing the Host's Interface. 586
Charting Printing Problems. 586
Diagnostic Software 587
Understanding Error Messages and Fixing Printer Problems 587
Other Things to Consider. 592
The Toner Cartridge. 592
Mirror 593
Vertical Lines. 593
Squeaking or Groaning Sounds 593
Maintenance Issues 593
Errant Toner. 594
Cleaning. 594
Improving Print Quality 596
Paper Quality and Feed Continuity 596
Image Formation 596
Laser Printer Rumors and Truth 596
Toner Is Made of Powdered Chicken Bones 596
Elvis Is in the Printer 596
Cartridges Are Designed to Self-Destruct. 597
Troubleshooting Recap 597

Chapter 21 • Troubleshooting Scanners **599**

Introduction 600
QuickSteps: Connecting a Flatbed Scanner 601
Types of Scanners and How They Work 602
    Scanner Types 602
    How a Scanner Scans 603
    Scanner/Computer Interface 604
    TWAIN 605
    Determining Image Quality 605
    Managing Scanned File Size 606
    Optical Character Recognition 607
Scanner Maintenance 607
Common Problems and Solutions 607
    Check the Connections 608
    Give It a Test 608
    Check the Port—and the Configuration 609
    Allocate Necessary Resources 610
    Sharing a Parallel Port 610
    Pick the Right Setting 610
    Edit Your Mistakes 611
    Fix the Original 611
    Viewing and Printing 611
Troubleshooting Tips 612

Chapter 22 • Modems and Other Communications Devices **613**

Introduction 614
Understanding Serial Communications 614
    How Serial Communications Work 615
    Why Is There RS-232? 617
    How RS-232 Works 618
    A Note on Reality 620
    Flow Control 620
    Common Cables: A Configuration Cookbook 620
Analog Modems 622
    Modem Speed 622
    Modem Standards 623
    Modem Maintenance 624
Welcome to Digital Broadband 625
    Choosing a Digital Technology 625
    Making the ISDN Connection 627
    Going Faster with DSL 628
    Digital Connections over Digital Cable 635
    Using a Satellite for Broadband Connections 637
    Wireless Connections via Microwave 639
Troubleshooting Tips 640
    Simple Problems, Simple Solutions 640
    Phone Line Noise and Quality Problems 640

Port Problems. 642
Modem Problems 642
Cable Troubleshooting. 643

Chapter 23 • Keyboards and Mice **645**
Introduction. 646
QuickSteps: Installing a Keyboard, Mouse, or Trackball 647
Keyboard Types and Components 648
  Keyboard Types. 648
  Switch or Contact Design 649
  System Board/Keyboard Interface 650
  Keyboard Connector 651
Keyboard Maintenance 651
What to Do When a Keyboard Fails You. 651
  Make Sure It Is Plugged In 651
  Make Sure BIOS and Windows See It 652
  Fix Bent Pins 652
  Connect It to Another Computer 652
  Check the Keys. 652
  Test Pin Voltages 653
  Check the Cable Continuity. 653
  Completely Disassemble It. 653
  Replace the Keyboard 654
Mouse Types and Components 654
  Mouse Types. 654
  Buttons and Wheels 655
  Mouse Positioning Methods 655
  Trackballs. 656
  Mouse Interfaces. 656
Mouse Cleaning 656
What to Do When Your Mouse Fails You 657
Wireless Input Devices 657
Troubleshooting Tips 658

Chapter 24 • Video Adapters and Displays. **659**
Introduction. 660
QuickSteps: Shopping for a Video Card. 661
QuickSteps: Installing a New Video Card. 661
How a Video Board Works 663
  The CPU and Video Images 663
  The System Bus 663
  The Video Memory 664
  The Video Imaging Chip. 667
Video Board Characteristics. 668
  Resolution and Colors. 668
  Vertical Scan Frequencies: Interlacing and 72Hz. 672
3D Video Boards 673

Video Monitor Characteristics. 674
    Monitor Mumbo Jumbo: Horizontal Scan Frequency 674
    Dot Pitch. 675
    Monitor Size 675
    Flat-Panel Displays 675
    Multifrequency Monitors 676
    Resizing Screens with Multisyncing Monitors. 677
Multiple Displays 677
    Issues Installing Multiple Display Cards. 678
Reference: Older Display Types 678
Troubleshooting Tips 681

Chapter 25 • Play It Loud: Sound Cards **683**
Introduction. 684
Sound Synthesis 685
    Sound Characteristics 685
    Signals to Bits: Sampling. 688
    FM Synthesis 691
    Wavetable Synthesis 692
Sound Card Characteristics 692
    8-, 16-, 32-, 64-, or 96-Bit Sound? 692
    IRQ or DMA Sound Recording? 693
    Pass-through and/or CD-ROM Interfaces?. 693
    What Types of Inputs and Outputs? 694
Speaker Systems 695
Installation Tips 696
New Applications for PC Sound 696
    MP3 Audio 696
    Digital Audio and Surround Sound 701
    3D Game Audio 702
    Streaming Media and the Internet 703
    Audio for Musicians 704
Troubleshooting Tips 707

Chapter 26 • You Oughta Be in Pictures: Video Capture. **709**
Introduction. 710
QuickSteps: Installing a Video Capture Board and a PC Cam 711
    Video Capture Board 711
    PC Cam. 712
Video Capture Overview. 713
    Video Capture System Components. 713
    The Video Input Device 714
    The Connection 721
    The Capture Board 730
    The CPU, Bus, and Disk Systems 733
Installing a Video Capture Board 734

Running the Video Capture Software 735
   Start from a Known Video Source 735
   Digital Video Capture and Transfer 735
   Analog Video Capture. 736
Using Offline Compression. 741
   Choosing a Codec: Don't Recompress Until You're Done! 742
   Setting Key Frames 743
   Setting Data Rate and Compression Quality. 743
   Padding for CD-ROM 744
   Using RealMedia Files for Internet Streaming 744
Getting around Bugs in the Video Capture Software 744
Troubleshooting Tips 745

Chapter 27 • An Overview of CD-ROM and DVD-ROM Drives 747
Introduction. 748
QuickSteps: Installing CD and DVD Drives 749
Types of CD-ROMs. 750
   Regular CD-ROM Drives 750
   CD-R and CD-RW Drives 750
   Cross-Platform Format Compatibility 751
Types of DVD Drives. 751
   Regular DVD-ROM Drives. 752
   Recordable DVD Drives 752
How a Drive Reads a CD 753
How CDs and DVDs Store Data 753
   Physical Composition of Regular CDs. 753
   Physical Composition of DVDs 754
   Physical Composition of CD-Rs 754
   Physical Composition of CD-RWs 754
Standards: An Issue of Compatibility. 755
   The Genesis of Standards 755
   Red Book. 755
   Yellow Book 755
   High Sierra and ISO 9660 756
   CD-ROM/XA. 756
   Multisession Capability. 757
Choosing the Right CD-ROM 757
   Physical Characteristics 757
   Performance Characteristics. 758
   Interface Type. 761
   Multimedia Kits 762
Installation. 763
   Physical Installation 763
   BIOS Configuration 763
   Drivers 764
Recording CDs. 764

Recording DVDs 765
   Recordable/Rewriteable DVDs 765
   Producing and Recording DVDs 767
Maintenance.. 768
   Dos and Don'ts of CDs and DVDs................................ 768
Troubleshooting Tips 768
   Common Reasons for Difficult CD-ROM Installations.............. 768
   DVD Troubleshooting... 769

Chapter 28 • Flash Memory **771**

Introduction.. 772
QuickSteps: Connecting a Flash USB Drive 773
How Flash Memory Works 774
   Storing Data.. 774
   It's Not Cheap 775
Different Types of Flash Memory Devices 775
   BIOS Chip.. 776
   CompactFlash... 776
   SmartMedia 777
   Memory Stick... 778
   MultiMediaCard... 778
   Secure Digital Card... 779
   Flash USB Drive 780
   PCMCIA Flash... 781
   Choosing a Card.. 781
   Non-Computer Uses... 782
Common Problems and Solutions 782
   Working with Drivers 782
   Recognizing the Device.. 783
   Formatting Cards 783
   Understanding Capacity 784
   Dealing with Multiple Flash Memory Devices 784

Chapter 29 • Networking Concepts and Hardware................... **785**

Introduction.. 786
QuickSteps: Installing a New Network Card 787
Basic Networking Concepts.. 789
   What Is a LAN?... 789
   Advantages of Networking 789
Understanding Networking Components, Protocols, and APIs 791
   Networking Components 792
   Networking Protocols and Application Programming Interfaces 803
Choosing a Network.. 814
   Office Networking Options...................................... 814
   Home Networking Options...................................... 815
Setting Up Your Network 818
   Installing Cables 818

Preparing a Wireless Network 821
Installing and Configuring Network Cards 822
Connecting Devices with Hubs and Switches 829
Hubs Connect the Dots 829
Switches 835
Internetworking and Intranetworking 837
Repeaters Extend the Network's Reach 838
Routers Connect Multiple Networks 841
Networking Security 842
General Security Tips 842
Use Passwords for Internal Security 842
Use a Firewall for External Security 843

Chapter 30 • A Buyer's Guide to PCs **847**

Introduction 848
Name-Brand versus Generic PCs 849
Parts of a Generic PC 849
Pros and Cons of Name-Brand PCs 851
Choosing PC Parts 852
CPU 852
System Bus Speed 853
Expansion Card Bus 853
RAM 854
ROM BIOS 854
Motherboard/System Board 854
Hard Disk Drives 854
Floppy Disks and Other Removable Storage 855
CD-ROM and DVD-ROM Drives 855
Video Board 855
Video Monitor 855
Sound Card 856
Speakers 856
Mice 856
Keyboards 856
Serial Ports 856
Parallel Ports 856
Universal Serial Buses (USBs) 857
Modems/Network Adapters 857
Printers 857
System Comparisons 857
Home 861
Student 862
Gamer 862
Audio/Video Enthusiast 863
Small Business 863
Corporate 864
Road Warrior 864

Where Should You Buy? 865
Shopping Tips 866

Chapter 31 • Notebook/Laptop Computers **869**

Introduction 870
QuickSteps: Upgrading and Maintaining Your Laptop 872
    Upgrading Your Memory 872
    Upgrading Your Hard Disk 873
    Replacing Batteries 874
Memory Upgrades 875
    Preparing for the Upgrade 875
    Doing the Installation 877
Hard Disk Upgrades 879
    Finding the Right Hard Disk 879
    Backing Up Your Data 880
    Preparing for the Hard Drive Upgrade 881
    Installing the New Hard Drive 881
    Installing a Second Hard Drive 883
    Installing PC Card Drive Cards 884
Other Kinds of Upgrades 885
    DVD Drives 885
    Laptop LAN Adapters 885
    Wireless LAN Cards 886
Working with Laptop Batteries 887
    Battery Care 887
    Charging a Battery 888
    Replacing a Battery 889
    Buying a New Battery 889
    Conserving Battery Power 890
Laptop Maintenance Issues 891
PC-to-Laptop Syncing 892
Syncing Data with PDAs 893
Troubleshooting Tips 894

Chapter 32 • Using the Internet for Hardware Support **895**

Introduction 896
QuickSteps: Getting Online Help 897
Problems with Traditional Support 898
    Journey into Faxback Hell 898
    Facing the Muzak: Technical Support Lines 899
    Making Friends and Influencing People 899
    Read All about It 900
Advantages of Online Support 900
    What's Out There? 900
    Why Online Support Is Better 902
Using the World Wide Web for Support 905
    Clicking and Linking 905

Finding Useful Web Sites 906
The Best Web Sites for Technical Information 908
Using FTP Sites for Support 912
Downloading via FTP. 912
Finding Useful FTP Servers 912
The Best FTP Servers for Downloading Files. 913
Using Usenet Newsgroups for Support 913
Understanding Usenet. 914
Finding Useful Usenet Newsgroups. 916
The Best Newsgroups for Technical Information 918
Using E-mail Mailing Lists for Support. 919
How Mailing Lists Work. 919
Finding Useful Mailing Lists. 919
The Best Mailing Lists for Technical Information. 920
Using Internet Relay Chat for Support 920
Chatting with IRC 920
Finding Useful IRC Channels 921
The Best IRC Channels for Technical Information 921
Cautions about Online Support. 923
Don't Believe Everything You Hear. 923
When in Doubt, Check for Viruses 923
Don't Give Out Personal Information 923
Troubleshooting Tips 924

Chapter 33 • This Old Computer **927**
Introduction. 928
The March of Technology 929
Worth Their Weight in Chips 931
What to Keep and What to Toss. 931
New Life for an Old Pentium? 932
Save Your Data! 933
Choosing an Upgrade Path 935
Upgrading a Computer. 935
Planning Your Upgrade. 936
Motherboards. 936
Making Final Decisions. 942
The Next Step 944

Chapter 34 • Building the Ultimate Computer. **945**
Introduction. 946
QuickSteps: Building the Ultimate Computer. 947
Step 1: Assemble All the Parts. 949
Computer Case. 949
Motherboard 951
Video Card. 952
Sound Cards. 953
Modems. 954
Hard Drive. 955

Zip Drive 955
CD-ROM/DVD Drive 956
Networking 956
Extra Interfaces 957
Step 2: Start with the Case 958
Step 3: Set Up the Motherboard 959
Installing the CPU 959
Setting the Clock Speed 960
Plugging in the CPU 963
Installing Memory 966
Step 4: Install the Video Card and Test the System 966
Plug In the Video Card 967
Providing Power to the Motherboard 967
The First System Test 967
Step 5: Install the Drives 968
Installing the Floppy Drive(s) 968
Installing the Hard Drive(s) 969
Setting Up the BIOS 970
Installing the CD-ROM or DVD Drive 972
Attaching the Keyboard and Mouse 973
Step 6: Install the Operating System 973
Step 7: Install the Sound Card 974
Step 8: Install the Rest of the Boards 976
Installing the Modem 976
Installing the DVD MPEG Decoder Board 976
Step 9: Put It All Together 977
Installing the Motherboard 977
Installing the Power Supply 978
Attaching the Add-on Boards 979
Installing the Drives 980
Another System Check 982
Install the Rest of the Boards 982
Parallel and Serial Port Connectors 983
Front-Panel Lights and Speaker 983
Troubleshooting Tips 984

Chapter 35 • Hardware Management via Software Solutions **985**
Introduction 986
QuickSteps: Using Control Panel 987
Set Accessibility Options 987
Set Up New Hardware in Windows 987
Add New Software 988
Remove Software 988
Add or Remove Windows Components 988
Change the System Date and Time 989
Choose a Different Video Driver 989
Change the Video Resolution or Color Depth 989
Test a Modem 990

Managing Your System via the Windows 9x/Me/2000/NT Control Panel 991
  Setting Accessibility Options 991
  Adding New Hardware 998
  Installing Boards That the System Can't Find 1001
  Adding and Removing Programs 1003
  Setting the Date/Time 1005
  Changing Display Options 1006
  Modems 1010
  System 1013
Managing Your System via the Windows XP Control Panel 1017
  Setting Accessibility Options 1017
  Adding New Hardware 1019
  Installing Boards That the System Can't Find 1020
  Adding and Removing Programs 1020
  Setting the Date/Time 1021
  Changing Display Options 1022
  Modems 1023
  System 1025
Using Windows' Other Utilities 1026
  System Monitor 1026
  Microsoft System Information 1026
  DirectX Diagnostic Tool 1027
  Windows Report Tool 1029
  Update Wizard Uninstall 1030
  System File Checker 1030
  Signature Verification Tool 1031
  Registry Checker 1031
  Automatic Skip Driver Agent 1031
  Dr. Watson 1031
  System Configuration Utility 1032
  ScanDisk 1033
  Version Conflict Manager 1033
Updating Your System with Windows Update and AutoUpdate 1034
  Running Windows Update 1034
  Using AutoUpdate 1035
Recovering Your System with Windows Me's System Restore 1035
  Setting System Restore Points 1036
  Reconfiguring and Disabling System Restore 1037
Using Other Software Tools 1038
  Windows Resource Kit 1038
  Third-Party Tools 1040
Managing the Windows Registry 1041
  Understanding the Registry 1041
  Backing Up and Restoring the Registry 1042
  Fixing a Corrupted Registry 1043
  Editing the Registry 1043
Troubleshooting Tips 1045

Appendix A • A Short Overview on Reading Hexadecimal **1047**

Introduction 1048
Counting in Hex 1049
Reading Memory Hex Addresses 1049
    Example 1: Counting in Hex—Determining the Size of a Range 1050
    Example 2: Comparing Overlapping ROM Address Ranges 1050
Converting Hex to Decimal 1051
Converting Decimal to Hex 1052

Appendix B • Sample A+ Core Module Exam Questions **1053**

Glossary **1075**

Index *1147*

Introduction

THIS NEW EDITION BRINGS TONS of new information. Over the years, each edition has seen chapters yanked out and completely rewritten, and that's true in this edition, in spades.

What's New in the 2003 Edition

In some ways, the PC hardware world doesn't change much. After 12 years, VGA is still the baseline video standard and floppies still hold only 1.44MB of data. But in other ways, it's moving all the time, and that has motivated this latest overhaul of *The Complete PC Upgrade & Maintenance Guide*.

As we do each year, we've updated this edition to cover the latest technologies that affect end users. Among the new topics included in this edition are the Pentium 4 processor and the newest technologies including flash memory, scanners, all-in-one printers, ADSL, satellite dish Internet access, video capture cards, and all of the new DVD recordable technologies.

NOTE *Be sure to check out the bonus chapter available on the Sybex Web site (*www.sybex.com*) that covers storage devices. Its topics include Zip, Jaz, and tape drives.*

NOTE *We have also included an electronic chapter, "Recovering Data and Fixing Hard Disks," on the Utilities CD. This chapter will help you find and restore data from dead drives.*

In addition to updating the chapters to include the latest technologies, we've added handy QuickSteps sections to the beginning of many chapters—these sections get straight to the point by providing step-by-step instructions for many major upgrade and repair procedures. QuickSteps sections also include a list of the items you'll need on hand and preparations you'll need in place before you begin.

In this edition, we have continued to include a Visual Upgrades section that will guide you through many of the common upgrades quickly and easily. As their name implies, the Visual Upgrades walk you through the process visually.

The combination of QuickSteps, Visual Upgrades, and the videos included on the CD will provide the confidence you need as you work through a particular procedure.

Finally, we have updated the Troubleshooting sections at the end of many chapters. You'll find workarounds to many common problems concentrated in these distinct sections. These sections also alert you to gotchas lurking within major hardware components and upgrading scenarios.

Why This Book?

I've been programming computers since 1973. But for years I wasn't a "hardware guy." After moving from mainframe programming to the early PCs that came out in the mid-'70s, I watched the micro-computer market, waiting for the computer that was useful and didn't require any soldering to get it up and running.

That's why I liked the IBM PC from the very beginning. Just take it out of the box, plug some stuff together, and *voilà!* A completely usable computer—and *no soldering*.

That was, of course, until I'd had it for nine months. Then, right in the middle of doing some work, all of a sudden, the floppy drive light came on for no apparent reason, the system rebooted itself, and the number 601 appeared on the screen. Nothing else happened—the machine refused to do any more. I turned it on and off again, and it did the same thing.

"What now?" I thought. It was 1982. Replacing *everything* was expensive. Floppy drives cost $500 apiece. A PC motherboard cost $1400. A floppy controller cost $275. Of course, all of this hap-pened shortly *after* the warranty on my PC ran out. I had an all-IBM machine, but some of the parts came from a dealer who was not an authorized IBM dealer, so IBM wouldn't even talk to me. I went to a service department of a large computer store chain seeking help. I looked at their hourly rates and *knew* from their high prices that they must know what they're doing (I was younger and dumber), so I confidently left my machine with them. They kept the machine for two months, said they couldn't find anything wrong with it, and charged me $800.

The problem, of course, persisted. I was scared. I mean, I'd just spent some big bucks for this computer, and then added to that $800 on some nonrepairs, and it still didn't work. So I figured, "What the heck, I can't make it any worse," and took the top off.

What I saw was that the drive was connected with a ribbon cable to a circuit board, a board I later learned was called the "floppy controller board." The controller board was new, the drive was new (the repair shop had already replaced them)—but what about the cable? You guessed it; $35 bought a new cable from a local computer supply place, and the problem went away forever.

I found out that I wasn't the only person with PC repair needs. On average, seven out of ten PCs suffer a breakdown of some kind. It takes an average of five days to fix, and the fix costs an average of $257. (This is according to a survey from the Business Products Consulting Group. The results were based on a survey of 500 business users. Besides, it was about time to throw in a statistic.) Even if you pay a maintenance company lots of money to keep your machines in shape, you should *still* do what-ever repairs you can. That's because the big cost of machine failures isn't the cost of the machine—it's the cost of the lost employee time, as employees must wait in line to use machines or forgo the services of a PC altogether. You may have to wait four hours for a service person, only to find that the fix was a simple five-minute operation. The result: four hours of lost employee time. Furthermore, and perhaps more important, service bureaus don't repair hard disks; they throw them away—along with your data. It's not hard to bring dead hard drives back to life, as you'll learn in this book.

Emboldened by my success, I read what few references existed about microcomputer repair, and I tried fixing a lot of things. Some things got fixed, some got "smoked." I asked a lot of questions and made a lot of mistakes, and finally got to the point where at worst I didn't do any damage and usu-ally met with success. I'd like to accelerate *you* to that point with this book. (But you'll still "smoke" the occasional device—everybody does.) Once I figured out how simple it was to fix PCs, I devel-oped a series of seminars on PC repair that I conduct in the United States, Canada, and Europe.

That's why you're reading this. (Unless you're thumbing through it in the bookstore. If you are, then *buy* the silly thing. Hundreds of thousands of people already have, so it's a good bet that you'll like it.)

This book won't teach you to fix *all* problems. Not all problems *can* be fixed—for instance, leaving your hard disk out in the rain will probably render your erstwhile data storage medium usable for little more than a paperweight. Nevertheless, even if you've never opened up a PC or installed an expansion board, this book can help you.

It will also help with terminology. Part of your job may involve talking to technical types. Some of those folks are good at talking to ordinary mortals, but there are some (and I'm sure you know a few of them) who can't seem to speak a single sentence without a liberal sprinkling of TLAs (you know, Three-Letter Acronyms). A thorough reading of this book will enable you to speak fluent "PC-ese," and the index will point you to definitions of most PC terms.

You'll also see a fair amount about installation in this book. Installation of new equipment often brings headaches: understanding how to do it and why it doesn't work once installed, testing the new equipment, and ensuring that it doesn't adversely affect already installed equipment. I'll also talk about how to take a tired old PC and soup it up to get better performance from it.

In the process of working with IBM PCs since 1981 and microcomputers since 1976, I have picked up or written a number of very useful utilities that assist in the diagnosis of PC problems. I'll discuss them in this book, and you'll find the programs on the book's CDs.

Who Is This Book For?

I'm writing this for the needy and the curious. Some of you *must* understand the machines that you depend on so much so that you can better keep them in top shape. Others may just wonder what's going on under the hood. Whoever you are, dig in and try something!

So don't let that useful little gray box on your desk control *you* when it goes down. Take control of *it*. (Remember who's supposed to be boss.) Even if you never take the machine apart (coward!), you'll still learn a lot about what goes on under the hood of your machine, and how to make it work faster and live longer.

Terminology

There are so many machines that it's hard to know how to refer generically to PCs. So here's the informal convention that I'll use in this book: when I say *PC* in this text, I include all PC-compatible machines—anything from an 8088 CPU to a Pentium 4, a laptop to a desktop, big to small, unless otherwise specified. Where necessary, I'll use *XT* to refer to XTs and XT clones—the 8088-based machines that you may still have hanging around. I'll use *AT* to refer to 286, 386, 486, or Pentium machines in general. More specifically, an *AT-type machine* is a desktop machine using a processor of 286 or later vintage. Most nowadays use a combination of expansion slots called *ISA* and *PCI* slots, but you may come across other kinds like EISA and VESA bus slots (and don't worry, I'm going to explain what those are in greater detail in Chapter 3, "Inside the PC: Pieces of the Picture"). Examples of those machines include not only the common clone, but also big names such as Compaq, HP, Dell, Gateway, and Packard Bell.

Back in 1987, IBM decided to go its own way in the PC market, so I'll usually be specific about discussing IBM machines. *PS/2* refers to the Micro Channel–based (again, another Chapter 3 term) PS/2s, the ones numbered from 50 up. They're not making them anymore (to my knowledge), but you'll probably come across Micro Channel machines now and then. Currently IBM is focusing on building machines pretty much like others', basically souped-up AT architectures.

My goal in developing this book is to include material of use to "techies" as well as to those who've never even opened up a PC. I'm not going to try to make an electrical engineer out of you; I'm not one myself. All it takes to do most PC maintenance is a screwdriver and some patience. I've made every effort to keep the jargon to a minimum and to define unusual PC terms when I use them. I *am* going to use jargon, however, as it will get you used to the "industry-speak;" this will equip you to read industry journals, Web sites, and other books.

Structure of This Book

First, you'll take a minute to survey the machines out on the market and look at the features that separate one type of PC from another. Then you'll look under the hood and see what's inside a PC. After that you'll step back and examine some preventive maintenance techniques and troubleshooting approaches. Next you'll look in detail at circuit boards, PC memory, and power supplies. Then you'll learn all about hard disks: how they work, how to install them, how to do data recovery on them, and everything you could ever need to know about viruses and virus prevention. The book then takes a look at floppy drives, printers, and multimedia essentials (modems, video capture boards, sound cards, and CD-ROMs). Next you'll learn about networking. You'll also get some great tips about buying a PC and all the latest on laptops. There's even a whole chapter on tapping into the vast sea of resources and information available on the Internet.

Safety Notes and Cautions

Before you get started, a few words of disclaimer:

Please heed the warnings that you'll see in the text. Read *all* of a chapter before trying surgery. The reason for this is simple. If I've put something in an order that isn't clear, you could damage the computer or yourself.

I mention many products in this text. I am not endorsing these products. Where I make note of them, they have been of value to me. However, manufacturer quality can vary, and goods can be redesigned.

In general, it's pretty hard to hurt yourself with a PC, short of dropping it on your toe. But there are a few exceptions:

- ◆ There's a silver or black box with a fan in it in the back of your machine. It's the power supply; it converts AC from the wall socket into DC for the PC's use. You can't miss the label, in five languages, that says, "If you open me, I'll kill you." *Do not open it.*

  If you were to open the top of the power supply while the machine was plugged in, or even if the power was off, you could get a full 120 volts (220–240 for those of you on the other side of the Atlantic) through you if you touched the wrong things. Even if the power supply is not plugged in, power-storing devices called *capacitors* can give you a good shock even after the machine has been unplugged and turned off. The same, by the way, goes for monitors: don't open them up.

WARNING   *Let me reiterate this: do not open the power supply or the monitor. Under the wrong circumstances* **it could kill you**. *There's always somebody who doesn't pay attention to the important stuff, but PAY ATTENTION TO THIS WARNING.*

◆   It is certainly safe to *replace* a power supply, although when doing such a replacement, again, be double sure that it is unplugged before removing the original power supply. More important, why go into the power supply in the first place? The only possible user repair I can imagine is to replace the fuse in the box, and again, don't even think of trying it unless you know how to discharge large capacitors safely.

◆   Another power supply item. Never connect a power supply to the wall socket and turn it on *when it is not connected to a PC motherboard*. Only turn on a power supply when the motherboard power connectors are in place.

Why? Back in the original PC days, some of the power supplies on the market would literally *explode* if you ran them like this (called "running it without a load"). Power supplies aren't glamorous things; no one touts the quality of their power supplies when selling PCs. Result? The cheapest power supplies get put into PCs. Your modern power supply is almost certainly not one of the explosive kinds, but I'd avoid the risk, myself. Besides, there isn't anything that you can test with a power supply just standing alone.

◆   Unless it's an emergency procedure, *back up* your data before doing anything drastic. What if something goes wrong and the machine never comes back?

◆   You can damage circuit boards by removing them with the power on. Don't do it. Turn the machine off before removing a circuit board.

◆   Take static electricity precautions; they're discussed in Chapter 4, "Avoiding Service: Preventive Maintenance."

The rest of the things you'll find in the PC are safe, but don't ignore these warnings.

Having said all of that, welcome! It's time for you to get to know your PC better and have some fun in the process.

Visual Upgrade

◆ Installing a CPU   2

◆ Removing and Installing SDRAM Modules   4

◆ Replacing a Power Supply   6

◆ Installing an IDE Hard Drive   8

◆ Installing a SCSI Card   10

◆ Replacing a Floppy Drive   12

◆ Installing a New Video Card   14

◆ Installing a Sound Card   16

◆ Installing a DVD Drive   18

INSTALLING A CPU

See Chapter 3, "Inside the PC: Pieces of the Picture," for more information.

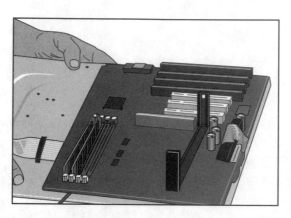

1. Black plastic guides help you slide the CPU cartridge into its slot.

2. Front view of the Pentium III. Note the fan power connector.

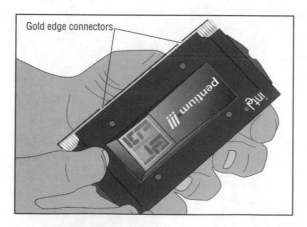

3. Back view of the Pentium III. Don't touch the gold edge connectors when handling or installing.

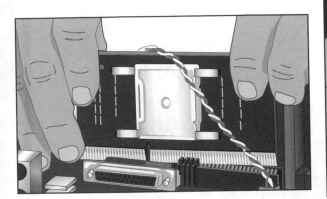

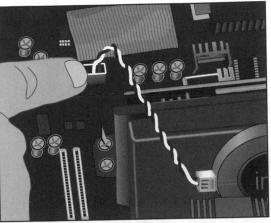

4. Insert the cartridge between the plastic guides and into the CPU slot.

5. Connect the cartridge fan's power cord to the power connector on the motherboard behind the CPU slot.

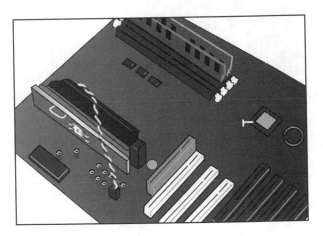

6. An installed Pentium III, with the fan power cord connected.

REMOVING AND INSTALLING SDRAM MODULES

See Chapter 8, "Semiconductor Memory," for more information.

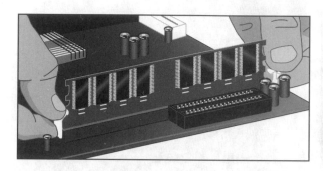

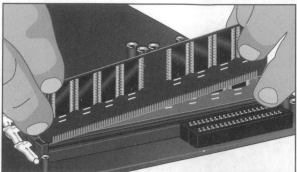

1. Pull the plastic clips at both ends of the slot away from the SDRAM module.

2. Gently pull the SDRAM module from its slot on the motherboard.

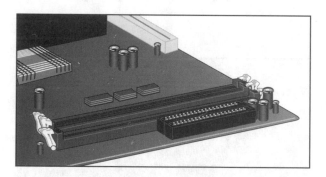

3. A motherboard with all of the SDRAM modules removed.

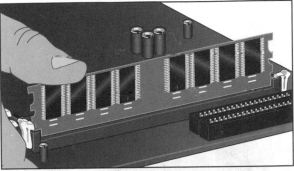

4. Carefully insert the new SDRAM module into the slot.

5. Press the SDRAM module into the slot until the plastic clips lock. If the module doesn't snap into place, press the lever inward.

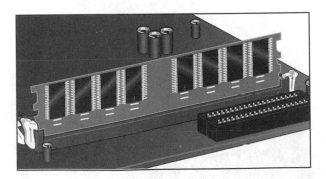

6. An SDRAM memory module properly seated in its motherboard slot.

REPLACING A POWER SUPPLY

See Chapter 9, "Power Supplies and Power Protection," for more information.

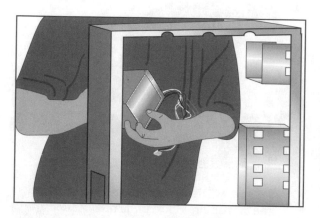

1. Position the new power supply unit at the rear of the case.

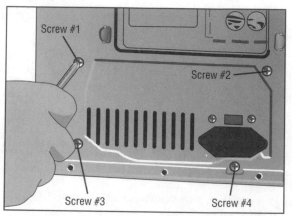

2. Fasten the power supply to the chassis with four screws.

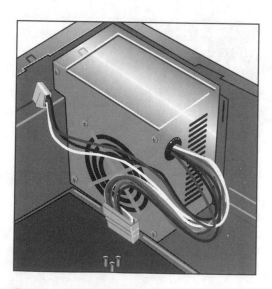

3. Connect the power supply's largest connector(s) to the motherboard. The connector(s) is keyed so that you cannot connect it incorrectly.

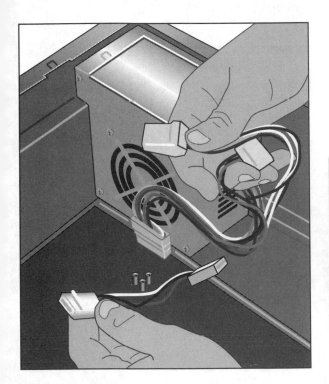

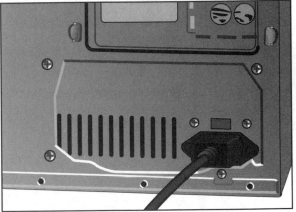

4. Connect the other Molex and Berg connectors to the fan, hard and floppy drives, CD-ROM drive, and other devices.

5. Plug the computer's power cord into the new power supply unit.

INSTALLING AN IDE HARD DRIVE

See Chapter 11, "Installing an IDE Hard Drive," for more information.

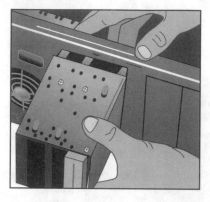

1. Mount the new drive in the computer chassis (or removable drive bay). Be sure to use two screws on each side!

2. If the computer has a removable drive bay, mount the drive bay in the computer's chassis and lock it into place.

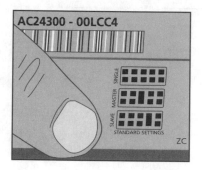

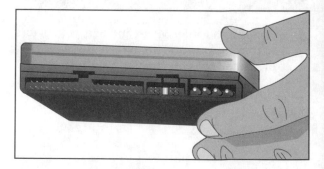

3. Check the drive's documentation (either in the manual or on the drive itself) for the drive's Master/Slave settings.

4. Set the jumper at the rear of the drive to either Master or Slave status.

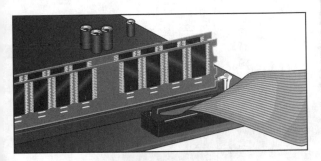

5. Connect the drive data cable to the IDE connector on the motherboard (if you are installing the first or third IDE in the computer).

6. Connect the free end of the IDE data cable to the connector at the rear of the hard drive.

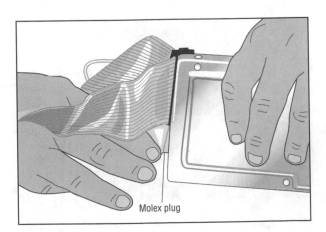

Molex plug

7. Connect the power supply's Molex plug to the power connector at the rear of the hard drive.

INSTALLING A SCSI CARD

See Chapter 12, "Understanding and Installing SCSI Devices," for more information.

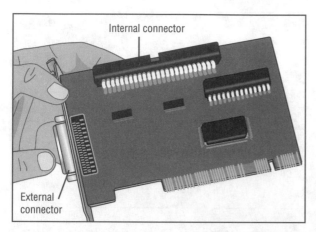

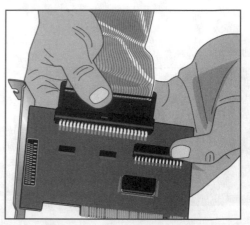

1. Locate the internal and external device connectors on the SCSI card.

2. Connect an internal device to the connector at the top of the card.

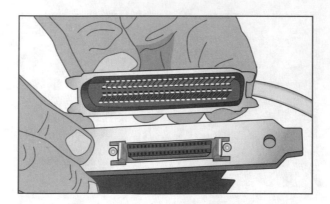

3. There are several types of external connectors for SCSI cards; be sure to match the correct cable to your card and device.

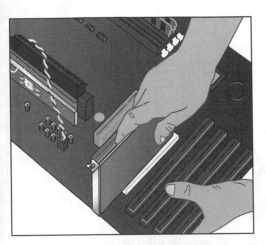

4. Insert the SCSI card into a PCI slot.

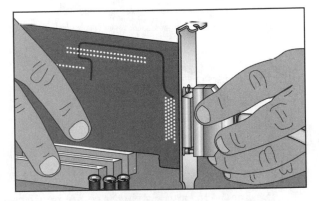

5. Insert the connector from an external device into the connector at the rear of the card.

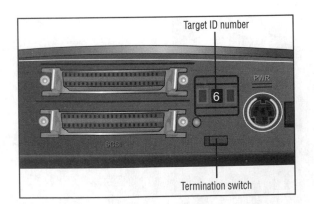

Target ID number

PWR

SCSI

Termination switch

6. Set the target ID number for the external device (in this example, a JAZ drive). Be sure the last device on the SCSI chain is terminated (in this example, the JAZ drive has a switch on the back that sets the termination).

REPLACING A FLOPPY DRIVE

See Chapter 17, "Understanding, Installing, and Repairing Floppy Drives," for more information.

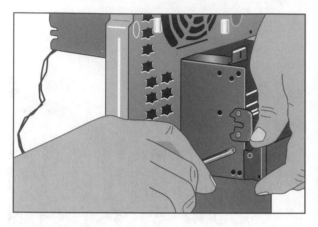

1. Mount the floppy drive in the computer's chassis or drive bay.

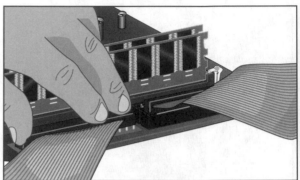

2. If you are installing the first floppy drive, connect the floppy drive data cable to the connector at the edge of the motherboard.

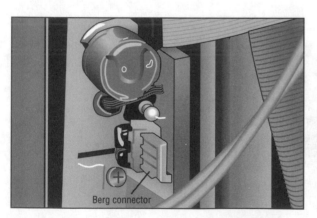

Berg connector

3. The power connector on the back of a floppy drive requires a Berg connector from the power supply unit.

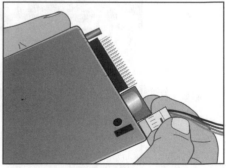

4. Connect the Berg connector from the power supply to the rear of the floppy drive.

5. Locate the gold connector pins at the rear of the floppy drive.

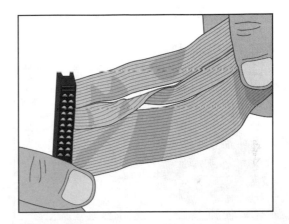

6. Choose one of the connectors on the floppy drive data cable to connect to these gold pins. If you are installing floppy drive A, use the connector with the twisted wires in the cable. If you are installing a second floppy drive, use one of the other data connectors on the cable.

7. Connect the floppy drive data cable to the gold pins at the rear of the floppy drive.

INSTALLING A NEW VIDEO CARD

See Chapter 24, "Video Adapters and Displays," for more information.

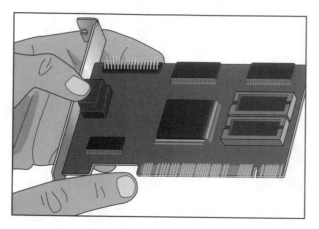

1. Never handle a circuit board by its edge connector; oils from your fingers can cause connectivity problems.

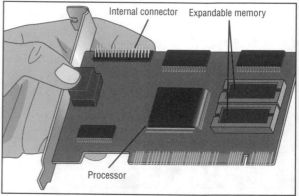

2. Most video cards have expandable memory, a processor, and an internal connector.

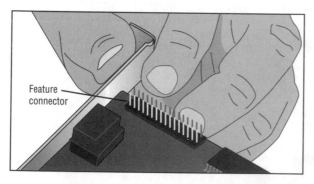

3. The internal connector on a video card is called a feature connector; you'll most often connect it to a television tuner or other video device.

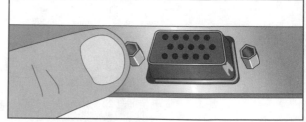

4. A video card's 15-pin D-shell connector is the standard plug for all computer video monitors.

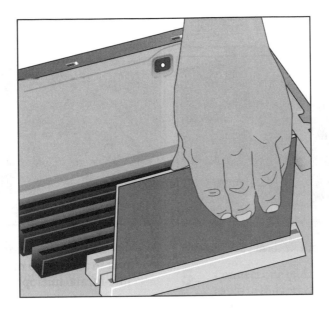

5. Align the video card with the slot and press down until it clicks into place.

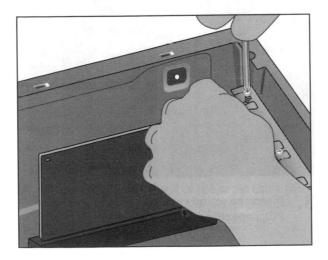

6. Mount the card securely by screwing the video card's rear plate to the computer's chassis.

INSTALLING A DVD DRIVE

See Chapter 27, "An Overview of CD-ROM and DVD-ROM Drives," for more information.

1. Install an internal DVD drive into an open 5¼" drive bay in your computer.

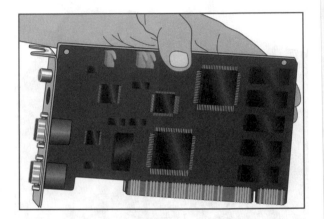

2. Install the DVD's hardware decoder card in an open PCI slot.

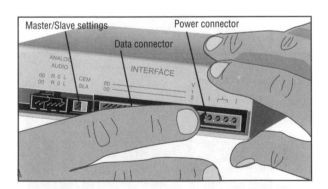

3. The rear of the DVD drive has several areas: the Master/Slave settings at the left; the data connector in the center; and the power connector at the right.

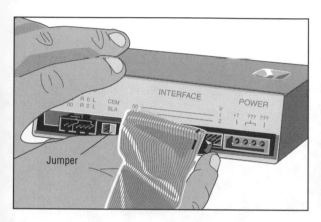

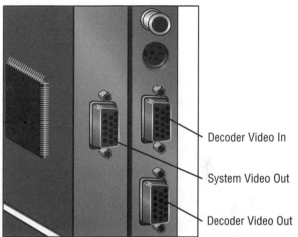

Decoder Video In

System Video Out

Decoder Video Out

4. Set the Master/Slave jumper; then connect the IDE data cable to the drive. Connect the power connector to the drive.

5. The hardware decoder card has two video connectors: one for input and one for output.

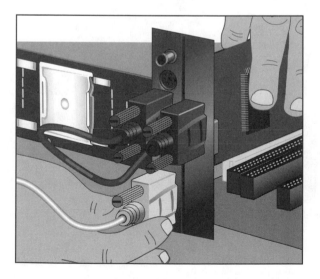

6. Attach a loopback cable from the computer video board's Video Out connector to the DVD decoder card's Video In connector. Then connect your monitor's video cable to the DVD decoder board's Video Out connector.

Chapter 1

Five Easy Pieces: PC Hardware in a Nutshell

◆ CPUs, Peripherals, and Controllers   23

◆ Buses and Interfaces   23

◆ The Sixth Piece: Drivers   27

◆ Other PC Components and Issues   28

Introduction

IF YOU HAVE ANY experience with buying, using, or fixing PCs, you've no doubt heard a bushel of strange terms—RAM, CPU, USB, PCI, FireWire, Athlon, Duron, Pentium, Itanium, you name it. And believe me, it's not going to get any better, because this business *loves* jargon.

Since their introduction in the 1980s, PCs have continued to evolve nonstop. The most recent changes are bringing them more closely in line with consumer hardware such as video cameras, DVD players, and televisions. Standards seem less chiseled in stone and more written in shifting sand. Until today, our consumer electronics and our PCs really didn't talk to one another or know the other existed. But technology is moving toward a wired home. With the advent of wireless technology, your notebook computer will automatically link up to your desktop, and while you are trying to figure out what's for dinner, the laptop will have updated the files on your desktop. You will also be able to turn on the TV with a click of the PC keyboard, and your PC's hard drive or recordable DVD drive will automatically record a TV show while you work on an Excel worksheet. Different companies are coming up with different ways to implement this type of technology, fueling a rapid-pace change in hardware and increasing the number of "standards."

There's also an increasing trend to put add-on hardware boards like video and sound cards, and even modems, right on the motherboard to save a little extra money in production.

The new millennium saw a major computer manufacturer introduce a computer with no expansion slots. The manufacturer's reasoning was that any add-on hardware that was required could be attached via the USB port.

If you don't know already, the motherboard is the central board in a PC to which everything else ultimately connects. The motherboard has a socket or slot for the central processing unit (CPU), expansion slots to add other hardware boards that control things like video and audio, ports to which devices like your mouse connect, sockets for adding extra RAM, Universal Serial Bus (USB) and FireWire ports for attaching a multitude of peripherals, and connectors called Integrated Drive Electronics (IDE) channels for plugging in hard drives, CD-ROM drives, and DVDs—phew! You'll learn a lot more about them in Chapter 3, "Inside the PC: Pieces of the Picture."

Seriously, PC hardware *can* be confusing because there are so many parts to a PC—and some of these parts change pretty quickly. I wish I could write this book so that it completely avoids the geeky details like, "The standard keyboard port uses I/O addresses 60 hex through 64 hex and IRQ1," but ultimately you'll *have* to know that stuff or you won't really be effective as a buyer, upgrader, or fixer. (A *keyboard port*, by the way, is the connector and circuitry in the computer that makes it possible for you to attach a keyboard to your PC.) And until they get those direct neural interfaces working in the next century or two, keyboards will remain kind of essential. I'll explain that "IRQ" and "I/O" stuff in Chapter 6, "Installing New Circuit Boards (without Creating New Problems)." Jumping in at that level right now, however, would probably convince the average reader that perhaps quantum physics would be a simpler course of study.

Knowledge really *is* power where computers are concerned. What we need, then, is some structure, along with a bird's-eye view of PC hardware. It's a lot easier to understand some new term if you have a classification system. What I'm going to explain in this chapter is the mental model that I use to understand PC hardware. It's not perfect—not *everything* will fit into this model—but I think you'll find it useful in your hardware education.

CPUs, Peripherals, and Controllers

Basically, PC hardware boils down to three kinds of devices: the *central processing unit (CPU)* (or, as more and more machines offer multiprocessor capabilities, the CPU*s*), *peripherals* (the input, output, and storage devices that the CPU needs in order to do actual work), and in-between devices that I'll generically call *controllers* or *adapters.*

For example, consider what makes it possible for the PC to put images on your video monitor. Every PC has a video monitor, and every PC also has a chip inside it called the CPU, often called the *processor,* which is essentially the "engine" of the PC. When you hear people say that they have a "Pentium 4 computer," they're describing the particular model name of the CPU around which their computer is built. Common CPU names you might hear are Pentium (in various flavors, such as II, III, or the non-Roman numeric 4) or Celeron; both of these are CPUs made by Intel. At one time, Intel had this market to itself, until other companies decided they could make CPUs faster and cheaper. These competitors include Advanced Micro Devices (AMD) and VIA Technologies, who market CPU chips with names like the Cyrix MII, Athlon, and Duron.

In between the CPU and the monitor is a kind of diplomatic device—a circuit that knows how to talk to both the CPU and the video monitor—called the *video adapter* or *video controller.* If you ever see a reference to an S3 graphics adapter, a Super VGA (SVGA) adapter, or a 3D adapter, this is a reference to a video adapter. Video adapters contain memory that they use to retain the current video image, as well as on-board electronics that know how to do many useful graphical tasks such as drawing lines, circles, and polygons. Why is this important? Well, if you are ever in the middle of a World War II dogfight fighting for your life (in a PC game, of course), you really want your graphics to be smooth. One of the most important specifications today for 3D video cards is how fast they can draw a simple geometric shape called a *polygon*—measured in millions of polygons per second.

Interestingly, there used to be a large number of companies that built video controllers, as well as the components for other manufacturers' video controllers. With the price erosion of high-performance graphics controllers in the latter part of the 1990s, many of these companies either quit making graphics controllers or made them only for sale to computer manufacturers for integration into their motherboards. The result: fewer third-party video adapter boards for sale at the consumer level.

You'll see this CPU-adapter or controller-peripheral connection throughout all PC hardware; for example:

◆ Figures 1.1 and 1.2 show speaker connections on the motherboard and a Creative Labs Sound Blaster Live sound card. These illustrate the two kinds of speakers used on computers today. One is the small PC speaker that's attached directly to your motherboard. The other is attached to special stereo sound circuitry that might also be built on the motherboard or on a separate circuit board that you plug into your motherboard. Once just cheap multimedia components, PC sound systems have risen in technology and performance, rivaling consumer audio.

◆ Most motherboards today have built-in circuitry to control Enhanced Integrated Drive Electronics (EIDE) hard drives, CD-ROM drives, and DVD drives. In fact, 80–85 percent of all drives being used in PCs today use the EIDE interface. Because of the prominence of the EIDE interface (which is discussed in more detail later in this chapter), you might have to install a special adapter if you want to connect another kind of drive to your system. For example, if you want to install a *Small Computer System Interface (SCSI)* hard drive, you'll need to install a special SCSI adapter (also called a *host adapter*) in one of the expansion slots on your motherboard.

◆ To connect a printer to the PC, you'll need a parallel port adapter or USB port.

◆ If you're connecting a scanner or a digital camera to your computer, you'll probably use one of your PC's USB ports.

◆ To use your computer as a video-editing bay, you connect your digital video camera to your PC's FireWire port—which is an ultra-fast way to transmit digital data from one device to another.

These are just a few examples of the different types of electronic components; you'll see tons more in this book.

FIGURE 1.1

The PC speaker and its connection on the motherboard

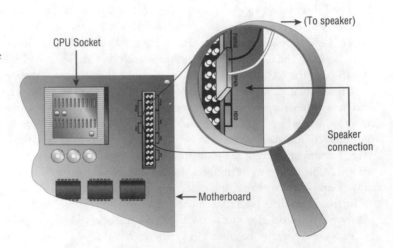

FIGURE 1.2

A Creative Labs Sound Blaster Live sound card

Buses and Interfaces

But wait, we're not done yet. We have three parts of my PC model down—CPUs, peripherals, and controllers/adapters. I'd better explain two more pieces that I've already mentioned: *buses* and *interfaces*.

Let's say that you're talking to a friend who has just bought a new computer. Lapsing into fluent computerese, your friend says, "Hey, I just got this 1.5-gigahertz Pentium 4 with 512 megabytes of RAM, a 50-gig hard disk, and AGP 2X video." Notice how your friend describes the computer—the first thing mentioned was a "1.5-gigahertz Pentium 4." As you've already read, "Pentium 4" describes the CPU, the chip around which the entire computer is built. Some people compare it to a car's engine—not a terrible analogy, with *gigahertz* being vaguely analogous to *horsepower*—but we'll take up CPUs in greater detail in Chapter 3.

The next part of the statement, "512 megabytes of RAM, 50-gig hard disk, and AGP 2X video," refers to hardware *other than* the CPU—hardware that helps to make the computer useful. *RAM* is the computer's memory, a bunch of electronic chips that the CPU uses to store the program and data it's currently working on. (RAM, by the way, stands for *random-access memory*, and no, it's not a very useful acronym. What we ought to call it is "chips that the CPU can both store data to and read data from," but I suppose that would make for far too long an acronym.) We'll take up RAM in some detail in Chapter 3 as well as in Chapter 9, "Power Supplies and Power Protection." What about "50-gig hard disk"? Well, *50 gigs* (*gigabytes*, or billion bytes) describes the amount of data-storage space the computer has on its hard drive. This is memory that will remain intact even after the computer has been shut down. Many explanations of computers show simple block diagrams that look something like Figure 1.3.

FIGURE 1.3

The CPU is logically connected to its memory (both RAM and hard disk), video display, and printer.

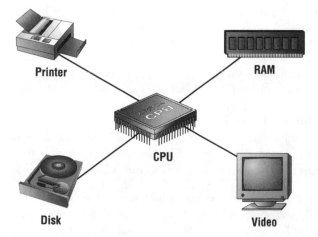

Printer

RAM

CPU

Disk

Video

So that PCs can be easily upgraded, PC manufacturers put empty electronic connectors inside each PC; most people call them *expansion slots*. The expansion slots are the easily visible part of the *bus*, which communicates with the CPU. Over the years, several bus types have become popular. The most common bus nowadays is PCI; don't worry about what "PCI" stands for—we'll take it up in detail in Chapter 3. Most motherboards today have these PCI expansion slots; some also include another (older) type of bus, called ISA. Figure 1.4 shows a motherboard with both of these kinds of slots. Notice which is which—you can really run into trouble if you try to plug an expansion board into the wrong kind of slot.

FIGURE 1.4

Notice the PCI and ISA expansion slots on this typical Pentium motherboard.

PCI

ISA

Why are there PCI and ISA bus connectors in this computer? Because they're both standards that computer system designers and computer expansion board designers can agree on. *That* is important because, just as the standard electrical sockets in your house's walls make it easy for you to buy appliances with electrical plugs and immediately use those appliances, a standard bus connector like PCI or ISA means you can buy your PC from one vendor and your sound card, display board, or internal modem (to name just a few examples) from another vendor and still be pretty sure that they'll work on your PC.

The mildly tentative tone of that last sentence reflects the fact that hardware compatibility in the PC world is sadly not a sure thing, and even the biggest names in the PC business sometimes sell hardware that just plain doesn't do what it's supposed to. It should be pointed out that the industry is getting much better and few hardware incompatibility issues remain—although software incompatibility is a different subject altogether.

Some other bus names you might come across in addition to PCI and ISA are *Video Electronic Standards Association (VESA)* and *Micro Channel Architecture (MCA)*. We'll cover the newer buses (current and upcoming) in Chapter 3, and we'll look at the older ones like VESA in Chapter 33, "This Old Computer."

TIP One piece of trivia you might find helpful to remember: the newer the PC motherboard, the fewer the number of ISA devices that will be supported by it. Many recent motherboards have just one dual ISA/PCI slot (along with lots of PCI slots) or no ISA connections at all. ISA has been provided all along for backward compatibility, but it's on its way out as it's replaced by faster buses.

By now you might be wondering exactly *who* sets the standards for how PCs are designed. Sadly, the answer in most cases is that there are a lot of cooks in the kitchen, and that makes standards seem less than... well, *standard*. Two of the most important cooks are Microsoft and Intel (sometimes referred to together as "WinTel"), who, almost every year, issue a set of design guidelines that spell out the minimum requirements that a PC must have to carry the label "Microsoft Windows compatible."

While most current video boards connect to the CPU through a PCI interface, one of the main things that drives innovation in the computer business is speed: the faster the CPU and the video controller can blast pictures onto the screen, the more popular the computer is likely to be. So when some in the industry became impatient with PCI's top speed (not fast enough!), Intel decided to add another bus—for graphics boards only—that the computer could use instead of a PCI. The new bus is called an *Advanced Graphics Port* (*AGP*). Thus, when you read an ad saying that a computer has "AGP video," it means there's a connector inside the PC that is designed to offer higher speed than PCI, and the system uses an AGP-compatible video controller.

NOTE *The first AGP controllers offered a speed of 1X or 2X, but the faster 4Xs are now on the market, along with the motherboards that support them. The fastest AGP specification is currently 2.0, with 3.0 (supporting 8X speed) currently in the draft stage. The original AGPs weren't a lot faster than using a PCI video board, though using AGP video meant you freed up a PCI slot. The 4X refers to a much faster rate of transfer from the video to the CPU and back again, something that is finally helping to end some of the video-speed bottlenecks that most people have experienced.*

We've seen CPUs, peripherals, controllers, and buses; now what about interfaces?

Just as standard buses like PCI make it easy for one vendor to offer a PC and another a disk controller, there's also a standard interface between the disk controller and the disk. For historical reasons, there is more than one way to connect a disk to a disk controller. Most PC systems nowadays use a disk interface called the *Enhanced Integrated Drive Electronics* (*EIDE*) interface. EIDE is so popular, in fact, that virtually all new motherboards have EIDE controller circuitry built right in. Typically, you'll find two EIDE connectors, each of which can accommodate up to two EIDE drives (either hard drives or CD-ROM/DVD drives). How are CPUs, buses, adapters, interfaces, and peripherals connected? Does one have to go with another? For example, will you find that SCSI adapters are available only for PCI? Not at all. As far as I know, SCSI adapters are available for every bus around, with the exception of AGP. Five easy pieces, then: CPUs, buses, controllers/adapters, interfaces, and peripherals. The CPU does the thinkin', the peripherals do the doin', and the controllers/adapters help them communicate. Buses and interfaces are just the glue that sticks them all together.

Actually, There's a Sixth Piece

Buying all of this hardware is of no value if you can't make it all work. As you probably know, computer hardware is of no value if there isn't *software* to control it. So, in a sense, there's a *sixth* piece to my five-piece model: software that's designed to control specific pieces of hardware. These pieces of software are called *drivers*.

The best hardware in the world is no good if your operating system and applications don't support it. The question of whether or not a particular piece of hardware has drivers for, say, Windows XP, Windows Me (Millennium Edition), Windows 2000, or Linux is of vital importance when you're buying new hardware. Most newer operating systems offer formal or informal hardware compatibility lists—a roster of hardware directly supported by that operating system version. At the very least, they'll have notes about devices known to have problems when used with that operating system (sometimes they include suggested workarounds too). You should find this information for your operating system before you shop for any new piece of hardware. Buying and using unsupported hardware can make for a long walk down a lonely road—such hardware might work just as well as one that's supported, but it might also require a lot more work on your part. So check with your software vendor before falling in love with some new doodad.

NOTE   *You can access Microsoft's hardware compatibility list for the entire family of Windows operating systems at* www.microsoft.com/hcl/.

Typical PC Components and Issues

At this point, you might be thinking, "Yes, I've heard of Pentium 4, gigahertz, EIDE, and AGP, but that's not *all* I've heard of—what about BIOS, or Ethernet, or FireWire connections?"

The intention of this chapter is to give you a very brief introduction to almost all basic PC terms and to help you start to organize the concepts of PC hardware in your mind—but first I needed to explain the five-part model. Now that you're comfortable (I hope!) with the terms CPU, bus, adapter/controller, interface, and peripheral, I can round out the chapter with five-second explanations of the PC terms I see as the most significant. (We'll take most of these on in greater detail in the rest of the book.)

What you'll see in Table 1.1 are PC features, a few common examples of each feature, and a brief bit of "why you care." Following the table, Figure 1.5 identifies some of the connectors you'll see on the back of your PC.

TABLE 1.1: PC PIECES

FEATURE	TYPICAL EXAMPLES	BRIEF DESCRIPTION
CPU type	Pentium, Pentium Pro, Pentium II, Pentium III, Pentium 4, Celeron, Itanium, K5, K6, Athlon, Duron, Alpha	The CPU determines how much memory the system can address, what kind of software it can run, and how fast it can go. The main difference in modern processors is speed, although newer ones add other capabilities, such as better graphics handling and multiprocessor support.
CPU speed	100MHz–2.2GHz (and getting faster every day!)	Megahertz (MHz) and gigahertz (GHz) are very rough measures of system speed. All other things being equal, a 1GHz processor would run twice as fast as a 500MHz processor. Because so many other components affect the speed of your computer, doubling the CPU speed never actually doubles the system speed.
Bus type	PCI, PC Card (also known as PCMCIA), CardBus, PC bus (8-bit ISA), AT bus (16-bit ISA), Proprietary 32-bit, 16- or 32-bit Micro Channel Architecture (MCA), EISA, Local or VESA bus, AGP, FireWire	The bus determines what kind of expansion circuit boards will work in the machine. As with a CPU, a major bus characteristic is speed. Boards built for one bus generally will not work on other buses, so the second main bus characteristic is compatibility. (Having a PC with the fastest bus in the world is no good if no one makes boards that work in that bus.) PC Card and CardBus are mainly used in laptops; most current desktops use PCI or ISA, or possibly AGP. You'll find that most controllers come in versions for any kind of bus.

Continued on next page

TABLE 1.1: PC PIECES *(continued)*

FEATURE	TYPICAL EXAMPLES	BRIEF DESCRIPTION
AGP bus	Your system either has it or it doesn't.	This bus is designed for use only with very fast video boards.
BIOS manufacturer	American Megatrends, Inc. (AMI); IBM; Compaq; Phoenix; Award	The *basic input/output system (BIOS)* is the most basic control software for your computer. The BIOS is what makes a PC IBM-compatible. It tells the computer how to look at the bus, memory, and floppy drive, and how to read other programs. The BIOS isn't a plug-in card, it's a chip that's mounted right on the motherboard.
Plug and Play compatibility	PC systems are identified as being either PnP compatible or not.	*Plug and Play (PnP)* is a standard that allows a computer to automatically identify and configure devices that you want to add to the system. Trouble was, early PnP devices were not quite compatible because they incorporated some older hardware (older is cheaper) that wasn't PnP compatible. Most computers made in the past few years have few if any problems with PnP. For fullest PnP compliance, your operating system has to support PnP (Windows 95/98/Me/XP/2000 do, Windows 3.*x* and Windows NT 4 do not), your motherboard's BIOS needs to support it (an upgrade might be available if it doesn't), and you must use only PnP-capable hardware (usually spelled out on the box or in the manual). Also, a newer type of PnP, called Universal PnP, is available in the new Windows XP operating system; Universal PnP extends the Plug-and-Play concept to the network, enabling automatic discovery and control of network devices and services.
Hard disk/ storage adapter	ATA/IDE, EIDE, SCSI	The interface controller allows your computer to communicate with your hard drive, CD-ROM, and DVD drive. Most systems today use EIDE because it is inexpensive, easy to install, and fast. EIDE uses a 40-pin cable to interface with drives. The terms *IDE* and *EIDE* are often replaced by *ATA* in common terminology, though they're all the same thing. An ATA-33 drive with 33 megabytes per second (MBps) throughput (simply put, how fast data moves to and from the drive) is the same as an Ultra DMA 33 drive, which is the same as an Ultra ATA 33 drive. Newer still are ATA-100 drives offering 100MBps throughput.

Continued on next page

TABLE 1.1: PC PIECES *(continued)*

FEATURE	TYPICAL EXAMPLES	BRIEF DESCRIPTION
CD-ROM speed, interface	EIDE or SCSI	CD-ROMs are the basic means for distributing programs and data today. For less than $1/disc, a vendor can provide the equivalent of about 600 books' worth of text. CD-ROM drives are the peripherals that make it possible to read those discs. With a CD-ROM, speed is a relative thing. If you're using it to read text files or load software, a slower drive (around 16X by today's standards) will do. But if you're using it to play games, then you want the fastest CD drive you can get (60X plus, today).
CD recorder (CD-R)/CD rewritable (CD-RW), also called CD burner	IDE, EIDE, SCSI, USB, FireWire	The CD recorder is a drive that permits either the one-time (recorder) or multiple (rewritable) writing of a CD-ROM disc, usually used for data storage or the writing of a program or music for distribution. A CD-ROM disc can hold over 720MB, but most CD-ROM recorder/writers write no more than 650MB (and rewritable CDs even less—440–550MB). These drives can also be used like a regular CD-ROM drive to install software and play audio CDs. USB versions are external and can easily be shared between multiple PCs (as long as all have at least one USB port).
DVD	IDE, EIDE, SCSI, USB, FireWire	As far as computers are concerned, a DVD drive is basically the next step after CD-ROM. DVDs look like CD-ROM discs, but DVDs can store more than 26 times as much data as CD-ROMs. While current CD-ROMs can store around 650MB, DVD drives can store as much as 17GB, depending on the model drive and disc you use.
DVD recorder, also called DVD burner	DVD-R, DVD-RAM, DVD-RW, DVD+RW	DVD-RAM drives are similar to CD-R drives, but for the higher-capacity DVD format. DVD-RAM lets you record as much as 2.6–3GB of data per disc side. In the current market, several competing recording/rewriting formats are slugging it out.
Video board	Video Graphics Array (VGA), Super Video Graphics Array (SVGA), 8514 Adapter, Extended Graphics Array (XGA)	The video board determines how images are displayed on your monitor. This in turn affects what kind of software you can run and how quickly data can appear on the screen. Video boards vary in the number of colors and pixels (the dots on the screen) that they can display. Most important in modern video boards, however, is whether they hold video data as a simple "dumb frame buffer," which requires that the CPU do all the video work, or they contain circuitry that can help with the grunt work of graphical screens. (Boards like this are called "bitblitter" boards.)

Continued on next page

TABLE 1.1: PC PIECES *(continued)*

FEATURE	TYPICAL EXAMPLES	BRIEF DESCRIPTION
Video board (cont.)		The main issues in video nowadays are speed, resolution, and color depth (the number of colors the system can display at one time). The interface between most video boards and their monitors is called an *analog RGB interface*, where RGB stands for *red, green,* and *blue*. Although some of the newer video boards interface with the new flat-panel displays with analog boards, more and more of the new flat-panel displays use a faster digital interface. Among today's fastest video boards are those including the 256-bit graphics processing unit for optimum 3-D graphics performance.
IEEE 1394 (FireWire)	Typically available as a built-in port	FireWire is a new external bus standard that's much faster than traditional bus options, allowing for a maximum data transfer speed of over 400MBps. FireWire has many possible uses, but it seems to be most popular for connecting digital video cameras, where fast real-time transfer of huge amounts of digital data is necessary.
Parallel port	Unidirectional, bidirectional, Enhanced Parallel Port (EPP), and Enhanced Capabilities Port (ECP)	The parallel port is the basic adapter for printers and external drives (such as Zip and CD-R/RW drives). The interface uses a connector called a Centronics connector at the printer end and what's known as a DB-25 connector on the computer end. In its simplest form, the parallel port is unidirectional (data goes from the computer to the printer and not the reverse). Most current parallel ports now also support bidirectional data flow (data can go back and forth between the computer and the parallel device) and higher data transmission speeds.
Serial port	COM1, 2, 3, 4, 5, 6	Serial ports are adapters that support a wide variety of low-speed peripherals, including modems, serial mice, digital cameras, Personal Digital Assistants like the 3Com Palm Pilot, and some kinds of scanners. They connect to peripherals using an interface called RS-232, which most commonly uses a male DB-25 or DB-9 connector.
Serial port UART	8250, 16450, 16550, 16650, 16750, 16950	The Universal Asynchronous Receiver/Transmitter (UART) is the main chip around which a serial port or internal modem is built. The 16550 UART is no longer the fastest of the lot, but it is still commonly used for high-speed communications and communications in multitasking environments. Software supports fast serial ports through a FIFO (first-in, first-out) buffer. The 16550 UART offers 16-byte FIFO, the 16650 offers 32-byte FIFO, the 16750 offers 64-byte FIFO, and the 16950 offers 128-bit FIFO.

Continued on next page

TABLE 1.1: PC PIECES *(continued)*

FEATURE	TYPICAL EXAMPLES	BRIEF DESCRIPTION
Universal Serial Bus	Available as a built-in port or an add-on interface card	This adapter (also called USB) was first introduced in 1995. It features both speed and flexibility; one USB interface can support up to 127 devices at speeds of up to 12 million bits per second. Keyboards, mice, scanners, digital cameras, and modems are examples of devices that USB can support. USB adapters use a small proprietary connector as their interface to USB-compliant peripherals, and can often be daisy chained together—although using multiple USB devices might require the use of one or more USB hubs. Virtually all new computer systems and all current operating systems now support the main USB standard. A new version of the standard, USB 2, is much faster and beats out SCSI and FireWire for drive throughput.
Main memory RAM	64, 96, 128, 256, 512MB	This is the workspace PCs use for the software they're currently processing. Newer software generally requires more RAM than older software.
Amount of L2 (level 2) static cache	256K, 512K, 1MB	Main memory is slower than most CPUs, making memory speed an important system bottleneck. Faster memory exists, but it's expensive. PCs compromise by including just a small amount of this faster memory, called *cache*.
Type of RAM	DRAM, EDO, SDRAM, RDRAM, DDR SDRAM	While main memory *is* slower than most CPUs, memory chip vendors have been working hard to try to bridge that gap. The fastest current kind of main memory is called *synchronous dynamic random access memory (SDRAM)*. It is preferable in new systems. While traditional RAM operates at 100MHz, newer forms operate at 200MHz to match faster motherboard clock speeds. Current forms of RAM are expected to be replaced by still-faster types, such as the Rambus DRAM (RDRAM) standard, or the less-expensive (but still fast) double data rate (DDR) SDRAM. By the way, memory usually connects to the CPU through a proprietary bus, rather than PCI or some other standard.
System clock/ calendar	Built-in on the motherboard or added on an expansion board on really old PCs	The system clock keeps the proper time and date and is used to "clock" various system operations.

Continued on next page

TABLE 1.1: PC PIECES *(continued)*

FEATURE	TYPICAL EXAMPLES	BRIEF DESCRIPTION
Keyboard	Key layouts vary	Keyboards have a controller on the PC's main board and most use either a mini-DIN (PS/2) or USB. There are still a lot of old keyboards that use a full-sized DIN interface called an AT style connector—a reference to the original IBM AT. Most new keyboards are compatible, and you have a choice about what kind of shape, color, size, and ergonomics you prefer.
Floppy disks	5¼-inch: 1.2MB; 3½-inch: 1.44MB, 2.88MB (unusual), LS-120	Floppy disks (also called floppies) are low-capacity removable media used to make your data portable. Today, since files are getting larger and larger, many computers are equipped with both a floppy drive and a Zip drive or some other high-capacity drive. The most common floppy drive today holds 1.44MB (just under a million and a half bytes) of data. Zip drives, by contrast, hold 100 or 250 million bytes—about the same as hundreds of floppy disks. Floppies are driven by circuits called (not surprisingly) floppy controllers, and they interface with these controllers through a standard connector on a 34-pin ribbon cable.
Cartridge storage devices	Iomega Jaz, Zip drives, Shark drives, Syquest drives, Castlewood Orb drives	These work like hard disks but are usually a bit slower. Their main feature is that they're reasonably priced backup devices. Some attach to a parallel port, some to EIDE, others to SCSI or USB.
Number of expansion slots	3–10	The more the merrier. Many big-name computers sport only three expansion slots. As the popularity of USB devices increases, expect to see fewer and fewer expansion slots.
Configuration method	Typically built into the system startup software	Computers won't work until you tell them about themselves, or *configure* them—which you do by changing the BIOS (CMOS) configuration operation for your system. Today, virtually all computers configure themselves using built-in software in the BIOS. In some cases, you might need to set a few jumpers to configure CPU voltage levels, bus frequency, and cache memory on the motherboard.

Continued on next page

TABLE 1.1: PC PIECES *(continued)*

FEATURE	TYPICAL EXAMPLES	BRIEF DESCRIPTION
Number of interrupts (IRQ levels) supported	8 or 16 (only very old PCs have 8)	For the computer to use its peripheral devices, it needs to know when a device has information for it. For example, if you press a key on the keyboard, the keyboard has to have a way to get that information to the computer. In the past, computers would get this information by "polling" their external devices (looking first at one device, then the next, and so on, repeating the process many times per second). Trouble is, this takes up a lot of computing time, and early microcomputers had little power to spare. So the engineers that developed the microcomputer changed instead to a new system that uses interrupts. Interrupts (also called *IRQs* or, more properly, *interrupt requests*) are associated with the external devices. When a device has information for the computer, it signals the CPU through its interrupt line. The problem is, generally no two devices can share an interrupt. This means that when you're configuring your system, you need to make sure that you don't assign the same interrupt to two or more devices. Doing so will cause those devices to have a conflict and can make the system crash—or at least not recognize the devices.
Number of DMA channels supported	4 or 8 (only very old PCs have just 4)	Usually, the only thing talking to your memory is the CPU. Information stored in RAM is read by the CPU, and the CPU uses RAM to store information. Some devices, however, such as hard drives, take a (relatively) long time to move data back and forth. And if the computer needs to act as the go-between for this data, the CPU can get bogged down in the process. *DMA (direct memory access)* allows certain devices to communicate directly with RAM (main memory), allowing the CPU to attend to other processes while the hard drive, for instance, transfers data to RAM. Using DMA to handle data transfer between many of the external devices and RAM really improves the overall processing speed of your computer.
Sound card	8-bit, 16-bit, 32-bit, 64-bit, 128-bit, FM, MIDI, and/or wavetable audio interface	Sound cards support music and sound reproduction on your PC, but music and sound are represented in an 8-bit, 16-bit, 32-bit, 64-bit, or 128-bit format. The 32-bit format is better, but it takes up more space. The sounds are recorded and reproduced either with FM synthesis, MIDI control, or wavetables. Additionally, with the right audio interface cable, a sound card in combination with the right software can play music on your PC. The newest sound cards even support Dolby 5.1, so you can watch your favorite movie using your computer's DVD drive and have the same heart-pounding sound you heard in the theater.

Continued on next page

TABLE 1.1: PC PIECES *(continued)*

FEATURE	TYPICAL EXAMPLES	BRIEF DESCRIPTION
LAN board	Ethernet, Token Ring, FDDI, ATM, ARCNet	*Local area networks (LANs)* allow PCs to communicate with each other and share data and printers. To do this, each PC on a LAN needs a *network interface card (NIC)*. There are several types of NICs, including Ethernet, Token Ring, Fiber Distributed Data Interface (FDDI), and Asynchronous Transfer Mode (ATM). Ethernet is the most common. Most businesses have LANs, and more and more homes are adding LANs as they acquire two or more PCs. Home and small business LANs are often *wireless*, which means that the LAN card connects to the network without cables—typically via radio frequency (RF) signals or your home phone line.
Printer control language	Epson codes, HPPCL (LaserJet commands), PostScript, others	Printer control languages tell your printer how to underline words, put pictures on the page, and change typefaces.

FIGURE 1.5

The connectors you'll see on the back of your computer

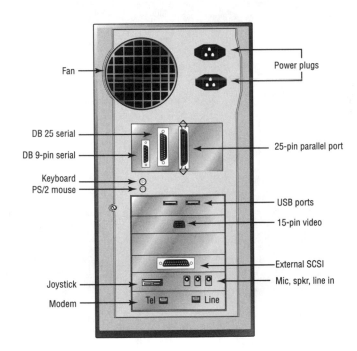

Whew! Look like a lot of stuff? Well, of course, it *is* a lot of stuff! If there weren't a whole bunch of things to learn in PC hardware this would be a pretty short book, right? But fear not, I promise we'll cover it all, nice and easy. First, though, let's get comfy with the inside of the PC in the next chapter.

Chapter 2

Disassembling the PC

◆ QuickSteps: Disassembling the PC   39

◆ Tools to Use, Tools to Avoid   42

◆ Some General Disassembly Advice   48

◆ Hints for Successful Reassembly   68

◆ Troubleshooting Tips   72

Introduction

IN THIS CHAPTER, YOU'LL take a look at how to disassemble a PC so that it can be reassembled. Sounds like fun, eh?

Now, it might seem that I ought to spend a few chapters just *talking* about PCs and PC repair before actually taking the thing apart. But that's *not* what I'm going to do. You see, in teaching PC repair to thousands of people, I've found that understanding PC repair and upgrade requires *two* kinds of knowledge.

The first kind of knowledge is a sort of "how it all fits together" knowledge—an understanding of things like how extended memory is different from conventional memory or what a superscalar CPU is. It's this knowledge of the components and interfaces—the connections between those components—that enables you to diagnose a problem or select the correct upgrade part. You'll learn about this kind of "microcomputer anatomy and physiology" throughout most of the rest of the book—in fact, the extended/expanded and superscalar stuff is in the next chapter, "Inside the PC: Pieces of the Picture."

The second sort of knowledge that you'll need is a different kind; it's a familiarity with tools and with some simple rules of disassembly. Perhaps it's my personal bias, but I prefer to teach these skills before getting into the concepts of Chapter 3. It may be that I do that because I'm kind of clumsy: I'm the kind of guy who forgets to put the plug in the bottom of the oil pan before I start refilling the engine with oil, so this is hard-won knowledge. That won't be true for all of you—if you're already someone who's comfortable with tools, then you probably *don't* have to be reminded that screwdrivers go "lefty loosey, righty tighty"—but us klutzes do, at least sometimes, and that's what this chapter is about. There are right ways to take a machine apart and there are wrong ways; this chapter shows you one of the right ways and talks about some of the wrong ways.

QuickSteps

Disassembling the PC

Here's a run-down of the procedure for taking apart your PC that I will discuss in detail in this chapter, plus a list of the tools you'll need in order to get the job done right.

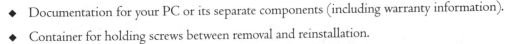

BE PREPARED

Before you start, there are some things you may need on hand. These include:

- Documentation for your PC or its separate components (including warranty information).

- Container for holding screws between removal and reinstallation.

- Appropriate screwdriver(s), such as a Phillips-head. (Today's machines offer a lot of diversity in the types of screws—and even the hard plastic retaining pins used in place of screws—that keep the cover in place and mount expansion cards inside the case. You may need to put a little effort into finding the right screwdriver—and it's possible that you'll need more than one size.)

- Paper and pen for taking notes and diagramming, or the ability to record information on another PC until you're done with the one you're fixing.

- Antistatic wrist strap.

- Chip extraction tool or L-shaped, slim piece of metal for removing the CPU if it's in other than a ZIF socket.

- Adequate room to work (with sufficient lighting).

WARNING *Make sure the PC and externals are not only turned off, but that the power cord is disconnected.*

Now you're ready to get started. The following are the *general* steps you need to take to disassemble your PC's system unit. For more specific instructions (to back up the system configuration, for example), read the rest of the chapter.

1. Determine whether your PC is still under warranty. If it is, call your vendor first—they have more experience, and you may invalidate your warranty by opening it up yourself. Next, determine whether you actually need to take apart your PC.

2. Find adequate, clean space on a tabletop, with good lighting in the work area.

3. Have the proper tools available, including a container in which you can store screws (or you can replace the screws in their holes in the part once it's fully removed) and other small hardware pieces. Also, be equipped with an antistatic wrist strap.

4. Back up the configuration before disassembly, noting the following regarding your hard drive(s):

   ◆ Some PCs don't permit the user to set the drive type, so you don't need to worry about storing the configuration because it should reset itself during the next boot.

   ◆ For most PCs that do let you set the drive type, record any information available on drive type and drive parameters (including cylinders, heads, and sectors per track)—you'll need this if your system can't be or isn't set to autodetect the drive(s).

   ◆ Most of the drives you're apt to see will be user-defined, or drive type 47. For these, you should record the parameter information (cylinders, heads, sectors), including the write precompensation cylinder and the drive's landing zone.

   ◆ The controllers of SCSI drives have their own BIOS that stores the configuration information, so you may see that (a) the PC BIOS doesn't see a drive of that type listed at all, and/or (b) you need to tell your BIOS not to worry about the SCSI drive.

5. Turn off the PC and anything attached to it.

6. Remove the monitor and put it aside.

7. Unplug the PC and remove the cover, setting screws into the container discussed in step 3.

WARNING   *Be careful that you don't rip cables when removing the top; the metal cases used on most PCs can have very sharp edges.*

8. Diagram the setup and internals before you begin removing anything, then rediagram as necessary to add information you couldn't see when you first began, noting in particular:

   ◆ Types and placement of cables

   ◆ Location and status of DIP switches and jumpers

   ◆ Motherboard connections, including power supply, power, speaker, and keyboard (detach the battery only if it's really necessary)

9. Start detaching connections.

10. Remove the boards. Set the boards in a clean, safe location.

WARNING   *Don't force things. If a part won't come out, stop and look again.*

11. Remove the drives, along with their various drive screws and cables. Set the boards in a clean, safe location and store the screws in a container.

12. Remove the power supply. (See the section "Understanding Advanced Power Management" in this chapter for information on the different types.)

13. Carefully remove the CPU by unlocking the locking lever on the ZIF socket or, if it's in a LIF socket, by using a chip extraction tool to gently pry the CPU from the socket.

14. Carefully remove the motherboard as necessary for the type of case in use, being cautious not to bend it or exert undue pressure on it. Put this aside in a clean place where it can't be jostled or knocked to the floor.

15. Evaluate the removed components, as desired.

16. Begin reassembling the PC while checking to make certain you're not making one of the common errors, such as reversing the way a cable should connect, forgetting to reconnect a wire, or failing to seat a board.

Choose Your Weapons: PC Repair Tools

Most PC problems can be fixed with nothing more complex than a screwdriver. But if you do a *lot* of PC work, you will no doubt want to add other tools to your toolkit.

What's the best kind of PC to work on? Ask me at different times and I'll give you different answers. If I'm fixing a PC when you ask me, then I'll tell you, "A PC sitting on the middle of a table, which is sitting in the middle of a room on a nice, low-static wood floor." Fixing PCs is a lot of fun; getting at the PC to work on it, however, is usually a pain. Computers are frequently shoved into corners—dark corners; connectors, if they are labeled at all, are labeled in the smallest print possible; and the machines get more and more tightly packed inside. (You'll find that PCs get darker inside and the lettering on the connectors gets smaller every year, for some strange reason. Maybe it's like my father's claim that snow gets heavier and more difficult to shovel every year; he's always speculated that it was due to variations in gravity.)

Screwdrivers

The basic tool.

Screwdrivers come in straight-slot, Phillips, and Torx varieties. You may also occasionally need a tool called a *nut driver*, which is a sort of screwdriver that has a hex drive at the end instead of a blade. The most common size nut driver for computers is ¼-inch. The *straight-slot screw* has, as its name implies, a single metal slot across its top. Be careful with these—it's easy for the screwdriver to slip from the slot, which makes it hard to bear down on a straight-slot screw and easy to jab yourself in the hand.

That's probably why Phillips screws were invented. *Phillips screws* have two slots at right angles to one another that taper in toward the center of the two slots. A corresponding peak in the Phillips screwdriver's tip fits nicely into that indentation, helping the screwdriver to stay centered and not slip as easily.

Or at least that's the idea.

There are two problems with Phillips screws, at least in the PC business. First, the screws that PC makers use are often made of some kind of soft, presumably cheap steel. And to make matters worse, the slots aren't very deep, making it easy to strip the heads of the screws. So be careful when removing Phillips screws from your computer.

The second problem is related to the first. It seems that half of the computers that I work on have previously been worked on by Ignatz the Strong Man, apparently on loan from the circus. People tighten PC case screws as if their data will leak out of the seams otherwise. It's a dumb practice for two reasons—first, it's unnecessary, and second, you'll strip the heads of the screws. Tighten screws to a snug fit; don't cinch them down as if they'll be subjected to a vibration test.

Another thought along those lines: there are several sizes of Phillips screwdrivers. I'm aware of sizes 000, 00, 0, 1, 2, and 3, and I'm sure there are more. Most PC screws are size No. 1. However, you may come across a case screw (one of the screws that secures the case to the chassis) that's a No. 2. The important point is to use the correct size screwdriver for the screw you're working with. Don't try to remove a No. 2 screw with a No. 1 Phillips; again, you'll strip the head. By the way, if you should happen to come across a screw that *has* a stripped slot, get out the ¼-inch nut driver I mentioned earlier. You can screw it in (or out) with that, since virtually all PC screws these days also have hex heads instead of round heads. See Figure 2.1.

FIGURE 2.1

The typical
hex-head/Phillips-
head PC screw can
be turned with either
a Phillips screwdriver
or a ¼-inch nut
driver.

Personally, I like electric screwdrivers. The Black & Decker that I got for Christmas was just about the most useful present I ever received.

Compaq, just to be difficult, sometimes builds their computers using a third type of screw, called a *Torx screw*. The Torx uses a six-sided, star-shaped hole in the head of the screw. Torx screwdrivers come in at least 15 sizes, which is a major pain for support people. You'll probably use only sizes T-10 and T-15. Why do manufacturers use Torx screws? Well, it's certainly not because of convenience—whatever they are, they are not *convenient*. I think it's because until about 10 years ago, most people couldn't easily buy Torx screwdrivers. The idea was probably that a computer company that used Torx screws could keep casual users from attempting to work on their computers. This was, however, a dumb idea. Things sometimes go wrong with PCs. Also, you may want to upgrade yours or replace a battery. If you can't get inside it, it can become useless junk before its time. Fortunately, anyone who's ever had to change the headlights on a GM car already *has* a set of Torx screwdrivers.

While I'm on this topic, let me tell you a quick story. Years ago, I bought a number of PCs from a PC configuration/sales company. We'd specified on the bid that we wanted 100 percent IBM components, as this was 1983 and the clone stuff was a bit iffy on compatibility. The company delivered the PCs with seals on the back of the boxes. When I had trouble installing software on one of the computers, I broke the seals, took the cover off, and discovered that the video board, floppy controller, and hard disk controller *weren't* IBM products. I called the vendor and explained that he had not fulfilled the contract when he sent us the non-IBM parts. His answer: I'd violated the warranty on the computer by removing the seals. (I suppose he would have used Torx fasteners if he'd thought of it.) My answer: after I thanked him for the first really good laugh I'd had in a while, I told him to either take the PCs back or outfit them correctly. He agreed to rebuild them with IBM components. Now, the moral of the story is *not* that IBM makes the best parts (although they're often quite good). The moral *is* that you should specify what you want in your PC and then make sure that you get it. And if you buy a computer and the vendor tries to keep you out of its insides, be suspicious.

Antistatic Wrist Straps

Repairing your PC can do more harm than good if you're not careful. I'll say this again in Chapter 4, "Avoiding Service: Preventive Maintenance," but it's worthwhile to mention it here (even if it *will* end up being a bit redundant). Remember that:

- Static electricity can damage chips.

- You generate static all the time.

- In order for you to *feel* a static charge, it must be in excess of 2,000 volts.

- You can destroy a chip with 200 volts or less!

We're all aware of static electricity on dry winter days, when walking across a carpet and touching a metal doorknob results in an annoying shock. But you're probably not aware that you generate static almost all the time, static that you don't even feel. It's entirely possible that you can reach over and pick up a board or a chip, not feel any tingle at all, and destroy the board or chip.

The answer to this problem is an *antistatic wrist strap*. It's an elastic, fabric band that fits over your wrist and then attaches to an electrical ground. Some antistatic wrist straps attach to a ground by plugging into a wall socket; they've actually got a plug on them! Since it *is* possible that a badly wired outlet could shock you, don't plug yourself in until you've read Chapter 9, "Power Supplies and Power Protection." In it, you'll find information about an outlet-wiring tester that you can use to check an outlet before hooking yourself up to it. Other antistatic wrist straps have alligator clips on them, which you connect to a piece of unpainted metal on your computer's case.

No matter what kind of antistatic strap you get, be sure to get *something* or you could end up breaking more things than you fix.

Now that you know the right way to handle the possibility of static, let's discuss the most common way people ground themselves to work on a PC: touching their hands to the outer frame of the PC before beginning to work inside the case. Why shouldn't you use this method? Because it's too easy to forget to ground yourself each time you go back in. It's also not foolproof. And, quite frankly, the wrist strap reminds you that you need to focus on the task at hand. So, use it.

TIP   While we're at it, here's a tip that doesn't apply only to women doing tech: remove any jewelry from fingers or wrists. Rings can catch on objects inside the case, as can watch straps, bracelet links, and long necklaces. Scratches may result on either internal components or the jewelry itself. Better to remove such items and pocket them while you work.

Interestingly, although newer computers use smaller and denser components, most current components are actually less susceptible to static damage than older ones because they are designed with buffers on the input and output lines. Although this can save you if you happen to make a mistake, don't use it as an excuse to be careless with your system and components—they can still be destroyed by static. Also, don't be fooled into thinking you'll see a big zap if this happens. As I said earlier, you may not even feel the kind of discharge that can ruin a piece of delicate electronics.

TIP   Here's something else you might not think about: if you happen to be wearing a loose bandage, rewrap it so it's snug and less likely to be caught on something. If you're not wearing a bandage yet, you might want to have one handy. The edges of some of these frames and controller cards are razor sharp.

Retrieving Tools

Here's the scenario: You're putting a PC back together and you're mostly done. You're threading one of the last screws into the back of an expansion board, and the screw slips... and drops into the bowels of the PC.

Arggh!

What do you do? Well, one approach is to pick up the PC, hold it upside down, and give it a shake. C'mon, admit it—you've done it. (*I* have. In IT circles, this is called the "spit it out!" technique.) But it's not a good idea. First of all, the silly screw will end up hitting the floor and rolling under something, so you'll never find it. Second, you'll probably rearrange something inside the cabinet of the PC.

Some people have screwdrivers with magnetic tips that they use to retrieve lost screws. This method works, but I'm awfully leery of having magnets around PCs. It's far too easy to forget that the screwdriver is magnetic and to lay it on top of a floppy disk or a tape cassette. Doing any of those things might erase data on the disk or tape (and, parenthetically, that's why you shouldn't put refrigerator magnets on your PC case).

Instead, pick up a little gadget called a *retrieving tool* (also known as a pickup tool or a multifinger tool). They look kind of like giant hypodermic needles, with a button or a plunger at one end and a set of little spring-loaded fingers on the other end (see Figure 2.2). Push the plunger, and the fingers pop out like a tiny hand; let go of the plunger, and the little fingers retract, grabbing anything within their grasp. Retrieving tools come in different sizes, ranging from the "too short" version, which doesn't quite reach as far as you need it to, to the "way too long" version, usable for oil refinery part retrieval, presumably. There are also versions with flexible shafts to aid with retrieval in hard-to-reach corners. You can find them in hardware stores.

TIP   If you're careful, you can also retrieve small parts with a long screwdriver and a bit of two-sided tape. Just fasten the tape on the end of the screwdriver, and poke at the part until it sticks to the tape. Just be careful not to become too attached to any other parts inside the case, in the event they're not as firmly fastened down as you'd like.

FIGURE 2.2

Retrieving tool

Hemostats

Some people call these *forceps*; they look somewhat like a pair of skinny pliers. Their tips are narrow, allowing you to grab things in hard-to-get-to spaces (like the extractors, mentioned later in this chapter). Additionally, this tool has a little clamp, so you can use it to hold things together. And, if you went to college in the early '70s as I did, then hey, you may even have one of these around from those days.

The retrieving tool (mentioned previously) is smaller, so it can get into a wider range of places. On the other hand, hemostats can grip better, making them ideal for removing things jammed into the wrong place, like the narrow space between your internal CD-ROM and disk drives.

Pliers and Diagonal Cutters

Retrieving tools, hemostats, and pliers make a kind of hierarchy. Pliers are not nearly as good at reaching difficult places as the other two are, but their gripping power is wonderful.

Another incredibly useful tool is known to techies as *diagonal cutters* or, for reasons I've never heard explained, *dikes* (see Figure 2.3). This tool is shaped a bit like a pair of pliers, but it has diagonal cutters at the business end instead of grippers. So, when someone says that they're going to "dike that chip off the board," they're not talking about water control devices, they're just saying that they'll use the diagonal cutters to remove a chip.

FIGURE 2.3

Pliers and diagonal cutters (dikes)

Long nose pliers

Diagonal cutter (dike)

Chip Extractors (PLCC and PGA)

As you'll learn in Chapter 3, there are many types of integrated circuits (chips). Some are rectangular, and others are square. The square chips come in two varieties. One is called a *Plastic Leadless Chip Carrier (PLCC)*, and the other is called a *Pin Grid Array (PGA)*. PLCCs are pretty tough to remove from their sockets without breaking them unless you have the right tool; it requires a special extractor. Today, most socketed PGAs (such as Pentium processors) are in zero insertion force (ZIF) sockets and don't require a tool. All you do is lift the locking lever and lift out the chip. For the older PGAs, you'll need a different extractor than for the PLCCs.

Where do you get those tools? You can find them at just about any computer parts store; for example, JDR Microdevices has a PLCC extractor for about four bucks (Part No. EXT-PLCC). I haven't been able to find a source of 273-pin PGA extractors; they're the type that you use to remove some of the older Pentiums. Jensen Tools does carry an any-size PGA extractor/inserter for $200, however. Fortunately, most current chips (from the Pentium II on) are large, and they are quite easy to insert or remove without special tools—but for those with "ancient" machines, chip extractors can be wonderful. JDR's PLCC extractor is shown in Figure 2.4; contact information for them is in the Vendor Guide on the Utilities CD that accompanies this book.

FIGURE 2.4

JDR Microdevices'
PLCC extractor

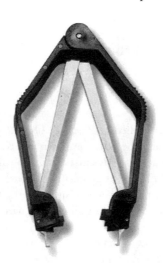

Lights and Mirrors

Poking around inside the dark, cramped quarters of a typical PC system unit can be made a little easier with improved lighting. For that reason, one of the best tools to add to your toolkit is a little flashlight like the Mini-Maglite. Flexible flashlights, like the SnakeLight, can be useful, too. You can find both types of flashlights at any good hardware store.

For peering into those hard-to-see places, you can't beat a small dental mirror. If you can't steal one from your friendly dental hygienist, you can probably buy one at a drug store or a hobby store.

Tools to Avoid

Many PC repair types start their tool collections with one of those 10-piece sets that you can pick up at computer stores for 10 bucks or so. Some of these are better than others—some super-cheap kits may not survive their first job. Overall, however, they're not a bad start, and they usually contain a few straight-slot, Phillips, and Torx screwdrivers, as well as a multifinger retrieving tool and the "chip-mangler twins"—DIP chip extractors and chip inserters. The manufacturers of these devices think they are useful extraction/insertion tools, but they are not. If you get them in a kit, throw them away. They do more damage than good and are to be avoided. The integrated circuit extraction/insertion kit is shown in Figure 2.5.

FIGURE 2.5

Integrated circuit
extraction/
insertion kit

Common rectangular-shaped chips are called *DIP chips*, or Dual Inline Package chips. The DIP *chip extractor* has two hooks that you snag under the DIP chip, then you pull up to remove the chip. The first problem with these tools is their inaccuracy. It's just as easy to yank a chip's socket off the motherboard as it is to yank the chip itself. The second problem is the lack of control that they offer. When removing a DIP chip with this extractor, you end up grabbing the tool as you would a pair of pliers, a hand/muscle configuration better suited to pulling *teeth* than to pulling delicate chips. You'll get the chip out, all right—or, at least, you'll get *most* of it out.

It is better to use a flat blade screwdriver to remove DIP chips. Just pry up one end of the chip a bit, then go to the other end of the chip and pry up the other end a bit, then return to the first end, and so on. Gradually work it out of the socket, and it'll come out whole and reusable.

The DIP *chip inserter* is a small cylindrical tool with a plunger in it. The idea is that you put a chip into the slot at the end of this tool, position the tool over the chip socket, push the plunger, and the chip slides right into the socket. The reality is that the chip smashes against the socket, mashing all the chip's legs and generally rendering the chip unusable. *Stay away from this tool.*

Now that you have the right tools (and gotten rid of the wrong ones), let's see what to do with them.

TIP   *Whatever kind of tool set you start out with, make certain you can manage it in your hands and that you can work both within and outside the case with the tools. Tools too large or too small for the job or your hands are ill advised. Check the grip, too. Some ultra-cheap kits have slippery handles—you don't want to drop a screwdriver on the card below—and tools that won't withstand much stress.*

General PC Disassembly Advice

It's quite important to keep a few basics in mind when disassembling computers. Something as simple as not having enough elbow room could cause you physical discomfort, and losing all your data because you forgot to back up your hard drive would certainly cause another type of discomfort!

Be Sure That Disassembly Is Necessary

New troubleshooters are always trigger-happy with their electric screwdrivers, but, as I'll discuss in Chapter 5, "Troubleshooting PC Problems," the vast majority of PC problems *aren't* hardware problems.

The most important thing you can do before opening the PC is to consider what else might be causing the problems aside from the hardware within the case. Although going inside the PC is not a big deal, it can be a hassle, and each trip inside increases the chances that you might unseat a cable or you might short out a board. So you want to avoid opening the machine when it's not necessary.

Here are some common things to check first:

◆ Is everything plugged in and otherwise connected as it should be? Is everything plugged into a wall socket; is the socket live (test it by plugging in something that you know is working)? The dumb little things we should have noticed can account for a lot of wasted time.

◆ Anything you added, removed, or modified just before the problem developed—this can be hardware, software, or drivers. Try to reverse the changes you made to see if the current problem "disappears."

◆ Outdated hardware drivers—particularly after upgrading your operating system, Web browser, or other major application. Updated drivers can usually be obtained from the manufacturer's Web site.

Even if you *do* have a hardware problem, you should stop before opening the machine and ask yourself an important troubleshooter's question: Is this thing still under warranty? If you can make the problem SEP (Somebody Else's Problem), then by all means do. If you're sure it's a printer that's dead out of the box, don't try to fix it—just send it back. Stuff that's dead right out of the box usually can't be fixed because it never worked to begin with. (There *are* a few exceptions to that rule, but it's true in general.) Always ask: Is this trip necessary?

Make Sure You Have Adequate Workspace

You will need a lot of room—most of a tabletop would be good; all of it would be better. Reduce the potential for static electricity. Raise the air humidity to 50 percent or so, use a commercial anti-static remedy, or at least touch something metal before you touch any PC component. (See Chapter 4 for more ideas on handling static electricity.)

Keep the Small Parts Organized

Get a cup or a bag in which to store screws and small pieces of hardware. If you leave the screws on the table, you'll eventually end up accidentally sweeping the screws off the table and onto the floor, where they'll roll down a floor register or under the heaviest object available. I knew a guy who kept the screws in the vent on top of the power supply—the one just above the fan. One day, he forgot they were there and turned the machine on. Power supply fans can *really* sling screws around!

NOTE   *An important goal of good PC maintenance is to end up without any spare parts.*

Since there will be at least two kinds of screws, it's not a bad idea to steal a page from car mechanics' books and use an egg carton to store them. Screws to secure the case, for example, tend to be a different size from the rest of the screws in the system, and sometimes you'll run across hard disks or CD-ROMs that require short screws. Anyway, egg cartons have a bunch of compartments, and you can label each compartment to correspond to the screw(s) you put there. Or if you want something even more secure, many hardware and sporting goods stores sell small plastic compartmentalized boxes with hinged lids. They aren't very expensive, and you can close the lid on each compartment as you fill it. That way, you'll know what goes where when you go to put the computer back together.

Or use yet another approach: After you've removed a part, put all the screws into the holes they came out of. You'll have to remove them again before replacing the part in its original location, so there's a bit of extra work with this method, but the chances of losing screws or getting them mixed up are much slimmer this way. This is particularly true because now and then you'll see a drive mounted in some kind of bracket in such a way that you *must* use the very short screws that came with the drive and bracket. If you use standard-length PC mounting screws instead, you'll end up driving the screw into the housing of the drive itself, making the drive unusable.

Back Up the Configuration

Virtually every modern PC stores a small bit of vital configuration information in a special memory chip called *CMOS memory*. That memory chip can't work—to be more specific, it won't "remember" its settings—unless it's hooked up to a working battery. If you end up removing the battery, the system will complain about not being configured when you reassemble it.

Let's take a minute and be sure that you understand what I'm talking about here, because there's a pretty common error that you may see when you reassemble your PC. When your computer's CMOS memory loses its information, your computer announces that with an error message on bootup. The message will say something like, "I've lost my configuration information, so I don't know what kind of hardware I've got. Please reload the setup information in my CMOS."

On some older computers, you'll see some pretty cryptic messages, ranging from 162 (accompanied by two beeps) to `Invalid CMOS information-run SETUP` and the like. I'll cover this later, in Chapter 6, "Installing New Circuit Boards (without Creating New Problems)," but the SETUP program is usually built into your computer and is accessed with different combinations of keystrokes. For example, on a computer with an AMI BIOS, you press the Delete key (Del) while the computer is booting. On an Award or Phoenix BIOS, you usually start SETUP by pressing Ctrl+Alt+Esc while the system boots; it's Ctrl+Alt+Ins for some other machines. You make a Dell computer run SETUP by pressing Ctrl+Alt+Enter at any time. Some computers (such as Compaq) flash a rectangular-shaped cursor in the upper-right or upper-left corner of the screen for a brief period while booting up; the computer will enter its SETUP if you press F1 or F10 (depending on the computer model) during that time.

By the way, do you see the extreme variation in methods of accessing SETUP? That's only the first of many, many reasons why it's essential to keep your computer's documentation someplace handy, something I'll harp on throughout this book.

TIP *Note that if you are running utility programs such as Norton Utilities, you may need to create and use special startup/system recovery disks to properly boot up your system and use the utilities. Refer to your software documentation for more information.*

No matter how you get into SETUP, seeing this error message is pretty unsettling for first-time PC explorers. Relax; if you end up getting this message when you reassemble your system, it's probably not something that you did wrong. More than likely, your computer lost its CMOS because you disconnected the battery while disassembling, or it may just be that the battery was failing. All you have to do is run SETUP and restore the PC's values.

In general, a PC that has lost its CMOS information can make pretty good guesses about what the correct values for the CMOS parameters should be. In many cases, it will beep at you and make you look over what it comes up with, and you'll be content with its choices. But one place where the computer might need a bit of help is in identifying your hard disk. This is more often true on earlier systems, because post-1995 PCs are pretty good at figuring out what kind of hard disk or disks they have. Still, even the newest PC might get confused, so it's a good idea to note the hard disk information on your PC before disassembling it. Run your PC's SETUP program and look in the "basic configuration" screen; you'll see information on up to four disks there.

TIP   In an effort to be "idiot-proof," some PCs don't let you set a drive type at all. By doing this, the designers of these PCs have severely limited the range of drives that you use in their computers—but maybe that was the idea, unfortunately. In any case, if you run across a computer that just plain won't let you examine or modify its drive information, then relax—you have nothing to worry about. The system will configure itself automatically if you clear the CMOS while disassembling it.

It may be obvious, but I'll say it anyway: write down the configuration information *before* you disassemble the PC. That way you can easily reset the configuration to the way it was before, no guessing required.

Again—access the basic configuration screen and write down everything you see there. Then you can proceed.

On some systems, hard disk type is represented as a number between 1 and 47. Some of the newer systems are able to autodetect the hard drive type. On those systems, you may be able to just boot up, and the computer will autodetect the hard drive(s) during bootup. On others, you may need to go into the BIOS setup and select the Autodetect option. Whatever your system does, it's a good idea to write down the drive type (if present) and the drive parameters (cylinders, heads, and sectors per track). Also, consider these two special conditions:

◆ SCSI hard disks are sufficiently unusual that the basic software that's built into the PC can't handle them. As a result, these unusual drives have their own built-in software (it's called a *BIOS*) to support themselves. However, because the basic BIOS that comes with the PC is of no use, you must tell the PC's BIOS to not worry about the hard disk. That leads to this seeming paradox: If you have a SCSI disk drive, your computer's SETUP program will probably indicate that you have no hard disks.

◆ It is likely that most of the drives you'll see will be "user-defined" (Type 47). That means you have to write down some extra information: the number of heads, cylinders, and sectors; the write precompensation cylinder; and the landing zone of the drive. Again, we'll get into all those things later in the book.

When you have all of that information written down, you'll be set in case you find that the CMOS data has dissolved.

TIP   If you own Norton Utilities, then take a look at the utility named DISKTOOL. Among other things, it will save CMOS information to a file as part of making what it calls a rescue disk.

Again, recording the CMOS information is important; you never know when you're going to need this information.

TIP   I will mainly cover hardware here, but you also need to be aware of a pesky little operating system matter. Whenever doing anything of this nature, it's wise to have a system boot disk, *also called a startup disk or system recovery disk, updated for whatever version of the operating system you're using. This helps you to boot the system even if the operating system is having a problem that precludes it from starting normally. Make sure that you have created a startup disk before you disassemble your computer. To create a startup disk in Windows, choose Start ➢ Settings ➢ Control Panel. Then choose Add/Remove Programs and select the Startup Disk tab. Follow the directions in each dialog box.*

Turn the PC and Associated Peripherals Off

This should be a relatively straightforward step. Just turn everything off!

By the way, when I say turn the peripherals off, I mean *all* peripherals—everything that's connected to the system unit. That includes printers, monitors, modems, you name it.

Take the Monitor off the PC and Set It Aside

If you don't have much work space, it's not a bad idea to put the monitor on the floor *with the tube facing into the room.* This might seem like exactly the wrong thing to do, since you might think that you could accidentally kick in the picture tube. In fact, just the opposite is true. It's very difficult to kick in the front of a picture tube. The glass in front is usually between ½ and ¾ of an inch thick! Kick the front and you're more likely to break your foot than the picture tube. The most vulnerable part of a monitor is the little stem that's at the rear of the picture tube. It's usually protected by only a thin wall of plastic, and the glass stem is only about ¹⁄₁₆ of an inch or so thick.

Unplug the Computer and Remove the Cover

First things first. Now that you have everything turned off, take the extra step of unplugging your PC. This protects you when you start messing around with all the electrical stuff inside.

Next, it's time to start taking things apart. Now, I don't know about you, but whenever I look at the back of a PC that I'm trying to disassemble for the first time, all I see are screws.

The problem then becomes knowing which screws help get the top off the computer and which screws will, when loosened, cause something in the computer to go "thunk!" (if the screw was supporting something big) or "dink!" (if the screw was supporting something small). You'll see case support screws on the back and sometimes on the side of PC cases. There are typically two to four screws on the back of a PC that don't hold the cover in place—they fasten the power supply to the inside of the PC. So look carefully and make sound decisions when removing PC screws.

TIP   The screws holding the case together aren't always screws. Sometimes they're larger thumbscrews that you can loosen and tighten by hand, no tools required. These thumbscrews are sometimes located on the sides of tower PCs.

PC cases come in several styles and sizes. There are basically two types: desktop cases and tower cases. *Desktop cases* are typically located on top of your desk (hence, the name), and come in two basic sizes—regular and slimline. Slimline cases usually have one or two removable faceplates for adding devices such as CD readers/writers or Zip drives. Regular desktop cases can have as many as five or six removable faceplates for additional internal devices. Desktop cases aren't as expandable as tower cases, and the slimline desktop is less expandable than the regular desktop case.

Tower cases are becoming more popular with newer PCs. Full-size tower cases offer the most expandability and are ideal for servers. Smaller towers are more popular for consumers and are available in mid-, mini-, and micro sizes. Some PC cases are specially designed for quick and easy access, while others can be a bit more cumbersome.

I can't detail how to get into every kind of PC case, but let's take a look at these two common case types. Let's start with a desktop case. Take a look at Figures 2.6 and 2.7.

FIGURE 2.6

Typical desktop case

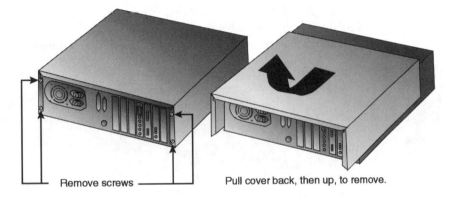

Remove screws

Pull cover back, then up, to remove.

FIGURE 2.7

Older "cable ripper" desktop case

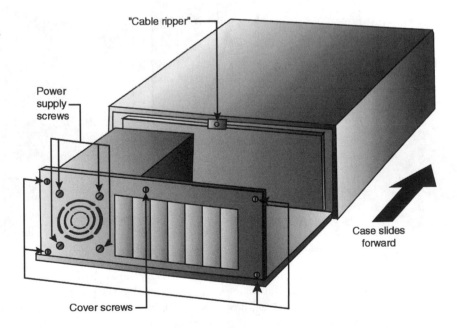

"Cable ripper"

Power supply screws

Cover screws

Case slides forward

Note that on the back of the PCs in Figures 2.6 and 2.7, there are four to six screws that hold the case in place and four others that hold the power supply in place. When you remove the screws, remember that you have to keep track of them somehow, so store them in one of the ways I recommended earlier (or use your own storage method if you're feeling adventuresome). Be careful not to knock the screws onto the floor. (If you're as clumsy as I am, you'll wait until there are more small screws and hardware and knock them all over at once.)

If you have a case like the one shown in Figure 2.7, slide the cover carefully forward and set it aside. And I mean *carefully*—don't rip the thin ribbon cables when you remove the top. The part of the case that mates with the middle screw is often a piece of unsmoothed sheet metal, and those of us who've met it before know it as the *cable ripper*. So be careful, because it is *very easy* to scratch a cable with the ripper. Just a nick can make your floppy or hard disk (the peripherals that use these cables) misbehave. I once saw a cable that had gotten the "rip the top open and scratch the cable" treatment, and although floppies could read and write fine, it caused them to refuse to format.

WARNING   *If the edge of a case is sharp enough to rip a cable, it's also sharp enough to rip your flesh. Be very careful when handling these cases—or keep a box of bandages nearby, just in case!*

Now let's look at how to remove the cover on a tower case, like the one in Figure 2.8.

FIGURE 2.8

Typical tower case

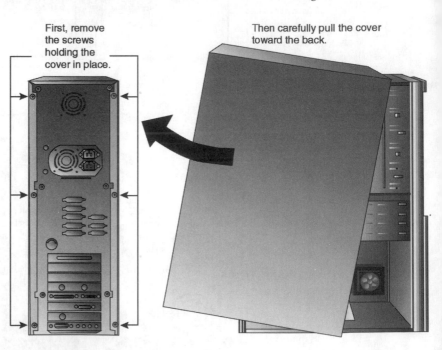

First, remove the screws holding the cover in place.

Then carefully pull the cover toward the back.

This is a full-sized tower, but all sizes come apart basically the same way. You remove some screws from the back and swing the cover off. Note that the power supply screws are on the inside of the back of the computer. The case screws, in contrast, sit outside of the metal lip that runs around the outside of the back of the computer.

It's usually tougher getting the cover back onto a tower than it is removing the cover in the first place, so keep an eye on how the cover comes *off*, so that you can figure out how it goes back *on*. Expect that the worst part of reassembling the computer will be convincing the cover to fit nicely on the case.

Now that you have the top off, take this opportunity to write your name on the inside of the case with an indelible marker, as a small extra bit of security. By the way, in desktop cases, the most important screw in the back is the top center screw—it holds the weight of the monitor. In normal usage, it is best to ensure that all five screws are in place. However, if you're going to be lazy, the one screw that *you must have* in place is the center screw. When you're reassembling, however, *don't* be lazy. Every one of those screws has a job. Look, PC companies are cheap, believe me. If they could save five cents on a screw, then they would. Those screws are in that case for a good reason.

Today's machines offer a lot of diversity in the types of screws—and even in the hard plastic retaining pins used in place of screws—to keep the cover in place and to mount expansion cards inside the case. So you may need to put a little effort into finding the right screwdriver—and it's possible that you'll need more than one size. A good tip here is to set aside any tools you find to be a good match so you can use them exclusively for doing PC hardware repairs. This helps ensure not only that you have the tools ready for troubleshooting, but also that they're clean and in good condition (and didn't just come in from repairing the lawnmower).

NOTE *I have five machines in my office. Two of them use hex screws (of different sizes) only at the four corners. The rest use an assortment of screw sizes and numbers (one has just one retaining screw, and the side slides off). Some of the cheap clones today use hard plastic retaining pins rather than screws to hold expansion boards in place. You have to pop the pin in and out—and try really hard not to fracture the board while doing so.*

Diagram!

Ensure that you have some paper and a pen so you can diagram what you disassemble. What order were the boards in? When you unplug something, it may not be simple to see how to reconnect it *unless* you have a good diagram. If there is no distinct marking on a cable, take a marker and *make* one. These machines aren't library books—it's okay to write on them. Remember that the game plan is to at least leave the machine the way you found it. You may not be able to fix the system, but you certainly don't want to leave it any *worse* off than you found it. If you're new in the business, pay special attention to the problem sources discussed in the following sections.

RIBBON CABLES

Ribbon cables (also called *data cables*) are flat cables connected to upright pins on circuit boards. There is a definite correct way to put them on a connector. As you can see in Figure 2.9, the ribbon cables have a dark stripe on one edge (usually red). Some manufacturers have begun using fine red speckles along one edge of the ribbon cables, so look carefully if you don't see the stripe at first.

The stripe on the ribbon cable corresponds to the position of pin number 1 on the connector. Trouble is, often the connector you're plugging the cable into will not be labeled. Therefore, it's a good idea to take a close look at how the cable is connected to the board/device. A few landmarks can be very useful. For example, does that dark stripe go up on the board? Down? Toward the speaker? Toward the power supply? (Note that I didn't say *left* or *right*—those can get you into trouble.) Make sure to note the current position of the cables in your diagram.

they are labeled P1 and P2, but labeling may vary from vendor to vendor. For example, you may also see them labeled P8 and P9. Newer computers using the ATX form factor use only one big connector, rather than two smaller ones. If yours has two connectors, be careful. Whether they're labeled or not, if you mix 'em up when you reassemble the machine, your system will go *poof!* Fortunately, all you need to do is remember two simple rules, and you'll never install the power plugs incorrectly: (1) Keep the black wires together. (2) Never force the plugs onto the connectors. That's it! If you don't force the plugs on, you can't put them on backward. Now the only thing you can do incorrectly is switch the left and right plugs. But if you always keep the black wires together, you won't make that mistake either.

FIGURE 2.11

The dual power connectors labeled P1 and P2 (labeling may vary from vendor to vendor)

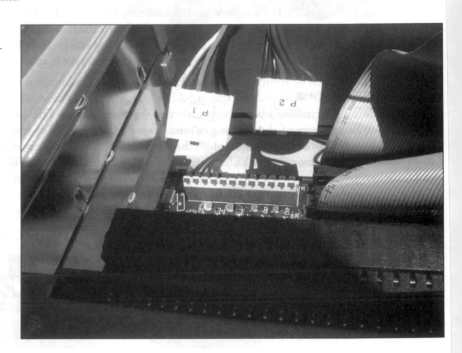

Speaker connection   This connects the timer (which generates the sound signal) to the speaker. It's generally a connector with yellow and black wires.

Keylock connection   On systems with front panel keylocks, a set of wires (two on some systems, four on others) connects the motherboard to the keylock. Fail to reconnect it, and the keylock feature won't work.

Power connection   Some PCs have "soft power" switches to allow software to control whether the computer is powered up. There's a button on the front of the PC that tells the power management software that it's okay to completely power up the computer. But the button must be connected to the motherboard for that to happen. Forget to reconnect the button, and the PC will look awfully dead, and that sort of thing can panic your clients—or you, if it's your PC and it's the first time you're disassembling it.

Remove the Boards Correctly

If you have never removed a circuit board, take a look at Figure 2.12.

First, detach all connectors from the board. When you do that, again, please be sure to diagram which connector went where. Don't just assume you can check the circuit board's schematic or diagram later, if needed, on the vendor's Web site. These diagrams are sometimes mislabeled or poorly displayed, so you want to be able to depend on your eyes and your diagram. Be very careful about forcing anything open or off. Remove the board's retaining screw (put the screw in the cup, remember) and grasp the board front and back with two hands. Rock the board back and forth (*not side to side!*), and it'll come out. *Don't* touch the gold edge connectors on the bottom part of the board—keep your finger gunk off the edge connectors.

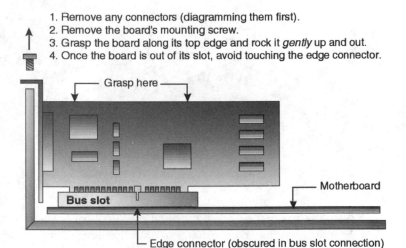

FIGURE 2.12

Removing a circuit board

1. Remove any connectors (diagramming them first).
2. Remove the board's mounting screw.
3. Grasp the board along its top edge and rock it *gently* up and out.
4. Once the board is out of its slot, avoid touching the edge connector.

Grasp here

Motherboard

Bus slot

Edge connector (obscured in bus slot connection)

Now that you have those boards out, you may be noticing how similar boards are. How do you keep track of the fact that *this* green-and-black circuit board with lots of jumpers goes into the first slot, but *that* green-and-black circuit board with lots of jumpers goes into the *third* slot? Take a look at Figure 2.13 for some hints.

When you get started in the PC disassembly business, all boards look the same. But after a while, you'll see that they have quite distinguishable characteristics.

As you know, circuit boards are covered with chips. And those chips may have a distinctive look, such as a company logo or the like. It's hard, for example, to miss Intel's logo on their CPUs.

Boards may also have some kind of writing on them. Sometimes it's a copyright or patent notice or the logo of the board designer. Sometimes it's even a label on the board that actually tells you what the thing does. Use these things to distinguish various boards.

Other boards have connectors that stand out, either on the board's face or on the back of the board. Use them, chip logos, and writing on the board to differentiate boards. You don't have to know yet what a board does; you've only got to be able to document where it came from and what it was connected to.

FIGURE 2.13

Various identification marks on boards

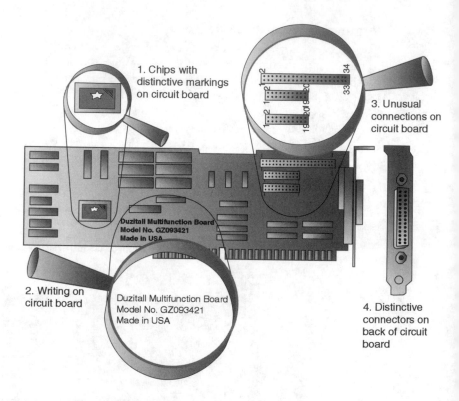

1. Chips with distinctive markings on circuit board

2. Writing on circuit board

3. Unusual connections on circuit board

4. Distinctive connectors on back of circuit board

Duzitall Multifunction Board
Model No. GZ093421
Made in USA

Duzitall Multifunction Board
Model No. GZ093421
Made in USA

Of course, if there's no other way to differentiate boards, you can always just put a paper label on the boards—printer-ready mailing labels are just fine, as long as you don't tape over any of the circuitry.

Remove the Drives

After you've removed the boards, you may want to take a bit of a breather—you've done some real work there, especially if it's your first time inside a system unit. As a matter of fact, in some classes we stop here, put the boards back in, power the system up, and verify that it still works. A gradual approach to exploration isn't a bad idea. (Remember, we *did* orbit the Earth for practice for eight years before going to the Moon...)

When you *are* ready to remove some drives, you'll find up to six main types in your computer:

- ◆ Floppy disk drives
- ◆ Hard disk drives
- ◆ CD-ROM drives
- ◆ DVD-ROM drives

- Tape drives

- Removable cartridge storage drives (Zip, Jaz, SuperDisk)

Of course, your computer probably doesn't have all six types of drives. But no matter what kind of drive you have, they all come out roughly the same way:

- They're secured to the chassis in some way.

- They get power from the power supply.

- They're connected to a board in the computer.

REMOVING DRIVE SCREWS

First, free the drives from the PC's chassis. Most drives come out something like the diagram in Figure 2.14.

FIGURE 2.14

Removing the hard drive

Remove mounting screws on both sides of case.

Pull hard drive out carefully.

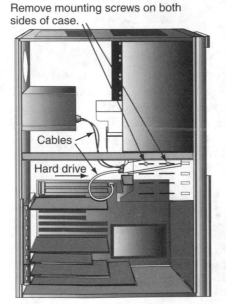
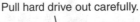
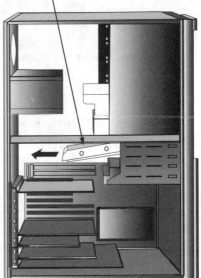

Cables

Hard drive

Part of the PC chassis is usually a metal cradle with holes drilled on either side of it. Screws threaded through the holes secure the drive to the chassis. Usually four screws hold a drive in place, two on either side (there are exceptions, but most computers work this way). Remove the screws, and you'll be able to move the drive around; that'll make removing the cables easier. After you have removed the screws, pull out the cables from the back of the drive and remove the drive.

Notice that most modern hard drives remove from the back. The floppy drives, CD-ROMs, and DVD-ROMs on most machines can be removed from the front or the back. Take a look at Figure 2.15. You can remove a floppy drive from the front or the rear of the computer.

FIGURE 2.15

Removing a 3½-inch
floppy drive

Floppy drive

Out

DISCONNECTING CABLES

Your drive will have a power cable and a data cable connected to it. Your CD-ROM drive will probably also have an audio cable. Remove those next. (Are you remembering to add these to your diagram?)

The first, and easier, cable to find and remove is the power cable. Power cables extend, as you'd imagine, from the power supply (the silver box with the big thick power cable on the back of it) to the drive. You'll see one of two types of power connectors, as shown in Figure 2.16.

FIGURE 2.16

Two types of power
connectors

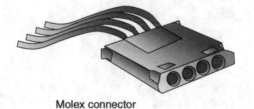

Molex connector   Berg connector

Most drives use the larger, more common Molex connector (named for the company that makes them). It's a milky white plastic connector with four relatively thick wires extending from its back; it has one yellow, one red, and two black wires. Just work the connector from side to side to remove it. 3½-inch floppy drives use the smaller Berg connector. On some machines, the drive power cables are labeled P10, P11, or P12. Remove them from the drive's circuit board *carefully*, as the connector tends to be a bit balky about coming loose from some drives. Now and then, I see some would-be Hercules who ends up breaking the connector right off the drive altogether. Just grasp the power connector and gently rock it from side to side. It'll come loose.

After you have the power connector off, take the data cables off. These are usually flat ribbon cables. Floppy drives and tape drives have 34-wire cables. IDE CD-ROMs (the most common type) have 40-wire cables, as do IDE hard disks. CD-ROMs can also have a three-wire CD audio cable that attaches to your sound card. SCSI drives have 50-wire cables. Again, diagramming is important. Replace one of these cables backward, and you could permanently damage something. In my experience, one of the top two or three mistakes that troubleshooting tyros make is to blithely remove cables without first noting where they should go upon reassembly, or in what configuration—red line up, red line down, or whatever. Every cable's layout looks obvious when it's removed, I know. But it's often *not* obvious when the time comes to replace it. (End of sermon.)

Remove the Power Supply

By now, the boards are out of the machine, and the drives are also gone. That'll make removing the power supply simple. At this point, the power supply's drive connections are detached, so you needn't worry about them. What you *haven't* yet detached, however, are the power connections to the motherboard. Some computers have two motherboard power connectors that must be detached. Others (those with advanced power management abilities) have just one big power connector.

UNDERSTANDING ADVANCED POWER MANAGEMENT

How do you know whether your computer has advanced power management? Simple. Look at the back of the computer. Is there a rocker switch for the system's power? Now look at the front of the computer. Is there a "power" button? If you answered yes to both questions—which describes most PCs made in the past five years or so—you're dealing with advanced power management.

Before 1990 or so, most computers had a single power switch, located on the back of the computer. The power switch was inconvenient there, but it was simple for the PC designers: the power supply was back there, and it was just easier to put the switch on the power supply.

Around 1990, PC designers decided that people wanted power switches on the fronts of their computers, so they routed a big thick cable from inside the power supply to the front of the PC, and the switch controlled that. It's a bit cumbersome for anyone building a new PC (as you'll read in a bit), but at least the switch was in a convenient place.

Around 1997, PCs got a whole new level of power management. If you're running Windows 98/Me/2000/XP (or even a late version of Windows 95), the operating system can shut down your computer or sort of put it into a light sleep when you're not using it. (Yes, I know, this isn't news in the laptop world, but it was sort of new for desktops at the time.)

These computers also have a power switch on their front panels—but it's not a *real* power switch. Follow the wires from the "power" switch and you'll see that it doesn't go to the power supply; it connects to the motherboard. The front power switch is a kind of "soft" power switch. You can power up your computer with it, or you can turn the computer off—but it doesn't *really* go off. It goes into a low-power suspended state. That way, when you turn on your computer, it doesn't have to go through the entire boot process; it needs only to "wake itself up" and it's ready to go. The *real* power switch is on the back of the PC.

So the quick and easy to way to figure out whether you have an advanced power management PC is to look at the power switches. If there's one on the back, it's old. If there's one on the front, it's medium-old. If there's one on the back *and* the front, it's relatively new, with advanced power management.

HANDLING ADVANCED POWER MANAGEMENT PCs

If you have a PC with both front and rear power switches, removing the power supply is actually quite like removing a power supply with a single rear switch. The power supply itself is held to the chassis with four screws. Take out the first three, and support the power supply a bit as you remove the fourth one. When you remove the last screw, the power supply just falls out of the case, which could be disastrous if it falls onto something delicate like the motherboard, so beware.

The front-panel power switch is really just a software-driven switch, and you'll notice that the wires from the motherboard to the front-panel switch are pretty small—which is another clue that it's not a real power switch. It'll be connected to the motherboard with a Berg connector. Diagram it and remove it.

REMOVING THE POWER SUPPLY OF A REAR POWER SWITCH PC

After you've removed the power connectors to the motherboard, you're ready to pull the power supply. Remove the four screws in the back of the chassis that hold the power supply in place. Then, if the power supply comes free, great; if not, try pushing it forward a bit to disengage it.

Again, be sure to diagram the power connectors! They look almost exactly the same... but put them on the motherboard backward, and you'll smoke that motherboard. You can see the typical power supply connections in Figure 2.17. Remember, keep the black wires together as shown in the illustration.

REMOVING THE POWER SUPPLY OF A FRONT POWER SWITCH PC

If you have one of those PCs with only one power switch located in the front, as I described earlier, you'll use a slightly different approach. Take a look at Figure 2.18 to see how.

FIGURE 2.17

Power supply
connectors

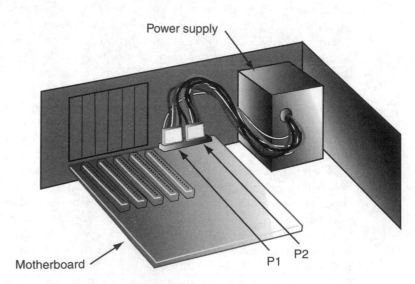

FIGURE 2.18

Removing the power supply from a PC with a front power switch

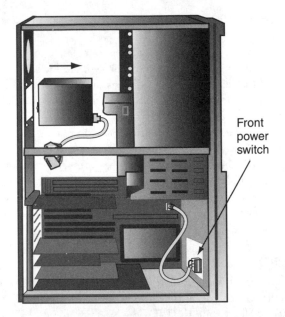

Front power switch

As before, remove any connections and remove the power supply case. But there's a middle step that doesn't exist on the power supplies with rear switches. A thick black cable extends from inside the power supply all the way to the front switch. There are four wires inside the thick black cable: a black, a blue, a white, and a brown wire. Now, AC power doesn't include positive and negative wires—there's a *hot* wire and a *return* wire instead. Ordinarily, the black is the hot, and the white is the return; older power supplies just ran a white and black into the power supply from the wall socket, and that was all that was needed—but the needs of the new power supply's front panel switches change all that. In order to build a front-panel switch, power supply/case makers decided to drag both the hot *and* the return out to the *front* of the case, and then send the hot and return *back* into the power supply.

◆ The *black* wire connects the *hot* side of the wall outlet to the switch.

◆ The *brown* wire connects the *hot* side of the power supply's power input to the power switch. When you push the switch on, you connect white and brown, providing a *hot* AC connection for the power supply.

◆ The *white* wire connects the *return* side of the wall outlet to the power switch.

◆ The *blue* wire connects the *return* side of the power supply's power input to the power switch. When you push the switch on, you connect black and blue, providing a return AC connection for the power supply.

If you disconnect the black, blue, white, and brown wires from the front panel switch, you should be able to see from the previous discussion how important it is to diagram your connections. This is one case where if you reconnect things backward, you could end up directly connecting *hot* from the wall socket right into *return* from the wall socket. That would cause a short circuit that could make your computer catch fire!

If you look at the front panel switch, you'll see four flat connection points called *spade lugs* where you can connect or disconnect the white, black, brown, or blue wires. You'll notice a very low ridge on the connector and that there are two spade lugs on either side of the ridge. Before disconnecting the wires from the switch, notice that the black and the blue are on one side of the ridge, and the white and the brown are on the other side. The ridge is just a "reminder" about which wires go with which other wires. Just keep the white and the brown on one side, and the black and the blue on the other side, and all will be well. The way I remember it is that one side is "black and blue."

I've been beating the drum of "diagram" for the entire chapter, but there is no more important place to diagram than this. Put simply, these wires run directly from the AC line current to the power supply. Mix them up when you put them back together, and you will create a direct short circuit on your house or office wiring. If you don't diagram this, don't put it back together. (Unless, of course, you need a reason for a fire drill...)

Remove the CPU

Just how you remove the CPU depends to some degree on the type of motherboard you have, but it depends more on the type of socket the CPU is situated in. Two major CPU socket types are used: the ZIF (zero insertion force) and the LIF (low insertion force). LIF sockets are sometimes called standard sockets. As its name suggests, the ZIF makes for easier installation and removal of the CPU.

A *ZIF socket* features a small locking lever. Gently push up on the lever, and the CPU is freed and ready to be carefully removed—you can just use your fingers. (Push down on the lever to lock the CPU back into place.)

A *LIF socket* requires a special chip extraction tool. This tool is sometimes packaged with CPU upgrades, but it can also be found at PC fairs, computer stores, and online PC specialty shops. Many hardware veterans, however, use (with great care, please) a strong but slender L-shaped (bent to shape, if necessary) piece of metal that they slide between the CPU and the socket and gently push up to lever the CPU slowly out. Patience and care are mandatory, because damaging any of the CPU's pins can mean having to replace it. You also don't want to drop the CPU into the belly of the PC as you're prying it free.

Starting back with the Pentium II and Slot 1, when the CPU stopped looking like a slender Lego block and changed to a tiny credit card–sized component you slip into place in a slot on the motherboard, it became all but impossible to insert the CPU into the socket in any other way but the right way.

Remove the Motherboard

Finally, the motherboard comes out. (Recall that the motherboard is the circuit board lying flat on the bottom of the case.)

Before you remove it, look on the motherboard for small wires and flat rectangular connectors; they usually lead to the keylock, speaker connections, status LEDs, a reset switch, and the front panel power switch, if you haven't removed it already. Take these connectors off but again, be *very, very, very sure* to diagram those connections before removing them.

DRAWER-TYPE CASES

If you have a system with the drawer-type case, look around the back of the case near the peripheral connections and see if you can find the latch that holds the drawer in place. It's usually a sheet metal tab you slide to the side that lets you then smoothly slide out the motherboard. *Smoothly*, if you've remembered to disconnect everything, that is—keep a watchful eye out for wires you've forgotten; it's easy to sever them with the often-sharp edges of the sheet metal of the PC case. If you're replacing the motherboard, you unbolt it from the drawer and bolt the new one in.

You can remove the motherboard from the drawer by removing two to six screws. They attach the motherboard to the drawer with metal standoffs.

STANDARD CASES

With standard PC cases, you'll have to unbolt the motherboard from the bottom of the PC case to remove it (or the side, if you have a tower case). You'll see from one to five small plastic connectors, depending on the make of the case. Most systems have a speaker cable and a keylock connector with four wires on a five-pin connector. You may also find a turbo LED and switch connectors, a reset switch connector, and a hard disk activity light connector (on motherboards that have integral IDE controllers). On most motherboards these days, the connections are labeled, as are the plugs on the ends of the cables.

You could remove the battery from the motherboard (assuming it has one), but if possible, remove the motherboard with the battery attached. It saves you the trouble of reconfiguring the system when you reassemble it. In Figure 2.19, I've diagrammed a motherboard.

Different motherboards are held in place in different ways, but the most common method involves a couple of screws and some plastic spacers.

Note that the motherboard is usually held down by only two screws. Your motherboard may be held in place with more than two screws, but two is most common. Remove and store them.

After you've removed the screws, you still won't be able to just pull out the motherboard. It is held off the metal case with some plastic spacers. In most cases, you don't need to remove the spacers. Instead, grab the board and carefully move it away from the power supply. The motherboard should slide over and out of the case. If it doesn't, work it *gently* until it does. Applying pressure or force will damage the motherboard.

FIGURE 2.19

Pentium mother-board with detail showing connection points

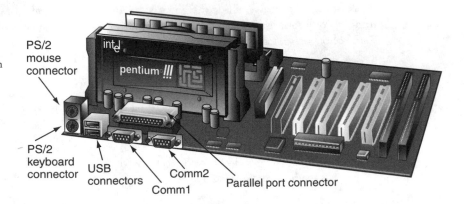

PS/2 mouse connector

PS/2 keyboard connector

USB connectors

Comm2

Comm1

Parallel port connector

NOTE   Some motherboards are too wide to slide over and out of the channels that hold the plastic spacers. With these boards, you'll need to use a pair of needle-nose pliers to pinch the tips of the spacers in the motherboard. This releases them, allowing you to pull the motherboard up and off the spacers. Figure 2.20 shows how to release the spacers.

FIGURE 2.20

Pinching the spacers to release them from the motherboard

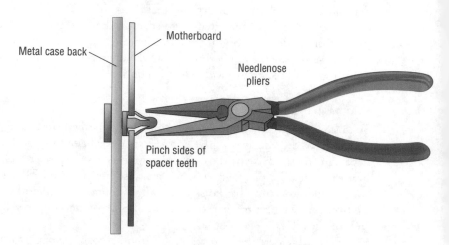

Metal case back

Motherboard

Needlenose pliers

Pinch sides of spacer teeth

Some motherboards use metal standoffs instead of plastic spacers. In that case, you'll remove from three to six screws, and the motherboard will lift right out of the case.

Did you get this far? Then congratulations! You've completely disassembled a PC. (And you've remembered to diagram everything, right?)

Reassembly Hints

A rock-climber friend once explained to me some of the ins and outs of rock climbing. The thing that surprised me most was that people get into the most trouble when climbing *down* mountains, not *up*. I guess that shouldn't have been all that surprising, though, since PC disassembly is pretty similar. It's during the reassembly that the mistakes get made.

Basically, when reassembling machines, just reverse the order of disassembly. Plan ahead. Don't be afraid to pull some things out and start over if you're in a corner. The important thing is to *take your time*. Follow these steps:

1. If you removed the spacers for the motherboard, set them in their original positions. Then reinstall the motherboard, using the original screws to hold it in place.

2. Reinstall the CPU onto the motherboard, and verify that you have seated it correctly in its socket.

3. Replace the power supply. Support it with your hand until you have enough screws in place to support its weight. Then, reconnect the wires to the motherboard according to the diagrams you made during disassembly.

4. Reinstall the drives and reconnect them to the power supply. Verify that you have inserted the power plugs in the right direction and orientation.

5. Reinsert the circuit boards into their original slots, taking care not to touch the gold edge connectors at the bottom of the boards. Use the diagrams that you made during disassembly to reconnect all connectors back to each board, including any connectors to the drives that you reinstalled in step 4. Secure the boards in place with the retaining screws.

6. Verify that you have no spare parts, and that all items have been reassembled according to the diagrams you made before you began to disassemble your computer.

Here are a few tips on putting your computer back together.

Connecting Cables and Edge Connectors: The Pin 1 Rule

Expansion boards in the PC are often controller boards for external devices such as disk drives or displays. Cables connect the boards to the displays. A common short cable type is a *ribbon cable*, also called a ribbon connector.

Most ribbon connectors can plug in either of two ways. Plugging in a connector upside down will usually not damage the device or the controller board, but it will keep it from working. Many cables are *keyed*—that is, a connector is modified so that it cannot be plugged in incorrectly. However, many aren't, so the following bit of information is valuable.

A ribbon cable consists of many small wires laid out flat in parallel to form a flat cable, hence the *ribbon* name. One of the wires on the extreme outside of the cable will be colored differently than the others. For instance, ribbon cables are usually blue, white, or gray. The edge wire's color is often darker, like dark blue or red. As you learned earlier, this wire—the colored edge—connects to pin 1 of the connector. This is the Pin 1 Rule. (Some cables are multicolored, looking like small rainbows. Use the brown wire for pin 1 there.) This information has saved me more times than I care to recount. (I learned it after incinerating a hard disk. If you're going to make mistakes, you might as well learn from them.)

How do you find pin 1 on the circuit board? Many labels are stenciled right onto the board—very nice. Others label only pin 2, as pin 1 is on the back of the board. So look for a 1, and if you can't find it, look for a 2. In the absence of a numeral 1 to indicate pin 1, some manufacturers will place a small, painted circle or short line next to pin 1 (see Figure 2.21). If you can't find either, turn the circuit board over. Notice the round blobs of solder where chips are secured to the circuit board. These are called *solder pads*. On some circuit boards, all the solder pads are round except for the pin 1s—they're square.

You'll find pin 1 on the circuit board of a hard or floppy disk, on disk controllers, or anywhere a ribbon cable connects to a circuit board.

Like most other convenient rules, there are exceptions. You may not find any indication of pin 1. Not all boards are labeled. Sadly, there are no Pin 1 Police. That's why diagrams are so important.

With ribbon cables comes one of the most common—and most dangerous—reassembly mistakes; you can see it in Figure 2.22.

Unfortunately, it's remarkably easy to put a ribbon cable back on and accidentally offset it by one pin or a row of pins, either vertically or horizontally. On one motherboard that I worked with, off-setting the pins by one destroyed the motherboard.

FIGURE 2.21

How to find pin 1
on a circuit board

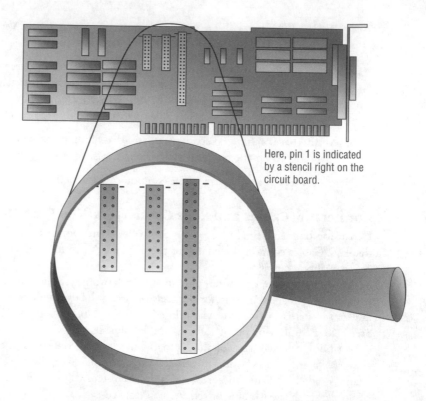

Here, pin 1 is indicated
by a stencil right on the
circuit board.

FIGURE 2.22

Examples of ribbon
cables installed
incorrectly

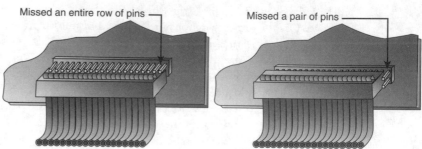

The diagram in Figure 2.22 shows the missed pins as being nicely visible, but bear in mind that it's just as easy to leave the naked pins *below* the connector, where it'll take close inspection to find them. So check your pin header connections closely.

Avoiding Common Reassembly Mistakes

In general, all you need for a good reassembly is patience and a good diagram. But here's what people tend to do wrong. Most of this stuff isn't fatal to your system *in the long term*, but it'll make you sweat until you figure it out. And if you take it to a repair shop to get it "fixed," the repair people will know who caused the problem (heh, heh).

SEATING THE MOTHERBOARD INCORRECTLY

Pay special attention when reseating the motherboard on its plastic spacers. Notice that the spacers are designed with a top disk and a bottom disk and a bit of space between. Then notice that the motherboard has raised metal slots with a V shape. The spacers are supposed to sit so that the V is between the upper and lower disks. Get a flashlight and check the spacers. Another way to test motherboard seating is to insert a circuit board—if it doesn't fit right, your motherboard is probably seated wrong.

In a related issue, make sure that the motherboard isn't sitting directly on the metal case; there must be a bit of air space between it and the case, or you'll short-circuit the board for sure. I tend to come across a lot of cheap cases whose screw holes don't line up exactly right, and I worry that some stray piece of metal on the (cheap) case will short out the (expensive) motherboard. So I tuck a sheet of cardboard between the motherboard and the case, punching holes in the cardboard to allow the screws and plastic spacers to pass through.

REVERSING DATA OR CONTROL CABLES

"Let's see, which side *does* this blue line go on?" Very common. If you don't diagram carefully, you may find yourself having trouble trying to figure out how a ribbon cable connects to, say, a drive. Well, if you didn't diagram carefully, use the Pin 1 Rule to help you.

MISHANDLING BOARDS

Don't stack boards. Lay them out separately. Occasionally, rough handling can scratch and remove a circuit board trace. This can be repaired by soldering a short (*as short as possible!*) wire across the cut in the trace. If you're unsure whether there's been a cut or scratch significant enough to make a difference (traces can be faint or thin to begin with), use your ohmmeter. Set to low ohms (Rx1 on the dial), then put the probes on either side of the suspected cut. The meter should read 0 if everything's okay.

TIP   When a board comes in an antistatic bag, inspect the board but then put it back in the bag until you're ready to install it. I have a miserable story about a hot new Matrox board I removed from the bag too soon: it was discovered by my cat with a queasy stomach before I had a chance to install it. Let's just say the cat christened the video adapter.

FORGETTING TO ATTACH POWER

This one's good for a heart attack. You forget to attach that Molex or Berg power connector to the hard disk, and—arggh!—you get disk boot failure.

NEGLECTING TO PLAN CABLING

Novice troubleshooters stuff the cables any which way to get them in the box. Then, the next time they open the box, the cables pop up and get caught on the tab for the center screw. Cables rip and bend, teardrops flow—you get the picture. Stuffed cables also impede airflow in the case and heat up the inside of the machine.

Put the drives part way in, attach their cables, then look and ask: How can I route these cables so they'll be out of the way? Sometimes the best way is to move the drives around, so don't hesitate to be creative.

As I mentioned, there's another good reason for watching your cables: heat. Fans in your PC try to remove warmer air from the hot components and circulate the cooler air drawn in through the vents. If a cluster of cables is allowed to block airflow within the case, you'll end up with a PC running hotter, and this makes delicate components more inclined to fail or report strange errors.

FORGETTING THE SPEAKER CONNECTION, KEYLOCK CONNECTION, AND BATTERY

The first two are minor, the last annoying. Forget to reconnect the battery, and your computer won't remember the configuration you set up. This can be very frustrating because the system will run when you set it up, but the next time you try to boot gives you the `Invalid Configuration` error.

PANICKING WHEN IT DOESN'T POWER UP IMMEDIATELY

I've seen students do this sometimes. They can't get the computer to boot up, so they tear it apart again, ripping cables and forcing boards out before removing their screws. Stay calm. If necessary, take a break and come back to it when you can evaluate the situation more objectively—you're more likely to catch something you've missed if you don't stare at it. No matter how important the machine is, you cannot fix it by rushing.

Troubleshooting Tips

One of the major mistakes you can make in working with hardware is to assume. And you run the risk of assuming when you don't follow some of the suggestions I offer you in this chapter and beyond, in the rest of the book.

One suggestion I've offered is that you diagram as you work, so you know how things were when you started and how to put them back together when you're done. Don't make the mistake of assuming you can go look up the schematics for a particular motherboard or other circuit board later. Many times, you'll be able to find what you need, but sometimes you won't find the board diagram at all, or worse, it may be mislabeled. If you're new to hardware, you may not be able to spot the mislabeling.

A user recently came to me, tearing out his hair because he bought a used system in which he wanted to upgrade the old ISA video adapter with a faster, better-featured AGP video adapter. He had the new adapter in hand, but with the PC apart for hours, he still couldn't find where to plug the AGP adapter in. His motherboard's age and chipset indicated he shouldn't have AGP support onboard, but his motherboard's documentation and the diagram of the motherboard on the manufacturer's Web site showed one. Indeed, the poor guy didn't have an AGP port on the motherboard despite what he'd read, so he had to go exchange his super new AGP adapter for a PCI.

With this in mind, consider these steps when you're looking at documentation and diagrams and trying to match them against the diagram you drew of the motherboard:

- Try to orient any diagrams and figures in the documentation to the way you're looking at the motherboard, to reduce confusion—this means try to look at the diagram from the same perspective you're looking into the case to view the motherboard.

- Always locate major components such as the CPU and the PCI slots in the diagrams or documentation—if your motherboard and your diagram show four PCI slots but the documentation shows three or five, you're probably not looking at an accurate diagram.

◆ When your computer's innards and your diagram look different from the documentation, consult the manufacturer's Web site first. Sometimes you'll find updated and/or corrected material there that was printed incorrectly in the paper manual.

◆ If there's still a discrepancy, use other sources to try to find out whether you have a different motherboard than you thought, or whether the manufacturer just provided the wrong model in the documentation. Some of the online hardware resources provided in Chapter 32, "Using the Internet and Online Services," are a good place to start for this information, since many of these resources review motherboards new to the market and provide pictures and specifics about them.

◆ When the differences between your diagram and the printed documentation are minor, note the differences on both the diagram and the documentation. That way, if you find just one (the diagram or the documentation) for a later troubleshooting session, you'll have a record of the correct information.

Now that you know how to take your PC apart, in the next chapter you'll examine the individual pieces you'll find inside the PC.

Chapter 3

Inside the PC: Pieces of the Picture

◆ QuickSteps: Installing a CPU   78

◆ Motherboard   79

◆ CPU Specifications and Applications   82

◆ PC Memory   118

◆ PC Expansion Buses   141

◆ Common Interfaces (Disk, Display, Network,
  Other Peripherals)   160

Introduction

GOT IT APART? EXCELLENT. Now let's see what's in there. The PC is a modular device—that is, it consists of a number of standard modules such as video cards, disk drives, and so on. This modularity is convenient to users and manufacturers because it enables computer systems to be compatible with each other and (as a result of standardization) inexpensive.

For our purposes, the PC's modularity also makes troubleshooting and repair much easier for regular people without thousands of dollars' worth of test equipment. Fixing your PC is much more tractable than, say, repairing your TV. (Also, your PC lacks the large *capacitors* that make the TV dangerous to fool around with even when unplugged.) If the problem is really bad, you may have to open the machine to fix it—but remember that most PC problems involve broken software or "broken" users, not hardware. Many repairs just require finding and replacing the faulty component. (Simply being able to go to a strange machine and identify the components impresses the heck out of a skeptical audience, including those folks who question your troubleshooting abilities.) So the first step is to identify what's in the box.

But before jumping into the components found within a PC, it's important to understand that PC hardware is undergoing changes as the technology and its designs become smaller, faster, and more integrated. Although PCs have traditionally been made up of separate components, the push is toward integration, or bringing more of the work of the additional expansion cards (such as those for audio and video) onto the motherboard itself. Your PC's motherboard may already include a sound or video chip in place of the separate cards discussed in this chapter.

A PC is composed of just a few components:

- A system board or motherboard; this usually contains these:

  - Central Processing Unit (CPU)

  - Main memory (DRAM, EDO, SDRAM)

  - Expansion slots attached to Peripheral Component Interconnect (PCI), Industry Standard Architecture (ISA) bus connectors, or Accelerated Graphics Port (AGP)

  - System clock/calendar

  - Keyboard adapter (interface)

  - Mouse adapter (interface)

  - Floppy disk controller

  - Primary Enhanced Integrated Drive Electronics (EIDE) interface, mainly for hard disks and CD-ROMs

  - Secondary EIDE interface

- Many motherboards also contain these:

  - Heat sink unit for the CPU

  - Serial port (RS-232C) or COM port

- ◆ Parallel (printer) port
- ◆ Static cache memory
- ◆ Universal Serial Bus (USB) connections (usually two on a desktop PC and one on a portable PC)

◆ Video card adapter (sometimes built into the motherboard)

◆ Sound card (many systems build this into the motherboard)

◆ Power supply

◆ Floppy disk drive(s)

◆ Hard disk drive(s)

◆ CD-ROM and/or DVD drive(s)—including recordable and rewritable drives

◆ Cooling fan(s)

In this chapter, you'll take a look at each of these components.

QuickSteps

Installing a CPU

All in all, CPUs can be one of the easier things to install and remove. The tricky part is making certain that the CPU and the motherboard you're installing it into are compatible. Try to install a PIII CPU into a Pentium motherboard—it won't fit.

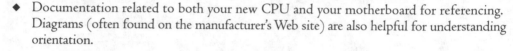

BE PREPARED

Before you start, there are some things you may need on hand. These include:

- ◆ Documentation related to both your new CPU and your motherboard for referencing. Diagrams (often found on the manufacturer's Web site) are also helpful for understanding orientation.

- ◆ Screwdriver(s) for opening the PC.

- ◆ Container for holding the screws.

- ◆ Antistatic wrist strap.

- ◆ Slender, flat bracket or similar tool for extracting the CPU (depending on CPU type).

1. Turn off the PC, disconnect the power, and remove any screws holding the PC cover in place.

2. Ground yourself using the antistatic wrist strap.

3. Locate your current CPU on the motherboard and remove it carefully. If still usable, it should be stored in an antistatic bag.

4. Consult the documentation for your motherboard and the new CPU (make sure they are compatible, see whether any adjustments need to be made for multipliers, etc.), and then gently seat the CPU into its place on the motherboard.

5. Replace the cover and screws, reconnect power, and turn on the PC.

6. Go into CMOS Setup (during boot, your screen will likely report `To enter Setup, press <key>`), and make certain that the new CPU is seen.

The System Board/Motherboard

Since their creation in 1971, microcomputers of all kinds have usually included most of their essential electronics on a single printed circuit board, called the *motherboard*. There are other ways of designing a computer, but the put-most-of-it-on-one-board approach is most popular, although even that goes through fads.

The first IBM PC in 1981 had a relatively simple motherboard and lots of expansion boards; modern computers tend to have more complex motherboards and a smaller number of expansion boards. (Integrating more components on the motherboard helps the manufacturer cut costs.) Eventually, the majority of PCs will have no expansion boards at all, because the functions that most of us need will be completely incorporated into the motherboard. In fact, that's the case with some laptops, such as the Dell Inspiron 8100, which has a motherboard that includes a 56K modem, a 10/100-megabit Ethernet card, 16-bit sound, a joystick interface, and a DVD drive.

I have mixed feelings about these heavily integrated motherboards: on one hand, they're tremendously convenient, but on the other hand, there's a "take it or leave it" aspect to them. Some of the newer-style integrated motherboards have components you can't disable in order to install a separate card. (Of course, many low-priced PCs aren't really designed to be upgraded or customized; the customers for these "plug and go" models will probably never open the case to poke around inside.)

As an example of the perils of overly integrated motherboards, a colleague of mine is having a devil of a time with hang-ups in his Web browser because of an integrated video chipset on his motherboard that refuses to be disabled so a free-standing video card can be used. Get in that situation, and when the video adapter fails, you don't toss the video card and buy a new one—you get to replace the whole motherboard.

The 1981 motherboards had room for a processor chip, 64KB of memory, a keyboard connection, and some expansion slots. The 2002 motherboards on the typical desktop PC also include a clock/calendar, serial port, parallel port, hard and floppy drive interfaces, mouse port, quite a bit more memory (512MB or more on some models), a couple of USB ports, and probably a FireWire port. Some manufacturers go even further by putting sound and video graphic accelerators on the motherboard, as well.

One unique form factor is called the *backplane* design. In the backplane design, the basic computer has *only* expansion slots, and the CPU sits on one of them. When vendors go through these backplane phases, they claim that it makes their PCs *modular*. By that, they mean that you'd upgrade your PC's CPU simply by removing the circuit board that contains the CPU and replacing it with a new CPU board—a five-minute bit of brain surgery that instantly transforms your PC from, say, a Pentium II to a Pentium III computer. What? You haven't heard of such a thing? While this design briefly appeared in the personal computer world back in the early '90s, it is almost entirely restricted to industrial computers that are mounted in 19-inch racks and are usually found inside of seismic trucks, remote radar stations, and such. Why didn't this easy approach to upgrades catch on? While the concept sounds appealing, the reality is less attractive: Because the board that the machine's CPU is on is not built to any kind of standard, you can't just buy a faster CPU board from anyone—you have to buy it from the original vendor. And in my experience, those vendors price their proprietary CPU upgrade boards quite high, often more expensive than just buying a whole new *faster* system!

If you want modularity, take my advice: the ultimate upgradable computer is a generic clone. It's based on a standard-sized motherboard that fits into a standard-sized case and takes standard boards and drives. When I want to upgrade it, all I do is buy a new motherboard and swap it for the old one. Motherboard prices are usually very high only when a new board is first introduced. Many Pentium 4 motherboards sell in the $100-$200 range, depending on make and model and special features (extra slots, faster front-side bus, whether it's jumper-less for fewer hardware hassles).

NOTE   *Now, I've been calling this board a* motherboard, *but some vendors have used different names for it. Over the years, IBM has called it a* system board *or a* planar board, *so don't be surprised if you hear those terms. I've also seen clone motherboard manufacturers call their boards* mainboards.

But enough talking about them—what do they look like? Figures 3.1, 3.2, 3.3, and 3.4 show three motherboards of old and newer machines and a Pentium 4 CPU.

FIGURE 3.1

Pentium
motherboard

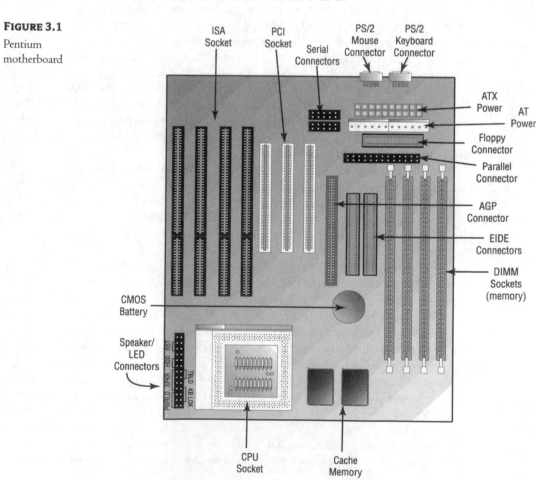

FIGURE 3.2

Pentium II
motherboard

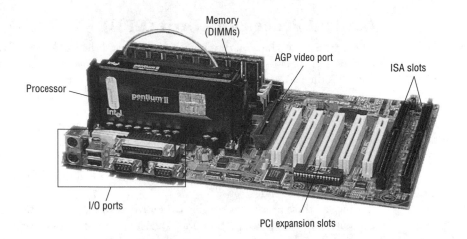

Memory
(DIMMs)

AGP video port

ISA slots

Processor

I/O ports

PCI expansion slots

FIGURE 3.3

Pentium III
motherboard

FIGURE 3.4

Pentium 4 CPU

Central Processing Unit (CPU)

There are a lot of chips on those motherboards, and they all kind of look alike, don't they? They may look equal, but some are more critical to the PC's operation than others. The big boss is the CPU. It's the part of the computer that knows how to do mathematics (and it's pretty smart; it can even do logarithms and cosines and that sort of thing) and logic, the two parts of all computer programs.

Since the first IBM PC in 1981, most PCs have been built around CPUs designed by Intel Corporation. Today, there are two other manufacturers whose microprocessors have made considerable inroads into the PCs we buy: Advanced Micro Devices (AMD) and VIA Technologies, which recently acquired chipmaker Cyrix. But both of these manufacturers' chips were based upon the processors that Intel developed.

Since all these processors are able to run Microsoft Windows, they have been nicknamed *Wintel* computers. In truth, though, they are also able to run other operating systems such as DOS, Unix, and Linux.

Intel has designed and created many microprocessors over the years, but the ones that interest us here are members of a family of chips starting with the 8086 and progressing to the Pentium 4 chips. Why is there a family? Why aren't people still using the 8086? In a word, *performance.* CPU performance determines, in large part, computer performance. A modern Pentium 4 is thousands of times faster than the original 8086, and differences of speed on that order change how you use computers. Back in the early 1980s, people started using spreadsheet programs, and those programs strained the power of then-contemporary chips such as the 8088. It wasn't unusual for a complex spreadsheet to require hours to recalculate. Nowadays, even the cheapest PC is so fast that I can't remember the last time I waited for a spreadsheet to recalculate.

Intel has been improving CPU performance in two main ways. First, they improved some micro components quantitatively, by just taking an old circuit and making it run faster. Simple CPU speed, measured in *megahertz* or *gigahertz* (both defined in a page or two), is an example. The second way that CPUs get snappier is through qualitative improvements, such as new manufacturing techniques that improve chip quality.

Whether improvements come quantitatively or qualitatively, CPUs vary in several ways that affect their performance. These variations are introduced in Table 3.1, which shows CPU properties. Take a minute to look over this table so that later you'll understand where a lot of PC limitations come from.

TABLE 3.1: CPU PROPERTIES

PROPERTY	DESCRIPTION
CPU speed	The number of operations that can be done per second
Microcode efficiency	The number of steps required to multiply two numbers (for example)
Word size	The largest number that can be operated on in one operation
Numeric coprocessor	Enables the CPU to directly perform floating-point numerical computations

Continued on next page

TABLE 3.1: CPU PROPERTIES *(continued)*

PROPERTY	DESCRIPTION
Number of instruction pipelines	The number of processes that can run simultaneously on this chip
Pipeline management	Enables the CPU to "look ahead" to future instructions so as to make the best of its power
Internal cache RAM	The amount of internal, high-speed memory that the chip includes
Data path	The largest number that can be transported into the chip in one operation
Maximum memory	The largest amount of memory that the chip can use

CPU Speeds (Megahertz/Gigahertz)

Computers are a little like clockwork devices. A clock strikes a beat, and a certain small amount of work gets done. Just like a beginning piano player plays to the beat of a metronome, computers run to the beat of a clock (although it's an electronic clock). If you set the metronome too fast for the beginning piano player, they will become confused and the music won't come out right; the player won't have enough time to find the next piano key, and the rendition will probably fall apart. Similarly, if you set the clock rate of a CPU too high, it will malfunction, but the result isn't discordant music; it's a system crash.

Normally, running a CPU too fast can damage the chip; at the very least, the computer may not function properly and the problems may not seem directly related to the CPU—for example, drive read and write errors. Part of the design of a PC entails determining a clock rate.

In some ways, the clock on a computer is like the coxswain on a rowing team. The coxswain is the person who holds up the megaphone, exhorting the rowers to "Stroke! Stroke! Stroke!" If he tells them to stroke too fast, they get out of sync and the boat slows down or stops. The coxswain is restricted to telling the team to stroke *no faster than the slowest rower*. In a PC, many chips all work to the beat of the computer's clock. That means that the computer's clock can't run any faster than the slowest computer component. CPU clocks generally "tick" millions of times per second. A clock that ticks at exactly one million times per second is said to be a one megahertz (1MHz) clock. The Apple II used a 2MHz clock. The early PCs and XTs (the first PCs with hard drives using an 8088 processor) used a 4.77MHz clock. IBM followed the PC with the AT, whose original model used a 6MHz clock, and later IBM offered a version that ran at 8MHz.

Modern PCs run so fast they have to be measured in gigahertz; one gigahertz (1GHz) is equal to one thousand megahertz.

Since the speed of a computer is used as a means of measuring how well it operates, the megahertz/gigahertz value of a computer is an important measure of its power. It's similar to looking at horsepower as an approximate measure of a car's power. All other things being equal, a faster clock means faster execution and better performance.

It's worth mentioning, however, that all things usually *aren't* equal. The CPU is only part of what makes a computer fast. A really fast CPU paired with an amazingly slow hard disk would turn in a mediocre performance. I once benchmarked a circa-1983 XT against a 1994 Pentium and found that the Pentium's hard disk and graphic boards were about 10 times faster than the XT's, but that the CPU was almost *300* times faster. A Pentium seems quick compared to an XT, of course, but not anywhere near 300 times faster, mostly because of the slower peripherals. If a computer were about 30 times faster than an XT in its disk, graphics board, and CPU, then it would probably feel faster than the Pentium system I benchmarked.

My advice, then—and I'll repeat it throughout this book—is this: When buying a computer on a budget, you might have to choose between a faster CPU and faster peripherals. I'd take the faster peripherals. That's because even the slowest new CPU sold today is plenty fast for just about anything you could think of doing with your PC. The bottleneck, then, comes in the other components.

Having said that, however, I should also mention that Intel and other CPU manufacturers tend to stop making any but the fastest CPUs at any given time, so you probably won't have the option to buy a really out-of-date, slow CPU anyway.

Nowadays, the slowest new computer you're likely to come across will be somewhere in the 1GHz range. The fastest computers will run at 2GHz—or faster.

Megahertz Revisited: Hot Chips, Clock Doublers, Triplers, Quintuplers, and In-Between

For many years, the maximum possible CPU speed determined a lot about the rest of the computer. Usually a PC manufacturer would design the entire motherboard to operate at the same speed as the CPU. When CPUs rose in speed from 5MHz to 8MHz, motherboards changed in speed from 5MHz to 8MHz. All the chips on the motherboard, including complex chips such as memory chips, had to operate at 8MHz to support an 8MHz motherboard. At the time, this turned out to be pretty difficult for speeds beyond 8MHz, so since about 1984, motherboards have been designed so that their different parts could run at different speeds. Coupling slowpoke components with speed demons means that some of the speed demons' power is wasted, but it's the only way to build economical systems.

From 1984 on, the section of the motherboard that supported memory was decoupled from the rest of the motherboard, speed-wise, as were the expansion slots or *bus slots* (you'll read more about memory and bus slot speeds a bit later in this chapter). But memory and bus slots constituted only a fraction of the motherboard real estate. Most of the chips and circuits on the motherboards of the mid-to-late '80s had to match the CPU's speed, so every time Intel came out with a faster chip, the motherboard designers had to go back to the drawing boards and design faster motherboards.

But building faster and faster motherboards is like climbing a mountain that gets steeper and steeper as you climb. Moving from 5MHz to 8MHz was easy; from 8MHz to 12MHz was harder. And 12MHz to 20MHz was even harder, as was the move around 1989 to motherboards that ran most of their components at 33MHz. In the closing months of the '80s, however, Intel started talking about producing 50MHz and 66MHz chips. Building motherboards that fast must have seemed just about impossible at the time.

CLOCK DOUBLER CHIPS

Intel needed to address several issues with their 50+MHz chips in 1989/1990. First was the motherboard question: what good is a 66MHz chip if no one knows how to build a motherboard that can use it? The second question came from the owners of existing systems. Weary of buying systems that seemed obsolete as soon as they were purchased, people wanted the ability to upgrade their systems without major surgery. So Intel came up with an alternative way to speed up CPUs: *clock doublers*.

The original clock doubler was a special 80486 (a processor I'll introduce later, but for the moment, understand that it was Intel's flagship processor between 1989 and 1993, the precursor to the Pentium family of chips) that could plug right into a CPU socket on a standard 25MHz motherboard. This special processor was designed to operate at 25MHz from the motherboard's point of view, but to operate internally at *twice* that rate—50MHz. Any internal action in the CPU, such as numeric calculations or moving data from one internal area of the CPU to another, was accomplished at 50MHz. But external instructions, such as loading data from memory or storing data to memory, happened more slowly, at 25MHz.

NOTE *Intel has names for these two clock rates, by the way. The external speed (25MHz, in the case of the preceding example) is called the* system bus frequency, *or front-side bus. The internal clock rate (50MHz, in the preceding example) is called the* processor core frequency.

Now, given that this chip ran at 25MHz for external instructions and 50MHz for internal instructions, what should Intel have called this chip—a 25MHz chip or a 50MHz chip? It's a bit of a conundrum, until you realize that the folks making the decision were, well, more oriented to the *marketing* side of Intel than the engineering side. So the new chip got the name 80486DX2-50—the *2* referring to the clock doubling, the *50* referring to its higher speed. They also offered an 80486DX2-66, a chip that plugged into a 33MHz motherboard but ran at 66MHz internally. *DX*, in those days, referred to a fuller, more capable system compared to its SX counterparts that were an interim upgrade (a 486SX was midway between a 386 and a 486).

At the time, Intel made an 80486DX-25 (a chip that ran both inside and out at 25MHz) and an 80486DX-50 (a chip that ran both inside and out at 50MHz), in addition to the 80486DX2-50. People often asked, "How fast is the DX2 *really*—is it more like the 'straight 25' or the 'straight 50'?" The answer was that it depended on what you were doing. CPU-intensive operations such as calculating spreadsheets or drawing complex graphics probably looked more like 50MHz, and input/output-oriented programs such as databases probably looked more like 25MHz. An in-between application, such as a word processor, fell somewhere in between. And, remember, Intel *also* offered the 80486DX-50 mentioned above. Many people *thought* they were buying a 50MHz DX but actually bought a "50MHz" DX2, and the difference in performance could be significant.

CLOCK TRIPLER CHIPS

In 1994, Intel introduced yet another variation on the 486 line, an 80486DX that was a *clock tripler*. Offered in 75MHz and 100MHz versions, these chips operated on motherboards that were 25MHz and 33MHz, respectively.

NOTE *Why does 33MHz tripled equal 100MHz? Why not 99MHz? Marketing reality again. After all, round up 99MHz and you get 100MHz. Well, kind of.*

Intel also took the opportunity to spruce up the internal workings of this new 486, and they added a bit more very fast internal memory (it's called *internal cache*, and I'll get to it soon), raising the amount inside the chip from 8KB (which the 80486 previously contained) to 16KB. That small amount of internal memory did indeed speed up the computer a bit in addition to the clock tripling, leading Intel to explore new realms of salesmanship by calling the new chip the *DX4*. That name is just DX4, by the way; there's no *80486* in the name. There's also a clock-tripled Pentium 200MHz chip that runs on a 66MHz motherboard.

CLOCK "ONE AND A HALFERS" AND SOME *REALLY* HOT CHIPS

We've seen clocks doubled and tripled. Are there clock-quadrupled chips? Yes, and quintupled chips, too: the 333MHz Pentium II runs 66MHz externally, and 333 internally, a fivefold increase. While figuring out how to build the 4x and 5x systems, Intel started playing around with noninteger multiples. Some CPUs have their clocks increased by *50 percent*, kind of a *one and a half clock*. The original Pentium models were offered in speeds of 60MHz and 66MHz. Later Pentium chips, code-named the P54C by Intel, were rated at 90 and 100MHz. They used 60MHz and 66MHz motherboards and increased their internal clock rates by half.

Which begs the question of why exactly there were two Pentium models with two clock rates so close. Why bother offering both a 60MHz and a 66MHz model?

The Pentium was a really tough chip to design. Every Intel chip design team is extremely limited in that no matter what the new chip's able to do, the one thing that it *must* do is run old software. This demand for backward compatibility makes for complex chips. *Complex* means lots of little components go into the chip, or, as insiders would say, the backward compatibility "needs a lot of silicon." Now, all that silicon generates heat. Put too much silicon in too small a place, and it starts to damage itself. Make the clock run faster, and the silicon gets even hotter. The Intel folks were just plain running up against some physical design barriers.

The Pentium's heat generation standards were shown in its technical specifications. According to Intel, the 66MHz Pentium should be expected to generate heat enough to bring the chip to 85 degrees. *Centigrade.*

That's about 185 degrees Fahrenheit. Good grief, you could toast marshmallows on that thing! (And, as I'll discuss later, heat isn't good for the electronics within a PC.) Intel tried its hardest to make a 66MHz Pentium chip work, but it was just so difficult that they ended up making Pentium chips that were mostly rejects. They *weren't* rejects, however, if they ran at a somewhat slower, *cooler*, rate, like 60MHz. So the 60MHz chips are, unfortunately, the rejects; Intel just lowered the standards to make them sellable.

Besides clock speed, however, another determining factor in chip heat is in the voltage that the chip operates on. The heat created by a chip is related to the square of the voltage. For a long time, most CPUs ran at 5 volts.

Intel decided to build the clock one and a half P54C chips with 3.3-volt power supplies. Five squared is 25; 3.3 squared is about 11. A 3.3-volt chip runs a lot cooler, which is why Intel uses 3.3 volts for the DX4, the newer Pentiums, and some later chips. Pentium Pros use 1.5 volts.

The DX4's use of 3.3 volts means that, paradoxically, it was the fastest 80486 chip, but was also the coolest.

CLOCK "TWO AND A HALFERS": THE PENTIUM OVERDRIVE

I know that all these chip speed permutations are getting a bit bizarre, but I'm not done yet. Intel also marketed a Pentium OverDrive chip, a chip that upgraded some existing 486 systems to Pentium-level speed.

A couple of caveats about this: First, this wouldn't work on all 486s; you had to have a 486 system that was designed with an extra-large socket. The extra-large socket had extra pins and was designed for the Pentium OverDrive chip. Second, it was kind of dubious how much like a Pentium the Pentium OverDrive could be, because the OverDrive is a 32-bit chip, whereas the true Pentium is a 64-bit chip (meaning it has a data path advantage because it's wider).

But enough bad news. The *good* news is that the Pentium OverDrive increased the internal speed of the OverDrive chip to two and a half times the speed of the motherboard. A Pentium OverDrive for a 25MHz 486 system runs internally at 63MHz. The OverDrive for a 33MHz system runs internally at 83MHz.

So What *Is* the Fastest Chip?

The past few years have seen record chip speed development, particularly with CPUs. It began in earnest in mid-1998, when Intel released two new Pentium II systems, the 350MHz and 400MHz chips. The next year brought the Pentium III (not a faster CPU by itself but with a faster clock speed) and AMD's first significantly different chip, the Athlon, which offered speeds of up to 700MHz. As I write this, we're now in the Pentium 4 era (Intel decided to stop using Roman numerals, apparently) with 2GHz systems on the market and 10GHz chipsets already in development. If you're feeling a bit of whiplash trying to keep up with hardware changes, you're not alone.

Intel was able to make the higher speeds work by using smaller components in a process first tested on the 333MHz chip, a design code-named *Deschutes*. (It was expensive to design, and Intel feared they were throwing all that research money down Deschutes… no, that's not true. Deschutes is a river in the West; that's where Intel gets its names for design projects, don't ask me why.)

Since the 300MHz and 333MHz systems both use a 66MHz system bus speed, the performance difference between a 300MHz system and a 333MHz system is quite small. The 350MHz and faster systems, however, have a system bus speed of 100 or 133MHz. The difference between a 333MHz (a 66 multiplied by 5—which actually comes out to 330, but, again, you'll see some variation like this) and a 350MHz (a 100 multiplied by 3.5) is quite significant, not so much because of the processor speed, but because the rest of the system runs at 100MHz versus 66MHz. One downside to the extra speed you get with the 100MHz bus, however, is that it runs a lot hotter than the 66MHz systems.

The heat problem is actually one reason for the Pentium Pro, the Pentium II Xeon, and the Pentium III Xeon chip. One of the Xeon's features is a built-in thermometer that monitors the chip's temperature. If the temperature gets above a safe level, the Xeon can safely close its process and shut down the system.

Before I move along, was your curiosity piqued by the mention of the 10GHz chips above? Those won't be seen for some time, although the rapid pace at which processor speeds are increasing makes this more of a *when* than an *if*. We're already at the point where you may not appreciate a great deal of difference between 800MHz and 1.5GHz in your usual day-to-day work at your PC. More times than not, you are more likely to get bottlenecked by your online communications speed (especially if you're using a dial-up connection on a traditional modem over analog phone lines) long before you feel your CPU is too slow for the task at hand.

So the power of the future may not be in the overall speed of the desktop processor, but in its capability to perform *parallel instruction processing*, or sharing work among multiple processors all working together.

But back to the 10GHz: analysts predict that speed like this will finally break the barrier between PC and human interaction. Even today, we're still experiencing problems making speech recognition and other human-to-PC interactions work as they should so that humans can work with PCs more naturally. Voice and handwriting recognition have come a long way from where they started, but the technology is still in a very rudimentary, slow form. Heavy-duty PC performance is required for success here, and that may be one of the chief roles played by processors faster than 2GHz.

A WORD ON OVERCLOCKING AND MATCHING CLOCK SPEEDS

Clock rates on chips and clock rates on motherboards are related. If the motherboard is built for 100MHz, then you should get a CPU that can handle a 100MHz clock. (Note I'm talking about the external or *system bus frequency*, not the internal rate.) Similarly, it's not a good idea to get a chip that's designed to run at a higher clock rate than the motherboard. The fit between motherboard and chip should be "just right."

Why is this true? Well, consider what happens if you get a chip that's too slow for the motherboard. For example, the Intel Pentium 150MHz chip had an external clock rate of 50MHz and was tripled. If you put it on a motherboard that is designed to provide a 66MHz clock signal to the processor, then the processor wouldn't be able to keep up with that rate. The result is that the chip would fail and overheat, possibly permanently damaging it. In the reverse situation, suppose you had a motherboard that put out a 66MHz clock signal, and you installed a 400MHz Xeon, which can handle an external clock rate of 100MHz. You wouldn't be driving the "400MHz" chip at 100MHz, you'd be driving it at 66MHz. It's a clock quadrupler, so the chip would dutifully quadruple that value, giving you a 266MHz Xeon. (Okay, again, we have a case where 66×4 isn't quite 266, but welcome to PC hardware!) That would be a waste of money.

This underscores a general point about chips and sockets: put a chip in that's too slow, and it will overheat and fail. Install a chip that's too fast, and it will work fine, but you're throwing your money away.

That all sounds logical, but some people point out that the difference between slow chips and fast chips is often luck anyway, because chip manufacturers just build a few thousand chips and then test them to see which ones are fast and which are slow. When testing, chip makers are conservative, goes the argument, so they might rate a chip at xMHz that could actually work at $1.3x$ or the like. Modern motherboards let you dial in any clock rate you want, so people buy a middle-rated chip and dial up a high clock rate. If the system doesn't crash immediately, they figure they've gotten lucky and bought a fast chip for the price of a slow one.

This is called *overclocking*. I don't recommend it, and basically here's why: Intel gets to charge more money for faster chips, and Intel's profit ratio indicates to me that they have no aversion to a healthy ROI (return on investment, that is). Yes, I suppose a few slip through the cracks, but in general a chip rated at x is no better than x. The symptoms of overclocking can be quite subtle and masquerade as problems with a hard disk, or keyboard, or something else. In addition, overclocking by its very nature invalidates your product warranty, so you're on your own. Overclocking can also cause other problems, as you'll read later in the "PC Expansion Buses" section. One thing you should be aware of is that Intel has now locked down the ability to overclock in most of its product line, driving true overclocking fans to other makes of processor.

Microcode Efficiency and Pipelines

As you just read, one way to make a chip faster is to simply drive it faster, by running up its clock in some way. Another way is to design the chip to make better use of each clock cycle.

MICROCODE IMPROVEMENTS

Microcode was a big advancement in that it allowed the CPU's instruction set to be implemented as a series of microinstructions. It's also called microprogramming. Microcode improvements have been an important part of Intel's strategy for ever-faster chips over the years; for example, the 8088 chip was succeeded by the 80188 chip, a chip that seemed to do all the same things that the 8088 does. Where's the difference?

In the case of the 8088 versus the 80188 (and also in the case of the 80386 versus the 80486), a lot of the difference lies in its *microcode efficiency*. Put simply, microcode efficiency just means: "How many clock ticks does it take a CPU to get a particular task done?" For example, an 8088 can calculate an integer division—that is, a division without any decimal places; divide 7 by 2 on an 8088 and you get 3, not 3.5. And to make matters worse, it can take the 8088 up to 70 clock cycles to get that done. The 80188, in contrast, can do it in only 25 clock cycles. Compare two machines that are identical except that one runs an 80188 and the other runs an 8088, and the 80188 will be able to do some things faster than an 8088.

The 80386 and 80486 are also similar in many ways, as you'll learn later in this chapter, but they differ in microcode efficiency. The simplest useful instruction that you can do with an 80386 is the MOV AX, BX, an assembly-language command that invokes a microcode instruction that moves data from a storage area inside the microcomputer, called BX, to another storage area inside the microcomputer, called AX. Technically, it's called a *register-to-register transfer*. All register operations on an 80386 require at least two clock cycles. The 80486 was designed so that all the two-cycle register instructions on the 80386 run in just one clock cycle on the 80486. One of the places that Intel is always looking to improve its chips is via the chip's microcode.

PIPELINING INSTRUCTIONS

By now, the folks at Intel had squeezed a lot of the "juice" out of improving microcode efficiency. So they needed some other tricks to continue to beat better speed out of newer chips. So starting with the Pentium, Intel has designed CPUs with smarter and smarter *pipelines.*

What's a pipeline? Well, if you peek inside the workings of a CPU, you'll see that it looks somewhat like an assembly line—I'll get specific about what happens in that line in a moment, but for now just visualize an assembly line, like one that builds cars. Instead of turning out cars, however, CPUs turn out executed instructions, and they don't call it an assembly line; they call it a pipeline. With pipelining, a bit of data goes to the first station in the pipeline; then after that bit moves on to the next station, another bit takes its place at the first station. With pipelining, there's a bit along every station of the process. So instead of each bit of data having to wait for the preceding bit to go through the entire pipeline before starting off, a bit moves to each station along the way immediately after its predecessor leaves.

Now, if you wanted to assemble more cars per hour, you could approach it in two ways. The obvious way is to just try to get all of the workers to do their jobs faster, enabling you to run the assembly line faster. That would be like taking an existing CPU and increasing its clock rate, upping its megahertz/gigahertz. It's not a bad approach to speed, but there's another way. Instead of just trying to do the same old thing, only faster, you could reengineer the entire process, streamlining the steps along the way.

What happens along a CPU's pipeline? It varies from chip to chip, but basically you can break down the execution of any instruction into five basic steps:

Fetch   Get the next instruction, either from random access memory (RAM) outside the CPU (on CPUs before the 486) or from the CPU's "instruction cache" memory (on 486 and later chips).

Decode   Instructions differ in length; some are 1 byte long, and some are several bytes long. A given instruction, such as a MOVE command, may come in several different flavors: move from one location inside the CPU chip to a location outside the CPU chip, move from one place inside the CPU to another place inside the CPU, and so on. Even though the instruction differences are subtle, they're important. The decode section handles that.

Get the operands   Most instructions require data to work on. Simply saying MOVE means nothing; the CPU must know *what* you want to move *where*. The *what* and *where* are operands. Similarly, if you tell the CPU, "Add 34 and 22," then *34* and *22* are the operands.

Execute   As the Nike guys say, just do it. Whatever the instruction said to do—add, move, divide, compare, or whatever—now's the time to get it done.

Write back results   After the operation has been done, the results of the operation—both the values created and any status information—get written to registers inside the computer.

By breaking up the task of executing an instruction into smaller subtasks, chip makers can divide the job of chip design into smaller chunks, and that in turn makes it possible to build these subsystems faster and faster. In other words, it's easier to build a CPU made up of five fast subpieces than it is to build a CPU out of one fast piece. This process of *fetch, decode, get operands, execute,* and *write back results* is called the *CPU pipeline*. Some CPUs use multiple pipelines, but I'll discuss that in a few pages.

Some of Intel's competitors tried to outdo Intel in the speed department by changing the structure of a pipeline. Cyrix made a chip called the M1 that used seven substeps rather than five. AMD made a CPU called the K5 with six substeps, and NexGen made an Nx586 with seven substeps. Intel even outdid itself with the Pentium Pro/Pentium II/Celeron/Xeon, which divided its pipelines into 14 steps!

Intel has stated a goal that, ultimately, some future member of the x86 family will execute each of its instructions in just one clock cycle. (Then again, world peace and funding Social Security are two goals that the government doesn't seem to be getting too far on, so don't hold your breath on the one-cycle promise either.)

Word Size

Every computer uses internal work areas, kind of like workbenches. These workbenches are called *registers*.

Any computer can be programmed to manipulate any size number, but the bigger the number, the longer it takes. The largest number that the computer can manipulate in one operation is determined by its *word size*. This is 8, 16, or 32 bits.

Think of it this way: If I ask you, "What is 5 times 6?" you'd answer, "30," immediately—you did it in one operation. If I ask, "What is 55 times 66?" you will do a series of steps to arrive at the answer. That's because 55 is larger than your word size and 5 isn't. If you had a bigger "workbench," a bigger word size, then you could get complex calculations done in fewer steps and therefore more quickly. That's one reason why a 386, with 32-bit registers, is faster than a 286, with 16-bit registers.

The 8088 through 80286 chips used 16-bit words. The 80386 through Pentium Pro/II and III/Celeron/Xeon systems used 32-bit words. The Pentium 4 also uses 32-bit words, but the floating point and multimedia registers of the chip have been increased to 128 bits to increase the speed of data transfers.

Data Path

No matter how large the computer's word size, the data must be transported into the CPU. This is the width of the computer's "loading door," or the *data path*. It can also be 8, 16, 32, or 64 bits. Obviously, a wider door will allow more data to be transported in less time than will a narrower door.

Consider, for example, an 8MHz 8088 versus an 8MHz 8086. The *only difference* between the 8088 and the 8086 is that the 8088 has an 8-bit data path, and the 8086 has a 16-bit data path. Now, both the 8088 and the 8086 have 16-bit registers, so a programmer would issue the same command to load 16 bits into either one—the command MOV AX,0200 will move the 16-bit value 200 hex into a 16-bit register called AX. That will take twice as long on the 8088 as it would on the 8086, because the 8086 can do it in one operation while the 8088 takes two. Note what's going on—although they're both 8MHz computers, the 8088 machine computes more slowly for some operations.

Now, you can see that the 8086 is a faster, more powerful chip than the 8088. But did you know that the 8088 was released *later* than the 8086? It's true; here's why.

When the 8086 was first released in 1977, it was one of the first microprocessors with a 16-bit data path. Almost every popular microprocessor-based computer available at the time was based on a CPU with an 8-bit data path. (*Almost* because the LSI-11 microprocessor had a 16-bit data path, and a few Heathkit computers used the LSI-11.) Because the CPUs all expected 8 bits whenever they *read* data and provided 8 bits when they *wrote* data, the motherboards of computers in those days contained enough circuitry to transport 8 bits around.

Now, the 8086 was a neat-looking chip, because its 16 bits seemed just the stuff to build a powerful microcomputer. But consider the *bad* side of a 16-bit CPU: it requires a 16-bit motherboard. An 8086's motherboard must contain enough circuitry to transport *16* bits around, so it could be *twice* as expensive as an 8-bit motherboard of the same type. That put the 8086 at an economic disadvantage. (It may seem like a trivial matter now, but in the late '70s, hardware was more expensive, and an 8086-based motherboard was significantly more expensive than an 8-bit motherboard.)

So the folks at Intel said to themselves, "How can we offer the power of the 8086 and still keep motherboard prices down?" And so they built the 8088, a year after the 8086's release. Inside, the 8088 is identical to the 8086. The only difference is in the size of its "front door"—the path that the 8088 uses to transport data into and out of the chip. Because it is only 8 bits wide, motherboard designers could easily adapt existing designs to the new chip. As a result, the 8088 enjoyed a moderate amount of success from 1979 to 1981. Of course, after IBM released the PC in 1981 based on the 8088, moderate eventually changed to amazing.

History repeated itself in 1988 with the 80386SX. The original 80386 was introduced in 1985—Intel's next-generation chip with a 32-bit data path. The 386 did fairly well fairly quickly, but not quickly enough for Intel. The 286 sold well also, but the 286 had a problem as far as Intel was concerned: Intel didn't *own* the 286. By that, I mean that while Intel invented the 286, it had also licensed several vendors to make the 286, so many 286s being sold were lining the pockets of AMD, Fairchild, Siemens, and a number of other chip builders. Intel wanted *all* the profit from the 386, however, so they refused to license the 386 to any other company.

The 286 was not only a cheap chip, it was also a 16-bit chip, and a pure 16-bit chip at that—both word size and data path. That meant that 286 PCs could be built around 16-bit motherboards, and 32-bit motherboards were going to be just plain expensive. Therefore, 286-based PCs would be *tons* cheaper than 386 PCs, so more 286s would sell than 386s; Intel didn't like that. So they embarked on a campaign of what has to be characterized as chip infanticide. They ran a huge advertising campaign advising people to stay away from the 286 and to buy 386-based PCs. They *also* answered the manufacturer's concerns about the costs of building a 32-bit motherboard by offering the 80386SX.

The 80386SX was an 80386 with one difference: its "front door" was 16 bits, not 32 bits. Vendors liked that because they could take their old 16-bit 80286 motherboards, modify their design a bit, and *voilà!* They could offer "386 technology." After a year, it became clear that the original 80386 needed a real name to distinguish it from its less powerful cousin's name, so it became known as the 80386DX.

The 80486 line of chips also included an 80486SX, but was it a 16-bit chip? No. It *was* a chip with reduced functionality, but the reduction was not due to changes in data path. Instead, the 486SX was different from the 486DX in the way that it calculated arithmetic. You'll learn more about that type of processing in the upcoming section "Numeric Coprocessors."

The Pentium, MMX, Pentium Pro, Pentium II, Pentium III, Pentium 4, Celeron, and Xeon chips actually have a data path *larger* than the word size; these chips have a 64-bit data path and 32-bit word sizes. What good is it having a front door that's twice the size of the workbench? Again, Pentium and later chips aren't so much faster because of higher megahertz, but because of internal design—to use an old phrase, you might say that they don't work *harder*, they work *smarter*. Once Intel figured that it could only do so much with a single 32-bit system, they decided to speed up the process by essentially giving the Pentium a *second* workbench, a second pipeline, as you'll read in a few pages. That second pipeline needs feeding, hence the value of a larger data path.

As I've stated earlier, the early Pentium line of chips also included an SX-like chip called the Pentium OverDrive chip. The Pentium uses a 64-bit data path, and 486 manufacturers wanted to include Pentium compatibility on their motherboards. However, 486 motherboards are 32-bit in nature. How, then, to offer Pentium compatibility? Simple: enter the Pentium OverDrive chip, which features a 32-bit data path. Kind of a Pentium SX, you might say. Was it a good idea? Sure, if your 486 motherboard could accommodate it (a few could). But, again, that'll all make sense when you get to the discussion of instruction pipelines, coming soon in the section "Superscalar and Instruction Pipelines." But first, let's look at yet another way to speed up your computer: give it a little shot of super-fast memory, *internal cache*.

Internal Cache Memory

When people talk of RAM on a computer, they're talking about chips that the CPU uses to store its programs and data as it works, chips external to the CPU. The increasing speed of CPUs has driven a corresponding need for faster RAM.

THE MEMORY TRADEOFF: SRAM VERSUS DRAM

RAM is commonly designed to be *dynamic* RAM, a simpler and cheaper design than its alternative, *static* RAM. I'll discuss static versus dynamic RAM in more detail in Chapter 8, "Semiconductor Memory," but for now, just understand that RAM presents a very fundamental tradeoff to system designers. Those designers can build computers to use either dynamic RAM or static RAM, and here's the tradeoff:

◆ Dynamic RAM (DRAM) is relatively cheap, but it is also relatively slow. In fact, no one makes DRAM that's fast enough to match speeds of modern CPUs.

◆ Static RAM (SRAM) is fast—it can be as fast as any of Intel's or AMD's chips. But it's expensive, up to 10 to 20 times as expensive for a given amount of memory as DRAM.

At this point, the only way to build RAM that is as fast as the CPU is to populate the entire PC with static RAM, but that would be much too expensive. So PCs use a lot of dynamic RAM, which unfortunately sacrifices speed. To get back some of that speed, Intel puts a small amount of fast static RAM right into the CPU. That way, oft-used data needn't be accessed via the relatively slow DRAM; instead, the CPU can keep the most important data right by its side, in this small cache of storage. In fact, that's what it's called—*cache RAM*. It first appeared in some of the faster 386-based systems, because designers included space on the motherboards of high-performance systems for a bit of SRAM.

L1 CACHE, L2 CACHE, AND THE 80486 FAMILY

Many computers designed since about 1987 have included cache RAM on their motherboards. The 80486 took the idea of cache a step further, however, in that the 80486 line of chips was the first in the x86 family to include cache RAM right on the CPU. With the exception of the DX4, they all contain 8KB of internal cache. The DX4 doubled that amount to 16KB. But even that small amount of extra, fast memory significantly improved CPU performance. Of course, while a few KB of cache is *nice*, it'd be nicer to have even more.

Most desktop motherboards today add from 64KB to 2MB more static RAM cache to the motherboard. That's not *internal* cache, however, because it's not internal to the CPU. It's *external* cache and it's commonly called *L2 cache*. The internal cache in the 80486 and later processors is called *L1 cache*. L1 cache is built into the processor and usually runs at a speed nearly equaling or equaling the internal processor speed (the *core processor frequency* in Intel-ese).

SOME SYSTEMS ARE "BROKE"

L2 cache is terrific for speed, but notice that I said most *desktop* PCs include cache. That's *very* important to anyone trying to compare the power of laptop computers to that of desktops. For example, back in 1999 I had a 166MHz clone Pentium desktop. I also had a 266MHz Digital Ultra HiNote 2000 laptop. The HiNote was a wonderful machine, but put it next to the 166MHz desktop and they seemed to be about the same speed; if anything, the "slower" 166MHz machine often seemed faster. Why? Because the 166 had 256KB of L2 static cache on its motherboard. The HiNote, like most laptops of its era, had no L2 cache.

This is less true today, of course, although the mechanics of a laptop still affect speed compared to desktop units with much fuller hardware. Basically, most laptop designs are "broke"—by which I mean that they have less cache overall than their desktop cousins.

By the same token, many inexpensive *store clones* (clones you could buy off the shelf when you bought your garden tools at Sears or your barbecue at Price Club) of the original Pentium era also eliminated the L2 cache as a cost-saving measure. Some enabled you (for a considerable price) to add an L2 cache later, if desired, while others did not.

TIP   Removing the L2 cache temporarily (on older systems that permit it) can sometimes help resolve problems. For example, on problematic installations or upgrades of Windows on PCs with an L2 cache, the short-term disabling of the L2 cache will let you install or upgrade Windows, and you can then reenable the L2 cache to working status.

PENTIUM CACHE

Speaking of the Pentium, part of how it produced better-than-486 performance was through its cache. The Pentium's cache system is better than the 486's in four ways. First, the Pentium has twice as much cache, with two 8KB caches—one for data, one for program code. (A later variation of the Pentium, the MMX chip, had double that amount, a 16KB data cache and a 16KB instruction cache.) Second, the cache's method of organizing its cached data is more efficient, using a *write-back* algorithm. The opposite of a write-back algorithm, a *write-through* algorithm (used by the 486), forces data written to the SRAM cache memory to be immediately written to the slower DRAM memory. That means that memory *reads* can come out of the cache quickly, but memory *writes* must always occur at the slower DRAM time. Reasoning that not every piece of information written to memory *stays* in memory very long, the Pentium's cache algorithm puts off writing data from SRAM to DRAM for as long as possible. Third, the cache controller wastes time in searching to see whether an item is in the cache—the Pentium reduces that time by dividing the cache into smaller caches, each of which can be searched more quickly; that technique uses a *two-way set-associative cache*.

To explain the fourth way in which the Pentium's cache is better than the 486's, I have to first make an important point about what a cache must do. You may know that a cache must guess what data and program code the CPU will need soon, and then go get that data before the CPU asks for it. But guessing what the CPU will need isn't a straightforward task, particularly when there are decisions to be made. For example, suppose the cache sees that the CPU is currently executing some instructions that mean, "Compare value A with value B. If A is greater than B, then set the value *maximum* to A; otherwise, set the value *maximum* to B." That simple statement boils down to a bunch of instructions, instructions in memory that had better be in the cache if the Pentium is going to be able to continue running without delays. But since the cache controller can't know whether the CPU will take the "A is greater than B" or "B is greater than A" fork in the road, it doesn't know which result's code to go grab and put in the cache. For years, *mainframe* cache controllers have used a technique called *branch prediction* to guess which way the CPU will go, and now the Pentium and later PC chips have cache controllers built into them with branch prediction capabilities. So that's *four* ways that the Pentium line of chips makes better use of your memory than the 486 did.

THE PENTIUM PRO, PENTIUM II, PENTIUM III, PENTIUM 4, CELERON, XEON, AND ITANIUM CACHES

What about the Pentium Pro and its more recent cousins, the Pentium II and III, the Celeron, and the Xeon, Pentium 4, and Itanium chips? Well, there's some good news and some bad news.

With the Pentium Pro, Intel introduced the revolutionary step of making a sort of double-sized chip, a chip that looked like two Pentium chips side by side. The second "chip," however, was a

512KB L2 memory, a built-in cache RAM. This cache was terrific in that it could talk to the CPU at half of the CPU's full internal speed (the core processor frequency), not the external bus speed. Motherboards could be designed with even more external cache, however, and some Pentium Pro systems sold with as much as 1024KB of external cache, a mix of the built-in L2 cache and some chips on the motherboard. Because any chips on the motherboard can communicate with the processor only at the external bus speed rather than the internal speed, you might call that on-motherboard cache a sort of level 3 cache. The Pentium Pro has 16KB of L1 cache, as did the original Pentium.

With the Pentium II, III, and 4, Intel created a larger rectangular package called a Single Edge Cartridge (SEC), which no longer allows external cache. You can see a Pentium III in Figure 3.5.

FIGURE 3.5

Pentium III in
SEC package

The result is that you couldn't design a motherboard for a Pentium II or III that contains any cache. The Pentium II/III had its built-in 512KB of L2 cache, but that's it. (The Pentium II/III also had more L1 cache than the Pentium Pro, 16KB of data and 16KB of instruction cache, for a total of 32KB.) And that leads to an interesting comparison of the older Pentium Pro versus the Pentium II/III. Some of the Pro motherboards had room for 1MB (1000 kilobytes) of cache. Therefore, you could benchmark a Pentium Pro at 200MHz (the fastest that they were built) versus a Pentium II at 333MHz—the Pentium Pro can actually be faster, because it's got 1024KB of cache versus the Pentium II and III's half megabyte of cache!

The Pentium II/III Xeon chip addressed that problem and offered considerably improved performance for two reasons. First, the Xeon communicated between its built-in L2 cache and its processor at full-core processor speed—a 600MHz Xeon talked to its L2 cache at a full 600MHz. Second, the Xeon came with up to 1024KB of built-in L2 cache.

But I haven't mentioned the Celeron. What kind of L2 cache does it come with? Originally it had none. But Intel's customers weren't very happy about the Celeron's missing cache, so current models of the Celeron also have cache memory (smaller than the Pentium II and III, but fast).

Table 3.2 summarizes the top speed and L2 cache of some of the more popular CPUs of recent years.

TABLE 3.2: MAJOR CPUS, THEIR SPEED, AND L2 CACHE

CPU	TOP SPEED	CLOCK SPEED (MHZ)	L2 CACHE SIZE
Pentium II	450MHz	66/100	256–512KB
VIA C3	800MHz	133	64KB

Continued on next page

TABLE 3.2: MAJOR CPUs, THEIR SPEED, AND L2 CACHE

CPU	TOP SPEED	CLOCK SPEED (MHz)	L2 CACHE SIZE
Xeon	800MHz	100	512KB, 1MB, 2MB
Pentium III	1GHz	133	256KB
Itanium	1GHz	100	4MB
Duron	1.2GHz	200	64KB
Celeron	1.2GHz	100	128KB
Athlon	1.6GHz	266	256KB
Pentium 4	2.2GHz	400	256KB

NOTE *That 2.2GHz top speed for the Pentium 4 is as-of Spring 2002. Intel has already announced plans for a 4GHz P4 chip to be released sometime in 2003—so things keep getting faster, almost every day!*

ITANIUM: NOW WE'RE TALKING L3 CACHE

You've already learned a little bit about the Itanium (formerly the Merced) IA-64 processor. Not only does the Itanium have the power of the Xeon-level L1 and 4MB L2 cache on board the chip itself, it adds up to 4MB of L3 cache (with an option for an L4 cache that can be added by an original equipment manufacturer (OEM). The L3 cache, smaller than a 3-by-5-inch index card, isn't on the chip itself but is contained in the processor package. The Itanium also has its own unique form factor, Slot M, and both the 800MHz and 1000MHz editions will operate on a 100MHz motherboard.

Numeric Coprocessors

Look at an early PC or XT, and next to the 8088 is an empty socket. From 1981 to 1983, IBM wouldn't say officially for what the socket on the PC was intended. But then they announced what everyone already knew: it was for the Intel 8087, a special-purpose microprocessor. The 8087 microprocessor is good for only one class of tasks: floating-point numeric operations.

Since then, all succeeding Intel CPUs offered some way of incorporating a floating-point computation unit. In fact, all the current processors have a built-in *floating-point processor unit* (*FPU*).

THE MMX: A MATRIX MATH COPROCESSOR

By the time the Pentium arrived, it seemed like there wasn't much to say anymore about coprocessors, because even the lowliest Pentium had the coprocessor circuitry built in.

But then a newer form of the Pentium arrived, the *MMX* (MMX, by the way, is purportedly not an acronym, because it doesn't officially stand for anything, but it basically means *multimedia extensions*). MMX technology is an enhancement to Intel CPUs that is designed to make PCs faster and more colorful when they're handling multimedia applications (interactive video, virtual reality, and high-quality 3D) and communications applications. The enhancement is provided by MMX versions of Intel chips, which, in addition to their regular features, respond to 57 instructions that are oriented to highly parallel operations with multimedia and communications data types. Multimedia apps do lots of computation, lots of tasks in parallel, and tend to use small integer data types. The 57 new microcode instructions that constitute MMX technology were designed to help speed up the core algorithms and thus improve overall application performance. Having the MMX instructions in a Pentium chip makes it easier to build code to do multimedia operations such as simultaneous, real-time activities. An example is multiple channels of audio, near-TV-quality video or animation, and Internet communication all running in the same application. And, in fact, MMX computers that I've worked on that have video capture boards can capture much higher-quality video than comparable non-MMX computers can with the same video capture hardware.

NOTE   *Every Pentium model since the MMX was introduced is MMX-compatible—meaning that the PII, the PIII, the Xeon, and the Celeron all support the multimedia instructions packaged into the Pentium MMX.*

The 57 instructions use a technique known as *Single Instruction, Multiple Data (SIMD)*, which means that a single instruction operates on multiple pieces of data in parallel. For example, with a single MMX instruction, up to eight integer pairs can be added together in parallel. This parallel operation uses 64-bit registers. Depending on the operation, these are defined as eight 8-bit bytes, four 16-bit words, two 32-bit double words, or one 64-bit quad word.

MMX technology was designed to simplify writing things that must manipulate matrix-oriented data, applications such as:

◆   Video capture programs

◆   Graphical manipulation programs such as Paint Shop Pro

◆   Graphics-intensive games

◆   2D and, to a lesser extent, 3D graphics

◆   Speech recognition

◆   Data compression

The MMX represents a specific policy goal for Intel: *let the system processor do all the computing.* Years ago, Intel sought to build terrific video capture boards around special-purpose chips designed to do one and only one thing: convert an analog video signal into a digital signal quickly. But Intel realized that they'd rather sell 100 million Pentium II chips a year than sell 50 million Pentium II chips, 5 million video capture chips, 10 million sound chips, and so on. So they started encouraging multimedia vendors to build cheaper boards that offload more and more of their work onto the main processor. The result is, of course, that people want faster and faster processors. The MMX's 57 new commands were added to the Pentium to make it easier for the processor to get those jobs done.

Does any software *require* the MMX? There are quite a few applications, but most of them are video games. Thus, if someone asks, "Is Windows XP (or 98 or 2000) MMX-compatible?" the answer is, "Yes." MMX CPUs have all the same operation codes (opcodes) as older CPUs, and the operating systems mentioned here have not been written to require the MMX opcodes.

What this means, of course, is that the new MMX-type processors should run all your old applications just fine. It doesn't mean, however, that you, personally, can somehow add MMX technology to your old-but-still-cranking 486 or Pentium chip. MMX instructions are new instructions directly incorporated into the processor, and this can be accomplished only when the chip is manufactured.

Which CPUs are MMX-compatible? The first MMX-capable CPU was *called* the MMX. It was a modified Pentium. But the Pentium chip didn't have enough room to be able to handle both the floating-point numeric coprocessor support as well as the matrix MMX support at the same time, so unfortunately when you're running MMX-specific software on an MMX, the floating-point support is disabled. That's too bad, because whenever you're doing matrix-specific calculations, you're likely to be also doing complex math (logs, sines, exponentials). The job still gets done, but without the floating-point coprocessor, complex math takes longer to do. Thus, the MMX gets faster on matrix operations but gets slower on floating-point. Is it a good tradeoff? Sorry, there's just no good answer to this one; it all depends upon the software you're running.

The next MMX was the Pentium II. The Pentium II is just a Pentium Pro with MMX circuits added. The good news is that the Pentium II has the power to simultaneously run both the MMX commands and the floating-point command—very cool! Clearly Intel regretted releasing a chip that made software choose between matrix and floating-point, leading some to wonder if the correct name of the Pentium II should really be the *Repent*ium chip. In any case, the Pentium II was soon joined by a lower-priced model (the Celeron) and a higher-priced model (the Xeon), both close cousins, and then by the Pentium III and Pentium 4—so close, in fact, that they have MMX circuitry as well.

Superscalar and Instruction Pipelines

Remember I said earlier that the Pentium and later chips try to "work smarter, not harder"? I'll explain that in a bit more detail here. As time goes on, Intel tries to speed up their CPUs. But they're greatly hampered by the need for backward compatibility. So they use another way to make the Pentium faster: basically, they put two CPUs into it.

THE PENTIUM PIPELINE STRUCTURE

As you read earlier, the circuitry that constitutes a CPU—registers, instruction decoders, and arithmetic/logic units—are all called *instruction pipelines* by CPU designers. All the Intel CPUs that I've discussed, up to and including the 486 family, had just one pipeline in each chip, which is a techie way of saying, "The 486 and predecessors could do only one thing at a time."

In contrast, there are essentially two CPUs in the Pentium chip. The first one is like a 486DX, a CPU with floating-point capabilities built right into it. The second is a 486SX, lacking a floating-point unit. (Why didn't they put two floating-point units in? It would have made the thing bigger, hotter, and more expensive.) That means that the Pentium is essentially a parallel-processing CPU, with the capability to do two things at once. Those two CPUs-within-a-CPU are called the *U and V pipelines*, and having more than one pipeline makes the Pentium a *superscalar* CPU. (Why not parallel processing or multiprocessing or dual processing, I don't know—*superscalar* is the buzzword.)

The neat part of this dual pipelining is that the Pentium uses both pipelines *automatically*. It takes a simple non-Pentium-aware program, reads it, and divides it into two pipelines. Now, that's not always possible, because some programs contain internal *dependencies*, but the Pentium does the best that it can.

For example, consider these three commands:

A = 3

B = 2

C = A + B

The first two commands, A = 3 and B = 2, are *not* dependent. You can manipulate A and manipulate B, and there's no interaction. Once they're done, then you're set to do C = A + B. As a result, A = 3 could go over the U pipeline while B = 2 goes over the V pipeline, and then C = A + B could run on the U pipeline once A = 3 was done. But now consider this sequence:

A = 1

A = A + 2

The second command can't be executed until the first command is done. Therefore, in this case, the Pentium would be forced to put the first command, A = 1, into one of the pipelines and then wait for it to finish before executing A = A + 2.

THE PENTIUM PRO/II/III/4/CELERON/XEON PIPELINE STRUCTURE

If two pipelines sound like a lot, then hold onto your hat, because the Pentium Pro/II/III/4/Celeron/Xeon chips contain an even more complex system with (depending on how you look at it) three or five pipelines. How does it work?

Think of the Pentium Pro family pipelines as being organized in three major pieces:

◆ Decode

◆ Execute

◆ Clean up

The decode section works as it does on earlier chips, just mainly fetching an instruction and figuring out what it needs to do—integer math, floating-point math, a memory read or write, or something else. There are three decoding pipelines, which means that the Pentium Pro can get three instructions ready at the same time. There aren't any interdependency problems with the decode phase.

The second phase executes the actual instruction. Because this takes the most time, Intel included *five* execution pipelines. Any one of them can perform very simple operations, but for more demanding (or time-consuming) tasks, there are specialists. Two of the pipelines can do only integer computations, like the V pipeline on a Pentium. Two of the pipelines can do both integer computations and floating-point computations, like the U pipeline on a Pentium. And one of the pipelines specializes in transferring data to and from memory. As with the Pentium's two-pipeline system, there's no guarantee that all five pipelines will remain active at all times, because interdependent code may, once again, make that impossible.

The Pentium 4 has made major improvements to the Pentium's two-pipeline system. Called the NetBurst microarchitecture, its features include hyper-pipelined technology, a rapid execution engine, a 400MHz system bus, and an execution trace cache. The hyper-pipelined technology doubles the pipeline depth in the Pentium 4 processor, allowing the processor to reach much higher core frequencies. The rapid execution engine allows the two integer arithmetic and logic units (ALUs) in the processor to run at twice the core frequency, which allows many integer instructions to execute in half a clock tick.

Recall that the older Pentium had to examine the incoming stream of program instructions and determine the dependencies within that stream; the Pentium Pro and later chips have the same need. For nonoptimized code, the Pentium Pro family has often proven to be fast but not amazingly so. In fact, in February 1996, *BYTE* magazine reported that the Pentium Pro ran 16-bit applications (including the 16-bit parts of Windows 95) *slower* than the Pentium did, because the Pentium Pro was "tuned" to run 32-bit applications better than the Pentium. That's why if you're still running Windows 3.1 or DOS programs, *or* if you're running several of those older programs like Word-Perfect 5.1 for DOS under Windows 95/98/NT, then you may not see particularly impressive behavior. You need *truly* 32-bit code (and code optimized for the Pentium Pro family) to see the performance improvements in the Pentium Pro, the Pentium II/III, the Celeron, and the Xeon (although the Celeron's lack of cache or limited cache makes it a pretty lame performer no matter what you do). And it's sadly true that there's not all that much code around that's really tuned to use 32 bits; even "new" 32-bit software such as Office 2000 and even Windows 2000 (as an operating system) still contains a lot of old 16-bit code. In my experience, the programs that are best tuned to use 32 bits are the high-end stuff—SQL database engines and file/print servers—and what some might call the low end—games. Personal productivity programs don't seem to be a priority for performance tuning; instead, the vendors seem more intent on adding thousands of features.

The Pentium 4 has almost three times the theoretical processor bus bandwidth of a Pentium III. A 400MHz system bus and *hyper-pipelined technology* (a 20-stage pipeline compared to the 10-stage pipeline in the PIII) increase overall CPU bandwidth to a theoretical maximum of about 3.2GB per second and raise the ceiling for clock speeds.

A final thought on superscalar architecture: it's now possible to take a second look at the Pentium OverDrive chip, the Pentium chip that fit on specially designed 486 motherboards. Was it a good idea? Well, consider what the Pentium really is: two 32-bit chips. As long as there are 64 bits feeding it, then the Pentium makes sense. But taking two 32-bit pipelines and forcing them to share a single 32-bit data path seems likely to end up creating a chip that only performs like a single 32-bit chip. (Maybe that's why Intel took so long to finally release it.)

Memory Addressable by a CPU

Megabytes are a unit of storage size—just about the amount of space needed to store a million characters. People use this term to talk about the size of primary memory—RAM, the kind of memory that goes in expansion boards, the kind of memory that Excel can run out of if you have a large spreadsheet—as well as secondary memory, which are disk drives. When most people say *memory*, they are talking about *primary* memory, so memory means chips or RAM. Folks usually just say *disk* memory when that's what they mean, rather than secondary memory.

Disk memory is also not *volatile*, which means that when you shut it off, it retains its data. Remove power from a memory chip (which happens whenever you turn the machine off), and it forgets whatever it contained. That's why you have to save your work to disk before shutting off the machine.

But using the same type of measurement (megabytes) for both disks and memory confuses people. I'll say, "I work with a Pentium 5 with 512MB of memory," and they'll think, "What good is *that*? Even I have *40 gigabytes* (40 billion bytes) on my PC." I was talking about primary memory— 512MB of RAM. I didn't say anything at all about how much hard disk space I've got. *They* were thinking of hard disk space and didn't tell me how much memory their PC has. (I hope it would be at the very least 64MB, and I wouldn't outfit a computer nowadays with less than 256MB.) End of digression.

You can't just keep adding memory to your PC indefinitely. A particular chip can *address* only a certain size of memory. For the oldest CPUs, this amount was 16,384 bytes—a 16KB memory. The original IBM PC's CPU could address 1024KB, or 1MB. Other, newer chips can address even more. The 80386, 80486, Pentium, and Pentium Pro families could address gigabytes, and newer ones still address terabytes.

Slots and Sockets

Are you feeling a bit confused about slots and sockets? If so, don't feel alone. The past few years, whenever a different approach to computer processors is taken, we end up with a different way in which the CPU is packaged for installation.

In recent modern CPU history, a *socket* was simply the place on the motherboard where the CPU plugs in—pins into holes. The Socket 7 standard created for the original Pentium-class PCs allowed for a simple insertion (or plug-in) of a CPU into the motherboard. Such CPUs feature 321 pins set in five staggered rows. A *slot* allows the CPU to slide into place, something like a tiny version of plugging an expansion card into a PCI slot.

Socket-type CPUs are cheaper to produce overall, while slot-type is an attempt to pack more speed and power into a CPU package. Put most simply, the closer you bring the cache to the processor, the better the system should perform, and the slot-type helps you accomplish that.

Although Intel moved away from the Socket 7 standard as it moved to the Pentium Pro (Socket 8, with 387 pins in five dual-pattern pin rows, and the cache built into the processor package) and the Pin Grid Array (PGA) 423-pin socket used by the Pentium 4, Socket 7 has stayed with us because alternative CPU manufacturers, particularly AMD, adopted it and used it for their line of K6 processors. Only with the Athlon has AMD broken stride, giving it a completely different Slot A insertion.

Intel, meanwhile, was shifting again. With the introduction of the Pentium II came the Single Edge Contact Cartridge (SECC), wherein the processor and cache are mounted on a *daughterboard* (secondary board) on the chip and then inserted into the motherboard. Pentium IIs and IIIs use Slot 1 technology, which has 242 pins set in two rows of 121 pins each. When Intel introduced the Itanium, change happened again, going from Slot 1 technology to Slot M.

Socket 370 was introduced during the PII reign as alternative packaging for Celerons (which in the beginning, had no L2 cache). But as Celerons were minted that included a 128KB L2 cache, the packaging turned to Slot 1, like the Pentium II itself, with an adapter available to fit a Socket 370 Celeron into a Pentium II–Slot 1–style motherboard. Table 3.3 lists CPUs and their slots or socket types.

TABLE 3.3: CPUs AND THEIR REQUIRED SLOTS/SOCKET TYPES

CPU	SLOT/SOCKET FORM FACTOR
Pentium (classic)	Socket 7
Pentium MMX	Socket 7
AMD K6	Socket 7
AMD K6-II	Socket 7
AMD K6-III	Socket 7
Pentium Pro	Socket 8
OverDrive	Socket 8
Celeron	Socket 370
Celeron	Slot 1
Pentium II	Slot 1
Pentium III	Slot 1
Pentium 4	423-pin socket
Athlon	Slot A
Duron	Slot A
Xeon	Slot 1
Itanium	Slot M

Details on CPU Chips

While I've talked a lot about various CPU chips in this part of the chapter, there are a few odds and ends that I haven't covered yet. I'll tie up those things here. I'll start by listing all the Intel and Intel-compatible CPUs and summarizing their characteristics—see Table 3.4. (The table is organized under abbreviated headings explained in the key that follows the table.)

TABLE 3.4: CPU SPECIFICATIONS AND APPLICATIONS

MODEL	ECF	ICF	WS/DP	IP	M	MC	IC	V	COMP
Intel									
8088	8	8	16/8	1	1	No	0	5	
8086	8	8	16/16	1	1	No	0	5	
80c86	8	8	16/16	1	1	No	0	5	

Continued on next page

TABLE 3.4: CPU SPECIFICATIONS AND APPLICATIONS *(continued)*

MODEL	ECF	ICF	WS/DP	IP	M	MC	IC	V	COMP
Intel									
80186	16	16	16/16	1	1	No	0	5	
80286	20	20	16/16	1	16	No	0	5	
80386DX	40	40	32/32	1	4096	No	0	5	
80386SX	25	25	32/16	1	16	No	0	5	
80486SLC	25	25	32/32	1	64	No	8	5	
	33	33							
80486DX	25	25	32/32	1	4096	Yes	8	5	
	33	33							
	50	50							
80486SX	20	20	32/32	1	4096	No	8	5	
	25	25							
	33	33							
80486DX2	20	40	32/32	1	4096	Yes	8	5	
	25	50							
	33	66							
80486DX4	25	75	32/32	1	4096	Yes	16	5	
	33	100							
Pentium	60	100	32/64	2	4096	Yes	16	5	
	66	133–200						3.3	
MMX	66	200–266	32/64	2	4096	Yes	32	1.5	
Pentium Pro	60	166	32/64	3	65,536	Yes	32	1.5	
	66	200							
Pentium II	66	233	32/64	3	65,536	Yes	32	1.5	
	100	266–450							
Pentium III	66	500	32/64		65,536	Yes	32	1.5	
	100	450–1000							
	133	533–1000							

Continued on next page

TABLE 3.4: CPU SPECIFICATIONS AND APPLICATIONS *(continued)*

MODEL	ECF	ICF	WS/DP	IP	M	MC	IC	V	COMP
Intel									
Pentium 4	100	400–2200	32/128	3	65,536	Yes	32	1.5	
Celeron	66	233–1200	32/64	3	65,536	Yes	32	1.5	
Xeon	100	350–800	32/64	3	65,536	Yes	32	2	
Itanium	100	500–1000	64/64	3		Yes			
NEC									
V20	10	10	16/8	1	1	No	0	5	8088
V30	10	10	16/8	1	1	No	0	5	8086
VIA/Cyrix									
80486SLC	25	25	32/32	1	16	No	1	5	386SX
	33	33							
80486SLC	25	50	32/32	1	16	No	1	5	386SX
80486DLC	33	33	32/32	1	4096	No	1	5	386DX
80486DX	33	33	32/32	1	4096	Yes	8	5	486DX
	40	40							
	50	50							
80486DX2	25	50	32/32	1	4096	Yes	8	5	486DX2
	33	66							
	40	80							
586		100–120	32/64	1	4096	Yes	16	3.45–5	Pentium
6x86	50	100	32/64	2	4096	Yes	16	3.3–5	Pentium
	55	110							
	60	120							
	66	133							
	75	150							
C3 (Cyrix III)	400	700–800	32/64	1	4096	Yes	64	1.6	Celeron

Continued on next page

TABLE 3.4: CPU SPECIFICATIONS AND APPLICATIONS *(continued)*

MODEL	ECF	ICF	WS/DP	IP	M	MC	IC	V	COMP
AMD									
386SE	25 33	25.33	32/16	1	16	No	0	3–5	386SX
386DE	33 40	33.40	32/32	1	4096	No	0	3–5	386DX
486DXLV	33	33	32/32	1	4096	Yes	8	3.0–3.6	486DX
486SXLV	33	33	32/32	1	4096	No	8	3.0–3.6	486SX
486DX	33 40	33.40	32/32	1	4096	Yes	8	5	486DX
486SX	33 40	33.40	32/32	1	4096	No	8	5	486SX
486DX2	25 33	50.66	32/32	1	4096	Yes	8	5	486DX2
486DX2-80	40	80	32/32	1	4096	Yes	8	5	486DX2
486DXL2	25 33	50 66	32/32	1	4096	Yes	8	5	486DX2
486SX2-50	25	50	32/32	1	4096	Yes	8	5	486SX
Am5x86	33	133	32/32		4096	Yes	16	3.45	Pentium 75
Duron	200	600–1200	32/64	3	4096	Yes	64	1.6/1.75	Celeron
Athlon	266	500–1600	32/64	3	65,536	Yes	128	1.6	Pentium III/4

ECF External clock frequency (in MHz)
ICF Internal clock frequency (in MHz)
WS/DP Word size and data path (in bits)
IP Instruction pipelines (how many)
M Physical memory addressability (in MB)
MC Math coprocessor
IC Internal cache (in KB)
V Voltage (in volts)
Comp Intel compatibility

Some of these chips are more powerful or less powerful. Some can actually allow you to improve the throughput of your existing PC, although most of these are in the past—CPU speeds are updated too swiftly now, so there is no real market for overdriving a CPU this way. Instead, many buy cheaper CPUs such as the Celeron and the K6-II and overclock them by manipulating clock/multiplier rates.

You'll see a bit of repetition in the following pages as I detail each processor, but that's intentional. I've thrown an awful lot of concepts at you so far; the intent in this section is to tie up all the CPU concepts before progressing on to memory, buses, and other hardware topics.

8088

The 8088 was the "Grand Old Man" of PC CPUs, although the 8086 came before it and was arguably a better design. It came in what was called a 40-pin DIP (Dual Inline Package) package, which means a rectangular plastic case with two rows of 20 pins. Older 8088s were called 8088-1s, because they could run at only low speeds (5MHz or slower). Turbo PC/XT clones ran at 6.66, 7.16, or 8MHz. To do this, they used the 8088-2, which was rated at up to 8MHz. The 8088 was the equivalent of about 29,000 transistors.

8086

The 8086 predated the 8088 by a year and was actually more powerful than it, but the 8086 was not as well known. The 8086 was different from the 8088 in that the 8086 not only had internal 16-bit registers (a 16-bit word) but also a 16-bit data path, the doorway to the outside world. Because that required 16-bit motherboards, however, the 8086 never really caught on. The 8088 was essentially a hobbled 8086, because it had only an 8-bit data path. But that made for a cheaper motherboard, so IBM went with the 8088—and the rest is history. But a few clone makers opted for 8086-based systems because the 8086 was 100 percent compatible with the 8088 *and* faster; one example was Compaq, with a tremendously successful computer called the Deskpro.

80186 AND 80188

You don't hear much about these chips, but they were souped-up versions of the 8086 and 8088. They didn't really have much in the way of new capabilities; they were just a polished version of the old chips, sort of similar to the way that the 80486 was not a big leap from the 80386, but rather a mildly improved version. The main differences were that the 186 and the 188 were manufactured in a PGA package (see the "80286" section for more on this) and had more efficient microcode. Tandy sold a computer called the Tandy 2000 that was 80186-based. It could have been a high-performance competitor to the Deskpro, but Tandy unwisely opted to make it only about 60 percent compatible with the IBM PC, forcing Tandy 2000 users to buy special versions of software. There weren't too many titles developed for the Tandy 2000, and it went nowhere.

The 80186 was the last member of what might be called the first family of PC CPUs, a family that started with the 8086.

80286

The 80286, introduced in 1981, was a major step forward for *x86* technology. It was packaged in a square ceramic PGA package. It also came in a cheaper package called a Plastic Leadless Chip Carrier

(PLCC). The PLCC is the more durable of the two and is mainly found in laptops, due to its lower profile. The PGA package has an inner and an outer square of solid pins; the PLCC has curved-under legs around its perimeter. The PGA "stands" on its legs. The PLCC is surrounded by its legs. You can see chip package types in Figure 3.6.

FIGURE 3.6

Chip package types

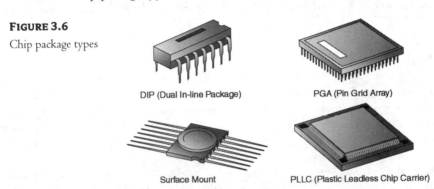

DIP (Dual In-line Package)   PGA (Pin Grid Array)

Surface Mount   PLLC (Plastic Leadless Chip Carrier)

The 286 packed a lot more power into a small package than the 8088 did: the 80286 was the equivalent of about 130,000 transistors in about the same volume. Because of this, the 80286 ran hotter, and some models required extra cooling provisions such as a heat sink. *Heat sinks* are small metal caps with metal cooling fins that fit on top of a chip and enable the chip to better dissipate the heat that it generates. You see them on modern CPUs, such as Pentiums, which produce even greater amounts of heat.

The 80286 was the sole member of the second family of PC-compatible CPUs. In many ways, it was a rough draft for the 386 family, the third family of PC CPUs.

80386DX AND 80386SX

The 80386, or as it was officially called by Intel, the 80386DX, was another quantum leap for the *x*86 family. Introduced in 1985, it came in a PGA package and was the equivalent of about 250,000 transistors. It incorporated a wealth of programming features, including the capability to multitask DOS programs with the help of operating systems such as Windows. The 32-bit data path sped up data access, leading to the design of buses such as the Micro Channel, EISA, VESA, and PCI buses (see the upcoming section on buses). It also differed from previous *x*86 designs in that it could address 4096MB of RAM.

The 386SX was identical to the 386DX except that it had a 16-bit data path to enable it to be more easily incorporated into AT-type hardware designs (recall that the AT's 286 had a 16-bit data path also). It was contained in a PLCC package.

The 80386 family brought a new set of instruction codes and a 32-bit programming model to PC CPUs that is essentially unchanged to this day. Look at the most modern PC programs not written specifically for a 32-bit Windows environment (32-bit Windows being Windows 95/98, Windows 2000, and Windows XP), and many of them will run on a circa-1985 386-based system, albeit slowly.

80386SL

The SL was part of a two-chip set that was basically a combination of a 386SX and a motherboard. The two chips together constituted almost all of what's needed to build an SX computer. What made it particularly interesting was that the chipset included power management. For example, the SL system could shut down the CPU between keystrokes, saving power. The SL mainly appeared in laptops; they were in PLCC packages.

80486DX

The 80486 (officially the 80486DX) was sort of an upgraded 386. Code-named during development *P4*, it combined a tuned-up 386 with two chips that sped up a 386 system: the 385 cache controller and the 387 numeric coprocessor. The microcode was larger and faster—there were the equivalent of 1.25 *million* transistors in this chip. Depending upon what the computer was doing, a 25MHz 386 with a 385 and a 387 (cache controller and external math coprocessor) would sometimes execute only half as many instructions per second as a 25MHz 486.

Better yet, the 486 chip was actually cheaper than a 386, 385, and 387 together, so eventually 486 computers were cheaper than fully loaded 386 machines. The DX appeared in PGA packages.

80486SX

The 80486SX was more of a marketing tool than a new chip. Intel took the 486DX chips that failed the math coprocessor analysis during product testing and sold them in a new package they called a 486SX. It had a specified maximum clock speed of 20MHz and no math coprocessor. Intel then offered a math coprocessor called the 487SX that was, believe it or not, a fully functional 486DX—a CPU chip with coprocessor and all. Once the 487SX was planted in its socket, it instructed the 486SX to just go to sleep; the 487SX then handled everything, including both general computing and numeric coprocessing, just as if it were a normal 486DX system running at 20MHz.

80486DX2, DX4, AND THE OVERDRIVE CHIP

The 80487SX, as it turns out, was a mere harbinger of the wide variety in CPUs that was to follow. With the 486, Intel first started experimenting with product diversification, taking a basically good product (the 486DX) and repackaging it in a variety of ways.

Recall that the 80487SX was *not* a floating-point coprocessor. It was a fully functional 80486DX, but packaged a bit differently—the pins on the bottom of the chip were arranged differently from the way they were arranged on the 80486DX, so you couldn't just pop an 80486DX in the 80487SX socket. Furthermore, unlike the floating-point coprocessors of yore (the 8087, 187, 287, and 387 families), the 80487SX didn't work with the erstwhile main processor—*it took over altogether*, effectively disconnecting the 80486SX. A bit of clever marketing, eh? Buy a "cheap" 486SX and then end up buying a whole 486DX disguised as a coprocessor, with the result that Intel gets to sell more chips than if you'd bought a 486DX in the first place.

Next stop in the 486-marketing universe was the original OverDrive chip. ("Original" because the term *overdrive* has since been recycled by Intel a number of times.) The OverDrive chip was a 486DX built for a 487SX socket, as usual, *except* that they made it a clock doubler like the 486DX2.

The net effect was that the OverDrive chip did everything at least as quickly as a 25MHz 80486DX, and many operations twice as fast! So the OverDrive chip would speed up your PC by about one-third to one-half. Was it worth it? An OverDrive chip cost around $300, not a small amount, but then not a budget-buster either.

Intel then took on the market of folks who had a 486DX and wanted more speed by offering the clock doubler 486DX2. Recall that the 80486DX2, like the OverDrive chip, ran outwardly at *x*MHz, but worked internally at 2*x*MHz. Thus, a so-called 66MHz 80486DX2 worked in a motherboard designed for a 33MHz chip, but ran internally at 66MHz. The value was, again, that a PC vendor needed only take one of its already existing 33MHz 80486DX models, replace the 33MHz 80486DX processor with a 66MHz 80486DX processor, and it instantly got a "66MHz 486."

The last in the Intel 486 line was the DX4, a clock tripler 486 that contained power management right on the chip, combining 386SL-like technology and clock tripling to produce a very nice processor. Its main role was in laptops, where it functioned extremely well.

486SLC AND 486DLC

This one wasn't an Intel chip. It wasn't even a 486. A 486SLC was a 386SX (no numeric coprocessor, recall) with just *1KB of cache* and, of course, a *16-bit data path*. The resulting chip was somewhere between a 386SX and a 486SX in performance. The 1KB was pretty measly, so you'd have to say that the performance was closer to the 386SX than to the 486. There was also a 486DLC, a 386DX with 1KB of cache memory added, and no coprocessor. These chips were pin compatible with the 386SX and 386DX, not the 486 line. My main gripe with them was the marketing baloney that went with them: people were told they were getting 486 technology when they bought one of these chips, but they actually got only 386 technology.

Micro technology improvement, macro sales pitches. Yup, you can always tell when a technological industry matures: the guys in the wheelhouse are marketing guys rather than engineers.

386DRU2

Another Intel competitor. It had an odd-looking name, but that was how it came to be known internally at the company. This Cyrix chip was a 386 clone, save that it was a clock doubler: you could make a 25MHz 386 into a 50MHz 386 with one of these.

That, in general, has been Cyrix's modus operandi: take what Intel does and do it better. It has not served them badly.

PENTIUM

In 1993, Intel introduced the processor they had code-named *P5*, known now as the Pentium processor. In some ways, it was just a souped-up 486—and, in fact, many in the industry expected Intel to follow their 80286/80386/80486 naming convention and call this new model the 80586. In other ways, it was much more, as you've seen from the earlier parts of this chapter. Here's a quick look at Pentium features besides the ones we've already examined.

Greater Raw Speed

The Pentium came in a variety of flavors: 60, 66, 75, 90, 100, 125, 133, 150, and 166MHz, and, in the newer MMX flavor, was available up to 266MHz. Intel offered an OverDrive upgrade for chips 100MHz and under that increased the chip's speed by about half.

The 120/133MHz OverDrive processor upgrade was designed to reduce the voltage used by the 60MHz and 66MHz chips from 5 volts to the 3.3 used by the more recent chips that took advantage of Intel's Voltage Reduction Technology.

NOTE *Counterintuitively, you may get better performance from a 133 than a 150, because the 133 is a doubled 66MHz chip, and the 150 is a two-and-a-halved 60.*

The Pentium was more difficult to make than its predecessors because, for one thing, it was much bigger than the 486. The 486 contained 1.2 million transistors; the Pentium contained 3.1 million— over two and a half times as many.

Fault Tolerance

The Pentium was designed to be used in conjunction with another Pentium on a motherboard specifically suited for fault tolerance (meaning, it would try to stand up to and operate under situations that might crash a less tolerant system). The second Pentium constantly monitored the first; if the main Pentium malfunctioned, the other one jumped right in and took up without skipping a beat.

Another purpose for two CPUs on one motherboard is *symmetric multiprocessing (SMP)*, the ability to divide the workload between multiple processors. Most dual CPU implementations are designed for SMP and not for fault tolerance.

First MMX Implementation

Another Pentium first was its so-called multimedia support, the matrix functions in the MMX. The MMX was just a Pentium with MMX instructions included and a larger cache.

THE PENTIUM PRO FAMILY: PENTIUM PRO, PENTIUM II, III, 4, CELERON, AND XEON

The Pentium Pro, Pentium II, III, Celeron, and Xeon chips are known as the P6 line of chips. The P6s differ from their predecessors for many reasons. But are they *faster* chips? Well, yes, kind of—but, like their predecessors, the P6 family is largely limited by its heritage: it's got to be *x*86 compatible.

Just looking at the P6 family shows how it's different. With the exception of the Celeron, the P6s are fairly large chips, because they contain lots of memory. The Pentium Pro chip, for example, is actually *two* chips. Inside the Pentium Pro, there is one chip (*die* is the actual word; it refers to the silicon wafer that is the actual electronics of a chip), which is the main processor. It has about 5.5 million transistors. Alongside it is a built-in 256KB external or L2 cache, about 15 million transistors' worth of static memory. You can see that in Figure 3.7.

The Pentium Pro incorporates three pipelines, rather than the two of the Pentium. By breaking up instruction execution into 14 steps, Intel has made it possible to do what they call *dynamic execution*. Explained earlier in the "Superscalar and Instruction Pipelines" section, dynamic execution works by using three parallel units to fetch and decode instructions; once prepared for execution, those instructions are tossed into a "pool" of waiting instructions. There's not much waiting, however, because the P6s have five execution units working side by side to try to shove instructions through at top speed. That helps because the Pentium Pro can handle groups of instructions *out of their original order*, which keeps as many of the fetch, decode, and execution units working at the highest capacity possible.

FIGURE 3.7

L2 cache on the
Pentium Pro chip

256K L2 cache

Main processor die

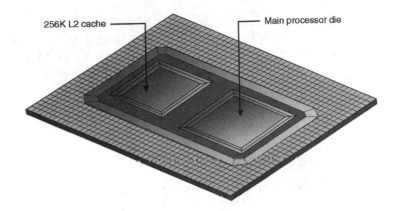

Oddly enough, the Pentium Pro has an L1 cache of only 16KB, the same as the standard Pentium, and in fact less than the Pentium MMX chips. That is offset by the large L2 cache incorporated into the chip. By putting the L2 cache on the chip, the Pentium Pro can more quickly access that memory, making it a faster "external" cache than the external caches found on Pentium and earlier chips. But 20 million transistors! That sucker is a mite toasty, so make sure there's a decent CPU fan on your Pentium Pro. Most come with a fan, as you see in Figure 3.8.

The other P6ers—Celeron, Xeon, and Pentium II—all have 32KB of L1 cache and can also suffer from heat exhaustion (the Xeon even has a sensor on-chip to detect overheating).

FIGURE 3.8

Pentium II package
with fan

The later P6s' heat problems weren't as terrible as they could be, however, because Intel again reduced the size of the transistors that make up the chip. Whereas the Pentium was built with 0.8-micron and 0.6-micron components, the Xeon is built with 0.25-micron components. That helps make the Xeon work at a decent reliability factor when running at 600MHz.

The Pentium III processors are very similar to the Pentium IIs; however, the IIIs run faster (450–550MHz), support 70 new instructions, and run on the 100MHz system bus with the original version and 133MHz on the newer Coppermines (more to come about Coppermines in just a bit).

Pentium II

The Pentium II (PII) made some impressive improvements to the original Pentium processor. Ranging in speeds from 233MHz to 450MHz, the PII improves not only speed, but also performance. The PII incorporates a 100MHz *front bus* interface (for the 350MHz, 400MHz, and 450MHz chips), allowing the processor to achieve greater speeds in interfacing with system resources.

The PII also has MMX technology built into the processor, thereby satisfying the new demands by users and software for faster graphics. The original PII came with 32KB of L1 cache (16KB for data and 16KB for instructions) and 512KB of L2 cache.

Pentium II Xeon

The PII processor was further enhanced by the creation of the Xeon family. The Xeon PII is designed for business applications and high-speed processing; up to eight processors can be combined to work together. The processor functions at 400MHz or 450MHz and can handle higher L2 cache. The 400MHz and 450MHz are available with 512KB or 1MB of L2 cache, but the 450MHz can handle up to a whopping 2MB.

Celeron

The Intel Celeron processor has become quite popular with home PC users. The reason for its increase in sales is due to its relatively low cost. Intel made a decision to lower processor costs (which in turn lowered PC costs) by making some changes to its existing processor families.

Recall that standard Pentium chips had 32KB of L1 cache and 512KB of L2 cache. The L2 cache is the expensive kind, so it makes sense that if you reduce its size, you reduce the cost of the processor, right? Well, that's what Intel did. The Celeron processor comes in speeds ranging from 300MHz to 550–650MHz (which operate at 66MHz bus speed and still have 32KB of L1 cache). But these processors come with only 128KB of L2 cache. Although this is a drastic cut in L2 cache size, the reduction in price for the processor and the PCs that use it make it a very favorable choice for buyers looking to save money on a new PC.

The Celeron also has a built-in booster market. As Intel sought to make it tough for ambitious overclockers to push PIIs and PIIIs to higher than rated speeds, the Celeron became the default preference of the overclocking crowd. If overclocking techniques fail, a cheaper CPU is a lot easier to burn up than a much more expensive PIII or P4.

NOTE *Check out the Celeron chip on Intel's Web site at* `http://www.intel.com/celeron`.

Pentium III

Intel released its Pentium III processor with a marketing blitz no one will soon forget. But was the new chip worth all the hype? Let's see.

First, the speeds offered by the Pentium III were higher than anything Intel offered before. Starting out at 450MHz–550MHz and ending up with chips in the 1GHz range, Pentium III chips also come with the MMX technology and (typically) 512KB of L2 cache. But other than the increase in speed, what was the big deal? Well, the Pentium III's strength lay in its capability to handle graphics faster and smoother than previous chips. Remember MMX? The Pentium III did MMX processing 70 instructions better! These new instructions were designed for real-time video, streaming video, and better graphics capabilities.

It's important to understand that the differences between a PII and a PIII are largely speed (the PII line stopped at 450MHz), and the 70 extra instructions already discussed. For the most part, the PIII CPU will drop right into a PII socket as a replacement on a motherboard, same as with the Xeon II/III.

The extra instructions included are useful in specific areas: streaming content delivered from the Internet (where the user doesn't have to sit and wait to receive *all* of a file before the audio and/or video begins to play) and in PC gaming. Depending on whose analysis you favor, performance with a PIII jumps about 10 to 15 percent over a PII in the areas where the extra instruction set counts.

However, the Pentium III isn't linear—there are actually two types of Pentium III. The original one was based on the same technology as the PII, but with those extra instructions. A change came about with Intel's Coppermine chipset in 1999, replacing traditional connectors with copper, and altering the process used from 0.25-micron to 0.18-micron, and offering a 133MHz system bus (original was 100MHz), as well as a 256K L2 cache on-chip, which runs at the same speed as the processor itself. One important difference with Coppermine is that it should finally support 4X AGP, critical to helping video performance hop forward. Before this, AGP video was limited to a 1X–2X data path, which fell short of allowing AGP to truly excite the serious gaming crowd that needs speed in video. All too often, AGP was chosen not because it was wildly faster and better than PCI video cards, but because it freed up a PCI slot for another type of expansion board.

Pentium 4

The Pentium 4 is the first truly new processor design from Intel since the Pentium Pro debuted at under 200MHz. Believe it or not, the Pentium Pro, Pentium II, Pentium III, Xeon, and Celeron processors were all based on the same P6 microarchitecture. Intel added some goodies like MMX, SSE, and integrated cache over the years, and they changed the way the processors were made, but they were all the same basic design.

The P4 is based on Intel's radical new NetBurst microarchitecture, and it's a different animal altogether. Remember that the P6 microarchitecture topped out at about 1GHz; to pass the 1GHz barrier, the Pentium 4's NetBurst microarchitecture is built to run comfortably at very high clock speeds. Not only that, but Intel's engineers had another hurdle to leap with this design. If NetBurst is going to stick around for as many years as P6 has, it will need to provide substantial performance gains as the years pass and clock speeds rise. So headroom and scalability were the orders of the day.

Intel's design philosophy gives the NetBurst microarchitecture a distinct character. For example, clock-for-clock performance, or the number of instructions per clock (IPC) the chip can process, should be relatively low. But clock speeds are very high.

The Pentium adds an execution trace cache. Contemporary x86 processors like the PIII and Athlon decode x86 instructions into smaller, bite-sized operations before processing them. (Intel calls them *micro-ops*.) This practice allows x86 processors to have much more RISC-like designs, but decoding x86 instructions takes time. NetBurst's execution trace cache takes the place of a conventional L1 instruction cache, and it caches micro-ops instead of x86 instructions. Intel is coy about the exact size of the trace cache, but they claim it can store about 12,000 micro-ops.

Smaller is faster. The Pentium 4 incorporates a small, low-latency L1 data cache. At only 8K, the NetBurst L1 data cache is only half the size of the Pentium III's, and just a fraction of the size of the AMD Athlon's 64K data cache. Intel chose this small cache size because smaller caches have lower latencies. While the Athlon and PIII data caches have a three-cycle latency, the P4's L1 data cache latency is two cycles. It's all part of the plan to keep that deep pipeline well fed.

The Pentium 4's L2 cache is 256K, just like the Athlon and PIII, but it's much, much cooler. The P4's L2 cache interface is 256 bits wide, and it sends data on every clock cycle. On a 1.4GHz Pentium 4, that works out to 44.8GB per second of bandwidth. That's almost four times the bandwidth of the L2 cache on a 1GHz PIII. As for the Athlon, its L2 cache is even slower still, but then I've seen AMD engineers claim the Athlon's L2 cache isn't really bandwidth-limited. Whatever the case, the P4's L2 cache is scary fast.

The NetBurst bus sends data four times per clock cycle, so you're going to hear us and everyone else talk about it as a "400MHz bus" from here to eternity. We'll also be talking about it as a 100MHz, quad-pumped bus, as well, just to keep you guessing. Whatever you call it, though, don't call it slow. This deeply pipelined, split-transaction bus is capable of transferring data at 3.2GB per second at 400MHz. Or at 100MHz. You get the picture.

Intel has added a set of 144 new instructions to the Pentium 4, dubbed SSE2. Like the original Streaming SIMD Extensions, SSE2 involves simultaneously executing a single instruction on multiple data targets (hence SIMD). Most importantly, SSE2 handles 128-bit, double-precision floating-point math. The ability to handle more precise floating-point numbers makes SSE2 just the ticket for accelerating a host of multimedia, 3D, engineering, and workstation-type tasks—once software is properly optimized to take advantage of it.

The Pentium 4's floating-point unit isn't as capable as the FPU in the Pentium III, and it's quite a bit less capable than the Athlon's FPU. To put it simply, the P4's FPU can't do as much work at once, and it has higher latencies in some cases. Programs optimized for SSE2 will be able to bypass the P4's FPU in many cases, but without special optimizations, the P4 will have a hard time keeping up.

Taken together, these design decisions are really radical. The depth of the P4's pipeline, combined with its less-than-stellar FPU, will keep its IPC—or clock-for-clock performance—relatively low. In legacy applications, especially those that lean heavily on conventional x86 ALUs and FPUs, the P4's performance may not be so exciting. But the Pentium 4 platform itself is very impressive, with gobs of bandwidth available all over the place. With the right optimizations for SSE2, multimedia apps positively scream on the P4.

NOTE   *The Pentium Pro family of chips did well sales-wise, but it's not entirely clear that it was because of their performance; more likely, it was a matter of their big megahertz numbers. The fact that the Pentium Pro line wasn't really all that much faster than the Pentium line underscores that speeding up CPUs gets tougher the higher you go. It's not enough to provide more megahertz and more raw speed. The winner in the CPU races will be the one that uses its time most wisely, with multiple pipelines, out-of-order instruction, data bypassing, and the like.*

NON-INTEL PENTIUM CHALLENGERS: M1/M2, NX586, K5/K6, C3, ATHLON, AND DURON

For many years, chip companies competed with Intel by making clones of its chips. But the Pentium was a different story, because its difference from the 486 was not tremendous—it's a fast chip, but it's not staggeringly faster than a 486. Add that to Intel's public relations disaster back in November 1994 over the Pentium's floating-point division problems (it was noted that math computations weren't being handled correctly), and computer manufacturers soon became more open to putting a non-Intel chip in their computers.

That was the opening needed to create Cyrix's M1, NexGen's Nx586, and AMD's K5. All three of these chips were intended to be "what the Pentium should have been." They were backward compatible with 486 software, but they all departed from the Pentium in slightly different ways.

Cyrix's 6x86

In October 1995, Cyrix announced the shipment of its rival to the Pentium, the 6x86 (formerly the M1). Although the 6x86 was a two-pipeline superscalar chip like the Pentium, the 6x86 offered a number of other features that were also offered by the Pentium Pro (released after the 6x86). However, the Cyrix 5x86, formerly known as the M1sc, was not a rival to the Pentium, although the numbering scheme made it sound like it was. 5x86s were pin compatible with an Intel 486, 6x86s with a Pentium.

The 6x86 featured the following:

Superpipelining   Instead of the Pentium's five stages, the 6x86 used a seven-stage pipeline to avoid lags in the execution process and increase the flow of information.

Register renaming   Provided temporary data storage for instant data availability without waiting for the CPU to access the on-chip cache or main system memory.

Data dependency removal   Provided instruction results to both pipelines simultaneously so that neither pipeline stalled while waiting for the results of calculations.

Multibranch prediction   Boosted processor performance by predicting with high accuracy the next instructions needed.

Speculative execution   Allowed the pipelines to continuously execute instructions that followed a branch without stalling the pipelines.

Out-of-order completion   Could process instructions out of order, making it possible to get faster-to-process instructions out of the way before spending time on the longer ones. This feature applied to the execute and write-back portions of the calculation process.

The 6x86 was a clock doubler or tripler (depending on the model). It stored calculation instructions and their results in a 16KB cache so that they could be called back into memory quickly, if necessary.

Cyrix also released the M2 processors, which were supposed to rival the Intel's Celeron processor line in power—but never rivaled them in terms of *selling* power.

AMD's K5/K6

The K5 was a fifth-generation processor offered by AMD. The K5 was distinct from AMD's 5x86, a souped-up version of the 486. The K5, a 64-bit version more like the Pentium, started shipping in

June 1996. The K5's most salient feature was its four instruction pipelines (twice as many as the Pentium).

The biggest difference between the K5 and the Cyrix 6x86 was that the Cyrix chip was a *CISC* (*Complex Instruction Set Chip*, an older approach to designing CPUs), whereas the K5 was a *RISC* (*Reduced Instruction Set Chip*, a newer approach). As such, the K5 had to translate the complex instructions it received to simpler ones that could be executed more quickly.

The K6 series offered some substantial gains over the K5 and has proved to be AMD's most popular chip design thus far, particularly after AMD introduced 3DNow! Technology to enhance Web surfing and game playing, much as the Pentium III did (AMD's released sooner). Because the K6 could be pushed in ways the PII and the PIII couldn't, and because it was priced below the Pentium II/III, the K6-II and K6-III represented a major alternative for many users as well as PC manufacturers.

NexGen's Nx586

This chip was the oddball of the crowd. First of all, it didn't support floating-point operations, which made it incompatible even with some programs that ran on an 80486DX. Second, it wasn't pin compatible with the Pentium, which required designers to create a whole new motherboard to use it. Third, it ran at 4 volts, which didn't match the Pentium's 3.3-volt requirement.

NexGen rates chips not by their speed, but by equivalent speeds for the Pentium. (The other non-Intel manufacturers do likewise.) For example, the 6x86 that was rated at 100MHz actually ran at 93MHz, but Cyrix claimed that it performed equally to a Pentium at that speed, and some benchmarks bore that out.

NOTE   *AMD now owns NexGen.*

VIA's C3

After several disappointing years (in terms of both chip development and sales), Cyrix looked to be down for the count. While AMD CPUs began to gain in overall popularity, Cyrix began to fade until 1999, when it was announced that VIA Technologies (the chipset manufacturer) would acquire the company and focus on making inexpensive alternatives to Intel chips. The latest VIA chip is the C3, formerly called the Cyrix III. (This chip was originally code-named Gobi, or Joshua.) The C3 builds upon the foundation Cyrix (pre-VIA) established with the M1 and M2.

The C3 is a Celeron-compatible chip with 128KB of L1 cache and a skimpy 64KB L2 cache. It uses a Socket 370 type connection, like the Celeron. Unlike the Celeron, the C3 supports enhanced 3DNow! and has a much faster 133MHz front-side bus. The initial units that shipped ran at 533KHz, and VIA claims that the C3 is the "coolest processor on the market." (I assume they're talking about low heat radiation, as opposed to really fab looks!)

AMD's Athlon (K7)

The Athlon, first introduced in 1999, has sometimes been called the first PC processor AMD didn't design wholly in Intel's shadow. Like a few new processors before it, the Athlon CPU was available in some supply before the motherboards needed to support it.

Oh, there are big similarities to Intel's PII, PIII, and P4, and these are necessary, too, because you need to be able to run the same programs regardless of which PC processor is being used. Like the

Pentiums, the Athlon is mounted on a module containing separate SRAM chips making up the L2 cache, with special connectors uniting the two. Also like the Pentiums, the Athlon offers a 512KB L2 cache that runs at half the speed of the processor itself.

But the differences are notable. First, the Athlon was designed around an entirely new processor core, uses a Slot A (rather than a Slot 1) socket, and offers a 200MHz front-side bus. The L1 cache is four times the size of what's available on a PIII, and an Athlon can decode any three *x*86 instructions at any given time. It also has the capability to dispatch up to nine internal instructions to its execution units per clock cycle, whereas a PIII can do just five. The Athlon is also credited with offering a better floating-point multiplying and adding capability for improved application and server performance, as well as enhanced gaming.

With the introduction of the new copper-interconnected Athlon, dubbed the Thunderbird, the integrated 256KB L2 cache runs at the full speed of the processor, instead of just half-speed. Thunderbird Athlons are smaller and faster than previous models, at a similar or slightly reduced cost.

AMD calls its latest Athlon chip the Athlon XP. The XP features what AMD calls *QuantiSpeed architecture*, which includes a fully pipelined microarchitecture and FPU, hardware prefetch, and translation look-aside buffers (TLBs), that prevents the processor from waiting when future data is requested. The XP is able to perform more calculations per second, thus boosting overall productivity from Thunderbird levels. (The XP designation is because AMD says the Athlon XP is ideally suited to run Windows XP—which means it's as much a marketing gimmick as anything else; AMD also changed the way they market their XP chips, no longer designating them by speed, but instead by how they compare to similarly fast Intel chips.)

AMD's Duron

AMD's Duron chip is their competitor in the price-sensitive low end of the PC market. Price-wise, it competes directly with Intel's Celeron CPU, although performance-wise it's right up there, in many ways, with the Pentium 4 and AMD's higher-priced Athlon chip.

Like the Athlon, the Duron fits into the Slot A socket. Its architecture is similar to the Athlon Thunderbird, except for a smaller 64KB L2 cache. It runs at a slightly lower voltage than the Thunderbird, so it runs a lot cooler than its big brother.

Comparing the Duron to Intel's Celeron, the Duron has a faster clock speed (200MHz versus 66MHz), larger L1 cache (128KB versus 32KB), and slightly smaller L2 cache (64KB versus 128KB). Its performance is actually closer to the Athlon/PIII/P4 level than it is to the Celeron, which makes it an excellent choice for budget-conscious consumers.

THE FUTURE: ITANIUM

The Itanium is Intel's first high-end, 64-bit central processor. Formerly code-named Merced, the Itanium is the flagship of Intel's IA-64 processor family, developed to go head-to-head with major professional server players such as IBM and Sun Microsystems' highly popular UltraSparc III—which are high-end RISC-based processors capable of performing some of the hardest tasks computers are called upon to do. In testing, this processor worked well with eight operating systems, including Windows NT 4, Linux, and various flavors of Unix. It's the capability to handle other than a strictly Windows-environment platform that makes Itanium a serious first entry for Intel into the powerhouse market. Intel processors have usually—intentionally or not—been designed around the

Microsoft Windows platform, whether it was lower-end consumer Windows such as Windows 95/98 or higher-powered Windows NT/2000/XP. Itanium's multiplatform support has gained the interest of major Linux distributors, for example, who formed a group called the Trillium Project to help bolster Itanium's roll-out.

To this end, the Itanium is not really designed for the typical home or corporate desktop PC. It's great for servers and processor-intensive tasks—as long as the software is written to take advantage of the Itanium's 64-bit processing. (Microsoft is shipping a 64-bit version of Windows XP, designed to do just that.) Intel's theory is this: with processing demand growing at an infinite pace, we need to find ways to wed the economics (lower cost) and the workhorse-usability of personal computers with the power of server technology. Their initial market is e-business, also known as Internet commerce, a market where the current choices are either to invest heavily in the RISC-based processor environment or to settle for a much less powerful server.

With all this said, you may be surprised to hear that this powerhouse, next-generation CPU (running in the 500MHz–1GHz range) is not a lot faster than the Pentium III—and, when running existing 32-bit applications, actually slower than a Pentium 4 or Athlon XP. But that's okay, because in a large, professional environment handling tens of thousands, if not millions, of records and files, and performing many functions, processor speed itself takes a back seat to parallel processing, whereby multiple processors work together to push through the work. Thus, an Itanium can process large databases and work with much larger amounts of memory than the 32-bit Intel chips commonly used in regular desktop systems.

As with the Xeon, PC vendors are initially offering the Itanium machines in two basic configurations: workstation and server (both high-end, meaning a lot of processing power). Workstations are fitted with a dual processor (two processors), whereas servers have four processors.

PC Memory

The PC, like all computers, must have *main memory*. Main memory's job is to be the place where the PC stores the programs and data that it is working on right now. It needs to be able to access these programs and data in *nanoseconds* (billionths of seconds), rather than—as in the case of secondary memory such as hard disks—*milliseconds* (thousandths of seconds).

The other name for main memory, which I've talked about before, is RAM, an acronym for the particularly unhelpful name *random access memory*. I say it's unhelpful because *random access* just means that it's as easy to get to the one-millionth location as it is to get to the first location. By contrast, with *sequential access*, like a tape drive, you have to fast-forward or rewind the tape to get to a particular location—the data is sequential. *Random* tells us very little because there's another kind of memory you'll meet later, named *ROM*, for *read-only memory*. That too is not sequential; the only difference between RAM and ROM is that you can both write data to RAM and read data from it, and you can only read data from ROM. Heck, even disk drives are random access. So a better name for RAM would probably be read/write memory, or RWM, but you can't pronounce RWM. You can pronounce RAM, so the term caught on.

How Memory Is Packaged: DIPs, SIMMs, and DIMMs

The most common way to find RAM today is as a series of dynamic RAM (DRAM) chips affixed to a miniature circuit board. The number of DRAM chips mounted on a side of the circuit board varies depending on type of RAM: sometimes there are eight, sometimes nine. Parity RAM adds an extra DRAM chip for error testing (for a total of nine), while non-parity RAM has eight DRAMs on a side.

If DRAM chips are mounted on only one side of a memory module, this RAM is packaged as a *Single Inline Memory Module (SIMM)*. SIMMs come in 30- and 72-pin types (with the 72-pin the "mightier" of the two, able to perform more work across less RAM). Earlier SIMMs had to be installed in pairs to work.

If, instead, DRAM chips are mounted on both sides of a memory module, this RAM is packaged as a *Dual Inline Memory Module (DIMM)*. DIMMs have 168 pins and don't need to be installed in pairs.

Most motherboards have room for four banks of memory. *Bank* refers to the actual sockets for memory you see on the motherboard, where *sticks* of RAM are installed. Some of the newer machines have no memory on the motherboard at all, but instead have a large circuit board with room for megs and megs of memory.

Over the years, memory packaging has changed. Before the late '80s, you'd buy memory as a bunch of small chips (called *DIPs* because that's the type of package used), and you'd plug them into chip sockets on the computer's motherboard or an add-in daughtercard. Depending on the processor type, you'd have to add memory in increments of 8, 9, 16, 18, 32, or 36 chips. Soon, the first generation of SIMMs appeared. Known as 30-pin SIMMs, one SIMM was the equivalent of eight or nine DIPs, and for a time most motherboards had sockets for 30-pin SIMMs.

Around 1992, a newer SIMM package that was the equivalent of 32 or 36 DIPs became more popular; this package is known as a 72-pin SIMM, and most modern motherboards' memory sockets are 72-pin SIMM sockets. Computers built around Pentium-class or Pentium Pro–class processors required that when you upgraded memory, you did it with pairs of 72-pin SIMMs.

Since 1996, a kind of main memory called a *synchronous dynamic RAM (SDRAM)* has appeared on the market. It too is a 72-pin SIMM, but it works differently and so requires yet another socket type. Some of today's motherboards have sockets for old-style 72-pin SIMMs and sockets for SDRAM modules; other motherboards only accept the newer SDRAM modules. You can see two kinds of SIMMs and a DIMM in Figure 3.9.

Solving the Memory Speed Problem: DRAM, Fast Page, EDO, Burst EDO, SDRAM, RDRAM, and DDR SDRAM

You read earlier in this chapter that it would be nice to have memory that ran as quickly as the processor, but that no one makes inexpensive, fast memory. It would seem, then, that slow memory speed would be an important pothole in the road to maximum speed, and that the smart PC buyer should be sure to spend all available money on the latest, fastest memory. PC hardware vendors have been eager to separate PC buyers from that money. In fact, fast memory *can* lead to a faster computer, but not *that* much faster.

But we have seen changes in memory bus speed over the last few years. Traditional SDRAM originally had a bus speed of 66MHz (once the PCI bus pushed up to 66MHz). Starting with the Intel BX chipset in 1998 (developed for PII and PIII processors with fuller support for newer hardware such as AGP and USB), bus speed jumped to 100MHz (PC100 RAM), which arguably provided a nice edge to overall performance as the CPUs were beginning to speed up as well. The latest Pentium IIIs have a 133MHz front-side bus and take 133MHz SDRAM DIMMs, while the Athlon K7 uses 200MHz SDRAM. The future is even faster, as you'll discover later in this chapter.

FIGURE 3.9

Single Inline
Memory Modules
(SIMMs) and a
Dual Inline Memory
Module (DIMM)

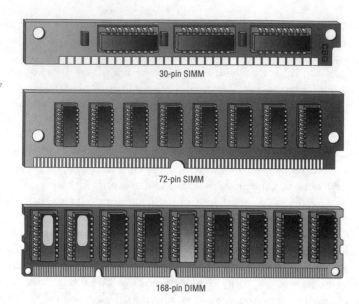

30-pin SIMM

72-pin SIMM

168-pin DIMM

Originally, main memory was simple dynamic RAM (DRAM), a good, inexpensive memory design that you don't see anymore. Recall that there is fast memory around called SRAM—static RAM. But it's too expensive to use for all system memory, so most PCs try to strike a balance by using a lot of cheap memory for main system memory and adding a little bit of the expensive SRAM to act as a memory cache. So PCs in the mid-to-late '80s tended to be a mix of a lot of DRAM and a bit of SRAM.

Memory makers wanted to build a DRAM that was faster (closer to SRAM speed), without making it too much more expensive. And that's when DRAM designers hit upon a couple of important concepts:

◆ It's impossible to make DRAM able to just grab data from any old location quickly.

◆ But once a DRAM has accessed a piece of data in *one* location, it is possible to design the DRAM so that it can quickly access data that is *nearby*.

A memory called *static column RAM* appeared in 1986 that used this information, and Compaq used it in their Compaq Deskpro 386 to squeeze good performance out of their computer. The early '90s saw another read-nearby-data-fast approach called *Fast Page Mode* memory, which was followed by *Extended Data Out*, or *EDO*, memory, which was followed by a slightly faster approach called *Burst Extended Data Out* memory.

Each memory type was faster than its predecessors, but they all shared the same basic characteristic: once a piece of data was read from a chip, nearby data could be read quickly. How near "nearby data" had to be varied from design to design, but it meant that at some point you'd exceed the "neighborhood" of the original data read. So, for example, let's assume that a "neighborhood" for a bit of data in a memory is 2048 bytes long. (Assume there's no static cache in this example.) It's the first thing in the morning, and the CPU's about to access its very first byte of the day. Because it's a

DRAM access that's not near the previous access (since there *was* no previous access), that first access is pretty slow. But suppose that the next thing the CPU needs is the byte right after that first byte (which is a quite reasonable assumption). It's "nearby" to the first byte, and so its access is fast. Assuming that the CPU keeps requesting data sequentially, it'll find fast response for the next 2046. But after that, access slows again as the CPU enters another "neighborhood."

The latest kind of popular RAM solves that problem. It's called, as I mentioned earlier, synchronous DRAM or SDRAM. How it works is interesting. The CPU tells it, "Go get some data at location 10,455," and the SDRAM goes to do that. That initial access takes a bit of time, as with earlier DRAM. But what the SDRAM does next is really unique: it just starts pumping data out of the memory sequentially until the CPU tells it to stop. After the data in location 10,455, it gets 10,456, then 10,457, and so on, and *all at SRAM speeds!* Basically, the memory just goes on "autopilot" and shotguns data sequentially at the CPU. Now, *if the CPU needs a big hunk of sequential data*, then this can be quite fast, and that's why if you look at current PC advertisements, they all trumpet how much SDRAM you get, as if it really made a difference in your system's performance. But the fact is, SDRAM or any other kind of RAM really won't affect system speed tremendously. You can see two SDRAM SIMMs in Figure 3.10.

FIGURE 3.10
SDRAM (with
Pentium III
cartridge socket
in background)

MORE RAM IS BETTER THAN FASTER RAM

To see why variations in system RAM type won't significantly affect your PC's performance, let's return to the notion of the static cache RAM. The idea with this 256KB–1024KB of memory cache is that it's obviously fast to access. So if the CPU needs the data from location *x* in main memory *and* the cache happens to already *have* that data, then the CPU can read the data from cache with almost no delay at all. If the data for location *x* isn't in the cache, that's fine—there's no hardware failure or anything like that—but access is slower, because the request for the data will have to go out to the slower main memory. But consider: if a system has, say, 256KB of cache and 32MB of main memory, then the cache has room for copies of only a small percentage of the data in the main memory. What determines which data is kept in cache and which data isn't? A memory controller circuit, either on the motherboard (in older systems) or the CPU (in modern systems). A cleverly built memory controller can get a lot of mileage out of a small amount of cache memory.

The key, then, to building a system that's both fast memory-wise and easy on the wallet is to add a small amount of expensive, fast memory as cache and then add a clever memory controller to get the most out of it. And that's what virtually every modern computer does (save for laptops, which generally don't have cache).

NOTE   *In modern computers, well over 95 percent of the CPU's memory requests are satisfied by the static cache.*

Let's do a little math to consider what that means vis-à-vis performance. Assume that about 25 percent of what the CPU does requires memory accesses. A slow memory system, then, could affect only 25 percent of the CPU's performance for good or ill. (This is a rough analysis and isn't completely accurate; it's just a back-of-the-envelope look at how memory affects performance.) But 95 percent of those memory accesses are satisfied by the nearly instantaneous static memory cache, so slow main memory could affect only 5 percent of the 25 percent of the CPU's tasks that are memory-oriented; in other words, *main memory speed affects about 1.25 percent of CPU tasks!* It may be that by the time you read this, some other new whiz-bang kind of memory has appeared to unseat SDRAM as the "fastest" memory technology, and you can be sure that its price tag will reflect its "latest and greatest" nature. But I'd suggest that rather than spending all kinds of money on faster memory, you spend that money on *more* memory. A PC with 32MB of blindingly fast memory would run Windows 98 far more slowly than a PC with 64MB of run-of-the-mill RAM.

With this said, understand that—particularly in a Windows 9*x* environment (Windows NT, 2000, and XP handle memory more precisely)—having the proper amount of RAM for your needs can be critical. For example, if you're working with an older machine of the Pentium or Pentium MMX type with just 16MB or 32MB of RAM and hitting serious performance issues, upgrading RAM to 64MB can improve the performance more than upgrading to a faster CPU.

RAMBUS DRAM (RDRAM)

As part of the move to the Coppermine (Camino) chipset, Intel wanted faster RAM not just for higher-end performance machines including servers, but standard desktops. Its choice was a new type of DRAM called *Rambus DRAM (RDRAM)*.

On paper, RDRAM sounds pretty good, although the actual product has been somewhat controversial. RDRAM, after all, is supposed to operate at twice the clock speed and be at least 10 times faster than current SDRAM technology. It's cited as perfect for any situation requiring both high bandwidth and low latency (where you need a lot of power up front, and you don't have the luxury of an often idle system). Three versions of it are intended: PC 600 (clock speed: 300MHz), PC 700 (actually 711 or 356MHz), and PC 800 (400MHz). Sounds fast, doesn't it?

Instead of SIMMs and DIMMs, Rambus comes in RIMMs, or Rambus Inline Memory Modules (see Figure 3.11). A RIMM differs from a SIMM or a DIMM in more than cost. Because these RIMMs can develop hot spots apparently related to their speed of operation, each RIMM has a heat spreader cover plate to try to diffuse the heat.

FIGURE 3.11

Rambus RIMMs

Beyond this, RIMMs can't be used on motherboards not designed with Rambus sockets in place. At the time of this writing, only the Pentium 4 with the Intel 850 chipset supports Rambus memory. PCs currently using 66MHz, 100MHz, or 133MHz SDRAM would need to overhaul both the motherboard and the processor chipset to use Rambus.

But the controversy develops from issues such as RDRAM's very proprietary 16-bit serial bus, and limitations on how it can be used. Thornier still is the matter of cost. Not too many RAM makers jumped on the bandwagon, so supplies are limited, production small and expensive. And test reports indicate the extra bang may not be worth the buck. AMD, for example, isn't embracing the Rambus route, and instead is looking at double data rate (DDR) SDRAM, which they say is fast enough and nowhere near as expensive.

At the time of this writing, with RDRAM still available on only a limited basis, the price difference between a Pentium 4 using SDRAM and one using RDRAM was about $200. This price differential is likely to push RDRAM into the upper fringe of desktop PC systems, with more mainstream models using the more traditional SDRAM or newer DDR SDRAM. It was estimated that more than 80 percent of the first Coppermine chipset-based systems shipped with SDRAM rather than RDRAM.

NOTE *PC users have only recently begun to enjoy a time when they could seriously stock their PCs with RAM without having to take out a loan. Old-timers will remember when 16MB of RAM cost over $1000 (and there are worse stories). The RAM business has also historically been hit with a good deal of instability. A fire at a chip-related plant in Korea a few years ago, and then the earthquakes in Taiwan in 1999, drastically increased prices for several months. If you add price instability to an already costly product, you potentially reduce the number of people who can afford the technology, and you make those who can afford it more inclined to consider the alternatives before they purchase a system. In today's world, you just can't do real work on an underpowered, under-RAM-supplied PC.*

Stay tuned to see if Rambus revolutionizes the RAM industry or disappears quickly as it's replaced with something that provides more performance for the price paid.

NOTE *You can keep up with the latest Rambus developments by visiting* `http://www.rambus.com`.

DOUBLE DATA RATE (DDR) SDRAM

If you want something faster than normal SDRAM but not as expensive as RDRAM, a good compromise is available in the form of *double data rate SDRAM—DDR SDRAM*, for short. DDR does exactly what it sounds like it does: doubling the rate at which standard SDRAM can process data. It does this by reading data on both the rising and falling edge of the clock signal; regular SDRAM carries data only on the rising edge. For example, instead of an SDRAM data rate of 133MHz, DDR SDRAM transfers data at 266MHz.

DDR SDRAM costs about $100 more than traditional SDRAM, but about $100 less than RDRAM. The performance boost over SDRAM is about 15 percent; RDRAM ups the performance level another 10 percent or so.

Unlike RDRAM, which few chipmakers (except Intel) are supporting, everybody appears to be jumping on the DDR SDRAM bandwagon. Intel is selling a DDR SDRAM version of its popular 845 Pentium 4 chipset; AMD has embraced DDR SDRAM for its Athlon and Duron chips; and VIA and Acer Labs are introducing DDR SDRAM for the Pentium 4.

The upshot is that you're seeing a three-tier approach to Pentium 4 computers. The bottom, lowest-priced tier uses SDRAM; the middle tier uses DDR SDRAM; and the highest-priced models use RDRAM. Clone chips from AMD and VIA are using either SDRAM or DDR SDRAM, and not supporting RDRAM at all.

SELF-HEALING RAM: ECC MEMORY

As you buy more and more memory, however, your PC becomes more fragile, because every memory byte is a circuit, and every circuit is something that can go wrong. A PC with 256KB of RAM has millions fewer failure points than does a PC with 64MB of RAM. This is not to suggest that you should buy PCs with 256KB of RAM; in fact, I'm not sure you *can* buy a machine with that little RAM. I think my microwave oven has a couple of megs these days.

From the original 1981 machines onward, PCs have been able to detect memory errors through a system called *parity*. Parity couldn't fix the error; it just knew that it was there. Once the parity error detection circuitry found a memory error, it made a sort of abrupt response to the problem: it just stopped the computer cold. That made people ask, "What good is parity if it just locks the system up—how is that better than just continuing to run with faulty memory?" (which is not a bad question). Parity also required a bit more memory. Early systems used either 8-bit SIMMs or 9-bit SIMMs—the difference was that the 9-bit SIMMs had parity. The same thing appears today with 72-pin SIMMs; they come in 32-bit or 36-bit varieties. The 36-bit variety includes parity.

Many systems nowadays opt not to use parity, and it's a shame, because parity has finally come into its own. Newer systems with parity memory cannot only detect an error, they can *correct* that error. This process is called *error correction code*, or *ECC*, memory. ECC memory's been around for mainframes and minis for years, but not for PCs save for a few expensive machines. With modern machines, however, all you need do is make sure that you buy parity memory (36-bit SIMMs rather than 32-bit SIMMs) and configure the system to use the memory for ECC—it's usually a software setting of some kind—and you get mainframe memory power for pennies. The shame is that many hardware vendors don't tell their customers about it.

NOTE   *It's worthwhile to note that 64-bit RAM is not ECC memory; 72-bit RAM is. If you want ECC memory, 72-bit is the type to buy.*

Managing Memory

So far, I've probably covered many of the terms that you come across when reading computer ads or tips on "powering up" your PC. Just remember the following three points, and you shouldn't have any problem distinguishing between them:

◆   RAM is volatile, meaning that it does not hold data when you turn a PC off, but disk drives retain the data stored on them even when the power is turned off.

◆   PCs tend to have a lot more disk space than they've got RAM space.

◆   As mentioned before, RAM is a lot faster than disk memory.

You'll also encounter another bunch of terms: *conventional memory*, *extended memory*, and *expanded memory*. These are more software-oriented terms than hardware-oriented, but they're worth going over in case you're trying to configure software that starts asking questions about how much memory you have.

MEMORY MANAGEMENT IN THE DOS WORLD

Many of the memory-related issues that we face today have their roots in the past, a past over 20 years ago. Trust me, this isn't just a history lesson—some things that IBM decided in the summer of 1980 affect how the latest version of Windows works today. So bear with all the DOS-era details in the sections to follow; there really is a point to all this!

Up until about a decade ago, memory management was a hot topic in the PC world. There were several reasons why:

◆   Memory chips were expensive—*very* expensive.

◆   DOS didn't do a good job of managing what memory it had.

◆   With limited memory space available, programs with a small memory "footprint" were highly valued.

◆   Many DOS programs and utilities were *Terminate and Stay Resident (TSR)*, meaning that they loaded into memory—and stayed there.

◆   The order in which programs loaded into memory affected program and system performance; if programs were loaded in the wrong order, system crashes would often result.

Memory management was *so* important that an entire subcategory of software (memory managers) was created, and several best-selling books were written about the topic. This might seem odd today, when memory is cheap and plentiful and the operating system actually does a good job of managing memory usage, but that's the way it was back then.

In the DOS world, you had to deal with the three distinct types of memory I mentioned earlier: conventional, extended, and expanded. The interaction of these different types (actually areas within the system's memory) determined what types of (and how many) programs your PC could run.

Conventional   This is the first 640KB of the first 1MB (1024KB) of memory, used for configuring the DOS program environment for games and such, and for loading DOS device drivers and programs that can be loaded into upper memory (640–1024KB).

Extended   This is memory beyond the 1MB barrier. Windows does most of its work with this type of memory.

Expanded   Also called *Expanded Memory Specification (EMS)* or *LIM*, this was used by a handful of programs written in the late '80s and early '90s; it isn't a factor today. (LIM, by the way, stands for Lotus-Intel-Microsoft, and was used primarily by Lotus 1-2-3 and certain Microsoft programs of the era.)

NOTE   *Expanded memory is only useful in trying to support much older machines, or much older software on more recent machines. Modern computer programs really don't make use of this any longer.*

Why so many kinds of memory? It's worth noting something before I go any further: nobody planned this. It just kind of "growed up that way." Nobody ever thought the PC would need more than 640KB of memory. (There's a famous Bill Gates quote from the early '80s along the lines of "No one will ever need more than 640KB of memory on a personal computer.")

Designing a Computer's Memory: Zoning the First Megabyte

In the summer of 1980, IBM commenced the PC development project. The goal of the small design team was to build a "home computer" (that's what we called them in those days) that could compete with the Apple II. The PC had a good start in that it was based around a much more powerful chip than the Apple's. The chip that IBM selected was, of course, the Intel 8088, and one of the powerful features was that the 8088 could address ("talk to") up to 1024KB—1MB, or 1,048,576 bytes—of RAM. That limit shaped DOS, the need for DOS compatibility shaped Windows 3.*x*, and Windows 3.*x* compatibility constrained much of the Windows 95/98 architecture. (Think of it as The Curse of Backward Compatibility.)

Planning a new computer is kind of like planning a new community. Before breaking ground on a new planned community, a zoning board or planning board determines what use will be made of all the land space. Thus, the planners of a new community start from some unused land, perhaps fallow farmland. After acquiring the land, the next step is to plot it out into lots and then determine which lots will hold residential buildings, which ones commercial buildings, industrial buildings, local government, and so on. You could say that before any buildings are built, a planner must allocate addresses. Before any buildings get built, the planner decides that any buildings built on address *x* must be residential, and any on a given address *y* must be commercial. In the same way, planning a computer requires allocating specific contents to "addresses." Now let's take a look at how memory in IBM's first computer was designated.

IBM, too, had to worry about traffic flow (the traffic isn't cars and trucks but instructions and requests running from hardware to CPU and back), about population density (too much equipment in one place affects the heat of the unit, and overheating affects a PC's performance), and resources (enough power to keep the drives, the video, and so on running).

Interrupt Vectors and DOS

The bottom 1KB of memory is an area used by the CPU as a kind of table of contents of hardware support programs called *software interrupts*. The table of contents is composed of pointers to those programs called *interrupt vectors*. This area is a fixed size of 1024 bytes—400 in hexadecimal. One interrupt points to the program that controls your disk drives, another to the video board, and so on. That 1KB is reserved for the interrupt vector table no matter what operating system you're running, and no matter which CPU you're using. Above that is DOS itself. I can't say exactly how much space DOS takes up in memory, simply because first, there are many versions of DOS, and second, different `CONFIG.SYS` options use more or less space, and that space adds to the DOS space requirements.

NOTE *Do you speak hexadecimal? If you don't now, you likely will as you develop more skills in PC troubleshooting, because hexadecimal (also called base 16) is part of the language of math making up the computer world. Simply put, hexadecimal takes the numerals 0–9 and then takes the letters A–F and sees and uses them as if they were numerals 10–15. These letters are multiplied on a base of 16. Depending on a letter's placement in a numeric statement, it may have extra weight, and be multiplied by powers of 0, 1, 2, or 3. For more information, turn to Appendix A, "A Short Overview on Reading Hexadecimal."*

Device Drivers

Directly above this bottom level, DOS loads a special class of programs called *device drivers*. Virtually every DOS-based computer uses at least one of these. (Similar programs in Windows are called *Windows drivers*, and they are files with an extension of either `.386` for Windows 3.*x* or `.VXD` for Windows 95 and above.)

Device drivers are programs that either allow DOS to support a new piece of hardware or add new capabilities to an existing piece of hardware. Device drivers are loaded in the `CONFIG.SYS` file with the `DEVICE=` statement.

Quite often, the order in which you load device drivers is important in DOS. In any case, device drivers change the way that your system reacts to information from your system's hardware. When you're trying to track down a problem, it's always a good idea to boot with as few device drivers as possible, whether talking about DOS, Windows, or Windows NT.

Command Shell

Every operating system has a program that accepts inputs from users and reformulates them in a manner that the operating system can understand. In the case of DOS, the most common command shell was and is (for those of us inclined to go to the command prompt) `COMMAND.COM`. It loaded after the device drivers, but before TSRs.

TSR or Memory Resident Programs

Under DOS, Terminate and Stay Resident (TSR) programs do much the same thing as device drivers, but they are loaded from `AUTOEXEC.BAT`, so they load after any device drivers.

DOS relied upon TSRs and device drivers, especially to load various types of utility programs, but they came with a price: they took up your precious 640KB conventional space that you needed to run DOS programs.

User Programs

Above the TSRs, you find the currently loaded program. The remaining memory is then available for the program's documents. Again, the top address is 640KB minus 1, rather than 640KB, because you start counting at *zero*, not *one*.

The vast majority of DOS programs claimed that they could run only in the low 640KB of your PC's memory, and that's largely true. That's why the 640KB conventional memory area is so important; if your program can live only in conventional memory, and the conventional memory is full, getting more memory won't help. One of my users once said of her computer, which had only 4MB of RAM at the time, "We need to buy more memory for my PC—I'm running out of memory." She was indeed running out of memory, but with an old application that couldn't use any more memory than 640KB. As far as that application was concerned, the memory beyond 640KB didn't even exist.

Video RAM

People used to say that DOS and DOS programs had a *640KB barrier* or *640KB limitation*, but that's not actually true. DOS programs were almost all written to run on the 8088 chip (and, of course, its successors, the 286 and later). Any 8088 program could address up to 1024KB of memory—in theory. There's nothing about DOS or the 8088 (or the Pentium II, for that matter) that requires the story to end at 640KB. Nevertheless, 640KB is a very real barrier for most systems. Why?

The blame for 640KB can be laid at the feet of those 1980 PC designers.

As used in the IBM world, the video board—the circuit board that acts as an interface between the CPU and the monitor—must have some memory on it. That memory is then shared between the circuitry on the video board and the CPU. The CPU "puts data on the screen" by putting data into this video RAM. The video circuitry sees the data in the memory and interprets it as graphical or textual information.

Video memory is memory used by video boards to keep track of what's to be displayed on the screen. When a program puts a character on the screen, or draws a circle on the screen, it is making changes to this video memory. IBM set aside 128KB for video memory, but most video boards don't need or use that much memory space. The answer to the original question, however ("Where does the 640KB limit come from?") is that the video RAM must go somewhere, and the original PC designers placed it from 640KB through 768KB. Even if there were more memory for user programs above 768KB, most programs could not use that memory, and *here* you see the DOS limitation: in general, DOS programs needed *contiguous blocks of memory*.

Thus, DOS programs could start grabbing memory just above DOS itself and then keep going until they hit a pothole of some kind—and in this case, that pothole is the video memory—at which point they stop looking for memory. In general, DOS programs aren't smart enough to use fragmented memory. (That's not true for Windows programs, by the way.)

You may be saying, "Why doesn't someone just build a PC with the video addresses higher up? Then there'd be more space for conventional memory." Unfortunately, that would not work. The reason is that a large number of programs are designed to directly manipulate the video hardware, and those programs are all written assuming that the video is where it's supposed to be—between 640KB and 768KB.

The current standard SVGA still uses the addresses from 640KB through 768KB (these addresses are numbered A0000–BFFFF). This is hexadecimal (check Appendix A if that's new to you).

Used memory address space differs from total memory on board because video board manufacturers use a technique called *paging* (explained further in the upcoming section "Video Memory and Paging"). Paging enables them to put lots of memory on the video board—lots of memory means better video—without taking up a lot of the CPU's total 1024KB memory address space.

Note that the video board can be convinced to disable memory usage from B0000 to B1000, the addresses that the MDA (Monochrome Display Adapter) uses. That's so your system could run two monitors. Although it's not common, some debugging systems for programmers let you test-run your program with program output going to a VGA monitor while displaying debugging information on a monochrome MDA monitor.

Newer PCI-based video boards are quite a bit smarter about using memory, so you can put multiple PCI-based video cards into a single computer.

Video Memory Layout   The 128KB set aside for video memory isn't just laid out as one big 128KB block; rather, there are three separate and distinct video memory areas, as seen in Figure 3.12.

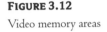

FIGURE 3.12

Video memory areas

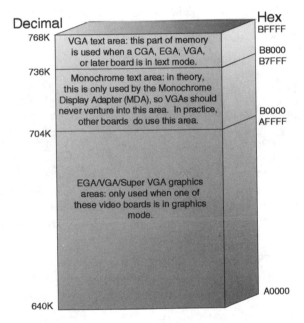

On current graphics boards, graphics activity takes place in the bottom 64KB of the video area. This is accessed only when in graphics mode. The 32KB area from B0000 through B7FFF was designated for the MDA, although IBM MDAs used only memory from B0000 through B0FFF, a 4KB area. Later MDA improvements such as the Hercules Graphics Controller and clones used the entire 32KB region.

Video Memory and Paging   As you look at the VGA graphics area, a question may be forming in your mind. Anyone who's bought a video board has heard of video boards with a megabyte or two or four of memory. Where does this memory go, given that there's only 64KB of addresses set aside for VGA graphics? The answer is in the technique I mentioned earlier, called *paging*.

Recall that the video RAM is not on the motherboard, but rather on the video board. (Of course, if the VGA is integrated into the motherboard, the video RAM will be also.) Paging hardware on the VGA board enables the video board to present only 64KB of its 256KB (the amount of memory found on a normal VGA) to the CPU at a time. There are then four 64KB pages on a standard VGA and, as it turns out, they each have a job. One page governs the blue part of the screen, another the red, another the green, and the final one the intensity of an image. The actual process of generating a complete VGA graphics screen looks something like the following:

1. Issue the command to bring in (page in) the blue 64KB.

2. Draw the blue part of the screen in the blue memory page.

3. Issue the command to page in the green page.

4. Draw the green part of the image.

5. Issue the command to page in the red 64KB page.

6. Draw the red part of the screen.

7. Issue the command to page in the intensity page.

8. Designate the areas that need high intensity and low intensity.

NOTE   *Paging is a process used commonly in the computer world to shoehorn a lot of memory into just a few addresses.*

You'll see this notion of paging in many places in the computer world. Now that you have a little insight into what's required to make *one small change* to what's visible on a VGA screen, it's easy to understand why Windows—or any graphical program—can run slowly even on a fast machine. There's just so darn much housekeeping that's got to be done every time you do so much as move the mouse! That's why a graphics accelerator (discussed in Chapter 24, "Video Adapters and Displays,") makes so much sense for today's software; in fact, most current video boards are accelerators.

The System Reserved Area

In addition to device drivers, user programs, and video, the PC needs to steal from the CPU's memory address space for the following:

◆ Small amounts of memory called *buffers* or *frames* used by some expansion boards

◆ Special memory-containing system software called ROM

ROM (Read-Only Memory)   I've talked so far about memory and RAM as if they were identical notions. As mentioned earlier, another kind of memory exists, which is not used as much as RAM, but is important nonetheless. Unlike RAM, which the CPU can both write data to and read data from, this other kind of memory cannot be altered. It can only be read, so it is called read-only memory. This is memory that someone (the computer manufacturer, usually) loads just once with a special device called a PROM blaster, EPROM programmer, or the like. So you can read information from ROM, but you can't write new information. (Well, you *can* write the information, but the ROM will ignore you. Think of ROM as a chip that can *give* advice, but can't *take* it.)

Why have a memory chip that you can store information in only *once*? Well, unlike normal RAM, the ROM has the virtue that it doesn't lose its memory when you turn the machine off—techie types would say that it is *nonvolatile*. You use ROM to store software that won't change. In essence, you can say that ROM on a circuit board contains the software that tells the system how to use a circuit board.

ROM chips are found on expansion boards such as LAN, video, or scanner interface cards, to name a few examples. ROM is also found on the system board. The ROM on the system board contains a piece of software called *BIOS*, the basic input/output system. You may recall from earlier in this chapter a reference to a set of low-level programs, called software interrupts, that directly manipulate your hardware. These programs are pointed to by the interrupt vectors at the bottom of RAM memory. Software interrupts work to help configure the working environment, while BIOS serves as something of the arbiter between the PC and DOS (or the PC and Windows). DOS relies on BIOS in that DOS doesn't communicate directly with your hardware; rather, it issues commands through BIOS. Thus, when DOS reads your floppy, it does it by calling on the BIOS routine that reads your floppy drive. That's why the BIOS is so important: The BIOS determines in large measure how compatible your PC is.

As you'd expect, IBM's BIOS is *the* standard of compatibility. Back in the early '80s, the first clone makers developed BIOS software that conformed in varying degrees to the IBM standard; so the question, "Does it run Lotus 1-2-3 and Microsoft Flight Simulator?" was the acid test of compatibility. Nowadays, I suppose it is "Does it run Windows XP?" Three companies—Phoenix Software, Award Software, and American Megatrends, Incorporated (AMI)—derive large incomes from their main business of writing *very* compatible BIOS software for clone makers. This has simplified the business of cloning considerably.

I've said that ROM contains software. As you know, software changes from time to time. Occasionally a problem can be fixed by "upgrading the ROM"—getting the latest version of the ROM-based software from the manufacturer. On older systems, it means opening up the system boxes and replacing a chip. On newer systems, it's easier—all you have to do is run a program that rewrites the ROM. You do need to be careful about this though, because the BIOS on some systems may be designed to run some specific hardware that is present on that computer only. If you replace the BIOS on a system like that, some of the devices on the computer may not function correctly (or at all).

For this reason, you have to know exactly what version of software is in the ROM chips in the computers that you are responsible for. In a maintenance notebook, keep track of the serial numbers or dates on the labels pasted on the backs of the ROM chips in your PCs, or look at the PC when it boots up for an opening message from the BIOS including the software version of the BIOS. Whenever you install a board, note any ROM identifying marks. It will save you from having to pop the top to find out when you call for service.

ROM chips can usually be easily identified because they are generally larger chips (24- or 28-pin DIP chips), they are socketed (so they can be easily changed), and they often have a paper label pasted on them with a version number or some such information printed on it. ROM chips are memories, albeit inflexible ones, so they require a place in the memory addresses in the reserved area from 640KB to 1024KB.

Flash RAM   As I just said, upgrading ROM on most modern PCs is a bit different from upgrading on older PCs. Newer PCs store their BIOS on a special kind of memory chip called *Flash RAM* or, as the chips were once more commonly known, an Electrically Erasable/Programmable Read-Only Memory (EEPROM, pronounced *double E PROM*).

Flash RAM is the same as a BIOS, with the one important exception: a *program* can modify the BIOS. BIOS upgrades can then be done by just running a BIOS update program.

Flash RAM modules are a great convenience on laptops, because laptops are so crowded inside that prying them apart to change a BIOS chip is an enormous hassle. With Flash RAM, however, it's child's play: just run a BIOS update program supplied by the laptop manufacturer, and the new BIOS is installed.

Ah, but there's one caveat. With added convenience potentially comes more risk. Some motherboards of today make Flash BIOS upgrading so easy, you don't even have to open up the case (a few years ago, you often had to move a jumper on the motherboard to get it to accept the "flashing"). While this innovation is a serious time-saver, viruses have appeared that are specifically written to do damage when you upgrade your BIOS (for example, the CIH virus, aka the Chernobyl virus, set to go off on the anniversary of the Chernobyl nuclear disaster or the 26th of every month, depending on the variant). The BIOS can't discern which is a good change and which is a bad one, so encountering such a virus and leaving it unchecked could damage your BIOS. When the damage is unchecked and runs its course, replacing the motherboard—or at least the BIOS chip on the motherboard—is warranted.

Buffers and Frames   A *buffer* acts as a sort of queue, or an area for storing computer messages. A *frame* refers to one complete scan of the active area of a computer display screen, containing a set number of horizontal scan lines, with a set number of pixels in each. *Frames per second (fps)* refers to the number of times the screen updates per second.

You've seen that video boards require memory to hold the current video image. They're not the only boards that use memory addresses, however; other boards also need a little memory space reserved for them. A LAN board, for example, may require some storage space. Here are a few examples:

◆   Token Ring LAN boards have 16KB of ROM that contains a sort of network-level BIOS. They also have a RAM buffer that can be adjusted to be as small as 8KB or as large as 64KB.

◆   Many Ethernet boards these days have a 32KB RAM buffer on them; that RAM buffer must have an address within the CPU's address range.

◆   Some old ARCNet cards (it's an acronym for Attached Resource Computer Network) have up to 64KB of ROM on them.

◆   Older VGA boards had 24KB of ROM on them, but super VGA boards usually have 32KB or 40KB of ROM.

◆   Many hard disk controllers have ROM, particularly hard disk controllers that offer some kind of high performance or unusual capabilities, like SCSI or enhanced IDE host adapters.

◆   Scanner interface cards, such as the one supplied with the old Hewlett-Packard ScanJet, included some ROM.

◆   An expanded, or LIM, memory board contains from 16KB to 64KB of page frame memory space to buffer transfers into and out of LIM memory.

All those memory pieces must fit somewhere in the reserved area from 640KB to 1024KB in the PC memory address space. Before you leave this section, let's add reserved areas to your memory map, as in Figure 3.13.

FIGURE 3.13

Memory map
with reserved
areas displayed

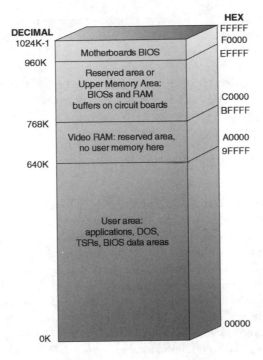

HEX
FFFFF
F0000
EFFFF

DECIMAL
1024K-1

Motherboards BIOS

960K

Reserved area or
Upper Memory Area:
BIOSs and RAM
buffers on circuit boards

C0000
BFFFF

768K

Video RAM: reserved area,
no user memory here

A0000
9FFFF

640K

User area:
applications, DOS,
TSRs, BIOS data areas

00000

0K

That's how the original PC designers laid out the first PC. The layout of that first 1024KB became a standard that no software or hardware designer dared violate, at the cost of 100 percent PC compatibility. But with more complex PCs came more memory—and a chance to get to more space.

Believe it or not, you've only gotten as far as the 8088 in this review of how software uses memory. But don't worry, the rest goes more quickly!

Extended Memory

Not content with the 8088/8086, Intel began in 1978 to develop processor chips with power rivaling that of minicomputers and mainframes. One thing micros lacked (then) that more powerful computers had was larger memory address space. So from the 80286's introduction in 1981 onward, Intel chips could address megabytes and megabytes. An 80286 could actually talk to ("address") 16MB. An 80386 or later could talk to 4GB (1GB is 1024MB) of RAM. The term for standard RAM above the 1MB level is *extended memory*.

Why did memory above 1024KB get a completely new name? Largely because the 286 and later chips had "split personalities": they could either address memory beyond 1024KB *or* run DOS programs. To use memory above 1024KB, the 286 and later chips had to shift to a new processor mode called *protected mode*. Protected mode had lots of virtues, but one big flaw: when a chip was in protected mode, it was incompatible with an older 8088 or 8086.

You see, most early CPUs used in microcomputers were more glorified calculator chips than computers—the 4004, 8008, 8080, 8085, 8086, 8088, 80188, and 80186 all fell into this category. Intel intended that the 80286 should have some powers that were mainframe-like, and in particular should be able to talk to more memory, and to *protect* that memory.

You're probably familiar with the notion that large mainframe computers can run multiple programs at the same time. Basically, the memory space of the computer gets parceled out to the applications ("Okay, text editor, you get 120KB, and database, you get 105KB, and spreadsheet, you get 150KB—no, you may *not* have more!"), and everyone's expected to stay in their places. But what about the odd program that accidentally strays from its area? If the text editor stretches a bit, it overwrites the database's area—what to do? Or, worse yet, suppose your computer were acting as a server on a LAN, and one program (a virus, or the like) tried to peek into the memory of the LAN server program itself—the *program that contains the system passwords?*

NOTE   *The 8088, 8086, and earlier chips cannot ever address memory above 1024KB, so they can never have extended memory.*

That's why memory protection is a good idea, and why mainframes have memory protection. The mainframe CPU has hardware built into it that keeps track of what application gets to use what memory. It's as if the CPU can put a "force field" around each program. As long as the program stays within its force field, it's okay. But if it tries to reach out of that area, it is stopped by the force field, and the CPU's "security system" is alerted that a protection violation was attempted. The operating system can then terminate the application (with extreme prejudice). In less colorful terms, if an application tries to reach out of its space, the protection hardware senses this and stops the application, probably by ending the program and informing the user.

This memory protection is essential for any multitasking operating systems, and Linux and all versions of Windows from 95 on multitask. Furthermore, they work with extended memory, so you'd think that they would exploit these "force fields."

They do, but in varying ways. The oddest approach to memory protection is the one that Windows 3.*x* used. You see, all this placing of "force fields" must be controlled by some program, which means that there's got to be some control over who gets to set up force fields and who doesn't. That leads to the notion in the Intel world of *privilege rings*, as you see in Figure 3.14.

FIGURE 3.14

Privilege rings

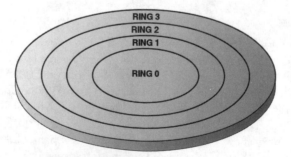

Programs in ring 0 can control anything. Programs in ring 1 can control other ring 1, 2, or 3 programs. Ring 2 programs control only ring 2 or 3 programs, and ring 3 programs can affect only other ring 3 programs. Logically, then, the operating system should be ring 0, and the applications should be ring 3. That's the way that most operating systems are built.

Sadly, Windows 3.*x* didn't do that. Under that operating system, all programs were granted ring 0 privileges. *All* programs. That meant that while all programs had memory protection, all programs also had the capability to override the memory protection. No Windows 3.*x* program was safe from any other Windows 3.*x* program, leading to an unfortunately familiar error called a *general protection fault (GPF)*. Other operating systems, including Windows 95/98, are built better, but Windows 95/98 really only works protection-wise when you use programs written for Windows 95/98; older Windows applications still aren't protected.

Anyway, back to the history: until 1981, none of the Intel CPUs had this built-in memory protection, but the 286 and later chips were all built with this feature. These chips could also address memory beyond 1024KB, but *only* while in protected mode. Again, the 8088, 8086, and earlier chips could not under any circumstances address memory beyond 1024KB, so they could not ever have extended memory.

Basically, programs that run while in protected mode don't try to do *anything* with memory without first requesting memory blocks from the operating system. Then, once the OS has granted them an area in memory, the programs load their data into their spaces, and stay there.

And *that's* the problem.

The basic problem with multitasking DOS programs is that they often live up to their nickname: the "spoiled children" of PC programs. This whole notion of first asking the operating system—DOS—for permission before using memory is totally unknown in the DOS world. Programs written for DOS pretty much assume that they're the only program in the system, so they just take whatever they want without asking for it. So for the 286 to have memory protection, it would not only have to be a *different* chip, it would have to be an *incompatible* chip—incompatible with DOS and DOS programs, in particular.

Now, designing and releasing a new chip that was totally incompatible with any previous Intel offerings would be suicidal. So Intel gave the 286 and subsequent chips split personalities: when they boot up, they act just like an 8088, except faster. They can talk to 1024KB, and no more: this 8088 emulation mode is called *real mode*. You'll sometimes hear people refer to DOS programs (when speaking of Windows) as *real mode programs*. That just means they were built for the 8088. Of course, despite the fact that no one buys 8088s anymore, software is still written for the 8088 every day because of DOS's popularity. With a few instructions, it can shift over to protected mode and talk to lots of memory beyond 1024KB. But, again, once the 286 or later chip is in protected mode, it can't run programs designed for real mode—DOS and DOS programs, that is.

You may be wondering, why didn't they just write an operating system that uses this protected mode? As I suggested earlier, they have—that was the whole idea of Windows 3.*x*, Windows NT, and Unix. Windows 3.*x* programs could address 16MB; some Windows programs—the ones that used Win32s—could address even more than that, although they required a 386 or 486 computer to do so.

Does that mean that DOS programs absolutely cannot use extended memory? By no means. A class of DOS programs uses software called a *DOS extender* to allow them to use extended memory. Basically, a DOS extender is a tiny operating system that unlocks the door to extended memory and provides tools that programmers can exploit to use that memory. Examples include Lotus 1-2-3 version 3.*x*, AutoCAD, and many database programs. This use of extended memory explains why, for example, 8088-based machines could run 1-2-3 version 3.

As XT-type machines were based on 8088/8086 chips, they *couldn't* have extended memory. ATs right up to the PIII and beyond *can*. When you see your computer count up to 16MB or 32MB or 64MB during the Power-On Self Test, you have some extended memory.

Let's take a simple example—an old 286 with 1024KB of memory. There is 1024KB of RAM, all of which must be given addresses. You recall from the earlier part of this chapter that the addresses from 0 to 640KB are intended to be filled so that conventional memory space exists. Addresses 640KB through 1024KB must be left alone, because they're intended for memory from other sources, such as the video board and add-in cards. So, of the 1024KB, 640KB gets put in the 0–640KB range. That leaves 1024KB – 640KB, or 384KB. Where does that memory get placed? It goes in the extended memory addresses, making it extended memory.

Figure 3.15 shows how it would look on your memory map.

FIGURE 3.15

Memory map with extended memory included

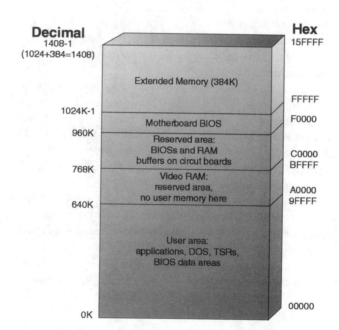

Not to belabor the point, but this breaking up of memory causes a lot of confusion for users, so let me emphasize again why the memory gets allocated this way. The key to understanding the answer is in understanding that there's a difference between *memory* and *memory addresses*.

Remember my analogy in the beginning of this section about designing a computer versus designing a town? Well, let's suppose you're designing a town built on 1024 one-acre lots (conveniently enough). Suppose you zone the first 640 lots for residential use, the next 128 for industrial, and the remaining 256 for commercial buildings. You now have addresses, and purposes for those addresses, but nothing in those addresses. Sure, there's now a lot called 200 First Avenue, but it's only a muddy rectangle of ground: send mail there, and it just sits outside and rots.

After the town has been zoned, you start putting houses in the residential addresses—filling your PC with memory. But suppose a vendor of prefabricated houses shows up with 1024 houses? That's the situation that a computer designer faces when building a computer with 1024KB of RAM. First, she plunks down houses in the first 640 lots, filling your "conventional" addresses. But the zoning board (that is, the requirements of PC hardware compatibility) precludes her from putting any of the houses in the top 384 addresses. (Here, the computer designer plays both the roles of the planning board and the prefabricated house vendor.) The top 384 lots do not have normal system RAM (houses) in them; rather, they have special RAM. That area is filled in for a PC with some RAM physically located on the video board, and perhaps some ROM located on the motherboard or add-in boards. That, too, is worth stressing: the memory in the video area isn't taken from the system's main memory; when you buy a PC with 1024KB of memory, none of that memory is ROM or video RAM. A PC with 1024KB of RAM actually has a fair amount *more* than 1024KB of RAM, if you count the RAM on the video board and the ROM and RAM buffers on the expansion boards—and that memory is *not* counted when your system does its power-up memory count. There is simply nowhere to put the extra 384 houses, which is why XTs and PCs—8088-based computers—didn't have more than 640KB of system RAM.

Now let's move along to the 286 and later chips. They have memory limitations of 16MB or more, so now you have to zone the addresses above 1024KB. Continuing the town planning analogy, suppose that this town has been in existence for 30 years, when a community springs up outside your original 1024 lots. You'd call that a suburb of the town; it might have a different tax rate, be governed differently, and have different levels of access to the privileges accorded town residents. For example, suburbanites might have to pay a fee to use the town parks, whereas the town residents might be able to use the parks for free. So it is with extended memory; the addresses above 1024KB are not accessible to the vast majority of DOS programs, as you've seen earlier in this discussion.

Return to the case of the vendor of prefab houses who finds herself with 1024 houses as she shows up in your new town. Again, she puts houses on the first 640 spaces and is then told that she cannot put houses on the top 384 addresses. "What will I do with these extra 384 houses?" she wails. "Take them out to the suburbs," she's told. So she puts the remaining 384 houses in the *extended* addresses, because the 384 addresses that she skipped from 640 to 1024 will be filled with buildings from another source.

So, getting back to the original question: what's happening with a 286 computer that counts up to 1024KB on power-up? First, understand that 1024KB is a count only of program memory. There is more memory in the computer—video RAM on the video board, system BIOS ROM on the motherboard, and ROM and perhaps small RAM buffers on add-in cards in the system—*that is not counted*. The 1024KB fills up the first 640KB and cannot fill up any of the addresses between 640K and 1024KB, or the PC will have program memory in the same addresses as video memory or ROM. Just as you can't put two houses on the same lot, so also two separate memories wired to the same address would both malfunction. So the extra 384KB of RAM gets addressed starting at 1024KB and going up to 1408KB.

TIP   *You do not have to fill a lower memory address before filling a higher address; that's why you can have extended memory before filling the system's reserved area.*

One more point that hangs some people up: I've said that the reserved area from 640KB to 1024KB contains memory, but it's not completely full. You'll usually find plenty of unused addresses between 768KB and 1024KB, a fact that created the memory manager market in the first place. Many people seem to feel that all the addresses from 0 through 1024KB must be filled by *something* before any addresses above 1024KB can be filled. But that's not true; you *could* build a computer with 128KB of conventional memory, video RAM between 640KB and 768KB, ROM between 768KB and 1024KB, and 6MB of extended memory above 1024KB. (You'd have trouble finding software that would run on it, but you could do it.)

Extended memory is simple for programmers to use, provided those programmers are working with an operating environment that supports extended memory. But extended memory wasn't always easy to work with, which led to *expanded* memory.

EMS, LIM, Paged, Expanded Memory

In 1985, Lotus 1-2-3 version 1A was the best-selling software package in history. People used Lotus for everything. And Parkinson's Law ("work expands to fill all available resources") seemed to become an iron rule—more and more users found the 640KB limitation a chafing one. Not as chafing, however, as the 1-2-3 copy protection scheme. Copy protection was a common practice among software vendors until around 1986. 1-2-3's copy protection required that you insert a key disk into your A: drive *whenever* you wanted to run 1-2-3. No key disk, no Lotus.

So, when Lotus announced 1-2-3 version 2, people were excited. At $495 a copy, it seemed a mite pricey; but Lotus made its users an upgrade offer. "Send us $125 and your version 1A key disk, and we'll send you 2," they offered. Well, at $125, that was hard to turn down. The downside was that you had to send in the key disk, which meant that you couldn't use 1-2-3 1A *or* 2 until the upgrade arrived; but Lotus FedExed the upgrades, and people saw only a day or so of downtime. (In case you're wondering, the world was a much different place then, and people didn't rely on PCs as heavily as they do today. Nowadays, of course, an upgrade offer that took a PC out of action for a day or two would be laughed off the market.) So hundreds of thousands of users got the 2 upgrade.

This is when it became clear that there was just one little problem: 1-2-3 version 2 took up more memory space than version 1A. Which meant that any spreadsheets that packed the memory up to the 640KB rafters—and there were plenty—would not run under 2 for love or money. Worse yet, the users couldn't revert to 1A (they'd turned in their 1A key disks), leaving them stranded. "Golly," those users said. (Well, they didn't actually say, "Golly," but this book is rated "G" for general audiences.) Lotus realized that they'd better do something *fast*, so they called up Intel, the chip designers, and asked what could be done. Lotus and Intel developed a paged memory system (recall paging in the video discussion) that they called *expanded memory*. Using this memory system required the user to buy a new kind of memory board that Intel built called an *AboveBoard*. (I'll explain the details on how it works in a bit.)

Let's finish your memory map by adding expanded memory off to the side of the standard memory column, as in Figure 3.16.

On 8088 and most 80286 computers, you needed a specific memory board to support LIM: two common examples of this kind of memory board were, again, the Intel AboveBoard and the AST RAMPage cards. On 386 and later machines, you could achieve LIM compatibility with just software. That means that a 386 could make extended memory behave software-wise like expanded memory. Part of what Windows 3.1 and up can do for DOS programs is to provide them with some extended memory that behaves like expanded memory. (The motherboards of some 286s could do that also, but not many.)

FIGURE 3.16

Memory map with
expanded memory

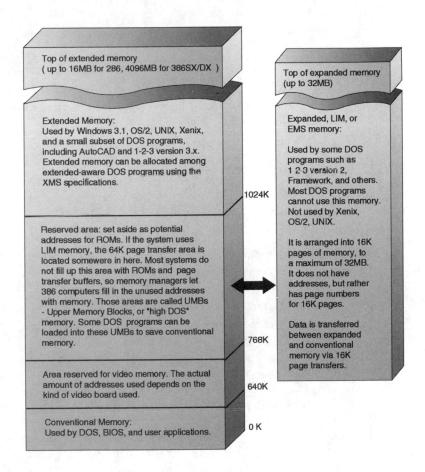

Reviewing Memory Types

So now you've seen conventional, extended, and expanded memory, and how they were used in the DOS era of personal computing. Let's review what you know so far:

- Conventional memory:
    - Available to all PCs.
    - Limited to 640KB.
    - Virtually every program can use this memory.
    - By default, DOS, device drivers, and TSRs are loaded in conventional memory.
- Extended memory:
    - Only possible with machines based on 286 and later chips; was impossible with XTs.

- ◆ A class of DOS programs could use it.

- ◆ Used by Unix, Linux, Windows.

◆ Expanded memory:

- ◆ Also called Lotus-Intel-Microsoft (LIM) memory or Expanded Memory Specification (EMS) memory.

- ◆ Could be used with PCs, XTs, ATs—any PC machine.

- ◆ Useful under DOS *with programs that can use it,* such as Lotus version 2.*x* and WordPerfect 5.1.

- ◆ 386 and later computers can make their extended memory act like expanded, as could a few 286-based machines.

TIP   If you have trouble distinguishing between extended and expanded memory, do what I do. I always pronounced the latter "exPanded," so I can remember that it is "Paged."

MEMORY MANAGEMENT IN THE POST-DOS WORLD

Early versions of Windows came with the same memory constraints found on DOS machines, primarily because those operating systems were essentially built on a DOS base. For example, Windows 3.1/Windows for Workgroups 3.11 were fairly needy of conventional memory—they wouldn't run without a certain amount of it.

Windows 95/98/Me is less dependent on the bottom 640KB—*unless* you are running old Windows 3.1 and/or DOS programs. When that happens, Windows 95/98/Me reverts to its old Windows 3.1 ways and gets needy of lower memory space. To be completely free of the need for conventional memory, you have to abandon DOS completely and move up to a 32-bit operating system, such as Windows NT, Windows 2000, or Windows XP (which is built on Windows NT/2000).

Different versions of Windows manage memory in different ways, although all use the Windows kernel to do the managing. The 16-bit Win9*x* kernel treats memory as one giant container; as you open new applications, the kernel sends data to RAM, where it's deposited in whatever memory location is available. The 32-bit WinNT kernel, on the other hand, sends the data to specific areas within RAM. Which means that memory management is more efficient—and more stable—on 32-bit versions of Windows.

This may not seem like a big difference—until you have a problem. When an application develops a fatal error, Windows "fixes" the problem by pulling the entire application (and all related data) out of memory. Since the Win9*x* kernel crams bits and pieces of application memory anywhere there's an empty space, pulling these bits and pieces out of their holes tends to make the entire system unstable. The WinNT kernel is much more orderly about where it puts application memory and thus can remove said memory without disturbing neighboring applications. The result is a much more stable system, where a single application crash doesn't crash the entire system.

In addition, Windows also takes advantage of *virtual memory.* By using spare hard disk space as a temporary memory storage area, Windows substantially increases your machine's effective memory—even though disk-based memory is noticeably slower than chip-based memory.

Another factor, of course, is the shrinking price tag on memory chips. Instead of worrying about how to cram two gallons of stuff into a one-gallon container, you can now solve your problem by buying a larger container. The days of PCs with (believe it or not) 1MB of RAM are long gone; now it's not uncommon for a new PC to come with 256MB or more memory. When you have that much memory to work with, micromanaging the use of that memory just isn't necessary.

The bottom line is that if you're running any version of Windows from Windows 95 on—and especially if you're running Windows NT, 2000, or XP—about the only memory-related issue you need to worry about is buying more of the stuff. Unlike the old DOS days, the easiest way to fix a memory management problem is to add more memory to your system. The more memory you have, the fewer problems you'll have, period.

PC Expansion Buses

"Pentium III 128MB system with 18GB drive and AGP video for sale," reads a computer ad. The Pentium part is clearly the processor. The 128MB is the RAM part, as you've just read, and everybody (well, anybody reading *this* book) knows what a hard disk is. But what's AGP? AGP is the name of one kind of *expansion bus*. What exactly an expansion bus *is*, why you want one, and why you have to worry about buses is the topic of this section.

What Is a Bus?

In order to be useful, the CPU must talk to memory, expansion boards, coprocessor (if the system has an external coprocessor), keyboard, and the like. It communicates with other devices on the motherboard via metal *traces* in the printed circuit, the copper lines that you'll see running around a board. That's how the SIMMs or DIMMs that probably live on your computer's motherboard communicate with the CPU, which is *also* probably on your computer's motherboard—they talk back and forth by shooting electrons along these thin metal traces.

But how can *expansion boards*, which aren't part of the motherboard, be connected to the CPU, the memory, and so on? Through the *bus*, or rather, through one of the buses—modern computers may have multiple expansion buses. And what are buses? Buses relate back to electrical engineering (as a lot of computer terminology does), and the term refers to a set of wires or tracks or conductors used to connect various parts of the PC.

Back in the early days of microcomputers, some computers didn't allow easy expansion. Take, for example, the early Macintosh computers. To expand a 128KB or 512KB Mac, you had to do some extensive engineering—which is why most people didn't mess around inside those computers. Any circuit boards that you wanted to add usually had to be mounted haphazardly inside the Mac's case; installing a hard disk required disassembling the computer, soldering connections onto the Mac motherboard, and reassembling the machine. Making modifications difficult puts the user at the mercy of the modifier, because virtually all such modifications are done at the expense of the manufacturer's warranty and service agreement, if any—and they're expensive, because they require a technician.

You don't have to do such brain surgery on a PC, thankfully. PCs have expansion slots that allow easy upgrades. (By the way, today's Macs also have expansion slots, fortunately; in fact, Macs built after 1995 have the same bus as some PCs, the PCI bus that I'll discuss soon.)

Another disadvantage of the old Macintosh approach was that the average Joe/Jane couldn't do the modifications themselves. This would be like you having to cut a hole in the wall of your house to find a main power line every time you want to use an appliance. Without standard interface connectors (that is, an outlet), you would have to find the power line, then splice the appliance into it to get power for the appliance.

This scenario, as you know, is silly, because you have standard outlet plugs. But it wasn't always unthinkable; when electricity first arrived, adding every new appliance entailed some fancy wiring work. (Kind of like adding a station to a LAN today.) Nowadays, however, you have an easy, standard way to add appliances. Any manufacturer who wants to sell you a device requiring electrical power needs only to ensure that the device takes standard U.S. current and add a two-prong or three-prong plug. "Upgrading" your house, then (adding the new appliance) is a simple matter: just "plug and play."

Many computers adopt a similar approach. Such computer manufacturers have issued a connector standard: any vendor desiring to offer an expansion board for this computer need only follow the connector specifications, and the board will work in the computer. Even the earliest computers included such a connector, first called the *omnibus connector*, because it gave access to virtually all important circuits in the computer. *Omnibus* was quickly shortened to bus, and *bus* it has remained.

So a computer bus is an intrinsic part of a computer's hardware communication standard, an agreement about how to build boards that can work in a standard PC. For various reasons, however, there are over a half-dozen such different standards in the PC world.

The First "PC" Bus

The PC wasn't the first computer based on a chip, not by about eight years. The first commercially available microcomputer was a computer called the Altair. It consisted of a case and a row of expansion slots. It was a backplane computer, with even the CPU on an expansion card. The bus that the Altair used became a standard in the industry for years, and it is still used in some machines: it was called the S-100 or Altair bus.

Although it was a standard, it wasn't ever true that every microcomputer used the S-100. The Apple II used a bus of its own, called the *Apple bus*. The original 1981 PC model used yet another bus, with 62 wires called lines. It came to be known as (you can see that this is something of a pattern, although a dull one) the *PC bus*.

The 62 lines mentioned above are offered to the outside world through a standard connector, as mentioned previously. These connectors are also called *expansion slots*, because expansion boards must plug into these slots. Some PCs have had no slots at all, so they weren't expandable; other machines have three, and most clone-type machines have eight slots. Some machines offer 10 slots. The more slots, the better: expansion slots equal flexibility and *upgradability*. (I know it's not a word, but you get the idea.) Let's take a minute, however, and look at what those 62 lines do.

DATA PATH

Now, remember that the original PC and XT were based on the 8088 chip. The 8088 had a data path (the "front door," recall?) of just 8 bits, so the PC bus includes only eight data lines. That means this bus is *8 bits wide*, and so data transfers can occur only in 8-bit chunks. Expansion slots on a computer with this bus are called *8-bit* slots. Eight of the 62 wires, then, transport data around the computer.

Consider the importance of data path in bus design. The 8 data bits supported by the original PC bus would be pretty inadequate for a Pentium-based system; recall that the Pentium uses a 64-bit data path.

Could someone actually *build* a Pentium computer with 8-bit expansion slots? Sure. But every time that the Pentium wanted to do a full 64-bit read of data, it would have to chop that request into eight separate 8-bit reads. *Really* slow. But it could be done, and in fact there are, as you'll learn later, designs almost as bad: most P5- and P6-based systems (which incorporate a 16-bit bus to this day), and the ISA bus you'll read about in a page or two, in addition to a 32-bit bus called PCI.

MEMORY SIZE

The original PC bus included 20 wires to address memory. What's that mean to us regular user types? Well, given that each one of those address wires can carry either a 0 or a 1 signal, then each wire can carry only one of two possible values. Since there are 20 of the address lines, the total number of possibilities is $2 \times 2 \times 2 \ldots$ 20 times. That's 2 to the 20th power, or just over one million. However, in a sense, you already knew that, because the 8088 can address only 1MB of RAM. All those address lines are duplicated on the PC bus, accounting for another 20 of the 62 bus lines.

MEMORY OR I/O ADDRESS?

The 20 address lines actually do double duty, because there are two kinds of addresses: the memory's addresses and *input/output addresses*. I'll discuss I/O addresses in greater detail in Chapter 6, "Installing New Circuit Boards (Without Creating New Problems)." However, at this point I'll mention that the computer must be able to tell when the address lines are transmitting a memory address versus when the address lines are transmitting an I/O address; one line on the bus designates which one it is.

Additionally, there are several other lines on the bus that tell whether the data on the bus has been read from memory (or an I/O device), or whether data is to be written to memory or I/O.

ELECTRONIC OVERHEAD

Some bus wires just transport simple electric power; there are +5 volts, −5 volts, +12 volts, and electric ground lines as part of the bus. Why are those lines there? Simple: to power a board plugged into a bus slot.

There are also a few control lines, like Reset (which, as you'd imagine, resets the processor), clock signals, and Refresh, which controls memory refresh (more on that in Chapter 8, "Semiconductor Memory").

INTERRUPTS AND DIRECT MEMORY ACCESS CHANNELS

Add-in cards sometimes need to demand the attention of the CPU; they do that via hardware interrupts or IRQ (interrupt request) levels. There are six IRQ levels on the PC bus, labeled IRQ2 through IRQ7. Each gets a wire on the bus. There are also IRQ0 and IRQ1, but they're not available on the bus.

Some of those add-in cards also need to transfer data to the system's memory quickly; they can do that via a direct memory access (DMA) channel. There are three DMA channels on the bus, labeled DMA1 through DMA3. There is also DMA channel 0, but, like IRQs 0 and 1, it's not accessible through the bus.

DMA and IRQs are both *extremely* important topics in PC upgrades, and I'm going to cover them in detail in Chapter 6.

I have given a somewhat in-depth look into the first PC bus so that you're ready to see why the many buses that followed are improvements on the original, and to help you decide which bus is right for any of the machines that you buy.

The first enhancement to the PC bus came with the IBM AT; let's take a look at that bus.

The AT (ISA) Bus

When developing the AT, IBM saw that it had to upgrade the bus. One reason was because the 80286 is a chip with a 16-bit data path. They certainly *could* have designed the AT with an 8-bit bus, but it'd be a terrible shame to make a 286 chip transfer data 8 bits at a time over the bus, rather than utilize its full 16-bit data path. So they thought that it'd be nice to have a 16-bit bus.

On the other hand, there was backward compatibility with the PC and XT to think of: it would be tough to sell a lot of ATs if they couldn't use the hardware (and software) of the existing, established PC/XT world. So IBM came up with a fairly good solution: they kept the old 62-line slot connectors and *added* another 36-wire connector, placing it in line with the older 62-line connector to provide some of these features:

◆ Eight more data lines, bringing the data bus to 16 bits in width.

◆ Four more address lines, bringing the address bus to 24 bits in width. Two to the 24th power is about 16 million, so the AT's 16-bit slots could support up to 16MB of RAM, in theory.

◆ Four more DMA channels, 4 through 7.

◆ Five more IRQ levels: IRQ10, 11, 12, 14, and 15. I'm getting a little ahead of myself, but I know that some of you will have an immediate question. You may know—and if not, you'll learn in Chapter 6—that there are *eight* more IRQs on a machine of this type; so why do we see only five on this newer bus slot? First, IRQ9 is wired where IRQ2 previously was, saving a bus line. What about IRQ2? It's off the bus now because it's the line that makes possible the new IRQ lines. Second, IRQ13 is dedicated to the math coprocessor, so there's no point in giving it any of the bus's wires. Finally, IRQ8 is connected to the system's clock/calendar, so it also does not require a line on the bus.

These two-part connectors are called, as you'd expect, 16-bit slots. You can see these two kinds of connectors in Figure 3.17.

For a while, this 16-bit bus was called the AT bus, and you'll still hear some people use that name. Since 1988, however, most people have referred to these types of bus slots as *Industry Standard Architecture (ISA)* slots. You can tell the difference between an 8-bit and a 16-bit ISA board by looking at the edge connector on the bottom of it. Take a look at an 8-bit board, as you see in Figure 3.18.

Notice that it has a single edge connector on the bottom. In contrast, look at a 16-bit board, like the one in Figure 3.19.

FIGURE 3.17

8-bit and 16-bit bus slots

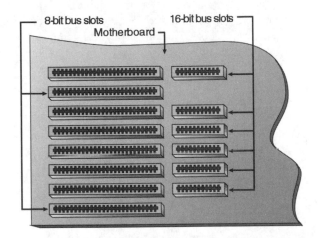

FIGURE 3.18

8-bit board

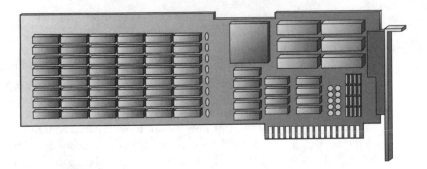

FIGURE 3.19

16-bit board

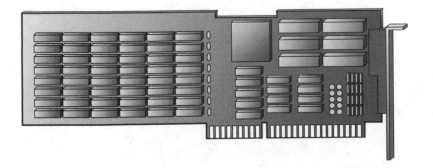

Since the 16-bit slots are just a superset of the 8-bit bus, 8-bit boards work just fine in 16-bit slots, which is a good thing—no modern PCs that I know of have the simple 8-bit slots. However, almost all *do* have the 16-bit slots, making 8-to-16 compatibility good in the unlikely case that you have an old 8-bit board around that you want to use.

Years ago, you would sometimes see a motherboard with both 8-bit slots and 16-bit slots. If the 16-bit slots can use 8-bit boards, why have any 8-bit slots on an AT-type machine at all? The reason is not an electrical reason, but a physical reason. Some older 8-bit boards have a *skirt* that extends down and back on the circuit board, making it physically impossible to plug an 8-bit board with a skirt into a 16-bit connector. You can see a board with a skirt in Figure 3.20.

FIGURE 3.20

8-bit board with a skirt

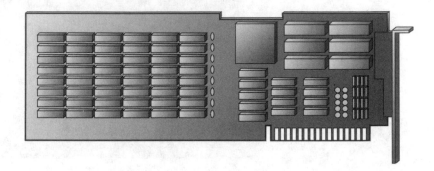

ISA has continued on our systems for backward compatibility. Even if we use some of the latest equipment on our PCs, some of us still have ISA sound cards and even modems and network cards either installed or sitting around as a backup.

But all reigns must come to an end, and ISA's has come. ISA is being eliminated in an effort to finally move away from the antiquated slowness of the bus, and to make room for USB and FireWire, though we continue to have slower serial and parallel ports supported under the design specifications.

Since January 1, 2000, ISA slots cannot be manufactured into a motherboard on a system that will bear the "certified Windows compatible" logo, as pronounced by the Microsoft-Intel PC design specifications. Even as Linux becomes more of a player in the PC world, Windows certification is important if you want to sell PCs.

JUST HOW FAST IS THAT BUS?

You learned back in the CPU section that different CPUs run at different speeds. You can't take a CPU rated to run at 25MHz and run it at 66MHz; it will fail. (You can *try*—recall that it's called overclocking—but it's not a good idea.)

Buses have clocks, as well, and those clocks drive the boards inserted into their expansion slots. That suggests a question: how is it that any board pretty much works in any kind of computer? Why does an ISA video board built for a 12MHz computer still work in a 400MHz Pentium II?

Part of the answer, you'll recall, is that the 400MHz Pentium II looks like a 100MHz chip from the motherboard's point of view; the 400MHz part is internal to the CPU chip. So the fastest bus you'd need for a 400MHz Pentium would be 100MHz. But for the rest of the story, let's return to 1985.

EARLY BUSES EQUALED CLOCK RATES

Prior to 1985, buses ran at the same speed as their CPUs. The PC ran at 4.77MHz, and so did the PC bus. Turbo XT clones that ran at 7.16MHz had buses that ran at 7.16MHz. When IBM released the 6MHz AT, then its bus ran at 6MHz, and so on.

But all this variation in bus speeds led to a major headache for expansion board buyers. A board designed for the 4.77MHz PC might not (and often *did* not) work in the faster machines. Part of a PC upgrader's job was to know which PC bus speeds a particular board would work in.

COMPAQ TRIES NOT TO MISS THE BUS

Then Compaq released its Deskpro 286/12.

In 1985, IBM was selling the AT, as you've already read. The fastest version ran at 8MHz. Compaq, as the number one IBM cloner, decided to seriously outpace IBM with their new Deskpro 286/12—the 12 stood for 12MHz.

Now, okay, 12MHz isn't such a big deal nowadays. But back then, it was like Compaq today offering a Pentium that runs at 800MHz. Nobody else even came close. But what to do about the bus? If they built a 12MHz 286 computer with a 12MHz bus, then in all probability no existing boards would work. Who'd buy a fast computer that wouldn't work with any of the add-in boards on the market?

Compaq's answer: decouple the main clock from the bus clock. They ran the CPU and much of the motherboard at 12MHz, but ran the bus at only 8MHz. Expansion boards sitting in slots would see only an 8MHz environment, so the new Deskpro could be both fast *and* compatible. And ever since, that's how everybody has built their ISA slots, at 8MHz. That's why you never have to worry about whether your computer is too slow for a particular board; from the board's point of view, every computer—including yours—runs at 8MHz. This *sounds* good, but...

The big drawback in having the expansion bus run at a separate clock speed than the external CPU bus is that some boards *should* run at CPU speed, such as memory boards. Imagine that you have a 100MHz Pentium. It communicates with its motherboard at 66MHz, because it's a clock-and-a-halfer. Suppose you want to put more memory on this system, so you buy an ISA memory card. (Please *don't* do this; this is just an example.) You pop it into one of the computer's 16-bit slots, and you'll have extended your memory, but *all memory accesses will be at 8MHz, not 66MHz*; every time you access memory on that board, your system will slow down to 8MHz. Yuck. And many of us use ISA boards on a daily basis to talk to our hard disks, video monitors, and local area networks. This is a major reason why we need something other than the ISA bus as a standard, and why there are so many kinds of alternative buses available.

ISA's Not Enough: Mesozoic Local Bus

The first folks to try to set a new bus standard were, again, Compaq, a year later.

In 1986, Compaq introduced one of the first 80386-based desktop computers. Because the 80386DX is a 32-bit chip, Compaq wanted to exploit that power with a new bus slot. Remember, *they* were the guys who saddled us with the 8MHz bus slots in the first place. Standard-speed bus slots were still a good idea, but how to offer memory expansion boards that were 32-bit in data path and 16MHz (the computer's clock rate) in speed, unless by building an entirely new bus?

Compaq decided to just include a new 32-bit slot on the motherboard, a slot solely for use with a specific memory card that Compaq (and later, third-party vendors) sold. Some 386 cloners adopted this new bus format, but it never really caught on. Instead, each vendor developed its own 32-bit "standard." Intel had one it pushed for a while in the late '80s, AT&T had another, Micronics a fourth, and so on.

These buses all had several things in common:

- They had a 32-bit data path.

- They ran at the clock speed of the 386 computer—usually 16MHz, 20MHz, 25MHz, or 33MHz.

- They supported only one particular board, sold by the motherboard's manufacturer.

These buses came to be known as *private* buses or, later, *local* buses, because they were "local" to the processor, since there was no extra clock circuitry between them and the CPU. From 1986 to 1991, the main value of local bus boards and slots was, again, to accommodate memory for their specific computer. These were the remote ancestors of what we now call the *VESA Local Bus (VLB)* standard— what I think of as the "Mesozoic" version of VLB. I suppose that if you used one of these on a hard disk controller, you'd "Jurassic *park*" the heads on your drive. (Yeah, it was a lousy pun. But stick around; they get worse.) Discussion of VLB, by the way, is coming up in a bit; I just wanted to keep this discussion in at least moderately chronological order.

The PS/2 Bus: Micro Channel Architecture (MCA)

Not to be outdone by Compaq in the trendsetting department, IBM attempted to change the rules again in 1987 when they announced the PS/2 line. The PS/2 Models 50 to 80 (*not* the 25 or 30) got a new bus called the *Micro Channel Architecture (MCA)* bus, in order to facilitate faster data transfer within the computer, and to lower noise levels. (ISA is a *very* noisy standard, which is another reason why it hasn't gotten faster over the years.) It didn't catch on, but IBM pushed it doggedly for years before surrendering in the mid-'90s.

Introducing a new bus was a bold move (although perhaps not a very bright one), in that the MCA bus was completely incompatible with the old ISA bus. ISA expansion boards didn't (and *don't*) work in the PS/2 line. PS/2 buyers must be sure when buying a board that it's an MCA board, not an ISA board, because the ISA boards are completely useless in MCA machines.

What prompted this bold move? Well, some of the things that I've already discussed and a few others. MCA never really caught on that strongly (and I'll talk about why that's true in a minute), but some of the features that it offered have become essential for any advanced bus.

BETTER SPEED AND DATA PATH

As you'd expect, MCA tried to better ISA by hitting its weak points. MCA runs at 10MHz, not 8MHz. Not a great improvement, but an improvement. MCA also supported either a 16-bit data path or a 32-bit data path. It actually has a streaming mode, wherein it can transfer 64 bits at a time.

SOFTWARE BOARD CONFIGURATION

Anyone who's installed an older ISA board (installation of boards is, again, the main topic for Chapter 6) has almost certainly struggled with small DIP switches and jumpers. These small hardware devices are used to configure older ISA boards. They're a pain in the neck, because they're often hard to change around, and you have to remove the PC's cover to get to them in the first place.

Micro Channel boards, in contrast, are software configurable—no jumpers and no DIP switches. You just run one central configuration program, and you can set up a computer by clicking with the mouse, rather than rooting around in the machine. This is a feature that was useful when it came out, but it's *essential* now—which is why Plug and Play hardware is becoming more and more ubiquitous.

BOARDS CAN SHARE INTERRUPTS

Once you start configuring boards, you'll find that the thing you're running out of most is interrupt levels. You can't put a mouse card on the same IRQ level as your local area network board, or your network connection could crash the first time that you move the mouse. That's because of how ISA was designed.

With MCA, it was *possible* to design a board that shares its interrupts with other boards. Very few Micro Channel boards *did* share interrupts, but it's possible. Why? Blame the people who write drivers. Even though several buses now support interrupt sharing, it's still almost unheard of, even in the most modern systems.

BUS MASTERING IMPROVES UPON DMA

I haven't explained *direct memory access (DMA)* in detail yet, but it's basically a way for expansion boards to quickly transfer data from themselves to the system's RAM, or from the RAM to the boards.

DMA's main goal in life is speed: it makes the PC faster.

DMA can't do one thing, however. Boards can transfer data directly to RAM, or RAM to boards, but *not* boards to boards. That's handled by a kind of "super" DMA called *bus mastering*. Bus mastering was not really supported by ISA (you can have one, but only one, bus master card in an entire ISA machine), but MCA supported bus mastering.

Bus mastering is another one of those features that first appeared with MCA, but is *de rigueur* for any modern advanced bus.

MCA was neat because it was cleaner, as I said before, so it could transfer data at higher speeds than the ISA machines of a few years back. (I said "could" because it has the capability, but that capability never became important in its market.) It also included something called *Programmable Option Select (POS)*. It allowed circuit boards to be a lot smarter about how they interact with the computer. For one thing, DIP switch and configuration problems lessened considerably. More on this in Chapter 6.

EISA (Extended Industry Standard Architecture)

Unfortunately, MCA turned out to be pretty unimportant in the market, mainly because IBM locked it up six ways to Sunday, patent-wise. Companies couldn't clone the MCA without paying a Draconian *5 percent* of their *gross* to IBM as fealty (oops, that's supposed to be *royalties*) for use of MCA. Five percent of gross is probably more than most companies are making as *profits*. For the 5 percent, you didn't even get the plans for MCA. *First* you had to spend hundreds of thousands of dollars figuring out how to clone MCA—IBM offered no help—*then* you got to pay Big Blue the 5 percent.

So Compaq talked eight other compatible makers (a group called Watchzone—Wyse, AST, Tandy, Compaq, Hewlett-Packard, Zenith, Olivetti, NEC, and Epson) into forming a joint venture to respond to MCA. They created yet another new bus, one called the *Extended Industry Standard Architecture (EISA)*, which was intended to have MCA's good features without sacrificing compatibility with the old AT (ISA) bus. Presumably, building it cost less than 5 percent of profits. It appeared in 1989 and still shows up on the motherboards of some systems that include both PCI and EISA slots.

EISA never got amazingly popular, but it was a kind of well-designed, solid bus that found its way into a lot of high-end servers. It was gaining some momentum around the mid-'90s, but it was overtaken by the newer, more powerful PCI standard.

What about EISA's features? Summarized, they include:

◆ 32-bit data path

◆ Enough address lines for 4GB of memory

◆ More I/O addresses, 64KB of them

◆ Software setup capability for boards, so no jumpers or DIP switches—similar to POS

◆ 8MHz clock rate (unfortunately)

◆ No more interrupts or DMA channels

◆ Supports cards that are physically large, making them cheaper to build (smaller cards cost more to design)

◆ Bus mastering

Note that EISA is *not* a local bus, because it runs at 8MHz. It runs at that poky speed because it must be, recall, hardware compatible with ISA, hence the need for slow bus slots. EISA will also run DMA at higher speeds than will ISA. The lack of local bus means, however, that EISA memory boards aren't a possibility. EISA machines either need enough SIMM space on the motherboard for sufficient memory, or the motherboard vendor must design a proprietary expansion slot for a proprietary memory card. EISA boards remain supported for use, but it's not a future standard.

Local Bus

In the XT and AT days, you expanded memory just by buying a memory expansion card, putting memory chips on it, and inserting the card into one of the PC's expansion slots. But by the time that PCs got to 12MHz, that easy answer disappeared. As I've already said, no matter how fast your PC is, the expansion slots still run at only 8MHz.

Now, I've been kind of beating up on slow buses, but they're not all *that* bad, in reality. Most boards in expansion slots communicate with components that are fairly slow anyway, such as floppy drives, printer ports, modems, and the like.

Only a handful of boards benefit from really high speeds. I've mentioned memory. Another board that really needs to be able to blitz data around is a video graphics board. Take a moment and calculate how many pixels (dots on the screen) you have on a 1024 × 768 video screen. Then consider that the CPU must shove them around perhaps dozens of times per second, and you can see that having fast access to the video board is a good thing.

Hard disk interfaces benefit from high speed, and in particular SCSI hard disk interfaces. Video capture boards are another type of fast board, and local area network cards are yet another candidate for local busing.

There are two main kinds of local bus around these days: the VLB bus and the PCI bus.

VESA Local Bus

As I've already told you, the local bus grew out of a sort of nonstandard. Some manufacturers designed a special high-speed slot for the motherboard that will accommodate only a memory board. That was the first local bus.

A bit later on, vendors started including local bus slots for video cards and then selling you the video cards that fit into those slots. The problem was one of noncompatibility: the local bus video card on one machine was incompatible with the local bus video card on another machine.

Since the lack of cross-compatibility was getting in the way of video board sales, an industry group promulgated and promoted a local bus standard called VESA after the group's name—*Video Electronic Standards Association*. It saw some moderate popularity for a bit in the early '90s but died out around 1993. It's not likely you'll run across a VESA motherboard with a Pentium or later chip on it; VESA's heyday was in the 486 days.

The VESA Local Bus (VLB) was an important step in the evolution of computers—having a 33MHz bus was cool!—but it wasn't enough. VLB is really just a 32-bit, high-speed extension of the older, dumb ISA architecture. Sometimes I describe VLB as a "big, dumb bus."

VLB actually hurt the PC world, in a way, because VLB offered improved speed but no better ways of *using* that speed: it just perpetuated the old PC approach of doing everything in a fast, brute force manner. *Brute force* here refers to the fact that the VLB did not offer most of the attractive features of the Micro Channel and EISA buses; it did not offer software setup of boards or bus mastering. VLB systems were still saddled with jumper-setting installations, and the CPU must baby-sit every single data transfer over the VLB bus. Forcing the CPU to manage each and every transfer keeps the CPU squarely in the middle of the system, making it a bottleneck to system performance.

PCI: Today's Bus

The PC world needed a better bus, because without a better bus there wasn't all that much sparkle in new CPUs. Intel was aware of this and was worried. Less sparkly new systems meant fewer new systems *sold*, and that meant fewer CPUs sold. Whatever hurts the PC world hurts Intel sales, so Intel designed an even newer, faster bus slot called PCI, short for Peripheral Component Interconnect. (Obviously, Intel believes in clinging to at least *one* PC tradition—dumb acronyms.) PCI is a good bus for several reasons, which are outlined in the following paragraphs. You can see a PCI board in Figure 3.21 and a PCI bus slot in Figure 3.22. The smaller and lighter-colored (usually white or cream or gray) slots are the PCI slots; the larger and darker (black or charcoal gray) slots next to them are ISA slots.

PROCESSOR INDEPENDENCE

The PCI bus doesn't directly interface with the CPU. Rather, it communicates with the CPU via a *bridge circuit* that can act as a buffer between the specifics of a particular CPU and the bus. If you've ever looked at Device Manager in Windows 9*x* and Windows 2000 and wondered what the heck a PCI bridge is, this is it.

What does that mean? It means really good news for non-PC computer users. Macintosh PCs and RISC-based machines such as the DEC Alpha are now coming out with PCI slots. That means a bigger market for PCI boards and an avenue for board makers to reach the PC, Mac, and RISC markets with a single board.

FIGURE 3.21

PCI board

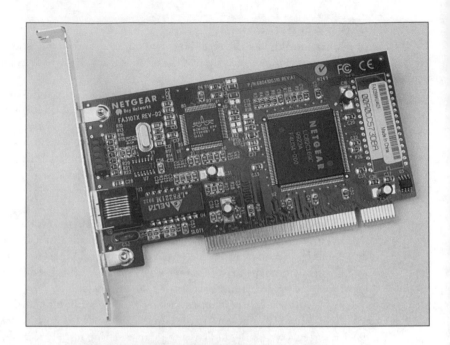

FIGURE 3.22

PCI and ISA bus
slots

WIDER DATA PATH

PCI distinguishes itself first because it is a 64-bit bus. PCI supports a data path appropriate for the newer Pentium-based computers, which require 64 bits at each clock cycle. PCI also supports a 32-bit data path, however, so it was used in some of the last 486 systems to be manufactured.

HIGH SPEED

Like VLB, PCI originally was developed to run to 33MHz. This made the net throughput of a PCI bus as large as 132Mbps with a 32-bit board, or 264Mbps with a 64-bit board. That's one of the bonuses of PCI: it can be configured as both a 32-bit as well as a 64-bit bus, and both 32-bit and 64-bit boards can be used in either.

In 1998, with the adoption of a new specification, the PCI bus moved to 66MHz. When 64-bit PCI devices are used at 66MHz, the throughput increases to 524Mbps. For the most part, 32-bit PCI devices and 64-bit devices are interchangeable (some types of BIOS types differentiate between the two under CMOS setup). Some nonstandard equipment, usually off brand, has presented some difficulties in configuration and use for the common user, but it has been, overall, one of the smoother transitions. The 66MHz PCI cards fit fine into the older PCI buses; they just won't operate at 66MHz. Meanwhile, 33MHz PCI boards go right into the newer motherboards, operating at their standard 32-bit selves.

Part of the changes in hardware over the past few years have centered around how to leave behind some of the slower buses and architecture to more adequately embrace faster technology and devices. Both Universal Serial Bus (USB) and FireWire/IEEE 1394 are part of that move.

PC manufacturers also wanted to extend the PCI bus to give it more longevity and usefulness (and at lower cost than FireWire), in a specification referred to as *PCIx*, or PCI Extended. However, don't look for PCIx devices (with their estimated throughput of up to 1Gbps) to appear in your next bargain PC system. PCIx is pretty much reserved for more serious business use, on servers and high-end workstations. It may filter down to the more modest system at a later time, but by then, we'll probably all be using FireWire and USB 2.

BACKWARD COMPATIBILITY

Although ISA or EISA boards cannot fit in PCI slots, the common chipsets that support PCI also support ISA and EISA. That means it's easy to build a PC with PCI, ISA, and EISA slots all on the same motherboard. Typical motherboard configurations either support PCI and ISA or PCI and EISA. For some reason, the PCI/ISA motherboards support only a single processor, and in general the PCI/EISA motherboards support multiple processors. There's no engineering reason for that; it's just that the Intel chipsets for single-processor systems support PCI/ISA, and the Intel chipsets for multiprocessor systems support PCI/EISA. Nowadays, almost all motherboard makers use the Intel chipsets.

BUS MASTERING

Like EISA and Micro Channel—and *unlike* VLB—PCI supports bus master adapter boards, paving the way for the "community" of processors that I referred to earlier.

Non–bus mastered data transfers require a lot of the CPU's time. For example, one author reports that a file transfer via an Ethernet network required over 40 percent CPU utilization when the Ethernet card was ISA, but only 6 percent with a similar setup and a PCI Ethernet card. Bus mastering is a good idea, and it's discussed in more detail in Chapter 6.

SOFTWARE SETUP

PCI supports the Plug and Play standard developed in 1992 by hardware vendors. There are, in general, no jumpers or DIP switches on PCI boards. There usually isn't even a board-specific configuration program. PCI setup is terrific on a Plug and Play system, but it can be a bit challenging on a non–Plug and Play system. There's an extensive discussion of that in Chapter 6.

PCI is a good architecture, and building PCI boards is relatively cheap. That's no doubt why it has become the premier PC bus.

Accelerated Graphics Port (AGP): Local Bus Returns

The original 33MHz bus was the VLB bus. And what created the driving need for a fast bus? Video. The two things that *always* seem to drive demand for faster buses are memory and video. 33MHz was a pretty fast speed for a video board back when CPUs ran at 50MHz and 66MHz. Of course, they soon ran faster than that, so it shouldn't be any surprise that video is again screaming for more speed.

This time, however, Intel wanted to be out in front and so, before some competitor could come up with a faster bus for graphics, Intel did. They call it the *Accelerated Graphics Port (AGP)* bus. (Note that the *A* stands for *accelerated*—some seem to want to rename AGP *Advanced* Graphics Port.) It accomplishes two things:

◆ It is four to eight times faster than PCI for transferring data. CPUs on systems with AGP video boards can, then, blast video images to their video board pretty quickly.

◆ It enables a video board to supplement its own video memory with some system memory.

Think of Accelerated Graphics Processing as just the latest local bus. In addition to speed, AGP allows a CPU to put a bitmap into regular old system memory and then be able to directly use and display that bitmap for the video board. You can see an AGP bus slot in Figure 3.23. The AGP slot is the one that's darker and slightly "offset" from the other, lighter PCI slots.

FIGURE 3.23

Accelerated graphics processing slot

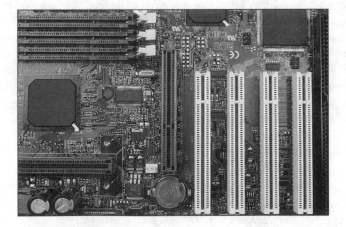

Intel clearly wants this new bus to be a very special-purpose bus. AGP motherboards have only one AGP slot, and as far as I can see, the chipsets allow only one AGP board. That's kind of a shame. In the past, new local buses *started* out as video or memory buses, but then SCSI host adapter vendors or other clever folks used the faster slots to do new and interesting things. More and more "interesting things" created a demand for faster buses, and soon large manufacturers responded with a new general-purpose bus. (That's how PCI appeared.) Because there's only one AGP slot essentially by definition, I suppose AGP won't turn out to be an intermediate step to a faster general-purpose bus.

When AGP first came out in wide market distribution in 1998, its speed (1X or 2X) was limited by other components on a PC system. The greatest issue was overall bandwidth. But changes to overall system speed, and the new forms of memory I've discussed, have finally allowed the production of 4X AGP cards. These new 4X AGP cards fit fine into existing AGP ports for 1X and 2X cards, but you won't have the speed and features over 1X/2X unless you have a sufficient system—including a motherboard/BIOS updated for 4X—to handle it.

PC Card (PCMCIA): The Portable Bus

Laptop computers are an absolute must for traveling professionals and are rapidly becoming basic equipment for more casual users as well (not to mention the explosion of non-PC, Internet-connected devices such as Web phones and Personal Digital Assistants, or PDAs). I have owned *15* laptops in the past 10 years. Laptops are great because they're almost 100 percent software compatible with their bigger cousins, the desktop machines.

But until about 1995, laptops had an Achilles' heel: add-in circuit boards. I've felt for a good long time now that eventually laptops will be *all* that we'll buy, because they're portable and don't take up as much office space as do other types of computer cases. Thankfully, lower prices on laptops have allowed more people to become mobile with their computers, but laptops still generally have a fairly short life expectancy since they are much more likely to break (being dropped, jarred in transit, you name it) and laptop theft has become a significant issue. However, the PC Card (called PCMCIA before 1995) helps to remove objections relating to upgradability, and the big 15-inch LCD screens on some laptops make working on a laptop not much different from working on a desktop system.

Over the years, it's been customary to add two kinds of hardware to laptops: an internal modem and more memory. But, because laptops never had standard expansion slots, laptop owners had to buy proprietary memory from laptop vendors—often an expensive proposition. But cost wasn't the worst part of this lack of a standard bus; in fact, cost was less important than the fact that lack of a standard bus led to the lack of a *market* for add-in boards for laptops.

Japanese vendors of memory products tried to address this problem in the late '80s by founding the *Personal Computer Memory Card Industry Association*, or, in its hard-to-remember acronym form, *PCMCIA*. (The head of the group once said, "If we'd have known how important the acronym would be, we would have picked another name." Some people just remember *People Can't Memorize Computer Industry Acronyms*.) After a few years of apologetic wincing, the association renamed the bus the PC Card bus; people still say PCMCIA, however, so you'll hear both names. A PC Card/PCMCIA board is about the size of a credit card, but a mite thicker. You can see some PC Cards in Figure 3.24.

TYPE 1, TYPE 2, AND TYPE 3 PC CARD SLOTS

The standard proved extremely popular—so popular, in fact, that hardware vendors said to the PCMCIA, "Why not also support modems or hard disks?" So the memory card interface became a "PC Card Type 1 slot." A Type 1 (or *release 1* in some references) slot is 3.3mm thick, with a 68-pin connector. Many Type 1 cards are memory cards, either standard RAM or "flash" memory cards loaded with a piece of software.

The need for internal modems drove the Type 2 slots. While developing Type 2, an important software standard called Card Services and Socket Services was developed—more on that later. Type 2 cards can be designed to act as an object placed directly into the PC's memory address space. Why is this different from Type 1 cards? If you bought a software-on-a-card Type 1 card, then the PC would have to copy the data from the Type 1 card into the PC's memory before it could run the software on the card. That took time, *and* used up some of the PC's memory. With Type 2, that's not necessary, making startup faster and increasing the amount of free memory available. Type 2 cards are 5mm thick, allowing more space for more complex circuitry. Type 1 cards will work in Type 2 slots.

FIGURE 3.24

PC Cards

Shortly after, the PCMCIA defined a Type 3 specification, one flexible enough to support removable hard disks. The main difference of Type 3 is that it's a lot thicker—Type 3 cards can be 10.5mm thick. Most laptops have room for either two Type 2 cards or a single Type 3. When purchasing Type 3 cards, be sure that what you're buying meets the standard—there are so-called "Type 3" hard disks that are 13mm thick. Xircom has also made a very cool combination modem/Ethernet card that has the connectors right on it. The connectors made it thicker, so they went to a Type 3 form factor. Yes, it takes up both slots, but it's convenient not to have to carry cables around to attach to the card.

SOCKET AND CARD SERVICES

The PC Card standard supports the capability to remove and install a PC Card *on the fly*. All other buses require that you power down the computer before installing or removing a card, but PC Card supports *hot swapping*—the capability to swap a card while the computer is running. The computer supports this capability with two levels of software support:

Socket services   The PCMCIA name for the BIOS-like software that handles the low-level hardware calls to the card. They are loaded like a device driver. Although cards can be swapped without powering down, changes in cards *do* require a reboot. (PC Card version 2.01 is the most recent version, but it is rumored that version 3 will allow changes without reboots.)

Card services A higher-layer set of routines that manage how the PC Card memory areas map into the CPU's memory area. They also provide a high-level interface supporting simple commands that are common to almost all PC Cards, commands such as ERASE, COPY, READ, and WRITE data.

In Windows 3.x and Windows NT, you usually have to reboot in order to enable or disable a PC Card. Starting with Windows 95, however, you can change most PC Cards at will, using them and removing them without rebooting.

PC CARD FEATURES

Let's compare PC Cards to the other buses that I've discussed, feature for feature. Take a look at Table 3.5.

TABLE 3.5: PC CARD FEATURES

FEATURE	RELATIONSHIP TO PC CARD
Memory address space	The PC Card supports a 64MB addressing capability. (This is because the bus uses 26 bits for addressing, and two to the 26th power is about 64 million.) This will be adequate for current machines, but will look sparse in a few years, as more demanding operating systems such as Windows 2000/XP become more popular.
Bus mastering	The PC Card does not support bus mastering or DMA.
Plug and Play setup	The PC Card not only allows—but requires—that hardware setups be done with software. Because of the physical size of a PC Card, you'll never see jumpers or DIP switches.
Number of PC Card slots possible in a single system	Most of the other buses support no more than 16 slots. The PC Card standard can, theoretically, support 4080 PC Card slots on a PC. In reality, most laptops have only two Type 2 slots. Some, like Digital's Ultra HiNote 2000 laptop, have four slots (yet another reason why I own one).
Data path	The data path for the PC Card is only 16 bits, a real shame, but one that is fixed in a later version of the PC Card called the CardBus.
Speed	Like other modern bus standards, the PC Card is limited to a 33MHz clock rate.

Years ago, it seemed to me that the smaller size of PC Cards, coupled with their low power usage, made the new bus quite attractive not only for laptops, but also for the so-called "green" PCs, desktop computers designed to use as little power as possible. I figured that for that reason, PC Cards could become an important *desktop* standard as well as a laptop standard. That didn't happen in the desktop world, but in the laptop world, be *sure* that whatever new laptop you buy has at least two Type 2 PC Card slots. Or, even better, if it's a relatively new laptop, make sure it's got two CardBus slots.

Mini PCI (Portable PCI)

Are you asking yourself, "Okay, why are we going back into PCI when we're in the middle of discussing PC Card information?" Because this is a special form of PCI device, with a much smaller form factor (actually, multiple small form factors), designed specifically for laptops and other portable devices.

Mini PCI devices are small (for example, 45-by-70-by-5.5mm for Type IB), internal expansion cards used for communications—either a modem or a network interface card. You won't see Mini PCI video cards, for instance.

This technology offers some nice advantages over the PC Card. For one, because they're smaller, they are cheaper to manufacture (PC Card technology still isn't cheap). For another, with such limited PC Card expansion in laptops, using Mini PCI frees up a PC Card slot for other needs. The Mini PCI specification also eliminates the need for dongles and proprietary I/O connectors.

Best of all, however, Mini PCI shouldn't need any special extras in order to be recognized by, or work with, your PC operating system. Your operating system should recognize the Mini PCI card as any other PCI device and work with it without a hitch. This is because Mini PCI is the functional equivalent of standard PCI, using the 32-bit PCI local bus and the same PCI BIOS/driver interface.

CardBus

First specified back in 1994, this is *PC Card: The Next Generation*. CardBus slots' main claim to fame is that they have a 32-bit data path rather than a 16-bit data path. They're also backward compatible: a CardBus slot can accommodate a PC Card without trouble. Other features include the following:

◆ They run at lower voltage—3.3 volts and lower, compared to 5 volts and lower for PC Cards.

◆ They can transfer data at up to 133Mbps (megabits per second)—they're 4 bytes wide and run up to 33MHz.

◆ In theory, you can do bus mastering and actually have a CPU on the CardBus card, although I haven't seen that in any cards yet.

If your laptop supports CardBus, buy CardBus cards when possible. I've run 100 megabit Ethernet with both PC Card and CardBus boards, and the CardBus is noticeably faster. But be sure your operating system supports CardBus. (Fortunately, just about all CardBus cards work under Windows 98/2000/XP.)

Table 3.6 summarizes the differences between the buses.

TABLE 3.6: BUS TYPES

BUS TYPE	MAXIMUM SPEED	NUMBER OF DATA BITS	NUMBER OF ADDRESS BITS	SOFTWARE SETUP?	BUS MASTER?
PC bus	10MHz (on some clones)	8	20	No	No
ISA bus	8MHz, faster on some clones	16	24	No	Only on one board
MCA	8MHz	32	32	Yes	Yes
VESA	33MHz	32	32	No	No
EISA	8MHz	32	32	Yes	Yes
PC Card	33MHz	16	26	Yes	No

Continued on next page

TABLE 3.6: BUS TYPES *(continued)*

BUS TYPE	MAXIMUM SPEED	NUMBER OF DATA BITS	NUMBER OF ADDRESS BITS	SOFTWARE SETUP?	BUS MASTER?
PCI	33MHz	32	32	Yes	Yes
CardBus	33MHz	32	32	Yes	Yes
AGP	66MHz	32	32	Yes	Yes
Mini PCI	33MHz	32	32	Yes	No

FireWire/IEEE 1394

Apple created the FireWire interface to replace serial ports, parallel ports, SCSI ports, and any other port that you'd use to connect a device to your computer. Apple owns the term *FireWire* and is protective of it, so this interface on a PC must be referred to by its IEEE specification number. (Which doesn't stop everybody and their brother—and me!—from referring to PC-based IEEE1394 connections by the FireWire name.)

Like the Universal Serial Bus (discussed later in this chapter), FireWire is based on a daisy-chain physical topology, meaning that devices will be able to cascade from hubs attached to the card in the computer. FireWire supports 63 devices, however, instead of the 127 that its cousin interface, USB, supports. This isn't a major issue because the chance that you would want to actually connect that many devices is remote. Although it's not required that a FireWire card be PCI, all the FireWire cards released to date *are* PCI. The FireWire bus needs all the speed it can get because it is designed to work with devices that require a lot of bandwidth, such as scanners, video cameras, and the like. Although, as I said, FireWire is designed to replace all other ports, it is also designed to cope with devices that require high and variable amounts of bandwidth. The standard is designed to support speeds of 100Mbps, 200Mbps, and 400Mbps, varying the path that the signal takes in order to avoid traffic problems.

At the time of this writing, FireWire (IEEE 1394) is the interface of choice for digital camcorders and is now appearing as an option on several high-end scanners and digital still cameras. Intel wants the newest version of USB (Version 2) to replace the need for IEEE 1394, but given that FireWire has been almost universally adopted for consumer electronics products (such as camcorders), it looks as if FireWire is here to stay.

FireWire (IEEE 1394) is positioned to be an important component in the integration of consumer electronics with our PC desktops, and that also might be a big part of the direction in which PC hardware is heading. The home and office of the future is likely to have the PC and its functions built into or connected into a whole complex of devices, and not separate from them.

Now configuring for FireWire sounds simple, but how about *powering* those dozens of devices? Well, two of the six wires in the cable are power lines, so your add-in devices can technically use your computer's main power supply. However, providing many devices their own power supplies is probably a good idea in order to keep the strain on the system power supply to a minimum.

A lot of how IEEE 1394 works depends on drivers, and these drivers must be OHCI compliant. OHCI stands for *Open Host Controller Interface*, a standard for how IEEE 1394 and USB devices communicate with other equipment to help ensure compatibility.

For example, I plan on replacing my slow but wondrously portable Sony USB CD-RW with an IEEE 1394 model also being offered by Sony. The speed is awesome! FireWire hard drives are already offered, because Macs have been ahead of PCs in that regard; USB and FireWire are old hat to the Apple crowd. FireWire should certainly simplify the process of adding or removing drives and other devices to your system, and it's meant to be fast. And there's another bonus: Like USB, IEEE 1394 devices can be used regardless of whether you're using a PC or a Macintosh. That bonus becomes serious when you're maintaining an office with multiple computers, especially if you have a mix of Wintel and Apple systems. But even if you are using PCs exclusively, you derive a benefit from equipment you can easily trade between machines. Windows 98, Windows 2000, and Windows XP all support both USB and FireWire.

System Clock

The system clock, mentioned before, is the metronome for the computer system. It was implemented on the early PCs on a chip called the 8284A. The 8284A was located near the 8088 on the system board of most XTs. The early AT-class machines had an 82284 chip.

Why would you care where the clock chip on your computer is? Well, in the old days, you could install a reset switch by using the clock chip. Nowadays, however, modern PCs have the clock circuit integrated with other chips on the motherboard.

Well, you've taken a good long look at what's on the PC's motherboard; now let's look at the other parts inside your machine.

Power Supply

U.S. line current is 120 volts *alternating current (AC)*. The PC, like most digital devices, is set up to use *direct current (DC)* at 5 and 12 volts. The conversion process is done by a *power supply*. The power supply is the silver or black box to the rear and right of the inside of the PC case.

Power supplies are rated by the amount of power that they can handle: The earliest PCs used 63.5-watt power supplies, and some servers ship with 375-watt power supplies. Your power supply determines in part how many peripherals you can put into a PC. Chapter 9, "Power Supplies and Power Protection," discusses selecting, replacing, and installing a power supply. The power supply can't always cope with environmental conditions, so that chapter also discusses add-on products: surge suppressors, spike isolators, and uninterruptible power supplies. You can see a power supply in Figure 3.25.

FIGURE 3.25

The power supply

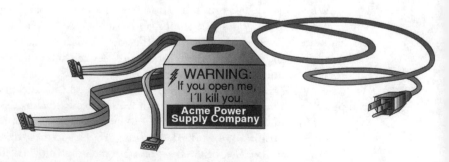

As I mentioned, the power supply is easy to find in the system: it's the silver or black box in the back of the chassis that has a label on it that warns you, in five languages, not to open the power supply.

Keyboard

The PC is useless without an input device, and the keyboard is one of the two input devices (the other being a mouse) used by most of us. The keyboard is subject to a number of hazards, however, so it needs maintenance—and sometimes replacement. The PC's keyboard actually contains a microprocessor of its own, called the Intel 8041, 8042, or 8048. Taking apart a keyboard isn't hard—but reassembling it *is*, and truthfully there's little point in it nowadays, because keyboards are very cheap. You can get a regular 101-key enhanced keyboard for under $20, or an ergonomic "broken" keyboard for under $75. You can even add wireless keyboards to your system; the RF receiver connects to your PC's keyboard connector, while the keyboard itself acts as the radio transmitter.

PS/2 and "standard" keyboards are electronically identical. The only difference is the connector. Most new keyboards have either a PS/2 connector and an adapter for the larger DIN connector, or the larger DIN connector and an adapter for the PS/2.

Mouse

Nearly every computer is equipped with a *mouse,* an input device used for pointing and selecting. The *graphical user interfaces (GUIs)* on modern operating systems can work with just a keyboard, but they are cumbersome without some kind of dedicated pointing device, and the most common is a mouse.

Mice come in the mechanical and optical variety. The mechanical is the traditional (and lower-cost) type, although improvements in optical technology may change that within the next few years. Mice interface with the computer either via a serial port (old), PS/2 port (which is also serial), a "bus mouse" port, or a cordless (usually serial) interface. USB mice and trackballs are also becoming popular choices.

You can learn more about the keyboard and the mouse in Chapter 23, "Keyboards and Mice."

Controllers in Your Computer

Other than the motherboard, power supply, and outside peripherals, the only important things left are the expansion boards in your computer. With the exception of memory boards—and the majority of modern computers don't use memory boards because they put all of their memory on the motherboard—most of the boards in your system are *controllers* of some kind.

What's a Controller?

Every peripheral device, whether internal or external, needs something to handle communications between it and the computer. These items are called controllers, interfaces, ports, or adapters. For example, a hard disk needs a hard disk controller, the keyboard needs a keyboard controller, and the video display needs a video adapter (controller). The main reason that controllers exist is to perform these tasks:

◆ Allow for well-defined industry standards (well, *fairly* well-defined industry standards) by creating a specification that all controller boards are designed to fit and operate in

◆ Match data transfer speeds between peripherals and the CPU

◆ Convert data from the CPU's format to what the peripheral uses, as well as amplify the electronic signals between CPU and peripheral

Adaptec's 2942W PCI SCSI bus mastering host adapter is as different from IBM's original XT-type hard drive controller as a Corvette is from a Chevette, yet 99 percent of the software that was written to work with the latter works just fine (or better) with the former. The underlying hardware is a lot better, and a lot *different*, so you'd imagine there would be big compatibility problems, but the hardware has been housebroken to respond to CPU requests in the same manner (although faster) as the old Xebec-designed IBM controller. Ditto video controllers designed by ATI or Paradise: they respond to the same software as IBM's original CGA, EGA, or VGA, but are cheaper and generally work faster. Using controllers with well-defined interfaces makes building compatible hardware possible.

Remember that notion of well-defined interfaces: together, all these interfaces define what is called *PC compatible*.

You can understand the value of well-defined interfaces and modularity by looking at an automobile. Perhaps (if you're my age) you learned to drive in an old '60s or '70s car, or, if you're my Dad's age, you learned to drive in a car from the '40s or '50s. Both of us now drive cars designed and built in the '90s. The old '67 Country Squire station wagon (okay, so now you know I grew up in the suburbs) was a radically different car from the Honda that I now drive. The Hudson my dad drove in the '40s was even more radically different from his current Toyota truck. But despite our education on different cars, we're both as well prepared to drive a 2000 model as someone who's only driven '90s cars, because the *interfaces* are the same. Because I don't interact directly with the car, but rather with the dashboard gauges and controls, I don't need to know the innards of the motor. If somebody stole into my backyard tomorrow and replaced my internal combustion engine under the hood with an engine that runs on air, I wouldn't know the difference.

Back to controllers, now: most peripherals are considerably slower than the CPU in transferring data. Even the hard disk, for example, is thousands of times slower than the CPU. Most microcomputers (like the PC) have been designed to control everything in their systems, to do *all* the computing work, but that's not necessary. One of the first examples of an all-encompassing microcomputer appeared with a company named Cogent Data Systems. Years ago, they made a hard disk controller for AT-class machines with memory and a microprocessor right on it: the main CPU just makes a request of the hard disk controller, then (with the right software) goes off to do something else while waiting for the controller to do the job. Eventually, the controller informs the CPU that it's finished with the data request and that in fact the controller has already transferred the data into the CPU's memory. Truthfully, the "speed matching" benefits of controllers haven't been really exploited in the PC world yet, because intra-PC *distributed computing* doesn't really exist—again, *yet*. The power of advanced buses such as PCI was supposed to change that, but the change is coming slowly—partially because board designers tend to keep doing the same thing over and over again, and partially because Intel encourages people to put work on the CPU's shoulders. That way, consumers will demand faster and faster CPUs or multi-CPU systems.

Another controller function is simple amplification. The CPU speaks its own electrical language to other chips on the motherboard. But it's a language without too much power—a CPU wouldn't be able to "shout" loudly enough to be heard any appreciable distance on a LAN. Devices such as video monitors need signals massaged into forms that they can use. Again, controllers serve this function.

A typical system will have a controller for the keyboard, a controller for the video display, controllers for the floppy and hard disks, and interface controllers for LAN, mouse, parallel, and serial ports.

Controllers Aren't Always Separate Boards

Here's a common misconception: a controller must be on a board all its own.

Not at all. The keyboard controller is generally not a board; it's just a chip on the motherboard. The hard and floppy disk controllers *used* to reside on separate boards in XT-type machines. Then, the earliest AT-class machines put the hard disk controller and the floppy controller on the same board. Another board held the parallel port, another the serial ports, yet another the joystick, and so on. Nowadays, motherboards incorporate all those functions and more in a single extremely integrated circuit board. These integrated motherboards can be terrific values in terms of price and performance.

Let's take a quick look at the common controllers in the system.

FOR THOSE WHO'VE READ EARLIER EDITIONS:

You may be raising your eyebrows at that last comment. What am I doing singing the praises of integrated motherboards? Didn't I once warn readers away from them? Yes, that's true: I *used* to be very much opposed to putting everything on the motherboard. So why the change?

Well, I *like* integrated motherboards now for the same reason that I disliked them before: compatibility. Nowadays there is an informal standard for these "do-it-all" motherboards; you can easily find a replacement motherboard for your Acme Clones computer from the Zudak Clones company. My old objection stemmed from the fact that the folks who used integrated motherboards (Compaq, Dell, Gateway, and those folks) all built integrated motherboards that were not interchangeable. Hence, if a Dell motherboard went bad, you were stuck buying a replacement from Dell, at a higher price than you would have paid had the motherboard been a more generic item. New manufacturing techniques have improved the quality of these motherboards, reducing the risk of failure of one or more of the integrated components.

However, there still is a downside: many in the PC industry see this as a cost-cutting measure and not very satisfactory for those of us more inclined to upgrade our PCs and customize them rather than buy the exact same unit as those belonging to neighbors and coworkers. The percentage of motherboards including integrated components is on the rise right now, but it's being tempered by a large dissenting audience who still feel this is a poor way to go.

Video Adapter

To allow the computer to communicate with a display monitor, either an integrated display adapter is used or an adapter card must be inserted in one of the PC's expansion slots. Also, you'll hear *video adapter, display adapter,* and *video card* used interchangeably. They all mean the same thing.

The basic kind of video board you find in the PC world even to this day is an enhancement of an old 1987 video standard called the *Video Graphics Array,* or *VGA*. It can display information either in a text-only form or in a graphical form.

Why is a 10-plus-year-old standard still current? Mainly because of the lack of a market leader. For years, graphical standards were created by IBM, video boards with names such as MDA, CGA, PGA, 8514, EGA, and the now-common VGA. You can see a video board in Figure 3.26.

FIGURE 3.26

Generic video adapter

But the lack of industry centralization has left us with no new standards; instead, there are a lot of video boards that exceed VGA's capabilities, boards generically called *super VGA* (SVGA) boards. Even though they're all lumped under the SVGA designation, they're all different, making it difficult sometimes to find *drivers* (the software that controls the video board) for a particular board.

Despite their variation, video boards all have several distinct components, as you see in Figure 3.27.

FIGURE 3.27

Video board components

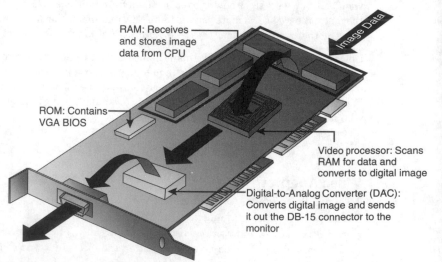

RAM: Receives and stores image data from CPU

Image Data

ROM: Contains VGA BIOS

Video processor: Scans RAM for data and converts to digital image

Digital-to-Analog Converter (DAC): Converts digital image and sends it out the DB-15 connector to the monitor

The video board contains video memory, as you learned earlier in the discussion on memory. The CPU places the video image into the video memory. A video chip on the video board then examines the data in the video memory and creates a digital image signal. That digital signal is then converted to an analog signal by a chip called the DAC, the Digital-to-Analog Converter, another chip on the video board, and the resultant signal goes out the connector on the back of the board and into your monitor.

Video boards are distinguished by their *resolution*, which is the number of dots (pixels) that they can put on the video screen, and their *color depth* (the number of colors they can display at one time). More dots means sharper pictures. They're also distinguished by how many colors they can display on those dots and by how much work the CPU must do in order to create images.

You see, on older video boards, the CPU had to do all the work of picture creation; it had to place each and every one of the pixels on the computer's screen. Nowadays, however, video boards include special circuitry called *accelerator* or *bitblitter* chips that can speed up video operations considerably. Many video boards also have hardware support for 3D rendering, allowing games to have a real-time realism that quite literally could not have happened in an under-$1 million machine 10 years ago. Other video boards include TV tuner support and/or video capture hardware.

SCSI Host Adapter

The *Small Computer System Interface (SCSI)* is a general-purpose interface that allows you to install just one circuit board in your system and use it to act as the "manager" for hard disks, tape drives, optical disks, CD-ROMs, digital cameras, scanners, and even a few kinds of printers. As you'll learn in Chapter 12, "Understanding and Installing SCSI Devices," SCSI can support up to seven devices, and more with SCSI-3.

Floppy Disk Controller and Disk Drives

The floppy disk drive is an essential peripheral, if an ancient one. The 1.44MB format has existed since the mid-'80s and has improved not a whit since then. Why? As with video, there's no market leader in the PC hardware area that can simply put a stake in the ground and say, "This *is* the new floppy standard." There are some great floppy technologies that store upward of 250MB on a removable disk, including the popular Zip drives, but none has really caught on and created a critical mass. And sadly, there may *never* be an industry consensus about high-capacity floppy drives, because most modern machines can boot from CD-ROM, allowing firms to bypass floppies altogether for distribution purposes and ship CDs instead, even for operating systems (which require the distribution media to be bootable).

Since they are peripherals, floppies require an interface. This interface is called a floppy disk controller. These will, in general, not give you many problems. They *do* fail occasionally, however, so you need to know how to recognize this and address it, since virtually all PCs have the floppy drive circuitry on the motherboard. In the case of a floppy drive controller failure, you'd have to either get a new motherboard (the excuse you've been looking for to upgrade to a newer processor!) or disable the floppy controller circuit and try to find a stand-alone board that can act as a floppy controller. (More info in Chapter 17, "Understanding, Installing, and Repairing Floppy Drives.")

The much more fertile ground for failure lies in the floppy disks and floppy disk drives themselves. Floppy drives can require speed adjustment, head alignment, and head cleaning. Speed adjustment and head cleaning can be done simply and cheaply. Alignment can require some specialized equipment and is not always cost effective. Floppy drives are so cheap these days that it's usually pointless to do anything but replace them, but it never hurts to know a bit about a component's innards.

Beyond adjustment is the problem of compatibility among drive types. There are three kinds of 3½-inch floppies, something you'll need to know if you're working with old floppies; for the past decade or so, the standard floppy has been the 1.44MB version. Chapter 17 talks about floppy installation and the kinds of maintenance that you can do on a floppy drive.

CD-ROM Drives

Once a nice add-on, a CD-ROM drive is now a necessity for any home machine and a recommended peripheral for a business machine. (Why don't all business machines need CDs? Because most businesses have networks, and CD-ROM drives can be networked, reducing the need for every machine on the network to have a CD-ROM drive.)

Not only are CD-ROMs basic equipment today, but more and more, CD drives that can write and even rewrite CDs (not just any CDs; the media has to be specifically rewrite-capable) are becoming common hardware in many offices and homes. In under 10 minutes, I can burn about 700MB of data to my Sony USB Supressa CD-RW. The USB connection means it's not physically installed in my PC (it plugs into a USB port as well as into the uninterruptible power supply), so I share it easily between various PCs in my office.

CD-ROM drives are essential because virtually every software package today is distributed only on CD-ROM. Chapter 27, "An Overview of CD-ROM and DVD-ROM Drives," examines these issues and explains how to choose and install a CD-ROM drive.

DVD Drives

Digital versatile disc (DVD) drives are the next technology level for CD-ROMs. Whereas CD-ROMs can store up to 700MB on a 4½-inch disk, DVDs theoretically can store up to 17GB (17 *billion* bytes).

DVDs use the same kind of interfaces as CD-ROMs, either IDE (as is most common) or SCSI. They are backward compatible, which means you can read CD-ROMs in DVD drives (but not vice versa).

Relatively new to the market are DVD recorders, in various formats. There are two record-only formats (DVD-R and DVD+R), and at least three rewritable formats (DVD-RAM, DVD-RW, and DVD+RW). As of this writing, no single format has become a standard, so you're likely to see recordable/rewritable DVD drives from different manufacturers embracing different, mostly incompatible formats.

Chapter 27 covers DVD drives as well, so turn there for more information.

Hard Disks and Hard Disk Interfaces

Most of your system's software and most of the data that you've created lives on your system's *hard disk*.

Years ago, you bought a hard disk by its size and by its interface. Normal-duty hard drives used an interface called ST-506. High-performance drives used a drive interface called the *Enhanced Small Device Interface*, or *ESDI*.

Nowadays, you still choose a hard disk by its size (see, some things never change) and by its interface; but the interface will either be the SCSI or the *Enhanced Integrated Drive Electronics (EIDE)* interface, usually called just *IDE* today. The vast majority of PCs currently use IDE, since virtually all PC motherboards have not one but *two* IDE interfaces built right on them. Each IDE interface can support two drives. As there are two IDE interfaces, then, the average PC can support four drives right out of the box. Most folks have at least one CD-ROM drive and a hard disk drive, so they have two "openings." Good candidates to fill those openings are perhaps more hard disk drives, a CD-R/RW or DVD drive, or perhaps a tape drive or Zip drive for backups.

When a hard disk fails, your main concern shouldn't be the hard disk. Hard disks are easy to replace and install, as you'll learn in Chapters 10 through 14. Your main worry should be the *data* on your drive. Data recovery is the subject of Chapter 16, "Care and Feeding of Hard Drives."

Older disk subsystems used hard disk controllers—ST-506 and ESDI interface boards were controllers—but the newer SCSI and EIDE interfaces do not use controllers; rather, they call them *host adapters* because their job is much simpler than the job of a controller. Basically, a host adapter just rearranges the data so that it can be accepted by the bus. Much of the circuitry that once sat on the controller now lives on the disk drive itself.

Some hard disk failures—precipitous drops in speed or loss of data—can be addressed at either the controller or the drive level. Problems such as head crashes can be avoided with some simple techniques, and even the ultimate disaster—a reformatted hard disk—can be reversed in some cases. Chapter 16 provides more information.

Tape Drives and Other Backup Devices

Thinking about skipping this part and going on to parallel ports, eh? It amazes me how many people don't have tape drives on their systems. It's quite common for PCs to sport 20GB or 40GB hard disks, but no tape drive. Once you bought that 40GB drive, how did you plan to back it up, anyway—with floppies? (Let's see, now; 40GB divided by 1.44MB per floppy equals... too many floppies.)

If your computer doesn't have a backup device, then ask yourself: Can I really afford to lose all this data? If the answer is *no*, then think about getting a tape drive. Tape drives install in the same kind of slot that you'd put a floppy drive into, and they have one of three kinds of controllers. Some tape drives run off a SCSI host adapter; others connect to the floppy disk controller; and a few have their own proprietary controller. Or consider the Jaz drive from Iomega, a tool I like and use quite a bit. It's a backup system that uses removable hard disk cartridges. The benefit to this drive is that if you have a hard disk failure, you can reboot with any drive, and run your programs and read your data directly from the Jaz drive the same way you would with a hard drive. I'll discuss backups more in Chapters 10 through 14.

Parallel (Centronics) Interfaces/IEEE 1284

The most common method of attaching a printer to a computer is through a simple interface called the *Centronics* interface. The interface was named after Centronics, the company that invented it in 1976. It's more commonly known today as the *parallel port*. Another way to connect printers to PCs is through a serial port, and I'll cover them in the next section.

PCs can support up to three parallel ports. They are named LPT1, LPT2, and LPT3; the name refers to Line PrinTer 1, 2, or 3.

Originally, parallel ports were unidirectional. They transported data only from the PC to the printer. *Control* lines led status information from the printer back to the PC, but data flowed in only one direction. For years, some parallel ports have had the option to move data backward, from the printer to the PC. That's important for two reasons:

♦ New printers can now send textual status information to the PC. Thus, it is possible with some printers for the printer to tell the PC, "I'm low on toner," or "I am a LaserJet 6."

♦ Modern PCs put things on the parallel port that aren't printers. Removable media drives and CD-ROM drives are two examples of peripheral hardware devices that can have parallel port options.

Some parallel ports not only support bidirectional data flow, they also support increased data transfer speed. These ports are called *enhanced* parallel ports, or EPP interfaces. Some parallel ports use a direct memory access (explained in Chapter 6) channel and become *extended capabilities ports (ECPs)*, offering even more speed. The IBM PC's parallel port was originally a proprietary interface, but it's become so widely used that there is now an "official" standard describing it, IEEE 1284. You'll sometimes see parallel ports or parallel cables referred to not as *parallel* but as *IEEE 1284 compliant*.

Most printers require only a simple unidirectional parallel port. But if you have a bidirectional, EPP, or ECP port, then those more advanced ports work fine with any kind of printer.

Parallel ports won't usually pose much of a problem, once you have them installed and configured. But the printers themselves, well, that's another story.

The actual printer is the greater source of failures: printers employ a large number of moving parts. While printers are much more reliable nowadays than they were in the bad old days of daisy-wheel printers, there's always the odd paper feed or black page problems.

Modems and Communication Ports

Besides parallel ports, the other common printer interface is the *serial port*. Serial ports are also known as *async ports, comm ports,* or *RS-232 ports*. They are bidirectional interfaces for low- to medium-speed data transfer; most serial ports can't transfer data faster than 115,000 bits per second, but there are some serial ports that can transfer data at 345,000 bits per second.

A serial port's main job isn't usually printers, however. The two most common uses for serial ports are to attach mice or modems to your PC. Modems enable your PC to communicate remotely with other computers via phone lines and to act as a fax machine.

The common names for these communications ports are COM1 and COM2. It's theoretically possible to have COM3 and COM4, but they're limited in their usefulness. (More on that in Chapter 6.)

RS-232 is a source of many cable problems: either the wrong cable is configured, or environmental problems (electronic noise) cause communication errors. Figure 3.28 depicts an IBM RS-232 adapter. Data communications troubleshooting is an entire book in itself—several books, in fact—but I cover the essentials in Chapter 22, "Communications Devices."

FIGURE 3.28
IBM RS-232
adapter

Serial ports are the PC's general-purpose input/output devices. Hand-held machines such as the PalmPilot attach to the PC via serial ports; digital cameras do; some scanners do, modems, mice, printers... it seems on many systems that there are too many things to attach to a serial port and not enough serial ports. *That's* why they invented USB.

The Universal Serial Bus (USB)

It's far too easy to run out of serial ports. For instance, say you have a serial mouse and a modem. No problem, right? The mouse goes on COM1, the modem on COM2. But what happens when you add a smart uninterruptible power supply (UPS), a device that can communicate with your computer for diagnostics and software control, to the mix? At this point, you have the choice of either losing your mouse (it's possible to navigate a graphical operating system with the arrow and Tab keys, but it's no fun), losing some of the UPS's capabilities, or adding another COM port with an add-in card and hoping that one set of software will function with a nonstandard interrupt. If you don't set up COM3 to use another interrupt, then it will conflict with COM1, but not all software is prepared to deal with that.

It's a puzzle, and the problems associated with adding serial ports could keep people from using some devices that need them. But there's a new type of port that alleviates the serial port overcrowding problem. That interface is called the *Universal Serial Bus (USB)*, and all new PCs come with one or more USB ports.

WHAT IS USB?

USB, developed by Microsoft, Compaq, National Semiconductor, and 25 other USB members, was designed to take the place of the keyboard port, parallel ports, game port, and serial ports by replacing them with a single connection from which you can daisy-chain *more than a hundred* USB-compatible devices. This single connection is even simpler than a nine-pin serial port, since it has only four pins. Physically, it looks either like one device (such as a keyboard) plugged into the computer, and then everything else plugged into a hub on the keyboard, or a hub plugged into the computer and then everything plugged into the hub. As in SCSI, each device can be plugged into up to seven devices and/or hubs at a time. You can see a USB connector and cable in Figure 3.29.

FIGURE 3.29

USB cable

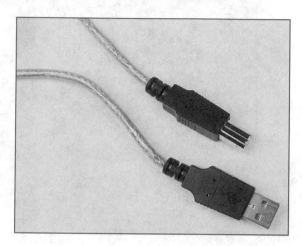

Either way, it's designed to be much simpler to put together; rather than installing cards for many of these devices, you plug them into a hub and call it a day. If they're true Plug and Play devices (which they *should* be), then your operating system should recognize them with very little help from you.

NOTE   Windows 98, Me, 2000, and XP have USB support with device drivers built into them.

USB is designed to be faster than serial ports, as well. The standard describes an interface that can transmit up to 12 megabits per second, as opposed to the 100+ kilobits per second of a serial interface. The speed is meant to keep up with telephony applications, such as low-resolution video conferencing. (For higher-resolution video, you'd need IEEE 1394.)

USB recognizes four types of data transfer, divided by the type of peripheral device that uses them: bulk, interrupt, asynchronous, and control. Printers, scanners, and digital cameras, which must send a great deal of information to the PC at one time, are bulk transmitters. Keyboards and joysticks, which people use to sporadically transmit small amounts of data that must be processed immediately, use interrupt transmittal. Telecom applications, which must be delivered in a steady stream and in a certain order, use asynchronous transmissions.

The hub determines which devices are plugged into it at any given time, and from that it deduces how much bandwidth each needs, based on the kind of data transmittal the device is trying to perform.

WHAT'S IT GOOD FOR?

Just about anyone should be able to benefit from the new interface. The ability to plug in a number of devices with only one port is particularly useful to laptop owners, since laptops have limited real estate into which to plug additional devices. You don't need lots of available ports, and the hub should be easier to get to than the back of your computer. It's intended to work for just about anything that you can plug into a port in your computer: speakers, modems, keyboards, and the like.

One of the things I like most about USB, besides the single IRQ use and the transportability, is the fact that I can happily shelve my printer or my scanner or graphics tablet when I'm not using it. When I need the device again, I just plug it in, and it's instantly found and available for use.

COMING SOON: USB 2

If you like USB version one, the next installment—USB 2—is about 10 times faster than the original USB implementation. USB 2 outperforms high-end SCSI *and* FireWire for throughput, although the difference in speed is inconsequential. At the time of this writing, USB 2 devices are few and far between—as are operating systems that support it. (Windows XP initially shipped *without* USB 2 support, although this support is scheduled to be added to the operating system at a later date.) The good news about USB 2 is that it is backward compatible with the two previous versions (USB 1.0 and USB 1.1). This means that you can use USB 2 devices with existing USB ports in your computer.

Slower devices such as mice, keyboards, and simple digital cameras won't need that kind of speed, but USB 2 might make an attractive option for those doing video editing or using high-speed drives, the same market as FireWire.

System Clock/Calendar and Configuration (CMOS) Chip

The system clock/calendar keeps the date and time even when the unit is turned off. Older XT-type systems required a separate board to support a clock/calendar, but virtually every modern computer has the feature built right into its motherboard as standard equipment.

THE CLOCK/CALENDAR AND CMOS BATTERY ISSUES

The clock/calendar is built on the same chip as the configuration memory circuit. *Configuration memory*, more commonly called the *CMOS*, is a small amount of memory that holds information that the computer needs in order to get started in the morning.

When you first turn your computer on, it must figure out what hardware it contains so that it can control that hardware. There's a list of the hardware in your system in the configuration memory. Most memory, however, is *volatile*, a 75-cent word meaning, "When you remove power from the memory, the memory forgets whatever was sitting in it." That's why the memory has a battery attached to it, so that the memory doesn't lose power, so it can remember while the rest of the PC slumbers.

Of course, with time, that battery will run down in power, the configuration memory will forget what kind of hardware is in your system, and the clock/calendar will no longer keep correct time. You'll have to install a new battery, of course, to fix the problem; but here's a common question about batteries and the clock.

People will tell me that their computer can no longer remember its configuration information, forcing them to reenter the configuration information into the computer every time that they turn the computer on. (They should just replace the battery but, for whatever reason, they haven't.) I explain that they've got to replace the battery, but they disagree, saying, "No, the battery's fine."

"How do you know that?" I ask.

"Because the computer keeps correct time," they respond. They're arguing that because the clock circuit still runs, the configuration memory circuit should still run. It's a good argument, but it misses the fact that running the clock requires less power *by far* than does running the configuration memory. As you may have learned from painful experience, it's possible for your car's battery to have enough power to run the interior lights and the radio, but not to crank the starter.

The vast majority of the time, the only problem from the clock will be with (1) the battery or (2) the software to use it.

The battery causes problems, of course, when it runs down and no longer keeps time. Replacement is no problem (usually $3–$10 at any decent electronics counter), save for some clock/calendar boards that *solder* the battery on the board. You kind of have to wonder if the people who designed this either (1) have parents who are first cousins or (2) want to be able to charge you $120 three years later to replace the battery. Many motherboard manufacturers nowadays have a soldered battery, but that may not be terrible news, because some of those motherboards also support a standard external battery; you just move a jumper on the motherboard to disable the soldered battery and enable the connection for the external battery. (More on CMOS and batteries in Chapter 6.)

NOTE *By the way, don't confuse the clock/calendar that I've discussed here with the clock that raps out the beat that the PC dances to—the one based on the 8284 or 82284 chip. They're different circuits. The CPU clock doesn't run when the power to the PC is off, in contrast to the clock/calendar, which continues to run all the time, courtesy of its battery.*

Local Area Network (LAN) Adapters

Put more than two PCs into an office, and soon you see the urge to merge: PC networks are everywhere. (Got one in your home yet? No? Don't worry; you will soon.)

Networks make it easy to share data, printers, modems, and access to the Internet. But the first step in networking your computer is to put a LAN board in every PC. They come in several flavors. The most popular kind of network is called *Ethernet*, and there are Ethernet boards for all of the PC buses. You can also create wireless networks based on RF, phone line, or even power line technology.

There's an awful lot to say about networks, and for more information you can check out Chapter 29, "Networking Concepts and Hardware." Check around the Internet, too, because you'll see all kinds of network setups today—for even the most casual of home users.

Sound Boards

Years ago, Creative Laboratories introduced the Sound Blaster, a board that allowed your PC to emit squeaks, squawks, squeals, and explosions. What good was that? Well, games, mostly. But sound cards have come a long way since then. Nowadays, you can buy sound cards that can produce quality superior to that of a CD player.

Sound cards are more than just a plaything. Multimedia in PCs is becoming a business tool—it's already an education tool. For many applications, clicking the OK button will bring up an animated window of a teacher explaining how to use a program's feature, rather than just the simple text screens that we used to see in older systems.

That will be a bit friendlier, but *understanding* what the person in the animation is saying in the first place requires good sound equipment. The wrong sound card/speaker combination can make voices sound like broadcasts from bad AM radios; the right combination can provide the audio version of virtual reality.

NOTE   *Chapter 25, "Play It Loud: Sound Cards," discusses sound cards in detail.*

Other Common Boards

That's about it for the most commonly found boards. You may also see the following boards:

3270 or 5250 emulation cards   Despite improvements in IBM's *Systems Network Architecture (SNA)* in the past few years, it's probably easiest to get your PC to talk to a mainframe computer by making it look like a dumb 3270 terminal, the familiar IBM "green screens" that you still see in offices around the world. (*Dumb* in terminal parlance means it lacks stand-alone processing power.) Attachmate, DCA, and others do a nice business filling this need. Plug one into your system, and your PC can hook up to the same old coaxial cable that's been serving IBM mainframe users for years. Just because you're attached to your company's AS/400, however, doesn't mean that you have an emulation board. Another way to get to your firm's mainframe or mainframes is over the LAN. In that case, your LAN has a machine on it acting as a *gateway*.

Tape controllers   If you want to install a tape drive for backup to your system, you'll need a controller of some kind. Many tape drives can use the floppy controller, but it's not recommended—such tapes are painfully slow, and remember that you bought the tape to quickly back up the hard disk. Some tapes are internal, some external. I'd recommend external because then you can buy a tape controller board for *all* of your machines, then buy only a few of the expensive tape drives themselves, and let the users share the occasional use of a tape drive. (That's "occasional" only when compared to the frequency of use for the hard disk. Backups should be near daily if you generate work of any importance at all. Yes, I know it's a pain, but can you *really* afford to lose a whole day's work? And are you sure you'd be able to re-create it if you did?) The higher-capacity tape drives all run off SCSI, but some cheaper tapes attach to the EIDE interface on your system.

Scanner interface cards   You probably won't see many of these, and you should be glad. In the early days of desktop publishing, some scanners connected to the computer via a proprietary SCSI interface card. Installing these cards was a nightmare that I would prefer to forget. Next, scanners shipped with SCSI adapters made for scanner manufacturers. In an attempt to avoid the nightmare of installing these interface cards, some scanners were then designed to connect to the parallel port—which was very, very slow. Now the scanner interface of choice is USB. Be thankful.

Finding Your Way around inside Your PC

Well, now you've learned some things about how your PC's put together. You know the names of some of the pieces in your system. But how do you figure out what's where once you take apart *your* computer? Trying to figure out what's in your computer for the first time can be tremendously disorienting. Here's my approach.

After you get the top of the computer off, find the easy stuff:

◆ Power supply

◆ Fan

◆ Floppy drives

◆ Hard disk or disks

◆ CD-ROM and tape drives, if present

After you've figured those out, only the boards are left. Figuring out the boards doesn't seem so difficult once the rest of the system has been identified.

Finding the Easy Stuff

The power supply is easy to find. It's a silver or black box with a fan on it, and it's attached to the power switch. As I've noted before, it probably has a label on it that says in five languages, "If you open me, I'll kill you."

The floppy drives should be simple to locate: just look at the slots in the front of the computer. The hard disk will be a box that whirs and has no slot in the front of it. CD-ROM and DVD drives are, I hope, also simple to find; they're usually well marked. (Although there's an apocryphal story about a tech support person who was called by a user because the user had broken his "cup holder." You know, the retractable one that CDs also happen to fit into.) Tape drives are likewise usually labeled.

That leaves the tougher-to-identify components: the circuit boards. Have you started drawing your diagram yet? If not, get cracking on it. It's really simple to screw up a computer by taking it apart and not being able to put it back together.

Locating Things on the Motherboard

Your system's motherboard, once you remove it, will have a few points worth noting. I'll use a typical Pentium II motherboard for examples.

THE POWER CONNECTION

Be sure to note where the power cables from the power supply go to the motherboard, as I mentioned in the last chapter. Putting the old style XT connectors back together backward will smoke the motherboard. You see the power connection in Figure 3.30.

FINDING THE CPU

The CPU on your system is often easily identifiable because many of them have a prominent Intel logo painted on them. If you're working with a much older system, look also for the distinctive names 80386, 80486, Pentium, and the like. Nowadays, finding a Pentium III or 4 is a snap; they're sitting upright in black plastic cases. You usually can't see the actual CPU, though, because it's surrounded by metal fins. Those fins are the heat sink that helps keep the chip from catching fire. (No, I'm not kidding.) You can see the processor in Figure 3.31.

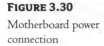

FIGURE 3.30

Motherboard power connection

FIGURE 3.31

Pentium II processor on motherboard

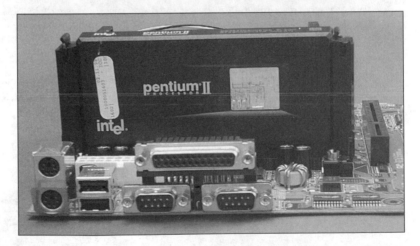

Older CPUs are also often socketed, and most Intel-type CPUs are in PGA packages. No matter what generation of PC you own, one good method for finding the CPU is to look for the largest chip in the box; that's often it.

REMEMBERING THE MEMORY

Your PC's motherboard has both RAM and ROM on it.

RAM memory is usually easy to spot, because it is typically in the form of a SIMM. If you have an older computer that uses separate chips, then the memory looks like uniform rows of small socketed chips. You see the memory in Figure 3.32.

FIGURE 3.32

SDRAM in Pentium
III motherboard

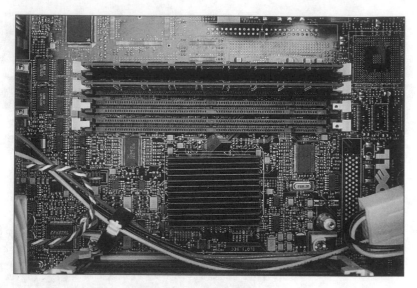

ROM memory is usually a large chip or pair of chips in sockets, *often with a label on the top* indicating a software version number. Newer systems don't have socketed ROM, because they're flash memory and should not need physical replacing—you can just download new versions of the BIOS programs.

SLOTS

The only other parts that you will be sure to want to find are the expansion slots in the computer. They're obvious, in that they're relatively long, narrow electrical connectors. Refer to the bus discussion earlier in this chapter to get an idea about the differences between bus slot types. Figure 3.33 shows (from right to left) two ISA slots, four PCI slots, and an AGP slot.

FIGURE 3.33

Expansion slots on a
motherboard

CMOS Battery

Keep a computer long enough, and you'll have to replace the battery or it won't be able to hold its configuration. Figure 3.34 shows that this motherboard uses a coin-type battery.

FIGURE 3.34

CMOS battery on a motherboard

DRIVE INTERFACE CABLES

Every motherboard I know of these days has the floppy drive controller and two EIDE host adapters integrated into its electronics. You'll have to attach and detach drive ribbon cables, so it's a good idea to locate the floppy and EIDE connectors, as you see in Figure 3.35.

FIGURE 3.35

Floppy and EIDE connectors on motherboard

Floppy connector

EIDE connectors

Identifying Circuit Boards

This is going to sound silly, but I use two basic approaches to identifying strange circuit boards.

The first rule is the "What is it connected to?" rule. Suppose you're trying to figure out what a board does. You notice that the back of the board is connected to a cable that goes to the video monitor. Heck, even a nonphysicist like me can figure out that the board must have something to do with video, so it's probably a video adapter.

Now, at this moment, you're saying, "Hey, wait a minute; I've disassembled the machine. Nothing's attached to it right now, so I have no idea what the board *used* to be attached to." Remember in the last chapter when I said that diagramming was essential? Here's an example of why that's true. (I hope at this stage in your PC exploration that this comment falls in the category of cautionary tale, rather than "I told you so....")

The second rule of board identification is the "What kind of connectors does it have on the back?" rule. There are different kinds of connectors on the back of a PC. Take a minute to become familiar with them.

Actually, with modern PCs, the issue is often not "What does this board do?" because most new systems have pretty integrated motherboards. Most new systems have *everything* on the motherboard save for a video board and (possibly) a LAN card and/or a modem. The more important question is, "What does this *connector* on my integrated motherboard do?" Well, again, a little organization, documentation, and observation can answer those questions.

THE D-SHELL CONNECTOR

The *D-shell connector* is called that because if you look at it the right way, it looks like a capital *D*. You can see a D-shell connector in Figure 3.36.

FIGURE 3.36

A D-shell connector

D-shell connectors come in male and female varieties. They also vary by the number of pins or sockets in their connectors. You'll see DB9 (nine pins or sockets), DB15, DB25, and DB37 connectors. They're used in serial ports, parallel ports, video adapters, joystick interfaces, and some LAN interfaces.

HP OR MINIATURE D-SHELL CONNECTOR

The *miniature D or HP connector* looks a lot like a D-shell connector, but the pins are all placed next to one another. The HP connector puts 50 pins in the same space that a normal D-shell puts only 25 pins. You can see an HP connector in Figure 3.37.

FIGURE 3.37

An HP connector

As I said, it looks like a D-shell connector. The main application that I've seen for HP connectors is in SCSI interfaces. A 50-pin version shows up on SCSI-2 interfaces, and SCSI-3 (a later version of the SCSI standard) uses a 68-pin HP connector.

Sometimes you'll hear people call the 50-pin HP connector a Centronics 50-pin since the pin configuration is similar to the Centronics connector discussed next.

CENTRONICS CONNECTOR

Made popular by its first big use in an interface created by a company of the same name, the *Centronics connector* looks like the drawing in Figure 3.38.

FIGURE 3.38

A Centronics connector

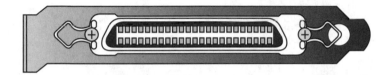

Don't confuse the Centronics connector with the Centronics interface, another name for the parallel port. The connector, which looks like an edge connector surrounded by a metal shell, is used on printers and in SCSI devices. In addition to parallel ports, Centronics connectors are used by some SCSI host adapters.

BNC CONNECTOR

A *BNC connector*, or *Bayonet Naur connector* (a bayonet is what they supposedly look like, and Naur is the guy who invented them), looks like a cylinder about 1 centimeter across with a thin tube down its center and two small bumps on its periphery. You can see several BNC connectors in Figure 3.39.

FIGURE 3.39

BNC connectors

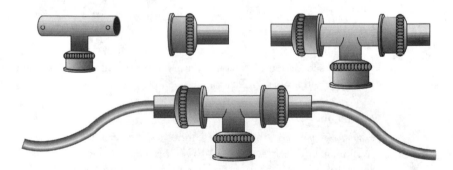

In Figure 3.39, you see (clockwise, from upper left) a T connector, used to connect a single BNC connector to two other BNC connectors. Next, you see a BNC plug, and then a T connector with two plugs. At the bottom of the diagram, you see two cables with BNC plugs connected to a T connector. The T connector would then be attached to a BNC connector on the back of a circuit board.

BNCs are most commonly used in a kind of LAN called Ethernet, although they are falling out of favor (because of the RJ-45, discussed next). Ethernet attaches in several ways, known as *thick*net, *thin*net, and *10Base-T*. It is the thinnet implementation of Ethernet that uses BNC connectors. Thinnet is also known as *10Base-2*.

BNC connectors have also been used in ARCNet and 3270 (a mainframe terminal interface) connectors.

RJ-45 OR RJ-13 CONNECTOR

These connectors look like the so-called *modular jacks* that you use to plug a phone into an answering machine or a wall jack. As a matter of fact, the connector that you use for a standard phone is called an *RJ-11*, or Registered Jack type 11 connector. Some networks use the slightly larger *RJ-45 connector*, which looks similar. The RJ-11 has four wires in it. The RJ-45 has eight wires in it.

RJ-45 is used in 10Base-T Ethernet connections, as well as LocalTalk connectors such as you'd see in a Macintosh network.

DIN CONNECTOR

The *DIN connector* comes from Germany; roughly translated, its name means *German national connector*. The DIN connector is a round, notched connector about an inch across, with from three to seven pins in it. DIN connectors are most commonly used in the PC world to connect keyboards to a motherboard.

MINIATURE DIN CONNECTOR

As the name implies, these are smaller versions of DIN connectors. You see a couple of variations on this in Figure 3.40.

FIGURE 3.40

Miniature DIN connectors

You'll see these used for bus mouse interfaces, InPort mouse interfaces, some keyboard interfaces, and some serial port applications.

MINIPLUG

A *miniplug connector* is the kind of connection that enables a set of headphones to attach to a Sony Walkman. You see these on CD-ROM players (not always, but often) or on the backs of sound cards, for microphone inputs or line input or output.

RCA PLUG

RCA plugs are the kind of connectors that you might see on the back of your VCR labeled Audio In or Video In. They were used years ago for simple video output on an old kind of video board called the Color/Graphics Adapter and a later board called the Enhanced Graphics Adapter. Nowadays, you usually see them only for sound inputs or outputs on some sound cards, or for video inputs on a video capture board.

USB CONNECTOR

Universal Serial Bus systems have a *USB connector*—a kind of flat connector with a tongue in its middle, as you see in Figure 3.41.

FIGURE 3.41

USB connector (in center; mini-DINs on left, D-shells on right)

FIREWIRE/IEEE 1394 CONNECTORS

FireWire must also have its own connectors installed on the machine or provided by an adapter installed into an expansion slot on the PC itself (available for under $100).

Boards and Connectors

Now let's put all this information together into some diagrams of common boards and connectors. Take a look at Figure 3.42.

FIGURE 3.42

Common boards and connectors

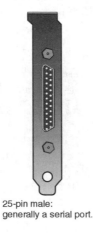

25-pin male: generally a serial port.

25 female: a parallel port.

EGA: 9-pin female, two RCA connectors, DIP switches.

Fifteen pins in three rows indicates VGA (Video Graphics Array) and graphics accelerators.

In Figure 3.42, you see the backs of some common interface boards. As I said earlier, note the extensive use of D-shell connectors.

Originally, video boards used a female DB9 connector to pipe out either color images, via what was called an RGB connector, or high-resolution monochrome images, via a digital monochrome video interface. That led to confusion, because it was possible to plug an RGB color monitor into a digital output; when that happened, little wisps of smoke would soon issue from atop the color monitor, and it would cease to function. Color video boards also output a kind of signal called *composite video*, which you can read more about in Chapter 26, "You Oughta Be in Pictures: Video Capture." If you see a female DB9 on a modern system, the board is most likely a Token Ring network card.

Nowadays, however, virtually all video adapters use a D-shell that is the same size as the old DB9, except that this D-shell has *three* rows of pins, not two, housing 14 or 15 pins. I say "14 or 15" because there is room for 15 pins, but some boards fill in one of the holes. You'll see those connectors on just about every video board, and *very* rarely you'll see a video board with several RCA connectors on the back; such a board is sending video out in multiple signals as is done on some high-end video equipment.

The parallel port usually employs a 25-socket female D-shell connector. I say "usually" because Tandy used a DIN connector for their parallel port for a while. And, just to confuse the issue a bit, some older SCSI host adapters use a female DB25 for attaching external SCSI devices.

Serial ports also use D-shell connectors—two kinds, in fact. Some serial ports use a male DB25. Others use a male DB9 connector. Note that oddity: most connectors you'll find on a PC are *not* male connectors, so the fact that serial ports use either 9-pin or 25-pin males is unusual. (My former girlfriend Sheila—she's mentioned in the acknowledgments—told me that she remembered that male 25s and male 9s were serial ports because most serial killers were male. A rather graphic way of remembering, for sure, but then again, Sheila is six foot one and was rated number one in the country in Tae Kwon Do, so I didn't argue with her about the little things, if you know what I mean.)

NOTE *Why are most connectors on a PC female? Well, designers of some kinds of interfaces have to put a connector of one gender on the PC and a connector of the opposite gender on the cable that the interface uses. Male connectors have a bunch of little pins, and pins break. Female connectors have a bunch of little sockets, and sockets don't, in general, break. Now, in the case of pin breakage, would you rather have to replace a cable ($) or an interface board ($$$)? That's why the female connectors go on the PC side rather than the cable side.*

Let's look at some more boards, as you see in Figure 3.43.

As I mentioned earlier, Ethernet comes in three guises: Thicknet, Thinnet, and twisted-pair versions. Thicknet is the oldest variety of Ethernet, and it's also called 10Base-5 Ethernet. It interfaces via a DB15 female connector, and is sometimes called an *Adapter Unit Interface (AUI)* or *DEC-Intel-Xerox (DIX)* connector. Thinnet uses a BNC connector; in the board pictured in Figure 3.43, you can use either the Thicknet connector or a Thinnet connector. The board next to it shows the third kind of Ethernet connection, a twisted-pair, or 10Base-T, connection, with an RJ-45 connector.

Next to that board is a modem. Modems have RJ-11 jacks for interfacing to phone lines, and the RJ-11s look like RJ-45s, so it might be easy to confuse an Ethernet card with a modem card. But modems have two connectors, and Ethernet cards often have an LED or two on their backs.

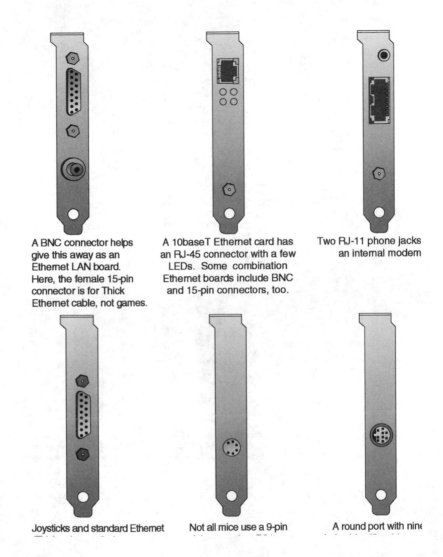

FIGURE 3.43

Additional boards

A BNC connector helps give this away as an Ethernet LAN board. Here, the female 15-pin connector is for Thick Ethernet cable, not games.

A 10baseT Ethernet card has an RJ-45 connector with a few LEDs. Some combination Ethernet boards include BNC and 15-pin connectors, too.

Two RJ-11 phone jacks an internal modem

Joysticks and standard Ethernet

Not all mice use a 9-pin

A round port with nine

Below those cards is a VGA, mentioned earlier, a joystick interface (a female DB15), and two types of miniature DIN connectors used to create a mouse interface.

Let's wrap up our look at the backs of common boards with a third group of boards, shown in Figure 3.44.

The top three boards in Figure 3.44 are varieties of SCSI interfaces, as I've mentioned earlier. Video capture boards take video inputs and convert them into digital data, and they can accept either simple composite video (like the kind that comes out the back of common VCRs), or they'll usually take the higher-quality super VHS–type connector, a miniature DIN. Below them are some backsides of some sound cards. Note that many sound cards have a joystick interface built right onto them.

FIGURE 3.44

Common boards

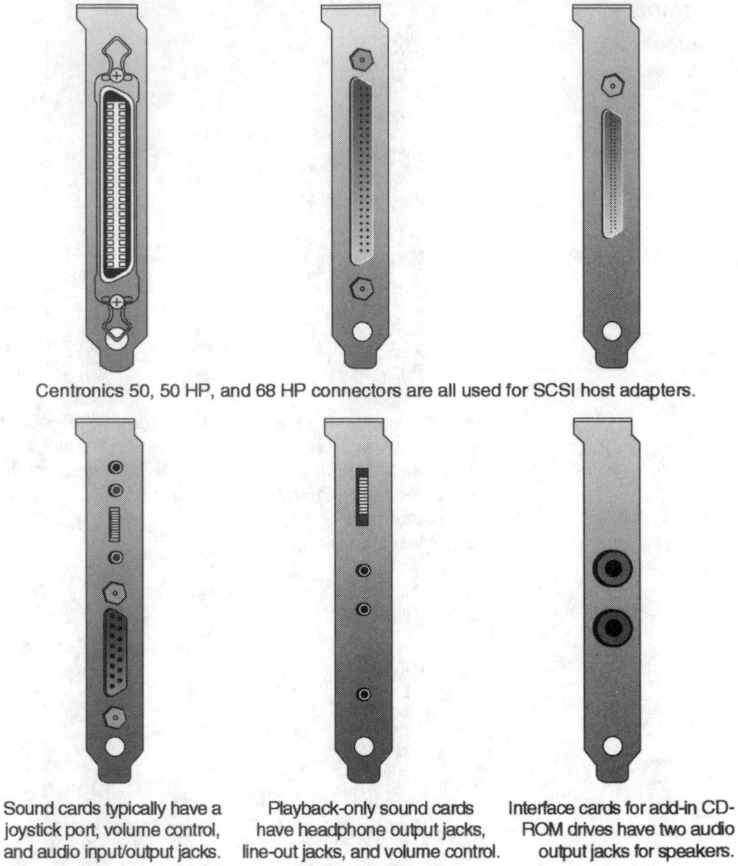

Centronics 50, 50 HP, and 68 HP connectors are all used for SCSI host adapters.

Sound cards typically have a joystick port, volume control, and audio input/output jacks.

Playback-only sound cards have headphone output jacks, line-out jacks, and volume control.

Interface cards for add-in CD-ROM drives have two audio output jacks for speakers.

Well, that was a long chapter, but now you're a certified "micro-biologist." The next chapter's a bit lighter, so don't stop now: turn the page and see how to keep all this stuff working!

Chapter 4

Avoiding Service: Preventive Maintenance

◆ QuickSteps: Checking the Environment   187

◆ QuickSteps: Preventive Maintenance   188

◆ The Menace of Heat   190

◆ Dealing with Dust   196

◆ Magnetism   197

◆ Stray Electromagnetism   198

◆ Damage Caused by Water and Liquids   208

◆ Troubleshooting Tips   209

Introduction

THE MOST EFFECTIVE WAY to cut down your repair bills is by good, preventive maintenance. There are things in the PC environment—some external, some created in ignorance by you through inattention—that can drastically shorten your PC's life.

Some of the things that affect your PC's life are common-sense things; I don't imagine that I have to tell you not to spill soft drinks (or, for that matter, hard drinks) into the keyboard. But other PC gremlin sources aren't quite so obvious; you'll get to all the environmental hazards, obvious or not, in this chapter. These are a few of the factors that can endanger your PC's health:

◆ Excessive heat

◆ Dust

◆ Magnetism

◆ Stray electromagnetism (including that found in electrical storms)

◆ Power surges, incorrect line voltage, and power outages

◆ Water and corrosive agents

There's an additional factor, which is people-produced and seen more and more as PCs become more common throughout the workplace and home. This factor—believe it or not—is grease, the kind that can be found in poorly ventilated kitchens, near cooking areas, or in workshop environments like a garage. Combine grease with dust and you have a sort of sludge that can form on and within the PC, effectively gumming up the works.

QuickSteps

Checking the Environment

Let's quickly run through the procedures and guidelines for protecting your PC that are covered in this chapter.

BE PREPARED

Before you start, there are some things you may need on hand. These include:

- ◆ Nonmagnetic Phillips- or Torx-head screwdriver for opening the PC case

- ◆ Container for holding the screws between removal and reinstallation

- ◆ Antistatic wrist strap for reducing the chance of stray electrostatic discharge damaging components inside the case

- ◆ Some type of temperature gauge for checking PC internal temperatures

1. Check power considerations:

   - ◆ No heating elements (coffeemaker, portable heaters) in the same outlet as a PC

   - ◆ No large electric motors (refrigerators, air conditioners) on the same line as the PC

   - ◆ Some kind of power noise protection

2. Check the computer's internal temperature ranges:

   - ◆ Maximum 110 degrees F (43 degrees C).

   - ◆ Minimum 65 degrees F (18 degrees C). (The minimum temperature can be considerably lower, as long as the computer remains *on* all the time.)

3. Prevent dust buildup—you can buy (from PC Power & Cooling; see the Vendor Guide on the Utilities CD for contact information) power supplies with a filtered fan that sucks air in through the *back* rather than the usual approach of pulling it in through the front.

4. Make sure there isn't a source of severe vibration on the same table as the hard disk.

5. Make sure you know or (if you're a support person) teach your users:

   - ◆ That you should leave the machines on all the time

   - ◆ That cables should be kept screwed in and out of the way

   - ◆ Basic "don't do this" things about your operating system—for example, formatting the hard disk

6. Protect against static electricity.

QuickSteps

Preventive Maintenance

Although this chapter mainly discusses the environmental problems that PCs face, I also want to talk about some preventive maintenance concerns. The fact is, preventive maintenance will save you time and headaches in the long run. These steps should take about two hours.

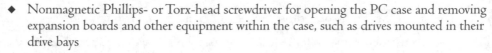

BE PREPARED

Before you start, there are some things you may need on hand. These include:

- ◆ Nonmagnetic Phillips- or Torx-head screwdriver for opening the PC case and removing expansion boards and other equipment within the case, such as drives mounted in their drive bays

- ◆ Container for holding the screws between removal and reinstallation

- ◆ Antistatic wrist strap for preventing static discharges while working inside the PC

- ◆ System backup software and available medium (Zip disks, CD-RWs, or tape cartridges) for performing a full or incremental system backup of the PC to protect the data

- ◆ Diagnostics software and commercial products such as a disk tools suite, a virus scanner, and other system check utilities in case you have problems identifying the source of difficulty

- ◆ Commercial connector cleaner solution and a lint-free cloth, or hard artist's eraser for cleaning the edge connectors

- ◆ Twist ties for binding cables together to keep them out of the way

- ◆ Slender, bent piece of metal for extracting a CPU (as described in Chapter 2, "Disassembling the PC")

- ◆ Can of compressed air for removing dust from components

---

1. Pick up the PC at its worksite. (Yes, this takes more time than having it delivered to your workplace, but you'll learn a lot just from observing its working environment.) Determine:

   - ◆ Are the connectors screwed in?

   - ◆ Have screws disappeared from the back of the machine?

   - ◆ What else is plugged into the PC's outlet? No other computer equipment? No cell phone rechargers? No coffeemakers?

   - ◆ Is the PC on a rickety table?

   - ◆ Is the PC near a window? Is it in a location that gets direct sun at some point in the day?

2. Ask if the machine is doing anything strange.

3. Ensure that the hard disk (if any) is backed up.

4. If the machine is running Windows Me or Windows XP, run System Restore to set a system restore point.

5. Run the machine's diagnostics. (If you're running a version of Windows *prior* to XP, it's a good idea to run ScanDisk; it's not included in the XP operating system.)

6. If it's a DOS computer, examine the `AUTOEXEC.BAT` and `CONFIG.SYS` files for any obvious problems—lack of a `BUFFERS` command, for example. If it's an older Windows machine (pre–Windows 95), look at the INI files for obvious tampering. Then run Windows and the programs a bit to ensure that they don't generate a lot of error messages (stating missing devices or conflicts) or return specific notes about stacks or buffers when programs crash. (This includes ensuring that the machine can print and can communicate over your corporate network or the Internet.)

7. Disassemble the PC.

8. Ground yourself.

9. Clean the edge connectors with a connector cleaner and a lint-free cloth or a hard, white artist's eraser.

10. Push the chips back into their sockets (this is discussed in Chapter 5, "Troubleshooting PC Problems").

11. Use canned air to remove dust from circuit boards—don't forget the circuit board under the hard disk.

12. Reassemble the PC. Ensure that all the cables are securely in place.

13. Rerun the diagnostics.

14. Ensure that all screws are present. If they are not, add the appropriate screws.

Heat and Thermal Shock

Every electronic device carries within it the seeds of its own destruction. More than half of the power given to chips is wasted as heat—and heat destroys chips. One of an electronics designer's main concerns is to ensure that an electronic device can dissipate heat as quickly as it can generate it. If it cannot, heat slowly builds up until the device fails.

More and more, heat can be seen as a by-product of overclocking, methods by which power users attempt to push their PC hardware for faster or otherwise more optimal performance. This is usually done through tweaking the motherboard and CPU, but it's increasingly being done with many video adapters, too.

There are several ways you can help control your PC's heat problem:

◆ Install an adequate fan in the power supply or add an auxiliary fan (or clean the one you have).

◆ Install a heat sink.

◆ Adjust your box design for better ventilation (including keeping cables from blocking proper air circulation within the PC case itself).

◆ Install a heat sensor device or monitor your existing one.

◆ Run the PC in a safe temperature range.

Removing Heat with a Fan

In general, laptops don't require a fan because enough heat dissipates from the main circuit board all by itself. (What you need to be careful of with laptops is that you don't block the vent(s) carrying warm air out of the unit.) However, most desktop and tower PCs will surely fail without a fan. Actually, many of today's PCs have several fans: one integrated into the power supply, one for the CPU, one for a high-performance video adapter, and sometimes more added to move heat from a hot hard drive.

When designing a fan, engineers must trade cooling power for noise. This is because the greater the capacity of the fan, the greater the noise produced—more air and more movement equal more noise. But it requires more engineering and costs more to make a very small fan that moves a fair amount of air—more than most of us would want to pay for a tiny fan. Years ago, power supplies were quite expensive, running in the $300 range for the cheapest power supply, so great care was exercised in choosing the right fan for protection. Nowadays, basic power supplies cost under $25, and I doubt that most PC company engineers could even tell you what kind of fan is sitting in their machines, any more than they could tell you who makes the case screws.

Now, that's a terrible shame, because the $3 fan that's sitting in most PC power supplies is a vital part. If it dies, your PC will cook itself in just a few hours.

And fans *do* die.

Fans range in quality, capacity, and purpose. As a general rule, the cheaper fans tend to wear out faster, sometimes in as little as six months to a year, while the more expensive variety made with bearings tend to endure. Such fans can often be removed, carefully cleaned of dust and debris (a pencil-sized paintbrush with a firm tip is ideal for this since you want to be careful to avoid damaging the fan), oiled, and returned to service without the need to replace the fan.

What causes all this heat that the fan is trying to remove? The more stuff that's in your PC, the hotter it runs. The things that make PCs hot inside include:

◆ Most chips, including memory chips, and CPUs in particular, because they have the greatest number of transistors inside them.

◆ Drive motors in some hard disks, floppies, and CD-ROM/DVD drives. Some CD-ROM/ DVD drives run quite warm, and large hard disks can run *extremely* hot. I've seen an old Maxtor 660MB ESDI drive run so hot that it almost burned my fingers. However, I saw the same thing on a more recent 1.7GB Fujitsu drive. Fortunately, drives in the 3½-inch half-height or third-height format run much cooler. Some circuit boards can run quite hot, depending on how well (or how poorly) they're designed.

Truthfully, heat buildup inside a PC is much less of a problem today than it was in the mid-1980s. In those days, every drive was a full-height drive, and every computer had 640KB of memory built up from 90 separate 64KB chips. Add one of those early hot 8087 coprocessors, and it was common to find the inside of a PC running 30 degrees F (16 degrees C) warmer inside its box than in the outside room.

Today's PCs, however, are much more energy-efficient. A standard 180- or 230-watt power supply handles far more devices hooked to it than do hardware designs from times past. But that doesn't mean you can't exhaust the power supply's range if you install many additional drives, for example. This can require a power supply upgrade to one of 300 watts designed for more professional needs.

Removing Heat with a Heat Sink

For years, electronics designers have had to struggle with hot components on circuit boards. Sometimes a fan just isn't enough, so they need more help cooling an internal chip. They do it with a heat sink. A *heat sink* is a small piece of metal, usually aluminum, with fins on it. The heat sink is glued (using a thick substance known as heat sink compound) or clamped to the hot chip. The metal conducts heat well, and the fins increase the surface area of the heat sink. The more area on the heat sink, the more heat that can be conducted off into the air and thereby removed from the PC.

The standard Pentium 4 processor packages have a heat sink and a fan integrated with the chip. The idea is that the heat sink pulls the heat off, and the fan disperses it. The Celeron doesn't come with a heat sink, but that doesn't mean that it's not a good idea to think about putting one on a hot chip. You can find heat sinks in electronics supply catalogs. Adding a fan can really increase the heat sink's ability to cool its chip. I've noticed that many modern motherboards have connections to power a couple of auxiliary fans, and you can buy fans that attach to those connections from PC clone parts places (look in the back of one of the PC magazines for them).

Understanding Good and Bad Box Designs

It's frustrating how totally unaware of heat problems many computer manufacturers are. The first tower computer I purchased was from a company named ACMA, and they put together an impressive machine. There were two fans in the case—a very nice touch—as well as a CPU fan. I have to say that they spoiled me. A later (1994) purchase, from an outfit called Systems Dynamics Group, was somewhat less enjoyable. The back of the PC chassis had room for two fans, but the system included only one fan. There's nothing intrinsically wrong with that, except that the cutout for the second fan—which is right next to the first fan—was left empty. The result was that the fan just sucked in air from the cutout a few inches away from it and blew that air back out. Made the fan happy, I suppose, but didn't do much for the CPU.

I noticed this pointless ventilation system pretty quickly, so I took some tape and covered up the extraneous cutout. Within seconds, the air being pumped out the back of the Pentium got 10 degrees warmer—which means that the CPU itself got that much cooler. If I'd left the extra cutout uncovered, the only ventilation that my Pentium system would have gotten was the simple convection from the heated boards and drives. Even at that, however, the Pentium system—which included a 1GB drive, 80MB of RAM, a CD-ROM, video capture board, video board, SCSI host adapter, and Ethernet card—ran only 10 degrees hotter inside the box than outside the box.

Things could have been a bit worse if the case was like some I've seen, with the fan *on the bottom of the tower!* This is not too common, fortunately, but it's worth asking about so you can avoid it when purchasing a PC. This setup puts the circuit boards on the top of the tower and the fan on the bottom. (Heat rises, remember—which means that a bottom-mounted fan is cooling the coolest part of the system.) I have no idea who designed this case, but it's nice to know that the banjo player kid from *Deliverance* finally has someone to look down on. The point I'm making here is to take a minute and look at the airflow in the box. Of course, even if you have a good box, you can still run into heat problems.

Living with Dead Fans

Several years ago (around 1995), I installed the Freelance Graphics program (remember Freelance Graphics?) on my system. Pulling the first floppy out of my A drive, I noticed that the floppy was warm. My memory flashed back to 1982, when something similar had happened—so I knew what was going on. My system's fan had died.

Fortunately, I found the problem early and shut down the computer. I had to travel to Europe for a few weeks to teach classes and consult, but I figured, no problem—I'll just leave the computer off.

Unfortunately, while I was gone, one of my employees helpfully started up the computer—reasoning that I always leave my computers on all the time, so what the hey? So, despite the "do not turn it on" sign I'd left on it, the computer merrily melted itself down while I lectured in Amsterdam. By the time I returned, the hard disk had self-destructed, as had the Ethernet card in it.

It's actually pretty amazing what *didn't* die in the system. The CPU (a 50MHz 486DX) ran for a couple of years afterward (until it became too slow to be of value), and the Adaptec 1742 SCSI host adapter is still in service in an old server.

Using Heat Sensor Devices

Now, I could have avoided this problem altogether if I had had a 110 Alert from a company called PC Power & Cooling. They're a name to know when you're buying power supplies. The 110 Alert, shown in Figure 4.1, is a circuit board about the size of a business card that plugs into a floppy power connector. When the PC's internal temperature gets to 110 degrees F, the alert starts making an annoying squealing noise. At 118 degrees F, it just shuts the computer down. The device costs around $15, and every network server should have one or one like it.

FIGURE 4.1

FIGURE 4.1

The 110 Alert thermal sensor device

While I'm on the subject of PC Power & Cooling, I should mention that this company also makes an interesting variety of power products for the PC, including power supplies with very quiet fans, power supplies with built-in battery backup, and high-quality PC cases. I use their stuff when I want to increase the odds that my PC will be running when I need it. If you have any questions about what rating of power supply to use, the company's Web site (www.pcpowercooling.com) will give you an analysis based on information you provide about your system and your needs. (Other contact information for the company is in the Vendor Guide on the Utilities CD.)

My introduction to PC Power & Cooling came with a hot 386. When I say "hot," I mean that this PC ran 25 degrees warmer inside than the temperature outside. PC Power & Cooling sold (and still sells) a series of Turbo-Cool power supplies that they claimed, at the time, would cool your PC by 35 to 40 degrees F. Now, obviously, my 386 could not be cooled by 35 degrees, because it was only 25 degrees over ambient (room) temperature—the best that a fan could do would be to lower the temperature inside the machine to the surrounding temperature. However, buying PC Power & Cooling's Turbo-Cool cooled my machine from 25 degrees over ambient to only *4* degrees over ambient.

Additionally, several motherboard manufacturers include a thermal sensing device onboard—meaning that it's built right into the board itself and can be enabled or disabled in the BIOS.

NOTE   *Intel's Pentium III and Pentium 4 processors include a diode that monitors the temperature of the CPU and shuts down the system if the CPU temperature exceeds 135 degrees. Some PIII motherboard manufacturers have incorporated a BIOS feature that allows you to check the CPU running temperature that the onboard diode reports. If your motherboard supports this feature, you'll find the CPU temperature readout in the hardware monitor setup screen.*

Keeping Temperature Ranges Safe for PCs

Electronic components have an ambient (room) temperature range within which they are built to work. IBM suggests that the PC, for instance, is built to work in the range of 60 to 85 degrees F. This is because the circuit boards can run as hot as 125 degrees, but a typical machine may be as much as 40 degrees hotter *inside* than outside. And 125 minus 40 yields 85 degrees, the suggested maximum temperature.

Obviously, if you have a good fan, the acceptable range of room temperatures expands considerably. If you have a really good fan, the inside of the machine is close to the same temperature as the outside. You don't want the inside of the PC to get any hotter than 110 degrees—hard disks can fail at that point, although, again, circuit boards can function in higher temperatures than that.

Heat also aids the corrosion process. Corrosion is a chemical process, and inside a computer, corrosion can roughly *double* in speed when the temperature of the process is raised by about 18 degrees F (10 degrees C). Chips slowly deteriorate, the hotter the faster.

Since the temperature inside the PC is the ambient temperature plus some constant, there are two ways to cool the inside of the PC—either lower the constant with a good fan, or lower the ambient temperature. Keep the room cooler, and the PC will be cooler.

How do you measure temperature and temperature changes in your PC? Simple: get a *digital temperature probe*. Radio Shack markets one for about $30. Or you can buy one from Edmund Scientific Corp. (www.edmundscientific.com), whose address is listed in the Miscellaneous Computer Products Vendors section of the Vendor Guide on the Utilities CD.

The easy way to use the probe is to tape it over the exit vents by the fan's power supply. An indoor/outdoor switch lets you quickly view the PC's inside temperature and the ambient temperature.

You may ask yourself, "OK, but what's the best operating temperature range for my CPU?" Intel and other chip designers and manufacturers provide optimum operating temperatures by CPU on their Web sites, along with other specific technical information.

Before leaving the subject of temperature ranges, I should mention one debate that never goes away: whether it's ever wise to leave the cover off a PC for any extended period.

Many of us leave the cover off short term, to make sure a new piece of equipment installed will work before we put in the screws. However, a considerable number of people, including seasoned computer veterans, believe that a PC functions better, overall, without the cover. Their theory is that much better air circulation is achieved with the bonus that you can better monitor and access the hardware.

The other side argues that today's systems were specifically optimized for overall cooling with the cover in place, and that you put the PC—and operator—at some degree of risk by leaving the cover off.

Indeed, during the summer, if you have your PC cover off for any period of time, you'll notice that the interior picks up almost as many dead insects as an outdoor light fixture. And, of course, operating a PC without a cover is ill-advised for anyone with small children, pets, or a crazy cousin who might decide to see what happens if he moves a switch or pulls a cable. As mentioned earlier, many surfaces inside the system can be razor sharp.

For peace of mind and a cleaner PC, you probably want to keep your cover on except when you're installing, removing, or checking a piece of hardware within the case.

DUTY CYCLES

I said before that a device should get rid of heat as quickly as it creates it. Not every device is that good, however. Devices are said to have a *duty cycle*. This number—expressed as a percentage—is the proportion of the time that a device can work without burning up. For example, a powerful motor may have a 50 percent duty cycle. This means that it should be active only 50 percent of the time. A starter motor on a car, for example, must produce a tremendous amount of power. Powerful motors are expensive to produce, so instead, cars use a motor that can produce a lot of power for a very short time. If you crank the engine on your car for several minutes at a stretch, you will likely damage or destroy the car's starter motor. Floppy drive motors are a similar example: run a floppy motor continuously and you'll likely burn out the motor. *Hard* disk motors, on the other hand, run continuously and must be designed with a 100 percent duty cycle.

Duty cycle is used to describe active versus inactive time for many kinds of devices. For some components, you control some of the overall duty cycle. For example, you decide how much work your printer will do in a single day. But many devices have internal cycles to keep them working on their own on a system that's up around the clock, just as many of today's PCs operate continuously.

THERMAL SHOCK

Because a PC is warmer inside than outside, changes in room temperature can become multiplied inside a PC.

This problem leads to a hazard called *thermal shock*. Thermal shock comes from subjecting components to rapid and large changes in temperature. It can disable your computer due to expansion/contraction damage. The most common scenario for thermal shock occurs when the PC is turned on Monday morning after a winter weekend. Many commercial buildings turn the temperature down to 55 degrees over the weekend; your office may contain some of that residual chill early Monday morning. Inside the PC, though, it may still be 55. Then you turn the machine on. Within 30 minutes some PCs can warm up to 120 degrees. This rapid, 65-degree rise in temperature brings on thermal shock.

This is an argument for leaving the PC on 24 hours a day, seven days a week. (You'll see some more reasons to do this soon.) The temperature inside the PC will be better regulated.

By the way, you can't leave portable PCs on all the time, so you should be extra careful with portables to avoid thermal shock. If your laptop has been sitting in the trunk on a cold February day, be sure to give it some time to warm up before trying to use it. And give it some time in a *dry* place, or water vapor will condense on the cold disk platters. Water on the disk platters is a surefire way to reduce your drive's life.

SUNBEAMS

Another heat effect is caused by sunbeams. Direct sunlight isn't a good thing for electronic equipment. A warm sunbeam feels nice for a few minutes, but sit in one for an hour and you'll understand why PCs don't like them. Direct sunlight is also, of course, terrible for floppy disks. Find a shadowy area for your PC and floppies, or use drapes or good window blinds/shades to protect them from the sun.

Dealing with Dust

Dust is everywhere. It consists of tiny sand granules, fossil skeletons of minuscule creatures that lived millions of years ago, dead skin, paper particles, and tiny crustaceans called dust mites that live off the other pieces. Dust is responsible for several evils.

First, it sticks to the circuit boards inside your computer. As dust builds up, an entire board can become coated with a fine insulating sheath. That would be fine if the dust was insulating your house, but thermal insulation is definitely a bad thing for computers. As you have seen, you seek to minimize impediments to thermal radiation from your computer components. To combat this, remove dust from inside the computer and from circuit boards periodically. A good period between cleaning is a year in a house and six months in an office. A simpler approach is to use the "while I'm at it" algorithm—when you need to disassemble the machine for some other reason, clean the insides while you're at it. A tool that can assist you is a can of compressed air. (*Compressed air* isn't actually compressed air; it's some kind of compressed gas.)

Just as effective for the case and inside support assemblies is a dust-free cloth wetted with a little water and ammonia (just a few drops). Don't use the cloth on circuit boards—get a can of compressed air and blow the dust off.

This should be obvious, but when you blow dust off boards, be aware of where it is going. If you can, have the vacuum cleaner nearby, or take the board to another area. *Please* don't hold the board over the PC's chassis and blow off the dust with compressed air—all this does is *move* the dust, not *remove* it.

The second dust evil is that dust can clog spaces, such as:

♦ The air intake area to your power supply or hard disk

♦ The space between the floppy disk drive head and the disk

To combat the floppy drive problem, some manufacturers offer a floppy dust cover that you put in place when the machine is turned off. The sad part of this is that you really need the cover when the machine is on. In addition, cathode-ray tube (CRT) displays have an unintended, unexpected, unpleasant, and unavoidable side effect—they attract dust. Turn your screen on, and all the dust in the area drops everything (what would dust particles drop, I wonder?) and heads straight for the display. Some of the particles get sidetracked and end up in the floppy drives.

One place that creates and collects paper dust is, of course, the printer. Printers should be vacuumed or blown out periodically, *away* from the computer. (Remember, dust goes somewhere when it's blown away.)

By the way, another fertile source of dust is ash particles. Most of us don't burn things indoors, *unless* we are smokers. If you smoke, fine: just don't do it near the computer. An old (1985) study by the U.S. Occupational Safety & Health Administration (OSHA) estimated that smoke at a computer workstation cuts the computer's life by 40 percent. How true that holds today is unknown. But it's still not a good idea to put anything smoky near the PC, nor is it wise to leave cigarette or cigar ash nearby, where it can be drawn into the machine. Greasy air isn't good either, so avoid setting up a PC next to a much-used stove or in a garage right next to where a vehicle pulls in.

NOTE   *Many people decide to put air cleaners/ionizers in the room where they use their PC(s). This seems to be especially true of smokers. Although that's fine to do, it's best to position the air cleaner at least several feet from the PC itself. Otherwise, smoke, dust, and other particles are apt to be drawn to the intake fan of the air cleaner. If the air cleaner is close to the PC, the PC's front vent may pick up some of the airborne debris instead.*

Magnetism

Magnets—both the permanent and electromagnetic type—can cause permanent loss of data on hard or floppy disks. Most often, the magnetism found in an office environment is produced by electric motors and electromagnets.

Don't think you have magnets around? How about:

◆ Magnets to hang notes on a file cabinet

◆ A paper clip holder with a magnet

◆ A word processing copy stand with a magnetic clip

◆ A magnetic screw extractor

TIP   *A frequently overlooked electromagnet is the one found in phones that ring using a real bell (which are not at all common these days). The clapper is forced against the bell (or buzzer, if the phone has one of those) in the phone by powering an electromagnet. If you absentmindedly put such a phone on top of a stack of floppy disks and the phone rings, you will probably have unrecoverable data errors on at least the top one. It's a good idea to get a phone with a ringer that is not a real bell to minimize the chance of erasing data inadvertently. (Plus, you'll have fewer people teasing you about your "old-fashioned" phone.)*

Another source of magnetism is, believe it or not, a CRT display. I have seen disk drives refuse to function because they were situated inches from a CRT.

X-ray machines in airports similarly produce some magnetism, although there is some controversy here. Some folks say, "Don't run floppies through the x-ray—walk them through." Others say the x-ray is okay but that the metal detector zaps floppies. Some people claim to have been burned at both. Personally, I walk through an average of three to four metal detectors per week carrying 3½-inch floppy disks and have never (knock on wood) had a problem. My laptops have been through x-ray machines everywhere, and I've never lost a byte on the hard disk because of it.

The fact of the matter is that airport metal detectors *should* be sufficiently gentle for floppies. Magnetism is measured in units called *gauss*. Metal detectors *in the U.S.* (notice the emphasis) emit far less gauss than that necessary to affect disks. I'm not sure about Europe, but the fillings in my teeth seem to set off the metal detectors in the Ottawa airport.

Another large source of magnetism is the motor in a printer—generally, it is not shielded (the motors on the drives don't produce very much magnetism, in case you're wondering).

And do you (or someone you assist) work in a word processing pool? Many word processors (the people kind, not the machine kind) use a copy stand that consists of a flexible metal arm and a magnet. The magnet holds the copy to be typed on the metal arm. The arm can sit right in front of the operator's face so that the operator can easily type the copy.

The problem arises when it's time to change the copy. I once watched a word processing operator remove the magnet to change the copy and slap the magnet on the side of the computer. It made perfect sense—the case was steel and held the magnet in a place that was easy to access. The only bad part of the whole operation was that the hard disk on that particular PC chassis was mounted on the extreme right-hand side of the case, right next to the magnet. You can start to see why I hate magnets....

A few years ago, I was a keynote speaker at a conference held in San Antonio, near the Alamo. As part of the "thank you" package that the conference organizers put together, we speakers got a refrigerator magnet in the shape of the Alamo. After almost placing my wallet (with my credit cards in it) on the magnet, almost laying demonstration floppies that I'd gotten at the conference on it, and almost storing the Alamo magnet in my laptop case (you know, next to the laptop's hard disk and any floppies that I had in the case), I finally gave up and threw the magnet away before I had a chance to *really* do some damage.

Oh, and by the way, *speakers* have magnets in them. Years ago, a friend purchased a home entertainment system that included a VCR, a stereo, and some monster speakers. That's when I noticed that he had stacked his videotapes on top of the speakers. I almost didn't have the heart to tell him, but I eventually advised him that his videos were history—and, sad to say, they *were*. Modern multimedia PCs all have speakers that claim to have shielded magnets, but I have a Sony woofer/satellite speaker system that makes my monitor's image get wobbly when I put the speakers too near the monitor. No matter what the manual says, I think I'll just keep the floppies away from there.

What about preventive maintenance? My advice is to go on an antimagnet crusade. Magnets near magnetic media are disasters waiting to happen.

A sad story: a large government agency's data center bought a handheld magnetic bulk floppy eraser. (I'm not sure why—they weren't a secret shop and thus did not have the need.) The PC expert in the shop tested it on a few junk floppies, then turned it off and didn't think about it. The next day, he remembered that he had left it on top of a plastic floppy file drawer. This meant that the eraser, even though turned off, was about an inch from the top of the floppies. He spent the next day testing each of the floppies, one by one. Most were dead. They got rid of the bulk eraser. I'm not sure what they did with the PC expert.

Stray Electromagnetism

Stray electromagnetism can cause problems for your PC and, in particular, for your network. Here, I'm referring to any electromagnetism that you don't want. It comes in several varieties:

◆ Radiated electromagnetic interference (EMI)

◆ Power noise and interruptions

◆ Electrostatic discharge (ESD)—static electricity

Electromagnetic Interference

EMI is caused when electromagnetism is radiated or conducted somewhere that you don't want it to be. In this section, I discuss two common types—crosstalk and radio frequency interference (RFI).

CROSSTALK

When two wires are physically close to each other, they can transmit interference between themselves called *crosstalk*. I'm not talking about short circuits here; the insulation can be completely intact. The problem is that the interfering wire contains electronic pulses. Electronic pulses produce magnetic fields as a side effect. The wire being interfered with is touched or crossed by the magnetic fields.

Magnetic fields crossing or touching a wire produce electronic pulses as a side effect. (Nature is, unfortunately, amazingly symmetrical at times like this.) The electronic pulses created in the second wire are faint copies of the pulses (the signal) from the first wire. These pulses interfere with the signal that you're trying to send on the second wire.

Crosstalk is not really a problem when applied to power lines, although I have heard of cases where the alternating current in power lines creates a hum on a communications line through crosstalk. The larger worry is when bundles of wires are stored in close quarters, and the wires are data cables.

There are five solutions to crosstalk:

◆ Move the wires farther apart (not always feasible).

◆ Use twisted-pair cable (varying the number of twists reduces crosstalk).

◆ Use shielded cable (the shield reduces crosstalk—don't even think of running ribbon cables for distances over 6 feet).

◆ Use fiber-optic cable—it's not electromagnetic; it's *photonic* (is that a great word, or what?). That means it uses light instead of electricity to transmit data, so there's no crosstalk.

◆ Don't run cables over fluorescent lights. The lights are noise emitters.

I once helped troubleshoot a network that had been installed in a classroom. The contractor had run the wires through the ceiling, but the network didn't seem to work. (Ever notice how often the words *network* and *not work* end up in the same sentence? A Russian friend calls them *nyet*works.) I pushed aside the ceiling tiles and found that the cable installer had saved himself some time and money by foregoing cable trays and instead wrapped the cables around the occasional fluorescent lamp. On a hunch, I turned off the lights and said to the people I was working with, "Start the network up again." Sure enough, it worked.

RADIO FREQUENCY INTERFERENCE

Radio frequency interference (RFI) is high-frequency (10kHz) radiation. It's a bad thing for computer communications. Sources are:

◆ Nearby radio sources

◆ Cordless telephones

◆ Keyboards

◆ Power-line intercoms (intercoms that use the power line's 60Hz as the carrier wave)

◆ Motors

Worse yet, your PC can be a *source* of RFI. If this happens, the FCC police come to your place of business and take your PC away. (Well, not really. But they *could* fine you, especially if your PC is interfering with someone else's equipment.)

RFI is bad because it can interfere with high-speed digital circuits. Your computer is composed of digital circuits. RFI can seem sinister because it seems to come and go mysteriously. Like all noise, it is an unwanted signal. How would you go about receiving a *wanted* RF signal? Simple—construct an antenna. Suppose you want to receive a signal of a given frequency. You would design an antenna of a particular length. (Basically, the best length is one-quarter of the wavelength. A 30-meter wavelength is best picked up by a 7.5-meter antenna. But it's not important that you know that—to learn more about it, pick up an amateur radio book.) Now, suppose that some kind of RFI is floating around. You're safe as long as you can't receive it. But suppose the computer is connected to the printer with a cable that, through bad luck, happens to be the correct length to receive that RFI. The result: printer gremlins. Fortunately, the answer is simple: shorten or lengthen the cable.

Electric motors are common RFI-producing culprits. I recently saw a workstation in Washington where the operator had put an electric fan (to cool *herself*, not the workstation) on top of the workstation. When the fan was on, it warped the top of the CRT's image slightly. Electric can openers, hair dryers, electric razors, electric pencil sharpeners, and printers are candidates. Sometimes it's hard to determine whether the device is messing up the PC simply by feeding back noise onto the power line or whether it is troubling the PC with RFI. Either way, the answer is to put the devices on separate power lines.

Your PC also *emits* RFI, which can impair the functioning of other PCs, televisions, and various sensitive pieces of equipment. By law, a desktop computer cannot be sold unless it meets Class B specifications—that is, the FCC requires that a device that is 3 meters from the PC must receive no more RFI than shown in Table 4.1.

TABLE 4.1: PERMISSIBLE RFI OUTPUT (FCC CLASS B SPECIFICATION)

MAXIMUM FIELD STRENGTH FREQUENCY	(MICROVOLTS/METER)
30–88MHz	100
89–216MHz	150
217–1000MHz	200

RFI became an issue when the personal computer was first introduced, because IBM had shielded its PC line in an effort to make life a little tougher on the clonemakers. By pushing the FCC to get tough on PCs, IBM had a bit of a jump on the market. Unfortunately, getting Class B certification isn't that hard, and just about every PC qualifies these days: clonemakers now say that their machines are "FCC Class B Certified." This has caused the reverse of IBM's original intent because the FCC certification seems a mark of legitimacy. In reality, FCC certification is not a measure of good design, quality components, or compatibility; it just means that the equipment doesn't produce excessive amounts of electromagnetic interference.

Protecting your PC from the devices around it and protecting the devices from your PC are done in the same way. If the PC doesn't leak RFI, then it's less likely to pick up any stray RFI in the area. Any holes in the case provide entry/exit points. Use the brackets that come with the machine to plug any unused expansion slots. Ensure that the case fits together snugly and correctly. If the case includes cutouts for interface connectors, find plates to cover the cutouts or simply use metal tape.

A simple AM radio can be used to monitor RFI field strength. A portable radio is ideal because it has light headphones and a small enough enclosure to allow fairly local signal strength monitoring. A cheap model is best—you don't want sophisticated noise filtering. Tune it to an area of the dial as far as possible from a strong station. Lower frequencies seem to work best. You'll then hear the various devices produce noises through the radio. I first noticed these noises when working ages ago on a clone computer that had an XT motherboard, a composite monitor, an external hard disk, and a two-drive external Bernoulli box. The quietest part of the system was the PC. The hard disk screamed and buzzed, the Bernoulli made low-frequency eggbeater-like sounds, and the monitor produced a fairly pure and relatively loud tone.

The PC sounded different, depending on what it was doing. When I typed, I heard a machine gun–like sound. When I asked for a text search, the fairly regular search made a "dee-dee-dee" sound. It's kind of fun (okay, I guess I don't get out much), and you might pop the top on your system and do a little "radio astronomy" on it.

NOTE *This is also a fairly effective way to "eavesdrop" on other people's PCs. Sophisticated detection devices are capable of tracking how a computer is used (and replicating a PC's monitor image) by monitoring a PC's RF emissions.*

I've also used the radio in a number of other ways. Once, I received a new motherboard, a 486 that I was going to use to upgrade a 286 system. I installed it, and nothing happened. No beeps, no blinking cursor, nothing but the fan. So I removed the motherboard and placed it on a cardboard box (no electrical short fears with a cardboard box). Then I placed a power supply next to it, plugged in the P8/P9 connectors, and powered up. I ran the radio over the motherboard and got no response, just a constant hum. Placing the radio right over the CPU got nothing. I reasoned that what I was hearing was just the clock circuit. I felt even more certain of my guess when I noticed that the CPU had been inserted backward into its socket. One dead motherboard, back to the manufacturer.

Power Noise

Wall sockets are a source of lots of problems. They basically fall into these three categories:

- Transients—spikes and surges

- Overvoltage and undervoltage

- No voltage at all—a power blackout

I'll cover these categories in depth in Chapter 9, "Power Supplies and Power Protection." Right now, however, let's look at a special problem—lightning—and then the fourth kind of power noise, the one that *you* cause: *power-up power surges*. In the process of discussing how to fix this, I'll have to weigh in on the Great PC Power Switch Debate.

WHEN LIGHTNING STRIKES

In many ways, lightning fits into what you've already read about here (transient electrical charges, for example), but it's a point worth discussing separately because of the PC damage caused each year by it.

Anyone who lives in an area prone to serious electrical storms during warmer months knows the damage a strike can cause to a television, particularly one with an external antenna wired into it. The charge from a strike on the antenna can travel into the house, into the back of the set, and can result in an explosion (if not a fire, too).

A PC can be at least as sensitive to lightning's effects and usually costs more to replace.

With PCs, you need to worry not only about the unit itself, but anything that wires into it from a source that could be affected by an electrical storm. In the most common situation, you use a phone line connected to a modem connected to your PC, which can act much like the TV with the lead wire from the antenna coming in. When lightning strikes phone lines in your neighborhood, the shock waves can travel along the connections and potentially travel into your home or office and into the back of the PC.

External modems, which have a separate power supply, tend to isolate the effects. Lightning may blow out the capacitors in the modem, but the damage usually stops there. Internal modems, however, are connected to the PC's motherboard. A charge occurring here could ruin not just the modem, but it could perhaps fry the motherboard as well. Think of what this means when you have a motherboard with the modem integrated right into the system board itself. Electricity felt on your phone line is delivered directly.

TIP Don't underestimate the potential damage lightning can cause when you're reading about protection methods in Chapter 9. Also take lightning into consideration if your PC develops some strange problems—a malfunctioning modem, no power up, or odd boot errors—immediately following a large storm.

LEAVE YOUR MACHINES ON 24 HOURS A DAY

I'd like to discuss one power-related item here: user-induced power surges. What user-induced power surges, you say? Simple: every time you turn on an electrical device, you get a power surge through it.

Some of the greatest stresses that electrical devices receive are when they are turned on or turned off. When do light bulbs burn out? Think about it—they generally burn out when you first turn them on or off. One study showed that when a device is first turned on, it draws as much as four to six times its normal power for less than one second. (This phenomenon is called *inrush current*.)

The answer? Leave your PCs on 24 hours a day, seven days a week. We've done it at my company for years. Turn the monitor off, turn the screen intensity down, or use one of those annoying automatic screensavers so the monitor doesn't get an image burned into it. Turn the printer off also. Modern power management techniques (check for a Power Management icon in Windows 98/2000/XP) let you put the hard drives and monitor to sleep on a set schedule. Leaving the machines on also regulates temperature and reduces a phenomenon called *chip creep* (which I'll discuss in Chapter 5).

What? You're still not convinced? I know, it doesn't seem intuitive—most people react that way. But it really does make sense. First of all, consider the things that you keep on all the time:

- Digital clocks, which obviously run continuously, incorporate some of the same digital technology as microcomputers, and they're pretty reliable.

- Calculators—I've seen accountants who use calculators that are kept on all the time.

- Mainframes, minis, and your phone PBX never go off.

- TVs—part of the TV is powered up all the time so that it can "warm up" instantly, unlike older sets.

- Thermostats—the temperature-regulating device in your home or business is a circuit that works all the time.

Most of the things that I just named are some of the most reliable, never-think-about-them devices that you work with.

Now, consider the hard disk. All disks incorporate a motor to spin them at high speeds (depending on the drive, they may spin at speeds ranging from 3600 to 10,000 rpm). You know from real life that it's a lot harder to get something moving than it is to keep it moving. (Ever push a car?) The cost, then, of turning hard disk motors on and off is that sometimes they just won't be able to get started.

For example, back in 1984 I bought my first hard disk, an external 32MB drive. It cost $929, and while it's dead and buried now, for years I was loathe to stop using it, because nine hundred bucks was a lot of money. (Still is, actually—although it can now buy a complete PC, not just a hard drive.) For a long time I kept it attached to a server and constantly running. The drive required a "jump-start" when it was turned off overnight: if the thing didn't want to work, we just removed it from the system, took off the hard disk's circuit board to expose the motor, and gave the motor a spin. After a couple of spins, we reassembled it, and it would start up fine. (No, I didn't put anything important on it, but it was a great demonstration tool. And it kept data just fine.)

Here's the point: as long as we didn't turn the system off, the hard drive worked quite well, at least as well as old 32MB hard drives work. This applies to hard disks in general, and in fact to anything with a motor. Yes, the motor's life is shortened when continuously on, but even then the expected life of the motor is beyond the reasonable life of a hard disk.

Leaving your computer on all the time heads off thermal shock, which is yet another reason to leave it on. Machines should never be power cycled quickly. I've seen people fry their power supplies by turning their computers on and off several times in a 30-second period to "clear problems," and they ended up creating bigger problems.

A word of caution, however: Leaving the machine on all the time is a good idea only if:

- Your machine is cooled adequately. If your machine is 100 degrees inside when the room is 70 degrees, it'll overheat when the building management turns off the cooling in your building on summer weekends and the room goes to 90 degrees. Make sure your machine has a good enough fan to handle higher temperatures.

- You have adequate surge protection, typically in the form of a surge protector strip installed between your computer (and its peripherals) and the AC power outlet. Actually, you should not run the machine at all unless you have adequate surge protection.

- You have fairly reliable power. If you lose power three times a week, there's no point in leaving the machines on all the time—the power company is turning them off and on for you. Even worse, the power that comes on just after a power outage is noise-filled. And even if you do have fairly reliable power, you may want to change your practice when there's a possibility of the kind of severe weather likely to cause temporary power problems.

Of course, if your operating system is prone to crashing, it's almost impossible to leave your system on continuously. For that reason, upgrading to a more stable operating system, such as Windows 2000 or Windows XP, will enable you to leave your system up-and-running even though individual applications may crash. In addition, older (pre–Windows XP) versions of Windows are prone to "memory leakage," and need to be rebooted about once a day to free up lost memory; Windows XP doesn't have this problem, which lets you keep your system running without constant rebooting.

Before moving on, let's take a quick peek at the other kinds of power problems—the ones you'll tackle in greater detail in Chapter 9.

TIP   *One more final word of caution: with broadband Internet connections through cable and DSL modems becoming increasingly popular and affordable, using a firewall to protect your PC from hack attacks is a necessity, most especially if you leave your PC on 24 hours a day. Consumer and professional firewalls, such as ZoneAlarm (*`www.zonealarm.com`*) and BlackICE Defender (*`www.iss.net`*), help you protect your PC or network from unwanted intrusion and virus attacks.*

TRANSIENTS

A *transient* is any brief change in power that doesn't repeat itself. It can be an undervoltage or an overvoltage. *Sags* (momentary undervoltage) and *surges* (momentary overvoltage) are transients. In brief, the transient may be of a high enough frequency that it slips right past the protective capacitors in your power supply and punches holes in your chips. (No, they're not holes that you can see, at least not without some very good equipment.) Transients have a cumulative effect—the first 100 may do nothing. Eventually, however, enough chickens come home to roost that your machine decides, one day, to go on vacation. (You might say that if enough chickens come home to roost, the machine "buys the farm." Permanently.) I'll talk about how to protect against these things in Chapter 9.

OVERVOLTAGE

You have an *overvoltage* condition when you get more than the rated voltage for a period of greater than 2.5 seconds. Such a voltage measurement is made as a moving average over several seconds.

Chronic overvoltage is just as bad for your system as transient overvoltage: the chips can fail as a result of it.

UNDERVOLTAGE

Summer in much of the country means that air conditioners are running full blast, and the power company is working feverishly to meet the power demands that they bring. Sometimes it can't meet the full needs, however, so it announces a reduction in voltage called a *brownout*, or an *undervoltage*.

Brownouts are bad for large motors, like the ones you'd find in a compressor for refrigeration. Brownouts make your TV screen look shrunken and they confuse power supplies. A power supply tries to provide continuous power to the PC. Power equals voltage times current. If the voltage drops and you want constant power, what do you do? Simple: draw more current. But drawing more current through a given conductor heats up the conductor. The power supply and the chips get hot and may overheat.

Surge protectors can't help you here. A *power conditioner* can—it uses a transformer to compensate for the sagging voltage. An uninterruptible power supply (UPS) also helps remedy a number of electrical problems that interrupted power can cause. I'll discuss power conditioners and UPSs in greater detail in Chapter 9.

Electrostatic Discharge

ESD—or, as you probably know it, *static electricity*—is annoyingly familiar to anyone who has lived through a winter indoors. The air is very dry (winter and forced hot-air ducts bring relative humidity to around 20 percent in my house, for example) and is an excellent insulator. You build up a static charge and keep it until you touch something like a metal doorknob—or much worse, your computer. On the other hand, in the summer, when relative humidity can be close to 100 percent (until 1998 I lived in a suburb of Washington, D.C., a city built over a swamp), you still build up static charges, but they leak away quickly due to the humidity of the air. Skin resistance also has a lot to do with dissipating charges. The resistance of your skin can be as little as 1000 ohms when wet and 500,000 ohms when dry. (This fun fact is courtesy of Jearl Walker's *Flying Circus of Physics*, published by John Wiley in 1977.)

You know how static electricity is built up. Static can damage chips if it creates a charge of 200 volts (sometimes even less). But for the average person to notice it, static discharge must be at least 2000 volts.

Scuffing across a pile carpet in February can build up 50,000 volts. This is an electron "debt" that must be paid. The next metal item you touch (metal gives up electrons easily) pays the debt with an electric shock. If it's 50,000 volts, why doesn't it electrocute you when you touch the metal? Simple: the amperage (which is the volume of electricity) is tiny. This is because even though the voltage is high, the resistance is up in the millions of ohms, and 50,000 volts divided by millions of ohms is a tiny amount of current. (As my physics professor used to tell us, "Twinkle, twinkle, little star; power equals I squared R." And people say physics is dull.) Different materials generate more or less static. Many people think that certain materials are static-prone, while others are not. As it turns out, materials have a triboelectric (the electrical discharge created when you rub two objects together) value. Two materials rubbed together will generate static in direct proportion to how far apart their triboelectric values are.

Some common materials, in order of their triboelectric values (from highest to lowest, reading the left column top to bottom, and then the right column top to bottom), are:

Air	Cotton
Human skin	Steel wool
Asbestos	Hard rubber
Rabbit fur	Nickel and copper
Glass	Brass and silver
Human hair	Gold and platinum
Nylon	Acetate and rayon
Wool	Polyester
Fur	Polyurethane
Lead	Polyvinyl
Silk	Chloride
Aluminum	Silicon
Paper	Teflon

Once an item is charged, the voltage potential between it and another object is proportional to the distance between it and the other item on the table. For instance, suppose I charge a glass rod with a cotton cloth. The glass will attract things below it on the preceding list, like paper, and it will attract more strongly things listed below paper.

Why does static damage PC components? The chips that largely comprise circuit boards are devices that can be damaged by high voltage, even if they're at low current. The two most common families of chips are complementary metal oxide semiconductor (CMOS) chips and transistor-transistor logic (TTL) chips. CMOS chips include negative metal oxide semiconductor (NMOS), positive metal oxide semiconductor (PMOS), and an assortment of newer devices that seem to appear on an almost daily basis. TTLs are an older family of chips. You can identify one common family of TTL chips by ID numbers that start with 74 (as in 7400, 7446, 74LS128, and the like). TTLs are faster-switching chips—so potentially faster chips (memories, CPUs, and such) could be designed with TTL. Ah, but TTL has a fatal flaw: it draws a lot of power. TTL chips need much more electricity than CMOS chips, so they create more heat. Therefore, although fast TTL CPUs could be constructed, CPUs are tough to justify because densely packed TTLs produce so much heat that they would destroy themselves.

CPUs and memories are generally CMOS chips. CMOS has a lower theoretical maximum speed, but it runs on a lot less power. Sadly, they are also more subject to static electricity damage. TTL chips can withstand considerably more static electricity than CMOS chips.

Even if static doesn't destroy a chip, it can shorten its life. Static is, then, something to be avoided if possible. Another effect occurs when the static is discharged: When the fat blue spark jumps from your finger to the computer case, a small electromagnetic pulse (EMP) is created. This isn't too good for chips. (EMP is the thing you've heard about that could cause a single nuclear explosion to destroy every computer in the country. It takes a lot less than a nuclear explosion to destroy the chips in your own computer.) The easiest way I get rid of my static is to discharge the static buildup on something metal that is not the computer's case. A metal desk or table leg is good.

For your business, however, you may want something a trifle more automatic. The options are to:

- Raise the humidity with a humidifier (evaporative, not ultrasonic—ultrasonic creates dust)

- Raise the humidity with plants or, perhaps, an aquarium

- Install static-free carpet

- Put antistatic "touch me" mats under the PCs

- Make your own antistatic spray (see below)

From the point of view of comfort, I recommend the first option strongly. Your employees won't feel dried out, and the static problem disappears. Raise humidity to just 50 percent, and the problem will go away.

You can make inexpensive, homemade antistatic spray. Just get a spray pump bottle and put about an inch of fabric softener in it. Fill it the rest of the way with water, shake it well, and you have a spray for your carpets to reduce static. Just spritz it on the carpet—the carpet will smell nice, and everyone will know that you've been busy. (I hear you asking, "How long does it last?" Don't worry, you'll know.)

NOTE   *In a similar vein, someone from a temporary services agency once told me that they tell their word processing operators to put a sheet of Bounce under the keyboard to reduce static. While this may make the area smell nice, it will have no effect on static around the computer.*

Technicians who must work with semiconductors all the time use an *antistatic wrist strap*, or *ground strap*, to minimize ESD. As you know from Chapter 2, the idea of an antistatic wrist strap is that you never create a spark—or, therefore, EMP—because you always have a nice ground connection that's draining off your charges. A good antistatic wrist strap is an elastic wristband with a metal plate built into it to provide a good electrical connection, attached to a wire with an alligator clip. You put the clip on something grounded—the power supply case is the most common place—and put the strap around your wrist. As you're connected to a ground, you continuously drain off your charges. A resistor in the ground strap slows down the discharge process a bit (from a microsecond to a few milliseconds), so you don't end up with one of the dangerous sparks that I've discussed before. If you do a lot of board work in a dry place, antistatic wrist straps are essential. Several Silicon Valley defense-contracting firms have a policy of firing employees for not wearing their ESD wrist straps when working on high-tech equipment such as satellites and military equipment.

When you must handle electronic components, take these precautions:

◆   Get an antistatic strap. They're cheap.

◆   Remember the high-tech equivalent of knocking on wood—touch unpainted metal periodically. One member of my staff has suggested handling chips only while naked on a wooden floor. While this might be entertaining to some of the staff, it would not, unfortunately, prevent static charges from building up since on a very dry day even the movement of your hair can build up a charge.

◆   Reduce the chances you'll have a lot of static in the air—even though you're wearing the antistatic wrist strap, you still want to avoid raising any more stray static in the area than you have to, so if you're wearing anything acrylic on a very cold day, remove it. Also, avoid standing on an acrylic carpet without a rubberized floor pad beneath your feet, and keep long hair tied behind your back.

◆   Don't handle components in areas that have high static potential, such as high-humidity environments or carpeted areas (unless the carpets are made of antistatic material).

◆   Consider what you're wearing. Don't wear an acrylic sweater when changing chips. Get leather-soled shoes. If your work environment allows it, you can really avoid static by removing your shoes and socks.

◆   Don't handle chips any more than is necessary. If you don't touch them, you won't hurt them.

◆   Use antistatic protective tubes and bags to transport and store chips.

◆   If possible, pick up components by their bodies. Don't touch the pins any more than necessary.

◆   Have I mentioned yet that you should have an antistatic strap and use an antistatic mat?

Use the proper precautions, and your PC won't get a big "charge" out of being touched by you.

Avoiding Water and Other Liquids

Water is an easy hazard to detect and avoid. You don't need any sophisticated detection devices. Shielding is unnecessary—you just keep the computer away from water.

Water and liquids are introduced into a computer system in one of several ways:

◆ Operator spills

◆ Flooding

◆ Leaks

Spills generally threaten the keyboard. One remedy—the one recommended by every article and book I've ever read on maintenance—is to forbid liquids near the computer. In most shops, this is unrealistic. Some people use clear, flexible, plastic covers on the keyboard, kind of like what some fast-food restaurants use on their cash registers. They have "normal" cash registers, but they have a plastic skin over the keys that allows the user to spill special sauce all over the keyboard without harming it. Use the plastic covers, and they can just hose down the keyboard (just kidding). With one of these keyboard "skins," you might say that you can practice safe typing.

A similar disaster, flooding, sometimes occurs. Don't assume that flooded components are destroyed components. Disassemble the computer and clean the boards by cleaning the contacts and edge connectors. You can buy connector cleaner fluids; some people use a hard, white artist's eraser—do not use pencil erasers! (A Texas Instruments study showed that they contain acids that do more harm than good to connectors.) Blow out crevices with compressed air. (And if you do disassemble, clean, dry, and reassemble your computer, and then find that it works, write the manufacturer a letter; they might put your face in an advertisement.)

Avoid damage caused by floods by thinking ahead. Don't store any electrical devices directly on the floor; not only are they at risk during a flood, but they'll be damaged when the floor is cleaned. Generally, flooding indoors is under 6 inches. In addition, be aware of leaking from improper roofing; when installing PCs, don't put one in directly under the suspicious stain on the ceiling. ("Oh, that—it was fixed two years ago. No problem now.")

Corrosion

Liquids (and gases) can accelerate corrosion of PCs and PC components. Corrosive agents include:

◆ Salt sweat in skin oils

◆ Water

◆ Airborne sulfuric acid, salt spray, and carbonic acid

Your fear here is not that the PC will fall away to rust; the largest problem that corrosion causes is oxidation of circuit contacts. When a device's connector becomes oxidized, it doesn't conduct as well, and so the device does not function, or—worse—malfunctions sporadically. Salt in sweat can do this, so be careful when handling circuit boards; don't touch edge connectors unless you have to. This is why some firms advertise that they use gold-edge connectors; gold is resistant to corrosion.

You don't believe that you have detectable traces of finger oils? Try this simple experiment. Pour a glass of soda or beer into a very clean glass—preferably a plastic cup that has never been used before. There will be a noticeable "head" of foam on the drink. (Diet soda seems particularly fizzy.) Now put your finger into the center of the head, just for a second. The head will rapidly dissolve, because the oils damage the surface tension required to support the head. It's the quickest way to eliminate a large head so you can pour a larger glass of beer. Or you could try buying a nice new flat-screen LCD computer monitor and see how many of your colleagues fail to understand that it is not a touch-screen device. You will end up with numerous thick, oily smudge marks on your monitor that are very visible and annoying when a dark background is displayed on it.

Carbonated liquids include carbonic acid, and coffee and tea contain tannic acids. The sugar in soda is eaten by bacteria that leave behind conductive excrement—like hiring some germs to put new traces on your circuit board. Generally, try to be very careful with drinks around computers.

Don't forget cleaning fluids. Be careful with that window cleaner that you're using to keep the display clean. If your PC is on a pedestal on the floor, and the floor is mopped each day, some of the mopping liquid gets into the PC. Cleaning fluids are very corrosive.

Again, you can clean edge connectors with either hard, white erasers (remember, don't use the pink erasers—they're acidic!) or connector cleaner products. One of the best-known vendors of these products is Texwipe (`www.texwipe.com`). Further contact information is available in the Vendor Guide on the Utilities CD.

NOTE *Although this chapter has discussed some preventive maintenance concerns, I've mainly talked about the environmental problems PCs face. But you should also do preventive maintenance, which means taking a machine off your desk at regular intervals, perhaps as often as every 6 months, and moving it to your "shop" to give it a good going-over so that you'll anticipate problems. If you missed the key preventive maintenance procedures listed at the beginning of this chapter, make sure you go back and check them out!*

Troubleshooting Tips

When troubleshooting PC problems, it's important not to overlook the very environmental factors discussed in this chapter (as well as whether the system has been "pushed" or overclocked to try to bolster performance).

Ask yourself these questions when you're working on a perplexing problem, particularly one where the difficulties occur at some times of the day but not others:

◆ Is the PC in direct sunlight or positioned in such a way that strong sunlight is hitting the case or monitor for a prolonged period of time? Install a shade or blinds, close the curtains, or move the PC where it won't have sunshine heating up the PC case, which in turn heats up the internal components.

◆ Is the room in which the PC is located prone to severe temperature changes? For example, in the winter, is the office quite warm during the day yet only has minimal heating during the cold nights? Such fluctuation isn't good for any system. If possible, move the PC into an area where the temperature remains more even throughout the day and night. If it must stay put, then the ambient temperature needs to be normalized before turning on the PC.

♦ Is the PC in a room shared with animals? Cats and other small critters like to huddle around warm things on cold days, and the hair they shed can gum up the works faster than a Kansas dust storm. In addition, a cat jumping on your keyboard can not only cause mechanical problems, but also introduce unwanted static electricity. If at all possible, isolate the PC from the animals. (And I know how impossible this is in most home office environments!)

♦ Are the problems occurring when the room temperature is very cold or very warm but not occurring at other times? Again, moving the PC to a more climate-controlled area is a good idea.

♦ Is hardware acting flaky after a particularly bad storm or power fluctuation? If so, the system needs to be evaluated, parts need to be replaced (as necessary), and the system then needs to be equipped with some type of power protection scheme, such as an uninterruptible power supply or surge protector.

♦ Is the PC located in an area where large appliances cycling up or down may cause a short flux in the power (noticeable by a brief flicker of the lights)? The PC should be moved to a different circuit from any other equipment that may interfere with it or its constant power supply. A power protection scheme such as a surge protector should be used.

♦ Is the area in which the PC is located prone to dampness? Dampness can cause odd behavior in a PC and can short out electronic components. Move the PC to a dry, temperate area.

♦ Have you or the PC's user recently "pushed" the limits of the system by adjusting clock settings on the motherboard or your video card? If so, such changes may potentially cause a heat problem inside the case, as well as account for other random errors and device failures. Reverse the "overclocking" and then either leave it alone or step it up very gradually.

By now, your PC is shined to a high gloss. But what happens when something goes wrong? For that, turn to the next chapter.

Chapter 5

Troubleshooting PC Problems

◆ QuickSteps: Troubleshooting PC Problems   213

◆ General Rules of Thumb   214

◆ Six Steps to Success   218

◆ Common Problems—and Solutions   232

◆ Handling an Emergency   237

Introduction

OKAY, SUPPOSE YOU DUST out your PC fortnightly. You clean and adjust your disk drives semiannually. You have a robot that zaps anyone carrying food or drink within 50 feet of your PC. But, one day, Microsoft Word refuses to print your purple prose. How do you proceed?

You might say that this is a chapter about religion. I want you to develop a process for dealing with computer repairs that you follow as dutifully as a zealot follows a religion.

Why get religious? Because people who fix PCs day in and day out—people who fix *anything* day in and day out, for that matter—have learned to do it by following some repeatable step-by-step procedures. That isn't the only approach you can take, of course; the alternative method is to attack each problem in a haphazard way.

Now, I'm somebody who's tried both the religious way and the haphazard way. As such, you might say that I'm uniquely qualified to offer you some advice on how to choose which approach to take.

If you find that you're plagued with too much free time, time you have to spend with the spouse and kids; if you just can't sleep at night and need something to fill those insomniac hours; if Saturdays and Sundays are painful tedium broken only by the occasional *Three Stooges* rerun—then, by all means, adopt the haphazard method. You'll be able to tackle all kinds of fascinating problems, most of which you created yourself while noodling around trying to fix the original problem. And, since the true haphazard fixer never takes notes, you'll get to experience the joy of problem-solving over and over, even when it's the same problem.

If, on the other hand, you want to do something with your days other than futzing around with balky PCs, then think about getting religion.

Don't get me wrong: there's nothing wrong with futzing around with a PC—you'll get some of your deepest insights and "ohhh... *that's* how it works" kind of knowledge through that kind of experimentation. All I'm saying is to keep the experimenting and the fixing as separate as possible. And when you *must* experiment, make sure that all your experiments are repeatable ones; taking notes should be gospel.

QuickSteps

Troubleshooting PC Problems

Here are the key steps you should take in troubleshooting most PC problems (while remembering to stay calm and positive). Several of these steps occur before you ever power down and remove the case.

BE PREPARED

Before you start, there are some things you may need on hand. These include:

- ◆ Documentation for your PC and/or its separate components (including warranty information)
- ◆ Container for placing screws between removal and reinstallation
- ◆ Appropriate screwdriver(s), such as a Phillips-head
- ◆ Antistatic wrist strap
- ◆ Boot disk and operating system installation CD (just in case)
- ◆ Connector cleaner or hard, white artist's eraser
- ◆ Diagnostic utilities

1. Check for operator errors—commands or configurations that you may have done wrong, software or hardware that you may have set up incorrectly, or instructions that you may have reversed (for example, literally reversing a cable or putting a jumper on exactly opposite from the way it needs to go).

2. Check to make certain that everything that should be plugged into either a direct power source or the PC itself is plugged in correctly, and that the connection is secure.

3. Check the software, including program files and drivers, to make sure you have the most current versions installed—and configured properly.

4. Check for external signs of trouble, such as flickering LED power indicators or those that don't come on at all, strange sounds or lack of sound, and lack of display.

5. Run appropriate diagnostic programs.

6. Only when all else fails, disassemble the PC. Shut it down, disconnect all power, remove the case, ground yourself, and go inside to check cable and power connections, the proper seating of expansion boards and memory modules, and anything out of the ordinary.

General Troubleshooting Rules

These rules have kept me out of trouble for a long time. I know they'll be of use to you.

PC TECHNICIAN'S CREED

◆ "Don't Panic" and "I Will Win"

◆ Wait... and Repeat

◆ Write Everything Down

◆ Do the Easy Stuff First

◆ Reboot and Try Again

◆ Simplify, Simplify, Simplify!

◆ Draw a Picture, Separate into Components, and Test

◆ Never Assume

◆ Trust No One: The Documentation Sometimes Lies

◆ Observe Like Sherlock Holmes

Although some of these suggestions are a bit tongue-in-cheek, there's a nugget of advice in every one, and they're all part of the philosophy of troubleshooting.

Remember: "Don't Panic" and "I Will Win"

You have to have confidence in yourself as a troubleshooter. Look, this stuff isn't that hard. My technical training is as a Ph.D. economist rather than as a computer scientist or engineer, I have 10 thumbs, and people pay *me* to fix machines. If I can do it, you can do it, too. There's not that much to these machines. When it comes right down to it, the only thing that you really can't replace for (at most) a hundred dollars or so is your data, and you can protect that with frequent backups.

If you don't go in there *knowing* that you're going to win, you're going to get beaten—these machines can *smell* fear. A former girlfriend, a black belt in Tae Kwon Do, told me once that an important tenet of Tae Kwon Do is to "have an indomitable spirit." Sounds good to me—practice some *Tech* Kwon Do, and don't forget that indomitable spirit.

Wait... and Repeat

It's a simple fact that the vast majority of "computer" problems are actually caused by human error. (That means you, bub!) If something goes wrong when you're using your PC, stop what you're doing, take a few deep breaths, and then try it again. Chances are you hit the wrong key or clicked the wrong button or just plain zigged when you meant to zag. There's a lot to be gained by having a little patience and perhaps going a little slower, so you don't repeat your mistakes.

Write Everything Down

If you read Chapter 2, "Disassembling the PC" (and if you didn't, go do it), then you've already learned about the hazards of not documenting. I tend not to write things down when I'm pretty sure that the operation will be simple (it almost never is), or when it's sufficiently traumatic that I'm certain that I couldn't forget (there's always another, bigger trauma waiting). I've found that I'm more likely to write down important notes if I keep my notebook—the paper kind—handy. These notes might include, for example, special location information or notations about a problem, such as a bent pin or the actual layout being the reverse of how it appears in the manufacturer's diagram. As a bonus, writing things in your notebook means that you'll be able to find them later.

Do the Easy Stuff First

I am, by nature, a lazy person. That's why I got interested in computers: they were machines that could free me from some drudgery. The *inexperienced* and lazy troubleshooter tries to save time by not making notes, by acting before thinking, and by *swapping* components or configuration information when he ought to be *stopping*. . . stopping to consider his next move.

What I've eventually figured out is that well-planned laziness is a virtue. An *experienced* lazy person looks ahead and says, "Oh, heck, what if I *can't* fix this thing? I don't want to create any more trouble for myself than necessary." And so the lazy person keeps diagrams and writes down everything that she does so she doesn't have to tear out her hair trying to put the PC back together.

The *experienced* lazy person does the easy stuff first; if it's a video problem, and it's not software, then four things could be swapped: the motherboard, the video board, the cable, or the monitor. What gets swapped first? The easy thing: the cable.

Reboot and Try Again

Your computer is affected by fluctuations in the power supply of as brief a duration as four milliseconds. That means that if your power disappeared for only $\frac{1}{200}$ of a second, you wouldn't see the lights flicker, the microwave would still work, and the TV wouldn't skip a beat—even the digital clocks wouldn't start blinking. But several bytes of your computer's memory (not a lot of the memory, or you'd see a memory error message of some kind) get randomized. The result is that a program that has always worked pretty well all of a sudden stops dead. You'll never find out why it locked up that one time in a thousand. Maybe everybody in the building was running their photocopiers at the same time. Maybe radiation from a solar storm assaulted your memory chips (yes, that can happen, although it's unlikely; when a technician blames something on "cosmic rays," she's being facetious). It doesn't matter; the quick answer to this problem is just to start over and reboot the machine.

Now, don't get too trigger-happy with the reboot if you're in the middle of an application. It's usually a really bad idea to do a hard reboot (the Ctrl+Alt+Del kind) out of Windows—try everything you can to get the machine to respond and let you do a graceful shutdown. If you reboot in the middle of an application, the application may leave files "open," and those files will be lost. (Such half-finished files lead to a phenomenon you may have seen called *lost clusters*. More on that when I discuss hard disks in Chapters 10 through 14.)

Simplify, Simplify, Simplify!

The average PC has about a bazillion screensavers, applications, background communications programs (such as fax receive programs), and of course driver programs for sound boards, network cards, video boards, and the mouse, to name just a few. Determining the source of a problem is really hard when there are innumerable interactions between hardware and software.

That means it's a good idea to eliminate as much as you can from a PC before trying to diagnose it. For example, boot without the network. If you're running Windows 95/98/Me, wait for the Starting Windows... message and press F8. That gives you the chance to boot Windows in Safe mode. In Windows NT/2000/XP, you can choose a configuration with a simple video driver at startup and then use Control Panel, under Services (or Control Panel ➤ Performance and Maintenance ➤ Services in Windows XP), to stop the loading of any unnecessary drivers or programs.

I've seen this happen over and over again. Programs or drivers or *whatever* that are loaded into your computer's memory—often without your knowledge—bump into other programs or drivers or whatever, causing a major conflict that can freeze up your entire system. Check out *everything* that gets loaded when Windows launches (don't forget to look in the StartUp program group) and eliminate those things that don't need to be there. Software troubleshooting is just like hardware troubleshooting: divide and conquer. Each piece of software that you're running is a piece of the system, and you want to minimize the number of pieces that you have to deal with.

Draw a Picture, Separate into Components, and Test

This is a true story: A friend was once a PC troubleshooter-type for a county government in Virginia, where I live. She tells this story about another PC troubleshooter-type—let's call him Ignatz. One day, their help desk got a phone call.

"Ignatz," the caller said, "Microsoft Word isn't printing with the new laser printer!"

Now, an experienced lazy person listens and says, "Gosh—how can I fix this without leaving my chair?" Many of us would probably zero in on that word, *new*. As in "*new* laser printer." The next questions might be something like, "What kind of printer did you have before the new laser printer?" "Have you ever seen Word print on this laser printer before?" (Probably not.) "Have you reconfigured Windows for the laser printer?" (A confused "What?" is the probable answer.)

Ignatz, on the other hand, attacked the problem by first swapping the motherboard on the PC that was attached to the laser printer.

Yes, that's right—you read that correctly. It even kind of fixed the problem, as Iggie figured that he would reload the user's software while he was at it. Yeah, we can observe that Ignatz is, umm, shall we say, "a couple sandwiches short of a picnic" when it comes to troubleshooting. But I see people do less extreme (but just as unnecessary) things all the time. Heck, I still do a lot of dumb things myself, playing Macho Man with a Screwdriver. But I hope to get better at remembering to be lazy when troubleshooting.

Now, if old Ig had stopped to think, then he could have diagrammed the whole system. Simplified, you could say that the laser printer is attached to a cable, which attaches to a parallel port, which is connected to the motherboard, which runs the software. That kind of divides the problem into: laser printer, cable, parallel port, motherboard, and software. Each of those components can then be isolated and tested. *Testing* most hardware just means swapping it, as most of us lack the expensive equipment needed to test hardware. But software can be played with in many ways, the most fruitful of which is usually in its setup and configuration. I'd look at the software first. I always look at the software before I go after the hardware. Why? Simple: I have a much better chance of finding the answer in software.

Never Assume

It's far too easy to assume that something is blameless. "How could the problem be the new version of PowerQuick? It's been clean for the last five versions!" Subject everything to your scrutiny, *including* the documentation. And while I'm on the subject...

Trust No One: The Documentation Sometimes Lies

Many years ago, I bought my first Video Graphics Adapter (VGA) board. It was made by Compaq Computer Corporation, and it wasn't cheap, but I bought it from Compaq because I knew that they made a compatible, high-quality product. Since it was in the early days of the VGA, many clones were kinda wobbly compatibility-wise, so I was playing it safe.

When I went to install the board, I took the time to read the documentation. About half of the booklet that came with the board discussed installation. In particular, several pages outlined how to properly set the three jumpers that were clearly marked and even illustrated in black-and-white photos. Before even removing the board from its antistatic bag, I studied the documentation and figured out how to set the three jumpers. Donning my antistatic wrist strap, I removed the board from its bag.

But it had only one jumper on it.

I looked and looked and *looked*, but there was only one jumper on the %$#@! thing. I picked up the manual again—and a lone piece of paper fluttered from between its pages. It basically said, "Your VGA is a new and improved model. It has only one jumper. Set it like this." Frustrating, yes, but at least Compaq provided the right documentation, albeit hidden. I've often wondered if the documentation's author didn't have a sense of humor, however: this 3-by-8-inch piece of paper is *copyrighted*.

Jumpers are usually not the real nightmare, however; the documentation is. Almost every one of these things is badly translated from some Pacific Rim nation's language to English and, worst of all, it's usually wrong. The jumper setting for the parallel port is usually off, and I've seen incorrect documentation for the serial port jumpers as well. If you're wondering, by the way, how I figure out the correct settings when the documentation is wrong, then I'm afraid that there's no single trick that I can share with you. When I run into one of these boards, I check my notes to see whether I've run into this particular model before. If I have, great; if not, all I can do is work by trial and error.

Today, more and more information about PC hardware (and software) is available from the manufacturers' online Web sites. If you haven't tapped this resource yet, stick with me through Chapter 32, "Using the Internet and Online Services," where you'll get a taste of some of the technical help riches out on the Net.

Observe Like Sherlock Holmes

In Arthur Conan Doyle's tales of the Great Detective, Sherlock Holmes sometimes exclaims about some new piece of evidence. He's obviously excited about it, but when Dr. Watson asks him *why* he's excited, Holmes gives nothing away. "Not yet, Watson," he demurs. "It's too early for theories."

What Holmes knew was that problem solving entails making theories, and then proving or disproving the theories with facts. But suppose Holmes had advanced an early theory aloud, perhaps in the company of the beleaguered Inspector Lestrade? Lestrade would like nothing better than to witness his harasser Holmes brought down by a faulty theory. Now, Holmes also knows that, so he has a subconscious aversion to finding any facts that disprove this ill-uttered supposition. By keeping his mouth shut until he has enough facts, he can offer a theory that he feels confident about.

You'll see this in your everyday troubleshooting life. Someone stands over your shoulder as you peer inside a disemboweled PC carcass. "What do you think it is?" he says.

This is a crucial moment. Learn to say automatically, "I don't know—there's not enough information yet." Otherwise, you'll find that now the game you're playing is no longer "fix the machine"; unconsciously, you're now playing a game called "prove you're right." So hang onto the theories until you have the facts.

When you open up a machine, you expose the machine to a certain risk that you'll do something dumb to it. PC troubleshooting differs from, say, automotive troubleshooting, in that the thing that's most commonly broken is the user. If you separate out the "user is broken" stuff (they forgot to turn it on, for example), software is the next most common problem. Honest-to-goodness hardware problems are actually quite uncommon compared to user and software problems. That leads me to the six specific troubleshooting steps.

Six Steps to Troubleshooting Success

The smart troubleshooter makes the troubleshooting job tractable by breaking down problems into individual steps. Don't panic, and remember to be methodical; otherwise, you will thrash helplessly about and get frustrated. Once you are frustrated, you are *lost*, and you start creating new problems.

Following is the method that I use. It looks a lot like methods suggested by other people, but it's not the only method. You certainly don't have to use *my* method, but find one you like and stick to it—even for the small or seemingly easy jobs. It's the "this'll take only five minutes" repairs that get me in trouble. (You know—like when someone gives you directions, saying, "You can't miss it." I *know* I'm in trouble then.) I'll assume for this discussion that you are interacting with someone else (the person with the PC problem), but you can just as easily interview yourself.

Before opening up the computer, do the following:

1. Check the nut behind the keyboard.

2. Check that everything is plugged in: power, monitor, phone lines, printer, modem, and so on.

3. Check the software.

4. Check external signs. Make notes of them.

5. Run an appropriate diagnostic utility.

Only then, if you still haven't solved the problem:

6. Disassemble the machine, clean the connectors, push the socketed chips back into their sockets, and put the machine back together.

Notice that the first five steps *aren't* hardware steps; let's take a closer look at all six.

TIP   If you're running Windows Me or XP and experience a problem after installing a new piece of software or hardware, consider using the new System Restore feature to effectively "undo" the installation and return your system to its previous (that is, working) condition. Once your system is back up and working properly, you can analyze what went wrong—and consider trying the installation again.

Check for Operator Error

Operator error is responsible for 93.3 percent of PC failures. (That's a made-up statistic. But it got your attention and probably isn't far from the truth.) There are lots of things that an operator can do wrong. But one real statistic from the PC retail industry is that up to 75 percent of hardware purchases returned as defective aren't defective and worked fine on retesting.

Regardless of how inflated that statistic may or may not be, that means a lot of folks aren't installing their hardware properly. Sure, some of it can be blamed on bad instructions, but many people flat-out admit that they never look at any documentation packed with the device they're trying to install—or read it after the first three to four times a device won't install "instantly."

And since the accompanying paperwork often ends up in the trash can with the packaging from the hardware, you can end up feeling isolated and uninformed a few months later, when the device stops working. Remember the old saying about how desperate people do desperate things?

There are three main sources of problems for PCs: hardware, software, and users. Guess which one is the most likely? Users. Software's second. Hardware is a distant third.

That begs the question of why the computer industry has so many people problems. In my opinion, it's mainly because the user interfaces still stink—even the "good" ones.

Frequently, people will ask me how to prepare a new hard disk to use in their PCs. I'll go through all the steps, and usually point them to a Web site or two that spells out the steps again for them, so they have something in print they can stare at. All too many times, however, one of these folks will come back to tell me, "It didn't work."

"What didn't work?" I'll ask.

The answer will come back, "I can't access my CD-ROM drive to install Windows" or "I followed all the instructions but the hard drive won't boot up!"

Invariably, I find that they didn't follow one—or more—of the steps. They either didn't FDISK or FORMAT (necessary to prep the drive) so it's not really ready for use, or they decided they didn't need to go to the trouble of installing a DOS CD-ROM driver on their boot disk, so they can't access their CD-ROM drive to install their operating system.

You see, computers are made up of hardware, and hardware for the most part is a pretty logical beast. Turn something one way, and a device becomes available for use. Turn it another way, and a device doesn't respond to you. You can't see a list of 10 steps and decide which 5 you might like to follow, because all 10 steps are likely required to get the result you want.

Still, the language of computers confuses people. You've heard the stories about users doing goofy things; well, they're true. I've seen them. Back in the old days of personal computing, I once watched a user follow the dBase III installation instructions: "Insert System Disk 1 in drive A and close the door." He inserted the disk in the drive, then got up (looking a little puzzled, I'll give him that), and closed the door to his office. If I hadn't been there to see it, I probably wouldn't have believed it. But before you giggle too loudly, consider: where was the "door"? Have you seen a door on a floppy drive lately? No, there's never been one, really—although old 5¼-inch drives did have a little latch across the drive opening. I mean, if you hired me to put a door on your house, and instead I installed a little plastic latch, then you'd sue me, and you'd *win*.

I teach quite a few computer classes, and now and then I've had some guy staring at the keyboard in puzzlement.

"What's wrong?" I'd ask.

"I'm looking for a key," he'd reply.

"Which one? I'll point it out," I would offer.

"The Any key," he'd say, still puzzled. I would look at the screen, where the software program was prompting `Press any key to continue`.... I had just finished with my "pay attention to what the computer is doing" lecture, and so this poor soul was trying his hardest to follow my directions. (Nowadays, there is an answer for the Any key searchers. You can buy an Any key kit: it's a keytop sticker that says, "ANY KEY." You install it on... well, any key.)

I've seen users "copy a floppy" with a photocopier. I once saw a bank organize their backup floppies by punching holes in them so they would fit into a small binder. True stories, all of them.

A friend at Microsoft tells the story of being called by someone who couldn't get Windows to do anything. "I've got my foot on the pedal," he said, "and it's not doing anything!" Well, mice are often found on the floor, but still...

Even worse, sometimes users will (horrors!) prevaricate slightly. "I didn't do anything. It just stopped working." Please note: I'm not one of those techie types whose motto is, "Assume that the user is lying," but sometimes it happens. More often, it's not that users lie. It's just that they don't know what's important, or they're embarrassed to tell you what they really did.

People feel defensive calling a support person (such as you). You want to collect as much information as possible. If you make them feel defensive, they'll misremember, or withhold information. Here's a trick that telemarketers are told: smile when you're on the phone with someone. It works. (As the late Sam Kinison once said, "It creates the illusion that you care.") Being a support person can be wearing. There's a tendency to feel like "These people must get up early in the morning to think up dumb things to ask," but you can't let it get you down. Remember, these folks can't be too dumb—after all, the same company that hired them hired you, too. (Heh, heh.)

Again, think *lazy*. How can you collect enough information while on the phone to fix the problem right over the phone? The key is to not act like so many support people, the ones who don't even let you get your question out before they break in with, "Are you sure your computer is plugged in?" Stop and think about how idiotic this phrasing is. Who's going to answer "No"? It's roughly equivalent to saying "Oh! Look at that. It's not plugged in. I *am* an idiot. Sorry to bother you."

Now, don't get me wrong: you have to ask the question—that's why it's step 2 in my six steps. But there's a right way and a wrong way. One right way is the "bureaucracy" approach: "I'm sorry that's happening to you. That must be really frustrating; I'll do whatever I can for you. But first, you know how it is here at XYZ Corp.; we have a form for everything. Forgive me, but I have to ask some dumb-sounding questions. Can you just double-check for me that the PC is plugged in..." Another good approach is to couch it in a self-deprecating way: "My asking you if the PC is plugged in reminded me of something dumb I did the other day. The PC was plugged into the surge protector, and the surge protector was plugged into the wall. It took me 15 minutes to figure out that the surge protector was turned off! Can you believe that I did something that stupid?" If the next sound you hear is, "Ummm, can I call you back? Someone just walked into my office," then you can be pretty sure you've just engineered another fixed PC.

Best of all, however, is that your *user* just fixed that PC. He's now had a success, so he'll remember that particular problem/solution combination. (Psychology tells us that people learn better with positive reinforcement than with negative reinforcement.) He'll probably end up feeling more capable, more likely to tackle the problem himself next time. "Success is a habit," said Vince Lombardi.

Another source of operator error stems from inexperienced operators. The PC isn't exactly the simplest thing in the world to master. The author of a book titled *Computer Wimp: 166 Things I Wish I Had Known Before I Bought My First Computer* observes in that book that learning to use a computer system may be the most difficult learning endeavor that people will undertake in their post-school life. (Things like raising kids are undoubtedly tougher, but they're different kinds of learning experiences.) It doesn't take a genius to recognize that most PC hardware and software manuals aren't the easiest things to comprehend. The answer? Good education. There are tons of good books, videos, college courses, and professional seminars on PCs, one for every budget. "If you think education is expensive," they say, "try ignorance."

Make Sure Everything Is Plugged In—Correctly

I know this sounds stupid, but we've all done it. A friend bought a modem and couldn't get it to work. It accepted commands all right, but could not dial out. The phone line was tested with a regular phone and worked fine. He was quite puzzled until he realized that he'd plugged the phone line into the *out* jack in the modem instead of the *in* jack. (The out jack is intended to be connected to the phone itself—not the phone line—so that the line can be shared between the modem and the phone).

As I just said, when you ask the user, "Is it plugged in?" be diplomatic. (Don't you hate it when tech support people ask *you* that question?) But don't be afraid to ask for firm answers to the following questions:

- Is the PC plugged into some kind of multi-outlet strip?

- Is the strip on? Did the user kick off the power switch?

- Can the user actually see that the power strip is plugged into the wall?

- Are the other devices that are plugged into the power strip working? Try having the user plug a desk lamp or fan into the power strip to see whether it works.

- If the PC or peripheral is plugged into an outlet controlled by a wall switch, is the switch turned on?

- Are the peripherals plugged in? Are they plugged *into the computer*? Are they plugged into the proper ports or connectors on the computer?

I know of a large communications company that kept sending technicians to try to determine why a LAN server kept dying at strange hours of the night. They'd set up the software at the user site, leave it running, and then eventually get called back to the site because after a day or two all kinds of files had been trashed. The techs would always ask, "Has this been turned off in the middle of an operation?" The users would solemnly (and annoyingly—this tech guy wasn't going to weasel out of fixing his company's buggy software *that* easily, they thought) shake their heads no. Finally, this large company sent its SuperTech—the guy who'd seen it all. He looked over the server and listened to the users' stories.

Now, this guy *knew* from the symptoms that the server was getting shut down improperly. (Remember that indomitable spirit. On the other hand, save the spirit for the machine—don't get snotty with the users.) So he looked for easy ways to turn off the machine accidentally. Noticing two light switches on the wall and only one fluorescent ceiling panel, he flipped both switches. You guessed it—the server was plugged into a switched outlet. The security staff, in making the rounds each night, would shut off the lights.

When you are checking whether peripherals are plugged in, you also need to make sure that they are in *tight*. Multiple-pin connectors slowly bend under gravity unless the mounting screws are tightened. As someone stretches their legs under the desk, a loose power cord could be moved enough to disconnect it, or disconnect and reconnect it. Connectors on the floor take a lot of abuse.

I think that people don't properly secure connectors because it often can't be done without one of those small straight-slot screwdrivers that are smaller than the one you have in the kitchen tool drawer, but larger than the one you use to adjust the screws in your glasses. (Of course, we true PC repair warriors are never without our small screwdriver with the pocket clip and the logo of some company on its side, but normal humans...) Nowadays, you can find a remedy: many cables are sold with big plastic screws that are easily hand-turnable. (Many folks call those screws *thumbscrews*, and I guess it's as good a term as any, but I find it a bit medieval.) Whenever possible, get cables with hand-turnable screws. They'll pay for themselves in the long run.

I'm one of the worst offenders in the cable screws department. As I install and reinstall various PC components a lot, I tend to just push my serial and video cables into their sockets, not bothering with the screwdriver. (I don't have the little screwdriver with the pocket clip when I don't happen to have my pocket protector around. You know, sometimes I want to work undercover, so I leave the pocket protector behind.) A few years ago, I had myself convinced that my serial port or modem was fried, because I was getting terrible error rates on my communications sessions all of a sudden. As I'd just finished giving a lecture on lightning damage to serial ports, and it was T-storm season in Washington, I figured ruefully that I'd just lost a serial port. "But," I thought, "who knows? Maybe when lightning toasted the port, it burned up some chips—I can at least take some pictures." So I got ready to take my PC apart. Of course, one of the first things I did was to remove the cables, and that's when I noticed that the serial cable just about fell off the back of the PC when I touched it. So I returned the cables to their interfaces—making sure they were secured tightly—and, as you've already guessed, the problems went away.

Check the Software

Remember I said that more problems are software problems than hardware problems? Software problems arrive in several guises:

◆ Operator error

◆ Keyboard/screen/disk/timer conflicts with memory-resident software

◆ Software that doesn't clean up after itself

◆ Software that requires hardware that isn't connected or activated

◆ Buggy applications

◆ Buggy driver programs

Software troubleshooting could be a book in itself. In fact, most of the books out there on supporting Windows, Linux, Novell NetWare, and the like are software-troubleshooting books. But let's tackle some of the broad causes of software problems.

VIRTUAL DEVICE DRIVERS AND DYNAMIC-LINK LIBRARIES

Modern operating systems, including Windows, are built in a kind of layer-cake fashion. The application programs (such as word processing, e-mail, and spreadsheet programs) sit atop the cake—they're the frosting. Your applications are supported by layers of cake and filling, layers that they need in order to work—heck, frosting all by itself is a bit much, right?

The bottom layer of the cake is the hardware. Application programs need services (such as printing, communicating with a network server, or saving files) done for them by the hardware (the printer, the network card, or the hard disk). How do applications communicate with hardware? How does your system prioritize and handle multiple requests without exploding?

Enter the operating system. If every application tries to use a piece of hardware at the same time, nothing works. What you need is a kind of traffic cop between the apps and the hardware. The OS is that cop, the piece that routes hardware requests between applications and hardware, keeping traffic jams to a minimum and "crashes" nonexistent (well, in theory, anyway). The OS acts as a "traffic cop" layer between your hardware and your applications.

Also in between your hardware and applications are two components that applications rely on to operate correctly. They are called *virtual device drivers (VxDs)* and *dynamic-link libraries (DLLs)*. Both act as filling between the layers, hidden from external view but key to the structure of the cake. I will discuss DLLs in a minute, but first let's consider drivers.

The lowest level of system software is the set of programs called *drivers*, which are customized to particular pieces of hardware. Drivers attach in a modular fashion to the main body of the OS (called the *kernel*). For example, in order to get Windows to recognize and use your Hewlett-Packard LaserJet model 5P, you must load a driver for that printer, adding it to the Windows system software.

Drivers can pose a bit of a problem for software stability. Most of the operating system is designed by a close-knit software development team; for example, most of the code in Windows 2000 was written by a handful of individuals working together at Microsoft. But most Windows drivers aren't written by Microsoft. Instead, the burden of writing driver programs usually falls to the hardware vendors: Diamond Multimedia writes drivers for its video boards, Hewlett-Packard (HP) writes drivers for its laser printers, and so on. Programmers working at these companies don't get the same kind of support (in terms of information, resources, and time) that they'd have if they were working at Microsoft, and so as a result they can't always write driver programs that are well integrated into an operating system. This is not a slap at programmers at Diamond, Hewlett-Packard, or any other hardware vendor; it's just a reality that the guy on Microsoft's Windows programming team who writes the Calculator code probably plays softball on the same team as the programmer who writes the Windows kernel code. And that has to mean that he'll get better answers to sticky programming questions than would someone from outside Microsoft.

Because of the way that drivers work in modern operating systems, they're usually called *virtual device drivers*. In the Windows world, the acronym for that is *VxD*. VxDs are sometimes designed to plug into a particular operating system (which means, for example, that you might not want to waste your time trying to use a Windows 95 VxD under Windows Me or Windows XP, unless you know that the driver will work in both of those operating systems).

The bottom line is that driver programs are often a weak link in an operating system. Windows may run fine for weeks, and then you install a new version of the driver for your ATI Mach 64 video card. You try to enter Print Preview mode from your favorite word processor, and something happens, whether it's an outright lockup or some garbage on the screen. The problem is most likely to be that new driver.

While this isn't gospel, most operating system designers do much of their initial development on "lowest common denominator" hardware, such as VGA for video. Keep those vanilla drivers around and use them when possible as a kind of "known good" baseline configuration.

And a final tip about device drivers: when a new version comes along, *keep the old one around for a while!* "Latest" isn't always "greatest" when it comes to drivers.

TIP   If you're running Windows Me or XP, you can use the System Restore feature to return your system to its previous state after you install a bad or incorrect driver. See Chapter 35, "Hardware Management via Software Solutions," for more information.

I recommend that you do what a friend of mine does, and use the baby food method of testing new drivers. The first time she mentioned this to me, I was puzzled.

"The *baby food* method?" I asked her. (I'm an excellent straight man.)

"Sure," she replied. "When a baby starts eating solid food, you don't know what he's going to be allergic to. So, suppose you want to see if he's allergic to carrots. You start feeding him carrots; if a few days go by and he hasn't swollen up, then carrots are probably okay.

"I do that with device drivers. I just pop 'em into the system, try out all my applications to make sure that none of them break, and then just live with the thing for a week to see if anything new and unpleasant happens to my system. If not, I keep the driver. If I have problems, then I document the problems, restore the old device driver, and see if those problems go away."

Good advice. But I'd add one thing to it. When you swap drivers on a piece of hardware, be sure to power down the system completely before restarting it. Some video drivers in particular don't work quite right unless you shut down the PC and restart after installing them

Another term you'll see turn up when troubleshooting software is *DLL*, short for *dynamic-link library*. A *library* is a file containing a bunch of small programs that get a particular task done. It's called a library for two reasons: first, there are usually many of those small programs in a particular library, and, second, the library file resembles a library in that it is publicly available; the programs in it are available to any application. For example, the program that tells Windows how to change the color of a part of the screen is almost certainly part of a library.

Now, the way a program finds a library is called *linking*. For most of the history of computer programming, libraries have become linked when a program called the *link editor* makes a copy of the desired library routines and incorporates those routines directly into the program. This is called *static linking*. Static linking is bad because (1) if you are running three programs that all know how to print (for example), then you're wasting RAM because you now have three copies of the print routine resident in memory; and (2) if the way that the OS wants an application to print (to continue the example) changes, then every application would have to be rebuilt.

Operating systems in use since the early '80s incorporate a different kind of linking, called *dynamic linking*. Under dynamic linking, a dynamic-link library is relinked every time the application calls for one of its library routines. Taking the example of printing, a program using static linking gets the whole library program inserted into it. A program linked dynamically to a library contains only a note that says, in essence, "When you need this routine, go out to `PRINT.DLL`, load it up, and link the routine before going any further." A DLL can also be shared; once one program has `PRINT.DLL` in memory, any other program needing `PRINT.DLL` gets the one copy that's already in memory, rather than loading another one.

What's this got to do with troubleshooting? Well, sometimes an incorrectly installed program may crash, complaining of a lack of a DLL. That may be fixable by reinstalling the program, or by editing the Windows Registry to include the correct path for the DLL. Or the DLL may have been accidentally erased. Or it could have been replaced.

Whenever you select File ➤ Open in any Windows program, your program calls up a DLL that contains a routine that knows how to put an Open dialog box on the screen. (In Windows, the DLL is called `COMMDLG.DLL`.) Now and then, I've installed programs that replaced the comes-in-the-Windows-box version of `COMMDLG.DLL` with their own, "improved" versions.

How do you find out whether you have a cowbird DLL in the nest? One simple way is to just compare the dates of the *other* DLLs that shipped with the OS to the suspect one. Or, as is more frequently the solution, you can simply reinstall the OS; it often saves more time than poking through DLLs looking for the "pretender."

Ill-Behaved Software

A number of mysteries can be linked to software that doesn't recover well from disabled or nonexistent hardware. Here are some common problems:

◆ Trying to print to a nonexistent printer

◆ Trying to print a non-PostScript formatted file to a PostScript printer—or vice versa

◆ Trying to print to a printer that is offline

◆ Trying to display high-resolution graphics data on a low-resolution monitor

◆ Trying to run a program that needs more memory than the PC contains

◆ Trying to install a program that insists on using your modem to dial into the mothership to register itself before it finalizes the installation—even if you don't have a modem connected to your system

These aren't really problems with the software—the problems all have something to do with the hardware—but the real issues arise because the software doesn't deal well with the hardware problem. The easy fix, however, is on the hardware side; you can't recode the program, but you *can* make simple hardware fixes.

Faulty Software

Sometimes the problem *is* just plain buggy software. Even the most popular programs can misbehave when faced with a full disk, insufficient memory, or some situation that the designer didn't anticipate or didn't test.

If you experience a problem with software, try to note exactly when the behavior occurs. Perhaps it always fails when you're trying to save to a network drive, but not to a local hard drive. Or maybe the software always crashes when system resources on the desktop run below 50 percent. Or maybe the software will run on any PC except one with a Cyrix CPU. Any behavior like this that you can reproduce can be very helpful to a team trying to debug a program.

If you have some experience with software and compiler/decompilers, you can sometimes check out the source code used to design the program and spot where an error might be (such as an incorrect command issued). Normal human beings can dismiss this possibility.

Finally, you can try uninstalling the suspect program to see whether that sorts things out. It always amazes me how often an uninstall/reinstall will fix even the most persnickety problems.

Check External Signs

If the computer has indicator lights, what do they indicate? Are all the lights glowing on the modem? Does the printer indicate "ready"? Is the hard disk squealing or grinding? Does the monitor image look bent? Your drives and other peripherals produce hums, whirrs, and clicks. After a while, these noises become familiar, and any variation in them signals a problem. Pay attention to these signs.

The first step in successful troubleshooting is to isolate the problem component. These signs can point the way.

It is important to document any signs here. Write down what lights are on and off, the positions of switches, and so forth.

Run a Diagnostic Utility

There is lots of help out there for your hardware problems—in the form of diagnostic software. Some computers ship with diagnostic programs that can help pinpoint various problems. Windows itself comes with a variety of diagnostic utilities, and other diagnostic programs are available from third parties or via downloading from freeware/shareware software archives.

Diagnostic programs can be quite valuable in helping to track down and fix both hardware and software problems—but only if your computer is up and running. If your computer is dead as a doornail, having a copy of the latest and greatest diagnostic program won't do you a lick of good, unless you want to use the CD as a drink coaster. (And by this point, having a refreshing drink might seem very appealing!)

Of course, if your computer is up and running, you might question the value of running a diagnostic program. After all, what must be functioning for you to run one of these programs? Well, the system board must be running, the video must be running so you can see the screen, the keyboard must be active to accept commands, and the floppy disk or CD drive must be working so the program can load. Merely loading the diagnostic program (or any other program, for that matter) tells you some things about your system.

Then there's the additional bonus that most diagnostic programs are visually impressive—they look technical as heck. My friend Dave Stang says that if nothing else, running a diagnostic on a customer's machine buys you a few minutes to think about what's actually wrong.

A DIAGNOSTIC WISH LIST

When assembling a set of tools to help you diagnose and fix hardware-related problems, you should consider the following types of utilities:

System inventory   These programs display and inventory what they can detect in your system. That can be useful not as inventory in and of itself; its greater value is in cataloging what the system can *see.* If you know darn well that you installed the mouse interface but it doesn't show up on the system inventory, then you have a problem. Before looking *too* hard for the answer, however, ask yourself first: is the driver for the mouse loaded? Diagnostic programs, like the operating system itself, usually can't detect an unusual piece of hardware unless the driver for that program is loaded.

Burn-in   When you first get a computer, it's a good idea to *burn it in.* This means to run it continuously for at least three days, running some kind of diagnostic software over and over again. Some PC manufacturers even offer a burn-in when buying a new PC.

Simple diagnostics are no good for this kind of process—for two reasons. First, most simple diagnostics insist on informing you of any errors, then *requiring* you to press a key to acknowledge that you've seen the error message. Higher-quality diagnostic programs allow you to run the diagnostic in a *logging* mode, whereby any error messages are saved to a file, and do not require confirmation of an error. Second, simple diagnostics tend to be of the "run once" variety; good programs let you run the diagnostic in a *continuous* mode, meaning it runs over and over and over until you tell it to stop.

Burn-in is an important step, so don't ignore it! Of the last 10 computers I've installed, two didn't fail until after four days of continuous testing. If I'd not done a burn-in on them, I probably would have ended up with a mysterious error appearing at a no-doubt inopportune time. (Mr. Murphy and his law seem to have taken up residence in my office.)

Interrupt/DMA/input/output address summary   As you'll learn in Chapter 6, "Installing New Circuit Boards (without Creating New Problems)," the hardest thing about installing a new circuit board is adjusting some things called the input/output port address, the DMA channel, the IRQ level, and the ROM address. (Don't sweat if you don't know what they are—they're all explained in the next chapter.) The reason that you adjust these settings is to make sure that they don't conflict with the port/DMA/IRQ/ROM of any other boards. For example, if you're putting a board in the system and that board must use either interrupt number 5 or interrupt number 7, but there's already a board in your system that uses interrupt 7, then you can't let the new board use interrupt 7. But the question arises, how do you find out what interrupts are in use on your system? Diagnostic procedures *try* to report this information. I say *try* because they unfortunately can't be trusted in this task, not due to inadequacies on the part of their programmers, but because of a simple fact: there's no way to reliably detect ports, DMAs, IRQs, or ROM addresses. How *do* you find out this information? You can look at the devices in your system by launching the System applet in Windows' Control Panel.

Hardware testing   A good diagnostic program should provide your hardware with a workout. It will test your computer's memory thoroughly, test every possible data pattern on your hard disk, run your serial port at its maximum speed—in short, a good diagnostic program should be a sort of cybernetic boot camp for your computer.

Setup   Some of these programs do things associated more with setup responsibilities than diagnostic ones. For example, most of these programs will low-level format a hard disk, an important step in setting up an older type of hard disk. Others may have a built-in system setup program that sets up the CMOS chip in a computer.

If you read these items carefully, you no doubt noticed a lot of *shoulds*, as in "a good diagnostic program should…" All this equivocation has a purpose, believe me: most diagnostic programs are junk. Look carefully before you spend the ton of money that you can easily spend on a diagnostic package.

TIP *One word of advice when running a diagnostic: although I told you to load all drivers before running the diagnostics, don't run your memory manager; it just confuses a memory test.*

THIRD-PARTY DIAGNOSTIC SOFTWARE

There's an entire subset of the computer software industry dedicated to providing software and hardware diagnostic utilities. Between the commercial publishers and the freeware/shareware publishers, you can find literally dozens of utilities, each designed to provide a variety of diagnostic functions.

It is said that one time the science fiction author Theodore Sturgeon was approached by a literary critic who said, "Ted, you write such good stuff; why do you waste your time writing science fiction?" Sturgeon asked, "What's wrong with science fiction?" The critic answered, "Ninety percent of science fiction is crap." (Well, he didn't actually say "crap," but this book is rated for general audiences.) Sturgeon is reported to have replied archly, "Ninety percent of *everything* is crap." I'm afraid that this truism, dubbed "Sturgeon's Law" by generations of science fiction fans, applies well to the diagnostics world. Let me then not waste ink beating up on this chaff; let's look at the wheat.

Technical Hardware–Only Diagnostics

The first class of diagnostics to consider is those that focus exclusively on hardware-related problems. These are often quite technical in nature, and sometimes include hardware (such as loopback plugs) to facilitate the testing of various hardware components. (Some of them are also quite expensive—the most comprehensive packages will cost you anywhere from $200 to $400.)

CheckIt   A fairly useful, extremely comprehensive set of hardware diagnostics from Smith Micro Software (formerly Touchstone Software). Actually, there are several different versions of CheckIt; for the most detailed diagnostics, you want the Professional Edition. Note that CheckIt does not include some of the hardware accessories that you need to do a thorough system check, such as loopback plugs for external port testing. (Smith Micro does have loopback plugs available as an extra-cost option, however.) That's not meant as a negative assessment; I like CheckIt and use it quite a bit. It has a good set of motherboard checkout routines (DMA, timer, IRQ, and the rest) as well as one of the better memory testers out there. See www.smithmicro.com/checkit/ for more information.

PC-Technician   An industrial-strength package from Windsor Technologies. I first looked at PC-Technician back in 1988, and I must truthfully say that I didn't think much of it then. But it's matured into a decent, general, inventory/setup/deep diagnostic routine. The full package includes the test disks, the loopbacks, a nice manual, and a carrying case for your tools. (Just make sure you don't put any magnetic screwdrivers next to the disks in the case!) Windsor also sells a program that will put your PC printer through its paces, as well as a plug-in BIOS POST code. The features that I like best about PC-Technician are the memory test—again, a good one in the same league as

CheckIt's—and the serial and parallel tests. All in all, PC-Technician is the best all-in-one tester. See www.windsortech.com/pctech.html for more information.

DisplayMate   A utility from DisplayMate Technologies (formerly Sonera Technologies) that checks only one thing—your display. But it does an extremely thorough job, testing aspects of your monitor that you probably didn't know were testable—*pincushioning*, for example. The accompanying manual is a tutorial on monitor problems and solutions. It won't test your memory or your printer, but it deserves a place on your diagnostics shelf. See www.displaymate.com for more information.

General Hardware/Software Diagnostics

The second class of utilities to consider includes those that perform both hardware and software diagnostics. These programs typically aren't as technical as the hardware-only diagnostics and therefore aren't as rigorous in their testing. They are, however, more consumer-friendly and thus easier for the average user to use.

I discuss these system tools—such as Norton Utilities and McAfee Utilities—in Chapter 35; turn there if you want to learn more.

WARNING   *Some diagnostic programs—such as McAfee's First Aid and Norton CrashGuard—are promoted as crash-prevention tools, meant to help prevent problems with your PC or with Windows. However, these programs require you to run them all the time; they attempt to create a buffer, or a shield, between the errors you might make and the machine itself. Although this type of software can keep you from making a fatal mistake, it also may interfere as you troubleshoot PC problems—the software may not allow you to make the changes that you need to make. Over time, you may also find that the rescue program isn't working as effectively—perhaps because it's configured wrong, or perhaps because you overrode it when it suggested you do or not do something. When this happens, whole new sets of problems can crop up that may affect booting your PC or Windows' proper operation. Thus, using this protection software may leave you needing protection from it. Use judiciously.*

As I've suggested, you can spend a *lot* of money on diagnostic programs, so it's a good idea to take advantage of the option that many computer dealers provide today whereby you can buy software and return it within a few weeks if it fails to live up to expectations or doesn't work properly with your PC setup. Better yet, check to see if there's a free 30- or 45-day trial of the program you can download and try, and then buy the full package if it works well for you.

WINDOWS DIAGNOSTICS

While not focused exclusively on hardware issues, all versions of Windows from Windows 98 on include a set of diagnostic system tools (accessed via Start ➤ Programs ➤ Accessories ➤ System Tools) that can help you track down many types of system problems. For example, ScanDisk enables you to perform either a surface or thorough scan of your drives and tries to fix errors it finds; Disk Defragmenter defragments and reorganizes your hard drive to make it run more efficiently.

Microsoft's System Information tool provides a host of indispensable data about various components of your system, and (via its Tools menu) serves as a gateway for several more "hidden" utilities. These utilities include the Dr. Watson logging tool, which keeps track of operations performed and error messages generated; System File Checker, which seeks out missing or damaged essential files and attempts to replace them; and the System Information Utility (a.k.a. MSCONFIG), which enables you to set up a troubleshooting bootup mode and select which items you really want to load at Windows startup.

These diagnostics are not available directly within Windows 95 or Windows NT 4. Windows 95 (as well as all later versions) does include Device Manager, one of the tabs available under the System icon in Control Panel. Although it's not a diagnostic checker, vital information gets reported there that you need to check when you're having a problem. You may see an exclamation mark or red *x* on a device, indicating a device in conflict or disabled entirely. Or you may find a needed device driver not present at all when it should be. Or you may find a note on your hard drive indicating that the drive is running in MS-DOS compatibility mode (meaning Windows feels the drive isn't set to run properly in Windows, so it's running in a slower mode compatible with MS-DOS).

I talk about all these Windows utilities—as well as some of the third-party diagnostic programs—in Chapter 35.

NOTE *Windows XP also provides several hardware troubleshooters that help you diagnose and repair hardware- or driver-related problems. A series of questions ask what the problem is and suggest solutions for you to try. For a complete list of these troubleshooters, search for the "List of Troubleshooters" help topic in the Windows XP Help and Support Center.*

Look Under the Hood

Assuming that you've worked through steps 1 through 5—and especially availed yourself of the appropriate troubleshooting utilities built into the Windows operating system—it's possible, if your troubles persist, that you may actually have a problem inside your PC's system unit. Fortunately, many internal hardware problems can be handled simply and without any fancy equipment. Step 6 just says:

- ◆ Take the PC apart.
- ◆ Clean any connectors with an artist's eraser or connector cleaner.
- ◆ Push all socketed chips back into their sockets.
- ◆ Reassemble the PC.

As you saw in Chapter 4, "Avoiding Service: Preventive Maintenance," edge connectors become dirty and make circuit boards fail. Sometimes "dead" boards will do the Lazarus trick if you clean their edge connectors.

If you examine most circuit boards, you'll see that most chips are soldered right onto the board. *Soldering* is a process whereby the chip is bonded to the printed circuits on the board by heating a mixture of tin and lead to the point that it is molten, then allowing the tin/lead mixture to flow over the printed circuit and chip leg, and finally solidify. Soldering is a great technique for mass-producing electronic components. The downside is that when you must fix soldered components, you must *first* de-solder the components. This isn't much fun, and most people don't have soldering skills.

Not all chips are soldered to boards, however. Some are put in *sockets*. A typical board might have 30 soldered chips and 4 socketed ones. Chips are socketed either because they've been voted "most likely to fail," or because the designer wanted to put off a decision until the last minute, or because the chip will likely have to be replaced periodically because it contains software that changes over time—remember ROM? So socketing chips makes our jobs as troubleshooters easier.

On the other hand, heating and cooling of systems make these socketed chips creep out of their sockets. That's why you should push socketed chips back into their sockets when inspecting a board for whatever reason. One particularly persnickety tech I know takes the socketed chips out of their sockets, cleans their chip legs with connector cleaner, and *then* puts the chips back in the sockets.

This should be obvious, but let me point it out anyway: don't push *soldered* chips. The best that it can do is nothing. The worst that it can do is damage a board and maybe a chip. When you push socketed chips back into a board, be sure that you are supporting the *back* of the board. If you just put a board on a table, then push down on the chips, you can end up bending and damaging the board.

I know that this kind of advice—"take it apart, clean the connectors, push the chips back in the sockets, and reassemble"—doesn't sound very dazzling. But, darn it, *it works!* Buying a board to replace a defective one is a pretty rare event for me as a troubleshooter, and I don't do much soldering. And besides, it impresses the people whose machines you're fixing—all they see you do is basically touch the boards. Eventually, you get the reputation as a person who can just "lay hands upon the board... and make it *whole!*" (With apologies to the evangelists in the crowd.)

When All Else Fails...

Don't feel ashamed if you can't diagnose every single problem you encounter. Even the best of us get stumped from time to time. When you've checked all your cables, run all the diagnostics, and disassembled/reassembled your entire system—and the darn thing *still* doesn't work!—it's time to turn to the experts for help.

One level of expert, of course, can be found on the Internet. A number of tech support sites are available on the Web, and most hardware and software vendors maintain tech support sections on their official Web sites. As I discuss in Chapter 32, it's likely that your problem has already been reported and documented *somewhere*, and the information available online might keep you from reinventing the wheel.

If the online help isn't any help, then you need to drop back 10 and punt—and call the vendor's official technical support line. This might cost you a bit, but at least you'll be getting advice from the horse's mouth. (Know that while some vendors still offer toll-free—and fee-free—tech support, others have eliminated 800-number lines and even make you pay them a fixed amount per call.) While e-mail support might be preferred by many vendors—and, in fact, may be just as effective—sometimes there's nothing like talking to a real human being in your quest to get your system back up and running.

Before you call tech support, make sure you've done your homework and have the following in front of you:

The vendor's tech support phone number   Don't laugh—you can't look up the number on the vendor's Web site if you can't start your PC!

The make and model number of your PC   Include other pertinent information—processor speed, amount of RAM installed, other peripherals attached, etc.

A detailed description of your problem   Note the operations you were performing just before the problem occurred.

A list of what other steps you've taken to track down the problem There's no sense doing the same thing twice.

A good book or a big, thick magazine You'll probably be on hold for a long, long time!

When you finally get through to a support technician, keep calm, cool, and collected, and be as polite as possible. As frustrated as you may be with your particular problem, the technician on the other end of the phone has already listened to dozens of complaining customers today. If you're nice to them, they'll be nice to you—and do whatever they can to help you find and fix your problem.

Common Problems—and Solutions

Enough with the theory and advice—let's get down to practical matters! This section looks at some of the more common hardware-related problems you may be unfortunate enough to encounter, and offers up the most-likely causes of those problems.

Your Computer Won't Start

This is perhaps the scariest problem you can encounter. Either nothing at all happens, or you hear a few familiar or unfamiliar sounds, or even see a blinking light or two, but it all leads to a big fat zero. What can cause your entire system not to work? Here are some things to look for:

- Make sure the power cable is connected, both to your PC and to either a power strip/surge suppressor or wall outlet. If the cable is connected to a power strip/surge suppressor, make sure the strip is turned on—and that other devices plugged into the strip are working. (The strip itself could be bad.) Make sure that the wall outlet has power. (Flip that wall switch—and check that circuit breaker—just to be sure.)

- Check to see whether the power cable itself is bad. If you have a spare cable or one from another PC, try swapping it for the current cable.

- If your system unit lights up and makes noise but nothing appears on-screen, make sure that the computer monitor is turned on and getting power, and that it is connected properly and securely to the monitor output on your system unit. If you suspect you actually have a monitor problem rather than a system unit problem, try connecting your PC to a different monitor.

- If your computer starts up but you receive an error message telling you that you have a non-bootable or invalid or non-system disk, you've accidentally left a floppy in drive A. Remove it.

- If your system *tries* to start but then locks up, it's possible you have some type of damage to your main hard disk. You could have a damaged boot sector, or an internal connection may have worked loose, or your key system files might have become corrupted. Try restarting with an emergency boot disk (or the Windows Startup disk) and then use ScanDisk to check for hard disk errors.

- If your system appears to start but then generates a series of beeps (with nothing showing on your video display), it's possible that you have a problem with your video card. (Consider this a *probability* if you've just installed a new video card!) Make sure the video card is seated firmly in its slot, and that you've switched the appropriate switches on your motherboard (if necessary) to recognize the new card. Try uninstalling the new card and reinstalling your old one—it's possible the new card is defective.

◆ A beeping-and-not-starting scenario can also be caused by incorrect settings in your system's CMOS setup. Check the video and memory settings, specifically. Another possible cause is a bad memory chip or faulty memory installation. A weak or dead CMOS battery can also cause this problem.

◆ If nothing turns on—no power lights light, no disk drives whirr, nothing—it's possible that the power supply transformer in your system unit is bad.

Your Computer Locks Up

In terms of causing extreme user panic, a frozen system is second only to a completely dead system. What can cause your system to freeze up? Here are some of the most likely causes:

◆ It's possible that it's not your entire system that's locked up—it could be your keyboard or mouse. Check the connections for both these devices, and make sure both cables are firmly plugged into the appropriate ports. If you're using a wireless keyboard or mouse, replace your batteries.

◆ Misbehaving software problems are, perhaps, the greatest cause of frozen systems. If a program is stalled, try switching to another open program, either from the Windows Taskbar or by pressing Alt+Tab to shuttle through all open programs. If things are still frozen, press Ctrl+Alt+Del (the old "three-fingered salute") to display the Close Program dialog box; highlight the program that isn't responding and click the End Task button. If, after trying all these actions, your system is *still* frozen, you'll have to reboot completely—press Ctrl+Alt+Del *twice* to shut down and then restart your entire system. If even this doesn't shut things down, you'll have to use the Power button on your system unit—or, in the worst of all possible cases, unplug the system unit from its power source.

WARNING   *Shutting down your PC by any method other than the standard Windows shutdown procedure runs the risk of damaging any currently open files—and, under some circumstances, of altering some of your system's display and operational settings.*

◆ Many computer lockups are caused by too many programs trying to use more memory than is available. It's possible that you'll get a kind of warning before a total lockup; if your computer starts to slow down in the middle of an operating session, it's a sure sign of an upcoming memory-related failure. If the problem recurs, try closing a program or two to free up system memory—or upgrade the amount of memory in your system unit.

◆ Since Windows uses free hard disk space to augment random access memory, too little disk space can also cause your system to slow down or freeze. Make sure you've gone through your folders and deleted any nonessential or unused files—especially TMP files in the \WINDOWS\ TEMP\ directory.

Finally, any time something weird happens with your system, consider whether the problem could have been caused by a computer virus. Make sure you're running some sort of antivirus program—especially when downloading files from the Internet or opening e-mail attachments—and run a full system sweep if you start experiencing performance problems.

A New Piece of Hardware Won't Work—or Messes Up Your System

It happens to the best of us. You install a new card or external peripheral, and all of a sudden your system either starts working funny or stops working completely. Obviously, something in the new installation caused the problem—but what?

◆ Make sure that the new hardware is properly installed. If you installed a new internal board, make sure the board is fitted properly in its slot, that any additional wires or cables are connected properly, and that any switches are set appropriately. If you installed a new external peripheral, make sure that it's plugged into the right port, that the cable is firmly connected, and that the device is hooked up to and is receiving external power (if that's required).

◆ Some new devices require you to reset specific jumpers or switches on your system's motherboard. Check the item's installation instructions and make sure you've performed this vital step.

◆ Check your system configuration. It's possible that Windows Plug and Play didn't recognize your new device, or didn't recognize it properly, or installed the wrong driver. Try uninstalling both the hardware and its associated software, and then reinstalling. Use the Add New Hardware Wizard to override the standard Plug-and-Play operation.

◆ Make sure you have the latest version of the item's device drivers. Go to the vendor's Web site and download updated drivers, if necessary. (While you're there, check the online support facilities to see whether any documented problems exist between this peripheral and your specific system.)

◆ Look for an interrupt conflict, which could occur if the new device tries to use the same IRQ as an older device. This happens a lot with COM ports—not only is sharing the same port a problem, but some devices (such as mice and modems) don't like to share even- or odd-numbered ports. (This means that you may have a conflict between COM1 and COM3 that could be fixed by moving one of the devices to COM2 or COM4.) If worse comes to worst, try reassigning the IRQ for your new piece of hardware.

◆ It's possible that your system's CMOS settings need to be changed. This is most common when you upgrade or change memory or disk drives. Enter the CMOS configuration utility on system startup and change the settings appropriate to the new hardware you added.

Your Hard Disk Crashes

Any problem you may encounter with your hard disk is a major problem. That's because everything—from your system files to your program files to your data files—resides on your hard disk. If you can't access your hard disk, your multi-thousand-dollar computer system is just that much more junk.

What are the most common causes of hard disk problems? Here are a few to look for:

◆ If your system can't access your hard disk at all, you'll need to reboot using a system disk or the Windows Startup disk. Run ScanDisk (it's built into the Windows Startup disk) or a third-party hard disk utility from a floppy to check drive C for defects, and then fix any found damage.

◆ If the hard disk utility doesn't get your hard disk spinning again, call in an expert. Even if your hard disk is seriously damaged, it may be possible for a professional technician to "rescue" the data on the damaged hard drive and transfer it to another disk.

◆ If you encounter frequent disk write errors, it's possible that you have some physical damage on your hard disk. Run the hard disk utility to check and fix any defects.

◆ If your disk is working but running slower than normal, it probably needs to be defragmented. Run a good disk defrag program (such as Windows' Disk Defragmenter) to get all those noncontiguous clusters lined up properly.

◆ If you experience a lot of disk write errors or your system runs much slower than normal, and if you're using DriveSpace for disk compression, the problem is probably in DriveSpace. DriveSpace gives your system a pretty good workout and can cause lots of different types of problems. You may find that disk compression is more trouble than it's worth; if so, uncompress the drive! (In these days of cheap hard drives, you're probably better off to install a second hard disk drive than you are to use DriveSpace or some similar disk compression utility.)

To avoid catastrophic hard disk crashes, make sure you perform all the activities outlined in Chapter 4. I know it's a cliché, but an ounce of prevention is certainly worth a pound of cure, especially where the valuable data on your hard disk is concerned.

Your Monitor Doesn't Display Properly

If your computer is working but your monitor isn't, look for these possible causes:

◆ Make sure the monitor is plugged in, turned on, and firmly connected to your PC.

◆ Try to determine whether it's a monitor problem or a video card problem. If you have a spare one handy, plug a different monitor into your PC; if it works, your old monitor has a problem. If it doesn't, the problem is most likely in your video card.

◆ Make sure that your system is configured properly for your video card/monitor combination. Right-click anywhere on the desktop and select Properties to display the Display Properties dialog box; use the Settings tab to select the correct hardware and configuration settings.

◆ If your monitor suddenly goes blank and emits a high-pitched whine, turn off your monitor—*immediately!* Leaving the monitor on in this condition could damage it. Now check the settings on your video card (or in Windows' Display Properties dialog box); chances are the configuration is set to a higher resolution than your monitor is capable of displaying. Reconfigure the settings for a lower-resolution display, and you should be fine.

- If your monitor pops and crackles and maybe even starts to smell (like something's burning), turn it off and go check the credit line on your nearest charge card. While it's possible that all this hubbub is caused by dirt building up inside your monitor, it's more likely that something major—like the power supply—has gone bad, and that it's time to invest in a new monitor.

Your Modem Won't Connect

In this interconnected world, we all need the Internet to survive. What do you do if your modem won't let you connect?

- Check your cables! If you're using an external modem, make sure it's firmly connected to the correct port on your PC, and that it's plugged into and receiving power from a power strip or wall outlet. If you're using an internal modem, make sure the card is firmly seated. For all modems, make sure that it's connected to a working phone line—and that you have the cable connected to the *in* jack on the modem, not the *out* jack!

- Make sure your modem is configured correctly. If you're using Windows 98, Me, or XP, use the Modem Troubleshooter to track down potential problems. Otherwise, go to Control Panel and start the Modems applet, then run the diagnostics in the Modem Properties dialog box. If problems persist, try uninstalling and then reinstalling the modem on your system—and then check whether an updated driver is available from the modem vendor.

- Check your dial-up configuration. Make sure you have the right phone numbers listed, that you've entered the correct username and password, and that any Internet service provider (ISP)–specific information (such as DNS numbers) is entered properly.

- Check your system network or TCP/IP settings. This isn't so much a problem with Windows 98/Me/2000/XP, but it can be an issue with Windows 95/NT and other operating systems.

Also, remember that just because you can't connect to your ISP doesn't mean that you have a modem problem. Many ISPs try to connect too many users through too few phone lines, resulting in busy signals, slow connections, dropped connections, or similar problems. See whether your connection problems ease up at different times of the day (the after-dinner period is a typical "rush hour" for most ISPs), or if your ISP has different numbers that you can use to connect. If the problem persists, consider changing ISPs.

Your Printer Won't Print

Printer problems are quite common—especially after you've just hooked up a new printer to your old system. Here are a few things to look for:

- It sounds so simple as to be insulting, but make sure that your printer is plugged in and has power, and that it is connected properly to your PC. A loose printer cable can cause all sorts of bizarre problems.

- Along the same lines, make sure that your printer isn't out of paper, and that it's online and not experiencing any type of paper jam.

◆ Make sure that Windows recognizes your printer—and that it recognizes the *correct* printer. (Recognizing a similar model from the same manufacturer doesn't cut it.) Make sure that Windows has the correct printer driver installed. You may even want to check with the manufacturer to make sure you have the latest and greatest version of the printer driver.

◆ If you have more than one printer installed on your system or network (including faxes and devices that your system sees as printers), check the Print dialog box to make sure you have the correct printer selected.

◆ Check for device conflicts. Fax machines and printers frequently interfere with each other, but any two devices, if not configured properly, can cause conflicts.

◆ Make sure you have enough free disk space to print. Windows will use temporary hard disk space (called a *cache*) to store data while a print job is in process. Try deleting old and unused files (including TMP files in the \WINDOWS\TEMP\ folder) to free up additional disk space.

Troubleshooting Tips for an Emergency

There really is a reason why I caution you to stay calm and not do anything desperate when you hit a snag. When people get scared, they do things they wouldn't even think about doing when their minds are clearer. If you lose your cool, you could end up having to fix several problems you created when trying to fix the first one.

Try to remember these considerations when troubleshooting a PC emergency:

Have an emergency kit handy.   Your kit should include a good screwdriver, a good flashlight, a boot disk or two (including the Windows Startup disk, if you're running Windows), a floppy-based copy of a virus scanner, and some key diagnostic utilities.

Have your operating system installation CD ready.   Many problems—both hardware and software—require you to have the installation CD to reinstall or fix components. This is especially true with the Windows operating system, though not entirely unique to it.

When you see the problem, stop!   At this point, you need to take a moment to shift gears from working to troubleshooting.

Ask yourself, "What's the last thing I did?"   Understanding the steps you just took to get you into the problem can help you identify the steps necessary to get you back out of it.

Do a first analysis of the "damage" before you try to change anything.   The first thing you spot wrong might not be the only thing wrong, and you need all the information you can gather to make a smart choice about how to proceed.

If you find yourself getting frustrated, take a break.   A good rest helps you keep your wits about you when you return to the computer.

When you finally put your hands on the PC to begin correcting the problem, take it one step at a time.   Try one procedure and see whether it fixes the problem. If not, undo it and try the next. Do too many things at once, and you'll start to forget what you tried or what your results were.

If you have another PC available, get on the Internet. Use the resources talked about in Chapter 32 to look for help.

Ask yourself why you have no backup system in place. (Apologies extended if you're one of the statistical minority who regularly backs up their files… or even thinks about doing so until they've lost data they sorely need.) Then, ask yourself whether the time you're going to waste doing work over again is better than the time you thought you'd waste making a backup. If backups are taking too long, the answer isn't fewer backups, but faster, more capable backup hardware.

Make sure you have the tech support number of your hardware manufacturer handy. Always have the number handy—just in case everything else you try fails!

Chapter 6

Installing New Circuit Boards (Without Creating New Problems)

◆ QuickSteps: Installing a New Circuit Board 241

◆ Configuring New Circuit Boards 243

◆ Resolving Installation Conflicts 246

◆ Understanding I/O Addresses, DMA, IRQs, and Bus Mastering 248

◆ Working with Plug and Play 272

◆ Troubleshooting Tips 280

Introduction

CIRCUIT BOARDS AND CHIPS are fairly reliable, as long as you keep them above water and don't subject them to the ol' 110-volt torture test. So, most boards that you handle won't be defective. Much more often, you'll be doing upgrades to existing machines, like replacing a video board with a faster, more powerful one; adding a sound card; or adding a LAN board to a machine that isn't yet on your company's network.

Putting a new board into your system and making it work involves five steps:

Installation   Put the board in the system and make sure all the cables are attached properly.

Configuration   Make sure the board and the rest of the system communicate.

Testing   Weed out any boards that either don't work or will soon stop working.

Loading and configuration of drivers   Load the software that will help the PC use the hardware.

More testing   Try out the new device to make sure it works with the drivers.

Getting those five things done will be the focus of this chapter.

This chapter begins with a QuickSteps section for those of you impatient for the basic steps of circuit-board installation.

QuickSteps

Installing a New Circuit Board

Now let's run through the procedures you'll need to follow when you install or replace a new circuit board.

BE PREPARED

Before you start, there are some things you'll need to perform the operation. These include:

- ◆ Nonmagnetic Phillips-head screwdriver

- ◆ Documentation for the new board

- ◆ Documentation for the motherboard on which you are installing the circuit board

- ◆ Installation disk for the new board

Unless the new circuit board is Plug and Play (PnP) and you're installing it on a recent-model computer, you might also need to:

- ◆ Determine available resources (IRQs, memory addresses, and DMA channels) that can be assigned to the device you're installing without causing any conflict.

Also, before installing or removing boards be sure that:

- ◆ You are wearing an antistatic wrist strap.

- ◆ The PC is turned off and unplugged.

---

1. Set any jumpers or switches on the new board to the resources you've already determined are available.

2. Install the board in an available motherboard slot of the correct type.

3. Boot to your operating system and install any setup software that came with the board. Even if the operating system automatically detects the device with Plug and Play, installing the setup software may add more capabilities.

4. Test the board's operation. If it doesn't work, check for resource conflicts.

5. Test all the other devices on your system to make sure that installing the new board has not caused a problem with any of them.

6. Document the settings for the new board, as well as any changes you made to existing device settings.

But I Have Plug and Play, So I Don't Have to Worry About This, Right?

For several years now, PC manufacturers have attempted to make our lives easier by designing PCs around a specification called *Plug and Play* (*PnP*). If you have a PC that was built after 1996, it's almost certainly a PnP system. PnP's designers intended that PnP systems would configure themselves automatically, as you no doubt guessed from the name "Plug and Play." You just pop a new board into your system and boot up the computer, and your PC automatically loads the drivers that it needs to use the new board. And now, with Windows XP, *Universal* Plug and Play allows your computer to discover and use network devices. In seconds, you're using your new hardware.

Older circuit boards and systems that are not PnP are called *legacy* devices and systems. Some newer systems will not accept legacy devices and have the dubious title of being legacy-free. According to Microsoft, "The term *legacy free* refers to the elimination of many elements of the original PC architecture—both hardware elements and firmware interfaces. The move to a legacy-free system architecture is impacting all of the PC industry, from component makers and IHVs to BIOS makers and PC system manufacturers." What this term actually means in most cases is that the motherboard doesn't have any Industry Standard Architecture (ISA) expansion slots, only PCI. Compaq computers that are legacy-free don't have any expansion slots at all; you add hardware through the Universal Serial Bus (USB) port.

Early PnP boards sometimes *did* work as advertised, but only if your PC met some fairly specific criteria—the right hardware, the right drivers, and the right operating system. If you *didn't* have all those pieces in place, however, you found that PnP systems were actually *harder* to configure than older systems. In fact, let's say that again, with emphasis.

WARNING   PnP needs both hardware and *software. So if you're not running a PnP-compliant operating system such as Windows 95/98/Me/2000/XP, your PC is not PnP, and hardware configuration can still be a real pain no matter whose PnP hardware you buy.*

Since some folks are running PnP hardware with a non-PnP operating system (like DOS or Windows NT 4), there's a section later in this chapter, "Making Plug and Play Work," on living with PnP's Dark Side. (In that section, you'll also learn about the "right" hardware, drivers, and operating system you need to make PnP happy.)

Installing boards in a PC of any kind isn't the toughest task in the world, but getting them to work once they're installed is made a bit difficult by a few different things. Some of the stumbling blocks are bad board documentation (and there's no shortage of that); insufficient information about the computer that you're installing the board into (that's usually *your* fault); address, IRQ, and DMA conflicts; and PnP woes.

Those challenges are what this chapter is all about. You'll learn what all of those things are and what you need to know in order to get new circuit boards into your system and make them work. It's not difficult stuff, but it *does* need some explaining, and I promise that I'll make the whole thing as understandable as possible. As an extra bonus, the knowledge you gain in this chapter about I/O, DMA, IRQ, and the like will give you a head start in troubleshooting other problems you'll learn about later in the book.

Configuring New Circuit Boards

Most circuit boards are fully functional when you take them out of the box. But many of those circuit boards seem not to work when you install them in a PC. Why? The main reason is that the new board may *conflict* with existing boards or, more specifically, with some resource on an existing board.

Put simply, you can't have two boards that claim the same identity in a system. If you were to insert two identical sound cards into the same system, neither one would work, even if both boards were in working order before you put them into the PC.

Configuration consists of:

◆ Assigning resources to the device, avoiding any conflicts with existing devices

◆ Providing software support for the device (through the BIOS and/or device drivers)

On older boards, you specify the resources that the device should use by setting jumpers or Dual Inline Package (DIP) switches. Newer PnP boards almost always set resources through the BIOS or operating system.

Depending on the board, your system, and your operating system, you may need to do some (but probably not all) of the following:

◆ Tell a memory expansion board how much memory is on the board (older boards only)

◆ Tell a modem which COM port to use (COM1, COM2, COM3, or COM4, or higher)

◆ Tell a printer port whether it is LPT1, LPT2, or LPT3

◆ Select DMA channels on a board

◆ Select IRQ lines on a board

◆ Select I/O addresses on a board

◆ Select RAM and/or ROM addresses on a board

◆ Load a driver for the board and tell the driver which I/O address you want the board to use

NOTE   We'll cover the last five items later in this chapter.

In many cases, the board is preconfigured at the factory to settings that will work in your PC, but not always. That's because it's impossible for the manufacturer to know what the proper settings should be for I/O addresses, DMA channels, IRQ lines, RAM addresses, and ROM addresses in your particular machine. Some older boards, unfortunately, are hardwired to a particular configuration that you can't change. The inflexible nature of those boards may mean that you won't be able to get them to work in your PC.

Solving Real-Life Configuration Conflicts

What does a hardware conflict *look* like? Here are a few common examples of installation woes.

Scenario 1   You install an internal modem in a PC; the modem refuses to work. Worse, your mouse, which used to work, doesn't work any more. What do you do?

Scenario 2   You install a sound card in your system and it seems to work pretty well. But now you can't print from inside Windows without crashing. What do you do?

Scenario 3   You're installing an Ethernet LAN card in a system, and it doesn't work. So you try an identical one. It doesn't work either. As you watch the *fourth* identical board fail, you begin to suspect a pattern. What's going on?

Scenario 4   You want to install a video capture board into a 2GHz PnP Pentium 4 system running Windows XP, but then you realize that the devices in your system have already used up all the IRQs. You need another IRQ (which I'll define later, but for now just understand it's a scarce thing). You realize that you have an internal modem in your system that you don't use and that it takes up an IRQ. So you remove the internal modem, install the video capture board, and fire up your computer. After Windows XP starts, it tells you that there's no way you can use the video capture board because there are not enough IRQs to accommodate the board. Clearly, Windows XP is delusional, so how do you medicate it properly?

Each of these problems is caused by *resource conflicts*. Here are some explanations of what caused the problems.

In Scenario 1, all modern computers come with two serial ports, named COM1 and COM2. But internal modems also need a communications port—in fact, they have serial interface hardware right on them, meaning that when you install an internal modem, you're *also* installing an extra COM port.

Now, that COM port built into the internal modem is probably set up at the factory to act like COM2, but you've already *got* a COM2 on your system. That means that the COM port will conflict with the existing COM2 on your system—and if your mouse isn't working any more, then it's likely that your mouse is a serial mouse on, as you've guessed by now, COM2.

What's the answer? There are two basic approaches. First, you could disable one of the serial ports that came with your PC. The second possibility is to configure the new COM port that's incorporated into the internal modem to be a third COM port (that is, COM3). Basically, you do that by assigning a spare IRQ (trust me, I'll explain IRQs soon) to the COM port. But that can be a problem if you've run out of IRQs (an easy thing to do) or if the communications software that you're running is too dumb to be able to work with anything but good old vanilla COM1 and COM2. That happens *less* with Windows 95/98/Me/2000/NT/XP software than it did with DOS software, but it happens.

Now, I hear you asking, "*How* do I disable one of the COM ports on my computer or assign a 'spare' IRQ to this internal modem?" The answer is the basis of configuration: you move a jumper (see Figure 6.1), move a DIP switch (see Figure 6.2), or run a program to shut off a COM port or assign different resources to it. Whether it's a DIP switch, a jumper, or a program depends on the hardware involved. Most modern systems configure all of the I/O ports in the BIOS, so that's probably where you'll go to change the settings for your built-in COM1 and COM2.

Note the symptom in that first example: you installed a new internal modem and, all of a sudden, the mouse stopped working.

NOTE   *Clue to device conflicts: if you've installed a new board and it doesn't work, don't just pull it out. Test the rest of the system with the new board in place. Does something that worked yesterday not work today? That's your clue that (1) the board is probably not broken but is conflicting with something, and (2) you now know what it's conflicting with, so it's easier to track down exactly what you have to change to make the thing work.*

FIGURE 6.1

Jumpers and how they work

Jumpers tend to be arranged by manufacturers in one of two ways. In the situation above, you see three sets of jumper pins. Moving from left to right, you see a jumper above the three pairs of pins, then connecting the leftmost pair, then connecting the middle pair. This might be interpreted as "jumper leftmost pins—enable BIOS" and "jumper middle pins—disable BIOS."

The alternative use of the jumpers is in triples. Here, you select an option by jumpering either pins 1 and 2, or 2 and 3. Here, you see the jumper above the pins, then jumpering pins 2 and 3, and finally jumpering pins 1 and 2. For example, jumpering pins 1 and 2 might mean "enable BIOS" and jumpering 2 and 3 might mean "disable BIOS."

FIGURE 6.2

Jumper and DIP switches example

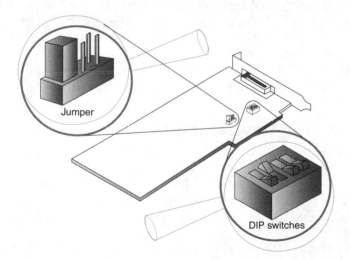

In Scenario 2, the sound card needed something called an interrupt, or *IRQ* (which is an acronym for *interrupt request*). Many sound cards are set to use IRQ7, but IRQ7 is preassigned to the first parallel port, LPT1. Under an operating system like Windows 95/98/Me/2000/NT/XP, you can't build a conflict like this into your system because the OS notices the conflict from the beginning and attempts to correct it during installation. In contrast, DOS and Windows 3.*x* don't worry about interrupt conflicts and will simply fail. The answer? Set the sound card to another interrupt. The answer to "How do I do *that?*" is coming.

In Scenario 3, the Ethernet card has some memory on it (16K), memory that must sit somewhere in the bottom 1024K of memory addresses. When you install the Ethernet card, you tell it where to place that 16K of memory—if you don't tell it where to put the memory, it just uses a default value. If a whole boatload of these cards don't work, then it could be due to one of four things. First, all of your Ethernet cards could be faulty. (It's unlikely, but possible.) Second, it may be that the default location of the memory is the same location that some *other* memory in your system is using; for example, you might have a SCSI host adapter that uses the same memory addresses for its BIOS. In that case, you've just got to find another location for the Ethernet card's memory. Third, if you're using DOS on your system, you may be using a memory manager like EMM386.EXE, and it may have grabbed the same address range for itself. If that happens, you have a software conflict rather than a hardware conflict, but it all boils down to the same thing: a nonfunctional board. The answer in that case is to tell the memory manager to stay the heck away from the LAN board's territory with an exclude statement (again, the answer to "how?" is coming). Fourth, if you're running Windows 95/98/Me/2000/NT/XP, then the network card driver may be looking for that 16K window in the wrong place: in actual fact, the board's working fine; it's just the driver software that needs adjustment. You usually adjust drivers in Control Panel in Windows 95/98/Me/2000/NT/XP.

Scenario 4 illustrates why PnP is sometimes called "Shrug and Pray." (It's also a bit technical, so if you don't follow it now, don't worry—we'll return to this a little later in the chapter.) You freed up an IRQ by removing the internal modem, which, by the way, was configured to behave as COM2. That freed up the IRQ associated with COM2, which is IRQ4. So why didn't PnP automatically assign the newly freed IRQ4 to the video capture board? Because the PnP system was designed to overlook IRQ4 when searching for IRQs; since all computers have a COM2 (which uses IRQ4 by default), it therefore assumes that IRQ4 must be occupied. How to solve this? Use the Windows Device Manager to force the computer to use IRQ4 for the video capture board. Then reboot, and the video capture board will work fine. (I'll explain how to do this later in the chapter, so hang on.)

And, in case you're wondering, yes, all four of these scenarios *are* true stories. Sadly.

Resolving Device Conflicts

The simplest kind of installation problem is a conflict with the I/O ports: COM and LPT. (By the way, *LPT* is an acronym for *Line PrinTer*.)

You are not allowed to have multiple COM ports with the same designation—each port must be uniquely named. For example, you can't have more than one COM1. But you can have a COM1, COM2, COM3, and so on. You can also have an LPT1, LPT2, and LPT3, although this is far less common.

A COM or LPT conflict arises when two boards have the same COM or LPT name. If two boards both want to be COM3, reconfigure one of them to be COM4. (You wouldn't want either to be COM1 or COM2 unless you had disabled the system's built-in COM ports in the BIOS, or you would create yet another conflict.) You can reconfigure a board in one of several ways, depending on how old your machine is.

On Newer Systems: PnP

PnP systems attempt to take software setup a step further by actually eliminating the need for it—in most cases you don't even have to run a setup program. The system detects new hardware every time you boot up your computer, and appropriate drivers are automatically installed. (You might be prompted to insert the Windows CD or a disk that came with the device so that the correct driver can be retrieved.) In the case of a board that wants a COM designation, it automatically picks the next available COM number and claims it for itself. So if COM1 through COM3 are spoken for, the new board automatically becomes COM4.

TIP   By the way, if you are using a PnP board under Windows 95/98/Me/2000/XP and it won't configure automatically, you may have to remove the board from the system (through Device Manager, I mean, not physically) and let Windows reinstall it for you (correctly this time, you hope). To do this, right-click My Computer on the desktop (or on the Start menu in Windows XP) and choose Properties from the shortcut menu. This will open a System Properties dialog box. Click the Device Manager tab (or click the Hardware tab in Windows XP and click the Device Manager button). Then, find the device that isn't working correctly, select it (by clicking once on it), and click the Remove button at the bottom of the window. Then, close the System Properties dialog box and restart your computer. When your computer reboots, it should reinitialize the device correctly.

On Older Systems

If you have an older machine, you will need to assign a COM port designation to each device manually, or disable the COM function altogether by doing one of the following:

- Alter the position of a jumper, as shown back in Figure 6.1.

- Alter the settings of a DIP switch.

- Run a program to adjust the board's "soft" switch settings. They operate just like physical switches but are modified via software rather than by physically moving them around.

But this really begs the tougher, more common question: how do you know which switch to move? I'm afraid there's no simple answer here; you've just gotta look at the documentation. People don't seem to believe this; they'll bring me a circuit board and ask me, "What does this do?" while pointing to a jumper. I just shrug my shoulders. There's no way to know without the documentation, so here's one of the best pieces of troubleshooting advice you'll ever get: become a documentation pack rat—but more on documentation later.

A Word about DIP Switches

Since we're discussing configuration, here are a few points about DIP switches. There are two basic types, diagrammed in Figure 6.3: the rocker switch and the slide switch.

FIGURE 6.3

Types of DIP switches

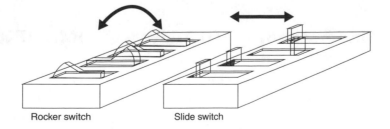

Rocker switch   Slide switch

DIP switches are chip-sized things that contain between 4 and 12 small plastic switches. You'll see them even on some of the most modern PnP-compatible systems. In a Perfect World, DIP switches are easy to access and labeled On or Off. Sadly, that's not always true; some say Open or Closed. If they do, just remember that Open = Off and Closed = On. Sometimes they say 1 or 0—1 = On, 0 = Off. Sometimes (grrrr…) they don't say anything at all. In this case, play around with them until you figure it out, and then write your findings in your notebook for future reference.

Second, if you have set the switches correctly but the PC refuses to recognize the settings, be aware that sometimes DIP switches are defective (it's happened to me). To test this, you can remove the system board and test the switches for continuity with an ohmmeter.

Finally, remember that sometimes manufacturers mislabel DIP switches or install them upside down. It *does* happen—rarely, but it happens.

Software Switch Setup Advice

Most boards in today's marketplace are designed without DIP switches. Such boards are designed to be set up through software provided with them or through PnP. Software setup has a good side and a bad side. The good side is that you can change settings on a board (such as making it COM1 rather than COM2) without having to open up the PC and mess with jumpers—you just run a program and you're done. The bad side is that now *you have to keep the setup program disk around forever*. What's that, you say? You're not that organized? You can barely keep track of the software long enough to get the board installed once? Okay, one solution is to get a big envelope and tape it to the side of your computer. Then put all of your setup disks in that envelope so that you'll always have them if you ever need them. Still think you might lose your disks? Okay, okay, maybe you don't *have* to keep the disk around forever, but it's a real good idea since you'll need the software that it contains to reinstall the board if your system ever fails. You may also want to make a copy of the disks or copy their contents to your hard disk in a folder created for that purpose. Of course, you can always burn all those setup disks, as well as downloaded drivers and hotfixes, to a CD-R or CD-RW disc to keep them all in one place, too. Then you'll have just one setup disc that you'll have to keep around.

So what happens if you *do* lose the disk? Check the manufacturer's Web site. Almost every board manufacturer maintains a database of the installation software for their boards online. As long as the company is still around, you should be able to get the software from the Web site. And, by the way, it might be a good idea to check that site once in a while anyway, since the companies often provide upgraded drivers there, too. Who knows—you might be able to improve your system's performance. For example, U.S. Robotics has a software upgrade for some of their 33.6K modems. All you have to do is download the new software for their 33.6K modem and it becomes a 56K modem! (See the Vendor Guide on the Utilities CD for U.S. Robotics' contact information.)

Understanding I/O Addresses, DMA, IRQs, RAM, and ROM Addresses

I've been promising to explain those "IRQ" things in detail, and if you made it this far, you've been patiently waiting for me to keep that promise. The time has come, this is the place….

The documentation that comes with circuit boards isn't always the easiest to understand. The folks who write circuit-board documentation assume that you understand five pretty important things. Those five things are:

I/O addresses   Addresses the circuit board uses to communicate with the CPU.

DMA channels   Used by some devices to speed up I/O to and from the system's memory. A system has only a few DMA channels, so a system is severely limited in how many devices requiring DMA channels it can have installed at once.

IRQs   Hardware components must interrupt the CPU to force it to service them in some time-critical fashion. Each device uses an interrupt request, or IRQ, to get the CPU's attention.

ROM addresses   Many boards include some of their low-level control software in ROM (read-only memory). The ROM requires a memory address, which cannot conflict with other ROMs or any RAM in the system.

RAM buffers   Some add-in cards maintain a little (8K to 64K) RAM on board to hold data temporarily. That RAM should not conflict with any other RAM or ROM in your system. Here's the scoop on these resources.

I/O Addresses

Stop and think for a minute about how the CPU talks to a piece of hardware such as a serial port, a disk controller, or a keyboard controller. You already know how the CPU talks to one kind of hardware—the memory. You know that the CPU can determine which part of what memory chip it's talking to because each location in memory has its own unique *memory address*.

Other hardware components have addresses as well, and although they're not memory addresses, the computer talks to them in more or less the same way it talks to memory. First, the computer puts the address of the device it wants to talk to on its bus, and then it either reads data from that location or writes data to that location. The address locations that the computer uses to talk to these devices are called *I/O (input/output)* addresses.

There are fewer I/O addresses than there are memory addresses—a lot fewer: any computer built with a 386 or later processor can address 4096MB of RAM or more, but only 64K of I/O addresses. That's not a serious limitation, however, since most of us won't be attaching (for example) a thousand keyboards to a single PC.

I/O addresses allow a CPU to tell its peripherals apart, as you can see in Figure 6.4.

FIGURE 6.4

Distinguishing peripherals with I/O addresses

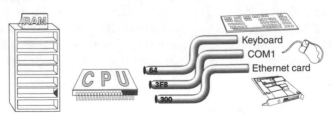

The CPU communicates with the RAM using memory addresses. It communicates with other peripherals—a keyboard controller, a serial port with a mouse on it, and an Ethernet LAN card, in this simplified example—via their I/O addresses. The keyboard controller sits at address 64, the serial port at 3F8 (there's an F in the number because it's a hex number, which I'll get to in a minute), and the Ethernet card is at address 300.

What this means is that when the CPU wants to send some data to the Ethernet card, it drops the data down the tube labeled 300, rather than the one labeled 3F8 or 64. (There aren't really tubes in a computer, of course; I just like the imagery of the CPU communicating with its minions via old-fashioned pneumatic tubes.)

IT'S HEX, BUT THERE ARE NO SPELLS

A quick word on the hex notation: you'll see that both memory addresses and I/O addresses tend to be reported in hexadecimal, an alternative way of writing numbers. There's no especially good reason for this; it's just something that techies prefer. To learn the gory details of hex, take a look at Appendix A, "A Short Overview on Reading Hexadecimal."

Briefly, though, hex is just another way to represent numbers. We're all comfortable with counting in the decimal system—the "normal" way of numbering: 0, 1, 2, 3, 4, 5, 6, 7, 8, 9... but what comes next? Well, we expect the next number to be 10, which is the first number—0—with a 1 at the front of it. We expect the number after that to be 11 (the number 1 with a 1 at the front of it), and so on.

The decimal system has 10 single-character number symbols, which is why it's called "base 10." Hexadecimal is based not on 10, but on 16. Why do we use hexadecimal? Because it's a lot easier for programmers to use than binary (100110110011101110110101010101), which is the way computers actually "think." Anyway, hex starts off with the familiar 0 through 9, so it's got the first 10. But after 9 comes the letter A—hex uses the letter A to represent its 11th digit. As you'd imagine, B comes next, and so on to F. You count in hex, then, like so: 0, 1, 2, 3, 4, 5, 6, 7, 8, 9, A, B, C, D, E, F... and then 10. See, hex has a 10 just like decimal, but it arrives later, and corresponds to the number 16 in decimal.

For example, suppose I were to tell you that the COM1 serial port uses an address range from 3F8 to 3FF. (I can hear Ford Prefect of *The Hitchhiker's Guide to the Galaxy* answer, "Why? Do you think you're likely to tell me that?") How many addresses does COM1 then take up? Well, you know that 3F8 is its first address. After 3F8 comes 3F9. Just like all the numbers you've ever known, the rightmost digit is the one that changes as the number gets bigger; 9 comes after 8, so 3F9 is the next value. You just learned that 9 is followed by A, so the next address would be 3FA, then 3FB, 3FC, 3FD, 3FE, and finally 3FF. Why *finally?* Because the range is from 3F8 to 3FF, so when you get to the 3FF, you stop. Go back and count them up, and you'll see that a serial port uses eight I/O addresses.

What does a serial port do with all of those addresses? Several things. First of all, a serial port can both transmit and receive bytes at the same time. One address holds received data and one holds outgoing data. Of the other addresses, some will be used for status information, such as, "Does the modem have a connection to another modem?" Some will be wasted—because, due to a peculiarity in the PC hardware, it's easier for a circuit designer to take 8 or 16 addresses than the actual number a device requires.

COMMON I/O ADDRESS USES

That's probably a bit more than you actually wanted to know. What you really need to know about addresses is, "How do you know which ones are currently taken?" Well, you can start off with Table 6.1.

TABLE 6.1: COMMON I/O ADDRESS USES IN PCS

HEX ADDRESS RANGE	USER
00–0F	DMA Controller 8237 #1
20–21	Programmable interrupt controller 8259A #1 IRQs 0–7
40–43	Timer 8253
60–63	8255 peripheral controller
60–64	Keyboard controller (8742)
80–8F	DMA page registers
A0–A1	Programmable interrupt controller #2 IRQs 8–15
A0–AF	NMI mask register
C0–DF	8237 DMA controller #2
CF8–CFF	PCI bus I/O port
F0–FF	Math coprocessor (integrated into modern processors but still reserved)
170–177	Secondary hard disk controller, if present (present in most modern systems)
1F0–1F8	Primary hard disk controller
200–20F	Joystick controller
210–217	Expansion chassis
220–22F	FM synthesis interface (WAV device), Sound Blaster default
230–233	Common CD-ROM I/O port
238–23B	Bus mouse
23C–23F	Alternate bus mouse
274–277	ISA PnP I/O Port
278–27F	LPT2
2B0–2DF	EGA (usually *not* used by modern video)
2E8–2EF	COM4 serial port
2F8–2FF	COM2 serial port
300–30F	Ethernet card (common location, not a standard)
320–32F	Hard disk controller (XT only)
330–33F	MIDI port (common location, not a standard)
370–377	Alternative floppy controller address

Continued on next page

TABLE 6.1: COMMON I/O ADDRESS USES IN PCs *(continued)*

HEX ADDRESS RANGE	USER
378–37F	LPT1 printer port
3B0–3BF	Monochrome adapter (also used on modern video)
3BC–3BF	LPT3 (uncommon)
3D0–3DF	Color/graphics adapter (also used on modern video)
3E8–3EF	COM3 serial port
3F0–3F7	Floppy disk controller
3F8–3FF	COM1 serial port
778–77F	LPT1 I/O port

NOTE *In PnP systems, PCI boards are assigned I/O addresses above 1000. A common I/O address for a PCI network board, for example, might be 1060–107F.*

You can also see what I/O addresses are in use in Windows by using the Device Manager. Double-click Computer in the Device Manager (at the top of the list of devices) and choose Input/Output (I/O) to see which addresses are occupied. You can also view I/O address assignments in System Information (Start ➤ Programs ➤ Accessories ➤ System Tools ➤ System Information) in Windows 98/Me/2000. (In Windows XP, you'd choose Start ➤ All Programs ➤ Accessories ➤ System Tools ➤ System Information.)

Many devices have only one I/O address that they can use. Using the example of COM1 again, part of the very definition of COM1 is that it uses I/O addresses 3F8–3FF. Other devices may allow you to use any of a range of addresses. For example, most sound cards default to address 220 but will allow you to reconfigure them to use another address if 220 is not available. Reconfigure a COM1 serial port, in contrast, and it's no longer a COM1 serial port.

The key to understanding why this information is important is knowing that an assigned address cannot be used by any other device; only one device is used per I/O address. To understand why this is so, I'll steal an old analogy.

I/O Address Conflicts

Think of I/O addresses as being like post office boxes. Say the keyboard has P.O. Box 64. When the keyboard has data for the system, it puts the data in Box 64. When the CPU wants to read the keyboard, it looks in Box 64. Box 64 is, in a very real sense, a better definition of the keyboard from the CPU's point of view than the keyboard itself is. If you plug a new device into your system and that device uses I/O address 64, then the new device won't work, and the keyboard will cease to work as well—because you can't run two devices off the same I/O address.

Now, in reality, no one's going to design a device that uses address 64, because everyone knows that it's reserved for the keyboard. But what about a case where you have a conflict over an optional address?

For example, I once installed a Sound Blaster 16 on a PC that was already equipped with an Ethernet card and a SCSI host adapter. The Sound Blaster 16 included a circuit called a Musical Instrument Digital Interface (MIDI) interface, and it happened to be set at I/O address 330. Unfortunately, 330 was the I/O address used by the SCSI host adapter, so I got a disk boot failure when I turned on my system. There actually was nothing wrong with the *disk*; it was the disk's host adapter board that couldn't work due to the conflict with the Sound Blaster 16. Checking the documentation, I found that the sound card's MIDI circuit offered either address 330, which it was currently using, or 300. I set the address to 300 (the Sound Blaster 16 uses a jumper to set its MIDI address), reinstalled the board, and had the situation shown in Figure 6.5.

FIGURE 6.5

Sharing I/O addresses between an Ethernet card and a sound card

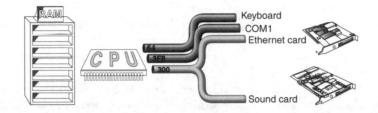

Now the CPU's I/O address 300—that particular "post office box"—is shared by the MIDI circuit on the sound card and the Ethernet card. The system didn't complain when I booted up, because my system doesn't need either the sound card or the Ethernet card in order to boot. But when I tried to configure the sound card, it failed. You can see why in Figure 6.6.

FIGURE 6.6

I/O conflict between an Ethernet card and a sound card

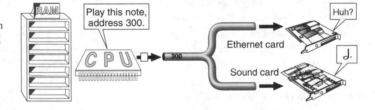

A "play this note" message went into I/O address 300. The Ethernet card has no idea how to respond to this request, and indeed may not be prepared for any requests at all. Worse yet, the electrical signal from the CPU gets split up two ways, so it may not be strong enough to actually get to *either* board.

Why did Creative Labs, the creator of the Sound Blaster 16, build a deliberate conflict into its card? The answer is, they did not. There is no official standard for SCSI host adapter I/O addresses; Adaptec uses 330 for some of their boards, Iomega offers a range from 320 through 350, and I'm sure other SCSI vendors have other options. Ethernet cards *tend* to sit at address 300, but that's not carved in stone. The problem is the lack of standardization. The most common conflicts occur between the types of boards that appeared after the mid-'80s, such as Ethernet cards and sound cards, because there's been no central coordinating force in the PC hardware industry since then.

How did I solve the conflict, by the way? Well, the Adaptec board offered me 330 or 300 as my only choices, as did the sound card. The Ethernet board offered 300, 310, 320, 330, or 340. I didn't want to mess with the Adaptec board, because it was the hard disk interface and if *it* became conflicted, I'd lose access to the hard disk—so I left the SCSI board at 330. That meant that the Sound Blaster 16 had to go to 300. The Ethernet board then played the peacemaker, because I set it to address 310.

More and more, I find that board manufacturers are moving from jumper settings to software settings, but in this case, the SCSI board and the sound card set their addresses with jumpers, and the Ethernet card set its I/O address with software. Which do I prefer? Well, software is, of course, nice. But suppose the sound card came preset to 330, as it did, and required that I run some software in order to get it to switch addresses? That would be a real pain. Think about it: I'd install the sound card at 330 initially, since I had no choice. That would disable my hard disk, requiring that I juggle floppies in order to run the program that would set a different address for the sound card. To add insult to injury, the setup program for the sound card works only after it's installed on the hard disk. I just might decide that getting past *that* gauntlet wouldn't be worth it and scrap the board altogether in favor of a different brand. In contrast, all I *actually* had to do was to move a jumper. So there are pros and cons to both sides.

I've already said this, but let me repeat: you probably won't have a clue which DIP switches do what without the documentation, so be sure to latch onto any switch-setting documentation you have. Or hope that the company that made the board whose DIP switches you're trying to set still has the switch settings on its Web site.

What would I have done, by the way, if the Ethernet card was set at 300 and wouldn't accept any other addresses? How would you resolve that problem? *You may not be able to resolve all I/O address conflicts,* because not all boards even give you the chance to change I/O addresses.

NOTE   *When working with very old computers, I occasionally run across OEM components (that is, parts that came with the computer when it was originally built) that were designed, as a cost-cutting measure, to work with only one I/O address. Some memory expansion boards were like that in 286-based PCs, as well as some modems. If you find a device like that, the best solution is probably to replace the device if possible with one that offers more flexibility.*

PROGRAMMED INPUT/OUTPUT (PIO)

Once a hard disk controller gets some data from the hard disk, that data's got to be stored in RAM. The same thing gets done when new data comes in on a LAN card. Big blocks of sound information must be zapped out to a sound card in a smooth, reliable fashion in order for that card to produce pleasant-sounding voice or music sounds. The data originates in the system's memory, and it must get to the sound card.

A fundamental problem in computer design is getting data from memory (RAM) to or from a hard disk controller, LAN board, video capture card, sound card, video card—in short, to transfer data between memory and a *peripheral.* (From this point on, I'll use the term *peripheral* to mean a LAN card, disk interface, and so forth.)

The easiest way to move data between a peripheral and memory is through *programmed input/output (PIO).* With PIO, the CPU sends commands to the peripheral through an I/O address or addresses; let's see how that's done with a simple example.

Suppose the CPU wants some data stored on one of the disk drives. Data on disks, as you'll learn in the disk section of this book (Chapters 10 through 17), is organized into sectors, which are blocks of data that can be anywhere from 512 bytes to as long as 32K (actually, 32,768 bytes), depending on the size and internal data organization of your hard drive. When a PC accesses data from a disk, it can't take it in 1- or 2-byte chunks; the smallest amount of data that the CPU can ask for is a sector of data (which, once again, can be from hundreds to tens of thousands of bytes long). Suppose the goal for the moment is to get sector 10 from the disk and to put it into RAM. The first step is for the CPU to tell the disk interface to get the data; it does that on I/O address 1F0 on many disk interfaces, as you can see in Figure 6.7.

FIGURE 6.7

PIO part 1: Requesting data from the disk interface using I/O addresses

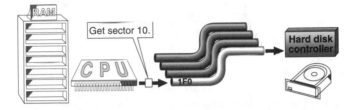

The disk interface responds to the request, pulling all of the data in the selected sector off the disk drive. The interface then tells the CPU that it's ready, and the CPU now has the task of getting the data from the disk interface to the RAM. The CPU begins by requesting the first 2 bytes of data, as shown in Figure 6.8.

FIGURE 6.8

PIO part 2: Requesting the first part of the data from the disk controller

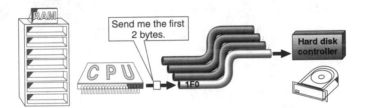

The CPU then stuffs that data somewhere in RAM, as you see in Figure 6.9.

FIGURE 6.9

PIO part 3: Putting the data into RAM

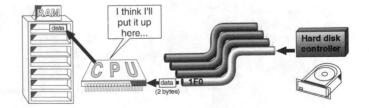

Moving those 2 bytes takes time, as does figuring out where to put the *next* 2 bytes. The CPU then requests 2 more bytes, puts them in RAM, figures out where the next bytes will go, and so on. Will this work? Yes, undoubtedly. Is it fast? Well, not always. Can we make this faster? Certainly; read on.

DMA (Direct Memory Access) Channels

Now, let's take a look at how PC CPUs access floppy disk drives. Suppose I want to read sector 20 from a floppy disk. Things start out very much the same as before, as you can see in Figure 6.10.

FIGURE 6.10

DMA part 1: Requesting data from the floppy disk controller

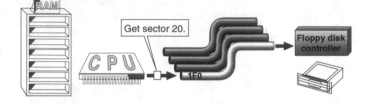

The floppy disk controller is at address 1F0, so the CPU sends the initial command out over that address. Ah, but when the disk controller has the data ready, it knows that having the CPU pick up 2 bytes and put them down and then pick up 2 more bytes and put them down (and so on) takes time. The idea is to get the data into the RAM, so why not cut out the go-between (as you can see in Figure 6.11)?

FIGURE 6.11

DMA part 2: Diversion of the CPU by the floppy disk controller

First, there's a diversionary tactic, allowing something other than the CPU to control the bus; then, as you see in Figure 6.12, the data is delivered to the RAM directly.

FIGURE 6.12

DMA part 3: Using the DMA channel to put data directly into RAM

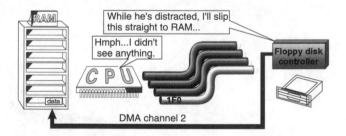

Okay, I admit that the disk controller doesn't really distract the CPU; actually, it says to the CPU, "May I have direct access to the memory?" Some of the wires on the bus are DMA request (DREQ) lines and some are DMA acknowledge (DACK) lines. A board requests direct access to the memory bus with a DREQ line, and the CPU responds with a DACK. The idea here is to allow only one peripheral at a time to control the bus. There are multiple DMA request/acknowledge lines, more commonly called DMA channels.

The original PC had a single DMA controller chip, the 8237. It allowed up to four DMA channels, and to this day 8-bit ISA slots have only four DMA channels available, numbered from 0 to 3, as shown in Table 6.2.

TABLE 6.2: 8-Bit ISA DMA Channels

DMA	DEFAULT FUNCTION
0	Dynamic RAM refresh
1	Available
2	Floppy disk controller
3	Hard disk controller

The original PC used DMA channel 0 for "dynamic memory refresh," and as such, was not associated with a bus slot. Briefly, here's how it worked. There are two kinds of memory: dynamic and static. *Dynamic* sounds better than *static*, but it isn't. When you tell static RAM (SRAM) something, it remembers it until you turn off the power or change it. Think of memory as a container of liquid, and static RAM is a ceramic mug. You put water in it, and it stays there. Dynamic RAM (DRAM), on the other hand, is like a water cup made out of a thin sheet of paper; it leaks. Put data into a DRAM and it will forget whatever you tell it within 4 milliseconds (ms).

As a result, old PCs had to drop everything and do a RAM refresh every 3.86ms. This took 5 clock cycles out of every 72, or about 7 percent of the PC's time. Of course, if the CPU was doing a lot of INs, OUTs, internal calculations, or the like, then you would not notice the slowdown; the whole idea of DMA is to work in parallel with the CPU. Wouldn't static RAM make a faster computer? Yes, in fact, it would make the computer much, much faster, but it's also much, much more costly. In more modern PCs, the RAM refresh is handled by a separate circuit. DRAM still needs to be refreshed in modern systems, but the CPU isn't involved, which means no DMA is required and channel 0 is free on most modern PCs.

On those old PCs, the hard disk controller used DMA channel 1, but most modern disk interfaces don't use DMA. Instead, they use PIO, for reasons I'll explain in a minute. As a result, channel 1 is available on modern PCs. The floppy disk controller has employed channel 2 since the old PC days, and it still does, so you should not assign anything else to DMA channel 2. Channel 3 is typically unused.

Any PC built after 1985 will have 16-bit ISA, Micro Channel Architecture (MCA), Extended Industry Standard Architecture (EISA), PC Card, PCI, or Video Electronics Standards Association (VESA) slots, all of which have *two* DMA controllers, and thus eight DMA channels to the XT's four.

Notice that this implies that you have only *one* free DMA channel on an old XT-type machine, but seven available DMA channels on most modern PCs—just leave channel 2 for the floppy disk controller, and you're in good shape. However, in reality, you may not have seven free DMA channels. PCs nowadays often require two DMA channels for the sound card, and many parallel ports can be configured to be an Extended Capabilities Port (ECP), which is basically just a parallel port with, uh, extended capabilities—it's bidirectional and faster than the standard parallel port—but ECP needs DMA. Table 6.3 shows the DMA channels on a 16- or 32-bit ISA/PCI system. Of these, all are associated with a bus slot except channel 4, which is a cascade to channels 0–3. As with the 8-bit system, channels 0–3 have 8-bit transfer capabilities, but the added channels, 5–7, are 16-bit.

TABLE 6.3: 16/32-BIT DMA CHANNELS

DMA	DEFAULT FUNCTION	TYPE
0	Available	8-bit
1	Available	8-bit
2	Floppy disk controller	8-bit
3	Available	8-bit
4	Cascade to first DMA controller	N/A
5	Available	16-bit
6	Available	16-bit
7	Available	16-bit

TO DMA OR NOT TO DMA?

You're probably wondering by now what I left out of the story. I just finished explaining that DMA allows for faster transfers of data between peripherals and memory, and modern machines basically don't use DMA. (You're supposed to go "*huh?*" at this point.)

DMA is pretty nifty, except for one thing. In order to assure backward compatibility, the AT's designers limited DMA operations to 4.77MHz—the original PC's clock speed. Lest you skim over this because it sounds like a history lesson, *ISA bus machines still do DMA at 4.77MHz*. Honest. If you have a shiny new 2GHz Pentium 4 system on your desk and you do a DMA operation on it, the whole shootin' match slows down to less than *1 percent* of that 2GHz clock speed. The best the other, now obsolete, buses (such as EISA and MCA) do when DMA-ing is 8MHz. Therefore, depending on the device, using DMA with an ISA device may actually slow things down rather than speed them up.

Fortunately, many modern ISA devices give you a choice about whether to DMA or not. Check the documentation—a device may have a jumper that turns DMA on or off, or you may be able to control DMA usage through the device's properties in Windows. You may want to try a device both ways and see which way you get better performance.

Generally speaking, ISA buses are becoming less common on new systems. Within a few years, you may be buying new systems with no ISA slots at all, so the question of whether to use DMA with an ISA device may be moot. PCI is the newer bus, and PCI doesn't use DMA at all.

So, in summary, if you have an expansion board that needs a DMA channel:

◆ On old PCs, the only one available is generally DMA channel 3.

◆ If you're installing a 16-bit board, try whenever possible to use the extra 16-bit-only DMAs, channels 4–7, so you'll leave room for the 8-bit boards in your system to use channel 3.

◆ Especially if you're out of DMAs, see if the board offers the option to disable DMA. It may be slower, or it may be faster. Try it both ways to see.

You can see common DMA uses in Table 6.4.

TABLE 6.4: COMMON DMA CHANNEL USES IN THE PC FAMILY

CHANNEL	USE
0	Dynamic RAM refresh (XT only)
1	Hard disk controller (XT only), or commonly used by sound cards in AT architecture
2	Floppy disk controller
3	Unused, but also used on many 16-bit sound cards (they use two DMA channels) or ECP parallel ports
4–7	Available on modern PCs

BUS MASTERING

This is a slight digression, but it's important, it fits in here, and I'll keep it short.

You just learned that DMA is a neat idea that is hampered by an historical error—4.77MHz. DMA actually has another problem, although it's not one that is immediately apparent.

DMA can transfer data from a peripheral to RAM, or from RAM to a peripheral, with neither transfer requiring the CPU's intervention. But DMA can't transfer data from a peripheral to a *peripheral*. Such an operation would actually be two DMA operations—peripheral 1 to RAM, followed by RAM to peripheral 2.

Many boards built for the EISA, MCA, or PCI buses can do *bus master transfers*, allowing them to bypass not only the CPU but RAM as well, transferring data between peripherals at the maximum speed that the bus supports. Bus mastering, then, can speed up a system in two ways. You see this diagrammed in Figure 6.13.

FIGURE 6.13

Bus mastering

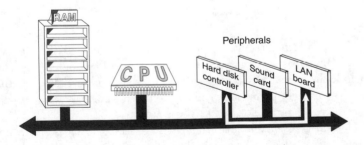

Peripherals

The ISA slots in your system support bus mastering but allow only one bus master board in your ISA system. The PCI slots, in contrast (as well as EISA or MCA slots, if you're working with one of those older systems), allow multiple bus masters. It's a feature worth exploiting. But bus mastering is useful for more than just peripheral-to-peripheral transfer; it's also terrific as a replacement for DMA. Designers of PCI-based boards use bus mastering to support fast peripheral-to-RAM transfers that aren't hobbled by the 4.77MHz limitation.

IRQ (Interrupt Request) Levels

In the DMA section, I described PIO. After the CPU made the request of the disk controller for the data, I said, "The interface then tells the CPU that it's ready..."—which was a trifle sneaky on my part. As far as the CPU is concerned, it initiates all conversations with peripherals; the peripherals "speak when they're spoken to." A peripheral gets the CPU's attention in one of two ways: *polling* or *interrupts*.

POLLING

Let's look at how DOS controls a parallel port in order to print data. (Don't worry, we'll get to more modern methods in a minute.) The printer is massively slower than the CPU, so there has to be some way to handshake the two. Things start off as you see in Figure 6.14.

FIGURE 6.14

Printing data through the parallel port

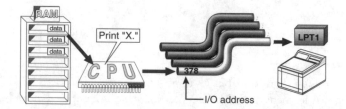

Data travels through I/O address 378, the address of LPT1, and is deposited from there into the printer. The CPU then keeps an eye on the printer, as you see in Figure 6.15.

FIGURE 6.15

The CPU watches the printer.

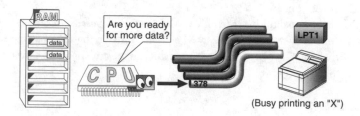

The CPU sits there at the "pneumatic tube" numbered 378, just waiting for the word from the printer, much as someone expecting a letter might run out to the mailbox every 10 minutes. (I'd include the lyrics for that song that goes "Wait a minute, Mr. Postman..." but then we'd have to get the copyright permission, and it's too much trouble. You might just want to hum along to get into the polling frame of mind.)

The CPU essentially sits on address 378, asking, "Are you ready now? How about *now*? How about NOW?" It's a big waste of the CPU's time, but this polling method of waiting for an I/O device to finish its work is simple to design. Besides, in a single-tasking world like you see in DOS, the CPU doesn't have anything else to do anyway; it is singly focused on servicing the parallel port. Eventually, as you see in Figure 6.16, the port responds.

The CPU now sends another byte to the printer, and it begins all over again. As I've said, the process is wasteful but simple, and it works fine in the single-tasking DOS world.

FIGURE 6.16

Response of the parallel port to polling

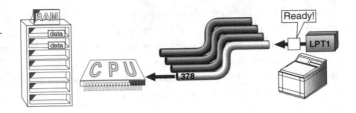

HARDWARE INTERRUPTS

But what about a multitasking world, such as the one most of us live in today? And even if you work in single-tasking mode, there are many peripherals on your PC, and the PC can't poll them all. That's why hardware interrupts are built into the PC.

You can see how interrupts work if we look back to the discussion of how the CPU gets data from the disk interface. Recall that the CPU stuffed a "get some data" request down I/O address 1F0. Now, it takes time for the disk to return the desired data. Why not let the CPU use that time to do other things? Take a look at Figure 6.17.

FIGURE 6.17

The CPU works on other things while waiting for the disk controller.

The disk interface is in its "own private Idaho," as is the CPU. But most modern disk controllers (I'm equivocating because some really high-performance SCSI host adapters don't do this) have a circuit running between themselves and the CPU, a circuit called an *interrupt request* level, or *IRQ* level. The disk interface wakes up the CPU, as you can see in Figure 6.18.

Once the CPU has been interrupted, it knows to start getting the information from the disk controller, as I described in the discussion of PIO a few pages back.

FIGURE 6.18

Using IRQ levels to get the attention of the CPU

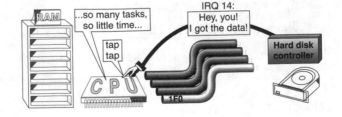

HOW INTERRUPTS WORK

PC interrupts were originally handled by an Intel 8259 prioritized interrupt controller (PIC). Nowadays, though, there's no discrete 8259 on your system; it's just built into the motherboard's chipset. The interrupt controller is *prioritized* in that the interrupt levels it controls are numbered from 0 to whatever (depending on which computer you are using). Lower numbers get higher priority. That means that if interrupt 3 and interrupt 7 both ring at the same time, it's interrupt 3 that gets handled first (*serviced*, in PC hardware lingo).

When an interrupt occurs, the interrupt controller forces the CPU to put its current work "on hold" and immediately execute a program that allows it to handle the interrupt. Such a program is called, appropriately, an *interrupt handler* or an *interrupt service routine*. For example, in the disk drive example, when IRQ14 occurs, the CPU jumps to a small program that tells it how to grab the data from the disk controller. The computer then stuffs the data into some RAM and returns to whatever it was doing before it was interrupted.

IRQs 2–7 in XTs (A Brief History)

The original PC had only one interrupt controller (the 8259), which had only eight interrupt lines. Interestingly, the 8259 implemented only lines 2 through 7. Lines 0 and 1 weren't even on the bus because they were preassigned. What is now IRQ8 (0 on the first 8259) was attached to a timer circuit that created an interrupt about 18 times per second, and IRQ1 was attached to the 8042 keyboard controller.

Driving the keyboard interface using interrupts is a good idea because the keyboard controller is pretty dumb. It has no memory to speak of, so every time a keystroke arrives at the controller, it must hand off that keystroke to the CPU (which then puts it in the keyboard buffer) before another keystroke comes in. Essentially, once the keyboard controller gets a keystroke, it wants to say to the CPU, "Hey! Stop everything! Come service me *now* before the user presses another key!" And so it "rings the bell"—okay, not really a bell; actually it just activates its interrupt line—and the CPU stops doing whatever it's doing and executes the program that moves the keystroke to the keyboard buffer. If it didn't do this, you would have a lot of dropped keystrokes. You can see a simple block diagram of how the bus, the CPU, and the 8259 interact in Figure 6.19. (I'm showing you how the XT did it because, as you'll see, IBM had to pull a bit of a trick to expand the number of interrupts on the AT, and—surprise!—that trick is still with us today and sometimes causes mischief.) Someone designing an expansion slot for the XT, then, could build a board to use IRQs 2–7; but not IRQ 0 or 1, because there simply weren't any wires running from IRQ 0 or 1 to the XT expansion bus slot connector.

Suppose a floppy disk controller wired to use IRQ6 wanted to interrupt the CPU to get serviced? Simplified a bit, here are the steps it would go through:

1. The disk controller sends a signal through IRQ6 on the bus.

2. The 8259 receives that signal on its input number 6.

3. The 8259 then looks to see if it is currently getting an interrupt signal from its higher-priority inputs—in other words, is the timer, keyboard, or anything attached to IRQs 2–5 demanding the 8259's attention?

4. Assuming there are no higher-priority interrupts, the 8259 then taps the CPU on the shoulder with the 8259's one "output" line, which is wired to the CPU's "incoming interrupt" line.

5. The CPU responds by putting a signal on the bus (not pictured) that says, "Okay, I'm willing to be interrupted; which interrupt number is it?"

6. The 8259 then seizes control of the *data* lines on the XT bus and uses them to transfer the value 6, the interrupt number.

7. The CPU has a table of locations where it keeps software to deal with different interrupts. There's a place there for servicing IRQ6, the floppy disk controller, so the CPU jumps to that location and executes that program, called the "floppy disk interrupt service routine."

8. Satisfied that its work is done for the moment, the 8259 resets the IRQ6 input line and is ready for the next interrupt.

CHOOSING IRQS

Eight IRQ lines with two preallocated for the timer and keyboard made configuring XTs a bit tricky, so PCs since the AT have all been equipped with a second 8259, bringing the total of interrupts on most PCs up to 16. *How* they added that 8259 is another story, one I'll tell you in a minute. Before I do that, however, let's take a look at which IRQs are usually free or taken; you can see the common uses for IRQs in Table 6.5.

TABLE 6.5: COMMON IRQ USES IN THE PC FAMILY

INTERRUPT LINE	DEVICE	COMMENTS
0	Timer	Not accessible by peripherals.
1	Keyboard	Not accessible by peripherals.
2	Cascade to IRQs 8–15	Used by second 8259 to signal interrupts; not available except on XTs.
3	COM2	Can also be COM4, but only one of the two.
4	COM1	Can also be COM3, but only one of the two.
5	XT hard disk controller, LPT2	Free on most PCs. Hard disk interface used only on XTs, or alternatively for LPT2 on the unusual machine with LPT2.
6	Floppy disk controller	
7	LPT1	
8	Clock	Not accessible by peripherals.
9		Generally available but can be confused with IRQ2; see text.
10		Generally available.
11		Generally available.
12	PS/2-type mouse port	If your PC/laptop has a built-in mouse port with a small circular connector, that port probably uses IRQ12.

Continued on next page

TABLE 6.5: COMMON IRQ USES IN THE PC FAMILY *(continued)*

INTERRUPT LINE	DEVICE	COMMENTS
13	Coprocessor	Interrupt required even for modern processors with integrated numeric coprocessors.
14	Primary hard disk interface	Taken in virtually all machines as the "primary PCI EIDE interface."
15	Secondary disk interface	Taken on most post-486 systems as the "secondary PCI EIDE interface."

If you're installing a board and need an IRQ, your best bet is to first look to IRQs 9, 10, 11, or 5, in that order (it's the order of descending priority, as you'll see in a minute). If they're not available, consider disabling your parallel port, if you're not using it, to recover IRQ7, or perhaps one of your COM ports if it's idle. If you're *still* in need, and you have only one hard disk and one CD-ROM drive, then you might ensure that the hard drive and CD-ROM are both on the primary EIDE interface (you'll read more about that in Chapter 16, "Care and Feeding of Hard Drives") and then disable the secondary EIDE interface, freeing up IRQ15. Be aware, however, that it can be a pain to consolidate a drive and a CD-ROM on the same interface if they're not already set up that way (you might have to set jumpers on one or both devices, for example), *and* not all systems even *allow* you to disable the secondary interface.

If you're configuring an XT (in a museum, perhaps?), your best bet for a free IRQ is either 2 or perhaps 7, but 7 is available only if you disable or remove your parallel port. And if you're configuring an 8-bit card in a modern system, the card can use only IRQs 0–7. Typically, 8-bit cards can use only IRQ5, because IRQ2 is not available.

Whatever you set your boards to, *write it down!* You'll need the information later.

Earlier, I suggested taping an envelope to the side of a PC and keeping important floppies there. Here are some other things to put in there. Each time I install a board (or modify an existing board), I get a new piece of paper and write down all the configuration information for the board. For example, I might note, "Intel EtherExpress 16 card installed 10 July 1999 by Mark Minasi; no EPROM on board, shared memory disabled, IRQ10 used, I/O address 310 set."

I hesitate to mention this, but you can sometimes solve device conflicts by doing surgery on the boards. Just lobotomize the chips that are performing the function that you wish to defeat. An example that I have seen a couple of times is with serial ports. A client wanted me to set up a multifunction board in a PC with clock, memory, printer, and serial ports. He already had a board installed that provided both serial ports COM1 and COM2. The jumpers on the multifunction board allowed me to set the multifunction board's serial port to either COM1 or COM2 but not to disable it altogether. What to do? A chip called the 8250 UART (Universal Asynchronous Receiver/Transmitter) is the heart of most serial ports. I found the 8250 on the multifunction board and removed it. The problem was eliminated. *Please don't try this unless you understand what you are doing.*

IRQs 2 AND 9: XT PROBLEMS THAT LIVE TO THIS DAY

Take a look back at Table 6.5 and you'll notice that IRQ2 is not available except on XTs. Why did those old dinosaurs have an IRQ we don't have? Recall that I said earlier that IBM had to do some fancy designing to add more IRQs to their AT. Unfortunately, that designing built a few quirks into the AT's IRQ structure—and every PC since has been designed in the same way, even your new 2GHz Pentium 4 system.

Recall that the PC/XT systems had a single interrupt controller, an Intel 8259 chip. The 8259 could support up to eight interrupt channels, and the original PC/XT systems hardwired channels 0 and 1 to the system timer (a clock circuit that goes "tick" every 55 milliseconds) and the 8042 keyboard controller.

The system was wired with those interrupts because IBM wanted to make sure that the keyboard and the timer had high priorities; recall that on an 8259, when two interrupts occur at the same time, the one with the lower number gets priority.

In 1984, the first 16-bit PC-compatible system was released—the IBM AT. The proliferation of add-in devices on the market made it clear that eight interrupt levels just weren't enough. So, how to add another 8259? Just slapping the extra 8259 onto the motherboard might present some backward compatibility problems, so IBM decided to kind of slip the extra 8259 in "through the back door," as you can see in Figure 6.19.

FIGURE 6.19

Adding an extra
8259 for more
IRQ levels

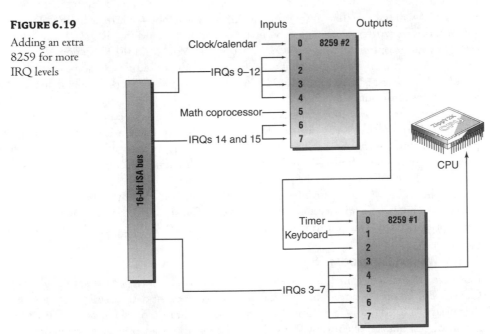

First, IBM added another 8259 and used its eight inputs to create IRQs 8–15. Just as the old 8259 had two IRQs that never showed up on the system bus (0 and 1), so also the new 8259 had two IRQs that the system bus didn't see: IRQ8 supported the clock/calendar, and IRQ13 supported the math coprocessor chip. But how to let the CPU know when one of the second 8259's IRQs fired? By *cascading* the 8259s: the second 8259's output—its way of saying, "Hey, I've got an interrupt!"—was connected as one of the *inputs* of the first 8259, IRQ2, in fact.

NOTE So, if an IRQ between 8 and 15 triggers, the second 8259 activates its output line. That shows up in the first 8259 as an IRQ2. The first 8259 tells the CPU, "I've got an interrupt for you," and the CPU of course asks, "Which IRQ?" When the 8259 replies, "IRQ2," the CPU knows that really means it now has to go to the second 8259 and say, "I hear from the first 8259 that you have an interrupt. Which line is it?" The second 8259 replies and the CPU services the second 8259's interrupt. Incidentally, all this talk about IRQs will become unimportant in the years to come, when ISA buses are no longer part of the average new PC. The PCI bus, when unencumbered by ISA, does not require each device to have its own IRQ, so this entire system will be going away when PC makers stop putting the ISA bus in their systems. In the interim, PCI buses can do a limited amount of IRQ sharing, if the operating system supports it; see "IRQ Sharing in PCI Systems" later in this chapter.

But now notice that IRQ2 is dedicated, as were IRQs 0 and 1 before. There would be no point in leaving IRQ2 available on the ISA bus, so IBM removed the wires on the motherboard connecting the first 8259's input number 2 and the pin on the ISA bus connectors. But, they reasoned, why waste that pin—so they recycled that bus pin, giving it to the newly created IRQ9. That's fine, in general, except for one thing—if you put an old 8-bit ISA board into a 16-bit ISA slot, the 8-bit board will think that pin is IRQ2, as was the case in the 8-bit ISA days. Even the jumpers on the 8-bit board will tell you that you're using IRQ2, but you're not—you're using IRQ9. And, generally, software drivers written to go with 8-bit boards don't understand the IRQ 2/9 confusion and don't even *give* you the option to choose IRQ9. What to do? Well, avoid IRQ2 on non-XT systems if you can; if you can't, then play around with the driver and jumper settings. In some cases, lying to the board and/or driver ("Sure, you're IRQ2, trust me") will make it work. The best answer? Get those ancient 8-bit cards out of your system!

And here's one more thought about how this cascaded 8259 structure affects IRQs: priorities. In the vast majority of cases, you don't really care which IRQ you assign a board to, as long as the board has an IRQ. But sometimes you'll see two boards that won't work together—the system works with either one but not with both—even though they have different IRQs. In that case, try swapping the IRQ levels. If that fixes it, then the problem was priorities.

But what is the order of priorities in IRQs? Well, you read earlier that back in the 8-bit XT days, IRQ 0 had the highest priority and IRQ7 the lowest. But since IRQs 8–15 snuck in through IRQ2, the priorities go from highest to lowest like so: 0, 1, 8, 9, 10, 11, 12, 13, 14, 15, 3, 4, 5, 6, 7.

So You Want a Third COM Port?

PCs were originally designed to support two RS-232 ports, which got the system names COM1 and COM2. But before the advent of the USB, serial ports were so darn useful that many people found they needed a third one—for example, on one of my PCs, I need a serial port for the mouse, another for my digital camera, one for my PalmPilot, and a fourth for an external infrared port.

If the PC was designed to support just two COM ports, how can you have more than two? By going *outside* of the basic PC design. You can add as many COM ports as you like beyond the first two, but the system treats them like any other "unusual" device—a network card, a SCSI board, or the like. What I mean is: whether you're running DOS or Windows 95/98/Me/2000/NT/XP, you don't need to load any drivers to configure your operating system to support things like a standard keyboard, LPT1, COM1, COM2, a floppy drive, or a hard disk. That's because those pieces of hardware are part of the "basic PC," so to speak. But add a network card, a sound card, or something else, and you take the PC beyond the bare minimum, requiring that you load drivers for the "unusual" hardware and perhaps configure those drivers. COM3 and beyond fall into the "unusual" category of hardware.

That means you'll need to do some more configuration to make a third or higher COM port work. Each COM port needs an IRQ, so be sure you have one free before trying to install an extra COM port. It also needs a range of I/O addresses, but there are usually enough of those around. Then you have to get the operating system to play ball with your new port.

If you're running Windows 95/98/Me/2000/XP, they do a pretty good job of detecting extra COM ports automatically. But if they don't, use Control Panel to tell Windows that you have a COM port. Open the System applet and choose Device Manager ÿ Ports (COM and LPT), then choose the particular port and click Properties. Click the Resources tab and deselect Use Automatic Settings. You can then tell Windows 95/98/Me/2000/XP what I/O address and IRQ your serial port is using.

Windows 3.1 also has a Control Panel, but in it, you should open the Ports dialog box and choose Advanced. There you'll find the dialog box to tell Windows 3.1 what resources the serial port uses. Windows NT 4's Control Panel works similarly.

IRQ Sharing in PCI Systems

Most modern systems today are PCI-based, and such systems can usually share a single IRQ among multiple PCI devices. For example, on my current system, IRQ11 is used for my PCI Ethernet card, my PCI sound card, and my PCI video card. PnP can set up this sharing automatically in Windows 95B (OSR2, a later OEM release) and Windows 98/Me/2000/XP, and will report "no conflicts" even though several devices are using the same IRQ. And it's true—there are "no conflicts"—because the devices share it peacefully without any infighting for control. Such is the beauty of PCI. On a non-PnP operating system, you must check the documentation for each device to find out whether it supports IRQ sharing and go through a trial-and-error process to see which PCI devices will share with which others.

Some CMOS setup programs (which I'll talk about later in this chapter in the section "PC Setup Memory: The CMOS Chip") have an option that enables or disables PCI IRQ sharing (sometimes called "steering"). I usually leave this turned on unless I'm experiencing problems with the sharing, because it makes the whole IRQ situation a lot easier to deal with.

For techies only, here's a behind-the-scenes look at how IRQ sharing works. Almost all PCI devices share a single IRQ called INTA#. (There are three other PCI interrupts, INTB# through INTD#, but they are not used except by PCI devices that require multiple IRQs.) However, the PCI interrupts must be mapped by the BIOS to ISA interrupts in an ISA system. And since ISA interrupts aren't sharable, each PCI device must be mapped to a unique ISA interrupt, so you're back where you started from—out of IRQs. When you turn on PCI IRQ sharing in the BIOS, though, it passes the interrupt assignment duty to the operating system, which (if it is capable of it) can map multiple PCI devices to a single ISA IRQ. Windows 95B/98/Me/2000/XP all support PCI IRQ sharing; the original version of Windows 95 and Windows 95A do not.

ROM Addresses and RAM Buffers

In addition to I/O addresses, DMA channels, and IRQ lines, there is a fourth source of potential conflict: ROM addresses. Some adapter boards require some ROM onboard to hold some low-level code; the most common examples are SCSI host adapters, video adapters, and some network cards.

Onboard ROM makes sense on some adapters. For example, the SCSI host adapters that I use the most are from Adaptec, and most of those have ROM on them. A program stored in that ROM causes any computer equipped with the Adaptec adapter to show at startup a message like "Press Ctrl+A to enter SCSI diagnostics." The diagnostics are a very useful set of utilities that you can access even if your hard disk isn't working (which is a good possibility, if you're installing a new SCSI adapter).

Other boards have some RAM onboard to provide memory that is *shared* between the system CPU and the adapter's circuitry. But RAM and ROM can present a configuration problem because, as before, a possibility exists that two different boards may require some software onboard, and if the two boards *both* try to locate their ROM or RAM at the same location in the PC's memory address space, neither one will work.

Some boards let you configure the start address of the ROM/RAM (through DIP switches, jumpers, or software). However, most of the major boards that include ROM/RAM, such as the EGA, VGA, XT-type hard disk controller, and the like, should *not* have their ROM addresses changed (if it's even possible). Too many pieces of software rely on their standard addresses. The boards you'll see that typically have ROM include the following:

- ◆ Video boards, which have ROM addressed at either address C0000 (yes, more hexadecimal; memory addresses are, like I/O addresses, expressed in hex) or E0000. It's usually not a good idea to move these addresses around.

- ◆ High-performance disk interfaces, like some special EIDE host adapters or SCSI host adapters, have ROM on them, but that ROM can be safely moved if the board permits.

- ◆ Token-ring network adapters have some ROM on them; it is moveable.

- ◆ Any kind of LAN board can have ROM on it, if the PC boots from the network and not from its local hard disk. It's unusual, but some companies use this "diskless workstation" approach. Some have RAM as well.

- ◆ Some high-end sound cards may have ROM on them; the ROM contains images of prerecorded sounds, like pianos, violins, or flutes.

- ◆ All PCs have some ROM at the top 64K of the first megabyte, the memory range from F0000 through FFFFF. That ROM is called the BIOS ROM. (BIOS stands for basic input/output system, as you read in Chapter 1, "Five Easy Pieces: PC Hardware in a Nutshell.")

You should be concerned about two things when configuring memory on add-in cards. First is the obvious one: make sure that two different boards don't have memory configured to the same address.

The second thing you have to be concerned about is the effect of adapter memory on your DOS memory manager, if you're using DOS. Memory managers must know exactly which areas of memory are already filled up with adapter RAM or ROM, or the memory manager will overwrite the RAM or ROM, potentially causing lots of system problems.

Most adapter RAM and ROM ranges vary, so I can't document them for you here, but you can see the ranges that don't change in Table 6.6.

TABLE 6.6: COMMON ROM AND RAM BUFFER ADDRESSES

FUNCTION	ADDRESS RANGE (HEX)	ADDRESS LENGTH
XT hard disk controller	C8000–CBFFF	16K
EGA	C0000–C3FFF	16K
VGA	C0000–C7FFF or E0000–E7FFF	32K

Another set of heavy users of onboard RAM is PC Card boards, which brings us to our next topic.

CONFIGURING PC CARD BOARDS

If you' have a laptop, it probably has at least one expansion slot designed to support a credit card–sized adapter card called a *PC Card* or, formerly, a *PCMCIA*. There are PC Card–format modems, both wired and wireless network cards, hard disks, Global Positioning System sensors, memory cards, SCSI adapters, and sound cards, just to name a few. Under some circumstances, PC Cards offer no trouble—but in certain situations you may have to struggle with them a bit.

PC Card Is Often PnP

In theory, PC Card boards are PnP in that they set up their own interrupts, memory, and so on. The idea is that any system using PC Cards should have some software called a *card services manager* that examines the cards in the system and sets their resources appropriately, making sure that no IRQs, I/O addresses, or memory addresses conflict. (DMA is not a problem because PC Cards can't use DMA.)

Of the popular operating systems available, Windows 95/98/Me/2000/XP handle PC Cards the best because they have a built-in card services management program. Windows 3.*x* has no native PC Card support, but some PC Cards come with Windows 3.1 software that will function as a card services manager, achieving essentially the same effect.

Using a PC Card without Card Services

People running DOS on laptops without a card services manager and people running Windows NT 4 or lower on laptops will have a tougher time configuring software to use the PC Cards. Let's see how you configure a PC Card in a system that lacks a card services manager.

First, install the PC Card into the laptop; let's say for example that it's a network card. Next, turn the laptop on and boot up the operating system, whether it's DOS or Windows NT. Then, load the driver for the network card. The driver's installation program will need to configure the driver, and it will ask you about the card—what IRQ is it using, what I/O address, and so on. Here's the hard part: *you have no idea what the answer is*. And the board ain't talking, at least not usually. You see, in the case where a PC Card powers up and there's no card services manager, the PC Card just picks its own resource values. That's the bad news, but it's not terrible news—these boards are usually designed to default to some set of IRQ, I/O address, and so on.

The good news is that because the driver for the PC Card was written by the same folks who made the board, the driver usually *also* defaults to the same set of IRQ, I/O address, and the like as the board. So if you pop a PC Card into a laptop with no other PC Cards, chances are that (1) the PC Card's defaults will work just fine, and (2) when you're installing the driver, you should just take the defaults. The card will then usually work. So even if you're working with a dumb operating system (one that isn't all that bright about PC Cards), a single PC Card in a system will usually work fine. If it doesn't, just be prepared to wait on hold with the PC Card's manufacturer.

Some PC Cards Make Life Easier

Some cards work better than that, however. Given the choice, I buy 3Com's PC Card Ethernet boards when purchasing network cards for my laptop because they come with a traditional software setup program. This program lets me set the PC Card Ethernet board to whatever I/O address and IRQ I want, and the board *stays* at that I/O and IRQ. It's way cool and I wish all PC Card manufacturers did this, because it makes setting up a Windows NT laptop leagues easier.

The 3Com cards aren't perfect, however. Recently I tried to install two 3Com 10/100 Ethernet cards in the same laptop because I wanted to use the laptop as an Internet router (it *can* be done and it actually works quite well, in case you're wondering, but it requires using either the Internet Connection Sharing [ICS] feature of Windows 98/Me/XP or NT Server, or using a third-party router program), but the 3Com setup program was unable to address two cards in the same laptop. This surprised me, because I'd installed multiple 3Com network interface cards (NICs) in a number of desktop systems, so I called 3Com tech support. The fellow on the phone laughed and admitted that no, the setup program couldn't distinguish multiple PC Cards in a single machine, but that they didn't get too many calls for that. I had no choice but to install a 3Com card and a Xircom card in the system. The Xircom brand is a bit more of a pain to install—you can't preset IRQs and such for Windows NT installation—but with the help of Xircom tech support, I got them both working.

Handling Multiple PC Cards

But what about a system with multiple PC Cards? Again, in Windows 95/98/Me/2000/XP you probably won't have a problem—the integrated card services manager handles the conflicts if it can. But in a DOS environment without a card services manager, or in Windows NT 4 and lower, you may see a situation where two PC Cards clobber each other. You can easily test this: try the system with just the first card. If that works, pull out that card and insert just the second card. If *that* works but they don't work together, then they're conflicting. What do you do about this?

Well, if one of the PC Cards is a well-designed one like the 3Com cards I mentioned a couple of paragraphs back, it's simple—just run the lame PC Card all by itself and note which IRQ, I/O, and possibly which memory it uses. Then pull that card out and insert the well-designed one, the one that lets you configure it. Set its resources to give the lame PC Card's desired resources a wide berth, and all will be well. And remember that whenever you configure a card to use particular resources, *write it down*. Put a mailing label on the PC Card and note what I/O, IRQ, and memory you set the card to.

Resolving Installation Conflicts: An Example

Ready for a real-world scenario? A few years ago, I needed to put some Ethernet cards into a half-dozen PCs. Each PC was different and had different add-on boards installed in it.

The first LAN card I installed was in a DOS-based PC with Windows 3.1. The Ethernet board I was installing used everything we've discussed—an I/O address range, a DMA channel, an IRQ channel, and some shared RAM. I left the I/O address at 300 hex, because that wouldn't conflict with the computer into which I was installing the board. The IRQ I chose was IRQ5, avoiding the more commonly used IRQ2. (I avoid IRQ2 because although it *can* be used in some systems, the fact that it cascades to IRQs 8–15 makes me a bit nervous; in the past, using IRQ2 had caused conflicts with Windows.) I set the DMA to channel 1 and put the shared RAM between CC000 and CFFFF, since I knew that it would not then conflict with the hard disk controller ROM between C8000 and CBFFF.

When I plugged the board in, however, it refused to function. A little fiddling around made me realize that the DOS memory manager I was using was placing its memory at the same addresses as the shared memory on my LAN board, which in turn was clobbering the LAN board. I told the memory manager to exclude the range of addresses from CC000 to CFFFF. (Consult your memory manager's documentation to see exactly how to do this.) The board worked fine after that.

I set the second board identically in another DOS/Win3.1 PC with the same memory management software installed, and it refused to work. A quick check of my notebook reminded me that this PC had a sound card that was using IRQ5, which caused the conflict. The LAN board offered only IRQs 2–7, and I didn't want to use any of them—I wanted to avoid 2 if I could, and 3–7 were busy—so I needed an alternative approach. A quick look at the sound card showed that it could support any IRQ up to IRQ10, so I reset the sound card to IRQ10, leaving IRQ5 free for the LAN board. Problem solved.

A third PC was a PnP system running Windows 95. I didn't worry too much about this one, because I figured that when Windows started up, PnP would kick in and reassign the sound card's resources. However, as it happened, this PC had a SCSI hard drive that also wanted to use IRQ5, so when I turned it on, the LAN board and the hard drive battled it out and neither one of them worked at all. I fixed it by removing the LAN board and rebooting, and then entering the SCSI drive's setup program and changing its IRQ assignment. Then I put the LAN board back in and things went smoothly.

I thought the fourth PC might be a challenge because it had all kinds of stuff installed—a sound card, a DVD drive, a CD-RW, a scanner, a printer, an internal modem—the works. A quick check in Windows 98 told me that all the IRQs were taken. So where was the LAN card supposed to go? I took a chance by installing it and booting up the system and, amazingly enough, Windows' PnP feature set it up flawlessly. Because it was a PCI system, several PCI devices were able to share a single IRQ, making room for the new device.

Still another PC was running Windows NT 4. I knew that I couldn't rely on PnP, since NT 4 doesn't support it. I started by checking out the current resource assignments in NT so I could avoid choosing resources for the new LAN board that were already in use. I did pretty well, and the LAN board installed and worked, but the user called me the next day to report that his ISDN terminal adapter was no longer working. Upon examination, I found an I/O address conflict between the two—and found that the terminal adapter had its own setup software that needed to be run to change its resource assignments. Of course, as luck would have it, the user had no idea where that software was, so I downloaded the latest version of it from the manufacturer's Web site. I ran the ISDN terminal adapter's setup program, made a change to its I/O address, and everything worked great.

I don't want to discourage you with these stories. I just want to underscore how important it is to keep documentation of what's installed in your current machines, keep the setup disks handy for every installed device, and be aware of the differences between PnP and non-PnP systems.

Where Do You Find Diagnostic Programs?

In Chapter 5, "Troubleshooting PC Problems," I mentioned the names of several generic diagnostic programs, including the Norton Utilities or Windsor's PC-Technician. You can use those to test a board, such as a motherboard or a memory board. They're perfectly good for that. But don't do what some folks I've seen do. I know of a group who bought a lot of PS/2s. They loaded up the Reference Diskette that came with the PS/2, told the diagnostics to run over and over, and left the machine. Hours later, they came back to see if there were any errors reported on the screen. No errors, so they shipped the machines to users. But the users complained that a lot of the machines had malfunctioning video. It turned out that the VGAs on Model 50s had a higher-than-average failure rate: I myself saw a classroom with 30 Model 50s develop video problems in about 20 percent of the machines. (If you have this problem, you might like to know that it seemed most prevalent when the room was above 75 to 80 degrees F. Maybe you could turn up the air conditioning.) The support staff was puzzled. How did this slip by them? Simple. Video diagnostics often require a user to look them over. If your reds are greens and blues are blacks, the monitor doesn't know. The video board doesn't know. You need an operator to audit the video tests.

Here's a cheap memory test. Build a Microsoft Excel spreadsheet that fills memory. It just consists of a single cell A1 with the value 1, then a cell A2 with the formula A1+1. Copy that cell until you run out of memory. Choose Tools ➤ Options and set Recalculation to Manual. Then write a short macro that loops continuously, recalculating and recalculating again. If you really want to add a level of elegance, calculate the sum of this large column of numbers and check it against the actual value. (The sum of 1, 2, 3, 4… N is equal to $N(N+1)/2$.)

If your board includes its own diagnostic testing programs, you should use them instead of the generic testing software, since they will be more likely to test the board more thoroughly. For example, Iomega supplies an RCDDIAG program that tests the controller. Alternatively, you can test a LAN board by putting a loopback connector of some kind on it to allow it to "hear" what it broadcasts.

NOTE   Windows comes with a System Configuration Utility that can help in disabling conflicting drivers and startup programs. You can run it from within System Information by choosing Tools ➤ System Configuration Utility (Windows 98 and Me) or running the program MSCONFIG from the `C:\Windows\System` *folder.*

Making Plug and Play Work

All of this fiddling-with-jumpers and rooting-around-for-setup-programs gets old quick.

I mean, *really* quick.

In a Perfect World, you'd just insert a board into your system and turn the system on, and the system would configure itself automatically, no muss, fuss, or greasy aftertaste. It would work something like this:

1. On bootup, the BIOS would recognize the board ("This is an Adaptec 2942W SCSI host adapter").

2. The BIOS would then ask the board what IRQs, DMAs, I/O addresses, RAM addresses, and ROM addresses it needs ("It requires an interrupt, a 256-byte block of I/O addresses, and a 16K ROM range").

3. *Then* the BIOS would ask the board what range of IRQs, DMAs, I/O addresses, RAM addresses, and ROM addresses it *can* use ("It can use IRQ 5, 7, 9, 10, 11, or 14, any 256-byte block from address 60K to 64K, and any ROM address from C0000 to E0000").

4. After that, the BIOS would set the resources (IRQ, and so on) so that they don't conflict with anything already in the system.

5. Once the board—and all others—were coexisting nicely, the operating system for the PC would load.

6. Early on, the operating system would note the existence of the new board and say, "Hey, this is an Adaptec 2940W , let's load a driver for it... ah, here it is, in `D:\WinDrivers`... ask the BIOS what IRQs and such it set the board to... configure the driver... done!" And the new board works like a charm.

Sounds cool, doesn't it? I mean, after all, that's what *you've* got to do to make a sound card, a SCSI host adapter, or a LAN adapter card work. Why not let the computer do it? Well, that's the whole idea behind Plug and Play (PnP).

Way back in 1993, Microsoft, Intel, and Compaq proposed a standard called PnP. The idea behind PnP was that board manufacturers would add circuitry to their add-in boards so that the automatic setup and resource query (*resource* here means IRQ, DMA, I/O address, ROM address, or RAM buffer address) capabilities of EISA and Micro Channel would become available to machines with ISA buses. In actuality, no one ever made a PnP system that included EISA, VESA, or MCA to my knowledge; every PnP system I've ever seen used either a hybrid of PCI and ISA or just PCI. Although PC Cards are not part of the PnP specification, most PnP systems can configure them. Laptops using just CardBus, a 32-bit bus, can be PnP.

PnP is a good idea, but it's a bit frustrating that you can't retrofit it on an existing system; it has to be built into a computer when you buy it. Today, fortunately, all new PCs are PnP-compatible, even if the boards you add into them aren't. In fact, in some cases, you can install one or two non-PnP boards, and the computer will build the rest of the system around them (as long as they don't conflict with themselves).

Booting on PnP Systems

Let's examine how PnP works. PnP starts off with a PnP-compatible motherboard. This motherboard has a BIOS that understands PnP and also contains about 16K of flash memory that is a part of the BIOS. Virtually all motherboards built in the past few years are PnP-compliant; I'd hazard a guess that anything since 1995 would be PnP-compatible.

You also must have add-in cards that are PnP-compatible. These cards are configured *every time you boot*, and that configuration is done by a routine called the *Configuration Manager*. The Configuration Manager is usually part of the BIOS. It's possible to build a PnP system that loads its Configuration Manager off a disk, but I don't recommend it, because you end up with an only mildly PnP system. In addition to a PnP motherboard and expansion boards, you need, as I've noted a couple of times already, a PnP-compliant operating system.

In the ideal world (that is, one in which everything is PnP), the system powers up, and the Configuration Manager assumes control. It asks each board what resources it needs and what range of resources it will accept. (For example, a board might say, "I need an IRQ, and I'll take either 2, 3, 4, or 5," in the same way that the Microsoft ISA bus mouse interface does; even though there are other interrupts, its circuitry for some reason will accept an IRQ only in the range of 2 to 5.) The Configuration Manager then assigns resources to the boards, avoiding conflicts.

This means that potentially installing one new PnP card to a PnP system could cause all of the other cards to move their resources around. What does that mean for the network, SCSI, sound card drivers, and so on, that must know which resources those boards use? Well, it implies that device drivers must be a bit smarter than they are now.

For example, any DOS-based client on a Windows NT network has a file called PROTOCOL.INI on its hard disk. In that file are often references such as IRQ=10, IOBASE=300, and so on. That DOS-based client doesn't work unless someone tells it what values to put in PROTOCOL.INI; in contrast, on a PnP system, the network software must take its cues from the Configuration Manager automatically, removing the need for operator intervention. If you venture into the BIOS setup for your computer, you will probably find a setting that is a trick question. It will ask if the operating system is a PnP O/S. The logical answer to this question is to say *Yes* if you are using Windows 95/98/Me/2000/XP. The correct setting is *No*. Why? Setting it to *No* ensures that the Configuration Manager built into the BIOS of the computer handles the assignment of system resources. The role of the PnP O/S is to tweak the resource assignments, not manage them.

Once all boards are taken care of, the system boots in the usual way. The main difference with PnP is that the hardware shuffling of resources (I/O addresses, DMA channels, RAM windows, and the like) happens every time you boot the system, and (one hopes) quickly and invisibly. Sometimes you install a new card and its resources won't be assigned by the BIOS. This results from the BIOS designers trying to please impatient users who want their computers to come up to speed as soon as possible. As a result, the BIOS Configuration Manager may not be aware that a new card was installed. When this happens, check and see if there is a Reset Configuration setting in the BIOS Setup. Changing this setting to *Yes* forces the Configuration Manager to read all of the installed cards the next time the computer is rebooted and to assign resources accordingly. Once this occurs, Reset Configuration returns to its normal and faster setting.

Oh, by the way, can you force a particular board to a particular resource? Yes—that's called *locking* the resource. The Configuration Manager on your system should allow that, or your operating system may; Windows 95/98/Me/2000/XP lets you do it with the Device Manager, which is in Control Panel (Control Panel ➤ System ➤ Device Manager). You can also get to it by right-clicking My Computer and choosing Properties, then clicking the Device Manager tab. In Windows XP, right-click My Computer and choose Manage to open the Computer Management window. Device Manager appears under the System Tools tree.

Be cautious in forcing your system to lock in resources. Today's PnP systems are pretty sophisticated in accomplishing resource management, so when you lock particular resources it may make it more difficult for the Configuration Manager to assign the other resources.

Configuring ATs and Beyond: Software Setup

Answering thousands of service calls that really just stemmed from incorrectly set DIP switches convinced IBM that they needed a computer that was easier to set up.

The main trouble with the XT and PC setup wasn't so much the switches as it was the fact that the PC owner would have to take the top off the computer and pull out some boards in order to get to the switches. So IBM came up with software setup on the first AT, back in 1984.

The AT wasn't totally set up with software; it had one DIP switch to set that configured its video. The rest of its motherboard configuration information was retained in a battery-backed memory. The add-in boards were left to fend for themselves configuration-wise; the bus was ISA and ISA does not support a standard method for doing software setup on a board.

Now, this isn't just an idle history lesson: *virtually every PC since then has used the same basic approach.* Let's see how it works.

PC SETUP MEMORY: THE CMOS CHIP

The nice thing about switches was that they conveyed information—if switch 3 was on, you had a monochrome video board, if switch 3 was off, you had a color video board, that kind of thing. This information was "nonvolatile," meaning that when you turned off the PC, switch 3 stayed where it was so that the PC could read its state the *next* time you turned on the PC.

Software setup wouldn't be as easy, the IBM engineers reasoned, unless they could either (A) put little robotic fingers in the PC's case to flip the switches when the software told them to, or (B) use some kind of memory structure to store the configuration information. Option B sounded like the better idea (I was just kidding about option A), so they decided to stuff the configuration data into a memory chip.

The problem with using a memory chip was that memory chips are volatile (as you recall from Chapter 3, "Inside the PC: Pieces of the Picture"), and as soon as you turn off the computer, the data in the chip evaporates. So the AT engineers put a small low-power memory chip into the AT and attached a battery to that chip to keep it powered when the system was turned off.

Like most memory chips, it was built around the complementary metal oxide semiconductor (CMOS) technology. The chip also contained a crude time and date/clock/calendar circuit. For some reason, the chip got the nickname "the CMOS chip," and that name stuck. It's a silly name on its face because *most* of the chips in modern machines are CMOS chips, but that's just what everybody calls it (and I'm surrendering and calling it that, since that's the term that others use).

The CMOS memory contains 64 bytes—not 64K, 64 *bytes*—of memory, as well as the clock/calendar. To read the data in the CMOS, your PC pushes the value's address—0 through 63—into I/O address 70 hex, and then reads it back in I/O address 71 hex. The PC writes new data by storing the requested address to I/O address 70 hex and then storing the new data to I/O address 71 hex.

The CMOS chip itself is often a Motorola 146818, 24-pin chip. It is volatile, like all semiconductor memory, and so requires a battery to maintain the integrity of its data when the system is turned off. When the battery runs down, the computer starts acting aphasic (look it up, but it means what you expect it to). The most common symptom of a failing battery is the incorrect time and date. Most systems use nonrechargeable lithium batteries (the same kind used in hearing aids) that claim to have lives of 3 to 10 years. Others use rechargeable NiCad batteries. Some systems use a memory and battery all-in-one chip from Dallas Semiconductor. It is distinguished by the alarm clock on its face and contains a battery that Dallas Semiconductor claims is good for 10 years. When you replace it, you also replace its battery.

It's worth mentioning that, as time went on, 64 bytes just weren't enough, so EISA, Micro Channel, and PCI machines usually have a different CMOS memory configuration.

MODIFYING THE SETUP MEMORY: RUNNING SETUP

The most important question in software setup is "How do you do it?" It depends. Since the AT's appearance in 1984, we've seen several approaches to setup programs:

◆ Early machines had a separate setup program on a 5¼-inch floppy disk that you'd run to modify the CMOS chip's memory or to set the time and date.

◆ Micro Channel and EISA systems usually require a setup program on floppy, because the setup program must incorporate information about new boards. Both of these architectures are nearly obsolete, however.

◆ Most 386 machines and above (including today's PCs) have a setup program in their BIOS, activated by pressing a certain key or key combination. Usually these keys must be pressed during startup, but on some older systems you can press them at any time to enter the setup utility.

◆ Pentium and higher PCI-based systems are usually a hybrid of built-in setup programs and PnP setup, wherein a system sets up at least some resources automatically with no operator intervention required.

The following sections outline some of the settings you can control from within the CMOS setup program.

Adjustable Bus Speeds

The standard ISA bus speed is, of course, 8MHz. Some clones allow you to increase the speed on that all the way up to 32MHz. It's a good idea to play with this feature, but do it carefully. I've found that most ISA cards can run just fine all the way up to 12MHz. On the other hand, if you want fast peripherals, you should invest in a machine with a PCI bus and use boards built for that interface. And ideally, your system should have an AGP bus for your video card, which further speeds up that component. Many of today's PCs have an ultra-high internal bus speed such as 66 or 100MHz; some can be adjusted, but most run at a fixed speed.

NOTE   *Turn back to Chapter 3 if you need a refresher on AGP.*

ADJUSTABLE MEMORY SPEEDS

In contrast, here's something I *wouldn't* mess around with. If you have memory that's significantly faster than the stuff that the documentation calls for, then go ahead and play around. But be sure you know how to restore the settings to their default state—or your system may not be able to get far enough into the boot process to even let you restart the setup program.

KEYBOARD SETTINGS

I prefer a machine that does not set the Num Lock by default when powering up. (I'm old and inflexible, and the first PCs left the Num Lock off by default.) Sometimes the BIOS lets you set this.

PASSWORDS

Be careful with these, as well. Many machines, laptops in particular, include power-on passwords as options. If you manage to forget your password, then there's usually no way to get into the machine, short of disconnecting the battery (better hope it's not soldered, like the batteries on most modern machines) and waiting overnight for the power to slowly drain out of the CMOS chip.

POWER MANAGEMENT

As onboard power management becomes chic in PC design, control of that power management often goes into the built-in setup program. You can use this to control when the computer turns itself off to save power and how often it does it. Just like the PnP management we discussed earlier, take the computer manufacturers' advice as to whether you let the O/S or the BIOS control power management. A poor choice in this setting can cause your computer to lock up every time the two sources of power management try to control the power state of the computer.

PCI CONTROL

Many PCI bus machines come with no control and configuration program for the boards in the PCI bus. It's an incredible oversight, but it's the case for hundreds of thousands of machines that use the PCI bus but don't support PnP.

These settings usually control a few things about the bus, but they're a sign of a poorly designed PCI machine. PCI machines should all be PnP-compatible and so should not require settings like PCI IDE interface enable/disable or the like.

Replacing the Configuration Battery

If your AT-type system insists on being set up anew every day, complete with reentering the correct date and time, you probably need a new battery. New batteries can be purchased in the $17–$30 price range. CompUSA and Radio Shack are two good places to find those batteries; so is your local PC hardware store. Alternatively, go to Radio Shack and get their Four AA Battery Holder (89 cents). Put four AA batteries in it and solder the wires from the holder to the AT battery contacts. This works, but it raises the question of where to put the battery holder (the power supply is a good place). If you are still using an AT-type system, this might be a good time to consider upgrading your system, since the batteries might cost more than the fair market price of your system.

NOTE   Just like any other type of battery, the AA batteries that you use in your computer need to be replaced before they get too old, or they can leak. This problem is more common with the cheaper brands.

There are several different kinds of batteries used in PCs. Some of them look like round, flat watch batteries, held in place with metal clips; others are little barrel-shaped contraptions that look like fat resistors. In some systems, the battery is built into the CMOS chip, and the battery and chip must be replaced as a unit. Check the motherboard's documentation to find out what kind you have.

TIP   Make sure you get the right voltage of battery. Your choices will probably be 3.6v, 4.5v, or 6v. Some motherboards allow you to set a jumper to specify what voltage of battery you are using, but it's easier to just replace the battery with an identical one if possible.

When the computer is powered up, it supplies the CMOS chip with the power it requires. Because the CMOS requires so little power to maintain its configuration information, it is possible to remove the battery and replace it without losing the data in the CMOS chip. This is because a small capacitor that is part of the circuit can supply the power needs of the CMOS chip for up to several hours. Still, before you replace the battery, it is a wise precaution to make note of any configuration information that is unique to your computer.

When you replace some types of batteries, you may notice that the battery is connected to the motherboard with two wires, one red and one white. If you don't pay attention when you take the old battery off, you may wonder how the new battery should be connected. In that case, remember RAP: *Red Away from the Power supply.*

Some motherboards have a lithium battery soldered onto the motherboard of the PC. When that battery runs out, you needn't solder a new one in place. Instead, these motherboards have a three-pin Berg connector that fits a standard battery. You usually have to find a jumper on the motherboard that tells the motherboard to stop trying to draw power from the soldered battery and instead pull from a battery attached to the Berg connector. Ensure that you have the polarity correct when installing lithium batteries. Having the polarity reversed can cause the battery to explode—no kidding.

For laptop owners, there is often another type of rechargeable configuration battery, sometimes called a "standby battery." This item is actually designed to hold a charge while you replace the main battery pack; this is in order to preserve any data you have in RAM. It is recharged from your AC adapter, just like your main battery, and since it works only during the few moments when you are in the midst of a battery change, it should always have enough power. In the event that it should fail, however, you will not be able to replace it yourself. This is a "manufacturer-only" replacement item, and you should not try to work on this yourself.

HEY, WAIT A MINUTE, MY PC DOESN'T HAVE A BATTERY!

Some computers do not have a CMOS battery at all. Instead they include a capacitor that gets charged up whenever the computer is plugged in. On such systems, you can leave them unplugged for up to a week without losing CMOS data. After that, they reload CMOS data from a backup on a flash ROM chip on the motherboard, which contains everything the PC needs to know about itself except the current date and time.

Other systems (especially newer, high-end ones) have a CMOS chip with a battery embedded in it. These batteries last 10 years or more, but when they die, the battery and chip must be replaced as a whole. Luckily, such chips are usually socketed, so it's easy to remove them from the motherboard. (Check the PC's manual to locate the chip.) You can order a replacement from the PC manufacturer or the motherboard manufacturer.

Parallel Port Configuration Anomalies

Here's a real PC configuration brainteaser you'll see on older systems. I have a PC with *only one* parallel port, which I configured as LPT2. There *is* no LPT1 in this machine. I boot it up. Once the system is running, what LPT port do I have on my system?

Answer: LPT1.

PCs have a strange feature when it comes to parallel ports. On bootup, the BIOS checks the LPTs. If there's no LPT1, it looks for an LPT2 or LPT3. If you have an LPT2 but no LPT1, it actually converts the LPT2 to an LPT1. This is, of course, a *software* adjustment. I'll repeat: it's flat-out impossible to have an LPT2 without an LPT1. If you *do* install an LPT2 without an LPT1, the LPT2 gets made into an LPT1 on bootup time.

Nice feature. I just wish the documentation had *told* me about it. You see, it was late one night, and—oh, heck, I don't want to even talk about it. Now *you* know.

16-Bit Boards with ROM May Conflict with 8-Bit Boards with ROM

Here's an oddity you may see in older systems with a mix of 8-bit and 16-bit ISA boards.

If you have two boards in your system—one 16-bit, and one 8-bit, both with ROM on them—the 16-bit board may cause the 8-bit board to malfunction.

Why? It has to do with a characteristic of the 16-bit ISA bus. It recognizes that it must talk to some boards that are 8-bit and some that are 16-bit. It doesn't know which are which. So the extended part of the 16-bit slots has three *cheater* lines, lines that are duplicates of three lines on the 8-bit part of the slot. The way the extra lines work is this: every time a memory access is to occur, the CPU sends out a warning message on the three cheater lines, describing roughly where the upcoming memory request will be going. "Roughly" means within 128K of the desired memory address. If a board has memory that is addressed anywhere in that 128K area, it responds with an "Okay, I'm ready" signal. *But* only the 16-bit boards have the cheater lines—so if the upcoming memory access is to/from an 8-bit board, the CPU will receive no response to the warning. In that case, it just conducts 8-bit transfers.

If, on the other hand, the CPU *does* receive a response, it conducts the memory access using 16-bit transfers. To review:

1. The CPU sends out a warning message: "I'm about to do a memory access. It will be some-where in the following 128K memory area...."

2. This message is audible only to 16-bit boards.

3. If a 16-bit board contains any memory—RAM or ROM—in that 128K address range, it responds, "*I've* got some memory in that range—do the memory access as 16-bit transfers." Any other 16-bit boards that happen to have memory in that range reply likewise.

4. On the other hand, 8-bit boards are deaf to the warning and so make no response, even if they do have memory in that 128K range.

5. If the CPU hears a 16-bit response, it conducts the memory access 16 bits at a time. Other-wise, it just transfers the data 8 bits at a time.

Where's the problem? What if there are *multiple* boards with memory in a given range? Well, if they're all 16-bit boards, that's no sweat. But what if, within a given 128K memory range, there were 8-bit *and* 16-bit boards? *Then* every time the CPU wanted to access the 8-bit board, it would send out a warning message that the 8-bit board, logically, would not hear or respond to—*but the 16-bit boards would!* Result: the CPU would send 16-bit data blocks to a board that could accept only 8-bit blocks—an apparent malfunction.

This sounds like a dire scenario, but it really only pops up in one area: the ROM reserve. The addresses from 768K to 896K are, you may recall, where the ROM is addressed: a 128K-sized memory area, notice. Every ROM access causes the CPU to issue a warning to the entire ROM area. If there are 8-bit boards and 16-bit boards with ROM on them, the 16-bit boards may respond to the CPU's attempts to access the ROMs on the 8-bit boards. This would result in the CPU again attempting 16-bit transfers to/from an 8-bit board. So, if adding a 16-bit board kills an existing 8-bit board, that may be a reason.

BOARDS THAT CONFLICT WITH INTEGRATED FEATURES

Another problem that used to plague technical support centers occurred when a customer would upgrade the sound or video card on a computer that had that feature integrated into the system. On the particular computer I was working on, this problem would occur when the customer went into the BIOS setup program and selected the Restore Default Setting. Unfortunately, the default setting reenabled the integrated audio features that were disabled by the company that added the new sound board as part of a promotional package upgrade. The result was that upon power-up, the system would lock up due to numerous conflicts. In this case, the lockup occurred before the computer reached the BIOS setup. The only solution was to remove the add-on board and then, when the system powered up, return to BIOS setup and disable the integrated features. After that, the sound card could be reinstalled.

Well, someday you'll just buy a board, plug it into a system, and you *will* be able to "play" with it instantly. That day is not here yet for those of us with older computers. But for now, master the concepts in this chapter and you'll be an expert installer.

Troubleshooting Tips

Here is a summary of some of the problems you might have when installing a circuit board, along with some possible solutions:

- ◆ If an old device stops working when you install a new one, there is probably a resource conflict. Reassign resources for one of the devices.

- ◆ Plug and Play devices can usually change resources through software, such as through the Windows 95/98/Me/2000/XP Device Manager. Go there first to work on resource conflict issues.

- ◆ IRQ conflicts are the most common resource problem, but they're not the only kind. Check also for I/O addresses, DMA channels, ROM addresses, and RAM buffers.

- ◆ If you run out of IRQs, it may be possible to enable IRQ-sharing through the BIOS in a PCI system. You can also disable one or both internal COM or LPT ports through your BIOS, freeing up their IRQs.

- ◆ On all except XT systems, you should avoid assigning IRQ2 to anything, because that's the IRQ used to cascade to IRQs 8–15.

- ◆ IRQ9 connects to IRQ2, so if you have a choice, avoid assigning IRQ9 to a device.

- ◆ If you are using PC Cards (formerly PCMCIA), Windows 95/98/Me/2000/XP has a built-in card services manager program to handle them. If you are using some other operating system, you should install a card services manager program if possible.

◆ If your PC forgets the date and time each time you turn it off, it may need its configuration battery replaced. Take the old one to a computer store to get an identical replacement if possible.

◆ On some systems, the old battery is soldered into place. You may be able to set a jumper on the motherboard to use an external battery instead.

◆ Be sure to get the right voltage for your replacement battery. Some motherboards allow you to select the battery voltage with jumpers; check the PC's documentation.

Now you know how to install a circuit board. But what if you just want to repair an existing one? That's what we'll cover in the next chapter.

Chapter 7

Repairs with Circuit Boards and Chips

◆ QuickSteps: Diagnosing and Solving
  Circuit Board Problems   285

◆ Finding the Problem Board   287

◆ When to Fix, When to Replace   294

◆ The PC Boot Process   295

◆ How to Find and Replace Bad Chips   302

◆ Troubleshooting Tips   307

Introduction

IF THE PROBLEM ISN'T software, if everything's plugged in, there are no resource conflicts, and it isn't something obvious like a burnt-out motor, a broken wire, a gummed-up printer, or an imploded display, then it's probably a defective circuit board. Step 1 is to identify the faulty part. I'll talk about diagnostic approaches in this chapter (they don't cost anything but time). Step 2 is repair. There are two levels of repair here: board level and chip level.

The more important as well as the more difficult of these operations is the first, *identification*. How do you know which board is bad? There are several approaches we'll examine here. Next, should you fix or replace the bad board? You'll see the pros and cons. Further along, as some repairs can involve chip replacements, we'll examine diagnosing and repairing memory problems—the chips you're most likely to install and replace.

QuickSteps

Diagnosing and Solving Circuit Board Problems

This section provides the key steps for figuring out what's wrong with your circuit board. For detailed information, refer to the chapter itself.

BE PREPARED

Before you start, there are some things you'll need to perform the operation:

- Nonmagnetic Phillips screwdriver
- Manual that came with the board (for checking resource assignments)
- Container to hold removed screws
- (Optional) A POST (Power-On Self Test) board, which reports a code indicating at what point in the boot process a problem occurs
- (Optional) A third-party utility program for troubleshooting hardware

Also, before you open up the PC and remove/add boards, make sure that:

- You are wearing an antistatic wrist strap.
- The PC is turned off and unplugged.

1. Before assuming you have a bad board, check for the following:
   - Conflicts between devices—see Chapter 6, "Installing New Circuit Boards (Without Creating New Problems)"
   - Software conflicts or faulty software installations
   - Hardware incompatibilities with certain programs

2. If the PC won't boot, and you have an extra identical PC, try swapping out components until you find the bad one.

   or

   If the PC won't boot and you only have the one machine, disconnect everything except the motherboard, power supply, and speaker. If the fan powers up and you hear beeps, turn it off and add a video card. Keep adding items until the machine fails.

Tools that may help in your diagnosis include:

◆ A POST (Power-On Self Test) board, which reports a code indicating at what point in the boot process a problem occurs. These dedicated pieces of test equipment are becoming rarer every year.

◆ A third-party utility program for troubleshooting hardware—like Norton Utilities.

◆ Pressing F8 while booting a Windows PC and choosing Step by Step Configuration from the Startup menu so that you can see at what point in the boot process the PC locks up.

3. Once you've found the errant item, do one of the following:

◆ Replace it with a new one (usually the best bet) or attempt to fix the board (not usually cost-effective, and sometimes not even possible).

◆ If the bad part is integrated on the motherboard, try to disable it in BIOS and add a board that takes over that function.

◆ If you can isolate the problem to a single chip on a board, you may be able to replace it. Chips in sockets are much easier to replace than those soldered into place. Don't spend more time diagnosing and replacing a chip than is worthwhile given the cost of a new board, however.

How Do You Find the Bad Board?

First, let's hunker down to the tough part—figuring out which board is the problem child.

To begin with, make *sure* you've checked the troubleshooting steps discussed in Chapter 5, "Troubleshooting PC Problems." You *know* by now that a switched outlet (or one with a tripped circuit breaker) isn't the culprit. You're not ripping the machine apart to figure out why it won't boot when the last thing you did was install a new expansion board (and the machine hasn't worked since you put the board in), without first removing the new board to see if the problem goes away.

Again, just be lazy and follow the beaten path. Don't get original. Make sure you've followed the seven steps. Also, make sure you have ruled out resource conflicts as the source of the problem. Turn back to Chapter 6 if you need help with this. Remember, if the PC worked fine before you installed some new component, the problem is probably a resource conflict between something old and something new.

Assuming the machine *does* boot, you can use the machine to help diagnose its own problems. Run the diagnostics to find out if it's the keyboard or video, and so on. That'll give you an indication of what's wrong.

Suppose the problem is clearly video. What now? Again, be lazy. Before you "remove the top and begin to swap," check the easy stuff. Swap the monitor first, before the video board.

Be even lazier—is the problem specific to something like a time of day, or, more likely, a piece of software? If the video works well enough to boot the system and runs some applications but dies when you're running a particular program (games are notorious in this regard), the problem is likely software, not hardware. This may mean any of the following:

◆ You've installed the program incorrectly (easy to do).

or

◆ There's a bug in the program's code that talks to your video board.

or

◆ Your video card or its software driver is not compatible with the program.

In this situation, if you have a second, identical computer, I'd take an exact same copy of the program and install it there. But in order to find a problem like this, it's important that the second computer be identical, right down to the version of the operating system, add-in boards, and so on. If the problem shows up on the second machine, common sense tells you that it's a software problem with the program or an installation problem or that the brand of video board that both machines have is not 100 percent compatible with the program.

If it's a compatibility problem, try updating the video driver, which will be available from the manufacturer's Web page. If updating the video driver doesn't help, try using a different video card. (In fact, if you have a lot of patience, you might even visit the Web site of the vendor who makes the program that is giving you the problem to see if they have a list of which video cards work and which don't.) If it's a problem with installation, try rereading the installation instructions. Maybe you made a wrong choice when you were installing the software. (Some programs require you to turn off your virus protection before installing, for example.) If you can't duplicate the problem by reinstalling the software, return to the company's Web site. Most companies have troubleshooting page(s) that list dozens or even hundreds of things that can go wrong and are easily corrected—and all of the instructions are usually right there.

If the machine doesn't boot at all, consult the next section.

Night of the Living Data: Making a Dead Machine "Undead"

Suppose the computer is completely unresponsive. You can't run the diagnostics because the machine won't talk at all. Here are two approaches to bringing your machine back from the dead, along with a few other possibilities and solutions.

IDENTIFYING THE PROBLEM BOARD I: TWO MACHINES

First of all, assume that there is only one problem. Ideally, you have two machines, one sick and one well. A simple strategy here is to swap boards one by one. Each time you swap a board, turn on *both machines* and note which machines are currently well. Ideally, you would like to induce the problem from the originally sick PC to the originally well PC.

By the way, did you check the old "intensity turned down on the monitor" trick? I'll turn down the intensity on my monitor for some reason, leave the machine, come back to the machine after a while (forgetting I've turned down the intensity), and panic, thinking that (at best) I've got a bad monitor.

Ghost in the Machine (Contagious Components)

Be careful here, however. Sometimes you end up with *two* sick machines. Why? I've seen components that, being damaged, damage other components. Suppose you've got a dead system, and you've stripped the system to the motherboard and power supply. You try to ascertain what's causing your problems, so you swap motherboards. Still no luck. So you try swapping power supplies. *Still* no response. What's happening?

You have a "demon" in the power supply: not only is it not working, but it also destroys motherboards. Originally it "ate" motherboard number one, and then you fed it another one. I've seen this in two situations: bad power supplies damaging motherboards and bad keyboard interfaces on motherboards damaging keyboards.

The moral is this:

1. Swap the power supply before the motherboard.

2. Before swapping the keyboard, test the keyboard interface with a voltmeter to make sure the keyboard interface on the PC is not the problem, as described in Chapter 23, "Keyboards and Mice."

IDENTIFYING THE PROBLEM BOARD II: JUST ONE MACHINE

If all you've got is one machine, here's a nice, minimalist approach. Some people call it the *min/max technique* (short for minimum/maximum).

Start with a machine that won't boot up at all and assume that there's only one thing wrong with it. Break it down to the bare essentials, then add pieces until the machine refuses to boot. *Once the machine refuses to boot, you'll know that the last item that you added is the trouble board.*

Start off by removing everything but the following:

- Power supply
- Motherboard
- Speaker

Turn it on. You should observe several things:

- The fan on the power supply should start right up. If it doesn't, either the power supply isn't getting power, or the fan's burned out. If the fan is burned out, and it *has been* burned out, then the problem's easy—you cooked your PC the last time you used it.

NOTE *There is one other reason that the fan might not start up. The power supply's pretty smart and can sense short circuits on the motherboard. If it senses such a short, it will shut down and refuse to do anything until the short's resolved.*

TIP *Here is a quick way to verify if a short in the motherboard is keeping the power supply from operating. With the computer shut off, unplug the power supply from the motherboard and then turn the computer back on. If the fan operates when disconnected from the motherboard, it is a good sign that the motherboard is destined for the motherboard graveyard.*

- The power supply might also produce a "click" on the speaker (you've probably never noticed it, but it happens each time you turn most PCs on). Another aspect of the "intelligent" power supply is that once it feels that it is up to the task of getting to work, it sends a signal to the motherboard that resets the system. The result might be a faint click. Once you hear that, you know that the power supply believes itself to be functional.

- Assuming that the fan starts and the power supply clicks, you'll probably get one long and two shorts beep out of the speaker—the motherboard's way of saying, "I can't find the video card." You may hear a different beep combination—different BIOS configurations respond differently to the "no video" condition.

If the three things outlined here have happened, congratulations—the machine booted. (It didn't do that before, remember?) If it didn't, there are only three possible culprits: the motherboard, power supply, or speaker. It's child's play now to figure out which is the offending component: just swap the speaker, power supply, and/or motherboard. Remember what I said before about swapping the power supply first, in case it's got a demon. Remember that in the PC repair business *the cheapest and most effective piece of test equipment is a spare part.* At this point, it's a quick swap.

Assuming that the machine booted, the next step is to add the video card. Try to boot the machine. Again, if it doesn't boot, try another video card. If it boots, you'll get error messages complaining about the lack of keyboard and drives—errors 301, 601, and 1701 on an older IBM or Compaq machine, and messages in English on pretty much any current machine. Keep adding boards until the machine fails.

When you assemble (or reassemble) your computer and apply power, sometimes the system will respond with a series of beeps. (Be sure to attach the system speaker so you can hear them.) Depending upon the system, the beeps can mean a number of different things. For example, usually a single short beep or a couple of short beeps will mean "everything's okay." On the other hand, if you get a repeating pattern of not-so-short beeps, the computer is probably trying to tell you something.

Phoenix and AMI are the two primary BIOS manufacturers in the computer industry. The beep codes for the AMI BIOS listed in Table 7.1 give you an idea of the wealth of information that can be conveyed by a series of beeps. These beep codes are not international standards, and you should check with the documentation that came with the computer to get an accurate interpretation of the beeps made by your computer.

TABLE 7.1: AMI BIOS BEEP CODES

BEEP CODE	MEANING
1 beep	Refresh failure
2 beeps	Parity error
3 beeps	Base 64K memory failure
4 beeps	Timer not operational
5 beeps	Processor error
6 beeps	8042—gate A20 failure
7 beeps	Processor exception interrupt error
8 beeps	Display memory read/write failure
9 beeps	ROM checksum error
10 beeps	CMOS shutdown register read/write error
11 beeps	Cache memory bad

Table 7.2 lists the Phoenix beep codes and their meanings. Again, even Phoenix changes its beep codes to meet specific testing requirements of computer manufacturers; check the documentation for your individual machine to ensure you are getting the correct beep definition. You will notice that the Phoenix error codes are a little different from AMI, in that the beeps occur in groups of three with pauses between the groups. So, for example, the first code would sound like this: BEEP (pause) BEEP (pause) BEEP-BEEP-BEEP (long pause), and then the pattern would repeat.

TABLE 7.2: PHOENIX BIOS BEEP CODES

BEEP CODE	MEANING
1-1-3	CMOS write/read failure
1-1-4	ROM BIOS checksum failure
1-2-1	Programmable interval timer failure
1-2-2	DMA initialization failure
1-2-3	DMA page register write/read failure

Continued on next page

TABLE 7.2: PHOENIX BIOS BEEP CODES *(continued)*

BEEP CODE	MEANING
1-3-1	RAM refresh verification failure
1-3-3	First 64K RAM chip or data line failure, multibit
1-3-4	First 64K RAM odd/even logic failure
1-4-1	Address line failure first 64K RAM
1-4-2	Parity failure first 64K RAM
2-1-1	Bit 0 first 64K RAM failure
2-1-2	Bit 1 first 64K RAM failure
2-1-3	Bit 2 first 64K RAM failure
2-1-4	Bit 3 first 64K RAM failure
2-2-1	Bit 4 first 64K RAM failure
2-2-2	Bit 5 first 64K RAM failure
2-2-3	Bit 6 first 64K RAM failure
2-2-4	Bit 7 first 64K RAM failure
2-3-1	Bit 8 first 64K RAM failure
2-3-2	Bit 9 first 64K RAM failure
2-3-3	Bit 10 first 64K RAM failure
2-3-4	Bit 11 first 64K RAM failure
2-4-1	Bit 12 first 64K RAM failure
2-4-2	Bit 13 first 64K RAM failure
2-4-3	Bit 14 first 64K RAM failure
2-4-4	Bit 15 first 64K RAM failure
3-1-1	Slave DMA register failure
3-1-2	Master DMA register failure
3-1-3	Master interrupt mask register failure
3-1-4	Slave interrupt mask register failure
3-2-4	Keyboard controller test failure
3-3-4	Screen initialization failure
3-4-1	Screen retrace test failure

Continued on next page

TABLE 7.2: PHOENIX BIOS BEEP CODES *(continued)*

BEEP CODE	MEANING
3-4-2	Search for video ROM in progress
4-2-1	Timer tick interrupt test in progress or failure
4-2-2	Shutdown test in progress or failure
4-2-3	Gate A20 failure
4-2-4	Unexpected interrupt in protected mode
4-3-1	RAM test in progress or address failure
4-3-3	Interval timer channel 2 test or failure
4-3-4	Time-of-day clock test or failure
4-4-1	Serial port test or failure
4-4-2	Parallel port test or failure
4-4-3	Math coprocessor test or failure

Note that this isn't gospel—your machine, depending on the manufacturer, may do something different from these expected outcomes. *Try it* sometime on your functioning PC. Note the outcomes. Do it *before* your computer breaks down, so you'll have a reference.

TIP   Again, I must stress this strongly: do this on a healthy PC so you can see what your healthy machine looks like at various stages of reassembly. If you don't know what healthy looks like, you can't recognize disease.

Now, you may get down to the last board, the machine may be booting fine, and you insert that last board, thinking, "Aha! Gotcha. Now to prove it…" But then the machine boots fine. (Grrrr…) Why? One of the following may be true:

+ It just wanted some attention.

+ It fails when boards are hot, and the disassembly and reassembly cooled it to the point that it works.

+ You didn't do the greatest job the first time you took it apart, cleaned it, and put it back together.

What Makes Boards Fail?

If you're reading this, you may already have a dead board. I've suggested that you just replace it, but in case you're interested, here's what generally zaps boards.

Most component problems boil down to either environmental trouble, damage due to mishandling, or faulty manufacturing. The most common ailments (and their antidotes) are the following:

+ Socketed chips can creep out of their sockets due to expansion and contraction. (Push them back in.)

◆ Bad solder joints can disconnect or cause short circuits. (Replace, or you can try resoldering if you feel up to it.)

◆ Weak components can fail under heat. (Replace them, if possible.) By the way, one easy way to find a component that is failing under heat is to put a handful of cotton swabs in the freezer for an hour (keep them dry). Then put the tip of a swab on the suspected component(s). If they come back to life, you've found your culprit.

◆ PC board traces can be scratched. This is something you can usually see if you look carefully (or use a magnifying glass).

◆ Dirt and dust can build up heat. (See Chapter 4, "Avoiding Service: Preventive Maintenance.")

◆ Edge connectors or chip pins can corrode. (Clean off corrosion with a pencil eraser.)

◆ Electromagnetic interference from other devices can cause impairment. (Keep unshielded devices such as speakers well away from PC components.)

Other Problems and Solutions

The remaining chapters in this book cover peripherals in depth, but here are some ideas for solving some kinds of problems, along with pointers to other chapters for more information.

HARD DISK PROBLEMS

If you seem to have a hard disk problem, look at the extensive discussions of drive recovery in the hard disk chapters (Chapters 10 through 14).

KEYBOARD PROBLEMS

Keyboard problems are covered in detail in Chapter 23, "Keyboards and Mice," but here are a few possibilities:

◆ The system board may be at fault. Test the keyboard test points (see Chapter 23 for more information).

◆ Is the keyboard plugged in securely? On some machines you need to push firmly to seat the keyboard plug in the socket. Never, ever remove a keyboard plug from, or insert a keyboard plug into, a computer that is energized. On older systems, this act is almost guaranteed to destroy components on the motherboard.

◆ Is it a PS/2 keyboard plugged into the PS/2 mouse port?

◆ Are you leaning on the spacebar (or any other key) accidentally, or is anything resting on a key?

◆ Are any keys stuck?

MANY BEEPS WHEN BOOTING, NO VIDEO

If you boot your PC and get one long beep and two short beeps and then the drive A light goes on but there's no display, the problem is most likely the display board. Assuming you have a bootable floppy in drive A, if the drive A light comes on, the system is responding—you just can't see it on the display. Swap the video board. Take a look at Chapter 24, "Video Adapters and Displays."

DRIVE A LIGHT STAYS ON

You try to access drive A, and the floppy light comes on and stays on. You probably put the drive cable on backward. Check Chapter 17, "Understanding, Installing, and Repairing Floppy Drives." Ditto if the drive A light comes on immediately when you start the PC, and it stays on.

There's another possible reason—are you loading a program from a floppy? The problem could be insufficient memory to run your application. Try your backup disk also.

PARITY CHECK ERROR (MEMORY ERROR)

See the section "Memory Tests" in Chapter 8, "Semiconductor Memory." Note that not all memory errors are caused by bad memory; see also the section "Causes of False Memory Errors" in that same chapter.

Fix or Replace Boards?

Assuming (as we'll discuss presently) that you can find the bad board, do you just replace it, or do you try to fix it? Sure, it's macho to get out the soldering iron and fix an errant board. But, in general, you won't find it cost-effective to repair a circuit board. This is basically because (1) the inexpensive boards are far cheaper to replace than to repair, and (2) the more expensive boards require even more expensive equipment to repair.

Inexpensive boards, such as one of those ubiquitous video or sound cards, can be had for a reasonable price. Chips on these boards are primarily soldered, not socketed, and so can only be fixed by someone trained to solder chips without destroying them. Add the hourly cost of this person to the cost of replacement chips, and it soon adds up to an amount in excess of the cost of a new $15 board. In addition, more and more boards are four-layer boards, which are tough to solder correctly. *Four-layer* means the board has not only printed circuit traces on the top and bottom, but two layers in the middle! Even if it is a simple two-layer board, don't forget that time is wasted inserting the board and powering up the computer after each chip replacement.

Maintenance Considerations for Integrated Motherboards

These days, most motherboards are of the all-in-one variety. The disk controllers, parallel and serial ports, mouse, and keyboard controllers all exist on proprietary chips that are mounted directly on the motherboard. Some of them even have built-in video and sound support. Arggh! Worst-case scenario for troubleshooting! If one of the onboard controllers fails, you may have to replace the whole motherboard!

But it's not *all* bad news. Now there are fewer boards to worry about and fewer DIP switches to fuss with. Also, reducing the chip count should produce a more reliable machine overall, and indeed it often does. But it can limit PC troubleshooting to an all-or-nothing matter because there's just one board in the system, and, as I've already said, it's just not reasonable to fix those kinds of surface mount components.

TIP   *What can you do if one of the onboard subsystems fails? In many instances, the BIOS on newer boards gives you the option of disabling one or more of the onboard circuits. So if, for example, your system board's IDE controller wanders off to the happy hunting grounds, you may be able to turn off the onboard circuitry and simply install a new IDE controller card in one of the available slots on your motherboard. Then all you have to do is move the data cable(s) (the flat, ribbon cables) to the new IDE card, and you're back in business.*

Understanding the PC Boot Process

Part of bringing a dead machine back to life is understanding how PCs get started in the first place. In this section, you'll learn in great detail what steps a PC goes through to boot, from the time you flip the power switch to the time that the operating system loads. Basically, three things affect whether or not a PC will boot:

1. The hardware must work.

2. The processor must start up and run a program in the BIOS called the Power-On Self Test (POST). (I mentioned BIOS in Chapter 6, and I'll cover it more thoroughly shortly.)

3. The BIOS must load the operating system from the active partition of the boot drive.

Let's start with a quick overview, and then we'll look at each step of the booting process in greater detail.

First, the system needs power from the wall (at least until solar-powered PCs appear) or a battery (in the case of a laptop), and the power supply had better be able to use it; a faulty power supply means a useless PC.

Second, at least a few pieces of the motherboard itself must work. In particular, the CPU, the system's cache RAM, the clock circuit, and the bottom 64K or so of system RAM must be functional, or you won't get anything on the screen at all.

Then, assuming that the basic hardware can function, you'll recall that each PC has a set of software built into a ROM, called the *basic input/output system*, or *BIOS*. That BIOS is a collection of important programs—programs that control the video board, the disk controller, the keyboard, and the system clock, to name a few—but perhaps the most important of those programs is the one that starts up the PC. That program determines what hardware is in the system, does a basic checkout of that hardware, and senses the presence of BIOS-like programs associated with expansion boards in the PC. If those programs exist on the expansion boards, the BIOS will yield control to them so that *they* can do the initialization.

Once the BIOS startup and checks work out all right, the BIOS then attempts to load the system software from the floppy, hard drive, or CD-ROM. Once the operating system gets loaded into the computer's RAM, the BIOS passes control to the operating system, and the computer is ready to use.

That's the overview; now let's look at the details.

Step One: PC Power

The computer first requires power. I'll handle that in greater detail in Chapter 9, "Power Supplies and Power Protection," so I won't elaborate on the point here. But remember: the power supply in the PC can be the culprit, rather than the power coming from the wall.

Step Two: Check the Hardware

Once your system is getting power, there's got to be some functioning computing hardware to use that power. The familiarity of computers and CPUs sometimes makes us forget exactly how many microscopic components have to work together in order for the PC to get up and running… but the PC doesn't forget. What I mean by that is that the BIOS software's first job is to look at what hardware is in your system and to check that it works.

THE ROM AND BOOTSTRAPPING

Why do we need BIOS? It has to do with how CPUs work. When a CPU powers up, it doesn't know how to communicate with anything—the keyboard, display, disk drives, you name it. Before it can communicate with, say, a hard disk, a CPU needs a program in memory that tells it *how* to communicate with a hard disk. Virtually all PC programs must be read from disk before the PC can run them. This kind of leads to a chicken-and-egg problem: the CPU needs a disk-reading program before it can read anything from disk, but it loads its programs from disk. From where, then, does the CPU read that first disk-reading program at the start of the day? It might seem like a good idea to just leave that program in memory in the first place, and that's the idea with ROM (read-only memory). Normal RAM chips are volatile, meaning they lose their contents when you shut down power on a PC; ROM does not forget.

One of ROM's most important jobs is to store low-level programs that control disks, keyboards, and the like. These programs are used not only at startup, but also throughout the day. The other part of the BIOS is the part that's used only when you first power up the computer, as seen in Figure 7.1.

All Intel chips have one feature in common: when they power up, they immediately start executing instructions located at an address 16 bytes below the 1024K level or, more specifically, at address FFFF:0000. That's why the main system BIOS chip gets a location up in the range of 960K through 1024K—so it can fill the need of the PC's CPU to have instructions to execute when it powers up. Take a look at Figure 7.2, which illustrates this concept.

FIGURE 7.1

Step 1 of the boot process

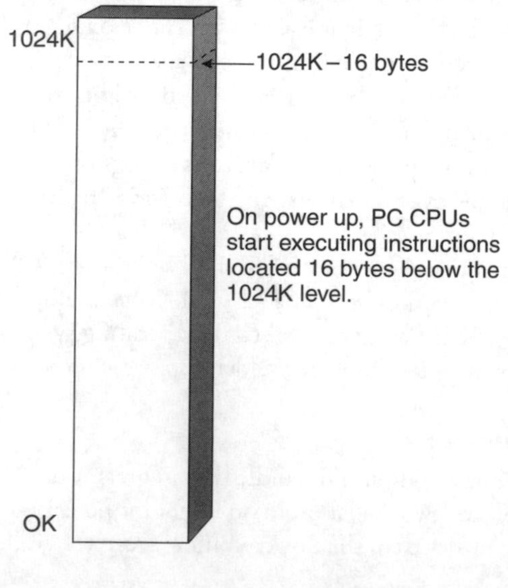

1024K

1024K – 16 bytes

On power up, PC CPUs start executing instructions located 16 bytes below the 1024K level.

OK

FIGURE 7.2

Location of BIOS in memory

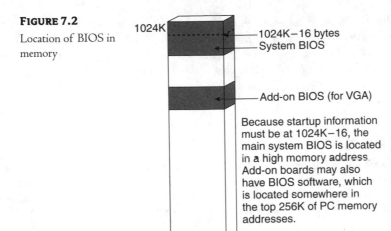

The BIOS's initial main job is to *inventory* and *initialize*: to figure out what's in your PC and then get it ready to do some work, testing it in the process. Now, this gets a little involved, so let's look at how BIOS does this in parts.

There are five steps to the BIOS initialization process:

1. Test some low memory.

2. Scan for other BIOS software.

3. Yield to other BIOS software.

4. Inventory the system.

5. Test the system.

Test Low Memory

In order for the BIOS to function, it needs some RAM to work with. So for most BIOS software, one of the first things done is to test the bottom part of the system's RAM. Now, if that test crashes, then most BIOS software can't recover. That leads to the following observation...

One major reason for a dead PC is that the lowest bank of RAM has failed. Therefore, one troubleshooting step is to replace the first bank of RAM.

NOTE *Replacing the first bank of RAM may not be possible on older machines because some motherboards have their first bank of memory soldered in place. (Thankfully, this is very rarely the case anymore except in a few proprietary systems.)*

Scan for Other BIOS Software

The BIOS in your PC can't support every possible piece of hardware—such as LAN boards, unusual video boards, you name it—so the important functions of inventory and initialization have to go somewhere else. That is why many add-on boards have some ROM on them, as you may have noticed when installing boards. What you may not know is that those ROM chips contain some initialization code for those boards. For example, a hard disk controller ROM might do a quick read of the hard disk—kind of an "Are you there?" test. A video board ROM might test the memory on the video board. A LAN board ROM might broadcast its network address over the LAN, testing that it has a unique network address.

ABOUT BIOS SIGNATURES

Add-on ROM chips are supposed to be easy for the main BIOS to find and should contain three signature bytes. The first bytes are hex 55, then comes AA, and then a number indicating how long the BIOS will be. That number is the length of the BIOS divided by 512. If you want to see this for yourself, try this little exercise, which shows you the BIOS signature on a video card. (This may not work in Windows NT/2000/XP systems.)

1. From the DOS command line, type **debug** and press Enter. You will see the prompt for DEBUG (-).

2. Your VGA ROM is either at hexadecimal address C000:0 or E000:0. To see it, type **d C000:0 L 3** and press Enter. If that doesn't yield a 55 AA *xx* code, try typing **d E000:0 L 3**.

The main system BIOS allows the add-on boards to do *their* inventory and initialization first. Now, before that can happen, the main system BIOS must *find* the other BIOS software. It does that by examining memory in the ROM area—the addresses between 768K and 960K. Once it finds other BIOS software, it can go to the next step.

Yield to Other BIOS Software

Once it has found a BIOS on the add-on board, the main system BIOS passes control to that BIOS so that it can do whatever inventory and initialization the add-on BIOS requires.

The main system BIOS allows every add-on card's BIOS to initialize itself before doing its own inventory and initialization. Notice what that means: the software contained in the ROM on an add-on board gets to run *before* the system BIOS, and it also runs before your operating system gets loaded—we haven't gotten near to loading the operating system yet. For an example, consider a VGA board. As you saw in the exercise above, it's got a BIOS chip on it, one that contains a setup routine. That setup routine usually announces that the board is up and ready by putting a copyright notice on the screen. That copyright notice is probably the first thing you see when you turn on your PC.

When your PC is booting, the VGA message appears *before* the memory test occurs and before the PC checks for the drives. Again, the point here is that this VGA ROM assumed total control of the system fairly early in the boot process, as will each ROM that's on an add-on board in turn. If anything goes wrong with a program in one of those ROM chips—and such things *do* happen—then a PC that functions properly before adding in the board will refuse to boot after that board has been installed. I'll come back to that notion in a minute, but let's finish up with the last two steps of this BIOS initialization.

Inventory and Test the System

Once all of the add-on ROM chips have gotten their time and, *assuming that their programs ran properly and returned control to the main system BIOS,* the main system BIOS will inventory the items that it will control, items that vary from system to system. At a minimum, one of the items that the system BIOS must inventory and initialize is the system memory.

What does "inventory and initialize" mean here? You've seen at least one example of it a million times—the memory test. Ever notice the quick flash of the drive lights on the floppy and hard disk drives? That's the "inventorying" of the storage devices.

HARD DISK TIME-OUTS

Now let's put this information to use. Ever seen a computer do the memory test, then seem to lock up and not boot? The problem may be the disk drive. The simple "Are you there?" test that the main system BIOS does every time you turn on the computer involves a quick disk read. But if the disk drive doesn't respond immediately, the BIOS doesn't give up—it waits, hoping that the drive will respond. The amount of time that it will wait is called the *time-out period.* I've seen more than one system BIOS with a time-out period of four minutes. That means that if the system has a bad hard drive, it could wait *four minutes* before reporting failure! The trouble is, most people aren't patient enough to wait four minutes—they just see the fact that their computer isn't doing anything. The logical verdict is that the computer is dead, and it's time for a new PC. So be *patient* when your computer doesn't respond on bootup; give it a few minutes, literally, to report a disk drive time-out.

If the hard disk does time out and report an error, the first thing to check is the cabling connections. Is the ribbon cable firmly plugged into the drive and into the motherboard's EIDE connector? Is it plugged in with the red stripe on the cable to pin 1?

NOTE   *You'll learn more about EIDE drive troubleshooting in Chapter 11, "Installing an IDE Hard Drive."*

INVENTORY LOCKUPS

Another manifestation of BIOS initialization problems that makes your PC look dead, is, as I've mentioned, the "inventory and initialize" function of add-on BIOS software. I once installed a SCSI host adapter in a computer and powered up the computer to test the system, which consisted of a matching controller board and drive. I turned the system on and it did almost nothing: the fan whirred, but that's it—nothing on the screen. This, of course, panicked me, as the system that I tried the board in was a $5000 high-powered workstation that I was trying to make even faster: the client wouldn't be very happy if I smoked her computer. So I tried removing the new host adapter and the system booted up just fine. Restored the board, and the system wouldn't boot. The problem was that the SCSI host adapter BIOS was set to act like the boot drive, so when the primary drive (which was the boot drive) tried to boot up, the host adapter tried to be the boot drive as well. No problem—I went into the SETUP utility during boot and turned off the BIOS boot feature.

CMOS SETUP INFORMATION READ

I've known people who thought that they had a bad drive because of a CMOS error, but what they *really* had was incorrect information in their CMOS. The CMOS has a battery that maintains startup information. If the battery dies, the system might not boot up, or it might boot up with default (and possibly incorrect) information about the hard disk or other components. When the CMOS battery fails, the computer goes back to the factory default BIOS settings. So, for example, if the default is "one floppy drive" and you actually have two, your second floppy drive will not function unless you go into the BIOS setup program and remind it about that other floppy drive. Your next step, of course, would be to get and install a replacement battery, as I described in Chapter 6.

LOAD MBR

First, the BIOS looks for a drive that's ready. The BIOS is usually set up to begin by first looking at A, your primary floppy drive. If there is nothing in drive A, the BIOS then looks at C, your primary hard drive. This default setup allows you to use a bootable floppy disk to boot from drive A if you want to run hard drive utility programs, install new operating systems, or run any program that needs to run before your installed operating system boots up. While this may not actually be the greatest idea in this virus-plagued age, sometimes you just have to boot from your floppy. (We'll look at virus issues in more depth in Chapter 15, "An Overview of Viruses.") Of course, to boot from drive C, just leave the floppy drive empty. Once the BIOS has detected a drive that's ready, it loads the first sector of data from that drive, the sector whose coordinates are cylinder 0, head 0, sector 1.

Some BIOS SETUP programs enable you to set a boot drive order, so you could, for example, set the system to check drive C first, check for a bootable CD-ROM second, and finally check drive A only if drive C and the CD-ROM do not contain the needed startup files. That makes the PC boot slightly faster, because it doesn't have to check drive A every time. However, if for some reason the startup files on the hard disk have a problem and you need to boot from a floppy, you will need to go into the BIOS SETUP program and change the boot order so that the PC will look in drive A before it hits C and becomes stymied.

Things work slightly differently for floppies and hard disks, but the hard disk procedure is actually just the floppy procedure with a few steps added, so let's focus on hard disks. That first sector on a hard disk is called the *Master Boot Record (MBR)*. It's just 512 bytes, so it should load easily into memory, although if it doesn't, the system won't boot and it probably will not show any error messages—it'll just lock up. Additionally, if the MBR is blank, the system will also lock up because it depends on that MBR to contain a meaningful program. If that happens, consult the troubleshooting procedure in Chapter 16, "Care and Feeding of Hard Drives," in the section "Recovering Data and Fixing Hard Disks."

FIND A BOOTABLE PARTITION

Once the MBR is in memory, the BIOS passes control of the PC over to it. The MBR contains a very small program that is the next link in the chain of events that leads to a successful boot. As you may know, PC hard disks can be *partitioned*, allowing you to make one physical hard disk seem like several hard disks, or perhaps to put multiple operating systems on a single hard disk. The MBR program just finds a bootable partition, loads the first sector of that partition into memory, and then passes control to the newly loaded sector. The MBR finds the bootable partition using a small table contained in the MBR itself called the *partition table*. That program is created and maintained by the DOS FDISK program, so you've probably modified a few partition tables in your time if you've set up hard disks. Anyway, if the MBR can't find a bootable partition, it'll issue a message that says Missing Operating System. Assuming that it can find a bootable partition, it'll load the first sector from that partition into memory and pass control to that sector.

By the way, you may know that the majority of computer viruses are called *boot sector viruses*. If your system is infected with one of these, this is the point where the virus becomes active. That's why cold booting from a floppy bypasses a virus if one exists on the MBR. (Of course, the floppy should be write-protected to prevent the virus from infecting it too.)

The DBR Loads and Executes

The first sector of the bootable partition goes by different names for different operating systems, but in the DOS world it's called the DBR, or *DOS Boot Record*. The DBR is another very brief program whose sole job in life is to find the two so-called "hidden" programs, called IO.SYS and MSDOS.SYS for those of you who use MS-DOS. Windows 95/98 also boots from IO.SYS and MSDOS.SYS, just like their DOS ancestors, but Windows Me, NT, 2000, and XP do not. You may have heard people say that Windows 95/98 runs on top of DOS or is DOS-based, but Windows Me, NT, 2000, and XP are not; this is what they mean.

Before loading the two hidden files, of course, the DBR must check to see that they're on your disk in the first place. If it can't find them, or encounters problems while loading the two files, it issues the possibly familiar message Non-system disk or disk error: insert boot disk and press any key when ready.

Assuming that all is well, the DBR yields the stage to the two hidden files.

THE HIDDEN FILES EXECUTE

Once the DBR loads the hidden files, the DBR passes control to the first hidden file (IO.SYS) and disappears. The first hidden file then *double-checks* that it has been loaded properly and checks the second hidden file. Once up and running, the first hidden file loads CONFIG.SYS. (The process is slightly different in Windows Me, NT, 2000, and XP systems, but they have their own hidden files that execute on the way to starting up.)

CONFIG.SYS LOADS AND EXECUTES

Assuming that you have a CONFIG.SYS file, the system executes the commands in CONFIG.SYS at this time. It first executes the BUFFERS, FILES, STACKS, DOS, FCBS, and LASTDRIVE commands, and then loads any device drivers. In a Windows 9x/NT/2000/XP system, you will not always have a CONFIG.SYS; those operating systems typically take their settings from WIN.INI, SYSTEM.INI, and/or the Windows Registry. (The same goes for AUTOEXEC.BAT.)

Error information on drivers is fairly sparse, but if CONFIG.SYS can't load a driver, it will say something like Bad or missing XXXX.DRV. If you're using Windows 95/98/NT, you can slow down the process by pressing F8 on bootup and then choosing Step by Step Confirmation from the Startup menu that appears. This forces the system to display one line at a time on the CONFIG.SYS, requiring a keystroke from you to continue to the next line. Some badly written drivers will simply crash the system without any error messages.

COMMAND.COM AND AUTOEXEC.BAT LOAD

The next step is to load something called the *user shell*; typically, it's the COMMAND.COM program. If CONFIG.SYS contains a SHELL statement, the hidden files will use that to locate a command shell, but, in the absence of a SHELL statement, the hidden files will next load COMMAND.COM from the root directory. Saying that COMMAND.COM is the "shell" of DOS means that it is the program that accepts user commands and loads programs at the user's request.

Your PC can run into trouble here if COMMAND.COM is missing or if it's not of a version that matches the hidden files.

Finally, COMMAND.COM loads and executes AUTOEXEC.BAT, executing any commands stored in there, and starts the graphical user interface of the operating system (Windows 9x/NT/2000/XP).

There are two common places where these last few steps can go wrong. First, CONFIG.SYS contains statements that can load device drivers, complete programs in their own right. Any bugs in a device driver can stop the system dead, so part of your troubleshooting approach might include temporarily renaming CONFIG.SYS to nullify its effects. If there's a SHELL statement in CONFIG.SYS, double-check that it makes sense: does it point to a bona fide copy of COMMAND.COM, and are all of the COMMAND.COM options correct?

NOTE   *If you have MS-DOS version 5 through 6.2, or you have upgraded to your current version of Windows from one of those DOS versions, onscreen help is available for DOS commands such as* COMMAND.COM. *To access it, type* **HELP** *and then the command name at a DOS prompt, like this:* **HELP COMMAND.COM**. *If you try this and get a* Bad command or file name *message, the DOS help file is not available on your PC.*

Second, if there's a SHELL statement, check to see if there is a corresponding SET COMSPEC statement in the AUTOEXEC.BAT file, as you see here:

CONFIG.SYS:

```
SHELL=C:\DOS\COMMAND.COM /E:512 /P
```

AUTOEXEC.BAT:

```
SET COMSPEC=C:\DOS\COMMAND.COM
```

Note in this example that the SHELL statement shows that the COMMAND.COM file is in the DOS subdirectory, and the SET COMSPEC statement agrees with it. If the two don't agree, you may see an error message like Cannot reload COMMAND.COM, system halted. That leaves AUTOEXEC.BAT as a source of troubles, and it's not without its share: load a buggy TSR program in AUTOEXEC.BAT, and the system will freeze at boot.

So, to review, you've seen how the PC starts up. A basic core of hardware must have power before anything can start. Then BIOS performs inventory and initialization. BIOS kicks off the DOS load process and, once DOS loads, your PC is ready to go to work. Now you understand the underlying mechanics so you can recognize where the boot process is failing. That, in combination with some of the other techniques in this chapter, should help you get a dead PC up and running.

Finding and Replacing Bad Chips

Okay, you *insist* on trying to fix some boards? Sometimes you *can* be a real hero and actually fix a circuit board. Most maintenance shops do very little board repair, instead returning boards to the manufacturer or, more often, just disposing of them. Board repair can be time consuming and therefore expensive, so it's not a great idea when most boards cost somewhere in the range of $100–$200 or even less. You'll spend a minimum of an hour and a maximum of forever fixing a board.

This is not to say that it should never be attempted. In fact, since the most expensive parts on your motherboard are usually socketed, the easiest chips you can troubleshoot are these:

- Memory chip
- Replacement microprocessor
- Coprocessor
- ROM (read-only memory)

If you're going to handle chips, please first take a look at the section on chip handling, "Chip Sockets and Chip Insertion/Removal," later in this chapter. In general, bad chips are found in one of the following ways:

- Manufacturer notification
- Software identification of chip malfunction
- Temperature testing
- Digital probe and pulse testing
- Use of specialized (and expensive) signature analyzers
- Exhaustive chip replacement

Chip "Recall"

Back in the early days of computers, the most common method of finding bad chips was manufacturer notification. That is, the manufacturer would send you a replacement chip and a notice that said something like, "Some boards built in 1996 malfunction due to a faulty 65X88 chip. Enclosed find a replacement 65X88...." Kind of like a car recall. Those days are gone for good.

Software Chip Testing

Software identification is possible when the chip is not so vital to the system that the system can't run without it. Many memory problems can be identified with software, as can some problems with some major chips, like the 8284 clock chip and the 8237 DMA controller. ROM often contains a *checksum* (an error check) that can be used to verify that the contents of the ROM haven't been damaged. You usually get the program that checks the checksum with the board that has the ROM in question. For example, most PC system diagnostics know where the checksum for the BIOS ROM is, and they check that as part of their routine.

Many boards now have flashable ROMs, which means that the manufacturer can make a program available from the Web site that will allow you to update the ROM on your board. Carefully read *all* of the instructions that come with these programs, as it is possible to permanently disable a card by improperly flashing the BIOS or attempting to apply the wrong BIOS to a card.

Temperature Chip Testing

Some faulty chips can be traced through their temperature or lack thereof. A properly functioning chip should be slightly warm to the touch—warmer, at least, than after a night of deactivation. A completely cool chip, particularly a large one (large chips tend to run warmer) is probably dead. Similarly, a very hot chip—the finger-burning variety—is probably dead or dying.

A worse situation occurs when the device works *sometimes*, then fails after a while (generally just before you were going to save your work). Heat can make a marginal component stop working, and the marginal component may not seem unduly warm. In this situation, how do you locate the bad component? By controlled application of heat and cold.

First, start up the device—PC, modem, whatever—with the cover off. Then blow warm air (I *did not say hot*—100 degrees will do nicely; I mean, we're talking a burn *in* process here, not burn *up*) onto the circuit board: use a hair dryer. The intermittent chip will fail eventually. Now get a can of component coolant and direct the cold blast directly onto the suspect chip. If there is no particular suspect chip, start with the big ones. Now try to restart the device. If it starts, there's a good chance that the cooled chip is the bad one. If it doesn't restart, try another chip. As always, keep notes.

Finally, there is the brute force method. Get a digital probe and pulser and test each chip, one by one. Surefire, but slow.

Identifying Chips

As long as we're trying to replace chips, let's see how to find the silly things in the first place, and let's look at what those numbers atop the chip mean. A chip can be described by its function, its identification number, and its manufacturer.

CHIP FUNCTION

Physical size is some indication of a chip's complexity, but it is not tremendously important. Memory chips are fairly small, but they are complex.

IDENTIFICATION NUMBER AND MANUFACTURER

When a manufacturer designs a new chip, they give it an identification number. For example, an 8088 is a particular microprocessor chip, and a 7400 is a quad two-input NAND chip. Generally, chip designs are patented, so another manufacturer must be licensed before it can offer a chip that it did not design. For example, back in the XT days, Intel designed the 8088, but Advanced Micro Devices (AMD) probably made more of them than Intel ever did. I do not know who developed the first 256K x 1 dynamic RAM chip, but virtually everyone in the chip business makes them now.

Prefixes and suffixes may be added to a chip's ID number. The suffixes refer to the package that it is in (usually DIP—Dual Inline Package, which is indicated by the suffix AN), or the temperature range (S is military specification, N is normal). Thus, 7400AN refers to a 7400 chip in a DIP package. A two-letter prefix refers to the manufacturer. Some manufacturer codes are HD for Hitachi, WD for Western Digital, DM for National Semiconductor, and R for Rockwell. Another code may be present, like B9544. This means (ignore the B) that the chip was made in the 44th week of 1995. Some vendors, like Intel, do not put a date code on their chips. Instead, they put a serial number on the chip (for example, a motherboard in front of me has a chip with serial number L5450275).

Other suffixes refer to performance, as with the old 8088-1 and 8088-2 microprocessors. The -2 ran up to 8MHz, and the -1 ran reliably only up to 5MHz. In the case of memory chips, there are more specific speed codes, as you'll learn in Chapter 8.

Soldering and Desoldering

If you're going to change chips, a few words about soldering.

It isn't hard, but it *does* take some practice. *If you have never soldered before, the place to learn is not on your PC!* Get some practice elsewhere, or just decide not to bother with soldering tasks. We PC fix-it people seek to minimize the amount of soldering required by choosing components that use sockets instead of solder whenever possible. More on sockets later.

The trick with soldering is to heat up *both* components to the desired temperature, then apply the solder. You want just enough heat to melt the solder, but not so much as to destroy whatever it is that you're soldering.

Soldering irons come in various powers or wattages. For PC work, you want a low-power iron, like a pencil iron fewer than 50 watts. Here are a few tips to remember when soldering:

◆ Use a 60/40 solder with rosin core (*not* acid core), ¹⁄₃₂-inch width.

◆ Do not apply the tip for more than 10 seconds—this should be more than sufficient.

◆ For desoldering, *do not* use solder suckers or vacuum bulbs unless they have grounded tips. They can build up static charges. Use wire braid instead.

◆ Remove the board first. Don't try to solder things on or off boards that are installed in the PC.

◆ When replacing chips or transistors, socket them first (see the next section).

◆ Buy a solder jig (sometimes called a "third hand") so that you have enough hands to hold the board, the soldering iron, the chip, and the desoldering tool. Many electronics stores sell different varieties of this product; Edmund Scientific (see the Vendor Guide on the Utilities CD) sells a reasonably priced one called the Extra Hands Work Station.

NOTE *By the way, a techie student once claimed that I was dead wrong about solder jigs, as true techies scoff at them. To the true techies, I apologize. I've used the things, and I like 'em.*

◆ If you are replacing a diode, transistor, or capacitor, draw a picture of how the original is installed. Memory (the human kind) gets faulty when faced with the normal frustration of soldering. It doesn't matter which way you insert a resistor.

◆ When desoldering a chip from a circuit board, don't desolder each pin in order. This builds up too much heat in one area. Jump around. Use a heat sink. Alternatively, use a solder tip designed for DIPs.

◆ As mentioned before, many system boards are now four-layer boards. They are *very* tough to work on competently with the usual inexpensive soldering equipment.

Chip Sockets and Chip Insertion/Removal

Most chips are soldered directly onto the printed circuit board, but they need not be. Chip *sockets* (as in light bulb "sockets") are available as an alternative. As long as you're removing and replacing a chip, think about installing a socket for the replacement.

The advantages of socketed chips are that they are easy to remove and replace, and it's a lot harder to damage a chip while inserting it in a socket than it is while soldering it in place. On the other hand, a soldered chip saves money—no socket must be bought. Also, it can't creep out of the socket.

As mentioned before, a socketed chip's problem may simply be that it has crept far enough out of the socket to impair the electrical connection. Recall that an early step in troubleshooting is to push all socketed chips gently back into their sockets.

Whether installing a socketed or directly mounted chip, you must be sure to install it with the correct side up. Chip pins are numbered with the farthest pin on the left side labeled 1, then counting down on the left side and finally up the right side (counterclockwise). You can see this in Figure 7.3.

FIGURE 7.3

Chip numbering

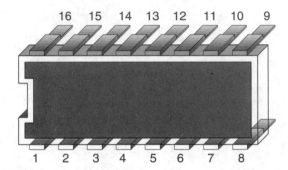

A chip can fit into a socket in one of two ways. The top of the chip generally has a notch to orient you when installing. To make things even easier, most circuit boards are designed so that all of the chips face the same way. This is *essential*: insert a chip with the notch facing the wrong way and you may destroy the chip. Figure 7.4 shows the correct orientation of the chip notches; consult the documentation for the chip if you cannot determine the correct alignment.

FIGURE 7.4

Chip notches

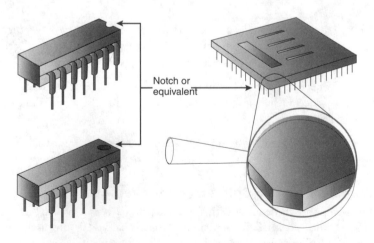

Notch or equivalent

Troubleshooting Tips

If you've tried everything else and finally determine that the problem you're having is indeed the circuit board, keep the following in mind:

◆ Beeps (more than one) when starting a PC usually indicate a problem with one of the primary components, such as the keyboard, video, or motherboard. Refer back to Tables 7.1 and 7.2 to find out what a particular string of beeps means.

◆ The power supply is more likely to be the problem than the motherboard in a no-power situation; further, a bad power supply can ruin a good motherboard, so do not swap a good motherboard into a system with a possibly bad power supply.

◆ Problems that occur only with one program usually signal an incompatibility between that program and your hardware. This problem can sometimes be overcome by a software patch from the manufacturer of either the hardware or the program.

◆ A heat source (like a hairdryer) and a cooling source (like spray coolant or a frozen cotton swab) can help you check for heat-related problems. If applying heat makes the component fail and cooling it makes it work, overheating is the culprit.

◆ Soldering and desoldering is not usually a cost-effective repair on a board, and it is difficult for beginners to do it correctly. If you do decide to solder or desolder, use a pencil iron under 50 watts and 60/40 solder with rosin (not acid) core, $\frac{1}{32}$-inch width.

Now let's move on to that essential part of everyone's PC: the memory.

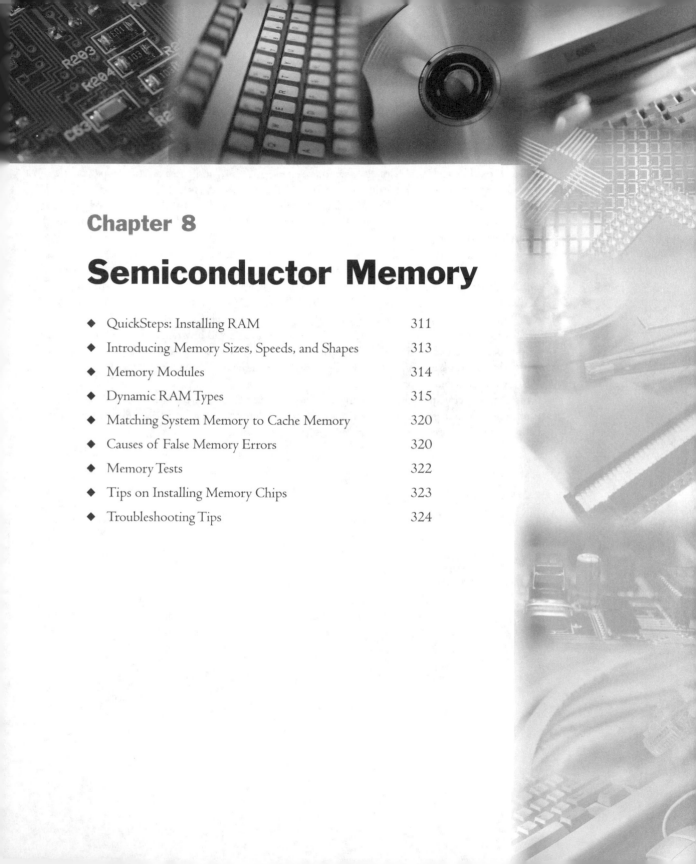

Chapter 8

Semiconductor Memory

◆ QuickSteps: Installing RAM   311

◆ Introducing Memory Sizes, Speeds, and Shapes   313

◆ Memory Modules   314

◆ Dynamic RAM Types   315

◆ Matching System Memory to Cache Memory   320

◆ Causes of False Memory Errors   320

◆ Memory Tests   322

◆ Tips on Installing Memory Chips   323

◆ Troubleshooting Tips   324

Introduction

I SAID IN THE last chapter that you generally won't handle troubleshooting down to the chip level. There are, as I noted, exceptions. Memory is one of them. So let's talk about the chips that you *will* replace. No discussion of circuit board and chip problems would be complete without some talk of memory chips. The technical name is *random-access memory (RAM)*, and these are the chips you are most likely to have to mess with. Typically, you'll work with *synchronous dynamic RAM (SDRAM)*, but some older computers use *static RAM (SRAM)*. The next few years should see SDRAM replaced by either the much faster *double data rate (DDR) SDRAM* or *Rambus DRAM (RDRAM)* as the most commonly used RAM in computers.

SDRAM and DDR SDRAM chips are sold mounted on several different-sized *form factors* (also called memory modules or memory sticks) that have their own unique names. *Dual Inline Memory Modules (DIMMs)* are, by far, the most common type of RAM memory modules sold these days. The capacity of RAM chips has increased dramatically since Bill Gates made his now-famous quote in 1981: "640K [about one-half of a megabyte] ought to be enough for anybody."

Prices for RAM can range from $50 for 128MB to over $500 for the newer 1GB modules. For some perspective, consider the 4GB (yes, *gigabyte*) RAM kit available for the Silicon Graphics (SGI) Onyx Reality. It was bargain priced from BuyComp.com several years ago at $19,321, a savings of over $7,100!!! Get yours today!

This chapter acquaints you with memory characteristics and tells you how to handle and install memory chips. You'll also learn about the kinds of problems that can lead to false memory errors and the tests used to detect memory problems.

QuickSteps

Installing RAM

Installing RAM is, in theory, easy, but is often an exercise in frustration. Why? Depending on the manufacturer of your computer, access to the part of the motherboard that contains the memory sockets can range from a simple operation to a complex process that might require dismantling the computer. I have a Packard-Bell that I purchased several years ago for $700 to use as a test server. You have to remove the motherboard power coupling to install or remove RAM if you want to put anything the size of a 3.5-inch hard disk in the lower drive bay, which I did. Then, even though the motherboard's IDE subsystem supports four devices, the cable had only one terminal on it, so I had to replace it in order to get another drive installed.

I've come across many systems like this, with wires pulled taut because the manufacturer probably didn't want to spend the extra $.0015 on an additional inch or two per cable, using unmarked IDE cables to save even more, and drive bays accessible only from the front (how do you get the cables attached?). One of my favorites is arbitrary power supply terminal length. There are usually a few extra terminals that snake from the power supply cable trunk that can be attached to drives and other internal devices. After you've cut off all the restricting zip ties, you find they are also intertwined in a way that allows most of the terminals to reach no more than 5 or 6 inches from the power supply. Everything is, of course, 6.5 to 10 inches away.

Ah. Fresh cynicism is great. A good bet here is that if you can take advantage of a super deal on RAM (128MB SDRAM DIMMs were going for about $25 in January 2002) and install it for free, do it. If nothing works, you can blame them. Let's press on, shall we?

BE PREPARED

Before you start, there are some things you may need on hand. These include:

- Phillips-head screwdriver to remove the case screws

- Small cup or other receptacle to place the screws in

- Antistatic wrist strap to prevent zapping (highly technical term) of the RAM, possibly causing failure

- Your motherboard's manual for settings, location, and jumper references

---

To install the RAM, follow these steps:

1. Shut down the system and remove the power cable.

2. Place the case on a flat, stable surface. Remove the screws from the rear of the case.

3. Slide off the cover. This is different for each maker, but new machines are starting to make it easier. Place tower systems right side down. Desktop systems should be oriented so that the ports on the rear of the case face left.

4. Locate the three DIMM or four RIMM slots. Note: *RIMM* is the trademarked name for a Direct Rambus memory module. RIMMs look similar to DIMMs but have a different pin count. They are approximately 4 inches (10cm) long, are very close to each other, are near the CPU, and have large white or gray tabs at each end. There should be a diagram in your computer user manual or the manual that came with your motherboard if you built your own.

   You should be wearing your antistatic wrist strap at this point; if you don't have one, touch the power supply case with your bare finger to discharge any static buildup that might be on your body.

5. Move the tabs away from the slot. They swing on sturdy hinges near the bottom of the slot.

6. Identify the pegs inside the slot. There will be two. Match those with the notches on the RAM and orient accordingly.

7. Lower the module into the slot. Apply only slight pressure to each end. This should kick up the tabs on each end.

8. Feel the module's positioning with your fingers along the top edge. If it slides or otherwise feels loose, reseat it.

9. When you feel confident that the notches match the pegs, the tabs are in the upright position from your slight pressure, and you feel comfortable that the module is ready, push firmly on one end of the top edge near a tab.

10. If all things go well, which is likely, you should feel and hear a taut snap as the module enters the pin array and the tab locks over the end.

11. Repeat with the other side.

12. Start the machine.

TIP   If you have a Dell, Hewlett-Packard, Packard-Bell, Micron, Gateway, Toshiba, Sony, Acer, IBM, or other top-tier machine, you will invariably view a company-specific splash screen when starting. To defeat this, tap the Delete key a few times. If this does nothing and the system enters Windows boot, reset the machine and try again with the F1 key. One of these will open the ROM BIOS settings applet. Check your BIOS material for the procedures needed to turn off the vendor-specific splash screen and to turn on verbose RAM checking. Turning on RAM checking will allow you to see the RAM Power-On Self Test (POST) when the BIOS checks for faults.

13. If the RAM is not recognized or the system does not start correctly, shut down, unplug, and reseat (stop, drop, and roll!). Verify that you have the correct replacement RAM for your computer. Next, check your documentation and verify that your computer supports the capacity of RAM you are installing. For example, the largest memory form factor that my Dell notebook can recognize is 256MB Small Outline DIMM (SO-DIMM); if I were to put in a 512MB SO-DIMM, it would not be detected. If everything is correct and repeated attempts to install the RAM result in failure, return the RAM for a replacement.

Introducing Memory Sizes, Speeds, and Shapes

You'll see memory referred to as *DIPs, SIPPs, SIMMs, DIMMs,* and so on. What do all these terms mean?

RAM memory is classified in the following ways:

- Package type, which refers to the plastic coating containing the actual silicon. With today's memory modules, the package type is a term rarely used, but in case you are working on a very old system, packaging for RAM can be any of the following:

  - *Dual Inline Package (DIP)* is the original memory chip used back in the days when individual memory chips were inserted in sockets on the motherboard. They are little, black, plastic bricks with two rows of metal legs, one on each of their long sides, hence the name *dual inline*.

  - *ZIP (Zigzag Inline Package)* briefly replaced DIP; all of the connectors were on one side, allowing the memory package to rest on its side rather than lying flat so that it took up less room on the motherboard. The Zip package departed with the appearance of memory modules.

- Form factor, which refers to the module that contains one or more of the following packages:

  - *Single Inline Pin Package (SIPP)* was the first attempt at a memory module. The SIPP is a small circuit board containing several memory chips and has a single row of pins across the bottom. You will find SIPP memory on older personal computers and workstations. The SIPP memory resembles SIMMs except that it has tiny pins instead of an edge connector. SIMMs eventually replaced SIPPs because the SIPP pins tended to bend or break easily.

  - *Single Inline Memory Module (SIMM)* is a modular circuit board with memory chips soldered on it. The SIMM has an edge connector that allows the entire SIMM module to be inserted into a socket on the motherboard. The early SIMMs had 30 pins and were 3.5 inches in length; the 72-pin SIMMs that later replaced them were 0.75 inches longer.

  - *Double Inline Memory Module (DIMM)* looks almost identical to the SIMM; however, the SIMM has memory chips on one side while the DIMM has memory mounted on both sides. To accommodate the extra memory, the DIMM has connectors on both sides of the module, giving it 168 pins. Another difference between the SIMM and the DIMM is the way that the modules are installed. The 72-pin SIMM installs at a slight angle, whereas the 168-pin DIMM installs straight down into the memory socket on the motherboard.

  - *Small Outline DIMM (SO-DIMM)* is the module that is now in common use in notebook computers. It is much smaller than the 168-pin DIMM and is available in either 72- or 144-pin configurations.

  - *Rambus Inline Memory Module (RIMM)* is a 184-pin module that looks a little like a DIMM. RIMMs offer faster access and transfer speed, and thus generate more heat. An aluminum sheath, called a heat spreader, covers the module to protect the chips from overheating. The RIMM is also available in a small outline form factor (SO-RIMM).

- *PC Cards* (also known as PCMCIA cards), SmartMedia, CompactFlash, and memory sticks are small, thin modules that plug into a special socket found mostly on notebook computers, digital cameras, and Personal Digital Assistants (PDAs).

- Various proprietary, vendor-specific chip packages.

- Access speed (how quickly the chip fetches data), which is measured in nanoseconds. Common access times are 40-, 50-, 60-, 70-, and 80ns for normal memories, and as low as 8ns for expensive, high-speed memories. Lower numbers are faster.

- Memory capacity; modern DIMM/RIMM capacity ranges from 32MB to 1024MB for memory modules.

Memory Modules

Let's take a closer look at the more popular form factors in which you'll find memory supplied.

Modern computers use 168-pin DIMMs or 184-pin RIMMs or, rarely, some kind of proprietary memory type. Early laptops in particular have made heavy use of proprietary memory modules, and there's rarely any rhyme or reason to the design. Before SO-DIMMs became popular, most notebook memory was developed using proprietary designs. It is always more cost-effective for a system manufacturer to use standard components. The SO-DIMM was designed to provide a standard form factor that fit into the small confines of a laptop. (More on that a little later.)

DIMMs have replaced SIMMs (both types are shown in Figure 8.1), primarily because they are simply more efficient and they can pack twice as much memory into the same space. And before you ask: no, you can't upgrade your computer simply by installing DIMM modules into your SIMM slots, because the actual package—the module board—has a different interface. Both the electronics and the connectors are different.

NOTE   The primary reason that DIMMs have a superior physical design over SIMMs is that they contain twice the contacts of SIMMs, a set on each side. This allows one DIMM to act as two SIMMs and eliminates the need to mount duplicate banks of RAM. In reality, modern systems with three physical banks for SDRAM DIMMs actually see six banks of RAM. One DIMM is already a pair. So simple, it's brilliant!

FIGURE 8.1

Memory banks on
64-bit computers

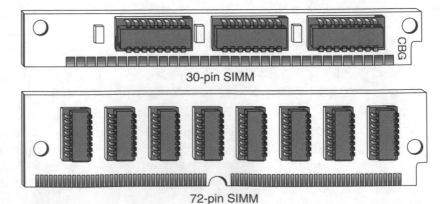

30-pin SIMM

72-pin SIMM

Will you need to keep increasing the amount of memory in your computer? Silly question. Speed and capacity largely drive the computer market. More is always better, and memory sizes thought to be really spiffy last year are called "brain dead" this year. Just stay tuned. Memory chips are a hot technology area and, other than CPUs, have the most influence on what you can do with your box.

Motherboard Chipsets

While the CPU in a computer gets a lot of attention, there is an equally important chip that determines what features and peripherals the computer will support. This all-important device is called the *chipset*, and it is this chip that ultimately determines what type and how much memory your computer supports.

Information about the chipset used in your computer is only important to those people who are purchasing motherboards to build their own computers. Although the chipset controls and provides many features on the motherboard, in this chapter we need be concerned only with the impact the chipset has on the type and amount of RAM that can be used with your computer.

Most systems being built today operate with chipsets made by Intel, VIA, or AMD, with Intel controlling the lion's share of the market. When the Pentium 4 originally was released, only one chipset family would work with it—Intel's i850 series—and it only supported dual-channel PC-800 RDRAM (I'll explain RDRAM later). At the time of its release, RDRAM was very expensive to produce, and many people chose to upgrade to a faster Pentium III computer that supported cheaper SDRAM memory rather than the Pentium 4 with its very expensive RDRAM. In 2001, chipsets for the Pentium 4 became available that supported the faster and cheaper alternative to RDRAM—DDR. Faced with losing market share, Intel released a chipset (the i845 series) that allowed the Pentium 4 to use DDR.

Until 2001, the most popular motherboard configurations came with three DIMM slots, and the chipset limited most of these systems to a maximum of 768MB of RAM (256MB DIMM × 3). Newer motherboards that offer support for DDR or RDRAM can accept up to four 512MB RDRAM RIMMs or two 1GB DDR modules, for a total of 2GB of RAM.

NOTE *Even though RDRAM comes in sets of two, in most configurations it can operate independently and does not require an operational partner.*

Before DIMM became the industry standard, nearly every Pentium or Pentium Pro–based motherboard used a proprietary memory module or 72-pin SIMMs. This caused confusion with many people who upgraded; you needed two 72-pin SIMMs to make a bank on these computers. This is because, as mentioned before, DIMMs are the logical representation of two SIMMs; one DIMM slot is the equivalent of two SIMM slots. Interleaving is eliminated, and since interleaving operations can be handled at the chip level and not handed off through a much slower bus, the speed increase is multifold. Many of these motherboards had four SIMM sockets, making two banks. However, the next generation of Pentium II/III/Celeron and AMD Athlon machines commonly used three banks of DIMM slots, and the DIMM slots did not require the addition of memory in pairs.

Dynamic RAM

As computers are built faster and faster, all the components must get faster and faster to make plopping a 2GHz Pentium 4 onto a motherboard worth it. Design a system around a 2GHz chip, and you need a lot of very fast components—including RAM.

NOTE *Static RAM (SRAM) is the simplest kind of memory to understand, because when you put data into it, the data stays there. Now, your response might be, "Big deal—isn't that the whole idea of memory? What good is memory that doesn't hold onto the data that you give it?" Well, to build that kind of memory, you have to build about six transistors into each bit storage location. That kind of memory—SRAM—can be quite fast, but also quite expensive. If you used SRAM for your PC memory, then there'd be no trouble with getting memories that kept up with your CPUs; but, on the other hand, you wouldn't be able to afford those computers, because SRAM is about 10 times more expensive than the DRAM that people are used to buying. SRAM is also physically larger than DRAM and generally runs much hotter. Of course, all these negative aspects drove the market to adopt DRAM and see SRAM move into a supporting role (it's typically used for Video RAM, L1 and L2 cache RAM, or other similar RAM needs). Fortunately, things have speeded up quite a bit over the past few years.*

Dynamic RAM (DRAM) was the economical answer to the earlier SRAM. Each DRAM bit is built of a single transistor and a capacitor, in contrast to SRAM's six transistors.

DRAM has two problems from the point of view of a PC designer. First, the *dynamic* in its name means that it forgets the data that you give it almost as fast as you can give it the data. That means that DRAM-based systems require refresh circuitry to get around this electronic amnesia.

Second, the way that DRAMs are built to be cheaper is that they are organized not simply into a set of addresses; rather, each bit in a DRAM has a row address and a column address. The slow part of accessing any part of a DRAM is in getting to its row. Once you're in a row, subsequent intra-row accesses can be quite fast. In fact, that's the area with the most advances recently: DRAMs that can access data quite quickly. This brings me to Table 8.1, which outlines the types of DRAM.

TABLE 8.1: THE MARCH OF TIME WITH DRAM

TYPE	FIRST USED	CLOCK RATE	BUS WIDTH*	PEAK BANDWIDTH	VOLTAGE
FPM (60, 70ns)	1990	25MHz	64-bit	200MBps	5v
EDO (50, 60, 70ns)	1994	40MHz	64-bit	320MBps	5v
SDRAM (66MHz)	1996	66MHz	64-bit	528MBps	3.3v
SDRAM (100MHz)	1998	100MHz	64-bit	800MBps	3.3v
SDRAM (133MHz)	1999	133MHz	64-bit	1.1GBps	3.3v
RDRAM (Direct Rambus)	1999	400MHz ($\times$2)	16-bit	1.6GBps	2.5v
DDR SDRAM (100MHz)	2001	100MHz ($\times$2)	64-bit	1.6GBps	3.3v
DDR SDRAM (133MHz)	2001	133MHz ($\times$2)	64-bit	2.1GBps	3.3v

* Indicates the maximum module data width, not its external bus width. 64-bit external pathways began with the 75MHz Pentium. Data courtesy of CMP TechWeb and Kingston Technology © 2000

As you can see in this table, it took four years to get from quite slow Fast Page Mode (FPM) RAM to Extended Data Out (EDO) RAM, which produced only a marginal increase in performance. At that time, adding 16MB of RAM to a 16MB system yielded an approximate 30 percent boost in overall performance. Going beyond that resulted in little more than an additional 5 percent, if even that.

That diminished return *ad infinitum* changed with SDRAM and its 66MHz bus. This also marked the point when RAM speed became tied to the CPU speed. This is important because timing is crucial to efficient data transfer in systems that are defined by time, such as our computers. 1998 ushered in 100MHz SDRAM, or PC-100. 1999 showed us 133MHz SDRAM, and RDRAM from a company named Rambus. The year 2001 was important because DDR became readily available, and the RAM war for market dominance between RDRAM and DDR is being fought in earnest.

NOTE *RDRAM is technically interesting, in that instead of increasing the size of the path that the data passes through, Rambus chose to make the path smaller. Quite a bit smaller, in fact. Most RAM operates using an internal 64-bit data structure and an external 64-bit data path. RDRAM uses a 16-bit data path. Now, this yields only a 500MBps-faster performance over 133MHz SDRAM, but its internal operations move at 400MHz. RDRAM I/O is doubled to two paths when it operates in dual-channel, which increases the effective speed to 800MHz, though that is only a theoretical speed limit and is diminished by the latency inherent with the RDRAM design.*

The dark gray section that encompasses the last three items in Table 8.1 is what appears to be the next major generation of RAM products: RDRAM and double data rate (DDR) SDRAM (which is properly referred to as DDR). Both SDR and DDR SDRAM look like ordinary DIMM modules with a difference in the notches so as to prevent it from being installed into a system that doesn't support it. As fast as DDR is, designers are already hard at work to produce a Triple Data Rate (TDR), and there is even talk of a Quad Data Rate (QDR). After the theoretical speed of QDR is reached, designers will then need to figure out ways to increase the speed of light.

Now that you have been doubled and tripled, let's look at the RDRAM a little closer. RDRAM comes in a package format called Rambus Inline Memory Module (RIMM). RIMMs come in 64-, 128-, and 256MB modules, error-correction code (ECC) and non-ECC, and at speeds of 600MHz, 700MHz, and 800MHz.

FPM AND EDO DRAM

FPM and EDO DRAM types are not used anymore. You may have one or the other in your PC that you are upgrading with the help of this book, but in the end, they will go the way of the woolly mammoth (unless you have another old machine that could use more RAM, but then that's another set of problems).

There is one instance where EDO DRAM can still be used, but it's mostly a crutch for backward compatibility. One motherboard I have worked with, the BIOStar MicroTech M6TLC PII, is capable of handling up to 384MB of SDRAM (128MB DIMMs), but can take up to 768MB of EDO DRAM (256MB DIMMs). As, however, with all pre-SDRAM DRAM types, EDO DRAM suffers from less efficient transfer speeds and reduced capabilities. If you need that much RAM, then you don't need a motherboard like this one and you certainly don't want EDO DRAM!

SDRAM

Synchronous dynamic RAM (SDRAM) is a variant of DRAM that includes an on-chip burst counter. This burst counter can be used to increment column addresses and increase the speed of memory access.

NOTE *SDRAM typically comes in DIMM formats, though they used to have the SIMM format as well. DIMM is the only format being manufactured today.*

Although faster is generally considered better and speed is pursued for its own sake, the reason behind the SDRAM was that CPUs were getting faster. With their increasing speed, they required ever-faster memory in order to function within earshot of their potential. With SDRAM, the CPU and RAM are locked together by the same clock. Thus, the speed of the RAM and the CPU are linked, or synchronized.

NOTE   *Another solution to the problem of speeding up RAM is cached SDRAM, which boosts the overall speed of the memory by adding a static RAM (SRAM) area on the dynamic RAM chip itself. This small amount of fast SRAM acts as a cache to the DRAM. The cached RAM briefly appeared several years ago but offered only minimal performance improvement and a chipset that supported it. Since none of the major chipset manufacturers supported it, it pretty much faded from the market.*

Normally, memory chips answer data requests. Cache memory can anticipate the CPU's needs. When the CPU asks for data, the memory already has it waiting and ready to go. Some cache memory implementations also include a pipeline. The pipelined architecture has a design in which one stage can fetch an address while other stages present the data for output. The cache memory concept has the advantage of being a simple, elegant replacement for older chips; it just plugs into the system and goes.

SDRAM modules come in 72-, 144-, and 168-pin packages and can range from 4MB to 512MB in capacity. There are generally two types of SDRAM DIMMs; *unbuffered* and *registered*. The 72-pin SO-DRAM was designed to meet the specific needs of portables and their space limitations. The problem was that upgrades required two modules, eliminating the savings in space. Thus was born the 144-pin SO-DRAM variant of the full-sized DIMM. The 168-pin packages are solely for use in systems that do not have space limitations.

NOTE   Unbuffered *memory is simple memory that relies on a controller to function predictably. This is the most common type of RAM and one of the reasons why RAM is inexpensive.* Registered *memory has a register array onboard, generally allowing for more orderly operations. It's also more costly to make, and that cost gets passed on to you, the buyer. Fortunately, it's really only important that you know which type your system requires. A general rule of thumb is, when in doubt, it'll probably take unbuffered. Don't worry. Nothing will break.*

TO ERROR CORRECT OR NOT TO ERROR CORRECT

You will probably note that some types of RAM are labeled ECC, which is short for error-correction code. If you have seen this, you likely wondered why it was more expensive than non-ECC RAM. Well, the answer is simple: ECC RAM does more than conventional RAM. Of course, if you need ECC RAM, you can probably afford to buy it, since it's mostly used to help prevent costly and damaging errors, faults, and mistakes. Now, if you're already buying ECC or if you already have it, then you don't need to read this sidebar and can move on. Computers that use ECC RAM automatically detect it and configure the system to use it. If you currently are using ECC RAM and add a non-ECC RAM memory module, the motherboard will detect it and disable the ECC features on both memory modules.

Good to see you stick it out. Now, how does ECC work? Good question. The answer is that ECC uses special algorithms to watch, evaluate, and fix various problems that appear in the data stream, either incoming or outgoing. This means greater stability for data-intensive applications such as CAD/CAM and audio and video editing, though I doubt you'll need it at home.

DDR SDRAM

As noted earlier, *DDR* is short for double data rate, and DDR maximizes output by using both the leading and following edge of the clock tick to perform operations. This means that DDR can locate and pass an address in one tick as opposed to two.

The physical dimensions of a DDR memory module are identical to those used by a standard DIMM except that the standard SDRAM (now called SDR, for Single Data Rate) module has two keys, or notches where there are no pins. The DDR DIMM has only one key because it provides an additional 16 pins to the space recovered by using only one notch. This gives the DDR module 184 pins compared to the 168 pins on the standard SDR SDRAM DIMM module. This means that a SDR DIMM cannot fit into a socket designed for a DDR module.

The logical names for DDR modules are PC-200, PC-266, and PC-333, which is a reference to their doubled bus speed. For example, a PC-100 doubled becomes a PC-200, right? Not exactly; for reasons that can only be attributed to blatant marketing propaganda, the new modules are labeled PC-1600, PC-2100, and PC-2700. Some have reasoned that this was so their numbers would be larger than the competing Rambus PC-800, but in fact the names are based on data transfer rates of the modules instead of their bus clock speeds.

SLDRAM

Synchronous link DRAM (SLDRAM) is what is called a protocol-based technology. Unlike other RAM, a *protocol-based technology* works on the premise of a facilitating object being involved in the transfer of data to and from one place and another. In this case, the data being transferred is stored in RAM. Think of the CPU as a client and the SLDRAM bus as a server. When the client requests data from the server, it's sent. Requests occur in both directions. This makes for a more intelligent data manipulation interactivity. To make it as fast as possible, SLDRAM uses a multiplexed bus to move data in and out, bypassing the limitations of traditional pins. SLDRAM can currently handle I/O speeds of up to 1.6GBps with a very fast theoretical cap of 3GBps. Its potential is very strong, but with the high speeds promised by DDR and RDRAM there is little effort to make this into a commercial product.

BLAST FROM THE PAST: MEMORY INTERLEAVING

Some systems attempted to minimize the loss of speed incurred by charging capacitors by arranging the RAM into *interleaved banks*. The idea was this: memory is organized into banks, or logical groups. With interleaving, memory subsystems always have an even number of banks. Memory addresses are then *interleaved* so that when one address (in the first bank) is being accessed, the following address (which is in the second bank) is being charged up. That way, when it's time to access the second bank, it needn't be charged, because the address that follows is ready to go. While reading that address in the second bank, its following address (back in the first bank) is being charged up, and so on.

Notice that this works only if the CPU's memory accesses tend to be in consecutive memory addresses. That's a pretty good assumption, but if the program running in the system jumps all around the RAM for data, then interleaving is defeated and memory accesses slow down.

Interleaving was a good idea for its time, but it was effective only for the first access in a row, and it required an even number of memory banks. It was rather awkward.

If you're upgrading an older system, keep track of whether it requires memory to be interleaved, or you might be confused as to why that old 80486 doesn't work, especially since you just put in fresh RAM.

Matching System Memory to Cache Memory

All the information mentioned earlier in this chapter on SDRAM and cache RAM points to one large problem in the personal computer industry: there is an increasing disparity in clock speeds between processors and DRAM. Combine this with an increasing degree of processor super-scalability, and you get a situation in which effective cache management becomes a critical factor in obtaining optimal application performance. System main memory access now can take anywhere from tens to hundreds of CPU clock cycles. Hence, the difference between finding information in the on-chip cache instead of in main memory can completely dominate the effective speed of an application, or even an entire system. There are a variety of techniques that make more effective use of the processor caches. These techniques can be divided into two types: those focusing on programs and those focusing on processors.

Better Programs

An important aspect in effective data cache management is how, and how well, an algorithm accesses the data that is in the cache. Since accessing memory whose addresses are adjacent or close together speeds up cache performance, structuring program code with the memory system in mind is often the best way to increase speed. Programmers can use a couple of design strategies to improve performance, such as making greater use of large element arrays instead of arranging data in multiple, individual structures. Additionally, code can be written to make use of processor-specific features. For example, most CPU instruction sets provide the user with the ability to manage the data cache via software.

Better Processors

Although writing better programs is a good place to look for better matches between system memory and cache memory, what about something for those of us up in the cheap seats—those of us who aren't involved in program creation? The best thing (perhaps the only thing) to do is look for systems that have already addressed this problem and look to the chip vendors to provide increasingly faster iron.

Some Pentium system designs use two or more processors with dedicated caches for each processor. The advantage of such a multiprocessor design is that each processor communicates freely with its own cache and thus provides highly efficient bus utilization. More efficient bus utilization equals more rapid cache access (equals a faster computer). Simple. The problem, of course, it that this kind of multiple-processor design tends to be expensive and complex. Each dedicated cache requires an additional cache controller and SRAMs, and each cache also requires its own data-path, memory-bus, and interrupt-control circuitry. Big money. Big headaches.

A bit different is a design that uses two processors that share a single secondary cache. This design is simpler and less expensive. You need only one cache controller and some SRAM. It's not as fast as dedicated caches, but according to Intel, it typically improves system performance by 50 percent to 80 percent with a secondary processor installed.

Causes of False Memory Errors

Memory often gets blamed for problems arising from other sources. In most cases, memory that has been working for a few weeks will work forever. While memory hardware failures were common up to the late '80s, the quality of memory chips has improved considerably since 1988. Reliability has increased substantially over the last 14-plus years as well. Rare is the case when RAM goes bad. That said, potential problems still exist, especially in older systems that are still in use, a growing practice in today's ever-more-common multi-PC home. These older systems still need to use the older RAM and, if these systems have had RAM augmented and not replaced, these older problems can still occur.

Power Drops and Surges

Memory is often falsely accused for a simple reason: the memory is so demanding in its need for constant, clean power. If the power drops out or surges for just a few millionths of a second, the memory loses its contents, causing a memory error. This wasn't an error caused by the memory—it was a power error that just *showed up* in the memory. Think of it as the canary in the coal mine of your PC.

Along the same lines, a static electric surge looks just like a power surge. Scuff across a pile carpet on a dry day, touch your computer, and you're likely to cause a memory error—but please *don't* try this out, because you may cause permanent memory damage. A failing power supply may, in the same way, cause apparent memory failures. So will noisy power being fed to a perfectly good power supply.

The telltale signs in this case are the addresses reported by the memory errors. If you've truly got a memory error, you'll see the same address reported as bad over and over. But memory errors that always report different locations—locations that test fine when tested a few minutes later—likely point to power problems.

Is there *enough* power? Insufficient power can cause parity errors. This problem can be a real pain, since it waits for some large disk access to trigger the parity error—for example, when you try to save your data to disk.

You see this problem with underpowered clones: your application works fine until you want to save the file, and then you get a parity check. The trouble is that you're running the power supply to the poor thing's limits and then want to fire up the hard disk. Not enough power, the memory gets shortchanged, and, BANG! A memory error happens.

And, while it's unusual, improperly shielded sources of RF noise can alter memory, causing parity errors. I remember a certain 64KB chip made back in the early '80s; this chip was built in a chip package that was accidentally made of a ceramic material that was a very low-level emitter of alpha particle radiation. Once in a while, an alpha particle would zip through the chip, causing a nonrepeatable error. I'm glad I don't have to troubleshoot *those* chips anymore.

Mismatched Chip Speeds and Manufacturers

If you need a chip that has an access speed of, say, 80ns, but you can get only a faster chip—say, one that runs at 60ns—can you use the faster 60ns chip to replace the slower 80ns chip? Yes, *but* you must replace the entire bank of chips when you do that. Putting a single 60ns chip into a bank of 80ns chips will often cause the 80s to appear to have errors.

Another issue that used to plague older memory was compatibility between manufacturers. Until the mid-1990s, whenever possible, I recommended avoiding mixing *manufacturers* in the same row. I flatly could not explain this, but I have seen cases where it caused problems. For instance, I had two rows of chips—one entirely Mitsubishi, another entirely Toshiba—that worked fine. Then I mixed the rows. Errors occurred. Restored the rows, and the problem disappeared. With current technology, the mixing of manufacturers should not cause problems.

Memory Tests

Modern RAM is pretty reliable, but you may come across a RAM failure of an odd sort on some SIMMs: *soft failures*. These are failures that show up only with very specific tests.

NOTE *DIMMs of SDRAM varieties rarely have faults. When they do, the faults can often be traced back to a fabrication error.*

Walking Bit Test

Years ago, a manuscript of an early edition of this book suddenly started growing typos. And odd typos they were, too: now and then, a letter would show up wrong for no reason. I first thought that the printer was failing, but checking in the file on the disk, I found that the typos were *there*, too. I thought this extremely odd, because I'd proofread the text—as had many others—and these obvious typos didn't appear. I began to be certain that the problem was machine induced.

I suspected my mass storage device, a Bernoulli cartridge system, and so I started saving the document on my hard disk instead. Still, the errors were cropping up. That's when I also noticed that some files were being corrupted when I copied them.

It was starting to look like the problem was in the system's memory. Whenever a piece of data passed through the system's memory, it would sometimes—very rarely, actually—become corrupt. Finally, I ran a *walking bit* test.

You see, standard memory tests just go to a particular location and test the heck out of it, stuffing different combinations of 1s and 0s into a particular byte and then reading them back. Tests of that kind were coming up zero for errors. But what about interactive problems? It turned out that there were two memory locations, at roughly 560KB and 600KB, that were in cahoots with one another, so to speak. Test either location, and there was no problem. But put a 1 into the 560KB location and, lo!, a 1 popped up in the 600KB location.

This kind of error is called a *walking bit* error, and it's a problem on the memory address circuitry rather than the memory itself. It really doesn't matter where the error originates, however, because the answer is the same: replace the problematic memory units. More on how in a little bit. It takes software to test this properly, and there are two programs that test a very wide range of things, including this.

Mountain/Valley and Checkerboard Tests

Here's another example of memory problems that will never be detected by single-byte testing. Consider a set of bit memory cells, as you see in Figure 8.2.

But suppose one kind of bit can "leak over" into another kind of bit, as you see in Figure 8.3.

The effect is that the 0 bits leak over into the 1s, eventually turning them into 0s. Filling each bit with a 0 and then surrounding it by 1s, and vice versa, is called the *mountain/valley* test. The *checkerboard* test lays out a pattern of 1s and 0s like the light and dark squares of a checkerboard.

All three of these tests are incorporated into the two memory tester programs (CheckIt and PC-Technician) that I recommended in Chapter 5, "Troubleshooting PC Problems." I strongly recommend running one of these programs overnight when you first install some new memory.

FIGURE 8.2

Set of bit
memory cells

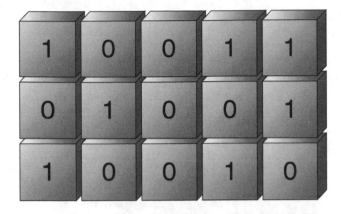

FIGURE 8.3

Set of bit memory
cells with a "leak
over" into another bit

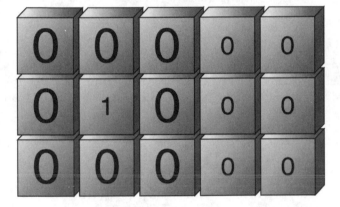

Tips on Installing Memory Chips

A lot of manuals include some really scary instructions for installing memory chips. I've probably installed a terabyte or so myself (512MB chips have made it easier to get to the 1GB level), so here's what works for me.

First, as always, be aware of static electricity. Your sweater and the soles of your shoes are powerful producers of it. If I'm worried about the static level of an area, and I'm not prepared with an antistatic strap, *I take my shoes and socks off.* I know it sounds a little bizarre, but I kill very few chips in my bare feet—probably less than a half dozen in all the time I've been installing memory.

Second, the memory chips go into slots on the motherboard. As before, don't insert a module into a board while the power is on. Push the white or gray knobs on the ends of the slot out from the center so you have room to slide in the module. Orient the module so that the notches in the pin array match the pegs in the slot on the board. Then push the chip into the socket firmly with your thumb.

TIP *Some people who have been around it long enough call any RAM package mounted on a printed circuit board a stick of RAM. Heck, I do. I will, for the sake of clarity, not refer to them here as sticks, but as modules.*

NOTE   Remember that patience *is the keyword here: look at what you're doing and take your time if you're new to the process.*

How do I upgrade my old 486? How do I remove SIMMs? Between removing and installing, removing SIMMs can be the harder task, depending on how chintzy the motherboard manufacturer was. Figure 8.4 shows you how to remove SIMMs.

FIGURE 8.4

Removing SIMMs

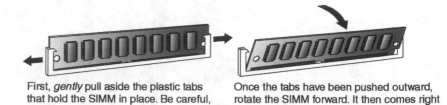

First, *gently* pull aside the plastic tabs that hold the SIMM in place. Be careful, as the tabs are easily broken.

Once the tabs have been pushed outward, rotate the SIMM forward. It then comes right out of its socket.

There is an unfortunately frequent occurrence in the classes I teach on PC repair that concerns SIMM removal. In every class, I tell students, "Don't remove SIMMs until I show you how to do it." Now and then, I'll get some prize idiot who decides that he'd rather figure it out himself. So he grabs the SIMM and yanks it out—and sure enough, he *did* figure out how to remove a SIMM! Unfortunately, however, that SIMM socket will never again hold a SIMM, because he has broken off the little plastic tabs that hold SIMMs in place. Even *more* unfortunately, that means memory can't be installed on the motherboard, which means someone—that student—is going to have to buy a new motherboard. So, unless you plan to exercise the old credit card when you attack SIMMs, follow this procedure.

The key to removing SIMMs (and DIMMs) is to push the little tabs outward *gently.* They hold the SIMM in place. If you push too hard, you can break them off. Some SIMM sockets are better designed and use metal spring tabs to hold the SIMMs in place—it's harder to break these off—but an unfortunate number of sockets use plastic tabs. Push the tabs outward either with the blade of a small screwdriver, or with your fingernails. Err on the side of caution. You'll feel the SIMM move a bit, and that will be your signal that you can try to pull it a bit forward. Once you have one tab and one side free, work on the other side.

Reinserting SIMMs is similar. You place the SIMM angled forward in the SIMM socket (do not angle a DIMM—they insert straight down), and then push it back into place. As the SIMM contacts the tabs, relieve the pressure on the tabs by helping them outward with your fingers. The SIMM will snap into place—start over if it doesn't—and all will be well. Memory is one of the most sensitive parts of your PC, both electronically and mechanically. Now that you know more about memory chips, your machine will run that much better.

Troubleshooting Tips

Before you start, this is where I get tough again. Now, I've already talked in detail about what can go wrong if you don't take the proper steps to protect yourself and your hardware before jamming your hands inside the case. I've also discussed the necessity of having any static discharge eliminated with an antistatic pad or wristband, so have your solution ready. Last, don't forget to disconnect the power cable completely. I cannot stress enough the importance of these precautions, unless, of course, you have money to burn on replacement parts.

TIP   *For more details on safety precautions, look over Chapter 4, "Avoiding Service: Preventive Maintenance."*

There can be only a few problems with RAM itself. Either it's bad or it's been statically "zapped." A few other problems can occur with installation. Here are some Q-and-A-type problems and solutions:

Q: I added a 128MB module to match my already installed one, but I still get only 128MB of RAM.

A: The module is not seated correctly. First, never put the case back on and screw it tight until *after* you have verified that all systems and subsystems are working properly. Second, using your fingertip, gently wiggle the top of the module. If it moves, remove and reseat it.

Q: My system had memory modules installed in two of the four SIMM slots. I just added a third SIMM module and the computer doesn't recognize it.

A: SIMM modules must be installed in banks of two. You will need to install a memory module in the remaining memory socket for the computer to recognize them both.

Q: I installed an additional DIMM memory module and the computer doesn't recognize it.

A: Verify that the computer doesn't require ECC memory. When non-ECC memory is placed in a computer that expects ECC memory, the result can be that the computer turns off the ECC feature or fails to recognize the new non-ECC memory.

Q: I installed new RAM a few *weeks* ago and everything worked fine until today, when I went from 64MB to 32MB. I reseated the DIMM several times but to no avail. What now?

A: Replace the DIMM with a new one. You can do this either through the retailer or the manufacturer. If this does not fix the problem, then it's likely a problem with your motherboard or another chip-level component. This is when you need to take the box in for service.

Q: I installed new RAM a few *months* ago and everything worked fine until today, when I went from 64MB to 32MB. I reseated the DIMM several times but to no avail. What now?

A: If something is going to go wrong with RAM (or any other chip component for that matter), it will happen in the first several weeks. Most manufacturers warrant their products for 3 to 12 months, others for the lifetime of the product. Make sure you keep all your warranty information in the same, easily remembered place and *register your stuff!* Once they officially know you bought it, it's hard for them to deny you service.

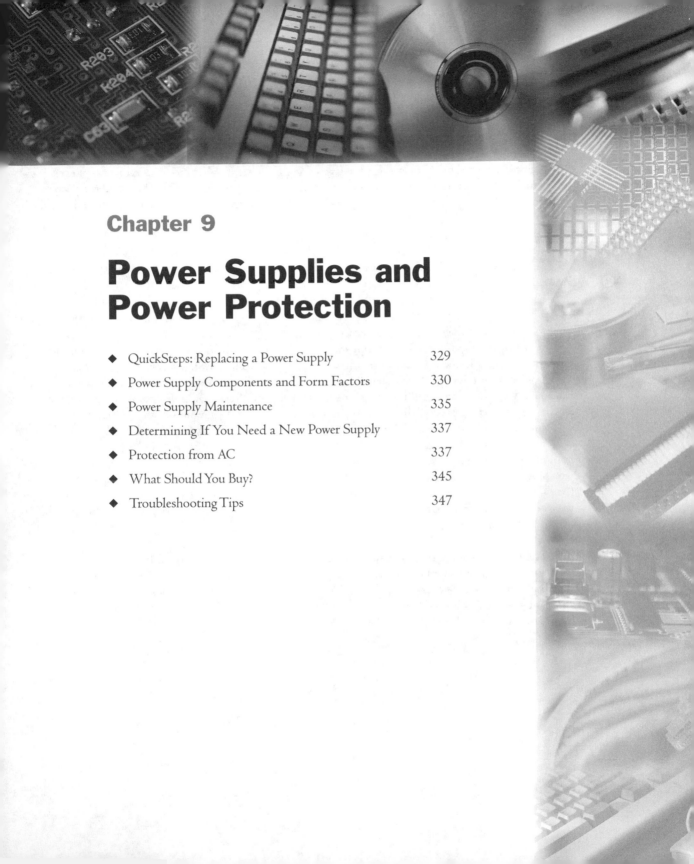

Chapter 9

Power Supplies and Power Protection

◆ QuickSteps: Replacing a Power Supply   329

◆ Power Supply Components and Form Factors   330

◆ Power Supply Maintenance   335

◆ Determining If You Need a New Power Supply   337

◆ Protection from AC   337

◆ What Should You Buy?   345

◆ Troubleshooting Tips   347

Introduction

PERSONAL COMPUTERS (AT LEAST, desktop PCs) don't come with batteries included. You plug them into the wall socket and they work. But the PC itself does not directly use wall current because it is 120-volt alternating current (AC) in North America, 220–240 in Europe and the U.K.

By the way, a word to European readers. Everything I say here applies to you *except* for references to the mains. As I just mentioned, your mains are not 120 volts, but more like 200+, and the power frequency is 50 Hz (cycles per second), not 60. *Do not* try any of the tests here that refer to the actual alternating current, unless you already know about working with the mains safely.

The PC doesn't need AC; it needs DC, usually 3.3 or 5 volts for its chips, 12 volts for the motors on older drives—newer drive motors run off 5 volts. But the wall sockets provide AC—so how does the PC convert the juice? With the power supply. The power supply actually doesn't *supply* power—it *converts* it from AC to DC.

There are two kinds of power supplies: linear power supplies and switching power supplies. The PC's power supply is, in every PC *I've* ever seen, a switching power supply. Both linear and switching power supplies have their positive and negative aspects.

Linear power supplies are based on transformers. That makes them hot, heavy, and impervious to changes in current levels, while rendering them vulnerable to voltage swings. Linear power supplies are an older design than switching power supplies, and you still find them on monitors and some external drive cases. Even small linear power supplies generate a relatively large amount of heat, which is why you should never cover the holes atop a monitor; you can fry a monitor quickly that way.

Switching power supplies are digital in nature. They step down voltage by essentially "switching" it on and off, hence their name. Think of how they work in this way: suppose you had a 1000-watt bulb in a lamp, but you only wanted the lighting value of a 100-watt bulb. You could get 100 watts' worth out of the 1000-watt bulb by switching it on and off but leaving it off 90 percent of the time. I know it sounds goofy, but if you could switch the light on and off quickly enough, then *you'd never see it flicker*. (In fact, that's how fluorescent lights work. They're actually very bright, but they flash off and on 60 times per second, too quickly for most eyes to register—and they're off over 90 percent of the time.)

Switching power supplies are less sensitive to fluctuations in input voltage, although that is still a problem. These power supplies generate heat—but a lot less of it than linear power supplies.

Why do we care about power supplies? Mainly because power supply troubles can be mysterious and annoying. Just as bad are similar-looking troubles with the supplied power itself. This chapter looks at both.

QuickSteps

Replacing a Power Supply

Here are the essential steps for replacing a power supply. The rest of this chapter provides more detailed coverage about power supply hardware.

BE PREPARED

Before you start, make sure you have the following handy:

- Nonmagnetic Phillips screwdriver
- Container to hold removed screws
- Antistatic wrist strap

1. Turn everything off and unplug the power supply from the wall outlet.

2. Unplug the power supply connectors from the motherboard and the drives.

3. Remove the four screws holding the power supply in the case and lift the power supply out.

    or

    If an AT, remove the screws holding the power switch to the case.

4. Insert the new power supply and secure it with the screws you removed in step 3.

    or

    If an AT, attach the power switch to the case with the screws removed in step 3.

5. Connect the power supply to the motherboard:

    - In an AT system, make sure P8 and P9 plug into the motherboard with the black wires next to each other in the center.

    - In an ATX system, the plug fits in only one direction.

6. Plug the power cord into the power supply. On an ATX system, flip the power switch on the power supply (if present).

7. Press the power button on the front of the PC. If you hear the fan(s) spinning up, the power supply is working. On newer systems, the fan(s) may not begin spinning immediately, so allow a few seconds just to make sure. Turn the power off again.

8. Connect the power supply connectors to the drives on your system. The floppy drive gets the little connector (the Berg); all other drives get the large ones (the Molex).

9. Turn the PC back on and confirm that all devices are working.

Components of the Power Supply

The power supply is the black or silver box in the back of the PC with the large yellow label telling you in five languages not to open the box and warning you that it is dangerous to do so. Despite the fact that I can only understand a few of the multilingual messages, I'm inclined to take them at their word.

The reason is mainly due to a thing called a *1000-microfarad capacitor,* which is inside the power supply. The capacitor is utilized to smooth out some power glitches. Big capacitors look like miniature soda cans, sized anywhere from about a couple of centimeters (about an inch) long to perhaps four times that size. Capacitors are kind of like holding tanks for electricity. If you've got some power that needs to go from point A to point B, but it tends to fluctuate a bit in the process, then an electronics designer can smooth it out a bit by putting a capacitor between A and B. The downside of a capacitor is that it's a part of a circuit that retains electricity even after you turn the circuit off. I once got a zap from a monster capacitor in a television that had been sitting unplugged in my family's attic for a few years, and I'm told that I'm lucky that I didn't do anything worse to myself.

The upshot of what I'm telling you is that the capacitors inside power supplies tend to argue against your trying to fix them. Power supplies can cost as little as $25 for an entire new unit, so just replace them if they're faulty. I recommend replacing and not repairing floppies just because it's a pain to repair them, but I recommend not repairing power supplies because they can hurt you.

NOTE   *Another reason not to open a power supply is that they are disposable and therefore cannot, in most cases, be repaired.*

Power Supply Form Factors

The motherboard needs power, and the power supply provides it. All power supplies are categorized by several characteristics, one of which is the *form factor.* This term describes the physical dimensions of the power supply and the types of power connectors it provides to power the motherboard. The form factors you will encounter in your PC work are described below.

PC/XT/AT Form Factors   The original power supply form factor got its name from the IBM PC/XT. In addition to the power connectors for the peripherals, the power supply also provided a motherboard power connection using two separate connectors, called P8 and P9, that plugged side-by-side into the motherboard. In 1984 IBM introduced the successor to the PC/XT: the AT. While the power supply's physical dimensions changed, the AT had the same motherboard and drive connections as the PC/XT form factor. The AT also featured a remote power switch. This feature, which appeared on the first tower-style case, allowed users to power up their computers from the front rather than having to reach around to the back or side. The AT form factor is no longer in use, except in very old computers running 286 CPUs. It was replaced by the Baby AT form factor.

Baby AT/LPX Form Factor   The Baby AT form factor got its name from the simple fact that it was a smaller version of the original AT form factor. With the exception of its smaller physical size, the Baby AT had the same power connectors as the AT and was used as a replacement for AT form factor power supplies. The Baby AT was extremely popular from 1985 through 1995, which means you stand a good chance of running into this form factor when you upgrade a computer.

Around the same time, another version of the Baby AT appeared under several different names, including *slimline* (because it was found in cases bearing the same name), *PS/2* (after the short-lived series of computers), and *LPX* (for low profile). While the LPX is physically smaller than the Baby AT, its output connectors are the same as the AT, with one small exception: the monitor pass-through power connector at the rear of the power supply began to disappear with the LPX form factor. As popular as these two form factors were, they were eventually replaced by the ATX.

ATX/NLX Form Factor   The year 1995 saw the introduction of the ATX form factor, and it was the first time that a genuine standard for both motherboards and their associated power supplies was created. Physically, the ATX power supply was almost identical to the Baby AT/LPX form factor, with the exception that the monitor pass-through power connector was now completely gone. Big changes occurred in both the output voltages and the connectors. A single 20-pin connector replaced the two separate connectors, P8 and P9. The ATX was the first power supply to provide 3.3 volts, and it introduced the first "soft power" switch, which allowed software to turn the computer on and off. The ATX power supply was designed for the NLX form factor motherboard, which is one of the reasons that the ATX power supply form factor is sometimes (and incorrectly) called the NLX power supply.

NOTE   *Some motherboards are designed for upgrading computers and have connectors for attaching to either AT or ATX form factor power supplies.*

Mini-ATX/Micro-ATX/SFX Form Factor   Mini-ATX, Micro-ATX, and SFX all describe a single form factor that is physically smaller than the ATX and does not have a −5 volt signal, which is only needed by some older expansion bus (ISA) cards.

ATX12V Form Factor   The newest form factor, a superset ATX called the ATX12V, was created for systems using P4 and high-end Athlon processors. The ATX12V adds an extra +12V power connector that enables the delivery of more current to the high-end processor-based boards. If you see a +12V 4-pin connector, you have an ATX12V power supply. If you don't find a +12V 4-pin connector, your power supply is an ATX version. A 6-pin Aux connector provides additional +3.3VDC and +5VDC current.

WARNING   *A Pentium 4 or AMD Athlon processor-based PC should use at least a 250-watt ATX12V power supply and a chassis that mechanically supports the processor heat sink assembly.*

Form Factor WTX   Any discussion of power supply form factors must include the WTX, which was introduced by Intel in 1998. This form factor is usually only seen on larger, more powerful systems (the *W* in WTX stands for *workstation*). The WTX is completely different from all earlier form factors. It is designed for multiple-CPU and multiple-drive systems, such as servers and high-end engineering workstations.

Form Factor Connectors

I've covered enough different form factors to make a large bowl of alphabet soup. Essentially, the motherboard requires either AT, ATX, or ATXV12 connectors. Table 9.1 summarizes the different form factors and their associated connectors.

TABLE 9.1: FORM FACTORS AND CONNECTORS

FORM FACTOR	MOTHERBOARD CONNECTOR
PC/XT/AT	AT
Baby AT/LPX	AT
ATX/NLX	ATX
SFX	ATX
WTX	Unique to WTX

AC power comes into the power supply from a wall outlet. On some systems (mostly the ATX ones), a power switch directly on the power supply turns this power influx on/off. Other systems don't have a switch on the power supply; whenever it's plugged in, it's automatically on.

However, just because the power supply is receiving juice from the wall doesn't necessarily mean that it is using that power to run the PC. The PC's on/off switch is separate, and on newer systems it's usually on the front of the PC. That switch controls the "soft power" feature described earlier and has a wire running from it to the motherboard; when you press the switch, the motherboard says to the power supply, "Hey, I want to turn on now, send me some of that power!" or "Okay, I'm ready to shut down, stop sending me power now." The point is, the power supply is the master of the power coming into the system—it receives it, converts it to DC, and doles it out as needed/requested to the components plugged into it.

As I mentioned, the connectors that plug the power supply into the motherboard are different depending on whether you've got an AT, ATX, or ATXV12 system. First, let's look at the AT model. P8 and P9 are identically sized and shaped; the only difference is the colors of wires and the order in which they appear. You have to get them plugged in right or you will irreparably smoke your motherboard. Just keep this in mind: *black together*. Both connectors have a black wire; when the connectors are plugged in properly, the black wire on P8 will be next to the black wire on P9. Figure 9.1 shows P8 and P9 connectors.

FIGURE 9.1

Power supply connectors to the motherboard for an AT system

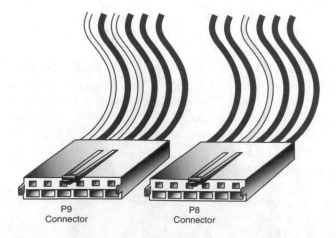

P9
Connector

P8
Connector

The ATX and ATXV12 design fixes that potential for confusion. On an ATX power supply, a single connector goes to the motherboard, shown in Figure 9.2. There's no way to get it plugged in wrong, because it fits in only one direction. The ATXV12 is similar, except for an additional four-pin connector for the extra power required by the newer, high-power processors.

FIGURE 9.2

Motherboard connector for an ATX power supply

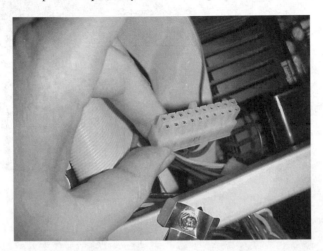

When you buy a computer, the case, the motherboard, and the power supply work as a team: they're all AT, or they're all ATX (this includes the ATXV12). Some motherboards can go either way, so they have both AT and ATX connector sockets. Figure 9.3 shows an example of such a beast. So if you ever buy a replacement for any of those components (a replacement power supply, for example), you need to make sure you get the right kind so it will work with your other pieces. You also need to make sure that you get a power supply with enough wattage (235 is decent for AT; 250 for ATX) to run all the devices you want to have in the system.

A bad power supply (either one that doesn't work at all or one that works erratically) can cause all kinds of problems in a system. If in doubt, test the power supply with a multimeter. The power supply lines can be tested against a ground (any of the black wires). If you are actually testing a power supply, all of the black wires should be tested.

You can then perform a resistance test of the motherboard. The tests are conducted on the power supply pins. Table 9.2 contains the *minimum* resistance for each connection. If the measured values are less than this, the motherboard is definitely faulty.

TABLE 9.2: SYSTEM BOARD RESISTANCES

COMMON LEAD (BLACK PROBE)	VOM (VOLTAGE-OHMMETER) LEAD	MINIMUM RESISTANCE (OHMS)
8	10	0.8
8	11	0.8
8	12	0.8
5	3	6
6	4	48
7	9	17

FIGURE 9.3

A motherboard with both AT and ATX power connectors

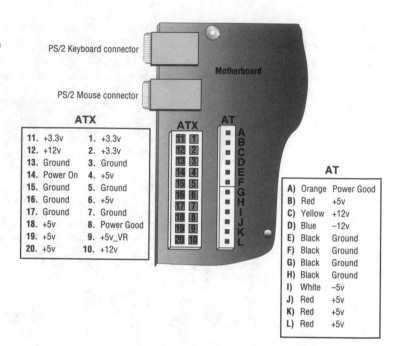

ATX		ATX		AT	
11. +3.3v	**1.** +3.3v		**A)**	Orange	Power Good
12. +12v	**2.** +3.3v		**B)**	Red	+5v
13. Ground	**3.** Ground		**C)**	Yellow	+12v
14. Power On	**4.** +5v		**D)**	Blue	−12v
15. Ground	**5.** Ground		**E)**	Black	Ground
16. Ground	**6.** +5v		**F)**	Black	Ground
17. Ground	**7.** Ground		**G)**	Black	Ground
18. +5v	**8.** Power Good		**H)**	Black	Ground
19. +5v	**9.** +5v_VR		**I)**	White	−5v
20. +5v	**10.** +12v		**J)**	Red	+5v
			K)	Red	+5v
			L)	Red	+5v

All power supplies, regardless of type, sport several identical Molex connectors for attaching to drives (hard disks, floppy disks, and tape drives). Figure 9.4 shows one of these. Most modern power supplies also include the smaller Berg connectors used to power 3½-inch floppy drives, shown in Figure 9.5. If your power supply doesn't have any Berg connectors, but you need one (or more), you can buy adapters at Radio Shack or a computer store that will convert a Molex to a Berg.

FIGURE 9.4

A Molex connector: your power supply has several of these.

You don't need to use all of the drive power connectors. Just because you've got four drive power connectors doesn't mean that you must have four drives. (I get asked that now and then.) Just make sure that the unused power connectors are tucked out of the way. I once saw a system freeze solid because one of the ground wires (the two black wires in the middle) on an unused drive power connector made contact with a test point on a motherboard.

Maintaining and Upgrading the Power Supply

Good news here: there isn't any maintenance required. The fan and the power switch are the only moving parts. If you suddenly notice that the PC is very quiet but still operating, your fan may have died. On newer systems, the fan(s) may be thermostatically controlled by the computer, so be sure the fan is supposed to be running before you panic. If the fan has failed, save everything and *shut down as soon as possible.* The computer's own heat can damage or destroy itself if the fan isn't working to dissipate it.

Don't block the vents that the PC uses for cooling. And take compressed air and blow the dust out of the fan now and then. (Remove the power supply from the PC case first so the dust doesn't immediately settle on the inside of computer.)

Years ago, desktop PCs lacked the power to drive all of their peripherals. It was common to find a PC start failing because it couldn't provide enough power to, well, *drive* its drives.

This experience led me to a preference for external peripherals, a preference that I retain to this day, even though today's PCs usually have power supplies with plenty of oomph. Whenever I'm buying a CD-ROM, large hard disk, or backup device, I buy it in an external case whenever possible. That means that every peripheral has its own fan and, as a bonus, its own power switch. Sometimes it's convenient to have the ability to disable a drive without popping the PC's top. It also means that the peripheral doesn't heat up the inside of the PC *and* it doesn't strain the PC's power supply.

Even if you don't have my "powernoia," however, you'll probably never have to worry about getting a larger power supply on your machine. *But,* if you're building a server with 512MB of RAM and a 100GB hard disk, as well as a CD-RW drive, a SCSI host adapter, and two LAN cards, you might think about one of the 300-plus-watt power supplies.

Better, however, is this advice: Don't just get a *big* power supply; get a *good* power supply, one of the ones made by the PC Power & Cooling people. I referred to them in Chapter 4, "Avoiding Service: Preventive Maintenance," and their contact information is listed in the Vendor Guide on the Utilities CD.

When buying a power supply, don't confuse "watts capacity" with "watts used." Will a 300-watt power supply use more power than a 150-watt power supply if it's put in a PC that draws only 100 watts? No. However, a 300-watt bulb uses more power than a 150-watt bulb because there, "watts" means watts used. The description "300-watt power supply" means a power supply that can convert *up to 300 watts*. Notice the *up to*—putting a 300-watt power supply on a system that only requires 50 watts will cause the power supply to convert only 50 watts. A lot of folks misunderstand that—even an IBM engineer in 1983 warned me that putting an XT's 130-watt power supply on an IBM PC would "burn up the motherboard." He was wrong, but I didn't know any better at the time.

But pushing a power supply too far isn't a good idea. How do you know how much power your machine is using? One simple way is to use a device like the Power Meter from PARA Systems. The Power Meter looks like a power strip with a gauge on it. You just plug it into the wall and then plug your system unit into the Power Meter. It has a wiring tester, so it tells you if your outlets are wired correctly. (See the section "Protecting the PC from the AC," coming up.) Then turn the system unit on and look at the needle on the gauge. It measures amperes of current flowing. You'll get a value between 0.5 and 3. Just multiply that ampere value by 58 and you'll get the number of watts that your system unit uses. If it is close to its rated power supply, it's time to get a bigger power supply.

Why 58? You may know that Power (Watts) = Volts × Amps, and that you ordinarily get 120 volts from the wall outlet. Why not multiply amps by 120? Simple—this isn't direct current, where amps and volts are always in phase. Instead, we're dealing here with AC, alternating current. In AC, current and voltage follow a sine wave–like path, a path that can fall out of step. That means multiplying amps by 120 would overstate the total actual power requirements. To calculate the correct wattage, you need to take a kind of "average" of the power used. This is called the *RMS power*.

When buying upgrade power supplies, consider the fan. I've seen far too many tower cases that put the drives and other hot things above the fan. And for heaven's sake, don't buy those dumb plug-in boards that have a fan on them. Your PC is built to circulate air in a particular direction. Those fans may actually work *against* the system's fan!

Also avoid the newer power supplies with fans that shut down "when they're not needed." They've got a thermocouple in them—a circuit that measures heat. If the heat in the system drops below some level, the fan shuts off. This is a terrible idea. PCs can suffer from "hot spots," areas that are considerably hotter than the average PC temperature. Just because the air going through the fan is, say, 100 degrees F, it doesn't mean that there isn't a 130-degree section over the processor. (And speaking of processor fans, if you've got one, check it occasionally. They're made incredibly cheaply, and tend to die after nine months or so, leaving you with a useless fan that actually *increases* the heat on the processor.)

Speaking of replacement power supplies, notice the first line on P8, which is called Power Good. This is a digital signal enabled by the power supply once it views itself as warmed up and ready. A flaky Power Good leads the computer to issue a long beep or short beeps or generally unusual noises. Some inexpensive replacement power supplies cause computers to emit a loud or long beep, then settle down to good service. I have experienced this myself, and I can only account for the beeps if the power supply doesn't wait quite long enough to first enable Power Good. A little initial up and down activity on the line induces the clock to issue a RESET command to the PC.

Determining If You Need a New Power Supply

You turn the computer on and nothing happens at all. It is plugged in, so it's not that—what next?

The Power Supply Troubleshooting Trail

First, check the wall outlet. The outlet should be providing between 104 and 130 volts AC current. Just set the voltage-ohmmeter (VOM) to read AC voltage and put one lead in each hole of the outlet. No VOM handy? Just plug in a lamp or appliance that uses AC power. In the United States, electrical power is very well regulated, so in almost all cases, if you have power at the outlet, you can assume it is within range.

Second, check the power cord. It should be firmly plugged into the power supply. If you have a spare cord, swap cords. Yes, power cords do fail.

Third, is power getting to the power supply? The fan gets it first, so if it isn't turning on, the power supply isn't getting power. When some power supplies are first turned on, the speaker emits a low click.

Fourth, check to make sure the power supply is connected to the motherboard using the right connectors, whether P8 and P9 (AT) or the single-piece, 20-pin ATX connector.

If all those things check out correctly, try swapping in a different power supply. The following section outlines how to remove and replace one.

Replacing a Power Supply

If you suspect the power supply, replace it. It's simple.

1. Open the PC case.

2. On the back of the PC, you will see four screws bolting the power supply to the chassis. Remove these.

3. Disconnect the power cables from the motherboard and drives. Draw a picture and make notes of what connects to what. Note wire colors: the black wires on the P8 and P9 connectors (if it's an AT system) are always next to each other.

4. If it's an AT, detach the screws that hold the power switch in the front of the computer. These screws may be difficult to reach without removing drives in some cases.

5. Install the new power supply by reversing the procedure.

6. To be extra careful, strip the PC down to the minimum circuit boards. Then power up and run whatever diagnostics you use.

Protecting the PC from the AC

You can control a lot of things in your environment, but you have little control over one aspect of the PC environment: the power delivered by the electric company. For various reasons, it may not come out clean and regular like it's supposed to. Worse yet, you can't always blame the power company—sometimes it's your fault or your building management's fault.

Do You Have Power Problems?

Power or wiring problems can show up as any of the following:

♦ The computer mysteriously "freezing up"

♦ Random memory errors

♦ Lost data on the hard disk

♦ Damaged chips on a circuit board

♦ Data transmission noise and peripheral errors

Years ago, I was at a hotel doing a presentation that involved a demonstration PC. The PC did the strangest things:

♦ Once, it stopped the memory test at 128KB and froze.

♦ Another time, it gave a memory error message around 400KB.

♦ The hard disk wouldn't boot about 30 percent of the time, despite a fresh format.

♦ It stopped talking to the keyboard a few times, requiring the "Big Red Switch" (the power switch).

What was the problem? The old "hotel power problem." When the coffee machine was on, the PC did strange things. Additionally, the PC shared an outlet with two 600-watt overheads in continuous use and a slide projector. I moved it to another outlet, and the problems disappeared.

Having said that, what can you do about power problems? The four steps to power protection are:

♦ Check that your outlets are wired correctly.

♦ Find out what else is on the power line.

♦ Provide a common ground for all devices.

♦ Protect against noise—surges, spikes, and under- and overvoltages.

Following are the facts to "empower" you to solve your line problems.

Check Outlet Wiring

AC outlets have three wires: a large prong, a small prong, and a center cylinder. The cylinder is the safety ground; the prongs are the "hot" or *phase* line (the official term is "phase," but anyone who's ever accidentally touched it calls it "hot") and the *return*, also called common, or neutral. The wires in the wall are supposed to be wired so that green is ground, white is return, and whatever's left (usually black) is phase.

It's not unheard of for the hot and the return to be reversed. This actually isn't a problem as long as *everything* is wired backward. But if you plug, say, the PC into a correctly wired outlet and a printer into a wrongly wired outlet, and if one of the devices connects the ground and the common—again, not an unusual occurrence—*and* there is a break in the neutral, then you'll get 120 volts across the cable from the printer to the PC. Lots of destruction will follow. Worse yet, miswired outlets can hurt you: if you touch both the PC and the printer at the same time, you are the electrical path.

You can buy circuit-wiring testers from most hardware stores. I got mine at Sears for $6 some years ago—they're probably a bit more now, but well worth it.

Check What Else Is on the Line

Ensure that there isn't any equipment on the same line as the PC that draws a lot of power. That includes the following:

- Large motors, like the ones you find in air conditioners, refrigerators, or machine tools

- Heating coils, such as in small space heaters or coffee makers—"personal coffee makers" are included here

- Copiers and their cousins, laser printers

Anything that draws a lot of current can draw down the amount of voltage being delivered to a PC on the same breaker or fuse. Worse yet, heating coil devices like coffee makers inadvertently create something called a *tank circuit* that can inject high-frequency spikes into the power line, noise that can slip through your power supply and go straight to the chips on the circuit boards.

One simple solution is to just get a dedicated power circuit to the computer. Another is to get an isolation transformer such as are found in a power conditioner. An RF (radio frequency) shield between the primary and secondary coils of the transformer removes the high-frequency noise.

Some large or old laser printers draw 15 amps all by themselves. That implies that, like it or not, you've got to put a 20-amp breaker in for *each* laser printer/PC combination. PCs *without* lasers don't draw much power and don't require a separate breaker.

Ensure Common Ground among Devices

Electrical ground is intended, among other things, to provide an electrical reference point, a benchmark value, like sea level. A computer communicates 1s or 0s to a modem, for instance, by varying voltage relative to ground: greater than +3 volts means 0, less than –3 volts means 1. Close to 0 volts means "nothing is being transmitted."

The problem arises when the two communicating devices don't agree on the value of ground. If, in the above example, the modem's ground is a 7-volts potential below the computer's ground, the modem and the computer each think that the other is sending data when actually neither is.

Generally, it's not that bad. But if the computer's ground is 3 volts different from the modem, the occasional bit will be lost or garbled.

The answer? Simple—just ensure that all devices plugged into your PC share the same ground. A simple six-outlet power strip will do this. There is one flaw in this approach, however: what about local area networks (LANs)? Basically, a LAN is one big ground problem. Some people have suggested grounding the shield of the network cables every hundred feet or so. The only true solution is to use fiber-optic LANs, but they're still a wee bit expensive.

NOTE   *Ensuring that all equipment has a common ground has nothing to do with having a proper ground. A proper ground is mainly for safety, not data protection. (If someone insists that you must have a good ground for proper data transfer, ask him how airplanes and spaceships manage it, hmmm?) We'll look at proper grounding soon.*

Protect against Power Noise

We've already discussed undervoltage, overvoltage, spikes, and surges in Chapter 4.

◆   *Undervoltage* is undesirable because the power supply reacts to too *little* voltage by drawing too *much* current. This heats up and may destroy components.

◆   *Overvoltage* can damage a chip because too much voltage destroys the circuits inside the chip.

When some outside force causes your power line to deliver more voltage than it is supposed to, this is called an overvoltage condition. Such conditions are, in general, dangerous to the computer.

The physics of it is this: the heart of the computer resides in its chips. A chip is a specially designed crystal. Crystals are highly structured molecules: many of them would be happier in a less structured environment. Applying electronic and heat energy to the crystals allows this breakdown in organization to occur. One spike might not do it, but it leaves damage that is cumulative. Even small spike damage is cumulative. Damage is proportional to energy. Energy is voltage, multiplied by current, multiplied by time.

Brief overvoltages of under a millisecond in length are called *spikes*. Longer ones—milliseconds to seconds—are called *surges*. *Spikes* may be of high enough frequency to introduce RFI-like problems.

You (or your boss) may be skeptical about the actual seriousness of power problems. This may all be, you suspect, a tempest in a teapot. If you don't think that you have power problems, spend $130 on a simple device that can monitor the quality of your power. Called the AC Monitor, you can get it from Milestek. They're listed in the Vendor Guide on the Utilities CD.

This device will continuously monitor the voltage that you are receiving at the outlet, and it will indicate power drops, surges, or spikes (no frequency variation, sadly) with a light and an audible warning.

The big three conditions that you wish to avoid are these:

◆   Surges and spikes

◆   Low voltage

◆   No voltage (power outages)

Solutions to Power Problems

Solutions to power problems fall into three categories:

◆   Isolation

◆   Shielding

◆   Proper grounding

Isolation means isolating the noise (surges, spikes, and so on) from the computer—draining it off harmlessly. This is done with filters, transformers, gas discharge tubes, and *metal oxide varistors (MOVs)*.

An MOV is an important part of a surge protector. When a surge comes in, an MOV shunts it off to ground. Unfortunately, the MOV is a kamikaze component—it "throws itself onto the grenade." Each MOV is only good for one big surge or a bunch of little surges. (No, there's no easy way to test to see whether an MOV is still working or not, at least not without a $2000 tester.) Power conditioners and surge protectors provide isolation in varying quality.

Shields minimize high-frequency noise. Shielding is evident in the filter capacitors in surge protectors, RF shields between the primary and secondary coils in a power conditioner, the metal case of the computer, and in the shield in shielded cable.

Some people view grounding as a magic answer to noise problems. Just run a wire from the device in question to a metal stake pounded into the ground (called a *ground stake*), and all of your ground problems go away! (Kind of like an electronic Roto-Rooter: "…and away go troubles down the drain.")

Nahhh.

First, having a proper ground *is* important. It makes electronic equipment safer (because it keeps you out of the circuit), but, as we've seen, a *common* ground is important to minimize communication errors between devices. So the main reason for a proper earth ground is safety.

The idea behind a ground stake (ya know, years ago, I thought ground stake was just hamburger…) is to provide a nice electrical path to earth ground. It *doesn't* eliminate noise, however: two ground stakes a few yards apart will pass current and noise between them. Ground stakes are less effective when there's a drought. I once heard of a ground stake that provided a better connection to ground than others on a particular site because it was, er, "watered" by local fauna. (No, I'm not sure I believe it, but ground *is* magic, and magical stories accompany it.)

A final thought on grounding: some companies are extra careful to ground their computer rooms, thinking that this will somehow protect their data. They're not so careful about the other areas in the building, however, so you've got a computer room with a cleaner ground than the rest of the building. Step back for a moment and ask what effect differential grounding would have on lightning protection. If lightning were to strike the building, it takes the easiest path to ground. If the easiest path to ground is through your computers, so be it. Basically, if you ground your computer room well and *don't* ground the rest of the building well, it's like putting a big "EAT AT JOE'S" sign on the computer room, as far as lightning is concerned.

Devices to Remedy Electrical Problems

Okay, now we've seen the problems and the approaches to solutions. Now let's look at what's available on the market to solve the problems.

If you're looking here for a recommendation, please understand that I haven't got good news. Electric power in the twenty-first century in most of the Western world is getting worse and worse due to aging equipment and lack of new capacity being pitted against ever-growing energy demands.

The PC really needs cleaner power than the stuff that you feed your refrigerator, Mr. Coffee, or desk lamp. The only absolutely reliable way to get clean power is to rectify the power, put it in a battery, and then use the DC power in the battery to reconstruct the AC power. A device that does this is a *UPS (uninterruptible power supply)*. A good one will cost you about a hundred bucks, but in the long run will save many hundreds on new computer components and lost data. On the other hand, there are some fairly effective alternatives like surge suppressors, *SPSs (standby power supplies)*, and power conditioners. Me? I'm building a faraday cage for my office (just as soon as I get some time and money…).

SURGE SUPPRESSORS AND SPIKE ISOLATORS

Many of us have purchased surge suppressors, or as they are also known, surge protectors or spike isolators.

The idea with suppression devices is that once they see a large surge coming, they redirect it out to the electric ground—kind of like opening the floodgates. The most common redirection device is an MOV, which I talked about a couple of sections earlier. It is an impassable barrier between the supply voltage and protective ground *until* the voltage reaches a certain level. *Gas discharge tubes* and *pellet arrestors* are slower but beefier devices. *Coaxial arrestors* fit somewhere in the middle.

The best suppressors use several lines of defense: MOVs, coax arrestors, and gas discharge tubes, for example.

Of course, an overzealous surge suppressor can redirect *too much* power for too long and create a worse surge of its own.

Another important question is *what* voltage level triggers the surge suppressor? They're not waiting for 120.00001 volts to get going: some will pass 1000 volts before calling in the Marines. By then, your PC is toast.

PC Magazine started doing tests of surge suppression devices years ago and published the results in the magazine. They created spikes and measured how much of the spike was allowed through. Some suppressors emitted smoke and flames when subjected to a real surge. Others died quietly, not informing the owner that they no longer protect the PC (they still pass electricity, so there's no way to know.)

THE BAD NEWS ABOUT SURGE SUPPRESSORS

As I've said, the best suppressors use several lines of defense, and the heart of those are MOVs. As we've said before, MOVs are one-time-only devices. One surge and they're history. Worse yet, they can't be tested.

Some surge protectors come with a little light that goes out when the surge protector doesn't protect anymore. But those little lights can't be trusted, either. The light is in series with a fuse, and the fuse is in series with the return from the MOV—it's called a *bleeder fuse*. Given a large enough surge, the fuse will blow (along with the MOV, you recall) and the light will go out. In that case, the case of a single large surge, the light *is* effective. But an MOV can also be destroyed by a number of smaller surges. In that case, the fuse would be unaffected, and the light would stay on.

Summarizing, there's no way to know whether or not your surge protector is still protecting. If you've got a light on your surge protector and it goes out, you definitely have a dead surge protector. But if the light's on, that's no guarantee of surge protector effectiveness.

Meanwhile, another company has built a renewable surge protector. The company's name is Zero-Surge, and their product is (likewise) called the Zero-Surge Protector. It's a good product, but be prepared to pay a bit for it, as you would for any quality device: models range from $150 to $200. Zero-Surge's contact information is in the Vendor Guide on the Utilities CD.

POWER CONDITIONERS

Between a surge protector and a backup power supply is another device, also in-between in price, called a *power conditioner*. A power conditioner does all the things that a surge protector does—filters and isolates line noise—and more. Rather than relying on MOVs and such, the power conditioner uses the inductance of its transformer to filter out line noise. An isolation transformer is a far superior device for removing noise to a capacitor or an MOV. Additionally, most power conditioners will boost up undervoltage so that your machine can continue to work through brownouts.

Recall that the surge protector's MOVs fail with no sign, so there's no good way to know whether your surge protector is doing any good. Power conditioners don't have that problem—when a transformer fails, you know it—the power conditioner just plain doesn't provide any power.

Which power conditioner is right for you? I have used the Tripplite LC1800. I've seen it in mail-order ads for as little as $179. One firm that sells them cheaply is Altex Electronics, which is also listed in the Vendor Guide on the Utilities CD.

The LC1800 even shows you your incoming voltage via some LEDs on its front panel. *Do not* plug your laser printer into the LC1800, as it is only rated for 6 amps. (Remember that lasers draw up to 15 amps.)

BACKUP POWER SUPPLIES

In addition to protection from short power irregularities, you may need backup power. I have lived in a number of places in the northeastern U.S. where summer lightning storms will kill the power for just a second—enough to erase your memory and make the digital clocks blink. Total loss of power can be remedied only with battery-based systems. Such systems are in the range of $150 to $1200 and up.

There are two types, a *standby power supply* (SPS) and an *uninterruptible power supply* (UPS). Figure 9.6 shows how UPSs and SPSs work. SPSs charge the batteries while watching the current level. If the power drops, they activate themselves and supply power until their batteries run down. A fast power switch must occur here, and it's important to find out what the switching time is—4ms or under is fine, and 14ms, in my experience, is not fast enough.

A UPS constantly runs power from the line current to a battery, then from the battery to the PC. This is superior to an SPS because there is no switching time involved. Also, this means that any surges affect the battery charging mechanism, not the computer. A UPS is, then, a surge suppressor also.

A UPS or SPS must convert DC current from a battery to AC for the PC. AC is supposed to look like a sine wave. Older and some cheaper UPS and SPS models produce square waves (see Figure 9.7). Square waves are bad because they include high-frequency harmonics, which can appear as EMI (electromagnetic interference) or RFI to the computer. Also, some peripherals (printers in particular) can't handle square-wave AC. So, when examining UPSs, ask whether they use square wave or sine wave. Some produce a pseudo-sine wave. It has the stair step look of a square wave, but it doesn't have as many harmonic problems. The good news is that most UPS and SPS models available in today's marketplace output pure sine waves.

Ordinarily, the purpose of a UPS is to allow you enough time to save whatever you're doing and shut down gracefully. If you are in an area where the power may disappear for hours, and may do it regularly, then you should look for the ability to attach external batteries to the UPS so that you can run the PC for longer periods.

Remember that a sine wave UPS is the only way to really eliminate most power problems. The reason *everyone* didn't have one was cost, and thanks to the advances in power conversion technology, everyone should have one.

FIGURE 9.6

How UPSs and
SPSs work

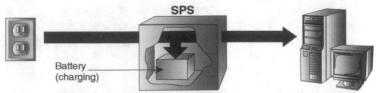

When power is normal, an SPS passes current through to the PC
– spikes and all – while siphoning off a bit of the power in order to keep the battery charged.

When the power is interrupted, the SPS supplies power to the PC from the battery for
as long as the battery lasts. The SPS must also sense the power-down condition and
get the battery on-line quickly enough that the PC can continue to work uninterrupted.

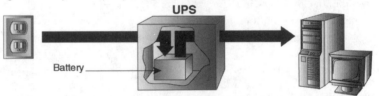

A UPS, on the other hand, sends power from the socket right into the battery, keeping it
constantly charged. The computer draws the power from the battery instead of the line.

When power is interrupted, the UPS continues to supply power to the computer
from the battery. Benefits: constant surge protection and zero switching time.

FIGURE 9.7

UPS AC waveforms

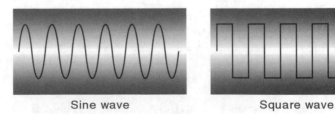

On the other hand, remember that a UPS is *always* online, and so must produce sine wave output. But UPSs do have the benefit that they provide surge protection by breaking down and reassembling the power, and SPSs *do not* provide this protection. You must still worry about surge protection when you buy an SPS, but that's not true if you buy a UPS. So make the choice that your budget allows.

Something to look for in backup power supplies—both UPSs and SPSs—is a serial port.

A serial port? Yes, a serial port. Most operating systems can monitor a signal from a serial port–equipped UPS/SPS. When power fails, the operating system is informed by the backup power supply of that occurrence, and the operating system does a graceful shutdown in the battery time remaining. This function is also called a *heartbeat.* Table 9.3 summarizes what I've covered about power problems and solutions.

TABLE 9.3: POWER PROBLEMS AND SOLUTIONS

PROTECTION METHOD	REMEDIES SURGES	REMEDIES LOW VOLTAGE	REMEDIES OUTAGE
Power conditioner	Yes	Yes	No
SPS	No	No	Yes
UPS	Yes	Yes	Yes

Before buying an SPS or a UPS, however, be aware of just one more thing—many people are selling SPSs under the name of "offline UPS." Real UPSs are nowadays being called "online UPS."

So What Should I Buy?

Sounds like you can spend a pile of money on power protection and, sadly, that's true: a real, honest-to-goodness UPS will set you back four figures. (As I mentioned, cheaper ones are SPSs that marketers call "offline UPS." Kind of like calling a car a "wingless ground-based airplane" or calling those salespeople "honesty-challenged.") The best compromise that I've come up with is a neat little combination of a power conditioner and an SPS with, of course, a serial port attached. Called the Smart-UPS 420, it's made by American Power Conversion (APC), and I've found them for about $210. It's a complete power solution, and they've worked wonderfully for me for the past four years, through storms and power company screwups. You can find contact information for APC in the Vendor Guide on the Utilities CD.

The Granddaddy of Power Problems: Lightning

When Thor's hammer falls near your site, you won't need any special equipment to note its passing. Curled-up, blackened circuit boards are pretty easy to spot.

I travel around North America and Europe teaching troubleshooting classes. You know what *everyone* tells me? No matter where we are, the natives tell me that they're in the "lightning capital of the world." (I know, hearing something *shocking* like that makes you want to *bolt.*) Take a look at Figure 9.8 to find out where you rate.

FIGURE 9.8

Mean annual number of days with thunderstorms

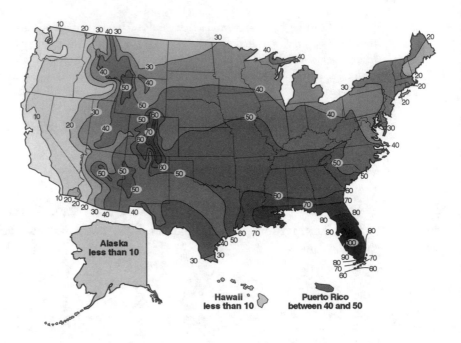

Looks like central Florida can lay claim to the "Thunderstorm Central" title. Here's what we know about thunderstorms:

◆ Lightning affects your system even if it doesn't strike your building.

◆ If the power utilities enter your house or office building above ground, you should consider unplugging any electronic device you can't afford to lose during a severe thunderstorm. If your utilities are below ground, the chances of a direct strike to the power is greatly reduced.

◆ As mentioned earlier, taking special care to ground the part of the building that the big computers are in just makes those computers more vulnerable. A better-grounded path is the one that lightning will take.

◆ Lightning arrestors can reduce the likelihood of lightning damage.

◆ Newer high-tech lightning rods are being used in some sites. They look like umbrellas built of barbed wire standing about 30 feet tall.

◆ A cheap lightning protection: overhand knots in the power cord.

Believe it or not, some researchers found this last one out. It makes the lightning surge work against itself and burn out the power cord, *not* the PC. And it works—Washington had the biggest thunderstorm it had in years in the summer of 1989, and the stuff with knots in the cords rode it out without a hitch. The TV didn't have knots in the cord, so I did have to buy a new TV.

The following year, a bolt hit my *telephone line*. It literally toasted the line from the telephone pole to my house; crispy brown little bits flaked off at the touch. But once inside, the bolt hit my five knots, and nothing inside was fried. Why did I tie the knots? I got tired of losing a modem every summer to lightning.

Since a lightning strike can send a spectacular power surge along power lines, damaging equipment that is plugged into nearby AC and phone outlets, you might want to consider something that provides a little more security than that provided by the knot-in-the-power-cord method. When it comes to lightning, the severity of these surges can only be neutralized by quality surge suppression. A good surge suppressor will provide surge protection on *all* AC outlets, not just one or two. Select models will include RJ11 modem/fax line surge suppression as well, preventing damage to modems and phone systems. These surge suppressors also feature indicators that inform you when the protection circuit has been compromised. The best part is that the good ones come with an insurance policy that ranges from $50,000 to $100,000, covering damage that is a result of the surge protector failing. While these are not cheap, they also are worth every cent you pay for them. At the time of this writing, you can expect to pay between $60 and $90 for a suppressor that offers all of the features I just described.

Power's not the sexiest part of PC hardware, but it sure can be the most troublesome. Get a Smart-UPS and a decent power supply, buy external peripherals, and you'll be electrified with the results.

Troubleshooting Tips

If you are not getting any power to the PC (no fans, no nothing), do the following:

◆ Check whether power is coming from the wall outlet to the power supply.

◆ If you are using a power strip, confirm that it is on. (Most power strips have a rocker on/off switch.)

◆ Check for loose connections from the power plug to the power supply or from the power supply to the motherboard.

◆ In an AT system, confirm that the black wires of P8 and P9 are together, not at opposite ends of the power connector on the motherboard.

◆ In an ATX system, make sure that the power switch on the power supply itself is on before you press the power button on the front of the PC.

◆ If the power supply has a voltage switch (110/220), make sure that it is set for the currency in the location in which you are working (110 is standard in the U.S.).

If you are having other problems with the PC that you suspect might be power-related, do the following:

◆ Check that your outlets are wired correctly.

◆ Make sure no other high-wattage devices are sharing the power line.

◆ Make sure that your outlets are grounded and that all your devices share the same ground (plugging them all into the same power strip will accomplish this).

◆ Install equipment that can protect against surges and spikes, low voltage, and/or power outages. This might include a surge suppressor, an SPS, or a UPS.

In the next chapter, we'll take a general look at the hard drive before moving on to specific types of drives.

Chapter 10

Hard Disk Drive Overview and Terminology

- ◆ Hard Drives and Interfaces 351
- ◆ What's in a Disk? 355
- ◆ Disk Performance Characteristics 365
- ◆ Getting Good Data Transfer Rates 374
- ◆ Size Limits 376
- ◆ Protocols for Transferring Data 381
- ◆ Modern ATA Standards 382

Introduction

HARD DRIVES ARE WHERE most of a PC user's data lives. Since your data is the most valuable part of your system, it stands to reason that the hard drive is, in some ways, the computer's most important part.

That's why this book has so many chapters on hard drives. In this one, you'll look at disk-ese and get a bird's-eye view of disk technology.

Disk Types and the Future

Before we begin, it's important to note that there are two basic types of disks: magnetic disks and optical discs. Examples of *magnetic disks* include floppy disks, hard drives, and hard drives with removable cartridges that you can mount either internally or externally.

Examples of *optical discs* include CDs, WORMs (Write Once, Read Many), DVDs, and erasable optical discs. Briefly, the disk controller writes data to an optical disc by using a laser to burn microscopic holes on the surface of the disc. The disk controller reads the data by shining a second laser on the disc surface and reading any changes in the reflection pattern that the holes cause. Refer to Chapter 27, "An Overview of CD-ROM and DVD-ROM Drives," for information about optical discs.

No single technology can provide the storage solutions for all segments of rapidly expanding markets. Advancing disk technology employed by some disk drives allows the storage of ever-increasing amounts of data on a disk and improves data transfer rates.

Special niche markets might consider using the holographic storage techniques that are currently being developed. A *holographic storage* technique stores data in two- or three-dimensional boundaries inside special containers. While not commonly used, this technique could be particularly useful in multimedia applications and for storing the many variants of image files.

Wet disk technology is another technology now being used by some manufacturers. Wet disk replaces the air cushion over the hard drive with liquid and allows the heads to get closer to the disk surface to read dense data.

As the number of individuals and businesses using computers (and the Internet) increases, so does the demand for larger storage capacity and higher disk access speeds. Disk technology will continue to improve and come up with innovative methods to meet these needs. Indeed, it is quite conceivable that a few years from now completely new and very different storage techniques may be available.

Hard Drives and Interfaces

All peripheral devices need some way of communicating with the computer. A hard drive subsystem consists of the hard drive itself, a disk interface, and the cable or cables connecting them. Disk interfaces are either host adapters or controllers, depending on the type of disk technology. Older drive technologies use controllers; newer ones use host adapters.

A *controller* is a device that controls the transfer of data (in both directions) between the computer and the peripheral device. Controllers can be built into a single chip or chipset, or they can be on expansion boards.

Host adapters are devices that contain the necessary circuitry to support another device. Host adapters can be built into the main circuitry of a computer, or they can be separate add-on boards.

Disk terms are relevant either to a hard drive or to a drive interface. For drives, Table 10.1 summarizes these terms.

TABLE 10.1: HARD DRIVE TERMS

DRIVE CHARACTERISTIC	WHAT IT MEANS, WHY IT'S RELEVANT
Number of cylinders	Part of capacity determination. Hard drives store data on a stack of aluminum or glass platters. Each surface of each platter (top and bottom) consists of magnetically divided circular tracks. A cylinder is a stack of corresponding tracks. For example, track 20 on each of the platters (tops and bottoms) would make up one of the cylinders of the hard drive.
Number of heads	Part of capacity determination. There are two heads for each platter of the hard drive (one on the top and one on the bottom). The heads read and write the data on the platters.
Number of sectors	Part of capacity determination. Each track on every platter consists of divisions or sections (the sectors). In general, each sector contains the same number of bytes of data.
Zone bit recording (ZBR)	Describes whether the number of sectors per track is constant. If the number of sectors per track remains the same on all tracks, the tracks divide the platters more or less like slices of pie. This makes the center tracks denser than the outer tracks. To make the data readable in the inner tracks, the data in the outer tracks is spread out; this compromises capacity. Therefore, most drives today vary the number of sectors per track to optimize the total disk area.
Head-positioning mechanism	A drive design element, a tradeoff of speed versus cost. Older hard drives use a stepper motor to move the heads back and forth so they can access each of the tracks (cylinders). Today, most hard drives move the heads using a voice coil. Refer to the "Voice Coil and Stepper Head-Positioning Mechanisms" section for more information.
Access time	Drive design characteristic. This is the amount of time it takes for the heads to locate a specific piece of data in the hard drive. The components of access time include controller overhead time, latency, and seek time. Usually manufacturers specify the "average access time," because the actual seek time varies depending on the location of the heads and the next bit of data.
Data transfer rate	The speed at which the system copies data from the hard drive to the computer or from the computer to the hard drive. Also called the *media rate*, it consists of two parts: first, the internal data transfer rate (the *sustained rate*), which relates to the amount of time it takes to read or write to the disk; and second, the external data transfer rate (the *burst rate*), which relates to the transfer speed over the interface between the hard drive and the rest of the PC.
Drive interface type	Configuration issues determine what kind of interface your computer will need to communicate with the hard drive. Most today employ Enhanced Integrated Drive Electronics (EIDE). The other popular interface in use today is Small Computer System Interface (SCSI), although the newer packetized SCSI interface (called Ultra160+ SCSI) promises even faster throughput, with full backward compatibility with older SCSI devices.

Continued on next page

TABLE 10.1: HARD DRIVE TERMS *(continued)*

DRIVE CHARACTERISTIC	WHAT IT MEANS, WHY IT'S RELEVANT
Direct memory access (DMA)	A popular hard drive interface data transfer method. DMA is a mechanism for transferring data between the hard drive and host memory that virtually eliminates the CPU from the transfer process. The use of DMA requires an operating system device driver and a basic input/output system (BIOS) that supports the DMA specifications. (For more information, refer to the "PIO and DMA Protocol Transfer Mechanisms" section in this chapter.)
Programmed input/ output (PIO)	The most popular hard drive interface data transfer method. It has five modes, each of which defines a different maximum transfer rate, and uses the CPU in the data transfer process. PIO transfers data to and from the disk controller through the I/O ports. The CPU manages throughput at the I/O ports. (For more information, refer to the "PIO and DMA Protocol Transfer Mechanisms" section in this chapter.)
Write precompensation cylinder	On older hard drives, the heads required higher current output to write to the inner cylinders because the data was so close together that the heads switched on and off more quickly there. Therefore, the platter needed more *oomph* to write the data reliably onto the inner tracks. The write precompensation cylinder specification told the computer when to boost the current to the write heads. Most recent hard drives don't need the boost because they keep sector lengths constant.

Drive interfaces have characteristics as well. Table 10.2 summarizes some of them.

TABLE 10.2: DRIVE INTERFACE CHARACTERISTICS

INTERFACE CHARACTERISTIC	RELEVANT TO HOST ADAPTER, CHARACTERISTIC CONTROLLER, OR BOTH	WHAT IT MEANS, WHY IT'S RELEVANT
Logical block addressing (LBA)	Host adapter	A method that allows computers to access all the data on hard drives larger than 528MB.
Onboard cache memory	Both	Some controllers have memory on them for keeping copies of data that the computer frequently requests.
Sector translation	Both	Alternate method of getting the computer to support larger drives.
Interface to system bus	Both	Indicates which PC bus this interface is built for. Possible types are ISA, EISA, MCA, PC Card, VESA, PCI, USB, and even parallel ports (see Table 10.3). Alternate method of getting the computer to support larger drives.
Max error burst/ECC length	Both	Indicates how many bad bits this controller can recover from.

In this chapter, you'll tackle everything in Table 10.2. After you've gone through this information, you should be ready to learn how to install, protect, and repair hard drive subsystems.

System buses provide pathways to move data and control signals between the various components within the computer. Current PCs can include several types of buses, including an expansion bus, a data bus, and a local bus:

Expansion bus   Also an external bus or input/output bus. Provides a path for adapter cards and external devices to the internal system bus.

Data bus   Provides for the transfer of data between system components and provides direct access to memory on the system board.

Local bus   Also an internal bus. Connects the microprocessor with the system controllers. Transfer rates over a local bus are close to the processor speed of the unit.

Table 10.3 briefly describes some of the system bus/interface types from Table 10.2.

TABLE 10.3: PC SYSTEM BUS/INTERFACE TYPES

BUS TYPE	ACRONYM DEFINITION	DESCRIPTION
EISA	Extended Industry Standard Architecture	An open standard PC bus architecture in systems with Intel Pentium, 80386, and 80486 that can transfer data at 32 bits per second. A few high-performance PCs use EISA. Most high-performance PCs use the PCI bus because it is more flexible (see the description of the PCI bus in this table).
ISA	Industry Standard Architecture	A standard PC bus architecture in IBM PC/XT and PC/AT systems that allows 16 bits at a time to flow between the computer, its expansion cards, and associated devices. ISA is usually used for slower peripherals. In the early '90s, the higher performance PCI bus started replacing ISA, and today ISA is almost obsolete as Intel and Microsoft continue to move the industry away from its use.
MCA	Micro Channel Architecture	An interface between one or more computers, their expansion cards, and other devices. A proprietary nonstandard system from IBM for its PS/2 computers.
PCI	Peripheral Component Interconnect	Originally a local bus interconnection, PCI is no longer a local bus architecture. Currently you can implement PCI (PCI 2 and up) as a 64-bit bus or 32-bit bus that synchronizes with the clock speed of the microprocessor. PCI uses all active paths to transmit both address and data signals and, in addition, supports burst data.

Continued on next page

USB	Universal Serial Bus	A Plug and Play interface between a computer and an add-on device. If a computer has a USB, you can add a new device without adding an adapter or turning off the computer. USB supports a data speed of 12Mbps. Today, most new computers and peripheral devices have USB.
VESA (VL Bus or VLB)	Video Electronics Standards Association	The first popular local bus. VESA is a technology that provides fast data flow between the expansion cards and the microprocessor. It is a 32-bit bus that is a direct extension of the 486-processor/memory bus. VESA is usually associated with systems with advanced video cards and is sometimes associated with disk controllers because it provides them with a more or less direct connection to the processor. With the advent of the Pentium processor and the PCI bus, VLB became obsolete for new systems. All Pentiums and higher use PCI.
IEEE 1394 (also known as FireWire)	Institute of Electrical and Electronics Engineers	The IEEE 1394 (or FireWire) bus is designed to replace serial, parallel, and SCSI ports with a universal six-wire connector. It supports up to 63 devices and is designed to support speeds up to 400Mbps, making it ideal for devices that require a lot of bandwidth (scanners, video cameras, hard drives, and more). Requires an operating system and drivers that support the Open Host Controller Interface (OHCI). Windows 98SE/Me/2000/XP include support for OHCI/IEEE 1394 devices.

Disk Geometry: Heads, Tracks, Cylinders, and Sectors

If I wanted to tell you how to get to my house, I might say something like, "Travel west from Washington, D.C., for 5 miles on I-6 to Dreller Avenue, then turn left on Dreller and take it south for another mile until you reach Garner Drive. Take a right onto Garner and I'm two blocks up on the right." In order to understand what I'm talking about, you'd have to understand *west, south, block, left,* and *right*. In the same way, you can't even think about doing disk work without understanding terms like *cylinder, head, sector,* and *track*—words that are basic to disk discussions.

Disk geometry refers to the electronic organization of any type of disk drive, the actual physical number of heads, cylinders, tracks, and sectors. The physical geometry of a disk stores data on disks in bytes and organizes the bytes into 512-byte groups called sectors. *Sectors* are the minimum unit of data that you can read from or write to a disk. A specific number of sectors group together into *tracks*, and tracks on hard drives are grouped together into *cylinders*.

A disk has at least two surfaces. The system addresses the sectors on a hard drive using a matrix of cylinders, heads, and sectors. You can see a cutaway view of a hard drive in Figure 10.1.

FIGURE 10.1

Cutaway view of a hard drive

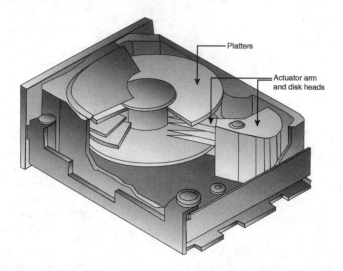

Before going into detail about hard drives, however, it's easiest to explain hard drive structure with a simpler storage medium—a 1.44MB floppy disk:

◆ A floppy disk is typically made of Mylar. Jackets covering the Mylar disk can be flexible or semi-rigid. The read/write heads access the Mylar surface through the drive gate.

◆ A floppy disk has two *sides* (surfaces), which require two *heads* to read them.

◆ Each side contains data.

◆ Each side has 80 concentric *tracks*. There is a related notion called *cylinders* (I'll explain them in a moment), so we say a 1.44MB floppy has 80 cylinders.

◆ Each track has nine divisions or *sectors* (like nine pieces of a pie).

◆ Each sector stores 0.5KB (512 bytes) of information.

In contrast to the Mylar of a floppy disk, a hard drive contains rigid metal or glass disks, called *platters*, stacked up on a spindle inside an air-filtered enclosure. For example, the original XT 10MB drive had two platters. Other drives may have fewer, some others many more. Again, a floppy disk is like one "platter," but it's not rigid.

The platters have a coating of a special material on both sides that allows the computer to store information in magnetic patterns. Each platter is capable of holding billions of bits of data per square inch. A special motor on the spindle drives the platters at high speeds.

A hard drive also has electromagnetic read/write heads and a logic board or controller. The sealed enclosure prevents foreign contaminants such as dust particles, fingerprints, or smoke particles from affecting the various components and operation of the disk drive. Foreign contaminants can cause a head crash, which can occur if the head makes contact with the disk surface itself or if the head touches particles on the disk surface.

Disk Heads

Like a floppy disk, the hard drive has an electromagnetic read/write *disk head* for each side of each platter. For example, some drives have four heads: two heads for each platter (one on the top and one on the bottom) × two platters. The read/write heads mount on an actuator arm that moves the heads over the surface of the platter on a very thin cushion of air to the proper track. A servo system generates feedback, which accurately positions the read/write heads. A rotary voice coil at one end powers each actuator arm. The actuator arms lock together and move from track to track as a single unit.

The disk controller (usually a microprocessor) controls the servo system and translates digital data into magnetic pulses that the read/write heads store on the platters. The read/write heads transfer the magnetic pulses back to the controller, which then converts them back into digital data for the CPU.

Remember, the disk drive is sealed and contains the mechanical components of the drive. You don't have to worry about aligning or cleaning these heads, and besides, you couldn't do those things even if you wanted to because the heads are inaccessible.

Manufacturers today are including magnetoresistive (MR) heads with separate read and write elements in disk drives. These heads make it possible to place more data under a single head. Having separate heads allows the construction of wider write and narrower read heads to suit differing operating needs.

Disk Tracks

Each side of each platter (each *surface*) contains concentric tracks, like a floppy and similar to the annual rings of a tree. A *disk track* is a path that contains the reproducible information on the magnetic media. Track counting starts at 0 at the outer edge and increases as it moves inward.

A floppy like the 1.44MB example I use in Figure 10.2 typically has 80 tracks; older hard drives start at 305 tracks, and newer drives go up from there. (Some drives today contain upward of 100,000 tracks!) Today, 3½-inch is the most common hard drive size in use. This means that the platters inside the drive are 3½ inches in diameter. Most laptop computers use 2½-inch drives. New technologies make it possible to store nearly as much data on one of these drives as on a 3½-inch drive.

FIGURE 10.2

A 1.44MB
floppy disk

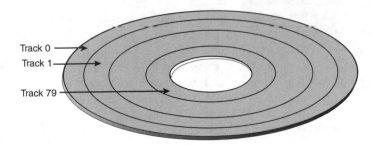

Track 0

Track 1

Track 79

Disk Cylinders

As I've said, a platter has two sides with concentric tracks. Two tracks that align exactly with each other (one on the bottom of the platter, and one on the top) form a *cylinder*. If there are two or more platters, all pairs of tracks that line up with each other make up the cylinder. If there are three platters, for example, each cylinder has six tracks (three pairs). In other words, taken together, the tracks become a virtual cylinder. You can see the relationship between tracks and cylinders in Figure 10.3.

The number of tracks per surface is identical to the number of cylinders; therefore, most manufacturers do not report the number of tracks, they report the number of cylinders. Although the two terms mean different things, people use *cylinder* and *track* synonymously.

FIGURE 10.3

The relationship between tracks and cylinders on a disk

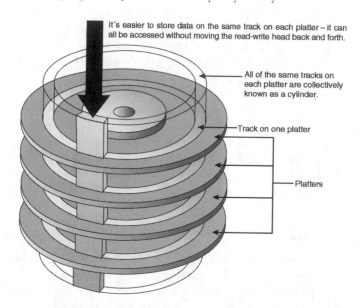

It's easier to store data on the same track on each platter – it can all be accessed without moving the read-write head back and forth.

All of the same tracks on each platter are collectively known as a cylinder.

Track on one platter

Platters

Hard drives usually have more than one platter, which means that most have four or more read/write heads. The heads lock together and attach to an *actuator arm*. This means that when the actuator positions head 0 (as in most of the rest of the computer business, here we count 0 to 3, not 1 to 4) over track 142 on surface 0, it also positions head 3 over track 142 on surface 3. Each head is always physically at the same track number or cylinder number. It is impossible to independently position the disk heads.

Here's how it works: To read a particular sector, the disk hardware goes through three steps. First, it must move the read/write head over the desired track. Second, it must wait for the disk to rotate so that the desired sector is under the head, and, finally, it must read.

In general, moving the head takes the most time. This means that the disk hardware can most quickly read a file whose sectors are all on the same track and *whose tracks lie above one another*—one head move can read a pile of data. Thus, if a large file starts out on, say, head 0, track 142, it's a good idea to make sure that the next track that file uses is head 1, track 142, and then head 2, track 142, and so on. There's no need for a head movement, but the disk can suck up a lot of data.

Disk Sectors

Each platter surface is figuratively cut into wedges like a pie. These wedges are called *sectors*. A sector is the smallest accessible unit on a disk. When you format a disk, the disk controller establishes the sector size. Floppies typically divide tracks into 8 to 18 sectors apiece, as shown in Figure 10.4.

FIGURE 10.4

Tracks and sectors on a floppy

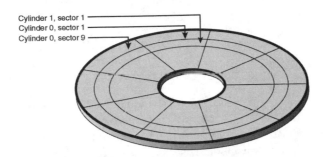

Both hard and floppy disk devices typically store 512 bytes on a sector—0.5KB of data, as 1KB = 1024 bytes. (See Figure 10.5.) In addition to containing data, each sector contains a few more bytes dedicated to error detection and correction and internal drive control.

FIGURE 10.5

Each sector typically contains 512 bytes of data.

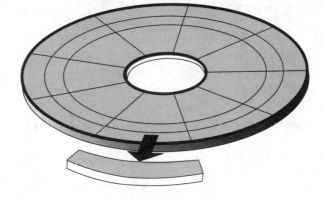

Summarizing, then, a 1.44MB floppy consists of:

◆ Two sides, or surfaces (and heads)

◆ 80 tracks and cylinders per side

◆ 18 sectors per track

◆ 0.5KB on each sector

So:

$$2 \times 80 \times 18 \times 0.5\text{KB} = 1.44\text{MB}$$

Now compare the specs on a 10MB XT hard drive, the simplest hard drive I've ever seen:

◆ Four surfaces

◆ 305 tracks on each surface

◆ 17 sectors per track

◆ 0.5KB on each sector

So:

$$4 \times 305 \times 17 \times 0.5KB = 10,370K \text{ bytes}$$

As you examine other disks, you will find that the 512 bytes per sector is constant. The number of tracks, the number of platters, and the number of sectors vary. Most manufacturers do not report the number of platters but instead the number of heads, which equals the number of surfaces. For example, consider a more modern disk:

◆ 16,383 cylinders

◆ 16 heads for storing data

◆ 3 platters

◆ 63 sectors per track

◆ 512 bytes (0.5KB) of data on each sector

Total all that up and you get a 60GB drive.

Zone Bit Recording

Before leaving the subject of sectors, it's worth mentioning that the diagrams that you've seen in this book so far have all shown drives as having a constant number of sectors per track. That's not always the case.

The outer track on a disk is typically double or more the circumference of the innermost track. With an equal number of sectors on each track, data on the outer track is quite loose, while data on the innermost track is quite dense.

Placing differing numbers of sectors per track on a disk surface is called *zone bit recording (ZBR)*. You will also hear the terms *multiple zone recording* or even just *zone recording* in place of ZBR. Consumer demand for greater and greater capacity on smaller and smaller drives, in combination with cheaper and faster electronics, has led to a growth in the use of ZBR.

Here's how it works: Based on their location on a disk, the ZBR program groups the tracks into zones. All tracks within a specific zone are given a constant number of sectors. Movement through the disk from the innermost zone to the outer zone passes you through multiple zones, each with a higher number of sectors than the one before.

Most software that you run on a computer won't know that your disk has ZBR. Because most computer software assumes that each track has a constant number of sectors, ZBR drives keep that software happy by pretending that this is true. One kind of disk that you'll run into that is *always* ZBR is a CD. Rather than concentric tracks, CDs have one long, continuous spiral similar to the grooves of a phonograph. CDs solve the varying numbers of sectors problem by varying the speed of the drive motor, depending on which part of the disk is being read; you'll learn more about CDs and CD-ROM drives in Chapter 27.

Physical and Logical Geometry

As mentioned previously, *physical geometry* refers to the electronic organization of any type of disk drive—the actual physical number of heads, cylinders, tracks, and sectors. In the '80s, the physical geometry of a disk was relatively simple, and the BIOS setup contained the number of heads, tracks, and sectors. The PC could easily access the drive.

There have been changes in disk geometry, but there have been very few changes in the original setup parameters in the system BIOS. The BIOS usually limits the number of sectors to 63 per track. This means that you need to fool the system to make sure that the old BIOS standards and the new disk drive are compatible.

Because the system BIOS handles only one number for the number of sectors per track, any drive that uses ZBR needs to hide the physical geometry of the disk from the system. The disk subsystem accomplishes this by using *logical geometry*. The manufacturer establishes the logical geometry, which is a set of bogus values for the cylinders, heads, and sectors on the disk. The disk controller gives these bogus values to the BIOS. The hard drive controller provides automatic translation between the logical and physical geometry. The physical geometry is totally hidden. Table 10.4 is an example of the difference between a drive's physical and logical geometry (it contains the specifications of one of my hard drives).

TABLE 10.4: SAMPLE HARD DRIVE'S PHYSICAL AND LOGICAL GEOMETRY

PARAMETERS	LOGICAL GEOMETRY	PHYSICAL GEOMETRY
Cylinders	7480	6810
Heads	16	6
Sectors per track	63	122–232
Total sectors	7,539,840	7,539,840

Sector Translation and Logical Block Addressing

Until around 1994, the BIOS on most PCs had a limit of 528MB for hard drives. Newer BIOS versions correct this limitation and theoretically work with hard drives in excess of 8.4GB. Early on, the biggest problem with the BIOS-driven constraints for disks wasn't that it was hard to support drives with 500 heads, because there weren't any of those around. The biggest problem was that there were a *lot* of drives with more than 1024 cylinders. A number of translation schemes address these problems, two of which include sector translation and logical block addressing.

NOTE *Refer to the section "BIOS and Operating System Capacity Barriers" for more information about disk capacity—and to your hardware and software specifications for details about your particular system.*

SECTOR TRANSLATION

When you install a hard drive in a computer, as you'll learn in the next few chapters, you have to tell the computer how many cylinders, heads, and sectors that new drive has. Strictly speaking, you're putting that information into your system's CMOS (complementary metal oxide semiconductor) chip.

Some older BIOS versions won't let you enter a value for cylinders above 1024, but most newer systems allow you to enter larger numbers. Now, suppose you have a drive that has 1600 cylinders and four heads. If you try to tell an older system that the number of cylinders is 1600, it'll just laugh. To compensate, some drive systems *fib* to the PC, saying that it's not 1600 cylinders and four heads, but rather 800 cylinders and *eight* heads. This cylinder/head/sector (CHS) translation divides the number of cylinders by an integer (in this case 2) and multiplies the number of heads by the same integer when passing CHS values from the drive to the operating system. Do the math, and you'll see that the capacity is the same either way, but now the BIOS is happy. The BIOS then issues commands to an 800-cylinder, 8-head disk, and the drive subsystem translates those imaginary coordinates into a 1600-cylinder, 4-head set of "true" coordinates. The name for this translation is *sector translation*, or *CHS translation*.

Some SCSI and IDE systems take sector translation to new heights by internally keeping track of only the total number of sectors on the entire drive. Ordinarily, system software would say to a disk interface, "Get me the sector on cylinder 100, head 3, sector 20." This is a "three-dimensional" sector address. But for these SCSI and IDE systems, the system software would just say, "Get me the 143,292nd sector on the disk." The numbering scheme for all sectors is sequential, one after the other, with no concern for their head or cylinder location. Such a sector-addressing scheme is a *linear addressing scheme*.

So why is this a problem? Usually, it's not. But if you're running a low-level disk fixer, the program may have to reformat particular tracks on the disk. When it requests the controller to low-level format, say, cylinder 10, head 5, the controller understands the request to mean, "Format the *real* cylinder 10 on the 1600-cylinder drive—not the *logical* 800-cylinder." In the process, the low-level format ends up destroying data that the disk fixer did not originally intend to destroy and could in fact render the hard drive useless. SpinRite (see the Vendor Guide on the Utilities CD) is a disk utility that detects sector translation and thus avoids these problems, but not all disk utilities do.

NOTE   *Disks smaller than 528MB use the CHS translation mode. The BIOS directly uses the logical geometry that the disk presents to it. Disks larger than 528MB use either Extended CHS (ECHS) mode or logical block addressing (LBA). ECHS takes the logical geometry of the hard drive and translates it into an equivalent geometry that makes the BIOS happy. LBA translates in a different manner from CHS, as described in the next section.*

LOGICAL BLOCK ADDRESSING

Sector translation gets a bit strange for larger drives that use logical block addressing (LBA). Instead of referring to a cylinder, head, and sector number, LBA assigns each sector a unique number starting at 0 and going up to the total number of sectors on the disk less 1 (that is, if the cylinder has 18 sectors, LBA would number them 0–17). The translation is similar to ECHS translation, but instead of translating to the drive's logical geometry, translation occurs directly to a logical block number (a sector number).

If you look at the BIOS listings for some of the newer drives, you'll find that some have specs that don't seem to make sense. For example, some claim to have *64 heads!* How huge is *that* drive? Well, physically, it's about the size of a pack of playing cards. How do they fit all those heads—let's see, 64 heads would be 32 platters—into a drive about an inch high? The answer, as you probably suspect, is that they *don't*. The drive claims to be 64 heads, 63 sectors, and 611 cylinders. That's a total of 1,231,776KB, 1203MB, or 1.17GB.

Remember that a megabyte isn't 1,000,000 bytes; it's 1,048,576 bytes. Similarly, a gigabyte isn't 1,000,000,000 bytes; it's 1,073,741,824 bytes. Don't be surprised, however, if manufacturers conveniently redefine the definitions to 1,000,000 and 1,000,000,000.

Let's say I have a drive with 2448 cylinders, 16 heads, and 63 sectors, which is about the same size as the drive described above.

Careful readers will be scratching their heads at this point and saying, "Hey, wait, 64 heads were definitely impossible for a drive that is one inch high, but *so are 16 heads*. What's the story?" It's true; the drive does not have 16 heads. But that's what I had to tell the computer when I set it up.

You see, this drive, like many modern high-capacity drives, uses ZBR encoding. That means that there are a variable number of sectors per track. The problem is that your PC's BIOS insists on knowing the number of cylinders, heads, and sectors per track on your drive and will refuse to use any drive until you provide that information. But my technical specifications for my drive say that it has 3854 cylinders and 6 data surfaces, and there's no information on sectors per track. There's no way a modern BIOS can just say, "It has 3854 cylinders, 6 data surfaces, and a variable number of sectors."

In response, the design of my drive's onboard electronics makes the PC happy and appears to provide a nice, consistent number of sectors per track. No problem, really—it's a kind of sector translation. The real problem is that the drive geometry that the drive exposes to the CMOS is 2448 cylinders, 16 heads, and 63 sectors. Sixteen heads and 63 sectors are no problem; 2448 cylinders are a problem.

My host adapter and my drive work together to solve the problem by using LBA. In the case of this drive, LBA rearranges the apparent geometry of the disk, which ends up producing an apparent drive with fewer cylinders and more heads than the system sees.

Usually, the disk interface supplies the LBA feature. Occasionally, however, I've seen jumpers on a drive that you must move in order for LBA to work with that drive. LBA's main job is to bypass DOS's quirkiness with drives over 504MB.

COMPARING TRANSLATION MODES

To reiterate, there are three translation modes: Standard CHS, Extended CHS, and LBA.

- Standard CHS uses
  - Physical geometry between the physical drive platters and the disk interface
  - Logical geometry between the disk interface and the BIOS
  - Logical geometry between the BIOS and operating system and applications
- Extended CHS uses

- ◆ Physical geometry between the physical drive platters and the disk interface

- ◆ Logical geometry between the disk interface and the BIOS

- ◆ Translated geometry between the BIOS and operating system and applications

◆ LBA uses

- ◆ Physical geometry between the physical drive platters and the disk interface

- ◆ Logical block addressing between the disk interface and the BIOS

- ◆ Translated geometry between the BIOS and operating system and applications

Voice Coil and Stepper Head-Positioning Mechanisms

Most of today's hard drives use voice coils in the actuator motor to move the heads back and forth. Earlier hard drives used a stepper motor mechanism to move the heads; many of today's floppy drives still use this mechanism.

VOICE COIL MECHANISMS

Named after the voice coil circuit in telephone electronics, the hard drive voice coil is a *closed control system*: it is self-correcting. The head moves, but it looks to the data on the disk to figure out exactly where to stop. A hard drive voice coil has a cylindrical rod at its middle. Energizing the coil moves the rod in or out of the coil, depending on how much energy the coil uses. The rod connects to the heads, so energizing the coil moves the heads in or out. The controller senses the position of the head by reading the magnetic servo pattern that the manufacturer prerecords on the drive. The magnetic servo pattern is in addition to any data on the disk. You can see a voice coil in Figure 10.6.

FIGURE 10.6

A voice coil

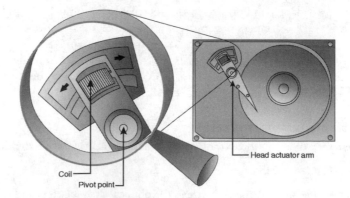

Coil
Pivot point
Head actuator arm

The actuator and control electronics determine how far to move the heads by reading the servo patterns and making the necessary adjustments for proper positioning of the heads. There are two types of servo systems: embedded servo and dedicated servo.

Some drives intersperse the head positioning information, allowing all surfaces to be used for data—this is an *embedded servo* positioning mechanism. The manufacturer lays servo information down on the disk by either restricting the servo signals to a wedge or sector of the tracks, or distributing the signals and embedding them into every sector.

Other drives dedicate an entire surface to this information—which is why you'll see some drives report an odd number of sides, such as the old Seagate 4096 that claims to have 9 surfaces but actually has 10. Such an approach is a *dedicated servo* positioning mechanism. A dedicated servo system is faster and has more accurate tracking than an embedded system, but it has the disadvantage of losing a whole disk surface to servo data and the requirement of a separate servo head.

When you turn off the machine, a spring holds the heads against the center of the disk. This means that whenever you shut down the computer, the drive parks itself! Note that if the system goes bad, all you can do is either buy a new drive or send it back to the manufacturer.

STEPPER MOTOR MECHANISM

Generally, the stepper motor system is found now only in floppy drives that read and write to disks with relatively low track density. The stepper is an *open* system: it is not self-correcting. A stepper system assumes that cylinder 40 will always be 40 clicks away from cylinder 0. As time goes on, its position drifts farther and farther from the actual data.

The stepper motor rotates in small, consistent increments and moves the drive read/write heads in individual steps. Specifically, the shaft of a stepper motor has magnets permanently attached to it. Energizing one or more of the coils that are around the body of the motor creates a magnetic field that interacts with the permanent magnets on the shaft of the motor. Turning these coils on and off in sequence causes the motor to rotate forward or backward.

Disk Performance Characteristics

One of the jobs of a hard drive is to read and write data as fast as possible. Some disk/controller combinations are faster than others. Many performance factors are interrelated. Drive speed is measured by two disk performance characteristics: how long it takes to find a particular piece of data (access time) and, once found, how quickly it can be read off the disk (data transfer rate).

The *access time*, or the time it takes to find the correct location or position on the drive, is a combination of the seek time and latency (terms I'll explain later in this section). The *average seek time* is the average time that the heads require to move from one track to any other track. The *data transfer rate* is the speed at which the drive reads and writes (transfers) data.

NOTE *A drive's average access time is the interval between the time a request for data is made by the system and the time the data becomes available from the drive. While the average access time metric is sometimes used to assess hard drives, it is more frequently used to assess CD-ROM drives.*

Seeks and Latency

How quickly you can find and read a sector is determined in part by access time. Reading a particular sector consists of two steps: first, move the head to the correct track. Then, once the head is over that track, wait for the sector to spin under the head, and then read the sector. You see this in Figure 10.7.

FIGURE 10.7

Reading a sector on a disk

Reading a particular sector involves two steps:

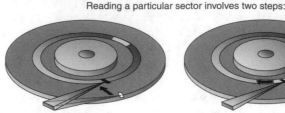

First, move the head to the desired track. That is called seek.

Then, once the head is over that track, wait for the sector to spin under the head. The wait is called the latency period.

Now, moving the head takes a lot longer than waiting for the sector to come around. So low seek times (the time to move the head) are critical to good disk performance.

The formula to remember is shown in Table 10.5.

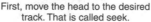

ACCESS TIME	=	**SEEK TIME**	+	**ROTATIONAL LATENCY PERIOD**
Time to find a sector	=	Time to move to the sector's cylinder	+	Time to wait for the sector to rotate around and appear under the head(s)

TABLE 10.5: ACCESS TIME FORMULA

The two components are called seek time and latency period or rotational latency period. *Seek time* is the time required for the head to position itself over a track. The *latency period* is how long it takes the desired sector to move under the head.

TYPICAL SEEK TIMES

Of the seek time and the latency period, the seek time is usually the longer wait. Seek time is normally expressed in milliseconds (ms). It varies according to how many tracks the heads must traverse. A seek from one track to the next track is usually quick—just a few milliseconds—but most seeks aren't so convenient. Remember, the lower the seek time, the better. Note that in current PCs, a millisecond is a long period, considering that the measure for modern PC memory is in nanoseconds. This means the system may have to wait for the hard drive.

A common measure of an average seek is the time the system requires to travel one-third of the way across the disk. Most benchmark programs use this measurement. You might wonder, "Why not halfway across the disk, rather than one-third?" The reason is that most accesses are short seeks—just a few tracks.

Years ago, companies sold hard drives with seek times of almost 100ms; by the mid-1980s, seek times were down to the high 30ms. Today, the average seek time on a new drive is between 5 and 10ms. In general, the low speed depends on what you're willing to spend.

For example, my 2001 desktop system has a 60GB Enhanced Integrated Drive Electronics (EIDE) hard drive with a seek time of 9.5ms—not the worst around, but not the fastest, either. If you were to buy this drive separately, it would cost you about $200, or just $3.32 per gigabyte.

Seek times are built into a drive. There's no way for you to improve a drive's seek time, short of getting a new drive.

ROTATIONAL LATENCY PERIOD

Once a head positions itself over a track, the job's not done: now the head has to wait for the correct sector to rotate under the head. How *much* time is a matter of luck: if you're lucky, the sector is already there; if you're really unlucky, you just missed it and will have to wait an entire revolution. As I mentioned before, this waiting time, whether large or small, is the *rotational latency period*. A common number cited is *average latency period*. This makes the simple assumption that, on average, the disk must make a half-revolution to get to your sector. Manufacturers calculate the latency period from the spindle speed. Latency, like seek time, is normally expressed in milliseconds.

Depending on the model, disk drives rotate between 3600 and 12,000 revolutions per minute (rpm). Most new hard drives have a spindle speed somewhere between 5400 and 7200rpm. For a disk rotating at 3600rpm, one-half revolution then takes 1/7200 of a minute = 60/7200 second = 8.33ms. This contributes to the amount of time that the system must wait for service (the rotational latency). The higher the spindle's speed (rpm), the lower the average latency. Reducing the latency improves system performance. Table 10.6 lists some standard spindle speeds and the corresponding average and worst-case rotational latency period (in milliseconds). Calculate the average latency based on a half rotation of the disk; calculate the worst-case latency on a full rotation of the disk.

TABLE 10.6: ROTATIONAL LATENCY AND SPINDLE SPEEDS

SPINDLE SPEED (RPM)	AVERAGE ROTATIONAL LATENCY (IN MS)	WORST-CASE ROTATIONAL LATENCY (IN MS)
3600	8.3	16.7
4500	6.7	13.3
5200	5.8	11.5
5400	5.6	11.1
6300	4.8	9.5
7200	4.2	8.3
10,000	3.0	6.0
12,000	2.5	5.0

Table 10.6 shows that the higher the speed of the spindle, the lower the latency; the latency rate of a new drive is probably going to be less than 3ms. As new technologies reduce drive costs, manufacturers are increasing the spindle speeds of the newer and more expensive drives. Reducing latency is particularly beneficial for users who frequently access random sectors on the disk.

NOTE   Manufacturers are also using cylinder and head skewing to reduce latency in today's high-speed disk and disk controllers. It is not possible for users to adjust the cylinder and head skewing.

Data Transfer Rates, Interleave Factors, and Skewing

After a disk has found the data, how fast can it transfer that data to the PC? As you've already read, this is called the *data transfer rate*. Specifically, the transfer rate is a measure of the amount of data that the system can access over a period of time (typically one second). It is determined by the external data transfer rate and the internal transfer rate. The *external data transfer rate* is the speed of the communication between the system memory and the internal buffer or cache built into the drive. The *internal data transfer rate* is the speed that the hard drive can physically write or read data to or from the surface of the platter and transfer it to the internal drive cache or read buffer. A number of factors can influence the data transfer rate, including interleave factors and cylinder and head skew.

THE INTERNAL DATA TRANSFER RATE

In a disk, the transfer rate is a measure of the communication between the CPU and the controller, and the controller and the disk drive. The internal transfer rate under discussion here is the rate that data is written to and read from the disk. Transfer rates vary depending on the density of the data on the disk, how fast the disk is spinning, and the location of the data.

NOTE *There are two types of density when discussing hard drives: areal density and track density. Areal density refers to how much data (bits) the disk can store in a square inch. Areal density affects the seek time and data transfer rates. Track density is a part of the calculation of areal density and is a measure of the density of the tracks on each platter.*

To calculate the density of the disk, multiply the bytes per sector by the number of sectors on the disk. Determine the number of revolutions of the spindle per second by dividing the spindle rpm value by 60. The following gives you the transfer rate in megabits per second:

Data transfer rate = (spindle speed/60 × sectors per track × 512 × 8)/1,000,000

Remember that there are only 512 bytes in a sector. This means that whenever an application requests, say, sector 1 of track 100 of side 2, it'll probably next need sector 2 of that track and side. In fact, most times when you need *one* sector from a track, you'll end up needing them all.

In times past, several factors affected the maximum data transfer rate of a hard drive, including the interleave factor and cylinder and head skew. Modern hard drives no longer have these variables (they're pedal to the metal for these factors), but it's still worthwhile to understand the challenges faced by hard drive designers in the past.

INTERLEAVE FACTOR

The *interleave factor* refers to the way sectors are organized on the disk. A 1:1 interleave factor means the sectors are arranged sequentially around each track. A 2:1 interleave factor means that consecutively numbered sectors are separated by an intervening sector around each track.

Modern hard drive controllers can handle a 1:1 interleave factor without any problem. It is not possible—or necessary—to adjust the interleave factor on modern disks.

NOTE *Interleaving is not a factor on modern IDE, EIDE, or SCSI disk drives. The following interleave factor discussion is included for historical purposes only.*

On older PCs, the process of low-level formatting a hard or floppy disk laid down milestones (sector IDs) that separated sectors from each other.

The numbering of sectors on a disk is logical so the system can address the sectors to read or write data. Logical sector 1 does not have to be the same sector as physical sector 1, nor does it have to be physically adjacent to logical sector 2. The number of physical sectors that occur between logical sector numbers is the interleave factor.

Interleaving was necessary because older controllers were not fast enough to finish reading or writing data for sector 1 until part of sector 2 was already spinning under the read/write heads. On 1.44MB floppies, the 18 sectors are laid out like numbers on the face of a clock, as shown in Figure 10.8.

FIGURE 10.8

1.44MB floppy
interleave order

That's because the floppy disk spins slowly enough so the controller can read all the sectors on a 1.44MB floppy in one pass. 1.44MB floppies have nine sectors on a track, and the disk rotates only five times per second. The most burden a floppy could put on its controller would be to throw it 0.5KB sector × 18 sectors/rotation × 5 rotations/second, or 45KB per second. Heck, the serial port on most PCs can run at almost that rate—consecutive sectors on a floppy are no big deal.

Early IDE and SCSI hard drives didn't work that way. The problem was that hard drives rotate many times faster than floppies. In addition, hard drives packed more sectors on a track. To see the problem, suppose you had a hard drive with a 1:1 interleave, meaning the sectors were in numerical order, as shown in Figure 10.9.

FIGURE 10.9

A 1:1 interleaved
hard drive

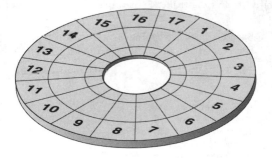

As the hard drive rotated, the minimum this disk would throw at the controller per second would be 0.5KB/sector × 17 sectors/rotation × 60 rotations/second = 510KB/second! Most hard drive controllers (and some computers) couldn't handle a half-megabyte per second. The computer had to both read the data and check the data for validity before transferring it to the computer's memory.

So let's look in detail at what happened when the computer read two sectors in succession on a 1:1 interleaved disk.

1. The operating system and BIOS request that the hard drive controller read a sector.

2. The controller instructs the disk head to move to the track and read the sector, as shown in Figure 10.10.

3. The head reads the data and transmits it to the controller.

FIGURE 10.10

How interleaving affects disk speed (part 1)

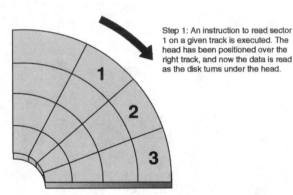

Step 1: An instruction to read sector 1 on a given track is executed. The head has been positioned over the right track, and now the data is read as the disk turns under the head.

4. Because hard drives are fragile devices, the controller always includes extra data when it writes information to the disk. This information, when read back, enables the controller to detect whether errors arose in the data. The information is called the *error-correction code (ECC)* and allows the computer to both detect and correct errors in the data read from the disk. It uses a mathematical function and takes a little while to compute: see Figure 10.11. (The microprocessors on hard drive controllers aren't the fastest things in the world. I mean, you don't find too many Pentiums on disk controllers.) Meanwhile, the disk continues to spin, as in Figure 10.12.

FIGURE 10.11

How disk error correction works

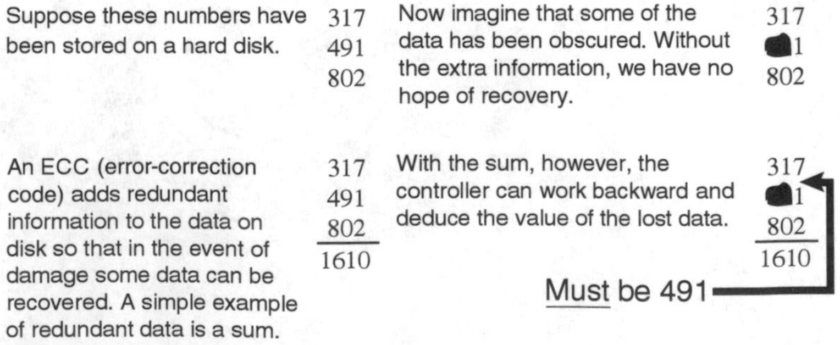

Suppose these numbers have been stored on a hard disk.
317
491
802

Now imagine that some of the data has been obscured. Without the extra information, we have no hope of recovery.
317
1
802

An ECC (error-correction code) adds redundant information to the data on disk so that in the event of damage some data can be recovered. A simple example of redundant data is a sum.
317
491
802
―――
1610

With the sum, however, the controller can work backward and deduce the value of the lost data.
317
1
802
―――
1610

Must be 491

FIGURE 10.12

How interleaving
affects disk speed
(part 2)

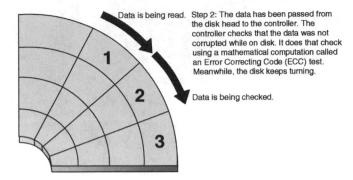

Data is being read. Step 2: The data has been passed from
the disk head to the controller. The
controller checks that the data was not
corrupted while on disk. It does that check
using a mathematical computation called
an Error Correcting Code (ECC) test.
Meanwhile, the disk keeps turning.

Data is being checked.

5. Once the controller checks the data, it passes it to the BIOS and the operating system, both of which are also paranoid about hard drive data loss. The BIOS and the operating system have their own small amount of overhead—proportionately less than the controller's, but relevant nonetheless. Meanwhile, the disk continues to spin; see Figure 10.13.

FIGURE 10.13

How interleaving
affects disk speed
(part 3)

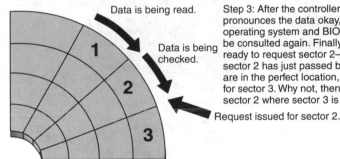

Data is being read.

Data is being
checked.

Step 3: After the controller
pronounces the data okay, the
operating system and BIOS must
be consulted again. Finally they're
ready to request sector 2—but
sector 2 has just passed by! We
are in the perfect location, however,
for sector 3. Why not, then, put
sector 2 where sector 3 is now?

Request issued for sector 2.

6. Now that everyone is happy with the data, the operating system wants the next sector. But the disk continues spinning while the controller, operating system, and BIOS take a long time with the last sector's data. If sector 2 comes right after sector 1, the controller always misses the subsequent sector. That implies that the controller has to wait a whole rotation to get the next sector.

Thus, on a disk with the sectors laid out clock-fashion, in numerical order, the controller always ended up reading only one sector per rotation. Because the disk rotated at least 60 times per second, the controller read 60 or more sectors/second. Each sector held at least 0.5KB, so the data transfer rate from this disk was 30KB/second, a rather poor transfer rate. (A 1.44MB floppy could outperform this disk because it transfers data at 45KB/second!)

But suppose the sectors were staggered to give the controller time to get ready for the next sector. IBM did that on the XT, as shown in Figure 10.14.

FIGURE 10.14

Hard drive with a
1:6 disk interleave

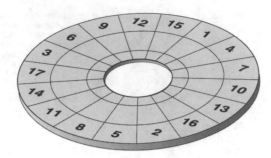

This is a 1:6 interleave. Start at 1, then count clockwise six sectors. You're now at 2. Count six more. You're now at 3. And so on. This gave the XT time to do computations and still catch the next sector. Inspection will show that the XT could read three sectors on the first rotation, or about 180 sectors/second. That means you could get three times the throughput from an XT by using a disk with a layout of 1:6.

As controllers got faster, they were able to compute error-correction codes faster. IBM interleaved the AT disk more tightly, as shown in Figure 10.15.

FIGURE 10.15

Hard drive with a
1:3 disk interleave

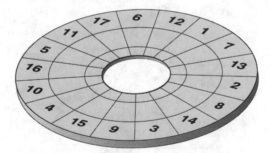

This is a 1:3 interleave factor. Here the computer could read six sectors on a single rotation. Remember why the interleave had to be a 1:3 disk—the sectors would be too close, and the controller would always miss the next sector. The net effect would be like getting only one sector per rotation.

Table 10.7 shows how the interleave factor affected a hard drive's maximum data transfer capacity. (Remember, all modern drives have a 1:1 interleave for the fastest possible data transfer.)

You can see that reformatting from IBM's default 1:6 interleave to a 1:5 interleave improved disk throughput by 20 percent. Changing interleave on an IBM AT from 1:3 to 1:2 increased disk throughput by 50 percent. The correct interleave factor means that the controller, the computer, and the disk are right in step, pulling data off the disk as quickly as is possible. The kind of controller you have determines the optimal interleave factor.

Remember, the interleave factor is set when you low-level format a hard drive. Some software writers used to offer interleave fixer programs. These measured the disk's optimal interleave, then allowed the disk's interleave factor to be reset without backing up, reformatting, and reloading. Their approach was really a simple one: just read a track, store it in memory, reformat the track to the proper interleave factor, and rewrite the original information.

TABLE 10.7: THE IMPORTANCE OF THE INTERLEAVE FACTOR

DRIVE TYPE	MAX DATA TRANSFER (KB/SECOND)	SECTORS READ/ROTATIONS
HARD DRIVE (17 SECTORS/TRACK)		
1:6	85	2.8
1:5	102	3.4
1:4	128	4.3
1:3	170	5.7
1:2	255	8.5
1:1	510	17.0

CYLINDER AND HEAD SKEW

Modern controllers eliminate the need for interleaving on modern disks. But other conditions can cause a less than optimal data transfer rate. For example, switching between tracks causes a time delay, as does switching from one head to another. Today's disk drive manufacturers design cylinder and head skewing to reduce latency when the read/write request causes a switch between consecutive heads or cylinders.

NOTE   *The design of modern disks makes it no longer possible for the user to adjust either cylinder or head skewing.*

Suppose the first sector of each track is physically in the same position on the platter. If you are reading the entire contents of two consecutive tracks, the controller reads all the sectors of the first track in order and then gets ready to switch to the first sector of the second track. At this point, the first sector of the second track is on top of the previous first sector, and the controller has yet to physically move the heads to the second track. This takes some time.

As the heads move to the second track, the first few sectors go by and the controller needs to wait an entire revolution of the platter before it can continue reading the data. To avoid this problem, the manufacturer might program the drive controller to offset the first, or start, sector of adjacent tracks from each other. For example, they could establish the first sector of track 2 to be adjacent to the third sector of track 1. This is *cylinder skew*, and movement is horizontal.

A similar time-delay problem occurs when switching from one head to another within a cylinder. Each track in the cylinder is accessible by one of the drive heads. Switching between heads is a purely electronic process and takes time, although there is no physical movement. Here too, the manufacturer might program the drive controller to offset the first sector of tracks within the cylinder from each other. This is *head skew*, and movement is vertical.

Error-Correction Code (ECC)

No electronic data transmission or storage system is perfect. Each system makes errors at a certain rate. Modern disks have built-in error-detection and error-correction mechanisms. While this isn't really a disk performance feature, I mentioned this in passing a few pages back, and I want to give you more of the information on how disks can self-correct errors.

Disk systems are great as storage media, but they're volatile. From the first second after you lay a piece of data on a disk, it starts "evaporating." The magnetic domains on the disk that define the data slowly randomize until the data is unrecognizable. The disk itself and the media may be fine, but the image of the data can fade after x years. Put another image on, and it'll last for another x years. (If you're taking videotapes of your baby in the hopes that you can use them to embarrass her in front of her dates in 15 years or so, physics may thwart you because the videotape is magnetic.)

Disk subsystems are aware of this and so include some method of detecting and correcting minor data loss. The disk subsystem can detect but not correct *major* data loss. The controller includes *extra* data when it writes information to the disk. When the controller reads back this information (the *error-correction code*, or *ECC*), it lets the controller detect whether errors have arisen in the data. You saw an example of ECC back in Figure 10.11. The basic idea is that the controller stores redundant information *with* the disk data at the time that the data is originally written to disk. Then, when the data is later read from disk, the disk controller checks the redundant information to verify data integrity.

The ECC calculations are more complex than a simple checksum. The ECC that most manufacturers implement in hard drives (and CD-ROMs) uses the Reed-Solomon algorithm. The calculations take time, so there's a tradeoff; more complex ECCs can recover more damaged data, but they take more computation time. The number of bits associated with a sector for ECC is a design decision and determines the robustness of the error detection and correction. Quite a number of modern disks use more than 200 bits of code for each sector.

Some controllers let you choose to use an x-bit ECC. In this example, x refers to the number of consecutive bad bits that the ECC can correct. The original AT hard drive controller, for instance, could correct up to 5 bad consecutive bits. That meant that it had a "maximum correctable error burst length" of 5 bits. Newer controllers, including drives in newer AT-type clones and many Pentium machines, can usually correct up to 11 bits (11 is better, if you can get it). Note that a newer controller may have to stay at 5 bits if you use it in an actual IBM AT—the IBM AT BIOS can support only 5-bit ECC. Some of the newest drives installed in the latest machines are using special high-speed controller hardware to do *70-bit* error correction! They can correct 70 bad bits in a row—quite amazing.

Getting Good Data Transfer Rates on Modern Systems

I said earlier that interleave adjustment is of value only on older systems. So how can you crank the maximum data rates out of your hard drive? Nowadays, most of it boils down to choosing good hardware and, to a lesser extent, to tuning device drivers.

Modern SCSI-3, Ultra SCSI, and EIDE host adapters can deliver megabytes and megabytes per second if they're set up right. Here are the big things to look for:

The drive must have a good data transfer rate.   Most drives nowadays have a small amount of cache memory on them. A small amount of cache can be useful to have, but note that that same cache can fool test programs into thinking that the drives are faster than they actually are. Read the sections "External Transfer Rate Dependencies" and "Caches in Drive Subsystems" later in this chapter for more information.

You need a fast disk interface.   On IDE drives, a host adapter with the EIDE interface is a good choice because it can transfer data more quickly.

Avoid using an ISA board.   If an ISA board is present, swap it out and use a PCI or VESA board instead. The fastest disk interface in the world will run slowly if it's an ISA board. Fast disk interfaces must be built on top of fast buses.

Avoid buying disk interface boards with tons of cache memory on them.   Read the "Caches in Drive Subsystems" section to see why.

Once you have the hardware in place, you may have to tune a device driver on your PC. My EIDE system, for example, will run just fine without any special drivers, but the performance that it turns in isn't stunning. Add the drivers that came with the disk interface card, however, and the data transfer numbers I get improve.

External Transfer Rate Dependencies

The external transfer rate depends on the type of drive interface in your PC and the modes that it supports. Support for modes existing in the drive interface need to be present in both the drive and the system BIOS. Higher external data transfer rates are possible if your EIDE interface supports the industry-standard programmed input/output (PIO) mode 4 and direct memory access (DMA) mode 2 protocols. Both of these protocols consist of a set of rules for operating the physical interface.

The system or host adapter BIOS needs to support these protocol modes. If this support is not present, the drive defaults to whatever slower transfer rate the BIOS and the disk drive support. The PIO and DMA transfer modes also require that the interface be running over a high-speed system bus such as PCI or VESA. You can read more about these transfer modes in the section "PIO and DMA Protocol Transfer Mechanisms."

Caches in Drive Subsystems

Disk drives are slow—I mean, really slow. Your computer uses RAM memory that responds to requests in tens of nanoseconds, but the disk drive responds to requests in tens of milliseconds. That's six orders of magnitude difference in speed! Most operating systems set aside a small area of memory as a disk cache.

A disk cache seeks to use the speed of memory to bolster the effective speed of the disk. The cache is held in memory chips and is usually one to a few megabytes. The operating system can access data previously placed in the disk cache on an as-needed basis. Using this disk cache can cut down on the number of physical seeks and transfers from the hard drive itself. Smart caching algorithms generally mean that there is no need to change the size of the disk cache.

The disk's adapter or controller board contains a cache that separates the internal read/write operations from transfers over the bus and holds recently accessed data. Most controllers now contain at least 64KB of cache RAM for these operations.

The amount of RAM on a disk drive itself is usually small, between 512KB and 2MB. This cache buffer acts as a holding area for one or more tracks or even a complete cylinder's worth of information in case you need it. The point of buffering an entire track is simple: managing one-to-one interleaving would be just about impossible otherwise, and besides, the built-in sector translation that virtually every drive does nowadays requires some buffer space to juggle sectors around. This cache buffer can be effective in speeding up both throughput and access times.

As an example, let's say a system has two drives: a high-performance EIDE drive and a lower-performance IDE drive. The EIDE drive turns in a buffered read value of 4688KBps, and the IDE transfers data at nearly the same rate, 4448KBps. Sounds like the two drives are equal—but they're not. It's just more likely that they both have 64KB of similar-speed RAM chips on them.

You can see the difference between the two drives when you compare the next transfer value: the sequential read value. There, the EIDE drive transfers data at 3664KBps, but the IDE falls way behind to 1280KBps.

A word of caution: if you increase the size of these caches, you could run out of memory to effectively run programs and manage data. This could force your PC to rely on virtual memory to run the programs.

Computers running modern operating systems have efficient caching algorithms built into them, so they have the benefits of caching. Onboard caches on disk interface boards just add another layer of data shuffling, and in my experience, real-world tasks don't get done any faster with them. Think of it this way: buying 4MB of cache RAM for your disk interface card costs the same as buying 4MB more for your system, but that interface card RAM does only one thing. Buying 4MB for the system is general purpose—you can use it for anything that computers need RAM for.

Another reason to avoid onboard caches on interface boards is write caching. Interfaces with memory on them will delay actually writing data to the disk in order to make the disk subsystem seem faster. It's not a bad idea *except* that sometimes your system resets itself without warning the disk interface. Because the system didn't warn the disk interface, it didn't write the data to the disk, and you have the equivalent of turning off the computer in the middle of a disk write. This is *not* mere paranoia; every "version 1.0" of an operating system that I've ever installed on a controller with delayed writes caused major problems. That's why my bottom-line recommendation on cached disk interfaces is: don't use them.

BIOS and Operating System Capacity Barriers

The BIOS and interfaces in older and modern PCs can impose limits on the size of the hard drive. Additionally, PC operating systems have some inherent characteristics that can limit disk size.

BIOS and Interface Limitations

The interface from the PC system to the hard drive controls the operation of the disk drive through the addresses and commands that it sends to the hard drive. On the system side of the interface, the BIOS provides software routines that let different applications access the hard drive. File manager routines provide the mapping from filenames to locations on the disk and then send read/write commands through the interrupt 13 (INT13) Application Programming Interface (API) to the BIOS. The INT13 is operating system independent and is the primary interface to the BIOS. BIOS routines convert INT13 requests into IDE/ATA interface requests for the disk drive to perform read/write functions. Note that manufacturers update the BIOS routines and INT13 functions from time to time. The size of IDE hard drive that the computer will recognize is dependent on a combination of requirements of the BIOS and the IDE/ATA interface.

NOTE   *ATA (Advanced Technology Attachment) is the real name of what is widely known as IDE.*

THE INT13 INTERFACE ADDRESSING

The use of INT13 requires specific hard drive parameters and exact head, cylinder, and sector addressing. Conventional INT13 functions use 24 bits to represent the disk geometry, as shown in Table 10.8.

TABLE 10.8: INT13 API 24-BIT ALLOCATION OF THE HARD DRIVE

NUMBER OF BITS ALLOCATED	FOR THE...	FOR A TOTAL OF...
10 bits	Cylinder number	1024 cylinders (2^{10}) that the system can address
8 bits	Head number	256 heads (2^8) that the system can address
6 bits	Sector number	63 sectors ($2^6 - 1$) that the system can address

Therefore, for conventional CHS addressing, using the values $1024 \times 256 \times 63$, it is possible to address up to 16,515,072 sectors. And at 512 bytes per sector, you get a theoretical disk capacity of 8.4GB. LBA addressing views the available address bits as a single number. Larger disks require a BIOS and operating system that support INT13 extensions or an operating system that bypasses the BIOS and INT13. INT13 uses 24-bit addressing.

INT13 EXTENSIONS

By the early '90s, the disk drive industry had increased the capacity and functionality of disk drives to such an extent that the BIOS INT13 interface specifications no longer provided adequate support. During the following years, a number of extensions were made to the specifications. These extensions permit

- The attachment of more than two drives to the system

- Accessing drives in excess of 528MB

- The use of BIOS translation algorithms (CHS and LBA)

- Commands to assign the order that the system is to access drives

INT13 extensions now make it possible to use faster versions of the PIO and DMA transfer modes. When the 8.4GB capacity barrier was encountered, BIOS developers included new extended INT13 functions that use 32 bits to represent addresses.

If a disk drive has a capacity greater than 8.4GB, using INT13 extensions requires changes both to the BIOS and to the operating system. Note that later versions of Windows 95 and all subsequent versions (98, Me, XP) already support these extensions, as do most other current operating systems. Windows NT and Linux do not. The Windows 2000 setup does not determine whether BIOS INT13 extensions are enabled or available for use before allowing the creation of a system partition with more than 1024 cylinders or typically larger than 8.4GB.

Few computer systems manufactured before 1998 support the INT13 extensions, although most newer systems *do* provide this support. The easiest way to add larger hard drive support to older PCs is to obtain a newer version of the machine's BIOS, or to install software (such as Ontrack's Disk

Manager) that links into the BIOS to add INT13 support. You can also install an intelligent host adapter with a BIOS that supports INT13 extensions, although adding this hardware to your system is probably the most complicated solution.

THE ATA INTERFACE ADDRESSING

The IDE/ATA interface recognizes a drive and figures out its capacity by looking at the logical geometry of the drive: the number of cylinders, heads, and sectors per track that it contains. Before 1994, drives and the BIOS supported only CHS addressing. Today's drives support both CHS addressing and LBA addressing.

Today's IDE/ATA interface uses 28 bits to represent the disk address, as shown in Table 10.9. The BIOS records the information in defined registers; it records the starting address of the data on the disk, the length of the data transfer, and the read or write command (read or write).

TABLE 10.9: IDE/ATA INTERFACE DISK ADDRESSING

NUMBER OF BITS ALLOCATED	FOR THE...	FOR A TOTAL OF...
16 bits	Cylinder address in the cylinder register.	65,536 cylinders (2^{16}) that the system can address
4 bits	Head address in the head register.	16 heads (2^4) that the system can address
8 bits	Sector address in the sector register. The first sector is number 1; there is no sector 0.	255 sectors ($2^8 - 1$) that the system can address

Therefore, for CHS addressing for the IDE/ATA interface using the values $65,536 \times 16 \times 255$, it is possible to address up to 267,386,880 sectors. And at 512 bytes per sector, you get a theoretical disk capacity of 137.4GB. IDE/ATA uses 28-bit addressing.

CAPACITY BARRIERS

As you have seen, the IDE/ATA and INT13 BIOS standards use a different number of bits for the disk geometry. It is necessary to observe the limitations of both standards, which means the system can use only the smaller of each geometry number, as shown in Table 10.10.

TABLE 10.10: COMBINED IDE/ATE AND INT13 ALLOCATION OF BITS

STANDARD	BITS FOR CYLINDER NUMBER	BITS FOR HEAD NUMBER	BITS FOR SECTOR NUMBER	TOTAL BITS FOR GEOMETRY
INT13	10	8	6	24
IDE/ATA	16	4	8	28
Smallest	10	4	6	20

The 528MB barrier   IDE/ATA (EIDE/ATA) disks have a limit of 16 logical heads. To compensate, these disks always have a large number of cylinders, but because of the INT13 limitation, they can see only 1024 of the cylinders and 63 sectors. When the system has a nontranslating BIOS, the capacity will be $1024 \times 16 \times 63 \times 512$, or 528MB. This is the well-known 528MB barrier.

To overcome this limit, BIOS designers implement one of two translating algorithms for converting the INT13 API address to the ATA address. The first is BitShift translation, which changes the cylinder and head values so that the total number of sectors remains the same. This is the most common translation method. The second algorithm is the LBA assist translation. A system can use this translation only if the drive supports LBA addressing.

The 2.1GB barrier   Although relatively rare, some older BIOSs can have a problem translating the disk geometry if the number of cylinders exceeds 4096. A BIOS with this problem could report the disk as 2.1GB although it could be larger. There is also a 2GB capacity barrier that is an operating system issue and has to do with the file allocation table (FAT).

The 4.2GB barrier   Some operating systems store the number of heads as an 8-bit value. This can cause a problem if the BIOS reports 256 heads and BitShift translation is in use. If this is the case, the maximum capacity is 4.2GB. Note that the LBA assist translation never reports more than 255 heads, so the problem does not exist where the drive and BIOS support LBA.

The 8.4GB barrier   The BIOS limitation of 8.4GB ($1024 \times 256 \times 63 \times 512$/per sector) causes this barrier. New extended INT13 functions have recently been added to overcome this barrier. The new extension passes a 64-bit LBA address in a device address packet. Extended INT13 passes the packet through host memory rather than through host registers. If the drive supports LBA, the BIOS passes the lower 28 bits of this address directly to the ATA registers. If LBA support is not present, the BIOS converts the LBA address to a CHS and passes that address to the ATA registers.

The 32GB barrier   Information about this barrier is still scarce. In some systems, the motherboard BIOS cannot address drives greater than 32GB. This is an LBA addressing limit in the particular BIOS code on the motherboard. Most BIOS manufacturers have now made corrections in their core BIOS. Contact your motherboard manufacturer for information and for a BIOS update if necessary.

Microsoft and others have found that the protected-mode (graphical) version of ScanDisk can misreport cluster sizes on IDE hard drives with a capacity exceeding 32GB and with a BIOS using the BitShift translation algorithm to report the disk's geometry. If the BIOS uses the LBA assist translation algorithm, there is no problem. (For the current status of a fix for this problem, search the Microsoft Knowledge Base for "ScanDisk Errors.")

CIRCUMVENTING DRIVE SIZE LIMITATIONS

You can circumvent this artificial limitation either by bypassing the BIOS or fooling the BIOS during CMOS setup. The bypass method is designed for operating systems such as NetWare and Unix and is referred to as *autoconfiguring*. It uses the Disk Parameter Table (DPT) instead of the BIOS to pass information about drive capacity from the IDE drive to the operating system.

The "fool the BIOS" method is called *autotranslating*. DOS and Windows machines can use auto-translating. When you choose this method during CMOS setup, you tell the BIOS to create an Enhanced Disk Parameter Table (EDPT) during the Power-On Self-Test (POST). The initialization process fills this table with the appropriate values for all the drive characteristics, along with a checksum value to ensure the accuracy of the parameters. This type of table allows the system to support drives with more than 1024 cylinders or more than 528MB.

The EDPT contains a set of drive parameters that come from two sources. The first set of drive parameters comes from the Identify Drive command. The second set of drive parameters is from the BIOS and includes a number of extended INT13 functions (see below). The EDPT provides information about the translation mode(s) that the drive and BIOS use. The information that the EDPT presents to the operating system is a translation of information taken from the drive. The information is not dependent on how the CHS and IDE bit fields match up.

BIOS TRANSLATION SUPPORT

The BIOS supports two types of translations based on information that the Identify Drive command returns:

◆ A straightforward translation of BIOS CHS information to IDE/ATA CHS information. This is referred to as *IDE CHS*.

◆ A translation of the CHS information that passes to the BIOS into a 28-bit logical block address (LBA). The BIOS receives this LBA information and sends it to the drive's task-file register, where it then sets bit 6 of the drive's select drive head register to indicate that the information in the task registers is LBA rather than CHS. From then on, the drive uses the LBA value to fetch the appropriate physical block from the disk.

The result of either of these translations is that the EDPT enables the enhanced IDE interface to access drives as large as 8.4GB. You need no software or operating system change to support high-capacity drives. The IDE CHS and the IDE LBA translations are mostly transparent to the operating system. Western Digital calls its IDE LBA-enabling driver *FASTDISK*.

Fortunately, virtually all newer systems have upgraded EIDE hard drive software, making it possible to use larger drives with no modifications at all.

Operating System Limitations

In the PC world, the operating system limits the partition size, which restricts installation of the operating system to the first 8.4GB of the disk. For example, the Windows NT bootstrap process has inherent hardware and software limitations beyond which Windows NT cannot operate. These limitations prevent Windows NT 4 from using a partition larger than 8.4GB as a system partition. Logical partitions in Windows NT can be much larger. Additionally, Windows NT limits the first partition, or boot partition, to a maximum of 4GB; because of this, a drive larger than 8.4GB must have at least two partitions.

Windows 98/Me/2000/XP were written after the development of the BIOS INT13 extensions and can boot from larger partitions. Windows NT 4 was developed before the INT13 extensions and is unable to use its features.

In the Windows world, operating systems that use the 16-bit versions of the FAT have an inherent limitation in the operating system that restricts a partition to 2.1GB. Because of this 16-bit FAT limitation, no version of Windows 95 supports hard drives that are larger than 32GB. If you want to use media larger than 32GB on a Windows 95 machine, Microsoft recommends that you upgrade to Microsoft Windows 98/Me/NT/2000/XP—all of which permit the use of a 32-bit FAT. (If you are using Windows NT, it must be Windows NT 4, and you must be running Service Pack 4 or higher.)

With 32-bit FAT and new technologies, the next limitation with the ATA interface is expected to occur at 137GB, when the 28 bits of addressing on the ATA bus run out. Possible solutions to this new limitation include increasing the size of each sector on the disk, switching to a completely different type of interface (such as IEEE 1394), or adopting the proposed ATA-6 EIDE protocol, which allows for 48 bits of address space—which would enable hard drives as big as 144 *petabytes*, 100,000 times bigger than today's biggest disks!

And bigger hard drives are coming. IBM has announced disks that store 100GB per square inch, thanks to the application of a material they're referring to as "pixie dust." This magic material is actually a three-atom-thick layer of the element ruthenium (a precious metal similar to platinum), which is sandwiched between two magnetic layers. This new antiferromagnetically coupled (AFC) media increases current areal density limits by a factor of four, and is already being used in IBM's Travelstar notebook hard drive drives. This pixie dust technology could, by 2003, enable desktop hard drives with a total capacity of 400GB, notebook drives with 200GB capacity, and one-inch Microdrives with 6GB capacity.

NOTE *A Microdrive is an ultra-small hard drive, introduced by IBM in 1999. The world's smallest hard drive, the Microdrive uses a single one-inch diameter platter and weighs just 16 grams. It's designed to be used in a variety of handheld devices, and currently comes in 340MB and 1GB sizes. The Microdrive rotates at 4500rpm and has a seek time of 15ms, an average latency of 6.7ms, and data transfer rates between 32 and 48MBps.*

PIO and DMA Protocol Transfer Mechanisms

The most popular hard drive interfaces that modern PCs use are ATA-2 (EIDE) drives running with PIO mode 4 or multiword DMA mode 2. Both PIO and DMA protocols consist of a set of rules for operating the IDE and EIDE interfaces. The PIO data transfer method depends on the processor to handle data transfers. DMA is a transfer mode for moving data between the hard drive and host memory that virtually eliminates the CPU from the transfer process.

The IDE/EIDE interface usually employs PIO because, back when IDE first came on the scene, PIO was faster than DMA. DMA was slower because it was tied to bus speed, and the ISA bus of the time was quite slow indeed. When interrogated with an Identify Drive command, a hard drive returns information about the PIO and DMA modes it is capable of using.

PIO Modes

PIO modes are a range of protocols for a drive and IDE controller to exchange data at different rates that the manufacturer implements in a chipset. PIO transfer modes use the CPU in the data transfer process. Because of CPU involvement in the process, PIO is ideal for lower-performance applications and single tasking. PIO modes do not require any special drivers.

There are five PIO modes (mode 0 through mode 4), and each one defines a different maximum transfer rate. Different IDE/ATA standards support some or all of the PIO transfer modes. PIO transfers data to and from the disk controller through the I/O ports to memory. The CPU manages throughput at the I/O ports.

For optimal performance, a controller should support the drive's highest PIO mode (usually PIO mode 4). The transfer rate of PIO modes is the external data transfer rate for the drive and represents the speed of the interface. It does not represent the speed of the drive itself. Note that modes 3 and 4 both require the use of a PCI or VESA local bus and specific BIOS support.

The VL Bus uses both PIO and block PIO (BPIO). Block PIO deals in larger chunks of data but otherwise works the same way as standard PIO. For example, whereas PIO transfers a single block of 256 words (512 bytes), BPIO transfers *n* blocks of 256 words. If you want to use BPIO, you need special drivers from Western Digital.

NOTE *VL Bus is an enhanced version of the VESA (Video Electronics Standards Association) bus.*

DMA Modes

Many IDE/EIDE drives support DMA transfer modes as an alternative to PIO. The DMA data transfer method lets the drive take care of data transfer after the processor takes care of initial setup. DMA allows the drive to move information directly to or from RAM, which is a boon for multitasking PCs. Early versions of DMA use a controller built into the chipset to make the transfer. Modern DMA uses the device itself to make the transfer.

Faster DMA and EIDE came along hand in hand with the introduction of faster buses. The EIDE interface supports these faster buses with Type B DMA (transfer rate of 4Mbps) and Type F DMA (for PCI local bus, transfer rates up to 8.33Mbps). Both Type B and Type F DMA require device drivers or BIOS changes that support the DMA specifications. Single-mode DMA is relatively slow and is now rarely used. Multiword DMA 1 and multiword DMA 2, however, are very fast and can use a transfer rate of 480ns or more. The Peripheral Component Interconnect (PCI) interface also supports a new type of DMA transfer called *scatter/gather*. Scatter/gather is useful in computers that use virtual memory management. In such a system, the computer can scatter a block of memory (four 4KB blocks) across the hard drive in many different physical locations. Normally, the interface would use four separate requests and DMA instructions to fetch that block of memory. With scatter/gather, a single I/O request "gathers" up the four 4KB blocks into a single 16KB block and delivers it. Since you're using one request instead of four, you get faster response.

Modern ATA Standards

ATA, or *Advanced Technology Attachment*, defines the standard drive interface as attached to an AT-style machine. ATA is a disk drive implementation that integrates the controller onto the drive itself. ATA defines the physical, electrical, transport, and command protocols for the internal attachment of storage devices and the communication between a PC and the hard drive.

ATA Specifications

The original ATA specification, commonly known as IDE, was an ANSI standard for connecting drives to the ISA bus. The interface was little more than a simple buffer. Today's AT Attachment interface (ATA-2), also an ANSI standard, is also known as Fast ATA-2 or Enhanced IDE (EIDE). ATA-2 pushes the data transfer rate up to 6.67Mbps, or 10Mbps for a cache-hit burst. It connects directly to the local bus that, in turn, has higher bandwidths than previously and, consequently, a higher throughput rate. The ATA-2 interface supports

- PIO modes 3 and 4 and DMA modes 1 and 2

- Block transfer commands

- Logical block addressing

- ATAPI support for non-hard-disk IDE/ATA devices

ATA is for hard drives only. The advent of tape and CD drives for PCs stimulated the development of the ATA Packet Interface (ATAPI) standard for non-hard-disk devices that plug into an ordinary ATA (IDE/EIDE) port. ATAPI requires BIOS and driver support. The ATAPI protocol allows these devices to share the ATA bus with traditional ATA disk drives.

ATA-3, also known as EIDE, adds some improvements to ATA-2, and ATA/ATAPI-4 and ATA/ATAPI-5 are later developments that push the data transfer rate even higher. ATA/ATAPI-4 (also known as Ultra ATA or Ultra DMA/33) incorporates support for a theoretical burst data transfer rate of 33Mbps, while ATA/ATAPI-5 incorporates support for a theoretical burst data transfer rate of 66Mbps. This version also provides support for the Universal Serial Bus (USB) devices through an Ultra Direct Memory Access (UDMA) ground bus 80-wire cable requirement and cyclic redundancy check (CRC).

Next on the drawing board is Ultra ATA/100 (also known as Ultra DMA mode 5), which is expected to be the final generation of the Parallel ATA interface. This new specification uses the same 40-pin, 80-wire conductor cable found in ATA/ATAPI-5, but increases the burst data transfer rates to 100Mbps by reducing signal voltage from 5V to 3.3V.

The industry is ultimately transitioning to Serial ATA, which will have lower signal voltages, a reduced pin count, and faster throughput than the traditional Parallel ATA interface. It will be completely compatible with existing ATA interfaces and provide support for legacy ATA and ATAPI devices. One of the biggest benefits of Serial ATA will be its thinner, more flexible cabling, which will replace the current wide ATA ribbon cable. This new Serial ATA cable can be up to 1 meter in length, and will be easier to route inside a PC's chassis. Initial Serial ATA devices should support data transfer rates of up to 150Mbps, with subsequent versions hitting 300Mbps and (eventually) 600Mbps.

EIDE and Fast ATA-2

ATA and ATA-2 are the interface standards. Fast ATA, Fast ATA-2, and EIDE are marketing terms invented by disk drive manufacturers. All use fast transfer PIO modes 3 and 4 and multiword DMA modes 1 and 2. EIDE is a Western Digital trademark. Both Seagate and Quantum use the term Fast ATA. Note that vendors tend to use these terms loosely, which can create some confusion.

Additionally, some manufacturers label hardware as EIDE even when they implement only a part of the EIDE features set. The difference between the two schemes is mainly in the scope of EIDE. Table 10.11 shows some of the differences.

TABLE 10.11: DIFFERENCES BETWEEN EIDE AND FAST ATA-2

FEATURE	EIDE DRIVES SUPPORT	FAST ATA-2 DRIVES SUPPORT
Fast transfer modes	Yes	Yes
LBA mode	Yes	Yes
Four devices on the interface	Yes	Sometimes
ATAPI support	Yes	Sometimes
Block mode	No	Yes
Western Digital's Enhanced BIOS	Yes	No

Installing an IEEE-1394 Hard Disk Drive

I've discussed the theory behind the hard disk drives; now let's move on to actually installing them.

Installation of an IEEE-1394/FireWire drive is relatively simple, providing you have the appropriate operating system and drivers. Windows 98SE/Me/2000/XP support the IEEE 1394/OHCI interface. Remember, however, that users of Windows 98 must upgrade to Windows 98SE for FireWire capability.

An IEEE-1394/FireWire connection is now offered as standard equipment in many new PCs, especially those that are configured for video capture and editing (for more information on that topic, see Chapter 26, "You Oughta Be in Pictures: Video Capture"). If your Pentium-class computer doesn't have FireWire capability, you can always get an add-on board that will fit into a PCI slot. Some add-on boards also give you the capability of adding two IEEE-1394 ports and two or more USB ports with a single card. The add-on boards come with the appropriate drivers if you need them. You will also receive the appropriate drivers with your FireWire hard drive.

To install the drive, you typically follow these steps:

1. Connect the AC power to the drive and then to an electrical outlet.

2. Turn on the power switch to the FireWire drive.

3. Connect the FireWire cable to the drive and to any FireWire connector on your PC.

4. Insert the installation CD that came with your FireWire drive. The installation software will step you through the process of installing additional drivers if your system needs them. The software may also optionally allow you to format your new FireWire drive.

TIP   *Even though FireWire devices can be hot-plugged and unplugged, they are not really designed to be portable devices in the way that Zip or Jaz disks are used. Take care before unplugging your FireWire hard drive, especially if you are in the midst of a data transfer. It could result in lost or corrupted data, and maybe even damage to the disk itself. You'll probably find an icon in your Windows system tray (at the right side of the Windows status bar) that allows you to prepare your FireWire drive for safe removal. As an example, in Windows Me, click the icon in the system tray that reads Unplug or Eject Hardware to stop or eject your FireWire drive.*

Installing an EIDE drive is a bit more complex. You're typically talking about an internal drive, so you have to insert the drive into the right bay, set the appropriate jumpers to acknowledge the drive, configure your system's CMOS for the new drive, set up the drive partitions, format the drive… in other words, it's a bit of work. Not necessarily hard to do, but definitely more stuff to do.

In the next chapter, then, you'll learn all there is to know about installing an EIDE drive.

Chapter 11

Installing an
IDE Hard Drive

◆ QuickSteps: Installing an IDE/ATA Hard Drive   389

◆ Deciphering the IDE Acronym Soup   391

◆ Obtaining Compatible Hardware   392

◆ Setting Jumpers and Cables   393

◆ Configuring the System's CMOS   396

Introduction

FOR AS LONG AS I can remember, hard drive prices have been in free fall. And that's good news for everybody—well, mostly. It's not entirely good news because just when I think I'm pretty happy with my computer, the drive prices go down, and I start eyeing a newer, larger, faster, cheaper (arggh!) hard drive. So, eventually, I give in, and I buy that new hard drive.

And then I've got to install it. Sound familiar? Then you've come to the right chapter. Here you'll learn how to put in an IDE/ATA hard drive. You'll learn how to jumper, cable, and install the drive, and how to set up a dual-drive system. You'll also learn how to configure the CMOS—where information about the hard drive installed in your system is stored.

QuickSteps

Installing an IDE/ATA Hard Drive

If you're in a hurry, you are in the right place. Collected here, for your convenience, are the basic steps that you will perform to install an IDE/ATA device.

NOTE *The terms IDE, ATA, and IDE/ATA have become generic and are used interchangeably throughout the industry. You will find these same terms used interchangeably in this chapter and the rest of the book, in keeping with industry standards. So when you read a description of an IDE drive, it also can be referring to an IDE/ATA and/or ATA drive.*

BE PREPARED

Before you start, there are some things you may need on hand. These include:

- Hard drive or other IDE device.

- Interface cable.

- Manual for the device and other configuration information.

- Adapter kit, if needed. Some systems come in small desktop cases and others in roomy tower cases. Regardless of which, check inside to see what drive bays you have free. All drives today are designed to fit either 5¼-inch or 3½-inch bays. Most hard drives are 3½-inch and most CD-ROM, CD-R/RW , and DVD drives are 5¼-inch. If you have only a 5¼-inch bay free for that new 20GB hard drive, you'll need an adapter kit.

- Flashlight—if not required, at least recommended.

- Phillips-head screwdriver with a medium tip.

- Small plastic cup for holding screws. Personally, I lay out screws in a pattern so I can return them to the place I removed them from. I work left-to-right, top-to-bottom. That way, I can just repeat the process and get the right screw in the right hole.

- Antistatic wrist strap—although not exactly necessary for installing drives and other similar devices, it's a good idea to have one handy. It's best not to harbor any stray static electricity if you happen to touch a component that you're not working on, which is altogether possible.

- Toenail or fingernail clippers— also not required, but handy. These are great for cutting those hampering zip ties (those plastic little strips that bunch wires together). Just be careful not to snip a wire or two. Of course, the cutting area of nail clippers is not very big, so there's little chance of this occurring if you pay attention.

Pardon me if this whole thing sounds like I'm a chef going through the throes of baking pastries for a big party, but there are ingredients (above) and clear-cut directions (below) for mixing it all together into a tasty digital treat.

1. Gather the ingredients and open the case.

2. Jumper the drive as appropriate. If you intend for the drive to become an adjunct to the existing main drive, set it to Slave as per the drive's manual. Almost all hard drives and CD-based drives ship with the drive jumpers set in Master mode by default. Many of the newer systems will require you to configure the drive as Cable Select. Use of Cable Select means that the drive's configuration is dependent on which IDE connector it is attached to. While you should check the system documentation to determine which configuration you should use, you can usually tell whether the drive needs to be Cable Select if the cable connectors are identified on the cable. Examples would be connectors labeled CD-ROM 1 and CD-ROM 2.

3. Insert the drive into its intended bay. This may be easy, or it may be nigh impossible. I've dealt with both many, many times. The newer budget systems are the worst—they were not designed to be upgraded. I've had to remove RAM, motherboard power taps, twisted cable, and other drives just to place a drive in a bay, sometimes all at once!

4. Locate an IDE cable terminal extending from the motherboard. The existing drive will likely be at the end of the cable, with another terminal several inches behind that. Also locate a power tap. These small, white blocks have four small holes and can be installed in only one way. Cable the drive.

5. *Now* you can put the screws in. Use the screws provided by the manufacturer. Using screws that go too deep can damage the drive. Allow the drive to be mobile while cabling or be content with the space there is between the back of a mounted drive and the power supply.

6. Leave the case open, check all your cable terminal points, and attach the monitor, keyboard, and mouse. The other cool stuff can come later. Power it up. You should see the drive being identified if you mounted and configured it correctly, although there are circumstances out of your control that could cause that to not happen (there's more detail further in the chapter).

7. Your system's CMOS should configure itself automatically; if it doesn't, enter SETUP during boot and configure the system's CMOS so that it knows a drive is there.

Of course, there's more to it than that. And that's why this entire chapter is devoted to the process and its details. First, though, you can work through these steps visually. That should help quite a bit.

Warnings and Apologia

Before you go on, however, let me warn you: hard drive installation has a lot of details to it. That's not because it's difficult—it's not—but because of the radically different types of hard drive subsystems that have grown up and become popular over the years.

Even though we generically call them *hard drive subsystems*, there are really two distinct kinds of drive installs you might have to do, in roughly descending order of likelihood:

◆ IDE

◆ SCSI

These drive types aren't as different as night and day, but significant enough differences exist that the actual installing of SCSI drives is covered in Chapter 13. "Partitioning and Formatting IDE and SCSI Drives" describes how to *partition* and *format* both types of drives once you've handled the hardware installation.

The IDE Mishmash

While the IDE interface is an excellent way to connect an internal peripheral to the computer, the many different labels by which it goes have confused many people. Let's take a moment and sort it out.

When hard drives first appeared in desktop PCs, it was necessary to install a separate controller card to connect the drive to the computer. It was an expensive and complicated arrangement that was made even more difficult by the incompatibilities of some controller and drive combinations. The hard drive industry decided there had to be a better way to attach a hard drive to a computer and, within a few years, specified a hard drive that had its own *Integrated Drive Electronics (IDE)*. It was an immediate success, and if that were the only name ever used, hard drive interfaces would appear far less confusing.

The biggest problem is that the specification that defines IDE is called the *Advanced Technology Attachment (ATA)* specification. So for a while drives with this interface were called *IDE/ATA*; then, around 1994 Western Digital made some improvements to the original specification, and rather than wait around for the specification to be updated, they called their version *Enhanced IDE (EIDE)*. This really muddied the waters since EIDE is not a specification and, to make matters worse, Western Digital redefines EIDE with each new release of the ATA specification. So, what EIDE meant in 1994 is different from what EIDE means today. The next year Seagate made improvements to the ATA specification and created their own snazzy name—*Fast ATA*, followed soon after by *Fast ATA-2*. Fortunately, Seagate and most other drive manufacturers quit coining their techno-babble names in the late 1990s (with Western Digital being the exception). Still, even though the label was a little long, drives were known as IDE/EIDE for a while.

Another term joined this never-ending name game when it was decided to use the IDE interface used to hook up CD-ROM drives. This process was more complicated than it sounds. You see, the IDE/ATA interface was designed to work only with hard drives. The first CD-ROMs and tape drives came with their own proprietary interface cards; the earliest combination I recall was a controller that was integrated into a sound card; some tape drives used the floppy disk interface, while some CD-ROMs attached to the computer using a SCSI interface. To make IDE work with non-hard-drive devices, a special protocol was developed called the *ATA Packet Interface (ATAPI)*. ATAPI enables these devices to plug into the standard IDE cable used by IDE/ATA hard drives and to be configured much like a hard drive would be. So, when you see a CD-ROM or other non-hard-drive peripheral advertised as being an "IDE device" or working with IDE, it is really using the ATAPI protocol.

The final confusing terms in the IDE name game are the terms used to describe the newest and fastest hard drives; I am referring to terms such as ATA-133, Ultra ATA-133, and Ultra DMA/133. Regardless of the letters used, the important part is the number at the end of the term, which is a reference to the speed (in megabytes per second) that the IDE interface can move data on to the computer's bus. So, if you have a drive labeled ATA-66, it means the drive can support data transfers up to 66MBps. The fastest hard drive available at the time this was written supports data transfers up to 133MBps.

Two major factors control how fast your hard drive can move data no matter what number is printed on the box the hard drive comes in. First, how fast is the IDE controller in your computer? If the IDE channel in your computer is designed as an ATA-33, even installing an ATA-133 drive won't make the drive move data any faster. The second factor that limits your drive's performance is less easily understood. No matter how fast the drive interface can go, the drive can only physically move data off the platter at a maximum of approximately 40MBps. In every throughput test I have run, the difference in performance among the ATA-66, ATA-100, and ATA-133 drives is minimal; you'll probably notice the difference only if you run a comparison test and read the results.

With all those names to choose from, in this chapter I'll refer to all of these devices by what has become their de facto name: IDE drives.

Steps in Hard Drive Installation

Installing an IDE hard drive requires following the steps outlined in the QuickSteps section at the start of this chapter, plus two more: partitioning the drive so that it will act as one large drive or several smaller ones, and formatting the drive to make it ready for your operating system. Again, for any given drive type, a step may vary or may be left out altogether, but the general sequence is the same.

As time has gone on, this process has sometimes gotten easier, and sometimes harder. Here's how to approach all but the last two steps. As I said earlier, I'll cover partitioning and formatting in Chapter 13.

Assemble Compatible Hardware

The hardest part about this step is just buying the right stuff. In the preceding chapter, you got some insights into the main decision points entailed in choosing the right drive subsystem. Remember to stress compatibility, size, and speed in making your decisions.

Since you have chosen IDE over SCSI (because you're reading this chapter), then your hard drive storage system will be based on IDE. When you're buying a drive, select one with as much disk space as you can afford; believe me, with the availability of broadband Internet access you'll fill it up quicker than you can imagine.

NOTE   *Remember, since it's IDE, chances are the drive will plug directly into the IDE cable that is attached to the motherboard. All motherboards made today have both primary and secondary IDE channels built into them.*

Now that IDE is an established interface, it is a safe bet that your IDE hard drive will work with your motherboard. There are some exceptions. If you can actually find a motherboard that doesn't have a built-in IDE interface, you can be assured it is at least five years old or even older; you would need to buy an IDE interface card. When you buy an IDE drive and interface, it's not a bad idea to check with the interface's manufacturer to ensure that it's compatible with the drive, and to check with the drive's manufacturer that the interface is okay. For example, if you buy a drive that supports the ATA-133 protocol (very fast), you will want an interface that also supports it to get the best performance out of the drive. While we're on the subject of the three faster drive protocols (ATA-66/ATA-100/ATA-133), it is necessary to ensure that you also have an 80-pin connector cable or the drives will automatically transfer data at a slower pace.

NOTE *All IDE interfaces are backward compatible. For example, if you install a newer ATA-100 hard drive on an IDE adapter that only supports ATA-33, it will still work—just not as fast.*

MASTER/SLAVE JUMPERS

The IDE controller is composed of one channel that can control two devices (hard drives, CD-ROM, etc.). Nearly every motherboard manufactured since 1995–1996 has two IDE controller channels built into it, labeled as the *primary channel* and the *secondary channel*. When two devices are attached to the same channel, one is configured as *Master* and the other as *Slave*.

Don't let the terms *Master* and *Slave* confuse you; they only represent an addressing scheme that allows both devices to share a common channel. The drive configured as Master is not any faster or better than the one with the Slave setting. The primary difference is that the drive configured as the Master on the Primary IDE channel is, by default, the boot drive. Even that is not set in stone on newer systems, because you can control which drive is the boot drive in your computer's CMOS configuration.

NOTE *Few systems leave the factory with motherboards that do not have IDE drive subsystems already installed and tested. The vast majority of these systems also have the capability to support up to four IDE drives, two Masters and two Slaves—one of each on the primary and secondary buses. My personal workstation (among my vast LAN system) has two 20GB hard drives, a 52X CD-ROM drive, and a 24X-20X-50X CD-R/RW drive, for a total of four drives. I do not have any controller cards in this system.*

The designation as Master and Slave isn't permanent and can be changed by altering a jumper setting on the drive. This gives you more choices when you're installing a second drive; for example, you may choose to retain your old drive as Master, adding the new drive as Slave, and then use a transfer utility to move your working OS to the new drive. Or you may opt to make your old Master a new Slave and install a fresh copy of your favorite OS to the new drive, a freshly minted Master.

Jumper, Cable, and Install the Drive

I'm going to combine some of my steps for discussion purposes, but they still happen in the order I originally described: First look at the drives and set their jumpers correctly, and then install them in the machine.

Cabling methods vary among the different drive interface types; I'll start out with the ones you're more likely to see, and then move to the older, less likely ones.

IDE CONFIGURATION

A typical IDE hard drive has connections like the ones you see in Figure 11.1.

FIGURE 11.1

Typical IDE hard
drive connections

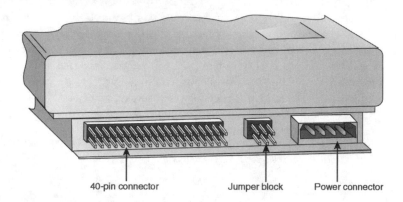

40-pin connector   Jumper block   Power connector

Like all drives, the hard drive needs a power connection. It uses the same old Molex connector that CD-ROMs, tapes, and other hard drives use. There is only one cable for data and control information, a 40-wire cable (unless the new drive is an ATA-66 or faster—then the cable is an 80-pin). (In case you were wondering why there appears to be twice as many wires, there isn't. To operate at the higher data speeds it is necessary to have shielded data wires—hence shielded wires.) The jumper block on the back of the drive enables you to specify whether this drive is a Master, Slave, or Cable Select; usually, if there's only one drive, use the Cable Select setting—but check the drive's documentation to be sure. In Figure 11.2, you see example jumper settings that could come from pretty much any IDE drive.

NOTE *Jumpers are little plastic blocks that have a bit of copper inside. They are formed so they can slide firmly over two posts. To close a pair of posts, you slide a jumper block over the two. They must be immediately adjacent to each other, and the hardware engineers design the post blocks to operate in this fashion. Common are two rows of three or four posts, with the leftmost posts in each row representing Master, Slave, or Cable Select configuration. The drive makers also often place a jumper on a single post with the same effect as not having a jumper; this is so you, the user, will have one if and when you want to install the drive as a Slave. The default, of course, is for the drive to be configured for Master status.*

When installing a multiple-IDE system, try to use the newer and faster of the two drives as the Master and the slower one as the Slave. The reason I say *try* is because not every drive will slave to every other drive. If one way doesn't work, try it the other way. The only other jumper you might have to set on an IDE drive would be an LBA jumper to enable or disable logical block addressing, provided on some drives to accommodate system BIOS issues. If your drive has this jumper setting, it is a very old drive. Hard drives don't have this setting anymore, but I ran across it on an IBM machine once a long time ago.

Once you have the jumpers in place, cable the hard drive to the host adapter. You'll see two kinds of cables, as shown in Figure 11.3.

A multiple-drive configuration would look like Figure 11.4.

FIGURE 11.2

Configuring drive jumpers

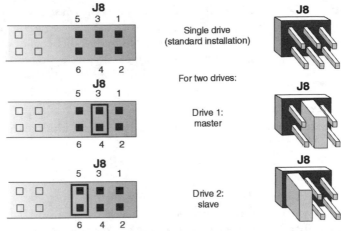

Single drive
(standard installation)

For two drives:

Drive 1:
master

Drive 2:
slave

Configuring drive jumpers for a Western Digital AT-IDE 540MB hard disk drive

FIGURE 11.3

Types of hard drive cables

Hard drive cable

Cable for two hard drives

FIGURE 11.4

Multiple IDE hard drives and a host adapter attached via a cable

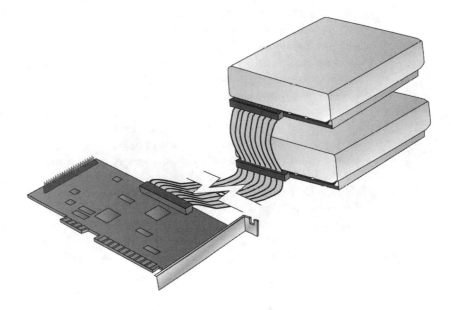

Note that it doesn't matter which connector the Master or Slave goes on unless the drives are configured as Cable Select. In such cases, the drive attached to the connector at the end of the cable becomes the Master and the drive connected to the other connector becomes the Slave. So, if you've put everything on right—no upside-down pin header connectors or forgotten Molex power connectors—then you're ready to proceed to CMOS configuration.

Configure the System's CMOS

I could have called this section "Introducing the Hard Drive to the Computer's Hard Drive BIOS." Your computer has low-level software, a set of built-in machine language programs whose purpose it is to control your hard drive hardware. That software must be in ROM on your system.

WHY MUST THE DRIVE STARTUP SOFTWARE BE IN ROM?

If you want to boot from a storage device (such as a hard drive), then the software to control that storage device must be already *built in* once you turn on the computer. Otherwise, the computer won't know how to access the storage device and load whatever operating system is on that device. It's kind of a chicken-and-egg problem: you need software to be able to read the hard drive, but you bought a hard drive in the first place so that you could put all your software there. This software "vicious circle" is broken, of course, with ROM, because it enables a PC designer to ensure that a small amount of software is automatically present in the computer's memory just as soon as the computer powers up. All that startup software is collectively called your computer's BIOS (basic input/output system), as you've read earlier in this book.

The BIOS doesn't contain software to control every possible peripheral, simply because it doesn't *have* to. There's no need for the BIOS to support a scanner or sound card; you don't need them to boot. Most LAN boards have no need of BIOS, unless you have a diskless workstation and therefore need to boot from the LAN card itself.

Unfortunately, there's more to making a drive work than some generic software. The BIOS software must know some of those intimate details of hard drives that you examined in the last chapter: cylinders, heads, write precompensation, and the like. Which leads to another chicken-and-egg problem: where to store the details of a hard drive?

Well, one obvious answer would be to put the information into some kind of ROM. But that's not a very good answer, because ROMs were a pain to make in the early '80s. It would be ludicrous to tell a PC buyer that she'd have to go find somebody with a ROM burner to make her a configuration chip every time she bought a new hard drive. Nowadays, flash memory is cheap enough that someone could easily design a little flash memory into a system to keep track of drive characteristics, but nobody had ever heard of flash memory in 1982.

Personally, I think the best answer would have been to store the drive's hardware configuration information on the drive itself, on the first sector. There wouldn't be a chicken-and-egg problem because every hard drive has a first sector with the coordinates cylinder 0, head 0, sector 1. But that didn't occur to the first PC hard drive system designers, and by now, you've probably figured out where the hard drive configuration information goes: into the system's CMOS. Most computers will store hard drive configuration information in the CMOS. *Most* computers? Sure. SCSIs don't need CMOS, and what about XTs?

THE EVOLUTION OF CMOS DRIVE TABLES

The first time I set up an AT-type system, I ran the SETUP program that came with the AT. Things started out pretty well, because it asked me easy stuff—"What day is it?" "How much memory does this computer have?" (Piece of cake—just count up the chips.) "What kind of floppy drives does this have?" (Still easy.) Then it asked what kind of hard drive I had.

"Heck, no problem," I thought, and typed in *Seagate ST-225*. (For the youngsters in the reading audience, that's a 21MB ST-506 drive that was just the cat's pajamas in 1983. I told you, I've been at this for a long time.)

After I typed *ST-225*, I swear snickering came out of the tiny little disk of metal and paper that thought it was a speaker. You see, the AT wants a *drive type number*, a number from 1 to 47.

In order to fully understand what a drive type number is, you should know a little history. The XT world usually saw controllers that could support only a very small group of drives. In an effort to combat this, the original AT had a table in its ROM describing 14 common drives of the time. Remember, a big difference between the XT BIOS and the AT BIOS is that the XT BIOS didn't come with hard drive support; ATs, in contrast, were all built assuming that they'd have hard drives, and so their BIOS contains support for hard drives. The idea was that when you bought a hard drive for your AT, the hard drive would look a lot like one of these 14 drives. If it didn't, then you couldn't use the drive.

Now, supporting 14 common drives sounded like a good idea; after all, 14 supported drives was better than the 4 to 8 supported by older XT controller boards. Of course, it seemed like a good idea only for a while, because drive types proliferated, and the next model of the AT had a BIOS that included descriptions of 25 common hard drives.

Do you suppose 25 drive types was enough? Nah, of course not, so the following generation of AT BIOS software included 47 drive types.

And then it stopped.

IBM's 1986 decision to use 47 built-in drive types has been adopted by most manufacturers to this day. And it has led to some troubles over the years. Today all computers come with a fixed drive table, an extra drive type called the *user-defined drive type*, and an Autodetect function. If the drive you're installing doesn't fit anything on the drive table, then you just select the user-defined type and specify the number of cylinders, heads, sectors, and write precompensation on the drive.

I suggest you select the Autodetect function. It's the easiest. All drives have identifying codes that enable them to be recognized by name. Current BIOS technology (and this has been so for the last several years) can detect the size of the drive installed and extrapolate the dimensions.

Pretty much all drives of all types are detected in this fashion today. CD-ROM, CD-R, CD-RW , DVD, LS120, Zip, and other such drives are all recognized by Phoenix and AMIBIOS CMOS BIOS chips. It's really much easier. The amazing variety of drive geometries today makes autodetection of user-definable drive types a necessity, and most computers designed in the mid- to late '90s include these options.

BLAST FROM THE PAST: IBM PC-AT DRIVE RECOGNITION OPTIONS

Just how far have we come since the halcyon days of the i386 and ROM BIOS that could not recognize a hard drive? Things have changed drastically since then, and thankfully, for the better (mostly).

Back in the old days, it used to be the case that if you tried to match your drive to your AT-type machine's drive table, and there was nothing on the drive table even remotely like your drive, you still couldn't match write precompensation even if you were willing to settle for a monstrous loss of cylinders. Or, if you were installing an RLL controller that formatted 26 sectors per track, nothing in your drive tables matched, because most of the drive tables out there were strictly MFM 17-sector entries.

In this case, you had three options:

◆ Get a new BIOS—one that included your drive type or a user-definable drive type—or get a BIOS custom-burned with your drive type. Again, that chip went on your *motherboard*, not the drive controller board.

◆ Buy an add-on ROM in addition to the BIOS ROM.

◆ Use a device driver such as SpeedStor or Disk Manager.

If you couldn't get a system BIOS ROM for your AT-type machine that allowed user-defined types (not everybody offered them), you might have discovered that a newer system BIOS was all you needed. A lot of old IBM ATs out there had only 14 drive types in their ROM: an upgrade to the more-common 47 types would do the trick (assuming that you needed this particular computer). Or you could have tried a custom ROM from the BIOS with any drive you liked. A custom ROM was about three times the cost of an off-the-shelf unmodified ROM. Most older 286- and 386-based AT-type machines had room for an extra pair of ROMs. Some vendors sold add-on ROM solely to enlarge the AT drive table.

Finally, there were software answers, such as products called SpeedStor or Disk Manager. The way they solved the BIOS compatibility problem was to format most of your drive as something other than a hard drive and then require that you load a device driver to read the drive.

The idea behind these device drivers was that they required only a small DOS-compatible partition on the front of the drive, a partition just large enough to boot from. The rest of the drive was invisible to the system's BIOS, but that was okay: the device driver handled that.

The strength of the device driver approach was that the device driver presented the remainder of the drive to DOS as a generic storage device. DOS was actually unaware that the device driver's space was a hard drive; all DOS knew was that there were lots of sectors that were available for storage. There was no limit on the number of sectors or tracks as far as the device driver was concerned.

The weakness of the device driver was that once you'd installed the driver, the system had to use the driver to access your hard drive. That posed problems for alternate operating systems or even for games that stretched the limits of the PC a bit.

The least desirable option was to use a device driver to communicate with your hard drive. One reason was that it was *another* piece of software that needed to function properly for your programs to use the hard drive and thus complicated your troubleshooting hassles. Another was that a ROM was usable for any operating system, so you'd have no trouble moving to Novell, Windows NT, or Unix at some point.

Chapter 12

Understanding and Installing SCSI Devices

◆ QuickSteps: Installing a SCSI Card   401

◆ SCSI Overview and Configuration   403

◆ SCSI-1, SCSI-2, and SCSI-3   404

◆ SCSI Physical Installation   412

◆ SCSI Software Installation   426

◆ Troubleshooting SCSI   428

Introduction

SMALL COMPUTER SYSTEM INTERFACE, or SCSI, is somewhat of the dark horse of system hard-ware. It's popular, but it has always remained just behind IDE in commonality due primarily to its higher cost and the difficulty that most people have understanding SCSI. Apple was enlightened for many years, having used two SCSI buses (one internal, the other external) in the vast majority of their systems. Recently, they too have turned to the lower cost of IDE despite the somewhat weaker performance and reliability. In this chapter, you'll learn about what SCSI does, how it works, how to physically install SCSI devices, and how to set up software to support SCSI devices. Once you know that, you will be better equipped to attack problems with SCSI.

QuickSteps

Installing a SCSI Card

If you're in a hurry, you are in the right place. Collected here, for your convenience, are the basic steps that you will perform to install a SCSI device.

BE PREPARED

Before you start, there are some things that you may need on hand. These include:

- ◆ Device's manual and other configuration information.

- ◆ Phillips-head screwdriver with a medium tip.

- ◆ Small plastic container for placing screws in. Personally, I lay out screws in a pattern so I can return them to the place I removed them. I work left to right, top to bottom. That way I can just repeat the process and get the right screw in the right hole.

- ◆ Antistatic wristband—though not exactly necessary for installing drives and other similar devices, it's a good idea to have one handy. It's best not to harbor any stray static electricity if you happen to touch a component that you're not working on, which is altogether possible.

- ◆ Hard disk drive or other SCSI device.

- ◆ SCSI host adapter, often referred to as a SCSI controller, if one is not already installed in the system.

- ◆ Adapter kit, if needed. Not to be confused with the SCSI host adapter, an *adapter kit* refers to the hardware mounting kit used to physically mount the hard drive. You see, some systems come in small desktop cases and others in roomy tower cases. Regardless of which, check inside to see what drive bays you have free. All drives today are designed to fit either 5¼-inch or 3½-inch bays. Most hard drives are 3½-inch and most CD-ROM, CD-R/RW, and DVD drives are 5¼-inch. If you have only a 5¼-inch bay free for that new 20GB hard disk, you'll need an adapter kit.

- ◆ Flashlight—if not required, at least recommended.

- ◆ Internal or external terminator, if your host adapter (internal) or external SCSI device doesn't have one built in.

- ◆ Toenail or fingernail clippers—again, not required, but handy. These are great for cutting those hampering zip ties (those little plastic strips that bunch wires together). Just be careful not to snip a wire or two. Of course, the cutting area of nail clippers is not very big, so there's little chance of this occurring if you pay attention.

If you went through the IDE chapter before this one, you'll note that I'm using pretty much the same recipe. Why? Because the installation of SCSI drives is similar to IDE drives. The differences are in setup and in the need to also install a SCSI host adapter card (most of the time), whereas IDE support is built into most motherboards. There are, however, some motherboards that have a SCSI bus built right in. Now, lets get to cookin' up some SCSI stew!

1. Gather the ingredients and open the case.

2. Jumper the drive as appropriate. If you intend for the drive to become an adjunct to the existing main drive, then set it to a higher SCSI ID number than the boot drive as per the drive's manual. Almost all hard disk and CD-ROM drives ship set to ID 0 or 1 by default. If you are installing a drive in an existing system, you need to ensure that you pick an ID number that isn't already in use—that includes the ID number used by the host adapter (usually 6 or 7).

3. Insert the drive into its intended bay. This may be easy, or it may be nigh impossible. I've dealt with both situations many, many times. A few of the newer budget systems can be challenging, as they were not designed to be upgraded. I've had to remove RAM, motherboard power taps, twisted cable, and other drives just to place a drive in a bay, sometimes all at once!

4. Now, either install the SCSI host adapter or, if you're installing a SCSI drive to a system with a SCSI host adapter already installed or with SCSI support built into the motherboard, move to the next step.

5. Locate a SCSI cable terminal extending from the motherboard. The existing drive will likely be at the end of the cable with more terminals several inches behind that. Also locate a power connector. These small, white blocks have four small holes and can be installed in only one way. Cable the drive.

6. Now you can put the screws in. Allow the drive to be mobile while cabling or be content with the space that exists between the back of a mounted drive and the power supply.

7. Terminate the last device on the SCSI chain if either the host adapter or built-in SCSI controller does not provide autotermination.

8. Leave the case open, check all your cable terminal points, and attach the monitor, keyboard, and mouse. The other cool stuff can come later. Power it up. You should see the drive being identified if you mounted and configured it correctly, although there are circumstances out of your control that could cause that to not happen (there's more detail further in the chapter).

Of course, there's more to it than that. And that's why there's an entire chapter on the process and its details. First, though, you can work through these steps visually. This should help quite a bit.

SCSI Overview

Prior to the mid-'80s, every type of storage device had its own kind of controller. If you wanted to add a scanner, a hard disk, a tape backup device, and a CD-ROM to your computer, then you'd have to install one board into the system that would act as the interface for the scanner, another for the hard disk, one for the tape, and one for the CD-ROM. That meant not only four controllers, it also meant having to *configure* four separate boards.

Most of the proprietary interface cards used a variation of a standard interface that is now known as the *Small Computer System Interface*, or *SCSI*. This interface first emerged in the 1980s. Designed by Shugart Associates (the people that introduced the floppy disk drive to the PC desktop), it was appropriately called the Shugart Associates Standard Interface (SASI). While SASI never caught on, it was modified and reappeared in the early 1990s as a proposed interface standard called SCSI. But the original SCSI standard (now called SCSI-1) proved to be too vague. It was possible for two devices to completely comply with the specification yet be unable to communicate with one another. During this time, companies began to make custom versions of the SCSI interface. Also during this period, SCSI earned a well-deserved reputation for being a difficult interface to work with. A company called Adaptec took the lead in the drive to create a SCSI interface that could become the standard interface for all peripherals. Adaptec believed that eventually SCSI would be used for all hard drives, and they might have been right were it not for the appearance of the IDE interface, which was inherently less expensive and complicated. SCSI remained the interface of choice for external peripherals until the Universal Serial Bus (USB) took over that job.

So, is SCSI going the way of beta? No, not at all. Even though it costs approximately 50 percent more than the equivalent IDE hard drive, SCSI drives still provide superior data throughput to IDE for large servers, and SCSI remains the interface of choice for servers and video editing.

SCSI Benefits

The benefit of putting a controller on each device in the SCSI world is that you know that the controller and drive are a matched set. In particular:

- The cables between the controller and the drive, which are a troublesome source of noise, can be extremely short, leading to much lower noise levels. In general, the longer the cable, the more opportunity to introduce interference.

- The controller and the drive (or the peripheral) can be more closely matched. When both the controller and drive come from the same maker, everything there becomes a known quantity and all external influences can be more easily dealt with (I'll get to those a bit later). That also means that built-in diagnostics can be included on the SCSI device.

SCSI peripherals can be focused to do a particular task, but they lack the capability to talk to any real-world bus. SCSI devices don't know what a Macintosh, a PC, or a Sun computer is. That's where the SCSI board that you install in your system comes in. The SCSI "controller," then, is not a controller at all; it's just a kind of universal translator that enables any SCSI device to communicate with a particular computer's bus. The SCSI *host adapter* (its true name) is, then, the glue that cements your SCSI devices and your computer.

The trick to SCSI is that it makes disk drives, all of which come in different shapes and sizes, into generic storage devices. That was the goal of the original SCSI. As time has gone on, SCSI has been expanded to include all kinds of storage devices, as well as printers and scanners.

NOTE   *As time has passed, traditional interfaces such as parallel have grown faster, and new ones such as USB are already fast enough for peripherals (for example, scanners and printers). Therefore, SCSI has become primarily the domain of those who want or need fast disk access or professional scanners.*

Some Basic SCSI Concepts

Understanding SCSI requires knowing a whole new bunch of terms. I'll describe some of them in a minute, as I take you step by step through planning and configuring a SCSI installation. But here's a quick introduction to some SCSI concepts.

SCSI-1, SCSI-2, AND SCSI-3

The original SCSI specification appeared in 1980 as a hard disk interface. It lacked agreed-upon standards, leading to a plethora of different—and incompatible—SCSI implementations. SCSI-2 made some big steps toward standardizing SCSI, improved the data transfer rate, and supported new types of devices. The original SCSI could only support eight devices (ID 0–7), and the host adapter took one of those. With the introduction of SCSI-2 came *Wide SCSI*, which supported up to 15 devices on a single SCSI cable. SCSI-3, or *Ultra SCSI*, increases the data transfer rate even more, increases cable lengths, and provides for simpler cable schemes. More on this below.

SINGLE-ENDED VERSUS DIFFERENTIAL SCSI

Some SCSI implementations use an electronic signaling system that is called *single-ended* in the SCSI world and is known as *unbalanced* in much of the data communications interface world. Single-ended SCSI systems will not work if the total length of their cables exceeds 6 meters. Differential SCSI uses a balanced approach that requires twice as many wires in a cable but can support up to 25 meters on a cable.

NOTE   *You may wonder why distance is important if all these devices are just sitting inside your PC case. Well, SCSI is a popular tool for network administrators as SCSI's format practically begs to be configured as a RAID (Redundant Array of Inexpensive Discs). A great number of these in a corporate server room or series of server rooms can start to create a wide gap. Consider the length needed to run a cable over a door frame as opposed to just across the carpet and you'll get an idea of how long cables can get.*

SCSI IDs

Because SCSI is a bus, multiple devices share it. One device is distinguished from another on the bus by its SCSI ID, a number from 0 to 7 on SCSI-1 or SCSI-2 (narrow) systems, 0 to 15 on wide SCSI-2 or single-channel SCSI-3 systems, and 0 to 31 on dual-channel SCSI-3 systems.

ACTIVE AND PASSIVE SCSI TERMINATORS

The electronics of SCSI require that both ends of the chain of SCSI devices contain a circuit that *terminates* the system. Older systems used a simple circuit called a *passive terminator.* Most systems nowadays require an *active terminator.* The problem is that many SCSI devices with built-in termination offer only passive termination, and that means that you've got to either buy an active termination device or put up with potential impairment of SCSI performance.

SCSI Underview

Sure, we've sort of glanced at SCSI, so now let's get our hands dirty. At this point, the different generations make little difference, because much modern software can't make full use of the modern SCSI generations. But some can, and that makes it worthwhile knowing about and purchasing more advanced SCSI. Here's a rundown on the SCSI generations.

SCSI-1: The Beginning of a Good Idea

As I mentioned earlier, in 1981, Shugart Associates—the company that eventually became Seagate—developed a parallel block-oriented transfer protocol called the Shugart Associates System Interface, or SASI.

SASI became the Small Computer System Interface, or SCSI, in 1984, when the ANSI's X3T9 committee formalized the specification.

SCSI-1 INTERFACE

SCSI is an 8-bit parallel interface between a SCSI host adapter and a SCSI device. (*Eight-bit* here has nothing to do—or very little to do—with your bus interface.) The standard runs at 5MHz, meaning a throughput of 8 bits, 5 million times a second, for a maximum data transfer rate of 5MBps. It incorporated a command set that could be only partially implemented by a vendor, but the vendor could still claim that its device was SCSI compatible. SCSI-1 is now obsolete, and older devices designed as SCSI-1 devices may not work with current SCSI host adapters.

SCSI-1 DEVICE TYPES

SCSI-1 defined several generic device types:

- Random access devices (hard disk)
- Sequential access devices (tapes)
- Printers
- Processors (host adapters)
- WORM optical drives
- Read-only random access devices

WARNING   *Even though SCSI-1 is obsolete, you will see references to it on SCSI cable descriptions because the term is used (incorrectly) to describe the original SCSI 50-pin Centronics connector.*

These types changed in SCSI-2, as you'll see later.

Asynchronous and Synchronous SCSI

SCSI-1 defined a SCSI notion that has remained with us, a set of rules for transferring data across the SCSI bus. You'll see references to it in some SCSI software, so let's take a minute and define asynchronous versus synchronous SCSI interfaces.

The most basic kind of data transfer over a SCSI bus goes something like this: the initiator requests a byte, the target responds by sending the byte over the SCSI bus, and the initiator says, "Got it," signaling to the target that the transfer went okay.

That "Got it" message is called a *handshake* or an *acknowledgment.* Each handshake takes time, however, and introduces a fair amount of overhead; in fact, one of the main failures of SCSI-1 was the amount of time spent on overhead.

This method of handshaking every byte is called *asynchronous SCSI.* There's a faster method, whereby the initiator acknowledges big blocks of bytes, rather than every single byte. That's called *synchronous SCSI.* It's essential for high-speed disk access. Double-check that both your host adapter and your drives support synchronous access.

You can have asynchronous and synchronous devices on the same SCSI bus, but nobody talks synchronous if the host adapter can't.

SCSI-1 left so much undefined that it was nearly inevitable that the actual SCSI-1 implementations on the market would be incompatible.

SCSI-2 Improves on a Good Thing

SCSI-2 was being developed even prior to formalization of the SCSI-1 standard by ANSI in 1986. The point at which SCSI-1 was finalized and SCSI-2 began was rather arbitrary and had more to do with simply deciding to get the standard published on a particular date than a quantum jump in specifications. The specification simply reflects where the state of progress was at the date of publishing. SCSI-2 enhancements include new command sets, wider data paths (8 and 16 bits), and command queuing.

SCRIPTING AND DISCONNECTS

SCSI-2 incorporates *scripting,* whereby a series of transfers can be "batched" across the bus. For example, a hard disk could be backed up to an optical drive—with no processor intervention.

SCSI-2 also allows *disconnects,* whereby the host adapter sends a command to a slow device such as a tape drive—a rewind command, for example—and then disconnects the drive from the SCSI bus, so that the whole bus doesn't have to remain idle while the tape rewinds.

KINDS OF DEVICES

SCSI-2 defines a slightly different set of generic device types than did SCSI-1:

- ◆ Random access devices (hard disk)
- ◆ Sequential access devices (tapes)
- ◆ Printers (even though it is defined, I've never seen a SCSI printer)
- ◆ Processors (host adapters)

- WORM optical drives

- CD-ROMs and CD-R/RW (which replaced the former)

- Scanners

- Magneto-optical drives

- Jukeboxes (the data storage type, not the music type)

- Communications devices

The first five are the same, the sixth changed, and the last four are new types.

FAST AND WIDE SCSI

As originally defined, SCSI is an 8-bit parallel interface between a SCSI device and a SCSI controller. Several variations have been defined in SCSI-2.

Fast SCSI doubles the data transfer rate over the existing data path. If SCSI-1 8-bit transfers are 5MBps, then Fast SCSI 8-bit transfers are 10MBps. Fast SCSI works on either single-ended or differential SCSI, but if you set up Fast SCSI on single-ended cables, your total cable length can be only 3 meters.

Wide SCSI uses an extra cable to increase the data path to 8 or 16 bits. Using nondifferential cables and interface, Wide SCSI can increase data transfer rate to 20MBps.

Fast-Wide SCSI uses a greater data transfer rate over a wider cable to support a data transfer rate of up to 40MBps, but 20MBps is more common.

SCSI-3, or Ultra SCSI

During the '90s, processor and data-transfer performance increased by factors in the hundreds. Now the disk subsystem has become a real bottleneck. Ultimately, Fibre Channel, with its incredibly high speeds, will resolve this problem. However, the solution will take time, will not be backward compatible, and will likely prove too expensive for many situations. In the meantime, Ultra SCSI serves as an interim solution. It's twice as fast as SCSI-2, multichanneled, and can use all that SCSI-1 and SCSI-2 hardware you have accumulated over the years.

For Ultra SCSI, ANSI separated the single SCSI standard into a collection of standards that are extensions of the SCSI-2 interface standard.

DEVICE TYPES

The command set has been expanded. There are now device types for Digital Audio Tapes (DAT) and for file server–type devices as well.

EXPANDED NUMBER OF I/O CHANNELS (MULTICHANNEL)

Give an Ultra SCSI drive an additional I/O channel, and you have MultiChannel SCSI, as it expands the number of I/O channels available to the system. For example, instead of a single channel supporting seven devices, the Adaptec 3940 has two channels, each with its own independent RISC processor. The 8-bit AHA 3940 Ultra SCSI version can support up to 15 devices and move data at up to 40MBps. The 16-bit AHA 3940 Wide Ultra SCSI version doubles this to 31 devices, and it can move data at up to an incredible 80MBps.

Performance is greatly enhanced by this strategy (as well as by doubling the internal clock speed), since faster devices can have their own channel. Slower devices can use another channel, so they are no longer a bottleneck impeding the speedier peripherals.

Another advantage of having multiple channels is the ability to use only one of your valuable PCI slots for hardware mirroring.

SHORTER CABLES

As data transfer speeds are increased with Ultra SCSI, transmission noise and signal quality become problematic over the entire length of the cable connecting the host and the device(s). To address this problem, the cable specification for Ultra SCSI was shortened to 1.5 meters. Bus extenders can be added to increase the total cable length to 7.5 meters.

MANDATORY ACTIVE TERMINATION

SCSI-3, as I've already mentioned, also forces the termination circuits to get a bit more complex. Instead of simple passive resistors, SCSI-3 termination must include voltage regulation circuits that keep the bus voltage between 4 and 5.25 volts. That means a less noisy bus, but it also spells trouble for a SCSI-3 configuration with an old SCSI-1 or SCSI-2 that doesn't support active termination. Again, many SCSI-1 or SCSI-2 devices do support SCSI, but there's no guarantee. And, like SCSI-2, SCSI-3 requires SCSI parity.

BRIDGING INTO SERIAL AND FIBRE CHANNEL SCSI

SCSI-3 introduces a lot more wires with a 68-wire connector. That's because of the parallel nature of SCSI, in combination with the new 32-bit data bus. But there's another approach, as well— serial SCSI.

Serial SCSI is a six-wire version of SCSI. It's easier to cable and used for greater distances; serial SCSI can run for over a kilometer of cable! Additionally, SCSI-3 is defined for optical fiber, paving the way for even faster systems. I'll talk more about Fibre Channel in a bit, but I mention it here because some aspects of this technology are included in the SCSI-3 standard.

Comparing SCSI-1, SCSI-2, SCSI-3

Table 12.1 compares SCSI-1, SCSI-2, and SCSI-3. Table 12.2 shows SCSI types and specifications.

TABLE 12.1: SCSI-1, SCSI-2, AND SCSI-3 COMPARED

STANDARD	BIT WIDTH	CABLE NAME	PIN COUNT	MAX TRANSFER RATE MBPS	MAX SCSI DEVICES	DESCRIPTION
SCSI-1	8	A	50	5	8	Asynchronous
SCSI-2	8	A	50	10	8	Fast

Continued on next page

TABLE 12.1: SCSI-1, SCSI-2, AND SCSI-3 COMPARED *(continued)*

STANDARD	BIT WIDTH	CABLE NAME	PIN COUNT	MAX TRANSFER RATE MBPS	MAX SCSI DEVICES	DESCRIPTION
SCSI-2	16	A+B	50+68	20	8	Fast-Wide**
SCSI-2	32	A+B	50+68	40	8	Fast-Wide**
SCSI-3	16	A	50	10	8	Fast
SCSI-3	16	P	68	20	16	Fast-Wide*
SCSI-3	32	P+Q	68+68	40	32	Fast-Wide**

*With one cable
**With two cables

TABLE 12.2: SCSI TYPES AND SPECIFICATIONS (NEW, COMBINED)

SCSI TYPE	MAX DEVICE	MBPS	BUS WIDTH	PINS	CABLE NAME	MAX LENGTH	NOTE
SCSI-1	7	5	8	25	A	19.7	Asynchronous
SCSI-2	7	5	8	50	A	19.7	
Fast SCSI-2	7	10	8	50	A	9.8	
Wide SCSI-2**	15	10–20	16	50+68	A+B	9.8	32-bit with 2 cables
Fast-Wide SCSI-2**	15	10–20	16	50+68	A+B	9.8	32-bit with 2 cables
8-bit Ultra SCSI-3	7	20	8	50	A	9.8 (to 4 devices) 4.9 (for 5 or more)	
16-bit Ultra SCSI-3*	15	20–40	16	68	P	9.8 (to 4 devices) 4.9 (for 5 or more)	
8-bit Ultra2 SCSI-3**	7	40	8	68+68	P+Q	39.4	16-bit with 2 cables
16-bit Ultra2 SCSI-3**	15	40–80	16	68+68	P+Q	39.4	32-bit with 2 cables

*Using one cable
**Using two cables

Fibre Channel

Hewlett-Packard, IBM, and Sun Microsystems began the Fibre Channel Systems Initiative (FCSI) in 1993. The goal of this initiative was to create an industry standard for I/O interconnection that would increase I/O performance and allow for more configuration flexibility. This technology is so complex that an entire book could be devoted to it. Therefore, I will give only an overview here.

Fibre Channel Storage Area Networks

Imagine for a minute that your current SCSI cable connects to your computer in the same way your network cable does. The other end of the cable connects to a hub, which in turn connects to a 100MBps "network" of hard drives (or other peripherals). If you are using copper cables, these other devices may be located up to 30 meters away. If you use fiber-optic, these devices may be in various buildings or even up to 10 kilometers apart. All your data I/O now travels through this cable rather than through the regular network. This configuration roughly defines a storage system implementation of Fibre Channel.

TERMINOLOGY

The concept of the interconnecting Fibre Channel network is called the *fabric*. Each point of connection, whether it be a hard drive or a server, is called an *N-port*, or *Node port*. When Fibre Channel is used to network storage devices, the term *SAN* is used, meaning *Storage Area Network*. Fibre Channel implementations that use a dual-loop configuration roughly analogous to Token Ring are called *Fibre Channel Arbitrated Loop*, or *FC-AL*.

NOTE Token Ring, *an IBM innovation, is a token-passing, ring-shaped local area network. Unfortunately it was more expensive than Ethernet and sort of worked itself out of the industry due to its higher costs. Those costs, however, were quite warranted as Token Ring (especially the FDDI implementation, which is like two Token Rings for the same workgroup) offered greater reliability and fewer dropped packets. Though Ethernet/802.3, at 100Mbps speeds, came out quite some time ago, it was only in 1999 that 100Mbps Token Ring was accepted as a standard.*

FIBRE CHANNEL AND CLUSTERS

Clusters are groupings of servers that are accessed by a common group of clients. The main benefit of clustering is *fail-over* capabilities. If a client is running an application from a server that fails catastrophically, another server in the cluster will dynamically take over, with no disruption to the client. Some applications can also scale by using clustering technology.

Fibre Channel complements clustering technology in several ways. Since it offers the ability to add more devices than other SCSI technologies, Fibre Channel offers the capability of creating larger clusters. Further, unlike older SCSI technologies, Fibre Channel can be configured not to give priority to any node, improving cluster performance.

Defining a SCSI Configuration

Making SCSI work requires understanding the following items and issues. This is just an overview; you'll examine each of these issues later in this chapter in detail.

SCSI Host Adapters

Issues:

◆ The host adapter must be compatible with the system's bus.

◆ The host adapter must be able to support the same level of SCSI (SCSI-1, SCSI-2, or SCSI-3) as the peripherals.

◆ When you're buying a SCSI host adapter, you're buying the ambassador between all those expensive, fast peripherals you bought and your CPU and memory. Now, more than ever, bus mastering and 32-bit interface SCSI host adapters are preferable.

◆ The host adapter must be assigned a SCSI ID between 0 and 7, or 0 and 15 on a single-channel SCSI-3 host adapter (most common for PCs).

◆ The host needs a SCSI driver that follows the same SCSI standard as the SCSI drivers on the peripherals. There have been three standards here: Advanced SCSI Programming Interface (ASPI), Common Access Method (CAM), and Layered Device Driver Architecture (LADDR). ASPI has become the primary standard. These are *not* related to SCSI-1, SCSI-2, and SCSI-3; this is a different dimension in SCSI compatibility.

SCSI-Compatible Peripherals

Issues:

◆ Each SCSI peripheral needs a SCSI driver that is compatible with the SCSI standard on the host's SCSI driver.

◆ All SCSI devices follow SCSI-1, SCSI-2, or SCSI-3 cable standards; it may be important to know which level the device follows when installing it.

◆ Each peripheral must be assigned a unique SCSI ID from 0 to 7, or 0 to 15 for single-channel SCSI-3.

◆ Devices can be mounted internally or externally.

◆ Some devices have optional built-in termination (see the next item); others may have termination that's *not* optional (this is *very* bad, but more common than you'd hope), and still others do not include termination of any kind.

◆ Terminated devices should support active termination, but some will support only passive termination.

◆ Devices should be able to be daisy chained, so they should have two SCSI connectors if they are external.

SCSI Cabling

Issues:

◆ There are several kinds of SCSI cables and even variations between SCSI-1, SCSI-2, and SCSI-3. (See Table 12.1.)

◆ You can't run cables more than a few feet, or the SCSI signal degrades and the peripheral doesn't work.

SCSI Termination

Issues:

◆ Each SCSI system needs two terminators, one on each extreme end of the chain of devices.

◆ There are two kinds of terminators: passive and active. You're supposed to be able to use either type for SCSI-1 or SCSI-2, but active is usually a better idea. SCSI-3 requires active termination.

◆ Some devices have built-in terminators; others require separate termination devices.

◆ The host adapter probably supports termination of some kind. This should be considered when terminating the system.

SCSI Drivers

Issues:

◆ The SCSI system needs a driver for each SCSI device, as well as a driver for the host adapter.

◆ SCSI hard disks may not require drivers; instead, they may have an onboard BIOS that serves that function.

SCSI Installation

Actually putting SCSI adapters and peripherals into your system is pretty much the same whether you're using devices that are SCSI-1 or SCSI-2. So let's look at physical installation first.

SCSI Physical Installation

Basically, putting a SCSI device into the PC requires the steps outlined earlier in the QuickSteps section. Software installation follows the physical end of a SCSI setup, but for the moment let's continue focusing on the physical part.

Choosing a SCSI Host Adapter

Many computers—more and more—have SCSI support right on their motherboards; others come with SCSI adapters in a slot as standard equipment. If this is true for you, then skip to the next section. But otherwise, just a few thoughts about choosing host adapters:

◆ There have been host adapters for just about every type of bus that has existed, including the 8-bit ISA, 16-bit ISA, and PCI. If you check around your favorite online auction, you can find host adapters for all of these now-obsolete buses, including the 16-bit MicroChannel, 32-bit MicroChannel, 32-bit EISA, and even the VL-Bus.

◆ Many SCSI host adapters use bus mastering to improve their performance. *Bus mastering* is very similar to direct memory access (DMA) in that it allows the host adapter to transfer data straight into memory without having to involve the CPU. But DMA allows only high-speed transfer from peripheral to memory or memory to peripheral—not peripheral to peripheral. Bus mastering makes peripheral-to-peripheral transfers possible without CPU intervention, often leading to higher-speed data access. Anyone who's heard of bus mastering has probably heard that the PCI buses support it. While it's not generally known, bus mastering is possible with ISA bus machines. Adaptec makes an AHA1542 controller that's almost jumper-free and that will do bus mastering on an ISA bus machine, providing some admirable data transfer rates.

TIP   By the way, there's another benefit to bus mastering: it means that your host adapter doesn't need to use one of your precious DMA channels.

◆ Some SCSI devices come with *optional cache RAM.* While it sounds like it'll make your system really scream, what it mainly does is make the benchmarks look good. A system that provides no hurdles between the bits on the platter and the CPU's RAM will provide pretty good data transfer rates that are real data transfer rates, not bogus ones. Bus mastering should reduce or remove the need for cache RAM on the controller.

◆ Look for an adapter that supports SCSI-2 or SCSI-3 if you have the budget, and potentially one that supports Fast SCSI, Wide SCSI, and Fast-Wide SCSI. If you don't need to support more than seven devices, you should select a narrow host adapter rather than a wide one, since the cables and connectors for the wide SCSI are more expensive than the narrow equivalents.

◆ If you need to support more than seven devices, or if you have a slow device that is monopolizing the bus and preventing faster devices from giving you the performance you need, consider a multichannel SCSI host adapter. That way, you can put the faster devices on one channel and the devices that are slowing things down on a separate channel.

◆ Make sure that your adapter has drivers that support the ASPI standard. (See "SCSI Software Installation" for more information.)

TIP   Choosing the wrong host adapter isn't the end of the world, but it can mean more installation and troubleshooting headaches.

Installing the SCSI Host Adapter

Putting a SCSI host adapter into the PC is pretty much the same as installing any board. SCSI adapters are a bit more of a pain than the average board to install because they typically require DMA channels, IRQ levels, I/O addresses, and a ROM address.

It's usually possible to connect SCSI devices to a host adapter both internally and externally. In Figure 12.1, you see that there is a 50-pin header connector on the SCSI host adapter for internal connections, and a Centronics 50-pin female connector for attaching external devices.

FIGURE 12.1

SCSI connectors

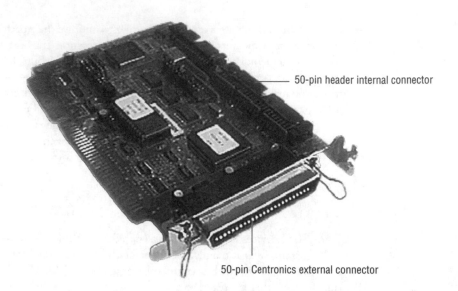

50-pin header internal connector

50-pin Centronics external connector

More recent SCSI adapters will use a miniature 50-socket D-shell connector. A note of interest here—some SCSI adapters with three interfaces (an internal Wide 68-pin connector, a 50-pin connector, and an external connector) will allow connection to only two of the three interfaces at the same time. Thus, if you have internal wide and narrow devices, the external connector cannot be used. You should consult your documentation for the particular adapter.

Assigning a SCSI ID to the Peripheral

Now consider the SCSI peripheral that you're going to install.

SCSI is a parallel interface. SCSI-1 (and most SCSI-2 implementations) defined eight wires to communicate data, an 8-bit data bus. Now, the SCSI designers needed a simple way for a number of devices on a SCSI bus to say, "I want to talk!" and they all needed a way to say that all at the same time—so they couldn't share a wire to signal that they wanted to use the bus. Every device needed a separate wire.

What, then, was the easiest way to let multiple devices signal that they wanted to use the bus? To let the data lines do double duty. Each data line is also a SCSI ID line, and, as the original SCSI design called for eight data lines, there are eight SCSI devices that can go on a SCSI bus.

A basic SCSI configuration assigns this identification number, called a SCSI ID, to each device on the SCSI system. The values for this ID range from 0 to 7, and the host adapter typically is set to 7. Other, more advanced, configurations can handle IDs from 0–15 and even 0–31. You typically can change the host ID from 7, or, in the case of the more advanced configurations, the last ID in the chain, but don't—you'll expose yourself unnecessarily to software incompatibilities.

You typically set a SCSI ID with a DIP switch, a jumper, a thumbwheel, or the like. There are just a few rules for setting SCSI IDs:

♦ Each device on the SCSI chain must have its own ID.

♦ The lower the SCSI ID, the higher the priority of the device. If two devices both want the bus at the same time, the one with the lower number wins. Hard drives need ID 0 or ID 1 because they should have highest priority.

♦ Do not use ID 0 or ID 1 for anything but hard disks. If you plan to boot from a SCSI hard disk, make it ID 0.

♦ Check your system documentation to see if it expects a device at a particular ID. For example, my advice to put a hard disk on ID 0 or 1 is really DOS- and Windows-based advice. Other operating systems (SCO Unix, for example) may not care about which ID you use for a boot drive. At the same time, SCO must see any CD-ROMs at ID 5.

♦ Regardless of what I recommend, or what your documentation says, the only way to solve some SCSI problems is to just try out different ID combinations until something works. I've never fixed anything by fiddling around with the adapter's ID, but I've fixed things by messing with other IDs.

♦ IBM PS/2 machines with SCSI drives use ID 6 for bootable hard disks (just in case you still have one of their antiques).

Does this sound a bit haphazard? Well, it is, to an extent: SCSI is still something of an evolving standard.

Something new to help us out is SCAM (SCSI Configure AutoMagically). With this newer functionality, devices and the host adapter configure SCSI IDs automatically. The hitch is that both the host adapter and devices need to support SCAM in order for this to work.

Targets, Initiators, LUNs, and LSUNs

So far I've been talking about SCSI IDs. But say that while installing my Adaptec SCSI hardware—Adaptec is the SCSI market leader and a manufacturer whose products I can recommend—I see a message upon bootup that says:

```
Host Adapter #0 - SCSI ID 6 - LUN 0: NEC CD-ROM DRIVE: 841 1.0
```

And a later message says:

```
Host Adapter #0, Target SCSI ID=6: NEC CD-ROM DRIVE:8411.0
```

First of all, `Target SCSI ID` is the same thing as `SCSI ID`. *Target* simply indicates that this device, a CD-ROM, is a target rather than an initiator.

In the SCSI world, any communication is initiated by one device and acknowledged by another device. The device that starts the conversation is called an *initiator*. The device that responds is called a *target*. In general, the host adapter acts as initiator and the SCSI peripherals act as targets. It is possible, however, for the two to reverse roles in some communications, but the *Target SCSI ID* message references the fact that the CD-ROM is usually a target.

The *logical unit number (LUN)* refers to the capability of a SCSI device to have subdevices. For example, consider the HP 6300 scanner, which is a high-end scanner that is SCSI and USB compatible. If I connect the scanner to the SCSI host adapter of one of my systems, I'll see a new SCSI ID, which refers to the scanner. If I attached an old Iomega 44+44 Bernoulli drive system, the two drives will be distinguished not by different SCSI IDs, but instead by different logical unit numbers under the same SCSI ID.

This is actually fairly unusual in the SCSI world and as a result will probably give your system heartburn—that is, your drivers may not be able to address the second 44MB drive. But now you'll know what *LUN* refers to. Again, the vast majority of devices include only one LUN.

In theory, each SCSI device can have up to eight LUNs. If one of the SCSI IDs is taken by the host adapter, that leaves seven for peripherals. If each peripheral had eight LUNs, there could be 56 SCSI logical units on a single host adapter.

To make things even worse, each LUN can have a sub-subdevice called an *LSUN*, or *logical sub-unit number*, which can range from 0 to 255. Let's see, 56 logical units, each with 256 logical subunits… that's 14,336 devices on a single host adapter! Not bad, eh? Well, actually, this wouldn't work for several reasons. First, a standard PC SCSI host adapter wouldn't get too far having to keep track of 14,000 devices. Second, there's a maximum cable length of 6 meters and a minimum cable length of 10 centimeters. Third, I don't know of any PC SCSI software that supports LSUNs.

Notice also the NEC CD-ROM . . . information. That's actual descriptive information in English that the CD-ROM gives to the host adapter about what it—the peripheral—is.

ENABLING/DISABLING SCSI PARITY

The SCSI bus can detect and use parity signals to detect errors in transmission over the SCSI cabling. Errors can and do occur, particularly as the cable gets longer from end to end.

TIP *To use SCSI parity, all devices must support it. If only one device does not support SCSI parity, then you must disable it for all devices on the chain.*

Some operating systems, such as Windows NT, will not work at all with a SCSI CD-ROM unless it supports SCSI parity. That implies that you should plan to support SCSI parity from the very beginning and buy only devices that support SCSI parity (and SCSI-2 and -3, by the way).

SCSI Daisy Chaining

Many of you will end up putting only one or two SCSI devices on a PC, but SCSI can easily support seven peripherals off a single SCSI host adapter (15 for Wide SCSI), or it could theoretically support hundreds of devices with a lot of rocket science. (The "hundreds of devices" concept works if you put eight SCSI adapters in a system, and each is connected in turn to eight SCSI adapters— that's possible; remember LUNs? The second-level SCSI adapters can be externally connected to other SCSI adapters, leaving the possibility of lots of devices. As I said a page back, it's impossible to find PC software that supports such a thing, so forget it.)

Multiple devices are attached to a single SCSI host adapter via daisy chaining. There are several kinds of cables in the SCSI world.

TYPES OF SCSI CABLES: SCSI, SCSI-1, SCSI-2, AND SCSI-3 (WIDE OR ULTRA WIDE)

External SCSI devices used to have two 50-pin female Centronics connectors, as you see in Figure 12.2, which shows the back of a SCSI device.

FIGURE 12.2

Connectors for
external SCSI
devices

A 50-pin male connector, such as you'd see on a SCSI cable, looks like Figure 12.3.

FIGURE 12.3

50-pin male connec-
tor for SCSI

Some external SCSI cables have a Centronics connector of this type on both ends of the cable. Such a cable is called a SCSI peripheral cable, or SCSI cable, and is pictured in Figure 12.4. Use it either to connect between SCSI-1 host adapters and SCSI devices or when daisy chaining from SCSI device to SCSI device.

FIGURE 12.4

SCSI peripheral
cable

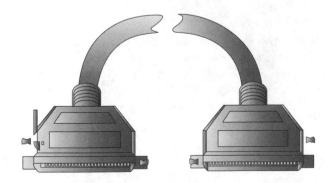

Other older SCSI cables have a male DB-25 connector on one side and a Centronics 50-conductor connector on the other side. Those are called Macintosh SCSI, or SCSI-1, cables and are pictured in Figure 12.5.

FIGURE 12.5

SCSI-1 cable

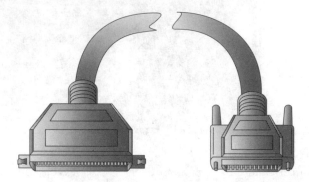

Newer SCSI adapters often do not employ a Centronics connector for external devices, but rather use a miniature 50-socket D-shell connector; some people call it an *HP-50 connector*. You can see the male version of that connector—the version that you'd see on a cable—in Figure 12.6.

FIGURE 12.6

SCSI connector—
50-socket D-shell
(HP-50 connector)

The cable incorporates two buttons on either side that you must squeeze together in order to connect or disconnect the cable to or from the adapter. You will see this connector instead of the Centronics on some peripherals (more and more, as time goes on) and more commonly on the backs of SCSI adapters. Since 1993, Adaptec has put them on the backs of their 1742 adapters in lieu of the more common Centronics 50. Such a cable—Centronics 50-conductor connection on one side, mini DB-50-pin connector on the other—is popularly called a SCSI-2 cable. Take a look at Figure 12.7.

FIGURE 12.7

SCSI-2 cable

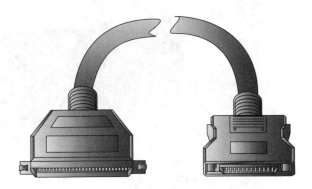

THROUGH THICK AND THIN: NOT ALL CABLES ARE EQUAL

While I'm discussing cables, let me relate a short war story that taught me an important lesson about cables.

I installed a CD-ROM onto a server so that I could install Windows NT 4.0 on my LAN. The CD-ROM was an external drive that used the 50-conductor Centronics connector, so I walked over to my cable pile and pulled out a standard SCSI cable with 50-conductor Centronics connectors on both ends. I plugged the CD-ROM into the SCSI adapter's interface port on the back of my PC, and the problems started. My existing tape drive and hard disk drive—both internal SCSI—started acting up.

After an hour or two of playing around with the system, I found that if I downgraded the SCSI system from SCSI-2 to SCSI-1 (I did this by reconfiguring my SCSI host adapter, an Adaptec AHA1542C), the problems went away. I had vague forebodings about losing SCSI-2 compatibility—SCSI parity doesn't work under SCSI-1, recall—but everything seemed to work, so I figured that I'd live with it.

Then came time to install NT. The README file said, "The SCSI and CD-ROM support built into Windows NT require that CD-ROMs provide SCSI parity to function properly." Great, I thought, and started fussing with the SCSI devices to get the CD-ROM to support SCSI parity. I mean, there was a jumper specifically included on the CD-ROM to control whether SCSI parity would be used, so why wouldn't it support SCSI parity?

Just on the off chance that I had a bad cable, I went back over to the cable pile to see what else I had. I found another dual 50 Centronics cable identical to the cable that I was using, and another dual 50 Centronics cable that was about twice as thick as the first two. I tried swapping the original thin cable for the other thin cable—no difference. But when I used the thicker cable, everything started working! I got full SCSI-2 support, as well as SCSI parity functionality.

A few calls around to cable places brought the information that, yes, there were two kinds of dual 50 Centronics cables. The thin ones work fine for SCSI-1 but not for SCSI-2. The thick ones are good for both.

INTERNAL SCSI CABLING

External devices, as you've read, tend to have two SCSI connections on them so that they can support the SCSI daisy chain. Internal devices, in contrast, use only a single 50-pin or 62-pin header connector. Internal SCSI cables are just ribbon cables with 50-pin or 62-pin IDC connectors, as you see in Figure 12.8.

FIGURE 12.8
Internal SCSI cable

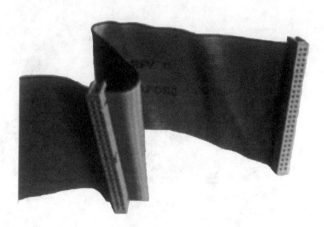

Because the connectors are sitting in the middle of the cable, one connector does the job for daisy chaining.

Terminating the SCSI Chain

Before popping the top back on your PC, there's one more thing that needs doing: you must terminate the SCSI chain.

NOTE   *SCSI-1 termination was a simple resistor. SCSI-2 termination requires a small amount of power applied by the SCSI device (600 milliamps at 4–5.25 volts). Some devices do provide termination resistance, but not termination power, making them potential troublemakers in a SCSI-2 setting.*

Whenever I discuss termination in class, people start referring to killer cyborgs from the future, but *termination* just means providing a voltage and resistance on either end of a cable, so that the entire bus has a particular set of electrical characteristics. Without this resistance, the SCSI cables cannot transport data around without significant error rates. (It will work sometimes, despite what some people claim, but it won't work reliably.)

NOTE   *Actually, on short SCSI chains, your peripherals might work, but there's no reason not to terminate properly. Problems occur in unterminated chains when packets "reflect" off of an inactive terminal point.*

ACTIVE AND PASSIVE TERMINATORS

SCSI-1 specified two kinds of termination, active and passive. Active was pretty much ignored until SCSI-2 became popular. Passive terminators are just a resistor network; if you're interested in how they work electronically, you can see that in Figure 12.9.

If you don't speak schematic, don't sweat it: the jaggy-looking things are resistors, *passive termination* refers to a source of electricity, and the triangle standing on its head represents electrical ground, the place that the power from Termpower is seeking to go. The main thing to notice is that the only thing going on here is resistors; there are no chips, and no amplification is going on. Passive termination is basically an adaptation of the simple terminators found in ancient floppy disk or ST-506 systems.

Back in the SCSI-1 days, the designers figured that the major use for SCSI would be to hook up a couple of hard disks to a host adapter, all with no more than 8 inches to a foot of cable.

FIGURE 12.9

Passive SCSI termination

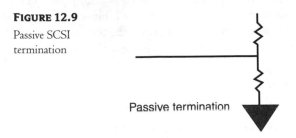

If, on the other hand, you intended to run longer cables and put a lot of stuff on them, then you need some kind of booster for termination power; that's active termination. It's represented schematically in Figure 12.10.

FIGURE 12.10

Active SCSI termination

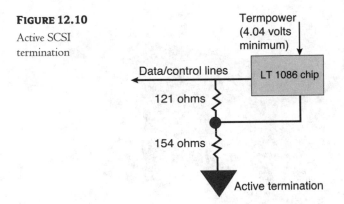

The LT 1086 chip's job is to provide amplification power when necessary. Active termination is, then, a bit more expensive than passive, but there is no more than a few cents' difference.

So, in a modern setup, do you need active or passive? As in the old SCSI-1 configuration, if all you're going to do is to hang a single drive on a host adapter, then it probably doesn't matter. But if you want to use longer cables, external devices (they usually need longer cables), and more than one or two devices, then active termination is a good idea. The problem, as you'll see in the next section, is that termination is built into the SCSI devices themselves, and some vendors get cheap and simply add passive termination.

You can mix passives and actives on a SCSI chain, putting a passive on one end and an active on another.

INTERNAL AND EXTERNAL TERMINATORS

You've seen that some SCSI devices are installed internally in the PC (and connect to the host adapter with a ribbon cable), and that other devices are installed externally (and connect to the host adapter with a SCSI cable of some kind). There are also internal and external terminators, as well as SCSI devices that have terminators built right in. As I have mentioned, some vendors build active termination into their devices, some build passive termination in, and some don't build in termination of any kind, forcing you to buy a separate termination device of one kind or another. Most SCSI devices with termination let you disable that termination, but some are boneheadedly designed without any provision for disabling termination, forcing you to put those devices on one of the extreme ends of the SCSI chain.

If you've got to disable a terminator, you'll find that devices let you do that in one of these ways:

◆ An internal, *Single Inline Pin Package (SIPP)* terminator on the host adapter and/or a hard disk.

◆ Some host adapters, such as the modern Adaptec adapters, let you enable or disable termination via software.

◆ Many devices adjust termination with a DIP switch or a jumper.

If you must buy an external terminator, then you'll need to choose the right one for whatever SCSI connector type you have. In Figure 12.11, you can see a Centronics terminator.

FIGURE 12.11

Centronics
terminator

They clip onto one of the Centronics connectors on the back of the last external device on your SCSI daisy chain. I've also seen external SCSI terminators for the mini DB-50/HP-50 connectors and the old Macintosh-style DB-25s.

SIPP-type terminators often show up on the host adapter itself, as it needs termination and SIPPs don't take up too much space. You can see a SIPP in Figure 12.12.

FIGURE 12.12

A SIPP-type
terminator

If you have a host adapter that uses SIPPs for its termination, then there are typically three of these SIPPs on a host adapter. You'll also find SIPPs on many internal SCSI hard disks. You just remove them (gently, as you may need to reinstall them one day) by working them out with needle-nosed pliers. Once you've done that, put them in an envelope, seal it, label it "SCSI Terminators," and store it somewhere.

If you look at the back of the external SCSI device, you may notice a switch labeled "termination." It can be flipped on or off, so if this SCSI device is the last on the chain, then all I need do is to flip it on; otherwise, I flip it off.

Sample SCSI Setup: One Internal Drive

When I say, "Put terminators on the end of the chain," it's worthwhile taking a minute and making sure that you know what I mean. With that in mind, let's look at a few sample SCSI applications. Take a look at Figure 12.13.

In this setup, you've got just a SCSI hard disk. There must be terminators on each side, but there are only two sides, so it's simple to figure out where the terminators go. Both terminators are probably SIPP-type terminators. The host is ID 7, the hard disk is ID 0; this means that you're intending to boot from the hard disk.

FIGURE 12.13

SCSI setup: one internal drive

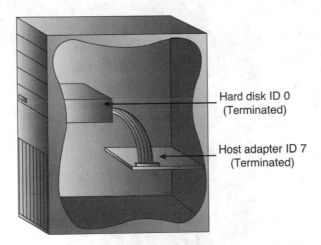

Hard disk ID 0
(Terminated)

Host adapter ID 7
(Terminated)

Sample SCSI Setup: Two Internal Devices

Now let's make it a bit more complex (see Figure 12.14).

Now I've added an internal CD-ROM. It needs to have a different ID, so ID 6 is good. Remember, I want to avoid the lowest ID number (ID 0) for anything other than a hard disk and I want to have a higher number and therefore lower priority. The CD-ROM isn't a high-priority device, anyway, so assigning it a higher SCSI ID versus a lower SCSI ID won't be that noticeable to a user. The hard disk terminators must be removed, as the hard disk is in the middle of the chain, and the CD-ROM is terminated.

FIGURE 12.14

SCSI setup: two
internal devices

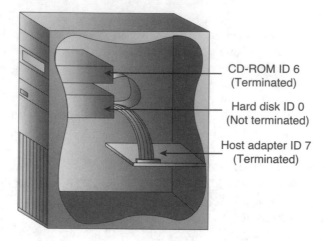

CD-ROM ID 6
(Terminated)

Hard disk ID 0
(Not terminated)

Host adapter ID 7
(Terminated)

Sample SCSI Setup: One External Device

Now let's do the same things, but with external devices, as shown in Figure 12.15.

FIGURE 12.15

SCSI setup: one
external device

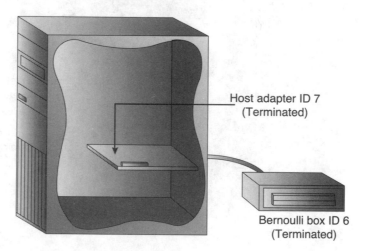

Host adapter ID 7
(Terminated)

Bernoulli box ID 6
(Terminated)

Now there's just one external device, a cartridge storage device that I won't try to boot from. I've set the Bernoulli box to ID 6 and terminated it, as it is the extreme end of the chain.

Sample SCSI Setup: Two External Devices

Continuing, I'll now add a second external device, as in Figure 12.16.

This time, I'll make the CD-ROM ID 5, as ID 6 is taken. The Bernoulli box shouldn't be terminated, as it is now in the middle of the chain, and the CD-ROM is terminated.

FIGURE 12.16

SCSI setup: two
external devices

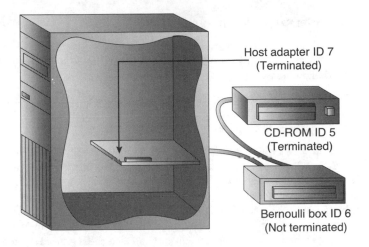

Host adapter ID 7
(Terminated)

CD-ROM ID 5
(Terminated)

Bernoulli box ID 6
(Not terminated)

Sample SCSI Setup: Internal and External Devices

For the grand finale, let's put two external devices and two internal devices on this system (see
Figure 12.17).

FIGURE 12.17

SCSI setup: two
external and two
internal devices

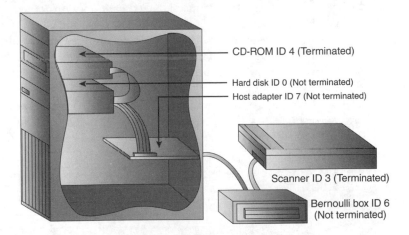

CD-ROM ID 4 (Terminated)

Hard disk ID 0 (Not terminated)
Host adapter ID 7 (Not terminated)

Scanner ID 3 (Terminated)

Bernoulli box ID 6
(Not terminated)

The important point to notice about this scenario is that the termination has been removed from
the host adapter, as it is now (for the first time) in the middle of the chain. The external devices are
attached to the external connector on the back of the SCSI host adapter (the Centronics or miniature D connector), and the internal devices are hooked to the internal 50-pin header connector.
Every device has a unique SCSI ID, and there's termination on the ends of the chain. Additionally,
I've assigned them SCSI IDs in roughly the order that their speeds warrant—the Bernoulli box is
faster than the CD-ROM and scanner, and so you assign it a lower priority than the peripherals,
resulting in equal access speeds.

SPECIAL TERMINATION ISSUES FOR SCSI-3

There are some special termination issues that apply to SCSI-3. On the external connector of a SCSI-3 host adapter, you can daisy chain both 8-bit (SCSI-2) and 16-bit (SCSI-3) devices. This can present some unique termination problems.

For example, suppose I attach to the external connector a SCSI-2 CD-ROM with a standard Centronics type SCSI-2 connector. To do this, I get an adapter that converts the 68-pin SCSI-3 connector on the host adapter to the 50 pins the SCSI-2 device uses. What is the result?

Think about it this way: a SCSI-2 device has 8 data bits or pins plus ground wires and other assorted signals. A SCSI-3 device uses two sets of 8 data bits, or 16 data bits total. You can call one of these two sets *a high order set* of 8 data bits and the other a *low order set*. When I connect a converter to the SCSI host adapter, I pass only the low order data bits to the SCSI-2 devices that are attached. Remember that the last device is terminated. What does it terminate in this scenario? Only the low order data bits! For that reason, it is critical that the adapter connected to the external port of the host adapter not only converts the 68 pins to 50, but that it terminates the high order data bits and associated ground signals.

SCSI Software Installation

Much of the SCSI installation process is like a normal hard disk's installation process: low-level format, partition, and high-level format. Doing those things isn't much different from doing them on non-SCSI hard disks, except that you may have to use a special program for the formatting and/or partitioning; check your SCSI software documentation for an example.

The tough part about SCSI software installation, however, is the drivers. There seem to be a million of them, and none of them appear to be on speaking terms with one another—and what do they do, anyway?

Until a few years ago, SCSI drivers were proprietary. You were crazy to buy a SCSI hard disk and host adapter unless you got them from the same vendor, a vendor that supplied drivers for the two of them. But since 1991, several *universal driver* standards have appeared. Figure 12.18 shows how they work.

FIGURE 12.18

Universal SCSI driver standards

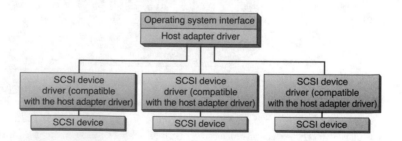

Rather than trying to create a hard disk driver, a CD-ROM driver, a scanner driver, and a tape driver that are all compatible with the operating system, a universal driver system defines an intermediate standard and supports that with a driver specific to the host adapter. The SCSI device drivers then need only be written to work with the intermediate standard defined by the host adapter's driver. The primary and exceedingly dominant standard is ASPI. Its two competitors, CAM and

LADDR, are gone. Additionally, no discussion of drivers can fail to include the INT 13 BIOS interface found on many SCSI host adapters.

The idea here is that you buy a host adapter from anyone and get a driver for that adapter that supports the ASPI standard. Since the driver on your host adapter board speaks ASPI, and your device's driver speaks ASPI, everything will work out fine. And if you decide to replace your current SCSI host adapter board with one that's faster or better in some way, then all you need is a new driver for that board—you don't even need to change the device driver for the tape drive. (It should be stressed that this is the idea; of course, ASPI compatibility is not a black-and-white thing in the real world. You should experience little incompatibility until you get into the really interesting SCSI drive farms, super-big device chains, or RAID arrays.)

With Bootable Hard Disks, You Don't Need SCSI Software

I'm going to discuss this in detail in a few pages, but if you are in the process of installing a SCSI hard disk on device 0 or 1, and in a hurry, then I wanted to note here that you needn't worry about SCSI software; you don't need it. Hard disks on device numbers 0 and/or 1 have built-in BIOS support and don't need separate SCSI drivers. Hard disks above device 1 or removable hard disks do require separate drivers.

Installing SCSI Software

If the system you are installing the SCSI drive on is using any Windows 9.*x* or later operating system, your host SCSI host adapter will be detected and the appropriate software should be automatically installed. If you are using DOS, be sure to read this section.

If your SCSI device didn't come with a driver, you can use the generic driver provided by Adaptec called EZ-SCSI. Here's a section from a CONFIG.SYS file built with EZ-SCSI:

```
DEVICE=C:\ADAPTEC\ASPI4DOS.SYS /D
DEVICE=C:\ADAPTEC\ASPIDISK.SYS /D
DEVICE=C:\ADAPTEC\ASPICD.SYS /D:MSCD001
```

Taken in order, these three device drivers (1) load the base ASPI support for the host adapter, (2) provide an ASPI-to-hard-disk interface for a removable SCSI hard disk (a Bernoulli box), and (3) provide an ASPI-to-CD-ROM interface for a SCSI CD-ROM. If the first driver didn't load, then the second and third drivers could not load.

EZ-SCSI comes with drivers for CD-ROMs, removable cartridge hard disks (such as Bernoulli boxes), and fixed hard disks. EZ-SCSI does not include drivers for scanners, WORM (optical Write Once, Read Many times) drives, WARM (optical Write And Read Many times) drives, scanners, or tape drives. If you get a device that supports ASPI later, then you can easily add it to a configuration that started out from EZ-SCSI. EZ-SCSI also comes with formatting and partitioning utilities for storage devices, a tape backup program, a scanning utility, and a benchmarking program.

WARNING *EZ-SCSI is not free, and it's doubtful that Adaptec will ever make it so. Neither does Adaptec, nor any other SCSI hardware vendor for that matter, make it easy to add SCSI to your system unless you buy something from them. Quite a distasteful attitude, I think. Why would you want SCSI if you don't have SCSI peripherals? IDE/ATAPI CD-R and CD-RW drives require an ASPI layer to be installed in order to be accessed and written to as such a device, and the makers of these devices are often asked to pay very large ASPI software licensing fees. Unfortunately, it's not always possible.*

The ASPI Standards

ASPI was invented by Adaptec, and the first time I read anything about ASPI, the A stood for Adaptec. But ASPI has been adopted by other hardware manufacturers, and, as you've read, it is the home of two very fine suites of SCSI drivers. I'd personally recommend that you stay within the ASPI standard, as it's easiest to find drivers that are ASPI compatible.

Let me underscore that there is no such thing as an "ASPI-compatible SCSI hard disk." The compatibility question relates to the drivers, not the hardware.

SCSI without Drivers: Onboard BIOS Support

After all this talk of mixing and matching drivers, you may be getting a bit queasy. But if all you're going to install is a hard disk or two, then you may never have to trouble with drivers.

WHY SCSI ADAPTERS HAVE BIOS

Using SCSI hard disks, if you think about it, can lead to a sort of chicken-and-egg problem. The SCSI device isn't accessible until the SCSI device drivers are loaded, and device drivers are generally loaded from the hard disk. But how can you load SCSI drivers from a SCSI hard disk? I suppose one answer would be to boot from a floppy and then not reboot, but it's a somewhat cumbersome answer.

The answer to the problem of, "How does my PC boot from a SCSI hard disk?" is that most SCSI adapters have an onboard BIOS that contains enough software to run the hard disk, even if there are no SCSI drivers loaded. That's a real lifesaver, enabling us to use SCSI hard disks without having to worry about drivers. However, they must be configured as SCSI IDs 0 and 1.

WHEN TO DISABLE A BIOS

Many SCSI installations that I do are not intended to support a hard disk. For example, installing a CD-ROM in an already running system means that I've already got a functional IDE drive in the system, so there's no point in replacing it with a SCSI drive.

In that case, I don't need the BIOS, so I disable it. You do that either with setup software or with some kind of physical setting, like a jumper or DIP switch. That's a real benefit, as it creates more space in my Upper Memory Area for larger Upper Memory Blocks. So disable your BIOS if you are not booting from a SCSI hard disk.

Troubleshooting SCSI

First, it's important to note that every version of Windows since 95 sleeps, eats, and breathes SCSI. In fact, they all need translation drivers to understand IDE/ATAPI, the type of drive shipped in a huge percentage of new systems for years!

Next, you'll be disappointed to find out that Windows 2000 does not have an ASPI layer built in, as NT did in previous versions.

Finally, the names *SCSI-1 cable* and *SCSI-2 cable* are misleading. What I've called SCSI-1 and SCSI-2 cables are not universal terms. Whenever you buy a SCSI cable, be extremely careful to specify the kinds of connectors you want on either side. Be triple careful about the mini DB-50 or HP-50 connector; everyone seems to have a different name for it, so make sure you're getting what you want.

NOTE   *Note that there is a difference between the terminology used and the physical characteristics of the cable. Although Wide SCSI has more pins (68 versus 50), the cable is not wider than a SCSI-2 cable. In fact, the SCSI-2 cable is the physically wider of the two. Wide refers to the data path—a 68-pin cable has 16 bits of data, whereas a SCSI-2 has only 8 bits or pins devoted to the data path.*

Installation Troubleshooting

Now that I've drilled into your head the idea that you should have only terminators on either side of the chain, let me offer some more suggestions to direct your troubleshooting.

NOTE   *The sum total of your SCSI cables should not exceed 18 feet. In general, the shorter your cables, the better.*

Sometimes a SCSI setup doesn't work. You check and recheck the SCSI IDs, but there are no duplicated IDs. You've terminated properly, but things still don't work. What do you do?

Remember that the sum total of cable lengths must not exceed 6 meters. Lower-quality cables mean that distance shrinks.

Things to try:

◆ Most SCSI host adapters display a sign-on message listing the recognized devices on the SCSI bus. Use that information as your first diagnostic. If the device is seen on the bus, but you can't get it to do tricks, then the problem is probably a driver problem rather than a hardware installation problem.

◆ If you encounter *phantom disks*—disks that you can see but cannot read or write—then you've probably put two devices on the same SCSI ID.

◆ Sometimes the ID-setting device is defective. I've seen a tape drive that, when set for ID 4, would show up as ID 6.

◆ Sometimes cables are defective, or combinations of cables don't get along.

To check whether it falls under the last item on this list, try this:

1. Install only the host adapter and its driver. Boot the system and make sure that the host adapter is working—no DMA/IRQ/IO address conflicts. It may even come with a host adapter diagnostic; run it.

2. Turn off the PC, add the first SCSI device, and power it up before you reboot the PC. SCSI devices often must be active before the host adapter can recognize them. (Also be sure that everything is terminated correctly.)

3. Once you've got that device in place, power down the PC and the existing SCSI device (if it's external), and add the next SCSI device. Test it as you just tested the first SCSI device.

I find it most convenient to install the internal devices first, then the external devices. I usually remove the SIPP terminators from the host adapter, and just place an external SCSI terminator on the connector on the back of my host adapter if it's a Centronics-type connector. Otherwise, I get a SCSI cable, attach it to the back of the host adapter, and then terminate that.

WARNING   *Remember to power down all the SCSI devices before adding or subtracting from the daisy chain.*

Chapter 13

Partitioning and Formatting IDE and SCSI Drives

◆ QuickSteps: Partitioning and
  Formatting a Hard Disk   433

◆ Low-Level Formatting   434

◆ Partitioning Drives   434

◆ Formatting Drives   444

◆ Using Third-Party Tools   445

◆ Troubleshooting Tips   445

Introduction

NOW THAT YOU'VE INSTALLED your hard drive, it's time to make use of it. If you were to boot up successfully into Windows at this point and go to My Computer, you would not see your drive. In order to use your hard drive, you have to perform two tasks: partitioning and formatting. (With a SCSI hard disk, you may need to perform an additional task first—low-level formatting—but I'll get to that in a minute.)

Partitioning a drive means that you tell the computer how the space on the physical hard drive should be apportioned to various drive letters (*logical drives*). You might choose to make your entire hard drive one big C drive, or to break up the physical drive into C, D, and E, or more. Partitioning also chooses a file storage system, such as FAT16, FAT32, or NTFS.

Formatting your hard drive structures the drive's space into well-organized compartments that can be used to store data. Each logical drive you create with partitioning must be formatted separately.

Take special care when using the information in this chapter on existing drives. Partitioning and formatting are "destructive" activities—they erase whatever data was stored on the disk. Once a drive has been partitioned and formatted, you will seldom need to redo it. You'll more likely find yourself partitioning and formatting a brand new drive you're adding to your system, or reformatting after some catastrophe (such as a virus) has trashed everything on the disk, leaving nothing left to lose.

QuickSteps

Partitioning and Formatting a Hard Disk

Whenever you install a new hard drive in your system, you'll need to follow several steps to prepare it to accept files.

BE PREPARED

Before you start, there are some things you'll need to perform the operation. These include:

- ◆ A bootable floppy, used to start the PC (unless you are configuring a second disk for the PC, and the primary hard disk is still bootable).

- ◆ If you're running Windows 9x, you'll need access to the MS-DOS programs FDISK and FORMAT. They're in the C:\Windows\Command folder. If you created a startup disk using Windows 9x, those programs will be there; otherwise, you can copy them from a working PC to your bootable floppy.

- ◆ If you're running Windows XP as an administrator, you'll need to use the Recovery Console (non-admins don't have access to this application). The DISKPART command partitions your hard drive, and the FORMAT command formats your hard drive. You can boot up your system with the Windows XP Setup CD to run the Recovery Console, or install it onto your hard drive to make it available as a bootup choice when Windows XP cannot start.

1. If you're configuring the PC's primary hard disk, boot your computer from a bootable floppy disk.

   or

   If configuring a new, secondary disk, you can start the PC from your hard disk normally.

2. Run FDISK and partition the new hard disk.

3. Exit FDISK and reboot your computer.

4. Format each new partition that you created in step 2.

5. Reboot your computer (not necessary in all cases but usually a good thing to do).

If you need to install your operating system, during your last reboot make sure you boot from the Setup disk required for installing your OS. If you are partitioning and formatting a secondary drive, you won't need to reinstall your OS. You may, however, need to reinstall certain programs if any new drive letter assignments change the location of previously installed applications.

TIP   As an alternative to FDISK and FORMAT, some hard drive manufacturers include a floppy disk with your new hard drive. This disk contains one or more utilities that help you partition and format your new hard drive quickly and easily. See "Partitioning Large Drives with Device Drivers" later in this chapter for more information about these utilities.

Low-Level Formatting

Low-level formatting divides the disk's tracks into a specific number of sectors, creating the intersector and intertrack gaps and recording the sector header and trailer information. It also fills each sector with a dummy value or a pattern of test values.

IDE Drives

Low-level formatting is typically done at the factory, so you should not have to worry about it, especially on IDE drives. There are utilities that will let you low-level format an IDE drive, but I don't recommend doing it because you'll mess up the optimal head and cylinder skew factors for the drive that were set at the factory, as well as the map of physically defective sectors on the drive. In fact, let me just say—don't low-level format IDE drives.

In the unlikely event that you should need to low-level format an IDE drive, check the manufacturer's Web site for a utility. Each IDE manufacturer has its own methodology for low-level formatting, and you can't get good results by using the utility for one brand with another brand's drive. Here are the Web sites to look for:

Seagate   `ftp://ftp.seagate.com/techsuppt/seagate_utils/sgatfmt4.zip`

IBM   `http://www.storage.ibm.com/techsup/hddtech/welcome.htm`

Quantum   `http://www.maxtor.com/maxtorhome.htm`

Western Digital   `http://www.wdc.com/service/ftp/wddiag/wd_diag.exe`

Maxtor   `http://www.Maxtor.com`

SCSI Drives

In the past, SCSI drives sometimes would come from the factory without low-level formatting, but this has changed in recent years. Should you need to low-level format a SCSI drive, you'll find a utility to do so built into the SCSI adapter's BIOS. As you boot your PC, you'll see a message on-screen about the SCSI adapter, telling you to press some certain key to enter its setup. Do so and then hunt around for the low-level hard disk formatting utility. But again, and I stress this strongly: don't low-level format a drive if you don't have to. Try partitioning it first (see the following section), and if that goes okay, just forget you ever heard about low-level formatting.

Partitioning

Partitioning a drive tells it how to allocate the available physical space among various drive letters. You must partition a drive in order to use it. Even if you're going to give the drive all to a single drive letter, you've still got to create a partition.

The program used most often to partition a drive is FDISK, a venerable old program that has been around since the early versions of DOS, and that still comes with versions of Windows earlier than Windows XP. You can use other, third-party programs, such as PartitionMagic, but the freebie FDISK works just fine for Windows 9x, Me, NT, and 2000.

HOW IT ALL BEGAN

In 1983, IBM ushered in the era of hard disks in PCs with their XT. Nobody was surprised that IBM would introduce a computer with a hard disk, but we *were* surprised by the large size of the hard disk—*10MB*! Back then, that was huge.

Why did IBM put the large drive on the XT? Because they wanted to sell us *two* operating systems—DOS and *Xenix*. For those who don't know, Xenix was a Unix variant that Microsoft was pushing for a while, back before they started selling OS/2, and *way* before Windows.

The problem with having both DOS and Xenix on the system was that they didn't get along. Xenix didn't like DOS's file format, and vice versa. So the only way to get them to peacefully coexist was to draw a line down the center of the drive, saying in effect, "This is *yours*, DOS, and that's *yours*, Xenix."

So Microsoft and IBM came up with a way to essentially split a 10MB drive into two 5MB drives. (Or a 6 and a 4, or a 2 and an 8, or whatever; you can chop up a drive just about any way you like.) That "chopping up" became known as partitioning.

Most people prefer to allocate all the physical space to a single hard disk letter (C). However, different situations may call for different configurations. For example, suppose you had a single 18GB drive. You could create two partitions, C and D, and install Windows 98 on one of them and Windows XP, or Linux, or some other operating system on the other. Then each time you started the PC, you could choose which drive to work from (and which operating system to load). This is called *dual-booting*, and it's possible only with multiple partitions.

Partitioning Options

Through the years, partitioning a physical hard disk into multiple logical drives has fallen in and out of fashion. Back when hard disks were small and MS-DOS was king, most people just partitioned their 20MB drives as one big drive and thanked their lucky stars that they had such a large drive. Then, in the mid-'80s, people started buying drives bigger than 32MB, which caused problems because DOS 3.3 couldn't support partitions larger than that size. As a result, people with drives larger than 32MB had to partition their drives into multiple logical drives that did not exceed 32MB. Real power users in those days had 120MB drives that they had to divide into a 32MB C, 32MB D, 32MB E, and 24MB F. It was a pain, but it was the only option.

Then DOS 5 came out, with support for larger partitions, and everybody started having single-partition drives again. Then hard disks got even bigger. Windows 95 and MS-DOS 6 supported hard disks up to 2.1GB in size, which seemed like plenty—but then hard disks got bigger again, and people found themselves carving up their 6GB drives. And so it's gone, over and over throughout the years, with hard disk capacity and operating system capability leap-frogging one another.

The latest versions of Windows (95/98/Me and above, and NT/2000/XP) provide *large disk support*, which allows you to have a single drive letter with up to 2TB (that's terabyte, which is the next step above a gigabyte), so there's virtually no operating system limitation anymore. Given that, people partition their drives into multiple logical drives for two main reasons: to support multiple operating systems, or as a matter of personal organizational preference. With Windows 95/98/Me as your operating system, there is also a related issue that fewer people consider: partition efficiency, as I'll explain in the next section.

Efficient Partitions: Clusters and Disks

What do I mean by *partition efficiency*? Well, first of all, I'm talking about systems using FAT16 or FAT32 file systems (essentially, MS-DOS and Windows 95/98/Me systems). Windows NT/2000/XP and OS/2 systems have their own native file systems and don't have the efficiency problem that I'm about to describe. For example, Windows NT/2000/XP, by default, uses the NT File System, or NTFS, although it can run on FAT16 or FAT32 if needed (not as efficiently, however).

The file system used in MS-DOS and Windows 95/98/Me is called the *file allocation table (FAT)* system. (You'll learn more about FAT in Chapter 14, "How Hard Drives Organize Data.") One of the cornerstones of FAT organization is that a FAT-based system allocates space to files in units called *clusters*. A cluster is an area on a hard disk ranging from 2KB to 64KB. (Floppies can have smaller clusters.) The important part about clusters is this: when a program writes a file to disk, it gets the disk space allocated to it by the operating system. When a FAT-based operating system allocates space, it does so cluster by cluster. Each cluster is allocated to one, and only one, file.

There are two variants of FAT: FAT16 and FAT32. *FAT16* is the older of the two. It's a 16-bit file system and has been used since the MS-DOS days. *FAT32* is a newer, more efficient 32-bit version that originated with Windows 95 and continues in Windows 98/Me.

The *size* of a cluster on a logical drive is determined by the size of the logical drive and the file system (FAT16 or FAT32), as you can see in Tables 13.1 and 13.2. Notice that the cluster sizes are smaller on a FAT32 system, making it a more efficient file storage method with less wasted space on the drive.

TABLE 13.1: RELATIONSHIP BETWEEN LOGICAL DRIVE SIZE AND CLUSTER SIZE: FAT16

SIZE OF LOGICAL DRIVE (IN MB)	CLUSTER SIZE (IN KB)
0–15	8
16–127	2
128–255	4
256–511	8
512–1023	16
1024–2047	32
2048–4095	64

TABLE 13.2: RELATIONSHIP BETWEEN LOGICAL DRIVE SIZE AND CLUSTER SIZE: FAT32

SIZE OF LOGICAL DRIVE (IN GB)	CLUSTER SIZE (IN KB)
< 8	4
8–16	8
16–32	16

To understand this whole thing about storage efficiency, and how the FAT system (more particularly, the FAT16 system) and your disk size play into it, let's look at an example. Suppose you save a 400-byte file on an 80MB logical drive. (I know that's a really tiny drive, but bear with me, just for the sake of discussion.) Clusters on an 80MB drive are 2KB in size, or 2048 bytes, and so those 400 bytes are placed in this 2048-byte cluster, wasting 1648 bytes in the cluster. That's wasteful, but consider the greater amount of wasted space if you stored that 400-byte file on a 3GB logical drive, where clusters are 64KB—65,536 bytes long. The cluster would have 400 useful bytes, and 65,136 bytes thrown away. Because cluster sizes are controlled by logical drive sizes, keeping logical drive sizes down keeps cluster sizes down, which leads to more efficient disk space usage.

Looking at Table 13.1, you see that with the FAT16 file system, the range of logical drive sizes that offer the smallest cluster is the range from 16MB through 127MB. If you had a drive that was 1024MB, then, you could divide it into eight logical drives—C, D, E, F, G, H, I, and J—each 127MB in size, and you'd even have a bit left on the end for a small logical drive K.

Is that the right way to divide up a disk? Well, yes and no. If you make one big logical drive of it, then you'd end up with clusters 32KB in size, and that's bad because of all the wasted space. On the other hand, one logical drive is easier to manage, search, and back up. Windows-based programs are so large these days, you might not be able to fit even a single program on one of those 127MB logical disks. So it's a matter of temperament and taste.

WARNING *DOS, early versions of Windows 95, and Windows NT 4 cannot recognize FAT32 partitions, so they will not be able to boot from a drive that has been converted from FAT16 to FAT32. Carefully consider your needs before proceeding.*

One attractive solution to the whole tiny-drive-versus-wasted-space dilemma is to use FAT32 instead of FAT16. FAT32 makes it much easier to use a single partition on your drive because of its enhanced capacities and smaller cluster size, as seen in Table 13.2. With FAT32, that 1024MB drive could be partitioned into a single logical drive and still have a cluster size of only 4KB. Most drives sold today are much bigger than 1024MB—they're more in the neighborhood of 20GB to 80GB, and power users go for even more. But when you have a drive that monstrously large, a few wasted clusters are probably not your biggest worry anyway.

NOTE *If you have installed Windows 98 as an upgrade over Windows 95, you can run the FAT32 converter included with Windows 98/Me to convert the drive from FAT16 to FAT32 without losing any data. (This is an exception to the general rule that you can't mess with the partitions without wiping out the disk content.) You can also buy third-party products such as PartitionMagic that can do the same conversion, plus some other nice things like change the allocation of the space between partitions.*

WARNING *One little caveat here: you can't convert a drive from FAT16 to FAT32 if you've run a disk compression program on it, such as DriveSpace or Stacker. The two technologies are incompatible with one another. If you have a compressed drive, the best thing to do is copy all your important files off it, then repartition it as a FAT32 drive and reformat it.*

FAT16 and FAT32 are by far the most popular file systems in use today, but not the only ones. NTFS is a powerful file system that provides many awesome features for NT/2000/XP users and system administrators. When you install Windows NT/2000/XP on an empty drive, you're prompted to choose whether you want to use FAT or NTFS. NTFS will make Windows NT/2000/XP run most efficiently, but if you later want to remove Windows NT/2000/XP and install Windows 95/98/Me on that drive, you'll have to repartition and reformat the drive in order to do so.

How to Partition a Drive

I've talked about the *why*, now let's look at the *how* of partitioning.

But first, I need to point out that all of the drive manufacturers offer some sort of utility that will do all of the steps in the following section for you. Most often, it will be on a floppy and/or CD that comes with the drive. If you got a drive that came in an OEM pack (as opposed to a retail package), you can download the needed utility from the drive manufacturer's Web site. Still, if you like doing it the manual way, here is how it is done on PCs that run Windows 9*x*, Me, NT, or 2000.

NOTE   *FDISK is not furnished with Windows XP. To repartition your drives using Windows XP, boot your computer with the Windows XP CD-ROM in your CD-ROM drive, and follow instructions to start the Recovery Console, which is a command-line utility. The* DISKPART *command allows you to add and delete partitions. For further information on the Recovery Console, search for the help topic Recovery Console in the Windows XP Help and Support Center.*

Let's suppose you have a 4GB hard disk that you want to divide into three logical drives of 1.5GB, 1.5GB, and 1GB. You use FDISK to partition the drive into two partitions initially, a *primary DOS partition* and an *extended DOS partition*. (Partitions that use the FAT16 or FAT32 file system are called DOS partitions, regardless of whether you will later load MS-DOS or Windows 95/98 on the drive.) The primary DOS partition can have only one logical drive, C, so you allocate 1.5GB for the primary DOS partition. But you can create as many logical drives as you want out of the space on the extended DOS partition (in this example, two), so you allocate the remaining space (2.5GB) for the extended partition and then create a logical drive D with 1.5GB and a logical drive E with 1GB out of it.

If you're working with an additional hard disk (not the system's main one), you can find FDISK in the C:\Windows\Command folder on your main hard disk.

If you're setting up the primary hard disk on a PC, you'll need to boot from a startup disk that contains FDISK. If you create an emergency startup disk using Windows 95/98, FDISK will automatically be included on it.

To partition a drive, follow these steps:

1.   At a command prompt, type **FDISK** and press Enter.

2.   If your copy of FDISK came from Windows 95b or higher, you'll see a warning like the one in Figure 13.1 asking whether you want to enable large disk support. Choose *Y* and press Enter.

      The main FDISK Options menu appears. Figure 13.2 shows the one from the version of FDISK that comes with Windows 98. Other versions are similar.

3.   First, check for existing partitions by choosing option 4, Display Partition Information. Existing partition information appears, if any. Figure 13.3 shows a single, primary DOS partition, for example.

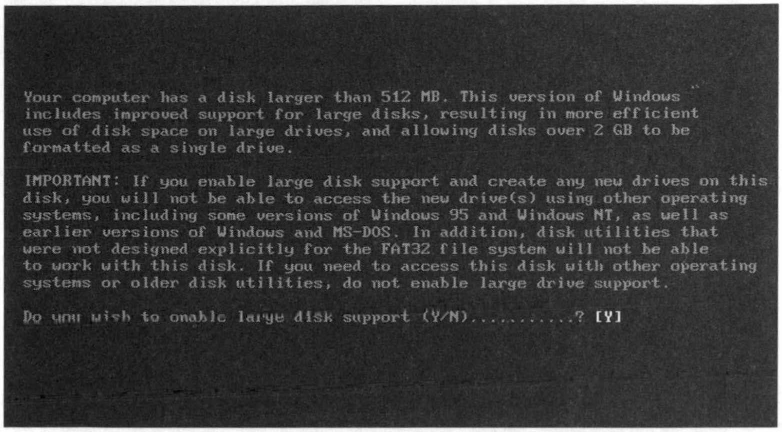

FIGURE 13.1

Enable large disk support if prompted.

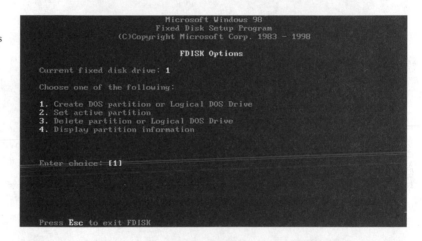

FIGURE 13.2

The FDISK Options menu

FIGURE 13.3

This drive has a primary DOS partition and no extended partitions.

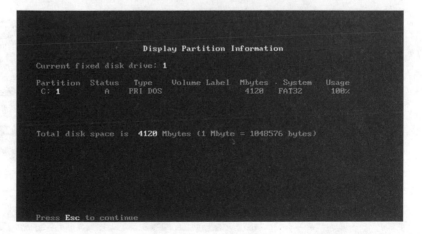

NOTE *If the disk already has a partition, you might not need to partition the drive again—you can simply press Esc until you exit the program and then format the drive(s) with the existing partitions.*

4. If you found existing partitions and you want to delete them and repartition, press Esc to go back to the FDISK Options menu and then do the following:

   A. Choose option 3, Delete Partition or Logical DOS Drive.

   B. If you have logical DOS drives on an extended partition, delete them first (option 3, see Figure 13.4). You can't delete an extended partition until you have first removed its logical drives.

   C. After you have deleted all the logical drives from the extended partition, delete the extended partition itself (option 2, Figure 13.4). You can't delete the primary partition until you have first deleted the extended one.

   D. After you have deleted the extended partition, delete the primary partition (option 1, Figure 13.4).

   E. After deleting all partitions, press Esc to return to the FDISK Options menu.

5. Now create the primary DOS partition by doing the following:

   A. Choose option 1, Create DOS Partition or Logical DOS Drive.

   B. Choose option 1, Create Primary DOS Partition.

   C. When asked whether you want to use the maximum available size for the primary DOS partition, choose Yes or No. If you want to follow along with the example I'm working through here, where you create three logical drives, you would choose No.

   D. If you answered No, enter the amount of space, either in megabytes or in percentage, that you want to allocate to the primary DOS partition (that is, the C drive). For example, to create a 1.5GB partition, type **1500**. See Figure 13.5.

   E. Press Esc to return to the FDISK Options menu.

FIGURE 13.4

Delete logical drives
and partitions here.

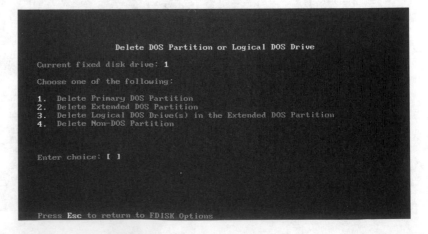

FIGURE 13.5

Allocate space for the primary DOS partition.

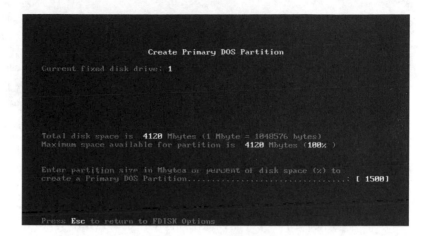

```
                          Create Primary DOS Partition
Current fixed disk drive: 1




Total disk space is   4120 Mbytes (1 Mbyte = 1048576 bytes)
Maximum space available for partition is   4120 Mbytes (100% )


Enter partition size in Mbytes or percent of disk space (%) to
create a Primary DOS Partition.................................: [ 1500]



Press Esc to return to FDISK Options
```

6. If you chose not to allocate all the space to the primary partition, it is not set automatically as the active partition. It must be active in order to be bootable. To make your primary partition active, do the following:

   A. From the FDISK Options menu, choose option 2, Set Active Partition.

   B. Type **1** to select partition 1 as the active one and press Enter.

   C. Press Esc to return to the FDISK Options menu.

7. Next, set up your extended partition using the remaining space, by doing the following:

   A. From the FDISK Options menu, choose 1, Create DOS Partition or Logical DOS Drive.

   B. Choose option 2, Create Extended DOS Partition.

   C. Leave the default setting for the extended partition size, which is all of the remaining space, and press Enter.

   D. Press Esc to verify the drive integrity. You're then prompted to define the logical drives.

   E. Enter the amount of space to allocate to the next logical drive (D). Leave the default to use the entire extended partition for it, or enter a specific size in megabytes or percentage. For our example, to make D a 1.5GB partition, you would type **1500**.

   F. Enter the amount of space for the next logical drive (E). For our example, leave the default to use all remaining space on the drive.

   G. When you are finished assigning all the remaining space on the extended partition, press Esc to return to the FDISK Options menu.

8. You're done partitioning! Press Esc to exit FDISK and then reboot your PC.

WARNING *Do not attempt to format or use the drives until you have rebooted. That's because drive letter assignments change when you partition, and the drive letters you booted with will no longer be correct.*

How DOS Names Partitions

Your operating system assigns drive letters to the various logical drives on your system, but how does it decide which logical drive gets what name? The answer may surprise you.

If you have one physical drive with three logical drives defined on it, as in the example in the preceding section, the naming is simple. The logical drive in the primary DOS partition is named C, and the two in the extended partition are named D and E. But suppose you have *two* physical drives that are each divided into three logical drives? How are *they* named?

Answer: it depends on whether there's a primary DOS partition on the second drive. It is acceptable for the second physical drive to contain only an extended partition, unlike the first physical drive, which *must* have a primary DOS partition before it can have an extended partition. It is also acceptable if the second physical drive has both a primary and an extended DOS partition.

- ◆ *If the second drive has both a primary and extended partition*, then the primary partition on the first drive is C, the primary partition on the second drive is D (surprise!), the two (in our example) logical drives in the extended partition on the first drive are named E and F, and the two logical drives in the extended partition on the second drive are named G and H.

- ◆ *If the second drive has only an extended partition*, then the primary partition on the first physical drive is C, again, and this time the logical drives in the extended partition on that first physical drive are named D and E. The three logical drives in the extended partition on the second drive are named F, G, and H.

Confused? Don't be. Regardless of what you name a volume during the partition process, you can rename it at any time under Windows by opening My Computer, right-clicking the drive, and choosing Properties. When the dialog box opens, you will find the volume name listed as *Label*. You can rename it to your heart's content at this point—however, you are still limited to the old DOS rule of a maximum of 11 characters.

Partitioning Large Drives with Device Drivers

If you have an old computer that you want to add a new, very large hard disk to, you may run into a little snag. Very old systems, which were built before gigantic hard disks were even dreamed of, can't recognize and take advantage of *logical block addressing (LBA)*. LBA is a method used to translate the cylinder, head, and sector specifications of a large drive (over 528MB) so they're usable by the system. In this case, we're talking about the physical hard disk, not a logical drive. Without LBA, a PC can't use a hard disk larger than 528MB (roughly half a gigabyte).

The solution is to use a driver that functions as a BIOS extender. It loads when the PC starts, and helps the PC recognize and work with the drive to its full potential.

Here's how it works: When you use a driver-type installer for a disk, it reworks your partitions so that you have a small primary DOS partition and a large non-DOS one. It then boots your PC from the small, recognizable partition and uses a driver in `CONFIG.SYS` to trick the operating system into thinking that the large, non-DOS partition is actually the primary, bootable drive.

Most hard disks sold today come with a SETUP disk that installs the needed drivers to configure the drive on an older PC. It's important to use the disk that came with the drive, because the program is often tailored to work specifically with that drive manufacturer's hardware. You can usually download the program for free from the manufacturer's Web site if you get a second-hand disk that no longer has a SETUP disk with it.

For the most part, this driver-based drive setup works fine. Here are a few caveats, however:

◆ Driver-based drive setup is not compatible with every old PC. Older PCs are worse than today's in terms of standardization, and some older PCs are not 100 percent compatible. I have run into systems that it wouldn't work with, notably some older Compaq PCs. You won't know until you try.

◆ Non-DOS operating systems, as I've mentioned before, cannot access these alien partitions set up by the driver-based drive setup. You would be unable to run OS/2 or Unix on a system employing it.

◆ It's one more source of bugs. I'm not saying any one brand of program in particular is buggy. But the more software, the more bugs and potential software conflicts.

◆ The driver requires a line in your `CONFIG.SYS` file in order to load. If `CONFIG.SYS` gets deleted, the drive won't be recognizable.

With slightly newer systems (circa 1995 or so), you may run into another problem: the BIOS does not support drives larger than 2GB or 8.4GB (depending on the system age), even with LBA. Such limitations can't always be overcome with the free utilities that come with the hard disk. It depends on the utility and its capabilities. On such a system, the BIOS may acknowledge the drive's existence but claim that it is a smaller size than it is, or it may not acknowledge the drive at all.

If you run into this situation, you have two choices. You can let the drive function as the size that the BIOS thinks it is, regardless of its larger actual size (if the BIOS sees the drive at all), or you can buy a third-party disk management program. There are several good programs on the market that overcome the BIOS drive size limitation. You may want to investigate Disk Manager (by Ontrack), Drive Up (by FWB Software), and EZ Drive (by MicroHouse). These programs work by telling the BIOS that the drive is a smaller size, and then using a driver loaded at startup to amend that data so that the full size of the drive can be recognized by the operating system when it loads.

WARNING *The only caveat you need to be aware of is when booting from a floppy. Usually drives that are installed this way need to self-boot to load the drivers they need to access all the space. Booting from a floppy can prevent this. So check the instructions on the driver. To boot from a floppy, you may need to press a key at boot time. This loads the driver and then returns you to a prompt that lets you run a floppy afterward.*

Backing Up Partition Information

Having gone through all that work to create the DOS partition, you may wonder, *what happens if the partition information is destroyed?* This is a real problem: in this situation, the PC will refuse to even recognize that a disk exists. The data's not erased, but it might as well be. The way you solve this problem is with prevention: back up the partition information. There are several ways to do this, and I'll show you a number of them in Chapter 16, "Care and Feeding of Hard Drives."

Formatting

Finally, you run the FORMAT program. Formatting a disk does not actually overwrite the data on the disk; rather, it wipes clean the record of what's stored on the disk, marking the data area of the disk as available for data storage.

What does that mean, exactly? Well, I'll get into all the details in Chapter 14, but for now, just understand that there are areas on a disk besides the data area, where data is stored that you copy to the disk. One of these areas is the FAT, which keeps track of which files are stored in which locations. When you format a disk, the FAT is re-created, along with a few other special system features of the disk, but the data area is left untouched. That means that your data is still there on the disk, even after reformatting. Utility programs such as Norton Utilities can sometimes be used to *unformat* a disk to retrieve some of that information.

The process for formatting a hard disk depends on the operating system. In MS-DOS, you use the `FORMAT drive letter:` command at the command prompt. You can do the same thing when booting from a startup disk created with Windows 9*x*.

NOTE   *In Windows XP, the* `FORMAT` *command is found in the Recovery Console.*

When you install Windows versions 95 and up, if the hard disk on which you are installing has not been formatted, the installation program will format it for you—no muss, no fuss.

To format a hard disk from *within* Windows 95 and up, you can right-click the drive icon and choose Format from the shortcut menu. Of course, you can't do this to your boot hard disk (that is, the one that contains the files that are running Windows); you can do it only with a secondary hard disk you are adding.

A Note about Bad Areas

You may have heard it said that reformatting a hard disk will get rid of bad areas on the disk. This isn't true—not exactly, anyway.

When you format a disk, it runs a cursory check of the disk for bad areas and excludes those bad areas from the formatting. However, not all bad areas are immediately obvious.

Bad areas have either *hard* errors or *soft* errors. Hard errors are problems in the disk surface itself, wherein it cannot record data at all. They are caused by manufacturing defects or later abuse. Soft errors, in contrast, occur when some data has faded on the disk to the point where it cannot be read. Disk repair programs, such as ScanDisk and Norton Utilities, fix such errors by retrieving any data they can from the area and then cordoning off the area as "bad" so it won't be used again (kind of like a hazardous waste dump for your system).

When you reformat a drive, it retains its memory of the hard errors, but not the soft ones. Some of the areas previously marked as bad therefore appear to be good again, but any data that you copy to them may be in peril.

Therefore, after reformatting a hard disk that contained many errors, you should run a disk utility such as ScanDisk in its Thorough mode to thoroughly check each physical sector of the disk for errors. ScanDisk comes free with Windows 95/98/Me/NT/2000.

Third-Party Partitioning and Formatting Tools

You may be surprised that you don't have to use the tools shipped with DOS and Windows to partition and format your drives. There are several very good third-party tools available, for a moderate cost, of course.

The leading third-party partitioning tool is PartitionMagic. Not only can you partition and format your hard disks, but you can also install multiple operating systems on your computer, each independent of the others, and choose which one to boot each time you start your PC. Partition-Magic also enables you to reallocate the disk space between logical drives on the same physical hard disk without losing any of the data on the drives. You can also switch between FAT16 and FAT32.

System Commander, by V Communications, is another top-notch tool with similar capabilities. You may also want to check out Disk Manager (by Ontrack), Drive Up (FWB Software), and EZ Drive (MicroHouse), all of which I mentioned earlier for partitioning help, but which offer a full range of partitioning and formatting utilities.

Troubleshooting Tips

Patience is said to be a virtue, and with hard disks that truism is, well, true. Basically, if you make a mistake while using FDISK or formatting a drive and catch it before you install an operating system and several hundred megabytes of software, you can pretty easily recover. If you don't find out until days later, well.... here are some tips:

- ◆ If your computer won't boot from your hard drive, run FDISK again and check to see that the partition you have your OS installed on is set as the active partition.

- ◆ If FDISK reports a disk size that isn't true, your BIOS may be incorrectly identifying your hard drive. Run your BIOS setup program and confirm that the size is correct, and try running FDISK again.

- ◆ An older BIOS may not recognize newer hard disks, especially those over 2GB or 8.4GB (depending on the system age). If this is the case, you should update your BIOS if possible. You may have to use special software provided by your hard disk manufacturer to fool your BIOS into recognizing the disk.

- ◆ No access to FORMAT? That may not be a problem. If you are planning to install Windows on the new hard disk, you may not need to bother with formatting the drive. Simply boot from your Windows CD (if your system allows you to boot from a CD—check the Boot Sequence settings in your BIOS) and let the SETUP program format the disk for you.

- ◆ Formatting a disk does not automatically make it bootable. If you've started the PC with a startup floppy made with Windows 95/98, use the /S switch with the FORMAT command (FORMAT C: /S) to copy the system files needed to boot along with the formatting operation.

Chapter 14

How Hard Drives Organize Data

◆ How DOS Organizes Disk Areas   449

◆ The FAT and the Directory   454

◆ Subdirectories   457

◆ Logical Drive Structure   458

◆ FAT32   460

◆ NTFS   461

◆ Backing Up Your Master Boot Record   462

Introduction

IN THE LAST FOUR chapters, I've talked about the details of how your disk hardware works. But disk repair requires understanding disk software more than disk hardware. In this chapter, I'll show you how DOS (and Windows of all varieties in one form or another, for that matter) stores data on your disk.

You may be telling yourself, well, even I know about FAT32. What's all this with DOS? That's a good question with a good answer. Understanding the low-level DOS file structure, FAT, is the easiest and fastest way to understand all other file systems. DOS is easy to learn and quick to understand. Get the basics in DOS and you'll move forward swiftly.

This chapter also covers NTFS, the file system native to Windows NT, Windows 2000, and Windows XP. We'll take a look at its main features and benefits.

The Basics

In simple disk-based systems, all you need to know about files is their location. In one early disk-based computer that I worked with, you'd keep track of files by noting their cylinder/head/sector location. It didn't have much of a user interface—you specified the address of a program, then the computer read it and executed it. You'd generally start up the system by loading the word processor (not a great one, as you'd expect, but better than a typewriter). This was a bit cumbersome because, you see, if I lost the address of my word processor, that meant I essentially lost the word processing program forever. I couldn't say "execute the program WP," which would have been preferable, but rather "execute cylinder 0, head 0, and sector 1."

After the word processor loaded, however, things looked much nicer. You could pick out a text file by name, load it, and work with it—you didn't have to know its address. That was possible because the word processor took a certain number of sectors for itself, sectors that it used to store documents. I didn't have to know the document's address because the word processor kept its own little directory to the sectors that it had taken over for documents. You'd ask for a file, say LETTER1.DOC. The word processor would look up LETTER1.DOC in its directory, see that LETTER1.DOC started in some cylinder/head/sector, and note how many sectors it was. Then the word processor would load up those sectors, and away you went.

That was a nice, simple system, but it had a few major drawbacks. The biggest problem was that only the word processor knew that the files existed. The BASIC interpreter or the simple database manager that came with the system was totally ignorant of the files because it was totally ignorant of the directory that the word processor kept for its own personal uses. The system also lacked most of the pieces of basic file maintenance. Space wasn't recovered well when files were erased, data-recovery tools didn't exist, and if the disks hadn't been small floppies, the system probably would never have worked. Using such a system to manage a hard disk would be silly.

That's a major reason why we have DOS and Windows. (Despite the Microsoft claims, up until FAT32 was introduced in 1995, DOS and Windows pretty much stored data in the same way.) DOS provided a central space and file management unit. An area that Lotus 1-2-3 sees as a file named FINANCE.WK1 is the exact same area that WordPerfect sees as a file named FINANCE.WK1. That way, any program can find any file, and no program will inadvertently write over another program's files (unless something goes very wrong).

NOTE *FAT32 doesn't change things drastically; it just allows for the space of larger drives to be used in a more efficient manner. It also allows for better long filename support, something DOS still doesn't do without help. I'll talk more about FAT32 later in this chapter.*

In this chapter, you'll learn that DOS manages files with a tree-structured directory and a construct called the file allocation table (FAT). You'll learn that space is managed with groups of sectors called clusters, a topic that I've discussed briefly already but that I'll go into in more detail shortly.

How DOS Organizes Disk Areas: Overview

You're now familiar with some terms: you know of tracks, cylinders, and such. Each OS organizes data in its own way. DOS sees data in the following way:

♦ Disks are divided into *absolute*, or *physical*, sectors.

◆ Absolute sectors map to *DOS* sectors.

◆ The DOS sectors are grouped into *clusters*.

◆ A file's *directory entry* includes the first cluster number in the file. That is the initial pointer into the FAT, which keeps track of where files are located.

◆ The FAT contains information that DOS uses to locate the remaining clusters. There's a FAT entry for each cluster.

A FAT entry can be any of the following:

◆ A number, which acts as a pointer to another cluster

◆ A zero, indicating an unused cluster

◆ A bad sector marking

◆ An end-of-file (EOF) indicator

Absolute Sectors and DOS Sectors

Identifying an area on a disk by its cylinder/head/sector refers to what DOS folks call its *absolute sector:* cylinder *x*, head *y*, sector *z*. This is illustrated in Figure 14.1. I have referred to this form of addressing as *three-dimensional* elsewhere in this book.

DOS doesn't directly use absolute sector locations. Instead, it refers to sectors with a single number called a *relative sector number* or *DOS sector number.* The number system is called *relative* rather than *absolute* because it numbers the sectors in order from front to back of a disk. There's no "cylinder 100, head 2, sector 1"; instead, there's "sector 15,421."

FIGURE 14.1

Three-dimensional addressing: identifying an area on a disk by its cylinder/head/sector

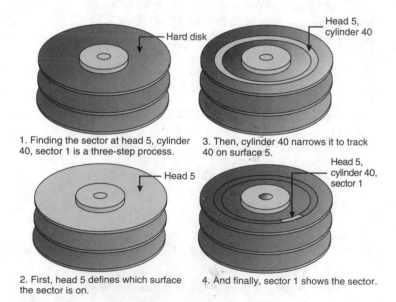

1. Finding the sector at head 5, cylinder 40, sector 1 is a three-step process.

2. First, head 5 defines which surface the sector is on.

3. Then, cylinder 40 narrows it to track 40 on surface 5.

4. And finally, sector 1 shows the sector.

When using relative sector numbering, DOS orders sectors by starting at cylinder 0, head 1, sector 1: this is *DOS sector 0*. (Note that cylinder 0, head 0, sector 1 does not have a DOS sector number designation: it is "out of bounds," as far as DOS is concerned.) The remaining sectors on the track are DOS sectors 2 through 16, assuming that a track has 17 sectors. DOS then moves to the next head, head 2. The 17 sectors on cylinder 0, head 2, are the next 17 DOS sectors, numbers 17 through 33. DOS keeps moving up the heads until the cylinder is exhausted, and then moves to head 0 of cylinder 1. It continues in this fashion, moving farther and farther inward toward the center of the disk.

You can relate the absolute address of a sector to its relative sector if you know the following information:

DH   Head that the DOS Boot Record (DBR) is located on (more to come on the DBR later in this chapter)

DC   Cylinder that the DBR is located on

DS   Sector that the DBR is located on

NS   Number of sectors per track on this disk

NH   Number of heads on this disk

Assuming that you have a C, H, and S (cylinder, head, and sector) address for a sector, you find its relative sector (let's call it RS) like so:

$$RS = NH \times NS \times [(C - DC) + NS] \times [(H - DH) + (S - DS)]$$

For example, suppose you have a logical drive D with its DBR on cylinder 100, head 1, and sector 1. The disk has 4 heads and 17 sectors per track. What is the relative sector number of the sector at the absolute address of cylinder 140, head 3, and sector 4?

$DH = 1$

$DC = 100$

$DS = 1$

$NS = 17$

$NH = 4$

Relative sector $= 4 \times 17 \times [(140 - 100) + 17] \times [(3 - 1) + (4 - 1)] = 2757$

The relative sector number is 2757.

How about computing the absolute location of a sector from its relative sector? Before you can do that, let me define some notation: DIV and MOD. *DIV* means do a division but throw away the remainder. For example, 7 DIV 3 equals 2, not 2.33. *MOD* means do the division but *keep* the remainder—throw away the quotient. So 7 MOD 3 equals 1, because when you divide 7 by 3 you get 2 with a remainder of 1.

Given the same definitions of RS, DC, DH, DS, NS, and NH, you find the absolute cylinder, head, and sector by using the following formulas. Remember, this time you already know RS, NS, NH, DH, DC, and DS, and you're looking for C (cylinder), H (head), and S (sector).

S = (RS MOD NS) + DS

Temp = RS DIV NS

Temp is a temporary variable you use and then throw away. It makes writing the formulas easier.

H = (Temp MOD NH) + DH

C = (Temp DIV NH) + DC

Let's try it out on the example you've already done. You've got relative sector 2757 on a disk with 4 heads and 17 sectors per track. The sector's logical drive has a DBR on cylinder 100, head 1, and sector 1.

Collect what you know so far:

DC = 100

DH = 1

DS = 1

NH = 4

NS = 17

RS = 2757

And then start calculating:

S = (2757 MOD 17) + 1 = 3 + 1 = 4

Temp = 2757 DIV 17 = 162

H = (162 MOD 4) + 1 = 2 + 1 = 3

C = (162 DIV 4) + 100 = 140

So relative sector 2757 turns out to be at cylinder 140, head 3, sector 4.

This sector-numbering notation is also known as a *linear sector address*. Why use DOS (relative) sector numbers in the first place? One reason is that they are hardware independent. All DOS assumes about the drive is that it consists of a bunch of sectors, and each sector contains 512 bytes. Another possible reason is that every four or eight sectors are grouped into a cluster, and it's easier to divide up a one-dimensional number like a DOS sector than it would be to have to constantly figure out that cluster 200 is on cylinder 40, head 2, sectors 15–17 and cylinder 40, head 3, sector 1. (I just made those numbers up, so don't try to figure out where I got them from.)

Clusters

Next, as I mentioned previously, DOS sectors are grouped into clusters.

A *cluster* is the minimum space allocated by DOS when DOS gives space to a file. For example, if you create a file that is 1 byte long, you don't take up just a byte on the disk, but instead the minimum allocation—a cluster. Cluster size varies with the disk type and size, as you can see from Table 14.1. Floppy disks use clusters that are just one sector long, but a 10GB hard disk uses clusters that are many sectors long—4096 bytes (4KB). That means that a 1-byte file on a single-sided floppy would take up 512 bytes on the disk, as would a 500-byte file. On the other hand, a 1-byte file would take up thousands of bytes on a 10GB disk drive. Note that Table 14.1 includes cluster sizes for NTFS, a non-DOS-based filing system, which I discuss later in this chapter.

TABLE 14.1: CLUSTER SIZES

DISK TYPE	CLUSTER SIZE (BYTES)	SECTORS PER CLUSTER
Single-sided floppy	512	1
Double-sided floppy	1024	2
3½-inch 720KB floppy	1024	2
3½-inch 1.44MB floppy	512	1
5¼-inch 1.2MB floppy	1024	2
0MB–15MB logical drive	4096	8
16MB–127MB logical drive	2048	4
128MB–255MB logical drive	4096	8
256MB–512MB logical drive	8192	16
512MB–1024MB logical drive	16,384	32
1024MB–2048MB logical drive	32,768	64
2048MB–4095MB logical drive	65,536	128
4096MB–8GB	4096 (FAT32 only)	* 64
9GB–16GB	8192 (FAT32 only)	* 64
17GB–32GB	16,384 (FAT32 only)	* 64
32GB and above	32,768 (FAT32 only)	* 64
2048MB–4095MB	4096 (NTFS only)	8
4096MB–8GB	8192 (NTFS only)	16
9GB–16GB	16,384 (NTFS only)	32
17GB–32GB	32,768 (NTFS only)	64
32GB and above	65,536 (NTFS only)	128

* *Note: FAT32 allows for cluster counts between 65,526 and 268,435,456 clusters.*

First there were floppies, then the 10MB disk drives, then the 1.2MB floppies, and now the 16+MB drives. DOS versions 4.*x* and later support drives up to 512MB in size—they use a 16-bit FAT (65,536 entries) and clusters of size 8192. Today, all new systems can support drives that contain many gigabytes of data.

You've seen that cylinders and heads are counted starting at 0, and that sectors start at 1, so it won't be *too* strange when I tell you that clusters start at number 2. By the way, clusters start only in the data area, after the FAT and directory.

Note that the largest logical drives available are the 4GB drives. That's because DOS is built on a processor architecture that can handle data objects up to only 64KB, and the 4GB drive requires 64KB-sized sectors. A bigger drive would require bigger sectors, and DOS can't handle sectors that big.

DOS Boot Record

The starting point in the DOS partition is the first sector, called, you will remember, DOS sector 0. That sector always contains an important piece of program code called the *DOS Boot Record (DBR)*. That's the code used to boot up the system, in combination with the partition record and the so-called "hidden" files. I'll explain in greater detail what the DBR does a bit later, but for now understand that it resides in the first DOS sector.

As DOS has evolved into its various versions, the DBR has also taken another important role. A table in the beginning of the DBR contains a bunch of disk ID information. Early versions of DOS pretty much ignored the table, but later versions need it. One byte on the table is pretty deadly—if set to a particular value, it keeps the system from booting from either the hard disk *or* the floppy. You'll see more about that in Chapter 16, "Care and Feeding of Hard Drives."

The FAT and the Directory

As I said earlier, the directory and the FAT work as a team in locating files. The directory tells you the names of your files, and the FAT tells you each file's location. Take a look at Figure 14.2.

The FAT immediately follows the DBR on the disk—it always begins on sector 1. The operating system then stores two identical copies of the FAT—the primary FAT and one for backup—right next to each other. In theory this would offer some sort of safeguard against damage to one of the FAT structures. Unfortunately, since both FATs are stored right next to each other, a problem with disk integrity would have a greater opportunity to corrupt both copies. Second, and this is my favorite part, if one copy is corrupted, Windows won't look at the second copy. The good news is that most file utilities will attempt to recover a damaged FAT by comparing the one suspected of damage with its copy. The FAT's size will vary according to how large the partition is.

The FAT is then immediately followed by the root directory. Directory entries are 32 bytes long, and the root contains space for 512 entries on a hard disk, or fewer entries for floppies, depending on the floppy type. The exact number of root entries is stored in the DBR. The data then follows the root on the disk.

Table 14.2 compares FAT/FAT32 and NTFS, Windows NT/2000/XP's file system that I'll discuss later in this chapter.

FIGURE 14.2

The FAT and the directory work together to locate files.

Each file has a directory entry telling DOS the file's name, size, last date altered, and the like.

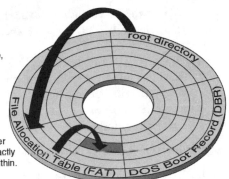

The entry then includes a pointer to the FAT, which tells DOS exactly which sectors the file resides within.

TABLE 14.2: FAT/FAT32 AND NTFS

FAT AND FAT32	NTFS
Cluster size determined by disk volume size	Cluster size determined by disk volume size and is adjustable
Files are placed in first free location on disk	No special areas on disk requiring file placement
Supports only READ-ONLY, SYSTEM, ARCHIVE, and HIDDEN attributes	Supports FAT/FAT32 attributes and additional Time Stamp and compression
Eight characters for a filename, and three characters for a file extension (255 for filenames in FAT32)	Supports long filenames and FAT 8.3 filenames
Only one file allocation table (increased chance of corruption/lost data)	Multiple copies of Master File Table kept on disk

A file's name and extension are self-explanatory. Of course, while DOS and Windows 3.1 are limited to 8 characters plus a 3-character extension, Windows 95/98/Me/NT/2000/XP can have filenames that are as long as 255 characters. You may not know about the attributes, however. The one-attribute byte is viewed by DOS as eight attribute *bits*, six of which are used:

ARCHIVE   Is set ($= 1$) if the file has not been backed up; reset ($= 0$) otherwise.

HIDDEN   If set, the file is invisible to most DOS functions.

READ-ONLY   If set, tells DOS not to allow changes or erasure of the file.

SYSTEM   Says, "Don't move this file."

LABEL   Indicates that this directory entry is not a file entry at all, but the disk label. That's why disk labels can be up to 11 characters—the label name uses the space taken up by a filename and a file extension.

DIRECTORY   Means that this directory entry does not point to a normal file, but rather to a subdirectory. Subdirectory information is stored in a file-like construct, hence the directory entry.

By the way, the read-only and archive bits can be manipulated by DOS's `ATTRIB` command. Set a file to read-only with `ATTRIB + R filename`, and you won't accidentally erase it (`-R` removes the read-only status).

The starting cluster number tells DOS where a file begins; the FAT tells where the rest of the file is. The starting cluster number is vital, then, because it is your link into the FAT. Finally, the last 4 bytes contain the file size in bytes.

Each cluster on the disk has a corresponding FAT entry. Given an entry for cluster *x*, the entry must be one of the following:

0   Indicates that the cluster is unallocated.

EOF (actually any value from hex FFF8 to FFFF)   Indicates that it is the last cluster in a file.

BAD (actually hex FFF7)   Indicates that the cluster contains a bad sector or sectors and should not be used.

Nonzero cluster number   Is a pointer to the *next* cluster in the file that *x* is a part of.

Figure 14.3 shows an excerpt from a FAT with entries relevant to the `ORDERS.DAT` directory being added to that directory.

FIGURE 14.3

Adding an excerpt from the ORDERS .DAT directory to the FAT

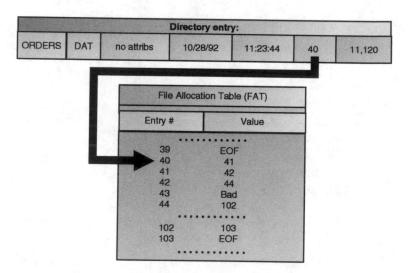

Reading this FAT excerpt, you can see that cluster 39 is the end of some file—you don't know which file. You start looking for `ORDERS.DAT` in cluster 40 because the directory entry *told* you to: entry 40 contains 41, meaning that 41 follows 40 as the next cluster in `ORDERS.DAT`. Entry 41 contains 42, meaning that 42 is the next cluster in `ORDERS.DAT`. Entry 42 contains 44, telling you to skip 43, which was skipped because it is a cluster with unusable areas in it—a bad cluster. Entry 44 tells you to skip to cluster 102 for the next cluster, and 102 points you to 103, which is the end of the file.

Note that each cluster's FAT entry in a file links to the next cluster's FAT entry in that file. This is called a *one-way linked list*, one way because you can follow it in only one direction. (If this is unclear, look only at entry 103, the EOF for `ORDERS.DAT`. Looking only at that entry, what would tell you that 102 was the previous entry? Nothing. On the other hand, the FAT *will* tell you to go from 102 to 103.)

Subdirectories

Now let's add subdirectories to the preceding example.

The subdirectory structure in DOS is implemented with very little change over what I've said so far. Subdirectories look like files, as far as DOS is concerned, except (1) they have a size equal to zero, and (2) their DIRECTORY attribute bit is set. The subdirectory itself resides in a cluster or clusters, and is arranged identically to the root directory, *except* for the first two entries. You know the "." and ".." files that you see whenever you type DIR in a subdirectory? They actually have file entries. The "." and ".." are stolen from old Unix terminology. The ".." entry refers to the subdirectory itself, and the "." refers to the parent of the subdirectory. Those entries, like other subdirectory entries, do not have sizes. The entry for "." (the self-referencing one), reports the *starting cluster* equal to the cluster that the subdirectory *itself* exists in. The entry for ".." reports the starting cluster of the parent directory. If the parent is the root, the cluster value is set to 0. I know that sounds complicated, so here are some examples.

Suppose you have a subdirectory called C:\JUNK, and the subdirectory was created on December 31, 2001. Let's further suppose that the subdirectory itself is in cluster 5000. This does *not* mean that the files in the subdirectory are in cluster 5000—it means that the actual information about the names and such of the files in \JUNK can be found in cluster 5000. The root entry for \JUNK in the root directory would look like this:

```
Name  Ext  Size  Date      Time     Cluster  Attribs
JUNK       0     12/31/01  8:03 p   5000     directory
```

Suppose further that \JUNK contains only one file, A.TXT, created on January 1, 2002, and that it starts in cluster 6000 and is 100 bytes long. If you looked in the contents of cluster 5000 to see the actual subdirectory structure of \JUNK, you'd see the following:

```
Name  Ext  Size  Date      Time     Cluster  Attribs
.          0     12/31/01  8:03 p   5000     directory
..         0     12/31/01  8:03 p   0        directory
A     TXT  100   01/01/02  7:00 p   6000     no attribs
```

Silly though they seem, those two entries must be the first two entries in a subdirectory, or CHKDSK says that the subdirectory is invalid. (CHKDSK's "cure" is worse than the complaint, so when CHKDSK offers to convert the subdirectory to a file, tell it to take a walk. More on this later in Chapter 16.)

A.TXT was a simple example; it takes up only one cluster. (Why? Because it's 100 bytes long.) If the file were longer than one cluster, DOS would simply follow the same procedure as with ORDERS.DAT— look in the FAT for entry 6000, read what's in there, and follow the FAT chain to the end of the file.

Let's summarize how a file in a subdirectory is read by DOS. Say you're reading the file ORDERS.DAT from the subdirectory you've just examined, C:\JUNK. DOS performs the following steps:

1. DOS looks in the root directory for an entry with the name JUNK that has its DIRECTORY attribute set. It notes the starting cluster of JUNK—suppose it is 5000, as in our example.

2. DOS goes to the FAT and looks up entry 5000 to see if the subdirectory information extends over several clusters. Most subdirectories can fit easily in one cluster, so DOS probably sees EOF in entry 5000. (Why do most subdirectories fit in one cluster? Most hard disk clusters are 2048 bytes, and each directory entry is 32 bytes long. That's enough space for 2048/32, or 64, directory entries. Most subdirectories don't have more than 64 files in them.)

3. DOS reads cluster 5000 and assumes that the data is formatted as in the root directory. It looks for a directory entry called ORDERS.DAT and notes the starting cluster. Suppose the starting cluster is 40.

4. DOS returns to the FAT and examines entry 40. Suppose 40 contains 41; that means that the file is not only in cluster 40, but also in 41.

5. Next, DOS continues examining the FAT, looking in entry 41. Suppose 41 contains 42; the file continues in cluster 42.

6. Assume that the remainder of the file search goes as in the earlier ORDERS.DAT example. Then DOS is done.

Notice that finding ORDERS.DAT in a subdirectory was the same as finding it in the root, except for the first two steps.

Logical Drive Structure

Ever since PC-DOS 3.3 (MS-DOS 3.2), it's been possible to create multiple logical drives out of a single physical drive. This section explains how they are organized.

In the case of a simple disk system, the PC looks first to the partition table to find where a partition exists; the partition entry then points to the first sector of the partition, which, by the way, contains the code to boot from that partition. You've already seen how that works with the primary DOS partition. Suppose there were a 16,384-cylinder, 16-head drive that contained a primary DOS partition in the first 8192 cylinders and a Xenix partition in the last 8192 cylinders. That's one 4.2GB logical drive for DOS and one 4.2GB logical drive for Xenix. (Note that the drive has 63 sectors per track.) The disk structure would then look like Figure 14.4.

It would seem that a similar arrangement occurs with a logical drive (let's call it drive D in this case) in an extended DOS partition: the partition points to the DBR of drive D, and everything is normal.

But it doesn't work that way. It *can't* work that way—there can be *multiple* logical drives in the extended partition. You would have a way to find the first logical drive, but how to find the others? There's a one-to-one relationship between partition table entries and DBRs for primary partitions, but not for extended partitions.

FIGURE 14.4

Disk structure of a 16-head drive with a 4.2GB primary DOS partition and a 4.2GB Xenix partition

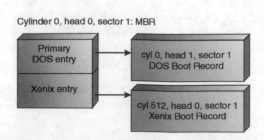

DOS makes one extended partition look like multiple drives by creating a set of fake Master Boot Records (MBRs) for the extended partition, one for each logical drive in the extended partition. The real MBR's partition table points to the extended partition. The first sector of the extended partition is not the DBR for a logical drive, but an extended partition table (EPT)—the first bogus MBR. Examining that EPT, you see a record pointing to the next track, where the DBR for drive D (the first logical drive in the extended partition) resides. Let's use the 16,384-cylinder drive again, but this time make the second 8192 cylinders an extended DOS partition with a single logical drive. Take a look at Figure 14.5.

FIGURE 14.5

Disk structure of a 16-head drive with a 4.2GB primary DOS partition and a 4.2GB extended DOS partition

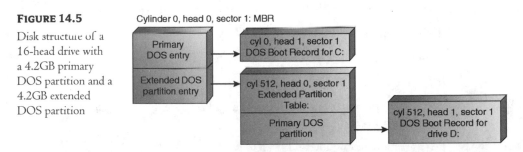

Note that, as in the case of the real MBR, the EPT wastes the rest of the track that the EPT is on. There is nothing in the sectors in cylinder 8192, head 0, sectors 2 through 63.

What if there are multiple logical drives in the extended DOS partition? Then there is a chain of EPTs. If the extended partition in our example were divided into two logical drives named D and E, the first EPT would contain two entries—the primary DOS entry for D and an extended DOS entry pointing to the start of drive E. Examination of the sector pointed to would show *another* EPT, this time with only one entry—a primary DOS partition for drive E. To illustrate this, assume that cylinders 8192 through 12,000 are used by logical drive D, and 12,001 through the end by logical drive E. Take a look at Figure 14.6.

FIGURE 14.6

MBR-to-DBR relationship with three logical drives

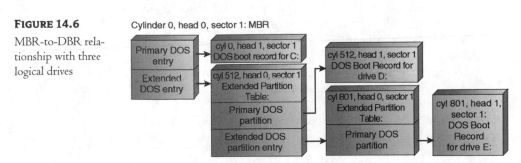

So the only way that DOS can find logical drives other than C is to wend its way through the chain of EPTs on the disk. That's why FDISK shows a slight pause when moving from the Create Extended Partition function to the Create Logical Drives part—it's searching the chain. Once FDISK is done, the hard drive is partitioned. After that, all you have to do is format the partitions, and it's ready to store data.

FAT32

Windows Me, Windows 98, and Windows 95 OSR2 allow you to choose between FAT16 and FAT32 when setting up a partition using FDISK. Of course, the message you receive doesn't ask if you want FAT16 or FAT32, which would quite honestly confuse many users. Instead, you are asked if you want support of large drives. If you say *No*, the disk will use a FAT16 file system. If you say *Yes*, it will be a FAT32 file system. While FAT32 provides a number of enhancements over any previous FAT, it is still lacking in areas of security and advanced data management compared with those that are available when using NTFS. Here's a quick look at what's been enhanced:

- ◆ It can see up to 2TB (terabytes!).

- ◆ Clusters are as small as 4KB for drives up to 8GB.

- ◆ It is not limited to storing the root directory at the top of the drive.

- ◆ Root directory limitations have been removed because it is now a cluster chain, which can be located anywhere on the drive.

- ◆ FATs are more recoverable and flexible.

- ◆ It can be dynamically resized.

Although FAT32 is *not* security-oriented the way NTFS is, most users choose to use FAT32—for several reasons, the most important being compatibility with just about everyone else on the planet. Okay, that might have been a little over the top, but I have been working on NT systems in U.S. corporations for many years, and few if any actually use the NTFS file system despite all of its technological advantages. Never forget that the Beta video format is technically superior to the VHS format but have you seen a Beta VCR lately?

We have mentioned the advantages of FAT32, yet for all of its advantages there is a particular situation in which you would not want to use it. If you intend to ever use Windows NT on the disk drive, you must use the FAT16 file system. This is because Windows 3.x, NT (both 3.x and 4), and the original Windows 95 cannot read or write files on a disk using a FAT32 file system. Many arguments used to be made of how wasteful FAT32 is because of its large cluster size when used with big drives. For this reason, the optimal drive size for FAT32 is considered by many to be 8GB, because it is the maximum-size drive that can be structured in 4KB clusters. While we could do a lot of math to show that larger cluster sizes are wasteful of disk space, in a world that sells 60GB drives for under $250, the point becomes moot.

One of the biggest problems older users face, though, is not thinking about drive compression. Most users of older systems used drive compression of one sort or another to optimize that tiny space as much as possible. FAT32 cannot be used with most drive compression software, including Microsoft DriveSpace 3. Once again, when disk drives were in the 10–30MB size category and selling for $100 per MB, compression was very important. It has been my experience in the past few years that most users don't even consider compression due to the performance hit versus benefit gained.

NTFS

NTFS, or NT File System, was developed specifically for Windows NT, and is now used as an advanced file system for Windows NT/2000/XP networks. Because Windows NT/2000/XP are not DOS-based operating systems, NTFS is not a DOS-based file system—you can only employ it if you're running NT, Windows 2000, or Windows XP. The main characteristics of NTFS are:

◆ System security; advanced file permission settings

◆ Supports Windows 2000/XP file encryption, disk quotas, volume mounting, and data compression

◆ Logging of activities in case the system goes down

◆ Inaccessibility if the computer is booted from a DOS floppy

◆ Maximum volume of 1024GB

◆ Filenames up to 256 characters long

◆ Extensive customization features that allow you to optimize disk performance

NTFS is based on a tree structure—all objects, files, and directories are treated as files, or records. The *Master File Table (MFT)* is a key component. The very first record, or file, of the MFT is named $Mft. It is essentially an index of all the files that reside in an NTFS volume. All filenames and their time stamps are included in the $Mft file. If a file is too large to fit all of its attributes in the $Mft file, the rest of the file is allocated to other parts of the volume. This approach provides more direct means of access to files than FAT and, therefore, faster access to directories and files.

The MFT also includes a mirror file, which provides a backup index of the entire volume in case the MFT is corrupted. Another difference between NTFS and FAT is that NTFS keeps track of all changes to the disk structure. Should your system go down, NTFS is able to recover the disk back to the last valid disk structure. Note that this tracking feature cannot recover user data that wasn't already written to the disk at the time a failure occurs, but the volume's structure will remain intact.

In a nutshell, this is how NTFS gets a file from disk to memory system: NTFS is file-based, as I explained above. When it is asked for a file reference, it looks up the file in the MFT and passes the parameters of the associated Logical Cluster Number (LCN) back to the controller so the file system driver can place the referenced LCNs in what's called a *run*, which is really just a chain of contiguous LCNs. (Nothing gets moved; just a bunch of run flags get turned on.) A full complement of runs makes a file, and the name of that file is the name under which the *runlist* is stored. When the file is called, the runlist is triggered, and all associated LCNs are read into memory.

NTFS 5 made its debut as part Windows 2000, and with it came these features:

Disk quotas Administrators can define the amount of space that a user is allocated. Additionally, they can define whether it is merely tracked or actually enforced by the server.

Encryption NTFS can now encrypt and decrypt data in real time as it is read and written to disk.

Reparse points   Applications are now able to capture data from open processes and perform operations on them before returning them to the system object that requested the initial operation. One of the key uses of this is for data redirection, allowing one object (that is, directory or file) to look like another. Hmmm, very Unix-like, that.

Sparse files   This is a rather interesting new capability. NTFS can allocate space to a file, but allow that file to remain very small. Okay, that's vague. VMWare, a virtual machine emulator for Windows NT and Linux, actually does this. If you tell VMWare that you want a 2GB drive container (a file that acts like a drive) to install Windows 98SE in your Windows NT 4 Workstation installation and use up only 800MB of that space, that's all it will use. If you look at the drive container file on your hard drive, it will say it's only 800MB.

Windows 2000 does this a little differently. First, when an object asks for space, the system checks to see whether there's room. The "No" is obvious, so I'll do the "Yes." The system then *soft* allocates that space to the object. The object can load anything into that space it wants, even if it's only a fraction of what it asked to be allocated. The system then keeps track of how much is being used of that soft allocation and will use the unused space as needed. Once the object starts asking for its requested space, the system makes sure it's available. This is a very useful feature.

USN journaling   USN journaling offers a more finely tuned way of tracking every minute operation transacted on the system. (USN stands for *update sequence number*, the format that defines and localizes file system changes.) As it stands with NT 4, there are a finite number of operations and activities that NT can monitor before it's swamped. Journaling is a way for the system to account for itself; each operation must log its activity as opposed to the system watching everything getting done and recording it. Journaling is much less CPU-intensive than *not* journaling; event traps are resource hogs.

TIP   If you're running a Windows NT or Windows 2000/XP network, the only time you really shouldn't use NTFS is when you need to support other operating systems on the same computer as Windows NT/2000/XP.

Preventive Tip: Backing Up Your Master Boot Record

I strongly suggest that you back up your Master Boot Record very, very often. I have found Ranish Partition Manager (RPM) to be the most useful utility in both protecting systems from boot record viruses and the silly ineptitudes I practice on occasion that seem to result in the destruction of a Master Boot Record. The last version I've been using is 2.40, and you can find it at this site:

```
www.ranish.com/part
```

It's stable, fast, relatively easy to use once you get the hang of it, and is very, very small. A 96KB download, to be exact. Save yourself gobs of trouble and add backing up your MBRs as a regular measure.

TIP   Since partitions and logical drives don't get changed very often on systems that are intended for consistent use, be sure to date the MBR copy on the floppy. It's also best to maintain an RPM disk for each machine instead of trying to remember which oddly named file was which machine's MBR copy.

Chapter 15

An Overview of Viruses

◆ Types of Viruses and How They Work   465

◆ Virus Hoaxes   471

◆ How to Protect Your PC from Viruses   472

◆ Antivirus Software and Other Resources   474

◆ How to Know if Your PC Is Infected   475

◆ Troubleshooting Tips   475

Introduction

WRITING MOST OF THIS book is a lot of fun. Fixing things is like putting together a puzzle—it's challenging and provides rewards in the end (a completed puzzle or a recovered hard disk). In either case, your only opponent is bad electrical power, buggy software, or (if you're supporting others) inattentive users.

Viruses are a whole different story. With viruses, you actually have a human opponent and sometimes a competent one.

Computer viruses are increasing at an alarming rate. In 1986 there was one known computer virus; three years later, that number had increased to six, and by 1990 the total had jumped to 80. Beginning in 1991, viruses were being discovered at the rate of one per week. As I am writing this, the rate is between three and five new viruses appearing every month (not including all of the variants). According to the Norton AntiVirus Research Center, between December 1998 and October 1999 the total virus count jumped from 20,500 to 42,000. And, according to information at McAfee's Virus Information Library, more than 57,000 viruses threatened our computers as of early 2002. While most of these new nasty viruses are variations of original viruses, they are nasty just the same.

A humorous anecdote came in the form of a technical support call I received a while back from a woman who claimed that her computer had 50,000 viruses. When I questioned how she knew this, she said she had just installed the latest Norton AntiVirus program and that was what it told her. As it turned out, she was reading the splash screen that appeared when the program was launched, which proudly announced that it could detect over 50,000 viruses—sigh.

People often ask at this point, "Why do people write viruses?" I wish I didn't have to answer this question. The answer is, viruses are written by computer criminals. Some people just plain get their jollies making other people's lives difficult, and they think it's clever to write viruses. The fact is, they're just childish. Virus authors exploit not cleverness but rather trust. Most viruses attack PCs via portals that exist because of *trust* in the computer community, not stupidity on the part of users. It's rather like this: Suppose you lived in a community where everyone knew everyone else, so folks didn't lock their doors. How clever need one be in order to be a thief? Not very—the thief *knows* that it's easy to get into any house. Would you applaud or be impressed with the skill of such a thief? Of course not. That's what today's virus authors are—mere children screaming for attention.

And that brings us to the topic of "ScriptKiddies." Instead of socializing with school friends, they're home wreaking havoc on the Internet. They use freely available virus-maker programs to modify existing viruses and code, which could translate into more attacks like the ILOVEYOU and Melissa viruses. They also scan networks to find computers that they can compromise. Once a target is found, they have no respect for privacy. They gain control of your machine through Trojan programs that have been installed on your machine (which are usually installed when you run unscanned executable files that you downloaded or received via e-mail). Once they get in, ScriptKiddies get their kicks by crashing your machine, playing with your CD-ROM door or your mouse, or stealing your password files so that they can crack them later.

There *are* people who get their kicks this way, and that's why antivirus software can be a nice support tool. It does the job that you and I have neither the time nor the knowledge for—monitoring the PC for common viruses and suspicious virus-like behavior. Good antivirus software should be able to prevent, detect, and remove viruses without destroying valuable data. It must also be easy to update, since new viruses are created every day, and software that can detect and clean every virus except the one you've currently got is less than useless. Good software, combined with educated users and regular backups, can make virus attacks less likely—and less serious.

This chapter provides an overview of viruses, including the most common terminology, the most common ways a virus enters your system, and tips on how to prevent and detect a virus.

Types of Viruses

What is a computer virus? A virus is a program that has been designed to replicate and spread on its own, preferably without a user's knowledge. *Virus* has come to be a generic term that people use these days to describe any of a group of programs designed to replicate themselves and spread (much like life, if you think about it). Some are pranks and do no damage, whereas others are intentionally destructive computer programs. Not all viruses are malicious or even intentional. While I was doing some contract work for IBM in the late 1990s, a virus shut down the entire IBM global network for the better part of a working day. What was this killer virus? It was a badly written program that was supposed to post a single Christmas greeting on everyone's computer screen in a single work area. Unfortunately, it wasn't written very well and it posted thousands of copies of the greeting on every terminal in the entire IBM worldwide network. By definition, it was a virus.

This section outlines various types of viruses, how they enter your computer, and the type of damage they do once they've infected your machine. You'll explore the following:

- ◆ File infectors and boot-sector viruses

- ◆ Macro viruses

- ◆ Worms

- ◆ Web applet viruses

NOTE *Myth: Viruses cannot harm your hardware—they affect only the data stored on your computer. Actually, a few viruses can and do attack the BIOS of a computer, rendering the computer useless and requiring that a new BIOS be installed.*

In the past, classifying viruses was much simpler than it is today. The two most common types of viruses a few years ago were file infectors and boot-sector viruses. But just as life continues to get more complicated as technology evolves, so do viruses. These days, a virus can be classified as, for example, a file infector macro virus, or a polymorphic stealth Web applet virus. Virus creators are constantly reinventing the wheel in order to develop the killer, undetectable virus. I'll cover how to protect your system from viruses later on, but for now let's take a look at the types of viruses and their techniques.

File Infectors and Boot-Sector Viruses

File infectors begin their dirty work whenever the executable file to which they are attached is run. They may proceed directly to certain areas of the disk where specific files sit (such as the partition tables or COMMAND.COM) or hide in memory for just the right moment. (File infectors are also called *program infectors*, or *parasitic viruses*.)

Another strain of file infector is made up of two split programs. One is the top program that will not register as a virus when a virus scanner runs, and the other contains an algorithm that, once the first program is resident, changes part of the first program's code to make it a virus.

The following lists the file types susceptible to viruses:

- EXE
- COM
- BIN
- DLL
- SYS
- DRV
- OVL
- VXD

Boot-sector viruses are not as common as they used to be. They infect your system when it reads an infected drive or floppy disk. Today, floppies are declining as a major source of virus infection, accounting for 68 percent of all reported infections in 1998, some 38 percent in 1999, and less than 5 percent today. These types of viruses generally prefer hard drives, but a minority, including the Stoned virus, infect floppies. They are loaded into memory when the PC is booted from a drive that contains an infected disk. You're probably wondering, "What if the disk is not really bootable (in other words, it has no COMMAND.COM file) and the screen displays the message Non-system disk error?" That doesn't stop anything, unfortunately. Once the computer attempts to boot from the infected disk, it's too late—the PC has to read the boot sector of the floppy to know it isn't bootable. During the read, the virus wakes up and springs into action.

Macro Viruses: Melissa Isn't the Girl Next Door

Macro viruses are one of the most widespread viruses around. Infections that spread through e-mail attachments—the source of macro viruses—increased from 32 percent in 1998 to 56 percent in 1999. E-mail attachments are the biggest source of macro viruses, while floppies are the typical carrier for boot-sector viruses. You can infect your system simply by opening a document with a macro virus attached. As their name implies, macro viruses reside as macros in a document.

How do macro viruses work? Macro viruses are written in the macro language of an application. Applications that currently permit the use of macros, such as word processing programs and spreadsheet programs, are at risk not only of infection, but also of infecting others. Macro viruses spread when infected documents are transferred. Most of the macro viruses around right now are designed to infect Microsoft Word (versions 6.x and later) and Microsoft Excel.

Many macro viruses do nothing or almost nothing: they spread, but that's about all. Some people believe that these relatively unobtrusive examples of macro viruses are not the product of hackers at all, but are mutations that first appeared as the result of random bit scrambling in somebody's download and wound up propagating, unseen and unnoticed, as time passed. On the other hand, there are destructive macro viruses that overwrite data, modify the contents of documents, and even send documents via e-mail.

Melissa, Concept, DMV, and *Nuclear* are names of some macro viruses. Melissa, which infected Microsoft Word 97 and Word 2000 documents, was so widespread that it brought computer viruses to the evening news. Once an infected document was opened, the virus attempted to locate the user's Microsoft Outlook address book, and if it found one, e-mailed a copy of the infected document to up to 50 people. Microsoft included security against macro viruses in Word 2000, but Melissa was intelligent enough to disable those security dialog boxes, so users would not be aware that the document they were trying to open was infected.

NOTE   *Melissa was not only a macro virus; she was a* worm, *too. To understand more about worms, see the section "Worms Wiggle Their Way through E-mail," later in this chapter.*

Concept and DMV worked in pretty much the same way: they forced you to save documents as templates and replicated themselves to your other documents. The main difference between the two is that DMV used the AutoClose macro to install itself in the Normal template, while Concept used AutoOpen. Nuclear could be destructive, however. On April 5, it deleted `COMMAND.COM`, and zeroed out `MSDOS.SYS` and `IO.SYS`, so that not only would your system fail to boot because it had no command shell, it wouldn't tell you what the problem was because the SYS files were missing.

That's the bad news. The good news is that Microsoft got on the ball and created the Word Macro Virus Protection Tool (available from `www.microsoft.com`) to alert you of the presence of macros in your documents (not macro viruses, just macros) and allow you to open documents without activating the macros. Once they're open, you can look at the list of attached macros. If you see anything called Insert Payload or Payload, you've got the Nuclear virus. AAAZAO and AAAZFS indicate the presence of the Concept virus. Other tools can clean the viruses from your system.

A DAY IN THE LIFE OF A MACRO VIRUS

Here's a relatively benign example of how a macro virus works: ShareFun is a Microsoft Word macro virus that attempts to spread over e-mail attachments. Every time somebody opens an infected file in Word, the chance of the virus becoming activated and spreading is one in four. You might open the document once, twice, or even a hundred times and you might luck out, but your odds each time are one in four that the virus will activate. If it does, and if Microsoft Mail is running at the same time, the virus will try to send e-mail messages to three people randomly selected from the local MSMail alias list. (It's harmless if you're not running MSMail.) The subject of the messages is always the same: "You have GOT to see this!" The message is empty of text, but it contains a link to a file attachment called `DOC1.DOC`, which is infected by the virus. If recipients double-click the attachment, they will get infected by the virus and could spread the infection further with their own MSMail. As of this writing, the virus does nothing destructive; it merely propagates, and only when the circumstances are there for it. (Incidentally, this virus is not technically an "e-mail virus," because the recipients do not literally get infected from your e-mail; rather, they get infected by trying to open the attachment.)

ShareFun also has code to protect itself: If you try to analyze the virus in Word for Windows by looking at the "macro" using either Tools ➢ Macro or File ➢ Templates, the virus will execute and infect your Word `NORMAL.DOT` template.

Worms Wiggle Their Way through E-mail

The major trait of a worm virus is its ability to propagate via e-mail. A worm program is sent as an e-mail attachment. Once you open the attachment, the worm locates your e-mail address book and sends out the infected attachment. You can imagine how quickly this type of virus can spread, considering how many of us rely on e-mail as a means to send documents, whether personal or work related.

As you learned previously in this chapter, our friend Melissa was a worm—she propagated by locating Microsoft Outlook address books and sending herself, infected Word document that she was, to your friends and colleagues. But alas, poor Melissa, she lost her place as the most popular worm. Another famous worm was the Love Bug virus. In simplest terms, thousands of people received e-mails with the subject line "ILOVEYOU." Thousands of people threw caution to the wind when they read the subject line and opened the attachment. Oooops. The ILOVEYOU worm went right to work, wiggling its way into users' Outlook Express address books and propagating itself. (At least it wasn't propagation without love.) Not only did the Love Bug virus propagate via e-mail, but it scanned users' PCs for passwords, which were sent back to the originator of the virus. It also copied itself over numerous file types, including MP3, JS, and JPEG.

The twenty-first century rang in a number of high-level worms, the most notable of which was Nimda (the reverse of Admin). It spread itself in multiple ways: by e-mail, open network shares, and vulnerable Microsoft IIS Web servers. Once a server was compromised, Nimda would create a local account with administrator privileges and copy itself to multiple locations. It used JavaScript to modify files with `.htm`, `.html`, and `.asp` extensions. When visitors browsed the infected pages, they were presented with a file named `readme.eml`, which then spread itself through Outlook Express as an e-mail attachment without the users' knowledge. And once the attachment reached the recipient, what made Nimda so dangerous was that a simple *preview* of the infected message could cause it to spread even further! As a result, the worm spread like wildfire and affected servers worldwide.

WARNING   A good way to avoid worms is to never open any file attachments from unknown sources and to listen to, or read, the national news. You can also visit the bug alert sites mentioned in this chapter. Viruses and their creators have been getting a lot of attention in the press lately. Press reports alerted computer users about the Love Bug and so limited the damage it caused.

Real-Time Messaging Viruses

As if e-mail viruses aren't enough, you also have to worry when you're talking with your friends in real-time. If you're fond of instant messaging (IM) services such as MSN Messenger, AOL Messenger, or ICQ, you'll probably notice an increase in viruses and worms there, too. If you see a flood of emoticons (smiley or winky faces and so on) and then receive a message that prompts you to open a file, don't open it!

MSN Messenger was attacked in May and June of 2001 by two worms. The first was the W32/ Hello worm, which was triggered when you received a message from another MSN Messenger user, or when you added another MSN Messenger user to your contact list. The worm attempted to spread itself by sending a message that read, "I have a file for u. its real funny." If you opened the `HELLO.EXE` file, the worm installed itself on your system and continued to spread. Soon afterward,

MSN Messenger users began to see the Choke worm, which operated in a similar manner. Its attachment was an executable file named with anti-political overtones.

Fortunately, these two introductory IM worms did nothing damaging—they only propagated themselves. But what they did do was open the door to using IM services as yet another vehicle for virus distribution (as if there weren't enough vehicles already).

Web Applet Viruses

Danger, Will Robinson—browsing the Web may be hazardous. The newest type of virus can exist in three popular Web scripting languages: ActiveX, JavaScript, and Java. While these languages allow for much of the gee-whiz features of the Web, such as 3D animation, it's possible for these languages to transfer virus programs to your system. The transfer is triggered by you simply opening a Web page that contains infected ActiveX controls or Java/JavaScript code. Once the virus makes its way into your system, it may corrupt files or directories, or do other types of damage—what happens depends on the actual virus.

To date there hasn't been an outbreak of a Web applet virus. However, as more and more consumers log on to the Internet, it's a safe bet that you'll be hearing more about this type of virus in the future.

NOTE   For information on how to protect yourself from Web applet viruses, see the section "Tips for Protecting Your PC against Viruses," later in this chapter.

VIRUS NAMING CONVENTIONS

How are viruses named? First, you'll see a prefix, such as *W97M*. This is normally the platform where the virus operates. W97M is a Word 97 Macro virus. Next, you'll see the virus family name, such as *Melissa*. Sometimes you'll see a suffix, such as *.a*. This indicates the variant of the virus. In certain situations, a virus will have an alias that is more commonly known than the official name. W32/Ska, also known as Happy99, is one such virus.

Here's a list of some common virus prefixes:

A97M   Access Macro viruses native to Access 97.

AOL   America Online Trojans.

Java   Viruses written in Java.

Trojan/Troj   Trojan horses.

W32   32-bit Windows viruses.

W95   Windows 95 viruses. These may affect Windows 98, too.

W97M   Word Macro viruses native to (and applicable only to) Word 97.

WNT   32-bit Windows viruses that can infect Windows NT.

X97M   Excel Macro viruses native to Excel 97.

VBS   Viruses written in Visual Basic Script.

Techniques of Attack

Virus creators get their kicks from tricking us—the more complex the virus, the longer it takes investigators to figure out how it works and how it spreads. A virus may use one or several sneaky modes of operation covered in this section.

Polymorphic Viruses

A *polymorphic* virus changes, or mutates, so that it cannot be detected by antivirus software. For example, back in 1998 a polymorphic macro virus named Excel8_Extras appeared. It created an infected spreadsheet in the Excel startup directory, then added a *randomly generated* macro and module name to infected documents. Because the virus was able to randomly generate new names, it took longer for investigators to pinpoint the virus.

Multipartite Viruses

Just to make things maximally confusing, some viruses have a boot-sector portion *and* a program-infector portion; these are called *multipartite* viruses. For example, researchers discovered that the Hare virus was a polymorphic, multipartite virus that infected COM and EXE files as well as Master Boot Records (MBRs) on hard drives and boot sectors of floppy disks. Upon execution, the virus infected the MBR and became resident, infecting any COM or EXE file that was executed.

Stealth Viruses

Some viruses are said to be stealth viruses. A *stealth* virus attempts to hide itself by keeping a copy of the parts of the disk that it infected, *before* it infected the disk. Then, when it detects that a virus scanner is looking for it, it shows the scanner the uninfected copy of the file, as if to say, "Nobody here but us chickens." Now, note that the stealth feature of a virus works only if the virus is active in memory, which will not be the case if you've first booted from a clean, write-protected DOS floppy. Always do that before running an important virus scan.

WARNING   *Many program infectors (and all boot sector viruses) become Terminate and Stay Resident (TSR) programs—which is a good reason to install a TSR scanner that can constantly monitor your system for viruses. TSRs take system memory, which tips you off that you may have a virus. If your system memory doesn't add up to 640K, then you might have a virus.*

Trojan Horses

A *Trojan horse* program acts like the Trojan horse of Greek mythology. A malevolent program is hidden inside another, apparently useful, program. While the "useful" program is running, the malevolent part does something nasty, like erase your FAT and directory.

The only good thing about Trojans is that they're self-limiting: once an evil Trojan erases your hard disk, it has erased itself as well. Today, instead of running on private e-mail systems like bulletin board systems as they did in the past, Trojans (which now typically have a replication component) are finding their way to the Internet and the World Wide Web.

Pure Trojans seem to have gone out of style. Trojans instead show up in the virus world as the initial source of infection for some viruses. A virus that injects itself into COM or EXE files is also a Trojan, because it is waiting for you to run that formerly useful program: once you run an infected copy of any application, you are waking the virus up.

Time Bombs and Logic Bombs

Then there is the bomb. There are *time bombs* and *logic bombs*. The *bomb* is a piece of code embedded in a program or the operating system itself that waits for a particular event to occur. When that event occurs, the logic bomb "goes off," doing some kind of damage.

Logic bombs have been around nearly since the beginning of computing. An early one showed up in a mainframe payroll program. The program's creator had inserted a clause in the payroll program that said, "If you find I'm not on the payroll, erase all payroll files."

Bombs show up as the more destructive part of viruses. They include instructions such as, "If it's Friday the 13th, erase the hard disk," or "If the worm has succeeded in making 10 copies of itself, erase the hard disk."

An Example of a Virus at Work

By now you know that a virus can use a combination of approaches in attacking your data. A virus might work in the following way:

1. Assume that you double-clicked one of those animated holiday cards sent to you in an e-mail as an EXE file—an executable program. The virus is then introduced to your system via the infected EXE file (an example is a Trojan horse). Either this Trojan is hidden in an application program that has been doctored by the virus creator, or it is the Trojan portion of a virus that is injected into a program file or the boot record by the worm portion.

2. Once the program with the Trojan is activated by a certain event, such as your running a particular application, the virus is awakened. It installs itself in the operating system as a logic bomb, waiting for an opportunity to (1) activate the worm and/or (2) activate the destructive portion of itself.

3. The logic bomb activates the worm portion whenever an acceptable host presents itself. Some viruses replicate only onto floppies from the hard disk. Other viruses infect any program file that gets activated, whether on the floppy disk or the hard disk. Every time the worm copies itself onto another disk or program, it activates a built-in counter that keeps track of how many copies it has made.

4. Eventually, the destructive part of the virus may be activated, either by an event, such as running a program, a date occurring (such as Friday the 13th), or by a certain number of replications. When the destructive portion activates, the virus may do something as innocuous as flashing a message on the screen or as damaging as erasing the hard disk.

Virus Hoaxes

As if viruses, and the very real threat they pose to computer users everywhere, aren't enough to cause you concern, there is a cottage industry springing up that is intended to cause panic and anxiety: hoaxes. Hoaxes are just that. They are fake virus warnings initially transmitted by a malicious person who relies on the likelihood that people will send them to everyone they know thinking they are doing a good deed. Sadly, no threat is averted, no virus is exposed, and no one is helped. What actually happens is a great deal of wasted time, confusion, and higher blood pressure.

To avoid falling into this trap, if you get a virus warning from anyone, you should first check with an authoritative antivirus Web site and do some research to see whether the message you are reading is about a real virus or a hoax. (See the "Resources: Stay Informed" section later in this chapter for a list of helpful Web sites.) If it's a hoax, please pass that on to the person who sent you the message and inform them of this tragic misuse of the Internet.

Tips for Protecting Your PC against Viruses

The most effective way to avoid catching viruses is to shut off your computer... permanently. Don't like that idea? How about just removing your floppy disk drives, disconnecting from your network, and never connecting to the Internet?

Effective as those means are, they're not much good in the real world. Never opening e-mails so as not to catch viruses is sort of like cutting off your hand so as not to get a hangnail. Sure, it prevents what you were trying to prevent, but it doesn't give you much good use of your hand—or your computer. In the real world, what can you do about viruses?

Purchase virus-protection software, install it on your system, and use it.   See the "Antivirus Software" section later in this chapter for a list of the best virus-protection/detection software.

Be sure to update your virus-protection software.   Some software will automatically link to the vendor's site and download detection code for the newest viruses. Or you can check the vendor's site from time to time to make sure your software is up to date. However you do it, do it.

Don't open e-mail attachments from people you don't know.   This is critically important because many newer viruses spread by sending infected files over the Internet as e-mail attachments. Sometimes, this includes people you do know, who may be unwittingly passing on an infected file to you. It's important to note that simply opening an e-mail with an infected attachment will not introduce the virus into your system.

Don't download files from the Internet unless you have virus-protection software that scans them for viruses.   Also, think twice about the site you're considering downloading from. Is it a company with its reputation at stake, or an unknown individual?

Consider disabling your browser's ability to handle pages that contain JavaScript, Java code, or ActiveX controls.   This doesn't necessarily mean that you won't be able to view the page—just the parts that contain ActiveX controls or Java/JavaScript. You can always reset your browser to handle those components if you need to.

If you don't want to disable your browser for ActiveX, Java, and JavaScript, consider the source before entering a site.   If you know nothing about the site, think twice before entering. There are a lot of people out there who have Web sites, a lot of time on their hands, and nothing to lose.

Keep up with the news.   Major outbreaks are reported on national, even local (depending on where you live) news, in newspapers, and on Web sites such as www.cnet.com.

Back up your data frequently.   I've already said this: viruses are scary, but not backing up regularly is scarier. Any of a large number of random external events—flood, fire, power surges, vibration—could destroy data on your hard disk, and it could happen at any time. Backing up regularly is more important than keeping up-to-date on the latest virus-buster programs.

If you're managing a network, centralize your applications. Install all programs used in the department on one computer (preferably one not used as a workstation) and then back up all the application software from that computer. Protect this computer from virus infection with your life. If you get a virus, you can use either the files from the computer or backup floppies to restore applications to the newly cleaned computer.

Don't use pirated software, especially games. First of all, it's not nice to use commercial software that you didn't pay for. Most software companies are fairly small operations, no more than 10 to 15 people. These are not large, faceless corporations that "deserve" (in the eyes of some people) being taken down a peg or two. Most software operations are Mom-and-Pop operations that just barely get by. Using copies of software you didn't buy is just plain theft. People who use illegal copies are thieves, plain and simple—and cowardly thieves, to boot. There's good, cheap software in all areas, so "just say no" when someone offers you a copy of a program. More relevant to the present discussion, many virus attacks that I've heard of seem to have come from pirated software—another good reason not to use copies.

Don't trust bundled CD-ROM software. Although you might think all software distributed on CD-ROM is virus-free and safe to use, there have been cases where companies inadvertently distributed a virus on their CD. Word macro viruses are a particular problem, so be sure to scan those files before opening them.

Avoid Web sites that cater to self-proclaimed "hackers." These sites tend to mainly have pirated games anyway, and the software generally isn't screened. The same idiots who think it's okay to crack the copy protection on a game and give it away free also think it's okay to insert a virus in the cracked game. In some odd Robin Hood manner, they view it as "just punishment" for anyone *else* who uses illegally copied software.

Be wary of shareware programs without documentation. If they don't tell you how to use it, maybe you shouldn't! Don't run the program.

Stick to big shareware download sites such as Tucows or PC Magazine, and Web sites that register their users. Most reputable Web sites these days ask that you register when you get on. Then they don't let you upload files until they've checked that you are who you say you are. That way, if you upload a virus, they can come after you. This makes people less likely to upload viruses.

Write-protect any floppy that you put in your drive, if possible. This is particularly important when installing a new piece of software: you don't want your master copy of a program to become infected. Some programs require that the disk not be protected while installing—I certainly hope that vendors move away from this practice. Also, get in the habit of leaving the floppy drive empty. Boot-sector viruses can't get at your hard disk if you don't boot from an infected floppy. You can read and write data on a floppy with an infected boot record for years and never be infected. But boot from the floppy—even if it's not a bootable floppy—and you've got the virus. If you're not careful, you'll find that now and then you try to reboot the machine with a floppy in drive A. Keep the drive empty and it won't happen.

Antivirus Software

Quite a few antivirus software packages are available that will search your PC for viruses and alert you if incoming files are infected. The following products are well worth consideration:

◆ Command AntiVirus (Command Software Systems Inc.; `www.commandcom.com`)

◆ F-Secure Anti-Virus (F-Secure Corp.; `www.datafellows.com`)

◆ McAfee Internet Guard Dog (McAfee Corp.; `www.mcafee.com`)

◆ McAfee VirusScan for Windows (McAfee Corp.; `www.mcafee.com`)

◆ Norton AntiVirus 2002 (Symantec Corp.; `www.symantec.com`)

◆ PC-cillin 2000 (Trend Micro Inc.; `www.antivirus.com`)

Resources: Stay Informed

First of all, understand that we're on shaky ground here. There are really no totally reliable sources of data on virus prevalence. As I said earlier, the people doing most of the yelling about what a big danger viruses pose to life on Earth are generally the people who stand to gain the most from the panic—vendors of antivirus products. Personally, I am concerned about viruses, but I have not panicked and I do not advise panic on your part.

The following URLs provide current lists of the top viruses, as well as virus descriptions and recent news about viruses, including hoaxes:

◆ McAfee AVERT Virus Information Library: `http://vil.nai.com/villib/alpha.asp`

◆ Symantec: `www.symantec.com/avcenter/`

◆ Trend Micro: `www.antivirus.com/pc-cillin/vinfo/`

◆ The WildList Organization International: `www.wildlist.org/WildList/`

◆ F-Secure: `www.f-secure.com/virus-info/`

◆ ICSA, division of TruSecure Corp.: `www.icsalabs.com/html/communities/antivirus/index.shtml`

◆ Virus Bulletin: `www.virusbtn.com`

Virus Hoax Lists

When you receive a warning in your e-mail to be on the lookout for the "latest and greatest" virus, and you can't find any information about it in the virus lists mentioned in the section "Resources: Stay Informed," it could be a hoax. Here are some sites that you can check for the latest virus hoaxes:

◆ McAfee: `vil.nai.com/VIL/hoaxes.asp`

◆ Symantec: `www.symantec.com/avcenter/hoax.html`

◆ Trend Micro: www.antivirus.com/pc-cillin/vinfo/hoaxes/hoax.asp

◆ F-Secure Hoax Warnings: www.f-secure.com/virus-info/hoax/

◆ Virus Hoax Listings: www.virusbtn.com/Hoax/hoaxlist.html

Viral Symptoms

How can you tell if your PC is infected with a virus? Here are some of the most common symptoms:

◆ Files or programs become corrupted or aren't working properly. For example, a Word document that was fine an hour ago now includes text or formatting that you did not insert.

◆ New programs or files appear mysteriously in a directory.

◆ Odd warning messages, error messages, or random dialog boxes appear on-screen.

◆ A drive name has been renamed.

◆ Programs or files suddenly disappear from directories.

◆ Memory problems occur—for example, not enough memory when you should have no problem running the applications and files that you're running.

◆ Visual elements appear; distortions of the screen and strange visual effects can suddenly start appearing on your screen.

Troubleshooting Tips

The following procedures have been helpful to me in coping with a virus attack. I recommend that you make a form for yourself from this list, arranging the list in two columns so that you've got one side free for checking things off and for your notes.

1. Calm down.

2. Grab a pen and pad so you can write out the diagnostic steps you take. It might be hard to believe that you could forget important details, but under the stress caused by a virus attack, anyone could be subject to bouts of amnesia. To keep from forgetting anything, make two lists. The first list should record what you've done in the recent past that may have allowed entry, such as opening an executable file from a friend of a friend. The second list should detail the steps you take to detect, isolate, and (you hope) destroy the virus. To remember what you've done as the hunt continues, you will want to reread your notes for the next few days—or months. Writing down what you are about to do also forces you to think about the next step. That mental pause may prevent you from taking an unnecessary step or making a dangerous error.

3. If you haven't already powered down the computer, record all information being displayed on-screen inside the virus dialog box: the type of virus reported, in which files it is contained, and the exact DOS or Windows message.

4. Note your most recent actions and computer symptoms (leaving the screen on for this step may help your memory).

5. In the rare case that your PC was infected by a floppy disk, note the names of all floppy disks lying around, and whether you received disks from anyone recently (if so, did you insert them in the floppy drive?) or gave disks to anyone else recently. Remove all floppies from drives and remember to discard all the floppy disks that were around the infected PC.

6. If you must save your on-screen data, save it to an empty floppy and mark the disk *immediately* as "Potentially Infected."

7. If at all possible, access the Internet on another system and look up the most recent virus list. Compare the reported symptoms with those manifested by the computer.

8. If there's a match, determine whether your antivirus software needs updating in order to detect the virus infecting your PC.

9. Power down (just rebooting may not oust the virus). Then reboot from the hard drive and run your antivirus software. Download the latest virus detectors from your antivirus software vendor's site.

10. Write down all files reported as infected. If no backups or hard copies exist for infected files, consider making copies to another floppy. If you make backups, mark those floppies as "Potentially Infected."

11. Rescan the hard drive with your antivirus program.

Don't let fear of viruses destroy your use and enjoyment of your PC. The analogies between safe sex and safe computing, although now trite, are very accurate. Have a good time, but use protection. At the very minimum, use antivirus software and back up data regularly. Don't put original program floppies in your PC's drives unless they have write-protect tabs on them. On a final note: if you know someone who's a virus author, report her to the authorities.

Chapter 16

Care and Feeding of Hard Drives

◆ Protecting Your Hard Drive 479

◆ Backing Up System Files 483

◆ File Defragmenters 492

◆ Recovering Data and Fixing Hard Drives 494

◆ Understanding and Repairing Media Errors 506

◆ Resurrecting Dead Hard Drives 508

Introduction

I DISCUSSED SOME OF these things earlier, but here's a summary of what you can do to make your disk hardware live longer. Some of these have been covered earlier; for the others, I'll expand upon them in a few pages.

As you read in Chapter 4, "Avoiding Service: Preventive Maintenance," leave your computers on all the time: it's easier on their drives not to have to start up every day.

Also, get good power protection. You read in Chapter 9, "Power Supplies and Power Protection," about buying power conditioners, UPSs, and SPSs to protect your hardware—and the hard disk is no exception. Surges go through the *whole* system, including the drive heads. And if the drive heads happen to be near the FAT or partition record...

A couple more tips:

- Use the proper mounting hardware for your drive, and mount it according to manufacturer's guidelines.

- Attend to squealing drives. Not only are they annoying, they may be trying to tell you something.

Let's take a closer look at how to care for your hard drive.

Protecting Your Hard Drive

There's not much to be done in the way of regular maintenance on the sealed hard drive: You can't clean the heads and you can't align them. If the drive itself is fried, then about all you can do with it is toss it and buy a newer and bigger one.

What kills hard drives? It used to be that hard drives were fragile devices that required a considerable amount of care and watchfulness, but current hard drives are all but bulletproof. Probably the single worst thing you can do to a hard drive is smack it around while the disks are spinning.

But hard drives do, on occasion, die. Which means that you need to have a protection plan for all your valuable data—just in case.

Data Protection

The essence of data protection is simple: back up your data. The different areas on your disk should be backed up at different intervals with different tools. A complete backup program consists of the following steps:

◆ Backing up the following:

- ◆ The drive type (if you are using an older system or hard drive)

- ◆ The MBR, including the FAT and directory (daily)

- ◆ System files (at regular intervals)

- ◆ The user data (regularly)

◆ Making an "emergency" boot floppy or CD for each system

◆ Taking whatever measures you can to minimize the probability of an accidental format

NOTE   *Although it may sound strange to accidentally format your hard drive, it's possible. Take my word for it, it's been done. Of course, if you're working in a "user-friendly" GUI environment like Windows or KDE for Linux, it's much easier to avoid such catastrophes, but there are still no guarantees.*

It also can't hurt if you do the following:

◆ Periodically defragment the data on your hard drive to ease any data recovery problems.

◆ Utilize the verification features of the operating system and some applications (if they exist).

◆ Understand the threat posed by computer viruses and know how to protect yourself from them. By the way, the best way to avoid computer viruses is to use one of the many excellent antivirus programs on the market and keep it updated.

It looks like a lot, but it's not really: let's take a look at each item.

Backing Up Your Hard Drive

NOTE   *Today, virtually all computers and hard drives autoconfigure when they are installed. As such, you never need to set the drive type in CMOS, and you can skip this section. If, on the other hand, you are using an older system, it's very important that you save the hard drive configuration data contained in your CMOS.*

The most important part of the CMOS information is your hard disk's disk type. Not that the other information in your CMOS memory isn't important, but it's that incorrect or missing hard drive data that will crash your system. The other information (like the time and date) will be nothing more than an inconvenience. To look at your CMOS data, run your computer's BIOS setup program and you'll see (among other things) the drive type displayed.

Looking at the list of information in the BIOS, you'll find a number of drive specifications (either two or four drives will be listed). Chances are that only one of the drives will have actual data. The others will generally say "not installed" or some other similar note.

Your drive will be either a predefined drive type, like drive type 15, or it will be a user-definable drive type. The user-definable drive type is usually numbered 47, although not all computers use 47; many older Compaq computers use a number in the low 60s.

If your drive is of a user-definable type, be sure to make a note of not only its drive number, but also the number of heads, cylinders, sectors, and write precompensation. Some computers require that you note the ECC length, so take that down if the Setup program shows it.

Better yet, stick a paper label on the drive with the drive number on it (or, if you're so inclined, a permanent marker works well, too). If you ever move the drive to another computer, however, you may not be able to use the same drive type number in the new one. Each computer's BIOS is different, and what is drive type 35 for one computer may be drive type 42 for another. But if you write down the specifications for the drive (heads, sectors, and so on), you'll always be able to enter the data into your new system and get the drive to work.

Backing Up and Restoring Your MBR with DEBUG

You may recall that the Master Boot Record (MBR) resides on cylinder 0, head 0, sector 1. Without your MBR, your computer will never boot. Unfortunately, because the head spends a lot of time there—the root directory and FAT are in that area, among other things—cylinder 0 is more prone to problems than most cylinders.

I have seen strange things kill cylinder 0, and when cylinder 0 is dead, the whole disk might just as well be dead. Lose the MBR, and the operating system has no idea how to communicate with the disk. So back it up.

As a matter of fact, it's a good idea to back up not only the MBR (which is the first sector of the first track), but the entire first track at cylinder 0, head 0. Various programs squirrel important information onto these otherwise-unused sectors: for example, a dual-boot system relies on sectors 2 and 3 of the track, and Disk Manager stores information about a drive's geometry on sector 8.

THE EXE FILES: USING DEBUG

Although DOS 5 included an MBR backup program, it was removed from DOS 6 and subsequent versions of DOS and all versions of Windows. So chances are you won't have an MBR backup program installed on your machine. Fortunately, you can back up the MBR with the Norton Utilities, if you have a copy. You can also back up your MBR if all you have is DEBUG (and that's available on even the most current systems). But be careful: DEBUG is a very powerful utility and can damage a file. If it is not used correctly, you will no longer be able to use the file. If you do use DEBUG, it's a good idea to use it on a copy, not an original file. That way, if you make a mistake, you still have an undamaged original. Use a bootable floppy that contains DEBUG.EXE (MS-DOS users) or DEBUG.COM (PC-DOS users). If you're using Windows, put a copy of DEBUG onto a Startup floppy before you begin. (You can usually find the file in the C:\Windows\System32\ folder.) Type the program lines into DEBUG as shown below in bold type. (The case doesn't matter, but I'm showing the words in caps for clarity's sake.) I've placed underscores where blanks should go. Line 1 starts DEBUG and creates a new file called MBR.DAT.

1. **DEBUG_MBR.DAT**. You will see a `File Not Found` message—because the file didn't exist before. Don't worry about the message.

2. **A**. This tells DEBUG that you want to assemble something.

3. **MOV_DX,9000**. This command tells DEBUG to move the value of segment 9000 to register DX. Since you can't write anything to a register, you have to move this information to an extra segment.

4. **MOV_ES,DX**. This command moves any information in register DX to the extra segment (called ES).

5. **XOR_BX,BX**. BX is the offset; Xor is a programming trick to set it to zero.

6. **MOV_CX,0001**. This command stores the value of track 0 and sector 1 in register CX.

7. **MOV_DX,0080**. Here, you're storing the information at head 0 of drive 80 (your A drive is drive 00, your B drive is drive 01, your C drive is drive 80, and your D drive is drive 81—these are all physical drives, not logical drives) into register DX.

8. **MOV_AX,0201**. This command tells DEBUG to read 1 sector.

9. **INT_13**. This is the BIOS disk call.

10. **INT_20**. This tells the BIOS, "I'm done!" and signals that it won't get any more commands and can leave memory.

11. Press Enter to stop entering commands.

12. **G** runs the program. When it's done, you should see a message that says `Program terminated normally`.

13. **R_CX**. This command asks DEBUG to show you the value of register CX and lets you edit it.

14. **200**. This is the size of the file that DEBUG will write.

15. **W_9000:00**.

16. Type **Q** to exit DEBUG.

Continued on next page

THE EXE FILES: USING DEBUG *(continued)*

Congratulations! You have just created a file called MBR.DAT. Here's a sample screen of this operation.

```
A:\>debug mbr.dat
-l 9000:0
-a
25A4:0100 mov dx,9000
25A4:0103 mov es,dx
25A4:0105 xor bx,bx
25A4:0107 mov cx,0001
25A4:010A mov dx,0080
25A4:010D mov ax,0301
25A4:0110 int 13
25A4:0112 int 20
25A4:0114
-g

Program terminated normally
-q

A:\>
```

The process of restoring your MBR is similar to that of saving it. To restore your MBR, first start from a bootable floppy that contains both DEBUG (.EXE or .COM) and the correct MBR.DAT—do not try restoring an MBR.DAT from one machine onto another machine unless the two machines are identical! Once you're set, change to the A drive and type the following (again, underscores should be typed as blanks):

1. **DEBUG_MBR.DAT.** This time, if you get a File not found message, stop and exit DEBUG (type Q) immediately! If you continue at this point, you could blast your MBR. (Seeing that message means that you didn't save it properly.)

2. Type L_9000:0 to direct DEBUG to load the information to 9000:0, where you'll tell the program to look for it.

3. Assuming that all went well, now type A to let DEBUG know you want to assemble a file.

4. MOV_DX,9000.

5. MOV_ES,DX.

6. XOR_BX,BX.

7. MOV_CX,0001.

8. MOV_DX,0080.

9. MOV_AX,0301. This command tells DEBUG that you want to write 1 sector.

10. INT_13.

11. INT_20.

12. Press Enter to stop entering commands.

13. G runs the program. When it's done, you should see a message that says Program terminated normally.

14. Press Q to exit DEBUG. Your screen will look like the previous graphic.

Backing Up System Files

It's no secret that operating systems are getting more and more complex these days. Your operating system's default system files, for example, include a bunch of configuration files that tell your operating system how to work and how your applications should work with it. Lose those files, and it's all over.

16-Bit Applications

If you're running an older computer, you'll have to deal with 16-bit applications and a less wieldy version of Windows. Newer versions of Windows use a totally different system file scheme, so this information may not be applicable to you.

For Windows 3.x and its corresponding 16-bit applications, the important files have the extension INI. Each application that you run has its own "innie" file that defines the environment in which it operates. For example, my copy of Ami Pro has an initialization file called `AMIPRO.INI`, which defines the default document template used, the default location to which files are saved, and so forth.

The Windows 3.x operating system itself has several initialization files:

SYSTEM.INI   Contains the hardware information for Windows.

WIN.INI   Contains the Windows user environment.

CONTROL.INI   Describes the color schemes and printers used with Windows.

PROGMAN.INI   Defines the contents of all Windows program groups and how the Program Manager works.

WINFILE.INI   Defines how objects appear in the File Manager.

This isn't the place for a complete discussion of the INI files, but if you'd like to know more, the Windows Resource Kit has a very good description of all the INI files and what they do.

NOTE   *INI files are generally kept in the* `Windows` *directory. You can view (and edit) an INI file in a text editor such as Windows Notepad. It's not a good idea to open it in a word processor lest you save it as a word processor file.*

What does all this mean in terms of rebuilding your system if necessary? When backing up, even if you normally only back up data rather than system files, it's a very good idea to back up all INI files as well. This way, if you must reinstall the operating system, you'll be able to restore your system exactly the way it was when you backed it up—application files and all. To restore INI files, just copy them back to the Windows directory, replacing any existing files. (Of course, be very sure that the backed-up files are the ones that you want to use.) The only restrictions are that this will work best if you're restoring the system information to the same computer you took it from. Other computers may not work with the memory configuration or fonts that you set up on the original system.

TIP   *If you've upgraded your system from Windows 3.x (or upgraded 3.x versions of some applications), you may still have INI files on your computer—even though the main system information is stored in the Windows Registry (discussed next). It never hurts to search for INI files on your system, just in case they exist and need to be backed up.*

Registry-Oriented Operating Systems (Windows 95 and Beyond)

Post-Windows 3.*x*, all versions of Windows from 95 on organize configuration information differently. Rather than having a bunch of INI files, almost all information relating to the operating systems and most 32-bit applications stored therein are stored in a central database known as the Registry. The exact files of which the Registry is composed depends on the operating system: for Windows 95/98/Me, it's two files, USER.DAT and SYSTEM.DAT; for Windows NT/2000/XP, it's a series of *hive* files, each of which describes a part of how the operating system works. But whichever operating system you're talking about, all the files are combined to make one Registry. The only exceptions to this are any 16-bit Windows apps on your system. They don't know how to look in the Registry for configuration information, so they maintain INI files and copy their contents to the Registry.

NOTE   There actually are a number of true 32-bit applications that still use INI files. The simple fact is that it's easier, faster, and more reliable to store information about an application's configuration in a local file, that is, an INI file that resides in the same directory as the application. Most commercial applications add entries to the Registry, but a fair number of shareware and freeware titles use INI files.

The good news about the Registry is that it's centralized: only one Registry to back up, not five or more individual text files. Most of the time, you make changes to the Registry in the same way that you usually make changes to INI files: by changing the settings in the Control Panel.

Your method of backing up the Registry depends on the operating system you're using. If you're using NT and have a tape drive, you can back up the Registry at the same time that you back up your other data. When you restore the data, you can choose to restore the Registry at the same time, so long as you restore it to the same drive that it came from. If you're using Windows 95 or its successors, you can export the Registry as a text file from the Registry Editor, and then import it as needed. Backing up the Registry on a regular basis is a *very* good idea, as the Registry is required to boot the operating system.

The structure of the Windows 98 Registry and the Windows Me Registry has not changed significantly from the Windows 95 Registry. What has changed is that the code that handles the Registry is faster, and the Registry now detects certain problems as they arise and automatically fixes them. Your system always keeps a backup copy of your Registry configuration (including user account information, protocol bindings, software program settings, and user preferences). You can use the backup copy if your current Registry encounters a problem. Each time you restart your computer, Registry Checker automatically scans your Registry. If Registry Checker notices a problem, it automatically replaces the Registry with the backup copy.

If you're using Windows 98 or Windows Me, you can start Registry Checker by clicking Start ➤ Programs ➤ Accessories ➤ System Tools ➤ System Information, and on the Tools menu, clicking Registry Checker. If your Registry contains an entry referencing a file that no longer exists (such as a .VXD file), it will not be fixed by Registry Checker.

Windows 2000 and Windows XP don't include the Registry Checker tool. Instead, if you're using the Professional version of the operating system, you can use the Backup utility to create a backup copy of the Registry. (You can also export a copy of the Registry from the Registry Editor utility, as mentioned previously.)

If you're using Windows XP Home Edition, Windows automatically saves a backup copy of the Registry whenever you create a new System Restore Point. You can restore an older version of the Registry by rebooting your system, pressing the F8 key when the system loads, and then selecting

Last Known Good Configuration from the startup menu. Of course, this doesn't help you if your hard disk is trashed; exporting the Registry from the Registry Editor (and then importing it again on a repaired system) is probably the best way to go.

Rebuilding the Operating System

Whichever operating system you're using, the process of rebuilding the system with its backed-up configuration is about the same:

1. Reinstall the operating system.

2. Install any patches (for example, Service Packs) that were installed when you backed up.

3. If necessary, restore or reinstall any applications that were not backed up.

4. Restore the data and the configuration files.

This should put your system back to the way that it was when you last backed up.

Backing Up User Data

If you're concerned about data integrity, I shouldn't have to tell you to back up regularly, but. . . quick, now, how many of you have backed up your hard disk in the last seven days? Hmmm. . . not too many. How about in the last month? Last year? *Ever?*

There are two kinds of hard disk users: the ones who have had a disk failure and lost data that wasn't backed up, and the ones who are going to.

You seek to stay in the latter category as long as possible.

I can't stress this strongly enough: at the first sign of unusual behavior, back up the entire disk.

Backup Options

When hard drives were smaller, it was semi-reasonable to back up an entire drive's data to floppies. These days, however, floppies just don't cut it for mass storage. Of my workstations, the one with the *small* disk has 20GB of storage space; one of the really monstrous systems has 80GB. For just a couple hundred dollars today, you can buy a drive with 60GB or more. There's no way that I'm backing up one of those drives to 1.44MB floppies—it would take more than 40,000 floppies!

Over the years, backup options have improved dramatically. In the past, you had three choices when it came to data protection: tape drives (controlled either by their own tape controller or from the floppy controller), removable drives such as Bernoulli boxes, or floppies. These days your options include:

- Tape drives

- Removable media drives such as Zip and Jaz drives

- Writable/rewritable CDs

- A second hard drive (hard disks are cheap now: why not?)

- Online storage

I'll discuss these options in the next several sections.

TAPE DRIVES

The traditional means of backing up a large hard disk is the tape drive. These devices are simple, they're a known quantity, and they're cheap. Although some tape drives still run off the floppy controller (which is bad, as it's slow), you can also buy SCSI or EIDE models that can plug into your system's host adapter. When looking for a tape drive, keep the following in mind:

- An external tape drive may cost a little more, but you'll be able to use it to back up more than one system.

- Preformatted tapes can save a great deal of time because some tapes (such as those for early Travan tape drives) can take up to an hour to format.

- The same tape software that works with one operating system may not work with another. Similarly, the data on those tapes may not be readable with tape software used on another operating system.

Tape drives come in a wide range of capacities and formats: consumer models range in size from 500MB to 40GB and higher using the Digital Audio Tape (DAT) format.

REMOVABLE MEDIA DRIVES

Removable media drives are exactly what they sound like: they're magnetic storage units that allow you to remove the media and put in a new set, giving you virtually unlimited storage capacity. They're not the fastest storage units out there, but they're cheaper than most and work pretty well. They have other advantages as well. Because they can connect to your computer via the parallel or USB port, you can use them to back up just about any system, even laptops. Plugging a removable drive into the parallel port doesn't necessarily mean that you can't use your printer, either: it goes between the parallel port and the printer.

TIP Removable drives are also a handy way of transferring data from a laptop back to your office workstation, if your laptop doesn't have a LAN connection to the other PC.

Iomega made the first popular removable drives for the PC in the form of the Bernoulli box. Although I've still got my Bernoulli box and like it, it's outmoded technology today; its cartridges are expensive, the box itself is bigger and heavier than a Zip drive, and it offers less storage capacity (150MB with the Bernoulli versus 250MB on a Zip disk). The cartridges are physically bigger, too.

The better alternatives to the Bernoulli also come from the Iomega company: Zip and Jaz drives.

For small systems, or for those users who only want to back up part of a drive, consider the Zip drive. These units, which plug into your parallel or SCSI port, use 250MB cartridges. (Older 100MB cartridges are also available.) Zip drives are about as cheap as you'll find in the realm of largish-scale backups: the new 250MB drives cost less than $150 and the cartridges typically run $10 or so—even less in quantity. Even if 250MB doesn't back up most modern drives, backing up your key data to a half-dozen or so cartridges isn't too bad. The Zip unit weighs about a pound, so you can even take it on the road. The cartridges are about the size of a 3½-inch floppy disk, except thicker.

For larger systems, Iomega makes Jaz drives. These removable drives have cartridges that can hold 1 or 2GB—not too shabby. They're pricier than Zip drives, but they're fast—faster, in fact, than most hard drives. (A Jaz drive backs up 1.5GB of data in about 5 minutes.)

NOTE *Another obsolete backup option is the magneto-optical (MO) drive. The MO looks a lot like a pygmy CD and is a little thicker. They often come in mountable cartridges to prevent direct handling, and they are slow. Quite a bit slower, in fact, than even the first, most basic 2X CD-R drives. Today, with 24X CD-R/RW drives available for under $200, the MO is not really a sensible option.*

CD-RW DRIVES

For those with larger storage needs, consider CD rewritable (CD-RW) and DVD rewritable (DVD-RW) drives. They range in capacity from standard CDs (650MB) to DVD-RAM and DVD-RW drives that can store up to 4.7GB (with 7GB versions on the way). CD writers are quite inexpensive, starting well under $200. The DVD drives are more expensive ($500 to $600—and falling) but are well worth the expense if you are managing enough data to merit their use.

ANOTHER HARD DRIVE

Hard disk space has gotten so cheap that it's feasible to just get a second hard disk and keep a copy of your data on both disks. Depending on which operating system you're using, you'll need to do this by periodically XCOPYing your data to the second hard disk, or, if you're running Windows NT, Windows 2000, or Windows XP Professional, you can use its Disk Administrator to set up the two disks as a mirror set.

NOTE *A mirror set is a group of two physical drives that are set up so that when data is written to one, it is written to the second as well.*

Of course, an extra hard drive isn't as portable as some of the other options that we've talked about here. Another disadvantage is that, unless it's an external drive, you can't switch it to another computer easily and, if it's part of a mirror set, you'll only be able to use it on a computer that has the compatible software installed. But for a high-speed and simple backup solution, it's very workable.

ONLINE BACKUPS

With broadband Internet connections more affordable (and more common), you now have an offsite option for your data backup needs. Several online services will back up data from your hard disk to their storage servers, via the Internet. The advantages of this kind of setup are that your data is safely stored offsite (good if your house or office burns down), and the backups can be scheduled to take place automatically. The main disadvantages are price (look to pay anywhere from $10 per month to $300 per year) and, if you have a slower connection, upload time. Some of the more popular sites include @Backup (www.backup.com), BackupUSA (www.backupusa.com), IBackup (www.ibackup.com), MIXvault (www.mixvault.com), and Virtual Backup (www.virtualbackup.com). The security of your data is ensured by using various encryption schemes.

Financial companies have even gotten into the game. Intuit offers Quickbooks customers the ability to back up their financial data over the Internet. Watch to see more and more application companies offering this specialized type of backup service.

What Software Do You Need?

The answer to this question really depends on what you're installing and what operating system you're using. For example, if you're using Windows 95 and up and decide to get a CD-ROM drive, the setup process is limited to telling Windows about the new hardware (this is either done automatically, via Plug and Play, or via the Add New Hardware utility in the Control Panel) and rebooting the machine.

Other hardware varies in its software requirements, for example:

Tape drives   You'll need to install the tape controller software. This may either come with the drive or be part of the operating system.

Removable drives   They'll have installation utilities.

A second hard disk   You'll need to set it up as you would any other hard disk.

CD and DVD Rewritable drives   Like CD-ROM drives, they'll have setup software. Some operating systems will be able to detect compatible types, but you'll need to see what types are supported first.

Once the software is installed, you'll be able to back up files. When using devices such as CD-Rs, removable drives, or optical drives, you could use the DOS XCOPY command to copy files and directories from your hard disk. However, it's easier to take advantage of the graphical interface of today's operating systems. Just drag the icon from the drive you want to back up onto the icon for your backup drive—or use the Copy command found in the My Computer window.

Backup Strategies

Having the tools to back up is only part of the solution. For complete data protection, you have to make sure that you use them. I know it's a pain, but you must back up your data on a daily basis if you generate anything of importance at all. Even losing one day's work can be bad, so how would you re-create a week's worth?

First, centralize your data as much as possible. If you're responsible for backing up more than one networked computer, consider storing all data on a file server for backup. It's much easier to back up one computer than ten.

Second, create a schedule and stick to it. I've found that a rotating backup schedule that combines full and differential backups works quite well. On Monday, for example, you might do a full backup of the system. Then, on each day of the rest of the week, you can do a differential or incremental backup so that you only copy the files that have changed.

NOTE   *A differential backup copies those files that have changed since the last backup of any kind; an incremental backup copies only those files that have changed since the last full backup.*

Name each backup tape, disk, or cartridge with its date, the machine it belongs to, and the type of backup it is. For example, a full backup of my workstation might be labeled "08/05/02 Full backup of INTEVA."

Finally, don't rely on your memory. Make yourself a backup schedule and put it on the wall or someplace very visible. Posting your backup schedule in a prominent place has two advantages. First, you know at a glance when you last backed up (initial each backup after you've completed it). Second, it reminds you to back up until it gets to be a regular habit.

CARBON COPIER

Ghost from Symantec and DriveImage from PowerQuest (see the Vendor Guide on the Utilities CD for contact information) are utilities that can make a complete copy of a drive and "paste" it to another drive (although it doesn't just paste—it can also format and resize the partitions). Think of it as software that acts as a Xerox machine for hardware.

The principle is simple; they copy every bit from the source drive, cluster for cluster, to a file that the program understands, typically with some sort of compression. When you're ready to create a duplicate drive, merely plug in the drive and tell the utility to copy the selected image to it.

Both DriveImage Pro and Ghost support multicasting for distributed network installations that cut down on excessive traffic. DriveImage even comes with a very cool little tool called MagicMover. Let's put it this way: Have you ever removed an application from one machine only to have to install it on another and reconfigure everything by hand? MagicMover allows you to migrate installed applications wholesale. It can track down every instance of a drive path that the application might require and reset it to the new drive's path structure.

But wait, that's not all! If you have media large enough (multigigabyte tape or DAT backup device) you can make an image of your drive and save it for restoring later. Test a lot of machines? When one bites the dust, slap a new disk image onto it. It beats having to reconfigure everything from scratch.

Pick one. They're both great buys.

Preparing Boot Floppies

Once you have the important places backed up, make sure that you can get your computer up and running without the help of your hard drive. This means that you must make sure you have a boot floppy for each of your systems, and it should be a bootable floppy with whatever device drivers you regularly use to boot your system. This is for emergencies when your PC won't boot from the hard disk.

If you're running Windows 98/Me/2000, you were required to create a boot disk when you first installed the operating system. If you're running Windows 95, you could have opted *not* to create a boot disk. If you *didn't* create a boot disk, all you need to do is to open the Control Panel, click Add/Remove Programs, choose the Startup Disk tab, and select the Create Disk option.

Note that I haven't mentioned Windows XP. That's because Microsoft's very latest operating system doesn't provide for the creation of a bootable floppy disk. Instead, Windows XP is set up to boot from its installation CD in case of a hard drive failure. So make sure you always have your original Windows XP CD handy, just in case.

The bottom line is that, no matter which operating system you're using, you should be sure that you have a boot floppy, the installation CD, or some kind of recovery disk handy.

There are a few caveats, though. For one, the boot floppy you use for pre-Windows XP systems has no clue about CD drives. So, for these older systems, a recovery by reinstalling Windows from CD is out. (Obviously, just the opposite is true with Windows XP.) Early versions of Windows, particularly Windows 95, did not come with a CD driver, even though it shipped on a CD. You were either expected to already have a CD driver installed in Windows 3.*x* or to create one from scratch. It was a pain.

Well, Microsoft heard and obeyed. With Windows 98/Me, they shipped a floppy disk that had generic drivers for most standard IDE and SCSI CD-ROM drives. It is *this* floppy that you must prize above all. It is the single most important tool you have in the recovery of any non-NTFS system, since it can boot pretty much any system that has CD-ROM support.

Now you have access to just about any utility that will run from a CD-R that you can cram into it. Do you have several utilities spread throughout CDs and floppies? This floppy will make most, if not all, of them available without having to reboot over and over again.

But what about NT and 2000? Windows 2000 is a complicated beast, but NT is almost as easy as Windows 9*x*. Just back up the Registry (those are the SYSTEM.DAT and USER.DAT files that are located in your C:\Windows directory). Unlike Windows NT, however, simply backing up the Registry in Windows 2000 isn't enough. There are a few more variables involved that Microsoft calls the System State. These items make up the System State for a domain controller:

◆ Active Directory

◆ Boot files

◆ COM+ class registration database

◆ Registry

◆ The SYSVOL

Just run a complete backup to tape or DAT and it will include *all* of the files necessary to back up your system. You should almost never back up just a handful of the important files—always back up everything you can.

If you don't have the space, however, back up the files that you cannot afford to lose. In a worst-case scenario, you'll have to reinstall the system and all of your applications, but that's not nearly as inconvenient as losing all your work and having to do it all over again.

NOTE   *If you're running Windows XP Professional (not the Home Edition, sorry), you also have the option of backing up the System State data with the Backup utility.*

Performing Media Tests Routinely

No disk medium is perfect. Greater use of voice coil head positioning and sputtered media has greatly improved disks, but there's always the chance that a part of a platter isn't coated perfectly. Worse yet, there's the chance that all that bad treatment most PCs get has led to a disk scratch or two.

That's why there are so many "disk tester" programs around. A popular example is the Norton Disk Doctor program that's been a part of the Norton Utilities for years. Basically, all these kinds of programs do is try to read your data, sector by sector. If there's a sector that they have trouble reading, they attempt to move the data elsewhere, then mark its cluster as bad in the FAT. Of course, once an area is marked bad, the operating system sidesteps it.

There are two problems with this approach. First—through no fault of their own—it is possible for these programs to miss some of the disk problems until they're just about disasters, and second, the way they mark bad areas (the FAT) is too transient. Take a look at Figure 16.1.

FIGURE 16.1

How the operating system handles disk errors

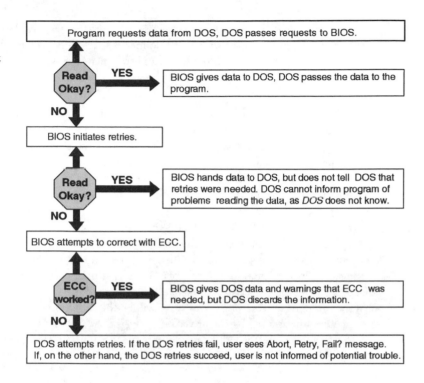

You see, with disks, there are a lot of problems that the operating system doesn't tell us about. If the operating system detects a read error, it performs several retries without informing the user. If the retries succeed, the user never knows there is a problem. Even *before* the operating system retries occur, however, the BIOS can retry. When the BIOS sees errors, it will respond by executing retries of its own or, if the retries don't work, employing the error correction hardware. (You may recall that hard disk controllers use an ECC—error correction code—that allows them to not only detect faulty data on the hard disk, but also to correct it—or a short burst of bad data anyway.) If BIOS retries have been sufficient, the operating system discovers nothing of the problem. However, if the BIOS had to use ECC to reconstruct data, it informs the operating system when it hands the data over. But believe it or not, the operating system actually has a small section of code whose job is to filter out these messages so that it can ignore the BIOS error messages.

"Ignore?" Yes. At boot, the system sets up pointers to various important areas in the BIOS. These pointers are called "software interrupts"—different from hardware interrupts, they're basically "canned" utility programs easily available to any program running on the system. One of them, INT13, points to disk routines. As provided by the BIOS manufacturer, read and write attempts with INT13 will return messages that inform INT13's caller of required error correction. During the boot sequence, however, the operating system actually substitutes some of its *own* INT13 code that ignores the fact that the sector had to be error corrected! That means that an application program can't even recover the error correction information if it *wants* to. This is dumb, as it would have been nice for Norton and the gang to be able to bypass the operating system and utilize INT13 directly, employing the fact that there had to be an error correction to warn users of disk areas that are causing problems. This also means the operating system ignores the early warnings of data and reports nothing until disaster strikes. It also means that it'll be tough for *any* tester program to do meaningful media tests, as both the BIOS and the operating system seem to discard the early warning signs.

Pattern Testing Methods

In order to generate the problems that prompt retries and ECC corrections, a program's got to *do* something—read or write the disk. So disk tester programs write and read data to/from the disk. You wouldn't think it would matter exactly *what* a test program writes, just that it writes—it seems that a test program has only to write out "Mary had a little lamb" or the like zillions of times all over the disk, then read it back, and the disk's tested. Believe it or not, however, there's a science to the choosing of test patterns.

Recall that data is encoded on the disk using either MFM (modified frequency modulation) or some kind of RLL (run-length limited). Both encoding schemes seek to merge the clock and data signals into a stream of pulses on the disk. It turns out that not all patterns are equally simple to encode and decode: some are less reliable. A read/write test writes out these problem patterns that are encoding method–specific. These patterns are called worst-case patterns, meaning that the pattern the program selects to test your drive will be the worst possible combination of 1s and 0s for the encoding that is used by the drive. This way, the sectors of the disk surface that are marginal will fail, the data on the sector will be read and moved to a different location, and the sector will be marked as bad.

File Defragmenters

After running for a while, the files on your hard drive can become *fragmented* or *noncontiguous*. This means that a given file may be stored partly in clusters 30–40 (one contiguous group) and partly in clusters 101–122 (another contiguous group). A file is said to be noncontiguous if (logically) it has more than one contiguous block of disk space.

Noncontiguous files are bad for two reasons, as demonstrated in Figure 16.2.

FIGURE 16.2

A fragmented and an unfragmented file

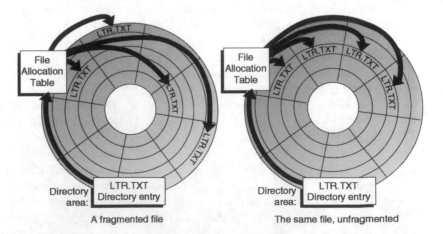

A fragmented file · The same file, unfragmented

First, noncontiguous files take longer to read. The fact that the disk head must go chasing all over the disk to read them slows down disk access. Putting the whole file together makes read operations quicker: move the head once, and all of the data can be read.

Second, you have a higher probability of recovering a deleted file if it is not fragmented. Keeping disks defragmented just pushes the odds a little further in your favor. Think of it this way: Suppose you have to find and piece together a file on a disk whose FAT has been zapped. Would you rather have to find a file in clusters 100, 120, and 1521, or a file in clusters 100 to 102? If the files are always defragmented, data recovery is easier.

NOTE *Most system utilities—and Windows itself, via the Recycle Bin—cache the most recently deleted files for improved recovery odds. It is not a good idea, though, to go about deleting things willy-nilly.*

How do files become fragmented? When the operating system needs a cluster, it basically grabs the first one available. When the disk is new, only a few clusters have been taken, and the rest of the disk is one large free area. New files are all contiguous. But as files are deleted, they create "holes" in the disk space. As the operating system looks for more clusters, it takes the first sector available. This can easily lead to a new file being spread out over several separate areas.

You can easily defragment files using the defrag utility that is included in all versions of Windows. It's located at Start ➢ Programs ➢ Accessories ➢ System Tools ➢ Disk Defragmenter (see Figure 16.3). Just fire it up and run an analysis on the disk first to find out if it even needs it. If it does, it's suggested that you do run the defragmenter. For FAT12, FAT16, and FAT32 file systems, I suggest that you close all running applications and anything else superfluous—especially screen savers. For NTFS 4 and NTFS 5, it's all right to leave things running since the defragmenter is designed to handle network server operations, but it's preferred to have as little running as possible.

FIGURE 16.3

The Disk Defragmenter utility in Windows 2000 Server

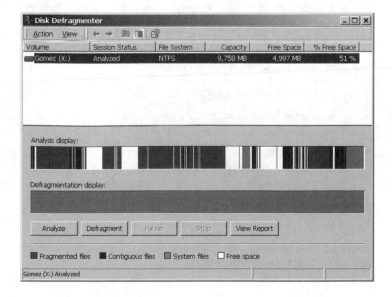

NOTE *Windows NT 4 does not come with a defragmenting tool, but ExecSoft is nice enough to offer Diskeeper Lite, a manually operated version of their award-winning Diskeeper. It's free of charge to anybody who needs it. If you want automation, you can pay for the big version and enjoy fast, convenient, nondestructive active defragmentation all the time. It even works over a network. See the Vendor Guide on the Utility CD for contact information.*

One last thing to keep in mind is that when using DOS and Windows 3.1, only fragmented files will be defragmented while the disk they are on is the boot drive. From Windows 95 on this isn't applicable, but with older systems, booting from a floppy or other device is essential if you want to defragment an entire drive, top to bottom.

Recovering Data and Fixing Hard Disks

The linchpin of the Windows space allocation system (not to mention DOS) is the file allocation table (FAT). The FAT and the directory structures allow Windows (and DOS) to keep track of the data stored on the device and where and how that data is stored. FAT troubles are what cause all of those cryptic CHKDSK woes. (And when I say CHKDSK, I'm also talking about ScanDisk, as it does basically the same thing except with a prettier interface.)

You see, CHKDSK *doesn't* check the disk, it checks the FAT. A lot of folks think that they're doing something good for their disk when they run CHKDSK. "I run CHKDSK now and then to look for bad areas on the disk," they say. That's totally wrong. CHKDSK just checks and reports on the state of the FAT. It doesn't do a new media check. ScanDisk in Windows 95/98/Me/2000/XP does perform surface testing of the entire disk, however, if the Thorough option is selected.

CHKDSK IN ACTION, SUCH AS IT IS

All the DOS command CHKDSK does when it reports numbers of bad sectors is to scan the FAT, counting up all the clusters marked as bad. Then it multiplies the number of bad clusters by the number of bytes per cluster and arrives at the number of bad bytes on the disk. Any new bad areas are not discovered by CHKDSK, but rather by one of the disk test programs that I discussed in Chapter 5, "Troubleshooting PC Problems." CHKDSK does only a few things:

- It counts up the available clusters, used clusters, and bad clusters.

- It searches the directory structure to ensure that it makes sense: all subdirectories must have the proper format (for example, the "." and ".." files must be in place). It examines the entire subdirectory tree.

- It examines all files' directory entries and FAT chains. The directory entry, you will recall, records the file size in bytes. The FAT chain tells how many clusters a file uses. Those two numbers must agree: there have to be enough clusters allocated in the FAT to accommodate the number of bytes referenced in the directory.

- It checks that all FAT chains make sense.

Understand before we go any further that CHKDSK errors do not point to hardware errors. They indicate either bad software or dumb operators.

The simplest kind of problem (simplest to repair, that is) is one where the directory or the FAT has been damaged or modified in some way that you don't want. For example, if you delete a file, it isn't really deleted—at least not at first, so it's easy to undelete it. Another directory/FAT problem is a formatted disk; believe it or not, you can often *un*format a hard disk! Yet another is something you've probably seen before, a *lost cluster.* You can repair all of these problems by manipulating the FAT and/or directory structure and leaving the data alone.

Somewhat harder to solve are the problems that come from actual disk damage in one part of the disk; these are the `Sector not found` errors. You usually fix them by telling the disk to avoid the affected area, then reloading backups on that area. Yes, I said backups; there's just no guarantee that you'll be able to recover data on an area that's been "cratered."

At the end of this chapter, we'll look in detail at how to resurrect dead drives. But first, the easy problems.

What Happens When a File Is Deleted

Sometimes carelessness and haste carry a painful price: accidental deletion of files. There are lots of ways to do this, and I need not dwell on them. Let's see how to recover from the problem.

Hold on a moment. Recover from *deletion*? Undeleting? Isn't that kind of like unpainting a house or unwatering a lawn?

Nope. First of all, understand that the operating system is lazy and doesn't really rub out much of *anything* when it deletes files.

Deletion is not done by blanking out clusters but instead by changing the first letter of the name of the file still stored in the directory. The operating system doesn't go to the trouble of erasing the clusters, so they just sit there, available for use the next time a new file is created (or an old file is expanded). *As long as you undelete before a new file is created, the file can be saved.* Figure 16.4 shows the FAT and directory entries of an example file, `HAMLET.TXT`, when it doesn't have any problems. `HAMLET.TXT` starts in cluster 100 and runs (contiguously) through cluster 104. Its file size implies that the file will be five clusters long, and indeed it turns out to be five clusters long.

FIGURE 16.4

FAT and directory
entries for a
normal file

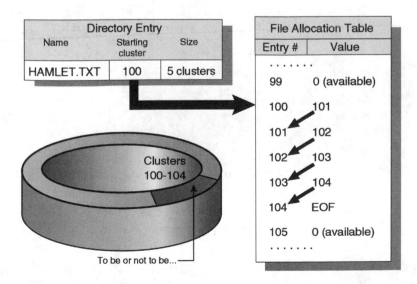

Figure 16.5 shows what HAMLET.TXT would look like if it was deleted. The first character is changed, and the FAT entries are changed to zero, making them available.

FIGURE 16.5

What happens when a file is deleted

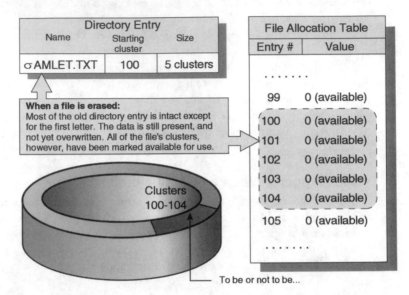

Basic Unerasing

For some reason, Windows does not have any undelete facilities except for the Recycle Bin, which only allows you to undelete files if you deleted them by putting them in the Recycle Bin. If you deleted a file from a DOS command prompt, there aren't any undelete possibilities. The process could be done by hand with a lot of patience and DEBUG, but fortunately, for both Windows and DOS, there are products to do this for you. The best known product is, of course, Norton Utilities. The original included UnDelete, and since version 3.1, it has included Quick UnDelete (QU).

NOTE *The Recycle Bin is really just another directory on your hard drive. When you trash files in Windows, you are moving those files from one folder to another.*

No matter how you undelete, please understand that it's not a guaranteed matter. Look back at the picture of what happens to HAMLET.TXT when it's deleted. The data's still there, and so is most of the directory entry, but the FAT chain has been zeroed out. What, then, does an undelete program know? Well, it knows this:

♦ By looking at the old directory entry, it can see how large the file was and so compute the number of clusters that must be reassembled.

♦ The directory entry also contains the number of the starting cluster. So you know, in the case of HAMLET.TXT, that it (1) occupied five clusters, and (2) started in cluster 100.

◆ Looking at the FAT, you see that cluster 100 is available, so you can attempt undeletion. If QU found 100 occupied, that would mean that the file had been overwritten. Not only is 100 free, but the next four clusters are free, too. Assuming that the file was contiguous before it was deleted (as most files are), QU would just reassemble HAMLET.TXT out of clusters 100 through 104. On the other hand, if HAMLET.TXT had actually been in clusters 100, 200, 250, and 301, the unerasing program would have reassembled the file completely incorrectly based on its assumptions.

It should be obvious that there's some guesswork here. Can you reduce the guesswork? Well, you've seen now that undeletion is mainly a matter of manipulating the FAT. An even easier and more reliable approach to reassembling the FAT chain would be to back up the FAT every day so that if a file were deleted, the old FAT image would be around and available to assist the unerasing program.

To summarize: when you have a deleted file that you want to undelete, don't create any new files, and undelete with a commercial program like Norton Utilities.

Here's a true story to underscore how important this is. I have a friend who's a PC support person. He worked in a department with a woman that he *really* wanted to get to know better—I mean, he wanted her to suffer a data loss in a *big* way. One day, Fate offered him his chance. She called up, explaining that she'd accidentally deleted a couple of files on her hard disk. He assured her that he could help her and raced over to her workstation with a copy of Norton Utilities. To make the program more convenient to work with, he (you guessed it) copied it to the hard disk. Arggh. The poor boy lost the data—*and* the date.

Unerasing Partially Overwritten Files

Someone calls you up. "I accidentally deleted a file," he says. "No problem," you reply, eager to don the cape and cowl and go save the day as Dataman, the finder of lost data.

"I'll be right over," you say. "Just be sure not to create any files until I get there." You arrive, and find him typing away at the keyboard. Dataman (that's you, remember) is aghast.

"I told you not to create any new files! What are you doing?" you cry.

"Oh, I lost a *PowerPoint* file. This is an *Excel* file I've just now created. That won't affect a deleted PowerPoint file, will it?"

"Users…" you mutter. No point in explaining now that there's only one FAT for the system and that it's not subdirectory-specific.

The previous is a true story, and it happened to me. Here's what I did.

1. First, as the new file was created in a different subdirectory, the original PowerPoint file's directory entry was not overwritten. I pulled it up with Norton and saw that the file was five clusters long and started in cluster 300. Thank goodness it was a file that contained text; partial text files are usually recoverable—partial spreadsheets often are not.

2. A look in the FAT showed that cluster 300 was, indeed, taken by the new Excel file. But clusters 301 through 304 were open.

3. I decided to create a directory entry with Norton and then string the FAT entries together by hand. Before I could do that, however, I needed to know which clusters used to contain the PowerPoint file. There are two approaches to getting this information: One is to just assume

that clusters 301 through 304 are the ones you're looking for. The other is to search the disk. I decided to search the disk.

4. Norton has a Text Search program. You give it some text to search for and tell it whether to search all of the disk or the deleted part of the disk. (Deleted here really means available areas. It will search just within a file, a range of sectors or clusters, or the whole disk, if you like.) In this case, I asked if there was a hard copy of the document around. There was, so I searched for random phrases that I typed in from the hard copy.

5. Once the match is found, Norton shows you exactly what it found and where it found it (cluster 20, sector 77). I kept notes on all the clusters that matched text from the hard copy and found that the text had probably been in clusters 300 (I knew that from the directory entry), 301, 302, 310, and 311—it had been fragmented!

6. Then I hand-assembled a file out of the remaining clusters.

Do be careful about using this search technique. There were also old versions of the document on the disk, and I kept finding them when trying to locate the remains of the deleted document.

So unerasing a partially overwritten file boils down to (1) finding out which clusters remain from the file and (2) building a directory and FAT chain by hand with Norton or the equivalent.

HOW PROGRAMS SAVE FILES

The way that most programs save files actually increases the chances that you can recover a lost file. Suppose I'm in Microsoft Word, working on a document called BOOK.DOC. When I tell Word to save the file, it goes through these steps:

1. It saves the file in its current state to a file with a TMP extension.

2. It waits for the entire file to be written out safely.

3. It deletes the previous BOOK.DOC and renames the TMP file to BOOK.DOC.

The effect is that not only do I have the current BOOK.DOC on disk, I've also got a whole bunch of "free" space that actually contains the previous version of the file. What about the next time I save the file—will Windows overwrite the old BOOK.DOC? Probably not. In order to minimize fragmentation, the operating system starts looking for free space after the cluster where it appeared previously. For example, suppose all of the disk's free space is contiguous. When I start up the PC in the morning, my BOOK.DOC might start at cluster 1000. Let's say that the free space starts at cluster 1500. Suppose also that BOOK.DOC is 50 clusters long. That means that the first time I save the file, the operating system will look for the first free cluster, which will turn out to be 1500. It will then save the file starting in clusters 1500–1549 and will mark clusters 1000–1049 as available. The next time I save the file, the operating system won't put the "new" file at cluster 1000; instead, it will look for a free cluster by remembering the last free cluster that it saw, which would be cluster 1550, and start from there. The net effect is that the space from 1000–1049 is left alone, at least until you run out of space on the disk or until you reboot.

I've used this to my advantage. Once, I accidentally managed to destroy both this whole book and my backups. (Don't ask.) As I very rarely reboot, I had all of my work for the past week or so sitting in the "available" part of the disk. A little search and stitch work, and it was all as good as new.

Recovering Accidentally Formatted Hard Disks

Formatting is kind of like erasing, only more so. Unformatting can be like undeleting, only a *lot* more so.

Accidental formats are a painful problem, as they zap the whole disk in one fell swoop. Remember that the DOS FORMAT command does not actually delete sector data but only deletes the boot record, the FAT, and the root directory, creating a set of blank FATs and a root directory in their place.

NOTE   One of the primary reasons disks are not completely formatted is because of the immense amount of time that would be involved in actually erasing the data. In reality nothing is ever "deleted" per se. To "erase" implies removal. Nothing is ever removed from a disk, just redefined. So, to make all data on the disk vanish you must convert the bits. Everything gets turned into 1s, and that makes the data unrecoverable and unreadable.

So the sectors are all there, but how to sew them back together? (A 40GB hard disk has millions of sectors.) There are two approaches, which I call Class I and Class II unformatters. Class I can recover an entire disk but requires some preparation *before* the format occurs. Class II, on the other hand, can't recover the entire disk but will work even if you haven't prepared the disk prior to the format.

CLASS I UNFORMATTERS

The Class I approach is to keep a copy of the FAT, the directory, and the boot record in a specific physical location. As long as you keep it up to date, the disk can be easily restored. See "Backing Up and Restoring Your MBR with DEBUG," earlier in this chapter, for how to do this.

CLASS II UNFORMATTERS

The alternative approach to unformatting, which I call the Class II approach, can only recover information in subdirectories, and even then there are no guarantees. Recall that subdirectory information is maintained in files, and those files are recognizable by their format: the ".." and "." directory entries. Unformatting programs first locate these files, then use the information in them to reassemble data files.

The subdirectory files contain a link to the first FAT entry. Since the FAT is a blank FAT, its only use is to tell you what the first sector was. It also tells you how many clusters the file used to take up. Unformatters just take a number of contiguous clusters and tack them together as the file. This means that fragmented files cannot be saved in their entirety, and garbage sectors may be tacked on the end of data files. But it's better than nothing, and your chances of success can be improved by running a defragmenting program now and then (see the "File Defragmenters" section). The defragmenting program should be run *before* formatting the disk. Defragmenting a freshly formatted disk accomplishes nothing. It also means that any files kept in the root directory cannot be restored.

Fixing Lost Clusters

Ah, yes. Lost clusters. These are the words in the CHKDSK error message that it seems everyone has seen in the past. People confuse lost clusters with bad clusters, so the lost cluster message strikes fear in users' hearts. It needn't, however: it generally just means some sloppy internal housekeeping on some program's part.

When CHKDSK reports lost clusters, it basically means loss of the pointer from the directory to the FAT. Recall that the *pointer* is just the "starting cluster" entry in a file's directory entry.

Lost clusters occur when the FAT entries for a file are written, but the starting cluster value for the file hasn't been put in the directory. Why would the FAT reflect a file's status while the directory would not? Generally, this happens because you can't report how large a file is until you've seen it and it's been stored on disk. Disk storage involves allocation of clusters, so as the clusters are allocated and filled, the FAT gets updated, little by little. The directory entry for a file, however, is the last part of the file to go on the disk, mainly because the directory contains the file's size, and the operating system can't know that until it's finished writing the file out.

As the directory entry with the starting cluster value is often the last thing written when the file is created, this means that a program that "died" in the middle of manipulating the FAT could easily have created some FAT chains without yet having written the directory entry. But why would a program "die"?

◆ The computer may have been shut off by a user in the middle of a file operation, perhaps because the user thought that turning the computer off would abort some mistake that was made. Shutting down during file operations is especially risky with Windows operating systems because they maintain a large number of temporary files when the system is operating.

◆ Buggy software. It either tries to bypass DOS and handle the FAT and directory stuff itself (incorrectly), or it just freezes up in the middle of the file write operation.

◆ Along the lines of buggy software, there are a fair number of programs that create "temporary" files for their own use. The programs are supposed to delete these files upon exit, but some don't do a very good job of erasing the files. Lost clusters result.

As I've explained, lost clusters are a chain of FAT entries—allocated clusters—with no directory entry. A lost cluster is, then, a "file with no name." (Sounds kinda like there's a country-western song in there: "Ah wrote a letter to my babe / but the disk went lame / an' now those purty words / are in a file with no name...." Okay, so I'm not Kenny Rogers.) You can see a chain of lost clusters in Figure 16.6.

FIGURE 16.6

A chain of lost clusters

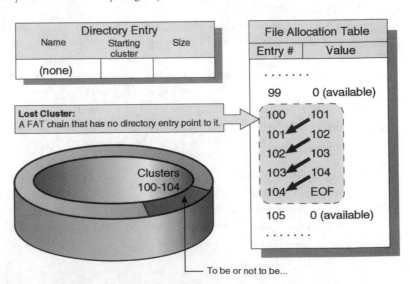

To be or not to be...

What do you do about lost clusters? First, remember that this is either a temporary file that's trash anyway or it's a file whose write operation was never finished properly. In either case, there's probably nothing of value there. The main reason that you want to clean up lost clusters is to make CHKDSK happy and to get the space back on your hard disk that those lost clusters are wasting.

If you run CHKDSK on a disk with a lost cluster, you'll see a message like this:

```
Errors found, F parameter not specified. Corrections will not be written to disk.
1 lost clusters found in 1 chain. Convert lost chains to files (Y/N)
```

Nobody ever knows what those first two lines mean, and they seem innocuous anyway. What gets people's attention, however, is the "lost clusters" part. First, CHKDSK is saying, "You have lost clusters." Most people are kind of panicky at this point, thinking, "Gee, I didn't even know I *had* clusters—much less that I could lose them." "Lost" gets confused with "bad" in most users' minds. They're not quite sure what's going on, but it seems that CHKDSK is offering to fix the problem with the "Convert lost chains to files?" question. So they say "Y" in response.

Those first two lines in the CHKDSK message *are*, in fact, important. CHKDSK, when run without the /F (Fix) option, does not actually do anything to the disk. What it's really saying is, "Even if I *say* I'm going to fix something, ignore me. I'm lying." If you tell CHKDSK to convert the lost chains to files, you'll get a response looking something like this:

```
XXXXXX bytes total disk space
XXXXXX bytes in XX directories...
2048 bytes would be in
1 recovered files...
```

You have to read the fine print: "2048 bytes *would be* in 1 recovered files." It didn't actually *do* anything. Run it again, and you'll get the exact same response. Since it's not doing anything, it can easily *keep* doing nothing forever. I know this all seems pretty obvious when I explain it, but you'd be surprised how many users wonder why there are lost clusters every single time that they run CHKDSK. The answer is simple: they always run CHKDSK, not CHKDSK/F, and so the few lost clusters that they have never get fixed.

How *would* you fix a chain of lost clusters? Just as CHKDSK says, it will convert the chain to a file. Lost clusters are just a file with no name, so CHKDSK creates a directory entry for the lost chain. The entry includes a bogus filename, FILE0000.CHK. If there's already a FILE0000.CHK, CHKDSK uses FILE0001.CHK, and so on. Those files are put in the root directory, by the way. For those people using DOS 6.2*x* and Windows 95 or later, ScanDisk will do the same thing, and you don't have to bother with the /F parameter.

NOTE *Just to make things particularly confusing, Microsoft removed ScanDisk from the latest version of their operating system. If you're running Windows XP, Microsoft recommends that you revert back to using good ol' CHKDSK. Go figure.*

Here's a *very important point:* If, for some reason, you have loads and loads of lost clusters, you may see a File creation error message when CHKDSK is trying to convert the chains to files. That's because CHKDSK puts all the files in the root directory, and the root, you may recall, only has room for up to 512 directory entries. So if you had 600 chains of lost clusters, CHKDSK would be able to create directory entries for the first 500-odd (depending on how many files you already have in the root), but would fail thereafter. The answer here is to handle the first 500-odd FILEXXXX.CHK files, then delete them, freeing up both their space and their directory entries. Then run CHKDSK again to handle their remaining lost clusters. Take a look at Figure 16.7.

FIGURE 16.7

Fixing a chain of lost clusters

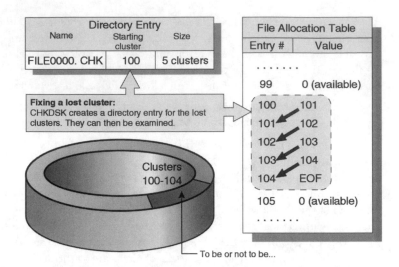

Once CHKDSK has put a filename on a chain, what can you do with this file? As I explained before, such files are usually temporary files and contain no valuable information. Data loss problems usually do not result in lost clusters.

On the other hand, it can't hurt to use a text editor or Norton to examine the file. There just may be some data that you thought you had lost.

Invalid Subdirectory Errors

As you've seen, a subdirectory's information is contained in a file. The subdirectory must have the "." and ".." files as its first entries. If they aren't there, CHKDSK assumes that the directory has been corrupted and issues a message like this one:

```
C:\PCNET Invalid sub-directory entry.
Convert directory to file (Y/N)?
```

CHKDSK is offering to take the actual subdirectory information and convert it to a file (not a particularly tough thing to do). The fact is, the operating system could work with the subdirectory without any trouble, even *if* the first two entries are corrupted.

CHKDSK, on the other hand, moves you from the frying pan into the fire. It is offering to *eliminate* the subdirectory as a directory. There are files in that subdirectory. Think about it: If we take away the directory, what do we have? FAT chains without directory entries because their subdirectory has been zapped. And what are they exactly? You got it—files with no name: lost clusters. Allowing CHKDSK to convert the subdirectory to a file instantly converts all the files in that subdirectory (and any subdirectories *under* that subdirectory) to lost clusters. Sheesh! Nice job, CHKDSK. Scan-Disk does the same dumb thing.

As I said, you can probably get to all the files even *if* the subdirectory is screwy. Try copying them elsewhere. Failing that, first print out the directory listing of the subdirectory.

Now CHKDSK sees a whole lot of FAT chains without directory entries because their directory is gone. It then converts these to FILE*XXXX*.CHK files. Your problem is to match up the CHK files with the former subdirectory contents. Your hints are the order and size of the files. The sizes may not match exactly, as CHKDSK just reports entire cluster size. The directory, which had more specific file size information, is gone, so the best that CHKDSK can do is to add up the number of bytes in the clusters and report that as the file size.

Here's an example. Imagine that you have the following files in an invalid subdirectory:

- ORDERS.TXT—2010 bytes

- NAMES.DBF—3000 bytes

Say that this is a hard disk, with 2048-byte sectors. After CHKDSK mauls the subdirectory, you find you have two new CHK files:

- FILE0000.CHK—2048 bytes

- FILE0001.CHK—4096 bytes

Notice that the file sizes have been rounded up to the nearest 2048 multiple. To finish the recovery job, first rename the files. Second, use Norton Utilities to revise the directory file size. *This is important,* as some software will refuse to read a file that has been completely recovered but has the wrong directory file size.

Or, try to fix the subdirectory yourself. You know what the subdirectory is supposed to look like—recall the ".." and "." files. Load the damaged subdirectory file with Norton Utilities and see if the damage is only minor. Perhaps you can do a little surgery and fix the problem without resorting to CHKDSK's extreme methods.

Allocation Error Message

Occasionally, you will see CHKDSK complain about an *allocation error.* That means that the directory and the FAT do not agree about how large a file is. CHKDSK's response is to assume that the FAT has better information than the directory and to just set the directory's size entry equal to the number of clusters times cluster size—the total number of bytes that CHKDSK can find for the file in the FAT. Take a look at Figure 16.8.

FIGURE 16.8

What an allocation error looks like

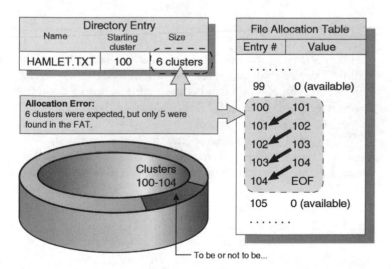

File Has Invalid Cluster Message

If a FAT chain leads to either a zero (an "available" cluster) or a "bad" marker, there's something wrong. CHKDSK responds by truncating the file at that point. For example, if a file were in clusters 100 through 104, a normal FAT chain would look like Table 16.1.

TABLE 16.1: THEORETICAL NORMAL FAT CHAIN

ENTRY NUMBER	ENTRY VALUE
100	101
101	102
102	103
103	104
104	EOF

However, if, through a software error, the value in entry 102 were converted to zero, the chain would look like Table 16.2.

TABLE 16.2: FAT CHAIN WITH A VALUE CONVERTED TO ZERO

ENTRY NUMBER	ENTRY VALUE
100	101
101	102
102	0
103	104
104	EOF

This poses two problems. The first is that 101 points to 102, indicating that cluster 102 is "taken." There's a conflict, however, because with a zero in its FAT entry, 102 claims to be available. Further, 103 and 104 have now been cast adrift: There's a chain from 103 to 104, but nothing in the directory points to it. So CHKDSK would report both an allocation error (because 102 contains 0) and a chain of lost clusters.

When CHKDSK reports an allocation error, ask yourself, "When did I last modify this file?" That's when the problem was created. If you can nail down what program or, more likely, what *combination* of programs caused the bad FAT chain to be written, you can keep it from happening again.

Cross-Linked Clusters

Another CHKDSK complaint is *cross-linked clusters*. It refers to multiple pointers into the same cluster. It means that more than one file thinks it owns a disk area: for example, cluster 14 is reported to be owned by more than one file. Figures 16.9 and 16.10 show a normal pair of files and a pair of cross-linked files, respectively.

FIGURE 16.9

A pair of normal files

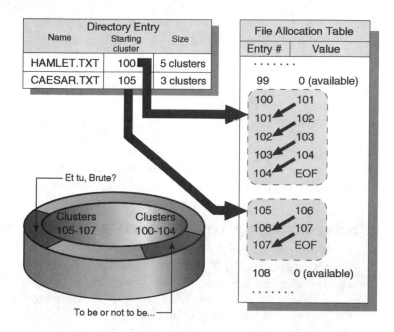

FIGURE 16.10

A pair of cross-linked files

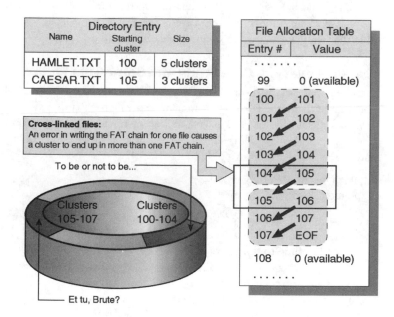

Files generally become cross-linked because there is more than one program running on the PC at the same time in some kind of multitasking mode, a mode of operation very common and familiar to Windows users today. There are different ways to handle multitasking. In an old approach, you ran two programs simultaneously by modifying DOS so that you could run two DOS environments simultaneously and then run each program under these copies of DOS. The problem starts when program 1 asks DOS copy 1 to write out a file, and program 2 asks DOS copy 2 to also write out a file. As both copies of DOS are running simultaneously, each grabs for the same cluster. Result: cross-linked files. This isn't supposed to happen with multitasking systems like Windows, Unix, and the Macintosh OS, but it still does, occasionally.

CHKDSK won't fix this for you; it'll just complain about it. To fix this, you first copy all affected files to other files, then delete the original affected files. In Figure 16.10, two files, HAMLET.TXT and CAESAR.TXT, are cross-linked. Copy them to HAMLET.BAK and CAESAR.BAK, respectively. Then delete HAMLET.TXT and CAESAR.TXT. The copied files will have as much data as can be recovered, although, in all probability, some data will be lost. Again, this is a software error, not a hardware one.

Understanding and Repairing Media Errors

Some problems aren't solved as easily as patching the FAT. Sometimes part of the drive just stops working. It could be that a part of the rusty coating on the drive that stores your data flaked off. Or perhaps the drive arm started to wobble a bit and can't get to a particular part of the disk. Whatever the reason, you may find yourself with a dead—or dying—part of a disk.

There are two very different problems facing a user of a hard disk with a media problem. First and foremost is data recovery. There *is* such a thing as "too late" when it comes to disk media errors, so, as I've said before, I strongly counsel adopting a religious attitude to backups. Second is the question, "Can I continue to use this drive?" The answer is, "Maybe," and, with some tricks you'll learn in this chapter, you can turn that into "Probably."

Data Recovery: A Case Study and Some Tips

Late one night in the distant past, I was working on the first edition of this book, concentrating on a fairly large chapter. I saved my document to my laptop's floppy disk drive (this was before laptops had hard disks) and tried to make a backup of my file (let's call it TEXT). The drive ran for a bit and then I heard a bone-chilling sound: the grinding noise of a misreading drive! Sure enough, seconds later I saw this:

```
Data error reading drive B:
Abort, Retry, Ignore?
```

What to do? I'd followed all the rules of good data integrity—I tried to back up as soon as I exited the application, but the dumb word processor hadn't verified the data when it wrote it out.

The first thing to try, of course, was *Retry*. It actually *does* work in some circumstances. Remember that your data doesn't actually disappear altogether, it just fades, albeit sometimes a *lot*. Before you get your hopes up, however, remember that Retry is almost always a wasted effort on hard disks, inasmuch as there may have been 90 retries even before you saw an error message. With floppies, it's a different story.

No luck. What now? Remember to go for the easy stuff first. I took the floppy out and resat it in the drive. (It works sometimes.) Still no luck. I tried another drive. Still no luck.

Now the chill began to grow down my back. But I knew what to do about that.

Get up and take a walk.

I'm serious. If you were in the position that I was in at that moment, you'd be panicked. Panic is a sure cause of problems.

Next, write-protect the floppy. Why? Simple. Most people do exactly the wrong thing at this point—they call in the big guns like Norton Disk Doctor. NDD is a nice program, but it's a surgeon. Surgeons get paid to *cut*. There's a time and place for surgeons, don't misunderstand me. But before you go to the surgeon, you get X-rays or MRIs, as a good doctor uses the most noninvasive techniques possible to figure out what the problem is before cutting.

And, for God's sake, *don't* run Norton SpeedDisk or Defrag! I have heard of no less than *five* cases in the last six months where someone wanted to recover data from a disk, so the "expert" first ran SpeedDisk. Arggh. In case it's not clear why this is an incredibly stupid idea, go back and read the "File Defragmenters" section. (Do I sound harsh? If so, it's because few things annoy me more than "experts" who don't have the courage to say the magic three words "I don't know," and instead just blunder along in the hopes that they can solve the problem. That may work with some problems, but, believe me, it sure doesn't work with data.) The job of these defragmenters is to move data that's in files so that each file is all in one place. That's data *in files*. In files means files that are good, readable, without problems. Delete data, and those areas that the data was once in are now available to be overwritten, and believe me, SpeedDisk will overwrite the data. Never, never, *never* run a disk defragmenter on a disk that you're trying to recover data from!

WARNING *One of SpeedDisk's features is the ability to erase all blank space. See how that could be a problem?*

Now, try to make a copy to work from. There are two approaches to copying a file, each with its own pros and cons.

◆ COPY the file elsewhere. When it gets to the bad part, and asks `Abort, Retry, Ignore?`, tell it Ignore. Ignore says to take the data, warts and all. Better to have a file with a creepy cluster or two than to have no file at all.

◆ Open a DOS window and `DISKCOPY` the disk. `DISKCOPY` "Xeroxes" a disk—it copies the disk sector by sector. The problem is that when it hits a bad sector, it skips the whole track. It doesn't try to copy it at all, and in fact if there were data on the target disk before, `DISKCOPY` doesn't even bother to delete the track. But the resulting disk has the same structure as the problem disk.

Sometimes the `DISKCOPY` command can get a few bytes that `COPY` can't, and vice versa. Remember, these are the noninvasive techniques, so you can play to your heart's content without making things worse. Try the following techniques on the copies first. If that's no good, only *then* do you actually work on the *original* damaged disk.

Again, I wanted to affect the disk as little as possible, so I first "disconnected" cluster 612 from the file. It was simple: I just used Norton Utilities' NU program and changed the FAT. The FAT previously said to go from cluster 611 to 612 and from 612 to 613. I changed it so that it went straight from 611 to 613, and I marked 612 as "bad," intending to look at it more closely later. Then I copied TEXT without a hitch. Terrific—most of the file was back, 1024 bytes to go.

Next, I went into NU and tried to read cluster 612. Now, as it turns out, clusters on a lot of floppy disks are just pairs of sectors—a sector on the bottom head and a sector on the top head of the floppy. No reason, therefore, to assume that the *whole* cluster was bad; it was quite unlikely that both sides would be damaged. So I asked NU to read the cluster, and sure enough, it got over half of it: one side (512 bytes) was totally undamaged, and some of the sector on the bad side was readable. Result: I got back about 800 bytes of the missing 1024 bytes, wrote them to another cluster, and again repointed the FAT to use the newly written cluster. Only 200 bytes remained of lost data, and 200 bytes is about a sentence or two, so it was a piece of cake to reconstruct. You'd nvr evn knw thr ws a prblem. (Just kidding.)

TIP   Of course, if you haven't changed much in your file since your last save, it may be quicker to skip all the troubleshooting, go back to the last saved version of the file, and repeat your work from there. (After all—why spend all that time fiddling with lost clusters if you only have to retype a paragraph or two?)

To summarize, when you get the dreaded `Abort, Retry, Ignore`? message:

1. First choose Retry. If that does it, copy the data and throw away the problem floppy.

2. Try another drive.

3. Stand up and walk around. Calm down.

4. Write-protect the problem floppy before going further.

5. Try to `DISKCOPY` or `COPY` the file before going further. Do the surgery on the copy if possible. Remember that `DISKCOPY` throws out entire tracks and `COPY` only loses a bad cluster.

   Do not run invasive utilities like Norton Disk Doctor or SpeedDisk. If you *do* run Disk Doctor, don't let it make any of the "fixes" that it offers to do unless you've exhausted all other possibilities. *Under no circumstances* should you run Norton SpeedDisk on a disk with files that you're trying to recover.

6. Run ScanDisk or the like to determine where the bad clusters are. Then run DiskEdit and try to read these clusters. DiskEdit will read the good data as well as the bad. Copy the cluster to somewhere else and rearrange the FAT to use that cluster. Don't forget to modify *both* FATs.

It bears repeating: as soon as your hard disk starts showing spontaneous new bad sectors, back up the whole disk *immediately* and get ready to replace it—it's on its way out.

Assuming you've recovered your data, do you throw the drive away? Sometimes, sometimes not. If you choose to keep it and try to bring it back to life, read the next section.

Resurrecting Dead Hard Disk Drives

`Unerasing` and `Sector not found` errors are really just the opening act for the big one—doing the Lazarus trick on your hard disk. Before you go further, you might review the section "Understanding the PC Boot Process" in Chapter 7, "Repairs with Circuit Boards and Chips."

Remember Your Priorities

Fixing a dead hard disk is really three different kinds of tasks. In order of importance:

1. You want to get your data off the hard disk.

2. You must make the disk hardware respond to the system.

3. You may want to make the disk bootable again and perhaps keep it in service.

Keep those priorities in mind. Many times, folks focus on the third and least important goal. Data recovery is the foremost goal, although you can't recover any data until the disk talks to the system in at least a minimal fashion.

The boot procedure is integral to the drive initialization process, the method whereby the system identifies the hard disk or disks in the PC. As I already mentioned, look back to the boot description in Chapter 7 for more information on that. I'll build on that information immediately by presenting a flowchart of the drive recovery process and follow that with a section on each phase of the recovery process.

This discussion assumes that we're talking about a drive that worked yesterday in the very same machine with the very same controller. You didn't drop it from the back of a truck, and you didn't add any new boards between then and now. If you're having installation problems, look back at Chapter 11, "Installing an IDE Hard Drive," or Chapter 12, "Understanding and Installing SCSI Devices," to find information on drive installation.

Tracing a Disk Failure

Understanding the boot process might lead you to try to first verify the hardware, then the partition, and so on—and that's how I'll do it, basically. But verifying the hardware involves popping the top, and I'd like to avoid that if possible. So I've arranged the troubleshooting steps into a master hard disk troubleshooting flowchart designed for minimum effort. You can see it in Figure 16.11. It's an overview, and I'll expand on each box, but it's still useful as a roadmap of the drive resurrection trail.

There's a lot of detail in the following sections, so it's easy to get lost. If you do, come back to this flowchart to orient yourself.

Recovery Step 1: Boot from a Floppy

Get your "toolkit" floppy ("panic" floppy, some people call it) that I suggested creating before. Boot from a floppy with whatever device drivers your system uses and then try to read C (or D or whatever). If the drive is accessible, just copy all the data off the drive. Then you can figure out why it's misbehaving with less stress. You also don't need to go any further in this chapter: just reinstall the drive.

NOTE   *If you're running Windows XP, you won't have a boot floppy, so you should boot from the installation CD instead.*

Recovery Step 2: Try to Read the MBR

The first and most important piece of data on the hard disk is the Master Boot Record (MBR) and the table that it carries within it, the partition table. Trying to read the MBR is a quick test of (1) the hardware's ability to recognize and read the drive, and (2) the integrity of the MBR data itself.

FIGURE 16.11

A simple flowchart example

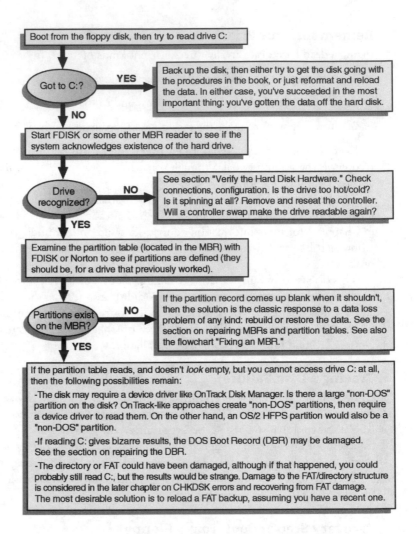

There are a number of programs that will read an MBR on a disk. The DOS FDISK program is one such program, although a fairly limited one. The Norton Utilities' DiskEdit program will also read an MBR. Even if you have one of the newer versions of Norton System Works, the DOS-based program DiskEdit is still on the CD.

Whichever program you use, fire it up and try to read the MBR. If there's something seriously wrong with the MBR, you'll get a message along the lines of, "You've asked me to read data off a disk, but the disk is not present," or the like. If you don't get that message, and it reads the MBR without complaint, skip the next subsection and go to "Recovery Step 3: Is the Partition Table Blank?"

BLAST FROM THE PAST: VERIFY THE HARD DISK HARDWARE

Many of the problems that this book talks about are hurdles that have been long cleared on newer computer systems. Of course, I still have a Toshiba T2200SX laptop (386SX20) and a 486DX33 desktop box in service that use hardware old enough to be this section's grandmother. (All right, maybe not grandmother, but aunt at the very least.) And these older machines still have those older problems. So here are a few tips on getting those old PCs back up and running—by verifying the hard disk hardware. (For tips on verifying modern drives, see the next section, "Verifying Modern Drives.")

If a cable's loose, the controller's got a couple of cooked chips, or the drive motor doesn't want to start spinning, you have a hardware problem. The BIOS generally detects that something is wrong during the initial POST (Power-On Self Test). You may see a message like one of the following. These messages are some of the first to appear when the system powers up, so watch carefully!

◆ `0 hard disk(s) found` message on boot

◆ `1701, 1780, 1781, 1790, 1791`, followed by `press F1 to continue`, and finally BASIC pops up on your screen

◆ `Drive failure, Hard disk failure`

◆ `Invalid configuration—press F1 to continue`

◆ `Run SETUP—configuration lost`

If you see one of these messages, don't panic. You can fix most hardware problems without a soldering iron and a schematic—a screwdriver and some patience will do the job in the majority of cases.

Try to resolve apparent hardware disk failures with the following steps:

1. Check that the PC has not lost its SETUP information.

2. Check that the drive has warmed to operating temperature: not too hot, not too cold. Simply touching it should tell you if it's room temperature or not.

3. Ensure that the cables are completely in place, or try swapping the cables. Also, make sure that cable terminals that do not have guide notches are matching pin 1 to pin 1.

4. Verify that the drive platters are spinning. It's not a good idea to open the case to take a peek, but you can still judge whether or not it's spinning. If it gets hot really quickly and there's no "rushing air" sound, it's likely had a catastrophic spindle crash and is not spinning. If you do hear the rushing air sound but it is interrupted by a "shingsh" sound, then you have either a head crash or a minor spindle crash. If none of these symptoms are detectable, it's either very good at hiding its own ailments or you need to look elsewhere for the problem.

5. If it is a band-stepper, watch the stepper motor to see if the head moves on power-up.

6. Reseat the chips.

Continued on next page

BLAST FROM THE PAST: VERIFY THE HARD DISK HARDWARE *(continued)*

7. Swap the controller. Older (and I mean older drives) had separate controllers. Modern drives, however, have controllers on them. Look underneath the drive and you will see a circuit board held in place by four to six screws. You'll need a #9 or #10 Torx wrench that you can get at your local hardware store for a couple of bucks. Take off the screws and remove the card, and you'll see that it's connected to the drive itself by pressure tabs. Swap in another controller from a drive of the same model (also match the revision) and plug it in.

CHECK THAT THE DRIVE HASN'T LOST CMOS

A drive won't work if it isn't recognized, as when an AT, PS/2, or 386 or later has lost its SETUP info or the information is wrong.

Did you see a message like "Invalid configuration information—press F1 to continue"? If the battery has run down on your 286/386/486 or later computer, it may have forgotten that it has a hard disk or, worse, it may misremember what kind of hard disk it has. Run the SETUP program for your computer to check to see that the computer remembers correctly what kind of hard disk it has.

But what if you've lost the drive parameters? Well, you should look it up in your documentation. You did keep track of your documentation, didn't you?

A 1790 or 1791 error almost always points to invalid configuration. AT-type systems first seek to cylinder 0, then out to the highest cylinder. If the seek to 0 fails, that's a 1780 or 1781, depending on whether it's the first or second hard drive. A 1780/1781 could be caused by a lot of things, so don't assume that the problem is configuration. If the seek to the highest cylinder fails, however, that's a 1790/1791—almost certainly a configuration problem. Why? Suppose a misconfiguration tells the system that the disk has 700 cylinders, when it actually has 500. The attempt to seek out to 700—200 cylinders further than the disk can handle—will fail, and 1790/1791 will result.

IS THE DRIVE TOO HOT OR COLD?

The drive won't work normally if it is too cold, or, less likely, too hot. Is it Monday morning? Did you just bring the drive in from the outside, if the computer is a laptop? Make sure the drive is warmed up to room temperature before you try to use it (this goes double if you're about to format it). Alternatively, could it be too hot? If a temperature probe indicates that your computer's insides exceed 110 degrees F (43 degrees C), your drive may be overheated.

One quick way to overheat the inside of a PC is if the PC's fan isn't working. Is air flowing through the chassis?

CHECK THE DRIVE CABLES

Perhaps the drive's cables have come loose or have been reconnected incorrectly, or they may just be bad. Do you have another set of cables? Give them a try. Have you been inside the computer recently? I know, I know—you didn't touch the hard drive. But removing the case could accidentally move cables around. Just reach down behind the drive and make sure the cables are snugly in place. I taught a "hands-on" class recently where we used 10 identical machines. One of the machines kept experiencing hard disk failures. In each case, all that was needed to fix the drive was to just reach around behind the drive and reseat the 34-wire edge connector, which kept slipping off.

Verifying Modern Drives

Drives these days are quite bulletproof. As such there are only a few things you need to do to check a drive. First, there's a preproblem checklist.

◆ Have you moved the drive to another bus?

◆ Have you changed any jumper settings?

◆ Was the drive, case, or anything containing the drive dropped or was it otherwise traumatized?

◆ Have you modified the BIOS settings?

◆ Did you change any drive letter or path assignments (Windows NT/2000 only)?

Then there's the post-problem checklist:

◆ Are the cables seated properly?

◆ Is the drive abnormally warm to the touch?

NOTE   *Keep in mind that drives already run warm. A drive that is uncomfortable to the touch should cause concern.*

◆ Is the drive recognized by the BIOS? That is, does the drive's name and model number appear in the POST information?

TIP   *Most big systems vendors (Compaq, Dell, Hewlett-Packard, and so on) ship their systems with a custom BIOS that displays their logo instead of the normal text-based startup. This is extraordinarily annoying to the seasoned user. If you have one of these systems, check your BIOS for a setting marked "Show POST Testing" or "Test RAM" that is disabled. Enabling the option should make the obnoxious advertisement disappear and the text visible.*

◆ Does it make noise above and beyond the normal?

◆ Does the drive click or make a scraping noise?

◆ Does the drive work but heat up quickly and become unreliable?

All of these factors may indicate a physical problem that could preclude any further steps at all. It's likely that you'll need a recovery service or, if you're extremely lucky, special disk recovery software that uses simplified drivers to minimize drive activity.

Recovery Step 3: Is the Partition Table Blank?

If the previous steps worked, stop: you needn't continue. On the other hand, if they didn't, we'll now examine the partition table (PT).

The previous step read the MBR mainly to see if the hardware was functioning in even a minimal way. Now we'll examine the PT to see if the partition definitions are still intact. (In the next step, we'll see if they make sense.) If the PT is blank, *you will not see any error messages at boot time.* DOS just ignores a nonpartitioned drive. If there isn't a bootable floppy in drive A, the system will request that a bootable floppy be inserted in drive A.

BIOS AUTODETECTION

Since all BIOS software is capable of autodetection routines today, vendors rarely, if ever, set specific drive values, instead relying on the BIOS to take care of that chore. As the BIOS recognizes and registers each drive, it prints the drive's vendor-specific information to the screen. For a typical system that has a CD-R/RW and an 8.4GB HDD, the BIOS POST might appear like this:

```
130,600KB RAM OK

ATA BUS0
Master - Maxtor 8.4GB 90845D4
Slave - None

ATA BUS1
Master - Ricoh CD-R/RW MP7040A
Slave - None
```

If you've paid attention to this over a long period of time, you'll notice immediately when something goes differently. Maybe the drive doesn't appear. Maybe it takes longer to be recognized. These two things are the biggest pointers to potential problems with a drive.

Returning to the flowchart in Figure 16.11, we're now at "Examine the partition table...." You have the MBR. Is the partition table blank—does FDISK report that there are no partitions?

The partition table should not be blank on a drive that was previously working, so something has deleted it. If it *isn't* blank, go to the next step. Perhaps the first thing you should do if you have a blank partition table is to just reboot. You fix a blank partition table/MBR as you would any data loss problem. Try to restore the data from a backup (or rebuild, if you didn't make a backup). If the drive won't take the data, reformat cylinder 0, head 0 to restore the sector IDs on that track. And if the format won't work, there's physical damage on 0/0, and you need to get a new hard drive.

The Final Step: Send Your Drive to the Mayo Clinic

Still can't get it to talk to you? Hey, look—even Dr. Kildare lost a few. If you *really* need that data, there is a last hope. It ain't cheap—from $500 to $20,000—but you can send it to a service. They disassemble the disk and remove the data, then send it to you on a CD or pretty much any media you require. These services can charge $200 to diagnose the problem, then you negotiate over the recovery cost. The negotiation will be colored by the time period you want it recovered in and how difficult the recovery is. Expensive, yes, but cheaper than going out of business.

NOTE   Note that I said, "...how difficult the recovery is." When you do send your drive to a service to be recovered, they take it and prepare the drive for recovery, making a list of recoverable files in the process. This means that they're already in a position to recover your data the instant you say go. Of course, you can opt to say no, and they'll return the drive to you, toss it out, or send it to the manufacturer. It's up to you. You only pay the $200 evaluation fee for testing, setup, and a list of files. If the list doesn't contain any files that you want to recover, at least you've only spent 200 smackeroos.

You'll find a list of data recovery services in the Vendor Guide on the Utilities CD. They may have specialties, so shop around a bit before sending your poor infirm hard disk to these wizards.

But I hope after getting through this chapter you needn't even contemplate bringing in outside help. You should now be informed enough to muddle through on your own!

Troubleshooting Recap

We obviously covered a lot of very technical information in this chapter. In case it's made your brain tired (it has mine, and I'm exposed to it every day!), here's a recap:

Remember your priorities You want your data back, you want your disk to work, and you'd like to use the drive again, if possible, in that order.

Step 1 Boot from a floppy. Try not to go too far without an emergency boot floppy. Give it time, and the "crash" will creep up on you when you least expect it.

Step 2 Try to read the MBR. This can rescue you from a lot of trouble. Remember to have a backup.

Step 3 Check to see if the partition table is blank. If you saved all of your partition table data, you can rebuild it.

The Final Step Send your drive to the Mayo Clinic. Wrap it up and send it off. These guys can often rescue data from seemingly unrecoverable drives.

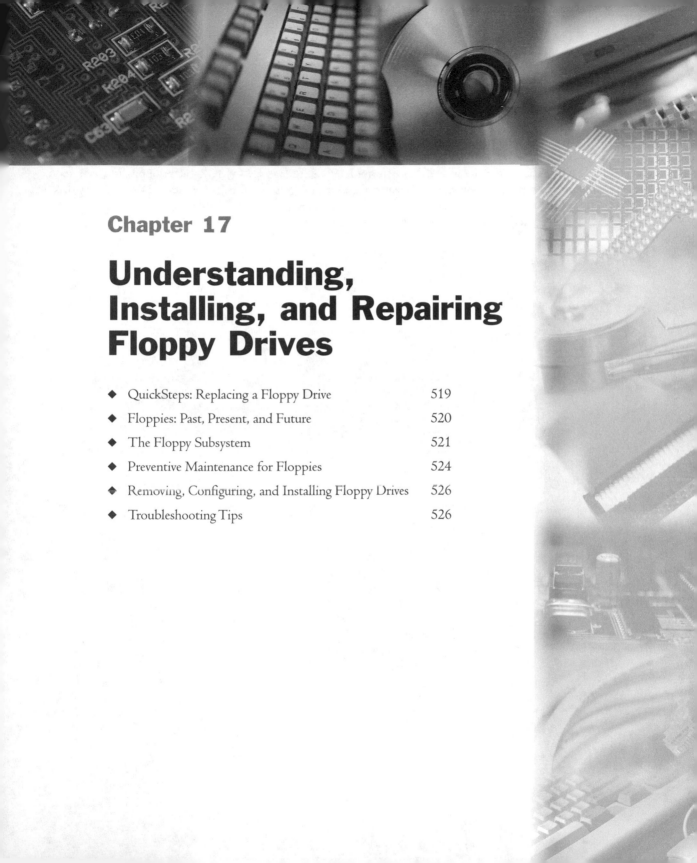

Chapter 17

Understanding, Installing, and Repairing Floppy Drives

◆ QuickSteps: Replacing a Floppy Drive   519

◆ Floppies: Past, Present, and Future   520

◆ The Floppy Subsystem   521

◆ Preventive Maintenance for Floppies   524

◆ Removing, Configuring, and Installing Floppy Drives   526

◆ Troubleshooting Tips   526

Introduction

NOW THAT WE'VE COVERED hard drives, let's take a look at floppy drives. Floppy drives are the venerable old grandfather of data storage; the original IBM PC stored data and programs using a 360KB 5¼-inch diskette. The technology has improved since then, but at its heart, floppy technology is the same as it has been since the mid-1980s. Today's 1.44MB 3½-inch floppy disks may soon be superseded by new, more efficient storage technologies, but for the next several years, floppy disks will continue to play a part in most of the computer systems that you service. In this chapter, you'll learn something about their maintenance and repair.

QuickSteps

Replacing a Floppy Drive

First, let's take a quick look at the procedures and guidelines for replacing your floppy drive.

BE PREPARED

Before you start, there are some things you'll need to perform the operation. These include:

- ◆ Nonmagnetic Phillips screwdriver
- ◆ Container to hold the removed screws
- ◆ Antistatic wrist strap
- ◆ New floppy drive

And as usual, before you work on a PC, ensure that:

- ◆ The PC is turned off and unplugged.

WARNING   Floppy drives are not especially sensitive to static electricity, but installing one requires connecting it to the I/O controller (usually the motherboard) with a ribbon cable, and the motherboard can be easily harmed by electrostatic discharge (ESD). Wear that antistatic wrist strap.

TIP   Before replacing a floppy drive, make sure the problem is not with an individual disk. Try the drive with several disks.

1. To replace a floppy drive, first turn off the PC's power and remove the cover.
2. Disconnect the ribbon cable and the power connector from the drive. Notice which direction the red stripe on the ribbon cable points (toward the center or the outside of the drive).
3. Unscrew the screws holding the floppy drive in place (unless it is held in place by clips and drive rails; in that case, release the clips). Pull the drive out of the PC.
4. Install the replacement drive by using screws or clips, as the case requires.
5. Connect the power cable (the small Berg one).
6. Connect the ribbon cable with the red stripe going to pin 1. The drive may have a little 1 next to one end of the connector to tip you off; if not, connect it in the same way that it was connected on the old drive (see step 3).
7. Turn on the PC and test the new drive by trying to read a disk from it.

Floppies: Past, Present, and Future

Believe it or not, floppy disks weren't always a standard part of the PC; and with program sizes and data storage requirements getting larger by the minute, there may soon come a time when floppy drives will be a thing of the past. For the present, however, you'll find that floppy drives are standard equipment in just about any desktop or tower PC that you buy. Laptop and notebook PCs provide built-in or optional external floppy drives.

In this section, you'll learn about the history, current status, and possible future of floppies. Later you'll get the details about the floppy subsystem and what to do when things go wrong.

In the Days before Floppies

I didn't buy my first four microcomputers (a Netronics Elf, a TRS80 Model I, an OSI Challenger 1P, and an IBM PC) with floppy disk drives. Floppies cost too much money at that time, so most of us micro users in those days used cassettes. *Cassettes?* Yup, cassettes. There was a standard interface called the *Tarbell interface* that let micros read and write data to standard $40 cassette machines at a rate of 600bps. They were a pain and not very reliable, but there wasn't much else available.

NOTE Cassettes were so popular, in fact, that the IBM PC was shipped with a cassette port, and the first PC I bought didn't have a floppy drive or floppy controller. I couldn't afford them anyway at first, but eventually I could. When the system booted up without an attached drive, it defaulted to a version of the BASIC language stored in ROM. This was, again, no great innovation—most microcomputers shipped with BASIC in ROM in the late '70s and early '80s. To this day, if you have a PS/2 that can't boot from the floppy or the hard disk, BASIC appears on the screen. You're seeing the same old cassette BASIC that's been part of the IBM PC system ROM since 1981.

The Post-Floppy Era

Virtually all PCs have included floppy drives since the mid-1980s. Floppies are a marvel of construction. Because they possess so many moving parts, it's surprising that they are the least bit reliable, but in fact they are fairly solid these days (with some exceptions). If you asked a PC repairperson in the early '80s, "What's the least reliable part of the PC?" you'd be told that it was probably a toss-up between the floppy drive and the daisy-wheel printer. But nobody uses daisies anymore, and their laser-based replacements are quite trouble-free. There's good news in the floppy department also, since floppies are less troublesome than they once were. This is partly because they are manufactured better and partly because they're used less; hard disks are the medium of choice for many home users and most corporate users. The floppy's role nowadays is mainly as a program distribution medium and an archival device. Since most hard disks can't travel, most computers still rely on floppies to get information from the outside world. (By the way, ask that repairperson what's the most troublesome part of *today's* PCs, and the answer will be the hard drive.)

Floppies used to be de rigueur in a system because they were the only removable disk type available. If you needed to "SneakerNet" a file from one PC to another, a floppy was your only option. (LANs and the Internet have introduced two alternatives to file transferring since then.) Over the last couple of years, a revolution has been afoot to omit regular floppy drives from the newest systems because better and more reliable removable storage devices have become available, including LS-120 (super-floppies), Zip drives, writeable and rewriteable CD-ROMs and DVD-ROMs, flash memory cards, and others. Flash memory cards have gained in popularity lately because they are the perfect go-between for PCs and PDAs, digital cameras, and MP3 players. The phenomenally popular iMac computers have led the way by making the floppy disk an external option rather than an integral part of the package. So you will gradually begin to see fewer and fewer floppy drives over the coming years, until eventually they go the way of the computer cassette tape drive. In that sense, we really are living in the "post-floppy" era!

Floppies Nowadays

Floppy disks are cheap enough these days that they're basically disposable; if a disk comes up with an error, just throw it away. Floppy drives are cheap these days too—it's cheaper to replace a floppy drive (around $15 to $20) than it is to spend an hour of a technician's labor troubleshooting the broken one.

Because of the popularity of CD-ROM as a program distribution medium, floppies are not used as heavily as they once were. Once, it was possible to ship commercial software on floppies. That still happens occasionally, but having to load 30 floppies to install one's word processor is a bit silly. A single CD-ROM is not only more convenient for the consumer, but also much cheaper to manufacture than the floppy disks required to hold the same amount of data.

The Future of Floppies

No discussion of floppies would be complete without a little look at where they are now. Several companies are vying to set the next standard in floppies. Toshiba, among other companies, has put forth a 2.88MB floppy disk standard, but it has received a less-than-enthusiastic welcome in the market, and you will seldom see such drives or disks for sale. (Most BIOS programs support them, however, so if you happen to have one, you're not stuck.) Another contender is the SuperDisk (a.k.a. LS-120), which can read and write to a 1.44MB floppy disk and can also read and write special "super floppies" that hold up to 120MB. Most computers made in the last several years include BIOS support for these. Zip drives, which hold up to either 120MB or 250MB per disk, have also cropped up as a popular floppy drive alternative.

However, the floppy drive as a whole may soon be a thing of the past. The newest PC standards do not even call for a floppy drive. Increasingly, rewriteable CD-ROM drives, Zip disks, and CompactFlash cards are taking over the functions that used to be relegated to floppy disks, including backup and data transfer. And, as I said earlier, new software almost universally comes on CD-ROM these days, rather than on floppy.

Will the floppy drive go the way of the dinosaur? It's likely. But for many more years, you will probably continue to upgrade and repair systems with floppy drives.

The Floppy Subsystem

Although floppy drives are an "aging" technology, you will still frequently encounter them in the systems you work with for many years to come, so you'll need to know something about how they work. In the rest of this chapter, I'll explain the mechanisms behind a floppy drive and its disks and tell you a little about troubleshooting and repairing floppy drives should you decide that it's worth your while to do so.

The floppy disk subsystem is, like the rest of the PC, modular. That's useful because you will see that you can use this modularity to "divide and conquer" in order to solve problems. The subsystem consists of four parts: the floppy disks themselves, the drive, the disk controller, and the cable connecting the drive to the controller.

Part 1: The Floppy Disk

A floppy, when extracted from its case, looks like a thin 45rpm record, only quite a bit smaller. It's a Mylar disk with iron oxide affixed to it. (Who would have imagined that we'd rely every day on a data storage medium made out of the same plastic that weather balloons are made of with rust glued onto it? Maybe that's why I can't read my backups on rainy days.) We worry so much about dust getting on our hard disk surfaces that we seal up the disk drive. Should we have the same concern about floppies? Is there some way to "clean" a disk? Those of us over, say, age 30 may recall getting out the Discwasher and cleaning an LP prior to playing it. For some people, a ritual like this was comforting. For those people, I must sadly report that no such ritual occurs with floppies.

Floppies are stored inside their own Discwasher: a semi-rigid case lined with fleecy material. As the disk rotates inside the case, the material picks up any dust. The case has a hole cut in it so that the disk can be read/written without having to remove it from the case. In general, there is no need to clean a floppy disk. You can see some floppy disks in Figure 17.1.

FIGURE 17.1

Floppy disks

A reasonable life expectancy for a floppy disk, according to disk manufacturers, is about three to four years. There are, of course, better and worse disks. There are different coatings on higher density disks, generally incorporating less iron oxide (a cheap ingredient) and more cobalt or barium (expensive ingredients). Table 17.1 lists the specs for the three types of 3½-inch floppy disks out there—double-density (DD), high-density (HD), and extra high density (ED), as well as the older 5¼-inch DD and HD models. Of these, you will probably encounter only 3½-inch high-density; the other standards are all but obsolete.

TABLE 17.1: FLOPPY DISK SPECIFICATIONS

	5¼″ DD	5¼″ HD	3½″ DD	3½″ HD	3½″ ED
Tracks per inch	48	96	135	135	135
Bits per inch	5876	9646	8717	17,434	45,868
Primary coating	Iron oxide	Cobalt	Cobalt	Cobalt	Barium
Thickness (micro-inches)	100	50	70	40	100
Recording polarity	Horizontal	Horizontal	Horizontal	Horizontal	Vertical

TIP *You should not archive data on a floppy disk that you expect to need after several years because floppies tend to develop surface errors over time that make certain sectors (it's a crapshoot which ones) on the disk unreadable. Try to store important archives on CD-R, or at least Zip disks.*

Part 2: The Floppy Drive

For many years now, 3½-inch, 1.44MB floppy drives have been the standard; you'd be hard-pressed to find one of the old 1.2MB 5¼-inch drives anymore except on the very oldest PCs. Even if you did find such a drive, finding a floppy disk for it that has not gone bad would be an even greater challenge! Remember, the average life of a floppy is only a few years. The very first 3½-inch floppy drives were 720KB in capacity, rather than 1.44MB, but again, such drives will appear only on systems 10 years and older.

A 3½-inch drive connects to the drive controller (normally built right into the motherboard) with a ribbon cable, the same as a hard drive or CD-ROM drive (except the ribbon cable the floppy drive uses is slightly narrower). It also requires power. Recall from Chapter 9, "Power Supplies and Power Protection," that a floppy disk uses the smaller, Berg connector from the power supply and not the normally chunky connector.

TIP *Most power supplies come with only one Berg connector, so if you have two floppy drives, you will need a power cable adapter. Your computer's motherboard or power supply/case may come with such an adapter; if not, you can pick up an inexpensive one at a computer store.*

Part 3: The Disk Controller

Whenever a computer wants to interface with an outside device, it needs a controller to act as a go-between to allow the outside device—a floppy, in this case—to talk with the CPU. XT-type machines generally had a separate controller board. AT-type machines usually put the floppy and hard disk controller function on the same board. Most motherboards today put the floppy and hard disk controllers right on the motherboard. A single floppy controller can handle up to two floppy drives.

Part 4: The Cable

The last piece in the floppy subsystem is the cable that connects the controller to the drive. Cables sound insignificant, but this one isn't: I've fixed a pile of floppy problems by swapping cables. The drive is connected to the controller by a 34-wire ribbon cable. Most of the cables have three edge connectors: one for the drive controller, one for drive A, and one for drive B (although very few computers nowadays have a second floppy drive). Since the cable is 34 wires wide, you'd think that the interface between the floppy and the controller is a parallel interface—8 bits wide—but it's not. Floppy-to-controller interface is serial, transferring 1 bit at a time.

It's important that you plug your floppy drive into the right connector on the cable. The connector from the drive controller to B (the middle connector on the cable) is a "straight-through" cable—that is, pin 1 on the drive controller side is connected to pin 1 on the floppy side, pin 2 is connected to pin 2, and so forth. The connector to A, at the other end from the controller, has a twist in it, however. This twist distinguishes A from B; you can see this in Figure 17.2. The ribbon cable has three connectors: one on one end and two on the other end. The lone end goes on the controller. The one in the middle goes on drive B. The one on the other end goes on drive A. If you're likely to forget (as I am), get a marker and write "controller," "B," and "A" on the appropriate connectors before disassembling the whole thing.

FIGURE 17.2

Floppy cable with twist for the A drive

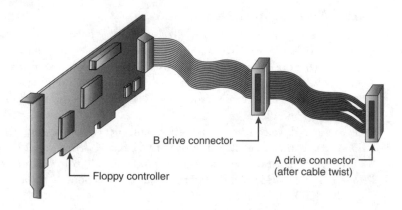

B drive connector

A drive connector (after cable twist)

Floppy controller

It never hurts to have a couple of extra ribbon cables around. The cables are inexpensive and available from many mail-order houses or computer discounters, so it's easy to keep an extra one around.

Simple Preventive Maintenance for Floppies

Failure of the floppy drive can be a scary, potentially disastrous thing if you have stored some critical data on a floppy disk. (That's not a very good idea, by the way. Never put your only copy of something important on a floppy.) What can you do to lower the probability of a floppy disaster?

Anyone who has a VCR and rents videotapes on a regular basis probably knows about the need to clean the VCR's heads. Something like that can be done for the floppy as well, although you'll probably never need to. And a few diagnostic tests can point out upcoming floppy problems.

To Clean Heads or Not to Clean Heads?

Like your VCR, floppy drives have an electromagnetic read/write head that does most of the drive's work. In the process of accessing the disk, the head may rub some of the coating off the disk and onto itself. It seems reasonable, then, to assume that head-cleaning kits are good things.

When you can't see something, you get superstitious about it. We can't see the junk on floppy heads (or the data on magnetic disks, for that matter), so we play it safe and purchase a floppy head cleaner to ward off floppy evil spirits. Once we've procured the cleaner, however, our first question is: *How often should I clean the floppy heads?*

The instructions on the head cleaner say to do it every week. That doesn't seem to be a good piece of advice; shoving a floppy head cleaner in a drive could misalign a disk head. The floppy cleaner is a relatively thick piece of cotton shaped like a floppy. Worse yet, some floppy cleaners are *abrasive*—they wear away some of the floppy head with every use. (One has to look askance at this procedure.

Scraping away some of the head to find a clean part seems somewhat like using sulfuric acid to clean one's teeth.)

Personally, I clean my heads only when the drive fails. I have some computers on which I've *never* cleaned the heads, and they work fine. My recommendation: clean the heads only when you start experiencing read/write errors. (Of course, for only slightly more money than a good-quality head-cleaning system, you could have a whole new floppy drive, so weigh your options.)

As I hinted before, *be careful* when choosing a floppy head cleaner! Don't buy an abrasive cleaner—make sure it uses a cotton floppy and some cleaning fluid.

By the way, there's an issue related to cleaning the heads called *demagnetizing* them; it's done with some audio recording heads. People sometimes ask me if floppy heads need to be demagnetized—they don't.

Defending Disks

Did you ever notice the "do not" cartoons on the back of a floppy disk jacket? Do not expose the disk to heat, cold, magnets, or dust, they warn. They lead you to believe that floppies are very fragile items. A little practical experience with disks teaches you that it isn't really true. Yes, disks must be taken care of, but you needn't get crazy about it. Don't put them on the radiator or leave them on a shelf that gets three hours of direct sunlight every day. Don't store them under the roof leak or use them as coasters. Given the choice, store them upright, stacked left to right rather than on top of each other. And keep them away from magnets.

When it comes to temperature extremes, you have to be concerned about *thermal shock* (which you read about in Chapter 4, "Avoiding Service: Preventive Maintenance"). If your portable computer has been sitting in the back of the car in freezing temperatures overnight, bring it in and let it warm up before using it. Just a little heat expansion/contraction can temporarily realign your drives or make the motors respond a little differently. In addition, condensation from rapidly warming items can build up on the electronics, and the moisture can cause electrical shorts. Extreme temperatures can damage the disks; vendors claim that disks should never be stored below 50 degrees or above 125 degrees. Cold isn't as much of a problem as heat. I've ordered software through the mail and had it sit outside in January in my mailbox for a week and have had no problem reading the disks.

Dust, smoke, and dirt can cause damage to the head and/or to a disk. Everybody knows smoking is not good for you, but you may not know just how bad it is for your drives. If you're in a dusty environment, think about getting a power supply with a filtered fan. Running the air through a filter before pushing it through the system removes the vast majority of the dust particles.

As you also read in Chapter 4, magnets—both the permanent and electromagnetic type—can cause permanent loss of data on hard or floppy disks. Something I have yet to understand is the little plastic paper clip holder with the circular magnet near the opening. Why is the magnet there? Are people afraid the paper clips will get out if not magnetically restrained? (As one of the members of Monty Python might say, "Are you suggesting paper clips are migratory?") One day, you'll put a floppy on top of the paper clip holder. It'll be sad. Or you'll use one of the paper clips—now magnetized by their proximity to the magnet—to clip a document to a floppy. Arggh.

WARNING *Watch out for less-obvious magnetic sources, too. Unshielded stereo speakers, for example, have powerful magnetic pulls. And some older telephones have magnets in them, too.*

Removing, Configuring, and Installing Floppy Drives

You generally won't repair drives; you'll replace them. That means it's most important to be able to rip 'em out and slap 'em in.

Removing Floppy Drives

Floppy drives are removed in three steps:

1. Remove screws from the mounting brackets.

2. Remove the power connection.

3. Remove the data connection.

I covered the physical extraction part pretty thoroughly in Chapter 2, "Disassembling the PC," so I won't repeat it here.

Installing Floppy Drives

Installing a floppy drive is just the reverse of removing one, except that the drive must be configured. To configure a new floppy, you must:

◆ Connect it to the twisted connector if it's drive A or to the nontwisted connector if it's drive B. You can't have a drive B in a system without a drive A, so your primary floppy should always be A, at the opposite end of the cable from the controller.

◆ Attach a power connector. Again, you want the smaller power connector, the Berg, for the floppy drive.

NOTE   *Most PCs use a standard size floppy drive, but some proprietary systems (the Compaq Presario is particularly notorious in this regard) use a nonstandard floppy drive with offset positioning that requires you to buy a replacement directly from the original manufacturer (and typically at two to three times the cost of a generic replacement!). So if you are replacing a floppy drive in someone else's PC, it pays to examine the old drive before buying a replacement for it.*

Troubleshooting Tips

The mechanical nature of floppy drives makes them prone to a host of ills. In this section, I'll catalog a few of them.

A Disk Cannot Be Read

Pop a disk in the drive, try to read it, and the message says `Data error reading drive A`, or `Sector not found reading drive A`, or perhaps the dreaded `General failure reading drive A`. Such a message is even better than your morning coffee to get the ol' blood pumping, particularly if the disk contains your only copy of the football pool.

What to do:

1. Press R for Retry. Sometimes it'll work. Ignore the painful grinding sounds. After three or four unsuccessful retries in a row, you may safely conclude that it's not going to work. But if

the drive seems to read a little bit of data before repeating the error, keep trying; you may be able to kludge the drive into reading the file—perhaps just this once—before it goes kaput completely.

2. Remove and replace the floppy disk. I've seen 3½-inch drives that are unreadable until you take out the disk and put it back in. The hub centering is fairly critical.

3. Take out the floppy disk and try it in another drive. The read/write head on one machine may be aligned just slightly differently than on another, and that little difference might make one drive read a disk that another cannot.

    If one drive can read a disk that another cannot, either the disk drive's head could be misaligned, or the floppy disk could have been formatted by a different disk drive and *that* drive's head was misaligned. Try to find the drive that created the disk. (If it's the one you've been fooling with, obviously this advice isn't too useful.)

4. If you *still* haven't solved the problem, you're basically in the same boat as someone who's suffered a media failure on his or her hard disk. See Chapter 16, "Care and Feeding of Hard Drives," for information on hard disk data recovery.

The Drive Refuses to Function

When the drive won't read or write properly, there are a bunch of possible causes. I am assuming here that this is a drive that worked fine yesterday and to which you haven't done anything that would obviously cause drive problems.

1. Did you see a floppy drive controller failure error on the screen when the system booted up? Such a Power-On Self Test (POST) error message means that drive A did not respond. The system no longer realizes that you have a floppy drive. This means that your CMOS battery has failed (in which case it would recognize only floppy drive A, not B), the floppy controller has failed (in which case both floppies would be dead), the floppy drive itself has failed, or the cable is bad.

2. If there was no POST error, try other disks in the drive. If only one disk gives the drive fits, the problem more likely lies in the disk.

3. Clean the disk drive heads. It's easy and takes only a minute. (But see my earlier caveats about drive cleaning in the "To Clean Heads or Not to Clean Heads?" section.)

4. Try to format a disk. If you can format a disk all right but that disk is unreadable by other drives, your drive head is probably misaligned. If it's misaligned, toss it. New floppy drives are about $15 to $20 today, and realigning a floppy drive is not a project, it's a career.

5. Finally, swap the relevant components: the controller, cable, and drive. Swap only one component at a time, and when swapping a component doesn't solve the problem, reinstall the original component and swap another one.

6. Again, don't overlook the lowly cable. Cables can get nicked when you're installing boards, replacing drives, or just removing the cover. How bad that is depends on which line gets

nicked. One cable on an old laptop that I once owned kept the change line from working, so that when I put in a different floppy, the file listing still showed the previous disk I was looking at. It takes only a two-minute swap with another cable to find out for sure. For more information about change lines, see the section "The Drive Shows Phantom Directories" later in this chapter.

INTERMITTENT DISK ERRORS CANNOT BE SOLVED BY CHANGING THE DRIVE

Or the controller, for that matter. Suppose you get periodic data loss and have changed the drive and controller—what next? The power supply. Malfunctioning power supplies often show up as gremlins in the system. Try swapping the power supply.

DISK ROTATION SPEED

Small variations in disk speed (plus or minus 1 percent) are okay, but greater differences can make the floppy nonfunctional or dangerous.

Dangerous? Yes. Many years ago, when copy-protection schemes were in vogue for programs distributed on floppy disk, I was asked to install a copy of a program I was using. It was a perfectly legal copy. When I went to install it, it informed me that it was an illegal copy and refused to load. I tried installing it on other machines. It didn't work. The software publisher first told me that I was lying or mistaken, and finally sent me another master disk.

What had happened was this: my floppy drive's speed was slightly off—not so different as to render it unusable for normal uses, but enough to upset the finicky copy-protection system on the program disk. Worse, the copy-protection system being used on the disk permanently altered disks that it saw as illegal copies so that they would always seem bad. That was why the disk wouldn't run on other computers.

The Drive Shows Phantom Directories

Imagine that you do something, give a DIR command, for example, on a floppy. Then you remove the disk and put a different disk in the drive. You do a DIR again, and you see the *directory of the previous floppy, not the one in the drive now!*

If you see this symptom on a computer, this is a RED ALERT! Don't use the thing until you get the problem fixed. Reason: say you put a floppy in the drive and do a DIR on it. Then you put a different floppy in the drive and write some data to the floppy. *The PC writes data to the new floppy using the old floppy's directory!* That means the newly written file is probably okay, but everything else on the floppy is trashed. (Let me tell you about how I lost four pages out of a chapter in a book I wrote many years back.) Where does this problem come from? It's something called the *change line signal*. I mentioned this earlier in the chapter, when I was talking about cables.

Time for a little history. Back in the old days, when floppies were the major storage medium for micros, software designers wanted to squeeze the most performance from those floppy drives, mainly because they were pretty low-performance. (I know, you were expecting one of those boring old-timer stories about how I used to have to write my own BIOS hacks and make cables using my teeth to bare the wires and so on. Not just now, but buy me a couple of Flowers' Bitters sometime, and I'll tell you about how I used a matchbook cover to repair a hard disk and saved the free world in the process.) One way to increase performance was to avoid, wherever possible, rereading information on a floppy. What information gets read the most? The directory and FAT. Way back before DOS even existed, there was an operating system called CP/M—Control Program for Microcomputers. To get better speed, some CP/M applications read the directory only when a disk was first inserted in a drive. That meant that if you were going to swap a floppy while in WordStar, you had to tell Word-Star about the switch, or it would trash your floppy. It was a real pain.

The original IBM PC folks remembered the CP/M experience and (I'm guessing) decided that they'd sacrifice a little speed for reliability. So the IBM PC and XT (but not all XT clones) BIOS always read the disk directory and FAT prior to doing anything dangerous—they didn't assume that the floppy stayed in the same place. And all was well with the world.

But some makers of compatibles, looking to outdo IBM performance-wise, sold computers with slightly different floppies; these floppy drives had something called *change line support*. No big revolution: in fact, it had been around since the CP/M days. One of the signals from the drive to the controller was a "change line" signal—it signaled that the floppy door had been opened since DOS had last looked at the drive. (Back then, floppy drives had little door flaps you opened and closed.) If the change line was activated, DOS would reread the floppy; if not, it wouldn't bother. That meant that writes did not need to be preceded by directory reads, as in the IBM XT case.

The IBM AT design team, looking to show the competition who was boss, added the change line feature to the AT. That means there is a minor difference between XT floppy drives and AT floppy drives: The XT drives don't really use line 34 on the floppy edge connector, but the AT drives use 34 as the "change line" line. To complicate matters, this question of whether change line support is really needed is determined by the type of BIOS in your computer. Some XT clones need it; some don't. Some AT clones need it; others don't. The IBM AT needs it, as does every other computer made since then—including the computers you work on today.

If you have a computer that needs change line support and you install a floppy drive that lacks it, the computer will display the phantom directory (and possibly trash a floppy someday). These days, however, it is virtually impossible to buy a floppy drive without change line support, so you don't need to worry about it. We're talking ancient history lesson here, with the XTs and ATs and such.

Now you know what change line support is and that some computers need it (including almost all the PCs that are still alive today). Suppose you find yourself with a change line problem—phantom directories. What do you do?

First, check the floppy cable. Try substituting a different floppy cable, and see if that doesn't clear up the problem. You can also try the following:

Fool the controller into thinking that there have been lots of change line signals. If you're a techie with cable-building capability, construct a cable that disconnects line 34 on the drive side and cross-connect lines 34 and 20 on the controller side. Line 20 is activated with each head step, so the controller will believe that it is seeing many change line signals.

Ctrl+C between disk accesses. This one works only if you're working at a DOS prompt (which few of us are anymore). Remember to do a Ctrl+C keystroke, and you've changed the floppy. It forces DOS to reread the disk directories. Not great, but a good emergency measure.

Floppy Troubleshooting Recap

There are several things to try before you give up on a floppy drive:

◆ Always try other disks in the drive before assuming that the drive itself is bad.

◆ If the floppy drive light comes on and stays on all the time, you have installed the ribbon cable backward.

◆ If the floppy drive light does not come on at all, check the power connector.

◆ If you see a floppy drive controller error at startup, check the BIOS to ensure that it recognizes your floppy drive. If the CMOS battery fails, it may forget about all drives except the first floppy drive (A).

◆ If you switch disks but the PC still shows the previous contents of the drive, check for a damaged ribbon cable.

◆ Intermittent disk access errors often indicate a bad power supply in the system.

◆ Data errors reading the disk can mean a bad disk. You might also try cleaning the disk heads by using a disk-cleaning kit.

◆ Try to format a disk. If it works but that disk is then unreadable by other drives, the drive head is probably misaligned. Throw the drive away and get a new one.

◆ If replacing the drive does not help, try replacing the cable. If that doesn't work, the problem is probably the disk controller. If it's built into the motherboard, you may need to disable it in the BIOS and install a separate I/O controller card to use instead.

Now, let's move on to the subject of printers. In the next chapter, I'll talk about troubleshooting printers in general. Then, in the following two chapters, I'll get specific about particular printers: inkjet and laser printers.

Chapter 18

Troubleshooting Printers

◆ QuickSteps: Connecting and Testing a Parallel Printer   533

◆ Printer Maintenance   534

◆ Printer Interfaces   537

◆ Common Problems and Solutions   542

◆ Troubleshooting Tips   545

Introduction

PRINTERS, LIKE ANY OTHER mechanical devices, can be real maintenance headaches. Whenever you have moving parts, they have the potential for wearing out, breaking down, or otherwise conking out.

However, it may surprise you to learn that most printer problems are *software* related. That is, the operating system or a particular program isn't sending the right information to the printer to get the desired printout. (You know the old saying—garbage in, garbage out!) For example, when a printer spits out endless sheets of paper with mysterious junk characters on them, it's a good bet that the printer driver is not speaking the printer's language.

I'll spend the next couple of chapters talking about printers. This chapter eases into the topic by discussing the general preventive maintenance you can perform on a printer, the various interfaces that printers use to connect to a PC, and some general printer troubleshooting. Then, in upcoming chapters, I'll cover inkjet printers and laser printers in greater detail.

QuickSteps

Connecting and Testing a Parallel Printer

Here are the basic steps for connecting a printer. For in-depth coverage on printers and how to troubleshoot printer problems, refer to the rest of this chapter.

BE PREPARED

Before you start, there are some things you may need on hand. These include:

- ◆ Printer's manual

- ◆ Computer's manual

- ◆ Printer's setup software, if you're running Windows

- ◆ (Optional) Extra parallel cable to swap with, in case there is any doubt whether the current one is working

    Before you connect a printer to a PC, make sure that:

- ◆ The computer is turned off.

- ◆ The printer is turned off.

1. Set up the printer and turn it on. Run its self-test to confirm that it's working properly.

2. Turn the printer off. Then connect the printer to the computer with a parallel cable. If you want to use ECP or EPP, make sure you have a parallel cable that is capable of that.

3. Turn on the PC. If needed, enter the PC's BIOS setup program and make sure the parallel port type is set correctly (ECP, EPP, Bidirectional, etc.).

4. If you're using Windows, run the setup software that came with the printer to install its printer driver.

    or

    If you're using a DOS-based program, configure the program to use the printer.

5. Print a self-test using the printer's Windows driver or utility program.

    or

    In a DOS program, create a simple document or drawing and print it as a test.

Printer Maintenance

Keeping your printer in top condition means giving it a little maintenance attention now and then. Printer maintenance varies depending on the type of printer, so let's look at the upkeep for some of the most common printer types.

Dot-Matrix Printers

If you're still using a dot-matrix printer, you are either seriously strapped for cash or you need to print multipart forms. I'll assume the latter. Because dot-matrix printers strike the page with small rods (called *needles*) that protrude from the print head (printers that use this type of technology are known as *impact* printers), they can print through multiple layers of carbon (or carbonless) copies, and some businesses need that capability.

NOTE *The only kind of impact printer you'll find for sale these days is a dot-matrix printer. Daisy-wheel printers, which used to rule the marketplace 10 to 15 years ago, are all but extinct. (Okay, you might find a daisy-wheel printer at an estate sale, or in a mysterious forgotten crate in a government warehouse.) And even dot-matrix printers are over the hill.*

To clean a dot-matrix printer, use a dry, soft cloth to clean both the paper path and the ribbon path. Most manufacturers suggest cleaning every six months, because the ribbon path can build up a film of inky glop that causes the ribbon to jam. Before doing this, go to a drug store and buy a dispenser box of clear latex gloves. Use them when working on the printer so that you don't have to wash your hands for hours to remove the ink. (But don't use them when you're working on chips and boards—that latex can build up some mean static.)

TIP *When you're working on a printer, it's easy to get ink on yourself and your clothes. Here's a tip that will help you clean up. A friend once told me that hairspray will remove ink from fabric. So another friend and I experimented with her hair mousse stuff—you know, the spray that you use to make your hair defy gravity? It did nothing. Then we tried some Aqua Net, a hairspray that hasn't changed since Jackie Kennedy used it in the White House. The result? We found that cheap hairspray works a lot better than the expensive stuff. Spray it on the fabric and rinse with cold water. A little soap will pick up the rest.*

You can also vacuum out the paper chaff periodically from the inside of the printer. The continuous-feed paper used in impact printers is somewhat more prone to leaving dust behind than single-sheet paper is. You may find it unwieldy to use the same vacuum on the printer as you use on the living room carpet. Purchasing a tech vacuum of some sort may be best because it is smaller and easier to use in tight areas, and it won't suck key tops right off your keyboards.

On an impact printer, the print head moves back and forth across the page, which means there is probably a drive belt. Determine if there is a belt-tightening mechanism for the printer and find the correct tension values. Keep a replacement belt on hand. (Believe me, they're no picnic to find in a hurry.)

WARNING *Some dot-matrix printers have ribbon cables that are used to carry the data to the print head. They often look like drive belts, but they are definitely not. Tighten these, and they'll usually break. If they do, you can say goodbye to your printer.*

Most impact printers never need to be lubricated. In fact, oil can do considerable damage if applied to the wrong places. If you thoroughly disassemble the printer, you will probably have to lubricate various points as you reassemble it. If you intend to do this, I strongly recommend that you get a maintenance manual from the manufacturer.

Here's a tip that will extend the life of both the ribbon and the print head: put some WD-40 lubricant on a used ink ribbon. Let it soak overnight. It'll produce good output the next day, and you won't damage the print head—WD-40 is a good lubricant for print heads. Let me stress, however, that this applies only to ink ribbons. If you have any other type of printer, this will not work. So don't go soaking that laser toner cartridge in anything, okay?

The expensive part of a dot-matrix printer that dies is the print head. Luckily, almost all dot-matrix printers these days have a *thermistor* (basically, a temperature sensor) that detects when the print head is getting too hot and shuts the printer down until it cools off. To avoid excess heat buildup around a dot-matrix printer, avoid stacking things around it—leave a clear path for airflow on all sides.

Replacing the print head is not economical on many printers because of the high price that manufacturers charge for replacements. For example, the print head replacement for a good-quality wide-carriage dot-matrix printer might cost $100 or more. Fact is, in almost every case, it makes no sense to replace a dot-matrix print head unless you need to print multipart forms or have one of the very expensive, high-speed dot-matrix printers. You can buy a brand-new printer for about the cost of a replacement dot-matrix print head.

Inkjet Printers

Inkjet printers have come a long way since their introduction back in the '70s. In fact, they've come such a long way that the next chapter will discuss them in more detail.

At one time, inkjet printers clogged pretty regularly because the ink would dry in the tiny holes that make up the print heads. Today, the jets are designed to resist drying, and some print heads are protected by a rubber boot that keeps the holes from drying out. Also, on some models, the heads are built into the ink tanks so that when you replace an empty tank, you're also getting new jets. This keeps the print on these printers looking like new.

Still, if you let an inkjet printer sit too long without using it, the ink in the jets (and/or in the ink cartridges) will dry out, and one or more colors won't print. This can result in some odd-looking printouts with amusing (but definitely not lifelike!) colored stripes. If this happens, run the printer's built-in head-cleaning utility. You can do this by pressing certain buttons on the printer itself, or in most cases through the printer's driver in Windows 95/98/Me/2000/XP. (Select Start ➤ Settings ➤ Printers, or choose Printers from Control Panel, then right-click the printer in the Printers window and choose Properties. Look for the cleaning command, usually on the Utilities tab.) After cleaning the heads, run a nozzle test, which you might be able to do by using the printer's buttons or through its Properties box in Windows. The nozzle test prints some basic geometrical pattern of lines on the page in each of its colors, so you can see which color, if any, is failing to print. Sometimes several cycles of cleaning (up to 15 cycles on an Epson) followed by testing are required to clear out the dried-up ink residue.

One trick I recently learned for clearing up Epson ink cartridges is relatively easy. If after several cleaning cycles the pattern still doesn't print correctly, try removing the ink cartridges and immediately replacing them. This has worked for me on several occasions when the print head wasn't printing correctly after the printer had not been used in several months.

You may see advertisements for refilled ink cartridges, or even kits that promise to let you refill the cartridges yourself, but this is seldom a good idea. True, it can save you money, but on many models, as I mentioned, the heads are built into the ink cartridges, so that you get new heads when you get new ink. This is by design. If you continue to print with the old heads tankful after tankful, the print quality will definitely suffer, and you may harm your printer.

NOTE *On some inkjet printers, moving the ink cartridges into view so you can replace them can be a real exercise in coordination. On certain Epson models, for example, you have to hold down two little tiny buttons simultaneously for several seconds, then press another button. Check the printer's manual to find out the procedure for your specific model—that's usually the only way to find out (other than visiting the manufacturer's Web site and searching for the info).*

All-in-One Combos

If space is a luxury to you but you need printing, faxing, copying, and scanning capabilities, you may have already considered an all-in-one combo. Some products that fall into this category are the Hewlett-Packard OfficeJet series, the Brother Multi-Function printers, and the Canon MultiPass series. Here, many options are available. The original designs of these machines had thermal printers that produced copies that were a little difficult to read, and you could count on the fact that they would fade within a few months. Today, most of these combos come with built-in inkjet printers (either black-and-white or color), but some of the more expensive models come with laser printers. Maintenance of the printer portion is similar to the methods discussed in the preceding section on inkjet printers, or in the following chapter, which discusses troubleshooting and maintenance of laser printers.

The all-in-ones also come with either a sheet-fed or flat-top scanner that also serves as a copier and fax input device. Some of the combos are designed to work with the fax modem on your PC, while others connect to the phone line directly so that you can receive faxes while your PC is off.

Although all-in-ones provide a space-saving advantage, there is one drawback. If you experience trouble with one of the components (printer, scanner, or fax) and need to send it in for repair, you also lose the ability to use the other features during that time. Still, all-in-ones are a convenient and cost-effective solution to purchasing each component individually.

Thermal-Transfer Printers

When you were a kid, did you ever make pictures by coloring with crayons onto a piece of heavy paper and then using an iron to transfer the colored wax to another piece of paper? (If not, just nod politely and keep reading—I'll get past the "when you were a kid" stories in a minute.) Thermal-transfer printing (known as "T-wax" printing in the trade) works something like that. Very hot pins are pressed onto a wax- or wax/resin-coated ribbon, and the wax or resin melts and is transferred to the paper beneath it. The difference is that the paper has to go through the process four times, once for each color (typically cyan, yellow, magenta, and black). This kind of printer produces excellent quality color images—better than an inkjet, and arguably better than color lasers—but are rather expensive in terms of consumables. You won't find them for sale in the typical office supply store— they're a specialty item. (Refills for them are also generally not available at your regular retail outlets.) Some of these also require special thermal paper, which of course is a lot more expensive than standard paper.

The issues involved with thermal-transfer printers are much like those with other printers: keep them cool and keep them plugged in. If you're having problems with print quality, such as smearing, you might try using another manufacturer's paper or ribbons.

Laser Printers

Laser printers are important enough that I'll devote an entire chapter to them later in this book. As a result, I'll limit my discussion of them here.

The laser printer is very similar to a copy machine and amazingly reliable. You may be surprised to learn that many different brands of laser printers operate using the same basic innards. The most common laser engine is made by Canon. Many of the HP LaserJets, Apple LaserWriters, and Canons (obviously), as well as the older QMS Kiss and others, are built around the Canon engine. They need very little maintenance except for a new cartridge every few thousand copies or so. The cartridges cost in the neighborhood of $70 to $120, and, according to HP, contain all that is needed for routine maintenance. So, every time you change your cartridge, you'll perform routine maintenance like cleaning the corona wires and paper pickup pawls.

It's okay to buy recycled toner cartridges, but make sure your refill company completely rebuilds the insides, including replacing the photoelectric drum. Avoid the "drill and fill" vendors—they don't replace the insides, and using that kind of refill will lead to a lower-quality print image and may damage the laser printer. If you don't refill the cartridges, many manufacturers provide a way to mail in the used ones for recycling (and sometimes a rebate).

Laser printers require proper ventilation and a fair amount of power. Other than that, don't pour any Cokes in them and they last a long time. Never ship a laser with a toner cartridge in place. It can open up and cover the inside of the laser with toner. And don't take the toner cartridge out and wave it around, or toner might spill out and make a mess. You will also want to wipe out any stray toner in the printer's insides every time you change the toner cartridge.

TIP   To get the last little bit of life out of a toner cartridge, you can take it out and shake it gently from side to side. But don't turn it on end, and don't shake it up and down, or toner might spill out.

On some models, a new toner cartridge comes with a long, thin felt strip mounted on a piece of plastic. You drop this into some slot or other on the printer, replacing the old and cruddy strip that was there before. Not all laser printers have this, though.

Printer Interfaces

For years the parallel port was far and away the most common type of interface between printer and computer, and even though it is slowly being replaced by USB, it's still important that you understand the basics of the parallel port. It's also important that you're aware of the other ways that a PC can communicate data to a printer.

Parallel Ports

The vast majority of printers connect to a PC via the *parallel port*, a female 25-pin connector that's typically built right into the PC. In an ATX design, it's a built-in part of the motherboard that sticks out of the back of the PC; in an AT design, it's a connector attached to the motherboard with a ribbon cable. As with other peripheral troubleshooting, you should start your diagnosis by checking this connection at all junctures. Is the parallel port functioning? Is the printer cable connected firmly at both ends? If it's an AT system, is the little ribbon cable inside the PC from the connector to the motherboard snugly plugged in?

THE HISTORY OF PARALLEL

The parallel port was originally devised as a high-speed, low-cost alternative to a serial port for printer interfaces.

Until 1976, serial ports were the established way of hooking up a printer to a computer. The problem was that serial port hardware was expensive. Adding a serial port to a computer could raise the computer's price by anywhere from $250 to $1000. That got in the way of selling printers, and so a printer company, Centronics, decided to do something about it—they created the Centronics parallel interface, which is essentially the parallel interface that PCs still use today.

There were some drawbacks to the parallel interface, however (and there still are today). While RS-232 (another term for serial cables) allows cables of more than 50 feet in length, the Centronics interface is reliable for only 15 feet—actually, less for modern ports. RS-232 is bidirectional and quite flexible as to the kind of things it can support. Originally, the Centronics parallel interface was designed to be unidirectional and was aimed only at printers. RS-232 is serial, employing only two wires for data; Centronics is an 8-bit parallel interface, with eight wires for data. The circuitry required to implement a parallel port, however, is much simpler than that required to implement a serial port because data in your computer is also parallel. The computer simply transmits the data as it is, so the cost of making a parallel port is much lower. The result was a Centronics interface that was easy to cobble together for just a few dollars and offered terrific throughput—as much as 500,000 bits per second (bps) compared to RS-232's 20,000bps.

TODAY'S PARALLEL PORTS

Since then, the parallel port has continued to evolve. First, some PCs and laptops offered bidirectional parallel ports. Then those bidirectional parallel ports were further modified to become *enhanced parallel ports* (*EPP*) and *extended capabilities ports* (*ECP*). ECP is more commonly used for printers, while EPP is more common for other parallel devices, such as Zip drives and scanners. These newer port types let you print with the speed of the wind, between 500,000 and 1,000,000bps. They also let printers form a lasting relationship with computers based on communication; the printer not only listens to the computer but also communicates its own problems—being out of paper or having a paper jam, for example. Using an ECP port, you don't need to go to the printer to discover that it didn't do its job—a message will pop up on your monitor telling you so.

To use an ECP port, you need four things: an ECP or EPP/ECP port, an ECP-capable printer, an IEEE 1284–compliant parallel cable, and Windows 9x/2000/Me/XP. Once you have these installed, you will begin to print with unparalleled speed (excuse the pun). If your parallel port's controller is built into the motherboard (as almost all are these days), you can set its mode in the BIOS setup program. Normally, the BIOS lets you choose a parallel port mode, such as Output Only (the old, unidirectional mode), Bidirectional (a simple bidirectional mode), ECP, or EPP.

The expanded capabilities of the parallel port have led to the parallel port's use in more areas than just printers. For a brief time, the parallel port saw use as a file transfer interface (for removable media drives or external CD-ROMs), as a connection to a local area network adapter, or as a connection to an input device such as a scanner. This arrangement usually caused more trouble than it was worth, and when USB devices arrived on the scene, the parallel port began to fall into disuse.

The biggest trouble with using the parallel port as a general-purpose port is that you have only one parallel port on most systems, so how can you have more than one parallel device at once? Well, you can continually switch cables, or you can attempt to share the port among the devices. Some nonprinter parallel devices, such as scanners, have a built-in pass-through that lets you connect the parallel devices in a sort of daisy chain, like SCSI. This arrangement works poorly on some systems and worse on others. Generally speaking, inkjet printers have a harder time sharing a parallel port than do other printer types, and different BIOS settings for the parallel port can sometimes make the difference between sharing success (marginal at best) and failure.

Windows 9x/2000/NT/Me/XP has support for up to three parallel ports, called LPT1 through LPT3. The term *LPT* is a carryover from the days of large mainframes, when the only printer that a computer would talk to (other than a Teletype typewriter) was a line printer (LPT). Parallel port addresses assigned to the parallel ports are hex 3BC, 378, and 278. The PC has a peculiar process for relating I/O addresses to LPT addresses. First, it looks for address 3BC. If there is a port at that address, it assigns it LPT1. If not, it looks for 378 and, if it exists, assigns *that* to LPT1. If that's not available, it finally tries for 278. Once LPT1 is assigned, it looks (in the same order) for LPT2 and LPT3. This means that if you put a first parallel port into a machine and the port has address 278, you'll end up with an LPT1, even though 278 is intended for LPT3. But install a second port at 378, and the next time you boot up, the 278 port will become LPT2. Most systems have only the one port, LPT1, but you can easily add expansion boards with extra ports (both parallel and serial).

USB Ports

Some newer printers will attach to your computer by a Universal Serial Bus (USB) port. You learned about the USB interface in Chapter 3, "Inside the PC: Pieces of the Picture." To use a USB printer with your PC, you need two things. First, verify that your PC has USB ports. Many Pentium II and all Pentium III/P4 motherboards support USB. You may find one or two USB ports on the back of your computer. If your motherboard doesn't support USB, you can also get a PCI USB adapter card. See Chapter 33, "This Old Computer," for more information.

Second, you need an operating system that supports the USB interface. Windows 98/Me/2000/XP offer USB support, while Windows 95/NT do not. USB supports Plug and Play installation, and you can unplug the USB cable from the printer to the PC while your PC is on. This is called *hot-swapping*. Typically, the first time you plug the printer into your PC's USB port, Windows 98/Me/2000/XP will automatically detect the connection and prompt you to install the printer drivers and related software. As a result, installing a USB printer is virtually painless. You have no IRQ settings to worry about, and you can be up and running in no time.

USB devices have some distinct advantages over serial or parallel ports, and it is expected that all other ports will be completely replaced by USB in the near future. Theoretically, you can connect up to 127 peripheral devices, such as mice, modems, keyboards, and printers, on a single USB port, and most newer PCs have two USB ports. However, there is a slight catch. Let's say you have a USB keyboard connected to one of your USB ports and a USB mouse connected to the other. Now you want to add a USB printer. Each USB device that you connect to your PC has to get power from somewhere. So you'll need to purchase a USB hub to connect additional peripherals.

Even though more USB 2.0 peripherals are appearing on computer store shelves every day, at this time USB 2.0 printers have not yet been released. While USB 2.0 is 40 times faster than USB 1.1, the main reason printer manufacturers continue to use USB 1.1 is that it is more than fast enough for printers. Still, it is inevitable that in the future all USB devices will be 2.0; so, if you find yourself with a USB 2.0 printer and a computer with an older USB 1.1 connection, it's no sweat. Just plug the 2.0 device into the older USB connector and it will work fine. One of the wonderful features of USB 2.0 is its backward compatibility with the previous USB.

QUICK USB TROUBLESHOOTING TIPS

Since a printer that is connected to a computer using a USB interface has a few wrinkles its parallel port counterpart doesn't, here are a few tips to use when you're troubleshooting USB-related problems.

Read the manual before installing. USB printers have one thing in common: they are very picky about how you install them. Some of the printers require that you install the software before connecting the printer; others ask you to connect and power on the printer partway through the installation. The key point here is that, unlike parallel printers (which you can typically install in just about any way, shape, or fashion without affecting the final result), USB printers will act weird or not print at all if you do not install them by the book. I just recently installed an Epson Stylus Photo 1200 without first reading the instructions. I ended up with a printer that could print the test page flawlessly but, when I tried to print from an application, the print job would disappear. Which brings us to the second aspect of the uniqueness of USB: you usually cannot correct a problem by reinstalling the printer correctly; you will need to visit the printer manufacturer's support Web page and read the detailed procedure for uninstalling the USB component of the printer (which is not deleted when you delete the printer in the printers folder). The procedure for my improperly installed Epson consisted of 40 steps (groan).

Check the version of Windows you're using. While most of the newer software will warn you if you are trying to install your USB printer on a version of Windows that does not support USB, not all installation software does. Put simply, if you are using Windows 3.1, Windows 95, or Windows NT, the USB connection won't work. Officially, Windows 95 (OSR 2.*x*) supports USB, but my experience has been that the USB support on any version of Windows 95 is questionable and not recommended by most printer manufacturers.

Check the USB controller. If your computer is relatively new, ignore this, but if you have one of the first computers to support USB, this step might be worth the effort. When Intel produced the first USB universal host controller chip for motherboards, they didn't have all of their ducks in a row, so to speak. As a result, the motherboard didn't support USB. At the time this chip was being used, no operating system supported USB and there were no USB-related devices, so nobody knew that the controller didn't quite work. To check it out:

1. Right-click on the My Computer icon and open System Properties.

2. In Device Manager, open the Universal Serial Bus and double-click on the Intel 82371SB PCI to USB Universal Host Controller entry. Does the controller have a different number? If so, you're okay; that means you have a newer controller. If not, go to the next step.

3. On the General tab, see if the hardware version is 000. If it is, you have the aforementioned chip. There is no workaround; you need to upgrade the motherboard.

If you can print but features are missing, try reinstalling.   While this issue isn't restricted to USB, it is seen most often with USB devices. You go to use some specific feature of the printer that is clearly described in the manual and discover that the feature is missing. This is what happens when you've installed the printer incorrectly. It occurs most often in later operating systems, such as Windows XP and Windows Me. What happens is that Windows detects the USB printer when it powers on and installs its own, somewhat primitive printer drivers. You will need to uninstall the printer and try again.

Now let's look at serial ports.

Serial Ports

The original printers connected to computers via serial (RS-232) ports. It's still possible to connect printers serially today, provided the printer has a serial interface (hardly any still do). But I don't recommend it. Serial port printing can be very slow, and with today's graphics-heavy print jobs, that can mean frustration and waiting around.

Some printers used to have both a parallel and a serial interface so, in theory, you could hook up two PCs to the same printer, each through a different interface. However, because of the speed issue with serial, I recommend instead that you share the printer through some other means—perhaps using a switch box or a network.

Infrared Ports

For members of the "virtual office" who have no desk but only a laptop to carry around and plug in as needed, there's a way to eliminate at least one of the cables you need to plug in: printers with infrared ports are available. Rather than requiring a parallel cable to connect the printer to your computer, a ray of infrared light shines between a transceiver on the computer and one on the printer.

NOTE   *There's no reason why desktop computers can't use infrared printers as well, but most desktop machines are not equipped with infrared capabilities. In contrast, most laptops, PDAs, and pocket PCs do have this capability.*

Data travels between the computer and printer via an infrared connection. Light and electric impulses all pulse at a certain rate per second; this rate is called the *frequency*—the more pulses, the higher the frequency. Signals with higher frequencies can transmit data more quickly (each pulse can carry a bit of data). However, they have a shorter range and are more prone to interference than lower-frequency signals because anything that interferes with the signal will affect more data than it would if there were fewer pulses per second. Infrared light has a high frequency. Thus, the computer sends a beam of infrared light to the receiver on the printer. The devices have a pretty good range, but it is usually limited to line of sight. (You can't print from an office around the corner.)

If you're having trouble with a wireless printer, check the following:

- Are the infrared ports on the printer and computer both clean and unblocked?
- If you're using a notebook, is the infrared port active? It is activated through the BIOS during startup. By default, it is off.
- Does it help to move the printer/computer to one side?
- Did someone stand between your printer and computer during the print job?

Other than that, troubleshooting an infrared printer is much like troubleshooting any other printer. The tricky thing about wireless printers is making the connections.

Network Printing

Most businesses today don't want to be tied down to providing a printer to every single PC—or, conversely, limiting each PC to printing on only one printer. Thus was born the network printer.

There are two ways to use your LAN to print. One is to connect the printer to a PC and then share that printer on the LAN. Although the printer "belongs" to the person using that PC, anyone on the network can send printer jobs to it. The other way to share a printer is to hook it directly into the network. This requires a network-capable printer. Some printers come network-ready; others can be made ready by installing an upgrade card in them. (This capability varies among manufacturers, but HP offers a JetDirect card for some models that make them network-capable.)

There are, however, a few caveats to using these marvels of technology. First, as with any network device, you must be using the same protocols on your server that you use on the printer's network interface, because the printer driver is installed on a server and then shared. Standard protocols supported are TCP/IP, NetBEUI, IPX/SPX, EtherTalk, and Data Link Control (DLC). Unlike other protocols, DLC is used only for printing and mainframe access in the Windows environment, so you may not have it installed. You must also be sure that the protocols are configured correctly—if you are using TCP/IP, for example, you must have an IP address and a subnet mask for the printer. It is also a very good idea to be sure that your network cable is securely plugged into the card and hub.

Common Problems and Solutions

It's hard to discuss printer problems and troubleshooting without delving too deeply into the specifics of the thousands of models out there. I don't have the space to do that (or, truthfully, the time to get to know all those printers), but I can pass along some generic pieces of advice. And, remember, I'll tell you more about lasers and inkjets in the next two chapters.

Isolate the Problem

As always, try to isolate the problem. Something in the computer or its software? The printer interface? The cable? The printer? Is the printer plugged in, cabled, and *online*?

The steps I use are as follows:

1. Check whether the printer is online, is plugged in, has paper, and is turned on.
2. Turn the printer off and then on again. Reboot the computer, and try it again.

3. If it is a network printer, check the network configuration (such as the IP address and subnet mask on TCP/IP).

4. Use the printer self-test to see whether the test page prints correctly. The printer's manual usually tells how to do this.

5. Check that the software is configured for the printer and that the correct drivers are loaded for it in Windows (if used).

6. Swap the printer cable to make sure your cable isn't faulty.

7. If it is a network printer, try printing from another computer.

8. Swap the printer with a different one of the same model, if possible.

Some other things to check right off the bat:

◆ Do a DIR from the command prompt, and then try a screen print using the Print Screen key.

◆ If you are troubleshooting a network printer, check the queue at the server to be certain there are no stuck jobs. If there are, then purge the queue.

◆ Check the printer manufacturer's Web site to see whether an updated driver is available for your version of Windows or for the particular DOS-based program you want to print from.

Check Cable Lengths

The role of cable lengths in noise and interference has been discussed before in this text. But another problem is overly long cables. Serial cables aren't supposed to be longer than 50 feet, and older parallel cables should not exceed 6 feet. Newer IEEE 1284 (ECP and EPP)–compliant cable can go to 15 feet. If you're using long cables and getting mysterious errors, the cables may be the culprits, but it's not very likely.

There are parallel port extenders—check Black Box (www.blackbox.com, or the Vendor Guide on the Utilities CD for additional contact information) to find them. An extender will let you run your parallel cable up to a kilometer.

Something I've noticed in recent years is that modern parallel port chips don't put out all that much power. I used to be able to share a printer between two computers with an A/B switch, but now it's often the case that it won't work unless the A/B switch has amplification power. The moral seems to be to keep those parallel port cables as short as possible. It is also not recommended to use an A/B switch with laser printers unless you have a powered switch.

Set Emulation Options Correctly

A common problem for DOS, Windows 3x, and some NT users was the selection of the printer's emulation mode. Many printers used to emulate a HP LaserJet of some kind. Unfortunately, some vendors' idea of "Hewlett-Packard compatible" was a blend of fact and fantasy. Anyway, in those days if you had your Acme Laser Printer set up for HP emulation, you didn't tell your software you had an Acme—instead, you told it you had an HP. This sounds simple, but you'd be surprised at the number of people who used to get tripped up on that one. With the current releases of Windows 9x/Me/2000/XP, the detection and selection of the printer driver is done automatically.

Another emulation option is international capability—that is, the ability to specify what country the output is being prepared for distribution in. Many printers speak foreign languages. If you set up your printer for British, you may get the pounds sterling sign rather than the dollar sign. Oh, and by the way, most printers nowadays don't have Dual Inline Package (DIP) switches; they support some kind of software setup. Many of the newer printers not only support multiple emulation modes, but they know enough to automatically switch modes based on the driver being used to print. Check the printer's documentation to see how your printer handles the emulation selection.

Check Ports, Their Settings, and Connections

As you know, printers can have a USB, serial, or parallel interface. On the PC, the only visible difference between the serial and the parallel port is that the parallel port has a female connector and the serial port has a male connector.

Electronically, they are radically different, however. The parallel interface uses different voltages and handshakes from the serial interface. Most printers today come with only parallel, or, less commonly, with both parallel and serial. As I mentioned before, given the choice, use USB or parallel because they are cleaner and faster interfaces.

As laser printers get faster and, more particularly, support higher resolution, more high-speed interfaces will appear. For example, Apple uses an AppleTalk 230,000bps interface to an Apple LaserWriter. Some printers interface with SCSI, and some use proprietary CPU-to-printer interfaces.

Some printer cables fasten with clips; others fasten with screws. You should tighten the screws if your cable uses them; don't just plug it in and hope nobody comes along to bump it. I once saw an Okidata printer that was printing consistently incorrect characters. I tried to understand the problem by comparing the ASCII codes of the desired characters to the codes actually printed. I found in each case that bit 6 was *always 1*. It turned out that the wire for line 6 was not fully seated. Securing the connector did the job.

I found a similar problem with a broken wire in a cable. Here's an example. Suppose I try to print *Hello* but get *Iekko*. Compare the codes of the desired and actual characters in Table 18.1.

The *E* and *O* aren't affected, but *H* and *L* are. Notice that in all cases the low bit is *1*.

TABLE 18.1: A SAMPLE PRINTER CABLE PROBLEM

DESIRED CHARACTER	CODE	ACTUAL CHARACTER	CODE
H	01001000	I	01001001
E	01100101	E	01100101
L	01101100	K	01101101
L	01101100	K	01101101
O	01101111	O	01101111

The serial port, being the versatile interface that it is, allows you to set several communication settings for it:

- Speed (1200, 2400, 4800, 9600, 14400, or 19200)
- Parity (Even, Odd, or None)
- Number of data bits (7 or 8)
- Number of stop bits (usually 1 or 2)

You can set these settings in the Properties box for the port (from Device Manager) in Windows. However, you are more likely to find a serial printer used in a very old system that doesn't have Windows 9x. In that case, you can do it at the command prompt, like so:

```
MODE COM1: speed,parity,data bits,stop bits,p
MODE LPT1:=COM1:
```

In the first case, an example would be:

```
MODE COM1:9600,N,8,1,P
MODE LPT1:=COM1:
```

meaning "9600 bits per second, no parity, 8 data bits, 1 stop bit." The *P* means that it's a printer.

If you are using an ECP parallel port for your printing needs, you may run into problems like garbled text or graphics. This is because some printers on the market haven't quite reached IEEE nirvana yet and therefore don't work so well with ECP. There are two things to do in this instance: in Windows, change the printer spooling properties from EMF to RAW; if that doesn't work, change the port back to Bidirectional or Output Only mode in your BIOS setup program.

If you're having other port problems, did you install something recently? Could something be conflicting with the printer port?

Consider the Weather

Everyone talks about it, but...

A printer repairman told me about a day that he'd had the previous October. He said that all over town a particular model of printer was failing left and right. He couldn't figure it out. We thought about it. Around the middle of October, we turn on the heat in Washington. That dries out the air and, in turn, the items in the work area. Chips don't mind being dried, but what about capacitors? Could a paper-type capacitor be malfunctioning because it was drying beyond a certain point?

A repair memo came around from the manufacturer a couple of months later. Sure enough, a particular capacitor didn't like it too dry. The answer: either put a humidifier near the printer, or change the capacitor to a similar, less dry-sensitive replacement. Moral: be suspicious when the seasons change.

Troubleshooting Tips

Like a bad cable TV connection on the night of the big pay-per-view fight, printers are notorious for going on the fritz when you've got two minutes to print and fax vitally important documents. Here are some additional troubleshooting tips to help you avoid resorting to the ultimate show of frustration: whacking your printer upside its paper tray as if it were a vending machine gone bad.

Printer Won't Print at All

If the printer won't print at all:

◆ Check that the printer is getting power, is online (check the Online button), and is connected to the PC.

◆ Turn the printer off and then on again. The same for the computer.

◆ Look on the printer for any error codes or flashing lights that could give a clue as to the problem.

◆ See that the printer has ink, toner, or ribbon, and that it's installed correctly.

◆ Turn off the computer and run the printer's self-test to see if it can print as a separate entity from the computer.

◆ Check to make sure the correct driver is installed on the PC.

◆ Check the printer queue and purge any print jobs that appear to be hung up.

◆ Turn the printer off, let it sit for 10 minutes, and try again. Overheating can shut down a printer temporarily.

◆ Try a different printer cable.

◆ Try hooking up the printer to a different computer to determine whether the problem is with the printer, the computer, or the software.

Printout Has Quality Problems

If the printout isn't all it should be:

◆ Ensure that the correct printer driver has been installed.

◆ Check the printer to make sure it is using the right print emulation mode if it has more than one available.

◆ On a dot-matrix printer, ensure that the belt is adjusted properly.

◆ Replace the ink, ribbon, or toner cartridge if needed, along with any other replacement parts, such as the felt pad in some laser models.

◆ Clean the printer according to the instructions in its manual.

◆ On an inkjet, clean the nozzles by using the printer's built-in utility for that purpose.

Now, just as I promised, I will delve more deeply into the workings of specific types of printers. Next up: inkjet printers.

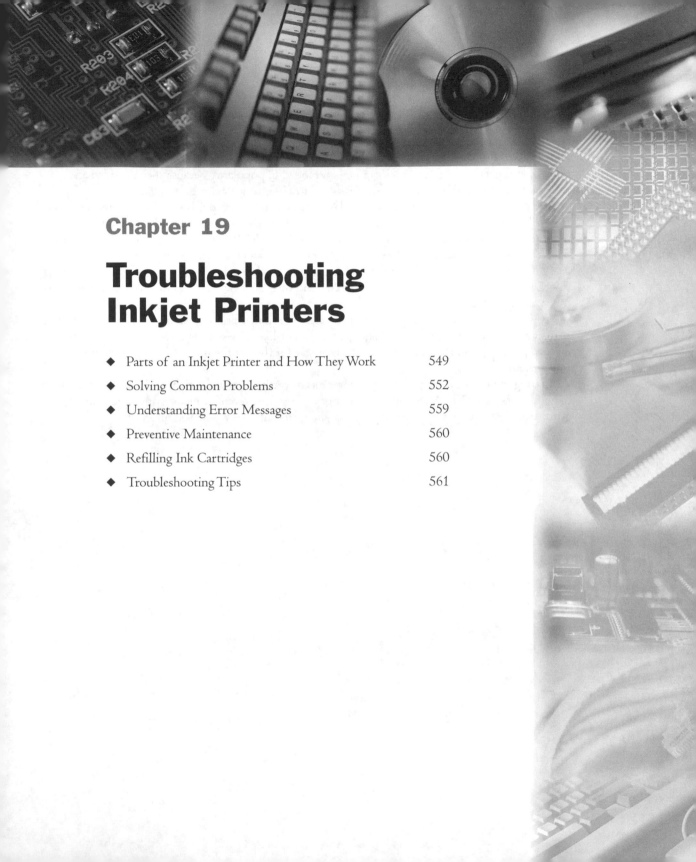

Chapter 19

Troubleshooting Inkjet Printers

◆ Parts of an Inkjet Printer and How They Work   549

◆ Solving Common Problems   552

◆ Understanding Error Messages   559

◆ Preventive Maintenance   560

◆ Refilling Ink Cartridges   560

◆ Troubleshooting Tips   561

Introduction

THE INKJET PRINTER BEGAN as a "poor man's laser," producing near laser quality black-and-white output at a fraction of the cost of a real laser printer. As the technology continued to develop, affordable color inkjet printers became available (while color laser printers were still way beyond the reach of ordinary people), and inkjet printers exploded in popularity because they provided an affordable way for the average home or small-business user to get color printouts.

Today, inkjet printers still cost less than laser printers. Inkjet output is not quite as crisp as output from a laser printer; you can tell the difference if you look closely with a magnifying glass. Inkjet output can also sometimes smear if you touch it immediately after it exits the printer. However, the difference is minor, and inkjet output looks professional enough for almost any home or business use. The drawbacks? Inkjet printing speed has traditionally been slower than that of laser printers (8–12 pages per minute, as opposed to 12–24), and their per-page cost (of the ink versus laser toner) is slightly higher.

As with laser printers, most problems associated with inkjet printers can be attributed to either human error or ignorance. You see, inkjet printers aren't like television sets. You can't just plug them in, turn them on, and expect them to work flawlessly for their entire life without a little Tender Loving Care.

Getting the most out of your inkjet printer means getting it to work right and then maintaining it in good working order. Once you learn the ropes of regular preventive maintenance and some emergency troubleshooting, you'll be able to get quality printouts every time you hit Print.

Parts of an Inkjet Printer

Inkjet printers are fairly simple machines in concept. They all have several common pieces:

- An outer case to hold the inner parts.

- A paper-feed mechanism.

- Ink cartridges, which hold the ink and can be black or a combination of black and color.

u Inkjets (collectively called a *print head*) that control the distribution of ink on the page. In Hewlett Packard printers, the print head is built into the ink cartridge; in other brands of inkjet printers, the print head is separate.

- A carrier that holds the ink cartridges and moves them back and forth over the paper.

- A paper-exit tray.

Some printers are multifunction devices that also include scanning, faxing, or copying capabilities. Such units will have additional parts; check the manual to learn more about them. Some of these devices are not inkjets, however, but rather simple laser or optical black-and-white printers.

The Case

Inkjet printer cases come in all shapes, sizes, and even a few colors. Ultimately, the type of case depends on the model of printer you have. Each manufacturer has designed its case to fit a variety of design and mechanical factors, so they aren't compatible with each other.

Most printer cases have some sort of lid or hatch that lifts up to give you access to the ink cartridges. You will not need to remove the entire outer case for routine operation. Should you need to perform more drastic operations on the printer, however, you can (on most models) remove a few screws and lift off the entire outer plastic shell.

You won't find any sort of manual for removing the printer's outer casing, as the manufacturer doesn't want you to do it. Instead, they want you to send your printer to an authorized repair center if there are problems that necessitate removing the case. However, I once took my Lexmark 5700 Color Jetprinter apart to clean the inner workings (it was all gunked up with ink) and was able to disassemble it and put it back together with no problems. The key is to work slowly and examine carefully how each piece fits with the others.

Did I mention that the case probably won't be just one piece? That's true. The Lexmark I took apart had something like eight pieces to its outer case. Two pieces make up the supporting base, three or four parts fit together to form the outer front of the printer, and a few more hold the paper-feed and paper-exit trays.

Whatever you do, don't force anything. Carefully note where all the screws are and remove them one at a time, putting the screws in a safe place so you don't lose them. If the screws are different sizes, write this on a piece of paper. When you try to put the case back together, this information is invaluable. After you take off one piece of the case, set it aside and move on to the next. As you remove the pieces of the case, look closely to see how they all fit together. Sometimes it seems like a jigsaw puzzle, so write some notes if you need to, so you remember the details.

When you disassemble your printer, you can clean each piece of the outer case with soap and water; if that doesn't work, try an alcohol-based cleaning solution and a soft cloth or paper towel. Be very careful in your choice of cleaning solutions, since some of them can damage the plastics used to make the case. This is a good idea if ink has sprayed on any inner surfaces or you happen to get inky fingerprints on any of the pieces (as I did).

The Paper-Feed Mechanism

The paper-feed mechanism usually holds approximately 100 sheets of paper or more (it really depends on your printer), and feeds the paper into the printer. On some printers, there is a separate, removable tray that holds the paper; on other printers you simply stack the paper up against the feed mechanism. Most inkjet printers allow you to use different sizes of paper, including standard letter, envelope, and greeting card–sized paper. An adjustable feed guide helps you position various types of paper correctly for feeding.

Some printers have the capability of feeding paper in from either the front or the back. Typically, HP inkjet printers are front loaders, while just about every other major printer manufacturer uses a gravity feed from the rear. The advantage of the front loader is a smaller footprint on your desktop. The disadvantage is the limitation in the thickness of the media supported. Some printers have a manual feed feature, which you can use to manually insert a single page at a time of some nonstandard paper size, like envelopes, that the printer doesn't normally support using the standard paper feed bin.

One of the most common problems with either type of paper-feed mechanism is in the rubber wheels that grab the paper—called grabber wheels. Through use, the grabber wheels begin to lose their traction due to becoming clogged with paper dust, resulting in misfeeds. The solution is simple—take a cotton swab and clean the wheels with denatured alcohol.

If cleaning the grabber wheels doesn't resolve the problem, it may be that the gears on the paper-feed mechanism have become worn and are starting to fail to pull paper into the printer smoothly and evenly. With newer printers, this happens very rarely. On some printers, the gears start making an annoying squeaking sound too, and oiling them doesn't help much. In such cases, it's usually worth it (to me, anyway) to take the printer to an authorized service center and have the feed mechanism refurbished. It's not that you can't do it yourself, but the authorized service centers have better access to the needed parts. Of course, with good-quality color inkjet printers costing less than $100, it is probably a better use of your money to simply replace the printer.

Ink Cartridges

The ink cartridges hold the ink that your printer uses. Make sure you use ink cartridges that are compatible with your make and model of printer, as they come in different shapes and sizes. Most look like little boxes, and some have carefully designed nozzles and electronic contacts built in. Other, more basic styles of ink cartridges are simply ink reservoirs that feed into the ink cartridge carrier, which has the more complicated parts.

Almost all color inkjet printers today have both color and black ink cartridges that you can replace separately. (On older models, cyan, yellow, and magenta were combined to make black, and it resulted in a somewhat muddy gray.)

Some color printers have the three primary colors in one cartridge, whereas other models allow you to purchase and install each of the three colors separately (magenta, yellow, and cyan). Printers that are used primarily for printing photographs will have five colors in the ink cartridge. The primary disadvantage to the "all colors in one box" type is that you may not use the colors at the same rate. If you run out of cyan, for example, you have no choice but to replace the entire cartridge to restore your color printing capability, or live with your inability to print blues. This is not an issue that should keep you up at nights, though, since the amount of ink you lose with this method is, in most cases, insignificant.

HP ink cartridges are manufactured with a protective piece of plastic and transparent tape that covers the nozzles and contacts. Most other manufacturers have a piece of tape that covers the air vent holes to prevent them from drying out. With these types of cartridges, inserting the cartridge into the holder the first time breaks the seal and allows the ink to flow into the print head. In either case, make sure to remove the tape prior to installing.

At the end of this chapter, I'll tell you more about cartridges, including how they can be refilled (and why you may *not* want to do so).

The Ink Cartridge Carrier

The ink cartridge carrier holds the ink cartridges and moves back and forth over the paper while ink is being sprayed onto the paper. On all inkjet printers except HP, this carrier also contains the print head. To install ink cartridges, you may have to move a lever, lift the lid, or press a button on the printer to put the carrier in a position to accept the cartridges, and then snap them into place. On some printers, the cartridge carriers come out of the printer completely, and then go back in with the new cartridge.

The Exit Tray

The exit tray holds the paper after it comes out of the printer. Many models of inkjet printers have sliding pieces to the exit tray, enabling you to retract the tray in order to save space when you're not using it. When you print, extend the tray to its full length to catch the paper.

A few printers have a lever you can flip to make the output come out at the opposite end of the printer from normal. For example, if the output normally comes out the front, you could make it come out the back. Why would you want to do this? Primarily to get a straight path through the printer. If you are printing on some stiff medium, such as cardboard, you can avoid the otherwise-inevitable curling by allowing the paper to exit the printer in a straight line from the spot where it entered, rather than curling around a roller on its way out. I am just joking about the cardboard—be careful about the thickness of paper you pass through your printer.

How an Inkjet Printer Works

At the most basic level, inkjet printers work by directing tiny droplets of ink onto paper. The older generation of impact dot matrix printers use a mechanical print head that physically impacts a ribbon, thereby transferring ink to the paper. In contrast, inkjet printer "heads" don't physically touch the paper at all. Instead, these printers force ink through nozzles and spray the ink right onto the paper. Depending on the printer and its technology, there can be between 21 and 128 nozzles for each of the four colors (cyan, yellow, magenta, and black). By mixing the colors, the printer can produce almost any color.

There are two types of inkjet printers: thermal and piezo. These are two different technologies used to force the ink from the cartridge and through the nozzles.

Thermal inkjets use the older of the two technologies. They heat the ink in the cartridge (to about 400 degrees Fahrenheit), causing vapor bubbles in the cartridge that rise to the top and force the ink out through the nozzle. The vacuum caused by the expelled ink draws more ink down into the nozzles, making a constant stream.

Piezo printing uses an electric charge instead of heat. It charges piezoelectric crystals in the nozzles, which change their shape as a result of the electric current, forcing the ink out through the nozzles.

The output of both technologies is essentially the same. The primary difference between the two is that, with the thermal inkjets (Hewlett-Packard), every time you replace the ink cartridge, you replace the print head. Traditionally with piezo technology, only the ink cartridge is replaced and the print head is a permanent part of the printer.

Common Problems and Possible Solutions

Just about all printer problems can be easily fixed if you know where to look. Although I attempt in this section to give you a good general sense of what problems might occur and how to prevent them, you should read the manual that came with your printer carefully.

The list of things that can go wrong with printing is fairly large, but you can organize them into general categories to help you troubleshoot. The point is to try to remove problems that might not be affecting you and to point you in the right general direction. Try thinking along these lines to categorize your printer problem:

- Your printer seems to be working, but nothing is printing.

- There are color problems.

- The printer appears dead.

- Printing seems very slow, but is working.

- The quality of your printouts is smeared or generally poor.

- The output is garbled or formatted incorrectly.

- The paper is jammed or not feeding correctly.

I'll cover each of these symptoms in turn.

Printer Appears to Work but Nothing Prints

This problem may be as simple as running out of ink. Most printers come with software status controls built into their Windows driver. Right-click the printer's icon in Windows, choose Properties (it works basically the same in all Windows versions), and look for a status monitor in the Printer Properties dialog box that indicates the ink level. Replace any cartridges that indicate they are out of ink. Figure 19.1 shows the ink levels for an Epson printer. Be aware that most status programs, like the status monitor shown in Figure 19.1, are separate programs that may or may not be installed at the same time as your printer driver. With the exception of the newest Epson ink cartridges (which have an electronic sensor in them), these status programs can only display an estimation of the amount of ink remaining. All of these status programs require that the printer be attached to the computer using bidirectional IEEE-1294 printer cables to work properly. You can also manually check HP cartridges by examining the ink cartridges, which have an indicator on the front that pretty accurately displays the amount of ink remaining.

FIGURE 19.1

This status monitor for the Epson Stylus Color 800 shows the color and black ink levels.

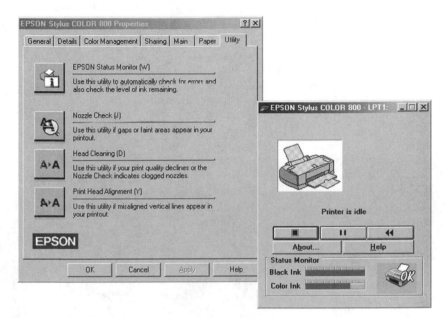

If you have sufficient ink, try running the nozzle check and/or the print head cleaning routine that is a part of your printer control program. Your nozzles might be clogged up. This is a common occurrence if you haven't printed in a long time. A nozzle check prints a test pattern using all the jets, so you can see whether any are malfunctioning. Head cleaning self-cleans each jet. You will want to run these two utilities, first one and then the other, to check the current nozzle functioning and to improve it. Head cleaning uses up a small amount of ink, however, so if you do it a lot, you'll end up wasting ink. Still, you will find that if the problem is clogged jets, running the head cleaning routines—sometimes up to 10 times—may restore the printer. If you haven't used the printer in over six months, there is a chance that the ink has dried up and you will need to replace the cartridge(s). Piezo technology print heads are a little more susceptible than thermal printers to this phenomenon. Because thermal print heads integrate the print head and ink supply into a single unit, you get a new print head each time you replace the ink cartridge. If the ink in your piezo print head should dry up, replacing the ink cartridge won't necessarily solve the problem.

True story: One time I was working with a printer that hadn't been used in over a year. Nearly all the nozzles were clogged, so I had to run the head cleaning routine 20 times in a row. The quality kept getting better and better, and I was feeling encouraged, but then the blue nozzles just quit. Kaput. Nothing. I panicked. Had I ruined the printer by repeated cleaning? Nope, I had just depleted all the blue ink. So I installed a new cartridge, and it worked perfectly.

If, after cleaning the print heads, you see intermittent output on the page, try cleaning them several more times; this can sometimes break loose the crud that's clogging up some of the jets. Most printers enable you to run the head cleaning routine by pressing certain buttons on the printer (check your documentation) or by choosing an option in the printer's Properties box (as shown in Figure 19.2).

FIGURE 19.2

Most printers have utilities such as nozzle checking and head cleaning built into the driver.

If that fails, take your ink cartridges out and check whether any obstructions might be blocking the ink. If you've recently replaced your ink cartridges, check them to make sure you removed all the protective coverings from the print nozzles and contacts.

WARNING   The documentation for some printer models claims that if you remove an ink cartridge after initially inserting it, it becomes useless and you can't reinsert it. I have reinserted a cartridge in one such printer successfully, despite the instructions, but if you have a printer that claims this, try all other troubleshooting first before you resort to removing the cartridge for examination and reinsertion.

Color Is Wrong

If the colors on your printout don't match what you see on-screen, the most likely problem is that one of the color jets is clogged or you're out of ink. Check the printout—do all greens look yellow, and is the blue missing? That means you're out of cyan. See the instructions in the preceding section for replacing an ink cartridge and/or cleaning the print heads.

If the color problem is more subtle (all colors appear, but they look too dark, too blue, or whatever), the problem might be with your monitor's color calibration. If your video card ships with a utility that allows you to calibrate your monitor's color, you should run it. There might also be a utility built into your printer driver or video card driver; try displaying the device's properties to look for one.

Sometimes the problem lies with the color management scheme selected by the application from which you are printing. For example, if you are printing from CorelDRAW , its color management profile is active by default. So, when printing to an Epson printer (whose color management is also on by default), the result of these two color management programs trying to out-think one another can be less than desirable output. I recommend turning off all color management except the one that came with the printer—which you might not be able to turn off anyhow.

Printer Doesn't Print at All

Ah, the dead printer. Fear not, the problem is usually simple.

First, check that the printer is plugged in and the power is on. Next, are any of the status lights on the printer blinking? Blinking lights can be an indication that either the printer is processing the print job or something is wrong that requires your intervention. Check your user manual to interpret the error condition. If you've ruled out any error conditions, check your printer cable connections. Try removing the printer cable and reseating it at both ends.

If these aren't causing the problem, make sure that the printer appears in your operating system and that it is online and currently selected as the default printer. In Windows, check the Printers list (Start ➢ Settings ➢ Printers); a checkmark next to the printer's icon indicates that it's the default. Right-click it and choose Set as Default if needed. Sometimes strange things happen and this gets messed up. I've seen cases of printers disappearing or suddenly going offline.

If your default printer is a network printer, make sure your network connection is up and running. If the printer appears "faded" or "grayed out" in the Printers window, it's because the printer is not available for some reason (usually due to a failure in the network connection to it).

Next, open the print queue for your printer (by double-clicking its icon in the Printers list or double-clicking the printer icon in the system tray) to see whether printing is currently paused. (The title bar will read Paused if it is.) Choose Printer ➢ Pause Printing to unpause it. You might have paused printing and forgotten to reset it.

If the printer's status is User Intervention, that means the printer is waiting on something. If it's a network printer, there could be a warning or error message on the host computer's screen, waiting to be answered. Or the printer could be out of paper or have a paper jam, although in such events, the computer usually displays an error message indicating the nature of the problem.

Printing Is Slow or Intermittent

Slow or intermittent printing could be caused by a couple of things. First, double-check your cable connection to the printer. If your printer is capable of bidirectional communications, make sure your printer cable is also. Bidirectional communications enable the printer to communicate with the operating system (and vice versa) so that your printer control program can communicate with the printer and return error messages and ink levels. Most printer cables available in stores today are bidirectional, but an old one you found in someone's junk drawer may not be. You can tell by looking closely at the actual cable. Somewhere along the length of the cable you will find lots of tiny letters and numbers; look for something that says "IEEE 1284," which indicates the cable is bidirectional. Any new printer cables will state whether they are bidirectional or IEEE 1284 on the packaging. If the cable is fine, check that bidirectional printing is enabled for the port that the printer is using (probably LPT1) in your PC's BIOS.

Slow printing could also be caused by your printer driver settings. In most cases, you can choose to print in draft, normal, or high-resolution mode. The higher the quality, the more time the printing will take. If you're printing at 2880dpi (dots per inch), your printout may take a very long time. If you want it to print faster and don't need the highest quality, lower your print quality settings through the printer's print settings. You can set these by displaying the printer's properties (right-click it and choose Properties), or, within some applications, with a PRINT SETUP command.

TIP When printing photographs on an inkjet printer, it isn't necessary to print at the highest resolution that the printer supports to get a good color photograph. When running some benchmark tests this year, I printed the same photograph at 720, 1440 and 2880dpi. While I noticed a slight improvement in quality between the 720 and the 1440dpi photo, I couldn't see any difference between the 1440 and the 2880dpi. Yet, the 2880dpi photo took three times longer to print and consumed twice as much ink.

Finally, slow printing can be the result of using the wrong driver for your printer. If you let Windows autodetect an older printer instead of running the setup software that came with the printer, you may not be using the best possible driver. Dig through the documentation that came with the printer and find its SETUP CD, and run that to install the specific driver for your printer. The autodetection of newer printers by Windows 98/Me/2000 and XP usually works fine. When given a choice between a driver provided by the Windows operating system and one provided by the printer manufacturer, always choose the one from the printer manufacturer. The one provided by the Windows OS tends to be a no-frills version and often does not support many of the advanced features of the printer.

Next, never ever assume that the printer driver that came with the printer you just bought is the most current driver. It may have been manufactured, boxed, and sent to the distribution warehouse several driver revisions ago. Always go the manufacturer's Web site to download the most current driver for your operating system. If the newest driver isn't for your operating system, don't use it. Only use the driver for the operating system you are using with your printer. Sounds obvious, right? If I had a nickel for every time that someone had selected the newest driver without regard to the operating system, I'd have a lot of nickels.

Quality Is Poor

If the printer prints, but the output isn't as good as you think it should be, you've got some investigative work to do to find out why.

First, check to see what quality mode the printer is set to operate in. As I mentioned earlier, the higher the quality, the slower the printing. Sometimes people set their printers to draft quality (the fastest, lowest-quality setting) and forget that they've done so. Check the printer's Properties box to view and change the quality setting. Figure 19.3 shows an example.

While you're there looking at the quality setting, see also whether there is a Media Type or Paper Type setting. With inkjet printers, plain old copy paper doesn't produce as good an image as special inkjet paper with a shinier surface and less porous "holes." The less porous the paper, the higher the dpi setting you can use for the printout. Using a very high dpi (such as 2400) with plain paper can actually result in a printout that looks *worse* than a printout at a lower resolution (720, perhaps) because the paper is too porous to handle the dots being that close together. For best results, buy paper made especially for inkjet printers, because it enables you to print at higher dpi.

FIGURE 19.3

Most printers enable you to choose from several quality settings.

Next, clean your print heads through the printer control program, as described in the previous "Printer Appears to Work but Nothing Prints" section. A clogged nozzle can result in stripes on the page (*banding*), or "bald" patches where there is no printing.

Your print heads may also be out of alignment. Run the print head alignment routine (if it exists—not all printers have alignment routines) for your printer. You'll probably find the alignment routine built into the printer driver, as with the other utilities you've seen so far in this chapter. The routine aligns the print heads and nozzles so that the black and color ink cartridges print at the same location on the page. This one does its stuff the first time, so you should not have to do it multiple times for best results (as with head cleaning).

Check your ink levels. Low ink results in banding or streaking. If you're low on color ink, your printout will appear washed out or oddly miscolored. You may be out of one of the three primary colors used in color printing.

Check the brand of the ink cartridges installed in your printer. I have tested several third-party ink cartridges and found that the blacks are not as dark nor the dyes in the colors as vivid as the original cartridges produced by the manufacturer.

If your HP printer appears to be smearing, remove your ink cartridges and inspect them manually to see if there is a buildup of paper debris. If there is, take a cotton swab and clean the print head portion of the cartridge and replace it in the holder. Reinstall the cartridges and make sure they are properly seated in the carrier. Remember that not all printers allow you to reinsert the same cartridge after removing it (at least not according to the documentation; you might still be able to do so). On some HP printers you will be requested to run the alignment procedure again, because the program thinks you have installed a new cartridge.

If you have problems at the edge of the page, such as output being cut off, you may be trying to print material outside of the effective print area of your printer. No printer will let you print across the full width of a standard sheet of paper. This is because the edge of the paper is used to hold it in place while transporting the paper through the printer. Most modern applications that support a Print Preview function are aware of the printable area of the selected printer and media and will show you exactly what will and will not print.

An exception to this paper edge issue is the newest line of Epson photo printers, which offer true borderless printing. This should not be confused with earlier borderless printing, which was accomplished using a special paper with perforated edges that you removed after the printing was complete.

Output Is Garbled or Formatted Incorrectly

If you print a nicely formatted word processing document, but it comes out with the wrong fonts, skewed margins, or junk characters, the problem is possibly a corrupt printer driver, but more than likely it is an interrupted print job.

If you interrupt a print job, the information header for the job is often lost. When the job is restarted, the printer begins receiving the control information about the print job, but it has no way of knowing that. Rather than using this control information to set up the print job, it prints all of that code gibberish—on many sheets of paper. The solution is to take the paper out of the printer and wait for the printer, and finally the computer, to realize it is out of paper. At that time you should receive an error message, which will give you the opportunity to cancel the print jobs.

If you have a damaged driver, you can repair the driver problem by deleting the printer from the Printers list and reinstalling it using the disk that came with the printer. If you don't have such a disk, download the needed setup software from the manufacturer's Web site. Windows comes with drivers for many popular printers, and you can use the Windows-provided driver in a pinch, if one from the manufacturer is not available. (The Windows version may not have as many features, so I try to always use the manufacturer-supplied drivers whenever possible.)

The driver is not always to blame, however. One time I had a very frustrating service call, in which the printer was printing the output scrunched up on the left side of each page. The printout would appear perfectly on-screen in Print Preview, but without fail, each page came out distorted. I tried reinstalling the driver. I tried resetting the printer. I tried printing from DOS. Nothing worked. Finally I checked inside the printer and noticed that the ink cartridges were not completely seated in their holders. I gave them a firm push into place, and *voilà!* Problem solved. Weird but true.

Paper Is Stuck or Not Moving

If paper jams in your printer, stop what you are doing and carefully but firmly pull the paper out of the printer. Try not to rip the paper as you pull it out, because you don't want to have small pieces of paper caught inside the printer. When you've removed the jammed piece of paper, throw it away and resend your job to the printer.

If paper fails to feed at all, check that the paper is seated correctly in the paper tray. If any obstructions are blocking the paper, carefully remove them. If a piece of paper is bent, it may not feed correctly. You'll have to throw it away.

You should also check to ensure that you haven't overloaded the paper feed tray. Too many sheets in the tray can easily cause jams or feed problems. Sometimes using very thick or very thin paper can cause feed problems too. Try to use a standard paper weight (20 lb or so) whenever possible.

Most printers also have paper guides that snuggle up against your paper and keep it straight as it feeds into the printer. These guides can be set for different sizes of paper. Make sure the guide is properly set and isn't loose.

Other issues that cause misfeeds or no feeds are media related. For example, most printers that can print to envelopes print one at a time or have a limit of five or eight unless you have a dedicated envelope feeder. Transparency material can be difficult for some printers to pick up and may have to be fed one sheet at a time.

Finally, make sure your printer is on a flat, stable surface. If it is tilted at an angle or on a shaky table, that might cause feed problems—I doubt it, but all things are possible.

Common Error Messages

Although each printer will have error messages that are unique to its particular make and model, here are a few error messages you might encounter.

Ink Low

This signifies that your ink cartridge is running out of ink. You should replace the ink cartridge soon. Some printer manufacturers recommend that you don't change an ink cartridge until the printer reports that the ink is completely out. You can make that call yourself, but it's nice to have the advance `Ink Low` warning so you can make sure you have a new cartridge available.

WARNING   *Ink cartridges tend to dry out on the shelf. Don't stockpile ink cartridges; after six months or so they lose their freshness.*

Out of Memory

Laser printers are page printers—they print entire pages at a time, so they must have a lot of memory in them to store a whole page. In contrast, inkjet printers are line printers—they print line-by-line, so they don't typically need a great deal of memory. You seldom hear of memory upgrades available for inkjet printers because it's simply not an issue.

Therefore, if you get an `Out of Memory` error message on-screen as you print to an inkjet printer, it most likely refers to a lack of memory on your PC, rather than on your printer. Usually it does not really mean that you should add memory to your PC; rather, it means that either memory-hogging programs running on your PC have allocated all the available memory or you have no space left on your hard drive. In either case, there isn't enough space left for the printer driver to spool its output to the printer. It's best to restart your PC and resubmit your print job after doing so.

Out of Paper

You are either completely out of paper, or if your printer has multiple paper sources, you may have designated an empty tray. You'll have to load more paper in your printer or switch to another paper tray to continue.

Paper Jam

Paper has jammed somewhere in your printer, preventing it from continuing. Carefully but firmly pull the paper out of the printer, hopefully in one piece. Depending on where the paper jam occurs, you may have to pull it out of the top (or paper-feed area) or the bottom (the paper-exit tray). If you can't reach the paper easily, you might have to open the access panel to reach inside your printer.

Print Head Failure

If your ink cartridges are not working correctly, you might receive a `Print Head Failure` error message. Dirty, fouled, or clogged ink cartridges can cause this problem. Clean your printer head through your printer control program, and if necessary, remove the ink cartridges and clean them with a clean cloth.

Preventive Maintenance

If you own a car, you're probably used to preventive maintenance. You change your oil every 3000 miles or every three months, check the air in the tires, check other fluid levels, and routinely put gas in it so it will run. Printers also require some regular maintenance, although it is far less troublesome than what you need to do for a car.

Clean the Print Heads

Although you don't want to overdo it, you should clean your print heads periodically by running the head cleaning utility (as discussed earlier in the chapter). This should remove any built-up "gunk" or ink on the print heads and help ensure consistently high-quality printouts.

Align the Print Heads

Every time you install new printer cartridges, you should also align your print heads. This keeps the color and black ink cartridges aligned so there are no gaps between black and color portions of your printout. Most printers do this automatically, but it doesn't hurt to do it manually by using the head alignment utility in your printer driver (covered earlier in the chapter).

Realigning print heads might also be necessary after moving your printer or bumping into it accidentally.

Refilling Ink Cartridges

Due to the cost of today's inkjet ink cartridges (usually over $30 for black and upward of $40 to $50 for color), a cottage industry of refillable inkjet cartridges has emerged. It should be said that most manufacturers do not recommend this, but what they don't know won't hurt them. In fact, some manufacturers make their ink cartridges very hard to get into by yourself, thus making it hard for you to refill them without special tools or equipment.

You should be able to purchase kits made specifically for your brand of printer and model of ink cartridges if your printer is popular enough. This method gives you some assurance that your new cartridge will contain ink with the same characteristics as the retail ink cartridge. If not, you may be stuck with buying the officially designated replacement cartridges.

Refilling ink cartridges involves removing the lid of the existing ink cartridge and simply refilling it. Due to the wide variety of existing ink cartridges, you should carefully follow the instructions provided with the kit you buy.

You should not refill a cartridge more than once. That's because, on HP printers, the print head jets are built into the cartridges. When you replace the ink cartridge, you also give yourself a brand-new set of jets. If you continually refill and reuse the same cartridge, you're never getting new jets, and your print quality can start to suffer. You'll get clogged jets more and more often, resulting in more head cleaning, which in turn wastes ink, and before you know it, you're caught in a vicious circle. Yes, it's okay to be a little thrifty and refill occasionally, but don't be so cheap that you cheat yourself out of decent quality printouts.

While all of the above is possible, I do not recommend buying generic replacement cartridges or refilling them because the color inks never look as good as the manufacturer's ink— regardless of what the ads tell you. I have compared many brand-name replacements, and the results have always been noticeably inferior to the results with the manufacturer's cartridge.

Troubleshooting Tips

Here's a summary of the troubleshooting procedures covered in the chapter:

- ◆ For print quality problems, check the utilities built into the printer's driver. (Right-click the printer and choose Properties to display the available tools and settings.)

- ◆ Use the nozzle checking utility to see whether any jets are clogged; then use the head cleaning utility to clean them. This uses ink, so balance the need for cleaning with your need not to waste ink.

- ◆ If the color is seriously off, one of the ink colors is probably out, or its nozzles are clogged. If the color problem is more uniform, check the color calibration for the video card and/or the printer. One or both may have a color correction utility.

- ◆ If the printer doesn't print at all, check all your connections, and make sure the printer is installed correctly in your operating system.

- ◆ Make sure the printer isn't offline, paused, or requiring user intervention (such as adding more paper).

- ◆ If the printer is accessed through a network, make sure your network connection is up and running.

- ◆ If the printer prints slowly, try decreasing the quality setting for a draft print. You can usually do this through the printer's Properties box. Slow printing may also be the result of using the wrong driver.

- ◆ Poor print quality can mean you are running out of one or more colors of ink, that the print heads are misaligned or clogged, or that you're using a draft quality setting.

- ◆ Garbled output indicates a problem with the printer driver. Remove the printer from Windows (or other operating system) and reinstall.

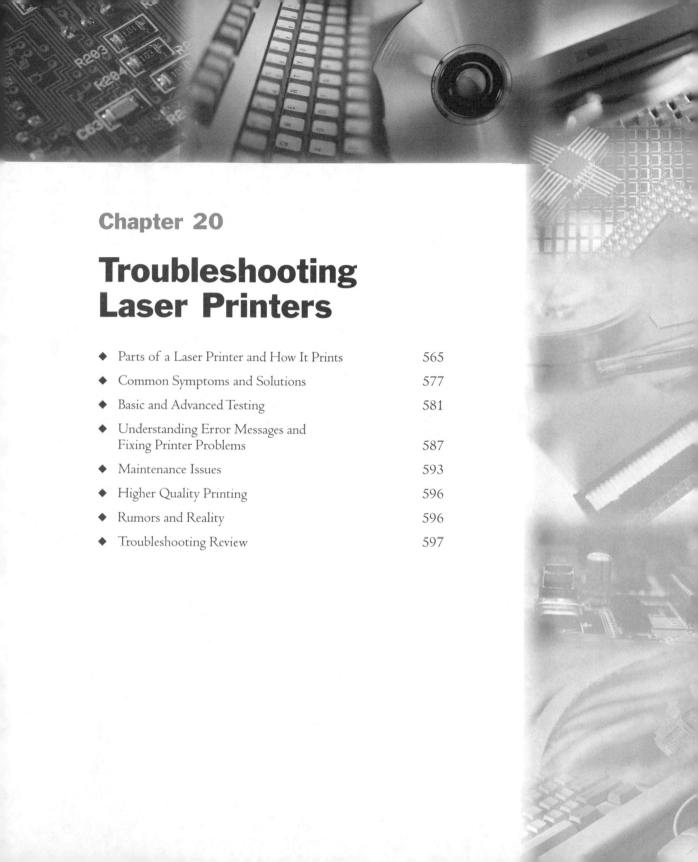

Chapter 20

Troubleshooting Laser Printers

◆ Parts of a Laser Printer and How It Prints   565

◆ Common Symptoms and Solutions   577

◆ Basic and Advanced Testing   581

◆ Understanding Error Messages and
Fixing Printer Problems   587

◆ Maintenance Issues   593

◆ Higher Quality Printing   596

◆ Rumors and Reality   596

◆ Troubleshooting Review   597

Introduction

LASER PRINTERS ARE ACTUALLY pretty reliable. Most of the printer problems you'll see are not printer problems at all, but rather problems with the humans trying to use them. As I told you in Chapter 5, "Troubleshooting PC Problems," you should first check the part of the equation that walks and talks.

Once the human component has been checked and cleared, exercise a methodical approach to testing the rest of the system. Break the problem down into its possibilities/probabilities, testing and eliminating them, one by one. Start with the easy stuff first. It's always possible that the only thing the printer needs is more paper.

Parts of a Laser Printer

Let's start out our discussion of a laser printer by looking at its parts.

Interface Controller

Much of a laser printer is actually a computer—that is, it's composed of the same basic stuff as your desktop computer: circuit boards, memory chips, ports, and so on. As in your computer, the laser printer has a large printed circuit board that receives, modifies, and outputs data. Different manufacturers call it by different names, but in this book I'll go with the generic name *interface controller*.

The interface controller is the printer's motherboard, and it handles some pretty important tasks. Here's some of what it does:

- ◆ Communicates with the PC that wants to print using an input interface (parallel, serial, network, or infrared)

- ◆ Manipulates incoming data for translation to the print engine

- ◆ Monitors the control panel (usually a button panel on its front) for user input

- ◆ Provides information on printer status at the display and through various LEDs

- ◆ Stores configuration and font information

Of these, the input interface is the one you will deal with most directly, so let's look at it more closely.

Input Interface

Depending on the printer, the input interface may provide only for parallel connection, or it may offer other options too, such as USB, serial, network, or some other special I/O such as infrared.

PARALLEL PORTS

As you learned in Chapter 18, "Troubleshooting Printers," parallel connectivity uses eight wires to transfer the data, with each bit traveling in parallel down a separate wire. A full byte (8 bits) of data at a time will travel the cable.

The Achilles' heel of the parallel port is the fact that it is limited in terms of distance. Most manufacturers want the parallel interface cable to be limited to about 35 feet for laser printer applications. The parallel interface is by far the most common printer interface type, and nearly all printers support it. In addition, if you want to run a Postscript driver on your computer, nearly every major provider of Postscript printer software requires that the printer be attached to the computer using the parallel port interface.

SERIAL PORTS

Serial, as the name implies, is used to send data in a bit-by-bit fashion, using one wire to send and another to receive. This is a rugged and flexible interface when compared to the parallel port. It can be configured to change several parameters, including speed, and can be found on everything from mice to modems.

When laser printers first appeared in the marketplace, many were equipped with dual interfaces—parallel and serial. The serial interface had several names. If it was meant to communicate only with a PC, it was usually labeled as an RS-232 port (the name of the serial interface specification used on the serial port). If the printer was designed to communicate with a Macintosh computer as well as a PC, the serial interface was labeled as an RS-422 port.

If a decent, shielded, twisted-pair cable is used in a quiet environment (one without lots of radio frequency or electromagnetic interference), it is possible to send and receive data through a serial port at distances of several hundred feet. However, its transmission speed is limited by its very nature—since it sends each bit one at a time, or serially, it can't rival a parallel port that sends 8 bits at once. Standard serial interfaces (RS-232/RS-422) pretty much disappeared from laser printers in the late 1990s.

USB

The Universal Serial Bus (USB) appeared as an interface for laser printers in the late 1990s. The USB interface has become increasingly popular with inkjet printers, but up until recently it was slow in being adopted into laser printer designs. Besides offering superior speed over the standard RS-232/RS-422 interfaces, the USB bus on a computer can support many devices, whereas the serial port can attach only to a single device. With the advent of USB 2.0, the USB may become the interface of choice over the next few years.

NETWORK INTERFACE

In Chapter 18, I explained the two ways a printer can hook into a network—through a networked PC or with its own network connection. You can connect to Token Ring or Ethernet, 10 or 100Mbps, coax, or twisted pair, depending on the network interface that your printer comes with or that you install in it.

OPTIONAL I/O

Some printers support additional I/O possibilities, such as an infrared or Macintosh connection. For example, on some HP laser printers, there's an expansion I/O (EIO) port located at the back of the printer next to the standard serial and parallel ports. This is the receptor of many upgrades and emulation enhancements. For example, the Design Jet module allows the printer to connect directly to a network without the need of a print server (a dedicated computer used to control the printer).

CPU

Just as your computer's motherboard holds its CPU, the printer's interface controller also holds the main brain of the printer, its CPU. No matter which port receives the data, the CPU controls its processing. Most laser printers today use a RISC processor (which, by the way, stands for Reduced Instruction Set Computer), as opposed to your PC, which uses a CISC (the C stands for *complex*). However, the basic processing concept is the same.

Printer RAM

It's important to remember that a laser printer is a page printer—it composes an entire page in memory first, and then transfers it to paper. So there must be enough RAM in the printer to hold an entire page, or it can't print. How much is "enough"? It depends on the page being printed. More and larger graphics, and more fonts, means more memory required.

When laser printers first appeared on the market, they came with a measly amount of memory (often only 512KB) that wasn't enough to compose a full-page graphic. People using those printers would get an error message when printing complex pages and, naturally, they complained about it bitterly to the manufacturers.

The manufacturers responded by offering to sell memory upgrades. But these upgrades were typically a proprietary type of memory, which cost quite a bit more than normal computer memory (which, at that time, was no bargain either!). Sometimes it was actually cheaper to buy a whole new printer with more memory than it was to pay for one of these RAM upgrades!

PRINT LANGUAGE

The printer communicates with the PC's software in a special language. When you install a printer driver, the driver knows what language that printer requires, and "speaks" it.

The most common language for laser printers is Printer Control Language, or PCL, developed by Hewlett-Packard in the early 1980s. The following table lists the various iterations of PCL and what printers they were originally used in.

PCL Version	Year Released	HP Printers
PCL 3	1984	LaserJet, LaserJet Plus
PCL 4	1985	LaserJet Series II, 3100 (all models), 3150 (all models)
PCL 4e	1989	LaserJet IIP, IIP Plus
PCL 5	1990	LaserJet III, IIID, IIIP, IIIsi, HP-GL/2, 4V, 4MV
PCL 5e	1992	LaserJet 4, 4M, 4L, 4ML, 4P, 4MP, 4 Plus, 4M Plus, 5P, 5MP, 5L, 5L-FS, 5Si, 5Si NX, 5Si MX, 5Si Mopier, 5Lxtra, 6L, 6Lxi, 6Lse, 6Lxi, 6MP, 1100 (all models)
PCL 5c	1994	Color LaserJet 4500, Color LaserJet 8500, Color LaserJet 5, 5M
PCL 6	1996	LaserJet 5, 5se, 5M, 5N, LaserJet 6, 6P, 6Pse, 6Pxi, 6MP, 2100 (all models), 4000 (all models), 4050 (all models), 5000 (all models), 8000 (all models), 8100 (all models)

You don't have to worry about which version of PCL a printer uses, in most cases. The driver will automatically handle the communication. If, however, you don't have the correct driver available for some reason, you can sometimes use a driver that speaks the same PCL version as the printer you have and get away with it. You can use Table 20.1, later in this chapter, as a guide for picking a substitute driver if needed.

The other major language that laser printers use is PostScript, which was developed by Adobe in 1985. PostScript offered many features that PCL lacked in the beginning, such as scalable typefaces, so it quickly became the standard in desktop publishing and graphics. It failed to catch on with the average mainstream user, however, because printers that used it were more expensive.

Nowadays, almost every laser printer supports PCL, and many support both PCL and PostScript. (You choose which language you want to use by selecting one driver or another in your software.)

Manufacturers have learned their lesson somewhat in recent years and have increased the amount of RAM in their printers to 4–8MB. They've also made printers that accept regular DRAM SIMMs or DIMMs (that is, the same type of RAM that computers use). That, combined with the dropping cost of memory in general, has made it a lot more economical to have a printer with a decent amount of memory (say, 20MB for an average home office printing at 1200dpi).

Printing Mechanisms

The parts I've talked about so far are all computer components but, obviously, a printer must have some mechanical parts too. The paper needs to be taken in, printed on, and spit back out again. Different laser printers handle the paper input/output in different ways, but the process of actually creating the printed image on the page is fairly standard among laser printers. You'll learn about this printing process in the following section.

How a Laser Printer Prints

Laser printing is a multistep process. Understanding the process is more than just a techie exercise; it's essential to understanding what can go wrong and how to fix it.

I'll explain this in detail shortly, but the overview on how a laser prints is roughly like this: the printing drum is cleaned, an image is "painted" onto it with electrostatic charges, print toner moves to the charged areas, the toner is transferred to a piece of paper, and, finally, the toner is fixed onto the paper permanently with a heated metal roller. You can see this in Figure 20.1.

Figure 20.2 shows a laser printer with paper ready to start running through the printing process.

FIGURE 20.1

How a laser printer works

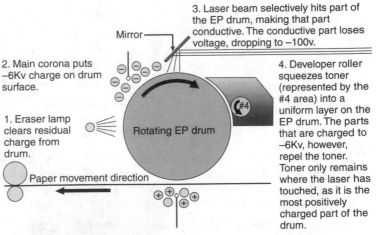

3. Laser beam selectively hits part of the EP drum, making that part conductive. The conductive part loses voltage, dropping to −100v.

Mirror

2. Main corona puts −6Kv charge on drum surface.

4. Developer roller squeezes toner (represented by the #4 area) into a uniform layer on the EP drum. The parts that are charged to −6Kv, however, repel the toner. Toner only remains where the laser has touched, as it is the most positively charged part of the drum.

1. Eraser lamp clears residual charge from drum.

Rotating EP drum

Paper movement direction

6. The image now only sits on the paper as fine, dustlike toner. The toner must be fixed to the page. The fuser roller actually melts the toner into the page with heat at a temperature of 180 degrees C.

5. The paper is pulled under the drum, which now contains the desired image written in toner. A second corona, the transfer corona, emits a positive charge, drawing the toner from the drum to the paper.

FIGURE 20.2

Laser printer beginning the printing process

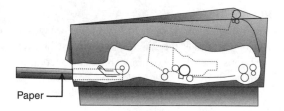

Paper —

The paper feeds from the left. The rollers and the print cartridge are on the right.

Data Input

When an application has data ready to be printed, it establishes communication with an output port in the PC. The PC then determines that there is indeed an output device attached to that port and satisfies itself that the device is waiting for data.

The laser printer responds in a favorable manner to the overtures of the computer by signaling on the strobe line (pin 1) on the parallel interface or DTR (line 20) on serial. This indicates that the printer is inactive but receptive.

When the application begins to deliver the data, it is received by the printer buffer—that is, its RAM. The printer's RAM holds the data until it can be processed by the printer's CPU and printed using the printer's print hardware.

Once the data is ready for printing, the hardware goes through a preparatory process before the laser actually begins to define the image.

A significant percentage of the printing process involves the electrophotographic cartridge. There are several things that need to happen within the cartridge each time that the interface controller receives data. The first of those things is drum preparation.

Drum Preparation

The heart of the print process is the photosensitive drum, an aluminum cylinder coated with a photosensitive material. The drum's job is to pick up laser printer *toner*—a fine black dust that is the "ink" of the laser printing process—and deposit it on the paper. Figure 20.3 points out the photosensitive drum.

FIGURE 20.3

Photosensitive drum in a laser printer

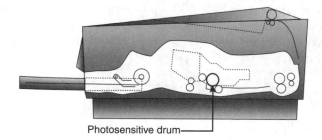

Photosensitive drum—

CLEANING THE DRUM

Since the same photosensitive drum is used to print every image (it actually rotates almost three times during the printing of each letter-sized page), it must be prepared for the newer image by completely purging the previous one. If the drum weren't completely purged, then subsequent pages would have ghostly images from previous pages. You know how hard it is to completely clean a blackboard when you erase it, and parts of what was on the blackboard previously kind of hang around? That's what we're trying to avoid in laser printing.

The cleaning process is accomplished in two parts. Physically, excess toner is constantly wiped from the drum by means of a rubber cleaning blade.

The drum is then cleaned electrostatically by five erase lamps found in the hinged top cover on the early printers and by another drum—a charged drum—in the later printer models. On the printers with lamps, the lamps can shine onto the photosensitive drum via one of the two narrow hinged covers on the top of the cartridge, which open automatically when the cover is closed. These lamps neutralize residual charges by illuminating the photosensitive component of the drum.

The photosensitive component can be permanently damaged by exposure to light; therefore, the illumination from the lamps is red filtered. Pop the top on certain laser printers, and you'll see red plastic; those are the filters for the lamps.

CONDITIONING

After the original preparation, the drum requires conditioning for the next image. This process involves the application of a uniformly negative charge to the surface of the drum by the primary corona assembly (the one in the cartridge) in the early printers or a charged drum in the later ones. The high-voltage power supply provides a −600v charge to the corona wire or charged drum, thus creating an electrical corona, kind of like some major-league static electricity. That −600v charge is applied by a very important thin wire called the *primary corona* located in the disposable laser cartridge. The corona must actually emit a *−6000v* charge in order to get the −600v applied to the drum.

Air is a natural insulator (it's true—in double-paned thermal windows, the air between the panes is as good an insulator as the glass panes are), and that could get in the way of transferring the charge from the corona wire to the drum. But when a corona wire produces a charge, it causes the air in the area of the wire to be ionized with the net effect so that it no longer provides insulation between the drum and the corona. The −600v charge is therefore transferred to the entire surface of the drum.

The voltage buildup on the surface of the drum is uniform because it is filtered by a grid that is attached to a varistor in the high-voltage power supply. Take a look at Figure 20.4.

A varistor is so named because it is a *variable resistor*. It will not conduct electricity until a specific voltage level is achieved. This, of course, is the characteristic that allows it to be useful in this particular application.

WRITING THE IMAGE ON THE DRUM

Now that it's conditioned, the drum is ready for the image.

First, the photosensitive drum is scanned by the laser unit. This is done in a fashion similar to that of a CRT, with a repeated horizontal sweeping motion of the beam. (As a matter of fact, the interface cable on PostScript and optional I/O printer interfaces is referred to in some HP technical documents as a *video cable.*)

FIGURE 20.4

Corona, varistor
grid, and drum

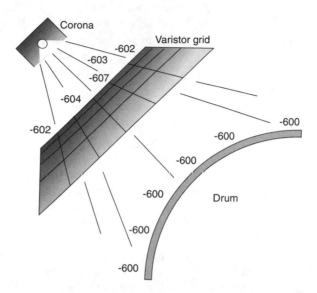

Once a character definition has been determined by the interface controller, the laser light is provided by turning a laser diode on and off at the appropriate times in the current beam position, which in turn is determined by its reflection from the rotation of a polygonal mirror.

On the LaserJet III and earlier, the on/off status of the laser diode could be changed 300 times for each inch of the beam's progress across the drum, hence the 300dpi resolution of those printers. This creates a map of the appropriate portion of the character on the drum by causing a discharge of the voltage potential in the affected areas, thus creating an invisible electrostatic image with the laser. More modern laser printers have even higher resolutions, up to 1200dpi or more.

The laser access to the drum is through the second hinged door on the cartridge, as you see in Figure 20.5.

FIGURE 20.5

Laser access to the
printer drum

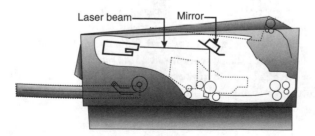

The beam continues its sweep in perfect synchronization with the rotation of the drum so that each incremental horizontal sweep of the beam is offset by ⅓₀₀ of an inch from the previous one. The process continues until the entire drum has thus been mapped.

The affected points of the drum are neutralized to about −100v.

The fact that the drum rotates ⅓₀₀ of an inch with each horizontal sweep of the laser and that the laser diode is able to change states 300 times per inch results in the 300 × 300dpi resolution of the printer.

How Color Laser Printers Differ

While color laser printers are expensive, they are gaining a following due to the glorious graphics and text they produce. The professional-looking output produced by these printers makes them a boon to people who do their own advertising or graphics printing.

Color laser printers work in much the same way as their cheaper black-and-white cousins. The technical details of the print process vary somewhat depending on the manufacturer. Some color lasers print each color on the page individually, making several passes (one for black and one for each of the toner colors), much like the color separation printing that's done by commercial presses. Because the printer has only one drum, the whole printing process repeats several times for each page, layering the toner.

A color printing method that is gaining more popularity is the "Direct-to-Drum" method used by many of the Hewlett-Packard color lasers. In this print method, the charging corona places the negative charge on the drum, and the laser then gently sweeps over the drum and creates an image for the yellow toner (the first of four primary printing colors) to attach to. After the yellow toner has made itself at home, the drum is again charged by the corona, and the laser works its art on the drum and creates an image for the next printing color, magenta. This same process happens again for the final two colors, cyan and black. After all four colors have been applied to the drum, the image is transferred onto the waiting paper. This method allows a single dot on the page to have a blended color, rather than the dithered colors of images produced on inkjet printers and cheaper color laser printers.

NOTE *An inexpensive alternative to color laser printing uses LED (light-emitting diode) technology rather than lasers. Okidata's OKICOLOR 8 printers use this technology. These printers print quickly because they make only one pass, as with an inkjet, but the quality is arguably not quite as good as with a real color laser.*

The problems people have with color laser printers are virtually identical to the problems with black-and-white models. One exception is color registration—that is, a failure of the colors to align properly on a laser printer that prints by making multiple passes over the paper. (Because fewer and fewer color lasers work that way these days, this problem is confined to only a few brands and models.) This problem is often a symptom of the paper not being fed through the printer precisely, so your difficulty is probably with the feed rollers rather than the printing process itself. Check your printer's documentation or the manufacturer's Web site to see what can be done.

The Paper Feed

When the drum has been conditioned, the paper sensor/feed roller assembly draws the paper into the printer. You can see this in Figure 20.6.

Notice that the paper is bowed slightly upward. You might have also noticed at some time that the printer draws the paper from the tray an inch or so and hesitates before continuing. Both occurrences are related to a procedure that ensures that the top edge of the paper is perfectly aligned with the top of the image on the drum.

FIGURE 20.6

Paper sensor/feed
roller assembly

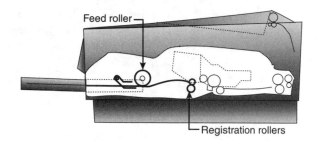

The paper is presented to the registration rollers, which impede its travel until a carefully timed release causes every part of the process to be synchronized.

Image Development

After the image is mapped on the photosensitive drum, there is then the simple application of a basic law of nature and of magnetic properties: opposites attract.

The developer component of the cartridge contains a rotating metallic cylinder with a permanent magnet running its length, a toner reservoir, and a toner height control mechanism. The height control is to regulate the amount of toner that may travel with the cylinder.

The metallic cylinder is situated adjacent to the photosensitive drum. Its sole purpose is to collect toner from the reservoir and present it to the drum in a usable form. This device is called the developing cylinder.

The developing cylinder rotates with a portion of its surface in contact with the toner in the toner reservoir of the cartridge. Its magnetic personality (not to mention the fact that its surface is given a highly negative −600v charge by the high-voltage power supply) causes an irresistible attraction to the tiny neutrally charged particles of toner, which then cling to the cylinder.

The toner that adheres to the cylinder adopts its charge by the time it travels to the image area of the photosensitive drum.

The toner is made of plastic resin particles (the part that melts) bonded to iron oxide (the part that is attracted by the electrical charges).

While the toner-laden developing cylinder rotates toward the image-ready photosensitive drum, a scraping blade removes the excess toner, thus delivering a uniform supply of it to the image process.

The electrical properties of the magnetized developing cylinder are further enhanced by a DC bias and an AC potential.

You can adjust the DC bias via the print density control knob on the printer. Its purpose is to regulate the density of the toner that ends up on the printed page. Counter-intuitively, selecting a *higher* number on the green wheel results in *less* toner being offered to the photosensitive drum and therefore results in a lighter image being put on the page. As the developing cylinder presents the now highly negatively charged toner to the laser-affected areas of the photosensitive drum, they are attracted to the invisible electrostatic image because it, although still negative in charge, is much less negative than the toner itself.

The remainder of the drum, not having been struck by the laser, remains at a −600v charge and effectively repels the similarly charged toner.

The AC component on the developer roller affects the DC potential, thus causing the toner, in a reciprocal process, to escape the negatively charged roller at the moment of highest potential, only to be reattracted to it when the AC component swings high. This happens 60 times per second, effectively presenting a fog of toner to the laser-affected areas.

Those particles of toner that find their way to the electrostatically defined image are not drawn back to the developing cylinder. Take a look at Figure 20.7 for an overview of the process.

FIGURE 20.7

Image processing (toner)

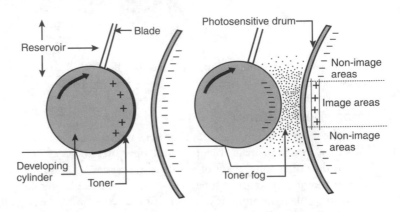

Image Transfer

The desired image now exists on the drum in the form of fine toner particles. Toner is about 50 percent iron oxide, 50 percent plastic. (You can actually get toner out of fabric by rubbing a powerful magnet across the surface.) Next, the laser printer transfers the toner to paper by giving the paper a strong (+600v) *positive* charge. That charge is applied by the *transfer corona*, another very important thin wire permanently mounted in the printer. The toner then jumps from the drum to the paper. Once the toner is on the paper, the paper runs past the *static charge eliminator*, which reduces the paper's charge. The image is now transferred to the paper. Take a look at Figure 20.8.

FIGURE 20.8

Transfer corona

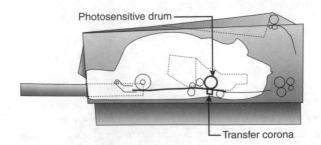

Fusing the Image to the Paper

Once the drum has yielded the image, separation of the paper from it (the drum) is not a foregone conclusion. However, as the paper advances, its natural stiffness facilitates the separation due to the fact that the drum circumference is relatively small. Thinner papers might adhere to the drum, however, so separation is also assisted by the static eliminator, a row of teeth with a highly negative charge that aids in the neutralization of the potential between the positively charged paper and the negatively charged drum.

The paper proceeds to the fusing station with its toner image in the precarious condition of being held to the paper by only gravity and a weak electrostatic charge.

The fusing station assembly is composed of a fuser roller, cleaning pad, thermistor, thermo-protector, and pressure roller.

The fuser roller is a Teflon-coated cylinder that has a high-intensity quartz lamp inside it to provide the heat for the fusing process. If the heat builds beyond acceptable levels, there is a detection/protection mechanism called a *thermistor*, located near the fuser roller, which will shut the printer down.

Just how hot are we talking about here? Well, the temperatures of the LaserJet III's fuser were 165 degrees C (330 degrees F) when on but inactive and 180 degrees C (355 degrees F) while printing. The temperatures are higher in the LaserJet 4 and later models. Given these temperatures, caution is advised in the insertion of any gummed, plastic-coated, inked, or raised image media (not to mention your fingers). I have heard multiple reports of people inserting nonrated Mylar or acetate to make overhead projection display sheets. Put simply, if you try to print on something that melts below 180 degrees C, you'll probably have to buy a new fuser roller. They make special transparency film just for laser printers, so make sure you buy that kind if you need some.

The cleaning pad is positioned so as to remain in constant contact with the fuser roller. It collects any contaminants that seek to become part of the process and provides the already slippery fuser with a silicone film. This ensures that the paper with its now fused image will continue as planned and not have a tendency to stick around (pardon the pun).

A critical part of the cartridge change is the replacement of this pad. It wears out, just like your printer runs out of toner, and needs to be replaced to maintain your printer's longevity and print quality. Without the silicone film, the hot fuser will be much more likely to receive permanent contamination. The replacement toner cartridge should come with a replacement cleaning pad; if it doesn't, check your printer manual to find out what to do.

The pressure roller is a rubber roller that is situated against the fuser roller in such a way that the paper is pressed between them as it passes through. The fuser roller is one of those strong personality types that leaves a lasting impression, so every few minutes the printer will rotate this assembly to keep the rubber roller from receiving a permanent indentation in the area where the rollers are being social. That's the odd noise that your laser printer sometimes makes for no obvious reason.

If you are unfortunate enough to get a paper jam prior to this point in the process, it will become immediately obvious that the image on the paper has not yet been fused. As you remove the affected sheet, liberal amounts of toner will remain on anything it gets in contact with.

As the paper proceeds along its path, it's very important that it not wobble off to the left or right, but instead cleave to the path of the straight and narrow. That is accomplished by the feed guide assembly.

As it passes between the fusing roller and the pressure roller, a combination of heat and pressure ensures that the deposited toner will not become random particles of plastic and iron at the slightest disturbance (see Figure 20.9).

FIGURE 20.9

Fusing roller and
pressure roller

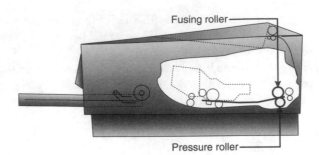

After the image is safely fused in place on the paper, the copy is ready for delivery utilizing the fuser roller and the exit delivery rollers. The exit area paper guides direct the paper to the facedown delivery tray at the top of the machine or the faceup delivery tray at the rear of the machine. Some printers have only one exit tray, usually the facedown one on top. Others allow you to choose by flipping a switch or lowering a tray.

When you're printing with heavy stock or fragile items, you can spare them the final turn by using the delivery tray at the back if your printer has one; just open the door and the paper comes out the back.

I've noticed that my envelopes don't wrinkle quite as badly if I let them exit at the back. This is because the exit delivery area at the top of the printer has the most acute angle that the paper encounters in the entire process. Unfortunately, the LaserJet 4 doesn't offer an option in paper delivery. It can be made to deliver out the back (check the printer's manual to find out how), but it can be tricky, particularly with older models. Take a look at Figure 20.10.

FIGURE 20.10

Rear exit for paper
on printers

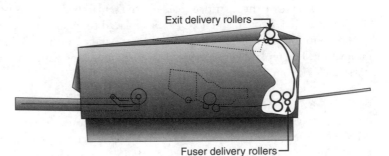

During this whole process, the printer uses sensors located throughout it, which report to the CPU as soon as they see the paper. The printer knows how long it should take to get from one sensor to the next; if a sensor doesn't report "seeing" the paper within a particular window of time, then the printer's CPU assumes that the paper's jammed, and it stops the printing process and reports a jam.

Printer Disassembly Dependencies

Now that you've got some feeling for how laser printers operate, we'll move along to handling some common repairs. If you find yourself disassembling a laser printer, use the chart in Figure 20.11 to determine what you must disassemble before getting to a particular piece.

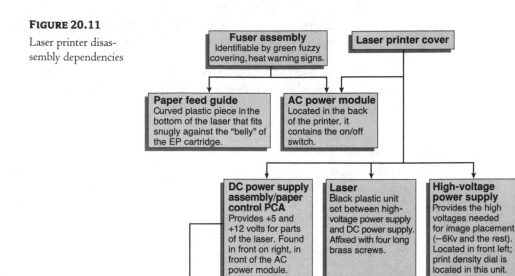

FIGURE 20.11

Laser printer disas-
sembly dependencies

Common Symptoms and Solutions

Now that you know how a laser printer works, you can see what can go wrong. There are lots of *potential* problems with lasers, but I'll confine this to the most common problems only; then we'll take a look at the more rigorous testing you can do.

Vertical White Streaks on the Page

Since the paper is transported top-to-bottom through the laser printer, the paper also passes the coronas top-to-bottom. If a part of the corona were covered with toner, it couldn't transmit all of its charge, leaving either the drum (if it's the main corona) or the paper (if it's the transfer corona) with insufficient charge. That would lead to a vertical stripe with little or no charge, thereby leaving no toner—a white stripe. The answer: clean the coronas.

The main corona is, recall, in the toner cartridge, so if you are being barraged with support calls at the time and you need a quick fix, you can just change the cartridge. But some printers come with a little brush or other cleaning tool with which you can clean your corona. On an HP LaserJet, for example, open the printer and you won't be able to miss the green plastic brush. Note that one side of it is gray and has a suedelike feel. That's for cleaning the main corona. Now remove the cartridge. Note the slot atop the cartridge. You'll see that the suede end of the brush fits nicely into the slot.

Just run it across the slot once and the corona's clean. Some cartridges don't allow you to clean the corona (notably the LaserJet 4 model and several non-HP models). Take a look at your manual for details.

The transfer corona is a permanent fixture in the laser, so it *must* be cleaned on *all* laser printers. Its exact position, again, varies depending on the make and model. On an HP LaserJet II, IID, III, or IIID, for example, open up the printer and, fairly close to the front of the printer, there's a metal trench that runs the width of the printer. It's protected with a webbing of monofilament threads. The monofilament keeps the paper from accidentally feeding into the trough and getting crunched up and snapping the delicate corona.

Shine a flashlight into the trench, and you'll see a hair-thin wire: that's the transfer corona. With the printer off, dip a Q-tip into some rubbing alcohol and carefully clean it end to end. (And, as my friend Brock Meeks says, "Once you clean the Corona, it's Miller Time.") Some printers don't let you get at the transfer corona (notably the HP LaserJet IIP and IIIP, among others), so check your printer manual if in doubt. And be careful with the wire! Don't break it, or your printer won't work and you're in for an expensive repair.

Smearing on the Page

Well, what keeps the toner from smearing? The fusing roller. It is covered with a Teflonlike coating to keep stuff from sticking to it, but it can become scratched or junk can just get baked onto it. In either case, the heat doesn't get transferred to the page. Try cleaning the roller with a soft cloth and some alcohol, but *let the thing cool down before you mess with it!*

Another cause of smears is trying to print double-sided on lasers that are designed to print single-sided. It seems tempting to create double-sided documents by running paper through the laser twice, but it's not a good idea. For one thing, there are rubber rollers that grip the paper so as to pull it through the printer. Ordinarily, they grip the underside of the paper and cause no trouble. But if you're printing on two sides, they end up gripping the underside of the paper—and the underside of the paper has printing on it. The rubber rollers smear the already printed side. This is less of an issue with newer laser printers than with some of the older models.

Horizontal Streaks on the Page

If you see a regular horizontal line on your output, it's more than likely caused by an irregularity in one of the many rollers that the paper must pass by on its journey from the paper cartridge to the output bin. The key to identifying *which* roller is in measuring the distance between the lines. If the horizontal lines are always spaced the same distance apart, then *that distance is the circumference of the bad roller.* Use the numbers shown in Figure 20.12 as a handy-dandy key: just measure the distance between the regular horizontal lines with a ruler and then read off the name of the bad roller. Whether or not you want to try to *replace* the problem child is up to you: getting to some of those rollers is a bit hairy. In my experience, however, the most common distance is 3.75 inches—the circumference of the photosensitive drum.

Cloudy, Faded Output

This sounds like an ad for a laundry detergent; it's what you see when the whites aren't white and the blacks aren't black. The probable cause is either low toner or a dirty or damaged corona wire.

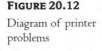

FIGURE 20.12

Diagram of printer problems

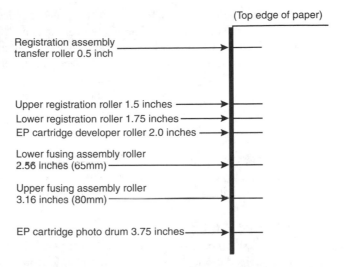

Recall that image creation and transfer requires two corona wires. The coronas attract toner, which can eventually get caked all over the wire and render it less useful. So you need to clean coronas now and then. Refer back to "Vertical White Streaks on the Page" earlier in the chapter for instructions on how to clean them.

Black Line Down the Side of the Page

I don't know why this happens, but you'll see it when the toner is low or the toner cartridge is faulty. Replace the cartridge.

Memory Overflow Error

If you get an out of memory error, or memory overflow, or 20 MEM message (on the LaserJets), it means that you asked the printer to do something that it doesn't have enough memory to do. One common reason for this is that you bought a printer without enough memory for the jobs you do. (Remember, I said earlier that many older laser printers came with only 512KB by default, which is not enough for a full-page graphic. Most laser printers sold today come with 2–4MB of RAM.)

The answer is generally to get more memory. But another possibility is that you've filled the printer's memory with *fonts*. They take up space in memory, too. I find that I can keep the printer from running out of memory under Windows 95 and up by making these modifications to the printer's properties (right-click on a printer in your Printers folder and choose Properties):

- ◆ Print TrueType as graphics.

- ◆ Use raster graphics rather than HP-GL graphics.

55 Error on Startup

Sometimes you'll get a 55 error when you turn a LaserJet printer on. It's pretty scary, particularly when you get out the shop manual and look it up.

There are two circuit boards—oops, PCAs—in lasers that are relevant to this problem. The DC controller board handles charging and discharging the coronas, and the interface board controls the parallel and serial interfaces. If you smoke your interface with a switchbox, just replace the Interface PCA. (In case you've never heard, HP says you can damage your LaserJet Interface PCA with a parallel port switchbox. If they catch you at it, they void your warranty.)

Anyway, when powering up, the two boards do a communications test to ensure that they're talking all right. If there's noise in their communication, the 55 error pops up. The HP shop manual says that you must replace the cards if you see this error, but don't sweat it too much: this error can just crop up due to the normal inrush surge that you get when you turn the machine on. I had a LaserJet Series II printer that was giving me 55 errors about every other day on power-up. I thought I'd have to do some surgery on the printer, but then I happened to move it to another outlet. Bingo! The error never returned. It seems that power noise of any kind on power-up shows up as a 55 error.

Fonts Do Not Appear on Page

Once you become a desktop publishing maven, you dazzle others with your documents—documents replete with fonts galore. But one day you find that a *really* font-intensive page will not print. What's going on?

You've come up against a printer shortcoming, I'm afraid. Older HP lasers (the II and III) can print only 16 different fonts per page. Remember, the printer defines *font* as a combination of typeface, size, stroke weight, and so on, so Courier regular 10-point is one font, Courier 10-point bold is another, Courier 12-point bold still another, and so on.

Actually, 16 fonts should not be a great hindrance. The strangest page in this book has no more than 10 fonts on it.

While we're on the subject, the LaserJet II can hold only 32 soft fonts in memory at any one time (that is, fonts other than the ones resident in the printer itself). That can be a real problem for a printer on a LAN, as it may have to serve *multiple* desktop publishing mavens. Can't you just hear it now? "I want four sizes of Helvetica, with italics and bold, and..." "But I *must* have Times Roman!" "*Times Roman*? You use *that* old woofer? You want to knock out my Palatino for Times Roman? Your name Gutenberg or something?" And the PostScript guys are just smiling in the corner... Luckily, almost all of the more modern laser printers can handle a lot more fonts, both per page and in memory generally, so you should seldom run into any walls.

Printer Picks Up Multiple Sheets

Believe it or not, this usually isn't the printer's fault. You need dry paper in order to get proper feed. Is the paper sitting in the tray for weeks at a time? Not good. When paper is removed from its ream wrapper, it's supposed to be dry. So how do you keep paper dry afterward? If it gets used in a day or two, there's no problem. But if it sits in the tray for longer, particularly in a humid environment, it could pick up some humidity. And make sure you've got the correct side of the paper up when you put it in the printer (look at the package for the arrow).

If you have a newer HP laser printer like the LaserJet 6 series, it could be your separator pad is getting worn out and you need to contact HP to see if your printer is eligible to receive a free replacement pad.

Paper Jams

Trying to print double-sided can cause this. The first time you run the paper through the printer, the paper gets a slight curl imparted to it. Turn it upside down and run it through the printer again and that slight curl can sometimes translate to a paper jam. Another cause of paper jams is printing on the wrong side of the paper. There are, believe it or not, two different sides to a sheet of paper, called the *wax* and the *wire*. Paper will have a "print this side up" indication on the wrapper: pay attention to it. Paper can acquire a curl in humid environments, but the wrapper keeps the paper dry, so don't take paper out of the ream until you're ready to use it. Using cheap paper can also lead to paper jams. Also, old laser printers may have rollers that get out of round, leading to jams.

New laser printers of the "small footprint with gravity paper feed" variety occasionally suffer from paper jams due to the printer grabbing several sheets at once. This problem was especially prevalent on the HP 5L series. It was possible to get this puppy jammed enough so that a technician was required to dismantle the printer to clear the jam. If you do get a jam, resist the urge to rip out the paper. Instead try powering the printer up and down several times. Each time the printer powers up it advances the paper a short distance. Try that to see if the printer will move the paper out for you. In case you notice that your printer does not have a power switch, you will need to resort to plugging and unplugging the printer.

Basic Testing

If you've got a serious laser problem, you may still be able to avoid taking the thing apart to fix it. Here are some tests to try before doing the heavy-duty screwdriver work.

Printer Power

Relative to your other office devices, laser printers are power hogs. Over 7 amps of constant current draw put this device in the same league as an entire well-equipped *kitchen*. Since the printer uses this much energy, it's critical that everything related to the electrical system be in top condition.

We've discussed outlet wiring before, back in Chapter 9, "Power Supplies and Protection." With lasers, however, it's doubly important because of all the power that they suck up. Ideally, you (as the technician) will have an electrical wiring diagram for each building you support, even if it's just your home. Then, when someone starts to plug a Mr. Coffee into an outlet on the same circuit as one of the workstations, you can offer appropriate and eloquent opposing arguments (all mainly consisting of "don't plug other things next to the laser unless you want to buy its replacement"), complete with documentation if necessary. You need to remember that it's a good idea to keep lasers on circuits of their own.

Resetting the Printer

Like the PC, the laser printer can become confused—it is a very complex piece of equipment performing very complex operations. Things go wrong. On occasion, you may find it necessary to reset the printer.

As with the PC, there are different levels of reset for a laser printer. The most severe reset of all for a PC is the power-down, or cold reboot. Cold reboots aren't usually the best way to handle PC problems because you might be using an application that must be shut down a certain way in order to start up again without problems. (Windows 95 and up is like that.) Printers don't have the same problem. As a matter of fact, the power-down reset for the printer only clears the print buffer; it doesn't clear any downloaded fonts or other system data. This can be a useful feature but, although it can temporarily get you past a difficulty, it won't always solve everything, and you'll still have to address the cause of the initial problem.

TIP If you reset the printer while your computer is still spooling data to it, when the printer comes back online the data may continue flowing to it. And since the first part of the job is now gone, you're likely to get garbage characters instead of your print job. Cancel the job from your print queue first, and then reset the printer.

You can also reset some laser printers using the buttons on their front panel. (Check the documentation to find out how.) If you do this, however, you'll lose any fonts or macros that you've downloaded to the printer.

On some color lasers, if the printer does not calibrate itself correctly at startup, the printer may work, but the colors will appear too dark. If you see this, turning the printer off and then back on again gives it another try at the color calibration routine.

The Cable and Ports

Next, take a look at the cable and the I/O ports.

SECURE CONNECTION

If your printer and computer don't seem to be communicating, check the printer's power cable and the data cable to make sure that they're both snugly seated. Pay special attention to the connections at both ends of the data cable: if the little screws on the cable hood aren't screwed in all the way and securing the cable, it's very easy to dislodge the cable, even by doing something as minor as stretching your legs under your desk and knocking the data cable aside.

CABLE LENGTH

So long as it can reach from your computer to the printer, it's not possible for a data cable to be too short. It can easily be too long, however. HP recommends that a parallel cable be no longer than 35 feet. As with many manufacturer standards, I have found that to be quite conservative. I've seen printers work fine with parallel data cables well beyond twice that length.

A serial cable can be much longer than a parallel cable because the signal voltages are higher.

WHAT WE HAVE HERE IS A FAILURE TO COMMUNICATE

If the printer is printing but isn't printing what you sent it, try swapping the data cable for another one. Cables can have flaws that show up only after you've handled the cable a little. If a data pin in a parallel cable breaks, the results could be something like the "Iekko/Hello" example from Chapter 18. If the cable is fine, check to make sure you are using the right driver for the printer.

Parallel Cable Type

In Chapter 18, you learned about the various modes for a parallel port—ECP, EPP, and so on. Not all parallel printer cables support these modes, so select one carefully. The original parallel printer cables were not bidirectional, so they did not include the needed circuitry to manage port modes in which information flows not only to the printer, but also from it.

Generally speaking, any new parallel printer cable that you buy today will work with an ECP or EPP port as long as the cable is labeled as being an IEEE-1284 cable. Don't go crazy and let someone convince you that you need a special cable with gold plating. Just make sure it says either bidirectional or 1284 somewhere on the packaging. Beware, however, of old cables fished out of someone's stash of extras.

You don't have to worry about this for serial cables, by the way, because they are by their very nature bidirectional. However, serial ports do not support ECP or EPP printing modes.

Environmental Considerations

You may not see these concerns on Greenpeace bumper stickers, but it's important that you consider them when setting up and using your printer.

HEAT

A laser printer can pump out some serious heat. This is one reason that it is important that it be placed in a well-ventilated area. Because of this, systems furniture, or any furniture that attempts to fit every part of your workstation into a neat little cubbyhole, can be bad news. It's sometimes built without regard for the fact that the equipment needs to breathe properly. While arranging a workstation, see to it that all your devices have air circulating around them so that heat can dissipate. If you use your printer when it's in an unventilated area, its heat-sensitive components are likely to cook and fail prematurely.

LIGHT

Always guard the toner cartridge from direct contact with strong light, as white light will shorten the useful life of the photosensitive drum. (The light that is used to bathe the drum for print preparation is red filtered, as in a darkroom.) Don't slide the toner cartridge's door open to see the photosensitive drum, unless, of course, you're planning to recycle the cartridge right away.

AMMONIA

Ammonia can be detrimental to the laser printer's ability to neutralize ozone (discussed below) and can also permanently damage the toner cartridge. The chief sources of ammonia in an office setting are the chemicals used for cleaning and those required in the blueprinting process. If you work in an office where blueprinting is done, keep a watchful eye on the fume hood fan and general ventilation in the area of the machine itself.

OZONE

In recent years, we've heard a lot about ozone and the ozone layer. Ozone is a pale blue gas naturally produced whenever a lightning bolt occurs. It's in the upper atmosphere as a by-product of the reaction of oxygen to solar ultraviolet rays. Ozone production doesn't require anything so dramatic as a lightning bolt, however. It's also a natural by-product of the ionization that takes place during the laser printing process.

Ozone is great stuff in the outer areas of the earth's atmosphere but is not good for humans and can be anything from a minor irritant to downright dangerous in significant concentrations. If it is present in concentrations greater than one part in 20,000, it is irritating to the mucous membranes and is poisonous. You can't generally see it, but its odor is most often described as pungent. Most people can detect the presence of ozone at a concentration as low as one part of ozone per 10 million parts of air.

Not only can ozone be harmful to humans, but, as a super-effective oxidizer, it can also cause deterioration of components in the machine itself. Therefore, ozone buildup is one more reason to make sure that your printer is properly ventilated. You're more likely to have problems with ozone in the following situations:

◆ There are several active laser printers and/or copiers in a small, confined area.

◆ The relative humidity is very low.

◆ There is improper or nonexistent ventilation.

◆ The ozone filter is in need of replacement.

◆ Any combination of the above conditions exists.

You should replace the ozone filter in the laser printer after about every 50,000 prints, if your printer has one that's replaceable (check the manual). If office ventilation leaves something to be desired, or if you've got a lot of laser printers in a small, enclosed area, I recommend that you replace the filters more frequently. Mind you, all of this only applies to printers that actually use a corona in the printing process; the LaserJet 4si, for example, would be exempt from this process.

Paper and Media Issues

Just think of this as an up-to-date version of "garbage in, garbage out."

PAPER TYPE

Every kind of laser printer has its own paper type and quality requirements. If you follow those requirements, you'll be less likely to run into paper jams and distortion problems. In general, the better the quality of the printer, the better the quality of paper it will require. At the very least, higher quality paper may give you higher quality printouts. High humidity can also affect the performance of paper in a laser printer (not to mention the fact that it can cause the printer to seal your envelopes).

THE PAPER FEED

You'll need to inspect the feed assemblies periodically. Over time, the feed rollers become glazed and thus less efficient at picking up one sheet of paper at a time from the paper tray. Replacing the rollers is not a major production, but many people that I have talked to find immediate (but temporary—isn't that always the way?) gratification by abrading the feed rollers somehow. You might try rubbing pencil erasers or *very fine* sandpaper over the rollers.

The separation pad (it's just beneath the feed rollers) plays a major role in letting the feed roller pick up only one sheet at a time. Over time, however, it wears thin. It's a good idea to replace the feed rollers and the separation pad about every 100,000 prints. You can buy them in a kit of other like items for those heavy-duty printer maintenance sessions.

CONTAMINANTS

Laser printers are powerful, yet delicate, machines. Foreign objects in the printer can really affect their performance for the worse. Therefore, you must be very careful about what you feed your laser printer: no foreign objects, only the paper recommended by the manufacturer, and no labels or other printables not intended for laser printers.

One of the nastiest things I ever heard of anyone feeding the laser printer was a piece of paper that had a staple in place. This is almost certain to do damage to the fuser assembly. If the Teflon of the roller has scratches in it, your prints will have vertical white lines on them. There's nothing to be done about this; you have to replace the fuser assembly.

Another common contaminant is any printable material not intended for a laser printer. If labels aren't specifically manufactured to be used in a laser printer, don't use them—this is one thing you really can't fudge on even if you've got extra plain labels. Also, letterhead that has raised ink may not fare well when run through the printer.

On a final note, there may be partial sheets of paper buried in the rest of the ream. They won't gum up your printer, but they could cause it to jam. Also, don't use textured paper since the toner does not stick to it.

NEVER JAM TODAY

Most laser printers have several paper jam sensors. Some of them are timing sensors, which make it highly unlikely that a jam could occur anywhere in the process without the printer alerting you. One major cause of jams is improper media; stock that is thicker or thinner than the printer is prepared to handle can cause a fair amount of difficulty.

If a jam occurs before the paper reaches the fusing assembly, you'll need to note two things:

- ◆ Any toner that has not gone through the fusing assembly will end up all over everything when the jam is fixed. The stuff is hard to get out of clothing or carpeting, so be careful when handling paper with loose toner on its surface.

- ◆ Carefully remove any paper jam in the area of the transfer corona, so as not to damage the wire or its attendant monofilament.

PAPER CURL AND WRINKLING

The major cause of curling is the effect that the fusion heat has on the paper composition—the amount of curl is generally directly proportional to the ash content of the paper. If you follow the manufacturer's recommendation for paper type, you're less likely to have problems with curling than otherwise.

Wrinkling will usually be the result of stiff paper negotiating the tight turn at the top of the printer near the facedown tray. It is most evident with heavy stock or envelopes. If the printer is equipped for it, you can avoid the problem by allowing heavy paper to feed from the faceup tray or output faceup to the rear of the printer instead of facedown at the top.

Advanced Testing

What you've already read are the easiest to fix and most common problems. Sometimes, however, the problem requires more work than a change in paper or a tap of the Reset button.

Voltage Tests

If, when you turn it on, the printer doesn't respond normally, the printer's power system is probably malfunctioning. To find out for sure, you'll need a voltage meter. A basic multimeter is a must for the printer technician, but a good digital unit is quite a bit more accurate; you should be able to obtain one for about $30. Using a digital multimeter makes it possible to check for high and low AC and DC voltages, resistances, and continuity.

Location of DC Voltage Test Points

The DC power supply provides three different DC voltages to the system's components. All three can be checked at an interface labeled J210; it is a 20-pin female interface with pin 1 located at the lower-left corner and the odd numbers along the bottom row, left to right.

Using the multimeter, check the indicated pins (every other pin along the bottom, left to right, starting at 1) for the following voltages (frame ground is the reference):

- Pin 1 = +5v.
- Pin 5 = −5v.
- Pin 9 = +24v.
- If *none* of the voltages are present, check the fuse on the DC power supply.
- The AC power.

If *one or more* of the voltages is missing, you'll need to do at least one of the following:

- Remove all optional devices, including memory.
- Replace the DC power supply assembly.
- Replace the DC controller PCA.

Testing the Host's Interface

When it comes to testing the host's I/O ports, a breakout box is a handy thing to have around. A breakout box is a diagnostic tool that will indicate with LEDs what the activity on the tested port happens to be. You can also use a breakout box to design a cable if you happen to be working with something that is nonstandard.

Charting Printing Problems

You can sometimes tell which printer component is causing problems from where the problem appears on the page. Figure 20.12, shown earlier in this chapter, can help you track down errant components.

Diagnostic Software

If you're having output problems and want to see exactly what is going from the computer to the printer, you can capture printer output in a file by means of a utility program. Your printer may have come with its own diagnostic software, or you may be able to download a testing utility from the printer manufacturer's Web site.

TESTING THE ENGINE

There are many things that could be wrong if you send a print job to the printer and nothing happens; one of the worst is a problem with the laser engine. To determine whether the laser engine is functioning properly, you need to bypass the interface controller where data is received and force the printer to do a direct print from the engine itself.

On newer Hewlett-Packard printers, beginning with the LaserJet 4, the engine can be tested by using the Self-Test menu on the printer (not the Print Test Page command from Windows).

But if you still have one of those older models hanging around, then look on the side of the printer that is opposite the memory upgrade socket for a hole (it's exposed on the LaserJet II but has a plastic cover on the LaserJet III). Push a ballpoint pen or the like into the hole. This will force a print direct from the laser engine circuitry. Try it now, while the printer's working, so you can compare it to tests you run when the printer is malfunctioning. Your good control test indicates the following:

- The laser engine and engine circuitry are functioning correctly.

- Laser alignment is correct (shown by side margins).

- Feed timing is correct (shown by top and bottom margins).

- There is sufficient toner.

- None of the major components is significantly damaged or contaminated in any way (there are no smudges or repeating anomalies).

SETTING A BASELINE

It's hard to get any information from a test print if you don't know what a good print looks like. Now, while the printer still works, you should print a test page using the Self-test menu on the printer itself. Some older models may not have menus to work with; in that case, you should consult your manual to find the exact instructions since they vary from printer to printer. Keep this test print somewhere, and you can compare it with your test prints later to see how the new print compares with the baseline test print. A test print shows various gray scales, text, horizontals, and verticals. The tightest horizontals and verticals will appear to the average viewer as single heavy lines but, if you look at them closely, you'll see multiple lines in those areas.

Understanding Error Messages and Fixing Printer Problems

One sure way to know that you've got a problem is for your laser printer to *tell* you that you've got one. In Table 20.1, I explain what each printer error message is on most HP LaserJets, what causes it, and what you should do to try to fix the problem that it describes. When the situation or the response required is not obvious (and sometimes even when it is), I have indicated the path to a (hopefully) happy ending. If your printer's manual has a similar table, consult it instead, as its codes will be specific to your printer.

TABLE 20.1: PRINTER ERROR MESSAGES

MESSAGE	MEANING	SOLUTION (WHERE APPLICABLE)
00 READY	The printer is ready.	
02 WARMING UP		Wait a few moments for the printer to signal "ready."
04 SELF TEST	Continuous self-test printing.	
05 SELF TEST	Self-test in progress (on some printers, this will result in a print).	
06 PRINTING TEST	Self-test printing.	
06 FONT PRINTOUT	Printing sample characters from all installed fonts. Or printing PS configuration pages.	
07 RESET	Printing sample characters from all installed fonts. Or printing PS configuration pages.	
08 COLD RESET	Returns both the Configuration and Print menu selections to the factory settings.	
09 MENU RESET	Returns all Print menu items to factory settings, clearing buffered pages, temporary fonts, and all macros.	
10 RESET TO SAVE (HP LaserJet only)		Press and hold Reset to confirm the acceptance of Print menu selections (you'll lose any temporary fonts, macros, or buffered data), or press Continue or On Line (no changes to selections will be made).
11 PAPER OUT (HP LaserJet only)		Add paper to the input tray.
12 PRINTER OPEN		Close the top cover assembly.
13 PAPER JAM	Sample jam codes (vary among printers): 13.1—internal jam, 13.2—input jam, 13.3—duplex jam, 13.4—output jam	Open the printer, clear the jam, and press Continue or On Line to reprint the page.
14 NO EP CART		Install the toner cartridge.
15 ENGINE TEST	Engine test with printout preceded by pressing the Test Print button.	

Continued on next page

TABLE 20.1: PRINTER ERROR MESSAGES *(continued)*

MESSAGE	MEANING	SOLUTION (WHERE APPLICABLE)
16 TONER LOW		Replace cartridge (rotating the existing cartridge briskly can result in more prints even if the message remains).
17 MEMORY CONFIG (HP LaserJet III only)	Indicates memory configuration in progress (happens when Page Protection is set to On).	
18 SKIP SELF TEST (HP LaserJet III only)	Skips the ROM and RAM tests on startup and is activated by holding down the minus key. Don't do this routinely.	
18 MIO NOT READY (LaserJet 4M or 4Plus)	The Modular I/O (network card) is not ready.	Power down the printer and make certain the card is seated properly in the socket. A new card may be needed if this persists.
20 ERROR	Indicates that memory capacity has been exceeded by the volume of data received.	
21 ERROR	Indicates that the memory received is too complex for the printer to process.	
21 PRINT OVERRUN		Enable page protection or reduce the complexity of the job (more printer memory may be required).
22 ERROR	Communication handshake was unsuccessful.	Rate of transmission or configuration may need changing.
22 I/O CONFIG ERR	Wrong handshake protocol (XON/XOFF, DC1/DC3, and DTR handshake protocols are supported).	
40 ERROR	An error occurred during data transmission (an error occurs if you power down the computer while the printer is online or an attempted transfer uses unmatched rates).	Turn the printer off and cancel the print job in Windows. Wait a few seconds and turn it back on again. Then resubmit the print job.
41 ERROR	A temporary page-creating error occurred.	Press the Continue key to repeat the page.
42 ERROR	Communications problem has occurred between the Interface/Formatter PCA and an optional interface device.	Reseat the optional I/O device and press Continue to resume printing.
43 ERROR	A communications problem has occurred between the Interface/Formatter PCA and an optional interface device.	Power off the printer and check your optional devices. Power on and try again. If the problem persists, contact the manufacturer for troubleshooting help.

Continued on next page

TABLE 20.1: PRINTER ERROR MESSAGES *(continued)*

MESSAGE	MEANING	SOLUTION (WHERE APPLICABLE)
49 REMOVE PAGE	Paper was in the manual feed guides when the printer was turned on.	
50 SERVICE		Power off the printer for at least 10 minutes. If the problem persists, you may have to repair or replace the fuser assembly.
51 ERROR	Indicates loss of laser beam for more than two seconds.	
52 ERROR	Scanner motor unable to maintain appropriate speed.	
53-x ERRORUNIT	Error detected on optional memory card.	Verify that the correct revision level (B or greater) is installed.
54 ERROR	Problem with the duplex unit shift plate.	
55 ERROR	Communications problem between the DC Controller PCA and the Interface/Formatter PCA.	Do a test print to verify functional DC controller. If the problem persists: check DC voltages at J210, replace the Interface/Formatter PCA, and replace the DC Controller PCA.
61 SERVICE	A checksum error in the Interface/Formatter PCA's ROM was detected during self-test.	
62 SERVICE	A checksum error in the Interface/Formatter PCA's ROM was detected during self-test.	
63 SERVICE	Error was detected in either the Interface/Formatter PCA's dynamic RAM or in optional memory.	Remove any optional memory and retest.
64 SERVICE	Indicates a laser scan buffer error.	Turn the computer off and back on.
65 SERVICE	An error occurred on the dynamic RAM controller.	Turn the computer off and back on. If that doesn't work, replace the Interface/Formatter PCA.
67 SERVICE	A miscellaneous hardware or address error has taken place on the Interface/Formatter PCA.	Reseat all cables, font cartridges, and optional devices. If that doesn't work, replace the Interface/Formatter PCA.
68 ERROR	A recoverable error has occurred in NVRAM (nonvolatile RAM).	Press Continue to clear, then verify the Control Panel menu settings; one or more items will have reverted to their factory defaults.

Continued on next page

TABLE 20.1: PRINTER ERROR MESSAGES *(continued)*

MESSAGE	MEANING	SOLUTION (WHERE APPLICABLE)
68 SERVICE	NVRAM failure has occurred.	Replace the Interface/Formatter PCA. You can temporarily operate the printer without VRAM, but all Control Panel volumes revert to their factory defaults and the 00 READY message becomes 68 READY/SERVICE.
69 SERVICE	Time-out error has occurred between the Interface/Formatter PCA and an optional I/O device.	Remove the optional device and retest. If the message persists, replace the Interface/Formatter PCA.
70 or 71 ERROR	Improper cartridge application.	Turn the printer off and back on. If the error persists, verify with the cartridge vendor that the cartridge was designed for that printer.
72 SERVICE	Font cartridge removal error. May also result from a malfunctioning font cartridge or poor connection.	Turn the printer off, wait a few seconds, and turn it back on again.
79 SERVICE	Miscellaneous problem.	Turn printer off and back on. If the problem persists, remove the memory modules and any installed font, macro, and personality cartridges one at a time. If the problem still occurs, and the printer has an optional I/O device installed, try a different interface (parallel or serial) if possible. If the problem continues, replace the Formatter PCA. If the problem is intermittent, temporarily remove any non-HP hardware/firmware and test the printer. If it keeps failing, replace the Formatter PCA.
CONFIG LANGUAGE	This message is the result of holding down the Enter key while powering on the printer.	Following the self-test, select a display language with the +, –, and Enter keys.
EC LOAD	You've requested an envelope size not currently installed in the printer, or the tray is out of envelopes.	Load the correct envelope in the (envelope size) envelope tray. Insert a loaded tray and select the loaded envelope size from the Control Panel or press Continue to override. Envelope size may be COM10, MONARC, C5, or DL.

Continued on next page

TABLE 20.1: PRINTER ERROR MESSAGES *(continued)*

MESSAGE	MEANING	SOLUTION (WHERE APPLICABLE)
PC LOAD	You've requested a paper size not currently installed.	Same as above, only for paper. Paper (paper size) size may be EXEC, LETTER, or LEGAL.
PE FEED or MF FEED	You've made a request to manually feed paper or envelopes of the indicated size.	
PE TRAY =	The printer wants to know the size of the paper or envelopes you're using.	Use the + and – keys to select a size (envelope size) and then press Enter. Press On Line or Continue to proceed.
FC	You removed font cartridge(s) while the printer was offline and contained buffered data.	Reinsert cartridge(s) and press the (LEFT/RIGHT/BOTH) Continue or On Line key.
NO FONT	The printer could not read the font cartridge(s).	Reinsert the cartridge(s) and try again.
FE CARTRIDGE	You removed a cartridge while the printer was online.	Turn the printer off, reinsert the cartridge, and turn the printer back on.
USER MAINTENANCE (LaserJet 4si only)	Has printed 200,000 pages.	
MENUS LOCKED	Administrator has a security lock on the Control Panel.	See your network administrator.

Other Things to Consider

If you're still looking for the source of a problem, one of these remedies may help.

The Toner Cartridge

If you install and maintain the toner cartridge properly, you shouldn't have problems with it. In these days of greenery, many people wonder whether they should use recharged cartridges. You're a lot safer using retreads than you used to be: the folks recycling them are either doing a better job or are using better components (or both); the recent efforts are far superior to many of the early ones. Still, keep an eye out for unscrupulous recyclers. A properly redone cartridge includes a new photosensitive drum. Beware of what are called "drill and fill operations," which drill a hole in the cartridge and refill it with toner but don't replace any of the parts inside.

Color laser printers require four separate toner cartridges, and the method for replacing them depends on the printer make and model. The printer should let you know when one of the cartridges needs replacing, but if you start seeing a particular color dropping out, check its toner level and replace as needed. Some color laser printers offer a color-by-color self-test, much as inkjet printers do, so you can gauge the quality of each individual cartridge's output.

Even first-time cartridges can cause print anomalies. If the cartridge is running out of toner, you might see vertical white streaks on your prints. Rocking the cartridge gently around its long axis usually lets you get about a hundred more prints out of the cartridge (depending on the amount of white space and toner density adjustment).

When new, toner cartridges sometimes make noises, don't worry too much about them—incidental printing noises are quite common and are not usually a matter of concern. Just watch for any print anomalies that might be related to the sounds you hear.

Mirror

In many laser printers, there's a mirror in the lid assembly. If it gets dirty, your prints may have fuzzy edges. Tobacco smoke is the most common culprit, so use a good glass cleaner and lens-cleaning material to get it back in shape, and chase smokers away from the printing area.

Vertical Lines

I talked earlier about what scratches on the feed rollers do to your print jobs: they will almost always leave vertical lines on the print. Scratches don't just appear—they're generally the result of someone running things through the printer that don't belong there (staples or labels or transparencies not meant for laser printing). Since even running paper through the laser printer twice generally isn't a good idea, there's no reason why staples should be anywhere near the printer paper in the first place.

DISTORTED IMAGES

If your printed images look stretched, the printer's feed components are probably slipping, or its gears are not functioning properly. The gears may not be gripping on the shaft, as they should be. To restore the printer's feed capability, get new feed rollers, separator pads, and assorted bushings in a kit, and replace the worn-out components.

Squeaking or Groaning Sounds

Laser printers can make some pretty bizarre sounds. Some of these sounds indicate developing problems, and should, therefore, receive appropriate attention, but a perfectly healthy and properly functioning printer can also make noises that sound as though the printer is malfunctioning. The most noticeable noises are generally part of the paper feed process.

A noise that I have been asked about more than any other is the one that comes every few minutes from an idle (but powered on) laser printer. This noise sounds like the printer's electric motor beginning, as though it's about to print, and then stopping abruptly. There's a good reason for that description: that's exactly what the sound is. Since the fuser assembly remains hot even when idle, the printer needs to rotate it every so often. Otherwise, the hot metallic fuser roller would burn a permanent depression into the rubber pressure roller with which it is in constant contact.

Maintenance Issues

Here are a few things you should check to keep your laser printer in good working order.

Errant Toner

When, in the course of printer events, you are called upon to clean up toner, the method will depend on the amount and location. You can clean up minute amounts on the inside of the printer along the paper's path with a slightly dampened cloth or a swab dipped in alcohol. If there are larger amounts of toner, more drastic measures are called for.

WARNING   Never, ever, ship a printer with a toner cartridge still inside.

If a cartridge is dropped or jostled improperly during shipment, you will likely have to clean up larger quantities of toner.

WARNING   Don't get out the Electrolux! Toner is a plastic resin bonded to iron particles, a deadly combination to hot electric motors (like those in vacuum cleaners). If you try to vacuum up the runaway toner, it will blow straight through a normal vacuum cleaner bag and into the motor, where the plastic will melt and the iron will play havoc with the armature and brushes. The particles that don't stop in the motor will fly through the air and cover the vicinity (and you) with tiny black particles that are very difficult to wash out of clothing.

If you get toner on your clothing or skin, remember its properties; use only cold water and plenty of soap. You're likely to get toner on you if you have to clear a paper jam that happened before the paper got to the fusing assembly, so be careful. If you have a large toner spill in the printer, take it outside and use a compressed air canister to clean out the printer.

Cleaning

Like getting exercise and balancing your checkbook, printer cleaning rarely gets done as often as the manuals recommend. Each of the printer's components needs to be cleaned regularly, however.

THE CLEAN COMMAND

Many printers, including most of the HP LaserJets, have a self-cleaning routine that you can run. One of the kindest things you can do for your printer is to run the self-cleaning routine every time you change the toner cartridge. If your printer doesn't have a clean utility, you might be able to download one from the manufacturer's Web site.

The clean command will usually print a large black box on a piece of copier grade paper. This sheet of paper is then placed facedown and sent through the process again. This is the only time you should refeed a piece of paper without the luxury of a duplex unit! Sending this sheet through again will reheat the toner that was placed on the paper the first time, causing it to become slightly adhesive. Any miscreant toner particles or small pieces of paper stuck to the innards of the printer will now be pulled out. The way to tell if the clean command has performed up to par is to check the black box that was printed on the first pass—if it is covered with shiny black specks, then you know it worked. You may need to do this more than once just to be sure you get all of the little varmints attached to your rollers.

CORONA WIRES

There are two corona wires in most printers. (Check your manual to find the exact locations.) You should clean both of them regularly or whenever there is a problem with the printer that might be caused by excess toner on the wire. Clean the primary corona in the toner cartridge once at the mid-point of the life of the cartridge—you've got no excuse to avoid doing so, as HP and many other printer manufacturers thoughtfully provide a plastic brush for the job. Insert the suede end of the brush into the slot in the cartridge and slide it from one end to the other.

The transfer corona is in the bottom of the printer beneath the paper path. On most printers, several monofilament lines protect it from damage in the event of a paper jam. Clean it with a cotton-tipped swab (which may come with your replacement cartridge), gently stroking it in each direction and on each side between the monofilament segments. I recommend that you do this in good light, so you can see how much pressure you are putting on the corona, as, if you break it, the entire corona assembly must be replaced.

Usually the products of your labor will be pretty innocuous: perhaps some toner or a little dust. The winner in the most-disgusting-corona-problem category, however, is the time one technician reportedly found several well-done roaches in the transfer corona channel. The only reason the users discovered the cockroaches was because the insects' bodies were making the pages turn black.

Some printers, such as the LaserJet 4, don't use a corona that you must clean; they use charging rollers. That's why it's important to check your printer's manual to find out exactly what parts you are expected to clean and how to access them.

REGISTRATION AND FEED GUIDE ASSEMBLIES

Here, maintenance is pretty easy: you need only occasionally wipe with a damp cloth to clean up that errant toner (unless, of course, some foreign object happens to stop in this area). You'll need to clear paper fragments away periodically, as it's here that paper fragments or partial pages will usually stop.

FUSING ASSEMBLY

I really can't overemphasize the importance of keeping the fuser roller free of contaminants. Because of the high temperatures at which it operates, this critical part of the printing process will have a tendency to hang on to a little bit of everything that touches it: paper curls up and stays with it, letterhead ink melts on it, and so forth. To keep this from happening, the roller itself is coated with Teflon and the brush that rides on top of it (on HPs, it's underneath the fuzzy green lid) is permeated with silicone.

I've seen people leave the cotton tip on the silicone pad that cleans the fuser. This is not a good idea, as this causes the pad to fit its slot too tightly instead of floating easily on the roller.

SEPARATION PAWLS

Push back the lid behind the fuser assembly, and you'll see a set of four clawlike things called *pawls*. The pawls facilitate the separation of the paper from the fuser. Over time, however, they get a gradual buildup of contaminants that could eventually begin to scrape the Teflon from the fuser roller. If they scrape off the Teflon, the effect is the same as that of a staple fed to the printer: broad vertical lines will begin to appear on the print.

You can't repair scratches on the fuser roller; you'll need to replace the entire fuser assembly. To avoid making a habit of this, regularly use an alcohol-dipped swab to clean each of the pawls thoroughly.

Improving Print Quality

There are some amazing differences between the printers that are available today and the ones we started with many years ago. Many of the best models today print at 1200 × 1200dpi and use ultra-fine toner to produce some impressive printing. No matter which printer you use, however, there are things that you can do to improve the quality of its output.

Paper Quality and Feed Continuity

The type of paper and the quality of the toner can differ along a surprisingly wide range. A close inspection will reveal the difference. And, as you read earlier in this chapter, the wrong type of paper can cause paper jams.

Keep the paper-feed mechanisms in top condition to avoid paper slippage and, with it, image problems. The key items are the feed rollers and the separation pad, located just inside the printer and near the paper tray receptor.

Image Formation

The image formation components are the laser engine, beam mirror, toner, developer roller, primary and transfer coronas, and photosensitive drum. With all these items involved, you might worry that the imaging components of the printer will be a troubleshooting nightmare. It's not that bad, though: if you keep the cartridge changed and the coronas cleaned, that's usually all you'll need to do to keep the print sharp.

A few last tips: As I've mentioned before, it's best to use a fresh ream of paper, not one that's been sitting in your laser printer's cartridge for the last two weeks soaking up moisture and developing a curl. Distribute the toner in the cartridge. Take the cartridge out of the printer and rotate it 15 times. Then shake it side to side 15 times. You can also help the laser's toner transfer process by "clearing its throat" and printing three to five *totally black pages*. You can do that with a little LaserJet program. Here's the command sequence; keep it handy:

```
esc&l0Eesc&l0Lesc*p0x0Yesc*c2400a3300B esc*c0PescE
```

That'll print a black page. The esc stands for the ASCII escape code, ASCII 27.

Laser Printer Rumors and Truth

I'd like to end this chapter with these rumors. I know they sound goofy, but I hear people ask this stuff in class, so here are the top laser rumors and, where I can supply it, the Truth.

Toner Is Made of Powdered Chicken Bones

When I heard this one, I thought I'd make a million bucks organizing a chicken bone recycling center. No go, though. (I *did* mention it to some execs at a well-known fried chicken chain, however, so if you end up seeing separate trash cans for the bones, you know whose fault it is.)

Elvis Is in the Printer

Rumor has it that, on HP LaserJets, if you press a certain set of keys on the laser panel, a full-page graphic of Elvis prints out, with the caption "The King Lives." So goes the tale.

HP swears it ain't so, and I believe them. Here's why: there isn't enough ROM on the laser circuit boards to store a bitmap of Elvis, even *before* he gained weight. I swear I heard this from someone in class, and others had heard of the rumor also. My guess is that HP brought it on themselves with the Secret Service Test Mode. (Why not tell everybody about it, anyway?)

Cartridges Are Designed to Self-Destruct

The rumor: There are pieces of glass in the toner of Canon-type cartridges that slowly chew up the print drum so it is completely unusable by about 8,000 copies. This supposedly is done to discourage rechargers.

I just don't know. HP denies it, but Canon's patent application for the toner includes "silica particles"—conceivably another name for pieces of glass. That's for the next book, I suppose.

The official HP spec sheet on toner says that toner is composed of the items listed in Table 20.2.

TABLE 20.2: LaserJet Toner Ingredients

COMPONENT	PERCENTAGE BY WEIGHT
Styrene acrylate copolymer	55–65
Iron oxide	30–40
Salicylic acid chromium chelate	1–3

Now, salicylic acid is *aspirin*. Maybe *that's* why it's no headache at all to set up a laser printer.

Troubleshooting Recap

Here's a quick review of the troubleshooting tips covered in this chapter:

- ◆ Vertical white streaks on the page can indicate a dirty transfer corona. Clean it with a cotton swab.

- ◆ Vertical black streaks indicate scratches on the feed rollers, perhaps caused by running staples or other hard foreign objects through the printer by mistake.

- ◆ Smeared ink could mean a scratched or dirty fusing roller. Clean it with a soft cloth and some alcohol (after it has cooled down). Ink sometimes also smears when you run double-sided pages on printers not designed for it.

- ◆ A distorted or stretched image probably means the printer's feed components are slipping or the gears are not functioning correctly. To restore the printer's feed capability, get new feed rollers, separator pads, and assorted bushings in a kit, and replace the worn-out components.

- ◆ Horizontal lines are usually caused by an irregularity in one of the many rollers that the paper passes through. To identify which roller, measure the distance between the lines. Figure 20.12 shows a chart to help.

◆ Cloudy or faded output usually means it's time to change the toner cartridge, or you've got a dirty or damaged corona wire.

◆ A black line down the side of the page can indicate the toner is low or the toner cartridge is faulty.

◆ Error codes that appear on the printer's LED panel can be looked up in the printer's manual or on the manufacturer's Web site. Table 20.1 lists the codes for Hewlett-Packard LaserJets.

◆ A printer that picks up multiple sheets is usually fine—it's the paper that's your problem. Make sure it is dry and well fanned. Dry it in a microwave if needed.

◆ Paper jams can result from trying to print double-sided or from curled or cheap paper.

◆ Many printer problems can result from using the wrong printer driver in Windows or other software you're using. Make sure you have the correct driver. Most printers come with a driver disk.

◆ If a printer that usually works fine gets an error or starts printing out garbage pages, try turning it off and then back on again after a few seconds.

◆ If you want the printer and computer to communicate using an ECP or EPP parallel port, make sure you have the parallel port defined in the computer's BIOS as ECP or EPP, and make sure you have an ECP- or EPP-capable cable.

◆ Avoid stacking anything that blocks the airflow around a laser printer. And avoid placing it in a low-ventilation cubbyhole in a computer desk.

◆ Keep toner cartridges away from strong light, as it's bad for the photosensitive drum.

◆ If your output is wrinkling, check the paper quality. You may be able to set the printer to eject the printed pages from the back, faceup, reducing the amount of turns the paper has to make to get to the exit, and perhaps reducing the wrinkling.

Chapter 21

Troubleshooting Scanners

◆ QuickSteps: Connecting and Testing a Flatbed Scanner   601

◆ Types of Scanners and How They Work   602

◆ Scanner Maintenance   607

◆ Solving Common Problems   607

◆ Troubleshooting Tips   612

Introduction

DUE TO THEIR SHRINKING COST, scanners are becoming an integral part of most home computer systems. You can get a decent scanner for well under $150 these days, and they're relatively easy to hook up and use.

Scanners are quite useful if you're doing any amount of digital photograph editing or storage. While you can shoot new photos with a digital camera, the only way to get your old photos into digital format is to scan them in. In fact, many camera buffs still prefer to shoot with a 35mm film camera and then scan the photo prints into their computer for digital editing, rather than compromise initial quality with a low-performance digital camera.

Scanners are also useful for scanning documents into computer files. Legal documents, credit card bills, monthly bank statements, you name it—you can use a scanner to make a hard copy electronic.

Connecting a scanner to your system is relatively easy, especially if you have a newer computer system, a newer scanner, and a recent version of Windows. (It's easiest with Windows XP, which includes a Scanner and Camera Wizard to handle most of the configuration for you.) Scanners are also fairly reliable machines, with most of their moving parts enclosed to reduce maintenance.

In this chapter, I'll discuss pretty much all you need to know about scanners—how to connect them, configure them, and troubleshoot them.

QuickSteps

Connecting a Flatbed Scanner

Here are the basic steps for connecting the most popular type of scanner—the flatbed scanner. For in-depth coverage on how to troubleshoot scanner-related problems, refer to the later sections of this chapter.

BE PREPARED

Before you start, there are some things you may need on hand. These include:

◆ Scanner documentation or user manual

◆ Scanner software or drivers ready to install, if required

◆ Your new flatbed scanner

1. If you're installing via a parallel or SCSI port, turn off your computer. (If you're installing via a USB port, leave your computer on.)

2. Plug your new scanner into a power source, then connect it to the appropriate port (USB, parallel, or SCSI) on the back of your computer. If your scanner shares a parallel port with your printer, power off your printer and connect the printer to the scanner to your PC, as directed in the scanner's instructions. If you're connecting via SCSI, you'll probably need to install a separate SCSI card in your computer and connect the scanner to that board.

3. Turn your computer on, then turn on your scanner.

TIP   Some scanners have a lock to protect the charge coupled device (CCD) from getting damaged during shipping. If your unit has such a lock, don't forget to unlock the CCD before you first use the scanner.

4. Windows should recognize the new scanner and install the appropriate drivers. You may be prompted to insert the scanner's installation disk or CD at this step.

5. If your scanner came with its own software (most scanners typically come with some graphics program or another), install that software now.

TIP   Some high-end scanners might require a manual calibration on installation. This is typically done by scanning a special shaded card that comes with the scanner, and then configuring various settings on the scanner's software control panel.

Types of Scanners and How They Work

A scanner works a little like a traditional office photocopier—except that the final result is a digital computer file, not a printed copy.

Scanner Types

There are five popular types of scanners you can install on your system:

Flatbed scanners The most popular type of scanner for home use is the flatbed, or desktop, scanner. Flatbed scanners, like the one in Figure 21.1, can be found for as little as $100, and make it easy to scan papers, books, and any other item that you can lay flat between a glass bed (plate) and the scanner's top cover. The image is scanned via a scan head that moves across the face of the original document. Most flatbed scanners scan in color.

Sheet-fed scanners Sheet-fed scanners are like flatbed scanners, except the scan head is fixed and the original document moves across the head. While flatbed scanners can scan just about any item that can fit on the glass plate, including three-dimensional objects, sheet-fed scanners can scan only flat pieces of paper. In addition, many sheet-fed scanners scan only in black and white.

Combo scanner/printer/fax A very popular option in home offices and small offices is the "all-in-one" machine that scans, prints, faxes, and copies. (It doesn't make coffee, though....) These units, popularized by Hewlett-Packard, effectively merge a black-and-white sheet-fed scanner with an inkjet or laser printer and a fax machine. You feed the original documents into a slot, just as you do with a freestanding sheet-fed printer, and then the scan head moves across the document.

Handheld scanners A handheld scanner is kind of a manually controlled flatbed scanner. In this case, the original document is placed on a flat surface (like a desktop), and you manually move the scanner across the face of the document. In essence, your arm becomes the moving scan head. This type of scanner doesn't deliver the best quality, but it is convenient—and very portable. Unfortunately, portable scanners have proved particularly problematic (and not very popular), and thus aren't in widespread use today.

FIGURE 21.1

Low-priced flatbed scanners—like this model from Visioneer—are part of many home computer systems.

Drum scanners   If you want high-quality black-and-white or color scans, like the kinds required by the magazine, newspaper, and book publishing industries, you need to go all the way up to an expensive drum scanner. This type of scanner mounts the original document on a rotating glass cylinder, called a *drum*. At the center of the cylinder is a sensor that splits light bounded off the document into three beams. Each beam is then sent through a color filter into a *photomultiplier tube* (PMT), where the light is changed into an electrical signal. Drum scanners are much more expensive than consumer-quality flatbed scanners, and they typically connect to a computer system via a SCSI interface.

Whatever method is used to scan a source document, a digital image of that document is then created. That digital image can be saved in a variety of graphics file formats (TIF, BMP, JPG, and so forth), or the text information can be extracted (via optical character recognition technology) and saved as a text file.

How a Scanner Scans

As shown in Figure 21.2, most flatbed scanners are composed of the following parts:

- Glass bed (or plate), on which the source document is placed facedown

- Lamp, used to illuminate the source document

- Mirrors, used to reflect the image of the source document

- Filters, which adjust the image of the source document

- Lens, used to focus the image of the source document onto the CCD array

FIGURE 21.2

The major parts of a flatbed scanner

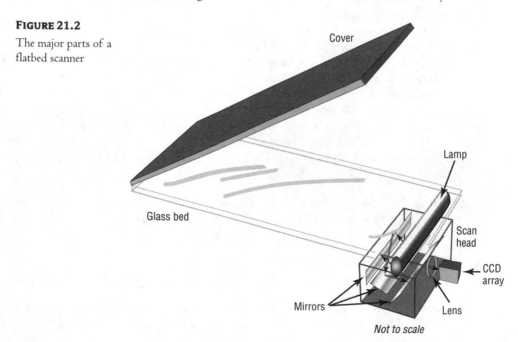

Not to scale

- CCD array, used to turn reflected light into an electrical charge
- Scan head, which contains the CCD array, mirrors, lens, and filter
- Stabilizer bar, to which the scan head is attached
- Belt, attached to the stepper motor and used to advance the stabilizer bar
- Stepper motor, used to drive the stabilizer bar
- Cover, used to provide a uniform background for the scanned document—and to keep you from being blinded by the scanner lamp

You prepare for a scan by placing the source document facedown on a glass plate. You then close the scanner's cover, which provides a uniform background that the scanner software can use as a reference point for determining the size of the scanned document.

When you press the button to start the scan, the lamp lights to illuminate the source document, and the stabilizer bar is sent rolling from one end of the document to the other. As the scan head—which is attached to the stabilizer bar—travels across the face of the document (in what is called a *pass*), light is reflected off the document, through a series of mirrors, filters, and lenses, and then onto the CCD array.

NOTE *Older scanners used a standard fluorescent lamp, while most newer scanners use either a cold cathode fluorescent lamp (CCFL) or xenon lamp.*

The CCD is actually a collection of light-sensitive diodes, called *photosites*. The photosites convert the reflected light into an electrical charge; since each photosite is sensitive to slight variations in light, the brighter the light that hits a photosite, the greater the electrical charge generated.

Most low-cost scanners use a single pass to scan the original document, while some higher-end models use a three-pass method. In the single-pass method, the lens splits the image into three identical versions of the original. These images are then passed through three color filters (red, green, and blue) to separate sections of the CCD and combined to create a single full-color image. In the three-pass method, each pass of the scan head uses a different color filter (red, green, or blue) between the lens and the CCD array; assembling the three filtered images results in a single full-color image.

Some inexpensive flatbed scanners use a *contact image sensor* (CIS) instead of a CCD array. The CIS replaces the entire CCD/mirror/filter/lens/lamp mechanism with rows of red, green, and blue LEDs. The image sensor is placed very close to the glass plate, and the LEDs combine to provide a bright white light. The illuminated image is then captured by the same sensors.

NOTE *While CIS scanners are smaller, lighter, and lower-cost than similar CCD scanners, they don't deliver the same image quality as their higher-priced CCD siblings. Look in the scanner's specs before you buy to see if it's CIS or CCD.*

Scanner/Computer Interface

There are three main interfaces used to connect scanners to personal computers: USB, parallel, and SCSI.

USB The USB interface is the easiest way to connect a consumer-grade flatbed scanner. Just connect a cable from your scanner's USB output to a USB input on your PC. Since USB is a "hot" interface, you don't have to turn off your computer to make your connection, and Windows should recognize the new device as soon as it's plugged in and turned on.

NOTE   *As this chapter was written, the very first USB2 scanners, such as the Epson Perfection 2450, were just hitting the market. These scanners should be at least four times faster than USB1.1 scanners—theoretically up to 40 times faster—while still maintaining USB1.1 compatibility.*

Parallel   The parallel interface is used by almost all sheet-fed and all-in-one scanners, as well as some older flatbed units. In the case of sheet-fed and flatbed scanners, the parallel connection is shared with a printer; the printer typically plugs into the back of the scanner (or into a special Y cable), and the scanner then interfaces directly to the PC. This type of connection can be problematic, especially if you try to use the scanner and printer at the same time. (You can't.) However, if you're connecting an all-in-one scanner/printer/fax/copier, the parallel connection is the only way to go, and you shouldn't encounter any problems.

NOTE   *Some consumer-grade scanners include both USB and parallel connections.*

SCSI   The faster SCSI interface is used for the high data transfer rates inherent with drum scanners. Most drum scanners include a dedicated SCSI card you have to install in your computer, although many also let you use a standard SCSI controller.

If you plan to buy a typical inexpensive flatbed scanner and you have a choice, go with a USB model. They're easiest to hook up and don't interfere with other peripherals in your system (such as your printer).

TWAIN

For your computer to communicate with your scanner, you must install a TWAIN software driver. The TWAIN driver acts as an interpreter between your scanner and TWAIN compliant applications on your computer.

NOTE   *TWAIN is that rare computer term that isn't an acronym. (It actually comes from the phrase "never the twain shall meet," because the driver sits between the software and the scanner.) For those of you who are acronymically inclined, however, feel free to use the following pseudo-acronym for TWAIN: Technology Without An Interesting Name.*

TWAIN enables applications to acquire images from your scanner without having to know all the details about your particular scanner. Recent versions of Windows are TWAIN compliant, as are most major graphics-editing programs, such as Adobe Photoshop.

Don't confuse the TWAIN driver with the image-editing software that comes with most scanners. The editing software may be TWAIN compliant (and probably is), but the ability to acquire images directly from the scanner is a function of the TWAIN driver, not of the image-editing program itself.

Determining Image Quality

Most flatbed scanners deliver a resolution of at least 300×300dpi. The dpi is determined by the number of sensors in a single row of the CCD or CIS array (which determines the x-direction sampling rate) and by the precision of the stepper motor (which determines the y-direction sampling rate).

For example, a scanner with 2550 sensors in each horizontal row delivers an x-direction sampling rate of 300. (2550 sensors divided by 8.5 inches = 300 sensors/inch). If the stepper motor can move the stabilizer bar in increments of ⅓₀₀th of an inch, the y-direction sampling rate is also 300—resulting in a 300 × 300dpi resolution.

Resolution can be artificially enhanced by the scanning software used by the scanner. Some software programs *interpolate* extra pixels between the actual pixels, thus increasing the apparent resolution. For example, software that puts one extra pixel between each real pixel turns a 300 × 300dpi scanner into a virtual 600 × 300 scanner.

The other factor in image quality is the sharpness of the image. Sharpness is determined primarily by the quality of the lens optics and the brightness of the light source. The higher-quality the lens and the brighter the light, the sharper the scan.

Color fidelity is measured in terms of *bit depth*. Almost all color scanners deliver 24-bit color, while some higher-priced models promise 30- or 36-bit color. While these higher-bit scanners process colors with the higher bit depth, they still output in 24-bit color, so you might not notice any measurable difference in the color of your scans.

Managing Scanned File Size

The higher the resolution of your scans, and the greater the bit depth, the larger the file sizes. For example, if you scan a 5 × 7 photograph at 600 × 1200dpi (and save it in the default BMP format), you end up with a whopping 74MB file. If you do a lot of scanning, you'll start to fill up that gigantic new hard disk—and then what do you do?

It's always a good idea to manage the file sizes of your scanned images. You can do this in several ways.

First, *don't* use the BMP format! Bitmapped files are the least efficient file types, period. Instead, configure your scanner acquisition software to use either the TIFF (if you intend to print the final file) or JPG (if you intend to use the file on the Internet) formats.

Second, if you don't need the full resolution, don't use it. For most purposes, 300 × 300dpi is just fine, and going to 600 × 600dpi (or higher) is overkill. (In fact, if you're putting a picture on the Web—or sending it via e-mail—then 72 × 72dpi is probably good enough.) Scan in as low a resolution as you can get by with, and you'll create smaller, more manageable files.

Next, if you don't need a big picture, shrink the scanned image. If that 5 × 7 photo you've scanned only needs to display as a 2.5 × 3.5 image in a newsletter or on a Web page, use your image-editing software to resize the picture accordingly.

In addition, you can usually reduce the color depth without affecting the way a picture looks. If you scanned at 24-bit resolution, you may be able reduce the color depth (within your image-editing program) to 8-bit or 16-bit color, especially if the scanned image is for online use. (You'll want to retain the higher color depth to print a photograph, of course—although anything higher than 24-bit color is wasted.)

Finally, check to see if your image acquisition software is saving duplicate or temporary versions of the images you scan. I have one program that saves a BMP file of every image I *preview*, before I do the final scan! You may need to track down these files in some temporary directory in either the Windows folder or the folder where the scanner software is installed. If you find any unnecessary files there, *delete them!* You may be surprised at the amount of disk space these temporary files use up.

NOTE *Some scanner software will save these interim files whether you want to or not; other software can be configured not to save interim files. Check the options menu on your software to discover what your software is saving while you're not looking.*

Optical Character Recognition

Many scanners also include optical character recognition (OCR) software, which enables you to convert scanned text into computer-based text. This way you can scan a document and import it directly into a word processor (such as Microsoft Word) as editable text, rather than as a graphic.

Most current OCR software does a fairly good job of translating printed characters to digital characters, although you'll still need to clean up any misinterpretations. The cleaner the scan, the better the job the OCR software does, so start with a clean original and make sure you take a good, high-contrast scan. (Also be sure the original document is centered and level on the glass bed and has no creases or blemishes.)

NOTE *Some advanced OCR software—sometimes referred to as page-recognition software—also captures fonts and page layout from the source document.*

TIP *OCR software works best when capturing black-and-white images. All the extra information in a color image only serves to confuse the software.*

Scanner Maintenance

Scanners don't require a lot of maintenance. (Unlike printers, scanners don't use up any consumables, like paper or ink.)

The main thing is to keep your scanner clean and as dust-free as possible. Use a soft cloth and glass cleaner to clean the scanner's glass bed. Take particular care to keep the glass free from smudges and scratches, both of which can affect the quality of your scans. You may also need to disassemble the unit to clean the *underside* of the glass, which can also get dusty.

As to mechanical maintenance, most consumer-level scanners don't have too many moving parts to which you have easy access. Depending on your scanner, even the light source (typically a lamp or small light bulb) may or may not be serviceable. Many manufacturers now use sealed lamps that can't be replaced by the user.

If you have a sheet-fed scanner (or an all-in-one unit that includes a sheet-fed scanner function), make sure the paper path is clean and free from jams and paper bits. Don't inadvertently jam the paper path by force-feeding paper that's too thick to fit.

The truth is, given the low price of today's scanners, if it breaks, you'll probably be tempted to just replace it.

Common Problems and Solutions

Before the dawn of USB, most scanner problems came from trying to share a parallel port with the printer. If you have a USB scanner, you automatically have an easier installation and fewer subsequent problems.

Beyond the parallel port problem, other common scanner problems include the inability to scan and poor-quality results.

Check the Connections

As with any peripheral device connected to your system, there are some basic things you need to check if you're having trouble with your scanner.

First, make sure the scanner is plugged into a live power supply and is turned on. You should see a light below the glass bed when the scanner is turned on and operational.

Second, make sure the scanner is properly connected to the correct port on your PC. Check both ends of the cable, just in case.

Finally, many scanners ship with their CCD and stabilizer arm locked down for transport. The scanner won't do much scanning if the stabilizer arm can't move, so check the manufacturer's instruction manual to make sure you've unlocked the CCD properly.

Give It a Test

When you're trying to track down a problem with your scanner, it helps to follow a step-by-step troubleshooting approach. For that reason, the first thing you should do (after you have the scanner connected and powered up) is perform a comprehensive test of your scanner to determine the nature of the problem.

TIP *Many scanners have a "self-test" mode that you can run to check out the unit's operation. In addition, some scanners come with software-based diagnostic utilities.*

Here's what you need to do:

1. Turn on your scanner and launch the scanner's image acquisition utility or software.

2. Place a black-and-white photo *facedown* on the glass bed. (If you're using a sheet-fed scanner, insert a black-and-white document into the sheet feed—and make sure it's facing the correct direction!)

3. Acquire the image with the scanning software.

4. If the scanned image is blank (either all black or all white), make sure the original photo or document was either placed facedown or inserted proper-side-up into the sheet feeder. (You could be scanning the back of the photo!)

5. If the acquired image is blurry or distorted, make sure the original photo or document was set firmly in place and that the cover of the scanner was closed. You may also need to select a particular type of scan in the scanning software. (You'll probably have choices like "B/W Photo," "Color Photo," "Line Art," and so on.) Choose the most appropriate image type.

6. Once you get a good preview image, go ahead and save the scan to disk. Experiment with scanning the document at different resolutions and image settings.

7. Now it's time to check the TWAIN driver. Close the scanner's software and open another graphics program—one that you know is TWAIN compliant. Do a File ➤ Open or File ➤ Acquire operation, and select your scanner from the "select source" option. Choose to acquire the image, and see if the graphics program actually acquires the image from your scanner.

8. If you can't acquire an image via the graphics program, you should check several things. First, make sure the program is TWAIN compliant; if not, use another program. Second, if your scanner doesn't appear on the "acquire source" menu, you may not have installed the TWAIN driver; try reinstalling the driver and testing again.

TIP   If, no matter how hard you try, you can't acquire scanned images from within your graphics program, you can always default to saving the images to disk using your scanner's acquisition software, and then opening or importing those files into your graphics-editing program as normal.

Check the Port—and the Configuration

If you've connected your scanner via a parallel port, make sure that your port is configured as an enhanced parallel port (EPP) or extended capabilities port (ECP). Many scanners require EPP/ECP operation, which utilizes high-speed, bidirectional data transfer to send data back and forth to your computer.

If Windows isn't recognizing your new scanner, your best course of action is to rerun the play. That is, unhook the scanner and try reinstalling it. (You may want to uninstall it before you reinstall it, although this isn't always necessary.) If Windows doesn't recognize the scanner when you reconnect it, try uninstalling the scanner, turning off your computer, and then reconnecting and rebooting. Windows should recognize the new device when it starts up again.

If Windows *still* doesn't recognize your scanner, run the Scanner and Camera Wizard (in Windows XP) or the Add New Hardware Wizard (in any version of Windows). Either of these options should let you install the scanner driver manually.

With some scanners, an even better approach is to install the unit from the scanner's installation CD. Some scanners include a robust installation program that will do everything from installing the drivers to configuring your system to installing the scanner's graphics-editing software.

TIP   When in doubt, read the scanner's manual for the recommended installation method—or visit the manufacturer's Web site for the latest drivers, installation instructions, and advice.

If your system recognizes your scanner after installation, but doesn't recognize it on subsequent use, you may have a configuration that requires your scanner to be powered up *before* Windows starts. That is, Windows won't recognize your scanner if you turn it on after Windows is up and running. Power down your computer, turn on your scanner, then power up your computer again. When Windows loads, it should recognize the already-running scanner.

Another related problem occurs when your scanner is set too far away from your computer. You should never use a cable longer than the one supplied with your scanner; long cable runs will not only degrade the image quality, but will also cause your computer not to recognize the signals coming from the scanner. Do not, under any circumstances, use an extension cable to lengthen the cable run from your scanner to your PC.

You might also be somewhat disappointed if you use a black-and-white printer to print a copy of a scanned color image. The problem here is how your black-and-white printer prints color images. The better solution is to use your scanner or graphics-editing software to convert the color image to grayscale, and then print the grayscale image. (Graphics-editing programs do a better job converting color images than most printers do.)

Troubleshooting Tips

Here's a summary of troubleshooting tips for your scanner:

- If your scanner is connected via the parallel port and isn't communicating with your computer (or if your scanner and printer are interfering with each other), check the order in which everything is powered up (scanner first, printer second, PC third) or consider installing a parallel port switch.

- If your scanner's stabilizer arm isn't moving, unlock it. (The lock is typically located on the bottom of a flatbed scanner.)

- If you can't acquire images from your scanner, reinstall the scanner's TWAIN driver.

- If your scans are slow—and you're connecting via the parallel port—make sure the port is configured as either an enhanced parallel port (EPP) or extended capabilities port (ECP).

- If your scans are slow (no matter how you're connected), consider increasing the size of your PC's swap file or adding more RAM to your system.

- If your scans are coming out blank, make sure you're placing the original facedown on a flatbed scanner, or in the appropriate direction in a sheet-fed scanner.

- If the scanned image is blurry or distorted, make sure the original document is placed firmly in or on the scanner, and that the flatbed scanner's cover is closed.

- If the quality of your scans is poor, make sure your scanner or scanner software is set to the appropriate setting for the type of image you're trying to scan.

- If you find minor errors in your scan—it's crooked, or off-center, or too dark or too light—use your scanner software or graphics-editing software to fix the errors in the scanned image.

In general, here's what you want to remember. If you can, connect your scanner via USB instead of the parallel port. Make sure the item to be scanned is in good condition and centered on the glass bed or in the sheet feeder. (While you're at it, make sure the glass surface is clean and the sheet feeder is clear.) Set your scanner or scanner software to the appropriate setting for the original image type. Then use your scanner software or image-editing software to edit any little mistakes that pop up in the scan.

Follow that general advice, and you'll minimize the opportunity for scanner-related problems.

Chapter 22

Modems and Other Communications Devices

◆ Understanding Serial Communications   614

◆ Working with RS-232   617

◆ How Analog Modems Work   622

◆ Migrating to Broadband Connections   625

◆ Installing and Configuring ISDN, DSL,
   Cable, and Satellite Modems   628

◆ Troubleshooting Tips   640

Introduction

WHEN COMPUTERS FIRST APPEARED on the scene many years ago, each was an island. But it didn't take us long to figure out how to connect to one another's machines, utilizing the PC's serial communications port, a modem, and the existing telephone network. The modem hooked up to the serial communications port and converted the PC's digital information into an analog format that could be transmitted over phone lines. On the other side of the connection, another modem converted the analog data back into digital format and fed it to another PC, via that PC's serial port.

This ability to "talk" computer to computer opened up an entire world of online communications, which has culminated in the enormous popularity of today's Internet. However, with the proliferation of multimedia content on the Internet comes the need for even faster connections that cannot be achieved with traditional analog modems. So-called *broadband* connections—through cable, DSL, and even satellites—make it less painful to access flashy Web sites and download huge files.

The tricky thing is, traditional serial communications are much, much different from the new technologies needed for broadband communications.

For example, a PC troubleshooter dealing with serial communications must understand:

◆ What RS-232 is

◆ How RS-232 is supposed to be used

◆ How RS-232 is actually used

◆ How to test RS-232 components

On the other hand, to troubleshoot broadband issues you need to understand:

◆ TCP/IP

◆ Ethernet cabling

◆ Network interface cards

◆ How to protect your PC from the outside world

In this chapter, then, I'll start by looking at traditional serial communication: how it works, what goes wrong, and how to make things connect right. After that, I'll show you the different broadband connections and technologies.

Understanding Serial Communications

IBM-compatible computers are typically equipped with two serial ports and one parallel port. Although both types of ports are used for communicating with external devices, they work in different ways.

A *parallel port* sends and receives data 8 bits at a time over eight separate wires. Parallel ports are typically used to connect PCs to printers—and are rarely used for much else.

On the other hand, a *serial port* sends and receives data one bit at a time over a single wire. While it takes eight times as long to transfer each byte of data this way, only a few wires are required. Serial ports are used to connect many types of devices, including modems—which are of primary interest in this chapter.

How Serial Communications Work

Let's start off with a look at each piece of the serial communications picture as it relates to your modem. Of course, analog signals from analog modems are not the only way of getting data to your PC—in today's broadband world, you also have digital modems and Ethernet to worry about. I'll talk about all these technologies in due course. But first, take a look at basic serial communications—and the RS-232 communications standard.

THE ASYNCHRONOUS PORT

Let's start on the computer end of the data flow, where your PC must be able to speak the language of asynchronous communications. A device that enables this to happen is called an *asynchronous port*, *asynchronous adapter*, *communications port*, or *RS-232* or *RS-232C port*. (RS-232 and RS-232C are the same thing. In fact, the "official" name nowadays is TIA/EIA-232D.)

NOTE *By the way, something that is* asynchronous *is generally the essence of all that is serial.* Serial *means one after the other, just like those old movie serials like* Rocketman *and* Superman. *It's the opposite of* synchronous, *also known as parallel, which means occurring at the same time. (You can think of it as that parallel universe in the old* Star Trek *episode where there was an insane, evil Kirk that got switched with the cool Kirk.)*

The connector type used is generally the standard 25-pin DB25 type, such as you would find on the back of most modems and that you can see in Figure 22.1. However, ever since the advent of the AT, some adapters have used a 9-pin connector instead. You won't miss the other 16 pins—asynchronous communication doesn't use them anyway. The signals are the same. (You *may* have a cabling problem, however. I'll discuss cables later.)

FIGURE 22.1

Standard 25-pin
DB25-type connector

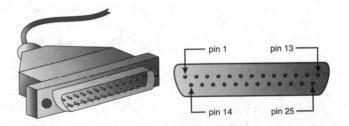

Most folks don't buy an asynchronous adapter on a board by itself. Instead, it usually appears as a connector (or two, for COM1 and COM2) right on the motherboard.

THE UART

This is going to sound like techie stuff, but it's important. You see, serial ports are not all created equal—even some of the newer serial ports.

Serial ports are based on a chip called a *Universal Asynchronous Receiver/Transmitter* (*UART*). The original was a National Semiconductor 8250 designed back in the late '70s. It worked great on the slow XTs and PCs. Unfortunately, computer manufacturers kept on using them all the way through to the 486-compatible computers, and thereby hangs a tale.

One of the big performance criteria with a UART is how quickly it resets after an interrupt. Interrupts occur whenever data arrives in the serial port, so you can imagine that they're pretty common occurrences. The 8250 took 1000 nanoseconds (ns) to reset, which was no problem when it was used by the older PCs. The PCs would access the 8250 in *2000*ns, so the 8250 taking forever to reset was no big deal from the PC CPU's point of view—the CPU was a lot slower.

Problems began appearing as soon as turbo XTs appeared. At 10MHz, an XT could access the 8250 in just about the same amount of time that it took the 8250 to reset, leading to a potential "not ready" problem for the UART. To correct this problem, a new chip, the 16450, was built by National Semiconductor, with a reset time five times faster than the 8250—200ns. That basically solved the bottleneck problem between CPU and UART.

Multitasking and higher transfer speeds, however, posed another problem. The CPU can be in only one place at a time, and if you're running five programs, the UART might find itself full of data with no CPU to transfer the data to. By the time the CPU would say to the UART, "Whatcha got for me?" the UART may have been forced to discard some data. The 16450 UART could hold only one byte. If that space was full, and the CPU hadn't come around to get the byte, any incoming bytes got discarded due to "buffer overflow." (The one byte in the 16450 is the "buffer.")

Enter the 16550. It has a 16-byte buffer. That may not sound like much, but have you done a file transfer under Windows and then opened a new program? The resulting disk access to load the new program means that the CPU ignores the UART for hundreds of nanoseconds, and you usually drop a block or two of data. That's not the end of the world—most communications software uses an error-checking scheme that detects the dropped block and resends it—but it still makes your system a bit slower and less reliable. And dropping a block at a critical time may mean losing your communications connection. The 16-byte buffer in the 16550 is the answer.

NOTE *As discussed in Chapter 3, "Inside the PC: Pieces of the Picture," the Universal Serial Bus (USB) has become a challenger to the "of course the modem goes in the serial port" mindset. This newer port type provides a single 4-pin connection for a number of devices (among them, compatible modems) to be daisy-chained from the computer, like a SCSI chain.*

THE CABLE

Communications cables are the bane of a PC expert's existence. The problem is that no manufacturer follows the RS-232 standard exactly. Many manufacturers use a different connector, or they rearrange the order of the pins. Neither is a fatal problem—just a pain in the neck.

Cables can have broken wires and loose pins, or they can be wired incorrectly. The section "Common Cables: A Configuration Cookbook" includes wiring diagrams for common PC cables.

NOTE *There are now two (different) common internal serial cables being used by motherboards, and they are incompatible. In general, motherboards will include the internal (ribbon) serial cables, so all you need to remember is to keep the cables that came with the motherboard together with that motherboard.*

THE MODEM

The most common use for a serial port is as an interface to a modem. A modem modulates and demodulates transmitted data (hence the word *modem*, a combination of *modulate/demodulate*).

The process is relatively simple. A modem accepts serial binary pulses from a computer and then modulates some property (amplitude, frequency, or phase) of an analog signal in order to transmit the digital data via that analog signal over an analog medium. The receiving modem performs the opposite process, enabling the analog information to arrive as digital pulses at the computer on the other end of the connection.

The bottom line is that modems enable computers (which are digital) to communicate via regular phone lines (which are analog). Modems aren't a new invention; they've been around for decades. In the PC world, Hayes Microcomputer Products introduced the Smartmodem in the early '80s, starting a whole new generation of communications devices. Today, so-called 56.6Kbps modems (actually 53Kbps—explained in the "Modem Speed" section later in this chapter) are pretty much the norm.

Why Is There RS-232?

You know, for a "standard," RS-232 sure provides a lot of headaches. Buy a device from Vendor A with an RS-232 port on it and a device from Vendor B with an RS-232 port on it, and try to hook them up. When it doesn't work (a common outcome), you start calling people.

Vendor A: "Trouble with our unit? Gosh, we don't really ever get bad reports on... Wait! What are you trying to connect to? *Vendor B?* That's your trouble. That guy hasn't designed an interface that follows specs since the day he got into business."

So you, reasonably, are annoyed by the temerity of Vendor B and call him. He is jolly.

Vendor B: "Vendor A? Is that old rapscallion (not the actual word used) still lying about me? His problem is that he builds 'em to the standard, all right—the *1964* standard. He's building RS-232-A ports. We follow the 1984 conventions, and..." (Soothing noises follow.)

If you could get these two guys in the same room, you know what they'd say?

"Your problem is the cable—it's the wrong one." You wait, expectant, for the solution. But they demur.

"Oh, no—we don't sell cables," they chorus, and then leave.

You'll probably face about two big RS-232 compatibility problems per year, and you'll be a happier person if you can take a swing at fixing them. Look, if a simple country economist like myself can do it, so can you.

So here's the world's shortest course on what RS-232 is and how it works.

Problems like the above aside, RS-232 exists so that vendors can offer equipment that can communicate with other vendors' equipment. I can buy a modem built before the PC was even designed, and it'll work with the PC just fine because they use RS-232 to communicate. RS-232 is an example of a *physical interface*—an agreement among vendors about how to make equipment communicate.

For a simpler and more familiar example of a physical interface, think of the plug in your wall socket. It supplies 120 volts, 60 cycles per second, also called hertz (Hz) alternating current. If you plug in something that uses, say, 220 volts, 50 cycles per second, you'll get very unpleasant results, up to and including burning your house down. So when did you last check to be sure that something used 120-volt, 60Hz current? Probably never: you just figure that if you buy something with a regular power plug on it, it'll use the juice okay. And you're right. There's a standards agency—Underwriters Laboratories (UL)—that concerns itself with power and safety, so you won't see a UL sticker on something that you could plug into a wall socket and damage yourself with.

So the plug itself seems important. Can I, for instance, use my U.S. microwave in London? Nope—they have different power. The first problem I'll run up against is, again, the plug—my plug won't fit into any wall sockets. Can I just snip off the plug, install a British-type power plug, and use the wall current? No again: it's 220 volts, 50Hz.

Why use different plugs, then? Simple: the plug is a *reminder* about where the equipment can and can't be used. The plug tells us something else, too: what devices *supply* power, and what devices *use* power. Female connectors indicate a device (like an extension cord) that supplies power. Male connectors indicate a device that uses power. This way, you don't plug a toaster into a microwave oven and think that something will come of the marriage.

Behind the plug lies a lot of information about the interface standard. Know what plug you have, and you don't have to worry about things like how many volts or hertz the power is. Well, RS-232 does something similar.

Just as there are two members of the power interface—the user and the supplier—so too are there two kinds of RS-232 interfaces. RS-232 was basically designed to allow computing devices called *data terminal equipment (DTE)* to talk to communications devices called *data circuit-terminating equipment (DCE)*. So there's a DTE-type RS-232 interface and a DCE-type RS-232 interface. RS-232 is designed to allow DTEs to talk only to DCEs. RS-232 uses DB25 and DB9 connectors. Male connectors go on the DTEs; female connectors go on the DCEs.

DTE-type interfaces are most commonly found on PCs and printers. Devices with DCE-type interfaces include modems, mice, and scanners.

How RS-232 Works

The original specification for RS-232 is a digital interface with 25 separate wires, each with its own task. RS-232 is defined for both synchronous and asynchronous communications, so there are a lot of lines in the 25 that you'll never use in asynchronous communications. In fact, for the most basic RS-232 applications, you need only three wires: transmit, receive, and ground. As mentioned before, lines are either "on" (with a voltage level of +3 volts or more), "off" (below −3), or "neither" (in between). Flow control is an important part of RS-232's purpose. *Flow control* allows a receiving device to say to a sending device, "STOP! My buffers (a small amount of memory in the receiving device) are overflowing—hang on a second and I'll get right back to you."

There are 10 important asynchronous lines in RS-232, as shown in Table 22.1. It's important to understand that each line is controlled by either one side or another. Line 2, for example, is viewed as input by one side and output by the other side. If both viewed line 2 as input, then both would be transmitting information that was never received, so each line (except grounds, which are just electrical reference points) is controlled by one side or another. Note, by the way, that there is also a 9-pin version of the RS-232 connector. When I refer to pin numbers in this chapter, I'm referring to the 25-pin numbers, not the 9-pin.

TABLE 22.1: RS-232 LEADS

DESCRIPTION	PIN # (25 PIN)	PIN # (9 PIN)	FROM	ABBREVIATION
Power On Indicator Leads				
Data Set Ready	6	6	DCE	DSR
Data Terminal Ready	20	4	DTE	DTR

Continued on next page

TABLE 22.1: RS-232 LEADS *(continued)*

DESCRIPTION	PIN # (25 PIN)	PIN # (9 PIN)	FROM	ABBREVIATION
Leads That Announce That an Outside Event Has Taken Place				
Data Carrier Detect	8	1	DCE	DCD
Ring Indicator	22	9	DCE	RI
Ready to Send/Receive Handshake Leads				
Request to Send	4	7	DTE	RTS
Clear to Send	5	8	DCE	CTS
Data Leads				
Transmit Data	2	3	DTE	TD
Receive Data	3	2	DCE	RD
Ground Leads				
Signal ground	7	5		SG
Protective ground	1			PG

Here's the sequence of events for a normal RS-232 session.

1. Both devices are powered up and indicate "power up" status. The DTE powers up line 20 (DTR, Data Terminal Ready). The DCE powers up line 6 (DSR, Data Set Ready). A well-designed RS-232 interface won't communicate further until these two lines are activated. The DTE waits to see a signal on line 6, the DCE on line 20. Lines 6 and 20 are supposed to be "equipment check" signals that indicate only device power status, but they're sometimes used as flow control lines.

2. The modem connects with another modem. This is where the communication in *data communication* comes in. In a modem/terminal situation, the situation envisioned by the RS-232 designers (see the section "A Note on Reality" for what often really happens), a distant modem is dialed up. The modems exchange carriers (the high-pitched whine that you hear when modems connect), and the modem (DCE, recall) tells the terminal (DTE, recall) about it over line 8, DCD (Data Carrier Detect). If you have an external modem with red lights, by the way, you see the preceding in the lights: line 6 is attached to the light labeled MR, Modem Ready; line 20 is attached to the light labeled Terminal Ready; and line 8 is attached to the light labeled CD (Carrier Detect).

3. The terminal (DTE) asks the modem (DCE) if it's ready. The terminal activates line 4, RTS (Request to Send). The modem, if ready, responds with line 5, CTS (Clear to Send). Now the handshake process is complete. Lines 4 and 5 are flow control lines.

4. Data is exchanged. The terminal (DTE) passes information for the modem (DCE) to transmit along line 2. The modem passes information back to the terminal along line 3.

And that's all there is to RS-232.

A Note on Reality

The above description is nice and complete so far as the standard goes, but most RS-232 interfaces aren't complete. Most PC software, for example, looks at only one handshake, such as 8 (Data Carrier Detect), 6 (Data Set Ready), or 5 (Clear to Send), and ignores the rest. Some software doesn't look at *any* control lines, so DTR, DSR, DCD, RTS, and CTS become irrelevant. That makes cabling easier, but it ignores the question of flow control.

Flow Control

Flow control is implemented in *either* hardware or software. *Software control* uses signals, such as the following, which are sent as data to the receiving computer:

◆ XON/XOFF

◆ ENQ/ACK

Hardware control sends control pulses along special wires (control lines) in the cable, and it's done with one or more of the control lines, usually one of the following:

◆ DSR

◆ CTS

◆ DCD

The software approach is to send "STOP!" characters back and forth when one side's buffers are overflowing. The hardware approach simply deactivates a line when the receiver needs a rest. Again, here's where your cable design is vitally important: if you neglect to include the particular handshake wire in your cable, there's no way for the computer to know that the device is overflowing its buffer.

Another handshaking problem shows up when one side is using one method and the other side a different one, as when the PC is looking at CTS and the other device is using XON/XOFF.

You can test your handshake easily. Say you're hooking up a serial printer. Have the computer send a bunch of information to the printer to be printed and then do something like pull the paper tray out or take the printer offline. Once that's done, see if the computer figures it out—does it stop sending information to the printer? Then put the paper tray back in or put the printer back online and see if it picks up where it left off. Keep switching protocols until one of them works for you (or refer to your product manual!).

Common Cables: A Configuration Cookbook

Well, now that you've had the complete RS-232 overview, here are a few basic cable diagrams, including:

◆ Serial DB25 connector to a modem (Figure 22.2)

◆ Serial DB9 connector to a modem (Figure 22.3)

◆ Serial DB25 connector to another PC or a printer (Figure 22.4)

◆ Serial DB9 connector to another AT or a printer (Figure 22.5)

◆ Serial DB9 to serial DB9 (computer to computer) or computer to printer (Figure 22.6)

FIGURE 22.2

25-pin DTE to
25-pin DCE cable

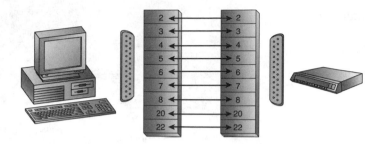

FIGURE 22.3

25-pin DTE to
9-pin DCE cable

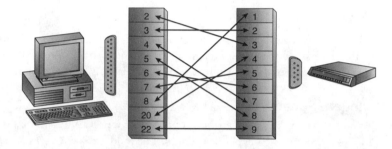

FIGURE 22.4

25-pin DTE to
25-pin DTE null
modem cable

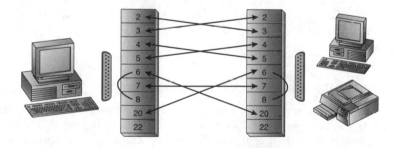

FIGURE 22.5

25-pin DTE to
9-pin DTE null
modem cable

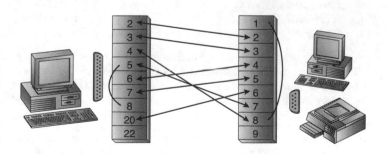

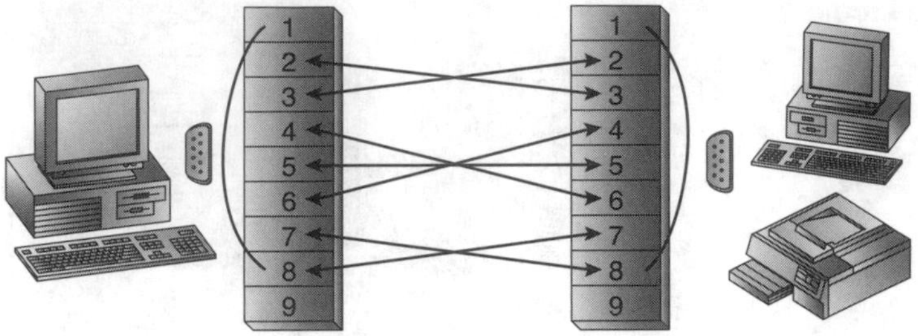

FIGURE 22.6

9-pin DTE to 9-pin DTE null modem cable

Analog Modems

The last several years have seen an immense leap in technologies surrounding the Internet. Certainly, as PCs have grown faster and relatively easier to use, the Internet has also become more usable. This is partly because of the near ubiquity of the (relatively) fast analog modem.

Modem Speed

As stated earlier, a modem enables your PC to connect to other computers and send and receive data files over the existing telephone network. The modem at one end converts digital data into a series of analog signals for transmission over the analog telephone lines, while the modem at the other end does the opposite, converting analog signals into digital data.

Modems come in two general types. An *internal* modem fits into an expansion slot inside your PC's system unit. An *external* modem connects to your PC via one of its serial ports (COM1 or COM2) or via its USB port. In today's market, internal modems are much more common than the external type.

WHAT HAPPENED TO THE EXTERNAL MODEM?

Nothing, per se. Well, I guess you could say that the Internet happened to the external modem. The more the Internet grows and shapes the way we live in very profound ways, the more the technology around us becomes Internet-enabled. And what's the most well known Internet appliance? Why, the personal computer, of course. With everyone wanting Internet access with their new systems and new PC sales even being driven by the Internet, a modem must be included or the vendor will not fare well against competition. It's expensive to add $50–$150 in plastic, cabling, and extra power supply to a new system that's going to retail for less than $700—especially when they can slot a $15 internal Winmodem into the box instead.

And, pray tell, what is a *Winmodem*? It's like an ancient mythological creature called a doppelganger, which could take the form of another and then take advantage of said imitation. Sadly, in the process, the copied individual or animal died. The Winmodem performs similar magic in that it mimics a real modem by acting like one, but in reality it is co-opting your CPU's precious clock cycles to do its bidding. The Winmodem is actually unable to do anything even vaguely modem-like on its own.

Of course, you can still buy "real" external modems and even internal versions of those expensive ones, but you typically don't have to, unless you plan on using an operating system other than Windows. The Winmodem, due to its "special capabilities," has limited support outside of Windows (hence the name). It is, however, unlikely that you will receive a "real" modem bundled with a system, even a system that costs more than $2000.

Early modems were asynchronous devices, operating at relatively slow transmission speeds. (Believe it or not, for a long time 9600bps was the top speed attainable for online communications.) Today's synchronous modems operate at transmission speeds approaching 56Kbps.

Of course, the actual speed at which a modem can operate depends on a number of factors, including:

◆ The throughput of the computer itself, and in particular its serial port

◆ The state of the telephone line (the cleaner the line, the faster the transmission)

◆ The kind of modem it is connecting to at the other end

The first potential bottleneck in your serial communication is the UART chip that controls the connection between the serial port and your PC's bus system. PCI bus systems operate in blocks of 32 bits, while serial cables transmit bits one at a time. The UART has to take all the 32-bit blocks coming from the computer and funnel the data, single file, into the serial port. Older UARTs have trouble keeping up with high transmission speeds; newer UARTs permit the faster speeds common in today's modems.

The next potential bottleneck is the phone line itself. First, it's analog, which is why you have to do the analog-to-digital (and back again) conversion in the first place. Second, the phone line has limited bandwidth—which means that there's only so much data that it can handle at one time. Third, analog phone lines are inherently noisy. While this may be only a minor annoyance for voice communications, it's a significant inhibitor to fast and clean data communications.

If the phone line is full of line noise (even noise that is inaudible to you), transmission rates drop until a reliable connection can be established. This may manifest itself in a modem capable of 56.6Kbps regularly connecting at 33.6Kbps or less. Removing external devices from the phone line may eliminate some of the noise, or you may need to contact your telephone company to do a line cleaning. (Of course, your telco may tell you—as mine told me—that it can guarantee connections of only 14.4Kbps. Your recourse at this point is to move to another state, so you can deal with a telco that is slightly more in tune with the times.)

The final potential bottleneck is the modem at the other end of the connection. In the early days of Internet service providers (ISPs), this was a major problem; few ISPs had installed 56.6Kbps modems, even though that speed had become standard on most new PCs. The result of a 56.6Kbps modem connecting to a 33.6Kbps modem is a 33.6Kbps connection; the transmission speed defaults to the speed of the slowest modem.

NOTE *Modem speeds have increased steadily since the early 1990s, to today's top analog speed of 53Kbps. Wait, you say—what about that so-called 56.6Kbps modem you think you have installed in your PC? Well, despite advertising claims and specifications stating otherwise, current modems cannot yet connect at a true 56.6Kbps. At best you may connect at a consistent 50.6Kbps, with peaks of 53Kbps. Why? Ask your local telephone company. Existing current (electrical, that is) limitations prevent telephone companies from extending beyond 53Kbps in total analog bandwidth per connection.*

Modem Standards

Modems are designed to follow certain standards so that they can communicate with other modems. These standards define not only the speed at which a modem may operate, but also determine how, exactly, a modem compresses data and performs its error control. The most common standards over the years—the so-called *V-dot* standards—are ratified by the CCITT (Comité Consultatif International Télégraphique et Téléphonique) and the ITU (International Telecommunications Union).

As with all technology standards, modem standards have evolved over the years. The initial V.22bis standard (2.4Kbps) evolved into the V.32 standard (9.6Kbps), which evolved into the V.32bis standard (14.4Kbps) and then the V.34 standard (28.8Kbps), which was upgraded in 1996 to the slightly faster V.34+ standard (33.6Kbps).

The next standard, V.90, was the result of a contentious protocol war that erupted in the late 1990s. At that time, two distinct technologies developed by two industry groups, X2 and k56flex, brought speeds up from their previous 33.5Kbps limit. After a bit of a spat, X2 disappeared and was replaced in 1998 by the V.90 standard—which has backward compatibility to k56flex, the apparent winner in the previously mentioned V.90 war.

The most recent attempt at standardizing, V.92, was instituted in late 2000. The V.92 standard includes several enhancements beyond those defined by the more established V.90 standard, including the following:

Modem on Hold   Suspends your online session for incoming calls and returns to your previous activity—without redialing—after the conversation is ended.

Quick Connect   Remembers line conditions from your last session to reduce the dial-up connection time (to about a third of what it was with V.90).

PCM Upstream   Boosts the maximum upstream data rate between you and your ISP (from 33.6Kbps to 48Kbps) to reduce upload times for large files and e-mail attachments.

As with all standards, both modems on a connection (yours and your ISP's) must support V.92 to take advantage of these new features.

Modem Maintenance

For the most part, modems are solid-state and so have no moving parts. Modems can tend to run hot, since many are designed around one or two fairly dense chips, so don't pile books atop an external modem—make sure the area around it is ventilated. Some ads show a phone perched on top of a modem, but I'm not sure that's such a good idea. I know that it's *not* a good idea to stack modems. I've had a fair amount of heat-related modem trouble. Be sure that you know where the modem's warranty information is. (Most modems have two-year warranties, so don't throw out that information.)

The usual stuff applies: Because they are large connectors with tiny pins, screw in the cables. Don't make the cables longer than they need to be; it increases the noise level in the cable, and if a loop of cable dangles down behind a table, it may get caught in something or be idly kicked. I know of an analyst who routinely braced his feet against the cable—just a nervous habit. The cable was even more nervous.

In Chapter 9, "Power Supplies and Power Protection," I mentioned power problems. *The same surge problems can appear on phone lines.* If the line from the phone company switching station to your computer is above ground at any point, think seriously about getting a *phone line isolator* (sometimes called a *modem isolator*). These are commonly featured on the standard electrical strips that you buy at your local national hardware or discount franchise. This isolator sits between the modem and the phone.

Another measure of prevention is an *RS-232 isolator*, which sits between the modem and the PC. I'd rather smoke a modem by itself than a modem and the rest of my system.

NOTE   *There used to be companies that offered optical isolators for RS-232, which solved all communications power surge problems, but they seem to have disappeared. I don't quite understand it, but it's certainly become difficult to find optical RS-232 isolators.*

You may be wondering why I beat up on surge protectors in Chapter 9 but am suggesting them now. Mainly, cost. Surges really don't occur that often over the phone line, save in the event of lightning strikes. When that unlikely lightning strike occurs, you want something that'll take the brunt of the impulse and (you hope) burn out in the process, cutting off the connection between your expensive equipment and the lightning. (I suppose you could also tie knots in the phone cord.)

Welcome to Digital Broadband

We all know one thing about the Internet—*it's slow!* More precisely, Internet connections are slow—or slower than you'd like them to be, especially if you visit media-rich Web sites or download large files or receive e-mails embedded with large JPEG pictures of your Uncle Jake's vacation to Myrtle Beach. Every little thing you look at or listen to online has to travel down that pipe to your PC, and the more things there are—and the bigger they are—the slower the Internet appears to be.

What is the solution to this World Wide Wait? A faster connection, of course.

If you're using a traditional analog modem connected to a standard phone line, you're stuck downloading your bits and bytes at 53Kbps. However, if you have a digital broadband connection—via DSL or cable or satellite—you can now receive data at 10 to 20 times that of your old analog speed. With broadband access, using the Internet is actually tolerable!

Today, however, broadband users remain in the minority. Most Internet users still connect at 53Kbps or less. Part of the reason for this relatively slow adoption is that broadband access isn't yet available in all areas of the country. (It doesn't help that several major broadband suppliers have gone belly-up in the past year, forcing their users back to standard dial-up connections.) But if the opportunity presents itself for you to trade in your slow analog connection for a fast digital connection, go for it!

Choosing a Digital Technology

So you want a faster Internet connection, do you? (You're not alone...) Unfortunately, it's not as simple as calling your current ISP and saying, "Speed it up!" No, you'll probably have to choose a new provider, based on the type of broadband technology that you want to embrace.

FIVE TYPES OF BROADBAND

For consumer and small business users, five main types of digital broadband connections are available. Each have their pluses and minuses, as follows:

Integrated Services Digital Network (ISDN)   ISDN was the first digital connection technology, offering speeds double that of existing analog modems. Unfortunately, ISDN technology is unwieldy, unreliable, and costly. In most areas, ISDN has been supplanted by the lower-cost, higher-performance DSL technology.

Digital subscriber line (DSL)   DSL is a digital connection that piggybacks on your standard phone lines. Costing not much more than a second phone line, DSL provides speeds that approach that of a T1 line (a long-established, very fast digital connection typically used by large businesses). T1 happens to cost about $1500 a month, which makes it prohibitive in cost and maintenance fees for the average Internet user. In comparison, a DSL connection at a minimum of 384Kbps downstream will run you about $40–$50 a month—including full ISP service.

Digital cable   Cable modems work just as you'd think they would, providing digital Internet access over the same cable that brings you your cable television programming. Since it has to handle all those channels, it's a big pipe to work with—and typically provides download speeds in excess of even DSL.

Digital satellite   The advent of these pizza box-sized satellite dishes opened up another interesting opportunity beyond crystal-clear television signals. The same type of satellite that delivers hundreds of channels of TV programming can also deliver high-speed data from the Internet. (In fact, some service providers let you use a single dish to receive both TV and PC data.) Plug a special card into your system, plug in and tune the dish, and go.

Broadband wireless   Also known as fixed-wireless connections, wireless systems use microwave technology to transmit and receive Internet data at broadband speeds. You'll need a special antenna on your roof, of course, but the link between your antenna and the Internet source is completely wireless.

PROS AND CONS

With all these broadband options, which is the best for you? Here are some factors to consider:

Availability   Not all types of broadband are available in all areas. If your cable company offers cable modems but your phone company doesn't offer DSL, the choice is easy. Likewise, if no land-based options are available, the satellite option is always there. (Broadband wireless is likely to be the least-available option—and probably not available at all in your area.)

Reliability   I'm not talking reliability of the connection here (although that's always an issue, no matter which option you go with). I'm talking reliability of the *provider*. For various reasons, many of the companies providing DSL and broadband cable access have gone out of business in the past year—including some very big companies, such as Excite@Home. I have trouble understanding how companies supplying such an in-demand service can fail to make money at it, but I'm just a computer guy, not a financial analyst. In any case, it pays to keep up-to-date with who's doing well and who's not, so you don't sign up with a provider that's close to shutting its doors—and stranding its users without service.

Faster—and easier—installation   Cable access is a snap to set up—many cable companies provide customer self-installation kits, and you can typically complete the entire procedure in an hour or less. DSL installation, however, is much more complex; it typically involves the interaction of three separate business entities and often requires some work on your existing copper wire phone line. Because of cable's relatively easy installation, you can probably obtain new cable broadband service a lot faster than you can obtain similar DSL service. Installation times for cable access are typically measured in days, whereas DSL installation times are often measured in weeks.

Speed   Even the best DSL connection is slightly slower than the same-priced cable connection (except during high network volume, as discussed in a few paragraphs). If you live far enough from the central office, you might find available DSL speed to be unacceptable. If this is the case, go with cable.

Upstream speed   For most users, upstream traffic consists of nothing more than requesting links for Web pages and sending the occasional e-mail. If, however, you send a lot of e-mail messages (or very large messages) or upload big files to FTP servers or newsgroups, you'll discover that many cable companies are using a very narrow band for return signaling, below all the space allocated for TV channels. This band is prone to RF interference and is very limited in capacity—with the result of delivering extremely slow upstream speed, or high latency (slightly delayed) uploads. This can be a major problem if you're participating in any real-time activities, such as multiplayer games, video conferencing, and the like. If upstream speed and latency is an issue, go with DSL.

Shared network traffic   One of the downfalls of cable broadband is that you share a network connection with many other users in your neighborhood. The more people using the network at the same time, the less bandwidth available for each individual user—and the slower the connection speed. You'd think this would be an easy fix (the cable company installs more network routers), but it remains a significant issue with some providers, so much so that connecting during prime time results in some very slow connections for users in highly connected neighborhoods. So check with your neighbors—if they're complaining about their cable connections slowing down, go with DSL instead.

Making the ISDN Connection

As I've said, the first type of digital connection available to home and small business Internet users was ISDN. For several years it was the *only* digital option—although it has been supplanted both in speed and cost by DSL and digital cable connections.

How ISDN Works

ISDN is a high-speed digital telephone line. ISDN utilizes two data channels that can each transmit 64Kbps, or the two channels can be combined for a single-channel throughput of 128Kbps. Not too shabby, especially when compared to the 53Kbps throughput of today's fastest analog modems. If you keep the channels separate, you can run two conversations (or two data sessions) via the same telephone connection. For example, you can use a single ISDN line to talk on the telephone while also using your modem.

ISDN is still available in most (but not all) areas of the United States. The cost of an ISDN connection varies significantly from state to state—so significantly, in fact, that it's difficult to quote usual charges with any amount of accuracy. Most often, the charges are based on a flat monthly fee plus a per-minute connection time charge. If you're connecting two places within the same calling zone or are able to wrangle a deal with your ISDN provider, you *may* have to pay only a flat monthly fee. If you can get such a deal, I highly recommend it; it will probably save you money if you're the kind of person who goes online enough to need a high-speed connection. In any case, you're probably looking at monthly ISDN bills in the $50–$100 range, and probably toward the high end of that range.

Besides being able to afford the connection, you'll need to make sure that your ISP has its own ISDN connection. Just as you can't make a 56.6Kbps connection unless the modems on both ends of the connection support speeds that high, you can't dial up using ISDN unless there are ISDN devices on both ends of the connection. (Really, it's a bit more complicated than that—an analog modem wouldn't know what to do with a digital signal if you did call it—but the end result is still the same: unless your provider offers an ISDN connection to the Internet, you can't have one.) These can be a little tricky to come by even if you live in an area that offers ISDN, so you may have to shop around a bit for a provider.

The bottom line is that ISDN is expensive and often difficult to obtain. Most users are better off investigating the availability of DSL or cable broadband.

INSTALLING AN ISDN CONNECTION

Assuming that you have an ISDN line and an Internet provider with an ISDN line, you'll need an ISDN modem (typically called a *terminal adapter*). This will let your analog modem use a digital line. (In the early days of ISDN, you would have needed another device called an NT1 to plug the terminal adapter into, but many new models are including the NT1 in the adapter itself.)

NOTE *If you intend to use additional devices, such as a telephone, on an ISDN line, you'll either need digital versions of the device or a converter. Converters are about $150. Considering that your analog phone is probably worth about that much, save some money by making sure the ISDN line is dedicated.*

If you plan to upgrade, you can replace your old modem with an ISDN model. These aren't cheap, but their cost is proportional to the increase in speed that you see. Some ISDN modems have more features than others do. Most ISDN modems have user-controlled band allocation so that you can combine the two data channels to get 128Kbps. If the telephone rings while you're connected, however, the channels will separate so that you can answer the telephone while keeping the original connection; they'll recombine once you hang up.

To recap, here's what you'll need to use ISDN:

◆ An ISDN telephone line

◆ Someone with an ISDN telephone line and associated equipment to call

◆ An ISDN modem and/or telephone, or a converter that you can plug analog equipment into

While this will get you up and running with ISDN, you should also investigate the other digital broadband options—all of which provide much faster connections, often at a much lower cost, than what you can get with ISDN.

Going Faster with DSL

DSL technology transforms a traditional phone line into a high-speed digital connection. Even the slowest DSL speeds are typically four to five times that of ISDN, or close to 10 times that of a traditional analog modem. And you get all this, plus traditional ISP services, for about $50 a month—less than what it would cost you to add a second phone line and subscribe to a traditional ISP.

Because of the average Internet user's need for speed, DSL has become a hot technology—so hot that DSL providers have had trouble keeping up with the demand. There's also been a problem with

DSL providers (especially the smaller players) staying in business. The result is that the biggest issue with DSL is availability. Still, while not all areas of the country have access to DSL service, the roll-out continues. If you can't get DSL today, chances are you'll have access soon.

How DSL Works

DSL is very cool, and it doesn't work much differently from ISDN—it's just a whole lot faster.

All forms of DSL are based on the ability to split existing phone lines into two or three frequency bands. This is called a *frequency spectrum*. If there are two frequency bands, one band is used to provide upstream data flow and the other is used to provide downstream data flow. If there are three bands, the third "channel" is used for standard voice. Plain old telephone service (POTS) takes up only a small portion of the total capacity of the available bandwidth, so adding this is trivial.

Physically, there has to be a connection between the provider and you. It's relatively easy enough for your local telephone company to pipe a T1, T3, or faster connection into your location, but they also need to add what's called a DSLAM, or DSL access multiplexer (just another fancy name for splitter). The Internet connection goes into the DSLAM, and the POTS lines pass through it. If there's no terminal adapter, your DSL modem on the other end of the DSLAM does nothing and simply acts as a fancy wire holder for the POTS lines.

On the other hand, if you *do* have a DSL modem, an ATM link (Asynchronous Transfer Mode, a very high-speed protocol link) is established.

It's in the so-called Last Mile that most of the problems with DSL can occur. The Last Mile, which is owned by the big telcos (such as Verizon, SBC Communications, Bell Canada, and Pacific Bell) is essentially just a simple POTS line, also known as twisted-pair, run from the switching facility (called a *central office*, or *CO*) nearest to your home. It's this stretch of POTS line that creates a distance limitation for DSL service. Copper wire can retain only so much cohesion for so long. After a certain point, the signal begins to degrade and it is no longer usable—which means that the further you are from a CO, the slower your DSL speed will be.

NOTE *It's worth noting that you don't always deal directly with the telco for your DSL service—even though they provide (and service) your POTS line. In many areas, you deal with a DSL service provider, who deals with the telco—typically through an intermediary called a* competitive local exchange carrier (CLEC). *The CLEC bundles large volumes of DSL service to multiple service providers; your individual service provider provides you with your Internet access. With the recent shakeout in the DSL market, however, a lot of service providers and CLECs went out of business—including two of the biggest, Northpoint and Rhythms. For many users, this leaves their telco as the sole available DSL provider. And, of course, the telco functions both as the CLEC and the service provider.*

Types of DSL

There are several types of DSL to choose from, each with its own advantages and disadvantages. Not all types are available in all areas, or from all providers. The most common types of DSL are:

ADSL Asymmetric digital subscriber line (also known as ADSL Full Rate or G.dmt), where upstream speed (from your modem to the ISP) is slower than downstream speed (from your ISP to you). With ADSL, downstream speeds can hit 8.5Mbps, with upstream speeds capped at 1.5Mbps. This type of pure ADSL is rather high-priced and targeted more at business users than home users.

ADSL Lite   Also called G.Lite, DSL-Lite, consumer DSL (CDSL), or universal ADSL (UADSL), this is a "notched-down" version of ADSL for the home market. ADSL Lite has a maximum downstream speed of 1.5Mbps, and a typical upstream speed of 384Kbps. Chances are if a company advertises home DSL service, they're talking about some version of ADSL Lite.

HDSL   High-bit-rate DSL, the original DSL technology. It uses four copper wires (two pairs) and delivers speeds of 1.5Mbps or so both upstream and downstream. HDSL was originally developed as a lower-cost alternative to T1 lines for large businesses.

IDSL   IDSL stands for ISDN digital subscriber line, and it's an ISDN service based on ISDN technology. It's slower than other types of DSL (144Kbps both upstream and downstream), but can be used over longer distances. Since IDSL uses ISDN transmission coding, it can go just about anywhere that ISDN can go—36,000 feet or more from a CO. If distance is a problem in obtaining ADSL-based service, IDSL is often a reasonable alternative. (I've heard, however, that some IDSL customers encounter a number of distance-related issues; the increased distance from the CO tends to result in a weaker signal, which is more difficult to keep in synch.)

RADSL   Rate-adaptive DSL—which means that the speed dynamically varies according to line conditions. When a RADSL modem first starts up, it tests the line and fixes the operating speed at the fastest rate the line can handle.

SDSL   Symmetric DSL (also called HDSL-2), an enhanced version of HDSL that works with only one pair of wires. Typically delivers speeds of 1.1Mbps in both directions.

VDSL   Very high-bit-rate DSL (also called BDSL), targeted at companies with high access demand, typically delivered over fiber-optic networks. Offers typical speeds of 34Mbps in both directions.

NOTE   *"Generic" DSL is sometimes referred to as xDSL, to embrace all the other leading acronyms.*

Table 22.2 compares the features of the various types of DSL. Two caveats: First, if you're at the far end of the distance range, expect your speeds to be substantially slower than the maximum. Second, the workable distance for each type of DSL varies considerably from provider to provider; the figures given here are reasonable averages.

TABLE 22.2: TYPES OF DSL

DSL TYPE	TYPICAL UPSTREAM SPEEDS	TYPICAL DOWNSTREAM SPEEDS	MAX. DIST. FROM CO
ADSL	1.5Mbps	8.5Mbps	18,000 ft. (9000 ft. for max. performance)
ADSL Lite	384Kbps	1.5Mbps	18,000 ft.
HDSL	1.5Mbps	1.5Mbps	12,000 ft.
IDSL	144Kbps	144Kbps	36,000 ft.
RADSL	Variable	Variable	18,000 ft.
SDSL	1.1Mbps	1.1Mbps	20,000 ft.
VDSL	34Mbps	34Mbps	4500 ft.
V.90 modem (comparison)	33.6Kbps	53Kbps	N/A

The most common type of DSL currently available is ADSL—or, for the home, ADSL Lite. ADSL's slower upstream speed is acceptable to most users, who download more than they upload, and enables the DSL provider to cram more users into their system.

While ADSL Lite is the most popular DSL for home use, some companies also offer home SDSL (which is preferable if you need a fast upstream rate) and ISDL (which is an option if you're too far from a CO for ADSL service) for home users. For business users, the faster (and higher-priced) ADSL Full Rate, HDSL, RADSL, and VDSL are popular options.

SPEED IS RELATIVE (TO DISTANCE)

Even if your area has DSL service, your particular location might not qualify. That's because your distance from your local telephone company's CO directly affects the speed of your DSL connection. The further you are from the CO, the slower the connection—and if you're too far away, you can't get service at all.

WARNING   The quality of your existing phone wiring will also affect your DSL connection. Even if you live close enough to the CO to get a fast connection, deteriorating wiring in your home or office may cause your DSL to either slow down or cease working. If this happens to you, see if your telco can clean or "condition" your line. You may also need to install a filter on your phone line so that your DSL connection doesn't interfere with your normal voice service.

Table 22.3 shows what types of DSL service are available, depending on your distance from the CO. (Because ADSL distance is dependent on speed, many service providers deliver a reduced-speed version for customers further out from the CO; therefore, I've included columns for both maximum-speed and reduced-speed ADSL.)

TABLE 22.3: DSL SERVICE BY DISTANCE FROM CO

DISTANCE (IN FEET)	VSDL	ADSL (MAX SPEED)	HDSL	ADSL (REDUCED SPEED)	ADSL LITE	RADSL	SDSL	ISDL
<5000	X	X	X	X	X	X	X	X
5000–9000		X	X	X	X	X	X	X
9000–12,000			X	X	X	X	X	X
12,000–18,000				X	X	X	X	X
18,000–20,000							X	X
20,000–36,000								X
>36,000								

INSTALLING AND CONFIGURING DSL

Having DSL installed is a process, to be sure. It took two months for mine to get installed, and that's in the D.C. area! The process, however, is pretty much the same everywhere and requires you to have no real technical know-how at all.

The first thing you do is call a DSL service provider—such as DIRECTV DSL (formerly Telocity) or EarthLink—or your local telco, and order service appropriate to your price range and needs. Most providers offer ADSL Lite service (1.5Mbps max downstream, although actual speeds may be slower than that) for $50 or less a month, often with a free modem and installation.

TIP   *To obtain a list of DSL providers in your area—and to confirm that your location qualifies for DSL service of any kind—visit the DSL Reports Web site, at* www.dslreports.com. *This site is a fount of information about DSL in general, and also offers tips and tweaks you can use to get the maximum performance from your DSL connection.*

Your DSL service provider will then contract with a CLEC (sometimes called a *partner*), such as Covad, which then makes arrangements with whichever telco owns your phone line. (Remember, if your telco is your DSL service provider, it's also your CLEC.) For those of you counting, that's a three-step process: service provider to partner to telco—which means that if you run into installation or service problems, you may end up dealing with three separate companies, each of which will undoubtedly point the finger at one of the other two companies. And, no, you can't go directly to the partner or the telco; you have to deal upstream in the proper pecking order. (This is sometimes referred to as "DSL hell"— and avoiding this unique type of purgatory is one reason to go with your telco for DSL service.)

Once you've placed your order (and waited the appropriate number of weeks—or months!), a representative of your local telco comes to your office or domicile to test the line to see if the "loop" is good. This means they are checking the POTS lines to see whether they can handle the connection and will pass clean data.

NOTE   *As mentioned earlier, DSL is limited to the distance from the central office and that CO's installed DSLAM. If that distance is exceeded, you cannot have DSL. If it were installed despite the long distance, it would be unreliable or not work at all.*

The CLEC that provides the DSL access is then notified by the telco that the line was tested and informed of its condition. If your line is acceptable, the process moves onward, and a technician from the CLEC makes an appointment to complete your installation. The telco marks the specific line tested for DSL, which is typically an existing phone line. The installer (from the CLEC) finds the line and prepares it, installs an RJ-45 jack at the wall plate you specify, and plugs it in to test it.

The installer will bring a DSL modem, unless you made arrangements to provide your own. They'll also need to plug into your network interface card (NIC). What? You don't have a network card in your PC? Don't panic—you may have other options available.

First, you could just go out and buy a NIC. (If you opt to go this route, make sure you buy and install the NIC before your DSL installer arrives.) Some DSL providers offer an internal DSL modem card (also known as a PCI DSL modem), which eliminates the need for a NIC. Another option is a DSL modem that connects through your PC's USB port (good) or serial port (problematic). Choose the option that works best for you—but know that the traditional Ethernet connection often works best, with the least installation and operational hassles.

Anyway, once the installer has the modem connected and everything appears to be working correctly, it's time to configure. You'll need a few things, which should be provided either by your installer or your DSL service provider:

◆ A static IP number (if your service provider provides static IP service—see the "Static IP vs. PPPoE" sidebar for more information)

◆ A gateway IP number

- ◆ At least two DNS IP numbers

- ◆ Your POP3 and SMTP server IP numbers

Now, write all these down and put the list in a safe place. Repeat this three times. Even fast minds like ours can get all in a twist and remember only one clever and crafty hiding place at a time, so it's best to hedge one's bets.

Now you can get to the configuration (this procedure assumes you're working with Windows 95/98/Me/XP):

1. Go to Start ➢ Settings ➢ Control Panel and open Network. (In Windows XP, select the Create a New Connection task.)

2. Enter the appropriate information. Do not activate WINS.

3. Click OK.

4. Restart the machine.

5. Enjoy your speedy connection.

STATIC IP VS. PPPOE

One of the early advertised benefits to DSL was an *always-on* connection (also called a *persistent connection*). Unlike connections via analog modem, where each session has to be started by dialing in and connecting to your ISP, a persistent connection is always there, always connected, no dialing in or connecting to required. (And I can tell you from my experience that having the Internet *always there* is a huge benefit.)

To deliver a persistent connection, a DSL provider must assign a static IP number to your computer. Think of a static IP as a permanent street address—it's a unique number, and it's always yours, no changing.

However, in the quest to maximize the use of their bandwidth, many DSL providers have quietly ceased offering static IPs. The reasoning is simple—if you have a static IP, your PC is always connected and you're always using a set amount of bandwidth, even when you're not surfing the Net. If, on the other hand, you were assigned an IP address only when you were physically using your connection, that would free up additional bandwidth that the DSL provider could then allocate to other users. It's a more efficient use of their pipe, if you want to think of it that way.

The alternative, then, to a static IP is something called *Point-to-Point Protocol over Ethernet (PPPoE)*. With PPPoE, you don't have a constant address—and you don't have a persistent connection. Instead, you have to log onto the DSL network each time you turn on your PC, and you're assigned a new and temporary IP address at that time, for the current session only. Not only is this a hassle (your Internet won't always be there, waiting patiently for you), it also eliminates the possibility of you hosting your own Web server (which you can if you have a static IP).

As much as most users hate PPPoE, it does have one distinct end user advantage—it's more secure than static IP. If your IP address is constantly changing, it's less likely that crackers will find their way into your system.

That slight benefit (which can be obviated via the use of firewall software) is, in most users' opinions, negated by the lack of an always-on connection. For that reason, if you have the choice between a provider offering static IP and another offering PPPoE, it's an easy decision to choose the static IP provider.

SECURING WINDOWS WITH A STATIC IP

As I've said, there is one big negative about DSL with a static IP: crackers. And, no, I don't mean the Ritz kind—I'm referring to the kind of mean and nasty people who use various technological means to "crack" into your system. (You've probably heard them called hackers, but *hacker* actually means someone who enjoys working with computers "very close to the metal." Hackers are not mean and malicious; crackers are.) Crackers like to gain access to systems that are not their own and destroy data, take things, or just leave evidence of their illicit presence.

To do this, they need what are called exploits, or shortcomings in the system that allow them to get around established security measures. Windows is very, *very* bad in this respect (bad, *bad* OS... BAD!) in that it practically broadcasts its presence. So, how do you prevent this from happening? Easy. Follow this very complicated list of instructions:

1. Turn off file sharing.

There is no step 2.

Obviously, this is a simplistic answer to a potentially complex problem, but if you have only one computer connected to the DSL, there is absolutely no need whatsoever to share your files with the world. Of course, there are more factors in real life and, hence, more options. To turn file sharing off, go to Start ➤ Settings ➤ Control Panel and open the Network item. Click the File/Print Sharing button in the lower half of the dialog box and deselect both items. You're done.

If you are sharing an Internet connection with a housemate via home networking of some sort (that is, peer-to-peer Ethernet, LAN, wireless, phone line–based, etc.), file sharing may be required. Some software packages are specifically designed to allow the sharing of a single modem connection (or DSL, of course) that also have built-in protection from caustic elements. Vicomsoft is a superb example of a company that provides a number of solutions at various price points for both Windows and Mac.

NOTE *You can find contact information for Vicomsoft in the Vendor Guide on the Utilities CD. If you have only two or three home-based users to consider, examine SurfDoubler and SurfDoubler Plus ($75 for two users, $100 for three). These products are also great if you have children around; they incorporate CyberNOT filtering service. For more complex jobs, consider the overwhelmingly cool Internet Gateway, also from Vicomsoft (it's woefully undernamed—it should be something like Internet Dazzler). A five-user package runs at about $250, but an unlimited user package is only about $730. For a small office, that's quite the bargain.*

Internet Gateway uses Network Address Translation (NAT) to make one IP address available to as many computers as are behind the server. The security benefit is that if the server is secure from attack, so are all the machines that it serves because they all appear to be one machine: the server. NAT works because the server records which internal machine sends a request, tracks the data from server to server, and delivers the data to the requesting client when it comes back. Only the server knows the real address of the machine that requested the data, and it just makes the translation for it.

If you're running Windows XP, a perfectly acceptable connection-sharing utility is built into the operating system. When you run the Network Setup Wizard, you'll be prompted to specify which computer is connected to the Internet; all your other computers can then automatically share that single connection, relatively safely. The safety is enhanced by the presence of the Internet Connection Firewall, which helps to shield your system from outside attack.

If you're not running Windows XP (or even if you are and want a more robust security solution), you should consider installing a third-party firewall program. A good firewall program, such as

BlackICE Defender, will stop all unauthorized traffic from outside your system and alert you to any severe attacks. See Chapter 29, "Networking Concepts and Hardware," for more information on modems and other security software.

Digital Connections over Digital Cable

The primary competitor to DSL is high-speed digital cable. The advantages are many: cable broadband is faster, easier to install, and—in many cases—more widely available than DSL. Depending on the deal offered by your local cable company, cable broadband may also be slightly lower cost than comparable DSL service. (Prices in the $$40–$50/month range—if you're also a cable TV subscriber—are common.)

I recently switched from DSL to cable, thanks to my DSL CLEC (Rhythms) deep-sixing on me. My experience is that cable is much easier to install, the cable company is easier to deal with and more willing to please than my old DSL provider, and the service itself is both faster and more reliable. (I was getting about 600Kbps downstream with my DSL connection; now I'm averaging close to 2Mbps with cable.)

Of course, I was lucky enough to sign up with a broadband cable provider that didn't utilize the Excite@Home service—which has since gone bankrupt, in one of the more dramatic failures of the dot-com era. Tens of thousands of Excite@Home users were left stranded by the service's shutdown, which left them scrambling for other high-speed connection options.

Like I said, I was lucky. I still have my fast connection, and nobody's gone out of business lately.

How Internet-over-Cable Works

Cable broadband works a little differently from either ISDN or DSL. Whereas ISDN and DSL piggyback over your copper phone lines, cable Internet occupies a *tunnel* within the cable signal that is sent via the cable company's fiber-optic or coaxial cable.

Internet signals are typically assigned a 6MHz slot within the cable signal, and deliver download speeds that can theoretically reach 5Mbps. (More common speeds are between 500Kbps and 2Mbps.) Upstream signals are assigned a smaller subset of that slot, resulting in slower upstream rates—typically in the 128–384Kbps range.

Some cable companies offer only one-way access. In this type of system, all upstream requests are sent via analog phone line and are limited to 33.3Kbps. As you can no doubt ascertain, this is a much inferior way of doing things, and you should opt for two-way cable (where both downstream and upstream access are via digital cable) whenever possible.

Fortunately, most cable companies support the Data Over Cable Service Interface Specification (DOCSIS). Any DOCSIS-compatible cable modem will work on any DOCSIS-compatible cable system—which means you can probably take your cable modem with you if you move. You can find cable modems from a variety of manufacturers, including Cisco Systems, Thomson Consumer Electronics (RCA), Motorola, Samsung, and others.

NOTE   Just because you have cable TV in your home doesn't mean that you have access to cable Internet. Not all cable systems support data service—in fact, if your system is an older one, chances are it doesn't offer Internet access. More modern systems, or older systems that have been upgraded to offer digital cable, are more likely to offer Internet access to their subscribers.

INSTALLING AND CONFIGURING CABLE ACCESS

While some cable companies still offer installation by a professional installer (and often charge you $50–$100 for the service!), many companies now provide self-installation kits. These kits include installation software, a USB-enabled cable modem, and enough instructions for you to figure out how it all fits together.

With this sort of self-install kit, the basic installation goes something like this:

1. Connect a coaxial cable from your cable outlet to your cable modem. (You may need to install a low-cost splitter so that the single outlet can feed both your PC and your television.)

2. Connect your cable modem to your computer's USB port.

3. Use the cable company's installation software to configure Windows' network settings to recognize the new connection.

And that's that.

NOTE   *Your cable company might not yet offer USB-capable cable modems. In that instance, you'll need to install a 10/100Base-T Ethernet card in your computer, and connect an Ethernet cable from this card to your cable modem. It's a trickier installation, but no worse than what you have with a typical DSL setup.*

THE ONE DOWNSIDE TO CABLE ACCESS—YOUR NEIGHBORS!

When you connect to your cable company's Internet service, you're connecting to a very large network. Since you're now a client on this giant client/server system, you're sharing various network services—which is not necessarily a good thing.

Too Many Neighbors = Slower Speed

While cable access is supposed to deliver much faster download speeds than DSL, in actuality the speed you receive on your connection is affected by the number of other users in your neighborhood. This is because your cable company provides a single 27Mbps connection to each node on its network. Since each node serves multiple homes, the more people accessing the Internet at any given time, the slower each connection will be. (Do the math—two users sharing a 27Mbps connection will have much higher transmission speeds than 10 users—or a hundred!—sharing the same connection.)

Of course, the cable company can alleviate this problem by installing more nodes and connecting fewer households per node. Nodes come in various sizes and can be combined differently for downstream and upstream use. While the typical cable company today creates 1500-user nodes, there's nothing stopping them from reconfiguring to just 500 users per node (nothing except the quest for higher profits, of course!).

Unfortunately, there's no way of knowing how many people your cable company assigns to a node, so it's impossible to know what to expect when you subscribe. (You can ask your cable representative what to expect, but they probably won't know.) The only sure thing is that your service *will* slow down during peak usage periods—typically during the early evening hours. If it gets too slow, you can always complain, but the results of such constructive feedback are, unfortunately, variable.

The shared network issue, however, might not be as bad as it once was. The latest version of the DOCSIS standard—DOCSIS 1.1—provides for modems with security enhancements and improved quality of service. Among these improvements is the ability to tie a specific data rate or percentage of total bandwidth to each user on the network. This enables cable companies to assign minimum bandwidth to users, if they so desire, which *should* help to alleviate the current bandwidth-sharing problem.

Nosy Neighbors in the Network Neighborhood

The fact that you're sharing a network with your neighbors creates another type of problem—that of security. Unless you take proper security precautions, it's relatively easy for nosy neighbors to peek at the folders and files on your computer. Because you're all on one big network together, all nearby computers will show up in Windows' Network Neighborhood. Clicking on a neighbor's computer will display the contents of their hard disk—and, in some cases, provide access to all the programs and data stored there.

To eliminate unwanted sharing, you want to disable Windows' file- and print-sharing features. (Use the Network applet in Control Panel; click the File and Print Sharing button and deselect the appropriate options.) You probably also want to install some type of firewall software, which will not only keep out your neighbors, but will also discourage more dedicated crackers from breaking into your system. (Like most DSL systems, cable broadband utilizes static IP.)

In addition, most cable providers are now managing the network security issue from their end. System software is used to isolate your connection from your neighbors on the network, so that you can't go peering into your neighbors' systems (or vice versa). Check with your cable provider to see how they manage this particular issue.

Using a Satellite for Broadband Connections

If you're too far away from your telco's central office for a DSL connection, and your cable company is not so state-of-the-art that it doesn't yet offer cable modems, there is still one broadband solution available to you—Internet via digital satellite.

Internet-over-satellite offers downstream rates of 400Kbps or so, about what you'd expect with a slower DSL connection—which is about eight times faster than analog dial-up. (It's much slower than typical cable access, however.) Upstream rates are capped at either 128Kbps or 256Kbps, depending on your service plan—or even slower (33.3Kbps) if you choose a one-way system that uses a standard analog phone line for all upstream transmissions.

The largest provider of satellite Internet access is Hughes Network Systems, the company behind the popular DIRECTV system. For Internet users, Hughes offers the DIRECWAY system (formerly called DirecPC), where Internet data is received by a 24-inch by 36-inch oval dish at 400Kbps speeds. The installation package (including dish and modem) will set you back about $200, with subscription fees in the $60–$70 range. Consult the DIRECWAY Web site (www.direcway.com) for more details.

NOTE   *The basic DIRECWAY dish cannot receive DIRECTV signals, nor can you receive DIRECWAY data on a DIRECTV dish. If you want to avail yourself of both services, Hughes offers the DirecDuo system, which uses a single dish for both Internet access and television programming. Aside from the sharing of the dish, all other aspects of DirecDuo are identical to that of DIRECWAY.*

EchoStar (a.k.a. the Dish Network) offers a service similar to DIRECWAY. The StarBand system offers 500Kbps (potential maximum—your mileage may vary) download speeds from a 24-inch by 36-inch oval dish. Their service is a two-way system, just like DIRECWAY's; pricing is about $70/month.

HOW SATELLITE INTERNET WORKS

The bits and bytes that make up the Internet's data don't have to travel to you via some sort of cable—they can also be beamed through the air. This, in essence, is how satellite Internet works, by beaming Internet data off an orbiting satellite down to a satellite dish that is connected to your PC. The data's the same as what you get via DSL or cable; it just travels a longer distance (about 22,000 miles from your dish to the satellite!).

Older satellite systems use the satellite to transmit data downstream, but rely on traditional phone lines (and a normal analog modem) to transmit data upstream. Newer two-way systems also let you send data upstream from your dish to the satellite, so you get the same transmission speed upstream and down. (This effectively makes you a satellite broadcaster—which sounds kind of cool, doesn't it?)

Let's look at how the two-way DIRECWAY system operates. When you access a Web page, the request to view that page travels is sent up from your dish to the DIRECWAY satellite (22,000 miles up), then down (another 22,000 miles) to DIRECWAY's Network Operations Center (NOC) in Maryland. The NOC sends a request to the Web page's server, and the data that makes up that page is then sent from that server back to DIRECWAY's NOC. (This request and fulfillment is all handled over multiple T3 lines.) The NOC then beams the data for the Web page up to the DIRECWAY satellite (22,000 miles up, again); the signal bounces off the satellite back down to your DIRECWAY dish (another 22,000 miles), at 400Kbps. The signal then travels from your dish to your PC.

Because of the huge distances involved, there is some delay (called *latency*) in the receipt of the requested page. Typical latency is around 0.5 seconds, with ping times averaging between 400ms and 600ms. This latency is virtually unnoticeable when you're dealing with typical Web viewing or e-mail communications, although it could be a problem when you're playing real-time multiple-player online games.

Still, the entire process—as complicated as it is—takes place in about a half-a-second. Not bad for an 88,000-mile trip!

WARNING   *DIRECWAY signals—as with any satellite signals—need direct line-of-sight from satellite to dish. If something gets in the way—even something as small as a leaf on a tree—the signal can be interrupted. In addition, heavy precipitation, in the form of either rain or snow, can disrupt the satellite signal. This can be an issue if you live in an area prone to heavy storms, such as southern Florida in the summertime.*

INSTALLING AND CONFIGURING SATELLITE ACCESS

Setting up satellite access requires installing a satellite dish (outside your house) and installing a PCI card modem (inside your PC). Let's start by looking at the dish installation.

Installing a DIRECWAY dish is no different from installing any other of the pizza box–sized dishes currently on the market. Although DIRECWAY recommends using a professional installer (and if free installation is offered, I recommend that you take it), installation is easy enough that if you're relatively handy with a screwdriver, you can probably tackle it yourself. You have to find a southern-facing space, not obscured by trees or other objects, and then mount the dish in a secure fashion. Following the instructions provided by DIRECWAY, you then aim the dish at the satellite; some dishes come with an LED indicator that lights up when you're on target. The better your aim, the stronger the signal; the stronger the signal, the more reliable your Internet connection.

NOTE   *The FCC mandates that trained professionals (not you or me) install any two-way satellite system.*

Now you run a special coaxial cable from the dish back inside your house, over to your PC. After you've installed the internal satellite modem card, connect the cable to the card. (DIRECWAY also makes an external modem, with USB connection, that may be preferable for some users.) Once the connection is made, run the installation software to set up your system, and you're ready for business.

NOTE *You must also have a normal analog modem—either internal or external—connected to your computer for the DIRECWAY service to work. DIRECWAY does not supply an analog modem with its system.*

Wireless Connections via Microwave

Broadband wireless access (BWA) provides wireless Internet connections—the only cable involved is from the microwave antenna to the back of your PC. This technology is probably the least-used of all broadband technologies, however; it's available only in a limited number of cities. You have to be within 35 miles of a microwave-transmitting tower to connect to the service.

Like most other broadband technologies, BWA is an "always on" connection. You'll find typical connection speeds to be between 512Kbps and 1.5Mbps downstream, with upstream rates in the 256Kbps neighborhood.

The problem with BWA is that it just isn't competitive with DSL or cable broadband—and it costs too much for the providers to roll out on a large scale. The largest provider of wireless broadband, Sprint, recently put a moratorium on signing new users, and announced that it wouldn't be rolling out its service to any new markets.

Dead in the water, in other words.

How Broadband Wireless Access Works

BWA uses a technology called *fixed wireless*. This technology is similar to cellular phone technology in that it uses cell towers to transmit and receive signals via microwaves. The microwave signals are received by a stationary antenna, called a *transceiver*. The transceiver is a diamond-shaped antenna about 13.5 inches by 13.5 inches. You point it at the nearest microwave transmission tower, then connect it to your PC via a modem and network card.

Installing and Configuring Broadband Wireless Access

Installation of broadband wireless is typically done by a professional installer employed by your broadband service provider. The installer will mount the transceiver on the outside of your house (on the roof, typically) and precisely aim it at the nearest transmission tower. The installer then runs a cable from the transceiver to your computer, and connects it to an external broadband modem. This modem is connected to your PC via an Ethernet card (yours to provide).

All you have to do is run the installation software to complete the connection.

Downsides to Wireless Broadband

Like cable broadband, BWA is a shared bandwidth technology. That means that when more users log on in your neighborhood, your download speeds will drop.

Like satellite broadband, BWA depends on a clear line of sight to the transmission source. While physical objects (like trees) don't obstruct microwave signals, you still have to aim the antenna carefully. If it's more than a few degrees off-center, it will miss the signals coming from the transmission tower.

Of course, the biggest downside is that the BWA infrastructure costs too much to roll out, with the result that it isn't widely available. Unless you're a current subscriber, you probably don't have wireless broadband as an option where you live.

Troubleshooting Tips

Communications troubleshooting can provide you with hours of mind-exercising delight, *if* you're the kind of person who likes puzzles. Let's see how to deconstruct the problem and isolate the bad component. There are a few possibilities to look at when you're troubleshooting communications:

◆ The phone line

◆ The port

◆ The modem

◆ The cable

In this section, you'll learn about troubleshooting each of these components. But first, I'll give you a quick overview of the most basic problems and solutions.

Simple Problems, Simple Solutions

You're set up to dial your ISP, but the modem doesn't respond. There are lots of possibilities:

Is the modem plugged into the phone jack? If you share the modem's phone line with a phone, you may have forgotten to plug the modem back in after using the phone.

Is the modem plugged into the computer? Did the serial cable fall out? (It won't if you screw in the connectors.)

Is the phone line working? Plug in a phone. Is there a dial tone?

Is it your phone system? If you have an in-house phone system, like a ROLM or Northern Telecom system, you may have to issue extra commands to dial out of your private branch exchange (PBX) system. Check with your telecommunications manager.

WARNING *Plugging an analog modem into a digital system will cause damage to the modem. If you plan on traveling, avail yourself of Hello Direct's LineStein digital adapter, which converts pesky digital jacks to analog in seconds. A mere $120 gets you the unit and another $40 gets you a battery pack (it normally plugs into the wall, but...). A few replacement laptop modems definitely cost more than that! The gizmo can "learn" the particulars of practically any digital PBX system. Just plug it into the wall and line and press the Learn button. A green light means a good line.*

Phone Line Noise and Quality Problems

Sometimes the problem isn't in your modem; it's the phone line itself. There are a couple of simple things you should try first. Can you try the call on another line? Is it a multiextension phone—could someone be picking up the phone as your modem tries to dial?

You should also check a few other areas:

◆ The quality of the communications provider

◆ The in-house wiring

◆ Whether call-waiting is interrupting modem sessions

The call-waiting is easy enough to check. Just make sure that you have a *70—or whatever your phone company's call-waiting turn-off arrangement is—in front of the ISP's dial-up access number. As for the first two items, experience and lots of dirty clothing are the only ways to solve them.

CHECK THE IN-HOUSE CABLE PLANT

You may find that line noise is being created by the wiring in your building. It could be that old wires don't transmit as well as they once did or that someone ran the wires near the high-voltage lines in the elevator shaft—any number of a million things could go wrong with the in-house cable plant. Inspect your cable plant periodically. I had phone noise trouble in my building, so I restrung my phone lines and the problem went away. (I actually found that my termination block was made out of four wood screws driven into a rafter in the basement!)

CHECK THE GROUND

Did you check that the modem and the PC share a common ground? You may recall from Chapter 9 that plugging the PC and a peripheral into different outlets can lead to slight differences in the value of "electrical ground," which in turn can lead to noisy communications.

CHECK THE VOLTAGE

The phone line has four lines, one each colored red, green, yellow, and black. Only the red and green lines are used. Each pair should offer 48 volts of DC power with all devices on-hook. Each off-hook device will draw about 3 to 9 volts (although some go as high as 12). Get seven phones off-hook on one line, and it will not have enough juice to power any of them, although the one closest to the main junction box might work. If your phone varies greatly from this, call your repair office.

WARNING The voltage on a normal phone line is enough to be felt. If you happen to measure the line while the phone is ringing, the voltage shoots up to almost 100 volts. Only do this test if you know what you're doing, please. We'd miss you.

Or you could try checking out the phone line with a phone-line tester. IBM makes one called the Modem Saver for about $30; it's not the greatest thing in the whole world, but it does the job. You just plug it into the modular phone jack and little lights tell you whether the line is working. You can find the information for this product in the Vendor Guide on the Utilities CD.

GOING FURTHER

Devices called *analog channel test units* will test the phone line between you and the other party. They are, however, quite expensive. You can also get an oscilloscope, which can help you measure the frequencies being produced by your modem to see whether they are within specification. Again, you may not want to go this far; the required investment in test equipment is not trivial.

Port Problems

Since the RS-232 port is a bidirectional device (it talks as well as listens), you can use a *loopback* to allow it to test itself. Serial ports *do* become ill. I don't know why—on my system, I presume it's something to do with the plugging and unplugging that I do. (I do a large amount of communications consulting, so I try out a lot of equipment on my system.) For instance, years ago I bought two Toshiba 1100+ laptop computers and they both had something wrong with the serial port: Receive Data in the first one, Ring Indicator in the second. Probably 20 percent of the expansion boards that I've worked with had a serial problem. So it's worthwhile knowing how to diagnose such a problem.

To test the port, you need to see what is happening on the various control lines. I recommend that you get a breakout box to assist you in testing the communications port.

A *breakout box* allows you to prototype a serial cable without soldering or pin crimping (the two most common methods of cable assembly). That's convenient because you can figure out what the correct cable configuration should be even if you don't know how to solder or crimp. Then you can give that cable configuration to someone in your company or a technical service house to make up the cable for you. You see, getting the cable made (soldered) isn't too hard, once you've settled on a cable design. But making sure that it's designed correctly *is* difficult, so you want to do it yourself; a breakout box makes that possible.

Regular 25-wire RS-232-type cables come in one side and go out the other. All 25 lines are represented on each side with large, round, metal posts. The breakout box comes with about a dozen wires that terminate in small plugs that mate with the posts. The way the box works is that you design a cable, run wires from post to post to make the connections necessary for the cable, and plug in the breakout box (it serves as the cable) to the two devices that you want to interface. The cable design either works or it doesn't.

As an example, say I'm trying to design a cable to allow my laptop to transfer data to my PC. The cables on either end are too short to connect the two devices, so I need to first run a couple of extension cables. I run a regular straight-through cable from the PC to one side of the breakout box and another regular straight-through cable from the laptop to the other side of the breakout box.

Now I'm ready to start prototyping. I figure I'll start my cable design with a cable that just connects 2 on the PC side to 3 on the laptop side, 3 on the PC side to 2 on the laptop side, and 7 on the PC side to 7 on the laptop side. (See the section "Common Cables: A Configuration Cookbook" for basic cable diagrams.) To set this up, I run one of the wires from 2 on the PC side to 3 on the laptop side, and from 3 on the PC side to 2 on the laptop side. I don't have to run a wire from 7 to 7—there are DIP switches for each of the 25 lines, and anytime I want a "straight-through" connection, I just have to close the DIP switch for that particular line. (Make sure the others are all set to "open," or you'll have lots of "wires" in your cable that you didn't intend to have.)

Some breakout boxes have red, and possibly green, lights to indicate activity levels for various inputs and outputs in the RS-232 connection. Red lights indicate the presence of voltage in excess of +3 volts (interpreted as 0), and green lights indicate the presence of voltage below –3 volts (interpreted as 1). The signal used to indicate "active" on the control leads is 0.

Modem Problems

Check the simple stuff first—such as, are the connections correct? Many modems have two phone jacks—one to connect to the wall and one to pass through to the phone. Connect the "phone" one to the wall and you'll dial up okay, but disconnect as soon as the other side answers!

Some modems have loopback capabilities built right in. In that case, you can do simple loopback tests, as described in the preceding section, "Port Problems." If not, the best first procedure is a modem swap. They're small and don't require much work to swap.

If you're using an external modem, do the front lights tell you anything? Put a breakout box inline between the modem and the computer. You should see the correspondence as shown in Table 22.4.

TABLE 22.4: MODEM FRONT-PANEL LIGHT/RS-232 LINE CORRESPONDENCE

MODEM LIGHT	RED LIGHT ON BREAKOUT BOX
TR	20
MR	6
RD	3
SD	2
CD	8

When a specific modem light is on, the corresponding breakout box light should be on.

If you're running Windows 98 or later, you can use the operating system to check your modem connection for you. From Control Panel, launch the Modems applet to display the Modem Properties dialog box. Select the Diagnostics tab, highlight the port used by your modem, and then click the More Info button. If you receive a series of OK responses, your modem is communicating properly and the problem is elsewhere. (Probably an incorrect configuration within Windows—check your COM port assignments and the modem's initialization string.) If, on the other hand, you *don't* receive positive responses, then your modem is not connected properly, not powered up (if it's an external modem), or just not working properly.

NOTE *Obviously, some things described here do not apply to an internal modem—the lights, for instance. Although some internal modems do have lights on their back panel, it's uncommon since most people don't orient the rear of their CPU case to point at them (although some do, and I've been known to keep a test unit uncased and backward for months on end). For an internal modem that is not a so-called Winmodem, make sure it's properly seated in its port and that the cable is working and properly seated in the correct jack. Also, double-check your driver installation. For Winmodems, do the same, but also make sure you're running Windows. Seriously, don't feel bad about reinstalling the drivers. That usually resets anything that was incorrectly modified.*

Cable Troubleshooting

To check out the serial cables, detach the breakout box from the computer, then connect the cable that you usually use to the computer. Connect the breakout box to the free end of the cable, and rerun the cable tests. If one fails, you have a broken wire.

Remember that with cables, speed trades off for distance. If you have a 100-foot RS-232 cable, you won't be able to run it at 38,400bps. But the exact same equipment and a 2-foot cable might be able to do it at that speed. The only difference is in the length of the cable.

On the other hand, if you're reading this because the cable has never worked, refer to the "How RS-232 Works" and "Common Cables: A Configuration Cookbook" sections.

Now that you know how to talk to other computers (via the Internet, specifically), it's time to go back to the one on your desk. In the next chapter, I'll discuss keyboards and mice.

Chapter 23

Keyboards and Mice

◆ QuickSteps: Installing a Keyboard, Mouse,
  or Trackball   647

◆ Types of Keyboards and How They Work   648

◆ Keyboard Maintenance   651

◆ Types of Mice and How They Work   654

◆ Wireless Input Devices   657

◆ Troubleshooting Your Keyboard and Mouse   658

Introduction

EVERY PERSONAL COMPUTER HAS a keyboard—and, with the near-universal acceptance of graphical user interfaces (GUIs), practically every PC has some kind of pointing device.

When it comes to keyboards, they all have pretty much the same keys, though there are some differences. You have the traditional IBM-type keyboard, the newer split ergonomic keyboards, and even wireless keyboards that let you do your typing from your easy chair. They're all the same to troubleshoot, however.

Turning to pointing devices, we've tried electronic stylus devices, light pens (I wanted to call this chapter "Of Mice and Pens," but I couldn't really justify it), and even a Headmouse that tracks the way that you are facing. Still, the most popular pointing device seems to be the mouse. Mice can be more of a pain than keyboards, however, so I'll tell you how to handle them, too, in this chapter.

QuickSteps

Installing a Keyboard, Mouse, or Trackball

Installing a new keyboard, mouse, or trackball is among the easiest installations you'll encounter.

BE PREPARED

Before you start, there are some things you may need on hand. These include:

◆ Documentation that came with the product, to ensure proper installation

◆ Software or drivers ready to install, if required

◆ Your new keyboard, mouse, or trackball

1. Turn off your computer.

NOTE   *USB devices are designed to be* hot-swappable *and should not require you to turn off your computer or reboot.*

2. Unplug the old device (keyboard, mouse, or trackball).

3. Plug your new device into the appropriate port (keyboard, mouse, or USB) on the back of your computer.

4. Turn your computer on.

5. Install any special software or drivers for non–Plug and Play devices. Windows should detect Plug and Play devices, and prompt you to install the correct drivers.

Keyboard Types and Components

With all of its moving parts, the keyboard has many potential sources of problems. Understanding those sources requires understanding the types of keyboards and their parts; here's a look at them.

Keyboard Types

There are a number of IBM-type keyboards, but you're most likely to come across one of these three:

Original PC or XT keyboard (generally called the XT keyboard) This has 83 keys and the benefit of a nice "clicky" feel. When you press a key, it offers some tactile feedback. Pretty much all IBM keyboards do that, but over the years many clone keyboards have adopted a mushy feel. The numeric keypad and the cursor control keys are integrated into one 5-inch by 3-inch area on the right side of the keyboard.

Original AT keyboard (generally called the AT keyboard) Improvements over the XT keyboard include a larger Enter key and the addition of a SysReq (or SysRq) key intended for use with OS/2. It also has 10 function keys either along the top or on the left side of the keyboard (labeled F1–F10). It's still my favorite keyboard layout, but it's been largely superseded in the marketplace by the 101-key keyboard.

The 101-key PS/2 keyboard (generally called the enhanced keyboard) This appeared in 1987 and has the big benefit of being compatible with every other keyboard interface. The extra keys were added by separating the cursor and numeric functions from the numeric keypad, as well as adding two more function keys, F11 and F12 (see Figure 23.1).

FIGURE 23.1

PS/2 keyboard

The main difference between the XT and AT keyboards is that the XT keyboard puts the keyboard microprocessor in the keyboard, and the AT keyboard assumes that the keyboard microprocessor is on the system board. They are generally incompatible: you can't use an XT keyboard on an AT, or vice versa. Clone keyboards generally get around this by putting an XT/AT switch on the keyboard. The enhanced keyboard, on the other hand, will work on any machine without modification.

NOTE *If you want to take your keyboard with you, a new type of flexible keyboard is available (from Man & Machine and other vendors) that is only about an inch high and made of a totally sealed rubbery material that can actually be rolled up like an old magazine. These flexible keyboards are ideal for use with PDAs, but are also finding converts among regular computer users who want a completely waterproof and dustproof keyboard—or something they can roll up and take with them!*

The "broken" keyboard designs (also called ergonomic keyboards), such as the Microsoft Natural Keyboard, look like a 101-key keyboard to the PC hardware. Figure 23.2 shows what they look like to the user. Because they're compatible with the existing hardware, they're easy to install, and although they take a little getting used to, they're easier on the wrists than standard keyboards. People who do a lot of typing might prefer these.

FIGURE 23.2

Microsoft Natural Keyboard

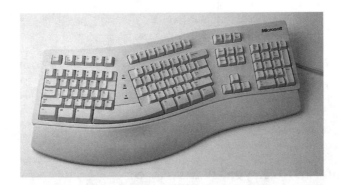

So-called Windows keyboards add three keys to the standard 101-key keyboard, typically on the same row as the spacebar. The new keys are two Windows keys (one on either side of the spacebar) that open the Windows Start menu, and an Application key that displays the same context menus you get when you right-click an item.

NOTE   Many newer keyboards have additional keys that can speed up your productivity. Some keyboards provide a large number of specialized keys that help you connect to and browse the Internet, and even operate your CD-ROM and multimedia applications. Some keys, through the help of drivers and special software, can be configured to perform your favorite tasks or to work with programs of your choosing; these are called hot keys.

Switch or Contact Design

The hardest part of designing a keyboard is in creating the right *action*—the right *touch*. Anyone who learned to type on a keyboard expects the keys to move about a third of an inch when pressed, and some keyboards do that correctly—I find those kinds of keyboards preferable. Newer keyboards, on laptops in particular, don't move as much ("don't have as much travel," is the actual lingo), less than half that amount. Let's see... this book is about 2 million keystrokes... one-sixth of a wasted inch per keystroke... comes out to almost 5 miles of extra finger work I'm doing with this old-fashioned keyboard! (And to think they say writing isn't strenuous.)

You'll find two basic kinds of keyboards:

◆ Switch-based

◆ Capacitive

The switch-based keyboard uses, as you'd imagine, microswitches (very small switches that turn on and off when a key is pressed) for each key on the keyboard. The switches can become dirty. They can be cleaned sometimes, but often it's easier to just replace them. They're sufficiently cheap that when a problem of any magnitude occurs, perhaps you should just throw away the keyboard and buy a new one—I've seen them for as little as $6. Clones tend to use this switch-type approach.

The IBM and AT&T keyboards are capacitive: in the bottom of the keyboard is one large capacitive surface. Each keyboard key pushes a spring, which in turn pushes a paddle. The paddle makes an impression on the capacitive module. The capacitive module sends out signals, which are interpreted by the 8048 microprocessor in the keyboard. It then sends the key's ID, called a *scan code*, to the PC. The PC then figures out what the key means.

NOTE   The capacitive design sounds more complicated (it is) and is more expensive than its switch-based counterpart. However, because a capacitive keyboard consists of one large module rather than a lot of prone-to-fail switches, it is less likely to fail. Unfortunately, your options for repairing a capacitive keyboard are limited; repairing a malfunctioning capacitive module is more expensive than repairing a switch-based keyboard if the problem lies with a switch or key. Truthfully, the most you can do to fix sticking keys on most keyboards is to clean them or just get a new keyboard.

System Board/Keyboard Interface

The interface between the keyboard cable and the system unit is the keyboard interface. This is a DIN (or mini-DIN if it's a PS/2) plug that has five (or six, for mini-DIN) pins. Figure 23.3 shows the connector *on the system unit side*. You can get adapters for DIN to mini-DIN, or mini-DIN to DIN, for a few dollars.

FIGURE 23.3

An old-style DIN keyboard connector with five pins (top) and a more current PS/2 mini-DIN keyboard connector with six pins (bottom)

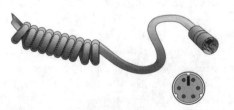

The Universal Serial Bus (USB) interface is becoming more popular for keyboards, and some models may, in fact, require you to use a USB port unless you have a USB-to-PS/2 adapter to make your USB keyboard compatible with the PS/2 keyboard port. The Microsoft Natural Keyboard and several Microsoft mice are examples of devices that are USB by design, although some versions may include a USB-to-PS/2 adapter with the product. USB devices have several benefits, which mostly derive from USB being a newer, faster technology. A USB connection is faster than the other, older

I/O ports on your computer, such as COM and parallel ports. In addition, a USB device doesn't require special device drivers for it to operate. (A driver is required, but USB drivers cover a wide range of devices, so, for example, a USB pointing device driver covers mice, touchpads, and writing boards.) You simply plug the device in and it works (ideally, that is). USB devices also require no conflict resolution for competing resources such as COM ports, which require IRQs and other precious system resources to operate.

About the only drawback to using a USB device is backward compatibility. Although Windows 98, Me, XP, and 2000 are USB "aware," Windows 95 and NT 4 are not, and are therefore incompatible with USB devices.

Keyboard Connector

The keyboard cable runs from a DIN connector, which attaches the system unit to a flat-jaw type connector inside the keyboard housing. The cable has five wires and can be checked for continuity quickly with an ohmmeter: disconnect the cable inside the keyboard and test each line. (See the "What to Do When a Keyboard Fails You" section in this chapter for details.) On the other hand, once you're inside the keyboard, then you're kind of making a choice: do you really want to spend four hours playing around inside a keyboard, four hours that may be totally fruitless, or do you just spend a few bucks on a new keyboard?

Keyboard Maintenance

The major aspect of maintenance for keyboards is *abstinence*—abstinence, that is, from spilling things into the keyboard. Protecting keyboards with plastic covers was discussed in Chapter 4, "Avoiding Service: Preventive Maintenance"; this is one approach. Another is just to be careful.

Periodically disconnect the keyboard and remove it from the general area of the PC. Pull the keytops off. (I hope this needn't be said, but I'll say it anyway: be sure you have a similar keyboard nearby so that you can put the keytops back in the right order, unless—heh, heh—this is a keyboard for someone you don't like.) Then hold it upside down and blow it clean with compressed air. The keytops aren't that tough to remove—I use one of those "chip puller" tools that come with PC toolkits (recall that they're dangerous to use to actually pull *chips* with), and find it to be *just* the tool for the job. If the keyboard is particularly messy, you can use a spray cleaner. In extremis, you can soak a sticky keyboard in water overnight—but make sure it's completely dry before you try using it.

What to Do When a Keyboard Fails You

Since most keyboards are so inexpensive (with the exception of some ergonomic and wireless keyboards), you may want to view the keyboard as disposable. There are some simple things you can do before throwing out a keyboard, however.

Make Sure It Is Plugged In

On the back of computers that use PS/2-type connectors are two identical ports: the mouse port and the keyboard port. Make sure you've plugged the keyboard into the correct port. You will get an error when turning on the computer if the mouse and/or keyboard are connected to the wrong port.

Make Sure BIOS and Windows See It

If there is a keyboard failure, you should see a message when your computer boots up. Pay close attention, and if you see the message, try checking the connection first before you move on to more drastic measures.

If the BIOS doesn't display any errors on-screen (such as `Keyboard not present` or `Keyboard failure`) when you boot up, make sure Windows recognizes your keyboard by checking Device Manager. You can access Device Manager in Windows by opening Control Panel and double-clicking the System icon. Select the Device Manager tab in the System Properties dialog box. Your keyboard should be listed in the Keyboard category. If it is listed, make sure it is the proper make and model.

To access Device Manager in Windows 2000, open Control Panel and double-click Administrative Tools. Next, double-click Computer Management and expand the System Tools category to find Device Manager. Your keyboard should be listed in the Keyboards category.

Fix Bent Pins

Check your PS/2-type connector that plugs into the motherboard for any bent or missing pins. This often happens if someone (usually children, although adults can do this too if they aren't paying attention) tries to force the connection in the wrong orientation. What happens is that the pins that aren't lined up with the correct holes on the motherboard connector get bent back as you force the connection. There's simply no place for them to go but sideways. If your pins are bent, carefully straighten them with a pair of slim, needle-nosed pliers. Be careful not to break off the pins as you straighten them.

Connect It to Another Computer

If you're fortunate enough to have more than one computer in your home (most businesses have several), you can try swapping keyboards with a machine that you know isn't suffering keyboard problems. If the keyboard that you suspect is having trouble doesn't work on the "good" computer, you know that keyboard is bad. If the new keyboard doesn't work on the machine you're testing, you may have a faulty keyboard connection on the motherboard. Unfortunately, there's not much you can do about this yourself. If your computer or motherboard is under warranty, or you have a maintenance agreement, you might be able to send your computer to the manufacturer and let them replace the keyboard connection. If you're doing the work yourself, you may have to replace the motherboard.

TIP   A good workaround for a faulty keyboard connector is to purchase a low-cost PCI card with a built-in keyboard connector; this is a good way to get a new keyboard connector without going to the cost and trouble of replacing the entire motherboard. (Similarly, you can just buy a new USB keyboard and connect it to your PC's USB port—bypassing the keyboard connection completely.)

Check the Keys

If only one key is malfunctioning, check the spring under the key to see whether it springs up and down, as a key should. Remove the key by grabbing it with your fingers and pulling up. For the tough keys, fashion a hook from a paper clip or, again, use a chip puller. You will see a spring under the key. Replace the keytop and see whether the problem goes away. If not, try pulling the spring out *just a little.* Then replace the keytop.

Some keyboards use rubber cups instead of springs. Either way, the cup or spring is designed to keep the keys from being "on" all the time.

Test Pin Voltages

The voltage between pin 4 and each of the other pins should be in the range of 2–5.5 volts DC. If any of these voltages are wrong, the problem probably lies in the PC—the system board in particular. If they're okay, the problem is probably in the keyboard. Note that the pins are not numbered consecutively for either a DIN or a mini-DIN.

If you hold a DIN so that the pins are at the top and count from left to right, the pins are numbered 1, 4, 2, 5, and 3; the number 2 pin is at the top-center point. Holding a mini-DIN with the single groove in the connector at the top, and starting from the bottom left and moving clockwise, the pins are numbered 1, 3, 5, 6, 4, and 2; the groove is between pins 5 and 6.

Check the Cable Continuity

Next, test continuity of the cable. Turn the keyboard upside down so that the cable is coming out of the back of the keyboard, to the right. Remove the two screws. The bottom plate will swing back and up for removal.

You will now see that the cable splits to a single wire, which is grounded to the bottom plate. You'll also see a cable with a flat-jaw connector. Push apart the jaws of the connector to release. You can then use an ohmmeter to test each of the five wires for continuity. An *ohmmeter* is a device that electricians (and computer technicians) use to test electrical circuits for power and detect short-circuits.

Completely Disassemble It

Not recommended for the fainthearted. You have a good chance of making things even worse, so don't do it unless there's no other hope.

WARNING *This step will take about four hours once you've taken the keyboard apart, put it back together wrong, figured out what you did wrong, taken it apart again, accidentally spilled all the pieces on the floor, etc., and then finally managed to reassemble the thing.*

Remove the main assembly from the keyboard case. With a vise or C-clamps, set up a support for the keyboard assembly on the sides. If you don't connect the clamps to the sides, you're in for a surprise when you remove the back metal plate. (Remember those springs on each paddle?)

Alternatively, you can make your life easier by removing all the keytops. But, again, don't do it unless you have another keyboard around that you can use as a guide to replacing the keytops.

NOTE *One way to remember which keys go where is to put the keyboard (keys facing down) on a photocopier or scanner and make a picture of the keys.*

A printed circuit board with capacitive pads on it is held against a metal plate by 10 metal tabs— 5 above, 5 below—and a hex screw. You must use pliers to unbend the tabs enough to remove the plate. Position the assembly so that the plate is on top (not the printed circuit board), then remove the metal plate.

The plate has been holding dozens of plastic paddles against the printed circuit card, one for each key. These are small, flat, easily broken pieces of plastic shaped like the outline of a castle turret, or the rook piece in chess. What you are looking for is a broken paddle. Replace any broken paddles and then put the metal plate back on.

The other reason to attempt this is if you've poured hot coffee into the keyboard. Very carefully remove all the paddles and clean them, as well as the bracket that they sit in. Then use alcohol to clean the capacitive PC board. Then reassemble and pray. I *have* seen this work—but only once.

Putting the metal plate back on is a bit difficult. Position it correctly, then use clamps to hold one side together while you bend the tabs on the other side into place. Again, it is easy to damage paddles at this point. Where do you get replacement paddles? No one that I know of sells them. Get them from the first keyboard that dies: it's good for 101 replacement paddles.

Replace the Keyboard

If you've gotten this far and have had no luck, don't despair. Many keyboard problems can't be fixed, and the things aren't that expensive anyway.

Logitech, KeyTronicEMS, Datadesk Technologies, and Northgate make good replacement keyboards. Datadesk's are a bit cheaper, and they have one that is programmable. This means that you can move that annoying Esc key somewhere else, set up your keyboard as a Dvorak keyboard, and the like.

NOTE   *The Dvorak keyboard has all the keys in different places than the traditional keyboard layout, which is derived from the typewriter and created in the 1870s. The Dvorak is supposed to make typing easier and faster.*

KeyTronicEMS offers a keyboard with an in-line bar-code reader. Other software enables you to print bar codes with a dot-matrix or laser printer. One firm I know of uses bar codes at the top of their document-tracking forms so that secretaries don't have to key (and sometimes miskey) a 12-digit document-tracking ID every time they have to update the document-tracking database.

Several companies are now offering ergonomic ("broken") keyboards designed to reduce hand and tendon stress, as I said earlier. I've used the Microsoft Natural Keyboard and Logitech's ergonomic model, and if you're looking for advice, I'd suggest that you find someone with one of these and borrow it for a while before you buy it. They definitely feel easier on my wrist and most of my hand, but my left index finger has to do enough reaching that sometimes it feels as if it's going to separate from the rest of my hand.

Mouse Types and Components

Mice are in some ways simpler devices than keyboards; after all, most have only two or three buttons and maybe a wheel as compared to the standard keyboard's 101 keys. (Some new mice do have up to six buttons.) But all mice have some moving parts that can go seriously wrong.

Mouse Types

Basically, mice work in this way: you move them, they figure out somehow how much you've moved them, and then they transmit that information to the computer. The "how they figure out how much you moved them" and the "transmit the data to the computer" parts are how mice vary.

Buttons and Wheels

All mice have at least two buttons: left and right. You can't go wrong choosing a two-button mouse, but a number of more modern mice have extra buttons and wheels to make scrolling, zooming, and selecting much easier. Microsoft's IntelliMouse Explorer (see Figure 23.4) has five programmable buttons that can be used with standard programs and Internet-related applications; it also has a small wheel (located between the left and right mouse buttons) that zooms in and out or scrolls.

Mouse Positioning Methods

Most mice are mechanical, meaning that they use some mechanical method for detecting motion. On most mice, the primary mechanical part is a ball on the bottom of the mouse. Take the mouse apart (remove the retaining ring, turn the mouse over, and the ball falls out, generally rolling under something), and you'll see three little wheels that turn when the ball moves against them.

Two of those wheels are monitored electronically; when they turn, they transmit to the computer how much they turned. The two wheels are perpendicular to each other, so one tracks X-axis motion and one tracks Y-axis motion. The third wheel just balances the first two.

The third kind of positioning mechanism is in the optical mouse, sold by Microsoft, Logitech, and others. This type of mouse has no moving parts. The mouse has optical sensors instead of a physical mouse ball, and can be used on any surface.

I recently purchased a Microsoft optical mouse for my laptop and simply love it. I can use the laptop downstairs while sitting on my living room couch and use the couch as a mouse pad, or travel in the car and use my leg. (Even better—there are no moving parts to get clogged up!)

Optical mice operate by using a red LED that takes 1500 snapshots per second of the surface below it. By comparing the images dynamically, they can determine speed, direction, and distance. You can use these mice on top of just about any surface that is relatively flat. However, you'll want to avoid using these optical mice on surfaces with solid color, or on glass or reflective surfaces. You'll also want to avoid patterns that are highly repetitive.

NOTE *The new Microsoft optical mice are a boon to gamers. In addition to having precise positioning, they are all USB mice. Normal mice operate at 40MHz (the frequency their position is updated by Windows) due to the interface, but USB mice operate at 120MHz. With frame rates of some games shooting well over 40MHz, having a mouse that can keep up with your game is a must.*

For those of you who like to navigate by feel, Logitech offers the iFeel mouse. This new little critter provides tactile feedback as you scroll around a Web page or desktop. You'll feel a gentle vibration when you roll over a menu or dialog box, almost as if your virtual computer desktop was physically real. Naturally, this type of enhancement increases the cost of the mouse—and introduces a new element to wear out or break down at a later date.

Trackballs

Trackballs are pointing devices that have the ball (normally located underneath and inside of a mouse) on the top of the unit. Instead of moving a mouse around, you move the trackball with your finger. It's just like the trackballs on some arcade machines—or like using an upside-down mouse, if you want to think of it that way.

Many people prefer trackballs to standard mice because you have fine control over the position of the cursor and don't have to move anything around on your desktop. Trackballs are ideal for certain professions, such as architects and graphic artists, who need a high degree of pointing precision as they work. Trackballs are also an attractive alternative for young children and people with certain disabilities because they often find them easier to use than mice. Some laptops even use this technology as their primary pointing device.

Mouse Interfaces

Most mice connect to a PC via a serial port. Some use a USB connection or proprietary interface.

There have been several proprietary mouse interfaces over the years, but the most common are the Microsoft bus mouse interface and the IBM PS/2-type interface, which is very like yet another Microsoft interface, the InPort interface. All three interfaces use a mini-DIN connector as a plug.

The Microsoft bus mouse interface is a bit brain damaged in that it works only with interrupts 2, 3, 4, or 5. The PS/2-type interface is typically integrated into a motherboard—I see it on a lot of laptops—and it's usually hard-wired to IRQ12.

Mouse Cleaning

On a mechanical mouse, the little wheels get gunk stuck to them or hair wrapped around them, so you must clean them. Just remove the mouse ball and examine the wheels. I've used rubbing alcohol, a toothpick, and a cotton swab to get the gunk off the wheels. You may also need to clean the ball with a bit of alcohol. Clean the mouse about twice a year—or more if your desk is covered with dirt or dust, which is just gunk in its fetal stages.

On an optical mouse, all you have to do is clean the sensors; you can often just polish them with a soft cloth.

What to Do When Your Mouse Fails You

You can troubleshoot a mouse by following these steps:

1. Make sure your mouse is plugged in securely.

2. Check the driver. Is the mouse driver set up correctly? Is it there in the first place?

3. Clean the mouse and shake any debris off the mouse pad.

4. Check the interface at the end of your mouse cable and at the motherboard, whether it is USB, PS/2, or the serial port. See if there are any obvious problems such as bent pins (for PS/2 and serial port mice only) that can be straightened.

5. Ensure that Windows recognizes the mouse and that it is listed in Device Manager as properly installed.

If all this fails, and your computer is not the culprit, you'll need to replace your mouse. Fortunately, mice are quite affordable; standard mice run around $10, with the fancy optical models starting at around $20.

Wireless Input Devices

I've talked about the issues involved with using cabled mice and keyboards. However, interest in wireless input devices has been picking up. What is there to know about these devices?

They work like this: you get a receiver with the wireless keyboard that plugs into your computer, usually through the keyboard port. Similarly, the wireless mouse receiver plugs into your mouse port. This cabled receiver then sits on top of your monitor (in the case of infrared systems) or anywhere within 30 feet or so of your keyboard or mouse (for RF models).

Some of these devices use infrared (IR) frequencies to transmit data, meaning that they have high bandwidth (not really an issue with something that transmits as little data as a keyboard or mouse does) and are pretty much immune to outside interference. Use a cordless telephone or other infrared devices (such as a TV remote control) in the same room, and it will have no effect at all. In order for the infrared frequencies to communicate, however, the receiver (on your PC) and transmitter (on your mouse or keyboard) have to be within the line of sight.

More common are radio-controlled wireless keyboards and mice. Newer wireless devices operate in the 900MHz frequency band and have a range of about 30 feet. Since RF signals pass through most objects, your mouse and keyboard don't have to be within the line of sight of the receiver—a big advantage over IR devices.

If you're using an RF keyboard or mouse, there is a slight risk of interference with other wireless devices (such as cordless phones) that also use the 900MHz band. Practically, however, this isn't much of an issue; if you do experience interference, just put a little distance between the two devices and the problem will probably fix itself.

Generally speaking, wireless devices are more expensive than wired devices, and input devices are no exception. Although one manufacturer's advertising extols wireless keyboards as a wonderful way to reduce cabling needs, the lack of one or two cables doesn't make up the price difference. You can find the cheapest keyboards for under $10, with wireless models starting at around $40.

Personally, I've grown to like wireless input devices. I've been using a Logitech wireless keyboard and mouse for about a year now, and I like being able to lean back in my chair, put my feet up on my desk (not good for my back, I know), and type away with my keyboard in my lap, not worrying at all about whether or not the cord will reach. If you don't mind replacing batteries every few months (and also don't mind the higher initial cost), doing away with the cords is a good thing.

Troubleshooting Tips

Here's a summary of troubleshooting tips for your keyboard:

◆ Make sure that the keyboard is plugged in and the connection is secure.

◆ Ensure that there are no BIOS warnings at bootup and that Windows recognizes the keyboard.

◆ Check the cable connector for any bent or missing pins.

◆ Swap the keyboard you suspect is malfunctioning with one that you are sure works to see if the problem lies with the computer and not the keyboard.

◆ Check the keys for proper functionality. They should all spring back to their original state when you press and release them.

◆ Test pin voltages on the keyboard cable.

◆ Check for cable continuity within the keyboard housing.

◆ Disassemble the keyboard and check all internal parts.

◆ Replace the keyboard if none of the above works and your computer is not at fault.

And here are a few things to try when your mouse isn't working correctly:

◆ Ensure that the mouse is plugged in securely.

◆ Check the mouse driver in Windows to make sure it's correctly installed.

◆ Clean your mouse to remove built-up gunk.

◆ Check for bent pins on the cable.

◆ Replace your mouse if nothing else works.

Chapter 24

Video Adapters and Displays

◆ QuickSteps: Shopping for a Video Card   661

◆ QuickSteps: Installing a New Video Card   661

◆ How a Video Board Works   663

◆ Video Board Characteristics   668

◆ Understanding and Comparing Monitors   674

◆ Troubleshooting Tips   681

Introduction

THE DISPLAY ON A computer is the primary output device. Because of that, your personal comfort when using a PC is wrapped up in the display, and video taste tends to be a personal kind of thing. What's behind the screen? How can you choose the best equipment for you? And how much can you fix when it fails?

This chapter will help you select and install a video card. We'll also take a look at the parts of a video board, as well as their image resolution, color depth, vertical frequency, and 3D capability.

QuickSteps

Shopping for a Video Card

1. Decide what your needs are—business, entertainment, gaming, or general purpose.

2. Budget yourself. Today's prices range from under $50 for a low-end VGA card to around $300 for a high-end consumer 3D card.

3. Pick your favorite 3D application programming interface (API), if necessary for gaming. Many games support multiple APIs (DirectX, OpenGL, and Glide), but some will specialize in one over the others. Check the requirements of the games you have or want to buy, and look for a card that supports those APIs.

4. Choose a manufacturer such as ATI or Matrox. (Contact information on these manufacturers can be found in the Vendor's Guide on the Utilities CD.) Check out online or magazine reviews of different cards to see how they match up.

5. Decide on an Accelerated Graphics Port (AGP) or PCI bus card. This depends on your motherboard; many older PCs do not have AGP. If you have an AGP slot, choose that type of card for better performance.

6. It's usually best to get the most memory you can afford, although general-purpose and business-computing video memory needs are less demanding.

QuickSteps

Installing a New Video Card

Here's a quick overview of the items you'll need and the steps you should take to install a new video card.

BE PREPARED

Before you start, there are some things you may need on hand. These include:

◆ A container for screws

◆ The manual for your computer

1. Begin with a clear tabletop so you have room to work.

2. Make sure your computer and peripherals are turned off, and ground yourself by touching something metallic.

3. Unplug all the connecting cables, including the power.

4. Remove the screws that hold the outer case of the computer, put them in your container, and carefully remove the case.

5. If you are replacing an old video card, find the old card inside your computer and remove the screw that attaches it to the computer chassis.

NOTE   *If you have a system with onboard video circuitry (you can tell if you do because the monitor will plug into the case of your computer rather than to an expansion card), you must disable the onboard video system before an add-on card will work. This usually involves moving a jumper on your motherboard or disabling it through the BIOS during setup. For computers that use jumpers, your computer's manual should have a jumper diagram that will tell you how to do this.*

6. Gently but firmly, ease the old video card out of the slot on the motherboard and remove the card from your computer.

7. Insert the new card into an open, compatible slot (AGP, PCI, or ISA) on your motherboard.

    ◆ If the slot is the same as the card you just took out, you can insert the new card into the slot you just vacated on your motherboard.

    or

    ◆ If your new card requires a different slot, you may need to remove a metal plate that covers an expansion card opening at the back of your computer. Unscrew the plate, remove it, and cover the opening that's left by the card you removed.

8. Mount the card securely by screwing the video card's rear plate into the computer's chassis.

9. Put the cover back on your computer and screw it on.

10. Reattach all the external cables.

11. Turn your computer and peripherals back on.

12. If your system and video card are Plug and Play compatible, when Windows boots up it should install the proper drivers for your card. You should have the disks or CD that came with the card handy at this stage. If Windows fails to detect your new video card, you should install the drivers manually. Either way, read through the manual that came with the video card for instructions on how to ensure the drivers are installed correctly.

How a Video Board Works

The parts of the board that you must understand in order to see how video works and how it can be tuned up include:

♦ The system CPU

♦ The system bus and its interface to the video board

♦ The video memory on the video board

♦ The video imaging chip on the video board

♦ The digital-to-analog converter (DAC) on the video board

Consider this: how does the CPU get an image onto the computer's display? I'll start from the CPU and end up at the monitor in this explanation.

A basic video board looks like the one shown in Figure 24.1.

FIGURE 24.1

An AGP video board

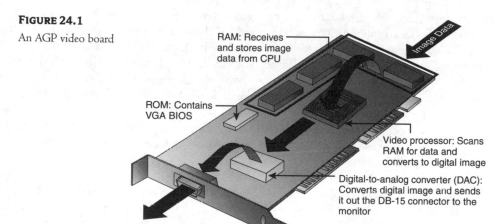

RAM: Receives and stores image data from CPU

ROM: Contains VGA BIOS

Image Data

Video processor: Scans RAM for data and converts to digital image

Digital-to-analog converter (DAC): Converts digital image and sends it out the DB-15 connector to the monitor

The CPU and Video Images

The primary objective of a video board is to take information from the CPU and display it on a monitor. When a program wants to display data, it does so by telling the CPU to store data in the video board. Exactly *how* a CPU does that varies. There are two basic kinds of video boards: dumb frame buffers and coprocessor/accelerator boards. I'll take up those two types in a bit, but for now just understand that the CPU controls the video board.

What that implies, for anyone trying to speed up a video subsystem, is that a faster CPU will make for faster video, all other things being equal.

The System Bus

The CPU is connected to the video board through the system's bus. The speed of that bus can be a constraint on how fast the video system can update. What's the fastest rate at which data might be zapped into a video board? Well, the video system need not update the picture on the screen much more often than 72 times per second, since you probably can't perceive images much faster than that. High-quality video boards have up to 64MB of RAM on them, so the maximum amount of data that a video board might have to work with would be 72 × 64, or 4608MB per second. The PCI bus runs at 33MHz and is 32 bits wide, so the maximum video data throughput for PCI video cards is 133MB per second. What does all that mean? Simply this: the faster your bus interface, the better for your video board. This suggests that when you buy a video board, you should buy a video board that uses an AGP bus, provided you have a motherboard that is AGP compatible. AGP runs at 66MHz and is 64 bits wide, providing a maximum video data throughput of 528MB per second!

Aside from its increased speed, the most distinguishing characteristics of an AGP bus are that it is a dedicated video bus and that an AGP video card can use system memory as an extension of its own local frame buffer memory. AGP 4X is the current version of AGP. The original version of AGP was referred to as specification 1.0. AGP 1.0 defined two different card speeds: 1X and 2X. The AGP 2.0 specification adds support for the 4X speed.

All AGP cards have a clock speed of 66MHz; the difference between AGP speeds is not the card's clock speed, but how many transfers the card makes during a cycle. AGP 1X makes a single transfer per cycle for a maximum data transfer rate of 266MBps—about twice as fast as the 33MHz PCI slot. AGP 2X makes two transfers per cycle, making its maximum data transfer rate 533MBps. The latest AGP 4X boasts a maximum data transfer rate of 1066MBps. Obviously when you're dealing with 3D animations or any other full-motion video environment, faster data transfer is better. AGP 4X is able to move data between the video card and your CPU at double the rate of today's standard AGP 2X speeds, to around 1GB per second.

In fact, the peripheral that probably benefits the most from a fast bus is the video board. How important is a local bus? Well, a video card in a standard ISA bus slot can only transfer data 16 bits at a time, at 8MHz. That's only 16MB per second. A video card sitting in an AGP slot can potentially transfer video data 128 times faster!

To fully take advantage of AGP 4X, you need an AGP 4X video card and an AGP 4X-compatible motherboard, or a system with integrated AGP 4X video on the motherboard, a CPU and memory modules that support 133MHz system bus speeds, and Windows 98 or a later operating system.

The Video Memory

The video image is then stored in the video memory. As with all memory, faster is better and more is better. (Why is more better? I'll discuss video resolution and color depth later, but the answer is, briefly: The more dots you want to put on your screen and the more colors that you want to be able to use for them, the more memory your video board needs.) But video memory has some special needs in that it is usually addressed in blocks, and it is addressed simultaneously by several chips—in particular, the CPU and the video imaging chip.

DUAL-PORTED MEMORY: VRAM

Let's look at that second characteristic first. Ordinarily, a RAM chip is addressed by the CPU and no other chip, unless there's a direct memory access (DMA) operation going on—and when that happens, the CPU doesn't access the memory.

In contrast, memory on a video chip has no choice but to talk to two chips at the same time; the CPU shovels image data into the video memory, and the imaging chip pulls it out. On video boards with normal RAM, this presents a performance problem; normal RAM can only address one chip at a time. Video boards with normal RAM just make the CPU and the imaging chip take turns, slowing things down.

Some video boards use a special kind of memory originally called Dual-Ported RAM, but which most people call VRAM, for Video RAM. There's nothing intrinsically video-ish about this RAM; it's just that its most logical application is in video boards.

DUAL-PORTED, BLOCK-ADDRESSABLE MEMORY: WRAM

But another thing about memory is its blocky nature. Modern graphical user interfaces tend to address memory in large blocks, rather than on a byte-by-byte basis. For example, to draw a colored background, the CPU must say to a whole large block of memory, "store value X," where X is the value that sets the desired background color. A CPU does that by arduously working on several locations one at a time.

Window RAM (WRAM) makes that task easier by allowing blocks, or "windows," of memory to be addressed in just a few commands. WRAM is a bit more expensive, but it's a good buy in video boards.

NEWER VIDEO MEMORY: MDRAM, SGRAM, AND DDR

Multibank DRAM (MDRAM) is aimed at the cost-conscious user who still wants good performance. MDRAM allows you to add memory in 32KB chunks, which lets you calculate exactly how much you need and install just that much. You therefore aren't wasting money on excess video memory that you may not need. MDRAM is much faster than VRAM and WRAM.

Synchronous Graphics RAM (SGRAM) operates at higher speeds than other video memory. It is capable of operating at speeds between 66MHz and 80MHz.

Double Data Rate Synchronous Dynamic RAM (DDR SDRAM) doesn't increase the memory clock speed, but it does move twice as much memory per clock cycle, thereby doubling the rate at which video data is moved.

VIDEO APERTURE

Some high-performance video accelerators (I'll discuss accelerators in a few pages) get their speed by mapping their video memory right into the computer's memory address space. This video is called the *video aperture*, and you have to understand it to solve some configuration problems.

Let's see how a video board uses memory. In graphics mode, an EGA, VGA, or newer video board only uses the addresses between 640KB and 704KB for video memory. But think for a moment, and you'll see that this doesn't seem to make sense. From 640KB to 704KB is just 64KB, and even a simple VGA board has 256KB of RAM on it. Super VGAs can have 1 to 16 or more *megabytes* of RAM on them. How does all that RAM fit into a 64KB address space?

Simple: a little bit at a time.

The VGA uses its 256KB of RAM within a 64KB constraint by taking the 256KB and chopping it up into *four* 64KB-sized areas. Most of the video memory is invisible to the CPU at any instant in time. To update the VGA, a VGA-aware program first asks the VGA to make the first 64KB area visible to the CPU. The 64KB is defined to describe the red part of the image. Once the red 64KB is made visible to the CPU—*paged in* is the correct term—then the VGA-aware program can modify the red part of the VGA image. The red 64KB—the *red page*—is then paged out, and the next 64KB—the green page—is paged in and modified. The same is done for the third page (the blue page) and the fourth page (the intensity page).

Stop and consider what had to happen just to update a single VGA screen: move in the red page, modify it, and move it out; then move in the green page, modify it, and move it out; then move in the blue page, modify it, and move it out; and, finally, move in the intensity page, modify it, and move it out. That's a lot of work. The reason so much work must be done is because of the severe memory address constraints of DOS-based programs, which in general must live in the bottom 1024KB of PC memory.

Now think about what happens with a Super VGA board with 2MB of RAM. If the Super VGA board is built like most Super VGA boards, the 64KB-page approach is still used. But 2MB is, however, *32 different 64KB pages*. That means that a Super VGA video driver for a 2MB video board must page in and out 32 different pages in order to update the video screen just once. *Now* it should be obvious why high-resolution Super VGA screens can be so terribly slow.

Some Super VGA boards take a totally different approach. They reason that they are not being used by DOS-based programs but by Windows programs. Windows can easily rise above the 1024KB address range, so some Super VGA boards place the whole 2MB of RAM right into the PC's address space, just like the RAM that the system uses to run programs. The value of this approach is that now the Video RAM can be updated in a straightforward, *fast* way, without having to wait around for 64KB-sized blocks to be paged around. The range of addresses used for this 2MB block of memory is called the *video aperture*.

Video aperture is usually an *option*; you can typically choose to just use the standard 64KB-at-address-640KB-page approach. While disabling video aperture and using the small page approach will slow you down, it might be the only way to get a system to work. IBM's accelerator board, the Extended Graphics Array (XGA), will optionally allow you to set its 2MB of Video RAM to a video aperture—*but* that aperture must be somewhere in the bottom 16MB of memory addresses. That's a shame, because many Windows "power users" will have at least 64MB of system RAM. The video aperture must appear in the bottom 16MB of addresses, but those addresses are already filled with RAM, so the XGA user would have to disable video aperture. That's not a problem for *every* high-performance board user, however. For example, the ATI mach32 system can use any address in the first 4GB.

The bottom line is that you should do the following:

◆ Look for video aperture as an option for high-performance video systems.

◆ Make sure that the video aperture can appear *anywhere* in the address range of 1GB–4GB.

◆ When experiencing video troubles, check to see if the manufacturer has already enabled the video aperture and perhaps accidentally addressed it on top of some system RAM. (I've seen that happen with an XGA system sold with 16MB of RAM and the XGA RAM addressed at the 8MB level. The system kept crashing Windows until the video aperture was disabled.)

The Video Imaging Chip

Once the image is in the Video RAM, that image must be converted into a digital video image format. That's done by the "display chip," "video chip," or "imaging chip," depending on who's talking about it. Over the years, there have been many different imaging chips. Nowadays, however, the main question to answer when looking at video chips is this: is it a dumb frame buffer or an accelerator/coprocessor of some kind?

FRAME BUFFER CHIPS

Most video chips in the PC world before 1992 were frame buffers. *Frame buffer* means that the board is populated with memory chips, as you've just learned, and the memory chips hold an image that closely resembles what shows up on the screen. Each dot (*pixel*) on the screen has a corresponding location on the video memory. Set it to one numeric value, and one color appears on the pixel. Another value, and another color, appears in its place.

The problem with frame buffers is that every one of those pixels must be arranged by the CPU. That can be a lot of work for one CPU—which is where accelerators and coprocessors come in.

SMARTER VIDEO CHIPS

Newer video chips take some of the burden off the main processor and put it on themselves. These kinds of chips are coprocessors called *video accelerators*.

Back in Chapter 3, "Inside the PC: Pieces of the Picture," you learned about numeric coprocessors, special-purpose CPUs that are particularly good at a small group of jobs.

Video coprocessors are just another kind of special-purpose CPU. As you'd expect, they're designed to shove pixels around quickly. Your math coprocessor is just a single chip, but video coprocessors are generally entire circuit boards. Coprocessors can be very fast, but unfortunately they're also expensive. It's not unusual to have to spend over $1000 on a coprocessor.

Accelerators typically include VGA circuitry onboard; coprocessors typically complement a VGA, requiring that you have both a VGA board and a coprocessor in your system. Coprocessors require that you link them to a normal video board via a "feature connector," a pin header or edge connector that you'll commonly see on video boards.

Related to a coprocessor is a less expensive alternative called an *accelerator*. The difference is that a coprocessor is a full-fledged microprocessor that's programmable to do just about any task that the main CPU can do. An accelerator, on the other hand, is not a general-purpose CPU, but rather a special-purpose chip that knows how to do a few particular graphical tasks quickly. Most accelerators are good at something called *bitblitting*. As you probably know, a term commonly used by GUI users for pictures is *bitmaps*. Windows wallpapers are bitmaps, screen captures are bitmaps, and any picture created with Paintbrush is a bitmap. Much of what slows Windows down is placing bitmaps on the screen, either transferring them from memory to screen, or moving them from one part of the screen to another part of the screen. Moving a bitmap is technically referred to as a *bitmap block transfer*, which is abbreviated *bitblt*. A number of inexpensive Windows accelerators are just VGA boards with a bitblitter chip onboard. The large number of bitblt operations that Windows does makes this combination of VGA and hardware bitblt support very cost-effective. Accelerators may also know how to build simple geometric shapes like lines or circles.

The fact that accelerators are a one-board approach in contrast to the video-board-and-coprocessor approach may make an accelerator a better buy. It's certainly a cheaper option, but be aware that an accelerator board's dual nature means that it has both generic VGA circuitry and accelerator circuitry, and the two circuits are unrelated. It's quite common to see incredibly fast accelerator chips paired with painfully slow VGA circuits, and the result is that running Windows is quite fast (the accelerator is at work) but games run very poorly, since the slower VGA circuit is now active. When looking at benchmark results for an accelerator, look for times for both the VGA circuit and the accelerator.

DIGITAL-TO-ANALOG CONVERTER (DAC)

The video board's work is almost done; the digital image has been produced by the imaging chip. Only one more thing to do—convert the image from digital to analog. That's done with a special chip called the digital-to-analog converter (DAC).

About all there is to say about the DAC is that it comes in varying abilities to produce color. The 15-bit DAC produces 32,768 colors; the 16-bit DAC produces 65,536 colors; and the 18-bit DAC produces 262,144 colors. The 24-bit and 30-bit DACs produce 16 million and 1 billion colors, respectively.

You usually can't upgrade DACs; whatever your vendor built in is what you're stuck with.

Video Board Characteristics

Now that you know the parts of a video board, how do you choose between video boards? RAM type, bus attachment, and video chip are all important, but so are image resolution, color depth, vertical frequency, and 3D capability. You'll learn about those in this section.

NOTE   If your needs are more specialized than for general computing or playing games, look for a video board that has a TV-out or digital flat-panel connection, video capture, or TV-tuner capabilities. Others support dual-monitor connections and may come with DVD software.

Resolution and Colors

Resolution on a video display is the number of horizontal and vertical dots that make up the picture. For example, the most basic resolution today is 640 × 480, which means that the image is 640 dots wide by 480 dots high. Most VGA boards nowadays are Super VGA boards, even the cheap clones. You can pick up a no-name VGA board for about $15–$30, and in addition to standard VGA, it will probably support 800 × 600 mode. The more expensive VGA boards support at least 1024 × 768 and usually 1280 × 1024 or higher. More resolution means more dots on the screen, which means that the video board needs more memory.

NOTE   Just because your graphic card and monitor can support high resolution doesn't mean you should use high resolution. For example, if you use 1024 × 768 on a 14-inch monitor, everything on the screen will look microscopic. Even if you own a huge monitor, beware of setting the resolution too high when playing certain games. Most of the games expect lower resolutions (e.g., 800 × 600) and may result in a fuzzy-looking game. Of course, with some of the games it may be difficult to tell if the display is distorted.

A video board's memory requirements are determined by two things: its resolution and the number of colors that it can display. For instance, the basic VGA can display a resolution of 320×200 with 256 colors, but when in the higher 640×480 resolution, it can only display 16 colors. That has nothing to do with the constraints of the monitor, or even of the VGA board, *except* for the amount of memory on the board. A normal VGA comes with 256KB right on the board. Table 24.1 shows a summary of resolutions available for common video boards throughout PC history.

TABLE 24.1: VIDEO BOARD RESOLUTIONS

Board Type	Resolutions Supported	Colors Supported
Color Graphics Array (CGA)	320×200	4
	640×200	2
Enhanced Graphics Array (EGA)	CGA resolutions	
	640×350	16
Video Graphics Array (VGA)	CGA and EGA	
	320×200	256
	640×480	16
Super VGA	CGA, EGA, VGA	
	$640 \times 480, 800 \times 600, 832 \times 624, 1024 \times 768, 1152 \times 870, 1280 \times 1024, 1360 \times 1024, 1600 \times 1200, 1920 \times 1080, 1920 \times 1200$	256, 32K, 64K, or 16 million+ (ranges from 4-bit to 32-bit color)

Resolutions like 1024×768 with 256 colors obviously require more memory—that's why you see ads for VGA cards with an option for 256KB, 512KB, or 1024KB on the board. If all you're doing is regular old VGA, you need only 256KB—there's no point in spending the extra money for 512KB or 1024KB. Table 24.2 shows the amount of memory that a video board needs for some sample resolution/color combinations.

NOTE *Note that cards can come with as much as 64MB of Video RAM built in, such as ATI's Radeon 8500. Most PCI and AGP cards ship with 8–32MB of Video RAM. At the time of this writing, nVidia's GeForce4 4600 video adapters will be shipping with 128MB of DDR memory.*

It should be explained that IBM did create several new video standards after VGA, which received *very* limited acceptance in the market—mainly because they were implemented on cards that used IBM's proprietary Micro Channel Architecture (MCA), which received *no* acceptance in the market. These were not included in most of the tables. Still, you may run across these acronyms from time to time (especially when looking at sales on old equipment), so here is a brief summary of these oldies-but-not-so-goodies:

8514/A This "professional" standard was actually introduced about the same time as standard VGA. It provided both higher-resolution/color modes and some limited hardware acceleration capabilities as well. By today's standards the 8514/A is quite primitive, supporting 1024×768

graphics in 256 colors but only at 43.5Hz (interlaced) or 640 × 480 at 60Hz (noninterlaced). You watch such a screen for prolonged periods and your friends will begin to call you blinky.

XGA This acronym stands for *Extended Graphics Array*. XGA cards were used in later PS/2 models; they can do bus mastering on the MCA bus and use either 512KB or 1MB of VRAM. In the 1MB configuration XGA supports 1024 × 768 graphics in 256 colors or 640 × 480 at high color (16 bits per pixel).

XGA-2 This graphics mode improves on XGA by extending 1024 × 768 support to high color and also supporting higher refresh rates than XGA or 8514/A.

TABLE 24.2: MEMORY REQUIRED AT VARIOUS COLOR DEPTHS

VGA AND APPLE 13″—640 × 480

RESOLUTION AND COLOR DEPTH	MINIMUM MEMORY REQUIRED
AT 16 colors (4-bit color)	256KB
AT 256 colors (8-bit color)	512KB
AT 32K colors (15-bit color)	1MB
AT 65K colors (16-bit color)	1MB
AT 16.7M colors (24-bit color) true color	1MB

SUPER VGA (SVGA)—800 × 600

RESOLUTION AND COLOR DEPTH	MINIMUM MEMORY REQUIRED
AT 16 colors (4-bit color)	256KB
AT 256 colors (8-bit color)	512KB
AT 32K colors (15-bit color)	1MB
AT 65K colors (16-bit color)	1MB
AT 16.7M colors (24-bit color) true color	1MB

NONSTANDARD SVGA—832 × 624

RESOLUTION AND COLOR DEPTH	MINIMUM MEMORY REQUIRED
AT 16 colors (4-bit color)	512KB
AT 256 colors (8-bit color)	1MB
AT 32K colors (15-bit color)	1MB
AT 65K colors (16-bit color)	1.5MB
AT 16.7M colors (24-bit color) true color	2MB

Continued on next page

TABLE 24.2: MEMORY REQUIRED AT VARIOUS COLOR DEPTHS *(continued)*

EXTENDED SVGA (XGA)—1024 × 768

RESOLUTION AND COLOR DEPTH	MINIMUM MEMORY REQUIRED
AT 16 colors (4-bit color)	512KB
AT 256 colors (8-bit color)	1MB
AT 32K colors (15-bit color)	1.5MB
AT 65K colors (16-bit color)	2MB
AT 16.7M colors (24-bit color) true color	2.5MB

NONSTANDARD XGA—1152 × 870

RESOLUTION AND COLOR DEPTH	MINIMUM MEMORY REQUIRED
AT 16 colors (4-bit color)	512KB
AT 256 colors (8-bit color)	1.5MB
AT 32K colors (15-bit color)	2MB
AT 65K colors (16-bit color)	2.5MB
AT 16.7M colors (24-bit color) true color	3.5MB

1280 × 1024

RESOLUTION AND COLOR DEPTH	MINIMUM MEMORY REQUIRED
AT 16 colors (4-bit color)	1MB
AT 256 colors (8-bit color)	1.5MB
AT 32K colors (15-bit color)	2.5MB
AT 65K colors (16-bit color)	3MB
AT 16.7M colors (24-bit color) true color	4MB

1360 × 1024

RESOLUTION AND COLOR DEPTH	MINIMUM MEMORY REQUIRED
AT 16 colors (4-bit color)	1MB
AT 256 colors (8-bit color)	1.5MB
AT 32K colors (15-bit color)	3MB
AT 65K colors (16-bit color)	3MB
AT 16.7M colors (24-bit color) true color	4.5MB

Continued on next page

TABLE 24.2: MEMORY REQUIRED AT VARIOUS COLOR DEPTHS *(continued)*

1600 × 1200

RESOLUTION AND COLOR DEPTH	MINIMUM MEMORY REQUIRED
AT 16 colors (4-bit color)	1MB
AT 256 colors (8-bit color)	2MB
AT 32K colors (15-bit color)	4MB
AT 65K colors (16-bit color)	4MB
AT 16.7M colors (24-bit color) true color	6MB

Vertical Scan Frequencies: Interlacing and 72Hz

Your video monitor displays information by projecting a narrow beam of electrons onto a phosphor-covered glass panel—your monitor screen. Wherever the beam hits, the phosphor becomes excited ("excited" here is a relative term) and the phosphor lights up for a brief period of time (see, excitement *is* relative here), then fades out. Because it fades very quickly—in hundredths of seconds—the electron beam must retrace its path constantly to keep the image on the screen. How often must it travel across the screen? Well, the electron beam in the back of a video monitor must repaint or *refresh* the screen at least 60 times per second, or your eye will probably perceive flicker. (Why "probably"? Hang on for a sentence or two.) And that brings me to a story about the IBM 8514 video system.

INTERLACING AND THE 8514

As mentioned earlier, the 8514 was an early IBM high-resolution (1024 × 768) video system; as a matter of fact, the 8514 video system is important because it was the first mass-market PC-based video system to support a resolution of 1024 × 768. But, in order to save money on the monitor, IBM cut a corner on the system. Now, to get high-resolution images, you need a high-quality (read: *expensive*) monitor. One way to get higher resolution out of a cheaper screen is to refresh it less often. The 8514 does not refresh 60 times per second, but rather at 43 times per second.

This isn't the first time we've seen this less-than-60-refreshes-per-second approach to high resolution; it's called *interlacing*. What was significant was that *IBM* did it, so the practice of interlacing became acceptable.

But, you see interlacing is *not* acceptable, at least not from a quality standpoint. The result of interlacing is a flickering screen and eyestrain headaches. That's why you have to be careful when buying a system with 1024 × 768 resolution. Check that it's *noninterlaced*.

By the way, if you do have an interlaced monitor, there may be a few things that you can do to reduce the effects of flicker. Several factors affect flicker—that's why I said "probably" a few sentences back. First, you see flicker better with your peripheral vision, because the center of your vision is built around low-resolution color receptors called *cones* on your retina. Surrounding the cones are high-resolution monochromatic receptors called *rods*.

Peripheral vision images fall on the rods. Sailors know this because when searching for a ship on the horizon, they don't look right at the horizon—they look below it, so the horizon falls on the high-resolution rods. In any case, the closer you are to your monitor, the more of its image falls on the cones, which are less flicker-prone. You can demonstrate this with any monitor. Stand so that your monitor is about 60 to 80 degrees to your left: If the direction you're facing is 12 o'clock, the monitor should be at about 10 o'clock. Hold a piece of paper in front of you and read the text on it. You'll notice that you're seeing the monitor out of the corner of your eye, and that it's flashing. This also suggests that you should buy a small monitor—a large image will end up falling more on your rods—but 1024 × 768 on a 12-inch screen is, well, suboptimal. Antiglare screens will also reduce flicker. Another antiflicker tactic is to keep your room bright. When the ambient light is bright, your pupils contract, which has the side effect of reducing the amount of light that gets to the peripheral rods. You'll also find that certain color combinations exaggerate the flicker—black and white is one problem combination—so play around with the Windows colors to make the screen more readable.

The Benefits of Fast Vertical Refresh Rates

Since I've brought up the subject of video with low refresh rates, it's worthwhile looking at the opposite end of the spectrum—video systems that refresh at more than 60 screens per second. The more common use of larger monitors means that more people notice flicker on normal 60Hz VGA. Furthermore, people nowadays use their computers all day, so anyone who has even the slightest sensitivity to flicker will get some eyestrain. As a result, vendors nowadays are offering VGA and Super VGA boards that put out much higher vertical refresh rates. Indeed, 72Hz, 80Hz, and 120Hz cards have flooded the market. Investing in the highest refresh rate you can afford is well worth it, in my opinion. My eyes rest much more easily on an 80Hz screen than a 60Hz screen.

There are, of course, a few caveats. First, you need a *monitor* that can handle the vertical refresh rate you want. The good news is, I surveyed about a dozen vendors and even the cheapest new 15-inch monitors support an 80Hz refresh rate. Since any new video board you can buy offers a wide range of support, you only need to exercise caution before you buy a used or discontinued video board. From the video board's Web site you will need to find out if your current monitor can use all of the video board's features. If not, either don't buy the board, or plan to buy a new monitor with your new board. (Don't you just love it when some computer expert tells you to go spend some money? Kidding aside, believe me, better video is worth it.)

The second caution is actually kind of funny or sad, depending on how you look at it. Every single computer I've set up in the past four years had a video system that came out of the box configured for a lower refresh rate than it could actually handle. Now, reconfiguring the video for a faster refresh rate usually isn't any harder than just running a short program that comes with the video board, so it's not like I unlocked some hidden feature of the video board. It's just plain inexplicable why a computer company would sell a superior video product as part of its PC but wouldn't take the two minutes to utilize those features.

So, if you have a recently purchased computer, take a close look at the video documentation that came with it. I've been able to bring more than a few surprised smiles to the faces of owners of PCs by running the video setup programs that were sitting right on their hard disks.

3D Video Boards

Three-dimensional graphics are all the rage today, especially in the gaming world. Although these video boards are also very important to a segment of the computer-aided design and graphics industry, it is through gaming that they have enjoyed their vast popularity.

Quite simply, 3D-capable video adapters are made for gamers. If you don't play games, you will see little to no improvement in the video displayed on your computer after investing several hundred dollars in one of these jewels. What is the draw of these expensive cards? They are able to make you believe you are seeing action in three dimensions in real time. They do this through the illusion of adding depth to a scene, creating powerful lighting effects, mapping textures to polygons, and other special effects.

While they share a common overall objective, there are different types of 3D video boards that implement 3D in substantially different manners. Each video board manufacturer relies on special chipsets, which are in turn created by other manufacturers. It is the video chipset that has the greatest effect on the 3D capabilities of the card. The prominent chip set manufacturer today is nVidia, which produces the TNT, TNT2, and GeForce chipsets. In December 2000 they bought out their major competitor, 3Dfx, which produced the Voodoo line of chipsets.

In addition to the chipset, the 3D API is also important. The top three APIs are DirectX, OpenGL, and Glide. DirectX is a 3D graphics API that was created by Microsoft for computers running Windows. A latecomer to the 3D party, DirectX now vies with OpenGL as the standard 3D API for Windows-based 3D applications. OpenGL, originally created by Silicon Graphics, is a 3D API supported by an independent industry consortium that is compatible with other operating systems besides Windows. Glide is a proprietary API used by 3Dfx's Voodoo line of chipsets.

Video Monitor Characteristics

Now that you have a board, what monitor goes with it? Monitors aren't as complex as video boards, but there are a few terms to work with.

Perhaps the most important thing to understand about the monitor/board partnership is that the video board calls the tune, and the monitor dances—if it can. Virtually all modern computers (except for some older laptops) have video circuitry that can produce 1024 × 768 signals, but some computers don't have monitors of a quality to actually *display* that signal. Having 120Hz is nice, but both the video board and the monitor must support it.

Monitor Mumbo Jumbo: Horizontal Scan Frequency

As I explained earlier, a monitor works by directing a beam of electrons against the inside of its screen. Phosphors on the inside of the screen become "excited" and glow. Making phosphors glow or not glow defines images on the screen. From a computer's point of view, a video display is just an array of pixels. *Resolution* is the number of dots that can be put on the screen. The electron beam sweeps across the tube, painting lines of dots. CGA uses 200 lines top to bottom, EGA used 350, and VGA uses 480. Since it uses higher resolutions, Super VGA uses even more lines.

Consider the number of horizontal lines that a monitor must draw per second. In a basic VGA, each screen has 480 lines, and there are 60 screens per second. So 480 times 60 is 28,800 lines per second. That is called the *horizontal scan frequency*; it is the number of times that the beam sweeps horizontally per second. It too is measured in hertz (Hz) or kilohertz (kHz)—thousands of hertz. Actually, a VGA has a somewhat higher horizontal scan rate than 28,800Hz (28.8kHz), because the monitor has extra lines that you can't see (they're called *overscan*). How *many* extra lines a monitor has varies from video mode to video mode. A CGA has a horizontal scan frequency of 15,750Hz, or 15.8kHz. EGA uses 21.8kHz, and VGA uses 31.5kHz. So the horizontal scan frequency your monitor needs to serve your board is determined in part by two important factors: the number of horizontal lines on the screen and the screen's refresh rate.

Dot Pitch

Some monitor ads tout "0.28mm dot pitch." What are they talking about?

We've seen that more resolution means more dots (pixels) on the screen. The distance between the centers of the dots on the monitor is the monitor's *dot pitch*, and it's measured in millimeters (mm). The smaller the dots, the closer together they can be and the higher the resolution that a monitor can show in a crisp and readable manner. A larger monitor can have a larger dot pitch without sacrificing resolution, simply because the monitor's screen is larger.

In reality, you'll see many different dot pitches for VGA monitors, including 0.34, 0.31, 0.29, 0.28, and 0.26 mm. Any new monitor you purchase will have at least a 0.28mm dot pitch. If buying a used/refurbished older monitor, avoid 0.34 on 12-inch VGA monitors, but you may find it quite acceptable on 14-inch monitors—go take a look at one before you buy it. You'll find 0.34 on a 14-inch or 0.31 on a 12-inch monitor is fine for VGA only, but buy 0.28 if you plan to use a Super VGA with 800 × 600 resolution, and buy 0.26 for a Super VGA using 1024 × 768 resolution.

Monitor Size

Monitors range in size from small 14-inch models to more professional-caliber monitors that have a display of 21 inches or more. While 19- and 21-inch monitors are more standard today, the factors you should weigh in choosing the right monitor for you are price, space, and use.

It almost goes without saying that the larger the monitor, the more money it will cost. Generally speaking, you can expect to pay between $200 and $1000 for a monitor, with the smaller monitors available at the low end of this spectrum. Seventeen-inch monitors fall in the middle, while 19- and 21-inch monitors can go off this scale.

In addition to price, space can be an important consideration. The larger monitors take up more desktop space—sometimes much more. Of course, the width of a 21-inch monitor will be larger than a 15-inch model, but the depth is of much more concern because of the size of the cathode ray tubes (CRT) used in larger monitors. If your computer desk space is limited, consider a flat-panel display, discussed in the following section.

Finally, how you plan to use your computer is an important factor in determining the right monitor to buy. If the primary role of your computer is general computing, you can get by with a 15- or 17-inch monitor, but if you spend much time with graphics, a larger monitor will help greatly. In some cases, you should use two monitors, which we will cover in more detail later in this chapter.

Another important point to remember when you choose a monitor is that the size of the screen you can actually use will be smaller than what is advertised. A 17-inch monitor, for example, may only have a viewable dimension of approximately 16 inches. This is caused in part by the fact that monitor sizes are based on the measurement of the CRT diagonally from one corner to the opposite, and also because computer monitors underscan. Underscanning creates an image that is smaller than the overall size of the CRT and leaves a black frame around your picture.

Flat-Panel Displays

Recently, flat-panel LCD displays (also called digital monitors) have emerged in larger numbers and are becoming quite popular for desktop computers. Their main benefit is their space-saving nature. Based on the technologies that power laptop displays rather than the traditional CRTs used in everyday monitors, flat-panel LCD displays take up significantly less desktop space.

These displays differ from their CRT counterparts in several ways. First, the dot pitch is determined by the physical size of the LCD elements that make up the LCD panel, rather than the size of the aperture grill or shadow mask of the CRT. Some flat-panel displays have a larger dot pitch than most CRTs. Another important difference is how the monitor size is measured. With CRTs, manufacturers must list the diagonal size of the CRT as well as the viewable area. This is because the geometry of the CRT curvature prevents the monitor from displaying information to the extreme corner edges. For example, a 19-inch CRT monitor may have only a 17.5-inch viewable area. Flat-panel displays don't have the same issues as the CRT, so a 15-inch diagonal LCD display has a viewable diagonal area of 15 inches. Flat-panel displays are costly, however. Even though the cost of the displays is dropping every month, at the time of this writing you can expect to spend over $500 for the 17-inch variety.

Please be aware that, as good as these newcomers are, they still present limitations when you're doing serious photo editing. The issue is based on the nature of the pixel display. When a phosphor dot is excited, it produces a glow with a soft edge. When a pixel in an LCD panel is energized, it creates the same colors as the CRT but it has a definite edge. The result is that in the soft areas of a photograph, like a shadow, it can be more difficult to accurately judge what the photo will look like when printed.

Multifrequency Monitors

The last monitor feature is *multisyncing*, the ability to handle multiple resolutions automatically. Recall that the horizontal frequency that you need to display an image is determined by the refresh rate (the vertical frequency) and the horizontal resolution. Until 1986, monitors were fixed-frequency in both the horizontal and vertical directions. When you bought a CGA monitor, it could only do one set of frequencies: 15.75kHz horizontal, 60Hz vertical. The EGA monitor had to be able to do double duty—it could be attached to either CGA or EGA boards, and so had two sets of frequencies: 15.75kHz/60Hz for CGA boards and 21.8kHz/60Hz for EGA boards. The VGA knows of three sets of frequencies: one for CGA modes, one for EGA modes, and 31.5kHz/60Hz for its native standard VGA mode. So a "vanilla VGA" monitor is a fixed-frequency monitor that only supports CGA, EGA, and VGA—no Super VGA modes.

In 1986, NEC changed that with its MultiSync monitor. The MultiSync could detect and synchronize with any horizontal frequency from 15kHz to 31.5kHz and with any vertical frequency from 50Hz to 70Hz. That meant that a single monitor could work on any kind of video board that was out at the time. More important, when IBM introduced the VGA in April 1987, the MultiSync was ready—it could handle VGA's 31.5kHz horizontal frequency with no problem.

Now all video vendors offer their own MultiSync-like monitors: they're generically called variable frequency monitors (VFMs). NEC doesn't sell the original MultiSync anymore, but they have Multi-Sync models from the 3FGX (31.5–38kHz horizontal, 50–80Hz vertical) to the 6FGX (30–66kHz horizontal, 50–90Hz vertical). The competition is not asleep, however.

At the moment, my pick for the best reasonably priced monitor is the ViewSonic E70. This is a terrific monitor for several reasons:

◆ It syncs up to a wide range of frequencies, including 1280 × 1024, and can do 1024 × 768 at 87Hz.

◆ It is crisp and clear.

- ◆ It automatically sizes itself. I don't have to play around with the size controls every time I change resolution or frequency.

- ◆ It's a 17-inch monitor, the smallest size I'd recommend for use day in and day out.

This is the monitor I'd pick for a new machine, without question. (Contact information for View-Sonic can be found in the Vendor's Guide on the Utilities CD.)

Resizing Screens with Multisyncing Monitors

You'll notice on some of the old MultiSync monitors that the screen size jumps around when you change resolution. Change from 640 × 480 at 60Hz to 640 × 480 at 72Hz, and the screen gets smaller.

That's due to the higher frequency of the beam writing the image on the screen. On those simple monitors, you must move size and position knobs in order to get the image just right.

This is normal, unfortunately. To combat it, you should buy "autosizing" monitors.

Multiple Displays

No matter how large your display is, it never seems large enough to let you see everything without scrolling or panning. The size of the monitors seems to have peaked at 21 inches, for several reasons. First, when you get a monitor larger than 21 inches, there is precious little room left on your desk. The second reason has to do with proper viewing distance. If you have a monitor with a 24-inch screen (yes, they make them and they cost about as much a late-model car), you should view it from a distance of 6 feet! The solution that has been gaining in popularity since the late '90s has been to have two or more displays hooked to the same computer. If this is the first you have heard of this, you might think that sounds a little weird. In fact, at the time I am writing this chapter it has become popular enough that major graphic card vendors offer dual-display support on their products.

So, how can you get your computer to use more than one display at the same time? There are two approaches, and both involve additional hardware and support from the operating system. One approach involves adding one or more additional graphic cards and monitors to your computer. If using Windows 98/Me/2000/XP, the computer will recognize the additional card and allow you to set up one as the primary display and the other as the secondary. From here it is possible to configure the monitors so that your desktop is spread between the two or more displays. This can be a very inexpensive solution when you consider that a decent used VGA monitor sells for around $70 and a new video card can be purchased for under $20.

The other solution is to either remove your existing graphic card or disable the integrated one in your motherboard and install one of the newer graphic cards that support dual displays. The fancy boards are not that expensive. One very fine example of a dual monitor card is the Matrox Millennium G550, which contains both a respectable 3D graphics accelerator and a dual-display capability called eDualHead; it can be purchased for a little over $100. With this installation it is possible to do a lot more configuring of the two displays because of the dedicated hardware in the graphic card.

An example of an enhancement offered by a dedicated graphic card is the eDualHead features of the Matrox G550. One of the browsing enhancements offered allows viewing information in virtual column format on several browser windows rather than having to scroll through a lengthy document. You can have each monitor displaying a different browser, which is a real time-saver.

My all-time favorite is the ability to have my photo-editing application open on both displays and to zoom in to do touch-up while the image in the secondary display remains at its original zoom level. This saves zooming back and forth, which is a common issue with photo retouching.

Issues Installing Multiple Display Cards

With the multiple-display support feature in Windows, you need to install the new graphic adapter(s) and monitor. The monitors and graphic adapters can be different—quite different. One of the systems I just tested had an AGP card as well as a PCI video card. Each monitor was set for a different color depth and screen resolution. One monitor serves as the primary display and will show the logon dialog box when you start your computer. In addition, most programs, when you open them, will display windows on the primary. The first time this happens, Windows will attempt to detect and install the drivers for the new graphic cards. Depending on the graphic card, it may reboot, so if you have added more than two graphic cards (you animal!) you may end up rebooting several times. If successful, all of the display adapters should appear in System Properties.

To configure the settings for multiple monitors, open Display Properties in Control Panel, or right-click the Windows Desktop and choose Settings. In Windows XP, right-click the desktop and choose Properties, then click the Settings tab in the Display Properties dialog box. You will see the icon of the monitors, and at the bottom there will be an Extend My Windows Desktop Onto This Monitor check box. Checking this will open a Compatibility Warning dialog box that essentially warns you that if your application doesn't support multiple displays, you should probably turn this feature off. Please be aware that not all graphic cards are supported—only those that work with Windows 98/Me/2000/XP. A good rule of thumb is, if the driver works with Win9x/Me/2000/XP, it most probably was shipped with your OS. When in doubt, check with the Microsoft Web site for a detailed list. When configuring the display settings, you drag the monitor icons so that the monitors are configured in Windows the same way they are physically aligned on your desktop.

Reference: Older Display Types

This section provides you with some background on pre-1987 displays. You may need this information if you ever find yourself working on an old system.

Before 1987, video standards basically came from IBM. Big Blue controlled the market, and whatever IBM did, everyone else would do. After 1987, however, the disastrous performance of the PS/2 in the market left the marketplace without a leader. The top-of-the-line video in 1987 was the VGA, which is the baseline standard today. But what preceded it?

There are several basic kinds of older monitors:

- Composite monochrome
- Composite color
- RGB
- EGA monitors
- Direct-drive TTL monochrome

Table 24.3 offers one way to understand these monitors.

TABLE 24.3: PC MONITOR TYPES

	ANALOG	DIGITAL
Monochrome	Composite monochrome	Monochrome TTL
Color	Color composite	RGB: CGA (640 × 200), EGA (640 × 350), VGA (640 × 480)

Composite monitors are a step better than a television set. They offer greater resolution than a TV, but that's about it. They offer low expense and good quality.

RGB (Red, Green, Blue) monitors offer better resolution for color text than do color composite monitors. The IBM Color Display and the Princeton Graphics HX12 are RGB monitors. RGBs are more expensive, offer somewhat better quality than composite color, and attach to a display adapter with a 9-pin D-shell connector. You see very few composite monitors in the PC world these days.

More expensive than regular RGB, EGA (Enhanced Graphics Adapter) monitors are RGB monitors with higher resolution. Characters are sharper and the display steadier. In addition, these monitors can display 43 lines of text on a screen rather than the usual 25. This isn't as great as it sounds: most programs won't support the 43-line mode. Notable exceptions are dBase and the IBM Personal Editor, but more and more are joining the crowd: OS/2 even directly supports 43-line displays with the MODE command. An example of an EGA monitor is the IBM Enhanced Color Display. As I've already mentioned, EGA has been supplanted by VGA, an even higher resolution display standard (it can display 50 lines of text, whereas EGA can only do 43).

Direct-drive TTL monitors are monochromatic (generally amber and black or green and black) and offer high-resolution, steady images. An example of this is the IBM Monochrome Display. They are connected with a 9-pin D-shell connector like the RGB, but don't plug one of these in where RGB is expected, or vice versa. You honestly will get smoke.

Fairly expensive, but most versatile, are the multiscan monitors. These can serve as an RGB or an EGA monitor—they sense at what rate data is coming in and adjust their scan rates accordingly. Most modern monitors are multiscan monitors.

The second part of a display subsystem is the controller board. Quite a few are in use currently, and they all have their characteristics. Table 24.4 summarizes them.

TABLE 24.4: COMMON PC ADAPTER TYPES

MAXIMUM ADAPTER	CHAR. RESOLUTION/ COLORS	MONITORS BOX SIZE	GRAPHICS SUPPORTED	SUPPORTED?
Color/Graphics Adapter (CGA)	640 × 200/2	8 × 8	RGB	Yes
			Composite	No
Monochrome Display Adapter (MDA)	720 × 350/3	9 × 14	Mono TTL	No

Continued on next page

TABLE 24.4: COMMON PC ADAPTER TYPES *(continued)*

MAXIMUM ADAPTER	CHAR. RESOLUTION/ COLORS	MONITORS BOX SIZE	GRAPHICS SUPPORTED	SUPPORTED?
Enhanced Graphics Adapter (EGA)	640×350/64	8×14	RGB	Yes
			EGA	No
			Mono TTL	No
Hercules Graphics Controller (HGC)	720×350/3	9×14	Mono TTL	Yes
Multi Color Graphics Array (MCGA)	640×480/2	8×16	Analog RGB	Yes
Video Graphics Array (VGA)	640×480/262,144	9×16	Analog RGB	Yes
Super VGA	Up to 1024×768/256	9×16	Analog RGB	Yes
8514/A	1024×768/262,144	9×16	Analog RGB	Yes
XGA	1024×768/262,144	9×16	Analog RGB	Yes

While we have discussed some of these before, here is a summary of several display adapters that were used throughout the late '80s:

◆ IBM Monochrome Display Adapter (MDA)

◆ Hercules Monochrome Graphics Adapter

◆ IBM Color/Graphics Adapter (CGA)

◆ IBM Enhanced Graphics Adapter (EGA)

◆ IBM Professional Graphics Adapter

The PGA   It never really caught on, but it was the first real attempt in the PC world to add intelligence to a video board. That led eventually to the graphic accelerator boards that are becoming standard equipment on many modern PCs.

The IBM Video Graphics Array   Sporting PGA-quality graphics and a much more reasonable price (the PGA ran around $3000), the VGA made its appearance in 1987 with the PS/2. This board is, as I've said, the baseline for video today.

The IBM 8514/A Very High Resolution Graphics Adapter   A video coprocessor in the tradition of the PGA. More successful than PGA, but still not a big smash hit. It was replaced by the XGA.

The IBM XGA (Extended Graphics Array)   Built to do Windows and OS/2 quickly. Never really caught on, but if you buy a modern PS/2, you'll have it built right into your motherboard. Refer to Table 24.4 for details about these boards.

Video is an important part of your PC, but its lack of moving parts means that the best medicine for video problems is to understand how it works and how to attack its problems. The wide variety of so-called Super VGA boards has led to a plethora of drivers and video setup programs. Make sure you have the most up-to-date drivers and a monitor that matches your board, and all will be well.

Troubleshooting Tips

Once you have a system in place, how do you attack video problems? Here are a few suggestions.
Some of the dumbest monitor problems are the easiest to resolve:

◆ Is it turned on?

◆ Is the brightness or contrast turned down?

◆ Is everything plugged in? Is it plugged into the right place?

◆ Did you hear one long and two short beeps indicating a bad video card?

◆ If the display is dead, do you hear the power supply fan? There are nonvideo reasons for a display "malfunction," such as when the power supply has killed the computer.

◆ If the computer is okay but the display is bad, you will see the drive light come on. Use a sound-emitting program to see if the computer is functioning.

The quickest test is a monitor swap. If that does nothing, swap the display cards. *Don't* try to service the monitor. As I've said before, you can hurt yourself doing that.

If the display is rolling and you can't see enough to check the video modes, restart the computer in Windows Safe mode (press the F8 key when you reboot and you'll be given a menu with Safe Mode as one of the options). This will start Windows in standard 640 × 480 in 16 colors, so you can use almost any card and monitor to test your system.

Speaking of drivers, sometimes you'll see a case where you reboot your operating system, only to lose synchronization—the screen turns into moving bands. That probably means that you told your video board to exceed the capabilities of the monitor. Drop back a bit in resolution and you'll be okay.

Now that we've talked about what you can see, let's talk about what you can hear on your computer. The next chapter is all about sound.

Chapter 25

Play It Loud: Sound Cards

◆ How Sound Synthesis Works   685

◆ Sound Card Characteristics   692

◆ Choosing the Right Speakers   695

◆ MP3, Digital Audio, and Other Applications   696

◆ Troubleshooting Tips   707

Introduction

IN THE EARLY DAYS of personal computing, the only way that a PC could make noise was with its built-in speaker. Even the best PC speaker is tinny, however, and the best we could hope for were squeaks, squawks, and the occasional boom (though even that was more like a crackle). One ambitious 1984 program called PC Parrot attempted to make the PC speak, but it was limited by the sound equipment possibilities.

That's not true anymore, of course, and it hasn't been for many years. Sound equipment on the PC is so good that millions of computer users are now using their PCs to burn MP3 files to CDs, listen to Internet radio stations, play audio-intensive PC games, and mix and record digital audio files. While the standard sound card that came with your PC might be adequate for office work and day-to-day Internet browsing, these special applications sometimes require a little more punch in the audio department, which a higher-end or more specialized sound card can deliver.

In this chapter, you'll learn how sound cards work, what features to look for when choosing one, and what you're likely to run into when you install one. You may notice that this chapter has no QuickSteps section. That's because installing a sound card is very simple and best explained through the Visual Upgrade guide at the beginning of this book. The tools you will need are listed in the following "Be Prepared" sidebar. You will not need anything special for the sound card itself.

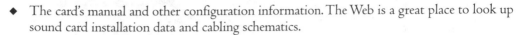

BE PREPARED

Before you start, there are some things you may need on hand. These include:

- The card's manual and other configuration information. The Web is a great place to look up sound card installation data and cabling schematics.

- Phillips-head screwdriver with a medium tip.

- Container for placing screws in. (I like to lay out the screws in the same pattern I removed them, working left-to-right, top-to-bottom. That way I can just repeat the process and get the right screw in the right hole.)

- Antistatic wrist strap.

- Flashlight.

- Nail clippers. These are great for cutting those hampering zip ties (those little plastic strips that bunch wires together). Because the cutting area of clippers is not very big, there's little chance of accidentally snipping a wire.

Sound Synthesis

The goal of sound cards is to record and play back sound. How they do it varies considerably, however. There are three main methods of sound reproduction:

- Sampling
- FM synthesis
- Wavetable synthesis

You'll look at these three methods later in this section. But first, let's discuss what sound *is*.

Sound Characteristics

Sound consists of a set of waves of varying pressure created in the air by our vocal cords, musical instruments, or natural forces. A picture of a sound is called a *sonogram*, and you can see one in Figure 25.1. It's a sonogram of the word *hello* being spoken (by me, in this case).

FIGURE 25.1

A sonogram of the word *hello*

Understanding a bit about sounds requires understanding a bit about signals. The dimensions of this signal are called *amplitude* and *frequency*. Amplitude and frequency probably conjure up visions of trigonometry and physics, but—I promise!—there's nothing tough about this.

SINE WAVES

In order to discuss signals in a bit more detail, I have to talk about another potentially scary topic—sine waves. Take a look at Figure 25.2.

FIGURE 25.2

Sine waves

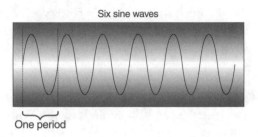

Six sine waves

One period

A wave starts anywhere, makes one upturn and one downturn (unless you start later in the signal, in which case it makes one downturn, *then* one upturn), and then ends up at the same height at which it started. That's one wave. But what does this have to do with data communications?

The imagery of waves works to describe signals because of the up-and-down (*periodic* is the more exact term) nature of waves. Turns out the sine wave is the building block of *all* waves.

What do I mean by *building block*? A mathematician by the name of Fourier proved that *any* wave phenomenon could be built by adding together the right series of waves. *Finding* the right series of waves to build any one signal is not a simple task—it's called a *Fourier decomposition*—but it *can* be done with the right tools (read: computing power). I won't do Fourier decompositions in *this* book; I just want you to understand why sine waves are so important to any study of signals. To see an example of sine waves adding up to a signal, look at Figure 25.3, which shows many sine waves superimposed on one another.

FIGURE 25.3

Several sine waves superimposed upon one another

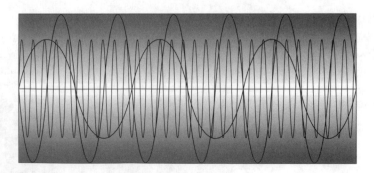

Notice that some jump up and down more quickly, some reach higher or lower, and some stretch a bit further left and right, but they're all sine waves. In Figure 25.4, you can add them all together.

FIGURE 25.4

Sum of the sine
waves in Figure 25.3

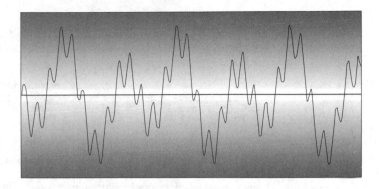

The sum is no longer anything *like* a sine wave. Any signal, no matter how bizarre, can be broken down into sine waves, which is why they're so important to a good understanding of signaling limitations. With that in mind, let's look at two aspects of a sine wave—amplitude and frequency.

AMPLITUDE

This should be a familiar concept, as we talk about amplitude all the time—we just call it *loudness* or *volume*.

In human voice communications, volume carries meaning, such as urgency, or it may be used so that a voice will carry far. From a sine wave's perspective, *amplitude* means *height*. Take a look at Figure 25.5.

FIGURE 25.5

Amplitudes of
sine waves

Smaller amplitude

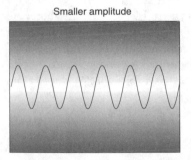

Greater amplitude

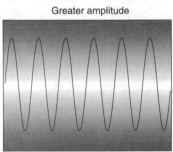

In signals, amplitude also relates to *power* used for transmission. When transmitting data, communications engineers must overcome the fact that transmitting data over a distance reduces a signal's amplitude, weakening it or *attenuating* it. You can partially restore a signal by *amplifying* it; all an amplifier does is try to boost the amplitude of the signal.

Communications systems use power, or amplitude, to describe two things:

◆ The raw transmission power of the communications medium

◆ Perhaps more important, the *clarity* of the communications medium—a ratio of the power of the noise to the power of the signal, known as the *signal-to-noise ratio*

FREQUENCY

The other sine wave characteristic is its frequency. *Frequency* describes how often a wave goes up and down in a given time. You can see this in Figure 25.6.

FIGURE 25.6

Comparative frequency of two sine waves

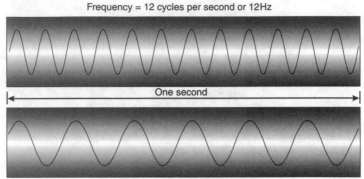

Frequency = 12 cycles per second or 12Hz

One second

Frequency = 6 cycles per second or 6Hz

In this figure, you see two waves diagrammed over the course of one second. The top wave goes up and down 12 times in that second, the bottom one only 6 times. That means that the top wave has a higher frequency.

Frequency is measured in *cycles per second*, which is abbreviated CPS, or, more commonly, the term *hertz* is used. Hertz is a unit that means, as you'd guess, "cycles per second," and is named after Heinrich Hertz, who was a German physicist. Hertz is usually abbreviated Hz. Look back at Figure 25.5, and you'll see that the two waves in that picture have the same frequency. Conversely, the two waves in Figure 25.6 have the same *amplitude* but different frequencies.

People talk about frequencies when talking about sound; if you say that someone has a high-pitched voice, you mean that person has a voice that produces a range of frequencies whose average is somewhat high, as human voices go.

Signals to Bits: Sampling

In order for your sound card to use a sound, the sound has to be converted from its analog self into a more bit-friendly format. The main method of converting analog sounds into digital is called *sampling*. (Before I learned how this was done, I called it *digitizing* the audio. I've since learned that expert types always say *sampling*, so file that in your list of good-stuff-to-know-at-cocktail-parties, and *never* say *digitizing*.) It's done with a method called Pulse Coded Modulation (PCM).

Suppose you are trying to convert the simple analog signal shown in Figure 25.7 into digital.

Under PCM, the signal is sampled many times per second, and the height of the wave is recorded. (Actually, what is recorded is the *logarithm* of the height—remember that sound volume is perceived logarithmically.) You can see an example of sampling in Figure 25.8.

The lines represent the height of the signal at various times. It's impossible to measure the height of the signal at all times, so you can measure only a limited number of samples—hence the *sampling* name.

FIGURE 25.7

A simple analog signal

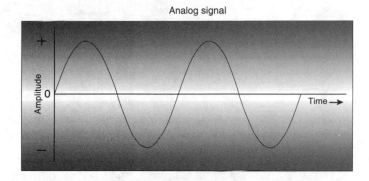

Analog signal

FIGURE 25.8

Sampling a signal

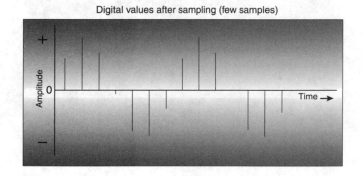

Digital values after sampling (few samples)

That doesn't seem like a lot of information about the signal, and it isn't. To get a better picture of how to reconstruct the original audio signal, you'd do better to get more samples in the same time period, as you see in Figure 25.9.

FIGURE 25.9

Reconstructing the original audio signal by getting more samples

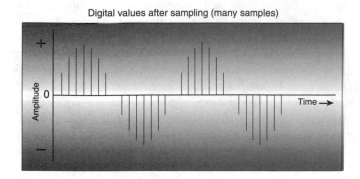

Digital values after sampling (many samples)

This underscores an important point, which is emphasized in Figure 25.10: more samples mean a higher-quality signal once reproduced. At the top of Figure 25.10, you can see an original signal for a second's duration. Below that is the result of sampling it 20 times in that second and the result of sampling it 40 times per second.

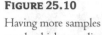

FIGURE 25.10

Having more samples equals a higher-quality reproduction of the signal.

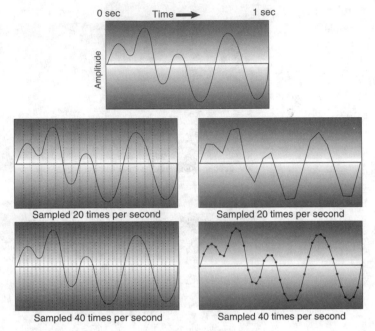

There are more values in the more frequently sampled signal, and so the reconstructed signal will be of higher quality.

How many samples do you need per second? For the answer to that, you need to turn to Nyquist's theorem. It says that to completely capture a signal, you've got to have N samples, where

$N = 2 \times$ signal bandwidth

The bandwidth of our ears is considered to be well within a 22,050Hz range. Twice that would be 44,100 samples per second, which is the sampling rate of a music CD. Higher sampling means more data must be stored per second.

But that's not all there is to sampling with PCM. Suppose the recorded values can range from −127 to +128, and they can be only integers. Since the total possible number of values is only 256, each signal value is encoded with 8 bits.

Why not use 16 bits per sample? Using 16 bits would allow for many more nuances of sound—65,536 values for 16 bits compared to 256 for 8 bits—but it doubles the amount of data needed to store a given audio signal. Of course, with the size of today's hard disks, there's little stopping you from using 16-bit encoding, at least as far as space goes. You can see the difference in bit sample sizes in Figure 25.11.

Music CDs sample 16 bits per sample, 44,100 samples per second, while the cheapest PC sound cards can sample at only 8 bits per sample; more expensive ones can sample up to 96 bits per sample. For most voice and music uses, 16 bits is fine, which yields about as much quality as the human ear can directly perceive.

NOTE *There is a popular use for this sampling technology today, and it's called MP3. You may have heard of it. I will cover MP3 technology, in detail, shortly.*

FIGURE 25.11

The difference in bit
sample sizes

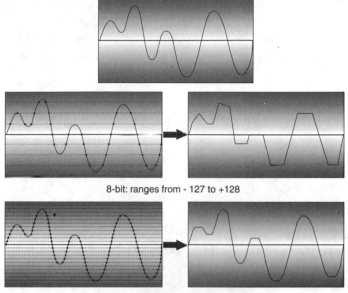

8-bit: ranges from - 127 to +128

16-bit: ranges from -32707 to +32708

FM Synthesis

Sampling works well for recording sounds. But to assemble entirely new sounds, PC software authors
need ways to tell a sound card, "Play an *A* as it would sound on a harpsichord." One method is to use
frequency modulation (FM) synthesis. It's usually implemented as a Musical Instrument Digital
Interface (MIDI) circuit.

I'm simplifying here, but the idea behind FM synthesis is that musical sounds follow a four-part
cycle, as you see in Figure 25.12.

FIGURE 25.12

The four-part cycle
of musical sounds

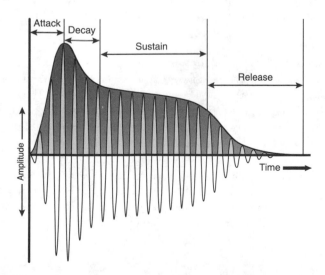

The notion in FM synthesis is to describe an instrument's waveform in terms of the size of the attack, decay, sustain, and release (ADSR) parts of the cycle. These four elements are generally the basis for sound in terms of waveforms. *Attack* is the speed at which a sound begins. *Decay* describes how the sound begins to release. *Sustain* describes the actual length of the sound. And finally, *release* describes when the note is "turned off."

Wavetable Synthesis

FM is an easy model to encode, and it allows for compact music files—several orders of magnitude smaller than sampled files. But the simplistic nature of the ADSR model limits musical fidelity.

Some sound cards get around that by storing entire instrument waveforms in a ROM on the board. That's called *wavetable synthesis*. If you want the best-quality musical synthesis, it's the way to go. (Of course, alternatively you could just buy CDs and play them on your stereo, but that wouldn't be as fun.)

Sound Card Characteristics

Sound cards vary in how they create sounds, how fine a resolution they use for sound, and what "extras" they carry onboard, such as a pass-through audio circuit or a CD-ROM interface. This section explains those options.

8-, 16-, 32-, 64-, or 96-Bit Sound?

So far in this book, a *16-bit card* has meant one that has a poorly aging 16-bit ISA slot connector on it. The card can pass 16 bits' worth of data at one time to the bus, but the only effect it has on sound is being a potential bottleneck when large amounts of data need to be passed at one time. When it comes to sound cards, *16-bit* means something else entirely: it refers to sample types.

NOTE *A sample is a recording of a sound, such as a musical instrument, for the purpose of playback. In this context, the sample attempts to reproduce an instrument's sound in a digital format. As you have learned, accurately reproducing an instrument's sound requires many samples that represent its entire scale of sonic capabilities. A typical collection of samples to cover a wide range of musical instruments is around 4 to 8MB in size, after compression. An accurate representation of a piano requires 16 to 24MB of space!*

Eight-bit samples are good for simple game sounds or music. However, you really need a board with the ability to play back and record 16-bit sounds (at a minimum!) to do good multimedia. The Sound Blaster 16 from Creative Labs was a good 16-bit card. Today there are 32- and 64-bit cards such as the AWE32 and AWE64, and they are commonly shipped in both OEM (original equipment manufacturer, or no-name parts that are built by companies that also build a model for consumer availability) and branded retail versions.

In terms of state-of-the-art consumer-grade sound cards, Creative Labs (the most ubiquitous sound card maker and the developer of technologies by which most other cards are defined) raised the bar when they released a line of Sound Blaster Live! 64-bit sound cards. Compared to older cards, even others from Creative Labs, the Live! card is intense. It is capable of up to 1024 discreet voice polyphony and hosting 32MB of samples. The Platinum version of the Live! card is available for a mere $150—which compares quite favorably to the professional boards of two years ago that ranged from $300 to $2000 with similar capabilities. More recently, Creative pushed the envelope even further when they released the Audigy series of audio cards. Costing about $100 for the gamers and MP3 versions and $200-$250 for the Platinum version (which comes with an Audigy Drive and front panel connectivity), you get incredible 24-bit, 96kHz, 5.1 channel surround sound, an impressive selection of multichannel sound processing capabilities, and a digital sound processing chip that is over four times faster than earlier models.

NOTE   *Keep in mind that the recent spate of sub-$500 computer systems has produced a new class of personal computer: the Minimalist. Gone are the days when everything was on a card so that if you wanted something new, you could simply add it. Most budget systems ship with video and audio subsystems built into the motherboard. Couple this with only two or three PCI slots and a single ISA slot (or none), and there's not much to work with there. Almost invariably, one of the PCI slots is taken by the modem, which leaves only one or two slots available for upgrades. See Chapter 3, "Inside the PC: Pieces of the Picture," and the section "PC Expansion Buses" for more detailed information.*

IRQ or DMA Sound Recording?

While capturing audio and video was often problematic under older versions of Windows, significant improvements have been made in recent years. Starting with Windows 98, the operating system now makes it fairly easy to get that total multimedia experience, due to a more efficient multitasking environment and improved conflict management.

Unfortunately, many simple sound cards are driven by interrupts, which chew up CPU time when the CPU needs to be able to just hunker down and pay attention to the video capture board. There are, however, some audio cards that aren't interrupt-driven, but are rather DMA-driven; Turtle Beach's cards are one good example. Because they don't lean on the interrupts, you'll get smoother audio/video interleaving on your recordings.

NOTE   *On a similar note, some older sound cards can handle only MIDI and can play back only MIDI files; others can play back only sampled files, typically in the WAV (pronounced wave) format. Most game music is MIDI, and most multimedia sound is WAV, so it would seem that having both capabilities in your card would be good, correct? Correct! No cards or chipsets shipping today in the consumer channel are limited to one or the other.*

Pass-through and/or CD-ROM Interfaces?

Many sound cards have a small Berg connector on them designed for a cable, like the one in Figure 25.13.

FIGURE 25.13

Berg connector on a cable

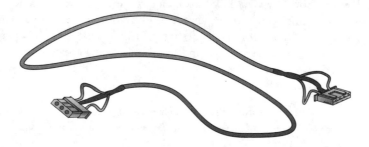

This is an audio pass-through cable. It lets you play music CDs from your PC's CD-ROM, through the speakers on your sound card. This used to be a problem because getting this audio cable required complying with each manufacturer's proprietary requirements. Things have settled down a bit these days, and you no longer need a veritable wig of cables just to make sure you have the correct one. CD-ROM drives coupled with standardized cabling for digital audio/video make it easier to install such devices.

So in a pinch, you can always install a poor man's (or woman's) pass-through cable: run a cable from the headphone output on the front of the CD-ROM to the Line In input on the back of the sound card.

Some sound cards have CD-ROM interfaces for proprietary CD-ROMs. I recommend that you avoid these, as they're a compatibility headache. Even the sound cards with SCSI interfaces implement slow SCSI interfaces. If you have a SCSI CD-ROM, my advice is to just get a good SCSI host adapter and hang the CD-ROM off that. On the other hand, with IDE/ATAPI drives as fast as 52X with bus speeds of anywhere from 4 to 33MBps (Ultra ATA), more expensive SCSI devices are often a waste of money for the casual user.

NOTE *SCSI is in no way a waste of time or money for the video or media specialist who needs SCSI's special capabilities, speed, and reliability. There's no match for SCSI when it comes time to record multitrack digital audio or edit live video, or for any number of the hundreds of other uses for SCSI drives and devices.*

What Types of Inputs and Outputs?

There's an interesting and very common "mismatch" found on almost all consumer-level sound cards available today. Whereas your home audio system uses line-level RCA jacks for input and output (two each for stereo, of course), most lower-priced sound cards use ⅛-inch stereo minijacks for line-level audio input and output. This means that if you want to send signals between any consumer audio device (cassette recorder, CD player, receiver, and so on) and your PC, you'll need an adapter cable to go from your audio equipment's left and right RCA jacks to your PC's single stereo minijack.

Although it's rare, some sound cards get around this problem by including left and right RCA jacks for input and/or output. If you intend to hook up your PC to your home audio equipment, look for this type of setup—or accept that you'll have to use an adapter cable.

Higher-end sound cards add Sony/Philips Digital Interface Format (S/PDIF) digital input and output jacks. Using digital input and output produces much higher-quality sound than the sound that has to be converted (on your audio card) from native digital to analog—and then, depending on the other device, back again. Digital jacks can be either coax (using an RCA jack and 75-ohm cable) or optical (using a TOSLink connector and fiber-optic cable); most cards opt for the lower-cost coax connectors. You can run the S/PDIF output and input to and from MiniDisc (MD) and Digital Audio Tape (DAT) recorders; if your PC includes a DVD player, you can also use the digital outputs to send surround-sound signals to a home theater system equipped with Dolby Digital surround processing. (Most stand-alone CD players, for copy-protection purposes, do not include any digital outputs.)

TIP *If you want to use the S/PDIF digital connections, make sure that your sound card includes the same type of jack (either coax or optical) used by your other audio equipment. Not all sound cards include both types of S/PDIF jacks.*

If you want your PC to play and record music (or feed sequenced music to synthesizers and other musical instruments), then you'll probably want a sound card that includes MIDI In and MIDI Out jacks. If your sound card doesn't include MIDI connections, you can use a special adapter cable to hook your MIDI instruments into your sound card's joystick port—which, in most cases, includes a "hidden" MIDI interface.

Speaker Systems

All this sound stuff is of no value unless you have some speakers through which to hear it. You *can* run some sound cards through the internal PC speaker, but *don't*: most built-in speakers are monaural and of pretty low quality.

Any add-on speakers you buy will most likely be stereo speakers. They can either be externally powered or run off the sound card's output; in general, a simple pair of speakers should not require power. More specialized systems may include a separate amplifier, so plan for an additional power outlet near the PC for the speakers.

Double-check that any speakers you use are shielded (most are) so that the magnetism they create is minimal. They'll be sitting near your PC, so it's quite likely that you'll end up putting floppies near them; an unshielded speaker can damage data on a hard or floppy disk if the disk is close enough to the speaker.

TIP *If you did not get a nice set of speakers with your last system, there is hope. You can buy some! Don't despair; they're quite reasonable. You can purchase a quality set of speakers complete with subwoofer for as low as $35 or pop for a complete surround-sound setup for only. . . hold onto your seat. . . $150! Just make sure your sound card supports all the features you want in a speaker system, or you'll incur another charge.*

If you're serious about your system's sound, it would behoove you to pick up a speaker/subwoofer combination system. These systems typically include right and left "satellite" speakers and a separate subwoofer, along with a separate power supply for the entire system. In most cases the subwoofer connects to the Audio Out minijack on your sound card, and then the left and right speakers connect to the subwoofer. The hookup is easy, and the improved bass from the subwoofer makes a significant difference in your system's sound.

Of course, if you're interested in a true surround-sound experience (especially nice if you're playing games that utilize so-called 3D audio, or watching DVD movies that include surround-sound soundtracks), you need more than two speakers. Just as a surround-sound system for a home theater system includes at least four speakers (plus a separate subwoofer), surround-sound systems for PCs include two front and two rear speakers, plus a subwoofer—and possibly a fifth center-channel speaker, for movie surround-sound. If you decide to go this route, make sure your sound card has an S/PDIF digital output and that you can figure out an efficient way to run cabling from the front to the rear of your computer workspace.

For the ultimate in sound reproduction, consider routing the sound from your PC to a separate, freestanding audio or home theater system. Look for sound cards that have the appropriate line-level RCA jack outputs (or relegate yourself to using an RCA-to-miniplug adapter), and then connect these to a free set of inputs on your stereo or audio/video receiver. (Make sure your cables are long enough to run from one unit to the other!) Alternately, if your sound card has an S/PDIF digital output, you can funnel this signal to the digital input on any audio/video receiver with Dolby Digital surround-sound decoding. While Windows' bleeps and bloops don't necessarily need this deluxe treatment, it's a joy to hear CDs and audio files in a way that only a full-sized system can deliver.

Sound quality isn't the only thing to consider when shopping for speakers. Today's computers come in a range of shapes and colors, and the same is true of speaker sets. You'll now see a variety of shapes and sizes that are more visually appealing and less "boxy" than the speakers of old. You'll find materials from clear to opaque and in an assortment of colors. Shapes range from streamlined and smooth to more artistic and sculptured.

Installation Tips

Truthfully, there isn't much to say about installing sound cards that is special, except for two things.

First, if you plan on using unshielded speakers, be careful where you put them. Depending on the size and type of magnets used by your speakers, they can have a profound effect on your viewing and storage pleasure. The magnets in unshielded speakers can literally bend the electrons away from their intended destination as they're fired at the glass, resulting in distortion. I briefly mounted my Sony satellite-and-woofer system atop my monitor, and the picture looked like it was melting around the edges. As for storage media, I only have one thing to say: magnets erase data.

Second, when you install that sound card on an older machine, document everything. The Sound Blaster 16 family of sound cards requires *three* I/O addresses, *two* DMA channels, and an IRQ ("in a pear tree...") to top it all off. Newer motherboards, BIOS chips, and architectures, as well as Windows 98/Me/2000/XP and a number of other operating systems, do quite well in allocating and managing the resources necessary to support all these features. Windows in particular is able to automatically sense and install the proper drivers for most Sound Blaster series products.

Nevertheless, things can go wrong, so make sure you take notes!

TIP   *If you are clueless about what's in your machine before you install such a board, then it's high time that you do an inventory. Whip out a pen and some paper and write down what you have.*

New Applications for PC Sound

Audio is an important component of the total PC experience. What used to go by the faded buzzword of *multimedia* is now an integral part of virtually everything you do on your PC. There are, however, specific applications that are more demanding than others, soundwise—and they aren't all related to music.

MP3 Audio

The hottest thing going in the PC world—soundwise, that is—is a relatively new audio format called MP3. As with most things computer-related, MP3 is an acronym of sorts, standing for MPEG Layer-3. This format deals specifically with compressing high-quality sound while retaining as much of the original quality as possible. It does this by removing those ranges of sounds that we cannot hear, which are produced in audio. There is always a measure of "waste" sound included in all recordings. Call it an imperfect world. Now, as more compression is applied, the complex algorithms used to determine what sounds a human is able to hear based on psychoacoustic models trim more and more inside of the human hearable range. So, the greater the compression, the lower the quality.

Needless to say, MP3 audio files have made quite an impact on the music industry. First, they're not secure—which means that they can be "ripped" from a CD and traded from user to user (and they are—with great vigor, I might add). Second, the files can get quite small and still sound acceptable. I'll do the numbers in a minute, but as an overview, you can get DAT-quality sound (that's right near CD-quality or White Book audio with slightly more dramatic losses in the higher spectrums) compressed down to a megabyte per minute.

Two factors make up the quality of MP3 files: kHz and Kbps (kilohertz and kilobits per second, respectively). The kHz is in direct relation to the bit depth of the sample. A 16-bit recording is on par with a 44.1kHz recording, also known as White Book or CD-quality audio. Making it 22kHz reduces its reproduction quality by only one-third. Kbps are the other piece to this two-part puzzle. Whereas kHz can be correlated to the sharpness of a picture, Kbps can be correlated to how smooth the sound plays back; Kbps are often referred to as *frames*.

To use a familiar analogy, in cartoons the more "frames" there are, the smoother the apparent motion. Simply put, 60 pictures showing the stages of a person moving their arm over a period of five seconds will result in a more natural movement than will 15 frames. Sound works the same way and, again, is represented in Kbps. 144Kbps at 44kHz makes for an MPEG Layer-3 file that sounds as good as digital CD audio but takes up only a fraction of the space. Considering this, Layer-3 can compress a CD-quality audio file to fit about a minute's worth of sound into roughly a megabyte of space. Your typical three- to five-minute song would end up being anywhere from 3 to 6MB in size.

PROS AND CONS OF THE MP3 FORMAT

The MP3 format has taken off like wildfire, embraced by both consumers (particularly college-age consumers) and the consumer electronics hardware industry. Why? Here are the facts, real quicklike:

- ◆ Near CD-quality sound.

- ◆ Very small files.

- ◆ As many options for storing the files as there are storage options.

- ◆ Can be extremely miserly on batteries.

- ◆ Everyone is getting on the MP3 train. Portable, home, and car MP3 audio components are either shipping or about to.

And then there are some non-hardware or software issues that make MP3 (well, any compressed digital audio format, for that matter) a very attractive format, indeed:

- ◆ It drastically reduces the requirements for publishing music to a worldwide audience. Artists don't have to wait for a record label executive to stumble along and fortuitously "discover" them. Instead, artists can record their music and publish it on sites like mp3.com and be heard by people everywhere.

- ◆ There are no additional costs (unless you don't have a computer, of course). Boatloads of freeware, shareware, and commercial software are available for doing pretty much anything you might want to with MP3s, and with the state of today's sound cards, even a bargain PC can serve as a low-end studio.

◆ CD collections can be a thing of the past. Think about it. You can move from your music shelf to the CD player, endlessly swapping CD for CD, or you can reach over, click a few times, and listen to as many albums as you have storage room for. That big hard drive is looking mighty nice.

WARNING   While a substantial number of MP3s are made available by musicians and their labels for promotional purposes (particularly useful for new and independent acts), it's not hard to find unauthorized MP3 copies of copyrighted material online. This type of illegal file trading, facilitated by Morpheus and similar Internet technologies, happens when users copy their personal CDs to MP3 files and then distribute those files over the Internet to people who do not own the CD. These acts of piracy prevent the original artists from receiving royalties earned for their performances, and add up to billions of dollars in lost revenue each year. While many in the recording industry blame technology for the piracy problem (witness the various lawsuits against Napster and MP3.com), the real culprits are end users who don't respect artists' rights—and the real victims are those artists who don't get paid for the music they make.

Unfortunately, the recording industry has not been as enthusiastic in its support of MP3—primarily because the MP3 format is not a secure format. This means that MP3s cannot be protected from theft and piracy, and explains why the major music labels (and some recording artists) regard the whole MP3 universe as nothing more than a pirate's trading ground or a home for unsigned bands.

This type of ostrich-like thinking flies in the face of the MP3 format's immense popularity, and ignores the wishes of a large audience for recorded music. So while the recording industry is pushing both new secure audio file formats and efforts to make the existing MP3 format more secure (through the Secure Digital Music Initiative), standard MP3s remain the format of choice among consumers today.

WHAT IS A CODEC?

When delving into the technical nature of various audio formats (including MP3), you may hear the term *codec* come up now and again. It's a fake word made up of two real words, *compression* and *decompression*. It's sometimes incorrectly used to describe either compression or decompression, so a codec can be a way of encoding media, decoding media, or (correctly) both.

One of the more secure codecs is Liquid Audio's format. These tracks can also be recorded in CD-quality but have the added ability to "time out" (meaning you can't listen to them anymore) after a certain period, specified either in days from first use or as a particular date. For example, the renowned art rock band Yes advance-released their single "Lightning Strikes" from their new album of the same name over the Internet in Liquid Audio. It timed out the day the album was released to the public. As you can see, this offers artists security and also acts as a great way to publicize a new recording and boost sales.

BURNING MP3s TO CD

What do you do with all those MP3 files once you've downloaded them to your hard disk? If you want to listen to them on your PC, you're pretty much all set—just use one of the MP3 playback programs (discussed next) and sit back and listen. If you want to offload the files to a portable MP3 player, just connect the player to your PC and use the included software to pick and load the songs you want.

A third alternative is to create your own personalized CDs containing the mix of songs that you select. To do this, you'll need to have a CD-R/CD-RW drive (sometimes called a *CD burner*) installed in or connected to your PC, and corresponding CD burner software. Use the software to assemble your track list, and then follow the program's instructions to copy the MP3 files from your hard disk to WAV files on a blank CD-R. The entire process is about as easy as using Windows Explorer to copy files from one drive to another.

TIP   *To play your new CD in a regular (non-PC) CD player, record in the CD-R format and use a blank CD-R disc specifically labeled for audio use. (CD-RW discs will not play in most CD players.)*

WARNING   *While the DVD players used in most home theater systems can play standard CDs, most DVD players cannot play CD-R discs. This has to do with the types of lasers used to record and play back the different formats—and means that you probably won't be able to use your DVD player to play back any MP3 discs that you create. Some of the newer DVD players, however, can read CD-R and CD-RW discs, and some will even play MP3 files from these CDs; when in doubt, check the player's specs to determine its playback capabilities.*

WHERE TO FIND MP3s

Numerous Internet sites specialize in MP3 files and software. Most of these sites offer large collections of MP3 files, as well as MP3 playback, editing, and storage software. The most popular of these sites include:

◆ AmpCast (www.ampcast.com)

◆ ARTISTdirect Network (www.artistdirect.com)

◆ Audiogalaxy (www.audiogalaxy.com)

◆ eClassical (www.eclassical.com)

◆ Emusic (www.emusic.com)

◆ GetMusic (www.getmusic.com)

◆ IUMA (www.iuma.com)

◆ Liquid Audio (www.liquidaudio.com)

◆ Listen.com (www.listen.com)

◆ Lycos MP3 Search (mp3.lycos.com)

◆ MP3.com (www.mp3.com)

◆ MUSICMATCH (www.musicmatch.com)

◆ Napster (www.napster.com)

◆ Scour (www.scour.com)

◆ Sonicnet (www.sonicnet.com)

◆ Tunes (www.tunes.com)

CONVERTING CDs TO MP3s

If you can put MP3s on a CD, what's to stop you from going the other direction—and converting songs on a CD to the more efficient MP3 format? Assuming you have the proper burner (or *ripper*) software, the procedure is as simple as ripping the CD audio into a WAV file, and then converting the WAV file into the MP3 format. Although the MP3 versions of your songs will lose a little in the way of fidelity, they'll take up a *lot* less disc space!

WARNING   Because of the rampant misuse and illegal distribution of MP3 files, many music CDs are coming out with protection features that prevent you from ripping songs. Also, Windows XP has some new built-in protection features that keep users from doing some of the audio tasks that are available in Windows 98 and Me.

MP3 PLAYERS (SOFTWARE)

There are a number of software solutions for playing and managing MP3 files on your personal computer. Here are some of the most popular MP3 players, jukeboxes, and rippers—listed (alphabetically) by platform:

Windows

eJay MP3 Station Plus   This versatile program is more than a player—it can also function as CD-burner software.

MAGIX mp3 maker   A combination MP3 player and CD ripper, complete with cross-fader, pitch, and other controls.

MUSICMATCH Jukebox   One of the best MP3 players/rippers—actually, a better ripper than it is a player.

PCDJ Phat   An MP3 player with an interface that looks like a DJ deck—and that offers basic audio mixing functions, such as cross-fading and pitch change.

RealJukebox   RealNetworks' premier player handles a variety of formats in addition to MP3, and has joined the ranks of the "skinners" and the "visualizers." No, these are not punk groups; they're ways of customizing the look of your player.

Sonique media player   One of the early commercial skins-based players with visualization capabilities. It works well but is more visually oriented, with its main highlight being animated menus and other controls. Sonique relies on Windows Media Player for its audio capabilities.

UltraPlayer   This relatively new player from UltraCo offers support for a wide variety of formats (including MP3, WAV, WMA, WMA, AVI, and various streaming audio formats), as well as a graphic equalizer and a number of digital signal processing (DSP) modes.

Winamp   Possibly the most well-known MP3 player there is—so much so that AOL bought the company. They also pioneered streaming MP3 with their SHOUTcast technology.

Windows Media Player   Microsoft likes to have its foot in as many doors as it can. MP3 media is no exception. Not surprisingly, it's taking on QuickTime and Real's two products by offering a staggering array of tools and features. Unlike most Microsoft software vying for leadership in an existing market, this is actually pretty easy to use.

NOTE   *Having trouble finding a manufacturer listed in this chapter? See the Vendor Guide on the Utilities CD for contact information on these companies.*

Unix/Linux

Kmp3   A very capable MP3 player for the popular KDE desktop manager.

mp3blaster   A console player that has an integrated playlist. Nice, fast, stable, and an app that only a Unix devotee could love.

mpg123   The granddaddy of them all (well, it's not *that* old) plays only from the console and doesn't have an interface, but there are many interfaces for X Windows and other Windows managers.

XMMS   Possibly the most well known MP3 player in the Linux world, it's an exact clone of Winamp. You'll need an X Windows server to use it.

MP3 PLAYERS (HARDWARE)

Remember that MP3 is a software phenomenon; you don't need any special hardware in order to download and play MP3 files on your personal computer. However, if you want to play MP3 files while you're *away* from your computer, you have several interesting options.

One of the most popular uses of MP3 files is for on-the-go listening, through a Walkman-type portable device. A number of these products are available for the MP3 buff, most of them storing the MP3 files in RAM (often via removable memory sticks) instead of on tape or CD. The trend was started by Diamond Multimedia with its popular RIO player; similar products are now available from Creative Labs, Frontier Labs, Iomega, Philips, RCA, Sony, and many others.

In addition to the portable players, some companies are releasing units that can be used in cars (remove the faceplate and stick in the cradle to upload files for the next day or for that road trip you've been planning on taking), outside (imagine a boom box that can play regular CDs and CD-Rs containing MP3s), and in the home (a 50GB hard drive makes a nice media storage component).

A good place to look up the latest MP3 player reviews is at www.cnet.com. Once there, click on Electronics Reviews, then Portable Music, and then MP3 Players. This site includes solid reviews and honest (sometimes scathingly so) criticism. It's worth a look just for its lowest price finder.

Digital Audio and Surround Sound

The audio in your PC is, by nature, digital audio. It's unfortunate, then, that most low-priced sound-cards allow only analog connections—forcing all input and output to go through a noise-inducing digital-to-analog or analog-to-digital conversion.

If you don't connect your PC to any other audio devices (save for your speakers), this probably isn't a big deal. However, if you do want to interface to another digital audio device, you don't want the sound to suffer from this unnecessary conversion—you want your audio signal to stay digital for as long as possible in the chain.

Fortunately, many higher-priced sound cards are coming with digital inputs and outputs (also called S/PDIF connections). Digital connections—in either coax or optical format—transmit audio data digitally, so that what goes into one device is sonically identical to what comes out of the preceding device. If you're recording to or from an MD or DAT, make sure your sound card has the proper S/PDIF digital connections.

Another use of digital audio is to transfer multiple-channel information for movie soundtracks. To feed this surround-sound signal to a Dolby Digital processor (found in most audio/video receivers), you need a DVD drive and a sound card with an S/PDIF output. (Again, either coax or digital will do.) Note that the digital 5.1-channel output from your DVD drive is fed directly from the drive and sent unprocessed to your card's S/PDIF digital output(s). Thus, when you connect the digital output from your PC to the corresponding digital input on your audio/video receiver, you get the true 5.1 surround-sound output, unvarnished.

Finally, surround-sound PC speaker systems—such as those designed for 3D game audio, discussed next—use the digital signal sent from an S/PDIF connection. If you want to play games in multiple-speaker 3D surround, make sure your sound card has the necessary S/PDIF connection.

3D Game Audio

It used to be that games were the stepchild applications for most personal computer users. Well, times have changed—PC games are now among the most demanding PC applications.

Most games use MIDI to play the game's background music, and WAV (or similar format) files to provide the rest of the game's voices and sound effects. Naturally, the better the specs of your sound card—and the better your PC speaker system—the better your games will sound. Since most games contain a lot of room-rumbling explosions, consider a speaker system that includes a separate subwoofer. (Better still, run the sound from your PC to your home audio system.)

The newest wrinkle in game sound is 3D audio. Normal 2D audio places the sound image across a flat sound field bordered by your left and right speakers. 3D audio attempts to position individual elements of the sound image relative to each other in a three-dimensional space that expands all around your viewing position. The amazing thing is that 3D audio can be achieved with just two speakers, using specially developed audio algorithms.

The confusing thing about 3D audio is that there isn't a single standard—one game might use Microsoft's DirectSound3D API (Application Programming Interface), while another might use Aureal's A3D API. These two APIs are not compatible, of course, which means you have to choose your 3D sound card based on the API used by your favorite games—and hope that all your games use the same API!

NOTE *Creative has developed a third 3D audio API—actually a set of extensions—that sits "on top of" the Direct-Sound3D API. The EAX extensions add reverb and chorus to the normal sound, providing more faithful mimicking of different types of audio environments.*

To date, Aureal's A3D API has been the more popular of the two competing formats. The A3D API is available on sound cards that utilize Aureal's Vortex chip, including models from Aureal, Diamond, Turtle Beach, and other manufacturers. Among the games utilizing A3D audio are Jedi Knight, MDK, Half-Life, and Heretic II. The DirectSound3D API hasn't garnered as much hardware support as has A3D (although Creative Labs is one notable supporter, with their Sound Blaster Live! line), so there aren't nearly as many games written for this standard.

Because the 3D audio formats use aural smoke and mirrors to trick you into thinking you're hearing sounds from behind you, you don't necessarily need a four-speaker system to hear 3D sound.

However, 3D audio from a four-speaker system (two in front, two in the rear) is demonstrably more effective than that from a standard two-speaker system, so if you're serious about 3D gaming, you may want to splurge for the extra speakers.

Streaming Media and the Internet

MP3, WAV, and other standard audio formats are great for storing music and other audio that you download to your hard disk and then play with an MP3 or other media player. However, there are many types of programming—especially live programming—for which downloading is impractical.

When you want to listen to something from the Internet without waiting several minutes for a large audio or video file to download, you want streaming media. Streaming media works around the problem of fitting a large file down a small pipe by enabling access to the first part of the file before the last part is fully downloaded, by downloading the large file as multiple smaller packets. This eliminates the long wait associated with typical media file downloads. Streaming audio (and video) files begin playing almost immediately, before the entire file is downloaded. In the case of live broadcasts—such as Internet radio—the streaming is continuous, as there isn't a complete "file" to download.

NOTE   One of the compromises made to enhance the streaming nature of streaming media is in sound and picture quality. Quite often, streaming audio and video programming is of lower quality than what you'd expect from other formats. (Some might describe the typical streaming quality as "poor.") Lower quality means smaller packet size, which helps the streaming media play back as smoothly as possible.

Numerous Web sites specialize in streaming media programming, the largest of which is Broadcast.com (`www.broadcast.com`). Here you can find hundreds and hundreds of Internet radio stations, music collections, live news and sports broadcasts, and even audio books—all in streaming media format. Many other sites also offer streaming media Webcasts; news and sports sites are big supporters of the format.

The following formats are the three most popular streaming media technologies:

RealAudio/RealVideo/RealMedia   RealAudio, from RealNetworks, is the granddaddy of streaming audio (introduced way back in 1994), and it is still the market leader. (RealVideo is the streaming video version; RealMedia is the catch-all term for all RealNetworks' streaming media.) RealMedia files typically have an RM extension, although so-called "pointer" files have a RAM extension. You play RealMedia files through the RealPlayer software.

Windows Media   Windows Media, from Microsoft, is the newest streaming media format— and it is coming on strong, thanks to the strength of Microsoft's latest Windows Media Player software. The Windows Media Player not only plays Windows Media files (with ASF, WMA, and WMV extensions), but it also plays RealMedia, MP3, and other audio and video file formats. You can also pick up radio stations from all over the world, in real time, and listen to any style of music imaginable.

QuickTime   QuickTime, from Apple, is an audio and video format suitable for both streaming and progressive downloading. QuickTime files—with either MOV, QT, or QTI extensions—are played via Apple's QuickTime Player.

You don't need any special hardware on your PC, beyond a standard sound card and speakers, to listen to streaming audio. (The same goes with viewing streaming video.) The biggest bottleneck is your Internet connection. Quite frankly, streaming media is problematic over a standard 56K modem. To ensure the highest-quality, uninterrupted streaming media performance, you really need a broadband Internet connection, such as that available via DSL or cable modem.

NOTE *If you're setting up your own Web site, you may want to offer streaming audio or video to your users. (Make sure your Web hosting service supports streaming media—most do, although they may charge extra for it.) To do this, you need to invest in the streaming development software for whichever format you choose to embrace. Basic authoring tools for RealMedia and Windows Media are available for free; QuickTime tools run $500 or more.*

Audio for Musicians

Computer technology has firmly invaded the world of music. Whether assisting playback (using software-based synthesizers and sequencers) or recording (using digital recording and mixing programs), the personal computer is an essential part of any professional musician's arsenal.

Since the audio needs of musicians differ from the audio needs of typical home or business computer users, specialized hardware may be required to achieve optimal results. This section evaluates the types of audio hardware you may need to invest in to turn your personal computer into a real-time musical instrument—or professional recording studio.

NOTE *You probably won't find sound cards, interfaces, and software for professional musicians at your local CompUSA. A better place to shop for these professional audio products is the electronics department at any large musical instrument retailer, such as Mars Music, Sam Ash Music, or Guitar Center.*

MIDI SEQUENCING AND PLAYBACK

MIDI—which is used not only to generate the sound of musical instruments on your computer, but also to control the playing of certain electronic instruments—is one of the most-used musical tools available today. Performing musicians use MIDI-compatible instruments and computer programs to sequence music—that is, to digitally record parts of songs (or even complete songs), and then play them back automatically, in real time, as if live musicians were present and playing. This way, the sound of a 40-piece ensemble can be re-created by a single musician, and complex recordings can be easily and accurately reproduced on the concert stage.

MIDI is also used by composers, who—using realistic-sounding samples of various instruments—can hear their arrangements played as they're written, without the trouble or expense of hiring outside musicians. The computer uses MIDI to generate the sounds of the instruments, which are then played in accordance with the written note values. In essence, MIDI-equipped composers have entire orchestras at their disposal, 24 hours a day.

Almost all sound cards sold today include some degree of MIDI functionality. At the very least, the card should include its own MIDI synthesizer, as discussed earlier in this chapter. More useful still is the capability to feed MIDI signals to other MIDI-compatible instruments, such as keyboard synthesizers, via a MIDI interface.

The most common interface used by MIDI instruments is Roland's MPU-401 interface. Most MIDI-capable sound cards today offer MPU-401 compatibility, but not all offer true MIDI inputs and outputs. Many consumer-oriented sound cards offer MIDI input and output only through the card's joystick port; a separate MIDI adapter cable is necessary to connect standard MIDI cables to this port. A sound card with a true MIDI connection includes separate MIDI In and MIDI Out jacks, which utilize five-pin DIN connectors.

Most MIDI musical instruments—and some professional sound cards—include a third jack, labeled MIDI Thru. By using the MIDI Thru jack, several MIDI instruments can be strung together in a series, all controlled by the same PC-based program. (The MIDI Thru jack on the first device is connected to the MIDI In on the next device in the series, and passes through the raw information fed into the first device's MIDI In jack.) Thus, a MIDI sequencer program can send one set of instructions to one synthesizer, another set of instructions to a second synthesizer, and a third set of instructions to a third sequencer—even though only the first synthesizer is hooked up to the PC.

Even though most sound cards today offer MIDI compatibility, not all offer the same level of MIDI performance. In addition, not all sound cards fully support all available MIDI operations. For example, some cards don't support *full duplex* operation, which enables you to record a new digital audio track and to listen to previously recorded tracks simultaneously. (Cards without this capability are called *half duplex* cards.)

That said, if you're working with MIDI in a professional audio environment, you'll probably want to replace your PC's standard sound card with a pro-level MIDI card. Cards of this type (such as the Aardvark Aark24 and the Digital Audio Labs CardDeluxe, typically priced in the $400–$700 range) often include additional features such as SMPTE (which stands for Society of Motion Picture and Television Engineers) sync, multiple MIDI input and output jacks, and S/PDIF digital input and output jacks (useful for sending output to MD or DAT recorders).

Another option is to plug a MIDI daughterboard and interface into an existing sound card. This option preserves your existing sound card environment (for normal PC audio) and adds additional MIDI capability and jacks. (Unfortunately, this option is also slightly more problematic, in terms of creating device conflicts and such.)

Once you have the right hardware on your PC, then you can install MIDI sequencing software to control your internal and external MIDI instruments. These programs let you create patterns and songs, store them on your hard disk, and then play them back in real time via your PC's MIDI outputs. With your synthesizers and other instruments playing automatically (as directed by your PC), you can just sit back and listen to the music—or use your sequenced tracks as backing for a live performance.

Among the most popular sequencing programs are Cakewalk Pro Audio, Cubase VST, Emagic's Logic Audio, Mixman Studio, and PowerTracks Pro Audio. Again, check out the Vendor Guide on the Utilities CD for company contact information.

PROFESSIONAL RECORDING AND MIXING

Whereas musicians of previous generations who wanted to lay down their tracks were forced to rent expensive recording studios (and employ expensive studio musicians), today's musicians can achieve comparable results in the comfort of their own living rooms, using PC-based recording and mixing software. Some of these programs are quite powerful, and when combined with the proper pro-level hardware, can turn your personal computer into a professional multitrack recording studio. In fact, digital recording offers numerous advantages to traditional analog tape recording, including the capability to perform seamless "punch-ins" of new material, add an almost infinite number of overdubs (without incurring noise loss or producing tape hiss), and digitally modify the sound of individual instruments or singers. It's no wonder that more and more musicians, at all levels, are modifying their personal computers to create their own home recording studios.

The first thing you need when creating a home recording studio is a computer with enough processing power and memory to do the job without locking up. Recording large digital files in real time is processor intensive, and you need a fairly fast system to ensure relatively painless recording. For example, Digidesign's Pro Tools—a very popular professional recording package—requires either a Pentium III or a Pentium II running at 300MHz or faster and 128MB RAM (minimum—256MB is recommended). Windows 98 Second Edition or Windows Me seem to be the operating systems of choice for most pro recording/mixing programs.

The second thing you need in your system is a very large, very fast hard drive. Audio files recorded for the highest possible fidelity are quite large, using the high-quality WAV format (rather than the rather lo-fi MP3 format). When you consider that five minutes of eight-channel CD-quality audio takes up about 200MB of space, you can see why disk size is important. Splurge for at least a 20GB hard disk, and consider a dedicated or removable hard disk drive. (The latter offers more storage flexibility, as well as the capability to take your music with you to another PC.) In terms of speed, you want a drive with a sustained transfer rate of at least 5MB per second and access time of 10ms or less. Most professionals choose a SCSI hard disk, as SCSI drives offer more efficient I/O than do IDE drives.

Third, you need a pro-quality sound card and audio interface box—which will typically set you back $1000 or more. Since you'll probably be recording multiple tracks simultaneously, you need more than a single input—which is where the audio interface device comes in. Most audio interface boxes provide eight or more inputs, with a variety of connectors—line level RCA, XLR, ¼-inch, S/PDIF digital, MIDI, and so on—and plug into the pro audio card. (Some newer interface boxes bypass the audio card by utilizing a USB connection.) The audio card should also include S/PDIF inputs and outputs, to receive input from digital playback devices and to send output to MD and DAT recorders. Look for these pro-level card/interface combos from Aardvark, Digidesign, Echo, EgoSys, Emagic, Frontier Design Group, Mark of the Unicorn (MOTU), SeaSound, Soundscape Digital Technology, and other similar manufacturers.

Finally, you need software that turns your PC into a recording/mixing console. Cakewalk Pro Audio, Cubase VST, Sonic Foundry's Vegas Audio, and similar programs are low-priced ($400 or so) alternatives, but the software of choice for most professionals is Digidesign's Pro Tools. Pro Tools enables musicians to record 24 or more tracks of digital audio onto their computers' hard disks, and then to digitally manipulate the pitch, tempo, and sound characteristics of each track—on a note-by-note basis, if desired. A basic Pro Tools setup includes the Pro Tools software, a special Pro Tools sound card, and a proprietary I/O box that contains eight channels of S/PDIF input/output and a MIDI interface. More advanced systems include additional I/O boxes (to increase the channel count), a SCSI accelerator card, and additional plug-ins to the basic software. Naturally, you can send the output from a Pro Tools system to any digital recording device, including MD and DAT recorders and CD-R/CD-RW burners.

NOTE *Some digital recording programs can also utilize a second monitor, with the recording data displayed on one monitor, and the recording and mixing controls displayed on the second monitor. Naturally, you'll need to install a second video card to take advantage of this feature. See Chapter 24, "Video Adapters and Displays," for more information on dual monitors.*

Troubleshooting Tips

There's nothing like troubleshooting a sound card, especially when you just installed it.

The first tip—one that you should regard as a very close friend—is to *limit yourself to doing only one thing at a time.* This way, if you get in a jam, it's much easier to backtrack and figure out what caused the problem.

The second thing to do—as you should with any new card you install in your PC—is to double-check all the connections. Make sure the card is seated properly and that all connections, both internal and external (to your speakers, for example), are solid.

The third thing to check is whether your computer system is configured properly for your sound card. Make sure you have the correct drivers installed and that you're using the latest, most up-to-date versions of those drivers. (When in doubt, check the manufacturer's Web site for new drivers, patches, and other utilities.)

If, after these basic checks, you're still having sound problems, chances are that you have some sort of port, IRQ, or DMA conflict with your sound card. Conflict problems are tough to track down, but the tools discussed in Chapter 35, "Hardware Management via Software Solutions," can help you find and fix any audio-related conflicts.

One of the most common problems occurs when setting up a Creative Labs brand Ensonique ES1371 or 1370 sound card (also called the Audio PCI64) for use in Windows MS-DOS mode. This is almost invariably a conflict with, oddly enough, LPT Interrupt Sharing, which is meant to resolve these kinds of problems. It's easy enough to disable. Go to My Computer ➢ Properties ➢ Device Manager ➢ Sound, Video, and Game Controllers and get the properties for your PCI64 card. Go to the Settings tab and uncheck the Allow LPT Interrupt Sharing check box. If that doesn't fix the problem and there are no other conflicts, it's likely that your card and game are simply incompatible.

A supposedly common problem with Turtle Beach's popular Monterey and Tahiti cards is that the microphone does not work. This is actually not the case. The microphones *do* work, just not in a way people expect. These cards require a line-level input, a state that is commonly mistaken for being nonpowered. Simple microphones don't output any significant amount of current, so, unless you have a microphone capable of producing line-level output (−10dBv to +4dBv) or a microphone pre-amplifier, you'll need another path to getting microphone input. You can buy a relatively inexpensive inline preamp made specifically for microphones, or you can get a mixer.

Cards are much more delicate than sound equipment and can fry easily. Make sure you place the correct current line to the correct jack, or you might end up with a card that doesn't do anything.

In addition, cheap sound cards are not always the best shielded cards available. This means that high-frequency interference from other components in your system can be a problem, in the form of an annoying buzz or hum. If you're experiencing this sort of problem, try repositioning the cards in your computer to separate the sound card from another card or another component generating the interference. (If you have the space, leave empty the slots on either side of your sound card.) You may even want to place a thin strip of aluminum sheeting around your sound card (being careful not to touch any other component with the sheeting) to better shield the card from interference. Of course, spending a few more bucks on a higher-quality sound card will also fix this problem.

Now you know how to get the most of your computer's sound—how about an accompanying picture with that? In the next chapter, I'll cover everything you need to know about video capture.

Chapter 26

You Oughta
Be in Pictures:
Video Capture

◆ QuickSteps: Installing a Video Capture Board
  and a PC Cam   711

◆ Digital and Analog Video System Components   713

◆ Installing Video Capture Boards   734

◆ Running Video Capture Software   735

◆ Using Offline Compression   741

◆ Handling Software Bugs   744

◆ Troubleshooting Tips   745

Introduction

JUST A FEW YEARS AGO, the state of the art in computer-assisted presentations was pretty color graphs. Now it's pretty color graphs with inserts of moving, talking figures. Video editing and production was the domain of the professional and the serious hobbyist. Producing your own feature movie was not even a fantasy. Now, however, the home user can capture, edit, and return to tape finished video productions that rival those done by professionals. With the advent of low-cost consumer digital camcorders in the Digital8 and MiniDV formats, as well as the high-speed FireWire digital connection found on most new computers, the quality can in fact equal professional results. One of the most famous examples of the desktop movie revolution was the creation of the movie *The Blair Witch Project*, shot on consumer analog and digital video camcorders and edited on desktop computer equipment. It grossed untold millions of dollars and launched a desktop video revolution.

You can also use video in e-mail: for less than $100 you can get a simple video camera that looks like a golf ball. You clip the camera to your monitor, hook the camera to your video capture board, FireWire, or USB port, and record your message in full motion video and sound. Then you package the video clip into an e-mail message, and your recipient can hear your voice and see you. With a product such as Microsoft's NetMeeting, you can hold interactive video conversations.

How do you accomplish all these moving-video feats? With video capture hardware and video-editing software. In this chapter, you'll learn what kinds of hardware and software you'll need, how to install them, and how to make them work.

QuickSteps

Installing a Video Capture Board and a PC Cam

Installing a video capture board is relatively simple in current PCI bus computers. Installing a PC cam on computers with USB ports is also easy. For both procedures, the main thing to remember is to follow instructions and take your time.

Video Capture Board

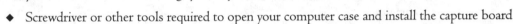

BE PREPARED

Before you start, here are some things you may need on hand:

- ◆ Screwdriver or other tools required to open your computer case and install the capture board
- ◆ Small container to hold removed screws
- ◆ Windows installation CD for any drivers required upon software installation
- ◆ Antistatic wrist strap
- ◆ Plenty of light so that you can see into the computer case when opened

1. Turn off your computer.

2. Put on your antistatic wrist strap and open your computer case.

3. Select the appropriate slot in which to place the capture board.

4. If there is a flange covering the opening for the slot, remove the screw holding it in place, and then remove the flange itself.

5. (If you don't have an antistatic wrist strap, drain any excess static electricity from your body by touching some bare metal on your computer's case before you pick up the capture board. Don't move your feet until the board is installed.) Place the board into the slot and press down firmly until it is seated. Use the screw that was originally holding the flange to hold the board in place.

6. Follow the board manufacturer's instructions for installing software drivers and other software utilities.

7. Follow the board manufacturer's instructions for testing and implementing the board itself.

PC Cam

Before you start, here are some things you may need on hand:

◆ PC cam documentation and installation software. Read the installation instructions thoroughly before you begin installation.

1. Plug the PC cam's USB cable into a USB port on your computer.

2. Plug the PC cam's power cable into the device and attach it to a power source.

3. Follow the PC cam manufacturer's instructions for installing software drivers and other software utilities.

4. Follow the PC cam manufacturer's instructions for testing and implementing the board itself.

Video Capture Overview

There's a lot to learn about doing video capture. Summarized, it looks like Figure 26.1.

FIGURE 26.1

Creating video
capture clips

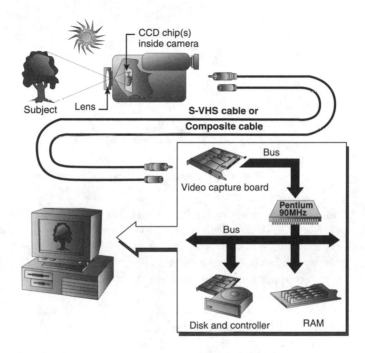

There's a lot to that; don't worry, I'll explain it all in this chapter. Briefly, however, creating video capture clips requires three main steps:

1. Connecting and configuring the video capture hardware and software

2. Capturing the image with video capture hardware

3. Running the resulting video file through an offline compressor for long-term storage

The last step is useful because video compression software today will enable you to make your files much smaller, thereby taking up less storage space, and still maintain pretty good sound and image quality.

Video Capture System Components

Let's go shopping for video capture stuff. I won't recommend too many brands of things to buy—at the speed that this business moves, many brand-name specifics would probably be obsolete by the time you read this. Instead, I'll highlight the kinds of equipment you'll need.

A video capture system includes four pieces:

◆ The video input device (typically a camcorder—either analog or digital)

◆ The connection (cable) between the input device and the video capture board

◆ The video capture board or digital video connections

◆ The rest of the PC doing the capture

These pieces are illustrated in Figure 26.2.

FIGURE 26.2

The pieces of a
video capture system

To do video capture you need a camera, cable, video capture board, and your PC.

All four pieces of this system rely on each other, making the whole process like a chain, no stronger than its weakest link. If you have lousy input (from a VHS-format camcorder, let's say), you'll get lousy images. Great cables and the world's best video capture system will ensure only that you get really full-fidelity reproductions of the camcorder's lousy images. And a million-dollar camera's super-high-quality images are useless if your capture board can't capture images bigger than 160 × 120 pixels.

In essence, you're wasting your time unless you have a high-quality video source, good cables, a good capture board, and a powerful PC to back it all up. The reality is that you can generate truly professional results if you invest in an all-digital video system, starting with a digital camcorder and ending with powerful desktop video-editing software. So-called digital video (DV) enables anyone with a personal computer (and the bucks for the rest of the system) to easily edit video footage in ways formerly available only to the pros. With a DV system, you can cut footage, insert footage, rearrange segments in a different sequence, add transitions and special effects, and overlay captions and titles—all without degrading the quality of the original footage. DV is definitely the way to go, and in today's market, the price for a complete system (from camcorder to computer) is within most families' budgets.

The Video Input Device

The first step in capturing and editing a video signal is the generation of that signal. Although most people use their PCs to edit videotaped footage shot with a camcorder, you can incorporate images from many other sources into your ultimate video masterpiece. Essentially, any device that generates a video signal can be fed into your video capture card and editing software—camcorders, stand-alone VCRs, DVD players, broadcast/satellite/cable television, even digital still cameras. Your video-editing software, then, can combine and edit video from any of these sources, and then output the result to tape or disc as desired.

CAMCORDERS

Out of all the components of a video-editing system, your camcorder (the word comes from the combination of *camera* and *recorder*) has the single most significant impact on your final edited masterpiece.

The optics and electronics of the camcorder's camera section determine the quality of the images captured, and the tape format of the recorder determines the resolution at which these images are captured.

Camera Considerations

It doesn't matter if the camcorder you select is analog (VHS, 8mm, Hi8, SVHS) or digital (Digital8 or MiniDV); the camera part of the system is governed by the same rules. While video cameras come with a lot of options these days (going by buzzwords such as Electronic Image Stabilization, autofocus, and autoshutter), don't let yourself get distracted by the doodads; camera image quality boils down to three facts:

- You must have good lighting and composition on your subject.

- You need good optics—that is, the lens or lenses—on the camera.

- The camera must receive the image with a high-quality imaging chip, an internal component in the camera.

The composition and lighting I leave up to you; but let's take a look at the optics and electronics end of image generation.

The light from your image goes first through the camera's lens. Some lenses are plastic; some are glass. Although glass is better, I wouldn't worry much about a camcorder's lens if you're doing video capture. Why? The low resolution of video capture (as compared to film) means that even the worst camera optics will deliver resolution beyond video capture's capabilities. (Naturally, higher-resolution recording formats—such as Digital8 or MiniDV—will utilize more of your camera's potential, as well as reveal any flaws in the camera's optics.)

Although plastic lenses can produce a credible video capture image, they are *much* easier to scratch than are glass lenses, so be sure to keep the lens cap on your camcorder when you're not using it, and clean the lens with a soft cloth and a lens cleaner. If you need to use special lenses for your video capture, then you might look into the higher-end camcorders that allow you to use standard camera lenses.

The lens focuses the image onto the part of the video camera that records it. While most video images are stored and transmitted in analog formats (the most popular videotape formats are analog, and so are the two most common video interfaces), the image is originally captured digitally. Modern camcorders capture video images with a chip that's similar to a memory chip, a chip called a *charge coupled device*, or *CCD*. A simplified version of how it works is something like this: a CCD is a memory chip that doesn't have a cover on it, just an array of memory cells. The camcorder electronics fill up all the memory areas, and then the lens applies the light to the exposed memory cells. Light affects how much data remains in the memory cells, so the camcorder circuitry figures out how much light is on various parts of the image by reading data in the various parts of the memory array.

CCDs vary in size, as measured by the total number of pixels that they detect. The total number of pixels on CCDs can range from about 250,000 to 570,000.

While that sounds like lots of pixels, it's really not. In order to store color information, the light from the lens is passed through a *stripe mask*, a colored filter that filters out all but red from some pixels, all but blue from others, and all but green from still others. As a result, some of the pixels then become red sensitive, green sensitive, or blue sensitive. Each complete *color pixel*, then, is composed of three of the chip's original pixels, so divide the original pixel count by three to get the total number of colored pixels that the camera truly has. Then, as the CCD is a square array of elements, take the square root of the resulting number to determine the CCD's horizontal and vertical resolution. You can see the composition of color pixels in Figure 26.3.

FIGURE 26.3

Three pixels make up a single color pixel.

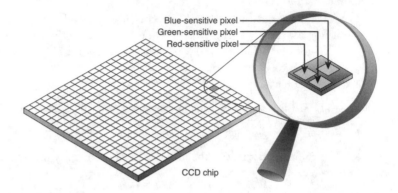

Blue-sensitive pixel
Green-sensitive pixel
Red-sensitive pixel

CCD chip

For example, one common CCD has 270,000 elements. That becomes $270,000/3 = 90,000$ color pixels. The square root of 90,000 is 300, so a 270,000-pixel CCD yields a color image with a resolution of 300×300 pixels.

Basic VHS-format camcorders usually have CCDs with 250,000 to 280,000 pixels, for resolutions of 300 to 306 pixels (horizontally and vertically). If you're going to buy a VHS-format camcorder, then it really doesn't matter which one you buy, as the CCD on one will be about the same as on any other.

Better camcorders, by contrast, utilize higher-resolution CCDs. It's not uncommon to find CCDs with pixel totals of 380K (356×356), 410K (370×370), 470K (396×396), and 570K (436×436), with the 470K chip most common.

If, on the other hand, you want much better quality and can afford to spend more money, you can get cameras with *three* CCDs: one for red, one for green, one for blue; *each* CCD has a resolution of about 640×640. Although a three-CCD system will definitely deliver a better picture, it may end up being a little bit of overkill since, as you'll see, the maximum resolution you'll see out of a video capture system is around 420×480.

When you're comparing the camera sections of various camcorders, note that no two chips and no two lenses are the same. Every year sees improvement in the CCD market. To find the best camcorder for your money, your best bet is to go to a showroom that sells lots of them. Connect different camcorders viewing the same image to the same monitor, one at a time, to get the best idea of which camcorder produces the best image—and don't presume that the most expensive camcorder is necessarily the best!

Recorder Considerations

Remember that a camcorder is more than just a camera—it's a camera *and* a video recorder. While you *can* feed a signal directly from a camcorder's camera to your PC, it's more likely that you'll use the camcorder to record images on videotape, and then feed the videotaped images to your PC.

When you're comparing the recorder sections of various camcorders, you have to navigate your way through a variety of mostly incompatible recording formats. When you see the terms VHS, VHS-C, SVHS, 8mm, Hi8, Digital8, and MiniDV, these do *not* describe the camera part of the camcorder; they describe the camcorder's recording format. And, as you will see, there are significant differences between formats, in terms of video reproduction.

The oldest and most established tape format is VHS, jointly developed by JVC and Matsushita back in the late 1970s. VHS camcorders are low-priced but bulky, and have fallen from popularity of late. VHS also delivers the lowest-possible resolution of all camcorder formats, with just 240 lines of horizontal resolution at its fastest recording speed—and 200-line resolution at the slowest speed. (Compare this resolution to the 330 lines available with normal broadcast television, and you can see why VHS is less than acceptable for most videophiles.)

VHS-C is a variation of the basic VHS format, delivering the same resolution but on a more compact videocassette. VHS-C cassettes typically provide 20 minutes or so of recording time, whereas standard VHS cassettes can deliver either two or six hours of recording, depending on the speed selected. VHS-C cassettes can be played on traditional VHS decks, via the use of a special adapter casing.

In the late 1980s, an attempt was made to upgrade the VHS format with better recording quality. The resulting Super VHS (SVHS) format uses a special tape formulation (and enhanced equalization in the VCR itself) to deliver 400 lines of resolution. If, for whatever reason, you feel bound to the VHS format, at least opt for a model with SVHS capability. The difference is easily visible.

Whereas the early camcorders were large and bulky (many were so big that they came with shoulder rests!), in the 1990s the trend was toward smaller and lighter units. To achieve the desired size and weight reduction, new recording formats were developed that utilized smaller, narrower tape and smaller cassettes. The first of these compact formats, developed by Sony, was the 8mm format. This format utilized tape that was only 8mm wide (hence the name), compared to the ½-inch-wide VHS tape. Because of its 2.5- or 5-hour recording capability (depending on recording speed) on a very small cassette, 8mm is the most-used camcorder format today—even though its picture quality, at 240 lines of resolution, is roughly equivalent to that of standard VHS.

Just as SVHS improved the picture quality of the standard VHS format, Sony's Hi8 improves the picture quality of the 8mm format—while using the same size cassettes. Utilizing a different tape formation, Hi8 can deliver 400 lines of horizontal resolution—roughly equivalent to SVHS quality. The differences in resolution are illustrated in Figure 26.4.

FIGURE 26.4

Comparing video resolution

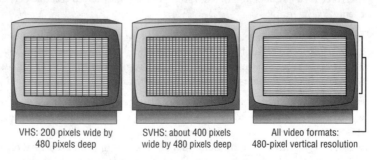

VHS: 200 pixels wide by 480 pixels deep

SVHS: about 400 pixels wide by 480 pixels deep

All video formats: 480-pixel vertical resolution

All of these older recording formats record video information in analog format. The newest formats, however, record video information digitally—thus delivering even higher-quality pictures, and interfacing quite well with the digital editing capabilities of today's personal computers. In fact, since digital copies are identical to digital originals, digital recording formats are the formats of choice for videophiles serious about taking advantage of their computers' video-editing capabilities.

The first of these new digital recording formats is Digital8, which delivers 500 lines of resolution along with true digital stereo sound. These recorders are more expensive than traditional analog recorders (in the $1000 range, although bargains can be found), and record (digitally, of course) on standard Digital8 and Hi8 cassettes. While this media compatibility is convenient (and makes for a relatively low cost per minute), digital recording puts twice as much information on the tape as does analog recording, effectively cutting the storage capacity of each tape in half.

LINES VERSUS PIXELS

When it comes to resolution, videophiles speak a different language than do computer geeks—so it's a little difficult to compare television-based measurements (which are based on "lines") with computer-based measurements (which are based on individual pixels).

First of all, traditional video formats—whether broadcast, VHS, SVHS, Hi8, DVD, or whatever—all share the same vertical resolution, 480 visible pixels from top to bottom. The TV paints 480 horizontal lines as its electron beam travels from the top of the screen to the bottom of the screen. (Actually, it paints 525 lines, but some of them get lost in TV overhead, making 480 the best number you can get for vertical resolution.)

The difference in video products is, as you saw in Figure 26.4, *horizontal* resolution. No one *ever* quotes vertical resolution because everything shows 480 lines top to bottom, at least in theory. But everyone quotes *horizontal* resolution. Horizontal resolution is defined something like this: if I were to point a camera at a piece of paper with a bunch of parallel vertical lines on it, how many of those lines could I fit on a screen before they blurred into each other?

The lowest answer to that question is VHS, which (at the fastest SP speed) delivers about 240 lines. Therefore, VHS (and 8mm) resolution, in computer terms, is about 240 pixels wide by 480 pixels deep. SVHS and Hi8 are about 400 × 480. The two current digital recording formats, Digital8 and MiniDV, are about 500 × 480. (In contrast, broadcast video is about 330 × 480 in resolution.)

As you'll see later in this chapter, the different types of video interfaces are designed for different levels of resolution, as well. The traditional composite interface can support about 240 × 480, and the Y/C (S-Video) interface is near 400 × 480 in resolution. Component video can deliver, at a minimum, 500 × 480—and, theoretically, more.

If you want something else to chew on, note that the 480 (actually 525, remember) top-to-bottom maximum measurement applies to traditional television signals only. The new HDTV digital TV format (actually several related standards) maxes out at either 720 lines (progressively scanned) or 1080 lines (interlaced). Horizontal resolution in the HDTV format is much improved, as well.

(Since I'm virtually certain that I'm going to get letters on this, I ask that the video experts in the audience please note: no one in the video industry publishes vertical by horizontal pixel equivalents, at least not ones that can be tested and agreed upon as standard. I spoke to four people who were all undoubtedly experts on video, and got different resolutions—sometimes *very* different resolutions—from each. Please don't write to tell me that I'm all wrong unless you've got a repeatable, definitive reference for your resolutions.)

The highest-quality consumer recording format today is MiniDV. This format records digitally on ultra-compact cassettes, delivers 500+ lines of resolution, and has a more accurate and color-rich picture than any other format. Many MiniDV camcorders include a host of computerized editing features, which you may or may not need if you'll be doing all your editing on your PC.

NOTE *Even though Digital8 and MiniDV are both digital recording formats, they should not be confused with digital broadcast formats, especially the new HDTV (High Definition Television) format. HDTV is a broadcast standard with a much sharper picture (more pixels, both horizontally and vertically) and a wider 16:9 aspect ratio. JVC and Matsushita have developed a digital recording format (dubbed Digital VHS, or DVHS) specifically for recording HDTV broadcasts. As I write this, DVHS recorders are not widely available, nor have any DVHS camcorders been announced.*

What are the differences between digital versus analog recording formats? The most significant difference between a digital and an analog camcorder, at least for the consumer, is that the digital camcorder captures the analog video from the camera, digitizes it, compresses it, and stores it as a digital computer file on the tape, whereas an analog camcorder records only the analog video on tape. In the case of the digital camcorder, the video file can be transferred directly to the computer's hard drive without any further capturing and compression process. In the analog system, the analog video collected by the camera and stored on tape still needs to be captured, digitized, compressed, and stored on the computer's hard drive.

In digital camcorders, much of the concern I discuss later about loss of quality in generational copying is not an issue. For that reason, the best possible formats for digital video editing are the two digital formats—Digital8 and MiniDV. If you *must* capture to analog tape, use SVHS or Hi8. Standard VHS or 8mm formats should be used only if no other options are available.

PC CAMS

Another inexpensive alternative to using a camcorder for video capture is the PC cam (short for PC camera). These devices are small, but fully functional, video cameras that plug into the computer's USB or parallel port, or into proprietary interface boards. They are designed to be used for video capture as well as to serve as live video sources for Web-based conferencing, e-mail video attachments, and other links to the Internet. These cameras range from $50 to $250 and all seem to deliver a similar quality. The results will not be adequate for serious video production but are fine for occasional use, as a video source for a Web cam, or for video conferencing as designed. PC cams usually don't have microphones, and if they do they are of poor quality. If you are capturing audio with video, you will need to provide an external microphone attached to the audio circuits of your computer.

Popular PC cams are the Intel PC Camera, Logitech QuickCam (either Express or Pro), Xirlink IBM PC Camera Pro Max, and 3Com HomeConnect. All are available in USB and parallel versions. The USB versions are much simpler to install and seem to have fewer conflicts with other hardware and software installed on the computer.

NOTE *A Web cam is a PC cam that is linked to a Web page to provide continuous streaming video via the Internet. Web cams (such as the almost legendary JenniCam, at* `www.jennicam.com`*) are used for fun, promotion, and security. Web cams generally use a PC cam device for the video source and utilize streaming video software (such as RealVideo) to establish the Web page component. Instructions for creating and maintaining a Web cam can be obtained from* `www.realaudio.com` *and other sources on the Internet.*

VCRs

A stand-alone videocassette recorder (VCR) is just like the recorder section of a camcorder—but in a set-top unit, without a camera attached. Most home VCRs are in the VHS format, with a few high-end models capable of SVHS recording and playback. There are few, if any, home VCRs utilizing any of the 8mm or digital formats.

Naturally, you can use your home VCR as a video source for your desktop video system. However, you'll be limited to the relatively low quality of VHS recordings, which will be readily apparent if this source material is mixed with footage from a higher-quality source.

If you do use a VCR as a video source, use the highest-quality connections available. For standard VHS decks, this means using the composite video jacks (labeled "video"); if you have an SVHS deck, use the S-Video connection.

DVD PLAYERS/DRIVES

You would think that DVDs would provide excellent source material for your desktop video system—and you'd be right, to a point. Horizontal resolution for DVD can approach 500 lines, with excellent color reproduction and low video noise, especially when using S-Video or composite video connections. (Equally superb picture quality is obtained when playing DVD movies on a computer's DVD-ROM drive.) So capturing video from a DVD *should* provide extremely high-quality material for your next video masterpiece.

The problem with capturing video from DVDs is that most commercial DVDs include one or more copy protection schemes, to inhibit illegal copying. The big movie studios are particularly concerned about prohibiting exact digital copies of their most popular movies, and have insisted that DVD hardware and software manufacturers provide measures that effectively prohibit this type of video piracy.

The first copy protection scheme employed on most consumer DVD players is the Analog Protection System (APS) developed by Macrovision. This system adds a rapidly modulated colorburst signal, along with pulses in the video blanking signal, to the composite and S-Video outputs of the DVD player. Thus, if you try to dub an analog copy from your DVD player to your VCR, the VCR's synchronization and automatic recording level circuitry will get confused, resulting in a distorted picture, color stripes, rolling, dark/light cycling, and other effects that make the picture totally unwatchable.

In addition to the APS scheme employed in DVD players, each DVD disc includes a serial Copy Generation Management System (CGMS) designed to prevent copies, or copies of copies. The CGMS information is embedded in the outgoing video signal, and tells the next device in line whether the information on the disc can be copied. If the disc is locked from copying, you'll see a message on-screen along the lines of `recording inhibited`.

As if all these measures weren't enough, a further copy protection requirement, called the Content Scrambling System (CSS) was written into the DVD standard. CSS is a data encryption and authentication scheme designed to prevent copying digital video files directly from a DVD. Data on the disc is encrypted with a special key; the same key must be present in the DVD player or drive to decrypt the file and allow normal viewing.

While all these copy protection schemes are optional, most commercial DVDs from major film and video studios utilize one or more of these methods to discourage piracy of their copyrighted content. The result is that it may be difficult, if not impossible, to feed a usable signal from your DVD player or DVD-ROM drive to your video-editing software. While cracks to the encryption code can be found on the Internet, these cracks are, of course, illegal—and you probably don't want to be engaging in illegal activities. You'll have to be content with simply watching your DVDs and not copying them.

WARNING   *Depending on the type of software decoder in your PC, you may not even be able to capture still frames from movies played in your DVD-ROM drive. Some decoder cards utilize a video overlay technique called colorkey to selectively replace a specified pixel color on your monitor with a pixel from the video source (DVD player/drive). Since this process appears downstream from your computer's video memory, when you try to take a screen shot, all you'll get is a solid square of the colorkey color. If this is an issue for you, you may want to switch to a software decoder that writes to normal video memory, or utilize a DVD player application (such as PowerDVD or the DVD player in Windows Me) that includes its own screen-shot capabilities.*

BROADCAST VIDEO

Programming from broadcast, cable, or satellite television can also be used as source material for your desktop video studio. If you want to record broadcast or cable video, you'll need to feed the signal through a tuner into one of the analog input jacks on your video capture card. (Some capture cards have RF inputs, but most don't, so you may need to feed through a VCR to utilize the composite video interface.) You can also install a TV tuner card in your PC and feed that signal internally to your editing software. Some video capture cards (such as the Matrox Marvel) even include a built-in TV tuner, which greatly simplifies this operation.

   Recording video from a direct broadcast satellite (DBS) system is easier, since most DBS receivers include both composite and S-Video outputs. Simply connect the highest-quality available output (normally S-Video) on your DBS receiver to the matching input on your video capture card, and you should be set.

NOTE   *Although the video on a DBS system is broadcast digitally, it is processed and output in an analog format. So even though it's a digital satellite, it's still an analog video signal—albeit with 425 or so lines of horizontal resolution, which is a good 25 percent better than standard broadcast television.*

DIGITAL STILL CAMERAS

You might not think of this, but the signal from a digital still camera can also be used as a source for your video-editing system. Many digital still cameras also have the capability to record short video movies, or to stay "on" continuously to function as a PC cam. In addition, interspersing still photos (downloaded from your digital camera) with video footage can make for an interesting approach to home movies and other video projects.

The Connection

After you've decided on the video source(s) for your next masterpiece, you need to connect that source to your computer. This should be a simple procedure, but there are several important options you need to consider.

THE VIDEO INTERFACE

Video input devices tend to have one or more of the following types of outputs:

◆ Some camcorders and all VCRs have a *radio frequency (RF)* output, the kind that goes directly into a television's antenna connection. Your video capture equipment probably won't support this interface, and because the image quality is very low, you wouldn't want it in any case.

◆ Most camcorders and VCRs have an interface known as a *composite video* interface. (This is normally labeled simply as "video.") It's one of two common interfaces on a video capture board—and is the minimum quality interface that you'd use to connect a video source (a camcorder or a VCR) to your PC.

◆ As I mentioned earlier, better-quality consumer camcorders and VCRs (as well as DVD players, DSS receivers, and other higher-end video components) have an output labeled *S-Video*—also known as an SVHS or Y/C interface. Given the choice, S-Video is preferred to composite video or RF when interfacing between a video source and a capture board.

◆ Some high-end video equipment types (typically *not* camcorders) utilize a *component video* interface—also known as a Y, Pr, Pb interface. Component video not only splits the luminance (brightness, or Y) and chrominance (color, or C) signals, it also breaks the chrominance information into its two main color difference signals (Pr, or red, and Pb, or blue). Component video delivers extremely high-quality video signals, with improved color accuracy and reduced color bleeding.

◆ If you have a digital input device (such as a Digital8 or MiniDV camcorder), the device will most likely have an *IEEE 1394/FireWire* interface. A FireWire connection is a digital connection, and it is ideal for transferring digital video between your video source and your computer. In essence, a FireWire connection transfers files from the video source to your hard drive, and back—which eliminates image quality loss and many of the other problems discussed below.

To understand these interfaces in detail, it helps to understand a bit about how video information gets shuttled around in the video and TV world—which is what I'll cover next.

From Black-and-White to Color

Before getting any further into this, let me warn you: understanding video interfaces is a bit difficult because the video industry "just growed that way." If the video business were starting out now, every piece of video equipment would probably use the simple, intuitive RGB (for red, green, and blue) interface. Like the muddle of extended, expanded, and conventional memory, no one planned this—it just turned out this way.

In addition, the technospeak of the video industry is different from the technospeak of the computer industry—and there are even differences between industrial and consumer video technospeak. So bear with me as I try to make some sense out of all the conflicting jargons and standards.

As you know, video didn't start out with *color* transmission; the first TVs were black-and-white, or monochrome. Actually, neither term is really correct; it's better to describe colorless video images as *grayscale*. In grayscale, video images are represented as pixels, as in color video, except each pixel can assume only a shade of gray. But what is "gray"? Technically, gray is any color created by mixing equal amounts of red, green, and blue light. Zero red, green, and blue yields black; full intensity red, green, and blue yields bright white. Varying intensities in between create lighter or darker grays. Although we're used to a world of color, we can easily interpret grayscale images; we do it whenever we see a black-and-white TV show or movie, or most pictures in newspapers. The combinations of red, green, and blue that produce some various shades of gray are illustrated in Figure 26.5.

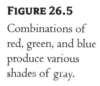

FIGURE 26.5

Combinations of red, green, and blue produce various shades of gray.

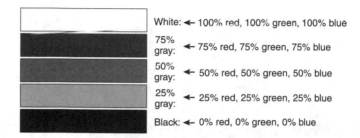

White: ← 100% red, 100% green, 100% blue

75% gray: ← 75% red, 75% green, 75% blue

50% gray: ← 50% red, 50% green, 50% blue

25% gray: ← 25% red, 25% green, 25% blue

Black: ← 0% red, 0% green, 0% blue

The original video equipment and TV broadcast equipment was designed in the grayscale-only days for grayscale-only signals. Basically, black-and-white TV signals consist of a series of information about the intensity of each pixel on the TV screen, information that tells the TV how much to light up each part of the screen, producing black-and-white images. A whole industry grew up in the '50s around grayscale TV: TV networks and studios invested millions of dollars in equipment that they obviously wouldn't want to see become obsolete. Millions of households invested hundreds of millions of dollars in TV sets that they wouldn't want to see become obsolete.

Which is why the advent of color TV in the 1950s posed a problem.

You see, everybody *wanted* color TV. Colorful pictures are more interesting than grayscale pictures to look at. But nobody wanted a new color system that would make the existing black-and-white TVs obsolete. NBC couldn't just say, "As of 1 January 1953, we're going to stop broadcasting old-style black-and-white signals and start broadcasting the new color signals. Now, the color signals won't work with your old TVs, so it's just too bad for all of you who've faithfully watched our network all this time—you'll have to go out and buy a new, expensive, color TV."

So the broadcast companies devised a method for transmitting color signals whereby the old grayscale signal still got transmitted, but with a separate color portion added. Old black-and-white TVs wouldn't look for the color information, and so they would still work fine, displaying grayscale images. But color TVs would know to look for that extra color information and display it. As the color information got pasted on the back of the existing grayscale signal, there wasn't much room for the color information. As a result, NTSC color video isn't of a very high quality. That's why the television industry recently adopted the new HDTV standard—which delivers more accurate color information and a higher-resolution picture than the current NTSC standard.

NOTE *NTSC stands for National Television System Committee. It's the North American standard video interface format for broadcast color TV and was developed in 1953 (an earlier black-and-white version of the NTSC standard was established in 1941).*

As I've said, color signals all boil down to three simple, or *primary*, colors: red, green, and blue. You can describe any color as a combination of those three colors, as you can see in Figure 26.6.

FIGURE 26.6

Primary colors combine to form other colors.

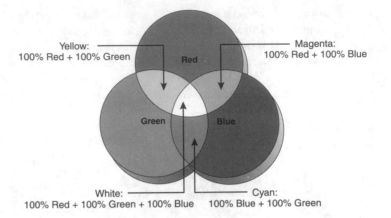

Yellow:
100% Red + 100% Green

Magenta:
100% Red + 100% Blue

Red

Green   Blue

White:
100% Red + 100% Green + 100% Blue

Cyan:
100% Blue + 100% Green

Basically, color video cameras record pictures by breaking down a picture into a grid of dots called *picture elements*, or *pixels*. The camera senses the degree of red intensity, green intensity, and blue intensity of each pixel, transmitting that information to the recording equipment (the VCR, tape deck, or whatever). Figure 26.7 illustrates how this works.

FIGURE 26.7

The camera records pictures as an array of pixels containing red, green, and blue color information.

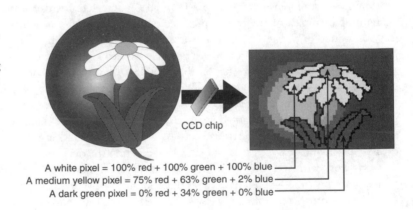

CCD chip

A white pixel = 100% red + 100% green + 100% blue
A medium yellow pixel = 75% red + 63% green + 2% blue
A dark green pixel = 0% red + 34% green + 0% blue

The color television signal, then, starts off with these three pieces of information: its red value, its green value, and its blue value. Each of those values is measured in *lumens*, a measure akin in some ways to voltage; it actually measures the number of photons striking some small area. Black-and-white TV equipment converts the red, green, and blue values to a single grayscale value called the *luminance* of the pixel, or the Y value. (Y isn't an abbreviation of any word, it comes from a 1930s color model that described colors in terms of a set of X, Y, and Z axes, rather than red/green/blue.) The formula used to create the grayscale pixel (depicted graphically in Figure 26.8) looks like the following:

Luminance of the grayscale pixel (Y of a video signal) =

$0.59 \times$ (luminance of green, or G) +

$0.11 \times$ (luminance of blue, or B) +

$0.30 \times$ (luminance of red, or R)

FIGURE 26.8

Formula used to
create the grayscale
pixel

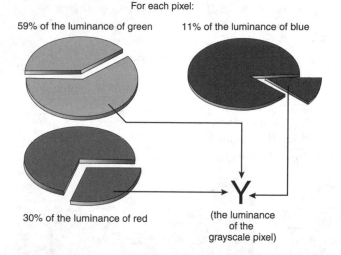

For each pixel:

59% of the luminance of green

11% of the luminance of blue

30% of the luminance of red

Y

(the luminance
of the
grayscale pixel)

You see that Y can be derived arithmetically from R, G, and B. Notice that green has the highest coefficient, 0.59—nearly 60 percent of the colors that you see depend on green!

Of course, no one knows exactly *why* we see green so well, but one theory works something like this: Most animals *lack* color vision, and see only in grayscale. Millions of years ago, however, our many-times-removed ancestors lived in trees as pre-primate, lemurlike creatures. Living in the green, leafy canopy of a jungle means having to detect predators who attempt to mimic the colors of the jungle, like the green of a tree-living python or the shadow-like stripes of a tiger. There are two ways to detect predators: by their movement and by color sense. Most animals detect other animals by motion. Our ancestors added a remarkable ability to see extremely fine differences in color, like the few-wavelengths difference in color between a green snake and the leaves that it hid in. Since a lot of their world was the green of leaves, green played a disproportionate role in their color sense, as it does today to *our* color sense. Notice also that you're most insensitive to blue; that's one reason why many people find blue to be a calming color. Looking at blues doesn't excite the optic nerve as much, which means that the ancient parts of our brains that are still looking out for predators can rest for a while.

Despite the fact that luminance contains red, green, and blue, it's not possible to deduce the original amount of red, green, and blue from a given luminance, any more than it's possible for me to ask you, "If I made $50,000 this year, some from consulting and some from writing, then how much did I make from consulting, and how much did I make from writing?" I haven't given you enough information to deduce the answer to my question. If you just transmit the luminance information, you haven't sent enough information to allow a color TV to reconstruct the R, G, and B.

But suppose I rephrase the question this way:

"I made $50,000 dollars last year from consulting and writing. I made half of my income from consulting and half from writing. How much money did I make from consulting, and how much from writing?" You see, I asked you to derive two values—consulting income and writing income. But when I gave you only one piece of information—the sum of both incomes—I didn't give you enough information to compute the separate income amounts. When I added the second piece of information, however—the ratio of the two incomes—you had enough information to solve the problem. So, to solve for two values, you need two pieces of information.

In the same way, the color-TV engineers knew that black-and-white TV was already using Y, so they wanted color TVs to *continue* to use Y (so that they'd be backward compatible with black-and-white signals). Y is derived from R, G, and B, but Y is only one piece of information. They'd need to add two more pieces of information onto the TV signal in order for a color TV to be able to reassemble the R, G, and B information.

Here's where it gets ugly: they decided to create two more signals composed of R, G, and B, but, unlike luminance, these two new signals, named I and Q, really don't correspond to anything in our experience. (Remember that Y corresponds to the grayscale part of the picture, the part you'd see if you turned down the color adjustment knob on your color TV set). For the curious, the formulas for I and Q are illustrated in Figure 26.9.

FIGURE 26.9

Computing values for I and Q

$$I = [0.74 \times (R-Y)] - [0.27 \times (B-Y)]$$

$$Q = [0.48 \times (R-Y)] + [0.41 \times (B-Y)]$$

The I and Q signals are blended so that they can be easily broken apart with a technique called *Quadrature Amplitude Modulation (QAM)*. The entire process of QAM is a bit complex, but you'll get the idea of how it works if you think of it this way: with QAM, you start with a baseline signal called a *carrier wave*. Like all waves, it has an *amplitude*, a *frequency*, and a *phase*. QAM modifies the carrier wave's amplitude to match the I signal, and changes the carrier's phase to store the Q value. Phase and amplitude are different characteristics of a wave, like the height and weight of a person, so they can be modified somewhat independently of each other. The combined I/Q signal is called *chrominance* (color), which is usually abbreviated C.

So, to sum up where you've gotten so far: R, G, and B don't get transmitted as R, G, and B, because luminance, or Y transmission, has been central to television broadcasting since TV was invented. Color television tiptoes around the limits of Y-based black-and-white transmission by creating separate I and Q signals, then combining them with the Y signal in such a way that they're separable by the receiving TV. The combined Y, I, and Q signal is the composite video signal illustrated in Figure 26.10.

Those composite signals are then converted into broadcast TV waves, where they are received by TVs, both color and black-and-white. Black-and-white TVs don't know to look for I and Q, so they see only Y, and are happy. Color TVs separate out (decode) Y, I, and Q; convert them to R, G, and B; and then display color on their screens.

FIGURE 26.10

The composite video signal

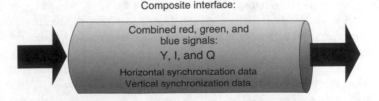

Composite interface:

Combined red, green, and blue signals:

Y, I, and Q

Horizontal synchronization data
Vertical synchronization data

Composite, S-Video, and Component Interfaces

Now let's see how all this technical theory is applied to consumer video equipment, in the form of different interfaces for different type of signals.

All video interfaces fall into one of two types: *component* (with separate connections for each color) or *composite* (which blends the red, green, and blue signals into a single signal). The two are contrasted in Figure 26.11.

FIGURE 26.11

Component versus composite video interfaces

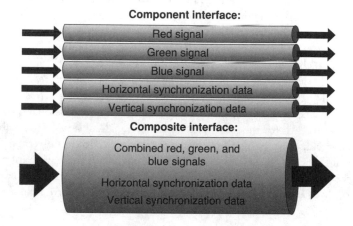

Component interface:
- Red signal
- Green signal
- Blue signal
- Horizontal synchronization data
- Vertical synchronization data

Composite interface:
- Combined red, green, and blue signals
- Horizontal synchronization data
- Vertical synchronization data

If you have the choice, a component interface is preferable, because keeping the color signals separate allows higher-quality signal transmission. Composite video, on the other hand, is cheaper to build hardware-wise, and so most consumer-grade video equipment in North America supports some type of composite interface. (Note that there are several types of composite video interfaces, only one of which is typically labeled "composite.")

The lowest-quality composite-type signal is the RF (for radio frequency) signal. RF combines all the video information (the Y, I, and Q) *plus* the program's audio information, and feeds it down one very cluttered pipe. This signal is broadcast over the airwaves (or piped through a cable system), and then interfaces with your television's tuner via an RF input, typically a coaxial cable connection. The RF signal is definitely the messiest of all possible interfaces: not only is it composite in nature, but it also has been modulated onto a radio frequency carrier, adding even more noise. Few video capture boards accept RF signals, although the TV tuner boards that allow you to view television in a window on your PC screen have RF inputs.

A better-quality composite signal is one that combines the Y, I, and Q values but does not incorporate audio (and is not modulated onto an RF carrier). This type of composite video interface uses a standard RCA connector and is typically labeled "video," "composite," or "NTSC." Although a composite interface delivers better results than an RF interface, separating the pieces and parts of a composite signal isn't a perfect process—and is not the preferred type of interface for either high-resolution picture reproduction or detailed video-editing work.

An even better video interface—not called composite, although still composite in nature—is the S-Video, or Y/C, interface. (This interface was once known as SVHS, for Super VHS, but that nomenclature has been dropped in favor of the less-confusing—and more universal—S-Video.)

Now you're in a better position to understand why it's called that: there are separate wires in the cable for the luminance (Y) signal and the chrominance (C) signal. This type of connection provides for a demonstrably sharper picture than what can be obtained from a composite video connection.

The best possible video interface, however, is a component interface. (Don't confuse component with composite—they're spelled similarly, but fall on opposite ends of the quality spectrum.) The Y, Pb, Pr interface (sometimes represented as Y, B-Y, R-Y) separates the video signal into three components, similar to the YIQ format. In this format, Y is the luminance signal and Pb and Pr are color difference signals, roughly representing the red and blue components of the signal (from which all other colors can be determined).

Video capture boards may store the capture data as Y, Pb, and Pr data rather than R, G, and B data—and typically have inputs labeled either Y, Pb, Pr or Y, B-Y, R-Y. High-end video components—including some DVD players—also utilize this type of component interface.

Moving beyond consumer equipment into the world of professional video, pro-quality video cameras connect to videocassette recorders of similar professional quality via an interface with *five* cables—one each for the red, green, and blue signals, and two more cables for synchronizing the signal. (Ever adjusted the Vertical Hold or Horizontal Hold knobs on a TV? That's what those cables transmit: vertical synchronization and horizontal synchronization information.) This type of five-connector component interface (some would call this the only pure component interface) would obviously be overkill for consumer-grade equipment, so you're unlikely to run into it—unless you happen across some pro equipment at some point.

NOTE   *The computer industry typically uses a variation of the Red Green Blue (RGB) component interface to connect video monitors to PC video cards. Not only do they have the common 15-pin VGA D-shell connector, they may also have five BNC connectors for the RGB component interface found in pro-grade video equipment.*

IEEE 1394/FireWire

If all this talk of component and composite and RGB confuses you, there is a simpler—and more efficient—interface available. The FireWire interface (also called an IEEE 1394 interface, after the standard-setting body that adopted it) is the fastest and most accurate way to transmit digital video signals from one device to another.

A FireWire connection doesn't transmit video signals per se—or at least doesn't transmit them in any type of traditional red, blue, and green format. Instead, FireWire is a high-speed connection for digital data, capable of transferring data at a sustained rate of 12.5MBps. By using FireWire, you can create video dubs with no generation loss whatsoever; all you're transferring are 1s and 0s, not a complex analog signal.

The full IEEE 1394 specification includes frame-accurate device control and the capability to read and write digital video, and thus is ideal as an interface to digital video recorders. Although not all Digital8 and MiniDV camcorders utilize a FireWire interface, most do.

IEEE 1394 was intended to make it easy to connect a wide variety of digital devices without the need for a central controller—typically a proprietary board plugged into the bus. It can be used not only for video transfer, but also as a high-speed connection for multimedia of all sorts, including digital still cameras. While there was initially talk of using IEEE 1394 for many types of connections (including for hard drives!), in reality IEEE 1394 has found its niche as the preferred interface for digital video applications.

NOTE *There are some slight variances in IEEE 1394 implementation. Technically, only Apple's version of the IEEE 1394 standard is called FireWire. However, there is no practical difference between generic IEEE 1394 and FireWire, and because of Apple's marketing program, FireWire has become the default name for the interface. Sony also has a marketing version of IEEE 1394 called iLink, and it is also compatible with other 1394 and FireWire products.*

Before FireWire, you had to use a component video, S-Video, or composite video connection to transfer video information in real time. With FireWire, that same information is transferred digitally—in a fraction of the time, and with no signal loss. The bottom line is simple: if your equipment has a FireWire connection, use it!

THE AUDIO INTERFACE

If you want to capture audio with your videos (and, unless you're making silent movies, you do), you'll discover that most video capture boards do not capture sound. Instead, you'll have to have a PC sound card of some kind—and you'll probably have to hook up the audio outputs from your video device to the audio inputs on your sound card. When transferring digital video, the audio tracks are already contained in the DV file and need not be captured separately and reintegrated into the computer file as they do in analog capture.

CABLES

Just one piece of advice: get good ones. The skinny composite or S-Video cables that come with most VCRs or camcorders can't provide the noise resistance that a third-party cable such as a Monster cable can. (Monster is the company that makes what are probably the best audio and video cables; you can find their stuff in higher-end electronics stores.)

For most applications, you'll be choosing from either composite ("video") cables or Y/C (S-Video) cables. They look like the ones in Figure 26.12.

FIGURE 26.12

Video cables

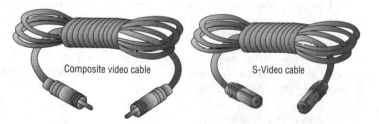

Composite video cable   S-Video cable

Even if you don't buy the really high-priced cables, buy *some* third-party cable. The cables that ship with video boards are usually of minimum quality, and even a place like Radio Shack can sell you a better cable.

In addition, the shorter the cable, the smaller the signal loss—so keep your cables as short as possible.

When selecting a FireWire cable for your systems, you should note that two types of connectors may be present on your digital equipment. Some connectors have four pins, and some have six pins. The result is the same, but in order to connect the cable to the device, you must have the proper number of pins on the connector. The cables come in four-pin-to-four-pin, four-pin-to-six-pin, and six-pin-to-six-pin. Check your devices before purchasing cables!

The Capture Board

The thing that makes your PC able to accept and record moving video is the video capture board. There are two fundamental types of capture boards: digital and analog.

The dominant trend today is toward full digital video capture and editing. In a completely digital system, you capture video directly onto digital videotape (via a Digital8 or MiniDV camcorder), transfer the video signal (digitally) to your PC via a FireWire connection, edit your video (digitally) via desktop video-editing software, and then transfer the results (again, digitally) back to your digital recorder via the FireWire interface. In this ideal system, you don't have to worry about any analog video capture at all.

In the real world, however, you probably still need some type of analog video capture capability. There are many reasons for this: you might not have a digital camcorder (there are lots of VHS, 8mm, and Hi-8 camcorders still being sold—and many more older models still in use); you may want to include video from other, nondigital sources (including standard VHS VCRs and DVD players); and you may want to output your results to VHS tape or to an external DVD burner. For these reasons, this section will cover both digital and analog video interfaces.

Before buying either type of board, of course, make sure that the capture board can capture *moving* video. A few video capture boards out there in the sub-$100 price range sound like a good deal, but they capture only stills.

Do stills sound like all that you need? Then these boards are *still* (no pun intended) not a good deal. Unless your image is totally still, then your capture gets a visual side effect that makes it look like you're viewing the image through venetian blinds.

CONSUMER VERSUS PRO

With all-digital video-editing systems becoming more affordable and offering near-broadcast quality results, where do you draw the line between professional and consumer video? Quite frankly, the output from a DV system (especially when utilizing a MiniDV camcorder as the source) *is* broadcast quality. So why don't the pros use the lower-cost consumer hardware and software for their work?

The biggest difference between consumer and pro video is speed. Professional video-editing systems are capable of rendering video in real time, while consumer products don't have the processing horsepower to do so. Instead, you edit your file (nonlinearly, of course) and then have your video-editing software batch-process your edits into a usable final file. In the professional world, you can edit while you're shooting—and the results are processed simultaneously. All that processing power costs money, however, which is why the pro gear is priced as it is.

Another difference between the consumer and pro worlds is reliability. Pro video systems are purpose-built to do one thing, and one thing well. Consumer video systems must share the hardware and peripherals of your computer system with lots of other applications, and thus aren't as bulletproof as the systems the pros use.

Bottom line, you can build a high-quality consumer video system for under $5000, while a pro video system will cost 10 times that. I think that makes consumer desktop video a terrific bargain—especially since the end result is pro-level quality.

DIGITAL INTERFACE BOARDS AND CONNECTIONS

The primary digital video interface that is used on consumer digital video and computer equipment is the IEEE 1394/FireWire connection. Since IEEE 1394/FireWire connectors are now standard equipment in even low-cost computers, both desktop and laptop, no additional hardware is required to transfer digital video from a digital camcorder to your computer. If your computer does not have a FireWire connection, you can add FireWire connectivity via a PCI board or, on a laptop, via a PC Card (PCMCIA card). This add-on FireWire connection can cost as little as $100 and include driver and video transfer software utilities.

If your desktop video is likely to include a mix of digital and analog inputs and outputs (input from a digital camcorder and output to VHS, for example), then you should consider a capture card that combines FireWire and analog interfaces. Examples of this type of hybrid digital/analog board are the Pinnacle Studio Deluxe and DC1000 integrated digital and analog capture/transfer cards, both from Pinnacle Systems (`www.pinnaclesys.com`).

NOTE   Don't confuse video capture boards with television tuner boards. The former captures video images from a variety of sources; the latter enables your PC to receive and display broadcast television signals (via a TV tuner built into the card) and typically has no capture capability. You can, however, use the signal from a TV tuner board as an input to your video capture software, and capture television programming in that fashion. (Which means, of course, that you can have both a video capture card and a TV tuner card in the same PC—along with your normal video card, of course!)

ANALOG CAPTURE SYSTEMS

Analog video boards differ from one another in a few ways:

◆   Some video boards support *overlay*, a feature whereby you can see video displayed in real time in a window on your computer.

◆   Most video boards support some kind of onboard real-time compression hardware. The exact method for doing that compression varies, leading to more- or less-effective compression options.

◆   Some video boards can't save moving video and are capable of grabbing only still pictures.

◆   Most video boards have both a composite and a Y/C connector—but be sure that whatever board you buy has a Y/C connector.

As always, a faster board requires a faster bus interface. Of the factors that I just mentioned, let's get the important ones out of the way.

Analog capture systems include boards that plug into a computer's bus, devices that plug into parallel, USB, and PCMCIA connectors. The boards have the fastest transfer rates and will allow the highest-quality capture with the least problems. There are, however, several very good systems that are external. The best example is the Dazzle Digital Video Creator device manufactured by Dazzle Multimedia (`www.dazzle.com`), and that comes in a USB version. This system captures MPEG2 compressed video that can be edited and transferred back to tape, used on CD-ROM or hard drive, or delivered on the Internet at a very good quality. In general, analog capture boards confront many issues not present in digital video transfer. These are considered in the subsequent sections.

Real-Time Compression Features

Compression is extremely important to video work. Even though a 320 × 240 window is pretty small, even at 15 frames per second (fps) this size picture produces about 3.5MBps of data in a completely raw format. Shove that much data down most hard disks' throats, and you'll end up with a lot of lost data. Although you *can* capture data to RAM, which is faster than disk by a good bit, most of us can't afford a few gigabytes of RAM with which to capture. How, then, to get high-volume video data onto a relatively low-speed drive? By precrunching the data down to size. Video capture boards do that with onboard compression hardware.

Virtually all video capture boards do some kind of real-time compression as they capture the video data. Most offer the option of a compression technique called YUV9, which is pretty standard, and another technique, which can compress data better, but which is specific to that particular capture board.

The downside of the board-specific, real-time compressor is that while it greatly improves your ability to capture long video sequences, it significantly reduces the video image quality. As I'll explain in an upcoming section, you usually *don't* want to capture data compressed by the video board, as the compression technique causes this degradation of image quality. If you can live with some image degradation, however, then the proprietary real-time compression support on most video capture boards will be useful; again, this will be clearer when I explain captures to memory versus captures to disk.

Overlay or Preview?

Analog video capture boards show you either the actual video signal as it arrives to the capture board, or the image that they're processing. In the first case—an *overlay* is the term—you see a window within your Windows screen (I'll assume that you're using Windows, although there are a few tools around for other operating systems) and full-motion video. In the second case, you see the image that's been processed by the video card, or the *preview* of the captured image.

Previews will always be inferior in quality to overlays, as previews are limited by the color depth of your video board—if your video board shows only 256 colors, then you'll see a 256-color rendering of the 16-million-color image. As I've said before, today's computers and capture boards can't keep up with the 30fps speed of broadcast video signals. Continuing the example of a 256-color video board, the colors will look "muddier" because Windows attempts to take the millions of colors in the incoming image and convert them into combinations of its 256 colors, a process called *dithering*. For example, if you had a video screen that could show *only* red, green, or blue in one intensity—each color was just "on" or "off," instead of capable of varying intensities—then you could fool your eye into seeing yellow by displaying a lot of green pixels interspersed with an equal number of red pixels. That would be a dithered yellow.

It sounds like an overlay board is more desirable than a preview board, but I'd tend to disagree. Overlay boards show you a nice, colorful, smooth picture, but that's usually not the picture that you end up with, so it's not very helpful. Further, overlay boards are more difficult to install.

When I described overlays, you may have wondered just how an overlay board can display 16-million-color video on a Windows desktop with a video driver that supports only 256 colors; sounds too good to be true, eh? Overlay boards accomplish this by modifying the way your video board works. Most every VGA board has an edge or pin-header connector on it called the *feature connector*. An overlay board requires that you run a cable from the feature connector on the VGA to a similar connector on the overlay board, and that you then disconnect the monitor from the video port on the back of the VGA and connect it to a similar-looking connector on the video capture board. This means that now the video capture board can "process" the signals from the VGA board before they get to the monitor. It is the hardware on the video capture board that allows full-motion video and 16 million colors. Essentially, it makes a window on your screen into a TV set. In fact, there are some boards available that are not video capture boards at all, but simply overlay boards. Equipped with an antenna input and tuner circuit, they allow you to watch TV in a window on your Windows desktop.

An odd side effect of the overlay is that the TV part of the window is not under the control of Windows (or whatever operating system is being used); it's just a kind of "hole" that the hardware fills. That means that if you try to capture an overlay window with the Alt+Print Screen or Print Screen key, then you won't get the image. Because the operating system doesn't control that portion of the screen, it cannot capture that part.

The CPU, Bus, and Disk Systems

I hope I've made clear by now that the whole name of the game in both digital and analog video capture is data transfer. There's lots of data to shovel around, and no room for your hardware to stop and "catch its breath," so to speak. That argues for a fast, wide bus.

Add audio capture, and you have an extra problem: now two boards with real-time demands are running simultaneously, throwing interrupts at the CPU, and, again, there's no time for either board to "catch its breath." That argues for bus mastering, so that both boards can transfer data to memory or disk without having to wait for the CPU. It would seem, then, that the optimal bus for video capture would be PCI, offering speed, width, and bus mastering.

The best hard drives to use for capturing video have traditionally been Fast-Wide SCSI hard drives that are audiovisual (AV) rated and can capture that highest-quality video at the lowest compression. In fact, a Fast-Wide SCSI system can capture, in a fast and properly configured computer, uncompressed full-screen video. Today's IDE drives, such as the Ultra ATA-100 7200 RPM models, rival SCSI drives for access speed and sustained data transfer rates.

More important than the peak transfer rate, however, is the drive's *minimum* transfer rate. If the sustained data rate of the hard disk drops below the required transfer rate of the video, the result is a herky-jerky playback, with stuttering audio and video and lots of dropouts and freeze-ups. Given the relative low cost of today's hard drives, spend a little more to ensure the performance you'll need for high-quality desktop video.

TIP   Total system throughput is also essential when dealing with digital video capture and editing. At a minimum, your system must deliver 3.5MBps sustained throughput to create and edit dropout-free video files.

An equally important consideration is the size of the hard drive. One hour of compressed digital video takes up 13GB of disk space. For this reason, you should invest in the largest hard disk you can afford (look in *at least* the 60–80GB range), but get as much as you can afford, and possibly in multiple hard disks. In fact, assigning a dedicated hard drive strictly for video storage is a good idea; this way, the reading and writing of video information to the drive won't be interrupted by standard system processes.

If you're thinking of multiple hard disk drives, consider an external drive with a FireWire interface for fast data throughput. If you're putting together a true pro-level system, you should consider using a RAID (Redundant Array of Independent Disks), which groups two or more drives together for greater storage and improved performance. (Depending on the size and number of disks in the array, a RAID will typically run you a minimum of $1000, on up into the five-figure range.)

DIGITAL VIDEO: SYSTEM REQUIREMENTS

If you're investing in a computer system specifically for desktop digital video editing, here are the minimum requirements to consider:

◆ Pentium 4 running at 1.2GHz or higher.

◆ 256 MB SDRAM (512MB or more recommended)

◆ 60–80GB dedicated hard disk (in addition to a separate hard disk for the rest of your system)

◆ 32MB graphics card

◆ IEEE 1394/FireWire and USB interfaces

Several streaming codecs are being optimized for the Pentium 4 processor, which will provide better playback and faster encoding—up to twice as fast as with similar Pentium III systems. (If you don't know what a codec is, don't worry—I'll explain it a bit later in this chapter.)

Installing a Video Capture Board

Installing a video capture board is just like installing any other board. Most video capture boards come with a software setup routine, and you must pick an I/O address, a hardware interrupt, and sometimes a memory overlay window. Virtually all the current boards and recent computer systems—certainly those that are up to the task of video capture and edit work—are PCI systems with automated installation processes. The next section points out some of the issues involved in manually configured systems.

Before you try to install the board, make sure that you've got a video source around that you can use to test the board. Every video capture board I've ever installed came with a self-test program; run it. The self-test will test for basic interrupt, memory, and I/O address conflicts. Then it will try to display the image coming in from the video source (the camera or the VCR). Now, if you pass the IRQ, I/O address, and memory test, then you still may not see an image. Here are some things to try if that happens:

◆ Check that the cable isn't loose or incorrectly connected. S-Video cables in particular seem to need to be firmly pushed into their sockets.

◆ If the video source is a camera and the screen is black, don't forget that most video cameras will shut themselves off after a while if they're not recording. Perhaps it's better to just run a tape in a VCR as a video source so that you don't have to worry about whether there's a test signal.

◆ Most video capture boards have both composite and S-Video inputs. They automatically figure out which input is active, but sometimes they guess wrong. The video capture software that comes with your board will usually allow you to force the board to use either the composite or the S-Video input.

◆ Even if you pass the I/O address, IRQ, and memory tests, double-check that you don't have a conflict on one of those. You can do this by using the hardware installation diagnostic in Windows.

Once the board is up and running, it's time to try out the video capture software.

Running the Video Capture Software

The point of all your hard work so far was to grab a video. Now let's try it.

Start from a Known Video Source

The best bet for your first time around is to use a fairly good-quality video to practice with. I'd recommend that you hook up a VCR to your video capture board and just continuously run a commercial videotape. It's only VHS quality, granted, but it's going to be correctly color balanced, show decent brightness and contrast, and will serve as a good reference point.

You should be able to see the actual video image on a video monitor in addition to your PC's monitor. Set up the VCR and a TV near the table. Most VCRs have both an antenna output and a composite video output—and Super VHS decks include S-Video outputs, as well. Use the highest-quality interface to connect the unit to the video capture board, and one of the remaining outputs to connect to the TV.

Naturally, as you gain experience with your video production capabilities, you'll want to input higher-quality video than what you can achieve with standard VHS tapes. The best-quality sources, of course, are digital tapes shot with Digital8 or MiniDV camcorders. Hooking up your digital camcorder is a snap; just use the IEEE 1394/FireWire connection to interface the camcorder with your PC, and use the composite or S-Video connection on your camcorder to feed a monitor signal to your television set.

Next, you will look at the capture and transfer process for both digital and analog video.

Digital Video Capture and Transfer

Digital camcorders (both Digital8 and MiniDV) capture video using the hardware-based digital video (DV) codec. This codec uses intra-frame compression to deliver 720×480 resolution at a data rate of 3.5MBps. Since the compression is done in-camera, no further compression is necessary in the transfer or editing processes—and you don't need a separate video capture card in your computer.

Transferring digital video is simple. Using the transfer and editing utilities supplied with your computer, FireWire transfer card, or video device, you copy digital video files in pretty much the same fashion as you copy data files from one hard drive to another. Most video transfer software can even control the operation of your digital recorder for starting, stopping, and fast-forward and reverse. With the cables properly connected and the equipment turned on, you need to use the controls to find the clip that is to be transferred, select a folder on the hard drive to store it, and begin the transferring process. Be sure to read the video transfer software and video device manuals for details of their specific features and processes.

During this copy process, the DV data is stored on your hard disk in either AVI (Windows) or QT (Macintosh) format. Files in either format can be easily edited by any popular digital editing program, such as Adobe Premiere, Sonic Foundry's Vegas Video, or ULead's Media Studio Pro. Windows XP users can capture and perform simple edits with Windows Movie Maker, which is part of the standard Windows XP installation.

After the file has been edited, you can then transfer it back to your digital camcorder; during this process, the AVI or QT file is translated back into standard video and audio, for offline viewing.

As you can see, the whole DV process is fairly simple. You also get the added benefit that the quality of your edited work is identical to that of your original footage. Subsequent copies will look identical, as well, without the degradation in quality (known as *generation loss*) inherent when copying analog tapes.

This is why DV has become so popular—it's both easy and delivers high-quality results! If you can afford a Digital8 or (better yet) a MiniDV camcorder, digital is definitely the way to go.

Analog Video Capture

Now I will cover the basics of the more complex analog capture and compression process—and you'll realize why it might be worth it to upgrade your old camcorder to a new digital model.

USE THE RIGHT VIDEO MODE ON YOUR PC

Before going any further, find a video mode that works well for your capture. You want a low-resolution driver, as high-resolution drivers must keep track of more pixels and so slow down the system. Because video is very colorful, however, you want a 16-million-color driver if possible. The best video mode is probably a 640×480 (or 800×600 on Windows XP) mode with 16 million colors. Whatever your options are, just pick the lowest resolution and then choose the most colors that your board will support.

ADJUST CONTRAST, BRIGHTNESS, AND COLOR

Now that you've got the TV showing you what the video *thinks* that it should look like, run the video capture software on your computer and take a look at the picture in the overlay/preview window. You're likely to see that the colors on the pictures are different from those on the TV. Use the video capture software's Video Source Options command or the like (every program has a different name for it) to adjust brightness, contrast, and colors.

Some systems provide separate slider controls for red, green, and blue. Others offer sliders with labels such as Saturation, Tint, or Hue.

Saturation refers to the purity of the color. Shine a red light on a white wall, and you'll see a red area on the wall. Shine a red light *and* a white light on the wall, and the resulting wall color changes; you'd say that it is "washed out." Adding white light *desaturates* a color. Pure colors are saturated; impure colors are desaturated.

Tint and *hue* are intended to mimic dials and knobs with similar names and functions on a TV set. They're compromises, and (in my opinion) not very good ones. As there are three things to adjust— red, green, and blue intensity—it's obviously impossible to provide all possible red/green/blue combinations on a single dial. Instead, then, these dials enable you to bias the colors between extreme red, extreme green, and anywhere in between. The bad news, then, about these controls is that they don't let you play with the blue setting. But, then, recall that blue is the least important of the three primary video colors.

CHOOSE FRAME SIZE AND FRAME RATE

Next, you'll actually capture some moving images. You must choose frame size and frame rate. You'll usually have frame size options up to 320 × 240 for moving captures and 640 × 480 for still captures. You can set any frame rate.

A 320 × 240 frame of 24-bit color will require 230,400 bytes to store. Using 15 frames per second would provide a raw data rate of 230,400 × 15, or 3,456,000 bytes per second, as I've said before. The relationship between frame size and data rate is illustrated in Figure 26.13.

FIGURE 26.13

Relationship between frame size and data rate

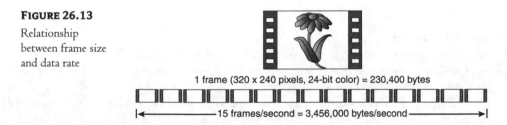

1 frame (320 x 240 pixels, 24-bit color) = 230,400 bytes

|←——————— 15 frames/second = 3,456,000 bytes/second ———————→|

That's a lot of data to shovel around. In contrast, 15 frames of size 160 × 120 at 24-bit color require transferring only 864,000 bytes per second. Assuming you had a high-performance hard disk that could, say, capture data at about 1.7MBps (not unreasonable for today's hard drives), then you'd be able to capture about 30 frames per second straight to disk.

The whole idea of 160 × 120 captures certainly sounds like it'll make your captures easy, and it will, because small frames don't require as much horsepower to record as do large frames. But you can't *see* small frames. My recommendation is that you do whatever is necessary to capture at 320 × 240 resolution, and at least at 15 frames per second. If you want to capture true full-frame full-motion video, however, you'll need to capture at 640 × 480 resolution, at 30 frames per second.

CAPTURE TO DISK

If you capture to disk, you'll have to reduce the flow of video capture data so that you don't overwhelm the maximum speed of the disk interface. You can do that in these ways:

◆ The capture process can't be slowed down by any extra operating system housekeeping. That means that it's much faster to allocate disk space on a defragmented disk drive, so defrag your disk before doing video capture.

◆ As I explained in the previous section, keep the frame rate low; 320 × 240 data at only 5fps produces a raw data rate of about 1.2MBps, which a fast hard disk can keep up with. Again, that's not the frame rate that I *recommend*, but if you must capture to disk, then it's one option.

◆ Again, use a smaller frame size; going from 320 × 240 to 160 × 120 cuts the data flow by a factor of four.

◆ Lower the audio sampling rate: try 16 bits per sample and 22,000 samples per second. If you capture mono instead of stereo, it cuts the audio requirements in half.

◆ Capture data with a compressing codec, so that there's less data to have to store to disk. The downside of this is that the compression technique will lose some of the video capture data; see the upcoming "Which Compression Format/Codec to Use with Capture?" section for more information. Compression is a tradeoff, so different applications will have greater or lesser compression requirements.

◆ The CPU's speed is important as well. An 800MHz processor can capture more data per second than can a 200MHz.

Disk capture imposes limits that you'd rather avoid, but unless you've got lots of RAM, it may be your only option.

CAPTURE TO RAM

In contrast, if you capture to RAM, you won't have to worry about dropping frames until you run out of RAM. You can address that by buying more RAM. Many computers today can accept as much as 512MB or 1GB of RAM or even more. In the final analysis, it is the best way to get captures done.

512MB can capture about four minutes of video data without data loss. Your system will, of course, be different from mine, and the numbers may be way off compared to your experience. Find out early on how much you can capture by just doing captures of different time lengths: try capturing five seconds. When the capture program is done, it will announce how many frames it dropped. Now, hopefully, a five-second capture will show no dropped frames; if it does, then you're probably capturing 640 × 480 moving video, or have very little RAM. Keep upping the length of time of the memory capture until you start dropping frames; you'll then know how long your captures can go.

WHICH COMPRESSION FORMAT/CODEC TO USE WITH CAPTURE?

You're almost ready to capture some video. You've got just one more decision to make: which codec to use.

Codec? As I explained in Chapter 25, codec stands for compression/decompression. Its job is to compress the video data as it's captured, and decompress it as it's being viewed or edited. The program that supports the compression and decompression—the codec—is kind of like a driver. (Just to make things more confusing, some very simple codecs don't compress at all; they're called codecs for simplicity's sake.) Some codecs are specific to particular boards; some are generic.

Lossy and Lossless Compression

Compression methods come in the lossy and lossless varieties. *Lossless* compression techniques enable you to compress data and then decompress it without losing any information. For example, expressing a price of forty-nine dollars and ninety-nine cents as $49.99 takes up less space, and yet you don't lose any information in translating from the one format to the other. *Lossy* compression techniques don't exactly decompress back to the original data. Storing forty-nine dollars and ninety-nine cents as $50 yields a terrific amount of compression, and is probably fine for many uses, but it's not exactly right when decompressed into fifty dollars.

Most computer data cannot be subjected to lossy techniques; you certainly wouldn't want a spreadsheet to store your financial data *almost* accurately. But image data withstands compression without corrupting its message terribly.

For example, on my hard disk I have an image of a forest. It is about 740KB. Stored in the Windows BMP format, there's no compression, so it ends up as a file that's 740KB in size. The simplest kind of compression is *run-length* compression, whereby you analyze the image for repeated bytes and represent them in a file as a formula. For example, if you've got a horizontal line of 500 blue pixels, you wouldn't store them as "blue, blue, blue... ;" instead, a run-length approach would store the information "repeat *blue pixel* 500 times." Stored in a run-length format, the file drops to a size of only 249KB. A run-length format is lossless, recall. A common *lossy* compression technique is called JPEG (after the group that invented it, the Joint Photographic Experts Group) compression. Stored as a JPEG file, the 740KB file becomes 95KB in size. Put the two images side by side, and you don't really see the differences.

There are many techniques besides run-length encoding and JPEG. One technique is *Variable Content Encoding (VCE)*, whereby the codec scans the image for repeated patterns of bytes. For example, if the pattern "r, r, b, b, r, r, b, b, r, g, g, g, g, g, r" appeared several times in the image, then the codec would build a *dictionary* of that and other common patterns. It would give each pattern a short identifier, which it would then use in the stored file. I'm vastly oversimplifying here, but it would be kind of like if the codec stored an image of a flagpole, calling it `image01`, and then encoded an image of the United Nations building. Instead of having to represent all the flagpoles in front of the UN building, the codec could skip all the pixels devoted to representing flagpoles, storing just the one image of a flagpole and putting the instruction `insert image01 here` wherever a flagpole went. This is related to another lossless method called *Huffman encoding*. If you've ever used a file compression program such as PKZIP or LHARC, then you've used Huffman encoding.

Yet another lossless technique is *delta encoding*. In delta encoding, video files are stored as groups composed of complete, or key, frames, followed by a series of *skeleton frames* that record only the differences from the previous frame. At 15fps, most of the screen does not change from one frame to another. If the video is of a person sitting and talking to the camera—what is known as a *talking head*, the phrase from which David Byrne took the name of his musical group—then the background remains unchanged, perhaps throughout the entire video. That background can be three-quarters of the entire image, meaning that the delta frames need not store information about those three-quarters of the screen. The delta idea applies not only from frame to frame, but also within a frame. A codec could, for example, encode a horizontal line of the image and then note that the next horizontal line of the image was almost identical; it wouldn't store the whole line, then, but just the changes—the *deltas*, in math and engineering terminology—for that line.

The idea of key frames matched with delta frames is common to many codecs, both lossy and lossless.

Codecs can do a lot of compression without loss, but the big gains are in lossy methods. Most lossy techniques rely on people's higher sensitivity to the grayscale image (the Y) than to the color (the C or the U and V, depending on the image encoding you're talking about).

The Intel Smart Video Recorder, for example, claims to record 24-bit data, but it doesn't; it uses a method that captures and analyzes a 4×4 pixel area. Consider that 16 24-bit pixels are 48 bytes. The Intel capture board views each 3-byte pixel as having a byte that describes the Y (luminance) part of the pixel, and U and V bytes that describe the color, the chrominance. The raw Intel capture codec doesn't touch the Y byte, but scrutinizes the U and V bytes, compressing them to 1 bit! How? Well, a 4 × 4 pixel area is pretty small. As a result, you're not likely to see large color changes from pixel to pixel. For that reason, Intel can do a kind of compression called *color subsampling*. It takes only the U and V bytes for the entire 4 × 4 "pixel group," and averages them. The average of the 16 U bytes is 1 byte, and the average of the 16 V bytes is 1 byte. There is now 1 U byte and 1 V byte, or 16 bits, to spread out over the 4 × 4 area. The 16 pixels in the group each take 1 bit, and so each pixel has its untouched 8 bits of Y information, and 1 bit of the communal U/V information. This process is illustrated in Figure 26.14.

FIGURE 26.14

Color subsampling

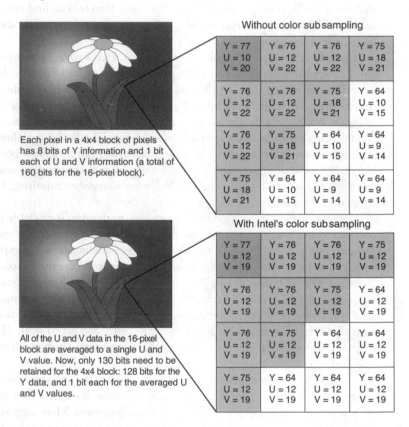

Each pixel in a 4x4 block of pixels has 8 bits of Y information and 1 bit each of U and V information (a total of 160 bits for the 16-pixel block).

All of the U and V data in the 16-pixel block are averaged to a single U and V value. Now, only 130 bits need to be retained for the 4x4 block: 128 bits for the Y data, and 1 bit each for the averaged U and V values.

Other boards do similar things. For example, you might find a YUV 4:2:2 option that also employs a 4 × 4 group, but that puts a bit more emphasis on the color information (two bits for U, two bits for V) and a little less on the grayscale image (four bits for Y).

The Intel Indeo codec takes things a step further by doing the 4 × 4 averaging not only on the U and V information, but on the Y information as well. If Indeo requires even greater compression, then it can average information over 4 × 8 or 8 × 8 pixel groups. The Indeo codec also drops 1 bit of the 8 bits of Y information, so that what was YUV9 information becomes essentially YUV8 information.

Vector quantization is yet another lossy technique related to the delta encoding lossless technique. Under the delta encoding technique, you store delta frames that vary from a key frame, and deltas within a frame. But if you examined the patterns of deltas, you'd see that *they* had some common patterns, as well. For example, imagine a picture of a sunset. A codec encodes each line of video image as pixels. But if you examined each horizontal line of the image, you'd see a gradient pattern from midnight blue to blue to reds to the orange of the sunset. That's a smooth gradient; even as the sky gets darker, the relative change in darkness as you go from the top to the bottom of the sky is pretty constant. That gradient can be expressed as a table of deltas, and the Intel Indeo codec contains a number of these prebuilt tables. The Indeo codec then tries to find one of these prestored delta tables that resembles whatever image it is working on, and essentially shoehorns the image into that delta table.

That's been a very quick look at compression. Here's what I want you to understand from all this: good compression involves a lot of analysis and a lot of CPU time. Video capture boards just don't have the horsepower to do a really good job of compression in real time; heck, nothing short of a massively parallel computer could do a really good job of compression in real time. Now, most video boards come with a video editor program that will subject your video to *offline* compression, which can take an hour to compress one minute of video. I'll talk about offline compression in a minute, but understand at this point that offline compressors can do a fairly good job of compacting your video data while doing the minimum damage to it; real-time compressors can't. It sounds like I'm saying that you shouldn't do any kind of compression when capturing, but that's probably not a realistic bit of advice.

Data transfer limitations on modern PCs mean that you'll probably have to accept *some* kind of real-time compression, but my advice is to play around a bit with the codecs that your system supports to find the one that does the least damage to the image as it compresses. As you'd expect, the codecs that reduce the data transfer rate the most also do the most violence to the original image. Start out with a no-compression codec, if that's an option. Record some reference data—something on a videotape, so you can ensure that you're getting identical recording conditions—and see how much data you can record with each codec before you start dropping frames. Then go with the lowest compression codec that you can stand to work with, and get to work. (I say "that you can stand to work with" because slower codecs mean shorter captures, which mean more time spent editing and splicing.)

If you're working with digital video, you'll be using the industry standard DV compression mode, which is based on the MotionJPEG (MJPEG) format. It's a lossy format, but at a level that is minimal and cannot be detected without laboratory test equipment. More important, DV compression is above the minimum broadcast digital video standards. Recompression can be done, once the basic DV file is on the computer's hard drive. This would usually be necessary for Internet playback, CD-ROM playback, and transfer to analog video tape.

Using Offline Compression

Once you have your video captured or your digital video transferred, you'll find that it's kind of huge. You may want to trim off some needless intro and exit frames. That's where a video editor is useful: it lets you take a subset of a capture file and then save it by using some kind of offline compression. The choices you must make at this stage include the following:

- The type of codec to use to compress the data
- Whether to set key frames
- Either the target data transfer rate of the output file or an index of quality
- Whether to pad the data for CD-ROM storage
- How to process video into a streaming format

Offline compression uses a codec, just as capture does; it may even have the same name as the capture codec. But offline compression can compress at much greater ratios than capture compression. There's a price to pay, of course—two prices, in fact. First of all, really dramatic compression rates require lossy compression techniques, with all of their tradeoffs. Second, compression takes time and ties up your computer. It takes time only once for each video, as you've got to capture each video only once, but it still takes time.

Let me revisit the reasons why you want to capture data in as pure a state as possible: The offline compression that you're going to do is lossy by nature. But if the data was first recorded with a lossy codec, and you compress it further with an offline codec, then you end up with data that's been "smeared" twice. That's why you should either capture without compression or with a codec that's as noninvasive of your data as possible.

Choosing a Codec: Don't Recompress Until You're Done!

After editing a captured video, you'll resave it to disk. At that time, the video-editing software will use a codec to encode the video data, just as the capture software did. Choosing a codec is easy. The big question is: are you done working on this AVI (audio/video) file? If you are, then use the codec that will give you the most compression. If not, then resave without any new compression. You'll compress even if you're not worried about the space that the file takes because of the data transfer rate required to play back the video clip. Playing back a raw Intel YUV9 video clip at full speed requires the computer doing the playback to read the file off its hard disk at about 1.3MBps, so it's a good idea to compress the data so it can be played on slower systems if you want to.

Suppose you're building a video out of five smaller clips. Each time you splice one of the smaller clips into the master clip, you save the intermediate result. If you use a codec with lossy compression to save these intermediate videos, then you'll end up reapplying lossy compression to your video several times, resulting in an awful-looking video. *This is very important.* For example, suppose you'd captured several small clips using a 24-bit RGB codec. This codec stores the entire image to disk or RAM, meaning that you won't be able to save very long clips before frames start dropping, so you'll be doing lots of editing. Suppose you've got pieces A, B, and C that you want to splice into video D, and suppose that your video editor lets you splice together only two files at a time. First, splice A and B, producing video IV1, for intermediate video 1. Also save it by using the 24-bit RGB codec. Then splice IV1 to C, saving it to D. Because D is the final product, it's fine to go ahead and use a lossy compression codec. The process is illustrated in Figure 26.15.

FIGURE 26.15

Reserve the lossy compression for the last save.

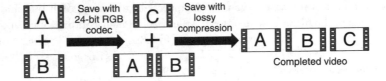

Setting Key Frames

Tell your video software that you want to set the compression type and options, and you'll probably see a dialog box something like the one shown in Figure 26.16.

FIGURE 26.16

Setting the compression type and options

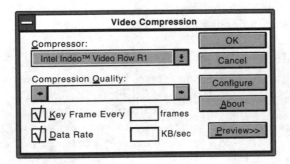

You can see the Compressor list box that lets you choose a codec. The compression software next lets you establish how often to set key frames, and whether you want to control the number of key frames. Tell the software that you do not want to control the number of key frames and concentrate instead on the data rate. Key frame adjustment is just fine-tuning. When you've got your video just the way you like it, try saving it with slightly different frame rates, and you can sometimes adjust the picture quality and data transfer rate. In general, however, you can unselect the box and forget it.

Setting Data Rate and Compression Quality

The example dialog box also shows a slider bar for Compression Quality and a check box for Data Rate. Actually, these options are the same thing. If you try to control one of them, you negate any control over the other.

Codecs have to make tradeoffs in order to compress data. Remember that less data means less data transferred per second. Putting the same image into less data means, logically, getting a lower-quality image; ergo, lower data rate equals lower compression quality.

The fact that the Compression Quality slider takes values between 0 and 100, and you can punch in any value that you like for the data transfer rate (from 10KBps to 16,000KBps) makes it seem that codecs must have infinite options in crunching your data. In truth, that's not the case. The Intel Indeo codec basically chooses whether to do its pixel averaging on the basis of a 4×4, 4×8, or 8×8 pixel group. That means that if you take the same video and save it with dozens of varying data rates, *you'll end up getting only two or three variations of the same file.*

This is important. If you tell a codec, "Make this a 405KBps file," then all the codec will do is examine the file and say to itself, "Well, I could *really* compress this, and get it down to 100KBps, or do a kind of average job, and get it to 267KBps, or do a really basic job, and that'd probably work out around 624KBps. I guess I'd better do the 267KBps job, as that's less than or equal to what I've been asked to do."

Padding for CD-ROM

One option that you see in video editors is Pad Output for CD-ROM, or something like that. This means to make sure that each frame's size is an even multiple of 2KB. CD-ROM drives read data from a disc in sectors of 2KB. For that reason, you'd like each video frame to come off right on a sector boundary. CD-ROM padding makes sure of that, writing enough zeroes at the end of each frame to ensure that it ends on a sector boundary, and so the next frame *starts* on a sector boundary. It's done to make the video play more smoothly.

Using RealMedia Files for Internet Streaming

If you want to deliver your video file over the Internet, chances are you'll want to recompress the file to a streaming media format, as discussed in Chapter 25, "Play It Loud: Sound Cards." (Streaming media enables users to view files while they're still being downloaded, thus eliminating long wait times.) The most common streaming formats today are RealMedia, QuickTime, and Microsoft's Windows Media (ASF, WMA for audio, and WMV for video). Of these, RealMedia has the largest user base, so it will probably be your format of choice. Several video-editing programs, including Adobe Premiere and Sonic Foundry's Vegas Video, provide the capability to save to the most common formats, including RealMedia.

Getting around Bugs in the Video Capture Software

This really isn't your job as a hardware fix-it kind of guy or gal, but you'll find that after you've done all the setting up, you'll have to deal with the worst part of analog video capture: software bugs.

Every programmer must grapple with memory when designing a program. Programs store all their data in memory areas called *heaps*, *arrays*, or *variables*, all of which must be properly allocated and provided for by the programmer. For example, if the programmer of a financial analysis program knows that he's going to allow the program to track just 10 people's portfolios, then he's got to allocate enough space to store 10 portfolios. If the user tries to input an 11th, then the program should contain built-in safeguards that would intercept that attempt and reject the request. If the program *didn't* reject the request to create an 11th portfolio area, then it would end up creating that 11th portfolio area on top of some other program's memory space, "clobbering" the program.

In the Windows world, the term for clobbering memory space is a *general protection fault*, or GP fault. GP faults happen when a program tries to utilize memory that it doesn't have the right to use, an area that may be in use by some other program. Similarly, a program may try to utilize memory that just plain doesn't exist, as in the case of a program trying to allocate the space from 32MB to 64MB on a 64MB system. Basically, GP faults happen because of sloppy programming.

NOTE *I bring this up because if you're running analog video capture software, you're going to run up against a lot of GP faults. Look at the kind of data rates that video can generate, and you can understand how the memory needs of video capture programs can easily exceed the amount of available memory or other system resources. The GP fault may be caused by the video-editing program, or it may be caused by the codec software, but no matter what's at fault, it still crashes your system.*

How do you avoid GP faults in your video capture system? First, have as much memory as possible on your computer. If the program never exceeds the available memory, then it's less likely to result in a GP fault. Second, allocate a big swap file to give your video program a little "elbow room." In addition, it's best to close any applications that you don't need to perform your video tasks. Third, believe it or not, some Windows programs are sensitive about the amount of conventional memory available on your computer; they can't run unless you've got a certain amount of conventional RAM available. Finally, I've found that one way to reduce the number of GP faults created by the Microsoft Video 1 and Indeo codecs is by previewing a few frames. Most video-editing programs have an option to allow you to select which compression codec to use, and in the resulting dialog box there's usually a Details button. Click it, and the dialog box unfolds, showing a Preview box and a slider bar that lets you control which frame you will see. Just let it build a few frames, and then the GP fault is less likely to occur. I have no idea why this works, but I've often found that it does.

Video capture can enable you to build some state-of-the-art presentations and programs as well as enable you to edit and produce video productions that range from montages of the kids to business marketing videos and even "desktop" movies. Now that you know how to do it, go try it!

Troubleshooting Tips

- To obtain the best-quality video, use the best camcorder you can obtain—in terms of both the camera and the recorder sections. A camera with three CCD chips is best, as is one of the digital recording formats—either Digital8 or MiniDV. If you can afford it, go with an all-digital system, from start to finish; DV delivers the best-quality picture and sound and provides the most (and easiest) editing options.

- If you are having trouble with cable connections, use the shortest and highest-quality cables for connectors. Cables wear out from use. Use fresh cables. Gold-plated connectors eliminate problems caused by corrosion.

- When considering video quality for analog capture, external capture devices are inexpensive, easy to install, and produce good-quality video. Plug-in boards, however, produce the highest-quality captures.

- If you drop frames when capturing to your hard drive, your hard drive is not fast enough. If possible, use a Fast, Wide, Ultra SCSI hard drive rated for AV for highest-quality analog capture. It's also possible that your hard disk is too fragmented, which will make it difficult for your hard disk to keep up with your video capture. Defrag your hard disk for best performance.

- Though external USB hard drives are okay for general file storage, the USB port is not fast enough to capture video to an external USB drive. Good results can be obtained with FireWire external hard drives, if a high-speed drive is selected. SCSI AV drives are still best.

◆ There is little difference between capturing directly from the camera and capturing from tape. Capturing video directly from the camera eliminates generational quality loss but lacks the convenience of multiple "takes" and portability afforded by capturing from tape. And, of course, if you're using DV recording, you eliminate any generation loss. Choose the method most comfortable to you—which will probably be taping first and capturing to hard disk later.

◆ MPEG, QuickTime, Windows Media, and RealMedia are all good file formats and all afford good-quality video. Select the appropriate format based on your target audience and its likely preference. If possible, give users a choice by providing more than one option.

◆ You get the best quality when you capture analog video at the same aspect ratio that your finished streaming file is anticipated to be. This helps reduce problems when you recompress your video from the original capture resolution to smaller streaming media formats for the Internet.

◆ If your streaming video jumps, drops frames, and leaves out chunks of video content, there may be too much action in the video. When shooting video primarily for use on the Internet, avoid pans, zooms, and scene and background changes. These effects increase the file size and result in dropped frames and poor-quality streaming video.

Chapter 27

An Overview of CD-ROM and DVD-ROM Drives

◆ QuickSteps: Installing CD and DVD Drives   749

◆ CD-ROM and DVD Types   750

◆ How Drives and CDs Work   753

◆ CD-ROM Standards   755

◆ Choosing a CD-ROM   757

◆ Installing CD and DVD Drives   763

◆ Recording CDs and DVDs   764

◆ Maintaining CDs and DVDs   768

◆ Troubleshooting Tips   768

Introduction

CD-ROM DRIVES ARE NO longer the luxury item they once were—having one is a necessity. Almost all software sold today comes on CD-ROM, so you'll need one to install any new programs you buy. CD-ROM drives also play audio CDs through your PC's speakers and let you play large, graphics-intensive games without making room on your hard disk for the entire program.

As CD technology continues to evolve, new kinds of drives are being made available. You can now purchase recordable and rewriteable CD drives (CD-R and CD-RW), or choose higher-capacity DVD drives. Even recordable DVDs are now within reach of the average consumer. In this chapter, I'll untangle the specifications of each drive type and tell you how to install, maintain, and troubleshoot all kinds of CD-ROM and DVD drives.

QuickSteps

Installing CD and DVD Drives

No matter what kind of CD-ROM you are installing (including DVD), the physical installation of the drive is basically the same. DVD requires a little bit of extra cabling if you are also installing an MPEG-decoder card (required to watch DVD movies on-screen), but other than that, they're very similar.

BE PREPARED

Before you start, there are some things you may need on hand. These include:

- ◆ Phillips-head screwdriver for mounting the drive in the case
- ◆ Small dish to hold the screws as you work
- ◆ Any instructions that came with the drive

---

1. If the drive requires a separate adapter card, install it in the PC. Most CD-ROM drives run off the motherboard's existing IDE interface, so this is probably not necessary.

2. If you're installing a DVD drive and you have an MPEG decoder card to install, install it in the PC. These are usually PCI cards. If it's an IDE drive you're installing, set the appropriate Master, Slave, or Cable Select (CS) settings. If SCSI, set the SCSI ID number and/or termination as needed.

3. Install the drive into an open bay.

4. Attach the power cable to the drive.

5. Connect the interface cable to the drive interface (on the motherboard or adapter card) and to the drive.

6. (Optional) Attach the sound cable from the CD-ROM drive to the sound card if you want to be able to play audio CDs.

7. If you're installing an MPEG decoder card as part of a DVD installation, attach a loopback cable from your computer's video board to the DVD decoder Video In port, then connect your monitor cable to the DVD decoder Video Out connector.

Types of CD-ROMs

Several types of CD-ROM drives are available:

♦ Standard CD-ROM drives, which read regular data and audio CDs

♦ CD recordable (CD-R) drives

♦ CD rewriteable (CD-RW) drives

♦ DVD-ROM drives, also called DVD players, which can read and play DVD movies

♦ DVD-recorder drives

NOTE *In this chapter, I'll use the term* CD-ROM *(or* CD-ROM *drive or* CD *drive) to refer to a drive, and the term* CD *to refer to a disc.*

When choosing a CD-ROM, think about how you'll be using it. Do you need to be able to read DVDs? If so, a DVD drive is your choice. Do you need to create your own CDs? Then go with CD-R or CD-RW. If you need neither of those capabilities, go with a regular old CD-ROM, and save yourself some money.

Regular CD-ROM Drives

You'll see a CD-ROM drive in virtually every computer sold today. These ubiquitous devices read data compact discs (CDs), just as you read the contents of any other disk on a PC. They also play audio CDs, provided you have a CD player program installed on your PC. For details about their mechanics, see "How CDs and DVDs Store Data" later in this chapter.

CD-R and CD-RW Drives

CD-R and CD-RW are two technologies for recording your own CDs. *CD-R*, the older technology, writes only once to a blank, writeable CD. After you write to the CD, it can't be written to again (except in the case of a multisession disc, which I'll get into later). It's great for data archiving or creating music CDs.

However, CD-R has its drawbacks. If the recording process falters, you've just wasted a blank CD (they cost about $1 apiece these days, much less if you buy in bulk). CD-R is also not great for backing up data that changes frequently, because you have to use a new CD every time something changes to make sure you have a current backup. That's where CD-RW comes in.

A *CD-RW* drive can write to a blank, rewriteable CD multiple times, just like with a hard or floppy disk. You can erase files stored on a CD-RW disc and make changes to them, so CD-RW is an ideal format for backing up constantly changing data, such as data files from an accounting program that you use every day. You can write to a typical CD-RW disc over 1000 times before it "wears out." Although CD-RW blanks are more expensive, they last longer because you don't have to throw one away when the data on it becomes outdated. The major drawback of CD-RW is the inability of many CD-ROM drives and CD players to read the CD-RW disc.

Most CD-RW drives sold today are dual-purpose drives that can do CD-R as well as CD-RW, depending on the type of blank you insert in them. I'll explain the specifics of both technologies later in the chapter.

Cross-Platform Format Compatibility

All the specialty types of CD-ROMs (CD-R, CD-RW , and DVD drives) can function as regular CD-ROM drives, in addition to their special functionality. Therefore, in theory anyway, you could replace your existing CD-ROM drive with one of these specialty drives. A lot of people do replace their CD-ROM with a DVD drive, in fact.

However, think twice before you replace your only CD-ROM with a CD-R or CD-RW drive. Think about it—what's one of the main things you'll want to do with a writeable CD drive? *Copy CDs.* And you won't be able to do that unless you have an additional drive in your system that can read CDs, or software that allows you to copy an entire CD image to your hard drive before you burn a copy.

In past years, compatibility between drive types has been a little shaky. The early CD-R drives produced discs that normal CD-ROM drives couldn't always read, nor could audio CD players in stereo systems. Things have gotten a lot better lately, however, so you should not have any problem playing a CD-R almost anywhere.

CD-RWs, however, are a different story. Because they are produced using a different type of encoding than CD-R discs, the resulting lower reflective capability of the CD-RW discs makes them difficult or impossible to read in some older CD-ROM drives and CD audio players. However, drives of 24X speed or faster can usually read CD-RWs. Look for *multiread* capability when shopping for a CD-ROM to determine whether it can read a CD-RW disc. The fact is that all CD recorders sold today support both CD-R and CD-RW. The expected growth in popularity of the CD-RW media never occurred—the price of the CD-R blanks is so low that the rewriteable solution doesn't seem all that attractive.

Types of DVD Drives

Like CD, *digital versatile disc (DVD)* is known mostly by its initials. Basically, the DVD format squeezes more data onto a single disc than is possible with a regular CD. CD-ROMs can fit about 630MB onto a disc, whereas DVD can fit as much as 17GB. DVDs are mostly used to distribute movies, but, increasingly, game manufacturers are releasing games and business applications on a single DVD that would otherwise have required multiple CDs.

A DVD drive can also function as a regular CD drive, so you don't need to have both in your PC; a DVD drive can replace your existing CD-ROM. In fact, DVD-ROM will eventually replace CD-ROM on the computer as a way to distribute software and high-capacity data. Some CD-ROM manufacturers are already planning to cease CD-ROM production in favor of DVD-ROM production, being that DVD drives can also read CDs.

The newest wrinkle in this evolving DVD market is a combination drive that is a both a DVD-ROM and a CD-ROM burner. This burner is becoming increasingly popular with newer systems and laptops. It usually goes by the name of *DVD/CD-RW (combo) drive.* As an add-on, it is a little pricey at the moment, but I expect the prices to drop as it becomes more popular.

TIP   When I bought my last PC, I shelled out the extra $150 to get a DVD drive instead of a regular CD-ROM. I thought it would be useful, but to be honest, except for the one time I played a movie on it just to see what that's like, I have not used the DVD capabilities. Since then, better and faster DVD drives have come out. If I had waited until I really needed one, I could have had a better DVD drive, not to mention spent less on it. Don't let the PC industry hype you into thinking that you need a DVD drive if you don't think you'll use one.

So far there have been several generations of DVD-ROM drives for computers. The first generation was 1X and could read only DVD format. The next generation was a 2X DVD-ROM that could also read CD-R format. The current generation of DVD-ROM drives offer speeds up to 16X, and some of them can read DVD-RAM or RPC2 (the current method used to encode and copy-protect DVD for several worldwide regions).

NOTE   *The speed of the DVD-ROM drive does not affect the quality of a DVD movie being played. For example, if you have a 2X DVD-ROM drive, replacing it with a 16X DVD-ROM drive will not improve the quality of the movie playback. The speed will have an impact on some DVD-based interactive multimedia games.*

Regular DVD-ROM Drives

There are two types of DVDs: DVD-video and DVD-ROM. *DVD-video* is what you buy at your local video store. These discs are optimized for the storage and playback of digital movies through a player connected to your television. These discs are analogous to audio CDs that you play in your stereo. *DVD-ROM* is the computer counterpart and, as such, is more similar to a CD that you use at your computer every day. The DVD-ROM drive in your computer will play both types of discs, and will play video that is digitized and saved in Windows-compatible formats such as AVI, MOV, and other streaming media formats such as Windows Media and RealMedia.

But in order to play DVD-video, you need either dedicated software or a special adapter card called an *MPEG decoder* to decode the movies. Some DVD drives you can buy come with the needed decoder card; others make you buy it separately. These decoder cards used to be very expensive, but they have recently come down in price. (You can buy a decent one for about $100 if you didn't get one with your DVD drive.) The good news is that if your computer is running at any speed above 200MHz, the DVD software solution works just fine. The best software available for this is Power DVD by CyberLink (`www.gocyberlink.com`). It offers support for a wide variety of features, such as DTS Digital Surround Decoder, Dolby Pro Logic II, and many others, and most important, it works really well on my slowest machine (a 200MHz IBM ThinkPad). A free download is available so that you can try before you buy it.

Recordable DVD Drives

In addition to DVD-video players and DVD-ROM drives, there's a third type of DVD drive. Several companies (Creative Labs, Panasonic, Hitachi, Hi-Val, and others) have developed DVD recorders, which will let you create your own DVDs that are entirely suitable for high-capacity data storage. In comparison to CD-R drives, they used to be very expensive, but this has changed dramatically over the past year. At the time of this writing, DVD recorders are selling in the $500 range. It is expected that the price will soon be competitive with CD-R/CD-RW drives. Recordable media for DVD-RAM drives is a bit more expensive in comparison to CD-R media, but its price too has dropped. A recordable DVD with 9.6GB capacity used to retail for as much as $45 to $50. The price is currently as low as $8.00 for a pack of three. With CD-R media currently costing less than a dollar apiece, there is still a significant price differential, but within a year blank DVD discs should almost be as low as CD-RW media.

How a Drive Reads a CD

After you insert a CD into the drive, the electronics within sense the disc, and a controller tells the spindle motor to begin spinning. A laser device (which uses a low-intensity gallium-arsenide laser mounted on a swing arm) is invoked, and focus-control circuits adjust the optical beam to the size of the pits on the disc (more on pits in a minute). The laser beam runs over the surface of the CD, reflecting light back to a photodetector, which measures the reflected light and encodes it into a digital signal. This signal then transfers to the drive electronics, which give the signal to the computer.

The key part here is what's on the surface of the CD, because that affects how the light gets back to the photodetector. The recorded CD has *pits* in it (or dots that look like pits to a laser—the pits are tiny indentations burned into the disc to represent data). To the CD player, however, the important part is not the pits, but the spaces between them, called the *land*. When the laser reads data, it senses the transitions between the lands and the pits. As you know, computers use the binary system (1s and 0s) to record data. A transition on a track is interpreted as a 1, and no transition is interpreted as a 0. The binary patterns are bounced back to the photodetector, which sends the data to a component that can interpret binary data back to its original format of sound, text, or graphics.

Now that you know how the readers work, take a look at how each type of CD (including DVD) stores the data to be read.

How CDs and DVDs Store Data

In order to understand how CDs and DVDs store data, you first have to understand several things about them: how the data is organized on the disc, what the disc is made of, and how discs are read and written. Those specifics are different for each of the CD types, so in this section you'll delve into each of them separately.

Physical Composition of Regular CDs

Compact discs are optical storage media that are read with laser light. The surface of the disc is arranged as a single spiral that begins at the inside of the disc and travels outward toward the edge of the disc. The commercially produced ones are made of injection-molded plastic formed from a stamper disc, coated with an aluminum film to make them reflective, and then lacquered to protect the surface. (CD-R and CD-RW are different, as I'll explain later.)

Compact discs aren't big (physically, only 4.72 inches in diameter), but from 527MB to 742MB will fit on a disc, depending on the number of sectors on the disc and the format used on it. Standard discs use the same size spiral as an audio CD (60 minutes) with 270,000 sectors and up to 99 tracks. The typical disc used in a computer-based CD-ROM drive stores 630MB using 333,000 sectors.

Compact discs are physically organized a little differently than hard disks. Whereas hard disks lay individual tracks in concentric circles, compact discs define a track by the length of a specific file; one file equals one track. The tracks on compact discs are laid sequentially on a continuous spiral. This spiral is a staggering 3 miles long and can contain more than 2 billion pits.

Commercially produced CDs are made up of a polycarbonate (plastic) wafer, about 1.2mm thick. This wafer is coated with metallic film, which is then covered, for protection, by a plastic polycarbonate coating. CDs are single-sided; the player reads data from only one side.

Regular CDs store data by arrangements of pits on the CD (about 0.12 microns deep and 0.6 microns wide). The pits produce areas of less reflectivity, so when a laser hits the disc, the light does not bounce back as strongly. Just like with 1s and 0s in binary computer code, this "pit/no pit" system stores binary data on the CD, as I said earlier.

Physical Composition of DVDs

A DVD is much like a regular CD. There are two kinds of DVDs: a single-layer kind that stores up to 4.7GB of data (or 135 minutes of video), and a dual-layer kind that stores up to 9.4GB in one layer or 17GB in two layers.

DVDs can store more information than regular CDs because they have a smaller pit length, less space between pits, a slightly larger data area (less wasted space around the outside and inside), and a few other minor design improvements. The primary difference is that the pits are much smaller and much closer together.

The new two-layer DVDs are a wonder of technology. The second data layer is written to a separate substrate below the first layer, which is semi-reflective to allow the laser to penetrate the top layer to read the substrate below. This enables the disc to hold more than twice the data on the same surface area. Is that cool, or *what*? And the technology is improving every day, so that in the future there might be many layers on a single DVD.

Physical Composition of CD-Rs

Recall from the preceding discussion that regular CD-ROMs are composed of metallic film on a plastic disc, and the disc is pitted to store the data by reflecting or not reflecting light from the pit/no pit areas.

Commercially available *recordable* CDs, on the other hand, are coated with metal in a process similar to electroplating and overlaid with photosensitive organic dye. When the laser burns data into the CD-R media, it heats the metal and the dye together, causing the area to diffuse light in the same way that a pit would on a mass-produced CD, so that CD-ROM drives are fooled into thinking that a pit exists. There is no pit, though—just a spot of less reflectivity.

Physical Composition of CD-RWs

So now you know that the dye on a recordable disc changes as a result of mixing with the underlying metal, into a nonreflective state. That change is permanent, which is why you can't alter a CD-R's content.

In contrast, CD-RWs also contain material that changes reflectivity when exposed to a laser, but not permanently. The CD-RW contains a silver-indium-antimony-tellurium alloy that is naturally reflective. When the CD-RW drive writes, the laser uses a high-power setting (called Pwrite) to heat the alloy to about 500 to 700 degrees Celsius, causing it to liquefy. After being liquefied, a spot loses its reflectivity when it hardens again, making an artificial pit. By reheating the area to a lower temperature (about 200 degrees Celsius, a setting called Perase), the laser makes the material revert to its reflective state. In this way, it is possible to write to CD-RWs many hundreds of times.

Before you can use a rewriteable disc, you have to format it—much like you format a hard disk, but with a special utility that comes with the CD-RW software. Early CD-RW drives took a long time to format discs (more than 30 minutes in some cases), but more modern drives can format a CD-RW in about 30 seconds. Formatting lays down a grooved spiral on the disc, ensuring accurate alignment of the burned-in data.

Standards: An Issue of Compatibility

If you've spent any time in the computing world at all, the concept of standards is not new to you. Parallel ports meet a standard, so that you can buy a parallel cable off the shelf and plug it into your printer. Data on your disks must follow the FAT format, so that your operating system and programs can read it. Internal hard drives follow standards that enable them to fit into drive bays, and so on.

Standards, both physical and logical, apply to CD technology as well, so that the discs can be read and the user can find the data on them. In this section, I'll discuss some of the particulars of those standards and where they came from.

The Genesis of Standards

So that all compact discs of a particular kind will work with a corresponding drive, data must be stored and indexed on all discs the same way.

The CD of today fared better than its predecessor, the *laser videodisc*, which was a large disc (about the size of a record album) that played movies on a TV. Philips and Sony were early, prominent developers of both videodisc and CD-ROM. They learned from their experiences with videodiscs that incompatibility can frustrate the user and subsequently restrict growth in the marketplace. Licking their wounds and vowing not to make the same mistake twice, they put their corporate heads together and developed a set of standards for CDs. Since that time, technology has progressed, necessitating the creation of new standards and extensions to existing standards. Before I jump ahead, let's briefly review and define the original standards.

A color system was used to designate CD-ROM primary standards: red, yellow, orange, green, and white. To simplify matters, think of these standards in the following manner:

Red Book   Digital audio

Yellow Book   Data storage

White Book   VideoCD (movies)

Orange Book   Writeable CDs, including CD-R and CD-RW

Green Book   Combination of Red Book and Yellow Book (for interactive presentations and kiosks)

Of these, Red and Yellow are by far the most important for PC users to know about. They're described in the following sections, along with High Sierra, ISO 9660, and CD-ROM/XA, which are all extensions of Yellow.

Red Book

The *Red Book* was the original specification defining how digital audio information is stored and indexed. It was developed for music CDs, which were the first CDs commercially available, and almost all music CDs conform to this standard today.

Yellow Book

The *Yellow Book*, also named *ISO 10149* (ISO stands for the International Organization for Standardization), extends the Red Book audio specifications and deals specifically with the more interactive requirements of CD-ROM: random access capability and multimedia. The specifications concentrate on storage and indexing of data and error correction.

This standard supports several file formats for the different computer platforms that use CD-ROMs. These include Native Macintosh hard disk format, Digital Equipment Corporation's (DEC's) VMS, Apple's Hierarchical File System (HFS), and ISO 9660 (which you'll learn about next).

High Sierra and ISO 9660

In 1985, CD-ROM companies formed an alliance to produce a standard CD file structure independent of the operating system. The result is commonly known as the *High Sierra* standard. After some modifications, the standard was formally accepted by the ISO and was named *ISO 9660*. It sets forth a standard file system with a hierarchical directory structure of eight levels. This *Compact Disc File System (CDFS)* is similar to the FAT architecture familiar to DOS users. It is the standard format for all data CDs produced today.

NOTE   *Theoretically, if a drive is an ISO 9660–compatible drive, it can, for example, read the information whether it is a Windows-based system or a Macintosh. However, this alone does not ensure compatibility because applications may contain instructions that use the resources of a given computing platform and that are not available on another platform. Thus, reading data and executing the program code is not the same; you can't execute programs written for Windows on a non-Windows machine such as a Macintosh, even if the Mac can detect the CD. Before you buy a CD, check its packaging to see what operating system it supports.*

CD-ROM/XA

The CD-ROM/XA standard is another extension to the Yellow Book. The *XA* stands for *extended architecture*, and this standard does exactly that. By defining the way in which different data types may be interleaved (that is, woven together) on a CD, the XA standard really makes multimedia CDs possible. It also allows for multisession recording.

A common application requiring the interleaving of sound and motion can be demonstrated through a multimedia presentation. Suppose you're giving a presentation with pictures of a person speaking and have sound to follow along. In order for the movement of the speaker's lips to match the spoken words, the sound and the pictures must be synchronized. To accommodate this, tracks on a CD-ROM/XA disc can contain interleaved video/picture, audio, and computer data.

Briefly, here's how it works. A standard CD track contains only Mode 1 data-type sectors. With CD-ROM/XA, a track contains only Mode 2 sectors. There are two form types within a Mode 2 sector: Form 1 contains user data (2048 bytes) and error-detection code (EDC) and error-correction code (ECC) data. Form 2 contains raw data (2324 bytes) such as audio or voice.

In order for a CD-ROM to be fully XA-compatible, it must have the following capabilities:

◆ Read data from two differently defined data streams. These streams are Mode 2, Form 1, which is static information, and Mode 2, Form 2, which is time-dependent information.

◆ Allow data from each stream to be buffered and delivered to the CPU and video subsystem as required.

◆ Translate the adaptive differential pulse code modulation (ADPCM). *ADPCM* is a standard for audio compression, usually a 4:1 ratio. In other words, the CD-ROM must be able to send the audio signal to the speakers properly decoded and decompressed.

Be careful of manufacturer claims that their drives are XA compliant. XA-compatible drives are still evolving, and unless they are able to read Mode 2, Form 2, they are not compatible. In addition, ADPCM translation is not always embedded in drives listed as XA compatible. To get full compatibility, you may need to purchase a new interface board.

The increased visibility of multimedia CDs has increased customer interest in XA compatibility, but to date most manufacturers have concentrated on interpreting images, not standardization. Although this is not really an issue now, expect it to become one as more titles with full XA functionality become available.

Multisession Capability

Recall from our earlier discussion of CD-R that you can write to a CD-R only once. *Multisession capability* provides a way out of that limitation, but at a price.

Say you have a 640MB capacity disc, and you write your daily backup of your data files to it. That takes up 100MB. The next day, you want to back up your data files again. You can create a second session on the same disc, and write the next day's backup to the new session. The only gotcha is that once you create the second session, the first session is gone forever. You can't access multiple sessions, only the last one written to the disc.

A multisession CD-R drive has the capability to write multiple sessions. A multisession CD-ROM has the capability to *read* a disc that contains multiple sessions. (That is, it can read the last session written to the disc. No drives can read the older sessions.)

If you want to use Photo-CDs (the kind you get when you develop your film at the local drugstore, that have your pictures in digital format), you will want to ensure that your CD-ROM has multisession capability, because of the way pictures are stored on the disc. Multisession capability is good to have even if you are not interested in Photo-CDs. In the corporate world, CD-R data discs are being used and recorded in multiple sessions for archiving purposes. In addition, the newer, portable CD-ROMs (such as Sony's MMCD portable) support XA format. If you intend to use a given CD on a portable and stationary drive, both should be XA compatible.

Choosing the Right CD-ROM

CD-ROM drives aren't all the same. They vary in terms of their hardware interface, speed, drivers used, access to additional hardware, and where they attach to the computer. So that you can select the right one for your needs, I'll go through the details of those characteristics now.

Physical Characteristics

Physically, most CD-ROM drives look pretty much alike. The front panel typically has a power-on indicator, CD busy signal, an Eject button, a manual eject hole, an audio jack, and a volume controller of some kind.

DISC LOADING

Not all computer-based CD players load discs the same way, as you may know from using the audio devices. Although no longer manufactured, some CD-ROM drives used to require that you place the CD in a *caddy* (a protective storage case that minimizes exposure to contaminants) for loading, and then insert the caddy into the drive. If your drive uses caddies, get a separate caddy for each CD, rather than sharing a caddy between discs. This avoids the hassle of finding a caddy when you need it, and will keep the disc protected. Other drives have a tray that the disc goes directly into. Once you put the disc into the tray, it slides back into place in the drive, and the CD starts spinning.

TIP   *If your CD-ROM player requires a caddy for its CDs, it is probably no faster than 4X. A new replacement 52X CD-ROM drive costs less than the price of additional caddies (if you can even find them).*

Although some caddy-style drives will play when the drive is on its side, so that the disc is positioned vertically rather than horizontally, some CD-ROM drives must be in a horizontal position to run. Do not attempt to run a CD player when it's on its side unless the drive is specifically listed as being able to support this position.

INTERNAL OR EXTERNAL

Many CD-ROM models are available in both internal and external flavors. If you have an empty drive bay and don't mind opening up your system to install the drive, internal drives are often the best choice. They tend to be less expensive than external drives, and more models are available. Additionally, some interfaces (such as IDE, for example) aren't available at all in external models, so if you have an IDE controller that you want to use with the drive, internal is your only choice.

External drives are good for those with a USB or SCSI interface who don't like cracking the case, don't have an extra drive bay, or are running into a bit of a power crunch from too many devices making demands on the power supply (external drives have their own power supply). They do tend to be more expensive than comparable internal drives, but (assuming that you have a USB port or a SCSI host adapter installed in your computer), they're much easier and faster to install. Plugging an external USB drive into your computer is as simple as it gets. If you plug a SCSI drive into an existing SCSI chain, first make sure your computer is off (SCSI isn't hot-swappable like USB). Then, plug in its power cable, make sure it's terminated properly, power the system back on... and there's your drive.

Performance Characteristics

All CD-ROM drives look pretty much alike (within the limits of being internal or external drives), but looks are not the measure of performance. You can buy drives with various spinning speeds, access/seek times, data transfer rates, buffering techniques, and so forth. All these features directly affect drive performance.

Some factors external to the drive can also affect its performance, such as CPU speed, physical interface, and the video system. However, unless you're planning to replace the entire system, there's not much you can do about system effects on CD-ROM performance, except to be aware of them. A slow processor or inadequate video system will keep the fastest CD-ROM drive from maximizing its potential. The fastest drive will not perform well on a slow 486—best to save your dollars for your Pentium system.

DATA TRANSFER RATE

If you're buying a CD-ROM drive, you have several choices: the slowest drives available today are 32X, and the fastest ones are 52X. Speeds are relative to the original (1X) CD-ROMs that were introduced back in 1981. The X factor measures the drive's capability to transfer data to the PC.

Faster is better, to a point, but as the speeds get higher, the difference becomes less apparent. You'll notice a big difference between a 2X drive and an 8X one, but very little between a 32X and a 50X, because other factors intervene, such as the limitations of the other system components.

Data transfer rate, measured in kilobytes per second, is the measure of the quantity of data supplied to your computer at the onset of the first read operation. I talked about the specifics of data transfer rate in Chapter 10, "Hard Disk Drive Overview and Terminology," and it works pretty much the same way on CD-ROM drives. Table 27.1 shows typical transfer rates. Please note that the bottom row of the table shows a drive speed of 100X; this is only to show the transfer rate at that spin speed—there are no 100X CD-ROM drives.

TABLE 27.1: CD-ROM Speeds and Data Transfer Rates

DRIVE SPEED	TRANSFER RATE (KBPS)
1X	150
2X	300
3X	450
4X	600
5X	900
8X	1200
10X	1500
12X	1800
16X	2400
18X	2700
24X	3600
32X	4800
36X	5400
40X	6000
48X	7200
52X	7600
100X	15,000

ACCESS TIME

Access time is the amount of delay between the drive receiving the command to read and the actual beginning of the reading. It's measured in milliseconds (ms). The measurement is just an average; the actual speed depends on where the data is located on the disc and how quickly the read mechanism can get to it. The closer to the center the data is, the quicker it can be accessed.

Don't expect an access time from your CD-ROM that even approaches the access time you see from your hard disk. I have one hard disk with an access time of 9ms, but a common CD-ROM access time is more than 100ms. Generally speaking, most hard disks are 10 times faster than most CD-ROM drives.

Table 27.2 lists some typical access times for various drive speeds. Lower numbers are better. Notice that unlike data transfer rate, the access time does not get better at a constant rate as the drive's X rating goes up.

TABLE 27.2: TYPICAL CD-ROM DRIVE ACCESS TIMES

DRIVE SPEED	ACCESS TIME (IN MS)
1X	400
2X	300
3X	200
4X	150
6X	150
8X	100
10X	100
12X	100
16X	90
18X	90
24X	90
32X	85
40X	75
48X	75
>48X	75

CACHING

Disk caching temporarily stores recently accessed or frequently accessed data to the hard disk, to take advantage of its higher access rates. Most CD-ROM drives have a small amount of memory in them for this purpose. Typically, the directory of the CD is cached. Caching the directory enables the computer to more quickly navigate subdirectories and makes the CD-ROM drive appear to be faster. However, the actual reading of the data is still slower.

BUFFERS

A cache uses some form of logic to figure out what to store: depending on how it's set up, it will temporarily store the most recently accessed or the most frequently accessed data on the hard disk.

Buffering is similar to cache, except that there's no logic to how data goes into it. Data is stored in the buffer until the CD-ROM drive is ready to send the data to the CPU for processing. Buffer sizes can vary from 32KB to 2MB. Although bigger is always better, you should look for a buffer of at least 512KB.

The efficiency of the use of the drive buffer is in part based on the firmware in the drive. Two approaches for buffering are used, one to increase throughput to the CPU, and one to reduce seek time. Circular buffer read-ahead enables the drive to continue reading with one interrupt to the CPU. As a result, the buffer is kept full, and throughput is increased. In the other approach, the root directory of the drive is copied into buffer memory, which helps to reduce random access time.

Interface Type

You can connect CD-ROM drives to the rest of your computer via an IDE, SCSI, USB, or parallel port. Although you should be familiar with these first interfaces from earlier chapters, I'll briefly review them here.

Before I begin, however, I'd like to point out a couple of things about CD-ROM drive interfaces. First, they work in pretty much the same way as hard disk interfaces or floppy interfaces, so if you have a handle on those, you're set. Second, most interfaces will do a credible job (with the exception of the parallel port, which is extremely slow). You can run into problems while installing CD-ROM drives with any of the interfaces, as illustrated in the upcoming "Troubleshooting Tips" section. Most conflicts will revolve around resource conflicts and outdated drivers.

SCSI drives have the best overall performance. However, the cost is higher, especially if you don't already own a SCSI controller. IDE drives cost less, and since most computers today have an integrated IDE interface, they are simple to install. Although proprietary interface drives were comparatively cheap, they didn't work with all operating systems and are no longer made for CD-ROM drives.

IDE

Integrated Device Electronics (IDE) came into being around 1985. IDE uses a superset of the Advanced Technology Attachment (ATA) specification called AT Attachment Packet Interface (ATAPI). The original ATA specification took form in 1984 due to the collaborative efforts of Western Digital and Compaq Computer Corporation, which developed the idea of building an AT-compatible controller directly into the drive electronics. More than any prior specification, IDE places drive- and host-interface electronics directly into the drive. As a whole, this significantly reduced the price of the hard disk subsystem. It also enabled vendors to make improvements to the capacities and performance of drives with less risk of incompatibility.

Historically, IDE drives worked well with the host adapters from other vendors. Problems still arose when users mixed drives from different manufacturers in a Master/Slave configuration. The ATA specification standardized the communications between the Master and Slave drives. Most current drives now follow this standard.

The motherboards of most ISA bus PCs and all PCI bus PCs include an IDE interface, but the drive houses the controller logic. The 16-bit parallel interface can support two drives (either two hard drives, or one hard drive and one CD-ROM). When you're attaching both a hard drive and a CD-ROM to the controller, you should configure the CD-ROM as the Slave device. (On an IDE interface, one drive must be designated as Master and the other as Slave. This prevents the two drives from trying to "talk" over each other.)

Since IDE interfaces are already on most PC motherboards, many CD-ROM drives use IDE. IDE drives are a good, cost-effective solution for text and graphics applications.

SCSI

If you're using a Mac or Unix system, you probably don't have any choice about using SCSI, because the OS requires it. You can either take this time for a soda break or keep reading to learn more about the interface. For Windows users, however, SCSI is not a foregone conclusion unless one of the following applies to you:

◆ You already have SCSI-compatible peripherals attached to your system.

◆ You plan to install multiple peripherals.

◆ You are looking toward the high-speed CD-ROMs (which normally have a SCSI interface).

SCSI is a good choice for those who need high performance and system flexibility. One SCSI host adapter card can provide a system interface for up to seven devices (one or more of which can be the CD-ROM), and SCSI devices have a high data transfer rate.

USB

Some external CD-R and CD-RW drives are connected to your computer through your USB port. This type of connection is fast and far easier to set up than the others. You simply plug your CD-R or CD-RW drive into your USB port, and that's about it. You don't have to worry about resource conflicts, and since USB is *hot-swappable*, you don't even have to turn off your computer to connect your drive. The only limitation of the USB interface is speed. The USB specification in current use is 1.1, and it only supports CD-R/CD-RW drives that are generally 4X. Now that USB 2.0 has become readily available, faster external CD burners using the new and faster interface are now becoming popular.

IEEE 1394 (FireWire)

Due to the speed limitation of the USB interface cited above, some companies are making external CD burners that use IEEE 1394 (called *FireWire* on the Mac). These burners offer great speed and the ability to swap between PCs and Macs; however, they cost two to three times as much as their USB counterparts.

Multimedia Kits

Back in the days when CD-ROM drives were first becoming popular, many people bought them as upgrades for their non-CD-equipped PCs. The problem was that at that time, standardization was a problem. Unlike today, when most CD-ROMs have an IDE or SCSI interface, back then there were way too many interface choices. Some CD-ROMs ran off proprietary SCSI-like interface cards; others used true SCSI; still others ran off a sound card. Beginning upgraders were often not sure of what they were getting and how it would fit with their existing systems.

Enter the *multimedia kit*. These package deals consisted of a CD-ROM drive, a sound card (usually one that doubled as the CD-ROM interface board), speakers, and a bundle of CD-ROM-based games and applications. The advantage: everything was guaranteed to work well together. The disadvantage: the CD-ROM often ran off the sound card, so if the sound card went bad, the CD-ROM sometimes wouldn't work either, and you had to scrap the whole kit (except the speakers, of course). These kits also tended to have cheap, tinny-sounding speakers compared to the sold-separately models.

These kits are practically nonexistent today, now that IDE is the standard CD-ROM interface and any sound card will work with any CD-ROM drive to produce multimedia; however, you may still find these kits for sale on eBay and at garage sales. Nowadays, they're often DVD equipped, too.

Installation

It's fairly easy these days to install CD-ROM or DVD-ROM drives. The procedure is similar for both types. The BIOS in most systems recognizes an IDE CD-ROM or DVD-ROM immediately upon startup, and most operating systems (including Windows 95/98/Me/2000/XP) automatically detect your CD-ROM without any prompting. Just hook up the drive to your IDE or SCSI interface, run the cables, and turn on the PC.

If you are installing a CD-ROM in a non-Windows environment or in an older PC, you may need to do some driver and/or BIOS setup after the physical installation to allow your system to see the new drive. But I'm getting ahead of myself here—first things first: the physical installation.

Physical Installation

Before you start the installation, think about where you're going to put the drive and set any jumpers on it accordingly. If it's an IDE drive, you'll need to connect it to one of your system's two IDE interfaces. If it'll be the only drive on that interface, it'll be the Master. If it's joining an existing device on that interface (on the same cable), it'll be the Slave. Set the jumpers on the drive accordingly. If it's a SCSI drive, make sure you set its ID number if there's a jumper on the drive for that, and make sure you have the termination for the chain set correctly. (This is just like the stuff you did for hard disks earlier in the book, so I won't belabor it here.)

You'll also need to free up a drive bay in your system if you're installing an internal model. Pop the plate off the front and slide the drive into the bay.

Next, connect the power plug and the interface cable (the ribbon cable), taking care to match up the stripe on the ribbon cable with pin 1 on the connector (usually indicated by a little *1* etched into the metal around it).

Finally, secure the drive in the bay with screws (usually provided with a drive) and fire up the PC to see if the new drive works.

BIOS Configuration

You may not need to tell your BIOS that you have a new drive—it may come up with that information on its own. As your system boots, you'll probably see a list of detected hardware; if your new CD-ROM or DVD-ROM appears on that list, the BIOS has figured it out.

Even if you don't see anything indicating that the BIOS has detected the drive, go ahead and let your operating system load. If the new drive appears there, you're fine—*no worries, mon*.

On some very old systems, you must enter the BIOS setup and set the drive type for the IDE interface to CD-ROM (or Auto, if there's no CD-ROM setting).

Drivers

On current Windows PCs, you do not need to load any drivers in CONFIG.SYS and AUTOEXEC.BAT to drive the CD-ROM. It should appear, ready for use, in My Computer. If it doesn't, you might try loading the device drivers and see whether that makes any difference. (Most CD-ROM drives used to come with a floppy disk that contained a SETUP program and drivers. If you planned to use the drive in MS-DOS or some other non–Plug and Play operating system, you had to run the SETUP program on this disk before you could use your drive.)

To operate a CD-ROM drive in MS-DOS, the following drivers need to be loaded:

◆ If it's a SCSI CD-ROM, there needs to be a line in CONFIG.SYS that loads the driver for the SCSI adapter. This driver comes from the SCSI card's manufacturer. It might look like this: DEVICE\C:\SCSI\SCSIDRV.SYS.

◆ In CONFIG.SYS, there needs to be a line that installs the driver for your specific model of CD-ROM. This driver comes from the CD-ROM drive's manufacturer. It might look something like this: DEVICE=C:\MYCD\NECCD.SYS /D:mscd001.

◆ In AUTOEXEC.BAT, the Microsoft CD extensions need to be loaded (MSCDEX.EXE). That would be something like this: C:\DOS\MSCDEX.EXE /D:mscd001.

If you need a driver for a specific SCSI card or CD-ROM drive, check the manufacturer's Web site. Generic drivers are also available that might work. You see them at work on a startup disk created with Windows 9x, for example; they enable you to start your system and use your CD-ROM drive when you are not in Windows. In a pinch, you can copy those drivers to your hard disk and use them for running in MS-DOS mode.

Recording CDs

The basic process of creating your own CDs is fairly straightforward. Of course, you need the CD-R or CD-RW drive. You also need special CD recording software. If you're lucky enough to be running Windows XP, you can enjoy the built-in CD-burning ability that comes with the operating system. Your drive should come with its own software, but other applications are available. Shop around and read a few reviews of other CD recording software if you are unhappy with what came with your drive.

Essentially, you create a CD by selecting the files and directories you want to write on the CD within the CD recording software and telling it to record. That's about it. You'll need to take special care that you choose the right standard so that your filenames appear correctly. Some standards support long filenames, whereas others do not. In addition, you can create hybrid CDs that can be read by both IBM-compatible and Macintosh computers.

One of the most frustrating parts about making a CD-R disc is encountering an error called a *buffer underrun*. This occurs when the drive you are reading from can't keep up with the CD writer's "need for speed" and makes it wait. The problem is—it can't wait. It has to keep moving, and writing, at a more-or-less continuous rate. If it's ready to write but the data hasn't arrived yet, a buffer underrun occurs, and you've just wasted a blank CD. With newer CD recorders this is no longer a problem—they have large built-in data buffers designed to prevent this. If you have an older system or CD burner, here are some things that can cause the dreaded buffer underrun:

◆ Some other application is hogging the processor's attention, so the processor can't tell the source drive to send the data to the CD-R fast enough. Try not to use any other programs, or even move the mouse around, while a CD is being created.

◆ The source drive can't operate as quickly as it needs to because of its own limitation. In that case, try transferring the files for the CD to your hard disk first, and then making the CD from there instead of going CD to CD.

◆ You don't have a large enough data buffer set up. A data buffer holds information read from the data source, so that even if there's a pause in the data reading, the writer can keep writing without a wait. You typically set this up in the drive properties.

◆ You don't have DMA enabled for the source drive. DMA modes transfer data with less CPU intervention. Try displaying the drive properties and turning on DMA transfer if possible.

◆ You are trying to record at too high a speed. Many CD-R drives advertise that they can record at up to 24X speed, but if you find you get buffer underrun errors at that speed, try a slower speed like 8X, 6X, or even 4X, and your errors may go away.

In general, SCSI CD-R drives are less susceptible to buffer underruns than IDE models. (But then they also cost more.)

Recording DVDs

One of the most confusing things about recordable DVDs is the myriad of different formats that recordable DVD drives can read and write; you can get lost trying to figure out what is compatible with what. The situation you have here is really similar to the early days of VCRs (remember the "Beta versus VHS" battles?), except that recordable DVDs are available in *four* basic physical formats: DVD-RAM, DVD-R, DVD-RW, and DVD+RW.

Most of the major DVD players have announced DVD home video recorders that will allow you to record video to DVD. However, it's a pretty tricky business to record analog video to DVD. At a minimum, you'll need a device that will record an MPEG video stream and a PCM audio track, but other options you'll probably want to see are Dolby Digital and MPEG audio tracks. Real-time compression requires really high bit rates for decent quality, and that lowers the capacity of the discs (which can cost as much as $10 apiece). It's an expensive proposition for a home video recorder. The costs involved to produce DVD home video recorders are much higher than those for VCRs, so you won't see DVD replacing the home VCR real soon.

Recordable/Rewriteable DVDs

First off, you can't play or record DVDs in a standard CD-R writer. The pits in the tracks of a DVD are smaller and closer together, which is one of the reasons why DVDs hold a lot more data. One recordable DVD can hold anywhere from 2.6GB to 17GB (depending on the format you are using).

Even though DVDs cost quite a bit more than CD-Rs, the large media capacity and fast read/write speeds make them particularly useful for digital audio, animation, video editing, and large system backups.

RECORDABLE DVD PHYSICAL FORMATS

As I've said, at present there are four major formats for DVD recording. But there's a problem: none of these writeable formats are fully compatible with one another, and there are even compatibility problems with existing drives and players. Using the old "Beta versus VHS" VCR analogy again, you couldn't play a Beta tape in a VHS player, and you couldn't play a VHS tape in a Beta player. (Well, maybe the analogy isn't quite perfect: Beta and VHS cartridges were different sizes, so it was pretty obvious which type of cartridge you had. With the exception of DVD-RAM, which requires a caddy for handling because it's sensitive, the other types of recordable DVD discs look pretty much the same.)

When you look at the specifications for current DVD recorders, you see a mixed bag of compatibility, so you'll need to do a lot of research into different recorders before you make your purchase. If you want to use the DVD recorder for your own system backups and data storage, any of the formats listed here will probably suit your needs. However, if you intend to share or distribute your DVDs, you should select a recordable DVD format that supports the needs of your intended audience.

DVD-R   First available in the fall of 1997, this format comes in two versions: DVD-R for general use, and DVD-R(A) for authoring. The general version uses a laser that is more compatible for future ability to write DVD-RAM. DVD-R(A) is intended for professional development and is not writeable in DVD-R drives. Both types, however, are readable in most DVD players and drives. Similar to CD-R technology, this format records sequentially to the disc and allows only one recording. The capacity of a first-generation disc was originally 3.9GB, and later increased to 4.7GB. A future version will support DVD-RW media. Discs will reportedly last 50 to 300 years.

DVD-RAM   Introduced in the summer of 1998, this rewriteable format has many manufacturers behind it, and is the format that is best suited for use in computers. However, DVD-RAM discs are not compatible with most existing drives and players because of format differences. This format is considerably more sensitive to handling than other formats. The double-sided disc must be enclosed in a cartridge, similar to the caddy used with early CD-ROM drives. For single-sided discs, the cartridge is optional but recommended.

Its initial capacity was 2.6GB per side, for a total of 5.2GB. Second-generation DVD-RAM discs have a capacity of 4.7GB per side, and are more suitable for editing and accessing movies and music. Second-generation drives are backward compatible with 2.6GB DVD-RAM discs, and can read other DVD and CD formats.

DVD-RW   Introduced in Japan in December 1999, this rewriteable format was created by Pioneer. It can be rewritten about a thousand times. DVD-RW is based on the DVD-R format and can record from one to six hours of video depending on quality. DVD-RW discs have 4.7GB capacity (the same as single-layer DVD-ROM). Though it is not usually required that you use a caddy or cartridge for the discs, some drives may require one. DVD-RW discs are playable in most DVD drives and players. However, when you insert a DVD-RW disc into some DVD-video players, the player may assume that it is trying to read a dual-layer disc (because of the lower reflectivity of the DVD-R disc). This little glitch can usually be fixed with a firmware upgrade for the DVD player.

DVD+RW   DVD+RW , a rewriteable format developed as a joint effort by HP, Mitsubishi Electric, Philips, Ricoh, Sony, and Yamaha, was the last format specified by the DVD forum. The DVD+RW discs are compatible with most existing DVD players, and they are able to write both CD-Rs and CD-RWs.

Producing and Recording DVDs

Development of DVD is different from CD creation, depending on whether you want to produce a DVD-ROM or a DVD-video.

You can typically use traditional multimedia development software (Macromedia Director, Click2learn ToolBook, or other similar software programs) to develop an interactive DVD-ROM that features MPEG-2 video and digital audio. Consumer and pro-level DVD-ROM formatting tools such as Adaptec Toast DVD (for the Mac OS), Daikin DVD-ROM formatter (for Windows NT and 2000), and Gear Pro DVD (for Windows 95/98/NT4) will allow you to write to DVD format.

Full-quality DVD-video discs, however, are another matter entirely. You develop a DVD-video in three stages. First you encode the video. Then you design, lay out, and test the interface. Finally, you pre-master a disc image.

If you want to go the distance, you can put your home movies onto DVD-video by following these steps:

1. Use video and audio capture boards to capture your video and audio from VHS, Hi8, or DV. You can use service bureaus or scanners to transfer slides to digital format.

2. Use a software encoder to encode the video into MPEG-2 format. Set the video frame rates to 29.97 frames per second (fps) for NTSC format (USA), or 25fps for PAL (European) format.

3. Use a software or hardware encoder to encode the audio into Dolby Digital. Format the audio as 48kHz PCM.

4. Import the video and audio clips into a DVD-video authoring program. Create menus and buttons that link to your media clips. You can also import your slides in TIF, JPEG, or Photoshop format.

5. Write your completed project to a DVD-R.

VideoCDs are easier (and cheaper) to create, especially since you can create them on CD-R or CD-RW drives. A VideoCD disc contains one data track that is recorded in CD-ROM XA Mode 2, Form 2. After the data track, one or more subsequent tracks contain video that is recorded in a single session. The MPEG-1 standard for VideoCD is similar to VHS-quality video, and the audio is hi-fi quality. Based on the White Book standard, VideoCDs should work on PCs, Macs, VideoCD players, and CD-I systems, provided they are equipped to handle this format. You can get MPEG-1 encoding software and write up to 70 minutes of full-motion video to standard CD-R or CD-RW format.

The quality won't be as good as DVD-video, but CD-R hardware, software, and discs are much cheaper than DVD.

Maintenance

The majority of maintenance entails caring for your CDs properly. By caring for your discs, you are doing preventive maintenance on the CD-ROM drive, reducing the opportunity for contaminants to enter the drive.

Dos and Don'ts of CDs and DVDs

Here are a few pointers to keep your CD-ROM and DVD drives up and running:

◆ Handle the discs only at the hub or the outer edge. Don't touch the shiny surface.

◆ When you insert a CD or DVD into the drive, make sure that you seat it properly in the tray.

◆ If a disc needs to be cleaned, use a soft, clean, *dry* cloth and wipe in a radial motion from the inner hub to the outer hub. Do not use a circular motion.

◆ Do not use cleaning agents—many solvents used in them can damage a disc.

◆ Do not use a wet cloth.

◆ Avoid cleaning the label side of the disc.

◆ Use a caddy to transport discs, and store them in their cases when not in use.

◆ Avoid exposure to extreme heat or cold.

◆ Avoid excess humidity.

◆ Avoid direct sunlight and high-intensity UV light.

◆ Don't put your CDs in a microwave. It'll make them unusable, and send up some spectacular sparks.

Troubleshooting Tips

First, I'll tell you about some problems common to CD-ROM drives. Then I'll move on to DVD drives.

Common Reasons for Difficult CD-ROM Installations

Installations of CD-ROM drives can be fraught with challenges for a variety of reasons, but the most common problems stem from balancing the needs of the drive against the needs of other peripherals within the system. The following list identifies some common reasons for difficult installations:

◆ Older BIOS may need to be told to look for the IDE CD-ROM drive.

- Problems with software drivers (applicable mainly if not using Windows):
    - MSCDEX not loaded in `AUTOEXEC.BAT`
    - Wrong version of MSCDEX
    - CD-ROM driver not loaded in `CONFIG.SYS`
    - Wrong CD-ROM driver being used
- Missing cables or forgotten cables:
    - Missing audio cable
    - Inverting the ribbon cable so it is connected upside down (Pin 1 Rule)
- Improper SCSI termination or SCSI ID.
- I/O, DMA, and IRQ conflicts.
- CD-ROM and host adapter incompatibilities. Check with the adapter's manufacturer for a list of supported drives.

If you've checked all the items in the preceding list and the drive still doesn't work, it's possible that either the drive or the controller is dead. (Obviously, it's the drive if something else is plugged into the controller and the other device works.) Check the following:

- Is the controller board seated properly? Reseat it, and if that doesn't work, try swapping it with an identical working board.
- Does the drive unit even work? If you have one, try connecting an identical working drive in its place.

SLOW INITIALIZATION OF THE DRIVE

This error message can be symptomatic of having the buffer parameter in the `MSCDEX.EXE` statement set too high. Set the buffers to 4 or 5 for each CD-ROM drive attached to your system. Modify the `/M:` parameter in the command line. If you're using `SMARTDRV`, try setting this parameter to 0. This is not an issue in Windows, because MSCDEX is not required. However, if you have Windows 9x and you are still using `MSCDEX.EXE` in your `AUTOEXEC.BAT`, you can save some startup time by disabling it there.

DVD Troubleshooting

Are there black borders at the top and bottom of the screen when a movie is playing? If so, this is normal if you're playing a movie in *widescreen* format. This is the same aspect ratio that you see in movie theaters. Because the widescreen presentation is wider than the aspect ratio of computer monitors (and most televisions), the black bands appear at the top and bottom of your screen.

If you have CDs that won't work in your DVD drive, first check to make sure the disc is clean. A dirty disc can be temperamental to read. If that fails, your DVD player might not be able to read the CD. Some CDs won't work in early DVD drives because the DVD laser isn't reflected off the dye used in creating the CD. In other cases, such as with Photo-CDs, you may be completely out of luck. Some DVD drives don't read Photo-CDs (the newer ones do, however). It's best to try a DVD drive before you invest a significant amount of time and money in a certain technology. If it works, stick with it.

If you have a DVD drive that has an external DVD decoder board, check to make sure you have the connecting video cables attached to the right ports. You should run a cable from your video card to the Video In port on the decoder card, then attach your monitor cable to the Video Out port on the DVD decoder card.

The sound quality of DVD movies on a computer system can be problematic. Most DVD movies have stereo surround sound and other hi-fi gimmicks, which may not be supported by your computer's sound system. If this is the case, you may experience unusual audio echoes and other oddities.

For DVD drives with software decoders, make sure you have the correct drivers installed. Visit the Web site of the drive's manufacturer to see whether updated device drivers and DVD player software are available. Manufacturers (good ones, anyway) continually refine their drivers and software to fix bugs and problems in previous releases.

Chapter 28

Flash Memory

◆ QuickSteps: Connecting a Flash USB Drive   773

◆ How Flash Memory Works   774

◆ Different Types of Flash Memory Devices   775

◆ Common Problems and Solutions   782

Introduction

THE LATEST RAGE IN data storage does away with the traditional hard disk, replacing all those moving parts and platters with solid-state memory—*flash memory*. Flash memory technology stores data on tiny, nonvolatile chips and cards that can easily be transported from one device to another.

The advantages of flash memory include the compact size of flash storage devices, the small amount of electricity necessary to power the devices, and the total lack of moving parts. These advantages make flash memory technology appealing for a variety of storage tasks.

You're likely to find flash memory used not just on your desktop computer, but also in notebook computers, handheld computers, PDAs, digital cameras, camcorders, portable MP3 players, cordless telephones, and other consumer electronics devices where space is at a premium. This chapter will tell you about all the different types of flash memory devices, and how they can be used with your personal computer system.

QuickSteps

Connecting a Flash USB Drive

Here are the basic steps for connecting one of the most popular types of flash memory devices, the keychain-sized flash USB drive. For in-depth coverage on how to troubleshoot problems with different types of flash memory devices, refer to the section "Common Problems and Solutions" later in this chapter.

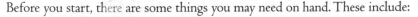

BE PREPARED

Before you start, there are some things you may need on hand. These include:

- Flash device documentation or user manual
- Flash device software or drivers ready to install, if required
- The flash USB drive

1. With your computer turned on, plug the flash USB drive into an open USB port on your computer.

2. You may be prompted to install the drivers for the new device; do so if necessary.

3. Your operating system should recognize the flash drive as a new drive, and assign it a drive letter. You can now start transferring data to and from the flash device, as if it were a normal disk drive.

How Flash Memory Works

Flash memory, sometimes called *flash RAM*, is a type of nonvolatile memory for your computer and for other electronics devices. Unlike traditional computer RAM, which is wiped clean when the power is turned off, the contents of a flash memory device don't evaporate when the host unit powers down. Flash memory data is always there, ready to be addressed whenever the power is turned back on.

The nonvolatile nature of flash memory makes it ideal for long-term data storage in portable electronics devices. When you take a picture with your digital camera, for example, that file is stored on a flash memory device, typically a CompactFlash or SmartMedia card. The data stays on the card, even when you turn off your camera or remove the card from the camera. When next you use the camera, or when you plug the card into a card reader (attached to your PC), the digital file is still there, ready to use.

You can't do that with normal RAM.

NOTE   *All erasable memory, including flash memory, is limited to a finite number of write/erase cycles. Early designs were only good for tens of thousands of cycles; today's flash memory can be written and erased more than a million times without a degradation in data integrity.*

Storing Data

Flash memory is actually a variation of electrically erasable programmable read-only memory (EEPROM). The big difference between the two is that EEPROM can be erased and rewritten at the byte level; flash memory can erase or reprogram blocks of bytes, not individual bytes.

Like all RAM, flash memory stores its data in cells within a memory chip. As you can see in Figure 28.1, a flash memory chip has a grid of columns and rows; each intersection is a cell, and each cell contains two transistors, separated from each other by a thin oxide layer. The first transistor, called the *floating gate*, accesses a row (called a *wordline*) via the second transistor, called the *control gate*.

FIGURE 28.1

Changing the value of a flash memory cell

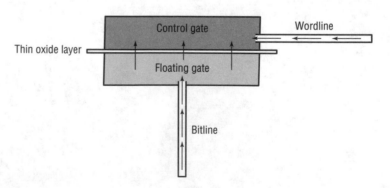

The default value of an empty cell is 1. Changing this value is done through a process called *Fowler-Nordheim tunneling*. In this process, a small electrical charge (10–13V) is applied to the floating gate. This charge (which comes from the column, or *bitline*) causes the floating gate to act like an electron gun and direct a flow of negatively charged electrons to the other side of the oxide layer. These electrons effectively act as a barrier between the control gate and the floating gate, breaking the connection (closing the gate) and changing the cell's value to 0. A cell's value can be returned to 1 by the application of a higher-voltage charge.

NOTE   *The memory cells in a flash memory device can be arranged in either a serial or parallel fashion. The serial arrangement is called NAND flash memory; the parallel arrangement is called NOR.*

Another defining characteristic of flash memory is that it is erased and reprogrammed in large chunks, called *blocks*. (Other types of memory are erased at the byte level.) That's where the name comes from, by the way; you erase one of these memory chips "in a flash," by working with large blocks of data. Erasing large blocks is faster than erasing individual bytes.

It's Not Cheap

By storing large amounts of memory—anywhere from several megabytes to 1GB—on a single chip, flash memory is starting to rival hard disks for sheer storage capacity. And since it's all done electronically, access times are typically faster for memory-based storage than they are for disk-based storage—and the amount of physical space required is significantly less.

So if flash memory can store data like a hard disk—but faster, and in a smaller physical space—why not replace your computer's hard disk with a flash memory device?

The answer is simple. It's because of the price.

Today's super-big hard disk drives cost less than $0.01 per MB of storage. A typical flash memory device, like a CompactFlash or SmartMedia card, costs between $0.60 and $0.90 for that same MB of storage. So you *could* use flash memory as your primary storage medium, but it would cost you dearly.

That said, the cost of flash memory is acceptable when you need to store lots of data in a small physical space—like in a digital camera, or PDA, or portable MP3 player. You can't put normal hard disks in these devices (both because of size and because of ruggedness), but you can use flash memory.

And, in fact, it's in these portable devices that flash memory really shines.

NOTE   *While normal hard disks are much bigger than flash memory cards, IBM's Microdrive is an honest-to-goodness hard drive the approximate size of a CompactFlash card. (The drive itself is just 1 inch in diameter.) Storage capacities range from 340MB to 1GB; you can buy the 1GB Microdrive for less than $300.*

Different Types of Flash Memory Devices

There are several different types of storage media that utilize flash memory technology. These media have several factors in common, including small physical size, low voltage requirements, and extreme portability and durability.

Most of these flash memory devices connect to your computer through add-on card readers or adapters. You can also access the data on a card by connecting the host digital device—such as a PDA or digital camera—to your PC.

BIOS Chip

While the concept of using flash memory for large data storage is a relatively new one, flash memory has been used in personal computers almost from the dawn of the PC era. The computer's BIOS code is held in flash memory, which is how your computer holds its settings even when it's powered off.

Flash memory makes updating your computer's BIOS chip relatively easy. When you make changes to your computer's settings, the new settings are "flashed" onto the BIOS, with the new data blocks overwriting the old data blocks in the chip's flash memory.

CompactFlash

CompactFlash (CF) cards are small, thin, squarish flash memory cards used in a variety of electronics devices, including portable PCs, handheld PCs, PDAs, digital cameras, digital voice recorders, set-top television boxes, and so on. Unlike SmartMedia, which is designed primarily for portable devices, CF is used in a variety of non-portable devices that have need of small, removable, high-capacity storage devices. Figure 28.2 shows a typical CF card from SanDisk, one of the primary manufacturers of flash memory devices.

FIGURE 28.2

A CompactFlash card from SanDisk—no bigger than a couple of tacks (Photo courtesy of SanDisk Corporation)

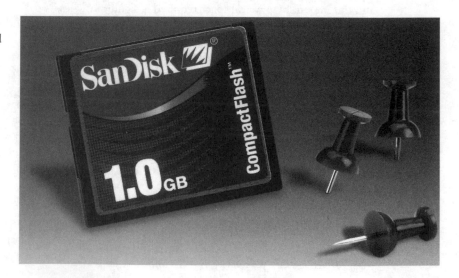

For example, if you have a DIRECTV satellite system, your satellite receiver unit (the box that sits on top of your TV) has a slot for a CF card. Your personal CF card stores your DIRECTV account information, and must be inserted in the box before you can activate your system. (You can also take your card with you to another DIRECTV box—and take all your personal information with you.)

Introduced in 1994, CF is fully compatible with the PCMCIA/PC Card format, so it can be used anywhere a PC Card can be used (with the proper physical adapter, of course). The original CF cards used an 8MB flash memory chip. Subsequent releases have expanded CF capacity all the way up to 512MB, with 1GB and higher capacity devices on the horizon.

Like SmartMedia cards, CF cards are widely used in digital cameras, as well as in various types of handheld PCs. CF cards differ from SmartMedia in that they're slightly larger and thicker, and they utilize a built-in controller chip.

SmartMedia

SmartMedia cards are small, lightweight, flash memory cards, designed for portable digital devices. You can find SmartMedia cards used in digital cameras, portable MP3 players, PDAs, and other similar devices. SmartMedia cards are available in sizes ranging from 2MB to 128MB. Figure 28.3 shows a typical SmartMedia card.

FIGURE 28.3

A SmartMedia card, used in digital cameras and other portable devices (Photo courtesy of SanDisk Corporation)

SmartMedia cards also conform to the PCMCIA/PC Card format used by all of today's portable computers—which means that you can use a simple PC Card adapter to insert a SmartMedia card into your laptop's PC Card slot.

NOTE *The original name for SmartMedia was Solid State Floppy Disk Card (SSFDC). The new name, SmartMedia, is a much better name, for marketing purposes, anyway. (It's also a registered trademark of Toshiba.)*

There are two different types of SmartMedia cards, operating at different voltages. Some equipment supports the 3.3V SmartMedia cards, other equipment supports 5V cards, and some devices support both. You can tell the voltage requirement of a SmartMedia card by the notch at the top of the card. If the notch is on the left side, it's a 5V card. If the notch is on the right, the card requires 3.3V.

Probably the most popular use of SmartMedia technology today is in digital cameras. While some cameras use CompactFlash cards (and Sony still clings to the memory stick format for most of its cameras), the majority of cameras today use SmartMedia cards to store their digital photos.

Memory Stick

The *memory stick* is a flash memory device used almost exclusively by Sony in its many different portable digital devices—digital cameras, portable MP3 players, CLIÉ handheld PCs, and so on. A memory stick is about the size and shape of a pack of chewing gum, and can range in capacity from 16MB to 256MB, with larger capacities expected soon.

Figure 28.4 shows a typical memory stick.

FIGURE 28.4

A memory stick storage device, used primarily in Sony electronics equipment (Photo courtesy of SanDisk Corporation)

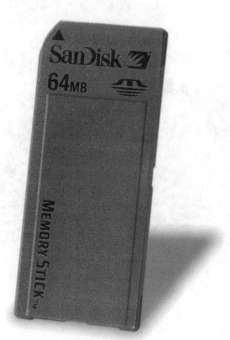

MultiMediaCard

The *MultiMediaCard (MMC)* is a postage stamp–sized flash memory card, originally targeted at the mobile phone and pager markets. (It was, in fact, co-developed by Siemens, one of the world's largest mobile phone manufacturers.) Because of its relatively high storage capacity, extremely small size, and miserly power consumption, it has found popularity in a variety of other devices, including digital video cameras, global positioning systems, portable MP3 players, and some newer PDAs. Figure 28.5 shows a typical MMC.

MultiMediaCards are available with capacities in the 8MB to 128MB range.

FIGURE 28.5

A MultiMediaCard, about the size of a postage stamp (Photo courtesy of SanDisk Corporation)

Secure Digital Card

Secure Digital (SD) Cards build upon the MMC format with additional capacity and a digital copyright security scheme. As you can see in Figure 28.6, an SD Card has the same form factor as an MMC, except that it's a little thicker. (The extra thickness enables the security features.) SD Cards are finding widespread popularity in handheld PCs, such as the PalmPilot and the Compaq iPAQ.

The big thing about SD Cards is the built-in cryptographic security for the protection of copyrighted data. Since SD Cards comply with both current and future Secure Digital Music Initiative (SDMI) requirements, the SD Card is the favored storage format of the large music companies.

SD Cards can also transfer data up to four times as fast as a comparable MMC. Current SD Cards can transfer data up to 2MB per second; future cards promise 10MB-per-second rates. Today, cards are available with capacities ranging from 8MB to 128MB.

All SD Card devices will accept existing MultiMediaCards, although the opposite is not true; the thicker SD Card can't fit into the thinner MMC slots.

Flash USB Drive

The latest implementation of flash memory technology is in so-called flash USB drives. These "drives" are actually flash memory devices designed to function like removable disk storage.

As you can see in Figure 28.7, these devices are small enough to be carried in your pocket or hung on your keychain, and connect directly to the USB port on your computer. Flash USB drives typically weigh less than an ounce, and many are instantly recognized as a new disk drive by Windows XP and other Plug and Play–compatible operating systems. (Some of these devices require the installation of a software driver to work; others don't.)

FIGURE 28.7

Big disk storage
in a small memory
device—JMTek's
USBDrive

Some of the more popular of these miniature storages devices include the Q Drive (Agaté Technologies), Flash USBDrive (JMTek), DiskOnKey (M-Systems), FlashDio (FlashDioUSA), EasyDisk (EasyDisk USA), and ThumbDrive (TREK). These drives are currently available in 8MB–1GB sizes, priced from under $50 to over $500, depending on capacity. Many users find them a good substitute for the bulkier Zip drive or other removable storage.

PCMCIA Flash

While most of the flash attention is on the smaller storage devices (CF, MMC, and so on), the *original* flash memory device came in the form of a larger PCMCIA card (PC Card). The advantage of PCMCIA flash, of course, is that you can use it in any device with a PCMCIA slot—which means most laptop PCs, and even some desktops. The extra size also enables larger storage capacities, so you can find PCMCIA flash cards with up to 5GB of storage.

There are actually three different types of PCMCIA flash cards; the difference between the types is the thickness of the card. Type I is the thinnest card, so it can fit into the most possible devices. It's also the format most used for flash memory—although you have to move up to the thicker Type II and III cards to get the larger capacities.

TIP   You can also purchase PCMCIA adapters for CF cards. These devices enable you to use your CF cards in your computer's standard PCMCIA slot.

Choosing a Card

With so many flash memory options around, which format is right for your needs? While which type of card you use is probably dictated by what slots your computer or other device has, you can also get a feel for the typical uses of each card from Table 28.1.

TABLE 28.1: TYPES OF CARDS

CARD TYPE	MAX. CAPACITY	DIMENSIONS (WIDTH × HEIGHT × THICKNESS, IN MM)	TYPICAL USES
SmartMedia	128MB	37 × 45 × 0.76	Digital cameras, PDAs, MP3 players
MultiMediaCard	128MB	24 × 32 × 1.4	Mobile phones, pagers, digital cameras, MP3 players, PDAs
Secure Digital Card	128MB	24 × 32 × 2.1	Digital cameras, PDAs, MP3 players
Memory Stick	256MB	21.5 × 50 × 2.8	Sony digital cameras, laptop PCs, PDAs
CompactFlash	1GB	43 × 36 × 3.3	Digital cameras, PDAs, MP3 players
Flash USB Drive	1GB	Varies	Desktop and laptop computers
PCMCIA Flash	5GB	54 × 85.6 × 3.3 (Type I), 5.0 (Type II), or 10.5 (Type III)	Laptop PCs

Non-Computer Uses

Obviously, flash memory—in the form of CompactFlash, SmartMedia, MultiMediaCards, and other media—is used in a variety of non-computer devices. From digital cameras and camcorders to cordless phones and answering machines, flash media is an essential part of many of today's consumer electronics devices.

A future use of flash memory technology is in the so-called *Personal Tag*, or *P-Tag*. Developed by SanDisk, the P-Tag is a removable electronic card capable of storing information about the person carrying it. Designed to be about the size of a 25-cent coin, the P-Tag could be used to store medical information about the wearer, for use by hospitals and emergency medical personnel. (In fact, the P-Tag was originally developed for use by the U.S. military, as a kind of universal ID card for military personnel.)

Which brings us to the concept of the *smart card*. The smart card is a device that looks like a standard credit card but that actually contains an embedded microprocessor and/or flash memory chip. The card can thus be programmed to contain various types of data—your personal ID information, the balance in your checking account, and so on.

While smart cards haven't caught on yet in the United States, they're big in Europe. The smart-card industry claims to have shipped more than one billion cards per year since 1998, for purposes as wide-ranging as accessing pay phones, managing banking transactions, and providing identification for health-care services.

The data on a smart card can be read and written to via contact or contactless methods. A contact smart card requires insertion into a smart-card reader; a contactless smart card contains a small, embedded antenna and transfers data via a wireless connection.

The flash memory in most smart cards is typically small—no more than 256KB. But that's enough to contain the basic numbers in a checking or credit account, or your name, address, and other personal information.

By the way, the national ID card concept that's been tossed around in the wake of the terrorist attacks on the World Trade Center would utilize this type of smart-card device. If some people get their way, we'll all be carrying flash memory around in our pockets—or maybe even embedded under our skin!

Common Problems and Solutions

Because flash memory devices have no moving parts, there's not a lot of maintenance required to keep them operating in tip-top shape. Just make sure the contacts are clean and that you don't bend or break them.

That's not to say you can't run into problems with these devices. Let's take a quick look at some of the more common problems you're likely to encounter when working with flash memory.

Working with Drivers

Most flash memory problems are driver related. Either the wrong drivers get installed, or the drivers become corrupted, or somehow Windows doesn't recognize the device and its drivers.

If you think you have a driver-related problem, the first thing to do is reinstall the original driver software. These files should be located on the installation disk or CD that came with your flash memory device. You can also check for updated versions of these drivers on the manufacturer's Web site.

When manufacturers increase card capacity, you probably need to update the corresponding drivers on your system. For example, if you started out with 64MB-capacity flash cards and recently upgraded to the new 128MB model, your old drivers might not recognize the new, higher-capacity cards. Whenever you move into something new, update your drivers as necessary.

Recognizing the Device

Some flash memory devices—flash USB drives, especially—are supposed to operate without the need to preinstall software drivers; Windows, theoretically, recognizes the device every time it's plugged into your PC. This USB-enabled device recognition actually works, sometimes. If you're finding that your system is *not* recognizing your flash memory device, you'll probably need to consult the device's instruction manual and install the drivers, anyway. (Also know that this automatic device recognition works only with newer operating systems, such as Windows XP; if you're using Windows 95 or an even older version, you'll definitely need to install drivers.)

NOTE   The vast majority of non-PC devices that use flash memory (digital cameras, MP3 players, etc.) have built-in support for the type of media they're designed for—no separate driver installation necessary.

If you have all the correct drivers installed and your system *still* doesn't recognize your device, make sure you're connecting it correctly. It's not uncommon for users to insert SmartMedia or Compact-Flash cards upside down—and your system definitely won't recognize an upside-down device. (And it should go without saying that you need to insert the memory card firmly—but not forcefully—into the card reader or card slot; poorly seated cards are also a common problem.)

Formatting Cards

SmartMedia and CompactFlash cards need to be formatted before use—although most cards come preformatted from the factory. (You can also format a card to "quick clean" the existing data.) However, it's possible for the format on a card to become corrupted, which can cause the card to appear to malfunction. This can happen when:

- A card is removed from a camera or other device before the camera has finished writing to the card.

- A camera is turned off before it has finished writing to the card.

- A camera's batteries run low or go dead.

- The wrong batteries are used in a camera or other device.

WARNING   Low batteries in a portable device (digital camera, MP3 player, etc.) will often result in flash memory devices not being recognized. Trying to use the device with low batteries could result in corrupted formatting or corrupted data on the memory device.

When a card is unformatted, formatted incorrectly, or has a corrupted format, that card probably won't be recognized by your PC or other electronic device. Sometimes the card will be recognized but inaccessible; other times the card will cause some sort of warning light or error message to appear. In any case, when you have a problem accessing or reading a flash memory card (and all your other cards work fine), then you probably have a formatting problem.

If you suspect that a card's format has become corrupted, reformat the card according to the device's instructions. If the card is connected to your PC (via a card reader or while inserted into a PC card slot), use My Computer to right-click the drive letter for that card, then select Format from the context menu.

If you're using a card reader of one sort or another, make sure that your card reader can handle the type of card you're trying to use. For example, if your card reader can handle cards up to 64MB capacity and you're trying to use a 128MB card, you may run into problems. Don't assume that cards from one manufacturer will work with another manufacturer's card reader.

Understanding Capacity

You might get a little confused when you go to check the capacity of your new flash memory card. It's not unusual for the actual reported capacity to be a little less than the promised capacity. For example, a 64MB card might report 60.9MB of free space.

Where did the other 3.1MB space go?

In this instance, it's a matter of definitions. Remember that a megabyte (MB) is actually 1,048,576 bytes—*not* 1,000,000 bytes, even. However, most flash memory manufacturers count a megabyte as an even million bytes, which results in the discrepancy. (Divide the advertised 64MB by 1,048,576 and you get 60,972,656 bytes—or the reported 60.9MB.)

Dealing with Multiple Flash Memory Devices

Not all devices use the same formatting for their flash memory cards. For example, Diamond Rio's MP3 players use SmartMedia cards but use a proprietary formatting for the flash memory—which means that you can't take a card from your MP3 player and use it in your digital camera without reformatting or adapting it first.

SimpleTech provides a free utility to convert Rio-adapted SmartMedia cards back to the standard SmartMedia format. Go to `www.simpletech.com/support/drivers/Photo_Readers/rio-diag.exe` to download the file.

If you want to transfer data from one type of flash memory device to another, you *could* copy it to your hard disk first, and then move the data to the second device. A more eloquent solution is presented by Addonics Technologies, which produces a neat little unit called the Pocket DigiDrive. Priced at just $90, this device connects to a single USB port on your PC and contains slots for most current types of flash devices—CompactFlash, SmartMedia, and memory sticks. You can plug in multiple flash devices and use the DigiDrive to copy data from one device to another, just as if they were separate drives on your computer system.

You might also want to strategize your equipment purchases around a specific type of flash card. Since these little buggers are pricey, it's nice if you can use the same cards in multiple devices—in your PDA, camera, and MP3 player, for example. That way, you can reuse your stash of cards, and not have to make duplicate purchases in multiple formats.

Chapter 29

Networking Concepts and Hardware

◆ QuickSteps: Installing a New Network Card   787

◆ Basic Networking Concepts   789

◆ Understanding Networking Components, Protocols, and APIs   791

◆ Choosing a Network—for Home or Business   814

◆ Installing Cables and Cards   818

◆ Connecting Devices with Hubs and Switches   829

◆ Internetworking and Intranetworking   837

◆ Networking Security   842

Introduction

OKAY, YOU'RE CONVINCED——YOUR HOME or office is never going to enter the 21st century until you get those PCs connected. Linking your computers means being able to share files, applications, peripherals (such as printers), and Internet connections—and brings other benefits, as well.

You already have the computers—what else do you need to make them start talking to one another? First, you'll need to understand some basic networking concepts. That's where this chapter comes in. Then, once you understand the basics, I'll tell you about all the components needed to set up your network—from network cards to cabling—and how to make them work.

If you've already set up a network, don't just skip over this chapter. I'll tell you what you need to extend your network or to link it to another one.

QuickSteps

Installing a New Network Card

If you have already installed any other type of card, installing a network card is straightforward.

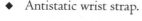

BE PREPARED

Before you start, here are some things you'll need to perform the operation:

- ◆ Antistatic wrist strap.

- ◆ Container to hold screws.

- ◆ Floppy disk or CD with software drivers that shipped with your card.

- ◆ Inventory of used IRQs, I/O address spaces, and (rarely) DMA channels so that you can be sure to assign your new card available resources and thereby avoid system conflicts. You can obtain this inventory by accessing Control Panel ➤ System ➤ Device Manager and double-clicking Computer at the top of the list.

If you're removing another card to insert the new one, follow these steps:

1. Power down your PC, open the computer case, and identify the card you want to remove.

2. Make sure that the card is disconnected from any outside cables.

3. Unscrew the small screw attaching the card to the PC case and lay it aside.

4. Pull gently on the card, using both hands to wiggle it back and forth slightly to disengage it from the connectors.

5. After you've pulled the card out, wrap it back up in its original sheath, if you kept it and plan to use the card again. Don't touch the gold connectors on the card; the oils in your skin can corrode the gold and degrade connectivity.

To install a new networking card, follow these steps:

1. Power down the PC, open the computer case, and find a slot in the PC that's free and fits your specific network card. Try to choose a slot that's not next to another card to maintain a good airflow.

2. Install your new card by first unwrapping the card, being careful not to touch the gold connectors, and setting it aside.

3. Unscrew the plate that covers the slot's opening to the rear of the computer and set the plate and screw aside. (You may need the plate later, and you'll need the screw in just a minute.)

4. Align the card with the slot in the PC and push gently but firmly to seat the card in its slot. You may need to push fairly hard, which can be somewhat intimidating if you're not used to inserting cards. If you have the right slot and push straight in, then the card should snap into place.

5. Using the screw that you set aside in step 3, screw the card in to hold it in place. This extra step will keep the card from sagging or working loose.

6. Close the case and, if the cables are already in place, connect them to the card.

7. Install the network card's drivers. The process for installing drivers depends on your operating system. Follow the instructions that come with the network card. (Check the manufacturer's Web site to make sure you have the most recent drivers for your card.)

8. Configure your card's interrupt, I/O address space, and (if applicable) DMA channels. (If your card is a PCI card, you won't have to worry about this step because it is Plug and Play.)

Basic Networking Concepts

In this section, I'll explain what a LAN is, help you choose from different types of LANs, and show you how to hook it all up.

What Is a LAN?

Strictly speaking, a *local area network (LAN)* is a group of computers connected within an enclosed area, such as a building. LANs can vary greatly in size. They can consist of two Windows PCs in your basement or several hundred workstations spread out over several floors in an office building. The key to the definition of a LAN is that all the computers on the network are grouped together in some fashion and connected somehow, and are in the same building. On most LANs, the medium of connection is some sort of cable. However, as I will discuss later in this chapter, some LANs use wireless communications to link their computers—and home networks are sometimes linked via telephone or power lines.

NOTE *Don't confuse a LAN (local area network) with a WAN (wide area network), which connects computers over extreme distances, typically utilizing the Internet as the networking backbone.*

There are two general types of networks that you can implement. A *client/server* network is comprised of a Master computer and multiple Slave computers. The Master computer, called a *server*, is a network-capable computer (with large storage capacity) dedicated to servicing requests for resources from the other computers on the network. The Slave computers, called *clients*, are the other computers that utilize (or subscribe to) the services provided by the server. In a client/server network, even if you have only two computers connected, one will be designated the server, and the other a client.

A *peer-to-peer* network is a simpler type of network. In this type of network—often used in home and small office environments—there is no designated Master computer. Each PC maintains its own identity, and is connected to the other computers primarily for file sharing, peripheral sharing, and (if you're into it) gaming. Whereas client/server networks typically require the use of an industrial-grade operating system, such as Windows 2000, peer-to-peer networks can be set up using the operating systems typically found on consumer PCs, such as Windows 98, Me, or XP.

Advantages of Networking

While setting up a network can be a time-consuming experience, there are many benefits to be gained by hooking all your computers together—benefits that far outweigh the hassles of configuring and maintaining the network.

SHARING APPLICATIONS

When all your computers are connected to a LAN, you gain the multiple advantages that come from application sharing. The way application sharing works is that one (and only one) copy of a software program is installed on the network server. When a client PC connects to the server, a copy of the application is loaded into the client computer's memory. As the client interacts with the program, it interacts with the copy stored in its own memory, not the one on the server, so that more than one client can access the same application simultaneously.

One major advantage gained by sharing applications in this fashion is that less disk space is needed on the individual client computers than if the application were installed on every PC. This is no small consideration in a world where the full installation of Microsoft Office now requires 2GB or more of disk space—before you create a single memo or spreadsheet! As common as large disks are nowadays, you won't necessarily have those large hard disks installed in every computer in your network.

Another advantage is that installing and upgrading applications is much easier if you can install the program files on a single point instead of on all computers in the network. Although this doesn't work for all applications or in all situations, when application sharing is feasible, it can save a lot of time and energy.

Finally, some applications are just meant to be shared—games in particular. Many of today's popular PC games come with multiple-player capabilities, which can be utilized only if you're connected to a network (or, in some cases, to the Internet). If you have two PCs, two avid gamers, and the right cards and cables, it's easy to set up an exciting Quake II contest.

NOTE One word of caution, however: installing applications on an application server for use by the rest of the network does not mean that you have to buy only one license for that application. Typically, you must buy one license for each user of the application, whether concurrent or total. (The requirements differ depending on the application.) If you don't have proper licensing for all your applications, you are guilty of software piracy, which is a federal crime. You don't think that anyone will know or care? Think again. The sole purpose of the watchdog organization called the Software and Information Industry Association (SIIA) is to care about piracy issues, and it will prosecute violations against its member organizations.

SHARING PERIPHERAL DEVICES

A *peripheral* (or *peripheral device*) is any piece of hardware that attaches to the motherboard of your computer, whether directly or indirectly. Not all peripheral devices are external to the computer case, and not all can be shared. However, for those that can be shared with the rest of the network, peripheral sharing can be a good way to make these devices available to everyone and make it easier for people to use them. For example, rather than having people line up at the PC with the printer attached, they can send print jobs to it as though it were attached to their machine and pick up those jobs at their leisure.

Sharing peripheral devices can save network users both time and money. It's true that even without a network, you don't have to buy printers or CD-ROM drives for every computer you own. One or two devices distributed throughout the office can work just as well if demand isn't high or people don't mind standing in line to use them. However, if people must waste time waiting for a device to be free, then the money saved by not having a printer at every desk may be spent in lost productivity.

Another advantage of peripheral sharing is the ability to connect multiple computers to a single high-speed Internet connection. If you have DSL or cable Internet service feeding into your house or small office, you can share all that Internet bandwidth with all the computers you've networked together.

Note that you don't have to make all shared peripheral devices available to everyone on the network—or give each user the same level of control. Thus, you can share that color printer (you know—the one that uses the really expensive cartridges) with the network, but protect it so that only the graphics people can access it—and keep all the other workers from using up those expensive cartridges by printing out rough drafts of their memos and to-do lists.

Enhancing Office Interaction

As offices get larger, it can be hard to keep people apprised of important events and to get them together all in one place. Networks can help encourage office cohesion by use of e-mail and group scheduling software.

Group scheduling was once probably one of your office manager's favorite ways of accumulating gray hair. It can be made much easier with the use of a network and some specialized scheduling software. Without these tools, organizing departmental meetings can be a nightmare as the organizer tries to sort through everyone's schedules to find a compatible time to meet. Group scheduling software can make this task much more approachable. The idea is this: everyone enters their schedules into a calendar program. Only they or selected people can see their own schedules, but the times are stored in a central database. When you want to call a meeting, you enter the names of the people you want to be present, then pick a time. If all the people listed are free at that time, the scheduling software will notify you. If not, it will notify you that there's a conflict and with whom, and (depending on the package) may be able to suggest the first time when all the people listed will be free. Once a time has been set, you can use the scheduling program to e-mail everyone invited to the meeting, telling them of the date and time.

Speaking of e-mail, it's useful for a lot more than just scheduling office meetings. In fact, e-mail is probably the most ubiquitous networking application today. And, since most e-mail systems permit you to attach files to e-mail messages, e-mail becomes another useful way to share files. Sending files via e-mail is like sharing the file with the network, but it has four main advantages (for some applications):

◆ You can explain anything confusing about the data in the e-mail message or emphasize the importance of the information.

◆ You can ensure that the recipient is getting the intended file, and you don't have to worry that they will open the wrong one by mistake.

◆ You don't have to worry about setting the proper permissions on the file or muck around with passwords because only the recipient of the e-mail message will get a copy of the file you send.

◆ You can send files to people with whom you don't share a LAN connection, such as those you can access only through e-mail via the Internet.

In short, the introduction of LANs is one of the best things to ever happen to office communication and information-sharing. Now that you understand the basics of what you can do with a LAN, you're ready to take a look at the pieces of the backbone that make all of this possible.

Understanding Networking Components, Protocols, and APIs

Before you dive right into the planning and implementation of your network, let's examine what exactly it is that makes a network work—the components, protocols, and Application Programming Interfaces (APIs) common to all network installations.

Networking Components

To create a simple network, you'll need hardware to connect your computers: network cards, some sort of cabling, and connectors to affix the cables to the cards inserted in each PC. I'll explain each of those items in this section.

DOOR TO THE OUTSIDE WORLD: NETWORK CARDS

The *network interface card (NIC)*, also known by such aliases as the network board or adapter, is the add-in card that you'll plug into the motherboard of your computer to provide an interface to the network. A network card really isn't fundamentally different from any other PCI card: it plugs into a slot on the motherboard, requires certain resources in order to operate, and has a built-in jack into which you can plug the network connection. If this were a sound card, you'd plug in speakers to produce sound. Since it's a network card, you plug in a network cable to produce connectivity.

You can divide NICs into categories in a few different ways. First, there's the type of network they support. As I mentioned in Chapter 3, "Inside the PC: Pieces of the Picture," the main type of LAN is Ethernet. Second, there's the type of cable that the cards support. The jack on the back of the card must be of a type into which you can plug the cable you want to use. Many Ethernet cards used to support the type of Ethernet that requires coaxial cable as well as the kind that requires unshielded twisted-pair (UTP) in a single card. For example, Figure 29.1 shows the back of a network card that includes ports for both types of interfaces, as well as an Attachment, or Adapter, Unit Interface (AUI) port. Because of the high initial cost, the coax Ethernet type of network has now pretty much been replaced by UTP (which uses an RJ-45 connector).

FIGURE 29.1

A dual-jack network card for both UTP and coax

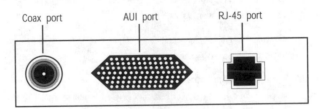

Coax port   AUI port   RJ-45 port

Third, there's the card's bus type, which governs how fast the NIC can talk to the motherboard. Most modern cards for desktop machines utilize the Peripheral Component Interconnect (PCI) bus. As noted in Chapter 3, Industry Standard Architecture (ISA) bus types still exist but are now obsolete. So it's a good idea to always use PCI network cards.

NOTE *Laptop users may use USB devices that provide UTP NIC capability or network cards that use the PC Card interface. (PC Cards were formerly called Personal Computer Memory Card International Association—PCMCIA—cards.)*

Fourth, there's the external data transfer rate, typically measured in megabits per second (Mbps). The data transfer rate that the network card you choose can support isn't the only factor that determines network speed, but it's one of them. Ethernet runs at 10Mbps (regular Ethernet), 100Mbps (called *Fast Ethernet*), or 1Gbps (*Gigabit Ethernet*). Although you can plug a PC with a 10Mbps card into a 100Mbps network, for example, the speed of the PC's connection to the LAN will be determined by the speed of the card connecting it to the LAN—or by the speed of the LAN, whichever is slowest.

Many NIC cards today operate at either 10 or 100Mbps and are identified by the designation of 10/100. Although they are a little more expensive than either the 10 or 100Mbps cards, the cost differential is very small, and these devices are more flexible and able to service your network needs for a long time. In fact, the fixed rate NIC cards are becoming less and less available. Today, you can purchase a cheap 10/100 NIC for $15.

NOTE *External data transfer rates are typically described in terms of bits per second (bps), whereas internal data transfer rates are typically described in terms of bytes per second (Bps). Remember, 1 byte equals 8 bits, and one ASCII character can be expressed in 1 byte.*

The faster version of Ethernet, Gigabit Ethernet, supports transmission speeds of up to 1 billion bits per second (Gbps). The NICs designed for these high speeds are very expensive and designed for the high-end server market, rather than for client PCs or ordinary servers.

THE SILVER LINK, THE SILKEN TIE: NETWORK CABLING

Sir Walter Scott may not have been talking about network cables when he wrote of these bonds, but the description fits: network cables are indeed the sometimes almost invisible but essential pieces for tying together a network. The types of information that will be sent between computers (text, complex graphics, video, or audio), the distance between computers, the kind of network that you want to create, and the environment in which those cables must operate are all determining factors for the type of cable you will need to use.

What are the options? There are several, divided between copper wire and fiber-optic. Each of them is designed to solve, in a different way, one of the most nagging problems facing any kind of transmission: interference, radio frequency noise, or RF noise (terms you may remember from Chapter 4, "Avoiding Service: Preventive Maintenance"). Copper wire was originally chosen as a medium for network transmissions because it conducts signals terrifically well, but that same capability makes it susceptible to interference from other sources of electrical signals, thus endangering the integrity of the original transmission. To get around this, the various cable types use one method or another of protecting the wire from outside interference or even making it immune to such interference.

NOTE *Copper wire, used within twisted-pair (UTP) and coaxial cable, may be either stranded or solid. Stranded wire is made of smaller wires combined, whereas solid is a single wire. Stranded cables are more flexible than solid and thus better for short runs requiring stress to the cable that might break a solid wire, but they are also more vulnerable to signal loss.*

The less susceptible cabling is to interference, the faster it is, because transmission speed along analog channels (such as copper wire) is a function of frequency. Before your eyes glaze over, understand that this is important. Copper cables are sometimes described in terms of the frequencies they can support, so if you don't understand what this means, then you're not going to understand those descriptions.

Frequency describes the rate at which electrical impulses travel through a certain area. As you learned in Chapter 25, "Play It Loud: Sound Cards," frequency is expressed in hertz, or cycles per second, the cycles being how fast the pulses can be created. They can be illustrated as sine waves (see Figure 29.2). In other words, a signal that runs at 8MHz can run 8 million cycles in one second. The higher the frequency, the faster the data is traveling because more 1s and 0s are being packed into a single second.

FIGURE 29.2

The more bumps of a sine wave in a given time period, the higher the frequency

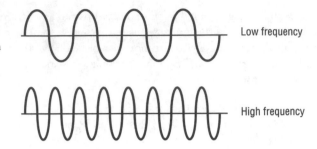

Low frequency

High frequency

Higher frequencies are more susceptible to interference than are lower frequencies because more data is compressed into a given instant. If you're unsure as to why this is so, take a look again at Figure 29.2. Suppose that something interfered with both the low-frequency signal and the high-frequency signal for a half-second (a long time, but this is to make the point, not to show precise measurements). During that half-second, the data transmitted along those channels would be corrupted and lost. In the case of the higher-frequency signal, you've lost a larger proportion of the data because more data was crammed into that half-second. The lower-frequency signal lost much less data.

The maximum frequency supported by a given cable does not imply that the data transfer rate of that cable always uses that frequency, but indicates only what the physical medium of the cable is theoretically capable of supporting, if undamaged and installed correctly. For example, Category 5 UTP (discussed in the following section) operates at a maximum frequency of 100MHz; but to support speeds of 100Mbps, a frequency of only 62.5MHz is required. That's just how fast the cable could transmit data under ideal conditions if the data were pushed through it that quickly. I'll discuss frequency and its relationship to signal strength and carrying power further under "Wireless Networking," later in this chapter.

INTERFERENCE VERSUS ATTENUATION

Although interference and attenuation have similar effects on data transmission (they're not good for it), they're not the same thing. *Interference* is a stray electronic signal that distorts the signal being transmitted, possibly corrupting the data being carried by adding extra humps in the sine wave or otherwise interfering with the signal. *Attenuation* is the increasing weakness of a signal as it travels. Just as a sound loses power from the time it leaves its source, but may still be audible at a given distance from its source, all signals experience attenuation. The problem arises when the signal is so severely attenuated (because it has traveled farther than it was meant to) that the fading signal can distort the data.

Both interference and attenuation work a lot like sound. Interference is the problem that you run into when a lot of people are all talking at once and it's difficult to sort out who said what, or even to distinguish the sound of one voice as it gets overrun by the sound of another. Attenuation is the problem you run into when someone is too far away for you to hear their voice properly and you may misunderstand them. Interference problems are resolved by shielding out other "conversations;" attenuation problems are resolved by boosting the signal.

Another variable in physical cable types is their reach. When reading the descriptions of the cable types, you'll notice that they vary in the length of the cable that they can use. That's due in part to a phenomenon called attenuation. Again, as you learned in terms of sound waves, *attenuation* is the degree to which a signal weakens over distance. The more vulnerable the cable is to interference, the more it will be affected by attenuation. The good news is that devices, such as repeaters, can rebroadcast the signal on long cables so they can run for longer distances.

Twisted-Pair Cable

If you wrap one good conductor around another one, they form a field that protects the conducting wires from RF noise. That's the approach taken by *twisted-pair cable*. There are two types of twisted-pair cable: unshielded twisted-pair (UTP) and shielded twisted-pair (STP).

These two types differ in two ways. First, UTP has four pairs of wires, and STP has two. Second, and the key to the difference in their names, STP has an extra conducting layer surrounding the twisted wires to give the cable an extra level of protection from interference. This does not necessarily imply that STP is always better protected from RF noise than UTP, but only that the two cable types take different approaches.

The theory with UTP is that the two wires wrapped around each other individually conduct noise, but cancel out each other's noise. The theory with STP is that the conductors are best protected with a layer of conducting wires rather than the two conductors being wrapped around each other. This extra layer of protection can make the STP cable hard to work with because it stiffens the cable, and the shielding works only as long as it's both properly grounded and not torn. Figure 29.3 shows the difference between UTP and STP.

FIGURE 29.3

Sections of UTP (top) and STP (bottom)

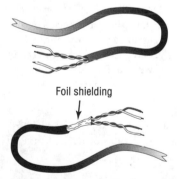

Foil shielding

NOTE *UTP is used in Ethernet networks (10Base-T and 100Base-T) and occasionally in Token Ring networks. STP cable is commonly used in Token Ring networks, which are not covered in this chapter.*

The Electronics Industry Association (EIA), Telecommunications Industry Association (TIA), and National Electrical Manufacturers Association (NEMA) established a five-grade standard for UTP. They then commissioned Underwriters Laboratories to certify and grade cable sold in the United States according to these standards. The higher the grade number, the more twists per foot and the more often the pattern of these twists must vary to throw off RFI. Thus, although no cable is entirely uninfluenced by interference, the higher the grade, the more immune that category of UTP is to RFI and EMI and the faster it can accurately transmit data. Technically speaking, Category 3 cable, rated for transmissions of up to 10Mbps and with at least three twists per foot, is LAN-capable and may be found in existing LANs. However, any new LANs using UTP will most likely use Category 5 cable, which in the trade is referred to as "Cat 5" cable. Cat 5 is rated for transmissions of up to 100Mbps and is capable of extending up to about 90 meters.

BEYOND CATEGORY 5

Note that Category 5 cable is the highest *certified* standard of twisted-pair cable. As of this writing, there are also a couple of not-yet-certified standards: enhanced Category 5 and Category 6.

Enhanced Category 5 cable is like Category 5 (high-speed UTP) except, well, it's enhanced. It's got more variance in its twist patterns and uses a higher grade of wire than does ordinary Category 5 cable and can typically support frequencies of up to 200MHz. It's not certain how the standard will define enhanced Category 5 cable—whether this will be the frequency rate required or if it will have to be as fast as 300MHz.

Category 6 cable is a kettle of fish of a different color because it requires a foil wrapping around the twisted-pair cable and is thus STP, rather than UTP. It's unclear as yet just how high its frequencies will be when and if a standard is defined. On the low end, one possibility is 350MHz, but on the high end, rates of 600MHz are bandied about. There are a lot of hang-ups attached to a Category 6 standard, such as what type of connector to use, the fact that it's STP instead of UTP, and the speed at which it's supposed to run. So Category 6 products are not likely to be widely available in the United States until some of these issues are sorted out.

Category 5 cable is able to keep up with the needs of Fast Ethernet, which supports data transfer rates of up to 100Mbps. Why are faster cables needed? Mostly because of the specter of Asynchronous Transfer Mode (ATM) and Gigabit Ethernet networks, which require frequencies in the hundreds of megahertz (350MHz for ATM) to keep up with them. These high-speed networks make Fast Ethernet look like your father's Oldsmobile. At a top frequency of 100MHz, Category 5 cable can't keep up with those needs, so the options are either to improve UTP performance or switch to fiber-optic cable.

IBM also maintains standards for a variety of types of twisted-pair cables (and two types of fiber), organizing them by function rather than in order of immunity to RFI. The twisted-pair types are as follows:

Type 1   Is solid-wire STP used for data transmission. It has two pairs of wires in each cable.

Type 2   Combines four unshielded solid wires and two shielded solid wires in the same sheath. The UTP is intended for voice transmission, and the STP is for data.

Type 3   Contains four pairs of solid-wire UTP to be used for voice or data.

Type 6   Contains two pairs of stranded-wire cable. It's essentially like Type 1 except that it uses stranded wire instead of solid.

Type 8   Is a special type of STP designed to be flatter than ordinary cable so it can be run under carpets.

Type 9   Consists of two pairs of STP covered with plenum rather than polyvinyl chloride (PVC) and is meant to be used between floors in a building. PVC emits toxic smoke when it burns, so plenum is required to meet some fire codes.

Twisted-pair networks typically connect each NIC to a centrally located switching area, either a hub or a *punchdown block* connected to a hub, which is a place to plug in lots of cables. I'll talk about hubs in the "Connecting Devices with Hubs and Switches" section of this chapter.

Coaxial Cable

Coaxial cable, often referred to as either *BNC cable* or *thinnet,* is made of a single copper wire encased in insulation and then covered with a layer of aluminum or copper braid that protects the conducting wire from RF noise. As you can see in Figure 29.4, coaxial cable has four parts:

- The central wire, called the *inner conductor*

- A layer of insulation, called the *dielectric,* which surrounds the inner conductor

- A layer of foil or metal braid, called the *shield,* which covers the dielectric

- The final layer of insulation (the part you can see), called the *jacket*

FIGURE 29.4

Coaxial cable

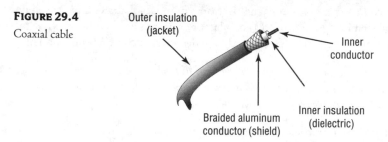

With a top data transfer rate of 10Mbps, coaxial cable is slow by modern standards, but it's got a couple of advantages over UTP for some installations. First, it can extend for longer runs. The top length for UTP cable runs is 90 meters, but coaxial cable can extend for more than 800 meters. However, after 185 meters you'll have to boost the signal with a device called a *repeater,* which I'll describe later in the chapter.

The second advantage is that you can use coaxial cables to connect PCs to each other directly (rather than to a central hub) in a daisy-chain effect. This can be handy for those who have only a couple of computers in the same room to connect and don't want to go to the expense of a hub.

NOTE   *There's a second kind of coaxial cable known as* thicknet, *which is used in older networks but not often installed new today. This cable can stretch for longer distances than can thinnet cable, but it's much harder to work with. One contractor I know who used to have to work with thicknet refers to it as "frozen yellow garden hose" because of its stiffness. Thicknet doesn't actually connect to the PCs themselves, but forms a backbone to the network that the PCs connect to with short patch cables.*

Fiber-Optic Cable

One way of getting around the problem of how to protect your data medium from EMI is to whack that Gordian knot in two. Make that cable utterly immune to EMI by not using electronic signals for transmission at all. That solution is called *fiber-optic cable*.

Fiber-optic cable is indifferent to RF noise because of the difference in its conductive medium; rather than using electronic pulses to send data, it uses light. The light is conducted through a hair-like glass or plastic fiber that is covered with a thin insulating layer called *cladding*. The cladding is then surrounded with a plastic jacket to protect the delicate fiber. You can see a drawing of fiber-optic cable in Figure 29.5.

FIGURE 29.5

Fiber-optic cable

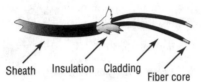

Sheath   Insulation   Cladding   Fiber core

As you'd expect, the fibers are the crucial element of data transmission. At each end of the fiber is a device called a *codec*, or coder/decoder. The codec is responsible for encoding the data into light pulses and then decoding them back into the electronic impulses that a computer can understand. To transmit data, a light-emitting diode (LED) or a laser at one end of the fiber sends signals along the cable. When those signals reach the other end, they're decoded into their original form.

NOTE *Astute readers will note from earlier chapters that I defined the term* codec *as "compression/decompression." You'll find it both ways, but generally the coder/decoder form is used to describe a hardware device, and the compression/decompression form refers to software used to encode and decode audio and video.*

It might sound as though traffic through a fiber-optic cable is limited to a single path of data, but this isn't true for a couple of reasons. First, fiber-optic cable may have more than one fiber in it, meaning that multiple data pathways exist. The more fibers a cable has, the more data can pass through it at once, just as a four-lane highway can carry more traffic than a single-lane road.

Second, there are two types of fiber-optic cable:

Single-mode fiber Sends transmissions along a single path, like a flashlight. This beam of light is intense, so single-mode fiber can carry more data for longer distances and is thus suitable either for applications that are traffic intensive or need to travel for long distances.

Multimode fiber Allows multiple modes to pass through the cable at once. There are two kinds of multimode fiber: step index and graded index. In *step index fiber-optic cable*, the light beams bounce around inside the cable in a zigzag pattern. *Graded index cable* has a more rounded pattern to the light movement, like a sine wave (see Figure 29.6).

NOTE *A* mode *is a ray of light entering a fiber at a particular angle.*

FIGURE 29.6

Multimode cable
sends more than one
beam of light down
the fiber at a time.

Step index system: Light bounces along an angular path inside the cable.

Graded index system: Light follows a more rounded path.

Both kinds of multimode fiber-optic cable are prone to *modal dispersion*—spreading of the received light impulse—due to the number of light beams traveling through the cable. When the signal spreads, it moves more slowly, so single-mode cable transmits faster than multimode cable. To understand this behavior, try imagining what would happen if you threw a ball down a pipe. If you threw just one ball and it went through without hitting the walls of the pipe, it would move faster and more accurately than if it bounced off the walls of the pipe. Just as bouncing off the walls of the pipe slows down the ball's travel speed, bouncing off the walls of the cable slows down the light signal.

NOTE   Single-mode cable is more expensive than multimode and can extend farther without requiring the signal to be boosted. Multimode cable is more often used within buildings; single-mode is reserved for inter-building use.

Fiber has had notable success as a LAN backbone, combined with UTP taps to each workstation, for those with high-traffic networks and deep pockets. Fiber's not often run to the desktop for a couple of reasons. First, it costs more per foot than does UTP and requires some specialized knowledge to install it, driving that cost up as well. Second, with the advent of Fast Ethernet (which, as I mentioned earlier, supports speeds of up to 100Mbps over copper wire), UTP is much faster than it used to be, not quite reaching fiber's speed when used in a Fiber Distributed Data Interface (FDDI) network, but rivaling it. However, as higher speeds are required for some applications and the costs of fiber drop, you can probably expect to see fiber run to the desktop more often.

If fiber is expensive to run to the desktop and no longer always hugely faster than UTP, then why use it at all? First, it *is* really fast and eminently suited to demanding sorts of traffic such as video. Second, since it transmits light, not electricity, fiber-optic cables are completely resistant to EMI and RFI, so signals are sometimes able to travel several miles without any degradation. Some kinds of fiber can transmit up to three miles in LAN environments and across the country via a high-powered laser device in WAN environments. Fiber-optic cable is also useful in hazardous environments because it can't spark (as electric transfer cables potentially could). Furthermore, it doesn't contain any metal, so it resists corrosion. Finally, fiber-optic cabling is harder to tap into than is copper-based cable, so it's more secure and therefore popular for top-secret communications.

A relatively new kind of high-end fiber network called *Fibre Channel* seeks to blur the distinction between individual devices and the network even more than the LAN does already. Fibre Channel can operate at even higher speeds than does FDDI.

CONNECTING A NETWORK—WITHOUT CABLE

While the vast majority of office networks are connected via some type of cable, there are other ways to connect your computers—without running all that wire. These alternate types of "wiring" are particularly popular in home networks, where it is often impractical to run long lengths of cable through walls and ceilings.

Power line networks enable you to send Ethernet packets over the electrical lines in your house. Power line networking uses Frequency Shift Keying (FSK) to send data back and forth. Two frequencies are used, one for 1 and one for 0; a transceiver unit attached between each computer and the nearest power outlet performs the frequency modulation. Although a power line network is extremely convenient and easy to set up, it is also very slow (data transfer can be as low as 50Kbps—compared to standard Ethernet's 100Mbps) and prone to disruptions from other electrical devices in your home.

Telephone line networks provide a similar level of convenience, but with higher data transfer rates (a minimum of 1Mbps) and greater reliability. With telephone line networking (commonly referred to as Home-PNA, based on the specifications developed by the Home Phone Networking Alliance), you connect each computer to an adapter that plugs into a standard phone jack. Then, utilizing a technology known as Frequency Division Multiplexing (FDM), data signals are sent through the adapter into your home phone line, and picked back up by another adapter and PC elsewhere on the network. Each adapter on the network sends its signal at a different frequency within the available band—enabling your computer network to effectively share the phone line with other voice and data traffic.

Finally, it's possible to connect a computer to a network without using any wires whatsoever. *Wireless networks* operate on the same principle as do wired networks, but without wires. Generally speaking, wireless networks can be divided into two classes: those using radio signals, and those using infrared signals. *Radio signals* have a wider range and (like radio) are relatively immune to most barriers, and with newer products using the 802.11 HR (High Rate) standard, are capable of transmitting at 11Mbps—slightly faster than regular Ethernet. *Infrared signals* have a very high frequency and high speed, but are easily disrupted, and thus impractical for most purposes.

In addition, the new *Bluetooth* specification could have important implications for wireless networks. Bluetooth uses a radio link to connect small mobile devices—such as PDAs—to each other, and to Bluetooth-equipped PCs. This would enable quick and easy network access for users with Palm, Handspring Visor, and other similar devices. (A network of Bluetooth-enabled portable devices is called a *personal area network*, or *piconet*.)

GETTING CONNECTED: CABLE-NIC CONNECTORS

Assembling your collection of NICs and cables is a large part of the business of putting together a LAN, but you still need something to make those NICs talk to those cables—which is where connectors come in.

Coaxial Cable Connectors

Three types of connectors are associated with coaxial cable:

- ◆ T connectors
- ◆ BNC connectors
- ◆ Terminators

You saw illustrations of these connectors in Chapter 3. I'll repeat some of those illustrations here as I describe how these connectors fit into a LAN.

T connectors (see Figure 29.7) plug into network cards, where they stick out the back of the PC and provide an interface for plugging in the BNC connector.

FIGURE 29.7

A T connector creates the interface into which you plug the BNC connector.

A BNC connector (see Figure 29.8) plugs into the T connector attached to the NIC. This links the card and the cable, with the cable forming the crossbars of the *T* (see Figure 29.9), and may also be used to link sections of coaxial cable.

FIGURE 29.8

The BNC connector may link coaxial cables to each other or to T connectors.

FIGURE 29.9

The BNC connector attaches the T connector to the coaxial cable.

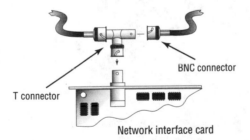

BNC connector

T connector

Network interface card

The terminators are the final piece of the coaxial puzzle; they are used to define the ends of the cable. If you don't have terminators at each end of a coaxial segment, then the signal will "echo" from the end of the cable and *shadow packets* will result. Shadow packets slow down network speed by increasing traffic and may corrupt data if confused with real packets. Terminating the segments ensures that packets will be destroyed when the signal reaches the end of the segment.

NOTE *Terminators are made for either 50-ohm or 75-ohm cable. The standard is usually a 50-ohm terminator. Pay attention when you're buying terminators because they won't work if you mix them up. Most coax network cable systems require 50-ohm terminators.*

Twisted-Pair Connectors

Most UTP cable uses RJ-45 connectors, which, as you learned in Chapter 3, look like chunkier versions of the connectors used to plug your telephone into the wall (see Figure 29.10). The RJ-45 connectors are attached to both ends of the cable; one end plugs into your computer card, and the other plugs into a hub or a punchdown block in the wiring closet. Essentially, it looks like a somewhat bulkier version of a telephone cord.

FIGURE 29.10

Each end of UTP network cable has an RJ-45 connector on it.

Okay, I lied—not all UTP cables connect a hub and a network card. You can use crossover cables in some implementations to daisy chain computers together. *Crossover cables* are wired to perform the function of a hub.

STP cable doesn't use the same connectors as UTP cable. You'll use a D-shell connector (see Figure 29.11) with STP to connect the cable to the NIC. You'll need an IBM Data Connector (Figure 29.12) to connect it to a multistation access unit (MAU) or hub.

FIGURE 29.11

A D-shell connector connects the cable to the machine's network card.

FIGURE 29.12

An IBM Data Connector connects the cable to the MAU.

WARNING   *You may notice that the D-shell connector used to connect to a Token Ring card is the same one that is used to connect to a video card. Be careful not to plug the network cable into your monitor.*

Fiber-Optic Connectors

Unlike copper-wire cables, in which the transmission medium is the biggest source of signal loss, fiber-optic is most susceptible to signal dispersion at its connectors. Fiber-optic cable uses two kinds of connectors: *screw-mounted adapter (SMA)* and *spring-loaded twist (ST)*. The ST connector uses a spring-loaded twist to clamp to the cable, whereas the SMA screws onto the end. ST connectors (see Figure 29.13) are more common than SMAs.

FIGURE 29.13

An ST connector and a connector cover

SUMMARY OF CABLE AND CONNECTOR TYPES

Having trouble assimilating all these cables and connectors? Table 29.1 lists the cable types discussed, their speeds, their maximum lengths, and the means they use to minimize electrical interference.

TABLE 29.1: CABLE AND CONNECTOR TYPES

CABLE TYPE	TOP SPEED	MAXIMUM LENGTH SUPPORTED	ANTI-INTERFERENCE MEASURES USED	CONNECTOR USED
Coaxial	10Mbps	800 meters	Copper braid around transmitting wires	BNC
Unshielded twisted-pair (UTP)	100Mbps	90 meters	Twisted-pairs	RJ-45
Shielded twisted-pair (STP)	100Mbps	90 meters	Twisted-pairs combined with metal shielding	D-shell
Fiber-optic	155Mbps or greater	10 kilometers	Transmission without electrical signals	ST or SMA

Networking Protocols and Application Programming Interfaces

For data to get from point A to point B on the LAN, you need not only hardware, but also networking software to package that data for transmittal. That networking software consists of three main parts, which work in tandem with the file system drivers of your operating system:

Redirector   Sends requests to the network instead of the local hard disk

Network card drivers   Provide communications between the operating system and the network card

Networking protocols   Send the data on its merry way and pick it up at the end of its journey

So, for example, if Fred tries to save a Microsoft Word file from his computer to a shared drive on the network file server, the following happens:

1. Fred clicks Save and chooses to save the document to his drive G, which is in fact a network connection to the physical drive D shared from the file server.

2. The redirector examines the request to save, notes that drive G is not locally available, and redirects the request to a part of the operating system called the *network file system driver.*

3. The file system driver passes the request to the network card driver.

4. The network card driver passes the request—and the data—to the network card.

5. The network card packages the data for transmission across the network and sends it.

6. The file server's network card notes that a package has arrived for it, and receives it.

At this point, the process is reversed: the server's network card driver passes the request to the file system driver in the operating system and writes the file to the local drive.

If you're building a network in an office, chances are excellent that sooner or later the network you create will be connected to another network in some manner or other. After all, that's how the Internet itself got started; local networks were given the means to connect to each other in a larger whole. Most networks grow in stages, rather than emerging full-blown in their final form, so they often include a hodgepodge not only of hardware but of network operating systems and communications needs as well. This, in turn, means that the network needs more than one type of redirector, must use more than one type of network protocol, and that not all the cards use the same driver. In short, sometimes even with careful planning it can be a bit of a mess as networks grow and merge. In this section, I'll discuss the various parts of the networking process so you can better understand what you're dealing with when it comes to managing networking software in all its varied parts.

First, I'll discuss the role of the redirector in arranging communications between applications and the operating system to reach network-accessible data. Second, I'll look at the role of the network card driver. Finally, I'll examine the three transport protocols used most often in PC-based networks.

THE ROLE OF REDIRECTORS

From the perspective of the PC initiating a network request, the first actor in the networking process is the *redirector*. Its role is to fool an application on the local machine into thinking that it is getting data from a local drive, rather than from a network drive. The point is that it shouldn't matter where the file being requested is stored; it should be accessible in the same way, no matter what.

For example, what happens if you are running Word and open a file stored on a network drive? From Word's point of view, there *is* no network. It knows only that there are one or more disk drives available with names consisting of a letter and a colon, as in A:, B:, C:, and so on. Like other application software, Word was not built to accommodate storage devices that aren't on the local machine. Thus, there must be a layer of software (placed just below Word) whose job it is to present a common drive-letter interface to Word when supplying data stored on the network. Word thinks that it is addressing local drives, but its requests for information from network drives must be *redirected* to network requests. So, if you tell Word to get the data from the directory DOCS on the server named BIGDOG, the redirector software initiates the request.

NOTE *Redirectors are often referred to as* clients *(as in, the Windows 98 Client for NetWare Networks) because they're a required part of a client machine.*

Therefore, before you can join a network, you must install a redirector that's compatible with the network type. Not all network operating systems use the same redirectors, so you must install the one that corresponds to the operating system on the network to which you're connecting. For example, Microsoft networks use Server Message Blocks (SMBs) to pass data back and forth, so they need a redirector that can phrase things in terms of SMBs. Novell networks use NetWare Control Protocols (NCPs) for the same job. So, to make requests of a NetWare server, you must use a redirector that can phrase requests in terms of NCPs. Note that having a transport protocol such as TCP/IP in common is not enough—you must have a redirector that works with the operating system to which you're connecting. The good news is that redirector support can overlap if the Presentation layer protocol is the same for more than one operating system. Thus, if you're using Windows 98, you can use the SMB-supporting Client for Microsoft Networks to connect to any operating system that supports SMBs.

REDIRECTORS AND APIS

Most user applications are unaware of the network or networks that they use. But some, such as e-mail or groupware programs, must be cognizant of the network and exist only *because* of the network. They need to be able to "plug in" and communicate with other programs running on other machines in the network.

Programmers build network-aware programs to be tailored to sets of commands that a network offers to applications programs. Those sets of commands are called APIs, or *Application Programming Interfaces*. Think of an API as being somewhat like the dashboard of a car. Your car's dashboard is the interface that you see, and you must learn to use it in order to operate the car. You have no idea while you're driving about what's under your car's hood—you just push down on the accelerator and the car goes faster.

Thus, you don't have to know precisely how a car works to drive it. Not only that, but once you know how to drive one car, you can drive just about any car because the controls—the API—are the same.

(I discovered while driving a friend's Volkswagen one night that Volkswagens do not use the same API for "reverse" that other manual-shift cars do, but this analogy generally works.)

A dashboard consists of just a few primitive commands: brake the car, accelerate the car, shift the car's transmission, and so on. There is no command for "back the car out of the driveway," and yet you can still back a car out of a driveway by just assembling a number of the primitive commands into the actual action of backing a car out of a driveway. You have, in a sense, built a program with your car's dashboard controls arranged in a certain order.

Your computer's API functions in pretty much the same way. Your network services, like the redirector, can sit on top of different transport protocols. Without an API, the programmers of your network software would have to develop one redirector program to connect Microsoft NT to IPX/SPX and a different redirector program to connect Microsoft NT to TCP/IP. It is the same redirector; it is just talking to different transport protocols. The way to avoid this is to provide a common "dashboard" for all the network services. Thus, the redirector service is not written to a protocol, but rather is written to an API (in our example, NetBIOS). NetBIOS can sit on top of IPX/SPX, NetBEUI, and TCP/IP. This means that the transport protocol can change, but you do not have to rewrite your network service because it is written to the API (NetBIOS).

Continued on next page

REDIRECTORS AND APIS *(continued)*

Sockets are a well-known type of API. They are temporary communication channels set up for passing information between a client program and a server program. These programs can be running either on the same machine or across the network. There are three network APIs that you'll probably come across in the networking world:

◆ Novell Sockets

◆ NetBIOS

◆ TCP/IP Sockets

The API will take your network request and perform the task through the proper transport protocol.

FILE SYSTEM DRIVERS

The redirector is the piece on the end of the connection that's making the request. Its counterpart on the end of the connection that's complying with that request is the *file system driver*.

File system drivers aren't used just for networking, but are part of any request for access to storage media. In Windows NT, for example, the network file system driver is one of the supported file systems: FAT, NTFS, CDFS, and the network.

NOTE   *I introduced FAT and NTFS in Chapter 14, "How Hard Drives Organize Your Data." CDFS is the Compact Disc File System, used by PC-based CD-ROM devices.*

In general, the role of *any* file system driver is to organize data on the storage media with which it's used. To take a commonly used disk drive file system that you're already familiar with, FAT numbers each cluster and notes which files are stored in which cluster. You will recall from Chapter 14 that if a file's data requires more than one cluster to hold it all, then each cluster will also include a pointer to the next cluster on the disk that's used to store that data; the final cluster has an end-of-file marker so the FAT file system knows when to stop looking. How does the file system know where the clusters are? When you format a disk, you're cataloging the space on it with the file system you use.

When you ask to retrieve a file, the FAT file system is in charge of finding the data you want and making sure that all of it is retrieved (as chances are excellent that not all of the data will be in the same cluster). Similarly, when you attempt to save a file to disk, the FAT file system finds the first free space on the disk and stores the data associated with that file in those clusters, marking the clusters to point to the next one used as required.

NOTE   *Depending on where disk space is available, those clusters may not be contiguous. The file system doesn't look for the first group of unused clusters that's large enough to store the file; it looks for the first unused cluster, period. If all the file's data won't fit into that space, then the file system will store the remaining data in the next free cluster, wherever that cluster happens to be on the disk.*

The network file system is just one more interface for reading disk space. The only difference is that it's used for network access instead of local access as are the other file systems. Thus, on the server end, when the server receives a request for disk access from some network client, the request goes to the network file system, which does what must be done—retrieve data, store a file, or whatever. The important aspect to this is that the network file system makes the local format of the server's hard disk immaterial to the client. Even if the file system with which the disk is formatted is not supported by the client, it doesn't matter because the local file system isn't the one used to satisfy network requests. So long as the client can talk to the server, the server will interpret the file system for the client.

THE ROLE OF NETWORK CARD DRIVERS

Now you know how a request gets from the application to the operating system, or is satisfied on the operating system side. How does that request get to the network? That's the role of a piece of software called a *network card driver*.

As you know, any device driver is a piece of software that lets an operating system and a piece of hardware talk to each other. Network drivers are responsible for managing any extra-computer communications, including those required to access the Internet. One network driver is installed for each model of card used. Thus, for example, if you have a PC with a cable modem connection to the Internet and a network connection, you'll need two drivers installed. If you have more than one network card installed (perhaps if your PC is acting as a router) and they're different kinds, you'll have one driver installed for each. However, if you have two network cards of the same type installed, you'll have to install only the one driver. Basically, these drivers install Data-Link network support for the PC, allowing it to access an Ethernet network, for example.

Network Binding Interfaces

Modern drivers use a tool to bind the network cards to the transport protocols. (I'll explain transport protocols more fully in the next section.) In general terms, this tool is called the *network binding interface*. It serves as the interface between a NIC driver and a collection of protocols called a transport stack.

NOTE *If you're familiar with the concept of binding a protocol to a network card, then the network binding interface is where the binding takes place. It's essentially a means of "marrying" a NIC driver and a network transport protocol.*

What's going on here is fairly straightforward. The network binding interface clumps each installed driver with each installed transport protocol. The name of the clump depends on the network type—for example, NetWare networks call them *modules*. Communication between modules is handled by a program called LSL under NetWare networks and PROTMAN.SYS under Microsoft networks. Any configuration information required for the binding interface is contained in a text file, such as PROTOCOL.INI for Microsoft networks, or NET.CFG for NetWare networks. However, if the default values for the drivers are used, there won't be much information in these configuration files.

THE TIES THAT BIND

One of the handy things about network binding interfaces is that they permit you to use more than one transport protocol with each network card driver. By default, all network transport protocols are bound with all installed network card drivers. When you attempt to send data across the network, and more than one transport protocol is installed, which protocol gets used? The answer depends on the order in which the transport protocols were bound. You can edit the binding order to place the protocol that will be used most often first, so as to reduce the number of retries required to find the protocol needed to access a particular server.

If you want to cut off communication to a server that's using a particular protocol, you don't have to uninstall it—just remove it from the list of protocols bound to the network card.

There are two competitors for the title of world standard network binding interface: Novell's Open Datalink Interface (ODI) and Microsoft's Network Driver Interface Specification (NDIS). These two binding interfaces have a lot in common in terms of what they do and how they do it. The main difference between them is that ODI-compliant drivers operate in real mode. As you know, this means that they must use memory in the first 640KB of the memory installed in your machine and that they can't cooperate with other drivers that may be installed in the system. NDIS-compliant drivers, in contrast, run in protected mode so they can multitask with other drivers and don't use scarce conventional memory.

Why use ODI-compliant drivers if they can't run in protected mode? Mostly because your redirector sometimes requires them. Not all redirectors will work with the NDIS-compliant drivers. If you're not sure, check the documentation for your operating system to find out the requirements of your particular redirector. Generally speaking, both NDIS and ODI work with all transport protocols; any limitation is on the driver side.

NETWORK TRANSPORT PROTOCOLS

Sneakily, throughout this part of the chapter I've been referring to transport protocols without ever really explaining what they are. Now's the time for the explanation.

Let's start with the concept of protocols. A *protocol*, quite simply, is a standard or set of rules. You are confronted with protocols in various aspects of your daily life. For example, if your phone in your house rings, you pick it up and say, "Hello?" Why do you say "hello" first? Why doesn't the caller identify himself first? The answer is that it's a tradition. It is the custom in the United States that the person answering the phone should respond first. In other words, this is the American protocol for answering the phone. If you were in mainland China, you'd pick up the telephone and wait for the other person to say, "Wei," to signal that they were there. When you meet someone, do you hug, kiss, or shake hands? Once again, the answer is determined by protocol.

How does this apply to networks? *Network transport protocols* determine how data is transmitted across the network, and how that data is packaged and addressed. For two computers on the same network to communicate, they must be using the same network transport protocols because the protocols used determine how the data is packaged and delivered.

The good news is that modern operating systems can simultaneously support more than one protocol, so you can use one for each type of connectivity you need. The bad news is that not all operating systems support all transport protocols; in fact, they tend to specialize, and even some like-named protocols are not usable across all platforms. However, today there's enough overlap that some degree of communication and interoperability is possible across all major operating systems.

TIP   Loading more than one network transport protocol uses up RAM, so even though it's possible to load more than one transport protocol with modern operating systems, it's a good idea to install support for only the ones you need.

Please be aware that the following sections are *introductions* to the three main protocols used in PC networking and are not complete. TCP/IP, for one, is an enormously complex protocol with sufficient configuration options to write a book about them, or a lot of books. What's here is simply intended to help you understand the basics of how each of these protocols work.

The NetBEUI Protocol

Back when IBM first started marketing their PC network, they needed a basic network protocol. They had no intention of building large networks, just small workgroups of a few dozen computers or less.

Out of that need grew the *Network Basic Input/Output System*, or *NetBIOS*. NetBIOS is just 18 commands that can create, maintain, and use connections between PCs on a network. IBM soon extended NetBIOS with the *NetBIOS Extended User Interface*, or *NetBEUI*, which is basically a refined set of NetBIOS commands. Over time, however, the names NetBEUI and NetBIOS have taken on different meanings. *NetBEUI* is the transport protocol, whereas *NetBIOS* is the set of programming commands that the system can use to manipulate the network; it is actually an API.

NetBEUI is one of the fastest protocols that you can use, in terms of its speed when slapping data into packets for transmittal and unwrapping said data on the receiving end. It's also beautifully simple to set up: you install it and bind it to a network driver, and it works. No configuration is required, and the address of the computer is an easy-to-remember name that you assign.

NOTE   Computer names on a network using NetBEUI are actually NetBIOS names. They can be up to 16 characters long and are not case sensitive.

However, there is one problem with NetBEUI, and this problem really limits its usefulness: you can't route it. In other words, if your needs are larger than those of a single segment, you can't use it to transport data beyond your local segment. (A *segment* is a piece of a network that can operate on its own or that has been subdivided simply for better management purposes. For example, within a network comprising several floors of a building, a segment might be on one floor.)

It's also supported only by some Microsoft operating systems and OS/2, so if you planned to communicate with the Unix file server or NetWare print server, well, you're out of luck.

Today, NetBEUI's usefulness is somewhat limited. First, Microsoft is not supporting NetBEUI with the newer releases of its operating systems. With both Windows 2000 and XP, NetBEUI must be manually installed off the CD. Second, TCP/IP is faster than it used to be, so NetBEUI doesn't have the performance advantage it did at one time. As Internet access becomes ever more ubiquitous, you need TCP/IP anyway, as it is the protocol required to use that network. Even though some NetBIOS applications require support that NetBEUI can give, you can now use NetBIOS over IP to get the same effect.

In short, NetBEUI's not useless, but its usefulness is limited to small, single-site networks that don't need Internet connectivity, and there aren't a lot of those around.

The IPX/SPX Protocol

IPX/SPX, Novell's proprietary transport protocol, is actually two protocols—IPX and SPX. IPX, or *Internet Package Exchange*, is a network-layer connectionless protocol. It's responsible for finding the best path for packets to take to reach their destination, or for picking them up when they arrive. *SPX*, or *Sequenced Package Exchange*, is a transport layer protocol that provides connection-oriented services between two nodes on the network.

Packet addressing and routing are handled by the IPX protocol. So, logical network addresses (as opposed to the hardware ones that are burned into the network card at production) are assigned at the IPX level. An IPX address consists of a 4-byte (32-bit) network number and a 6-byte (48-bit) node number.

What do these numbers mean? The *network number*, also called the external network address, identifies the physical segment to which the computer is attached. If two or more servers are on the same network segment, then they'll all use the same external address.

NOTE *External network addresses are assigned only to NetWare servers. Client machines on a NetWare network inherit their external network addresses from the server they log into.*

The *node number*, or internal network address, is usually the hardware address of the network card inside the PC. This is handy, as it means that no translation has to take place from software-assigned names to hardware-assigned names. When installing a Novell NetWare server, you are asked to accept or change the internal IPX number. It then becomes that server's ID number. If you type **slist** from a workstation, you'll see this ID for each server listed.

Figure 29.14 shows the format of a complete NetWare IPX address.

FIGURE 29.14

A NetWare logical address

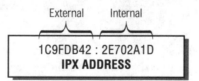

The TCP/IP Protocol

The TCP/IP Protocol

Working at the network level, the *Internet Protocol (IP)* provides a standard set of rules and specifications for the different networks to follow if they want IP to route their packets from one network to another. IP is designed for communications between both LANs and individual machines. The *Transmission Control Protocol (TCP)*, on the other hand, takes network information and translates it into a form that your network can understand. In this way, it supports process-to-process communication between two machines or clients. You could think of IP as the part of the protocol that sets the rules of communication and TCP as the part that does the interpreting.

NOTE *Strictly speaking, TCP/IP has more than two parts—it's a suite of protocols. However, the best known are IP and TCP, so I'll concentrate on them here.*

You can tell how good TCP/IP is at its job by its current task. It's the transport protocol for the Internet, the system that connects thousands of individual computers and networks across the world. Although originally designed for use by universities and the military, TCP/IP is becoming more popular for business applications. It can be used to connect LANs, Unix hosts, DEC VAX minicomputers, and many other kinds of computers.

What happens when a Mac in a remote office wants to send data to a PC in headquarters? First, TCP establishes a connection that provides full duplex error-checking (error-checking of data in both directions) between the two platforms. Second, IP lays down the rules of communication and connects the ports of the PC and the Mac. At this point, TCP has prepared the data, so IP takes it, breaks it into smaller pieces if the original was too big, and puts a new header (a "forwarding address") on the packet to make sure it gets where it's going. The TCP packet is also labeled with the kind of data it's carrying and how long it is. Next, IP converts the packet into a standard encoded format and passes it to the PC at headquarters. Finally, the PC's TCP translates the encoded packet back into "PC-ese," that is, its own networking protocol. You can see the process in Figure 29.15.

FIGURE 29.15

Sending data from a Mac to a PC through a TCP/IP network

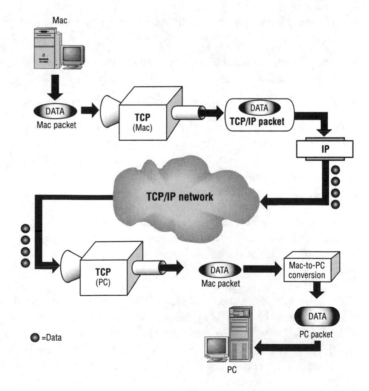

TCP/IP has become the default protocol for many of the world's networks. It's the only universal communicator that permits computers of all types—PCs, Macintoshes, and Unix workstations—to communicate, and, as I've said, it's required for communication on the Internet. It is a little slower than NetBEUI, but its wide support more than makes up for any performance hit. It's better to be a little slow and able to talk to the whole world than really fast and able to talk to only small groups.

Configuration Requirements for TCP/IP

One catch to TCP/IP is that it can be difficult for novices to set up, as there are so many addresses and servers to assign. As I've discussed already in this chapter, NetBEUI and IPX/SPX are pretty simple to set up addresses for. In the case of NetBEUI, you assign a computer name, and in the case of IPX/SPX, you assign a network identifier and let the system assign its own node identifier based on the hardware address of the PC's network card. However, TCP/IP can require a whole slew of addresses, including these:

- A local IP address
- The IP address of the Domain Name Service (DNS) server, which translates an easy-to-remember name, such as `computer.company.com`, into an IP address, such as `192.168.0.100`
- On NT networks using NetBIOS names to identify computers, the IP address of the Windows Internet Naming Service (WINS) server, which translates NetBIOS names into IP addresses
- The default gateway (that is, the portal to the next network segment), which is required even for Internet access
- The number (called the *subnet mask*) that identifies the network segment to which your computer is attached
- If dynamic IP addressing is enabled, the IP address of the server assigning IP addresses

If you've spent any time on the Internet at all, you're probably familiar with the concept of IP addresses. Simply put, they're a 32-bit (4-byte) number that identifies a computer on the network. This is the software address of the PC, as opposed to the hardware address burned into the network card. In its binary form, an IP address might look something like this:

```
11000000 01101010 01111110 11000001
```

It's not wildly easy to read by anyone but a programmer or a computer, so for the convenience of humans, IP addresses are written in what's called *dotted quad* format, converting each byte of the 32 bits into a number using the base-10 system, as shown here:

```
192.106.126.193
```

Each network card attached to a TCP/IP network has a unique IP address that identifies it on the network—not just the physical segment to which it's attached, but the entire network.

Where does this IP address come from? How do you know what numbers to include in it? The answer depends on the scope of your network. If you're creating IP addresses for a local TCP/IP network that will never have any contact with the Internet whatsoever, then you can more or less make them up if you want to, just so long as no two network cards have the same IP address. However, if you want to connect to the Internet, you'll need to get unique IP addresses, and that's where an organization called the InterNIC comes in.

The *InterNIC*, simply put, is an organization in charge of assigning Internet addresses to companies and organizations that request them. In broad terms, it assigns groups of IP addresses to organizations based on their sizes, by assigning specific numbers for the first byte (or first two, or first three) and then letting the organization use any numbers they like for the other addresses. So, for example, if you requested a set of Internet addresses from the InterNIC, they might give you the set 192.106.X.X. This would mean that all your IP addresses would have to start with the 192.106. prefix, but that you could assign numbers (up to 255) as you chose for the final two quads of the address. The parts assigned by the InterNIC are called the *network* portion of the address, and the parts assigned internally are called the *host* portion.

NOTE   *If your eyes aren't boggling at the idea of having to assign an IP address for each computer in your organization, they should be. Not only must you assign the numbers, but you must also create a file that maps computer names to the IP addresses. The file with the name mappings must be kept up-to-date on every computer on the network. To reduce the complexity of this problem, you can run a Dynamic Host Configuration Protocol (DHCP) server to assign IP addresses from a pool, and then use a WINS or DNS server to resolve name-address mappings. WINS servers take care of NetBIOS names, and DNS servers take care of domain names.*

A key part of Internet addressing lies in identifying not just a specific computer, but identifying the *subnet*, or part of a network, to which it belongs. That's done not with an external network number, as with IPX/SPX addresses, but with the subnet mask. The subnet mask is a number that can be overlaid onto the IP address. If the network portions of the IP address match the subnet mask, then the IP address is on the same subnet. If the network portions don't match, then the two IP addresses are on different subnets.

It's easy for two computers on the same subnet to communicate with each other; TCP/IP broadcasts the data, and the computer with the destination address that matches the one in the IP packet picks up the data. If a computer on one subnet wishes to communicate with a computer on another subnet, then the request must go to the router that connects the two subnets. The router looks at the network address of the destination address, decides whether that address is on the local subnet, and if it isn't, forwards the packet to the next subnet. Then that router examines the destination IP address, decides whether the address is on *that* subnet, and either broadcasts the message for pickup or forwards the packet again to the next subnet. This procedure continues until the correct subnet is found.

When a packet arrives at its destination, a protocol called the *Address Resolution Protocol (ARP)* resolves the IP address to the network card's hardware address. ARP is also responsible for translating the addresses for outgoing data.

Multiple Transport Stacks

Two things should be obvious by now. First of all, there is no single best network protocol. Second, you may conceivably want to run all three of the protocols (NetBEUI, IPX/SPX, and TCP/IP), each for a different reason, and the good news is that you can. One of the values of the current networking model is that it supports multiple transport protocols. This is shown in Figure 29.16.

In this example, you see that the client machine has three transport protocols loaded, and the server has one. This could happen if the client machine connected to more than one server. The IPX stack might talk to a Novell server, the TCP/IP stack might talk to an Internet server, and even NetBEUI might be used for local access with Microsoft machines. Each transport protocol binds to the drivers and redirector installed on each machine. As discussed earlier in the "Network Binding Interfaces" section, you can change the binding order for the various protocols so that IPX/SPX (or a compatible protocol) may be used first when connecting to a NetWare server, or TCP/IP for connecting to the Internet.

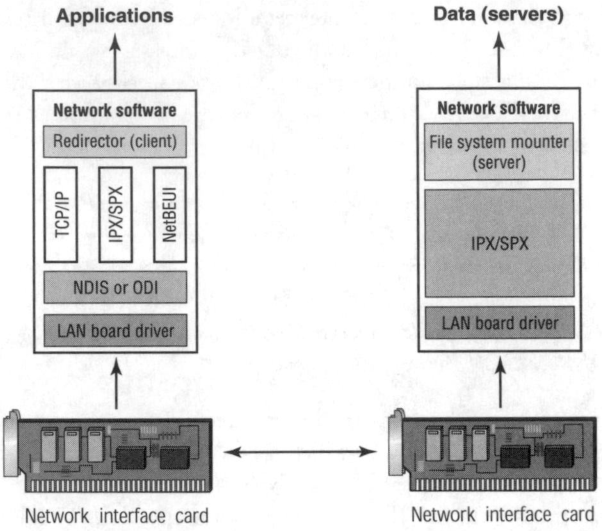

FIGURE 29.16

A network using multiple transport protocols

Choosing a Network

Now that you know how a network works, how do you choose what type of network to use? If you're in a traditional office, your choice is simple—an Ethernet network, perhaps with wireless capability for specific users. If you're building a home network, however, the choices are more numerous. Do you go with a more complex and costly (although faster and more reliable) Ethernet network, or do you embrace one of the non-Ethernet technologies, such as wireless or phone-based connections? This section will help you make the right choice.

Office Networking Options

When installing a LAN in a corporate environment, your big choices will be what transfer speed to support—and whether you want to include wireless accessibility.

ETHERNET NETWORKING

If you're installing a network in a medium or large office, Ethernet is the LAN of choice. Only a cabled connection provides the security and speed you need for an effective corporate network. In addition, phone line and power line networks are impractical if you share a large building with other businesses; it's too easy for your packets to get mixed in with those of another business using the same technology.

The most common type of Ethernet connection used in most corporations is 100Base-T, which transmits data at 100Mbps. You could use 10Base-T, but 10Mbps will seem sluggish, especially if you have a lot of users connected to the network. Conversely, if you have a large network (and a big budget) you may want to splurge for the 1Gbps speed of a Gigabit Ethernet.

WIRELESS NETWORKING

If your employee base includes telecommuters or outside sales reps who often stop by the office (and want to use their laptops while they're there), consider adding wireless capability to your network. Each remote PC must be outfitted with a wireless LAN card, and you need to add an access point to your network hardware, to enable wireless access up to 11Mbps. If you're considering this type of wireless access, check out offerings from several companies, including LinkSYS, NETGEAR, Intel, and Proxim.

VIRTUAL PRIVATE NETWORKING

Something else to consider when setting up your corporate network is how to provide access to the network to employees not in the office. This issue of remote access is addressed by a new networking technology, called *virtual private networking*. With virtual private networking, employees working from home (or away on a business trip) can dial into your corporate network and access their office computers, as well as other resources on the network.

In essence, a virtual private network (VPN) connects the resources of one network over another network. A typical VPN consists of authenticated and encrypted "tunnels" through a shared data network—in most cases, the Internet.

To enable this type of extra-LAN access, VPN uses what is called a *tunneling protocol*, such as Point-to-Point Tunneling Protocol (PPTP), Layer 2 Tunneling Protocol (L2TP), or Layer 2 Forwarding (L2F). When one of these protocols is installed on your network, any remote client can configure their Dial-Up Networking connection with the proper information specific to your network (including IP addresses and passwords) and then gain secure access to the corporate network.

Home Networking Options

When you're setting up a network for your home (or home-based office), you have the same options available as you would in a corporate environment—plus a few more. Whereas speed and security are the two main considerations for a corporate LAN, ease of setup is probably the main concern for most home networkers—especially the ease of cabling. Let's face it—unless you had the prescience to have Ethernet cabling strung when your home was under construction, the prospect of running long lengths of expensive cable from room to room (and through walls!) might be a tad daunting. In this likelihood, implementing an easier-to-set-up phone line or wireless network might have greater appeal.

ETHERNET NETWORKING

Yes, you can build an Ethernet-based home network. An Ethernet network is still the fastest, most reliable network you can construct—and many new PCs are coming with built-in Ethernet capability. In terms of add-in cards, you can choose from either 10Base-T or 100Base-T cards.

NOTE *Many Ethernet cards are billed as 10/100. This means that they're capable of Fast Ethernet's 100Mbps transmission rate, but can also operate at the slower speed if connected to a 10Mbps hub. The 10/100Mbps cards cost a little—although not much—more, but provide 10 times the data transfer rate.*

Note, however, that hooking up an Ethernet network requires a small degree of technical know-how—expertise that not all home users may possess. Not only do you need to install an Ethernet card in each PC, you also have to install a *hub* (discussed later in this chapter) to physically connect the machines. While this isn't necessarily costly or complex, you do have to know what you're doing. Plus, you have to physically run the Ethernet cabling between the machines, which, depending where your PCs are located, may or may not be a piece of cake—and could require complex and costly installation.

POWER LINE NETWORKING

Connecting your computers via your home's power grid is one cable-less option—although probably not a practical one. This technology has always been relatively slow (around 50Kbps); with the release of new products from NETGEAR, it now transfers data at speeds of up to 14Mbps. Even with this speed improvement, power line networking is still considered slow.

TELEPHONE LINE NETWORKING

An easier way to construct a cable-less network is by using your home's phone lines. Phone-line networking (called HomePNA) is based on specifications produced by the Home Phone Networking Alliance (HPNA). Even though you use the phone lines to transmit data on your home network, your telephones can still function without interfering with the network. HomePNA networks have not enjoyed huge success because the original equipment could only transfer data at an unacceptably slow rate of 1Mbps. The current specification, HPNA 2.0, can transfer data at 10Mbps, and the specification in development (3.0) will allow the phone lines to reach speeds of 100Mbps.

There are several HomePNA products on the market, many for less than $100 per PC. The most popular product is Intel's AnyPoint Home Network kit. The standard AnyPoint adapter plugs into a parallel or USB port on your PC and then connects to the nearest phone line (no hub necessary). It's about that easy—and the software bundled with AnyPoint makes setting up the network a snap. (If you don't want to tie up an external port on your PC, you can install a PCI card AnyPoint model.)

In spite of the enormous efforts of the HPNA, the advantages of HomePNA have been over-shadowed by wireless network solutions that cost the same amount of money, offer the same or better data rates, and do not require the installation of phone wires.

WIRELESS NETWORKING

The highest-tech cable-less network solution is to set up a wireless network. Several solutions are available, all at a relatively low cost.

If you're a Macintosh owner, many new Macs include support for Apple's AirPort wireless networking technology. AirPort runs just as fast as 10Base-T Ethernet (10Mbps), is easy to set up and configure, and works fairly well.

On the PC side of things, you can choose from four possible wireless solutions: HomeRF, IEEE 802.11b, IEEE 802.11a, and Bluetooth.

HomeRF is sold by both Intel (AnyPoint) and Proxim (Symphony); Proxim manufactures both products. The original HomeRF products were limited to the same low speed as the networks that used existing phone lines (1.6Mbps). HomeRF has greatly improved and can now transfer data at 10Mbps at ranges up to 100 feet.

Of all the wireless standards, IEEE 802.11b can be considered the de facto standard. Eight companies currently manufacture products using 802.11b, which is also referred to as *WiFi*. (WiFi sounds much more appealing from a marketing standpoint. Consumers are not fond of any product name that resembles the part number of a brake drum.) A WiFi network transmits data at a snappy 10Mbps and, due to the way the standard communicates between units, offers several advantages over HomeRF. The most important advantage is the compatibility of equipment made by different manufacturers. Another advantage is the greater sustained throughput of the WiFi solution over HomeRF.

An even faster version of WiFi is the IEEE 802.11a standard (as of yet, it doesn't have a snappy name). Proxim began shipping this product in the first half of 2002, and for a slightly higher price than WiFi, the 802.11a moves data at speeds up to 100Mbps. Until other companies begin shipping 802.11a products, however, I recommend sticking with WiFi.

A wireless solution that receives an enormous amount of press is Bluetooth. This specification is different from the first three in that it is *not* designed to hook local computers together. Rather, Bluetooth enables your computer to connect to the Internet from anywhere using Bluetooth service providers, much like cell phones connect to their service providers. The only problem with the Bluetooth solution is the general unavailability of Bluetooth service providers. The actual Bluetooth specification is also in limbo as the IEEE committee tries to resolve some technical issues.

SHARING A BROADBAND INTERNET CONNECTION

One of the most popular uses of a home network is to connect multiple computers to a single broadband (DSL or cable modem) Internet connection. If this is your goal, you may have several options available to you.

If you're using a DSL connection, note that some DSL modems also function as network hubs. To use a DSL modem/hub to connect multiple PCs, you'll have to connect each computer to the modem/hub via an Ethernet connection. (Many DSL modems can also be connected via a USB or parallel port, although you can't use these ports for multiple-PC connections.) If your DSL supplier offers this hardware and service, it's an easy-to-use option.

The other option, of course, is to connect all your computers to some sort of home network (Ethernet, phone line, power line, or wireless). The lead computer will connect to your DSL or cable modem, and then all the other computers on the network will also have access to that connection.

Due to the growing popularity of broadband Internet, a feature called Internet Connection Sharing (ICS) was added to Windows 98 Second Edition, Me, 2000, and XP. With ICS, it's relatively easy to configure one PC to be the Connection Sharing computer, and then to route Internet access from other networked computers through this lead PC.

With ICS, the only computer on your network that is visible to the Internet is the Connection Sharing computer, which provides private IP addresses and name resolution services for all the other computers on your network. When an individual PC accesses the Internet, that computer's private IP address is transmitted to the Connection Sharing computer, which then translates it to the IP address of the Connection Sharing computer and sends it out to the Internet. Translation back to the initiating PC is made when information is downloaded from the Internet to that PC.

Setting Up Your Network

Now that you understand the technology behind networking and have decided on the type of network you want to install, let's get to it!

Installing Cables

Most of what I'm going to talk about here concerns how to prepare for a contractor's help and what you need to know about your physical installation before the cabling process begins. This is not a complete tutorial in cable installation. First, I don't have room. Second, it's difficult to tailor such instructions when you can't see the environment in which the cable will be installed. Third, complex cabling is often a specialist's job. Therefore, I'll talk about the basics, so far as you need to know them for simple cabling jobs or for overseeing someone else doing a more complex one. After reading this, you'll be better prepared to instruct the cable installer in what you need done. Outsourcing this kind of work isn't cheap, and the meter's always ticking, so it's best to be prepared.

PLAN AHEAD

This is one of those really obvious but easily overlooked hints: don't just think about what your needs are now, think about what they'll be five or ten years down the line. Cabling a building is not so much fun that you're going to want to do it twice, so plan ahead.

First, know your situation. Get the blueprints for the building you're in and study them. Where is the ductwork? Where's the electrical wiring and how is it shielded? Are there any surprises waiting to happen? What are the fire codes for your area? What do they say about where you can use PVC-coated cable and where you must use plenum?

Get the fastest cable you can afford. Even if you don't need it now, the chances are excellent that sooner or later you'll use it, when your company starts implementing databases or video to the desktop or some such thing. Buy that 100Mbps Category 5 now, or even fiber if you can justify it, and you'll save yourself money later in not having to pay for two cabling installations.

GIVE YOURSELF SOME SLACK

Don't plan out your cabling needs to the last foot, but anticipate quite a bit of extra cable. First, you'll need this because you can't just plug PCs into the network on top of each other.

TIP   Conveniently, some coaxial cable comes with markings every 10 feet, so you can tell how far apart to make the connections.

Second, the extra room will give you flexibility. If you have just enough cable for your needs, then sooner or later Joe User is going to want to move his PC five feet to the left, and that's going to completely throw off your entire network if your plan has no flexibility built into it. When running the cable along the ceiling or floor, leave a few loops (6 to 8 feet for backbone cable) at each corner, or each doorway, or anywhere that there's a permanent physical feature in the building so you can find it again. Secure the loops with electrical tape to keep them neat and out of the way. When you need a little more length in your cable, you'll have it.

Otherwise, you'll have two options: splicing the cable yourself, or paying someone else to do it. Contractors typically charge not only for the length of the cable they run, but also for the number of terminations they must do. Splicing the cable means paying for two useless terminations that don't do anything but give you more length that you could have had from the beginning with a little planning. Similarly, when running taps from a backbone or hub, give yourself a spare 10 to 15 feet so that you can move the PC at a later time if you need to do so.

WARNING   *If you haven't planned for flexibility and need to extend your cable, splice it rather than attempting to stretch it. Stretching can damage cable—especially stranded cable—and damaged cable is far more prone to interference.*

Giving yourself elbow room applies to conduit, too. In big installations with high security needs, you'll often have a central backbone run in a large duct, with smaller conduits branching off from it. This is an expensive configuration, and larger conduits will make it more expensive yet. Regardless, you should seriously consider getting conduit a little larger than you need now. For example, if the ½-inch variety will let you run two taps from the backbone, get the ¾-inch variety so that you can run three or four taps if you need to do so. Once again, even if it's more expensive up front, giving yourself room to grow will save you money down the road, when you don't have to buy new conduit, pay to have it installed, and scrap the stuff you already paid for.

NEATNESS COUNTS

Keep in mind that you're going to have to deal with this cable at some point after it's installed, so make it as easy to get at as possible. When it comes to ceiling installations, you may be tempted to just throw the cables across the "floor" of the ceiling because it's less work. It's true, this is less work initially, but when you have to work up in that ceiling later, you're not going to like it if you have to trip over cable snaking across the floor. To avoid this, tie the cables to something such as the supports of the drop ceiling; clamps are made for the purpose, or you can use the plastic snap ties. You may also want to consider attaching the cables to air conditioning or heating ductwork.

As a last resort, leave all the cables on the floor of the ceiling, but bundle and tie them so that they're out of the way. That way, if you have to move them, you have to move only one lump, not six individual cables all tangled up together.

NOTE   *Not all drop ceilings can support cable, so you may have to tie the cables to the supports or ductwork to make this work at all.*

Running cables under the floor requires similar planning. Again, lay the cables neatly so that they're easy to get to. If you have the money, consider getting ductwork to run the cables in so that they stay in one place. Also, put the cables somewhere that you can get to them *after* the furniture has been put into the room. It might look neater to have the cables running along the wall, but chances are excellent that cubicles or an extremely heavy table will be along the wall. The middle of the room, where there's less likely to be furniture, is a better bet.

If you're running cable *on* the floor, then the rules are a little different. In that case, you'll do well to keep the cables against the wall and out of harm's way. That way, people will be less likely to trip over them (injuring themselves and/or the network in the process). Also, janitorial staff are less likely to damage them with enthusiastic cleaning. Tape down cables as best you can to avoid the chances of them being tripped on or wandering away.

Finally, label *everything*. At troubleshooting time, you're going to want to know which cables go where without doing this routine: "Okay, Karen, when I say 'Go,' shake the cable so I can tell which one it is." That exchange is typically followed by this routine: "Okay, it wasn't that cable. When I say so, shake the one next to it."

To avoid this, you can use different colors of electrical tape wrapped around the ends of the cables, or little adhesive numbers, or (if you have deep pockets) color-coded cables themselves. These make it easier to tell which cable you have at the end and also make it possible to tell which cable you're holding when you're crouched in the ceiling. I don't recommend hand-printed labels, as they can be hard to read. Unless you have a really complicated cabling system that requires extensive description, symbols are probably the way to go. You can identify them at a glance and don't have to decipher someone else's handwriting or turn the cable over to read the whole thing. A little more than 10 percent of the male population can't tell red from green, so consider using symbols or avoiding green and red cables.

TIP   *Keep a legend of cable codes around so people can tell what they're looking at even if you're out of the office.*

PLAY WELL WITH OTHERS

Finally, think about what's going to be running in the same place as your network cable. Got lots of interference-producing devices around? Consider cable with extra shielding, such as coaxial or STP, or, better yet, RFI-immune fiber.

TIP   *Fluorescent lights emit a lot of EMI, so don't run cables over the top of them.*

Are electrical cables already in place? Don't run your network cables parallel to them, particularly if you're looking at big bundles, such as those leading up to a fuse box. If new electrical cables are going in after the network has been installed, avoid introducing new interference problems by asking for armored cable (run in a metal sheath) rather than the ones enclosed in the plastic sheath. Once again, it will cost more up front, but these extra precautions may save you money later.

THINGS TO KNOW AHEAD OF TIME

I've talked about some of the specifics you need to be aware of before the cabling process begins. Here are some questions for your contractor. Figuring out these details early in the process can save you time, money, and lots of headaches.

Do you have wiring conduits?   Many buildings provide you with built-in places in the walls and ceilings where you can run your cable. Often, these wiring conduits are themselves plenum-rated. This means that you *may* be able to use a cheaper PVC cable.

How are you testing your cables?   You will want to know the precise method that is being used to test the cables after they are installed. Common sense reigns supreme on this issue. (Keep in mind that common sense really isn't that common.) Make sure that you get a written description of the testing method and follow the testing logic from start to finish to ensure that it makes sense for installation.

How are you documenting your cables?   Make sure that the cables are being documented and labeled according to your company's set standard. If your company has not set one, then it should do so. You want to be sure that the labeling system makes sense to you, so I recommend that your company set the labeling standard, not the contractor.

What is the repair policy for the cable installation?   You will want at least a 24-hour on-site response from your contractor. Many contractors say they have a 24-hour response to cable problems, when what they mean is, "We will call you back within 24 hours, and it may take us up to a week to get there." You don't want that; you want the contractor at your site in 24 hours or less. Cable problems are mission-critical problems.

Can you get at least three local references from the contractor?   You will want three local references from your contractor so that you can personally see the quality of their work and documentation of it. Most companies will not mind taking you on a tour of their cable systems if they are happy with the work the contractor has done. Don't forget to reciprocate when prospective clients call you to come see your expertly designed and installed cable system.

Are you following building and fire code requirements?   To ensure the safety of all your employees, follow all local building and fire codes. You want to select a contractor who can demonstrate by experience and references that they are well versed in the local regulations. When in doubt, call the city or county offices and ask questions.

Do you need to notify anyone else in your building or locale of your plans?   You may need to check with other tenants in your building to make sure that the cable installation will not conflict with their workflow. This is usually more of a courtesy than a requirement. Often, if you notify building management, they will notify all the other tenants in your building.

How long is the guarantee on the cable installation valid?   Verify the length of time the contractor will guarantee their labor and the cables. A one-year service contract is advisable. Reasonable costs for an annual service contract should not exceed 12 percent of the overall cable installation cost.

Preparing a Wireless Network

Preparing for a wireless network—or, more likely, a wireless portion of a wired network—isn't significantly different from preparing for a wired one. You still have to think about environmental factors and how the data is going to get from point A to point B.

As I said earlier, two kinds of wireless networking are used in LANs. Most common are the *radio-frequency (RF)* wireless networks, which can be used to connect PCs and servers over a fairly wide area—even though some have relatively low transmission speeds (as low as 1Mbps, but more commonly in the 10Mbps range with 100Mbps soon to be widely available). More specialized applications, such as wireless printers and keyboards, use *infrared (IR)* technology to create a high-speed, short-range link.

Interference is the biggest problem you're likely to encounter with wireless networks. Infrared communications have an extremely high frequency, so in order to use them, the sender and receiver must be close and in the line of sight. If you can't stretch a piece of string between the sending device and the receiving one, they can't communicate. Therefore, if you have an IR printer, it's a good idea to place it somewhere that IR notebook users can access it without people walking between the two devices.

RF devices are less prone to interference because their lower frequencies mean that the signal can more or less go around obstacles instead of being blocked by them. For this reason, although IR devices are confined to the room in which they operate, RF wireless devices can roam up to about 100 to 150 feet away from their source if indoors, or 800 to 1000 feet away if outdoors. Thick walls or metal barriers will interfere with the signal, but otherwise they're pretty flexible.

Installing and Configuring Network Cards

The cables are in. Now, you're ready to attach them to something. If you're not familiar with cable installation and configuration, read on. You'll learn how to get the card in the box in the first place and how to make it work with the other cards in the box once it's in there.

INSTALLING NETWORK CARDS

If you have any experience installing cards in a PC, the mechanics of installing a network card are pretty straightforward. Power down the PC, don your antistatic strap, open the computer case, and find a slot in the PC that's free and fits the kind of card you have.

TIP   If you can, choose a slot that's not next to another card in order to keep the airflow inside the PC's box as open as possible.

If you're removing another card to insert the new one, follow these steps:

1. Make sure that the card is disconnected from any outside cables.

2. Unscrew the small screw attaching the card to the PC case and lay it aside.

3. Pull gently on the card, using both hands to wiggle it back and forth slightly to disengage it from the connectors. This may take a little tugging, but if the card doesn't come fairly easily, stop and make sure that the card is indeed fully disconnected from the PC.

4. After you've pulled the card out, set it aside. Wrap it back up in its original sheath, if you kept it and plan to use the card again. Don't touch the gold connectors on the card; the oils in your skin can corrode the gold and thus reduce the card's connectivity.

Installing a card is much the same process, in reverse:

1. Unwrap the card, being careful not to touch the gold connectors, and set it aside.

2. Power down the PC and open it up.

3. Find an open slot on the motherboard that matches the bus required by the card. An ISA card needs an ISA slot; a PCI card needs a PCI slot.

NOTE   PCI is the card type you're most likely to be dealing with. MCA and EISA cards are very rare, and I'd be surprised if you found a network card that required that you use either bus type. It's possible to find EISA network cards, but they're fairly uncommon.

4. Unscrew the plate that covered the open slot's opening to the rear of the computer and set the plate and screw aside. You may need the plate later, and you'll need the screw in just a minute.

5. Align the network card with the slot in the PC, and push gently but firmly to seat the card in its slot. You may need to push fairly hard for this to work, which can be somewhat intimidating if you're not used to inserting cards. If you have the right slot and push straight in, then the card should snap into place.

6. Using the screw that you set aside in step 4, screw the card into the little hole in the case to hold it in place. If the card is in all the way, this extra step won't affect the card's positioning all that much, but will keep it from sagging or working loose.

7. Replace the case and, if the cables are already in place, connect them to the card.

INSTALLING NETWORK CARD DRIVERS

The process for installing the drivers for the card depends on your operating system. Like other add-in cards, network cards come with a floppy disk containing drivers. To install these drivers, follow the instructions that come with the network card. The setup process is usually initiated with really complex operations, such as running INSTALL from the A drive. This type of installation program will have an interface like the one shown in Figure 29.17.

TIP The operating system may include drivers for the card, but if the operating system is more than a year old, the drivers that come with the card itself are likely to be newer.

FIGURE 29.17

Installing network cards from a floppy disk

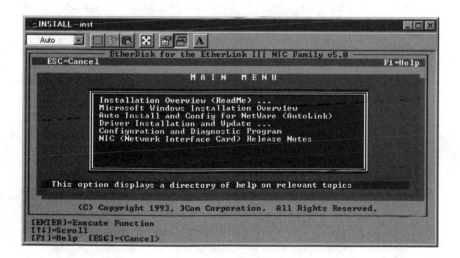

More recent versions of operating systems may include drivers for the cards that you can load by using an interface within the operating system. For example, Windows 95/98 includes the Add New Hardware Wizard, which you can use to detect the card and automatically load the required driver. In most cases, you will not need to use the wizard as Windows 9x/2000/Me/XP supports Plug and

Play, which will automatically detect and install the necessary drivers. That said, you may end up using the disk anyway, as the drivers on the floppy disk may be more recent, or may be better optimized for the card than are the drivers included with the operating system. Consider the 3Com EtherLink III NIC used for the previous example (see Figure 29.17). When installing the card for use with NT, you're not supposed to use the drivers that come with the operating system. Instead, you should manually select the card to be installed and install the drivers from the floppy. Not sure what you should do? Read the documentation for the card included in the package or (often) on the manufacturer's Web site.

Speaking of Web sites, it's a good idea to bypass the drivers provided on the floppy disk or in the operating system. This is because any drivers supplied on disk are likely to be outdated by the time the disk gets in your hands for installation. Instead, go to the Web site for the network card's manufacturer and find the section for software downloads. Select the type and model of card you're using. There will often be a page from which you can connect to download sites for that particular model of card.

Any responsible company will prominently display the date that the drivers were released. Compare the dates listed on the site with the dates of the drivers on the floppy disk in order to determine whether there are more recent versions of the drivers for your particular card. This tip about downloading drivers from the Internet applies not only to network cards but also to any device you're installing. Not all device drivers are frequently updated, but it's always worth looking.

CONFIGURING CARD RESOURCES

In a lot of ways, installing the card physically is the easy part: you plug it in and you're ready to go. Configuring it is another matter entirely. In the "Networking Protocols and Application Programming Interfaces" section, I talked about the logical addresses that the cards use. I also discussed how those addresses must be unique on the network, but that's not the hard part. The hard part lies in making sure that the network card has access to the CPU and a place to store its data while it's waiting for the CPU to process that data. In other words, it needs its own interrupt, I/O address space, and (rarely) DMA channels. You should recall these terms from Chapter 6, "Installing New Circuit Boards (without Creating New Problems)," where they were covered in detail. In the next few pages I will review what they mean in terms of configuring your network card.

TIP   On PCI cards, interrupts, I/O buffers, and DMA settings are software configured by automatic detection in the operating system. On older cards, some of these settings may be set with hardware jumpers or switches on the card itself. So, before installing a card in the machine, note whether the card is software configurable or hardware configurable.

TIP   If you're using only PCI cards and have installed an operating system that supports Plug and Play (Windows 9x/Me/2000/XP), you don't have to worry about any of the configuration issues mentioned in the remainder of this section. PCI cards support Plug and Play, in which the cards are self configuring. The cards still use the same resources described here—you just don't have to hand-configure them.

Getting the CPU's Attention: Interrupt Requests

The network card is in charge of sending and receiving information across the network. However, it can't *do* anything with that information. All number crunching, moving to main memory, or data manipulation must be handled by the CPU.

This is fine, but every other device in the PC or attached to it—the keyboard, hard disk, video card, sound card, and what have you—is also contending for access to the CPU. As you know from Chapter 6, the CPU uses *interrupts* to manage this communication.

When the network card has packets waiting to be processed, they're stored in the NIC's memory. When a packet arrives in the "waiting room," or memory, on the NIC, the NIC goes over to the CPU, taps it on the shoulder, and says, "Excuse me, CPU, but there is some information sitting in the memory of the NIC. When you get a chance, will you please interrupt what you are doing and process this information or move it over to main memory?" When the NIC does this, it is making an *interrupt request*.

Once the CPU receives this request, it goes ahead and continues working. However, when it gets a free moment, the CPU will then go over to the NIC and start processing the information or move the information from the NIC to main memory.

Generally speaking, each device on your network that needs an interrupt must have a different IRQ line assigned to it. If you assign the same IRQ to both the network card and the LPT2 port, sometimes one won't work, sometimes the other, and sometimes neither will work.

How do you find out which interrupts your network card can use and which of those are free? The first question can be answered by reading your network card's documentation. Somewhere, it should list supported interrupts. Most network cards support two or three interrupts, one of which is likely to be IRQ5.

If no supported interrupts are available for your network card but some interrupts are available, look to see whether a device in your system could switch to the one that's free. For example, suppose that your network card supports only IRQ5 and IRQ10, but IRQ7 is the only one available. If your sound card is using 5 but will support 7, switch the sound card's interrupt to 7.

You can answer the second question in a couple of ways. One method is to meticulously document each interrupt, I/O buffer area, and used DMA channel and write them on a sheet of paper that's kept in an envelope taped to the computer case. There are a couple of advantages to this method. First, you can always get a good idea of your system's configuration, even when the computer is turned off. Second, it's easy to see the configuration at a glance—something not always true when dealing with software diagnostics. The only catch to this method is that you *must* keep it updated, or you're lost.

Well, not entirely lost. Although software diagnostics have historically not been all that great at correctly identifying which devices were using which resources (including IRQs), beginning with Windows 95 the situation got a lot better. The Device Manager tab in the System applet available in the Windows Control Panel can tell you what resources some devices are using. As shown in Figure 29.18, select the device for which you want information, then click the Properties button. You'll move to the Properties sheet for the device. Turn to the Resources tab, as shown in Figure 29.19, and you'll be able to see the system resources that a particular network card is using. (Note that the Resources tab is not available for every device in the Device Manager window.)

You can use the Device Manager not only to determine current system configuration but also to change it. To change the interrupt a device is using, click the Change Setting button on the Resources tab and enter a new IRQ number in the space provided. If you choose an interrupt not supported by that device, Windows will tell you and offer you another option. If you choose an interrupt that *is* supported but is already in use by another device, the Device Manager will alert you to the problem, as shown in Figure 29.20. If you insist on making the devices conflict, the Device Manager will show the problem device in the list with an exclamation point next to it (see Figure 29.21).

FIGURE 29.18

The Windows
Device Manager

FIGURE 29.19

The properties of a
network card

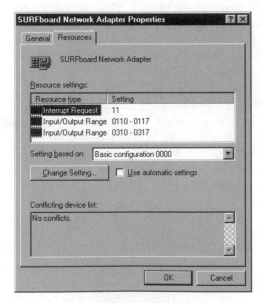

FIGURE 29.20

The Device Manager will warn you if you assign an interrupt already in use by another device.

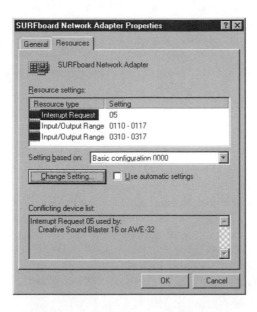

FIGURE 29.21

Devices currently not working will have an exclamation point next to their entries in the list of installed devices.

An exclamation point next to a device in the list of installed devices doesn't necessarily indicate a resource conflict, but could herald some other problem with the device that keeps it from working.

WARNING   *Another option for Microsoft Windows users is Microsoft Diagnostics (MSD), the DOS-based system information tool. You can use it to get configuration information about your system, but unless you run it from DOS (not from a DOS window in Windows), then it's likely to be inaccurate. For example, note that the network adapter shown in the previous example is using IRQ5. When I run MSD on the same computer, it reports that IRQ5 is free and open for use; that is a troubleshooting nightmare waiting to happen.*

Where Does This Data Go? Choosing a Base I/O Address

Now you know how the network card gets the CPU's attention when it has information to pass along. Where is this information stored? For that matter, when the CPU passes instructions to the peripheral device, where are those instructions stored?

The answer to both questions lies in the I/O addresses. Remember, they're like a mailbox that the CPU can use to pick up data waiting for it and to drop off instructions for the device to which that I/O area belongs. Each device must have its own I/O area so that the CPU will drop off the appropriate instructions to each device; it's going to cause no end of confusion if the CPU asks the network card to play a sound. Therefore, you'll either need to tell the device which I/O addresses to use or let the system configure itself to avoid conflicts. The *base* I/O address is the one defining the bottom of the range.

NOTE   *Normally, you'll configure the base I/O address, and the rest is taken care of for you. However, some cards require you to define a range, letting you pick from one of the ranges supported by that card.*

CONVERTING HEXADECIMAL ADDRESSES

As you learned in Chapter 6, I/O addresses and memory addresses are written in hexadecimal, a base-16 numbering system like the familiar base-10 numbering system. You can do conversions if you want to, but for most of us, the simplest way to convert hexadecimal to decimal is to break out the Windows calculator and run it in Scientific mode. Make sure that the calculator is set to display in the number system you're starting with (say, hexadecimal), type in the number, and then change the display to the numbering system to which you're converting. This doesn't impress people the same way that converting in your head does, but you don't have to *tell* anyone you used the Windows calculator.

Getting Information to the CPU: Direct Memory Access

Once the CPU knows that there is a packet of information sitting on the NIC, how does the information get from the NIC to main memory?

By using *direct memory access (DMA)*. You already know that when a packet arrives at your workstation, it goes to the memory of the network card. At that point, the network card issues an interrupt to the CPU to ask it to do something with this data that it's just received. The next step is for the CPU to tell DMA chips on the motherboard, "Please move this information for me and let me know when you're finished." The real power of direct memory access is that the DMA chips can move information back and forth while the CPU is busy with other tasks.

When the DMA chip is finished moving the information, it lets the CPU know that it is done.

As with IRQ lines, every device on your network that needs to use DMA must use a unique DMA channel to avoid traffic jams and system crashes. No software utilities document this information well. The best way to keep track of your DMA channels is to document the settings of your cards as you install them. As most cards—especially newer ones—don't use DMA channels, this isn't too hard to do.

DMA isn't just for motherboards. A special type of network card known as a *bus-mastered network interface* card (actually, as you should recall from Chapter 6, this could be any kind of card) has a DMA chip on the card itself.

With its own DMA chip, a bus-mastered network card can communicate with main system RAM without additional processing intervention by the CPU.

Connecting Devices with Hubs and Switches

Now that you have all your computers and other devices connected to the network, it's time to get them talking to each other. To connect devices within your network, you use hubs and switches, which are discussed here.

Hubs Connect the Dots

Hub is a catch-all term for a device that connects networked devices to each other. The term is used most often to apply to devices used in Ethernet networks. Token Ring networks use *multistation access units (MAUs)*, which, like the network itself, function differently from the Ethernet hubs. However, both hubs and MAUs serve the same basic function of joining the PCs on the LAN.

THE TYPES OF HUB MODELS

Most hubs come in one of three forms:

- Stand-alone
- Stacked
- Modular

Stand-alone hubs are what they sound like—powered or (more rarely) unpowered devices that may or may not include the capability to connect to other hubs with a short run of cable, perhaps fiber or twisted-pair, in which case they're *stacked*. Stand-alone hubs, both alone and in stacked form, are shown in Figure 29.22.

TIP *Unmanaged stand-alone hubs are generally pretty inexpensive (I picked up one LinkSys hub with five PC ports for $59), but hubs get more expensive as more ports are added. If you don't need management capabilities, buying two stand-alone hubs and linking them may be cheaper than buying one big one.*

Modular hubs are built with a backplane that hub cards can plug into, as shown in Figure 29.23.

FIGURE 29.22

Stand-alone hubs may be used alone or linked to other hubs.

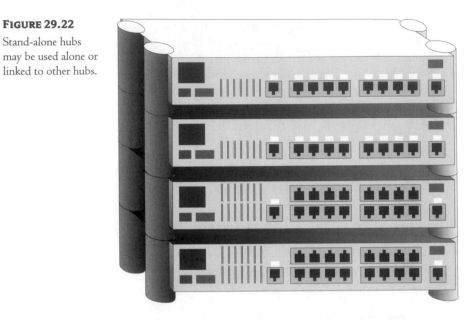

FIGURE 29.23

Modular hubs look like add-in cards plugging into a motherboard.

Add-in card for additional ports

If built to be "intelligent" (I'll explain that further in just a moment), the hubs in a modular or stacked design may be managed by one hub that's the Master, while the rest are Slave hubs. Why choose a modular or stacked hub? Mostly, it will depend on how your network will grow. You can add modules to a hub chassis, or you can get stackable hubs to distribute them throughout your building, wherever they happen to be needed.

SOME HUBS ARE MORE EQUAL THAN OTHERS

Hubs come in a variety of forms, ranging from extremely simple designs that act as a cable interface to those that offer some advanced management techniques. You can theoretically divide hubs into three categories:

◆ Passive

◆ Active

◆ Intelligent/managed (two terms for the same thing)

Passive hubs are unpowered devices, such as patch panels, that provide an interface for cables to transfer data back and forth. They're appropriate for some applications, such as wiring a house for a network, but you're more likely to find an active and/or managed hub in most LANs.

NOTE   All completely passive devices are unpowered, as a powered hub regenerates the signal and is therefore active.

An *active hub*—that is, any powered hub—has repeating qualities, repackaging and regenerating the signal (as described in the upcoming section on network repeaters). Otherwise, active hubs serve the same functions as passive hubs, blindly making sure that data put on the network is broadcast to each connected segment so that whomever the data is for can pick it up. One advantage that most powered hubs have is *status lights*. If a PC's connection to the network is working, then the light for the port it's plugged into comes on. If the PC isn't connected to the network, then the light is out. Another status light on one hub I have shows a scary-looking red light whenever collisions take place, but recall that some collisions are a normal and expected part of Ethernet operations.

Intelligent, or *managed, hubs* have a module that allows them to do a bit more than just shove data along the network; they can be used to help you troubleshoot or keep tabs on your network. If you see a hub sold with a managed device interface (MDI), it's an intelligent hub.

Management protocols, such as the Simple Network Management Protocol (SNMP), have two parts. A monitor runs on a management server, and an agent runs on the devices to be managed. The monitor and the agent can communicate. In the case of SNMP, the most common generic management protocol, the monitor queries the agent and collects information from it, perhaps including the following:

◆ Hub and/or port-level status and activity information

◆ Performance statistics on a per-port basis

◆ Network mapping of all SNMP-capable hardware on the network

◆ Event logging of network errors and activity

You can also use management software to do things to managed devices, such as:

◆ Change network security by denying unauthorized people access to the hub

◆ Set tolerances for activity, error levels, and performance so that you know if those tolerances are exceeded

NOTE *This is a sample of the kinds of information that may be available with managed hubs, not a complete list or one that will apply to all managed hubs. The precise information that the management software delivers depends on the agent installed and may vary with the model.*

Managed hubs aren't always necessary. If your network has only a single hub and this hub is easy to get at, you can probably check it out in person as easily as you can call up diagnostic software. The more PCs that are on the network, and the harder the hub is to get at, the more complicated troubleshooting gets. What's simple with one hub becomes a nightmare when you have 10 hubs with 16 PC ports each. In that case, some kind of management software can help you keep your sanity when it comes time for troubleshooting.

TIP *When choosing managed hubs, look for management modules that can be upgraded with flash ROM. That way, when improvements become available, you can upgrade the module rather than replace it.*

HUB ARCHITECTURE

At its most basic level, a hub is a device that offers an electrical connection for cables that can't be hooked into each other directly. *Ports,* or the little holes you stick the cables in to connect them (see Figure 29.24), are relevant to the definition of any hub.

FIGURE 29.24

Inserting STP cables into a hub

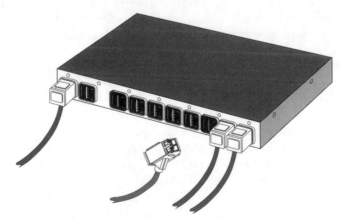

Ports are important; the ports in a hub determine the following:

◆ The cable type that the hub supports

◆ The number of PCs that may be connected with a single hub

◆ Whether the hub is expandable and may be remotely managed when the network is down

Like network cards, hub ports are designed to accommodate only particular kinds of cable connectors. For example, thin coaxial cable and UTP require different ports, and STP requires ports different from those used by fiber. Like other network devices, hubs can be used only with the type of cable with which they're compatible. Also like other devices, they're logically compatible once the cables fit. That is, if you buy a hub that supports connections to RJ-45 connectors like those used with UTP, then you should be able to use that hub for your 10Base-T network whether the hub came from Ye Olde Hub Shoppe or 3Com—the physical interface remains the same. To make a live network connection, you provide power to the hub and plug in the cables.

NOTE *Some hubs have ports for various sorts of cables. This allows them to connect to more than one type of network so that you can physically connect, say, an AS400 to your PC-based 10Base-T LAN. Or, you can connect hubs with backbone cables made of thick coaxial cable or fiber-optic cable.*

Those ports won't do you any good unless there's some mechanism to connect them internally so that packets from one cable may be passed to the rest of the network. To let ports—and thus the nodes plugged into those ports—communicate, there's an internal bus system inside the hub providing each port with a receiving connection and a sending connection. The way that data is sent to each port depends on the type of network involved. For example, Ethernet networks broadcast data to all parts of the network, leaving it to the nodes to sort out whether a packet is intended for them or should be ignored. Thus, data coming into a hub from a PC on a 10Base-T Ethernet network is broadcast to all segments plugged into the hub, as illustrated in Figure 29.25.

FIGURE 29.25

Data sent on a 10Base-T network is broadcast to each PC plugged into a hub via the ports.

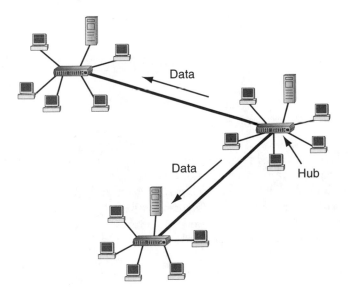

Some intelligent hubs note the physical address of the network card associated with a particular port. These hubs may either be preprogrammed with a static list of address-hub mappings or they may create mappings through discovery. Static address mappings can be used to keep unauthorized people off the network. As shown in Figure 29.26, if a hub is given a static list of port-address mappings, and a PC with a physical address not found in that list attempts to connect to the network, a smart hub can isolate that port. Once isolated, the unauthorized PC can't connect to any of the other PCs plugged into the hub.

FIGURE 29.26

Intelligent hubs can use static lists of authorized physical addresses to keep unauthorized PCs off the network.

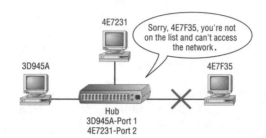

The internal bus of the hub operates at the same speed as the network, or, more precisely, the speed of the network is determined in part by the speed of the hub. Therefore, if you want to run a 100Mbps network, you'll need a hub with an internal bus that supports that speed.

Not all the ports in a hub are for plugging in computers. One, the AUI port, may be present to let you connect the hub to another hub or to another device such as a bridge or router, as shown in Figure 29.27.

FIGURE 29.27

Use the extra port to link hubs to each other or to internetworking devices.

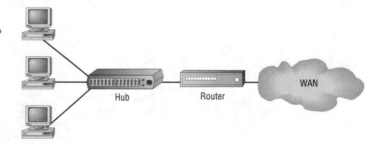

Models with AUI ports typically list the number of ports like this: 5 + 1, meaning that the hub has five ports for PCs to plug into and one AUI. The type of cable that plugs into the AUI port depends on the hub; some models may use fiber or thick coaxial, while others may use RJ-45 and look like one of the PC ports. More expensive hubs may have fiber AUI connections. However, even the cheap $59 hub that my network supports can connect to other hubs at 100Mbps because its AUI supports Category 5 cable.

TIP   *The more ports a hub has, the more expensive it's likely to be. Check costs—it may be cheaper to attach two hubs with their AUIs rather than to buy a single hub with the number of ports that you need.*

In addition to their AUI ports, some hubs will have a serial port interface. This interface enables you to connect the hub to a PC or modem and thus get remote management capability that isn't affected by network crashes not related to the hub itself. Such management is referred to as *out of band* management, as it takes place independent of ordinary network transmissions.

Switches

You'll notice that some smart hubs don't just blindly shove data onto all the segments of the network that are plugged into them. Instead, they notice the MAC addresses of the network cards associated with each port and can discriminate based on those addresses. Switches carry this capability somewhat further to identify the destination's MAC address and forward the packet only to the segment on which that address is located.

The distinction between an ordinary hub and a switching hub is the difference between the office switchboard operator getting an incoming call and paging the intended recipient to pick up the call, and calling a specific office and patching through the call directly. Figure 29.28 illustrates this concept.

FIGURE 29.28

Switching the signal (top) versus broadcasting the signal (bottom)

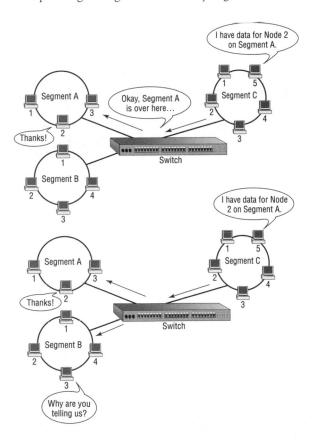

Why bother switching the signal instead of broadcasting it? One major reason is traffic control. If every time there's a telephone call into the office, the switchboard operator makes everyone listen to the page and then decide whether to pick up, that's more of an interruption to the office than it is to directly notify the call's target. Similarly, when a hub broadcasts all frames to all segments attached to it, then every PC on the network has to stop and "listen" and can't "talk" lest they cause a collision. If the signal is switched only to the part of the network where it needs to go, then the rest of the network isn't bothered. It can transmit data on the other segments without interfering with the first transmission.

Switching also makes it possible to reserve more bandwidth for high-traffic applications. With ordinary hubs or repeaters on a 10Mbps network, all ports share the same 10Mbps pipe. With switching, each port can have its own 10Mbps pipe, unencumbered by traffic from other ports. Switching makes it possible to connect multiple LANs to get all the advantages of being linked without the disadvantages of sharing bandwidth.

The role of a switch is a bit more complex than simply that of a hub with a little more on the ball than average. As illustrated in Figure 29.29, you typically don't plug individual PCs into a switch, but plug hubs into the switch's ports so that each segment of the network has its own port. Depending on where you put the switches in the LAN, you can use the switch to isolate portions of the network at the workgroup, departmental, or backbone level.

FIGURE 29.29

Use switches to isolate parts of the network, not to isolate individual PCs.

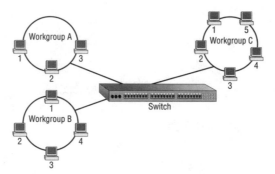

NOTE *Although switches are often used to connect LAN segments, you can connect an individual PC to one if you want to devote a large amount of bandwidth to a single power user or server.*

SWITCHING METHODS

Most switches use one of two methods to accomplish their mission: cut-through or store-and-forward. In *cut-through switching*, the switch reads only the MAC address in the frame to be switched. (*Framing* is the act of packaging data into segments called packets, or *frames*.) The switch starts forwarding the frame to the appropriate port on which that MAC address is to be found as soon as the switch knows where to send it—usually after only 20 to 30 bytes of information have entered the switch. (Recall that an Ethernet frame has about 1500 bytes of information in it, so this pause to inspect 30 bytes of the frame represents very little latency.) Thus, cut-through switching operates essentially at line speed.

Store-and-forward receives the entire frame and then inspects it to determine its destination MAC address and to check the frame for errors. Only frames that are in good shape get forwarded.

Figure 29.30 illustrates the difference between the two methods.

Which method is better? Cut-through switching is generally faster, as the frames can be shoved onto the appropriate segment as quickly as they arrive at the switch. However, this method carries the hazard of forwarding damaged frames and thus increasing network traffic with useless bits. Store-and-forward switching is slightly slower, as each frame must be inspected for errors before it's forwarded, but is less likely to propagate errors on the network. It's not slow, exactly, but there's a degree of latency found with store-and-forward switching not found with cut-through switching, and the larger the frame, the greater the delay.

FIGURE 29.30

The switching method you choose depends on whether it's more important for your network to be error free or very fast.

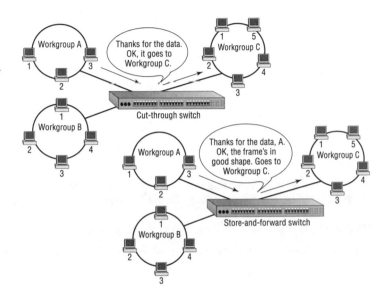

Therefore, cut-through switches are best for networks that need high throughput more than they need to reduce the chance of error propagation; smaller, simpler networks can benefit from them. Store-and-forward switches may be necessary for more complex networks that can't take the chance of wasting time on garbage frames.

NOTE   Some switches support both methods. Ordinarily, they use cut-through switching and monitor error rates without storing the frames. If error rates exceed a predetermined tolerance, the switches change to store-and-forward switching.

Internetworking and Intranetworking

Sometimes it's not enough to create a single LAN. These days, the chances are excellent that your LAN will either start out connected to another network or it will be connected to another network at some future time. That's when you have to move on from simple networks and start dealing with intranetworking and internetworking devices.

Intranetworking and internetworking devices? Yup. The basic difference between the two is that *intra*networking devices extend your LAN, and *inter*networking devices connect two different LANs or networks of any size or breadth. This isn't a perfect division, by any means. Why? Because it's sometimes hard to tell where one network ends and another begins. Some devices include both extending and linking capabilities, but the internet/intranet division is a start for organizing networking hardware.

MODELS OF NETWORK FUNCTIONALITY

You can fit some aspects of networking hardware into a simple model, so long as you don't strain the model overmuch.

Physical layer devices, such as repeaters, operate like an extension of network cable, allowing the network to transmit its signal farther than would otherwise be possible.

A *Data-Link layer device* has some functions specific to a particular kind of network, such as Ethernet or Token Ring. The degree of complexity of these functions varies with the device. For example, hubs are mostly concerned with connecting the members of a network indiscriminately; switches may forward information to only the particular segment where a frame's destination address may be found; and bridges may actually permit two disparate network types to be connected. However, the basic idea remains the same; they're concerned with hardware only. A Data-Link layer device doesn't know or care what networking protocol is in place on the network, what network operating system is in place, or what applications are running on the network.

The Data-Link layer is divided into two sublayers: the *Media Access Control (MAC)* and the *Logical Link Control (LLC)*. The MAC layer is concerned with hardware addresses and connectionless data transfer, whereas the LLC layer makes connections before passing along data. Most Data-Link devices are more concerned with MAC functions than with the LLC functions, but bridges may use some capabilities defined at the LLC level.

Network layer devices, such as routers, are concerned with networking protocols, such as IPX/SPX or TCP/IP, not with network type.

Repeaters Extend the Network's Reach

Repeaters are devices that regenerate an electronic or photonic signal so as to increase the distance that that signal can travel—basically, to boost it at some point after its original transmission. All repeaters do is strengthen the signal by repackaging and rebroadcasting; they do not connect disparate networks, filter packets, or route data to other subnets.

The sole purpose of a repeater is to reduce the effects of attenuation. As you may recall, that's the tech-ese for "signals get weaker as they travel." As signals get weaker, they're more easily corrupted by other signals. This shouldn't be news to anyone who's ever used a radio while on the road. Say you're driving along, listening to Bela Fleck. As your drive approaches the end of the broadcast area, Bela doesn't immediately disappear, but has a disturbing habit of suddenly breaking off and sounding like the Bee Gees, because the radio station in the new broadcast area is having a "Best of Disco" show. Bela fades out, and the Bee Gees fade in. What happens with radio also happens to networks; no matter what type of signal it is, how well it's shielded, or how immune to interference, sooner or later it will fade to the point at which it's no longer intelligible at its destination.

You can take two approaches when it comes to solving the problem of attenuation. First, you can boost the signal with increased voltage, which is what your radio station is doing when they start boasting about getting a new transmitter. The new transmitter will have no effect on the signal's quality for the original broadcast area. However, it will improve it on the outer edges of the broadcast area and extend it to new areas. Sooner or later, the signal will still fade, but with the stronger original signal, it will travel farther before doing so.

The second approach, and the one taken by networks and inherent in repeater design, is to repeat the signal, so as to start it out fresh again.

WHAT CAN REPEATERS DO FOR YOU?

In repeating the signal, repeaters can have a couple of beneficial effects. First, in Ethernet networks they can help you avoid collisions, or allow you to have a bigger network and spare you from worrying as much about collisions. Second, they can allow you to isolate parts of your network.

NOTE *All segments of a network connected with repeaters must be using the same Data-Link and Network protocols. That is, you cannot use a repeater to connect a Token Ring network to an Ethernet one, or to connect an Ethernet network running IPX/SPX to one running TCP/IP. Both networks must be of the same type (Ethernet) and running the same transport protocol.*

Avoiding Collisions

Like other baseband networks, Ethernet networks have only a single "path" on which data can travel at a time. Collisions occur on Ethernet networks when two or more PCs' network cards begin transmitting data on the network at the same time. Therefore, before a PC on an Ethernet network begins transmitting, it listens to the network to make sure that all's quiet on the western front before it begins. However, a PC can hear only so far, and if a node too far away to hear—but on the same segment—is already transmitting, then they'll collide. Admittedly, collisions are inherent in the Ethernet design and to be expected on a properly functioning network, but they can slow down the network by requiring retries. You don't want to have collisions more often than is strictly necessary. Repeaters can help you avoid excessive collisions by boosting the signal so that all PCs on the network can "hear" each other.

Isolating Segments

Ethernet segments are vulnerable to downtime caused by breaks in the cable connection. If you have some parts of the network that are more prone than others to network downtime, then a repeater could isolate those segments, letting them go down in flames without affecting the rest of the network. For example, say that you're running a PC training firm and want your instructors to get lots of hands-on experience. Therefore, you set aside part of the network to let them mess with it and with test-bed servers. After all, the last person you want within reach of the mail server is someone playing, "What happens if I do *this*?" However, if that segment is connected to the rest of the network, then removed cables, forgotten terminations, and other network problems could have a bad effect on network functionality elsewhere. That is where the repeater can help you; even if the cable segments are shorter than the 185m maximum, you can still use a repeater to keep the dead bits of the network from affecting the living ones.

HOW DO REPEATERS WORK?

So now you know that the function of a repeater is to regenerate a signal so it can travel farther. Strictly speaking, this isn't quite true; rather than just boosting the signal, repeaters repackage a signal and rebroadcast it. Essentially, what happens is this: when data packets arrive at the repeater, the device takes them apart and repackages them in the same form in which they started out. The repeater isn't affecting the data or touching the addressing information. However, it is revitalizing the signal from scratch, not just resending the original signal. That said, there's no error control built into this process. If a packet is corrupted when it gets to the repeater, it will be corrupted when it leaves the repeater.

NOTE   *On Ethernet networks, every device is a repeater.*

REPEATERS VERSUS EXTENDERS

It's a given that repeaters don't just repeat, but actually repackage. There *is* a device that just repeats; it's called a LAN *extender*, and this device fulfills the function that you'd expect from something called a repeater. Extenders function similarly to repeaters in that they permit you to have longer networks without increasing the chances of collisions, but they don't add to your repeater count. What's repeater count? You can have up to only four repeaters in a single network, and the number you have is called your *repeater count*.

There's no reason to *not* use a repeater in place of an extender, except that you can use only so many repeaters in a network, and you're not limited in the number of extenders that you can use.

Again, you can have up to only four repeaters in a single network, or else Bad Things (such as network failures or delays) can happen. There are two reasons for this.

First, overuse of repeaters can actually increase the number of collisions on the network. Every time a package is disassembled and reassembled, there's a tiny delay. This delay isn't long enough to matter when a package is being reassembled only once, but the more repeaters on the network, the more tiny delays you'll have. Eventually, the delays will accumulate until, at some point, a sending node is waiting too long to receive any acknowledgment of its transmission and resends its data. The trouble is that when the sending node does this, its original packet is still in transit. If the sending node resends the data while the original transmission is still limping on toward its final destination, then the two packets will collide. Once again, collisions are to be expected in an Ethernet network, but you don't have to go looking for them.

The second potential problem with too many repeaters is data corruption. Each time a repeater breaks down and reassembles a packet, the repeater might put the data back together incorrectly, perhaps substituting a 0 for a 1 at some point along the line. (If that doesn't sound like a big deal, then consider this: 11001100 binary is 204 decimal, but 11101100 is 236 decimal. Someone just got an informal raise.) It's like the old game of Gossip that perhaps you played in grade school. Person A whispers something in the ear of person B, and person B whispers what they heard in the ear of person C, and so forth around the circle. Finally, person O says what they heard, and it turns out to be an extremely garbled version of what person A said in the first place. Funny then (at least fourth-graders get a big kick out of it), but not good when what's getting garbled is not tongue twisters but your network's data.

The four-repeater rule is not carved in stone; your network will not work perfectly with four repeaters, then crash in flames as soon as you add the fifth. However, it will become more unreliable as you increase repeater count, and four hops is the recommended upper limit.

Routers Connect Multiple Networks

Routers are used to connect two or more separate networks as well as to connect multiple computers on a network to a single shared unit, like a DSL or cable modem. Whereas bridges forward data packets *within* a network, routers forward data packets *between* networks.

Since routers operate based on protocols that are independent of the specific technology used for the network itself, routers can easily interconnect networks that employ different technologies. This capability to "bridge" different networking technologies has led to the widespread deployment of routers throughout the Internet.

NOTE *Because a router is a logical boundary for the network—Ethernet data doesn't cross a router unless instructed to do so by the router itself—a router can also be used to divide a single network into two logically separate networks.*

If you're responsible for only a single network, the only router you're likely to encounter is the one between your network and the Internet. If you're responsible for multiple networks, you'll have routers between each network.

When data arrives from one network, the router decides—based on its *routing table*—where to forward that data. A routing table (also called a configuration table) contains information on which connections lead to particular groups of addresses, priorities for connections to be used, and rules for handling both routine and special types of traffic. In small routers, a routing table might contain only a half-dozen lines of instructions. In large routers handling significant amounts of Internet traffic, routing tables can be staggering in their size and complexity.

NOTE *If you're interested in how many routers are involved in a typical bit of Internet traffic, use the Traceroute utility (included with most versions of Windows). Go to the MS-DOS prompt, change to the* **WINDOWS** *directory, and type* **tracert www.sitename.com** *(where the second part of the command is a specific site name). Traceroute will return a list of the routers that were utilized to get from your computer to that site, along with their addresses and the time (in milliseconds) it took a packet of information to move from one router to another. Don't be surprised to see dozens of routers involved in even the simplest connections!*

Routers are also responsible for optimizing, as much as possible, the routing paths for internetworked data. A router uses a routing algorithm to determine the optimal path to a destination, attempting to reduce the number of hops and delays between the originating point and the destination point. However, since network data travels in packets—and since the optimal route between two points is in constant flux, especially over the Internet—different packets from the same message might travel completely different routes. This route determination, on a packet-by-packet basis, is made by each router the packet encounters on its trip.

Remember that, unlike bridges, routers deal only in networks, not in individual hosts. Even though the IP address of a host contains both the host's network address and the host's specific number on that network, a router will extract only the network address—and decide, based on the network address, where to transfer the data being routed.

One additional responsibility of the router is to keep unwanted visitors and data *out* of the network to which it's connected. Most routers have rules limiting how computers from outside the network (either from another LAN or from the Internet) can connect to computers inside the network. In addition, rules within the router will determine how your network appears to the outside world, as well as execute various security functions.

Networking Security

Any time you connect two or more computers (or connect a single computer to that global network we call the Internet), you run the risk of unauthorized access. In an ideal world, a computer will be accessed only by its designated user; in the real world, the possibility exists for any given computer to be accessed by users who don't have appropriate authorization.

The only surefire way to keep the data and programs on a computer safe from unauthorized access is to never connect that computer to a network—including the Internet. Of course, in today's networked world, that sort of isolation is impractical, if not impossible. That means that, at some level, you have to apply some degree of security measures to the computers on your network. Of course, too much security makes the computer inconvenient to use; too little security opens up the computer to potential unauthorized use. Like most things in life, networking security becomes a game of risk versus reward—with the safety of your programs and data in the balance.

General Security Tips

Whenever you have valuable data stored on a network, you should take certain common-sense precautions, just in case something bad happens:

- Keep backups—off the network, if not completely offsite!—of all your important files.

- If data doesn't have to be accessed by the network, don't store it on the network—store it on a non-networked computer, instead.

- Make sure you're up-to-date with recent operating system updates—these updates often patch holes that allow unauthorized access.

- For greater security, keep your server and other key equipment locked up in a separate room; the fewer people who have access to the hardware, the less likely it is that your hardware will be vandalized.

Beyond these basic advisories, let's look at some more-specific security measures you probably should be evaluating.

Use Passwords for Internal Security

Within the boundaries of a local area network, the biggest security concern is the illicit access by one user of another user's computer. This is why every user of the network should be assigned a password, and every computer on the network should be password protected. Theoretically, if a computer can be accessed only by a specific password, and that password is known only to a single user, unauthorized access should pretty much be shut down.

Unless a password is stolen.

Stolen passwords are the most common cause of network security breaches. That's because the human beings who use your network are sometimes careless.

Sometimes they use a password that's too easily guessed. (Birthdates, Social Security numbers, children's names, and pet's names are common ones.) You can combat this problem by requiring passwords to be a certain length (the longer the better) and to contain a combination of letters and numbers. In short, the more complex the password, the harder it is to crack.

Sometimes they leave their password lying around for prying eyes to see. (Really—take an after-hours walk around the office and observe how many passwords you see attached to computer monitors via Post-It notes.) You can try to combat this problem by yelling at the offending parties—a lot of good that will do!—or by requiring users to change their passwords on a frequent basis. (This doesn't eliminate sloppiness or prying eyes, but does minimize the amount of time a "borrowed" password is usable.)

Sometimes they can use their password to access parts of the network that they really shouldn't be accessing. This, of course, is your problem, not theirs. Make sure that the computers or drives or folders that contain sensitive data are designated as off-limits for all but the most essential personnel—meaning that not all employees need password-level access to everything on the network. The fewer people who know the password to your most sensitive data, the less likely it is that that password will be compromised.

One last thing you can do to improve your network's password security is to limit the number of tries a user has to enter a password. Password-cracking software exists that keeps feeding (at a rapid clip) hundreds and thousands of different combinations into a password field in an attempt to guess the password; limiting the number of retries effectively defeats this type of software.

Use a Firewall for External Security

When you open your network to the Internet (or to any external network), your security concerns multiply by several orders of magnitude. Just look at the types of security threats you can potentially encounter:

Viruses and Trojans A computer *virus* is a piece of malicious code that can infect your computer system. A *Trojan* (as in *Trojan horse*) is a type of virus, such as NetBus or Black Orifice, that is planted on your network and surreptitiously takes control of the host computer. Trojans can be programmed to do just about anything to your system—such as change the computer's IP address, install destructive scripts or programs, and so on. This is particularly damaging if the computer accessed is the network server, as any damage inflicted could affect the entire network.

Denial-of-service (DoS) attacks These easy-to-launch attacks involve the sending of more requests to a computer or network than it can handle. If, for example, a host computer is capable of answering 25 requests per second, and an attacker sends (via automated programs) 40 requests per second, the host will be unable to service all the attacker's requests—let alone any legitimate requests. In essence, the host computer (and often the host computer's network) gets overloaded.

E-mail bombs Similar to a DoS attack, this type of attack is caused by someone sending you the same e-mail hundreds or thousands of times, until your network's e-mail system can't accept any more messages.

Redirect bombs This type of attack changes the path that information takes by sending it to a different router—essentially letting hackers erase their steps by using computers on your network to do their dirty work.

IP spoofing A spoof occurs when the attacker's computer claims to have the IP address of another computer, thus enabling the attacker to gain access and execute operations based on the authority of the spoofed computer.

IP session hijacking   This sophisticated type of attack enables the attacker to take over and control individual computers on your network. Whatever the user is doing at the point of the hijack is visible to the hijacker; it's a great way to read confidential e-mail and other information. When a computer is hijacked, the user sees only that their session has been dropped; more often than not, they'll log back in, even as the hijacker (still logged in as the hijacked user) continues poking around the network, typically unnoticed.

SMTP session hijacking   SMTP is the most common method of sending Internet-based e-mail, and SMTP session hijacking occurs when an outsider redirects a large volume of e-mail (typically spam) through the SMTP server of an unsuspecting host.

Buffer overruns   This type of attack occurs when an infiltrator hijacks an application running on the host computer and then inserts rogue executable code—effectively rendering the application unusable.

Data theft   One of the more common results of unauthorized access is the "stealing" of confidential data. This might not sound like a big thing, but industrial espionage is big business—and trade secrets are meant to be kept secret.

Data diddling   Even worse than data theft, this occurs when an unauthorized user accesses confidential data—and changes it. Think of the repercussions if someone broke into your network and moved a few decimal points in the master spreadsheet, or transposed some of the digits in the numbers used in the automatic payroll system. Not only is the data changed, but you might not notice the change until something *really* bad results!

Data destruction   Some attackers just want to cause damage—and deleting and corrupting files are particularly high-tech forms of vandalism.

Short of disconnecting your Internet connection, how do you guard against these types of unwanted intrusions?

The best protection against Internet-based attacks is to install a *firewall* between your network and the Internet. A firewall is simply a collection of components—either software- or hardware-based—that forms a barrier between two networks (such as your network and the Internet) and selectively filters the information that is passed between the networks. Hardware-based firewalls typically take the form of routers with built-in filtering capabilities. Software-based firewalls can be installed on any computer with the proper Internet connection.

NOTE   *A firewall (software-based) is also recommended for any home computer connected to a constant Internet connection—such as that provided by a DSL, cable, or ISDN modem.*

The most obvious place to install a firewall is where your network connects to the Internet—typically a T1 or T3 line. (If you have multiple T1/T3 lines, you'll need to install a separate firewall at each access point.) If your company utilizes several LANs (one for each department or floor, for example), you may also want to install firewalls between the individual networks.

Firewalls use one or more of three methods to control traffic flowing in and out of the network:

Proxy service   A proxy essentially serves as a "middleman" between computers on your network and the Internet. Instead of data being sent from the Internet to an individual PC, the data is sent to the firewall (proxy), where it is *cached.* Users on your network thus access the cached data on the proxy server, instead of actually going out to the Internet.

Packet filtering   In this scheme, individual data packets are fed through a set of administrator-assigned filters. Packets that pass the filtering are sent to the requesting system, and packets that don't pass the test are discarded.

Stateful inspection   This method doesn't examine the contents of each packet, but instead compares certain key parts of the packet to a database of trusted information. If the comparison results in a match, the information is allowed through. Nonmatching data is discarded.

Almost all types of firewalls are customizable, to one degree or another. In essence, you can add or remove filters based on IP addresses, domain names, protocols, ports, and specific words and phrases. (In the last instance, the firewall will *sniff* each packet of information looking for an exact text match; you can program this type of filter to block packets that contain the word *dork,* for example.)

TIP   *You can assess the vulnerability of your network to outside attacks by availing yourself of an online security service. These services—such as WebTrends' Security Analyzer—essentially try to hack into your network (via the Internet), and then report back to you where your weaknesses lie.*

If you value the information stored on your network, you'll take the appropriate steps to protect that information—by protecting the security of your network. Strict password management and firewalls are your two best defenses against unauthorized access, and should be part of the arsenal of any network administrator—no matter how large or how small the network!

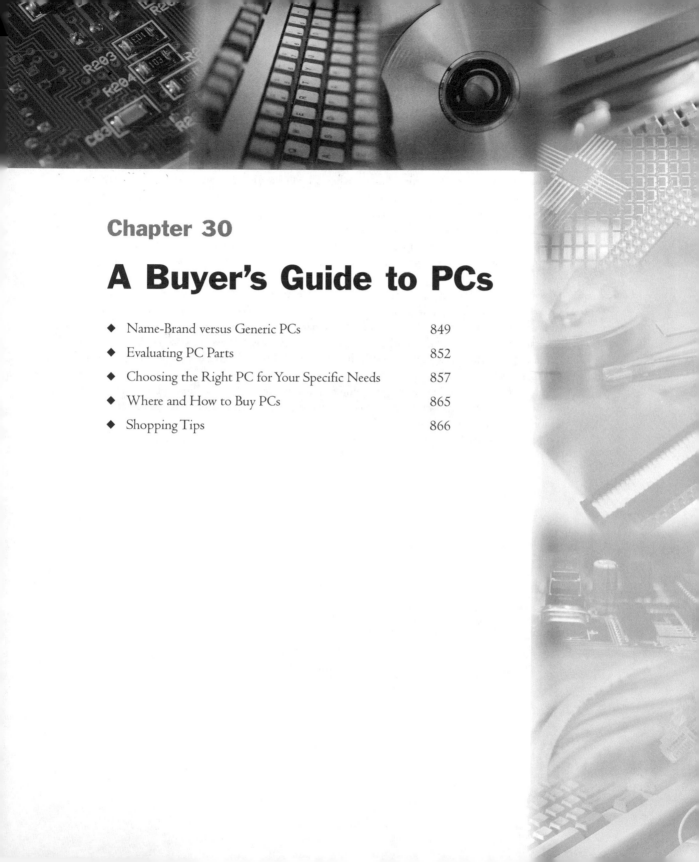

Chapter 30

A Buyer's Guide to PCs

◆ Name-Brand versus Generic PCs   849

◆ Evaluating PC Parts   852

◆ Choosing the Right PC for Your Specific Needs   857

◆ Where and How to Buy PCs   865

◆ Shopping Tips   866

Introduction

IF YOU'RE THE KIND of person who fixes your own or someone else's PC (and if you aren't, why would you be reading this book?), you're likely to be the kind of person who's often looking to the next PC, the latest and greatest machine. Perhaps your palms itch when you see that someone else owns a state-of-the-art Pentium 4 system when all you can afford is an entry-level Celeron. You eye 80GB hard drives the way some teenage boys (and many grown men) eye Corvettes.

Or maybe you're not that way. Maybe your computer is just a tool for you, a platform upon which to get some work done. But you've found that your current platform just isn't fast enough or versatile enough to support your computing needs, and you want to know how to either upgrade your existing machine or buy a new one that won't offer as much trouble when it's time to upgrade again in a few years.

Now is a good time to upgrade; with prices these days, everybody can own some of the fastest PCs on the planet. In fact, today's lowest-priced machines perform better than high-end systems sold just a few years ago. The truth is, in today's PC market, buyers with tons of money don't have much advantage over the rest of us. (Unless, of course, you just *have* to have a 2.2GHz Pentium 4–based system with the flat-panel screen, 80GB drive, and DVD burner. You *will* pay a lot of money for that kind of system!)

But *which* one to buy? Well, I'm not going to tell you *that*: there are zillions of honest vendors out there who deserve your money. I'd just like to give you some advice on how to make sure that your vendor is one of the good ones.

I'll tell you what I tell my clients: When you're going to buy a PC, you should consider four things: compatibility, upgradability, serviceability, and price/performance.

Name-Brand versus Generic PCs

What type of PC are you going to buy? As with any consumer product, there are differences between "name-brand" computers and those that are "generic."

Name-brand, or proprietary, computers are built by well-known companies such as IBM, Compaq, Hewlett-Packard, Dell, and Gateway, and can be found in most computer retail outlets. You can also buy them directly from the manufacturer by using a toll-free number, the Internet, or mail order. Some of these companies shoot for top-notch quality, service, and other value-added options, so you may not get much of a bargain price-wise. Others target price-conscious consumers and offer some pretty good deals. With almost all major manufacturers, however, you'll get a name-brand computer that is supported by a company that is visible in the marketplace and that has a significant service and support operation.

Generic computers, on the other hand, are a mixed bag. You *might* get a lower price than you will with a comparable name-brand computer (that isn't a given, in these days of fierce competition—especially at the low end of the market), and you *might* get a machine that is more easily serviced or upgraded, but you probably won't have access to 24/7 customer support or a bunch of extras, such as extensive software bundles.

Many generic computers do use high-quality components, so the overall quality of the computer and its compatibility with other components is often comparable to name-brand computers—although you should do some research to make sure this is the case. When you hit the lowest end of the generic spectrum, however, you'll find some computers you definitely should stay away from. They are built from the cheapest components and are more unreliable than computers from other manufacturers that I've mentioned here.

If you're confident of your technical skills and actually enjoy poking around inside your computer's system unit, a generic computer might be a good choice, since generics typically require a little more assembly than name brands do. On the other hand, if you consider computing a utility rather than a hobby—and don't like fiddling with the technical stuff any more than you have to—then buying a proprietary PC from a name-brand manufacturer is probably a better decision.

Parts of a Generic PC

Generic machines are typically built from a few separate industry-standard parts. Those parts include:

Standard case If you buy a computer with an unusually shaped case, such as the "slimline" PCs or the micro-towers, you may find that all the boards inside the computer are unusually shaped as well. That means that you probably won't be able to easily locate affordable replacement parts should you need them. It also means that you can't put an industry-standard (generic) power supply in your system. That's undesirable because there are some very nice power supply options these days, such as larger fans or power supplies with built-in battery backup. The choice of whether you get a desktop case or tower model is completely up to you. Desktop cases tend to save space on your desktop (you can put your monitor on top of them), but towers are nice and roomy inside. You can also place tower cases on the floor if you want to.

ATX case This is a newer case style, which rotates the processor and expansion slots 90 degrees inside the case, giving you room to add more cards. A side-mounted fan on the power supply does a better job of cooling the system than the standard version. But the most visible difference is the double-height aperture in the back where the keyboard, mouse, and ports are located; these ports are all piled on top of one another. A standard motherboard will not fit in an ATX case, nor will an ATX-specific motherboard fit in a standard case. Some cases have additional buttons (usually located on the front of the case): a Turbo mode button, a reset button, and a power switch. The Turbo button, now obsolete, does the opposite of what it says: it actually slows down your computer. The reset button enables you to "warm boot" your computer. (In other words, press the reset button to reboot your computer without turning the power off.) The power switch/button, obviously, turns your computer on or off. Power switches that are located on the front of the case are the most convenient. It is sometimes a pain (especially if you have a tower case under your desktop) to reach around and grope for the power switch just to turn your computer on.

Motherboard   The largest circuit board in the case, the motherboard holds the CPU, memory, and expansion slots. On that motherboard there should be *eight* expansion slots, rather than the three that you find on some computers these days, so that you can add expansion boards to your PC now and in the future. Three slots just aren't enough. Today's motherboards should have mostly (or all) PCI slots and one AGP slot. You can't tell how many or what kind of expansion slots there are from looking at the back of the computer. You'll have to ask a salesperson or read the marketing material closely.

Pentium III processors have a distinct performance advantage over older, 66MHz bus systems. Motherboards built at around a 100MHz bus speed will feature Pentium III processors and better performance than the older 66MHz bus systems; 133MHz bus systems are also available, if you're willing to shell out big bucks for them. Pentium 4 motherboards feature blazingly fast 400MHz system buses and can hold up to 2GB of RAM.

New motherboards may also support the AGP 4X standard, which is an improvement over the widely deployed AGP 2 standard, resulting in faster video performance if you have an AGP video card that supports AGP 4. Finally, look for a system that has USB ports, and FireWire if you're into desktop video and audio production. Better yet, look for USB2 ports, which are backward-compatible with the older USB ports and just as fast as FireWire.

I/O   This used to be a separate entity, but now it is built into most motherboards. It's good to get a motherboard with two EIDE controllers that support Ultra ATA/100 transfer rates. EIDE controllers allow your hard drives to talk to the CPU, and two controllers let you have up to four hard drives or CD-ROMs. Since there are two EIDE channels, if you put more than one device on a channel they will be in a Master/Slave configuration. The parallel port resides here as well; get one that is ECP/EPP so that you can connect to a nice, fast printer. There should be PS/2 or USB ports for your mouse and keyboard so that you don't need to waste a perfectly good serial port. Speaking of which, serial ports and floppy drive connectors are considered I/O as well; not much to concern yourself with here—just be sure you have the standard setup of one floppy controller and two COM ports.

Video adapter board   This is the component that allows the PC to display images on the monitor. Look for a video board that can display screen resolutions of at least 1024 × 768, support true color (16 million colors), and is a 3D board if you play games. AGP video boards are faster, so look for that as well.

That's just a generic overview. In "Choosing PC Parts," I'll zoom in on particular features you should be looking for.

Pros and Cons of Name-Brand PCs

How does a generic PC differ from a name-brand PC? Well, you find all the same functions in a name-brand PC, but you most often find all of them on a single circuit board, a kind of "workaholic" motherboard.

The big problem with name-brand computers is that, because of that proprietary motherboard, they are not often as easily upgradable and sometimes are more expensive to repair. Proprietary computer motherboards are typically shaped differently from each other and from generic motherboards, making it impossible for you to replace an old or damaged proprietary motherboard with anything but another motherboard of the exact same make and model. Because motherboards of that particular make and model are available only from that particular vendor (by definition, since the motherboard is proprietary), it may be expensive or impossible to get a replacement. Likewise, it's almost certainly impossible to get an upgrade.

Of course, none of these issues may be important to you. If you do all your upgrading outside the case (via USB ports), the number or position of slots inside the system unit are irrelevant. And, given the super-low prices of today's PCs, if something as major as a motherboard fails, you're better off trashing the whole system and buying a new one, rather than spending a similar amount of money to fix the broken machine.

When you consider the benefits of a name-brand PC—especially the 24/7 technical support and longer warranties—you can see why there are many more Dell and Compaq and Gateway PCs sold today than there are generic machines built by no-name manufacturers. Also, today's hyper-competitive market has driven the prices down on name-brand models to a point where buying generic won't save you much, if any, money. If low price is your motivating factor, spend your $699 on a cheap Compaq or HP, where you'll get a relatively high-performance box with reliable support. Yeah, you won't have much in the way of upgrade options, but that may not be an issue.

That said, let's take a closer look at how the average name-brand PC matches my four purchasing criteria.

Compatibility could be an issue, because if the vendor did anything wrong (for example, if the company chose a mildly incompatible video chip, as AT&T did for some of their systems several years back), you must either throw away the computer or hope that the designer was farsighted enough to allow you to disable the built-in video function so you can go out and spend more money on a separate video board. Realistically, however, you probably won't run into many (if any) compatibility issues from the most popular manufacturers.

Upgradability is a concern because not all boards are built alike. Take, for example, the Compaq Deskpro systems. Although they worked very well, they were difficult to upgrade (the motherboards especially, because they were not a standard shape). You had to buy a new motherboard from Compaq, as opposed to running to your local vendor and picking up a newer, faster one when it came out. In terms of adding peripherals, however, you were okay, because you could add newer devices via the PC's USB ports.

Serviceability is probably the least of your problems. While proprietary PCs often use proprietary parts, unless the manufacturer goes out of business (and if they do, did you really buy a name brand?) the parts should be readily available from the manufacturer or an authorized repair center. Yes, the generic parts in a generic PC can be bought at any technical supply house, but it isn't that hard to find name-brand parts, either. (Besides, you'll actually be able to find an authorized technician for a name-brand PC; the number of shops servicing no-name clones is diminishing.)

And what about *price/performance*? First of all, notice that I put this last. That's because compared to what computers used to cost, *any* current PC is a bargain, even if you pay list price for one made by IBM. In this regard, neither name-brand or generic PCs hold an edge. Competition is such that if you pick a price point, you'll find PCs from dozens of manufacturers that offer almost identical performance specifications. You should base your purchase decision, then, on other factors—such as historical brand reliability, ease of service, and any extras that might be thrown in to get your sale.

Choosing PC Parts

When choosing a PC, I look at what it's made of in order to decide whether it's the kind of machine that I'm looking for. Let's look at the important parts of a PC and summarize the factors you should consider when buying a PC. All of these items are discussed elsewhere in the book; this is just a summary. Consult the index to find out where to read more about any given topic.

TIP   Don't rely on Windows' system requirements to dictate the performance parameters of your new PC—these numbers are the bare minimum you need to operate and don't reflect true operating reality. For example, if you check out the system requirements of any version of Windows, they'll appear ridiculously low. Windows 98 can supposedly run on a 486DX/66 machine with 24MB of RAM, and Windows XP's minimum system requirements are a 233MHz Pentium-class CPU with 64MB of RAM. Don't fool yourself into thinking that these machines will be even remotely satisfactory—unless you look forward to getting a lot of napping done while you wait for your computer to finish even the most menial tasks.

CPU

Today, most PCs are equipped with a Pentium 4 or an equivalent processor from another manufacturer. For the best performance, go with the Intel Pentium 4 or AMD Athlon chip. For the best value—and if speed is not an issue—consider an Intel Celeron or AMD Duron processor. Whatever the case, get the most that you can afford so you won't have to upgrade for a while.

How fast a processor should you buy? It all depends on what you're using your PC for. If you're a typical user, you use your PC to run a few Microsoft Office apps (Word, Excel, etc.) and browse the Web. This type of use doesn't require a lot of power, and even the slowest chips available today (such as the 1.2GHz Intel Celeron or the 1GHz AMD Duron) will do the job without working up a sweat. If, on the other hand, you do a lot of graphics or video work—or if you play a lot of high-end, graphics-heavy games—then you might benefit from a faster chip. You'll find mid-level systems sporting 1.6 to 2GHz Pentium 4 chips or 1.47 to 1.67GHz AMD Athlon processors.

At the time of this writing, the fastest performance will come from systems built around the Pentium 4 chip. This chip (running at a minimum of 1.3GHz) is ideal for the most hard-core gamers and those doing digital video editing. If all you do is surf the Web and send e-mail, you'd be wasting your money. (It would be like owning a Ferrari and driving it only once a week to church—the next block over.)

The bottom line is that while processors are getting faster, applications that use or need that speed are few and far between. Save your money and buy something in the low to mid-range—it'll be more than fast enough for most applications.

While processors keep getting faster (even though they're more than fast enough already), what's *not* getting faster are the peripherals. CPUs today are hundreds of times faster than XT-level CPUs; modern peripherals, however, are only dozens of times faster than XT-era peripherals. Take the money you're saving by not buying the latest and greatest CPU and spend that on a faster bus and faster peripherals.

Also be certain to get enough cache memory. There are two types of cache memory: L1 (or level 1) and L2 (level 2). Cache memory is used by the processor to access frequently used pieces of data and can speed up your system. L1 cache is resident on the CPU and doesn't require a bus to transport data between the cache and the processor. L1 cache is usually 32KB. L2 cache also resides on the CPU but requires a bus to transport data, slowing it down by comparison to L1 cache. L2 cache sizes range from 128KB on the Intel Celeron to 256KB on Intel's Pentium 4 chips.

System Bus Speed

Faster is always better, but faster is also more expensive. System bus speeds are used with the speed of your CPU and a clock multiplier to determine the ultimate speed of your system. Bus speed also affects the type of RAM you can install later on. RAM chips are compatible only with the system bus speed they are originally designed for.

Just for comparison's sake, Pentium III chips typically have a 100MHz bus speed. The AMD Athlon runs between 200MHz and 266MHz, and the latest Pentium 4s top out at 400MHz. As I said, faster is better.

Expansion Card Bus

You need a fast bus to drive fast peripherals. You want a *smart* bus so that your system works with Plug and Play and so that you can set up new boards easily. There's really only one smart and fast bus: PCI.

Most new motherboards are coming out with more PCI slots (which is good—you should look for this in a board), a few EISA slots for backward compatibility, and an AGP slot, which is currently reserved for high-speed video. Which brings me to my next bus requirement: Plug and Play. Make absolutely sure that your new machine will support Plug and Play (through its PCI and AGP slots) as implemented by Windows 98/Me/XP.

Not every board you plug into your system needs to be a PCI board, although that is preferable. You should be sure, however, that the following adapters are PCI:

◆ SCSI host adapter

◆ Any LAN cards

◆ Any video capture or sound capture hardware

Note that some low-end PCs come with *only* PCI slots. This may not be an issue (it's easy enough to find PCI versions of most internal cards), but you'll have to take special care to buy only PCI cards if you need to upgrade. I mention this because I spent an entire day driving back and forth to various stores after purchasing an EISA serial port card for a friend's new PC—only to find out that it was a PCI-only machine.

RAM

Remember this simple mathematical equation to help you buy the right amount of RAM: More = Better. Today's operating systems like RAM—especially Windows 2000 and Windows XP. I consider 128MB of RAM the bare minimum these days and recommend that you get 256MB, unless you're totally cash-strapped. Do not, in any instance, accept the 64MB that might come with an ultra low-end machine; that's not enough to run Windows applications with any sort of acceptable speed or reliability.

TIP   If you're doing professional graphics or digital video work, go for at least 512MB of RAM, preferably more—these applications need the extra headroom.

The bottom line is, you can never have too much RAM!

ROM BIOS

This is an important part of compatibility. Make sure your system has one of the big three—Phoenix, Award, or AMI. That way, it's easy to get upgrades. Nice BIOS features include:

◆ User-definable drive types

◆ Bus speeds that can be specified in the setup

◆ Processor cache enable/disable

◆ Plug and Play capable

◆ Flash upgradable

Motherboard/System Board

Motherboards come in a variety of flavors, depending on the number and type of ports you need and the form factor of the case. They also have different bus speeds. The system bus speed determines the speed at which the CPU and the motherboard communicate. (400MHz is state of the art today.) You'll also need to ensure that the motherboard has USB ports if you plan on expanding your system in the future with USB devices, and it should also have an AGP slot for an advanced video card. If the USB ports and AGP slot are built in, and the PC has their associated devices already installed when you purchase it, you won't have to worry about it.

Hard Disk Drives

You're probably going to end up buying EIDE-type drives, mainly because they're so amazingly cheap, fast, and reliable. Just back the silly things up *regularly*, because a limited array of repair options are open to you. Since storage is becoming more affordable by the day—and since you'll *always* find a way to fill up the extra space—go for a minimum size of 40GB for most applications.

TIP   If you do digital video editing, consider buying a second 40GB hard drive just for your video files.

Floppy Disks and Other Removable Storage

You probably won't have much of a choice in terms of 3.5-inch disk drives. Although most users experience few if any problems, no matter what kind of drive they have, if given the choice I prefer the high reliability of a TEAC over other, more problematic brands.

To supplement your floppy drive, you might also consider getting an internal Iomega Zip drive—which makes it easier for you to transfer large files from PC to PC when CD-R is not available. (They're also great for backing up files from your hard disk.)

CD-ROM and DVD-ROM Drives

At a minimum, you should have a CD-ROM drive in any computer you buy. If you don't (come to think of it, I don't know if they even sell systems without them nowadays), you won't be able to install any software. Virtually all software these days is distributed on CD-ROM, except for some unique system utilities that require you to boot from a floppy drive.

Because DVD-ROM is becoming more widespread, I suggest you go for a DVD-ROM drive—which can also read CD-ROMs. That way, when software and games are more prevalently distributed on DVDs, you'll be able to buy them without worrying about being able to use them. As an added bonus, you'll be able to play DVD movies on your PC. Not a great productivity-enhancer, but they are fun! For more information about these drives, refer to Chapter 27, "An Overview of CD-ROM and DVD-ROM Drives."

NOTE *The one trade-off you'll make if you get a DVD-ROM drive instead of a CD-ROM is a bit of speed. CD-ROM drives max out at 48X or more, while DVD-ROM drives tend to be a bit slower. Most of the time, though, you'll never know the difference.*

You should also consider buying a CD-R or CD-RW drive, so you can burn your own CDs. (This is good for collecting MP3s, backing up your essential data, and transferring large files to other computers.) Although you can use the CD-R/RW drive as your sole CD-ROM drive, you're probably better off considering the CD-R/RW as an auxiliary drive. Use the DVD-ROM as your main *playback* drive, and the CD-R/RW as your *recording* drive.

Video Board

Get an AGP video accelerator board to support modern graphical operating systems, applications, and games. If you're a heavy graphics user, make sure you get a card with at least 64MB of high-speed SDRAM. (See Chapter 24, "Video Adapters and Displays," for more about video.)

Video Monitor

Buy at least a 17-inch monitor—and consider a 19-inch monitor if you have desk space for it. You'll save on eyestrain, regardless of the resolution you choose. If you consistently work in high resolutions such as 1024 × 768, this size monitor is a must.

Alternately, consider a flat-screen display—especially if desk space is an issue. Flat-screen displays have generally been more expensive than traditional monitors, but their prices are coming down. I was at my local Office Depot earlier today and saw that 15-inch flat screens have finally hit the $300 mark, which is a lot cheaper than the $1000 I paid just a year ago.

NOTE *Remember that inches don't translate exactly between tube-type and flat-screen displays; a 15-inch flat screen has exactly the same viewable area as a 17-inch traditional monitor.*

Sound Card

All PCs will come with some sort of sound card, typically partnered with some sort of basic external speaker system. If all you do is browse the Web, write memos, and crunch spreadsheets, the standard sound card is probably good enough for you.

However, if you listen to a lot of MP3s or CDs or Internet radio stations, consider upgrading to a 64-bit card with an extra complement of built-in voices. If you play a lot of games, go for a card that offers 3D sound.

Speakers

Most PCs ship with some sort of speaker system to complement the sound card. The common little cubes are perfectly functional, but if you actually listen to audio through your PC, you'll want something better. Spending a few extra bucks for better speakers will provide a substantial payback. Definitely go for a system with a separate subwoofer, and make sure you evaluate the rated output (in watts) of the left and right speakers—the higher the better. Because sound is subjective, this is one component of your system that is worth evaluating in person before you buy.

Mice

Any of the Microsoft mice seem the best of all the ones I've worked with—although Logitech makes some sweet little rodents, too. The newest mice don't have balls—they use infrared pulses to determine how far, how fast, and in what direction you move the mouse. They come in USB versions and don't even require a mouse pad. You might also want to consider a wireless mouse (sometimes paired with a wireless keyboard), which offers a lot of positioning flexibility.

Keyboards

The standard keyboard that ships with your new PC is a perfectly acceptable input device. However, if you do a lot of typing—and want to avoid the onset of carpal tunnel syndrome—consider upgrading to an ergonomic keyboard, such as Microsoft's Natural Keyboard. Even though the split-keyboard design might take a little getting used to, it's a lot easier on the wrists.

Serial Ports

Look for serial ports based on the 16550 UART chip—which is just about any serial port available today. It's built for multitasking.

Parallel Ports

Make sure that your parallel ports are enhanced parallel ports or ECP/EPP interfaces. They're faster and bidirectional. Bidirectional parallel ports are essential for modern printers, which send status information back to the PC over those ports.

Universal Serial Buses (USBs)

How many things do you currently have attached to your computer? A monitor, sound card, printer, scanner, card reader, more? Eventually, on a standard system, you'll run out of room for more additions. USB is designed to solve this problem; you can have up to 127 devices attached to a USB port. Not only that, you can simply plug in the device and forget it—no messy configurations or even reboots. When you get a system, look into one with USB ports on the motherboard, since so many people are coming out with compatible add-ons. The newer USB2 ports are backward compatible with the older USB and are 40 times faster than the older version.

TIP   Many systems come with two USB ports, which works great if that's all you need. But if you need more ports and can't daisy-chain devices together (many USB devices for PCs do not have USB ports on them, so you can't connect them together), you should consider buying a USB hub. These connect to a USB port on your computer and offer more open ports for you to use.

Modems / Network Adapters

Many systems come with an internal modem so you can connect to the Internet. Don't take anything less than a 56K modem that supports the V.90 standard—even if you'll be using a DSL or cable Internet connection. You might even want to hold out for a modem that supports the new V.92 standard, which—while not increasing the speed at all—does add a few minor bells and whistles that can make connecting a little easier. (You'll find that there will always be a need for a traditional analog modem—for when your broadband connection goes dead, for example, or to send PC-based faxes, or to let your new software applications dial into the mothership for registration.)

If you're working on a network, you'll need to get a network adapter card. These come in a wide variety of flavors, and the type you get depends on the type of network you have. The most common type is the Ethernet network, which operates at speeds of either 10Mbps or 100Mbps. Go for a 10/100 card for the most flexibility.

You can also get dual modem/network adapter cards, which will enable you to connect to the Internet over a phone line and be connected to your network at the same time.

Printers

Although laser printers used to be the standard for high-quality output, today's inkjet printers are also excellent. Even the lowest-cost inkjet printers support up to 1200×1200 dpi resolution, and some color inkjet printers can produce photo-quality printouts. Color inkjet printers usually cost only a few hundred dollars, whereas color laser printers still run several thousands of dollars. That said, a good-quality laser printer is probably a necessity if you're using it for your business or printing a lot of high-volume black-and-white jobs. An inkjet is more of a home or lighter-duty printer—but a necessity if you want four-color output.

System Comparisons

Ultimately, the type of system you buy should do the tasks you need it to do. If you are just going to connect to the Internet, you'll need a much less powerful (which also means less expensive) system than someone who wants to play the most advanced games on the market. Before buying your new PC, see if you fit into one of these categories:

Home   You use your computer for everyday tasks such as financial planning, writing letters, and connecting to the Internet.

Student   You use your PC for homework, for research (on the Internet), for instant messaging and chat (on the Internet, again), and for some game playing and MP3 downloading.

Gamer   You want to play all the great games out there—including the latest ones with the very best graphics and sound.

Audio/video enthusiast   You want to hook up your digital video camera to your PC to edit your movies—and to create your own musical soundtracks.

Small business   You use your PC for your business and for a little personal use; you may even be connected to a small network.

Corporate   You use your computer in a networked environment—and you have to use the same applications as everyone else in your office.

Road warrior   Your computer is a laptop and you take it on the road—so it has to be light, yet powerful enough to be your sole PC.

I'll explore each of these categories in more detail in just a minute. First, though, let's compare the recommended systems for each type of user. Table 30.1 lists what pieces, parts, and performance are typical of these systems, and gives you a general price range you can expect.

Of course, you can play with the components and go up or down the technology scale. Buying more advanced components will raise the price of the system—some dramatically. Another area to watch for is other peripherals that I haven't listed in Table 30.1. These might include printers, scanners, external storage drives, tape backup drives, and so on.

TABLE 30.1: COMPUTER FEATURES VERSUS NEEDS

USER CATEGORY	SYSTEM FEATURES	COST
Home	Intel Celeron 1GHz or AMD Duron 1GHz processor	$500–$1000
	128MB of RAM	
	20GB hard drive	
	48X CD-ROM (or a DVD-ROM drive)	
	Generic sound card	
	Generic speakers with optional subwoofer	
	15" or 17" monitor	
	16MB AGP video card	
	56K V.90 modem	

Continued on next page

TABLE 30.1: COMPUTER FEATURES VERSUS NEEDS *(continued)*

USER CATEGORY	SYSTEM FEATURES	COST
Home	Standard mouse	
	Standard keyboard	
	Microsoft Windows Me or Windows XP	
Student	Intel Celeron 1GHz, AMD Duron 1.1GHz, or Intel Pentium III 1GHz processor	$700–$1200
	256MB of RAM	
	40GB hard drive	
	CD-R/RW drive	
	Generic sound card	
	Two speakers with subwoofer	
	15" or 17" monitor	
	16MB AGP video card	
	56K V.90 modem	
	Standard mouse	
	Microsoft Natural Keyboard	
	Microsoft Windows Me or Windows XP	
Gamer	Intel Pentium 4 1.7GHz or AMD Athlon XP 1.6GHz processor	$1200–$2200
	512MB of RAM	
	40GB hard drive	
	16X/40X CD/DVD-ROM	
	3D sound card	
	Two (or four) speakers with subwoofer	
	17" or 19" monitor	
	32MB or 64MB AGP 3D video card w/graphics accelerator	
	56K V.90 modem	
	10/100 Ethernet network interface card (if connected to broadband Internet)	
	Microsoft IntelliMouse with IntelliEye	
	Standard keyboard	
	Microsoft Windows Me or Windows XP	

Continued on next page

TABLE 30.1: COMPUTER FEATURES VERSUS NEEDS *(continued)*

USER CATEGORY	SYSTEM FEATURES	COST
Audio/video enthusiast	Intel Pentium 4 1.4GHz to 2.2GHz or AMD Athlon XP 1.6GHz to 2GHz processor	$2000–$4000
	1GB of RAM	
	60GB or 80GB ATA-100 hard drive	
	16X/40X DVD-ROM drive plus CD-R/RW drive	
	64-bit sound card with MIDI input and output	
	Two (or four) speakers with subwoofer	
	17″, 19″, or 21″ monitor	
	32MB or 64MB AGP 3D video card w/graphics accelerator	
	56K V.90 modem IEEE 1394/FireWire interface Analog video capture card	
	10/100 Ethernet network interface card (if connected to broadband Internet)	
	Microsoft IntelliMouse with IntelliEye	
	Standard keyboard	
	Microsoft Windows Me or Windows XP	
Small business	Intel Pentium 4 1.8GHz or AMD Athlon 1.8GHz processor	$1200–$2000
	256MB of RAM	
	40GB hard drive	
	CD-R/RW drive	
	Generic sound card	
	Generic speakers with optional subwoofer	
	17" monitor	
	16MB AGP video card	
	56K V.90 modem	
	Standard mouse	
	Microsoft Natural Keyboard	
	Microsoft Windows Me, Windows 2000, or Windows XP	

Continued on next page

TABLE 30.1: COMPUTER FEATURES VERSUS NEEDS *(continued)*

USER CATEGORY	SYSTEM FEATURES	COST
Corporate	Intel Celeron 1.3GHz, AMD Duron 1.3GHz, or Intel Pentium 4 1.4GHz processor	$800–$1400
	256MB of RAM	
	40GB hard drive	
	48X CD-ROM	
	Generic sound card	
	Generic speakers	
	15" or 17" monitor	
	16MB AGP video card	
	Standard mouse	
	Microsoft Natural Keyboard	
	Windows 2000 or Windows XP	
	10/100 Ethernet network interface card	
Road warrior	Notebook PC with Intel Pentium III 1GHz or 1.2GHz processor; consider Transmeta's new Crusoe chip	$2000–$3500
	256MB of RAM	
	30GB hard drive	
	8X/40X CD/DVD-ROM drive	
	Built-in speaker(s)	
	12" or 15" active matrix display	
	56K V.90 modem (may be software based)	
	Pointing device	
	Keyboard	
	Windows Me, Windows 2000, or Windows XP	
	10/100 Ethernet capability (built-in)	

Home

For the home, you need a PC that can run basic Microsoft Office applications, surf the Internet, and possibly play a few games. None of these activities are particularly demanding, so you should start your search at the low end of the PC price scale—between $500 and $1000.

In this price range you'll be looking at a 1GHz Celeron or 1GHz AMD Duron processor, either of which is plenty fast. Make sure your system has 128MB of RAM (some might come with just 64MB standard), and consider spending a few extra bucks to upgrade from a 15-inch to a 17-inch monitor. In the hard drive department, 20GB should be adequate for your needs. You'll also get a CD-ROM drive standard; if it isn't too much extra, you might want to splurge for a DVD-ROM drive instead.

If you think you'll be listening to a lot of music on this machine (either on CD or over the Internet), consider upgrading the speaker system to include bigger fronts and a separate subwoofer. Make sure the sound card is Sound Blaster compatible.

As with all noncorporate PCs, expect to have Windows XP preinstalled on your hard drive—probably along with Microsoft Works Suite. If you prefer to use Microsoft Office, you'll have to upgrade.

NOTE *If Microsoft Word is the only Microsoft Office application that you use, you're in luck—Microsoft Works Suite includes Word as its word processor.*

If you have more than one PC at home, you might want to consider networking them together. A wireless or power line–based network is easiest to install, especially if the PCs are in different parts of the house, but if you decide to go with a traditional Ethernet-based network, don't forget to add a 10/100 Ethernet network card to your system.

Student

Student PC use isn't a whole lot different from standard home use—with the possible exception of heavier music playback and some CD burning. You'll be looking at the same Celeron 1GHz processor, or possibly an 1.1GHz AMD Duron or 1GHz Intel Pentium III. You'll want to trade up the standard CD-ROM drive for a CD-R/RW burner, and consider going to a 40GB hard drive. (Those MP3 files take up a lot of disk space!) And make sure you get a speaker system that will do your MP3 files justice—which means larger front speakers and a separate subwoofer.

Since you'll be writing a lot of reports and term papers, make sure you upgrade to an ergonomic keyboard, such as the Microsoft Natural Keyboard. If you'll be using this computer while you're away at college, you'll probably need an Ethernet card, so you can plug into the campus network. Windows XP will be your operating system, and you'll probably get Microsoft Works Suite as your standard software.

Expect to pay between $700 and $1200 for a fully decked-out student PC.

TIP *It's a good idea not to buy a new PC before you head off to college. Always check with your college or university to see (1) what type of computer and software they recommend—some schools require Macintosh, not IBM compatibles—and (2) what kind of deals they're offering for purchase through the school. You might find that you can pick up a comparable PC for a lot less money through a school-sponsored buying program than you can at a traditional retail outlet.*

Gamer

Believe it or not, PC games demand extremely powerful PCs to deliver the ultimate gaming experience. You'll want a fairly powerful processor, and the AMD Athlon is probably a better choice than an Intel Pentium 4; go for a chip running in the neighborhood of 1.5–1.8GHz. You'll also need a lot more memory than with a typical home machine; 512MB should provide you with a machine that has minimum lag during those firefights with players from across the globe.

Since games take up a lot of disk space, go for a 40GB hard disk, and make sure you get a DVD-ROM drive. (Many new games are coming on single DVDs rather than multiple CDs.) You'll want a high-quality 3D sound card, and either a 32MB or 64MB 3D video card with graphics accelerator. You definitely want a good speaker system with a powerful subwoofer; you might want to consider going with a full surround-sound system. And you'll need a big monitor for the full gaming experience, so think about either a 17-inch or 19-inch model.

You'll also want to replace (or supplement) the standard mouse with a high-quality joystick or similar game controller. In addition, if you have a broadband (DSL or cable) Internet connection, you may need to include a 10/100 Ethernet card so you can network this and any other PCs together to share the connection.

You'll pay for this performance, of course. The lowest-price gaming machines run around $1200, with the high-performance models topping out around $2200.

Audio/Video Enthusiast

The most demanding application for a computer today is digital video editing. You need the fastest processor, the fastest video, the most versatile audio, a lot of memory, and a huge hard disk. All this power will set you back at least $2000, and possibly $4000 or more.

In terms of speed, go for the fastest Pentium 4 (1.4 to 2.2GHz) or AMD Athlon XP (1.6GHz to 2GHz) you can afford. Cram the sucker full of memory and don't stop until you hit at least 1GB, and then make sure you get at least a 60MB or 80MB ATA-100 hard disk. You may even want to consider adding a second SCSI hard disk, just to store your digital movie files.

You'll want to include both a DVD-ROM drive and a CD-R/RW drive, so you can play back (and possibly record) DVD movies and burn your movie files to CD. A big monitor will be helpful, so don't shy away from the 19-inch (or even the 21-inch) models. Make sure you match the monitor with a 32MB or 64MB video card with graphics accelerator.

It's imperative that a system designed for digital video editing have an IEEE 1394/FireWire interface. You'll also want a separate analog video capture card (for input/output from and to VCRs and other nondigital devices) and possibly a separate MIDI sound card/controller for mixing multiple audio signals.

In this price range, you'll probably have your choice of Windows Me/XP/2000; Windows XP is the better choice for video editing work today. (Most digital editing software runs on Windows Me or XP; fewer programs run on Windows 2000.) You'll probably also get Microsoft Office preinstalled, whether you want it or not.

Small Business

The typical small business PC looks a lot like the typical home PC, but with less emphasis on multimedia features and more emphasis on storage. You'll probably be looking at a system powered by either a Pentium 4 1.8GHz or AMD Athlon 1.8GHz chip, and you should definitely upgrade to 256MB of RAM. Since you'll be storing all your business data on this machine, at least a 40GB hard drive should be a good investment.

A CD-R/RW drive is a nice touch, considering that you'll probably be trading large files (such as PowerPoint presentations) with clients or other workers. Don't worry too much about the audio or video cards, but make sure you go for a 17-inch monitor.

If you'll be typing for long periods of time, upgrade to a more ergonomic keyboard, such as the Microsoft Natural Keyboard. Finally, if you'll connected to other PCs on a network, make sure you get a 10/100 Ethernet card installed.

Given a choice of operating systems, it's okay to stick with Windows Me—although Windows 2000 or Windows XP might be better if you're in a networked environment. Pass on the free copy of Microsoft Works Suite and upgrade to the full version of Microsoft Office.

All this will cost you just a bit more than a typical home PC. Expect to shell out between $1200 and $2000.

Corporate

A corporate PC isn't much different from a small business PC—except that you definitely need network access, and you might be able to get by with a lower-cost processor and smaller hard disk. (More of your stuff will be stored on the network server, so why spend money on disk space you won't be using?)

Start with a 1.3GHz Celeron or 1.3GHz AMD Duron processor (or possibly a 1.4GHz Pentium 4), add 256MB of RAM and a 40GB hard disk, and you have your basic corporate system. If your company is cheap, you might be forced to accept a 15-inch monitor, although you should hold out for a 17-inch model. Don't expect to get anything fancy in the way of audio or video, though—and don't be surprised if the IT person hands you a set of headphones so you can compute without disturbing your cube-mates.

The standard operating system for the corporate environment is still Windows 2000 (Windows NT if your company hasn't upgraded yet, and Windows XP Professional if they are upgrading to the latest). Make sure the machine comes with a 10/100 Ethernet card, so you can connect to the corporate network.

Expect to pay between $800 and $1400 for this rather bland machine.

Road Warrior

This last computing category is slightly more complex. If you're one of the millions of telecommuters or traveling salespeople out there, you'll have to forsake a traditional desktop computer for a portable model. When you're talking portables, you're faced with a whole new set of considerations, including:

- ◆ Size (the smaller the better—unless the screen gets too small to use)
- ◆ Weight (the lighter the better—until you start sacrificing functionality)
- ◆ Features (how much stuff do you really need to take with you?)

If you're only a part-time portable user—that is, if you rely on a desktop PC as your main machine and use the portable only for an occasional trip—then you might want to consider a thin, light, less-fully featured notebook. These portables typically offer a 12-inch screen and a slightly smaller keyboard, and make the floppy and CD-ROM drives external and optional. The result is something small enough to comfortably carry, with enough functionality to check your e-mail and do some *very* basic Office work. Expect to pay between $2000 and $2500 for one of these mini-marvels.

If, on the other hand, your portable is your *only* computer, you need to get it as loaded as you would a desktop model. You'll want a larger screen (15-inch, at least), full-size keyboard, integrated CD/DVD-ROM drive, big hard disk (20GB is nice), and plenty of memory (128MB should suffice). One of these puppies, while packing on the pounds (8 lbs. or so is typical), can do just about everything a decent desktop PC can. This is especially so if you purchase a docking station, so your laptop will have full port functionality when you're not traveling. Expect to spend between $2500 and $3500 for a full-featured laptop—docking station not included.

Whichever type of portable PC you choose, you'll definitely want Ethernet access built in, so you can plug into whichever corporate network you're around on any given day. Naturally, you also want a built-in modem—or else you'll never be able to check your e-mail!

Where Should You Buy?

When I ask this question, I don't mean whether you should buy from Dell, IBM, or Jeff and Akbar's House of Clones. Instead, I mean, "Should you buy directly from the manufacturer, via mail order, the Internet, or at a store?"

Well, if you're a really large company, then it probably makes sense to go straight to Compaq or whomever and negotiate a specific deal. But if you're an individual or a small business, then you'll have to examine your strategies.

Of course, going to a big computer or office supply retailer, such as CompUSA, is always an option. Sometimes you can find competent sales help there, and sometimes you can find decent prices. Sometimes you can't. If you get a good deal, go for it; if not, consider other options.

One of those other options is to go to one of the many small businesses whose main line of work is to sell computer parts, software, supplies, and systems. These local vendors often offer prices that are a tad cheaper than what you find at the big-box boys. And patronizing your local PC store means that when you need that disk drive on Saturday, you need only run down the street to get it, rather than waiting a week for it to ship from the manufacturer. (To be honest, the real reason I like dealing with local retailers is because I like my vendors within choking distance.)

You can probably get the best prices by purchasing via mail order or over the Internet (à la Gateway, Dell, and others). *But* if you do that, then returning defective merchandise involves shipping things around, getting RMA (Return Merchandise Authorization) numbers, etc. That can be a hassle (as can obtaining technical support).

That's not to say that dealing with mail order firms or e-tailers doesn't make sense. Mail-order and Internet firms are more likely to have the latest and greatest software and hardware. Their prices will, again, sometimes be lower than the local store's. They may even know more about the product than a local vendor might—*if* you get the right salesperson on the phone. But take it from a veteran—there are a few things to look out for. Read on for some shopping tips.

Shopping Tips

The two essential laws of buying a new PC are to never sign anything and never hand over any money until you're absolutely sure you are getting the system you want and need. Knowledge, as they say, is power. Make sure you read all the literature (and do the appropriate online research) concerning your prospective PC, and make sure you understand everything you read. It's also very helpful to perform a cost-tradeoff analysis. Sit down and decide what you absolutely need and calculate the price of the system, then start upgrading components and recalculate the price. Stop when you reach the top limit of your budget and decide whether you'll be happy. If not, can you reduce anything to make room for that component you really, really want?

You can also purchase with an eye toward future upgrades. For example, you may want a 60GB hard drive but can't afford it right now. Hard drives are relatively easy to upgrade, especially if you plan on adding a second one in the future. Maybe you can compromise on a 40GB hard drive now and get another 40GB drive within a year. Your total storage space would reach 80GB—more than the 60GB you would have originally purchased.

WARNING   *One thing you definitely don't want to buy is a long-term Internet service contract. Many PC manufacturers and retailers will try to lure you in with a "discounted" price that is actually derived by subtracting a $100 (or more) rebate that you earn by committing to a year or more of Internet service. The truth is, Internet access is cheap ($20 a month or less) and getting cheaper. If you sign up for three years of Internet access, there's no telling how cheap that access will be by the end of your contract. Remember that you went into the store to buy a computer, not an Internet plan—and stick to it!*

Other components, such as the CPU, are more expensive to upgrade later. I recommend getting the fastest CPU and the most amount of memory you can afford the first time around.

When you're ready to order, especially from a mail-order firm or e-tailer, take these precautions:

Use a credit card.   It's your first line of defense when mail-order or Internet companies get nasty. If you didn't get what you wanted, just box it up, ship it back, and cancel the charge. Years ago, some PC manufacturers used to charge a 15 percent "restocking fee." One sent me a hard disk that had clearly been dropped. When it worked, it registered seek times in the hundreds of milliseconds, despite what their ad promised. They tried to convince me that the drive was just what I wanted, but I knew better and sent it back. They tried to charge me a restocking fee, so I just complained to Citibank, and they backed off.

Find out whom you're talking to.   If the person responds, "Operator 22" (I suppose his friends call him "22"), ask to speak with a supervisor. You're about to give this guy your name, address, phone, and credit card number, and he won't even tell you who he is? Write the name down. Also get a confirmation number or order number.

Buy the product only if it's in stock.   Back-ordered things can take months to arrive, and by the time they do, you'll be charged the older (and higher) price. Get the salesperson to check that it can ship today. If not, don't place the order.

Ship it overnight or second-day.   By default, most mail-order and Internet companies use UPS ground, which can take anywhere from one week to a millennium to arrive. Second-day is usually only a few dollars more, and that way you can get a guaranteed delivery date out of the salesperson.

Once you have the product, keep the carton that it came in for 30 days. That way, if a problem arises, it's easy to ship it back. And if you do have to ship something back, then by all means insure it.

You should follow these same precautions when purchasing from a manufacturer or retailer Web site. What's nice about buying direct from the manufacturer over the Web is that you can custom-design your own system right online, choosing your CPU, memory, video display, and so on. Once you've ordered, the company builds your system and ships it to you within days.

Just follow those rules and you should have good luck getting your computer through the mail.

When you take your new PC home (or when it arrives via mail order), the first thing you should do is to carefully unpack it and read through the documentation that comes with it. Then, find a place to set it up and put it together. Be sure to connect everything to the correct ports. Turn it on and give it a test drive. In fact, test all the components so you know they are all working. Print something, connect to the Internet or your network, play a game that makes use of your 3D video card, etc. If something doesn't work, recheck all your connections and reread any manuals. If you can't resolve the problem, call the service/support division of the company you bought the PC from and start getting their help. The bottom line is, if something doesn't work and it's not your fault, you need to get it fixed or replaced by the manufacturer/reseller immediately.

TIP   It's also a good idea to leave your new system on for two to three days straight, even if you would normally turn it off each time you're done using it. This helps the components to get "settled." This little endurance test will weed out components that have flaws and are going to fail anyway. Better to get it over with sooner rather than later.

Once you're sure everything works and you're happy with your new system, start installing other applications that you own and have fun with your new PC!

Chapter 31

Notebook/Laptop Computers

◆ QuickSteps: Upgrading and Maintaining Your Laptop   872

◆ Upgrading Your Memory   875

◆ Upgrading Your Hard Disk   879

◆ Recharging and Replacing Batteries   887

◆ Maintaining and Protecting Your Laptop   891

◆ Syncing Data with Your PC or PDA   892

◆ Troubleshooting Tips   894

Introduction

IN SOME RESPECTS, UPGRADING and maintaining your laptop or notebook computer is much simpler than taking care of a desktop machine. On one hand, the jobs you can take care of on your own usually are plainly indicated in your owner's manual and often require nothing more than unplugging an old module and plugging in a new one. On the other hand, you must leave some things in the hands of experts with specialized equipment. Again, your task is simple: put your laptop in a box, ship it off, and pay the nice people who are taking care of you.

In between these two clear extremes are upgrades and fixes that require taking the laptop apart and doing the kind of minor surgery that, with a little instruction, you can typically handle on your own. In this chapter, I'll identify which types of upgrades and fixes fall into each of the above-mentioned categories, and give you instructions for accomplishing them. Here are some examples of all three classes of upgrade:

- Say you want to add a modem. For most laptops, the process is simple: you locate the PC Card slot on your laptop, open the cover, and slide in your new credit-card-sized modem. Okay, you'll need to install the drivers too, but with PC Cards it's almost automatic.

- Say you've decided to install a larger hard disk or more memory. These are two tasks you *can* handle yourself, but both entail opening a system that might not have been designed to be taken apart easily. If you're adventurous, handy with small tools, and want to save some money, you can do the job. If you have a lot invested in your laptop and don't feel that experimenting is such a good idea, companies that specialize in laptop upgrades will do the job quickly and for relatively little money, and will usually guarantee their work.

- Say you want to upgrade your Pentium II laptop to a Pentium III processor. This you cannot do on your own. Reason: Laptop CPUs are generally surface mounted rather than socket mounted. You cannot remove a surface-mounted laptop CPU on your own. It takes special tools and expert skills.

I'll be spending time in this chapter on the first and second categories in the preceding list. Let me also reiterate that such items as hard drives and memory modules, while designed to be easily replaced, do involve opening your system. Whenever you do your own upgrading, be mindful of several important factors:

WARNING   You should read and reread the terms and conditions of any service agreements and/or warranties that came with your laptop. In some cases, opening up your laptop and tinkering with its innards can void such agreements.

- Depending on which brand of laptop you have, opening the system could mean removing the screen and/or the keyboard before you can get to the object of your replacement tasks. Getting from point A to point B in a laptop usually requires a detour or two, so don't get frustrated. Plan your moves carefully, but expect to be sidetracked.

- Refer to your owner's manual early and often. If you've lost it, write to the manufacturer and get a new one.

◆ In all cases, be even more aware than usual of cleanliness and antistatic precautions. Real estate inside a laptop is cramped; loose bits of dust, crumbs, and pet fur really need to be kept out. Not only can they cause components to not fit right, they can cause electrical shorts and trap and hold excess heat. You can get away with a little dust in a big desktop box; there's usually enough room to let the system fan work and enough space to dissipate the heat. Laptops don't give you that luxury.

◆ Always assume that cables and connectors have no slack. Again, space is so tight inside a laptop that everything has been measured down to the last millimeter. Never tug, bend, or twist anything.

◆ Never handle new parts anywhere but along the edges, if at all possible (and, if there's a choice, along the plastic edges instead of the metal edges). Latex hospital gloves are really handy, as well as cheap; consider wearing one glove for basic moves such as picking up objects and taking them out of a bag, and keep your other hand free for performing the moves that require more dexterity.

◆ Go out and buy the correct tools if you don't already have them. A set of jeweler's screwdrivers with rotating barrel bodies will save you more grief than you can even guess at, and for $5 or $10 a set you don't have to break the bank to add them to your toolbox.

Modern laptops have been purposely designed to keep those of us who love to tinker firmly in the back seat. The parts you can mess with are clearly marked. The parts that are off-limits should be scrupulously avoided. In a lot of respects, these are delicate, precision instruments, and the best way to really screw one up is to start hacking around with the assumption that you can make something fit by pushing just a *little* bit harder.

QuickSteps

Upgrading and Maintaining Your Laptop

These QuickSteps summarize how to upgrade your laptop's memory, install a new hard drive, and replace your battery.

Upgrading Your Memory

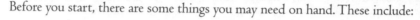

BE PREPARED

Before you start, there are some things you may need on hand. These include:

- ◆ Small Phillips screwdriver, for removing the cover over the memory panel on the laptop
- ◆ Documentation for the laptop, to tell you where and how to insert the memory
- ◆ (Optional) Antistatic wrist strap, to guard against static electricity damage
- ◆ Memory purchased from laptop manufacturer or reputable third-party vendor

1. Turn off the PC and unplug the power cord.
2. Consult the laptop documentation to find out where the memory goes.
3. Open the computer to gain access to the memory. On many laptops, there is a panel on the bottom that you remove by sliding off a small plastic cover or unscrewing a few small screws. On some others, you must remove the keyboard and place the memory underneath.
4. Remove the old memory, if needed. Consult the documentation; the procedure varies from system to system.
5. Insert the new memory. Again, see the documentation.
6. Put everything back together, replacing any components or panels you removed to get access to the memory.
7. Turn on the PC. It should detect the new memory automatically.

Upgrading Your Hard Disk

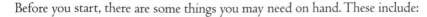

BE PREPARED

Before you start, there are some things you may need on hand. These include:

♦ Bootable floppy disk, to restart the PC after installing the new hard disk.

♦ Documentation for the laptop, to tell you where and how to insert the hard disk.

♦ Small Phillips- and flat-head screwdrivers, to remove screws on access plates (if necessary) and mounting hardware (if necessary).

♦ Needle-nosed pliers, in case you drop something into the system and need to fish it out.

♦ Pencil and paper, to write or sketch the current physical layout of cables and connectors.

♦ (Optional) Antistatic wrist strap to guard against static electricity damage.

♦ Hex or Torx screwdriver on some computers, to remove screws on access plates (if necessary) and mounting hardware (if necessary).

♦ Software to partition and format the new drive, if you have bought what is known as a *bare* drive, which has not been partitioned and formatted by the manufacturer.

♦ Hard disk designed to work with your laptop. (Consult the manufacturer to find out what you need.)

1. Back up your important data on your hard disk.

2. Open your laptop's case. Refer to the laptop documentation to find out what you need to remove for access to the hard disk.

3. Remove the existing hard drive. The exact method varies; the documentation should tell you how.

4. Install the new hard drive.

5. Boot from your floppy startup disk and partition/format the new drive.

6. Install your operating system.

Replacing Batteries

BE PREPARED

You don't usually need any special tools to install a battery, because on a laptop batteries are designed for quick swapping in and out. But before you start, there are some things you'll need to perform the operation. These include:

◆ New battery, specifically chosen to work with your laptop. (There are many kinds out there, only a short list of which will work with any one particular laptop.)

◆ The documentation for the laptop, to tell you where the battery is located and how to access it.

1. Turn off the computer.

2. Disconnect it from the AC adapter and remove any cables to printers, modems, networks, etc.

3. Find out where your battery is located by checking the laptop documentation, and remove any panel or flip open any hatch needed to access it.

4. Pull the old battery out.

5. Insert the new battery quickly. Some older laptops can't hold their BIOS setup configuration for more than a few minutes without a battery, but nearly every laptop made since 1990 has a separate battery for maintaining the CMOS configuration.

6. Close up the laptop.

7. If this is a brand-new battery, keep the machine off and connect the AC adapter. Fully charge the battery before you turn on the computer.

Memory Upgrades

Upgrading the computer's memory is probably the most common improvement that people make, as well as one of the easiest to accomplish. Most laptops come with specific instructions on how to do it and provide the specifications for exactly what kind of memory to buy.

Early laptops used proprietary memory modules, rather than standard SIMMs or DIMMs. This meant you had to buy very carefully, and only after consulting your laptop documentation and/or its manufacturer. Now, most laptops use a standardized SO-DIMM (Small Outline DIMM) form factor, which has been responsible for reducing the price and availability of RAM for laptops. For most laptops, you can order a memory module from a company that specializes in various brands of memory, but as a fallback plan you can order it from the laptop's manufacturer.

Many laptops use a modular system for memory. A certain amount of memory is built into the system, and you can't remove it. (On modern laptops it's usually some basic amount like 32MB.) Then there is an expansion socket into which you can plug one additional memory module, of whatever size you want. So, for example, suppose your current PC has 128MB of memory—64MB built in and a 64MB expansion module. You will need to remove the 64MB expansion and replace it with a higher-denomination expansion module to increase your overall memory.

Preparing for the Upgrade

As long as you follow some basic, preliminary precautions, you should have little to worry about when it comes time to upgrade the memory on your laptop.

BACK UP YOUR IMPORTANT DATA

Making sure that you back up your important data from your hard disk before you do any work on your computer is always a good idea. The chances that you'll do some damage are slight, but you have to lose everything only one time to understand the value of backups.

PREPARE YOUR WORKSPACE

Before you start, clear off your workspace. The kitchen table will do just fine (wipe it down first). Have a flat surface to work on with plenty of room to lay things out. You don't want your screwdriver rolling onto the floor just when you need it. I like to work on a clean, white towel (not a terrycloth towel, though—you don't want to introduce lint). The color provides contrast, and the softness reduces ricochets and adds a little traction for fast-moving, small items such as screws. Lay out your tools (a small flat-blade screwdriver, small- and large-head Phillips screwdrivers, and maybe small needle-nosed pliers just in case). Some systems require little hex-head screwdrivers, but most do not. The tools will vary; just make sure you've got your toolkit close at hand. You may want an antistatic strap that you can wrap around your wrist or ankle to keep static from building up while you work, but for a short job like this you probably won't need one.

DISCONNECT EVERYTHING

When installing any kind of internal components in your laptop, including memory modules, always double-check that the computer is turned off and disconnected from the AC adapter. Remove the battery pack from the computer. Remove all cables to components such as printers, external modems, and so on, and any PC Cards.

GROUND YOURSELF

Make sure that you are well grounded and always touch something metal before you touch the delicate stuff inside the laptop. That way, if you've collected any static, you'll discharge it onto the metal object instead of into your computer. Those little blue sparks that come off your fingers can have hundreds or even thousands of volts, and that's definitely not good for electronic components that run on 2.2–5 volts. Filing cabinets, light fixtures, and door frames are good things to touch to see if you're sparking.

Also, please make sure that none of your tools are the magnetized kind that come in so handy in other situations around the home. They're good for fishing lost screws out of the sink, but you don't want them anywhere near your computer.

KEEP IT CLEAN

So, touching some things is good to get rid of static. On the other hand, there are other things you never want to touch at all. For example, do not touch the metal conductors on the memory modules. Even minute amounts of dust, grit, skin oils, and sticky crud left over from lunch can be a real problem. Also, try not to touch cables, wires, and other components you're not working on. Maybe it's picky, but the fewer things you mess with, the fewer things you'll have to check later if the system doesn't work the way it's supposed to. Remember the latex gloves I mentioned earlier? This is a good time to take them out and put them on.

MAKE A MAP

With some laptops, you may need to unplug something else (such as a hard drive or a battery) before you can get to the memory module adapter, or slot. If you do, sit back for a minute, grab a pencil and paper, and make a sketch of what plugs into what before you start pulling things apart. Don't worry about making it pretty or exactly to scale; just make sure everything in the sketch is accurately identified and labeled. This is especially important for any wires you need to move out of the way. You can't rely on your remembrance of things past to make sure they all go back exactly the way they need to go back. With bigger machines, such as desktop computers or car engines, you can get away with tagging wires with masking tape. You won't have that kind of room inside a laptop, and you really don't want gummy tape glue inside your system.

GET MOTIVATED!

At this point, you may be asking yourself whether you really want to do this kind of upgrade on your own. You may think that all these precautions signal something difficult or dangerous. That is really not the case. All I'm trying to do is point out that you need to take your time and proceed in a careful, well-planned manner.

Look at it this way—installing memory in your laptop will take you 10 to 15 minutes. These things are made to be upgraded, after all. Now, if you pay people at the local computer store to do the upgrade for you, it will take them the same 10 or 15 minutes to do the job. It will also cost you about $85. That's the going hourly rate for most PC repair jobs, and you'll pay for a full hour regardless of how little time the upgrade really takes.

At the very least, you should try doing the installation yourself, and if you get to a place where you really don't want to go any further, then take it down to the shop. But first give it a shot yourself. You'll be surprised at how easily most of these systems come together—and you can use the $85 you save to treat yourself to dinner and a movie.

Doing the Installation

Increasing the memory on your laptop is probably the easiest upgrade option available. The following sections detail the steps involved.

ACCESS THE MEMORY MODULE

The first thing you have to do is open up the computer so you can get at the memory modules. Most laptops have access hatches that you open from the bottom, so close the screen, turn the laptop over, and work from the bottom of the laptop system unit. Sometimes you have to unscrew a cover plate to open the memory hatch; with other laptops, you push small locking tabs and lift the cover plate away from the body of the machine. In either case, the correct hatch should be marked with something that indicates which is the correct one. It might say *memory*, it might have a stylized drawing of a memory module, it might have something arcane, like the term *exp*, but it will usually have something to indicate that this is where the memory lives. If there are other hatches, they too will be marked. You're smart—you'll figure it out.

Some laptops require you to remove or simply lift up the keyboard in order to access the memory area. For these systems, open up the screen, unlatch the keyboard (by sliding the unlocking latches on the side or at the back), and work on the system from the top.

The top-access systems usually still have the memory modules down at the bottom of the system, so you may also have to move the disk drive or hard drive to get at the memory. If you have to move a drive, it will usually come equipped with a plastic tab that you use as a handle. Always use the tabs or handles they give you. Do not put a screwdriver under the drive and try to lever it out. Look before you pull. There may be little plastic or metal devices that the manufacturer used to hold the drive in place. There may be small screws that hold it down. Refer to your owner's manual to see whether you need to remove any of these things or whether the whole unit should slide out as a single piece.

Even on systems you access from the bottom, you may still have to move something else out of the way before you can reach the memory area. Some laptops, for example, require that you remove the hard drive by sliding it out of its socket and removing it from the machine.

LOOK AROUND

Once you have exposed the memory area, you'll want to stop for a minute and study what's in front of you. Does your system have slots that accept SO-DIMM memory modules, or is it the kind that uses prepackaged proprietary memory modules?

If you have the latter, you'll simply insert the new, two-plug memory module into the sockets that are provided. These machines are usually limited to accepting only one upgrade module, so if something is already in the upgrade sockets, you'll have to remove it before you can add the new module.

Do you have empty slots, or are all of them filled? If you have empty slots, you can go ahead with the addition of your new memory. If your slots are all filled, you'll have to empty one or more of them so you have a place to put your new memory.

OUT WITH THE OLD

If you have to remove memory, look for something that indicates which slot has the highest number (for example, there might be a small 0 or 1 printed on the board next to the slot). You will usually want to replace existing memory starting with the highest numbered slot. (This is where your owner's manual or the company's tech support people can be most helpful, by giving exact instructions if you can't find a clear indicator just by looking at the slots.)

To remove any memory modules you have to get rid of, look for the locking latches on both edges of the socket. Unhook the latches from the module by pressing them away from the module. These latches can sometimes be fairly tight, but don't get carried away and apply too much force; you don't want to snap them off. Just a gentle push outward should be enough. Once the latches are released from the edges of the module, you can tilt the module upward and slide it out. Do not touch the gold or tin connectors.

Set aside any modules you've removed and save them for possible future use. You never know when they might come in handy. You may be able to sell your old memory. My local computer store has a bulletin board for people to advertise old parts that they want to sell or buy, including used chips. Failing that, try giving them to a school. Taxpayer revolt being what it is, the school's probably pretty desperate for any charity you care to offer, and you can probably take a tax break by deducting the value (or a percentage of it) when April rolls around. (Ask your tax preparer, just to be sure.)

IN WITH THE NEW

If you have empty slots and don't have to take anything out before you add the new memory, or if you've freed some room by following the previous instructions, pick up your new module by the edges and slide it into the socket. It will go in at an angle and then pivot down until it locks into place. Make sure it's fully seated in the slot before you pivot it down.

Most memory modules are keyed by having little notches cut into the side so that they will fit into the slot only one way. If you have any doubts (for example, if the module seems really hard to fit into the connector), take it out and try it the other way. (This is also why you took a few minutes to make a sketch of what things looked like before you started.) Never try to cram something into a place where it doesn't seem to want to go. It might be misaligned, something might be blocking the way, or it might be upside down. These things slide in easily. If yours doesn't, it's the wrong way around. Turn it and try again: dust it off, line it up, and make sure it goes in straight; just don't force it.

PUT EVERYTHING BACK

Once you have the new memory correctly installed, by whichever method your laptop requires, replace whatever you took out, or off, in exactly the same way you removed it. Replace the drives, battery packs, and access covers in reverse order from the way they came off. Reconnect any cables you disconnected and turn the machine on. It will go through its normal boot cycle, only this time you should see a bigger number on your screen when it does the memory check. If all goes well, you're done. For example, if you installed a 64MB module in a computer that already had 32MB of memory, the boot sequence should confirm that all went well by showing that you now have 96MB of memory.

If you get an error message or if the amount of memory the computer recognizes does not match the amount you should now have, don't worry about it. Sometimes the BIOS gives you that, and you enter the BIOS program, and then exit it, and everything is fine from then on.

If you continue to get BIOS error messages regarding the memory at startup, however, you'll have to turn off the machine and go through the installation process again. If you have to reopen the computer and do it all again, it'll probably be because the new memory module isn't fully inserted into the slot. Make sure that it's straight and fully seated, so the locking tabs snap into the notches on the module. And if that doesn't fix it, send the memory back, because it's defective.

Hard Disk Upgrades

The capacity of your laptop's hard disk drive can be increased by installing compression programs, such as Microsoft's DriveSpace, that will effectively double the amount of space you can use but at the expense of precious system resources. At some point, you may decide that you've compressed everything as far as you can and you still need more room. You have these options:

◆ You can attach a removable media drive, such as a Zip drive or CD-RW drive, via your laptop's USB or parallel port.

◆ You can slip a PC Card hard drive into your laptop.

◆ Some laptops will let you swap the floppy disk drive or CD-ROM drive with a second hard disk.

◆ You can remove your current hard drive and completely replace it with a new, higher-capacity model.

The last of these options is the one most people choose. The others have certain drawbacks. External removable media drives force you to carry extra gear and, although they're good for special occasions such as hauling around huge graphics files, they tend to be cumbersome and somewhat slow. PC Card hard drives are handy and work quite well, but using one means giving up, at least temporarily, access to PC Card modems and other devices that use the same slot or slots. Replacing your floppy drive or CD-ROM with a second hard drive is a tempting solution, and some people are happy to trade their floppy for something bigger. However, others rely on their floppies to load new files and programs, or need to keep their CD-ROMs for the large reference works they have in their CD libraries. Additionally, not all laptops have controllers capable of supporting a second hard drive. If you have one that will, such as an IBM ThinkPad, I'll go into that upgrade option shortly. For now, though, let's take a look at what you need to do to replace your current hard drive with a new one.

Finding the Right Hard Disk

The only real trick in replacing your hard drive is getting a new one that will work with your laptop—and that isn't really much of a trick. Almost all laptop computers use 2½-inch hard drives. If your laptop was made before 1996, it probably has a *full-height* hard drive, about 18 millimeters high. If your laptop was made after 1996, it probably has a *slim-line* hard drive, about 11mm high.

A slim hard drive will usually work in an older (pre-1996) laptop, but a full-height drive won't fit in a laptop made for the 11mm drives. If you find a really good deal on a full-height drive but aren't sure whether it will fit into your newer laptop, the best way to check is to remove your current drive (see "Taking Out the Old Hard Drive" later in this chapter) and take a ruler to its height. Just measure the height of the drive, not its supporting brackets. If it's 18mm, you can use a new drive that is either 11mm or 18mm. If it's 11mm, you need to specify the same (a slim-line model) for your new drive, too.

VERIFYING THE BIOS

Another factor you have to watch out for is what kind of BIOS you have. Some older BIOS chips will not let you have a hard drive larger than 540MB (or, on slightly newer systems, 4GB or 8.4GB is the limit). If you have this kind of BIOS, you will need a software BIOS *extender* (software that enables the BIOS to recognize larger hard drives) for your notebook/laptop, or you will need to send your laptop to an upgrade company that will update your firmware BIOS. I talked about this in great detail in Chapter 13, "Partitioning and Formatting IDE and SCSI Drives."

The good news is that most mail-order sources either will include the BIOS upgrade software as part of the price, or will upgrade your firmware BIOS if you send them the computer. The bad news is that if you have to send your laptop away to be upgraded, you're going to be without it for a few days. Generally speaking, however, most laptops will do just fine with a software BIOS extender, and you won't have to send your machine out into the cold, cruel world on its own.

OBTAINING MOUNTING HARDWARE

Finally, some laptop hard drives are manufactured in such a way that their supporting brackets are built right into the drive itself. If you have this kind of hard drive, you will need to get new mounting hardware along with your hard drive, and you may have to hunt to find it. A lot of retailers don't carry a large variety of brackets. Your best bet in such a case is to call your laptop's manufacturer, or the hard drive vendor, and find out where you can get the hardware you need to attach the new drive to the laptop. Seems like such a minor item, but details like these can give you the biggest headaches.

NOTE   *Need some pointers on how to locate a source for laptop hard drives? Again, the best way to find one quickly is to use one of the search engines on the Internet. Just run a search for* laptop + hard drive.

Backing Up Your Data

Things can go wrong—remember Murphy's Law? It's always better to be safe than sorry when messing around with your hard-earned data. Do not remove your old hard drive until it is entirely backed up, either on the new hard drive or by some other means.

To back up your data, you have a number of options, as presented in the following paragraphs.

NETWORK BACKUP

If you have access to a network, the easiest way to back up your hard disk is to copy everything from your laptop to the server and keep it there until you have finished installing your new hard drive. You will need to make sure you have all your configuration software on a floppy disk, however, or your machine won't be able to access the network to let you download all your files when you are ready for them.

EXTERNAL DRIVE

If you have an external tape drive, CDR-RW drive, or a Zip drive, you can use MS Backup or some other backup program (the Backup program that comes with Windows 9x/Me/XP is good) to move all your files to the external drive and then restore them to the new hard drive after you finish installing it.

SECOND LAPTOP OR DESKTOP COMPUTER

You can use a commercial program such as LapLink to copy all your files to another machine and then restore them to the new hard drive after you finish installing it.

SECOND HARD DRIVE

If you have a laptop that will accommodate two hard drives (by removing the floppy disk drive or CD-ROM, for example), you can install the new hard drive, XCOPY everything from the old drive to the new drive, remove both drives, install the new drive in place of the old drive, and finally, reinstall the floppy drive or CD-ROM. This is a lot of work, but sometimes you have to get creative if you want to get anything done.

Alternatively, you can use the Seagate FileCopy program. FileCopy will make an exact, bootable duplicate of the original hard drive on another hard drive that has as large or larger capacity.

Programs such as Norton Ghost and Drive Copy make complete copies of your hard disk content, onto whatever media you choose (another hard disk, a CD-R/RW, etc.). That way, you can back up everything just as it is and then "transplant" it onto the new drive later. Such a program can save you hours in reinstalling Windows and all your Windows programs and recopying all your files.

Preparing for the Hard Drive Upgrade

You've got the hard drive and mounting hardware. You've backed up all your files. You have a bootable floppy disk at hand and another floppy with all your network access software. If you've backed up your old hard drive to a server and removed all boisterous children and pets to another room, you're all set to begin. Before you start, however, make sure you have all the necessary tools handy. Refer back to the QuickSteps at the beginning of this chapter for a list of what you might need.

Installing the New Hard Drive

You're all ready to go. You have your hard drive. You have your laptop. You have a flat, clean surface on which to work. Your tools are all laid out where you can reach them. You have grounded yourself. Let's get started.

OPENING THE LAPTOP

In order to get to the hard drive of some laptops, you need to completely open them up. With others, you may just have to lift off the keyboard by unsnapping it. And some have drives that simply slide out (my favorite).

First, make sure you know the location of the hard drive.

You may be lucky and have a drive caddy that slides out from the computer, no screws required. Another easy replacement job is for machines in which the keyboard or other piece unsnaps or lifts up to reveal the hard drive. Only slightly more involved are laptops in which a top or bottom piece is unscrewed and removed to get to the hard drive. More difficult are the laptops that have a top or bottom piece that is unscrewed and removed, and then require that one or more components be removed to get to the hard drive. The hardest type is the kind of laptop in which a top or bottom piece is unscrewed and removed, and most components, including the system board, are removed to get to the hard drive.

If you have a computer that comes with a hard drive caddy, you can ignore most of this information because you just slide out the old drive and slide in the new one.

Work slowly and carefully. Don't try to pry apart your computer once the screws are removed. Many of the notebook computers have extremely thin plastic snaps that align the top and bottom and help to hold them together. In addition, some types of notebooks also require you to remove a keyboard mask, while others may have this keyboard mask built into the top cover piece. Slowly pull away the plastic cover while carefully looking for connecting cables. If you find any, you will need to disengage them before you can completely open the system.

Finally, many laptops have quite a bit of mounting hardware, which has to be removed before you can gain access to the drive.

Taking Out the Old Hard Drive

Once you can see the hard drive, find the proper screwdriver among the tools you have thoughtfully laid out within reach and unscrew the mounting bracket. Remove the mounting bracket along with the drive.

Be sure to carefully detach the drive interface from the interface connector, and remember which way the drive was positioned. Consider drawing a sketch to help you remember the proper position.

Remove the hard drive from its mounting bracket. It will probably just slide out, but you may have to push it a little. Never push at an angle, and be careful not to push too hard. If you don't detect any movement while applying moderate force, check it for small screws or plastic tabs that may be holding it in place.

Putting In the New Hard Drive

First, install the new hard drive in the mounting bracket. Next, carefully place the new hard drive (in its mounting bracket) into the same spot where the old one was positioned. Pull out the sketch you made when removing the old drive and make sure you're putting the new one in the same way the old one came out. Also, be extra careful that the drive interface pins are properly aligned with the cable or connector to which they attach. These parts are really small and often quite delicate, and it's easy to wind up with the top row of pins in the bottom row of the connector.

That's really all there is to it. Carefully align and replace any covers, keyboard masks, plastic snaps, and so on, in the same order you removed them, but don't try to permanently close up the system just yet. Make sure any screws you do install go in all the way, but don't over-torque them. You shouldn't have any pieces left over. If you drop a screw and it rolls down into the system, get it out before you do anything else. These are small machines—it didn't go very far. Pick the system up and roll it from side to side (like one of those kid's toys with little ball bearings that you try to roll into the clown's nose). The little screw will eventually rattle into a place where you can see it and grab it with your nonmagnetized needle-nosed pliers. Dental picks and hemostats are also handy for this kind of work, although they're usually not things most people have in their toolboxes and are too expensive unless you do this kind of thing a lot.

Finally, while you have everything open, you could spray it with a can of compressed air to get out any dust. Don't try to wipe away the dust with a cloth or a paper towel, though—you'll likely scratch something or leave lint or paper fibers behind. Also, don't blow on the inside of your laptop. Your breath may be minty fresh, but it's also very humid.

TESTING THE NEW HARD DISK

Now, before you put the system completely back together, put the battery pack back in and turn on the laptop. If the system runs through its memory test, you can breathe a sigh of relief. If the system won't run the memory test, the most likely culprit is the hard drive interface or one of the other connections. Check all the connections. If you don't find anything obvious, try replacing the old drive and try again. If this works, something is wrong with the new hard drive.

If the memory test succeeds, you'll probably get an error message such as `HDD Configuration Error`. Don't worry. You want it to say this. Your CMOS is looking for the hard drive you took out and just doesn't recognize the new one yet. Get into your CMOS setup routine (with the SETUP disk, or by pressing one or more keys while the system is booting) and set the hard drive to the correct type as indicated by the information that came with the new unit. You may have to identify it by number, and you may need to fill in several parameters, such as number of heads, number of cylinders, and number of sectors. All this information should be in with the packing slip and the bubble wrap in the new drive's shipping box. On the other hand, you may not need to do anything except reboot.

Now that there is nothing on your hard drive, you'll need to boot your computer from your bootable floppy disk (a floppy that has `COMMAND.COM` on it). After you've formatted the drive, you should be able to boot right from the new hard drive.

If you've transferred your `CONFIG.SYS` and `AUTOEXEC.BAT` files from your old hard drive, your system may not boot from the new hard drive because something in these files is not configured correctly for your new drive. Refer to Chapter 11, "Installing an IDE Hard Drive," and Chapter 13. Dealing with a laptop hard disk is the same as with any other computer.

CLOSING UP

Once everything seems to be working, you can close up your computer. Put the keyboard back in place. Screw down any access hatches you had to remove. Connect your laptop to the network, Zip drive, external tape drive, or whatever you used to hold all your backup files, and then partition and format the drive, as described in Chapter 13. Reinstall the operating system and copy your data onto your new drive.

Installing a Second Hard Drive

With some laptops, such as the IBM ThinkPad 760, you can replace the floppy drive or CD-ROM drive with a second hard disk. Often, however, you will need to buy a second hard disk holder since you can't just let the new hard drive rattle around in there. Other laptops, such as the Dell Inspiron 7500 series, have additional bays for sliding in an additional hard drive (or extra battery).

When you put your secondary hard drive into its caddy, make sure that any slots, connectors, or projections on the hard drive match the corresponding slots, connectors, and projections on the caddy. Then press it firmly into the caddy until you hear it click into place. If it doesn't seem to be going in after you've applied a moderate amount of force, don't keep pushing. It's probably not lined up right. Take it out and reinsert it. You may have to wiggle it a little to make sure everything is lined up correctly.

Next, remove the disk drive or CD-ROM drive. On laptops that have removable keyboards, this requires the following steps:

1. Make sure that no disks or CDs are in the drive you're taking out.

2. Turn off the power.

3. Disconnect the AC adapter.

4. Unplug any cables that attach to printers and modems.

5. Unlatch the keyboard and swing it up out of the way.

6. Remove the battery.

7. Use the attached handles, tabs, or straps to remove the CD-ROM drive or disk drive.

If you're replacing a disk drive with a hard drive, you will have a hole in the front of the laptop where you used to insert disks. You can cover this with a shaped piece of plastic called a *bezel*. Remember the baggie with all that unidentifiable stuff from when you brought your laptop home and unpacked it? Your bezel's in there. If you saved the box, go rummage around in the closet until you find it. If you threw the box away, you can usually get a bezel at your local computer store. Generally, they are shipped with new hard drives, but you might make a note to ask just to be sure. Some bezels are made to be installed from the inside of the computer while the drive bay is empty. Others are designed to be pushed into place from the outside. Either way, make sure you cover the hole in the front or side of your laptop. Holes like that are invitations to all sorts of problems.

If you're replacing a CD-ROM drive with a hard drive, you can usually just slide the new hard drive into the space vacated by the old, unwanted CD-ROM. If that space was previously unoccupied, you may have to remove a bezel so the front of the hard drive can be seen from the outside (so you can see the drive's activity light) and then finish up with the following steps:

1. Firmly press the new hard drive holder until it clicks into the connector.

2. Replace the battery.

3. Reattach the keyboard and reconnect the AC adapter and whatever cables you just took off.

Installing PC Card Drive Cards

PC Card hard drives, sometimes also called hard cards or credit-card hard drives, offer an extremely simple way to add storage capacity to your laptop. They generally come in the size known as a Type 3 PC Card, which means that they take up two card slots in your laptop and can store upward of 1GB. You can get Type 1 and Type 2 PC Card hard drive cards, which take up only one slot but tend to be small in terms of capacity. However, IBM now offers a series of Microdrives in the Type 2 format that have a capacity of up to 1GB. Although they were primarily designed for use in digital cameras, they can be used in most laptops.

Installing a PC Card hard drive requires nothing more than making sure you have installed the device driver software that comes on a disk with the card and that you have the card pointed the right way. Make sure the notched edge on the card goes in first. Press the card firmly into the connector. Usually, there will be an Eject button either inside the PC Card opening or on the side of the computer next to the card slot. You'll know when the card is fully installed because the Eject button will pop out. On some laptops—the IBM ThinkPad for example—you then pull the Eject button out a little bit and fold it toward the front of the laptop. If you need to eject a PC Card while the laptop is operating, you should ensure that a PC Card manager program isn't running. If a program is running, eject the card using the program before physically removing it.

Other Kinds of Upgrades

Now I've covered upgrading memory and hard drives, but what if you want to upgrade your laptop in different ways? Say you want to increase its utility in the office instead of just using it at home or on the road. The following sections go into some of the other things you can do to put more life in your laptop.

DVD Drives

This is my favorite upgrade because my job requires long flights to the Far East and there is nothing like watching movies on your laptop to make the time fly by. If you are looking to justify the expense, remember that you can use the DVD drives for reading reference DVDs (like Microsoft's Encarta) as well as watching movies.

There are two ways to add a DVD to your laptop: installing an internal DVD drive (which replaces your CD-ROM drive) and attaching an external DVD to the laptop using a USB port. The latter is cumbersome (involving a lot of external stuff), and the internal solution must be made specifically for the laptop. Regardless of which type of DVD drive you have, there are a few other considerations.

Once you have resolved the inny or outy (internal/external) question, your next decision is whether to get a DVD that has hardware decoding or software decoding. Hardware decoding places no performance burden on the CPU but costs more. Software decoding uses the laptop's CPU to do the decoding. If CPU in your laptop is slower than 266MHz, you should consider hardware decoding. If your laptop already has a DVD drive that uses software decoding and you discover that your CPU is really having difficulty doing the job, you can get a hardware decoder that plugs into the PC slot. MARGI makes an excellent decoder called DVD-to-Go, which I use in my Dell Inspiron 7000 to watch movies.

As you are having wonderful warm fuzzy thoughts of long flights with endless movies, remember that watching a movie on your laptop puts a continuous load on your battery and you might be surprised how quickly it can dissipate your laptop's battery. The solution is to either bring several (heavy) batteries or invest in an airline/car power adapter. Most airlines now have power outlets available (even in coach). In fact, on my last flight to Greece, when I was selecting a seat I specifically requested one with a power outlet. It took the reservations representative a while to figure it out, but I ended up with my favorite films on the 12-hour flight.

Laptop LAN Adapters

You can connect your laptop to the company network by connecting a LAN adapter to the parallel or SCSI port of your laptop or inserting a LAN adapter card into your PC Card slot. Some have telephone jack–type connectors (RJ-45) for 10Base-T connections, and some have coax cable connections (BNC). You'll have to find out which kind you need, and you'll have to ensure that your laptop is configured with the correct software for networking. Prices can range from about $45 to $100, depending on the type of network you have and which vendor you choose. Also, prices change rapidly, as with everything else involving computers, so be sure to get the most recent price quotes from whomever you choose.

You can find dozens of resources on the Internet that make information about LAN adapters easy to find. Computer Shopper has a wonderful set of utilities that enable a person to select, compare, and choose which system they want peripherals for. CNET has similar information, as does ZDNet and dozens of other sites, both retail and editorial.

PC CARD LAN ADAPTER CARDS

A different type of LAN adapter is the PC Card type. Instead of plugging a cable with an attached adapter into a port on your laptop, you insert the PC Card LAN adapter card into the PC Card slot in the side of your laptop and connect to the network by means of attaching the network cable to it. There are many kinds, from many manufacturers. Lots of current information about them is available online. See Figure 31.1 for an example of a network adapter/modem combo.

FIGURE 31.1

PC Card (Xircom network adapter/ modem combo FR)

Wireless LAN Cards

If you're the type of person who thinks it's more than a little pointless to have a walkabout computer that's shackled to a desk by its LAN connection, you can upgrade to a wireless LAN card. These cards are more expensive than the ones discussed in the preceding sections, but they do give you more mobility.

There are two general categories of wireless communication devices for laptops: *HomeRF* and *Wireless LAN* (IEEE 802.11*x*), which is also called *WiFi*. The wireless LANs are themselves divided into several categories:

◆ IEEE 802.11b (data rate: 10Mbps)

◆ IEEE 802.11a (data rate: 100Mbps)

◆ IEEE 802.11g (which, when finally published, will be able to communicate with both of the two previous standards)

◆ IEEE 802.15, also known as Bluetooth

All offer ranges of about 100–150 feet.

The original version of HomeRF wireless had a slow data throughput, restricted to about 1Mbps. That version has been replaced with the newer HomeRF, which operates in the 2.4GHz frequency domain and moves data along at a brisk rate of up to 10Mbps.

At the time of this writing, wireless products that use 802.11b are becoming increasingly popular—over nine different companies offer a wide range of products and feature data rates around 10Mbps. The latest commercially available products use the 802.11a standard, which is intended for enterprise applications and offers data rates at up to 100Mbps. To date, several companies offer products that support this protocol, and since they are able to deliver this faster data connection for only about a 25 percent increase in price, I expect this to become more popular than 802.11b.

The problem with the two standards is they operate at two different frequencies and data rates, so they cannot talk to each other. Also, since the 802.11b standard uses the same frequency spectrum (2.4GHz) as wireless phones and microwave ovens, it is more susceptible to interference than 802.11a, which operates in the 5GHz region of the RF spectrum. But a solution is on the horizon: 802.11g. When this standard is implemented, the wireless devices using it will be able to talk to both 11b and 11a wireless devices.

Another standard that's being talked about is IEEE 802.15 (known better as Bluetooth). Due to the popularity of 802.11a and 802.11b protocols, Bluetooth, which was thought to be next new wireless standard that would replace all other wireless standards, has been a little slow out of the gate. Some printers offer Bluetooth wireless connections, but to date, Bluetooth hasn't become as popular as predicted.

As mentioned earlier, your best source for current and accurate information about wireless LAN cards is the Internet, since technology and pricing changes so rapidly.

Working with Laptop Batteries

When you're on the road, without access to AC power, your laptop battery is your lifeline. Without it, your laptop is just another seven-pound paperweight. This section looks at charging, replacing, and extending the life of the battery's charge.

Battery Care

Most laptops come with specific instructions on how to deal with their batteries. They are not all the same. In general, however, you will have a recharger and/or AC adapter you can use when your battery power runs low. The AC adapter will recharge the battery at the same time that it provides power to keep your laptop running. Some batteries will fully recharge no matter when you plug in the AC adapter. Others will not. The IBM ThinkPad, for example, carries this warning: "Repeatedly charging a battery pack that has not been completely discharged shortens the battery operating time. To preserve battery operating time, discharge the battery pack completely, then recharge it."

Always be especially careful that the adapter you use with your laptop is the one that came with the computer or is a replacement specifically recommended by the manufacturer. The plug from your cordless electric drill's adapter may very well fit your computer, but there is little chance that the voltage and amperage requirements will match as well, and you'll be really sorry if you use it to recharge your laptop.

WARNING   A battery is not just something that can hurt your computer. It is something that can hurt you. Batteries can and do explode if you handle them carelessly—like throw them in a fire or use a battery charger that wasn't designed for the type of battery you are charging.

Keep these tips in mind when handling your laptop battery:

◆ Keep the battery away from fire.

◆ Keep the battery away from water.

◆ Never try to take it apart.

◆ Don't drop it, throw it, or bang it on the table.

◆ Always use only the battery designed especially for your particular make and model.

Something else to pack into your carrying case is a small, one- or two-socket surge protector. If you're going to be using your laptop from hotel rooms, conference centers, airport lounges, and other such places, you'll need one. You can't be any more confident of the quality of the electricity out there than you can back in the office—and you've got a surge protector on the floor under your desk, right?

Finally, it's a good idea to have more than one battery for your laptop. This is not just to let you keep working when you're out of reach of electricity. Many batteries need to be completely depleted before being recharged, so an extra battery lets you completely drain a battery, swap it out, and plug it into a recharger while you use the laptop with the backup battery. Completely draining a NiCad battery before recharging it often adds significantly to its useful life. The same is not true of NiMH batteries, which seem to deliver more power and have less of a charging issue than any battery technology before or since.

Charging a Battery

Keep your battery healthy by following the manufacturer's guidelines for first use and for when and how to recharge it. For example, the battery pack in many computers will be low or "dead" when you first buy it. You have to plug in the AC adapter and let it take a charge before you can use it. Furthermore, most NiCad batteries require that you charge them, drain them completely, and charge them again (sometimes repeatedly) before they will accept and hold their maximum charge.

New batteries and those that have not been used in a long time will not take a full charge the first time you connect them to the AC adapter. With some types of batteries, such as the lithium-ion battery pack that IBM uses in the ThinkPad, you will have to fully discharge and then recharge the battery up to a half-dozen times before the battery is operating at peak performance.

NiCad batteries work best when they are completely discharged before you recharge them, while NiMH and lithium-ion batteries couldn't care less. You might have thought that you were helping the NiCad battery to a longer life by keeping the laptop connected to the AC adapter all the time, but just the opposite is true. Because of a phenomenon called *memory effect*, they eventually lose their ability to hold a full charge. With some much older laptops, you are advised not to run them while their batteries are charging. The competing demands of accepting a new charge while simultaneously losing charge as part of normal operation cause internal problems that shorten the battery's life. Nearly every laptop made after 1996 has either NiMH or lithium-ion batteries, so this is not an issue.

Some batteries need to be completely discharged and then recharged from time to time. It cleans them out, so to speak, the same way you sometimes drain and refill the radiator in your car. Some power-management utilities that come with the laptop, or that you can buy at your local computer store, have discharging functions as part of the program. For example, the discharging program for the IBM ThinkPad works like this: (1) Connect the AC adapter to the computer. (2) Click the Discharge button on the Fuel-Gauge program. (3) The battery automatically drains. (4) When it hits bottom, it starts to charge up again automatically.

Replacing a Battery

Regardless of how well you care for your battery, there will come a time when you have to take it out and put in a new one. Since this is one of the things most people will have to do fairly routinely, most laptops make it pretty easy.

1. Turn off the computer.

2. Disconnect it from the AC adapter and remove any cables to printers, modems, networks, etc.

3. Find out where your battery is located. On some laptops, you will access it through a hatch on the bottom or the front of the computer. Generally, the hatch will simply slide out, but in some cases you will need to take out some screws or release a locking mechanism. On other laptops, you reach the battery from the top by first lifting off the keyboard. Check your owner's manual if you're not sure how the keyboard comes off.

4. The battery is usually right on top. Once you get the hatch or access panel off, the battery is the first thing you see. Make sure, however, that you don't need to remove something else before you go to work on the battery. If your laptop has a CD-ROM, for example, you may have to remove it before you can pull the power pack.

5. Some batteries have plastic tabs or handles that you use to pull them away from their sockets before lifting them out. Others are unplugged simply by sliding them out of the connectors by hand. If yours has tabs or handles, use them.

6. Don't pull out the battery and then go home for the evening. Put the new one in right away. Some laptops depend on their batteries to hold their CMOS configurations for more than a few minutes or seconds.

7. Close up the laptop in the reverse order you opened it.

8. If this is a brand-new battery, keep the machine off and connect the AC adapter. Fully charge the battery before you turn on the computer. Also, you may have to completely discharge and then recharge the battery a few times before the battery will operate at maximum capacity.

Buying a New Battery

Sometimes the information printed on the side of the battery can be confusing or obscure. The Internet has a plethora of information about batteries for just about every laptop and notebook available.

NOTE   *Several good online sources are available on the Internet for finding more information about batteries for your laptop. Just run a search on* laptops + battery.

If you still can't find a battery for your machine, the technical support people who work for the online supply houses will generally be able to locate the information (and the battery) you need. For some of the more obscure or older makes, you may have to send your old battery to the supplier and have it rebuilt. Doing so can sometimes take a week or more.

Conserving Battery Power

Many laptops now have power-management functions, either built into the BIOS, operating from within Windows, or available by using special drivers. These functions monitor whether the system is on and whether anybody is using it. After prescribed periods of no input from the keyboard or mouse, the laptop "goes to sleep." It doesn't turn itself off but slumbers until you wake it up. The advantage is that power-consuming features of the unit, such as the screen display, are no longer drawing down the charge in the battery. Preserving the life of the battery is obviously preferable to replacing it, so there are several things you can do to make sure you get the most use out of yours.

Most laptops today have power-management features in the BIOS. When you enable power management, you allow the laptop to help you save battery power by shutting itself off in various degrees when you leave it running without AC power. My laptop, for example, has three degrees of power management to choose from in the BIOS: Max Performance, Balanced Power Saving, and Max Power Saving. They control when and if the hard disk will stop spinning, the display will turn off, and so on.

Some laptops come from the factory with a small, non-DOS partition on the hard disk that they can use to Suspend to Disk. This copies the contents of memory to the small partition when you issue a command to do so, or when the battery power gets critically low, so you can stop using power completely without having to shut down your PC.

Windows 9x/NT/2000/XP provide power-management functionality too. Use the Power applet in Control Panel to control how long Windows waits before turning off the display and/or hard disk action to save power. See Figure 31.2.

FIGURE 31.2

Windows 98's power-management controls, accessible through Control Panel. Windows NT/2000/Me/XP have similar controls.

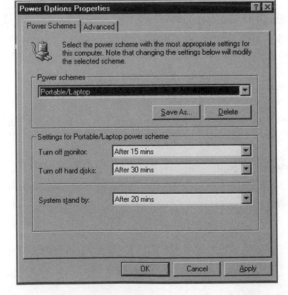

Laptop Maintenance Issues

Although keeping your laptop in good condition requires many of the same considerations as a desktop machine (for instance, keep it clean and dry, and feed it high-quality electricity), its portability adds a few factors to the equation and makes some of the ordinary issues especially important.

One of the most important things you can do to keep your laptop in good shape is to make sure you have a good carrying case. Sounds trivial, maybe, but it's not. Your laptop is a traveling companion, and as with any situation where you leave a secure, controlled environment, it will be subject to the same bumps and knocks as you.

Modern carrying cases are especially designed to save you and your notebook lots of grief, and it's well worth the investment to get one you can count on. I don't necessarily mean you have to spend hundreds of dollars for one of those aluminum suitcases, either. A good padded shoulder bag will give you all the protection you'll usually need; will make it easier for you to get through doors, into cars, and onto airplanes; and will keep you from having to reinvest in new laptops.

So, don't carry your laptop outside without a case. It may look power-chic in a TV commercial, but it's probably the worst thing you can do. People drop things, even important things, and no ordinary laptop will survive a tumble onto concrete.

When you're looking at carrying cases, check that it's made of a nonporous material. Even if you like the look of a canvas-type bag, make sure there's some kind of inner liner that will keep it from transferring moisture to the inside. Raindrops on the outside are okay. When they soak through and fizzle your laptop, they're not okay.

Check the hardware between the bag and the carrying strap. If the connection is a simple spring latch, never pick up the bag with the computer inside without first making sure the "tongue and groove" pieces are straight before pulling on the strap. Sideways pressure on many of the latches that I've had experience with will cause most of them to release. You will get to find out how much a new case (or perhaps a new computer) costs when the case opens and the computer lands on one of its corners or slams into something hard (such as airport steps).

You also want to make sure that the case you get has separate compartments for things you carry with you. Pens, pencils, mice, and modems rattling around and bumping into your machine can cause damage.

Make sure the outer walls of the case are well padded. The padding doesn't have to be extremely thick, but you want something between the case walls and your computer to distribute the shock of accidental bumps.

Finally, don't put anything in your case that doesn't belong there. I know people who have packed socks, toothbrushes, and candy bars into their carrying cases and treated them as overnight bags for emergency business trips. These people also tend to buy more new laptops than my other acquaintances. Putting anything in the bag that is damp, pointy, or crumbly is always a bad idea.

The weakest link on your laptop is the hinge that flips the screen up and down. It's not that the hinges are designed badly; it's just that they get the most exercise, and unlike with people, exercise makes them weaker instead of stronger. Unfortunately, the only thing you can do to keep a hinge from croaking before its time is just don't fool with it too much:

◆ Never pick up the laptop by the open screen.

◆ Don't slam it shut because you're in a hurry.

◆ Don't yank it open and bend it too far.

◆ Don't open and close it repeatedly as a way to ease nervous tension.

Generally, you should not oil the hinges. They really weren't made for that kind of maintenance, and oil is a tremendous attractor of dust, grit, and pollen, all of which will only gum things up even worse.

The other areas you have to watch are the openings in your laptop's case. The floppy drive has a latch, flap, or door that closes when there's no disk in the drive. If this gets stuck in the "open" position, you'll collect lots of dust and your floppy drive, at least, could be ruined. On many laptops, the floppy drive flap is pretty flimsy and can be quite easily pushed aside (which is another good reason to have a laptop carrying case that gives you separate compartments for business cards, paper clips, and pencils). You don't want a stick of chewing gum wedging into your floppy drive after you've packed up your laptop for a business trip.

The other area that exposes the inside of your laptop to the outside world is the bay with your PC Card slot openings. Your computer probably came with plastic covers to seal up any slots that are not in use. Or it may have hinged flaps that come down when the slot is empty. Make sure these slots are closed or sealed. The connectors inside the slots are especially tiny, and even minute amounts of foreign material can cause big problems.

When it comes to the monitor screen, there are only a couple of precautions you have to keep in mind. First, when you clean it, use a soft, lint-free cloth. Dry is best; very slightly damp is okay if you have really sticky garbage caked onto the screen; wet is never recommended. Try not to use paper towels—the cheap kind can scratch. Second, don't twist the monitor, which means don't grab it when you want to swivel the computer around to show somebody what's being displayed. You can damage the screen as well as the hinges that hold it to the computer. If your computer uses one of the film technologies for display (such as a thin-film transistor, or TFT, display), then pushing, hitting, or twisting the screen can warp the film. Screens are not repairable items. If yours gets broken, you have to replace it.

PC-to-Laptop Syncing

Most people who have a laptop also have a desktop PC. Keeping files updated between them can be a real challenge.

If both PCs are on a network together, you can transfer files between PCs using the network connection. If not, you can connect them directly with a null modem cable (basically a straight pass-through serial cable) and then use special software to manage the connection. Windows comes with a Direct Cable Connection utility that does the job just fine.

Windows 9x also comes with a synchronization feature called My Briefcase that's specifically designed for keeping files matched up between your desktop and your laptop PCs. For example, suppose you are working on a report at work, and you want to take the latest draft home with you over the weekend. You copy the report from your desktop computer to the Briefcase on your laptop (using either a disk or your LAN). Then, you work on the report at home, and when you return to the office, you synchronize your Briefcase, copying the latest version back to the desktop to overwrite the older version.

You can use My Briefcase either with a floppy disk or on a network. To do it on a floppy, first copy the files on your main PC into the My Briefcase icon on your desktop in Windows. Then drag the My Briefcase folder onto the floppy drive icon to move it there. On a network, start at the remote PC (the laptop) and access the files on the main PC through Network Neighborhood (or My Network Places, depending on the Windows version you have). Drag them to the My Briefcase icon on the remote PC to copy them there.

Then, to sync the files from a floppy, copy the My Briefcase folder back to the desktop from the floppy disk. Then open the My Briefcase window and click the Update All button. Or, on a network, make sure both PCs are connected to the network and open the My Briefcase folder on the remote PC. Then click Update All to update the copies on the main PC.

Syncing Data with PDAs

Many people these days use Personal Digital Assistants (PDAs), made by 3Com, Handspring, and other well-known companies. Popular models include the Palm IIIc (see Figure 31.3), the Palm VII and Vx, and the Visor. All use the same Palm operating system. Models running the Microsoft Pocket PC operating system include the iPAQ, Cassiopeia, and Jornada.

FIGURE 31.3

Palm IIIc

The primary purpose of a PDA is to store addresses, appointments, and task lists in a portable, easy-to-update format. You can use a PDA as a stand-alone tool, but it's most effective when combined with a computer. You can enter and update your data on the computer, and then transfer it to the PDA by syncing. *Syncing* updates the information on both sources—the PDA and the computer—by comparing the dates of various additions, edits, and deletions and placing the most current information in both places.

Palm OS–based PDAs come with their own operating system, called Palm Desktop. You can use it to store and edit your information if you like, or you can use any of a variety of other programs instead if you prefer. The PDAs work with Microsoft Outlook, Lotus Notes, and several other popular programs through special drivers called conduits. Most Palm OS–based models come with conduits for popular applications that you can install when you run the setup software for the device on your PC. Pocket PCs ship with ActiveSync, which lets the device synchronize with Microsoft Outlook.

To sync a PDA, simply place it in its cradle (which is attached to the PC via a serial or USB port) and press the button on the cradle. (There's only one button; you can't miss it.) You can also initiate a sync from the PC by clicking the Synchronize button in the program you have set the device up to sync with. In Outlook, for example, installing the conduit places a Synchronize icon on Outlook's toolbar, and you can click that icon to begin the sync.

Troubleshooting Tips

Troubleshooting laptops and handheld computers involves some techniques similar to those you would use for a desktop computer, but there are some important differences. The similarities (at least for laptops) lie mainly with the operating system and software you use. The version of Windows running on a laptop is the same operating system that you have on your desktop. The main difference is that all your components are connected together internally, and you have an internal power supply (that is, your battery). You don't really have to check cable connections or mess with add-in cards as you do for a desktop model. Instead, the trouble might have to do with configuration and battery issues.

If your computer won't turn on and is unplugged, your battery may be dead. Try plugging in the laptop's A/C adapter so you know you have power and try it again. Most of the time, that's the problem. If your laptop still won't turn on, it may already be on but it might be in a power-saving sleep mode. Try pressing a key on the keyboard to wake it up, or move your mouse/cursor around a bit (or touch your finger on the touchpad). In some cases, you may have to press and hold the power button down for a few seconds to get it to wake up.

As with desktop computers, make sure all your drivers are updated. On my Dell Inspiron 7500, I regularly check for updates at the Dell Web site for my major components:

♦ Integrated video system

♦ DVD-ROM drive

♦ Touchpad drivers

♦ Modem/network adapter PC Card

♦ Sound card

Laptops are the computer of choice for more and more people every day because of their unique combination of features and convenience. Now that you know how to keep yours in good repair and to care for it properly, you're ready to join the ranks of the computing road warriors.

Chapter 32

Using the Internet for Hardware Support

◆ QuickSteps: Getting Help Online   897

◆ Problems with Finding Help the Old-Fashioned Way   898

◆ Advantages of Online Support   900

◆ Searching the Web   905

◆ Using FTP, Usenet, Mailing Lists, and IRC   912

◆ Cautions about Online Support   923

◆ Troubleshooting Tips   924

Introduction

Do you know the single most important reason you need to get online if you own a computer? Because going online gives you the tools you need to master the PC—from the hardware to the operating system to the software—as well as tips on future technology that you need to prepare for now to handle tomorrow.

You see, there's only one place where you can obtain help for your computer-related problems, find the latest drivers for your hardware and peripherals, and learn about the latest developments in the technology field. That place is the Internet—and it should be an essential component of your information and support strategy.

I just spent one hour on the Web (I'm not joking—the time spent was 62 minutes, 11 seconds) and quite literally solved a week's worth of PC hardware concerns. In that hour, I grabbed two brand-new drivers for equipment I use, researched the pros and cons of a motherboard I'm planning to buy, read a couple of articles on Rambus memory, arranged to beta-test some new diagnostic software, looked up technical notes on terminating some network cable, exchanged messages with a friend at 3Com who pointed me to a solid DSL modem for my new office, and performed a bandwidth test to see whether my current modem is operating at maximum speed for my phone line. That's a lot of necessary ground to cover in an hour, all made possible because of the phenomenal amount of material available on the Internet today.

QuickSteps

Getting Online Help

Gathered from the information presented in this chapter, here are the steps for getting online help for problems you may experience with your PC.

BE PREPARED

Before you start, there are some things you may need on hand. These include:

◆ Paper and a pen/pencil, for taking notes and for keeping information you need handy (or maybe you already have these things stored in a database or text file on another PC).

◆ Basic information about your PC (type of CPU and motherboard, video card chipset used, exact version of your operating system) so that you can provide these necessary details when posting or calling to get assistance.

◆ Prepared short synopsis of the problem (for example, what you may have installed, removed, or modified just before the problem cropped up; exact symptoms you're seeing; what you've already tried and what behavior changes, if any, you saw as a result) so that you can report it when posting or calling for technical assistance.

◆ Product registration information and/or the model and serial number of the malfunctioning device, to give the manufacturer if you're reporting the device (and especially if you need to return it for a working one).

◆ The problem PC or device nearby when you research, post a message online, or call for support so that you can double-check settings and walk through a set of steps. Troubleshooting is a lot harder when you don't have the system right there.

1. Connect to the Internet as you normally would.

2. Select one of the resources mentioned in this chapter—CNET, for example.

3. Search the site for relevant information—in FAQs, or via interactive troubleshooters, or in previous messages on forums or message boards.

4. To post your own question to a forum or message board, prepare your post by giving necessary information about the problem you're having, including exact error messages and relevant background information about your PC (such as which operating system and version you have, recent changes you've made to the configuration, and your type of PC). Post your message on the board, then wait a few hours (or perhaps a few days, on less-busy sites), and then check back to see what responses you may have—and respond appropriately.

5. Analyze the information you've received and proceed with your troubleshooting.

Problems with Traditional Support

Getting the information you need through traditional means can be difficult—or, at times, virtually impossible. You have problems to solve, new drivers to track down and acquire, newer and fancier hardware to install, and new software versions to learn about. Where do you turn?

If you're looking for technical or industry information, many good trade magazines are available—and some are free to computer professionals—but these periodicals give you too much to look at. It's easy for me to accumulate a dozen magazines and journals in a week while I'm out of town. How can I read all of that and pull out the information I need in time to get through the next lot when they show up the following week?

Some problems can't be solved by magazines, either. A lot of knowledgeable people read them and write for them, but the problem is the time lag. If I'm installing a new board, and it's not working no matter what I do, I want to know how to make it work *now*, not weeks or months from now. Writing a letter to an advice columnist at my favorite computer magazine, waiting for the letter to be published, and then waiting for a reply isn't going to help me.

Another option is to call the board manufacturer's tech support line, but that approach is problematic as well. First, the manufacturer might not have a support line—or the line might not be available during hours convenient to you. Even if a support line is available, it's probably not free—you might have to foot the bill for the call (ever notice how few tech support lines these days are 800 numbers?), or you may even have to pay the manufacturer to get a response. If you do happen to get through to a real live person (after listening to the all-Muzak version of "Raindrops Keep Falling on My Head" for an hour or more), that person might not have the answer you need, or may have to "check it out and get back to you." Good luck with that one.

Then there's the problem of acquiring updated drivers, software patches, hardware documentation that the maker assumed we wouldn't need, and just plain new product information. Working with computers often involves a fair amount of isolation and not a lot of free time, and it's hard to keep up with all that stuff. I need a way to throw questions into the ether for anyone and everyone to answer, to acquire drivers without waiting for the manufacturer to get around to sending me a disk, and to learn about new products.

Here are some examples of the frustrating situations you can run into when trying to get information you need *now*. At the very least, these are some reasons why *I* learned to use online services for tech support and getting software.

Journey into Faxback Hell

In concept, faxback services are a nice way of answering common customer questions. Why hire staff to run a telephone line when 75 percent of the people who call have the same question? It's much simpler to prepare documents that answer the most frequently asked questions, and then make those documents available via fax to those who request them.

The catch is that you usually have to know exactly what you want before these services work, and be able to provide a document number for it. No document number, no fax. Even if you get one of the rare faxback services in which real people handle telephone questions, that real human probably doesn't know which document you need. Usually, the only way to get a document number is to order the catalog from the faxback service, at which point you have a list of titles with document numbers next to them. In other words, you still can't be sure that you're ordering the document that you need.

Facing the Muzak: Technical Support Lines

I don't want to pick on those who staff tech support lines. Tech support has to be one of the most thankless jobs around. Callers are stressed out from worrying about their problem, probably snappish from being kept on hold, and prone to ask what sound like stupid questions because the tech support rep has answered that same one six times already that day. (See where faxback services come from?)

But tech support lines aren't usually any fun for the caller, either. Many people have a hard time explaining a particular chain of events to someone they can't see. Others wait on hold for 20 minutes (or longer!) to hear a tech support person tell them, "Gee, I've never heard of that problem before—can you hold on a minute (or 2, or 10) while I get my supervisor?"

Having to "upgrade" your problem to the next level is also annoying. The folks on the first line of support (the so-called *level 1* reps) often have little or no technical knowledge. These are the folks who tell you to defrag your hard disk when you're actually experiencing some sort of interrupt conflict (as if defragging your disk is the magic solution to all possible computer problems!). If you want *real* technical support, you need to ask for a *level 2* rep, who might—if you're lucky—have some technical experience and access to the company's tech support database.

To make matters worse, the handful of phone lines that feed into the tech support department—unlike the large number of sales lines available for taking orders—are often not toll-free, which means that if you're at work, you may have to explain to the business manager all those long-distance charges on your code, or if you're at home, you have to swallow the long-distance bill yourself. In addition, far too many tech support lines are 9-to-5 propositions, which means that weekend warrior types can be stuck until Monday if they have a problem.

And then there's that period of being on hold. I'm never sure whether it's more annoying to hear violin renditions of "Purple Haze" or a comforting voice repeatedly assuring me that my patience is appreciated. (How do they know that I'm being patient? Maybe I'm grinding my teeth smooth while waiting to get back to something productive.)

True story—during one recent patch of dismal service from my DSL provider, who shall remain nameless, users were forced to wait on hold for *over two hours* before getting connected to a tech support rep. I know one user who was so fed up over this intolerable wait that he decided to cancel his service—and then had to wait on hold for another hour to reach an account representative in the customer support department!

Finally, there are the tech support lines that won't even talk to you until you've given them $250. I ask you—what other industry ships such a large percentage of shoddy, barely working products—and then charges you even more money to restore the products to what should have been a normal working condition?

The *idea* of a tech support line is wonderful—that a company will provide a team of experts to answer your questions on demand. The reality is often less wonderful, for both the caller and the tech support person.

Making Friends and Influencing People

Often, one of the best ways to answer a question is to find someone who has more experience than you do. Unfortunately, this is sometimes easier said than done. You may not have anyone around to ask (often the case for home PC-ers), or *you* may be the person with the most experience. Sometimes your circle of personal resources just doesn't have experience where you need it—or they may profess a great deal more expertise than they actually have, and some of the poorest PC tech support is done over the water cooler. If you've been a NetWare person all your life, and all the people you know are NetWare people, then you could be stuck when setting up that Windows NT Server machine and something obscure goes wrong. At this point, you need more friends and work associates.

Then, too, friends don't always give you written instructions when answering your questions. Either you try to remember what they told you or you write it down yourself, but there's always the possibility of misinterpreting or outright forgetting what they told you. I leave it to your imagination to envision how ugly *that* can get.

NOTE *Fortunately, there's a way around having to write things down when friends answer your questions. Windows XP includes a Remote Assistance feature that allows a trusted friend or associate to connect directly to your computer over the Internet, and he or she can actually help you fix your PC remotely. In fact, you can even connect directly with a Microsoft technical representative. Basically, you send out an invitation to this person to connect to your computer, and he or she accepts the invitation. Once the connection is established, your friend or associate can control your desktop as if he or she is sitting right at your side.*

Read All about It

As I noted at the beginning of this section, the computer industry produces too much information for one person to keep up with—hundreds of pages show up on my doorstep every week. Then there's the problem of money. Not all these magazines come cheap, especially if you can't demonstrate that you work in the industry (not difficult to do, but a consideration) and therefore warrant a professional courtesy rate. And some magazines require you to pay full price, no matter who you are. Even if the subscriptions are tax deductible for you, it adds up.

Advantages of Online Support

So if obtaining technical support through traditional methods is so problematic, what do you do? Fortunately, many companies have turned to the Internet to provide technical support for their customers—and many third-party sites now offer much better (and easier-to-find) information than what has been historically available in the "real world."

What's Out There?

One of the advantages of going online is the massive amount of information that's available. So what help can you get from cyberspace? Take a look at the kinds of support you can find.

NEW PRODUCT INFORMATION

Not surprisingly, there is a lot of new product information on the Web, as people try to make the idea of the marketplace on your desk a reality. Most reputable manufacturers provide detailed product specs online for your pre- or post-purchase perusal—and if the manufacturer's information is lacking, it's likely that one of the many online e-tailers for that product will have the facts you need.

Finding this type of information online is a lot easier than trying to appropriate a much-coveted and exceedingly rare product brochure from your local PC retailer!

PRODUCT DOCUMENTATION

Complete product docs are not *always* available in cyberspace, but manufacturers are more frequently posting this information online for anybody to read. Since a lot of hardware is sold without documentation (as if you didn't need the documentation to set up the hardware?), going online is often the easiest—and sometimes the *only*—way to get it. Many times, too, documentation updates will be posted online, covering ground missed in the original docs—or features documented incorrectly. Going online is often the only way to get this updated information.

REVIEWS

Product reviews—both professional and real-user anecdotes—are available everywhere on the Internet, often ahead of similar reviews in traditional print journals. The lack of print delay means the reviewers are working with later versions or drivers, especially when reviewing a product in testing. When new hardware, a new driver, or a patch debuts, you don't have to be a guinea pig by being the first to buy and try it. Instead, you can take a few days to read about the response the item is getting from users posting to newsgroups and Web-based message boards—before you invest your money and/or time.

WHITE PAPERS AND BACKGROUND INFORMATION

White papers are wholly different from short question-and-answer help and quick troubleshooting pieces: they're sort of the mini-thesis or novella of the tech world. They take a specific topic (the effect of older analog phone lines and wiring on a modem's dial-up connection speed, or the configuration of Windows NT/2000/XP for optimal security, for example) and explore it in some detail. Sometimes such papers include an industry-wide perspective, and sometimes they provide in-depth comparisons of different chipsets or features.

Typically authored by an expert in the field (a senior project manager, a senior product developer, etc., at a company responsible for the product or issue being discussed), they can provide quite a bit of background that several short technical articles or product information churned out by a company's marketing department don't provide.

FREQUENTLY ASKED QUESTIONS (FAQS)

Because certain topics come up as questions again and again ("How do I update a driver?" or "How do I get this device to work under Windows XP?"), one Internet information resource stable is frequently asked questions (FAQ) pages, listing the most common questions about a product along with their answers.

TECHNICAL SUPPORT DATABASES

Chances are that you're not the first user experiencing this specific problem with this particular product. If the manufacturer is on its toes (and not all are...), it has kept a record of previously reported problems and assembled them into a searchable technical support database. (One terrific example of a technical support database is Microsoft's Knowledge Base—an indispensable resource for anyone using a Microsoft product— located at `search.support.microsoft.com`.) Searching for your problem in a database of problems is often the best and easiest way to find the "official" solution.

INTERACTIVE TROUBLESHOOTERS

Many manufacturers have automated the question-and-answer format of a typical tech support phone call and put it online, in the form of an interactive troubleshooter. Answer the branching questions posed by the troubleshooter, and the troubleshooter will present what it thinks is the appropriate solution to your problem.

ADVICE

Today on the Internet, more and more technical sites are cropping up that provide step-by-step how-tos and advice for hardware installation and troubleshooting. One big advantage to these sites is that you can often learn from people who use a product much like you do. The downside tends to be that there are a lot more so-called "experts" out there than there are people who can actually fix a PC. One tip is to look around such sites for people who seem to be well respected and able to explain things clearly. A good tech tends to have a big following, so with a little reading, it often becomes clear which "experts" you should listen to and which ones you should ignore.

WARNING   *Advice you'll get from other Internet users is not any more universally accurate than advice you get from people you run into in the "real world." Check your sources before doing anything drastic based on anyone's posting!*

DEVICE DRIVERS AND UTILITIES

The Internet is the primary resource for the latest versions of these necessary files. Device drivers are crucial to getting your old hardware to work with your new software. For instance, when Windows Me first came out, some peripherals wouldn't work with the old drivers, so users eagerly awaited the arrival of new Windows Me drivers from their hardware manufacturers—which were promptly made available for downloading at the manufacturers' Web sites. Shareware and freeware PC utilities are also commonly available.

Why Online Support Is Better

Now that you know what types of resources you can find on the Internet, let's look at why you'd want to use online support—instead of the traditional phone-and-paper-based support.

IT'S OFTEN CHEAPER

There are two types of costs: money that you *spend*, and money that you *lose*—or, as we old-country economists would have it, explicit and implicit costs. Let's assume that you have a telephone and a modem (or some other type of Internet access), and compare what you'll find online with what you typically receive via phone-based support.

If you call tech support with your problem, the process goes like this:

1. Call the tech support line (almost certainly long-distance), probably between 9 A.M. and 5 P.M. (*their* time zone, not necessarily yours), when phone rates are highest.

2. Wait on hold. (Get a cup of coffee, order a pizza, do a crossword puzzle, hum along to Montovani…)

3. Talk to the tech support person.

4. Possibly wait on hold again while the tech person looks up the problem or consults with someone else (the old level-1-to-level-2 upgrade).

5. If all goes well, get the answer.

Not only is the process time consuming, but every single bit of that process occurs while the meter—*your* meter!—is ticking.

To find the answer to your problem online, on the other hand, the process looks more like this:

1. Go to the manufacturer's Web site.

2. Search the support section of the site for your particular problem—this can include searching pre-prepared FAQs, using interactive troubleshooters, or browsing through previously posted messages on the site's message boards.

3. If the answer to your question has not been previously addressed, go to the site's message board (sometimes called a *forum*) and post your question as a new message. Optionally, you can ask your question of the site's tech support staff via a Web-based form (if available) or e-mail message (if e-mail support is offered).

4. If you don't receive a direct response to your question (via a return e-mail from company support staff), return to the site's message board to read any responses to your question.

None of this costs you anything above the monthly service charge for your ISP (usually about $20). And at no time do you have to sit on hold and listen to elevator music or some inane greeting.

IT'S CONVENIENT

One of the biggest hassles of tech support lines is the time spent on hold. If you have something else that you could be doing, it's annoying to have to wait, tied to the telephone, for someone to answer your call. If instead you seek support at the manufacturer's Web site, or post your question to a newsgroup or forum, then you can do something else while waiting for an answer—assuming you can't find a solution on your first trip online.

WARNING   If you need an answer now, *posting a question to a newsgroup may not be good enough—you may get the answer you need in 10 minutes, tomorrow, next week, or never. (It all depends on whether other users see your question—and have an appropriate answer.) But if it's something that you want to know but don't have to know right this second, newsgroups and similar forums are great.*

Another aspect to the convenience of the Internet is that it runs on a 24-hour clock. People are online all the time, not just from 9 to 5. For instance, I've found that one of the best times to post a question to a newsgroup is after the normal workday. This may have something to do with geography—I live on the East Coast, so 5 P.M. comes earlier to me than it does to most of the country. But it's also because a lot of techies check into their newsgroups (or Web-based message boards) when they get home from work, or late at night. If I post a question at 5 P.M. EST, then by morning I often have a collection of answers.

Here's a real-world example: I once posted a message to a Usenet newsgroup about a problem that I was having installing Windows NT Server on a new machine. All the hardware conformed to NT's compatibility requirements, but on reboot the dratted installation would tell me that it couldn't find NTLDR, one of the required components for starting the system. NTLDR was on my hard disk—I could see it when booting from a DOS floppy—but darned if the installation program saw it. I gave up late that night (trying to fix things when you're tired can be a great mistake), posted a message that outlined the problem and described the error messages that I saw, and resolved to check in the following day. When I returned to the newsgroup the next day, I discovered that three people had posted responses to my original posting, and one of those responses did the trick. I updated the system BIOS, and the installation worked just fine.

The Internet's 24/7 convenience isn't limited to question-and-answer sessions, either. Want to see what applications are out for Windows 2000/XP but it's 3 A.M.? How about looking up the technical specs on Advanced Micro Devices' latest CPU—on Christmas Day? You can often find this type of information listed at the manufacturer's Web site, or you can use a search engine to search the Web for other sites containing information about the subject at hand. You can also download drivers and evaluation software at your convenience, not at the convenience of someone else.

INITIAL RESULTS MAY BE BETTER

One of the nasty truths about today's very inexpensive (relative to the past) hardware, coupled with the burgeoning population of first-time PC users, is that a lot of tech companies have had to scale back some of their support services, or at least not beef them up as much as might be needed to handle a high volume of user phone calls. (Kind of counterintuitive, isn't it—just when they need to provide *more* support, they provide *less* of it!)

As one cost-saving measure, many manufacturers *outsource* their first-tier product support, meaning they hire an outside support firm to handle initial calls from users. Additional follow-up, if such a thing exists, is provided by more experienced technicians supplied by the manufacturer.

This means that during your first call for support, it's possible you won't reach someone employed by the manufacturer. In some cases, you may not even reach someone who has ever used the product for which you need help. Heck, the person you talk to may be more of an operator than a technician. Many agencies use script books or computer databases to look up your question and offer an answer based on the closest match they can find. Throw them a question not in the script, and you may be in for a long wait or several calls.

However, when you access support resources on the Internet, you can go right to the good stuff— no level 1 techs here! Some manufacturers provide public access to a database of known issues and problems, and some even provide very detailed technical documents and white papers. If you need this higher-level information, you can go right to it, without having to pass through several levels of tech support personnel first. (Goodbye, level 1 techs!)

FOLLOW-UP IS OFTEN BETTER

One of the best aspects of the Internet's many newsgroups and forums is that those people who answer your questions are generally doing it not because they're getting paid for it, but because they're trying to help you. I've found that that translates to good follow-up. Until you post a message saying that all is well with your problem, you can almost certainly count on people trying to help you through the process, if you're polite and respond to messages posted to you.

For example, on one occasion I was helping a friend figure out how best to deliver Microsoft PowerPoint (a PC application) to people in a largely Unix-oriented office. We were trying to decide whether it would be better to provide the users with individual machines that could run the application, set up a PowerPoint workstation or two for those times when they needed it, use some kind of PC emulation on the SPARC 5s and 20s that the users already had, or what. (For those of you raising your eyebrows at the thought of buying users a second computer just to run an application, this office was an intelligence shop that had some money to spend on the project.) I posted a message outlining the situation on a couple of relevant forums, one for the PowerPoint side of the problem and one for the organizational side of the problem. The answers that I received about the organizational aspects of the problem sparked some new questions, which I asked, and then some other people got into the question and raised some more issues. By the time things wound down a couple of days later, I had what I needed and far more background besides.

Using the World Wide Web for Support

Originally a method devised by a Swiss think tank to make its papers on physics available to other scientists, the World Wide Web has become the most-used portion of the Internet. (In fact, to many users the Web is synonymous with the Internet.) The graphical side of the Internet, the Web offers papers that you can read online, files that you can download, and links that you can follow to related sites. In short, the Web offers you the world—at the click of a hyperlink.

Clicking and Linking

I don't need to tell you how to use a Web browser (such as Internet Explorer) to navigate the Web. I will point out, however, that there may be more uses for your browser than you currently know about.

For example, you know that clicking an underlined hyperlink will jump you to the Web page referenced in the hyperlink. But did you know that hyperlinks don't always link to other pages? Web developers can use hyperlinks to link to pictures, sound files, video files, and any type of file that you might wish to download.

On most manufacturers' Web sites you can find lists of drivers, patches, and other programs for downloading. If the developer of the site has done his or her work well, when you click the link for one of these files, that file will be automatically downloaded to your hard disk. (Actually, you'll see a dialog box asking you if and where you want to save the file, but you know what I mean.)

If clicking the link doesn't download the file (if, for example, clicking a link to a graphics file simply displays the graphic in a new window), you can still use your browser to download the file. Just right-click the link to display the pop-up menu, then select the Save or Save to Disk option. This will display the old familiar Save As dialog box, which will enable you to save the linked file to your hard disk.

Your Web browser can also be used to access and download files from FTP sites; more on that later.

NOTE   *Many drivers and other utilities are relatively small files, easily downloadable via a normal 56K modem. However, some manufacturers embed drivers and utilities in larger files and make you download the whole shebang just to get the little driver you need. Some of these files can be huge (1MB or more), and are easier to deal with if you have some sort of high-speed (DSL or cable) Internet connection.*

Finding Useful Web Sites

The Web is big—really, really big. Out of all the millions and millions of pages out there in cyberspace, how do you find the ones you need to solve your PC hardware problems?

I've put together a list of the best technical Web sites, which I'll get to in a minute. But before you hit these general sites, it's probably a good idea to go to the source of your problem—the hardware or software manufacturer.

FINDING MANUFACTURER WEB SITES

A good rule of thumb when seeking support via the Internet is to go to the manufacturer's Web site first, learn everything you can, and then expand your search to related sites (tech sites with reviews of a product, or sites where users may be asking questions and getting help with that product) and newsgroups. You hit the manufacturer first because—in theory, anyway—that's where the most accurate and most up-to-date information should reside.

NOTE   *The relevancy—in terms of both applicability and timeliness—of technical information on manufacturers' Web sites is variable. Some manufacturers take Web-based support very seriously and update their sites daily. Others view the Web as more of a marketing tool and let their Web support pages languish unattended for weeks and months on end. As with all things Internet-related, YMMV (your mileage may vary).*

There are several ways to find the URL for a specific manufacturer. First, many manufacturers list their Web address (and e-mail address, for direct contact) in their product documentation. If the address is not listed there, try typing the manufacturer's name into the middle of a URL, surrounded by a `www.` and a `.com`—for example, if the manufacturer is IBM, you would give `www.ibm.com` a try. (This one happens to work!) Finally, you can use a Web search engine (which I'll discuss in a moment) to search for the manufacturer's Web site; Yahoo! is particularly good at this type of manufacturer search.

Sometimes it's quicker to go to unofficial Web sites that link to the official ones, rather than going to the opening page of an official site and then wandering through a maze of linked pages. For example, if you need HP scanner drivers, you might go first to a third-party site that contains links to a bunch of different manufacturers' scanner download sites. When you click the HP link on that page, you'll jump immediately to the specific part of the HP site where drivers are stored.

On some occasions, the manufacturer's site might not contain the documentation or the drivers that you need. For example, when I needed documentation for an Adaptec SCSI host adapter, the AHA-2490, I went first to the official Adaptec site. Unfortunately, all that was available on the site was a phone number that I could call to order the docs—not exactly what I was looking for! My response was to use one of the Web search engines to search for *Adaptec documentation*, which led me to the Memory Lane Computers site, which had the documentation I wanted, online and immediately accessible. My point is that when a manufacturer's site doesn't contain the documentation you need, a third-party site might.

TIP   Two of the best sites to find updated drivers and related information are Drivers.com (`www.drivers.com`*) and DriverGuide.com (*`www.driverguide.com`*).*

USING SEARCH ENGINES AND DIRECTORIES

If you don't know the exact URL for the Web site you want—or don't even know what site it is you're looking for—then your best bet is to use one of the Web's many search sites. Literally hundreds of search sites are available, of which a dozen or so generate the bulk of the overall traffic.

There are two types of search sites—search engines and directories. A *search engine* uses high-powered software to automatically crawl the Web and compile huge indexes of available sites; when you search a search site, you're actually searching the millions of pages currently listed in that index. A *directory* consists of a smaller number of handpicked (by human beings!) listings, often organized into easy-to-navigate categories.

Google, Northern Light, HotBot, Excite, Lycos, and AltaVista are all search engines. Many search engines also include supplementary directory listings; for example, Yahoo! (a popular directory) also provides listings generated from a search engine (Google, for example).

Which type of search site should you use—a search engine or a directory? In general, a search engine delivers *more* results, whereas a directory delivers *more targeted* results. Many users prefer directories because of their organization; other users prefer the quantity of results delivered by search engines. It's really a matter a personal taste.

TIP   To generate more efficient results, enter precise search criteria. For example, if you need a driver for a particular video card, enter the vendor's name plus the word driver. *Some search engines (Google and AltaVista, for example) offer advanced search results that allow you to search for specific strings, or with Boolean operations such as "and" or "or" conditions.*

That said, here are some of the features that I find desirable in a search site:

A report of the total number of hits generated from a search   While a smaller number of hits are easier to read through, a larger number of hits may yield a lot more information for you. A Web search engine that generates only a few hits on a major topic may not be a very robust search engine.

A large number of hits displayed simultaneously   I find it faster to scroll down a page than to move to another page to see the next 10 hits. This parameter can be adjusted on many sites.

As little extraneous text surrounding the hits as possible   This is so that the links are easy to see. An option is the capability to customize the query results to show more or less surrounding information.

NOTE   Before deciding that a particular topic isn't referenced on the Web, make sure that you've tried more than one search site. Different search engines and directories index different parts of the Internet (or index the Internet using different criteria), so an identical search might generate totally different results at different search sites.

The following search sites, while a small subset of what's available, happen to be the ones that I've used most or like best.

Google   Google (`www.google.com`) is one of the best search engines—and my current favorite. In my experience, it produces the most accurate results of any search engine and delivers those results faster than any other site. Unlike the Excites and Lycos of the world, Google has resisted the urge to become a bloated "portal"; the only thing Google does is search, and it does that exceedingly well.

Interestingly, Google uses a slightly unusual method to rank the pages in its index. Whereas other search engines tend to rank their results on the frequency or predominance of the search term on the page, Google ranks results based on how many other pages link to that page. This sounds kind of like a popularity contest, but it works—you're more likely to find the official manufacturer site listed at the top of a Google results page than you are with other search engines. Chances are good that when you enter the search term and click the I'm Feeling Lucky button, you'll get there.

Northern Light   Northern Light (`www.northernlight.com`) is a hidden gem. Not only does it have one of the largest indexes of any search engine, it also features a "special collection" of additional documents (available for a fee) that you just can't find on any other site. I also like how Northern Light automatically categorizes its results into folders and subfolders.

AltaVista and HotBot   AltaVista (`www.altavista.com`) and HotBot (`hotbot.lycos.com`) are both big, powerful search engines. Both provide lots of search options, including advanced Boolean operations, that you can use to refine your search. As a bonus, AltaVista also offers specific searches for Usenet postings and multimedia files. They're both good, general search sites, worthy of everyday use.

Yahoo!   Yahoo! (`www.yahoo.com`) is one of the most popular search sites on the Internet—and one of the most popular sites on the Web, period. Yes, it offers the fewest results (it's a directory, not a search engine), but those results are typically high quality and well organized. If all you're looking for is the URL for a specific manufacturer's site, Yahoo! is the place to go. Yahoo! also offers supplemental results from the Google search engine (just click the Web Site Matches link at the bottom of any results page), as well as quick links to other search sites.

The Best Web Sites for Technical Information

Since the Internet was born on a computer and initially populated by computer enthusiasts, it makes sense that many Web sites focus on topics of interest to computer users. Some of these sites offer news and reviews, while others incorporate discussion forums where you can post questions, get answers, and maybe even help someone else. Still more sites offer drivers and utilities for downloading, deliver online tutorials and how-tos, or provide free or fee-based technical support from experts (both real and self-professed).

That said, here's a short list (organized alphabetically) of some of the better technical sites on the Web. The next time you need help or information, check these out!

WARNING   Web sites and other Internet resources tend to come and go—which means that any specific URL listed in this book may, at some point in time, go dead. Also, the character of existing groups or Web sites may change over time. This information is not guaranteed.

Active-Hardware   As you can tell from its name, Active-Hardware (`www.active-hardware.com`) is a PC hardware-oriented site, complete with tech news and reviews. The site also includes a robust section of downloadable drivers.

AnandTech   This site (`www.anandtech.com`) focuses on hardware news and reviews, and includes a number of discussion forums.

Ars Technica   The Ars site (`www.arstechnica.com`) combines tech news and articles, product reviews, a buyer's guide, how-tos and tweaks, and a discussion forum for computer enthusiasts.

BohTech   Short for Bohemian Technology, BohTech (`www.bohtech.com`) provides an online community for computer users with problems. The site includes a user-driven forum as well as a growing list of FAQs for key topics.

Click & Learn   Click & Learn (`www.mkdata.dk/click/`) offers hundreds of illustrated guides and tutorials for all manner of technical topics, from adapters to Zip drives. It's a terrific resource for learning about any new computer-related technology.

CMPnet   CMPnet (`www.cmpnet.com`) offers a multitude of resources for technical professionals, culled from the CMP magazine group.

CNET   The CNET family of sites (`www.cnet.com`) is a true one-stop shop for computer industry news and technical information. This tech portal includes links to other full-service sites that offer tech news, file and driver downloads, hardware and software reviews, and how-to and help information. It's a key site for anyone serious about computing.

Computer Hope   If you're having problems with your computer, there is hope—Computer Hope, that is. Computer Hope (`www.computerhope.com`) offers free computer help, questions and answers about common problems, listings of hardware and software vendors, and quick links to computer magazines and a computer dictionary.

Computing.Net   Computing.Net (`www.computing.net`) bills itself as "the industry's first technical support site." I don't know about being first, but it's one of the best; Computing.Net does a good job of centralizing technical support for all operating systems and types of computers. The support forums, which organize information by operating system (Windows 9x, Windows 2000/XP, Linux, etc.), are the best part of the site. Also useful are the numerous FAQs that contain answers to the most common questions asked in the forums, a huge listing of downloadable hardware drivers, a number of how-tos for solving common problems, and a section just for novices.

CPUReview.com   CPUReview.com (`www.cpureview.com`) presents the latest news in PC microprocessors and related hardware, and includes articles, reviews, and editorials.

DriverGuide.com   DriverGuide.com (`www.driverguide.com`) is *the* place to look for updated device drivers. The site consists of a massive database (compiled by the site's users) of drivers and related resources. Follow the links from this site to download and install the latest drivers for your system. The site also includes discussion boards, utilities, and helpful tutorials.

Drivers.com   Drivers.com (`www.drivers.com`) is another great site for the latest device drivers. Between DriverGuide.com and Drivers.com, you're practically guaranteed to find the right drivers for any device on your system.

EarthWeb   EarthWeb (www.earthweb.com) is a network of sites targeting IT professionals. It includes individual portals for IT management, networking and communications, Web development, hardware and systems, and software development.

Expertcity.com   Although Expertcity.com (www.expertcity.com) offers some free assistance, most of the help on this site comes from experts who "bid" to help you—for a fee. You ask your question, then choose your expert and price.

Experts Exchange   Experts Exchange (www.experts-exchange.com) is billed as "the number 1 professional collaboration network." It works on a type of bonus system—you answer questions on a topic for another user and then earn points toward getting *your* questions answered by other experts.

HardwareCentral   HardwareCentral (www.hardwarecentral.com) is a terrific source for in-depth computer hardware information. It includes news, reviews, previews, opinions, tips, and tutorials—as well as a discussion section and a variety of driver and utility downloads.

HotHardware   HotHardware (www.hothardware.com) is another hardware-oriented site, based on the following claim: "Only the hottest PC hardware tested and burned in." Includes news, reviews, and a user discussion forum.

Microsoft Personal Support Center   This site (support.microsoft.com/) serves as the gateway to all of Microsoft's support services, including the indispensable Microsoft Knowledge Base. If you're having any sort of problem on a Windows-based machine, chances are a Microsoft product is somehow involved—which means that this site should be at the top of your Favorites list! You can also find a ton of FAQs, service releases, patches, and updates in the Microsoft Download Center, accessible from the main Support Center page (or you can go there directly at www.microsoft.com/downloads/).

The PC Guide   The PC Guide (www.pcguide.com) offers step-by-step how-tos, discussion forums, and tips on a variety of hardware-related topics.

PC Mechanic   This site (www.pcmech.com) offers articles, columns, and tutorials for various technical topics.

PCsupport.com   PCsupport.com (corporate.pcsupport.com) bills itself as "the leader in eSupport solutions." This translates into a combination of automated online support tools, searchable "knowledge directories" of more than 2200 hardware and software products, and 24/7 live support from certified technical experts. Some of this is free; some is fee-based. (Note that PCsupport.com recently acquired MyHelpDesk, another top-rated tech support site, and integrated that site's content and services into the PCsupport.com site.)

PCTIPS.com   This site (www.pctips.com) presents articles and forums that focus on online help for major PC hardware, software, and operating systems.

Protonic.com   Protonic.com (www.protonic.com) is an online community that provides free technical support to computer users. You can ask questions directly to site personnel or visit the site's many discussion boards.

SelfHelpDesk   SelfHelpDesk (www.selfhelpdesk.com) is run by Unisys and offers a variety of free online technical support, targeted primarily at corporate computing.

TechTutorials.com This site (`www.techtutorials.com`) contains a huge directory of more than 1500 free computer and networking tutorials and white papers, targeted at the IT professional.

TechWeb TechWeb (`www.techweb.com`) offers news and downloads for IT professionals. Use this site's Advanced Search option to investigate various computing topics—and check out the links to related sites, at the bottom of the home page. (TechWeb is associated with CMPnet.)

Tom's Hardware Guide Tom's Hardware Guide (`www.tomshardware.com`) is one of the best PC hardware sites on the Internet, and includes plenty of information you can use to either troubleshoot or soup up your system.

VirtualDr VirtualDr (`www.virtualdr.com`) offers technical support and information for all major operating systems, as well as many types of hardware. Also included are numerous discussion groups and online tutorials.

WebTechGeek WebTechGeek (`www.webtechgeek.com`) presents news and guides on a variety of technical topics, including PCs, PDAs, MP3s, and digital cameras.

WinDrivers.com The main feature of this site (`www.windrivers.com`) is a huge library of downloadable Windows device drivers from practically every vendor in existence. It also features Windows-related hardware support.

ZDNet ZDNet (`www.zdnet.com`) is a high-tech portal that combines all the technology news and information from *PC Magazine*, *Macworld*, and other Ziff-Davis magazines. Includes news, online help, how-tos, and lots of useful downloads.

DOWNLOADING PATCHES, DRIVERS, AND UTILITIES

You can find drivers, utilities, and patches available for downloading at any number of Web and FTP sites, as well as in newsgroups devoted to binary files. In addition to driver-only sites (such as DriverGuide.com and Drivers.com), almost all hardware and software vendors that have a Web site have some sort of "support" link on their home page and a relatively easy way to locate driver downloads.

When downloading files, keep these things in mind:

◆ It's rare that a virus is uploaded to a moderated forum or commercial Web site, but it can happen. Before running any program on your system, it's a good idea to virus-check it first. (PC viruses, recall, can exist only in executable files or Microsoft Office documents containing macros, so other binary files and message threads don't need to be checked for viruses.)

◆ Downloading large files can take a long time, and if there's an error in your connection during the download, you may have to repeat it. Therefore, if you're connecting to the Internet over a phone line that has call-waiting activated, you may want to disable that feature before you connect by prefacing the phone number with *70.

◆ Shareware is not freeware. If you use a shareware product, then you're implicitly agreeing to pay the shareware's author for the software once the evaluation period has expired.

◆ Copyright laws apply to electronic documents. You can't, for example, download a white paper that someone has written, remove their name, and substitute your own.

NOTE   *No doubt that I've left out dozens of useful sources of information, but this is meant to be a starting point, not a definitive guide of every single technical resource available online. If you know of a newsgroup, forum, or Web site that I haven't mentioned here but you think could be helpful to those repairing or upgrading their PCs, please* don't *e-mail me with the information. I'll find it.*

Using FTP Sites for Support

FTP sites are dedicated servers, connected to the Internet, that hold collections of files available for downloading. Although Web sites are now the most common places to find files for downloading, some Web sites link to FTP sites for their file storage and downloading—and FTP sites are still good places to find software, utilities, and drivers.

Downloading via FTP

FTP (File Transfer Protocol) is an Internet protocol that predates the World Wide Web. In essence, an FTP site is a server optimized for file downloading, using either specialized FTP client software or a Web browser.

When you use your Web browser to access an FTP server, the directories and subdirectories on the server are displayed in a directory tree in the browser's main window. You turn your browser into a de facto FTP client by entering the address of the FTP site into the address box in your browser—but with *FTP* (instead of *HTTP*) in front of the address. For example, the full address of the Megatrends FTP server looks like this: `ftp://ftp.megatrends.com`. (For the curious, you can pull down utilities and Windows NT information from this site.)

Unless you have an account on the FTP server that you're trying to reach—if you're not sure, you probably don't—you'll have to log in anonymously, providing your e-mail address for a password. (Supplying your e-mail address isn't always necessary, but it is polite because that lets the FTP administrator know who's been there.) Not all sites support anonymous login, but most of the ones that you're likely to need do.

NOTE   *When you use a Web browser to FTP, you are automatically connected to FTP sites with anonymous login—no extra steps required. If a site does not support anonymous login, then you'll know it: you'll be prompted for a password that you won't have and have to cancel out in disgrace.*

Finding Useful FTP Servers

There are two ways to find FTP sites: through the lists of sites built into popular FTP clients, and through Web-based FTP search engines and directories.

If you want to use a dedicated FTP client for downloading, check out CuteFTP (downloadable from `www.cuteftp.com`) or LapLinkFTP (downloadable from `www.laplinkftp.com`). These programs include comprehensive lists of public and corporate FTP servers, built right into the software.

If you prefer to access FTP sites from your Web browser, you can find directories of FTP sites (categorized by topic) at TILE.NET/FTP (`tile.net/ftp`) and at the LapLinkFTP Web site. If you have a specific file that you're looking for, you can search for filenames across a range of FTP servers at FtpFind (`www.ftpfind.com`).

NOTE   *As the Web continues to become more popular, the number of FTP sites is beginning to decrease—so don't be surprised if you run into a dead link or two on any list of FTP servers.*

The Best FTP Servers for Downloading Files

As a kind of head start for your quest for online support, here's a short list of FTP servers that have plentiful archives of drivers, utilities, and other downloadable software programs:

- ◆ FUNET (`ftp.funet.fi`)
- ◆ Megatrends (`ftp.megatrends.com`)
- ◆ Microsoft (`ftp.microsoft.com`)
- ◆ PC World (`ftp.pcworld.com`)
- ◆ PIPEX (`ftp.pipex.net`)
- ◆ ProtoSource (`ftp.psnw.com`)
- ◆ Universitat Duisburg Archive (`ftp.uni-duisburg.de`)
- ◆ University of Illinois Archive (`ftp.cso.uiuc.edu`)
- ◆ University of North Carolina/ibiblio Archive (`ibiblio.org/pub/`)
- ◆ Washington University Archives (`wuarchive.wustl.edu`)

In addition, most hardware and software vendors maintain their own corporate FTP servers. Try accessing these sites by adding an `ftp` to the company name and dot-com. For example, the address for Gateway 2000's FTP server is `ftp.gateway2000.com`.

TIP   *When you're navigating through FTP sites, you're most likely to find downloadable files in the* Pub *or* Files *directories.*

Using Usenet Newsgroups for Support

Newsgroups are discussion groups that are part of a service called *Usenet.* (Usenet, like the World Wide Web, is part of the larger Internet.) Newsgroups are available on all kinds of topics, from bicycle maintenance to cat stories to problems associated with configuring hard drives to... you name it. If you haven't found a group that covers exactly the topic that you want to discuss, either you should look a little harder or one will probably pop up soon enough.

NOTE   *An unspoken rule of the technical Internet is that in exchange for getting help from those more knowledgeable than you, you in turn help someone else less experienced than you are.*

Understanding Usenet

Usenet (also called NewsNet and NNTP) is similar in many ways to e-mail, except that you don't have a dedicated address and you don't exchange messages on a one-to-one basis. Instead, you "post" messages (called *articles*) into a forum for all other users to read and perhaps respond to.

In essence, each Usenet newsgroup (and there are tens of thousands of them) is a collection of topic-related messages that are stored on special NNTP servers. You access the messages using an NNTP-compliant client, such as Outlook Express. Usenet groups have names similar to Web site domain names, but they are often longer and, hence, more descriptive. An example of a Usenet newsgroup name is `comp.os.ms-windows.apps.compatibility.win95`, a group dedicated to discussing application compatibility issues with Windows 95. Other newsgroup names can get quite silly, such as the obvious dislike for a beloved purple dinosaur shared by the list members of `alt.barney.dinosaur.die.die.die`.

Due to their interactive nature, newsgroups are good places to get problem-solving advice. (Message boards on computer-oriented Web sites are also good sources for this type of advice.) Sometimes you can get lucky and find that someone else has asked a similar question before you did, but most of the time it's easiest if you go ahead and ask anyway.

TIP *If the forum or newsgroup in which you plan to post a question has a list of FAQs, read the FAQ before posting to make sure that your solution isn't in it.*

NOTE *While newsgroups are great sources for advice, they're not really good sources for downloadable utilities. That's because newsgroups don't archive information; most messages remain "live" for only a few days or weeks before they're cleared away to make space for newer postings. However, there is a way that you can take a trip down memory lane. Check out Google Groups (`http://groups.google.com`), which lets you search through a complete 20-year Usenet Archive of over 700 million Usenet messages. In addition to finding threads of a more technical nature, imagine finding such items as the first Usenet mention of Microsoft (28 May 1981, `net.general`), MTV (22 March 1982, `net.music`), or Madonna (13 July 1983, `net.audio`)! More about Google Groups later in this chapter.*

HOW NEWSGROUPS WORK

Most newsgroups are unmoderated, meaning that no one's watching the message content to ensure that subject discussions stay on track, or that people are polite (or even not downright obscene) to one another, or that people don't post totally irrelevant messages in the wrong forums (called *spamming*, and considered to be impolite). Although there's a lot of garbage in newsgroups (on the order of offers of nude celebrity pictures or discounted prices on your next order of Viagra), newsgroups have been around for a long time and are good places to find people with lots of technical experience. Technical newsgroups, after all, are frequented by those interested enough in talking shop to do it online.

WARNING *Know that Usenet is frequently used by unscrupulous individuals to pass material with mature content, and/or illicit and illegal information, including child pornography. Newsgroups that carry this type of information often have descriptive names with sex in the title. If you are careful, you'll never see such material, but be aware that it is out there (the Internet is anonymous, remember—especially Usenet). Also remember that many people cross-post (distribute the same message to a number of other groups) and send such material to groups that do not dwell on those things.*

Normally, your access to newsgroups works like this: your ISP maintains a news server that stores as many of the postings in all or selected newsgroups as possible. (Note that this means that you may not have access to all available newsgroups—if a group isn't on your news server, you can't reach it.) Rather than connecting directly to Usenet, then, you connect to the news server and read the messages posted there. Any messages that you post to a newsgroup will be uploaded from the news server to Usenet itself, and then propagated to other Usenet servers across the Internet.

NOTE   *The more traffic a newsgroup or forum experiences (that is, the more new messages are posted each time you visit), the more likely it is that someone will see your posting and reply to it.*

NEWSGROUP HIERARCHIES

There are more than 30,000 newsgroups on Usenet (although not all may be available on your ISP's server, as noted earlier). Browsing through this many newsgroups takes more time and energy than even I have, so there has to be a way to organize the groups. There is, of course, since all newsgroup names adhere to a simple hierarchy. You start with one of several major domains (the part of the name to the left of the first period), and then move down through the hierarchy (much as you'd move down through a list of folders and subfolders) as you move past each additional period in the name.

The major newsgroup domains include the following:

`alt.`   Stands for *alternative*—the discussions here are probably a little weird, as just about anything goes in these groups.

`biz.`   These newsgroups are host to discussions about various business products and services.

`comp.`   These newsgroups are, broadly speaking, computer-based. They may be computer-related humor or Sound Blaster installation hints. The exact nature of the discussion depends on which group you're talking about, but the discussions should in some way touch on computers (even if it's about how evil they are). This is probably the best domain to browse through for computer-related information and help.

`humanities.`   This is the place to discuss literature, fine arts, and other humanities (but *not* popular entertainment—see the `rec.` domain for that!).

`k12.`   This domain includes education-related discussions about kindergarten through grade 12.

`misc.`   Hard to fit into any particular category, these groups might cover such topics as good techie books, militia activity, and home schooling.

`news.`   These newsgroups generally cover network- and newsgroup-related technical issues.

`rec.`   These groups are recreation oriented, covering just about any topic that you could think of for recreation.

`soc.`   These groups deal with social and cultural issues.

`sci.`   This is where you'll find science-related discussions, for both professionals and laypersons.

`talk.`   These groups are for those who like debate. Whatever you feel like arguing about, it's probably covered here.

NOTE *There are also many regional and company-specific Usenet domains. (For example, the* `japan.` *domain contains Japanese-oriented newsgroups, and the* `microsoft.` *domain includes newsgroups about Microsoft products.) Some of the larger regional domains include hierarchies that resemble the overall Usenet hierarchy in their complexity.*

There's a lot of crossover between domains. If you're so inclined, you can probably start a flame war on a `comp.` newsgroup that would do credit to an `alt.` newsgroup. (Just post an "NT is better than Linux!" message to see what I mean.) That said, the above domains represent how the usual topic hierarchies shake out, more or less.

NETIQUETTE

This chapter is about research, not manners, but manners can play a significant role in determining whether your research results pay off. Remember, no one *has* to answer your questions.

◆ DON'T WRITE IN ALL CAPITAL LETTERS. THIS IS CONSIDERED SHOUTING AND IS RUDE.

◆ Be specific in message headers. "Help!" is too vague to grab my attention; "Need to restore hard disk configuration information" is more effective.

◆ Explain your situation briefly, but completely, at the beginning of the message. If it's a troubleshooting question, describe what you've done so far and any relevant parts of your configuration. People are more likely to reply to your posts if they know the background.

◆ Don't make posts longer than they need to be. First, reading on-screen is harder than reading hard copy, and paging through messages is wearisome. Second, people are paying to download and read your messages—don't give them junk.

◆ Don't post a question in more than one section in an online forum, or in more than one newsgroup. If it's in the wrong section of a forum, the forum sysop will move it to the correct one. Posting the same question to more than one newsgroup is sometimes acceptable if the groups are not too similar in topic and the question fits into more than one category, but keep it to a minimum.

◆ Be polite. The people who are replying to your posts are doing *you* a favor. For heaven's sake, don't be rude to them, even if you disagree with their conclusions. Everyone can see your posts, not just their intended recipient.

◆ If you encounter anyone breaking these rules, don't lecture them about it. If the forum or newsgroup is moderated, the moderator will do so. If it isn't, I assure you that someone else will take care of it and you won't have to look like a scold.

Finding Useful Usenet Newsgroups

Even if you browse Usenet by hierarchy, you still have tens of thousands of individual newsgroups to sift through. That's a lot of list scrolling, so it's useful to have a newsgroup reader that includes a search function. (Most do.)

As an example, searching for the word *computer* generates a list that includes a lot of newsgroups in the `comp.` or `news.` domains—as well as groups *not* in those domains. It's also important to note that the results of this search do not include some newsgroups that I know (from personal experience) are computer related, because those newsgroups don't have the word *computer* in their names. In other words, don't assume that if the keywords you enter to find information about your SuperSender modem don't net anything, then no one is talking about your SuperSender modem. You just need to start surfing the groups themselves to see what people are talking about.

When you need help with a problem and you don't know where to start looking, think about keywords associated with your difficulty. In your newsreader, you can see the way that newsgroups are named. Based on that naming scheme, identify the parts of your problem that might be in the name of a newsgroup. For instance, if you want to ask advice about choosing a SCSI controller to work with your system running Windows NT Workstation, that gives you several good potential keywords: *SCSI*, *NT*, and *configure*. (In this case, I'd probably start with SCSI, since that's really what your question is about.)

From the results of this keyword search, you can choose a newsgroup that looks likely (perhaps `comp.periphs.scsi`), go to it, and read a little of the message traffic already posted to see whether people are talking about subjects related to your problem.

If no SCSI newsgroups seem to fit the bill, you can try *NT* instead. There's a trick to this one, though: newsreaders aren't case sensitive, and most don't let you distinguish between searching for whole words only and searching for part of a word. Therefore, if you search for *nt* only, you'll get the NT hits, but you'll also get any other newsgroups with names that have *nt* in any form. (Obviously, this point doesn't apply to just NT, but to any combination of letters that have significance on their own but can also be part of a word.) So this time, if you search for *.nt* (note the period before the *nt*), you'll get a more targeted list of results.

This search still found some newsgroups not focused on Windows NT, but it's better than the results you would have received by searching for *nt* by itself. Scrolling down the list, you notice that there's a newsgroup called `comp.os.ms-windows.nt.setup.hardware`. That looks more promising, so you go to it, read some of the messages already posted, and post your question if it hasn't been asked recently. Then, you can check back into the newsgroup at intervals to see whether anyone has replied to your posting.

TIP   *If you post to a newsgroup using your real e-mail address, you're likely to find yourself on multiple mailing lists for get-rich-quick schemes—even ones having nothing to do with what you posted about. The quick and dirty workaround for this little problem is to use a phony address for your Usenet postings. (Some users insert the term* nospam *somewhere in their real address; any thinking human being who wants to respond directly to you will see the* nospam *and remove it, thus revealing your real address.)*

As I've discussed, there are tens of thousands of newsgroups out there. Not all of them will be available from your news server (some servers subscribe to only a limited number of groups, and there's not much that you can do about that), but there are enough that you should be able to get help with almost anything.

SEARCHING NEWSGROUP ARCHIVES AT GOOGLE GROUPS

Because there are so many newsgroups, a server that subscribes to all the groups may be able to store only a few days' worth of traffic at a time. To keep current with a newsgroup, then, you'll need to check in fairly regularly.

What do you do if you want to read messages that were posted more than a few days ago—messages that are no longer available on your ISP's newsgroup server? When this need arises, it's time to access the Usenet archives, which are available on the Google Groups Web site (http://groups.google.com).

For several years, a full archive of postings from all Usenet newsgroups was maintained by Deja.com (formerly called DejaNews). Early in 2001, Google, the search engine site, acquired the Deja.com site and all its archives. So now you can search the Usenet archive at Google Groups in any number of ways—including, if you click the Advanced Groups Search link, by keyword, by newsgroup name, by date, by username, and so on. (If you want to avoid the nasty stuff, you can also choose to filter out all adult-oriented newsgroups from your search.)

Google Groups is *the* site for serious newsgroup research. Not only can you search multiple newsgroups with a single query, you can also view all the messages in related threads—or even read all messages from a specific user. If it's ever been posted to a newsgroup, chances are that you can find it at Google Groups.

The Best Newsgroups for Technical Information

Here is a short list of individual newsgroups and newsgroup hierarchies that might be of interest if you need technical computer information or support. A wildcard (*) at the end of a name indicates that some or all of the groups in that particular hierarchy might be worthwhile.

- `alt.comp`
- `alt.comp.hardware.*`
- `alt.comp.periphs.*`
- `alt.computer`
- `alt.sys.pc-clone.*`
- `comp.misc`
- `comp.os.linux.*`
- `comp.os.ms-dos.*`
- `comp.os.ms-windows.*`
- `comp.periphs.*`
- `comp.sys.ibm.pc.hardware.*`
- `comp.sys.intel`
- `microsoft.public.*`
- `misc.forsale.computers.*`

TIP   *Some of the best computer troubleshooting groups seem to have the word* hardware *in them. This keyword nets you a plethora of useful newsgroups. Why* hardware *and not more specific words? Traffic levels, mostly. Newsgroups devoted more specifically to particular hardware questions (such as I/O transfer) seem to have too little traffic to do much good.*

Using E-mail Mailing Lists for Support

Similar to Usenet newsgroups are e-mail mailing lists. The major differences are that newsgroups are public and unmoderated (generally), whereas mailing lists are mostly private (by invitation only, in some cases) and often moderated. The result, typically, is a more focused forum with less extraneous "noise" from off-topic posts.

How Mailing Lists Work

E-mail mailing lists operate through the convenience of e-mail. Members of the mailing list send e-mail messages to the list moderator; those messages are then re-sent (either individually or combined into a more manageable daily *digest*) to other members of the list. This means, of course, that you have to *subscribe* to the list and provide the list moderator with your e-mail address. Some lists allow just about anyone with an inbox to subscribe, while other lists have more stringent membership requirements—necessary, in some cases, to keep out the riffraff and improve the quality of the list.

TIP   *If you're uneasy about giving out your private e-mail address (and you should be, given the huge quantities of unsolicited spam that result from public address postings), consider opening a separate e-mail account solely for mailing list use. Hotmail, Yahoo!, and other free e-mail services are worth considering for this sort of "buffered" e-mail account.*

While different mailing lists have different methods of subscribing (and some even have their own Web sites, for both subscription and archival purposes), most use some sort of automated e-mail registration. The way it typically works is that you send a blank e-mail message to the designated address, with the single word *subscribe* in the subject line. Unsubscribing is usually the reverse: you send a blank e-mail with the word *unsubscribe* in the subject line.

Using a mailing list to obtain advice and information is similar to using a Usenet newsgroup. You begin by sending an e-mail message containing your question or comment to the list moderator. Your message is then immediately sent to the other list subscribers—or, for those lists that offer digest services, combined with all other messages received that day and then sent as one large message to the digest subscribers. When other subscribers choose to respond, they send a reply to the list moderator; that reply is then sent to all other subscribers or added to the daily digest. Naturally, if a fellow subscriber chooses to make their e-mail address public, you can bypass the rest of the list and reply directly to that individual.

Finding Useful Mailing Lists

Since many mailing lists are run by individuals (or by individual organizations), where can you find a list of all the lists that are available?

One good listing of mailing lists is the Liszt (www.liszt.com). You can use this Web site to search for mailing lists by keyword, or you can browse through Liszt's hierarchical directory of topics. To give you an example of what you'll find, if you go to the Computers topic, you'll find listings for 40 subcategories (from 3D to Windows), with several lists in each subcategory. (The Hardware subcategory, at time of writing, included 18 mailing lists.)

Another good source of mailing lists is Yahoo! Groups (`http://groups.yahoo.com`), which serves as a hosting service for tens of thousands of lists. As with Liszt, you can search through Yahoo! Groups' mailing lists or browse through their organized categories. (Yahoo! Groups' Hardware category, at time of writing, included more than 1000 mailing lists.)

The Best Mailing Lists for Technical Information

To give you a head start on your hunt for the perfect mailing list, here are lists to consider for computer hardware help and support:

1PCBuilder   A list for people who build, upgrade, or repair their own PCs. See `http://groups.yahoo.com/group/1PCBuilder/` for more information.

compuhelp   Provides help for hardware and operating system problems. Contact `compuhelp-owner@lists.spunge.org` for more information.

computertalkshop   A general computer discussion list. See `http://questforcertification.com/cts/` for more information.

pchelp   Provides help on computer hardware and software issues. See `http://groups.yahoo.com/group/pchelp/` for more information.

pchelp4u   Specializes in help for hardware and Windows-related problems. See `http://groups.yahoo.com/group/pchelp4u/` for more information.

pctoolbin   Offers discussions about PC maintenance, tools, and utilities. See `http://groups.yahoo.com/group/pctoolbin/` for more information.

survpc   A list for users of older DOS and Windows-based PCs. See `http://groups.yahoo.com/list/survpc/` for more information.

TIP   Using Liszt and Yahoo! Groups, you can also find mailing lists devoted to specific vendors or types of equipment. Just search by vendor name.

Using Internet Relay Chat for Support

If you can't wait the hours or days it might take to generate a response from a question posted to a newsgroup or mailing list, you have a real-time alternative: Internet Relay Chat.

Chatting with IRC

Internet Relay Chat (IRC) is that part of the Internet that facilitates real-time text-based conversation between groups of like-minded users. Think of IRC as being kind of like CB radio; different *channels* are dedicated to specific topics, and once you're in a channel, you're talking publicly with everybody else who is currently in the channel. It's also possible to hold private conversations with other users logged on to a specific IRC network; these conversations are not visible to other users in a channel.

NOTE   IRC operates on a traditional client/server model. You (and your software) are the client, and the IRC computer you and other clients connect to is the server.

IRC is a collection of individual chat networks, all connected to the main Internet backbone. To participate in IRC, you have to connect to an IRC *server* dedicated to a specific IRC *network*; you can connect to only one network at a time. (You'll often find similar channels on different networks; these channels operate independently from each other, however.)

You can find a complete list of available IRC networks (and their associated servers) at www.mirc.com/servers.html. The most popular IRC networks include ChatNet, DALnet, EFnet, Galaxy Net, IRC-Net, NewNet, Starlink, and Undernet.

Since each IRC network is composed of multiple servers, you connect to a specific server that is itself connected to the larger network. (You access the server over the Internet, of course.) You have to log on to the server with a unique *nickname* (of your own creation), and then you can access specific channels on that network.

To use IRC, you need a piece of software called an IRC client. The most popular IRC client is mIRC, a shareware program you can download from www.mirc.com. mIRC enables you to connect to any IRC server (and includes a full list of servers for all major IRC networks), and then chat in multiple channels simultaneously.

NOTE *IRC is one of the largest and most accessible forms of online chat on the Internet. You can also find similar-working chat rooms on proprietary online services (such as America Online) and on many individual Web sites. (For example, Yahoo! has a thriving chat section.) Web-based chat can be either HTML- or Java-based and typically requires no other software beyond your Web browser.*

Finding Useful IRC Channels

The best place to search for IRC channels is the same place you search for e-mail mailing lists: Liszt (www.liszt.com/chat/). Liszt lets you search for specific topics and then lists channels that match those topics—and the specific IRC networks where you can find those channels.

WARNING *Of all the flaky components of the Internet, IRC is the most flaky. IRC channels come and go with the wind, and you never know what's going to be there from one day to the next. Take any lists of IRC channels (including the one coming up next) with a grain of salt—there are no guarantees with IRC!*

The Best IRC Channels for Technical Information

There are tens of thousands of IRC channels, devoted to everything from general chat to kinky sex to local sports teams. Naturally, you're interested in those channels where the best and the brightest computer gurus hang out, so you can learn from their expertise.

The first thing to do is to identify those IRC networks with the most traffic, since more traffic equals more people chatting equals more of a chance that you'll get your questions answered. For hardware support purposes, those channels are DALnet, EFnet, and Undernet.

What follows is a short list of the busiest hardware support channels on those three networks. Obviously, other channels touch on the topic at hand, but these channels are probably the best places to start if you need a quick answer to a problem.

DALnet The best hardware-related channel on the DALnet network is #computers.

EFnet   There are three good support-oriented channels on the EFnet network: `#computerhelp`, `#computers`, and `#hardware`.

Undernet   On Undernet, the busiest hardware and support channels are `#computerhelp`, `#computers`, and `#hardware`.

NOTE   All IRC channels start with a #.

PROPRIETARY ONLINE SERVICES AND SUPPORT

All the resources listed so far in this chapter are available to anyone with an Internet connection. In addition to these public sources of information, several proprietary sources of online information are available to you—providing you subscribe to the services that supply the information, that is.

The largest source of proprietary online information is *America Online (AOL)*. With more than 27 million users, AOL is the world's largest ISP—and the largest provider of proprietary online content.

Unfortunately, AOL doesn't develop a lot of its own content, but rather licenses content from other sources. For example, much of the content on AOL's Computing channel comes from CNET—and mirrors what you can find for free on CNET's regular Web site. (You can check out some of AOL's computing content for free on the AOL Web site, at www.aol.com/webcenters/computing/.)

The second-largest proprietary online service is *MSN* (The Microsoft Network). Unlike AOL, most of MSN's computer-related content is freely accessible over the Web, and it includes a good deal of unique information—including news, reviews, downloads, forums, and so on. You can access MSN Computing Central at http://computingcentral.msn.com.

MSN Computing Central maintains more than two dozen computing forums, running through a range of operating systems (not just Microsoft based: Unix, Linux, and OS/2, too), telephony and PC communications, games, and safe computing (virus and network security). For the purpose of researching how to upgrade and maintain your PC (check the title of this book), Computing Central's Hardware forum is probably your best bet; it has an active membership, and a variety of question topics and skill levels are represented. (I haven't seen anyone laughed at for asking a newbie question yet.) In fact, one very basic question about what RAM was got some people out of the woodwork admitting that they didn't know either; thanks for asking. The traffic there is not as heavy as some hardware-related Usenet newsgroups, but it's not bad.

The third proprietary online service, *CompuServe*, used to be *the* online service to join if you were into computers or wanted access to the people shaping the computer industry. A decade ago, it was pretty easy to join a whole host of computer forums (available exclusively on the CompuServe service) and rub elbows with top decision-makers and senior support brass at companies such as Microsoft, Novell, Lotus, and Digital Equipment Corporation (DEC). You paid for the privilege, too; for a very long time, you paid a hefty monthly subscription fee—in addition to hourly connection fees (as high as $24/hour!).

Today's CompuServe, however, is a pale image of what used to be—and CompuServe's supremacy in online technical material has faded considerably. CompuServe is now owned by America Online, and its technical content has become somewhat limited. Most of the old CompuServe contingent of experienced professionals—those folks who could answer almost any computer question—have migrated to the World Wide Web. Today, you can still join and participate in computer forums and download files, but it's usually easier to locate the same—or better—material on the Web.

Cautions about Online Support

Throughout this chapter I've been talking about how the Internet can be a marvelous help to you when you're trying to research something related to your computer or to get help with a problem. Now it's time for some cautions to go along with the cheerleading. (Most of this stuff will probably seem really obvious, but bear with me.)

Don't Believe Everything You Hear

There's a lot of misinformation in the PC world. It's not actual lying, but it's stuff that's misheard, or corrected later but the person telling you missed the correction, or misunderstood because the listener didn't have enough background to remember the information correctly. The trouble is that a lot of this misinformation gets repeated until it has a life of its own. Some is harmless, such as an assertion that I saw repeated that Microsoft was responsible for changing the PCMCIA card's name to the PC Card (they weren't), but some is not.

If someone suggests a drastic measure in response to a problem that you've posted a question about, I suggest that you hang on for a little while and see whether you get any other responses. Surely you've met people in person who claim to know more than their experience covers; well, they exist in cyberspace, too—and they're harder to strangle when you follow their suggestion and something goes desperately wrong.

When in Doubt, Check for Viruses

First, a dose of reality: viruses aren't a problem for most commercial sites. FTP sites, for example, rarely allow anonymous logins to upload files to their sites. Manufacturer-supported Web sites provide official files (and only official files) for downloading, and go to the extra effort of virus-checking those files. No company wants the public relations nightmare of being responsible for a virus infection.

That said, you should be careful of sites that are not related to a particular company or that cater to those who might enjoy a little rule-breaking before breakfast. If you come across a site that offers to let you download games and (possibly) pirated software, or quite openly caters to hackers, it's a good idea to check the files that you download before running them. Once again, only executable files can contain PC viruses, so you needn't worry about document files (with the exception of Office documents that have macros in them) or messages.

NOTE *Macro viruses are both cross-platform and capable of being contained in a document. This class of virus is discussed in more detail in Chapter 15, "An Overview of Viruses."*

Don't Give Out Personal Information

When posting in public areas such as newsgroups or forums, don't give out any personal information that you don't want the world to know about, such as your home address, your telephone number, credit card or checking account information, or the like. This information isn't impossible to find or figure out (especially for those who have a little time on their hands and nothing better to do), but that doesn't mean you have to make it easy for them.

Troubleshooting Tips

Getting assistance from a remote source always presents some degree of difficulty, just because the person who is helping you can't see your system. This puts the responsibility squarely on your shoulders to present your problem as clearly as possible, erring on the side of offering too much rather than too little information.

In a recent informal survey of several managers who run online technical support forums for MSN Computing Central, almost all reported the same thing: users often don't give enough information when first presenting their problem to get useful help.

These are real examples taken from just one morning's online help requests:

"Help. I'm getting an error message. What do I do?" is all one user writes, not mentioning *which* error message, let alone where it was observed, or what might have happened as a result.

"Why doesn't the drive I just added work?" writes another, failing to provide even basic details about what kind of drive, how it was prepared and configured, or what operating system is being used.

"My PC beeps. What do I do to stop it????? Also, why does it crash when I use my favorite program??? Huh???? That's really dumb!!!!!!!!!!!!!!!! And why couldn't I install Windows 2000 or Windows XP???" types another person. All PCs beep unless they're dead, but because no information is provided, we don't know if it's beeping unusually. We don't know what program is causing the user's PC to crash, or whether the user is getting any error messages before the crash that might give an indication of what's wrong. As for why Windows 2000/XP wouldn't install, we're left wondering here, too, because there's no information on what happened when the person tried to install. Finally, this exemplifies a common myth about online tech support: that more punctuation—like exclamation marks to highlight frustration—will take the place of providing details about the PC and its problem. Sadly, it doesn't.

If you find someone able and willing to help you, the last thing you want to do is force the person into a position of having to pull teeth to extract information from you—it's a waste of their time and yours, and you probably want to solve this sooner rather than later. So present basic details about your system and the problem at hand when you post the first time, and if you reply, reference the previous messages. You don't have to write a book, but you need to offer basic facts. Important details to include are:

- Type of machine, such as Pentium III, and a quick overview of what you have installed (that is, 64MB of RAM, 10GB hard drive with 5GB free, and so on).

- Operating system used—check your version and report it. (And yes, Windows 98 Second Edition is distinct from the original Windows 98; Windows XP Home is also distinct from Windows XP Professional.)

- If receiving an error message, provide the *exact* wording and whether it can be reproduced when it occurs.

- The last thing(s) you were doing before the problem was noticed or reported, including any hardware, software, or upgrades installed or removed.

- Exact steps you've taken already to try to resolve the problem (important in case something you tried was in error, and a second problem could mask the solution of the original problem).

♦ Any other relevant information, such as noting an LED power indicator not on when it should be, or your machine's failing to boot, or the PC beeping a specific number of times on bootup.

That's about all there is to obtaining support online. At this point, you should have a good idea of the tools available to you, and how to find what you need. Just remember these basic rules:

♦ The answer is probably out there somewhere. Don't give up too easily.

♦ Most people like nothing more than to give advice, so never be afraid to ask.

So have fun out in cyberspace—I'll see you there!

Chapter 33

This Old Computer

◆ Understanding How and Why Computers Evolved   929

◆ Deciding What's Worth Keeping and What's Not   931

◆ Making a Game Plan   935

◆ Upgrading Your Computer   935

Introduction

I'VE BEEN WORKING WITH computers in one way or another now for decades. As a result, I've seen computers evolve from giant, room-filling monsters such as the Univac that predicted the presidential election results in the early days of television, all the way to computers so small that they fit easily in the palm of a hand. And in all that time, one thing I've learned has been universally true: every new computer is faster, smaller, and cheaper, and has greater capacity than the last.

What does this mean to you? Well, for starters:

◆ Any computer you buy today will already be becoming obsolete while you're taking it home.

◆ The options you buy for your computer today will be cheaper tomorrow.

◆ No matter what your computer can do today, you'll want it to do something new tomorrow.

What can you do? The answer is actually pretty simple: *never buy anything for your computer that you won't be using now.* Why? Because (as I just mentioned) the thing you want today will be faster, cheaper, and generally better tomorrow. So if you won't need it until tomorrow, wait until tomorrow to buy it.

A common mistake newcomers to computers make is assuming that they are buying an appliance, like a refrigerator, that will be good for 10 years. Computers just aren't like that. While it's true that the computer you buy today will be capable of performing the same *tasks* in 10 years (assuming nothing breaks), *your needs will be different.* If you buy your computer and never upgrade its components, your computer will become obsolete in two to three years. If you're adventurous, however, you (or your favorite service rep) can selectively upgrade your components over time and extend the life of your computer and its capability to make your life easier.

The March of Technology

Back in the "good old days," personal computers were not a business at all. They were a hobby. They were the hobby of people who loved technology. They dabbled in electronics. Actually, a lot of them did much more than dabble. Most were also engineers—engineers who designed and built radios, TVs, and just about any kind of electronic test equipment that you might be able to think of.

These people were engineers because they loved the technology. So back in the mid-'70s, when Intel produced the 4004 chip, the first microprocessor (they originally called it a microcomputer), it opened the door to a new world for us. Interestingly, Intel really didn't know what they'd done at first. They developed the 4004 processor to solve a problem for one of their customers. Figure 33.1 shows the 4004 processor.

FIGURE 33.1

Intel's 4004 micro-processor chip

The problem Intel needed to solve was that their client, Busicom, was competing with several companies that were producing new versions of their circuits very quickly. Busicom needed a new way to bring their new designs to market faster. Intel found a way.

At that time, whenever a company developed a new circuit design, it took them months to lay out new circuit boards and manufacture them. It was a process that had been refined and refined, but they had hit a wall. They couldn't get any faster.

Intel proposed something revolutionary. To understand what they did, you need to know that electronics firms were beginning to use components called Programmable Array Logic (PAL) integrated circuits. These devices contained small arrays of logic circuits that could be customized to perform specific tasks by burning certain circuit paths in the chip. The PAL enabled companies to bring new products to market faster because they could include a number of these customizable parts in the design and make changes to the circuit without redesigning the board.

Trouble was, the PALs had limitations. First, they were small and contained only a few logic gates. And second, they could be customized only once. After that, they were as unchangeable as any other chip; so if you wanted to make another change, you had to get new PALs. (Today's PALs are a *lot* more powerful than the ones we had back in the old days.)

NOTE *Computers compute with the help of logic, and* logic gates *using Boolean algebra are the components on the chip that make this possible. The logic gates are hardwired into the chip while Boolean algebra dictates the form of the gate and how we use it. Electrical signals (the things that make up bits) go into the logic gates and are compared using logical operations such as AND, OR, and NOT. For example, an AND gate compares at least two values and results in TRUE (or 1 using binary notation) if they are both identical. If not, the result is FALSE (or 0).*

Intel's idea was to use a programmable device that could perform many tasks based upon programming. And that device could be reprogrammed at any time, even when it was running another program. They had developed a part that was designed to replace a lot of logic chips. In fact, though, what they had invented was the first single-chip computer. (Well, not quite, since it required some support chips, but it was amazing nonetheless.)

The 4004 was programmed in products to couple the processor with a ROM chip. The program was stored in the ROM, and the computer did whatever task was programmed into the ROM. Later, EPROM (Erasable/Programmable Read-Only Memory) chips were developed. To erase one of the EPROMS, you exposed the logic wafer inside the chip to ultraviolet (UV) light passing through an open window on the top of the chip.

Intel's programmable chip (the 4004) was a great idea, but in the end Busicom backed out, and Intel was left with a part that was developed but had no customers.

What could Intel do?

They sold it to hobbyists, engineers, and anyone with the "bug." Remember the people I was talking about before? The ones who loved technology? They became the first real customers for Intel's 4004 chip. But it wasn't long before they wanted more. You see, Intel never intended to make computers—just a chip that enabled circuits to be made faster and easier. Now they were being asked to take their relatively simple, 4-bit processor and turn it into something that hobbyists could use to make a real computer... a *personal* computer.

So Intel made the 8008—the first 8-bit microprocessor—and the rest is history.

Hobbyists who were passionate about technology were initially Intel's primary customers for this new class of product. Intel sold parts faster than they could make them, because they had customers who were obsessed. Their own engineers joined in the frenzy, which resulted in newer, faster, more capable parts streaming out of the new technology. Computers doubled and tripled in speed and power in a heartbeat. Initially, it was passion for technology that drove the market. But in the end, it was money that drove the market.

More and more people in the computer business were becoming multimillionaires, and soon the drive was on to make better, faster, and cheaper parts because it meant making more money. That's why the computer industry moves so quickly. It's designed to make the makers rich.

But it also makes the end users confused. In the early days of computing, most people had no interest in computers. In fact, most people were only barely aware of them. But with the introduction of a single computer program—VisiCalc, the first "killer app"—people found themselves compelled to buy computers. A company, noticing that its competitors had computers, felt compelled to buy them so as to compete more effectively. And once again, the rest is history.

The whole point of this history lesson is to show how (and why) computers got here as they are, and to explain why technology has advanced so quickly. This is a business in which the only way you can stand still is to "run as fast as you can." So grab your hat, your checkbook, and your old computer—we're going to start running.

Worth Their Weight in Chips

Okay, so now you have a decision to make. Is your computer an old computer?

C'mon, didn't you read the previous section? If you have a computer, you have an old computer. The question is, *how* old is your computer? There's a saying I used to hear when I was a kid: "worth its weight in gold." It meant that something was very valuable. Nowadays, gold is worth about $300 an ounce. That's about the weight of a silver dollar. Today, we have a new measure of value: silicon. Well, not exactly silicon, but the circuits that we implant onto the surface of silicon. Figure 33.2 shows a microprocessor on the tip of a finger, weighing maybe 1/50 of an ounce. Depending upon the actual part, one of these can be worth more than $1000! And sometimes much, much more.

Computers are made of these silicon chips with circuits built into the very structure of the chip (hence, integrated circuits). How much they're worth depends on a lot of factors, but nothing has more influence on the value of a microprocessor than its age. For example, when 80286s were first introduced, they were worth hundreds of dollars. Today they are worth only a few cents.

FIGURE 33.2

A microprocessor on the tip of a finger

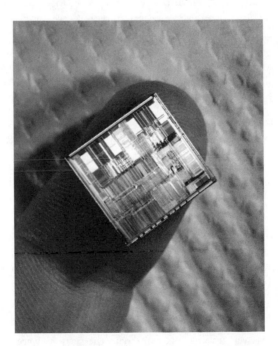

What to Keep and What to Toss

The fact that a computer is old doesn't necessarily mean that you should throw it away lock, stock, and barrel. Let's take a look at which components you can salvage and which ones you should consider replacing.

New Life for an Old Pentium?

Let's take a look at an old 90Hz Pentium system. It includes a Pentium motherboard; 32MB RAM; a 1.2MB, 3½-inch floppy drive; a 124MB hard drive; a 14,400bps modem; a 15-inch VGA monitor; an early inkjet printer; a 4X CD-ROM drive; and ISA sound and video cards.

Why did I start with an older Pentium? Because anything older wouldn't be worth upgrading, and there are almost no parts that you can use to upgrade them. And everything newer can be upgraded. Of course, the newer they are, the easier they are to upgrade.

So what can you do to make this system more current? Here's the list, but be aware that upgrading all these components will cost about the same as putting together a totally new system, will be more trouble, and will not work as well.

"All right," I hear you asking, "if it's a bad idea to upgrade an old Pentium, why should I even read this information?" Because you don't need to replace all the components. The best advice I can give you for a computer as old as one of the early Pentiums is to keep using it, as it is, for as long as it does what you need and as long as the parts keep working. This, by the way, is good advice for any computer that you have. If you need a faster computer, save your data and get a new system. In Chapter 34, "Building the Ultimate Computer," I'll talk about the benefits of buying a new computer versus building one yourself.

If you decide to keep using your old computer but parts such as your CD-ROM drive or monitor start to fail, you can replace some of the parts one or two at a time to keep it alive. So if your old Pentium is still adequate for your needs, but something is broken, here's what you can replace:

Video card   If your old VGA card bites the dust, you can replace it with a new card, but most of the new ones are PCI and AGP. You'll need to search for an old ISA video board to replace your bad one.

Floppy drive   Standard 3½-inch floppy drives haven't changed much over the last several years except that the price is now less than $20, so you should be able to replace a defective one with a minimum of fuss.

Hard drive   If you need to replace your hard drive, make sure to get one that is compatible with your BIOS, or upgrade your BIOS at the same time. Some older machines don't recognize drives larger than 512MB, and an old BIOS may not even recognize your new drive. You should also make sure to purchase the same type of hard drive that you are replacing. Replace a SCSI drive with another SCSI, or IDE with an IDE.

Power supply   This component fails more often than any other in older systems. This is primarily because the power supplies that came with the systems were often designed to meet the needs of the basic system but had very little to spare. So when users added boards or drives, they exceeded the capacity of the supply. Note that the newer P4 requires a power supply with additional power connectors that don't exist on the older power supplies. If the power supply on one of the older systems dies, you may need to get a new case as well, since many of the new power supplies won't fit in older cases—they're too small.

Motherboard   This is it. The big upgrade. When you're done with this one, your faithful old Pentium that ran at a blinding speed of 90MHz will have a new brain. It can even become a Pentium III. But since you'll probably want to replace a lot more than the motherboard if you do this upgrade (putting old, slow parts with a new, fast motherboard is a bad idea), you should probably read the next chapter before proceeding. There you'll learn how to build your ultimate computer from scratch. If you do choose to replace the motherboard, you might have to replace the power supply because there is a good chance the power connectors will be different.

Save Your Data!

When people think of a computer, they generally think of the actual physical equipment—the CPU, monitor, keyboard, and so on. But the fact is, the most important part of your computer is the information that it contains. You can always replace the CPU, the keyboard, or the mouse. But once data is lost, the only way to get it back is to reconstruct it. The process of reconstruction can be, by far, more expensive than the entire computer. It's the information in the computer that makes it *your* computer. It has your bookkeeping, your addresses, your letters, your taxes, and your games—everything that you do with your computer that *makes* it your computer lives in the data.

So when you upgrade your system, make sure that your data follows you. Here's how you do it.

BACKING UP TO REMOVABLE MEDIA

There are a few kinds of removable computer media. There are cartridge hard drives such as the Zip and Jaz drives (shown in Figure 33.3), tape drives such as HP's Colorado drives, and CD writers (and read/write CDs). All of these have their upsides and their downsides. The real benefit to removable media is that you can easily transport your data from one place to another. The only real downside to removable media is that it loads more slowly than it does from your primary hard drive.

FIGURE 33.3

Removable media drives

To move your data to a removable drive such as a Jaz or Zip drive, install the drivers for the unit you have and reboot with the drive connected and powered up. In Windows, it will appear as another drive in your My Computer window. Once installed, every removable drive behaves essentially like another hard drive.

You can also use Windows' Backup Wizard to save your data to a backup drive. To access Backup from Windows 95/98, choose Programs from the Start menu. Then choose Accessories ➢ System Tools ➢ Backup. If it is not there, don't panic. From the Control Panel choose Add/Remove Programs and select the Windows Setup tab. Open the System Tools category and select Backup. If you are using Windows Me, Backup must be installed as a separate application from the Microsoft Windows Me CD. Make sure that you have your backup drive plugged in and ready to go before you begin. Once there, the Backup Wizard will guide you through the process.

BACKING UP TO TAPE

Backing up to a tape drive is similar to backing up to removable media, but since it's a serial device, not random access, it has some subtle differences. You can't just drag and drop files with most tape backup systems. You have to use a backup program to manage the process. Most tape drives come with some kind of backup software. If you don't like the features of the backup program that came with Windows, there are plenty of alternative programs out there to select from.

BACKING UP DIRECTLY TO ANOTHER HARD DRIVE

If you're going to be upgrading to a new hard drive, the fastest and probably best approach is to copy files directly from your old drive to your new one (see Figure 33.4). Most new drives include software to facilitate this. For example, Seagate drives have a program called FileCopy. This program creates an exact duplicate of your old drive's data on your new drive, where it can be run as if it were the original.

FIGURE 33.4

Hooking up both your new and old hard drives to the same system is probably the best way to transfer files from the old drive to the new drive.

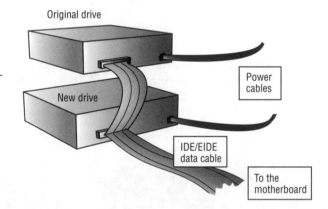

When you install a new drive without removing the old one first, you need to run a program that tells your computer which drive is the old one and which is the new one. Then you set up the drive parameters (it's mostly automatic), partition and format the new drive, and go into Windows. From there, run FileCopy or a similar program, and the computer automatically transfers the files.

Once you're done, you can either remove your old drive or leave it in as a secondary drive. Either way, you switch the new drive to primary (since the newer one is usually both larger and faster), and off you go. If you remove the old drive, you can hold onto it as it is, and you'll have an image backup of your system for emergencies.

You can transfer the entire contents of the old drive to a new one, even if the new drive is not the same capacity, by using a program such as DriveCopy or Norton Ghost. These programs make a sector-by-sector copy of the complete contents, so the new drive looks identical to the old PC. This can be a great time-saver, because you don't have to reinstall Windows and all your programs on the new drive. After copying the old drive onto the new, you can then remove the old drive from the system and discard it, or reformat it and reuse it elsewhere.

Choosing an Upgrade Path

There are many reasons why you might want to upgrade your computer system. Many people upgrade because they learn about a tool or program and decide that they must have it, for one of these reasons:

- Their friend has it.
- They saw it in an ad.
- A salesman said it was cool.

These, by the way, are all the wrong reasons to upgrade. If you find yourself considering an upgrade because you want another "thing" on your computer, you're asking for trouble. The more "things" you have attached to your system, the slower it will perform and the more likely it is to crash. Every time you add another device driver or use up another IRQ or address line, there's a chance that all the other stuff on your system will stop working. (By the way, this is also true of any software you install.)

Most people add software and peripherals to their computers much as they would add a new CD to their music collection. Trouble is, unlike a music CD, programs alter the way your system works. Before you add a program (or anything else) to your system, make sure you really want it and will have a good use for it.

The right way to choose a peripheral or a new program is to find that you need your computer to be able to do something that it can't, then do some research to be sure that the new item will actually provide your computer with that new capability. For example, let's say that you have a true color ISA SVGA card in a machine without PCI or AGP slots. If you go out and buy the latest 3D 4X AGP video card and try to install it in your system, you're in for a nasty shock. It won't be possible. You'll have to take it back to the store and reinstall your older, less capable card.

Getting the picture?

In the preceding scenario, you went to a lot of trouble just to wind up in the same place you began. You logged wasted time and maybe lost money as well. If you had done a little research up front, you could have saved yourself all that time and effort.

If you really need an upgrade, then it's worth it. But if you don't *really* need it, look out—you may be asking for a lot of trouble for nothing. So be careful not to upgrade your computer just because you see or hear of something that sounds interesting. The best decision-making process to use for upgrading your computer is as follows:

1. Decide whether you need new functionality.
2. Research products/tools/techniques to determine which one(s) best meets your needs, and be sure they will integrate easily with your existing system to provide the functionality you seek.
3. Acquire new products/tools/techniques and install necessary components.

Ready to start upgrading? Okay then, let's go.

Upgrading a Computer

Before you begin any type of upgrade to your system—even installing a new software program—be sure that you've backed up all necessary data on your hard drive. If you haven't, stop reading and do it now. Skipping this step would be a terrible mistake.

Planning Your Upgrade

Computer owners usually have one of two basic types of computer systems—a home PC or a business PC (or a combination of the two). While these two categories often involve basically the same hardware, the computers tend to do different kinds of things. One is optimized to do home applications, and the other is optimized for business applications. When planning an upgrade, the decisions you make should be based on the type of system you have.

First, make a checklist of what you need the computer to do. Should it be faster? I know the answer to this is always "yes." But you need to ask yourself how much you're willing to pay for increased speed. Do you need new capabilities? Components that can provide these would include modems, networks, printers, scanners, and video cameras... you get the idea.

The following list includes most traditional computer hardware and peripherals; use it as a guide to create your own checklist for planning your upgrade. You may choose to add other unusual or esoteric components to your own list.

- Motherboard
- Microprocessor
- Memory
- Hard drive
- Floppy drive
- Removable media drive
- Tape drive
- Modem
- Home networking components
- Scanners
- Printers
- Cameras
- TV tuners (enabling you to receive television signals through your computer just like in a television)

The sections that follow discuss some of the individual components that you might consider upgrading.

Motherboards

Although your microprocessor is really the heart of your computer, virtually everything plugs into the motherboard. And today's motherboards have most of the I/O circuits on them as well. Current motherboards have the following:

- IDE controllers for these components:
  - Hard drive(s)

- CD-ROM drive(s)
- Internal removable media drive(s)
- Floppy controller
- Serial ports
- Parallel port
- USB port(s)
- PS/2 keyboard port
- PS/2 mouse port
- Video chipset (on some boards)
- Sound chipset (on some boards)
- PCI expansion slots
- ISA expansion slots (becoming very scarce)
- AGP video slot (on most boards)
- Cache memory
- Memory slots
- Microprocessor socket and support circuits:
  - ZIF socket (on some boards)
  - Variable voltage circuitry
  - Variable processor bus speed

Although some of these items are pretty obvious, some are not so obvious. Let's take a look at what each of these does.

Before going out to buy a brand new motherboard, make sure it will fit your existing case. There are several different form factors for motherboards, which are all designed to fit the various cases that exist. These are broadly classified as AT or ATX.

IDE CONTROLLERS

Most motherboards have two of these, labeled Primary and Secondary. Figure 33.5 shows a typical pair of IDE connectors. By the way, as you may recall from earlier in the book, IDE adapters will talk to both IDE and IDE/ATAPI drives. When you connect the data cables to the IDE connectors, make sure that you align pin 1 of the cable with pin 1 of the connector.

The other end of the data cable goes into the connectors on the appropriate drive. They are also labeled, usually on the bottom of the drive.

When you connect your drives, connect your boot hard drive to the Primary connector. Also, be sure to set it to Master. There's a jumper that determines whether a drive is the Master or the Slave drive, or you can enable Cable Select (CS) and the BIOS will make the decision based on which connector the drive is attached to. In that case, make sure it is attached to the connector at the end of the cable. Every drive has a host adapter built into it that has the capability to control two drives. This allows two drives to share a single data cable. So when you set one of the drives to Slave, it turns its host adapter off. Setting it to Master sets it up to control two drives. On some drives, you need to remove all jumpers for a single drive. Others can control one or two drives if they are set to Master.

FIGURE 33.5

Typical IDE connectors on a motherboard

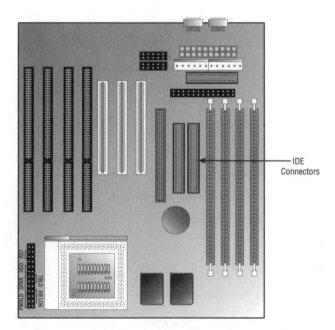

IDE Connectors

MICROPROCESSOR

Choosing an upgrade microprocessor can be a tough decision. At any given moment, a variety of processors are available from several manufacturers. The top two manufacturers are Intel and AMD. Intel, of course, is the market leader. They invented the microprocessor and they lead the pack. That is, they set the standards. Everyone else has to follow the leader. AMD traditionally makes compatible processors that are almost always a little (or sometimes a lot) faster in one way or another than comparable Intel processors.

Another fact to be aware of is that the newest, fastest processors are almost always much more expensive than those that are just a bit slower. For example, recent pricing for a 2GHz Intel Pentium 4 (which was the fastest processor at the time this book was being written) was about $900. The 1.6GHz AMD Athlon, which is rated at 90 percent as fast as the Intel Pentium 4, was about $350—about a third of the price.

FLOPPY CONTROLLER

The floppy controller on the motherboard can control up to two floppy drives. The floppy drives also use a single cable, but instead of setting jumpers on the drives to select which is drive A and which is drive B, the cable itself is modified. The A drive must be plugged into the connector that has a twist in the middle (see Figure 33.6).

FIGURE 33.6

The floppy cable that has a twist in it is for drive A.

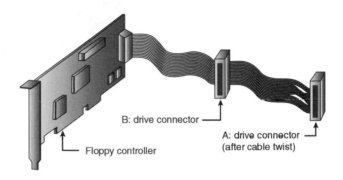

B: drive connector ———

A: drive connector ———
(after cable twist)

Floppy controller

SERIAL AND PARALLEL PORTS

The serial and parallel port cables should be plugged into the motherboard in the same way as the IDE connectors are plugged in (be sure to align pin 1). The trick to installing these connectors is that most are supplied on a metal bar that attaches to a slot in the back of the computer that could hold an expansion card. To avoid losing a potential expansion slot, take the connectors off the metal bar and mount them in the mounting holes in the back of the case, as shown in Figure 33.7.

FIGURE 33.7

Installing the serial and parallel port connectors in the back of the computer

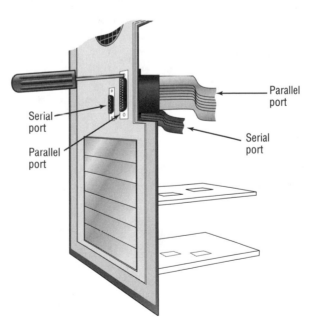

Parallel port

Serial port

Serial port

Parallel port

USB PORTS

Two varieties of USB ports are available. For motherboards that have the USB circuitry onboard, you'll get a pair of connectors, mounted on a metal bar, just like the serial and parallel ports described earlier. In this case, however, leave the connectors on the metal bar—there's no place to attach the USB ports individually on a standard case. The newest version of the USB specification (2.0) is starting to appear on some of the more popular motherboards. If you have the opportunity, opt for the 2.0 USB. It is backward compatible with earlier versions, which means all of your existing USB devices will work on it as well as the newer and faster devices.

For motherboards that don't have USB circuitry onboard, and precious few don't, you can get a USB adapter card that will plug right into a PCI slot.

KEYBOARDS, MICE, PS/2, AND DIN

Now this is a confusing bunch of connectors. Depending on your motherboard, either you will have a single, large DIN connector or you'll have two mini-DIN (PS/2) connectors. The older style keyboards use the larger DIN connectors that haven't been manufactured in years, and new ones use the smaller PS/2-style connectors. The main problem you may run into is that the PS/2 keyboard and mouse connectors look almost exactly the same, so look for the labels before you plug anything into them. And *never, never* force them!

VIDEO AND SOUND

Years ago, personal computers were text-based and had no sound. Then one day Mr. Sim came to America. He brought with him the first Sound Blaster card and he, not Steve Jobs, changed computers forever. In essence, he created multimedia. Today almost every application uses some kind of sound and graphics. Even Microsoft uses multimedia. People understand sound and graphics, and if your system isn't capable of multimedia, you should probably consider upgrading your capability with new sound and video cards. Lots of motherboards today actually have sound and video right on the board. If they do, then all you need to do to set them up is plug them in. All Windows versions from 95 on will identify these ports automatically and prompt you for the included driver disk(s).

PCI, ISA, AND AGP

These are the expansion slots that you'll find on your motherboard. Most new boards are PCI boards. They are the standard for expansion slots because they are much faster than the older-style ISA slots. For several years, even new motherboards included at least a few ISA slots to accommodate some of the older ISA expansion boards. These days, ISA slots have gone the way of all things. The AGP slot on newer motherboards is a high-speed expansion slot that you can use for the new, fast video cards. Figure 33.8 shows the ISA sockets, PCI sockets, and an AGP connector on a motherboard.

Most new motherboards have several kinds of memory and memory slots, such as DIMMs, SIMMs and cache memory (see Figure 33.9). Some of the new P4 boards also have RIMM memory slots. Most boards have at least 256KB of fast cache memory. In most cases, you can increase that to as much as 1MB, and sometimes even 2MB.

NOTE   *Although new motherboards with SIMM memory sockets have become pretty rare, if you have the option of using DIMMs or SIMMs, always choose DIMMs. They are available in faster speeds, and some motherboards that will run at only 66MHz using SIMMs will run at 133MHz with DIMMs.*

FIGURE 33.8

PCI, ISA, and AGP connectors

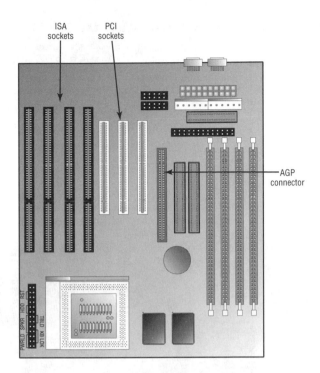

FIGURE 33.9

DIMM sockets and cache memory on the motherboard

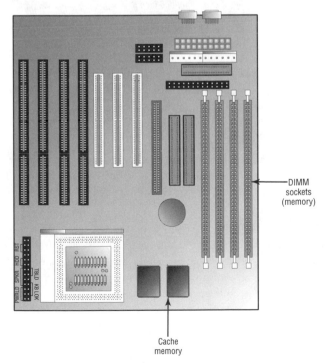

THE MICROPROCESSOR SLOT AND CONTROL CIRCUITRY

The microprocessor socket is very special. It's called a zero insertion force (ZIF) socket, and it's shown in Figure 33.10. It enables you to insert or remove your expensive microprocessor in the socket without putting any stress on its leads. If you look at it closely, you'll see that there's a lever on the side of the socket. When the lever is in the up position, the holes in the plastic top align with the electrical connections below them, so the socket will slide in easily. Once the chip is in place, move the lever to the down (locked) position, and the top of the socket slides over and presses the leads of the processor tightly against the electrical contacts inside the socket.

FIGURE 33.10

A ZIF socket with the microprocessor out and the lever up

Near the ZIF socket, you'll find a few groups of jumpers. By putting the jumpers in the right places, you can set both the voltage and the frequency for the processor. Details are printed in the motherboard manual and often on the motherboard itself.

Making Final Decisions

Okay, so now you're familiar with your motherboard, you know what goes where, and you know how to plug things in. Time to make the final decisions. What new capabilities do you want to add to your system? In this section, you'll take a look at the choices you have and what each does for you.

COMMUNICATION OPTIONS

No matter what kind of computer you have today, you're almost certainly going to want to have communications capabilities. These include Internet access, e-mail, perhaps a home network, and possibly even video conferencing. All of these things are forms of communication.

For the most part, computer communications consist of sending and receiving digital information between computers. In addition to a requirement that both computers be compatible, there are two other limiting factors when it comes to digital information. First, can the computers handle both the type and the speed of the data being sent? Second, can the medium used to connect the computers support the data speed? The *medium*, as you probably know, is the vehicle that carries the data, such as phone lines, cable, or satellite.

Modems

The most basic kind of computer communication today is modem to modem. Modem, by the way, is a word that was created from the term *modulator/demodulator*, which describes what a modem does. During modem communication, the signal is initially digital. The modem receives data from your computer and converts that data into a series of tones (which, by the way, are what you hear as screeches and beeps when the modem is connecting—sometimes referred to as *white noise*). Once the modem connects, the speaker is usually programmed to shut off. It makes that lovely sound only so you know it's trying to connect.

Choosing a modem is pretty easy if all you want to do is connect to your ISP. There are basically two kinds of modems: internal and external. Internal modems plug into a card slot in your motherboard, and external modems connect to a serial port on the outside of your computer. That is, unless you have a USB modem (not common yet). Actually, if I were choosing an external modem, I'd get the USB kind since they won't use up any of my precious COM ports. But frankly, I almost always choose internal modems because they are more convenient. No extra wires to fall over, no extra power connectors to deal with.

Home Networks

Home networks are becoming more and more common these days. Quite a few homes today have more than one computer. A home network enables you to share data as well as resources. For example, with a home network, everyone can print using the same printer. And if you do have more than one printer, any computer connected to the network can print to any printer that is also connected to the network. So if you have a laser printer in your home office, for example, then your son could write a report on his computer and print it on your laser printer (if you'll let him). Similarly, if you want to print some color photos, you could load glossy paper into junior's color inkjet printer and print your photos on that printer.

There are a couple of kinds of home networks. One connects your computers via standard Ethernet cables. Another, which is gaining more acceptance these days, is the phone line network. With the advent of USB technology, home networks that run through USB connections are now possible, although they are typically slower than a conventional 10Mbps Ethernet network.

NOTE *To learn more about USB connections, go back to Chapter 3, "Inside the PC: Pieces of the Picture." And for more information on home networks, check out Chapter 29, "Networking Concepts and Hardware."*

Ethernet networks connect computers via special cables and sometimes hubs. There are two popular Ethernet cabling systems, *twisted-pair* and *coaxial*. Twisted-pair cabling looks like phone wires with a gland problem. The wires are thicker, and the connectors are the same basic shape as telephone cable connectors, only larger. Coaxial cabling is similar to the cable used for cable TV, and uses bayonet-type screw-on connectors. For most home installations, twisted-pair or phone line networks are the best choice. They are far easier to install, and generally are quite a bit less expensive than coaxial.

Phone Line Networks

Phone line networks use your existing telephone wiring. The assumption is that you already have telephone wiring to the same places that your computers will be located. Each computer in your network will need a phone line adapter card. The cards transmit and receive data over the same lines as your phone without interfering with phone service, because they operate at a different frequency than the phones.

As an example, consider Intel's AnyPoint Phone Line Network. They offer all you need to network all of the computers in your home or small office. (Actually, you may need to use your Windows setup CD to load some of the network protocols, so keep it handy.)

To set up the network, all you need to do is plug the cards into the system, use the cables to connect the cards to a nearby telephone jack, and run the setup software. Once the network's installed, you can share files, resources (such as printers and modems), and even drives (including removable media drives).

PLAYING GAMES

Did you know that game playing is the second most popular reason that people buy computers? (The top reason is Internet access.) What do you need to have in order to really get the most out of game play on your computer?

You need a high-performance computer. In fact, video games are really "pushing the envelope" of multimedia. So if you're planning to play games, get a fast 3D video card with at least 16MB of video RAM. You should also get a great sound card, such as Creative Labs' Live card, speakers, the best monitor you can afford, and whatever game controllers you will need to make your game playing more realistic.

The Next Step

Well, that's about it. If you have an older system and you want to convert it to a new system, go through your checklist and replace the parts you want to upgrade. But choose carefully. Remember, never buy more computer than you expect to need right now. Buying parts that you think you may need in the future is usually a waste of money, since those parts will probably be faster, smaller, and less expensive then. And by the way, when it comes to computers, the future can be as soon as tomorrow… or even later on today.

And one final note: If, after reading this chapter, there's more you want to do to your system, read on. As I said earlier, in the next chapter you'll look at building the ultimate computer. Of course that, too, is a moving target. So all I can really do is give you the basics, since by the time you get this book, there's almost certainly going to be yet another generation of components.

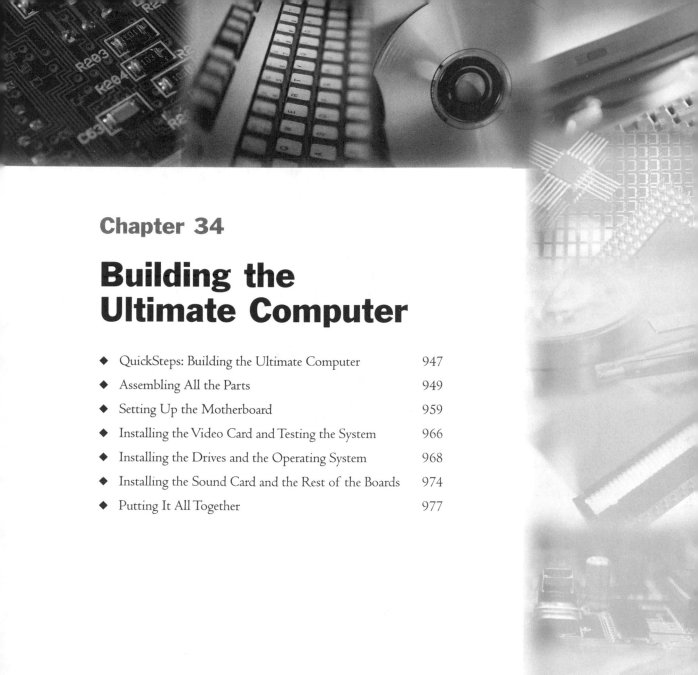

Chapter 34

Building the Ultimate Computer

◆ QuickSteps: Building the Ultimate Computer   947

◆ Assembling All the Parts   949

◆ Setting Up the Motherboard   959

◆ Installing the Video Card and Testing the System   966

◆ Installing the Drives and the Operating System   968

◆ Installing the Sound Card and the Rest of the Boards   974

◆ Putting It All Together   977

Introduction

WELL, FOLKS, THIS IS it. In this chapter you're going to build the ultimate computer. Sound like a tall order? All right, I'll admit that building any system from scratch is a big project. But by now, you've already done the toughest part: figuring out what to put into your ultimate system. (You have decided, haven't you?)

In fairness, I must make you aware of the fact that the ultimate computer may not necessarily be one you build from scratch. Due to the tremendous price pressure put on PC manufacturers, you now can buy a name-brand computer for less than the cost of building one. In the heyday of computers, there was a high profit margin in the name-brand computers—not any more. At the time I am writing this, I priced out a custom-built (by me, that is) 1.7GHz Intel Pentium 4 computer with 128MB of RDRAM, high-performance 20GB hard drive, etc., for about $1100. When I browsed around the online inventory at the Dell Factory Outlet, I found the same system (with a three-year warranty) for about $1000. The Dell computer arrives tomorrow. Still, there are a lot of compelling reasons to build your own computer, so let's jump into it.

QuickSteps

Building the Ultimate Computer

Because so many components are involved, this series of QuickSteps is only an overview of the steps necessary to build a computer. Refer to the appropriate section in this chapter for the details of each step; refer to the appropriate chapter for more information on the individual devices and hardware being installed.

BE PREPARED

Before you start, there are some things you may need on hand. These include:

- ◆ The documentation that comes with the components. I can't emphasize this strongly enough. Although the procedures I lay out are correct in the general sense, the manuals that come with your hardware give you a lot more specific information that you should abide by.

- ◆ Containers for screws and other small objects you don't want to lose.

- ◆ Software, including an operating system such as Windows 98SE.

- ◆ Lots of room to work with.

- ◆ A clean tabletop.

- ◆ All of the hardware that is going to become your new computer.

- ◆ Patience.

- ◆ More patience.

- ◆ Device drivers required by individual components, such as a modem or video card.

---

1. Gather all your parts.

2. Open the case and remove the power supply and drive chassis.

3. Set up your motherboard.

    - ◆ Install the CPU.

    - ◆ Install main memory.

TIP   It's a good idea to connect everything you can outside the case first and test each component as you install it. Only when you're sure everything works should you disassemble the test setup and install everything inside the case. (That's why, even though you're putting everything together here, the last step is to "put it all together.") This approach makes troubleshooting much easier.

4. Install the video card (if the motherboard doesn't have integrated video) and test it.

5. Install the hard drive(s) and floppy drive.

6. Configure the BIOS.

7. Install your CD-ROM or DVD drive.

8. Install the operating system.

9. Install the sound card (if the motherboard doesn't have integrated audio).

10. Install your other expansion boards, such as an internal modem and DVD decoder board.

11. Put it all together:

   ◆ Install the motherboard.

   ◆ Install the power supply.

   ◆ Attach the add-on boards.

   ◆ Install the drives.

   ◆ Conduct another system check.

   ◆ Install the rest of the boards.

   ◆ Install the parallel and serial port connectors.

   ◆ Connect the front panel lights and speaker.

Step 1: Assemble All the Parts

The first thing to do is look over all the parts you have, just to make sure that you've got everything you need. I'll briefly recap what you should look for when you go out to buy the items discussed in this section, but almost everything listed here has already been covered in more detail earlier on in the book. So if you want more information, check the index or table of contents for pointers.

Computer Case

There's more to this important item than meets the eye. The case provides a framework for your whole system. It's the main part of the computer that you'll see, and it includes the power supply that will run your computer. So choose one that looks nice (if that is important to you), has lots of room to work in, and is sturdy and solidly built. You can choose from a wide variety of case styles these days. There are even cases with translucent plastic case covers reminiscent of the iMac. Another feature that is finally becoming popular with case manufacturers is the tool-free modular case. This kind of case usually costs a little more than the standard sheet-metal wonder, but it makes assembling and reconfiguring a breeze. For example, a common feature in this style of case is a slide-out compartment to hold the hard drives, CD/DVD ROM, and floppy drive. It allows you to assemble everything outside the case and then slide the entire module into the case as a single unit. Figure 34.1 shows an excellent case. The power supply is up out of the way of the rest of the system, and the metal module frame that holds the drives is removable.

FIGURE 34.1

Computer case with removable drive frame

Notice that the power supply is at the top of the case. Always make sure that the power supply is near the top if you are getting a tower case. This is important because heat rises, and the fan in the power supply pulls air out of the top of the case; cooler air is pulled in through the bottom. A power supply near the middle or bottom of the case would draw heat across the CPU, drives, or whatever is between the fan and the top of the case.

Depending on your personal taste and needs, there are several different types and sizes of cases you can purchase. Above all, make sure you match the case with the motherboard you plan to purchase. Here is an overview of common case styles:

Desktop   This type of case lies flat on its widest side, and people typically set their monitor on top of it.

Slim-line   Like a desktop model but squashed so it's not as tall.

Mini-tower   This case stands up (think monolith) and is fairly short with perhaps two large and two small externally accessible bays.

Midsized tower   Like a mini-tower but slightly taller, with a few more bays.

Tower (or full tower)   A big tower case with lots of expansion bays, suitable for power users or network servers.

Plan ahead and get a case with enough bays to hold all the equipment you plan to install, such as hard drives, floppy drives, and a CD/DVD-ROM drive. Table 34.1 shows the common types of computer cases and how many internal and external bays they have.

NOTE   Table 34.1 has two columns, Internal Bays and External Bays, which warrant further explanation. Internal bays hold devices that don't require external access to operate, such as a hard drive. Once you install a device in an internal bay and put the computer case back together, you can't get at that device without removing the cover. Internal bays are primarily used for additional hard drives. An external bay is designed to hold a device that requires external access to operate, such as a floppy or CD-ROM drive. Both of these examples require access to "the outside world" because you must be able to insert and extract floppy disks and CD-ROM discs to use the drives. For example, if you plan on installing two hard drives, a floppy drive, a CD/DVD-ROM, and an internal Zip drive, you will need at least two internal and three external bays.

TABLE 34.1: COMMON COMPUTER CASE TYPES AND SIZES

CASE	SIZE	EXTERNAL BAYS (HARD DRIVES, ETC.)	INTERNAL BAYS (FLOPPY DRIVE, CD-ROM)
Full tower	Large	6+	3–5+
Midsized tower	Medium	5	2–4
Mini-tower	Small	4	2–3
Desktop	Small	4	1–2
Slim-line	Smallest	3	1–2

Finally, you must consider what motherboard form factor you will be using and buy a case that it will fit into. Cases are classified by motherboard form factor categories: AT, Baby AT, ATX, and Mini ATX. An AT motherboard will fit only into an AT case. It is large and only seen on 386 motherboards or earlier. The AT motherboard was replaced by the Baby AT form factor, which was the most popular case and motherboard until 1997. Baby AT motherboards have a single, full-sized keyboard (DIN) connector soldered onto the board. The serial and parallel port connectors are almost always attached using ribbon cables to a connector on the motherboard. The Baby AT board has been replaced by the ATX and Mini ATX form factor board.

Motherboard

The motherboard serves as the basis of your PC, so it's important that you choose one with the features you need to put everything else in place. Here are some factors to consider when choosing a motherboard:

Processors accepted This is your primary decision factor. Choose the processor model and speed that you want to build your system around first and shop only for motherboards that accept that processor. Both the AMD and Intel Web sites offer listings of approved motherboards for their processors.

Baby AT versus ATX form factor Make sure the motherboard matches up with the case in this regard. ATX is the newer type and has a number of advantages over the Baby AT, including better cooling, better power management, and onboard parallel and serial port connectors (so you don't have to run ribbon cables from the motherboard to the connectors inside the case).

Type of memory used If you want to reuse memory from an old system, make sure the motherboard will support it. Many new motherboards support only a certain memory form factor and speed of memory, such as 100MHz or 133MHz; your old SIMMs and DIMMs may not work in such a motherboard. Remember that our goal is to build the ultimate computer, so don't downgrade the computer too much to accommodate your old memory. The cost of memory, like everything else, has plummeted in the past few years.

Number of ISA and PCI slots Newer motherboards have phased out ISA slots. That's fine, unless you have old ISA devices, such as a modem, network card, or sound card that you were planning to reuse in this system. If you are considering reusing your ISA cards, keep in mind that this chapter is about building the *ultimate* computer—any ISA cards you have are nearly four years old and, most important, do not support Plug and Play. Before you agonize over losing your ISA cards, remember that replacement PCI cards don't cost as much these days as the ISA cards they are replacing.

USB support This is almost a no-brainer these days—all motherboards have it. But some motherboards offer two USB ports, while others offer four. Four is better, obviously. Try to get a motherboard that supports the newest version of USB, version 2.0.

Built-in video Some motherboards come with a built-in video card. If the motherboard is made by Intel, the integrated graphics card is excellent. If you buy a cheaper off-brand motherboard, ask about the graphics capability of the integrated graphics chip. If it is really poor, you can usually disable it in the BIOS if you want to use a third-party video card. Many motherboards offer an AGP slot into which you can put a replacement video card (see below). Remember that unless you are building this computer to play really high-end 3D graphic games, the integrated video is usually more than adequate.

AGP slot   AGP is the latest and greatest (and fastest) system bus type, used only for video cards. Make sure the motherboard has an AGP video slot unless you plan to use built-in video. The current version for AGP is called either 4X or version 2.0.

Built-in sound   Some motherboards have a built-in sound card, often an Ensoniq model (a division of Creative Labs, the Sound Blaster people). It's good enough for casual use, but those with serious sound demands, such as gamers or musicians, may find it inadequate. Like with the built-in video, you can install a high-end card and the integrated sound can usually be disabled in the BIOS if you don't want it.

Video Card

Video cards are one of the hidden bottlenecks in computers. You can have the fastest system (you're building one), but if you use a slow video card, it'll still perform like it's on vacation in the Bahamas.

For your ultimate system, you'll use an AGP video card with lots of built-in video RAM. Recall that AGP is a type of system bus corresponding to a slot on the motherboard. You may see both PCI and AGP video cards for sale when you shop. If your motherboard will accept an AGP model, that's what you want; if not, PCI will do. AGP performs somewhat better because it has a faster path to the processor than PCI.

When you go to buy a video card, the three basic things you should look for initially are speed, memory, and 3D capability.

Speed on video cards is measured in lots of different ways. One is a measurement of "millions of polygons per second." Polygons are the shapes used to create 3D graphics. The more polygons per second, the faster the card can produce images.

Another speed measurement that is often listed is something called the "frame rate." A frame in computer graphics terms is the same as a single frame on movie film. To get smooth, realistic, full-motion video, you should have a frame rate of at least 30 frames per second, which is comparable to the number of frames per second you see in a movie at the theater. As the frame rate goes down, the image gets jumpy. For a business system that isn't going to be playing a lot of graphic-intensive games, a rate of 15 frames per second would be minimally acceptable.

Video cards have their own built-in memory that's used for video processing. The higher the resolution and the greater the color depth, the more video memory is required for that operating mode. For example, a video card with 2MB would be able to display 16.7 million colors at 800×600 resolution, but only 256 colors at 1024×768 resolution. The amount of memory a card has nothing to do with its speed of performance.

In case you're interested, here's how the maximum resolution/color depth is calculated. If you have a 16-color display, you need 4 bits to control each dot because 16 combinations are possible with a 4-digit binary number (2 to the 4th power, or 16). If you multiply the number of dots in the resolution by the number of bits required for each dot, you have the amount of memory required to display that resolution. For example, 640×480 with 16 colors would be $640 \times 480 \times 4$, or 1,228,800 bits. There are 8 bits in a byte, so that would be 153,600 bytes (approximately 154KB). Therefore, if your video card had 1MB, you could have any of the following combinations: 640×480 in 24-bit color, 800×600 in 16-bit color, 1024×768 in 8-bit color (256 colors), or 1280×1024 in 4-bit color (16 colors). Most video cards today come with a minimum of 4MB, which should be plenty unless you have a huge monitor that you want to operate in very high resolutions with 24-bit color depth. (If that's the case, get out your calculator and use the formula I just described to decide what you need.)

You also need to think about inputs and outputs. The basic function of a video card is to accept data from a computer and to output images to a video display. But many video cards today do a lot more. Some accept video input from video cameras and output to television sets, and others will output to the new digital flat-panel displays. If you think you might be interested in any of those capabilities, make sure you shop with them in mind.

Sound Cards

People love for their PCs to make noise—to play music, to make game sounds, to talk back to them. And who do we have to thank for it? Creative Labs and their amazing Sound Blaster cards. Okay, there are other sound cards out today. But the Sound Blaster was the first, and for a long time, it's been the best. They made the rules for sound cards, much as Hayes made the rules for smart modems. So today, even though Hayes is long gone, their modem's AT instruction set is still the standard (along with a lot of new extensions). And, as far I can see, Creative Labs will be with us for a long time to come, and the Sound Blaster's standard will continue to be the template for all other sound cards.

When you go out to buy a sound card, the first thing to look for is Sound Blaster compatibility (unless, of course, you're getting a genuine Sound Blaster of some sort). If you get a card that isn't Sound Blaster–compatible, there's a chance it won't work with some of the programs you may want to run.

The next thing to look for is the card's specifications. There are three factors to be concerned about with a sound card—its number of bits, its wavetable capability, and its input and output jacks:

Number of bits   Almost all sound cards today are 16-bit or 32-bit cards. Don't accept an 8-bit card.

Wavetable capability   There are two kinds of sound cards: FM synthesis and wavetable synthesis. The latter is preferable. Wavetable cards have prerecorded, built-in sounds, such as the sounds of various instruments playing different notes. (FM synthesis cards simulate those notes instead, which doesn't sound as good.) Wavetable cards commonly have 32, 64, or 128 voices that they can play at once.

NOTE   *If you hear of a sound card that has 16 in its name, it is probably referring to its bits and it probably does not contain wavetable synthesis (check the box to be sure). If, on the other hand, there is 64 or 128 in the name, the numbers probably refer to the number of wavetable voices.*

Input and output   The important question is this: does the card have the jacks you want? Jacks come in many varieties, and not everyone needs every kind. You will, at the minimum, want a speaker output, a microphone port, and line in/line out. You may also want to look for MIDI input, which enables you to plug in a keyboard or other digital instrument, and an auxiliary input.

Most sound cards also have a built-in joystick port like the one shown in Figure 34.2. Joysticks are primarily for games, but they can also be used for some accessibility programs that let people with disabilities use a PC. Joysticks don't really have anything to do with sounds but have traditionally appeared on sound cards because people who like sounds usually like games too.

FIGURE 34.2

Joystick port on the sound card

Modems

Want to connect to the Internet? To get on, you need a device that will connect your computer to it. For most of us, unless you have broadband access (cable modem or ADSL), this is going to be some kind of modem. You really need a fax modem if you are using your computer as a fax machine. One of my clients also needs a dial-up modem to access an older-style state service that tracks bills going through the state legislature.

The traditional type of modem is a modulator/demodulator that translates digital signals from the PC to analog format for transmission over a phone line. That's the kind that most people have, and that's what I think of when I hear the term "modem." Other kinds of modems are available today, such as cable modems and DSL modems, but these are not really modems in the strict sense of the word. Like a modem, they do connect you to the Internet or other online service, but they do so differently. Rather than converting between analog and digital signals, they simply pass along the digital information as-is across a network or digital phone line.

If you're getting a standard modem, the things you should look for are the speed (almost all are 56K), data-translation capability (these days you should get V.92), and any extra features you may want to have, such as voice and fax. Most modems today do faxing, but not all have voice capabilities. This allows you to hook up a speaker and microphone so that the computer will operate as a speakerphone or answering machine. You may also want to get a modem that can handle a video camera so you can have two-way videophone communications.

The final decision you need to make regarding your modem is whether to get an internal or external one. External modems have LEDs on them (see Figure 34.3) that let you see what the modem is doing from one moment to another. They also don't use any of the system power or system slots. On the other hand, most of us don't need to know exactly what the modem is doing and rarely use up every slot in our systems. Also, an external modem uses up either a serial port (there are only two of them) or a USB port, which will cost you more money.

For these reasons, and because I don't like to have so many extra things hung on the outside of the computer, I usually recommend internal modems. For this system, that's what you'll use.

By the way, don't think you can save a few dollars by using a generic modem. Why? When using a modem, the driver is very important, and brand-name modems tend to have better-written drivers than the off-brand ones. In my opinion, 3Com offers some of the best available.

For my dream PC, I wouldn't go with a standard modem at all—I'd spring for a cable or DSL connection. But if that's not available (it depends on your location), my choice would be a 3Com V.92 56K modem.

FIGURE 34.3

External modem showing indicator lights

Hard Drive

The hard drive holds the most valuable thing in your computer—your data. Choose your new drive carefully. The drive should be fast, reliable, and large enough to handle more than double the data you'll need to store.

"Double?" you say? Yep, double. Fact is, once a drive gets half full, it starts to slow down. So (for example) if you think you'll need 20GB, get a 40GB or larger drive.

NOTE *When you get a hard drive, buy it as a complete kit. That way, you'll get all of the extra bits and pieces you need to install it easily. For example, mounting rails are not always needed, but they're great to have on hand if you discover you need them for the slot you're trying to mount the drive into in your case.*

Hard disks have two critical performance measurements:

Average access time   The time it takes for the drive head to reach and read the average bit of data, measured in milliseconds. Lower is better. A decent speed is 8ms.

Data transfer rate   How quickly data moves from the hard disk to memory is expressed as the rotational speed of the hard drive. Higher is better. At this time, the two rotational speeds being offered on hard drives are 5400 and 7200 rpm. While higher rotational speed can produce higher data transfer rates, the difference in performance isn't as directly related as it may appear. As the rotational speed increases, there is an increase in latency, because it is more difficult for the drive to extract the data sequentially from the faster spinning disk. The result is that the 7200-rpm drive transfers data faster, but the increase isn't earthshaking.

Floppy drive   Floppy drives are being used less and less these days. Still, they're cheap and you should have one installed if only for the purposes of having a way to boot the system up for diagnostic purposes.

Zip Drive

Although the Zip drive is more of a marketing achievement than an engineering achievement, it is, nevertheless, useful for transferring large files. Depending on the model, Zip disks hold either 100 or 250MB of data, which is more than enough capacity to transfer even the largest graphic files, Power-Point presentations, or other files for business or pleasure.

When you buy your Zip drive, I recommend getting at least one 10-pack of disks. First of all, most dealers will give you a deal if you buy them when you're getting the drive. And second, you'll want them later. I usually get the ones that come in a variety of colors. This makes it easy for me to see quickly which disk I want.

CD-ROM/DVD Drive

Now this is something that always gets me excited. Don't ask me why. I guess that I'm still a kid when it comes to movies, but the technology of DVD movies is just plain incredible.

DVD drives can hold more than two hours of high-quality, full-motion picture video as well as CD-quality, 3D stereo sound! And I can watch it on my computer (my own personal movie theater) or connect it to a big-screen TV and hi-fi stereo system and share it with my friends.

So if you get a DVD drive, you can use any of the standard-format CDs or DVDs. The kinds of things to look for when you go out to buy a DVD drive are speed and features.

Now, when I say "features," I'm not kidding. DVD drives can be purchased as a drive only or they can be purchased as a kit. With the speed of today's processors, it is no longer necessary to buy the kit that contains the hardware decoder. The software decoder that is included with nearly every DVD-ROM drive is more than capable of providing all of the features found in hardware decoders. In fact, hardly anyone sells the DVD hardware bundles (kits) anymore.

So, why do you need decoding? When the DVD image is put onto the disc, the information is compressed so that the manufacturer can fit more stuff on it. This stuff includes alternate languages (yes, Kermit the Frog speaks Cantonese on some DVDs) and different screen proportions, such as standard and wide-screen (also called letterbox). They also usually include the promos and trailers, and sometimes feature extra goodies, such as a director's cut of the movie or behind-the-scenes information.

Anyway, the data on the DVD disc has to be decoded. Two kinds of decoders are available: software and hardware. In practice, as long as your computer is running at a speed of 200MHz or better, you will see excellent results with the software decoders. I highly recommend the PowerDVD by CyberLink (`http://www.gocyberlink.com/english/index.asp`). This software application is hands-down the best you can get for your DVD drive. Of course, you can pay more and get a hardware decoder.

The hardware decoder decodes the data on the DVD with very little burden on the CPU. Remember that even though this is the ultimate computer, your computer is fast enough to produce excellent movies with software decoders.

Networking

You may think that just because you have a home system or a small office system, you don't need networking. Well, you may want to think again.

The only people who don't really need a local area network are people with just one computer. Everyone else will benefit from it. This is true even if the other computer is your kid's computer. A second system can really save you if you ever crash. One of the best things you can do with your network is back up the data from one computer onto another. Or better yet, back it up onto a removable media drive that's connected to another computer. Then, if one of the systems goes down (I should say *when* it goes down, since eventually they all do), you can go over to the other computer, download the files you need from the removable media drive, and continue working while the sick one is being revived. And, by the way, be sure to install the drivers for the removable media drive on both machines so that it can be run from either computer.

Now, getting back to networking. A lot of options are available for networking (as you may recall from Chapter 29, "Networking Concepts and Hardware"). The fastest of these today is Ethernet. So, as you probably guessed (ultimate computer, you know the routine), you're getting Ethernet.

To set up a small Ethernet network, you will need the following, most of which can be purchased together in some sort of network starter kit at your local PC store.

A network interface card (NIC) for each PC Two speeds are available: 10Base-T and 100Base-T. 100Base-T is better and faster, but most of these cards support both speeds and are called 10/100. This is the best choice and they are not expensive.

Hub You'll need a hub to connect the various PCs and networked devices together. Be sure you get one with room for expansion. For example, if you currently have three PCs, get a five-device switch.

Cables You'll need a network cable to run between each NIC and the hub. Check the plugs on the NIC and the hub, but you'll probably want RJ-45 plugs on the cable. The cable is referred to a Cat-5 cable. The *Cat* part has nothing to do with furry felines but rather the standard, which is Category 5.

Extra Interfaces

The idea of extra interfaces might surprise you. Don't worry, you'll use them later—for now, just get them. One is USB, pictured in Figure 34.4, which you may already have built into your motherboard. It has become the standard interface, like serial and parallel, and all of the new motherboards have them. A lot of new devices are being offered with USB connections, and they make adding other devices to the system very simple—no IRQs or other complications to consider. Just plug it in and the system recognizes it.

The other connection I'm recommending is FireWire, also known as IEEE 1394. This new interface is quite fast, and for now, it's the only way to get (for example) full-motion digital video from a DV camera. If you aren't concerned about getting the video as a digital signal, you can use a standard NTSC or S-video interface, but neither is as sharp as digital.

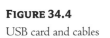

FIGURE 34.4

USB card and cables

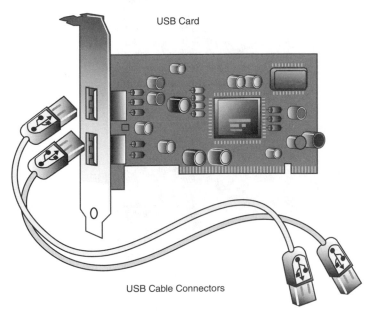

Step 2: Start with the Case

Now that you have everything you need and you're ready to roll, you need to find a large, open space that's big enough for you to open the case and work on any side of it easily.

Get a couple of cups, an egg carton, or some other convenient containers to hold all of the loose screws that you'll be taking out of the computer case. Typically, there are at least two sizes of screws used in computers. If you have more than one container, you can keep them separated by size.

You're using a tower case for the ultimate computer. Find the cover screws and take them all out (see Figure 34.5). Leave the screws for the power supply in place for now.

TIP   *The power supply screws will generally be only in the back panel of the case, while the case screws will go through the cover and the back panel and will be nearer the outer perimeter of the back.*

You can mount the motherboard directly into the case and do all your diagnostic testing from there, but it can sometimes be difficult to work with a motherboard when it's down inside there. That's why I like to test the motherboard before I mount it in the case. To do so, you may need to remove the power supply from the case, because the power supply is required for testing (you've gotta have some power to fire it up and see if it works). You can try leaving the power supply in the case and see whether the cables will reach to where you have the motherboard sitting, but it's probably easiest just to undo the couple of screws holding the power supply in the case and pop it on out. On an AT case, the power switch is screwed to the front of the case; you can remove it or leave it in place if the cables will reach.

Once the cover is off (put it somewhere you won't trip over it), you can see inside the cabinet.

FIGURE 34.5

Removing the
cover screws from
a tower case

TIP   During the initial configuration and diagnostics (before putting the motherboard into the case), some people like to set it on a book or box that is about 2 inches high and roughly 9 × 11 inches. You can even use the box that the motherboard came in for this purpose. This will help later when you're installing circuit cards in the motherboard because it allows you to press a card down firmly without bending the little metal lip that may hang down from a circuit card past the bottom of the case when the cover is off.

Step 3: Set Up the Motherboard

Now remove your motherboard from its protective plastic bag and open up the motherboard manual that came with it. This is an extremely important document. When you're done here, put it in a safe place. It contains information that you must have to be able to use the motherboard.

Installing the CPU

Take a look at your CPU. It is essential that the CPU socket on the motherboard match the CPU form factor that you have chosen.

Open up the motherboard manual to the page that shows a diagram of the motherboard layout. It should be labeled with all of the locations of the various control jumpers, interface connectors, and components. Find the jumpers that control the CPU and system voltage. Figure 34.6 shows a motherboard with a Super7 processor slot; your motherboard may look different.

FIGURE 34.6

The motherboard layout showing all of the major components, connectors, and jumper locations

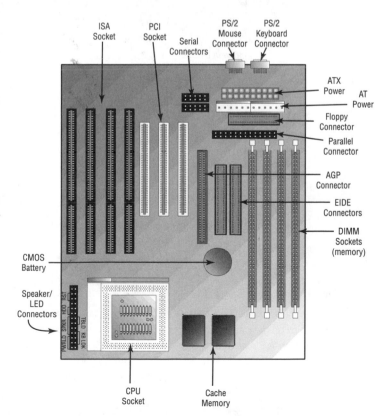

SETTING THE VOLTAGES

Now take a look at the page that shows the jumper positions for different voltages on the motherboard. Most motherboards do not have voltage selections, but just in case you have an older motherboard, the following information will be of great help to you. The *core voltage* is the voltage that the CPU uses for its internal operation. The *I/O voltage* is the voltage it uses to communicate with the rest of the system. Depending on your motherboard, you will need to set either one or the other of these voltages.

To set the voltages, you'll need to put some jumpers in the right places on the motherboard. You should find a table in your motherboard manual that looks a lot like the one in Figure 34.7. Placing or removing these jumpers sets the correct voltages for the CPU and system I/O. Set them incorrectly, and you can say goodbye to your expensive CPU—so set the jumpers carefully.

FIGURE 34.7

The motherboard's voltage settings table

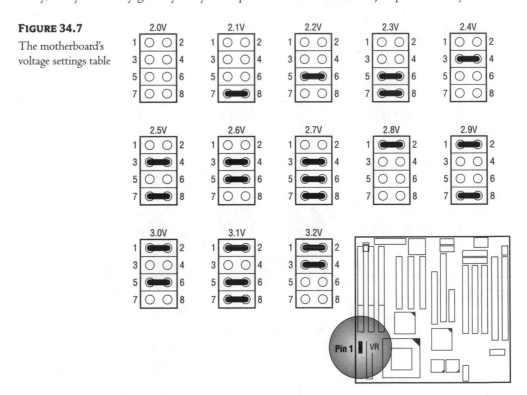

Setting the Clock Speed

Before you go any further, on the outside chance that your CPU isn't imprinted with information about which frequency at which to set it, the motherboard manual usually contains a table that covers that information for most current processors. Table 34.2 is an example of such a table. (This is just an example; you should use information relevant to your CPU.)

TABLE 34.2: OPERATING FREQUENCIES AND MULTIPLIERS FOR CPUS

CPU TYPE	FREQUENCY (MHZ)	SYSTEM BUS CLOCK (MHZ)	MULTIPLIER
Intel			
Pentium 166 MMX	166	66	2.5
Pentium 200 MMX	200	66	3
Pentium 233 MMX	233	66	3.5
Celeron 400	400	66	6
Celeron 433	433	66	6.5
Celeron 466	466	66	7
Celeron 500	500	66	7.5
Celeron 533	533	66	8
Pentium ll 233 MMX	233	66	3.5
Pentium ll 266 MMX	266	66	4
Pentium ll 300 MMX	300	66	4.5
Pentium ll 333 MMX	333	66	5
Pentium ll 350 MMX	350	100	3.5
Pentium ll 400 MMX	400	100	4
Pentium ll 450 MMX	450	100	4.5
Pentium lll 450 MMX	450	100	4.5
Pentium lll 500 MMX	500	100	5
Pentium lll 550 MMX	550	100	5.5
Pentium lll 600 MMX	600	100	6
Pentium lll 533B MMX	533	133	4
Pentium lll 600B MMX	600	133	4.5
Pentium lll 550E MMX	550	100	5.5
Pentium lll 500E MMX	550	100	5
Pentium lll 600E MMX	600	100	6
Pentium lll 650 MMX	650	100	6.5
Pentium lll 700 MMX	700	100	7
Pentium lll 750 MMX	750	100	7.5
Pentium lll 800 MMX	800	100	8

Continued on next page

TABLE 34.2: OPERATING FREQUENCIES AND MULTIPLIERS FOR CPUS *(continued)*

CPU TYPE	FREQUENCY (MHz)	SYSTEM BUS CLOCK (MHz)	MULTIPLIER
Intel			
Pentium III 533EB MMX	533	133	4
Pentium III 600EB MMX	600	133	4.5
Pentium III 667 MMX	667	133	5
Pentium III 733 MMX	733	133	5.5
Pentium III 800EB MMX	800	133	6
Pentium 4	900	200	4.5
AMD			
K6-166	166	66	2.5
K6-200	200	66	3.5
K6-233	233	66	3.5
K6-266	266	66	4
K6-300	300	66	4.5
K6-II-300	300	66	4.5
K6-III-300	300	100	3
K6-II-333	333	95	3.5
K6-II-350	350	100	3.5
K6-II-366	366	66	5.5
K6-II-400	400	100	4
K6-III-400	400	100	4
K6-III-450	450	100	4.5
Athlon 600	600	200	3
Athlon 650	650	200	3.25
Athlon 700	700	200	3.50
Athlon 750	450	200	3.75
Athlon 800	800	200	4
Athlon 850	850	200	4.25
Athlon 900	900	200	4.5
Athlon 950	950	200	4.75
Athlon 1000	1000	200	5

Setting the clock speed is very similar to setting the voltages. Let's say that the CPU runs at 900MHz. If the motherboard manufacturer tried to make all of the components operate at 900MHz using today's technology, you'd have a system either too expensive to buy or one that would work only if it were all on a single chip. Bottom line: the rest of the system has to run slower. How much slower? Well, bus speeds in today's systems range from 66MHz to 200MHz. On a 900MHz Athlon system, for example, the bus speed is 200MHz (as you saw in Table 34.2).

The Multiplier

Most motherboards sold today can autodetect the processor speed, but you must tell others by setting a multiplier jumper on the motherboard. You can refer to Table 34.2 for some processor and multiplier settings; always check the documentation for the correct setting for your motherboard. Figure 34.8 shows some sample jumper settings you might find in a motherboard manual. The multiplier for a 900MHz processor running on a board with a 200MHz bus, for example, would be 4.5.

FIGURE 34.8

A sample CPU clock multiplier settings table; check your motherboard manual for yours.

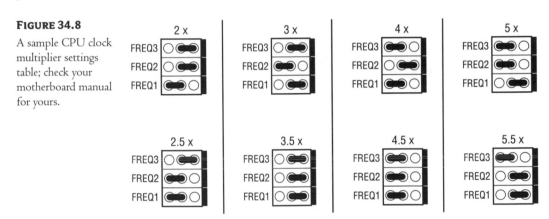

Plugging in the CPU

All your CPU settings should be complete now, so get ready to install the CPU. Two main types of CPU connectors are in use today, and you should have already chosen the correct motherboard for the type of CPU you have.

Pin Grid Array (PGA) A PGA is a square, zero insertion force (ZIF) grid of holes with a little handle that lifts up to open and goes down to close. The processor has little pin "feet" that fit down into the holes. There are various sizes of these:

◆ Socket7 is what the original Pentiums used.

◆ A variation called Super7 is the current standard and is used by many AMD and Cyrix processors.

◆ There is also a Socket PGA-370 version that some of the newer Celeron processors use.

Slots These slots look somewhat like the slots in the motherboard that circuit cards fit into, but they're designed to accept only a processor. The processor is in a rectangular cartridge that fits snugly into the slot. Sometimes there are plastic support brackets at either end of the slot to ensure that the processor doesn't fall over. You typically mount a cooling fan to the outside of the plastic cartridge.

- Slot 1 holds Pentium II processors, which come in a cartridge. Inside the cartridge are the processor and the L2 cache, both mounted on a common circuit board. It can also accept the older type of Celeron and the Pentium III processor, which was mounted on a bar circuit board (no plastic cartridge around it), with a fan strapped directly to the processor chip.

- Slot 2 holds higher-end Pentium II, Pentium III, and Pentium 4 cartridges and also Xeon processors. It's the same design but a larger slot and a larger cartridge.

To install a PGA-type processor, lift the lever on the CPU's ZIF socket. Then carefully align the pins on the CPU with the holes in the socket, as shown in Figure 34.9.

FIGURE 34.9

Aligning the CPU pins with the holes in the ZIF socket

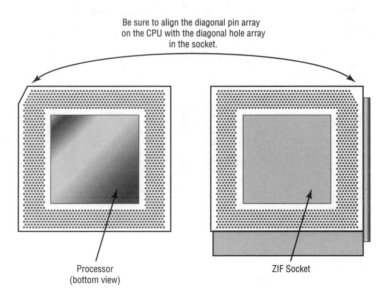

Be sure to align the diagonal pin array on the CPU with the diagonal hole array in the socket.

Processor
(bottom view)

ZIF Socket

WARNING *Be sure to align the holes correctly. One corner of the CPU has a pin missing and one corner of the socket has a hole missing. If you don't align the CPU properly, it won't go in correctly, and you may damage one or more of the delicate pins, making the CPU unusable.*

The CPU should fit into the socket with absolutely no resistance. If it's tight, check the locking lever to make sure it's not partly locked. It should be up and back, as shown in Figure 34.10.

Once the CPU is fully seated in its socket, lower the lever and lock it into place. It should click into position behind a molded clip in the socket's side.

FIGURE 34.10

Opening the locking lever fully

Next, squeeze a bit of heat sink compound from its tube into the center of the metal top of the CPU and put the heat sink/fan on top of the CPU, as shown in Figure 34.11. Finally, clip the heat sink/fan on both sides, and you're done installing the CPU.

FIGURE 34.11

Installing the heat sink/fan on the CPU

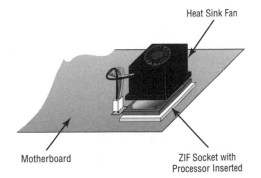

To install a slot-type processor (Slot 1 or Slot 2), first install the plastic mounting brackets that came with the motherboard. This can be frustrating because the directions are often vague as to where and how the brackets should be positioned. But persevere—this is often the hardest part of a Slot 1 or Slot 2 installation, and once it's over with, you're home free.

Align the cartridge over the slot, making sure it's facing the right way. Note the positioning of the trench in the slot and match it up with the edge of the circuit card sticking out of the bottom of the cartridge. Then firmly press the cartridge into the slot so that the mounting brackets hold it in place.

Installing Memory

The next thing you need to do is plug the memory into the motherboard. Today two kinds of memory are used: Dual Inline Memory Modules (DIMMs) and Rambus Inline Memory Modules (RIMMs). RIMM is the high-performance memory type that can be used with Pentium 4. Some newer Pentium 4 motherboards can use single data rate dynamic RAM (generally just called DRAM) and double data rate RAM (DDR-RAM), depending on the chipset that the manufacturer designed into the motherboard. RIMMs look similar to DIMMs, but have a different pin count. RIMMs transfer data in 16-bit chunks. The faster access and transfer speed generates more heat. An aluminum sheath, called a *heat spreader* or *heat sink*, covers the module to protect the chips from overheating. To get maximum system performance, use either DDR-RAM, which uses a DIMM socket, or Rambus DRAM (RDRAM).

So how much memory should you get? Memory used to be a very expensive item, but not anymore. Even the frighteningly expensive RDRAM is coming down in price so as to be competitive with DDR-RAM. Even though memory is cheap, these new motherboards can support up to 2–4GB of RAM. I recommend that you install 512 MB or 1 GB of RAM if you are using Windows Me/2000/XP. If you are using Windows 9x, then 256–512 MB will suffice, but the price differential between 256MB and 512MB is only a few dollars. So if you are going to err, err on the side of too much RAM.

NOTE *The most important thing about installing memory is making sure you buy the right kind. Either DIMM or RIMM memory sockets are the standard for new motherboards today, and there are two kinds. The older kind, synchronous dynamic RAM (SDRAM), was standard in most PCs. The newer memory technologies are RDRAM and DDR-RAM. RDRAM is more expensive and more efficient and speedy, but not all motherboards accept it. The fastest non-Rambus memory is DDR-RAM, which is twice as fast as the fastest SDRAM and is now almost as cheap.*

To install the DIMM, first take a look at the DIMM and then look at the DIMM socket.

Although it's not initially obvious, there are small notches in the edge connector of the DIMM that align with mating plugs in the DIMM socket. Turn the DIMM so that it lines up correctly and press it straight down into the socket until the latching levers on either side start to lock into position. Once the DIMM is fully seated, pull the latches up the rest of the way to lock in the DIMMs.

Step 4: Install the Video Card and Test the System

At this point, I feel I should tell you about a good friend of mine. This friend—we'll call him Jim—loved to build computers. Trouble is, most of the time they didn't work—well, not at first, anyway. I don't know if it was the parts he bought, a negative attitude, or what, but if he ever assembled a computer right into the case without testing the parts first, it never... I mean *never* worked.

I can't tell you why. He'd take the same parts, lay them out on the test bench, and plug them together first, and they'd work just fine. But skip the test, and the system would be doomed. Oh, he'd get it running eventually, but in the end, he always wound up taking it apart and putting it together again piece by piece on the test bench first.

So let me give you some advice: put the whole thing together first outside the case. Once you're sure everything is working, *then* assemble it into the case. This, by the way, is good advice even if you don't have the same little black cloud following you around that my friend had.

Plug In the Video Card

The next step in building your computer is to plug in the video card. Although the philosophy at this point is to plug the system in and test it with as close to nothing plugged into it as possible, without a video card you'll have a real hard time telling what's going on in the computer. This system has an AGP video card, so find the AGP slot. (If your motherboard has built-in video, you won't have an AGP slot, of course, but neither will you need to plug in a video card.) Press the video card firmly into the slot.

Next, connect the monitor to the video card. Before you test the system, you'll need to make sure the monitor is plugged in and powered on, of course, but that'll come a bit later.

Providing Power to the Motherboard

First, you'll need to plug the power supply into the motherboard. Look at the wires coming out of the power supply and locate the long one (ATX). That's what plugs into the motherboard; refer to Chapter 9, "Power Supplies and Power Protection," if you need more assistance.

Next, find the little pair of wires that run from the case's power button and hook them up to the corresponding pins on the motherboard. The motherboard manual's layout diagram will tell you which ones to use.

TIP You may also want to connect the wires for the speaker (mounted in the case) to the appropriate pins on the motherboard so that you can hear any warning beeps that the motherboard may emit during the startup process. They can help you in troubleshooting problems.

On many ATX systems, there are actually two power switches: one on the power supply itself and one on the case. The one on the power supply is the "hard shutoff" that turns power off or on to the whole shebang; the button on the front of the PC controls whether the motherboard *thinks* it's on or off. When you turn on the power switch on the power supply, you may hear the PC's fan kick on for a second and then back off again. That means that the motherboard is receiving power but has not gotten the signal from the power button to turn on.

Some power supplies have a power switch permanently connected to them with a long, thick wire. That switch mounts in the front of the case and functions as the sole power switch for the system. If you have such a switch dangling on a wire from your power supply, be careful with it. The wires are not always well insulated on these. You might want to wrap it with black electrician's tape before you go further.

Finally, plug the power supply's power cable into the wall and flip the power switch on the power supply. If there is a separate power button on the case, push that too, and the system should begin to start up. You'll hear the power supply fan, and you should see some messages on the monitor indicating that something is happening.

The First System Test

Take a look at the monitor. Did the name of the video card come up? Did it count up as much memory as you installed? (Note that 64MB comes up to about 65 million, and 128MB reaches about 131 million.) If the system got that far, it's doing well. Turn everything off and move on to the next step. If it didn't make it, you need to recheck all the steps you've taken so far.

The most frustrating problems to troubleshoot can be those where you don't see anything on-screen at all. Here are some tips:

- No power supply fan noise:
  - Are both power switches on? Some systems have two, as noted earlier.
  - Is the processor installed correctly?
  - Is the memory installed correctly?
  - Are the fans controlled by the computer and therefore don't come on immediately?
  - Are you sure the power supply is not defective?
- The fan goes on but nothing appears on-screen:
  - Is the video card installed correctly?
  - Is the memory installed correctly?
  - Is the monitor on and connected to the video card?

In my PC-building career, I have spent more time troubleshooting at this point in the process than any other. Fortunately, there are a finite number of things that could be causing the problem. Sometimes swapping out the motherboard, processor, memory, video card, and power supply, one by one, and replacing them with known good ones is the only way to pinpoint the problem.

After you get something on-screen, you might choose to go ahead and mount the motherboard in the case. (Skip ahead to the section "Put It All Together" for details.) Everything you add from that point on can be added directly into the case, although less intrepid persons may decide to continue adding components outside the case and putting it all into the case only after the entire system has proved itself.

Step 5: Install the Drives

Now that you're sure the motherboard, memory, and video card are all working, the next thing you need to do is install the drives. Well, okay, not all the drives—just the floppy drive, hard drive (you're only using one in this system), and the CD-ROM or DVD.

All these drives need to go in next because it takes one or more of them to install the operating system.

Installing the Floppy Drive(s)

Figure 34.12 shows a floppy drive and its data cable. See the dark stripe along one edge of the data cable? This marks the wire that goes to pin 1 on the connectors. Another thing you should look for is a twist in the cable. The twist is positioned just before the connector for drive A. The floppy drive controller is wired to detect this twist and assigns the drive nearest the twist to drive A. Except for the cabling, there's no difference between an A drive and a B drive unless one is a (shudder) 5 ¼-inch drive.

FIGURE 34.12

A floppy drive and its cable (notice the twist near one of the connectors)

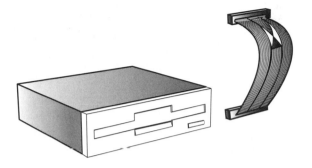

If you look at the back of a floppy drive, you'll see two connectors. One is the data connector and the other is the power connector. Although many drives print where pin 1 is on the circuit board, some don't. When that happens, just plug the data cable in so that the dark stripe (usually red) is nearest the power connector.

Installing the Hard Drive(s)

Like floppies, two hard drives can also share a single flat ribbon data cable. These, however, are not twisted to define the drives. Instead, they are set up as Master and Slave. Figure 34.13 shows the back of a typical IDE/ATA hard drive. There are three connector areas. The largest area is for the data cable, the area with large pins is the power connector, and the center area is the control block where you place the jumpers for the Master and Slave settings. The exception is when you have a ribbon cable that is marked for operation of Cable Select. With both devices set to Cable Select, then the connector mated to the drive determines if it is Master or Slave.

FIGURE 34.13

Location of the connectors on a hard drive

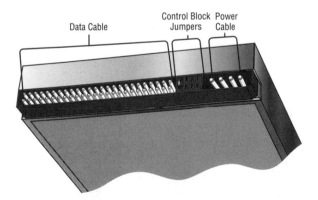

There are usually two IDE/ATA connectors on the motherboard. One is called Primary and the other is called Secondary. To specify a hard drive as drive C (also called the boot drive), plug its data cable into the Primary connector and set its control block jumper to Master.

Now plug in the data cable and the power cable. Be sure to position pin 1 of the data cable nearest to the power connector and to align the angled corners of the power plug with the angled corners of the power connector.

Setting Up the BIOS

As you may recall, there are a number of different ways to get the computer to go to the BIOS setup screen. Since this one has an AMI BIOS, it's very easy. Shortly after the computer begins to boot up, it displays a message on the screen like the one shown in Figure 34.14.

FIGURE 34.14

The main BIOS setup screen

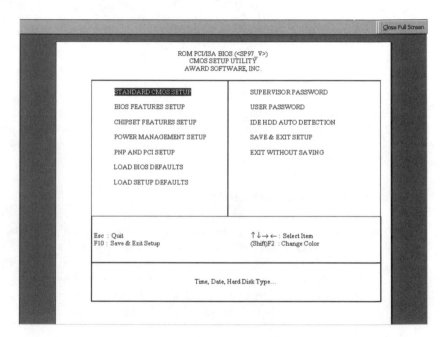

If you're like me, you're probably thinking that there are way too many options in the BIOS. But don't let it intimidate you. The first screen is just a table of contents. Every listing in the table of contents takes you to another page of options in the BIOS. Once you get into it, you'll find changing the BIOS options pretty easy.

In fact, some people get so comfortable with the BIOS setup that they start to change things they don't understand. *Don't do this.* If you don't know what you're doing, making changes to the BIOS can get you into more trouble than you even want to think about. Fortunately, there really aren't that many things you'll have to do in the BIOS under normal circumstances. So let's move on to the things you need to do.

SETTING THE TIME, THE DATE, AND A FEW OTHER ESSENTIALS

The settings you program into the BIOS will be saved by CMOS memory so the computer will know how to boot up each time you start it. The BIOS contains information on your hard drive, your built-in peripheral controllers such as the floppy, COM ports, and so on.

If you're using an AMI BIOS like the one pictured in Figure 34.14, the first place you should go is to the Standard CMOS Setup page. To do this, just highlight it with the up or down arrow on the keyboard and press Enter. The Standard CMOS Setup screen is shown in Figure 34.15.

FIGURE 34.15

The Standard
CMOS Setup screen

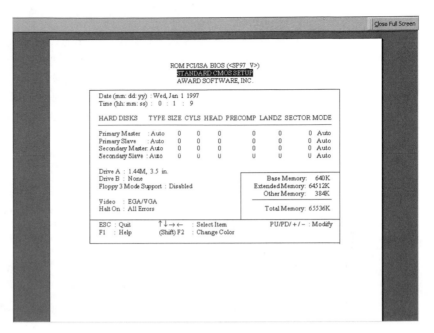

Take a look at the bottom of the screen. There you'll find the basic controls for the BIOS setup. Since it's text based, you'll need to press different keys to make changes. To move from one item to the next, use the arrow keys on the keyboard. This moves the highlight around the screen. Once the item you want to change is highlighted, press the Page Up or Page Down key to change the value in the highlighted area. To get an idea of how it works, move the highlight to the month at the top of the screen and press Page Up.

One thing that you should be aware of as you set the time is that the computer uses military time. This means that 12:00 (12 hundred hours) is noon and 0:00 is midnight. Hours between 0:01 and 11:59 are A.M. hours; hours between 12:01 and 23:59 are P.M. hours.

Another thing you may notice is that many of the items in the list are already filled in for you. This computer is set up to automatically detect quite a few devices. It found the 1.44MB floppy drive, the VGA display, and the memory. You may also notice that the hard drive is not listed. The BIOS, however, can automatically detect the hard drive. In the old days, you had to tell the BIOS that you wanted it to autodetect the hard drive, but in this day and age, you may not even be able to prevent it from performing autodetection. Once you're satisfied with all of the other settings on this screen, exit by pressing the Esc key on your keyboard to go back to the main screen.

Now move the highlight to IDE HDD Auto Detect (if it is there) and press Enter. The computer will immediately begin to autodetect your drives. Once it finds one, it will display the drive's parameters in the box near the bottom of the screen. Sometimes it will give you two or three options for how you want the drive set up. Generally, it's best to just press the Enter key to accept the default settings.

Once the system has detected your drives, exit the autodetection screen by pressing the Esc key and go back to Standard CMOS Setup to confirm that your drives match what you have in the system. Finally, check the time and date.

OTHER BIOS SETTINGS

On most motherboards, you can leave all the other settings as they are and your system will function pretty well. But in case you get curious, here are some of the other common settings you might find in your BIOS setup program:

ECC Specifies ECC or non-ECC memory, two different types of RAM memory. You'll have this option only on a motherboard that supports both types of memory. ECC stands for error-correction code. Non-ECC is usually the default.

L2 Cache ECC Support If enabled, allows error checking to occur on data accessed from the L2 cache. Disabled is the default.

Plug and Play OS The default is *No*. Specifies whether a Plug and Play operating system is being used. *No* lets the BIOS configure all the devices; *Yes* lets the operating system configure them. You don't have to set this to *Yes* in order to use a PnP operating system. In almost all circumstances, leave this option set to *No*.

Reset Configuration Data When set to *Yes*, clears the Plug and Play BIOS configuration data on the next boot and then resets itself to *No*.

Peripheral Configuration Opens a screen in which you can configure your parallel, serial, and USB ports.

DMI Events Logging Lets you log any startup error messages and view them through the BIOS program.

Resource Configuration Lets you tweak the memory block usage for various system resources. Not recommended unless you know what you're doing.

There are many other specialty settings that have to do with RAM, caches, recover time, aperture size, and so on, but you should not change these unless you have a specific reason for doing so. Such settings are set by default to standard values that work in almost all cases.

EXITING THE BIOS SETUP

If everything checks out, press Esc to get back to the main menu, move your cursor over to the item that says Save & Exit Setup, and press Enter.

This will reboot the system. Of course, it won't be able to boot up unless you already have a system on your hard drive, and you don't. But you're still not quite ready to install Windows. Remember that Windows is generally supplied on a CD-ROM, and so far you don't have a CD-ROM drive in the system. So let's do that now.

Installing the CD-ROM or DVD Drive

Installing a CD-ROM or DVD is pretty much the same as installing a hard drive. In fact, it's almost identical. You set the control block to Master, Slave, or Cable Select (in this case there's only one other IDE-type drive, so make it Slave), plug in the power and data cables (remember, red stripe nearest the power connector), and you're done. You'll install the little audio cable later when you put everything into the case. To help you visualize the whole thing, Figure 34.16 shows a picture of the back of a typical IDE DVD drive (CD-ROMs look essentially the same).

FIGURE 34.16

The connectors on the back of a DVD drive

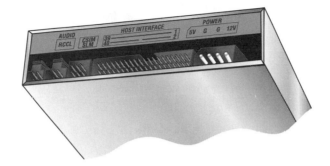

Attaching the Keyboard and Mouse

Okay, there's one more thing you have to do before you fire up the computer to install the operating system: you need to attach a keyboard and mouse. First, plug the keyboard into the keyboard connector. There used to be two types of keyboard connectors: AT (larger) connectors, which are very rarely seen except in computer museums, and PS/2 (smaller) connectors. With the newest connector, the Universal Serial Bus (USB), all you need to worry about is whether you have the right keyboard connector type for the plug on the motherboard. If not, you can use an adapter to change it to the right type of plug.

All new systems today come with a PS/2-style mouse port, which looks identical to a PS/2-style keyboard port. You'll need to check the motherboard documentation to determine which is which.

Now, turn on the PC, and see whether the lights on the various drives you've installed come on briefly and then go off. If they do, it's a sign that they're working. Then turn the PC off again and go on to the next step.

Step 6: Install the Operating System

Ready to install the operating system? If you choose Windows as your operating system (and just about everybody does these days), it'll take between 30 and 60 minutes... at least, that's what Microsoft claims. Of course, as fast as this system is, you should be able to cut off quite a bit of that time. For home or small business use, Windows Me or XP is your best bet; for corporate use, you'll want Windows 2000.

The best way to install Windows on a brand-new system is to boot from the CD. You may need to go back into the BIOS setup program and set the Boot Sequence setting so that it checks the CD-ROM drive for a bootable CD, but that's an easy matter to take care of. Then insert the CD into the CD-ROM drive, turn everything on, and follow the on-screen prompts. Installation is painless and for the most part self-explanatory, with very clear instructions and explanations on-screen.

If you can't boot from the CD for some reason, boot from a floppy disk, switch to the CD-ROM drive (by typing its drive letter and a colon and pressing Enter), and type **SETUP** to begin the install process. As part of its setup, Windows will partition and format the new drive as needed. See Chapter 13, "Partitioning and Formatting IDE and SCSI Drives," for more information about drive setup. Some notes on the process:

♦ As part of the Windows setup process, you'll be presented with Microsoft's terms and copyright notice. You'll have to accept these to continue. If you like, you can even read them all. On the other hand, almost no one does read them. Boiled down, they're telling you that you're not allowed to make extra copies of the program and that you may not modify it and distribute it or transfer the copy you have without deleting it from all your systems. There are a few other details, but that's basically it.

♦ Once you've agreed to abide by Microsoft's copyright, you need to prove that you are the rightful owner of the program. To do this, you must enter the excessively long product code that is on the original sleeve or on a sheet of paper that came with the CD.

♦ The setup program asks you where you want to put the Windows files. It offers you the opportunity to put them into a subdirectory called Windows. Personally, I recommend you use that one. All of the programs you get for the system will expect it to be there.

♦ All versions of Windows now prompt you to create a boot disk as part of the install. You'll use this to boot up your system if, for some reason, you can't get your hard drive to cooperate some day. Think of it as a little insurance policy. It takes only a few minutes to make it, but it could really bail you out some day. For this step, you'll need a blank 3 ½-inch disk, labeled so that you'll remember what it is.

♦ After Windows installs itself, it goes through your system, searching for any Plug and Play devices. Of course, many of the things that you'll be adding are still lying on the table a few feet from the system, so it won't detect those. Don't worry; it'll notice them when you put them in later. For now, just relax and let it do its thing and reboot itself.

At the conclusion of all this installation fervor, you'll end up with a basic system that can boot from the hard drive and load Windows. At that point, it's time to shut it all down again and add in the rest of your hardware. Onward to step 7!

Step 7: Install the Sound Card

For this system, you're using Creative Labs' Sound Blaster Live! sound card. It provides 3D sound and 64 voices—it can play up to 64 sounds at once and can handle up to eight speakers.

NOTE *If you chose a motherboard with built-in sound support, you won't go through this step, of course, because the sound is already there.*

It's a PCI board, so it needs to go into one of the PCI slots. This, by the way, is very important. It's actually possible to plug a PCI board into an ISA slot, but do not do this! You can fry the board and/or the entire system, motherboard and all, if you are unlucky.

The PCI plugs are short, and they are white or light colored. The ISA slots are much longer and are generally black or a dark color.

Now plug the sound card into one of the PCI sockets and plug in at least one set of powered speakers. These are speakers that have a built-in amplifier. They're necessary because the output from the Sound Blaster Live! card is not amplified. If you tried to play it through unpowered speakers, you would have a hard time hearing anything.

NOTE *Notice that when you plug in a card, there's a stem that goes down below the edge of the motherboard. This would normally engage in the bottom of the computer case to help secure the card. Here, however, if you've got the motherboard up on a box or book, as I suggested at the beginning of this chapter, it won't get in the way.*

Turn on the computer and wait for it to start Windows. This time you'll probably get a lot of messages as you boot up, telling you that Windows has detected motherboard resources, the video card, and your sound card. It will also ask you for the disk(s) or CDs that came with the boards. Go ahead and install the drivers by putting in the disks it asks for, and let it continue booting up.

Once the system has finished booting, you should hear the Microsoft sound. If you don't, open Control Panel by selecting it under Settings in the Start menu. Then double-click the Sounds icon and you'll get a window.

This window has a large area near the top labeled Events. This is a list of the different things that can trigger a sound in Windows. Next to the events that have sounds associated with them are little yellow speaker icons (see Figure 34.17). If you click one of the little speakers, the name of the sound associated with it will appear in the Name text box below the Events window.

Once you've selected one of the events, you can hear the sound it'll make by clicking the right arrow button to the right of the Preview window. Do that now.

FIGURE 34.17

The Sounds Properties window

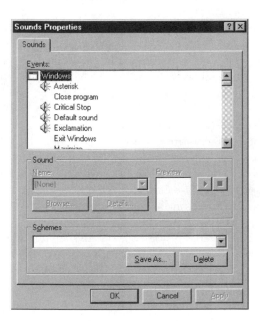

Did you hear a sound?

If you did, the sound card is working correctly. Now, make sure the CD that came with the sound card is in its drive and run the setup program that came with it. This will install some additional drivers and a number of sound applications on your hard drive.

Step 8: Install the Rest of the Boards

Now you can pat yourself on the back and heave a deep sigh of pleasure—you're almost halfway through building the ultimate computer! You have only a few more things to install and test, so let's get to those right now.

Installing the Modem

If you haven't already done it, power down the computer and plug in the modem. It also goes into a PCI slot.

Now power up the computer again; wait for the system to detect your modem and request the driver disk. Insert the disk into the floppy drive and press Enter. This will install the drivers for your modem and prepare it for connection to the Internet.

Installing the DVD MPEG Decoder Board

Shut down the system again and plug in the DVD MPEG decoder card. To understand what this card does, you have to understand how movies are digitized and put onto a disc. Moving video images produce huge data files, and to make matters worse, they must be read at an incredibly fast rate to provide smooth full-motion video on the screen.

As big as they are, DVD discs would not be large enough for a full two-hour movie if the video data were not compressed. DVD movies are compressed using a method called MPEG (Moving Picture Experts Group, the folks who created this method of compression). This compressed data is then stored on the disc and must be decompressed (also called decoded) before it can be viewed.

The computer has two methods of decoding the MPEG data—hardware and software decoding. The DVD decoder card you're installing will do hardware decoding, which takes a burden off the CPU.

The DVD decoder card works in conjunction with the video card. To install the DVD decoder card, plug the card into another open PCI slot. A special video feed-through cable is included in the package with the video card. Connect the mini-DIN connector at one end of the feed-through cable to the DVD decoder card (shown in Figure 34.18). Then connect the other end of the feed-through cable (the end that has a 15-pin D-connector) to the video output of the video card. (You'll need to remove the monitor's cable first.) Finally, connect the monitor to the video output on the back of the DVD decoder board.

Power up the computer again. This time the system should recognize the new DVD decoder board. Install the software that came with the board and then, as a final check, insert a DVD movie into the DVD drive and check it to make sure the video plays correctly.

Figure 34.18

The DVD decoder card and its cable connections

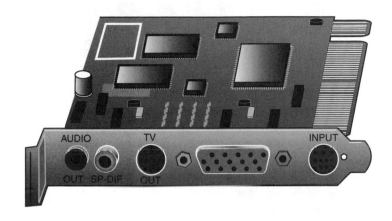

Step 9: Put It All Together

Now it's finally time to put all of the pieces into the computer case. Take the system apart; put all of the cards, cables, and connectors aside; and get ready to put it all into the case, piece by piece. The first thing you should put in the case is the motherboard. It's easiest to do this when the case is empty.

Installing the Motherboard

The motherboard is held in the case by a couple of small brass nuts and screws and small white plastic standoffs like the one pictured in Figure 34.19.

One thing you may notice is that there are more metal clip locations than there are holes in the motherboard. This is so that one case design can accommodate a number of different board designs.

Figure 34.19

A motherboard standoff

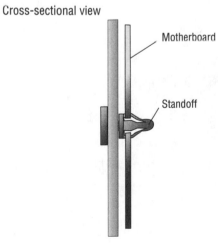

Cross-sectional view

Motherboard

Standoff

Holding the motherboard at an angle, note the locations of the clips and holes in the case that line up with holes in the motherboard. Some of the locations on the motherboard that line up will correspond to threaded holes in the case bottom. Screw the nuts into those holes (usually only one or two per case).

TIP   Use a nut driver to make sure the nuts are tight, but do not tighten them so much that you strip their threads or break them off.

Next, insert the white standoffs into the clips that aligned with holes in the motherboard. Then, very carefully, put the motherboard over the standoffs, making sure they all are showing through their respective holes, and gently press the motherboard down onto the standoffs. They should all snap into place.

Once the motherboard has been clipped to the standoffs, get a couple of the smaller screws and screw them into the nut(s) you installed earlier.

Most bags of screws that come with a case include several rust-colored paper washers. Install these between the motherboard and each screw to help prevent electrical shorting. This is not a problem in high-quality motherboards because the boards are manufactured with plenty of blank space around each screw hole, but on a cheaper board it can be a problem. Some people also put the paper washers *under* the motherboard around each screw hole, though it can be very awkward to do.

Installing the Power Supply

Once the motherboard is in, you can reinstall the power supply. The box itself goes in the same bracket it came out of near the top of the case, and depending on the model, the power switch may need to be reinstalled in the front of the case. You'll probably need to take the plastic front piece off first so you can get to the screws that hold the switch on. This is all illustrated in Figure 34.20.

FIGURE 34.20

Installing the power supply

Attaching the Add-on Boards

If you look at the rear of the computer case, you'll see that there are a number of metal covers that line up with the various slot positions of the motherboard. You need to remove the covers that line up with the places where you'll be installing boards into the motherboard.

TIP *When you unscrew the covers, be sure to put the little screws that come out into the container you set aside for them so that you can use them to attach the new boards you'll be installing.*

There are two kinds of board connectors on the motherboard: AGP (for your video card) and PCI (for all the other boards). Ideally, the boards should fit straight down into the connector in the motherboard. Some, however, will be tight. There are a few tricks you can use to get these boards to cooperate. First, try rocking the board back and forth along its length, as shown in Figure 34.21. *Never* rock it across its length; that could break the connector (see Figure 34.22).

FIGURE 34.21

The right way to rock an expansion card

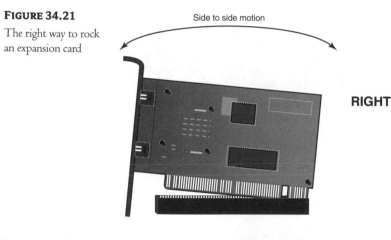

Side to side motion

RIGHT

FIGURE 34.22

The wrong way to rock an expansion card

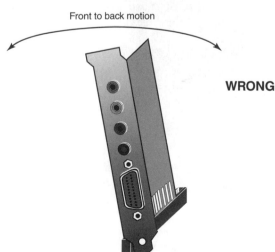

Front to back motion

WRONG

Install the video card into the AGP slot (it's the one that's a bit behind the other slots). Be sure to line up the metal tab at the bottom of the bracket so that it goes between the motherboard and the case. Then, using one of the screws that came out of one of the cover plates, secure the board into the computer case.

The one rule you should never break when you're installing a board is *don't force it!* If it doesn't go in easily, look around. You'll eventually find the culprit. Once I was installing a board and didn't know about the "don't force it" rule. So I leaned into the board to make it go in. Two things happened: (1) The connector cracked (this is not a replaceable part); (2) I cut the wire that was under the board, between the board and the connector—but not before jamming the board and wire into the connector so tightly that I couldn't get the board out of the connector without a pair of pliers. Needless to say, I had no choice but to buy a new board and start all over again.

Once you've installed the video card, plug the power connectors into the motherboard. I know I've said this before, but I think it's important to remind you, just in case you've forgotten—be sure you're plugging connectors into the correct spots.

Okay, now it's time to test the system again. Plug in the mouse and keyboard. If you have a serial mouse, you'll need to plug in the serial adapter before you can attach the mouse. Don't worry about mounting the adapter in the case—just plug it into the motherboard for now.

Next, plug in the power cord and monitor and switch on the system. After a few seconds you should see some activity on the display. If you do, you're ready to put in the rest of the boards and the drives.

Installing the Drives

Although there are several different arrangements you can use for the drives, I usually suggest that you put the DVD or CD-ROM in the topmost position in the case. This makes it easy to see and easy to reach over and put in CDs, since there's nothing on top of it. Next item down should be the Zip case, then the floppy drive, and finally, the hard drive.

Whichever drive arrangement you choose, be sure to reattach the smaller drive frame before you install any of the drives. Then grab the CD drive. Since the space at the top of most tower cases is a bit cramped, I suggest you plug the data and audio cables into the drive while it is still outside the case. Then feed the loose ends of the cables through the front opening of the drive bay, followed by the drive itself (as shown in Figure 34.23).

Once the CD drive is in the case, plug its power connector into its power receptacle, plug the end connector on the data cable into the motherboard, and screw the drive into the mounting. Make sure that the audio cable is routed into the computer so you can plug it into the sound card later.

The next drive to install is the Zip drive. The Zip drive is a 3 ½-inch drive, so you can put it into the top 3 ½-inch drive bay, or you can put it into a 5 ¼-inch bay using mounting rails and put it under the CD drive, as shown in Figure 34.24.

In this case, you'll put it in the 3 ½-inch bay. It should be installed just like the CD drive was. First, set the Master/Slave jumper to Master (it'll be the first drive on the secondary IDE connector). Then connect the data cable to the drive while it's still outside the case and feed the data cable through the open bay. Slide the drive in behind it, push the drive most of the way in, and attach the power cable to its connector. Then push it in the rest of the way and screw the drive into the side frames like you did with the CD drive. Oh, and don't forget to plug the other end of the data cable into the Secondary IDE connector on your motherboard. Also, check to make sure that pin 1 (the side of the data cable with the red stripe) is connected to pin 1 on both the drive and the motherboard connectors.

FIGURE 34.23

Installing the
CD drive

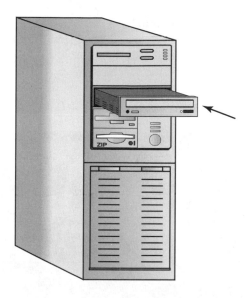

FIGURE 34.24

The Zip drive can go
in the location
shown or in the bay
above (shown with
floppy drive)

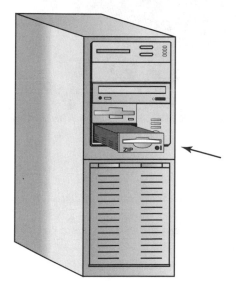

Now get the floppy drive and attach the twisted end of its data cable to the back of the floppy drive. Since there won't be a second floppy drive in this system, the second connector will be empty. Feed its cable through the open floppy bay and plug the far end of the floppy cable into the floppy connector on the motherboard just as you did with the Zip drive.

Installing the hard drive is similar to installing the other drives, but there is one small difference: it's installed from the inside of the computer. It doesn't show on the front of the system.

Unlike with the other drives, do not install the data cable yet. You'll be installing the connector in the center of the cable you used to connect the CD drive. Put the drive into the lowest position in the drive bay and push it forward into position, as shown in Figure 34.25.

Next, find the middle connector of the data cable you used to connect the CD drive. Plug it into the data connector of the hard drive, aligning pin 1 on the drive with the red stripe on the data cable. Then plug the power connector into the hard drive and screw the drive into the drive frame.

FIGURE 34.25

Installing the hard drive

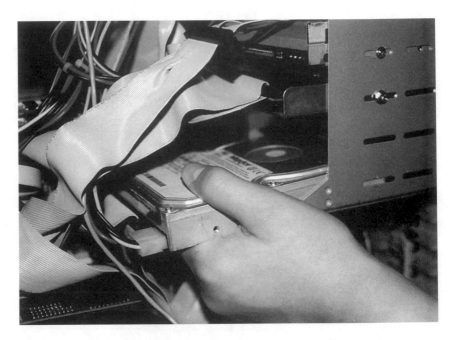

Another System Check

Before you go any further, it's a good idea to test the system again. This will confirm that you installed all of the drives correctly. So make sure the video cable is plugged into the monitor, your mouse and keyboard are connected, and your power plug is in. Then turn on the system.

The computer should boot up, read the hard drive, and go right into Windows. When it's finished booting, double-click My Computer and make sure that all of your drives appear in the window.

NOTE *If your system won't boot after you've put the motherboard in the case but it was working fine before, check to make sure there is no metal (besides the brass pieces) connecting the motherboard to the case. An errant screw is all it takes to create a short and make everything stop working. Check also to make sure there are paper washers around each of the screws holding the motherboard into the case.*

Install the Rest of the Boards

Once you know that the system works with the drives, you can install the remaining boards. Insert them, one at a time, and then screw them down.

After you've installed all the boards, you should see one or more little wires dangling down from the back of the CD drive. This is the audio cable that feeds sound from the audio portion of the CD drive to the sound card, so you can play audio CDs and the sound from games that use audio tracks (like Diablo II and Age of Empires II).

Parallel and Serial Port Connectors

Getting tired of connecting wires? Well, hang on—you're almost done. Remember the serial and parallel cables? On an ATX system, they're built right into the motherboard and have been there from the start of the process.

But wait! Don't start popping yet. Notice how one of the cutouts is larger than the others? The larger one is for the parallel port and the smaller one is for the serial port. I've had a few overzealous students pop out two large or two small cutouts. Do this, and you'll find yourself taping a cutout back into the case.

Front-Panel Lights and Speaker

Okay, that's it! Only one more, tiny task left: connecting the LEDs and the system speaker. The front-panel LEDs tell you if the system has power, when the hard drive is reading or writing, and so on. And the speaker beeps at you when the computer wants your attention. You may have connected a few of these earlier, when you were connecting the power switch and/or the system speaker for testing purposes.

The LED and speaker connections on the motherboard are all labeled—in tiny, almost unreadable letters. Unfortunately, there's always stuff around them that makes them hard to read. And of course, it's dark down in there. And to keep things interesting, the motherboard manufacturers change the positions of the connectors periodically, just to keep us on our feet (so to speak). Luckily, the motherboard manual often includes a chart that tells you what's what.

So get out your flashlight and magnifying lens, pull up close to the motherboard, and let's dive in.

In most cases, the bundle of little black connectors is rubber-banded together near the front of the case. Take off the rubber band (if it's there) and look closely at the connectors. Most of the time they'll also have labels. The following list tells you what wires you should have and what they are labeled:

HDD   This is the hard disk drive activity light. The circuit that runs the hard drive turns this on whenever it writes to or reads from the hard drive.

TBLD   This is the Turbo LED, a holdover from the old days when some systems had two speeds at which it could operate. This is not used today. Ignore it.

SPKR   The speaker beeps once when you boot and many times if there's an error. It also provides the sound for some applications, although more and more programs use the real sound card found in most systems today.

KEYLOCK   The keylock is not commonly used because it is so easy to overcome. The idea behind the keylock, which was introduced back with the original IBM AT computer, was to prevent the keyboard from entering data unless the key was inserted and turned. Trouble is, all anyone needs to do is remove the cover and pull off this connector. The keylock is rarely if ever seen today.

PWR   This is often grouped together with the keylock connector. It lights when the system has more than five volts of power available.

How do you plug these in? Simple; just shove the appropriate connector onto the pins. There is, however, one minor thing you need to look out for. Since they're LEDs, the connectors are polarized. That is, they need to go on one particular way. And the way is almost never labeled. So you may need to experiment until you get it right. You can sometimes tell from the chart in the motherboard manual. The little connectors usually have writing on one side and indents on the other, and they all go the same direction. So if you figure out one of them, just face all the others the same way and you're home free.

Well, that's it—you've finished building the ultimate computer! All you need to do now is put the cover on and secure it with screws. Be sure to hang onto all the documentation that came with your components, both for future reference and in case you need them for warranty service or replacement.

Troubleshooting Tips

The list of things that can go wrong when you build your own computer can be rather large since you're working with so many different components. However, if you find yourself in trouble, try these suggestions:

- Make sure you've properly installed all the components.
- Check to see that all your data cables are seated correctly and the pins line up.
- Consult the documentation for all your components to make sure you're following their installation and setup instructions.

Aside from these general troubleshooting tips, you might find these additional suggestions helpful:

- Do your research. Read everything that comes with your hardware, and if you can, visit manufacturer Web sites for FAQs, helpful hints, and more.
- Take your time. Block an entire day (or more) if you've never done this before.
- Plan on things going wrong. All but the most experienced technicians usually make mistakes. If you do, back up and—if you have to—start over.
- Don't get too frustrated. When things don't work, relax and take a deep breath. You won't be very productive if all you can think about is throwing your computer out the nearest window. If you need to, put it away and come back when you've calmed down.
- Give yourself plenty of space. Don't try to build a computer on a very small or crowded desktop. Use a large table or workbench so you can spread all the pieces around and everything isn't in one large pile.
- Be organized. Use separate bins for your different component subassemblies, screws, and other parts. If you have to, label your bins so you don't get confused. You might also label your data and power cables so you know where you want them to go. Organization also helps you not lose parts.

Well, now that you've got the computer built, it's time to use it! In the next chapter, we'll cover some basics about setting up Windows so that it works best for you.

Chapter 35

Hardware Management via Software Solutions

◆ QuickSteps: Using Control Panel   987

◆ Managing Your System via Control Panel   991

◆ Using Windows XP's Control Panel   1017

◆ Using Windows' *Other* Utilities   1026

◆ Windows Update and AutoUpdate   1034

◆ Windows Me and XP's System Restore   1035

◆ Using Other Software Tools   1038

◆ Managing the Windows Registry   1041

◆ Troubleshooting Tips   1045

Introduction

THE HARDWARE AND SOFTWARE of a computer system are mutually dependent on each other. For a new piece of hardware to work, your software (in particular, your operating system) must be aware of the new device and must be configured appropriately. This means that whenever you're working on your system's hardware, you're also interfacing with the operating system—which introduces an extra level of complexity to the operation.

Because of this interrelationship between hardware and software, you need to be aware of and know how to use various configuration and system management utilities that are built into your operating system. If you know what you're doing, you can use these built-in Windows utilities to manage the installation and operation of your hardware, and to track down any hardware-related problems that may develop.

NOTE   *Although the content in this chapter is based primarily on Windows 98 Second Edition (SE) and Windows Me (Millennium Edition), many of the features discussed here are also available in Windows 95/NT/2000/XP. The majority of screen shots in this chapter represent a system running Windows 98 SE. If you're running a different version of Windows, the look and feel of your screens may differ slightly from those shown here.*

QuickSteps

Using Control Panel

In the following QuickSteps, instructions not indicated as Windows XP apply to most previous versions of Windows, and to Windows XP if you are using the Classic interface. Where Windows XP instructions are given, they apply to the instructions that you should follow when using the new Windows XP interface.

Set Accessibility Options

1. In Control Panel, double-click Accessibility Options, or in Windows XP, choose Control Panel ➤ Accessibility Options ➤ Accessibility Options.

2. Set keyboard accessibility features on the Keyboard tab:

   StickyKeys   Makes the Shift, Alt, and Ctrl keys function as toggles

   FilterKeys   Ignores brief or repeated keystrokes

   ToggleKeys   Plays sounds when Caps Lock, Num Lock, and Scroll Lock are pressed

3. Set Sound accessibility features on the Sound tab:

   SoundSentry   Generates visual warnings when Windows makes a sound

   ShowSounds   Displays captions (in compatible programs) for the sounds it makes

4. Choose a High Contrast display option on the Display tab.

5. Set up the mouse to be controlled by the keyboard on the Mouse tab.

6. Set general usage options on the General tab.

7. Click OK.

Set Up New Hardware in Windows

1. Install the new hardware and start the computer. Windows may detect the new device automatically.

2. If Windows does not detect the new device, run the Add New Hardware Wizard from Control Panel, which will attempt to detect new devices. (In Windows XP, choose Control Panel ➤ Printers and Other Hardware, and then select Add Hardware from the See Also section in the left pane.)

3. If the device cannot be found, perhaps there is a device conflict. If you can determine which device is conflicting with the new one, remove it from the system and restart.

4. Go to Device Manager by clicking the System icon in Control Panel. (In Windows XP, right-click My Computer and choose Properties. Select the Hardware tab, and click the Device Manager button.) From Device Manager, remove the old device you took out. Then restart the PC again with the new device installed. Windows should detect it.

5. After you get the new device up and running, reinstall the old device. To avoid conflict, Windows will probably assign it a different resource than it had used before.

Add New Software

1. Insert the disk or CD in your PC. Some CDs have an AutoRun feature that starts the installation program automatically.

2. If the installation program does not start, choose Add/Remove Programs from Control Panel (Add or Remove Programs in Windows XP) and click the Install button on the Install/Uninstall tab.

3. Follow the prompts that appear.

Remove Software

1. Open Add/Remove Programs (Add or Remove Programs in Windows XP) from Control Panel.

2. On the Install/Uninstall tab, select the program to uninstall from the list; if you're using XP, select the program to uninstall from the Change or Remove Programs list that appears in the first window.

3. Click Add/Remove (or Change/Remove in Windows XP).

4. Follow the prompts that appear.

Add or Remove Windows Components

1. Open Add/Remove Programs (Add or Remove Programs in Windows XP) from Control Panel.

2. Click the Windows Setup tab, or in Windows XP, select the Add/Remove Windows Components icon.

3. Double-click a category to see the programs in it.

4. Place or remove checkmarks beside the program names to install or uninstall them.

5. Click OK. You may be prompted to insert your Windows CD.

6. Follow the prompts. You may be prompted to restart Windows.

Change the System Date and Time

1. Double-click Date/Time in Control Panel, or double-click the clock in the system tray. In Windows XP, choose Control Panel ➢ Date, Time, Language, and Regional Options ➢ Date and Time.

2. Change the date and/or time as needed.

3. Click OK.

Choose a Different Video Driver

In Windows versions previous to Windows XP, or when running Windows XP with the Classic interface, follow these steps:

1. Double-click the Display icon in Control Panel, or right-click the desktop and choose Properties.

2. On the Settings tab, click the Advanced button.

3. Click the Change button.

4. Work through the Update Device Driver Wizard to choose a different driver.

If you are running Windows XP with its new standard interface, the steps are slightly different:

1. Choose Control Panel ➢ Appearance and Themes ➢ Display.

2. On the Settings tab, click the Advanced button.

3. On the Adapter tab, click the Properties button.

4. On the Driver tab, click Update Driver.

5. Follow the steps in the Hardware Update Wizard to update the driver.

Change the Video Resolution or Color Depth

1. Double-click the Display icon in Control Panel (in Windows XP, choose Control Panel ➢ Appearance and Themes ➢ Display), or right-click the desktop and choose Properties.

2. On the Settings tab, choose a color depth from the Colors list (the Color Quality list in Windows XP).

3. Drag the Screen Area slider bar (the Screen Resolution slider bar in Windows XP) to choose a different resolution.

4. Click OK.

Test a Modem

For versions of Windows before Windows XP, follow these steps:

1. Double-click Modems in Control Panel.

2. Select the Diagnostics tab.

3. Click the modem to test.

4. Click More Info.

In Windows XP, follow these steps to test your modem:

1. Choose Control Panel ➤ Printers and Other Hardware ➤ Phone and Modem Options.

2. On the Modems tab, click the modem you want to test.

3. Click Properties.

4. Click Diagnostics.

5. Click Query Modem.

Managing Your System via the Windows 9*x*/Me/2000/NT Control Panel

Control Panel is one of the most useful features of Windows. It gives you access to utility programs that can make the difference between finishing an installation and total frustration. (Trust me; I've been there.) In this section, you'll take a short tour of the utility programs in Control Panel for Windows versions older than Windows XP—what the utilities do and how to use them. (I'll cover the Windows XP Control Panel later in this chapter.)

To open Control Panel, click the Start button, click Settings, and then click Control Panel. By the way, since some applications produce their own icons in Control Panel, yours may look a little different from the one in Figure 35.1. Don't worry about it. I'll explain the most common utilities you'll need (or at least find useful).

FIGURE 35.1

Control Panel in Windows 9*x*/Me/2000/NT

Setting Accessibility Options

The Accessibility Options are a set of controls that can make it easier for people with certain disabilities to use their computers. Double-click this icon and you'll see a window that looks like the one pictured in Figure 35.2.

This control window contains five pages that are accessible via the tabs along the top of the pages. Each tab is labeled according to the options it provides.

NOTE   *In addition to the Accessibility Options, there are Accessibility Tools. These include a magnifier, high-contrast mouse pointers, and a wizard for setting up the Accessibility Options. These Accessibility Tools are not installed by default in versions of Windows prior to Windows XP; you must use Add/Remove Programs in Control Panel to install additional Windows components such as these. See the section "Windows Setup" later in this chapter.*

FIGURE 35.2

Accessibility
Properties

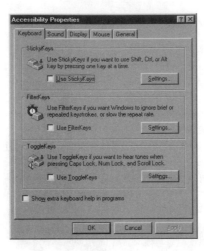

KEYBOARD FUNCTIONS

Use the Keyboard tab of the Accessibility Properties window to manage the settings for keyboard functions. Keyboard functions let you control your interaction with the keyboard and its interaction with your computer.

StickyKeys

StickyKeys are keys that stay in effect until you press them again. This is useful for people who find it difficult to press two keys at once. For example, if you turn on StickyKeys and then press and release the Alt key, the system will behave as though you were holding down the Alt key until you press the Alt key again. The Alt key, in this case, is the modifier key, because it modifies the meaning of the other keys you press in conjunction with it. Other modifier keys you can use are Ctrl and Shift.

To enable the StickyKeys feature, select its check box in the Accessibility Properties box.

To use StickyKeys, press the desired modifier key twice in a row. To cancel the sticky key, just press the modifier key one more time.

To configure how StickyKeys works, click the Settings button next to it in the Accessibility Properties window. For example, you can specify whether StickyKeys will make a short tone when you turn on a modifier key and when you turn it off again. Another option, which is disabled by default, is Use Shortcut. If you turn this on, you can enable StickyKeys by pressing the Shift key five times in a row. There are four other options you can adjust in this window; they're pictured in Figure 35.3.

FilterKeys

Take a look at the FilterKeys option in Figure 35.2. Click its Settings button to display the dialog box shown in Figure 35.4, in which you can set two functions. First, you can program it to ignore multiple keystrokes of the same key. This is useful if you tend to accidentally press some keys twice or more when you type.

FIGURE 35.3

Settings for
StickyKeys

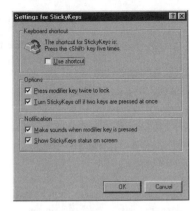

FIGURE 35.4

Settings for
FilterKeys

Second, FilterKeys can ignore quick keystrokes and slow down the keyboard's key repeat rate. This is an especially useful setting if you find that you often get several repeats of a character as you're typing when you intended to type only one.

You can even choose the repeat rate and the rate at which multiple keys are detected. In the Settings for FilterKeys dialog box, select the Ignore Quick Keystrokes and Slow Down the Repeat Rate option, then click its Settings button. Set the rate on the slider in the Advanced Settings for Filter-Keys box (see Figure 35.5). In Windows XP, you specify similar settings by choosing options from the Repeat Delay, Repeat Rate, and SlowKeys drop-down lists.

FIGURE 35.5

The FilterKeys con-
trol slider

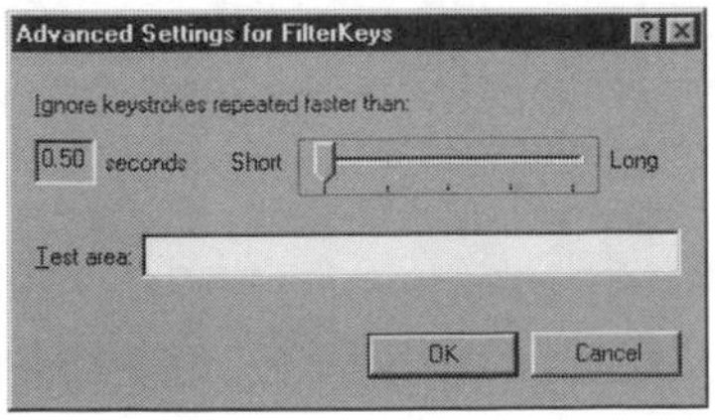

NOTE   After you've chosen a new rate, it's a good idea to test the repeat speed by typing in the Test Area below the slider.

As with all the other Accessibility Options, you can tell the system to beep or flash the screen (or both) when the computer activates the function. To do so, choose that option in the Notification section of the Settings box for the selected function.

ToggleKeys

This simple function makes a sound whenever the Caps Lock, Num Lock, or Scroll Lock key is pressed. It's useful for beginning typists who may accidentally press one of these without realizing it. If you enable it, you can then use a shortcut to turn ToggleKeys on or off as you work.

To enable the shortcut, click Settings in the ToggleKeys section of the Accessibility Properties window. Then select the Use Shortcut check box in the dialog box that appears. Once the feature is enabled, you can turn on ToggleKeys by pressing and holding the Num Lock key for 5 seconds.

SOUND

The Sound tab of the Accessibility Properties window contains options for controlling sounds (see Figure 35.6).

FIGURE 35.6

The Sound tab includes the Sound-Sentry and Show-Sounds options for controlling the sound of your computer.

SoundSentry

This feature is useful for hearing-impaired users. It flashes parts of the screen when the computer would normally generate a sound. To set this, check the Use SoundSentry check box in the Accessibility Properties window and then click the Settings button. This opens a window like the one in Figure 35.7.

The controls in this window enable you to choose which part of the screen will flash when the system generates a sound. For windowed programs (those that aren't full screen), you can select the title bar, the window itself, or the entire desktop.

FIGURE 35.7

Settings for
SoundSentry

NOTE   In general, it's better to choose the active title bar (the colored bar across the top of the active window) as the flashing element because the desktop can be obscured by the active window in some cases.*

ShowSounds

ShowSounds is an add-on function for SoundSentry that displays short text messages describing warnings that might have audio messages or signals.

DISPLAY

The Display tab of the Accessibility Properties window contains options for controlling what appears on your computer monitor (see Figure 35.8).

FIGURE 35.8

The Display tab
includes the Use
High Contrast
option for control-
ling the display of
your computer.

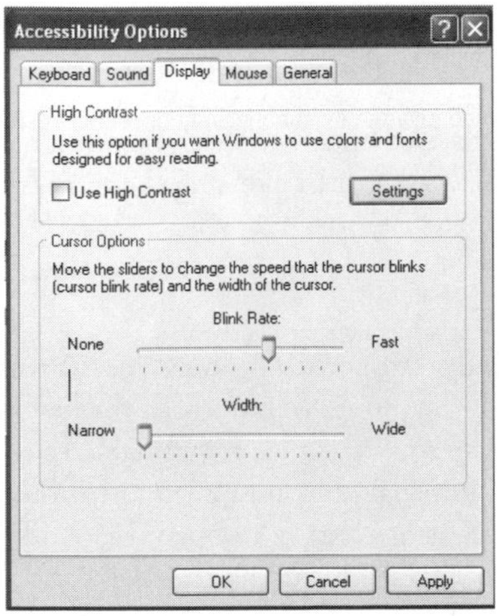

This page has only one option in versions of Windows prior to XP: Use High Contrast. However, there's more to this setting than meets the eye (so to speak). Click the Settings button to display the window in Figure 35.9 and you'll see what I mean.

FIGURE 35.9

Select one of the High Contrast color schemes.

NOTE   *In Windows versions prior to XP, use one of the two primary default color scheme options (White on Black or Black on White) to get a display that can be more easily seen by people with visual problems. The Custom option lets you choose any of the standard Windows color schemes.*

NOTE   *In High Contrast mode, some system fonts may appear larger.*

All Windows versions display a Use Shortcut check box that allows you to switch between two color schemes (as your mood dictates) just by pressing the Left Alt, Left Shift, and Print Screen keys at the same time.

MOUSE

The Mouse tab of the Accessibility Properties window doesn't really control mouse functions. Instead, it enables you to control the mouse pointer with the keyboard (see Figure 35.10). It's designed to help people who have trouble with (or are unable to use) a mouse.

Selecting the MouseKeys option enables you to move the mouse pointer by pressing the arrow keys on the keyboard. Click the Settings button to open the window shown in Figure 35.11, and you can control the way the mouse behaves—including the speed and acceleration of the mouse pointer. You can also specify whether you want to be able to change the pointer speed on the fly by pressing the Ctrl key to speed up and the Shift key to slow down.

FIGURE 35.10

The Mouse tab includes the Mouse-Keys option, which enables you to control the mouse pointer by using the keyboard.

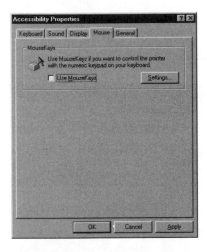

FIGURE 35.11

The Settings for MouseKeys window

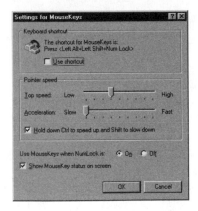

GENERAL

The General tab of the Accessibility Properties window has three functions: Automatic Reset, Notification, and SerialKey Devices (see Figure 35.12).

Automatic Reset turns off the accessibility features if you don't use the computer for a while. The default time is 5 minutes, but it can be set to any time you like (in 5-minute increments), up to 30 minutes.

Notification gives you a warning message and/or sound when one of the accessibility features is turned on or off.

SerialKey enables you to use special add-on devices through one of your serial ports as an alternative interface to the mouse and keyboard. Because of his degenerative nerve disease, Dr. Stephen Hawking, the famous physicist, uses one of these controls (among other things) to control his computer.

FIGURE 35.12

The General tab of
the Accessibility
Properties window

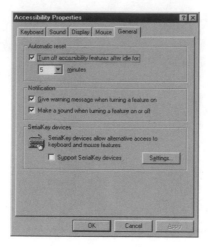

Adding New Hardware

When you install a Plug and Play board in your system, Windows will generally detect it automatically and either install its drivers from those already in your system or ask you to insert a driver disk from the manufacturer.

Some boards need a little help, however. You'll find that help in the Add New Hardware control. If you've installed a new board in your system and Windows didn't notice, double-click Add New Hardware to open a wizard that will walk you through the installation (see Figure 35.13).

FIGURE 35.13

The Add New
Hardware Wizard

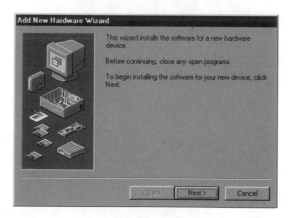

Click the Next button to move through each step of the process, as Windows examines your system and detects first Plug and Play, then non–Plug and Play devices. Running this wizard can take a while, since the computer will check every possible hardware configuration. Once it's done, though, it will usually find any new devices that have been added.

Of course, there will always be exceptions. Sometimes the Add New Hardware Wizard will find the wrong things. And sometimes it won't find a new board because there is some kind of conflict.

For example, if you have a new board that is designed to use IRQ15 and you already have a device using IRQ15, the wizard may be unable to find the new board.

Read on to learn how to install Plug and Play devices *manually*.

MANUALLY INSTALLING PLUG AND PLAY DEVICES

Most modern devices are Plug and Play compatible, and can have their IRQs assigned on the fly by Windows when it first detects them. If a particular device requires one particular IRQ, you should install it first, let it have its persnickety pick of the IRQs, and then install more congenial devices afterward. That may mean removing some of your existing devices temporarily, then reinstalling them.

To do this, first determine which existing device is conflicting with the new one. Check the new device's documentation to find out which IRQ it needs and then use Device Manager to find out which device is using it.

To access Device Manager in versions prior to Windows XP, double-click System in Control Panel to open the System Properties window (shown in Figure 35.14). (You can also right-click the My Computer icon on the desktop and choose Properties to get to the same place.) This is another one of those windows that has four tabbed pages. The first page, called General, shows a brief list that describes the computer and lists your operating system version, owner's name, manufacturer, processor, and installed memory.

FIGURE 35.14

The General tab of the System Properties window

Click the Device Manager tab, and a list of installed devices appears. Double-click Computer at the top of the list. The Computer Properties window opens, listing the system IRQs and the devices assigned to them (see Figure 35.15).

Now return to the Device Manager tab (see Figure 35.16). Device Manager shows all the devices that are installed in your computer. Since everyone's computer is a little different, chances are your list won't look exactly like this one, but it will have most of the same devices. The information in the list is organized like an outline, listing categories of devices. The devices themselves appear within each category. To see the devices, click the plus sign beside the category.

FIGURE 35.15

Check out IRQ allocation here.

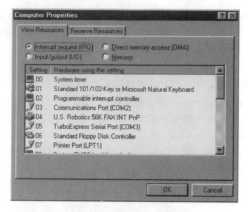

FIGURE 35.16

The Device
Manager tab

You'll find categories for your drives, controllers, keyboard, and so on. If you click the plus sign next to the Modem category, for example, you might find US Robotics 56K V.90. You'll take a closer look at Device Manager a little later in this chapter, in the "System" section. Right now you're here to do one thing: delete the item from this list that corresponds to the hardware that you need to remove. Once it's gone from here, the computer can assign its resource to the uncooperative device you're trying to install. Let's say the conflicting device is a scanner. Go down the list until you find the scanner (hint: it's probably in the Imaging Device category), click it, and then click the Remove button near the bottom of the window. Click OK to close the System Properties window.

Windows should ask if you want to reboot, but if it doesn't, you need to shut down (choose Shut Down from the Start menu) and power down the system. Make sure the older device in the conflict is unhooked, removed, or turned off (so that Windows won't immediately redetect it at startup) and that the newer device is in, on, and ready to go. Now power up the system again. This time, the system should have little trouble installing the new board and its driver(s). Once the new board is installed, shut down the system again, plug in the old board, and let the system redetect it. It should find a new IRQ for it, and you'll have installed both boards.

Installing Boards That the System Can't Find

Sometimes you'll want to install a legacy board that the system just can't find at all. If the Add New Hardware Wizard is unable to detect the new device, try running it again, but this time, at the screen shown in Figure 35.17, choose No, I Want to Select the Hardware from a List.

FIGURE 35.17

Tell the Add New Hardware Wizard that you will select the device yourself.

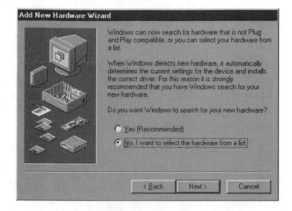

Now when you click the Next button, you'll be asked to choose a hardware category (see Figure 35.18).

FIGURE 35.18

Select the device category.

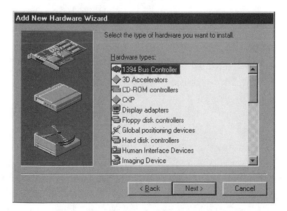

Click Next again, and one of two things will happen, depending on the category you chose:

◆ You'll immediately see a list of manufacturers and models of that hardware type, from which you can select your model. Figure 35.19 shows an example for network cards.

◆ A specialized wizard runs for that type of hardware. Work through it, making one last-ditch effort at autodetection, before the list of manufacturers and models appears.

FIGURE 35.19

Select the make and model of your device.

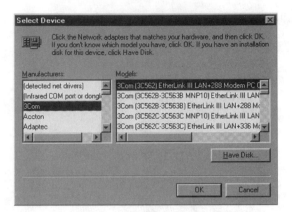

Select your make and model, or, if you have a disk that came with the hardware, insert it and select Have Disk to use the drivers from the disk instead. (You can also use Have Disk if you have downloaded drivers from the Internet, as described in the following section. Just point to the drive and folder on your system where you stored the download.)

If the manufacturer isn't listed and you don't have a driver disk, choose the top item in the Manufacturers list, Standard Types, and click the item in the right-hand list box that most closely matches the device you're installing (good luck). This will install a driver that we hope will do an adequate job of running your device. Sometimes you'll get lucky and it'll work. Sometimes you won't be so lucky and... well, you may need to spend some time finding the right drivers.

GETTING THE DRIVERS ONLINE

At one time, if you needed a driver and you didn't have it, you had only one recourse—call the manufacturer. Sometimes, if you were lucky, they would be able to send you the driver(s) you needed within a short period of time (a week or so). But all too often, it took longer—much longer. And you'd have to wait and wait to install your board. And sometimes, if you were really unlucky, the manufacturer was out of business or simply didn't support that board any more.

Today, things have improved because of the Internet. If you need a driver, generally all you need to do is go to the manufacturer's Web site, find their support page, and download any drivers you need on the spot. (You can read more about the availability of Internet-based resources in Chapter 32, "Using the Internet for Hardware Support.")

What's really amazing, though, is that not long ago, I needed a driver for a board that was made by a company that had gone out of business. In the old days, I'd have been out of luck. With the manufacturer gone, my chances of finding the driver were about zero.

But with the Internet, I was able to get the driver with almost the same ease I would have had if the company were still around. Once I found out that the company had disappeared, I went to a search engine (you could use Google, Alta Vista, or Yahoo!, for example), entered the name of the device I was looking for (I used its actual part number), and waited a few minutes.

I got about a thousand hits! I looked down the list and found a Web site that was operated by a users group that maintained a file of what they called "Obsolete Drivers."

They had exactly what I was looking for. Within minutes I had downloaded the driver and installed it in my system. Thanks, Internet!

TIP   *It's a good idea to run a virus check on any file you download from the Internet before you install it in your system. Even the best-intentioned Web site operators can inadvertently use files that have become infected.*

Adding and Removing Programs

Like the Add/Remove Hardware feature in Control Panel, the Add/Remove Programs feature has multiple tabbed pages (see Figure 35.20). The Install/Uninstall page found in Windows versions prior to Windows XP lists all the programs that are currently in your Registry. The *Registry* is a file that contains a record of all the programs in your system that are Windows-compliant. These programs use an assortment of resources, and the Registry keeps track of them. (I'll talk about the Registry in more detail later in this chapter, in the "Managing the Windows Registry" section.)

FIGURE 35.20

The Install/
Uninstall tab of
the Add/Remove
Programs Properties
window

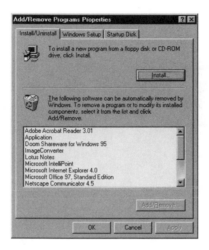

Since the resource files for any given program might be scattered in any number of folders (which is why you need the Registry—to keep track of where all those files reside), it's likely that if you try to manually delete an installed program, you'll wind up leaving a lot of the program files behind (which, needless to say, wastes a lot of space on your hard drive). By using the Add/Remove Programs utility, you can get rid of all the parts of a program when you delete it.

REMOVING (UNINSTALLING) A PROGRAM

To remove a program, select it from the list box on the Install/Uninstall page and click Add/ Remove. An Uninstall program will run that removes the program. (The Uninstall program will be different depending on the program; most programs come with their own.)

Sometimes the Uninstall Wizard can't delete pieces of a program because they are in use or have other active components in them. In that case, the wizard will tell you that pieces were left behind and that you must remove them manually. To see which pieces were left behind, click the Details button.

During the uninstall process, Windows may occasionally display a message that tells you a file is no longer being used by any other program. Windows asks if you want to delete the file or keep it on your system. It's probably safe to delete the files if they reside in folders that are specific *only* to the program you're removing; however, if Windows asks about files in your System folder, or other folders that are shared by one or more programs, keep them on your hard drive just in case.

After you uninstall the program, double-check to see if any folders were left behind. In some cases, software programs store your data or work in subfolders underneath the installation folder, and they may still be there after you uninstall the software.

INSTALLING A PROGRAM

To install a program, insert the CD or disk containing the program and click the Install button on the Install/Uninstall page. Windows searches all your removable disk drives for programs to install and suggests an installation program to run, as shown in Figure 35.21. Click Finish to run that program and install the software.

NOTE   Some CDs will AutoStart. This means that as soon as you put them into the drive, they are read and begin their installation process. If you insert a program CD and it offers to install itself, go ahead and let it.

FIGURE 35.21

The Run Installation Program window asks if this is the program you want to install.

WINDOWS SETUP

Windows Setup lets you install additional Windows components that were not installed when you initially loaded Windows. When you select the Windows Setup tab, you'll see the page shown in Figure 35.22.

FIGURE 35.22

The Windows Setup tab

The list contains program categories. The ones with checkmarks in white boxes are fully installed (that is, all the programs in that category are installed). Those with checkmarks in gray boxes are partially installed (that is, some but not all of the programs in that category are installed). To see what programs are in a category, or to select individual programs from a category, double-click a category or click once and then click Details.

To install a program or an entire category, click its check box and click the OK button. (You can check more than one item before clicking OK.) To delete an item, deselect its box by clicking it. The check will disappear, and Windows Setup will remove those items when you click OK.

When you click OK, you may be prompted for your Windows CD, so be prepared for that.

STARTUP DISK

The last tab in the Add/Remove Program Properties window opens the Startup Disk page (see Figure 35.23). Creating a startup disk is pretty simple—put a blank disk into your floppy drive and click the Create Disk button. You can use a startup disk to start the PC if it won't boot from the hard drive for some reason.

FIGURE 35.23

The Startup Disk page is used to create a boot disk.

Setting the Date/Time

Clicking Date/Time in Control Panel opens the Date/Time Properties window (shown in Figure 35.24), which is used to adjust the time and date of your computer.

TIP   You can also open the Date/Time Properties window by double-clicking the time display in the Windows system tray.

There's a calendar on the left and a clock on the right. To set the date, choose the month and year you want from the selection lists and click the day you want from the calendar. To change the time, click the item you want to change in the numeric list box and either type in a new time or click the up/down arrows to scroll to the correct time.

The Time Zone box tells your computer where it is so it can tell you the time and date of other countries accurately. To change time zones, just open the Time Zone drop-down list and choose one.

FIGURE 35.24

The Date/Time
Properties window

Changing Display Options

The Display Properties window has more options than I need to cover in an upgrade and maintenance book, but there are a few things that you should look at. Double-click the Display icon in Control Panel and you'll see a window that looks like Figure 35.25. You can also see the same window by right-clicking the desktop and choosing Properties.

FIGURE 35.25

The Background tab
of the Display Prop-
erties window

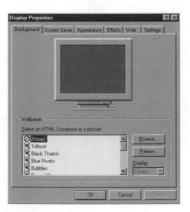

Display Properties lets you change your screensaver, background, and quite a few other items that can be fun, but the only thing that you'll need to look at now is the Settings tab. This is where you can change the resolution of your screen, the number of colors displayed, and the type of display adapter and monitor you use (see Figure 35.26).

Directly under the picture of a monitor, you'll find a description of the current display adapter and monitor. Below that are two areas that let you change the color depth and screen resolution. Depending on the display adapter and monitor you're using, you'll be able to choose anything from 16-color to True Color, which may be either 24-bit or 32-bit, depending, once again, on your display adapter and monitor.

FIGURE 35.26

The Settings tab

To set other properties for the display, click the Advanced button. The tabs that appear in the resulting dialog box vary depending on your video card's driver (Figure 35.27 shows a typical one), but they all have at least these four tabs: General, Adapter, Monitor, and Performance. I'll cover only the four basic tabs, since there's no way I can guess what extra tabs you have.

GENERAL

The General tab (see Figure 35.27) lets you change the system font size and decide whether the system restarts after you change any of the display parameters.

FIGURE 35.27

The General tab of the advanced Display Properties window

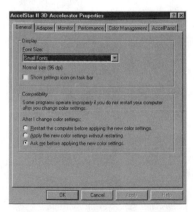

Display (Font Size)

You can choose small, large, or custom font sizes. Large fonts are 125 percent the size of the Small (normal) fonts. If you select Other, a window like the one in Figure 35.28 will open.

You can change the font size by typing a percentage value in the text box at the top of the window or by dragging the ruler in the graphic below it to the left or the right. Dragging to the right makes the font larger, and dragging it to the left makes it smaller.

FIGURE 35.28

The Custom Font Size window

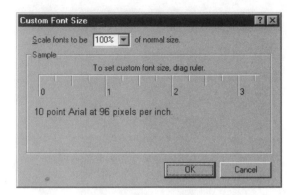

Once you've chosen a size, a sample of the text size will appear in the graphic window below the ruler (see Figure 35.29).

NOTE *Changing the font size can have a profound effect on the appearance of your computer display and the programs you run.*

FIGURE 35.29

Viewing the new font size

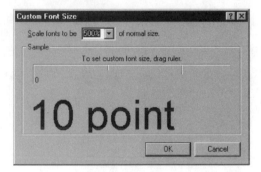

Show Settings Icon on Task Bar

Select or deselect this check box to choose whether you want an icon in the system tray that provides quick access to the Display Properties dialog box.

Compatibility

When you change the color depth of the display (from the Color palette list on the Settings tab, as shown in Figure 35.26), Windows will prompt you to restart, or not, depending on what you choose here. If you do not restart after changing the color depth, some programs may not look quite right, or the icons on your desktop may appear in odd colors.

ADAPTER

The Adapter tab helps you control the settings for your video card.

Driver

To choose a different driver, click the Change button and work through the Update Device Driver Wizard.

Just like when you install new hardware (as you learned earlier in the chapter), Windows may correctly detect your video card, or it may not. If it detects it as Standard VGA or some variant of that, but you have a better card, you may need to tell it to look for drivers on disk and then provide the driver disk that came with the video card. To do that, in the Update Device Driver Wizard, choose Display a List of All the Drivers in a Specific Location, So You Can Select the Driver You Want (see Figure 35.30), and then choose Have Disk.

FIGURE 35.30

Choose to confine the search for drivers to a specific location.

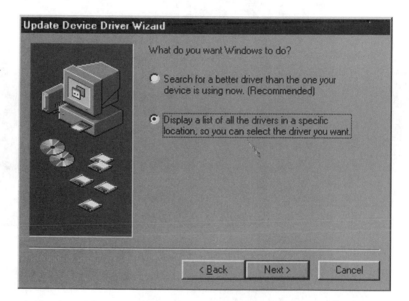

Refresh Rate

The *refresh rate* is the frequency at which the display is repainted, or refreshed, on the monitor. This is limited to the highest rate that both the monitor and the video card can agree on.

The default setting is Optimal, and that's the setting I recommend in most cases. However, if your monitor is not directly supported by Windows (see the following "Monitor" section) but you know that it can support a higher refresh rate than a generic monitor, you might want to choose a specific refresh rate.

After setting the refresh rate, Windows makes the change and gives you the opportunity to return to your previous settings. If you do not click Yes to accept the new settings within a few seconds, it reverts automatically, so you are not stuck with an unusable setting. You can tell if the refresh rate is too high because the screen will look distorted, especially around the edges.

MONITOR

On the Monitor tab (see Figure 35.31), you can click the Change button to change the monitor that Windows thinks you have. This works just like changing the video card's driver, as you learned earlier.

You can also choose whether the monitor is Energy Star–compliant (a power savings standard), whether to automatically detect Plug and Play monitors (recommended, usually), and whether to reset the display when it resumes after being suspended (a power management issue).

FIGURE 35.31

Configure the settings for your monitor.

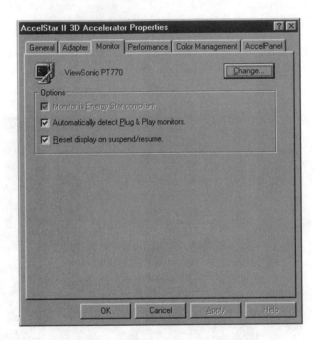

PERFORMANCE

There is only one control on the Performance tab (see Figure 35.32): a slider that sets the hardware acceleration. The higher the setting, the better video performance you get. You should leave this set to Full unless you are having problems with video compatibility with a specific program. (Games are usually the worst offenders here.) In that case, crank the Performance down one level and try the program again; keep doing this until you can run the program without errors.

I have found that video problems associated with running certain programs can be corrected in most cases by installing the most recent DirectX drivers for your video card. You can usually download these from the video card manufacturer's Web site, either separately or as part of a complete driver update.

Modems

Now skip to the Modems properties in Control Panel. You use this window to configure and test your modem.

In classic Windows applications (that is, pre-XP), when you double-click the Modems icon you'll see the Modems Properties window, shown in Figure 35.33. There are two tabbed pages in this control window: General and Diagnostics.

FIGURE 35.32

Use Full hardware acceleration unless you are experiencing problems.

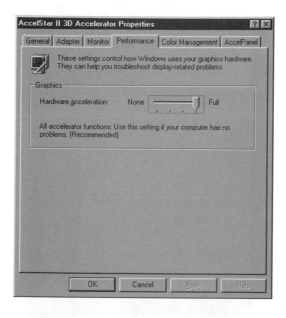

FIGURE 35.33

The Modems Properties window in classic Windows applications

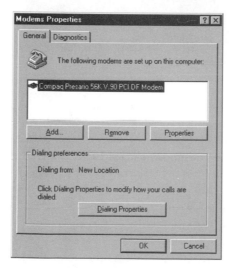

CONNECTED MODEMS

In classic versions of Windows, the first tabbed page, General, shows you the modems that are connected to your computer. Although most people don't have more than one, you can connect several if, for example, you want to use your system as a dial-up e-mail server or have an ISDN modem for your Internet connection and a fax/modem for sending faxes.

Dialing Properties

Click the Dialing Properties button at the bottom of the General tab to open the Dialing Properties dialog box (see Figure 35.34). From here you can configure your location, including area code, the number to dial for an outside line, and so on. Incidentally, you can get to this same dialog box by choosing Telephony directly from Control Panel.

FIGURE 35.34

The Dialing Properties dialog box in classic versions of Windows

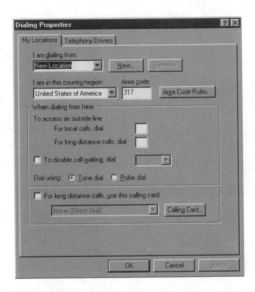

Adding or Removing Modems

Using the Add and Remove buttons in the Modems Properties window, you can install modems or remove them from your system. The Add button runs the Add New Modem Wizard, which is a specialized version of the Add New Hardware Wizard you saw earlier in the chapter.

The Remove button removes a modem's driver from the system. After you remove a modem's driver, you also need to physically remove the modem from the PC (if it's internal) or disconnect it (if it's an external model). Otherwise, Windows may redetect it and reinstall its driver the next time you start the PC.

Modem Properties

Choose a modem and then click the Properties button to open the modem's Properties box. In classic versions of Windows, this box has two tabs: General and Connection.

From the General tab, you can choose or view the modem's COM port, adjust its speaker volume (if it has one), and set its maximum speed.

From the Connection tab, you can control the connection and call preferences. Connection preferences control the number of data bits transmitted, as well as the parity and stop bits. Of course, most modem programs automatically set these parameters for you, so you'll rarely have to make any changes here.

Call preferences control how the modem dials. The default values (which you shouldn't change unless you really know what you're doing) are Wait for Dial Tone before Dialing and Cancel the Call if You Can't Get Connected within a Minute (60 Seconds). If you're in a country that has a lot of trouble connecting, you might want to increase this value to give the modem a chance to eventually connect.

DIAGNOSTICS

The Diagnostics tab of the Modems Properties window lets you communicate with your modem and try a few standard commands to see whether it will respond correctly. Although the test isn't conclusive, it does tell you if the modem is connected and can receive commands. Figure 35.35 shows the Diagnostics tab in classic versions of Windows. Choose the modem and then click the More Info button. After a few seconds, a report appears. If at least some of the lines report "OK," then the modem is installed and working correctly.

FIGURE 35.35

The Diagnostics tab

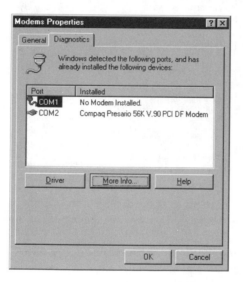

System

Although I mentioned the System feature of Control Panel earlier, I really only touched on its capabilities. This is where you can look at and change any of the devices in your computer. Double-click the System icon and you'll see the System Properties window.

The System Properties window has four tabs: General, Device Manager, Hardware Profiles, and Performance. In classic versions of Windows, the first tab, General, displays general information about your system—which operating system you're running, who your computer is registered to, and that sort of thing. The second tab, Device Manager, is an important system management tool, and I'll discuss it in more depth starting in the following paragraph. The third tab, Hardware Profiles, enables you to set up different startup configurations and is seldom used. The final tab, Performance, displays important system status information—and I'll talk more about this one later, too.

DEVICE MANAGER

As you read earlier in this chapter, if you click the Device Manager tab, you'll see a list of all the devices installed on your system. Click a listed device type that has a plus sign beside it, and it will display a list of all the devices that are in that category. For example, when you click the Ports category, you'll see a list of all the ports on your system, including your serial ports and parallel ports (see Figure 35.36). The serial ports are called Communications ports, and the parallel ports are called Printer ports.

FIGURE 35.36

The Device Manager tab with the Ports list

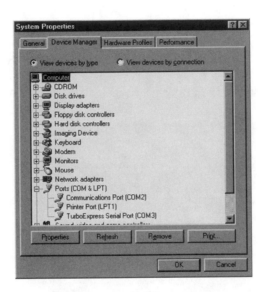

There are two ways you can organize the devices in the Device Manager: by device type or by connection. Generally, it's easier to organize them by type because it organizes the devices by *what* they are, not *where* they are.

If Windows is reporting a problem with a specific device driver, you'll see a special symbol next to that device. A black exclamation point (!) on a yellow background indicates that the device is in a "problem state." A red X indicates that the device is currently disabled—probably because the correct driver isn't loaded. A blue *i* on a white background indicates that the device is using a manual configuration instead of the default settings (not necessarily a bad thing).

NOTE *A device can be in a "problem state" and still be functioning. In this instance, the device still has some sort of problem (although the problem isn't knocking the device all the way out), which should be explained in the accompanying problem code.*

To look at the properties of a device, you can double-click the device or you can select it and then click the Properties button. If you do this, you'll open a Properties window that shows the device specifications and the driver that's running it.

For some devices, you can look at and set which port, IRQ, and memory it uses. However, generally it's a bad idea to mess with those settings because it prevents Windows from reassigning resources should you decide to add or remove devices later.

If you have a device conflict, open that device's Properties window and select the General tab. You'll now see a message that explains the basic problem and presents the steps Windows recommends to solve it. The message may also display a problem code and number that can be useful when you're consulting with a technical support specialist.

Sometimes you can resolve a resource conflict by choosing an alternate IRQ and/or memory configuration for the problem device. For example, suppose you have two devices that both want to use IRQ11, and one of them isn't working because of it. You can display the properties for one of the devices by double-clicking it in Device Manager and viewing its Resources tab. At the bottom of the screen, it will report the conflict with the other device. To fix the conflict, deselect the Use Automatic Settings check box and choose a different configuration from the Setting Based On list. Be sure to choose a configuration that results in No Conflicts being reported in the Conflicting Device List. See Figure 35.37.

FIGURE 35.37

Choose an alternate set of resource settings for the device.

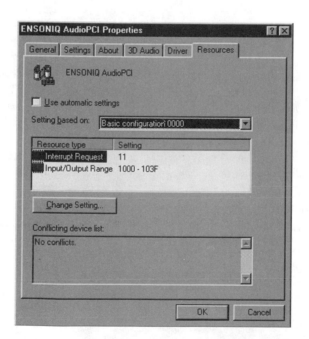

If there aren't any suitable configurations to choose from in the Setting Based On list, you can assign an IRQ or memory address manually. To do so, click the one you want (IRQ or Input/Output Range) and then click Change Setting. A box appears in which you can make your selection. See Figure 35.38.

If you see a message that the resource cannot be modified, try the other side of the equation—that is, try to change the resources for the other device involved in the conflict. (This process is covered in more detail in the section "Adding New Hardware.")

FIGURE 35.38

Manually assign resources to a device to eliminate a conflict.

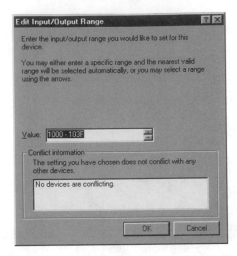

In other cases, you may need to update to a newer version of a device driver. To do this, go to the device's Properties window, select the Driver tab, and then click the Update Driver button. This starts the Update Device Driver Wizard; click the Next button and then select Search for a Better Driver. Click Next and you'll be asked *where* you want to search for an upgraded driver. If you have the driver on disk (hard, floppy, or CD-ROM), select the appropriate option. If you prefer to go out on the Internet and search Microsoft's Web site for an updated driver, select Microsoft Windows Update. Once a new driver is found, you can use the rest of the wizard to install and configure the new driver.

PERFORMANCE

The Performance tab of the System Properties window, shown in Figure 35.39, enables you to review the performance of your system.

FIGURE 35.39

The Performance tab

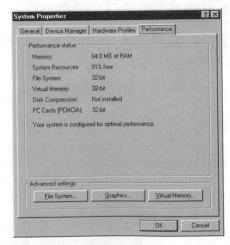

The top part of the window (grouped under the heading of Performance Status) displays key information about your system's performance:

Memory   Shows the amount of random access memory (RAM) on your system.

System Resources   Displays the percentage of system resources (such as windows, images, icons, and virtual memory) currently available for use. The higher the number, the better.

File System   Specifies whether you are using a 32-bit or MS-DOS compatibility mode (real-mode) file system.

Virtual Memory   Specifies whether you are using 32-bit or 16-bit disk-based virtual memory.

Disk Compression   Specifies whether you have enabled disk compression on your hard disk.

PC Cards (PCMCIA)   Specifies whether you have any PC Card sockets installed on your system.

Below the Performance Status section are three buttons, grouped under the Advanced Settings heading. Clicking the File System button displays the File System window, where you can configure settings specific to each of the drives attached to your system. Clicking the Graphics button displays the Advanced Graphics Settings window, where you can adjust your system hardware's graphics acceleration. Clicking the Virtual Memory button displays the Virtual Memory window, where you can adjust the size of the virtual memory cache for your system.

Managing Your System via the Windows XP Control Panel

Windows XP users will immediately notice that the default Control Panel interface in Windows XP is much different than that found in previous versions of Windows (that is, unless the Switch to Classic View option is selected in Control Panel). The icons and options that you see in Windows XP may be slightly different. But for the most part, the windows that you see in Windows XP will be fairly similar to those discussed in "Managing Your System via the Windows 9X/Me/2000/NT Control Panel." The following sections highlight where the differences occur, so you'll need to refer back to previous sections where indicated.

To open Control Panel in Windows XP, choose Start ➤ Control Panel. The default Control Panel interface (also referred to as Category View) is shown in Figure 35.40.

Setting Accessibility Options

By default, Windows XP installs accessibility tools (the Magnifier, high-contrast mouse pointers, and the Accessibility Wizard). To make use of these tools, click the Accessibility Options icon in the main window to open the Accessibility Options category window. From there, click the Accessibility Options control panel icon to see a window that looks similar to the one previously shown in Figure 35.2.

KEYBOARD FUNCTIONS

The Keyboard tab of the Accessibility Options window manages keyboard settings. The options and settings that you choose for StickyKeys, FilterKeys, and ToggleKeys are very similar to those discussed previously for earlier versions of Windows. Refer to Figures 35.2 through 35.4 and related discussions for further instructions on how to use these features.

FIGURE 35.40

Control Panel in
Windows XP

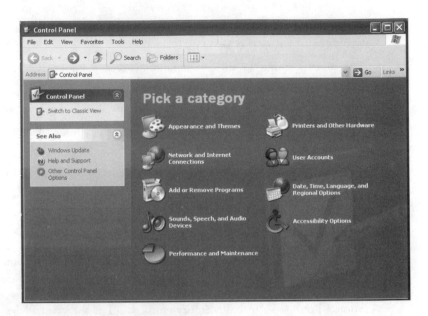

The procedure to enable or disable ToggleKeys is slightly different in Windows XP, however. On the Keyboard tab of the Accessibility Options window, check the Use Toggle Keys option and click the Settings button. This opens the Settings for ToggleKeys window, where you can elect to use a keyboard shortcut to enable or disable this feature.

SOUND

The Sound tab of the Accessibility Options window contains options for controlling sounds. The SoundSentry and ShowSounds options are similar to those discussed and shown previously in Figures 35.6 and 35.7, with the exception that you select a visual warning option from a drop-down list on the Sound tab instead of in a separate window. The visual warning setting determines which part of the screen will flash when the system generates a sound. For windowed programs (those that aren't full screen) you can select the title bar, the window itself, or the entire desktop.

DISPLAY

The Display tab of the Accessibility Options window controls the high-contrast and cursor options. To specify high contrast settings, check the Use High Contrast option and click the Settings button to display the Settings for High Contrast dialog box. In addition to several different high-contrast black and high-contrast white options with varying font sizes, you can choose from a good selection of Windows color schemes. All choices are available from the drop-down list shown in Figure 35.41. Windows XP also presents some cursor options on the Display tab that allow you to adjust the cursor blink rate from None to Fast, and the cursor width from Narrow to Wide.

MOUSE

The Mouse tab of the Accessibility Options window allows you to enable or disable the MouseKeys feature and to configure its settings. Refer to Figures 35.10 and 35.11 and related discussions for instructions on how to configure this option.

FIGURE 35.41

Select one of the High Contrast color schemes

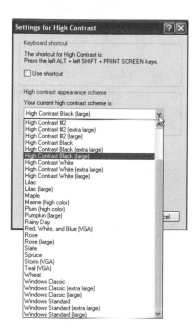

GENERAL

The General tab of the Accessibility Options window includes the Reset, Notification, and SerialKey Devices settings previously shown in Figure 35.12. In addition, it provides two options if you are logged on as an administrator: you can apply all settings to the logon desktop, or apply all settings as defaults for new users.

Adding New Hardware

In Windows XP, you add new hardware with the Add Hardware Wizard. Its features and options are similar to those discussed for the Add New Hardware Wizard found in previous versions of Windows (see Figure 35.13).

MANUALLY INSTALLING PLUG AND PLAY DEVICES

In the event that you need to manually install a device, you use Device Manager as discussed for previous versions of Windows. To determine which IRQs are being used in Windows XP:

1. From the Start menu or from your desktop, right-click My Computer and choose Properties.

2. Click the Hardware tab, and then click the Device Manager button to open Device Manager.

3. From Device Manager, choose View ➤ Resources by Type.

4. Expand the Interrupt Request (IRQ) list to view the system IRQs and the devices assigned to them.

Once you determine if any devices conflict with the new hardware, you can fix the conflicts in Device Manager. Choose View ➤ Devices by Type to return to the device list. For further discussion about how to use Device Manager, refer to Figures 35.14 through 35.16 and the related discussion.

Installing Boards That the System Can't Find

Sometimes you'll want to install a legacy board that the system just can't find at all. If the Add New Hardware Wizard is unable to detect the new device, try running it again, but this time, at the window shown in Figure 35.17, choose No, I Want to Select the Hardware from a List.

NOTE *The steps are similar in Windows XP. The Add Hardware Wizard presents two options: Search for and Install the Hardware Automatically (Recommended), and Install the Hardware That I Manually Select from a List (Advanced). Choose the second option.*

Now when you click the Next button, you'll be asked to choose a hardware category. See Figure 35.18; the window in the Windows XP Add Hardware Wizard is similar, as are the steps that you need to follow.

Adding and Removing Programs

The Add or Remove Programs window for Windows XP is shown in Figure 35.42. To open this window, choose Start ➤ Control Panel ➤ Add or Remove Programs. You'll find the program list by clicking the Change or Remove Programs icon.

REMOVING (UNINSTALLING) A PROGRAM

To remove a program, select it from the Currently Installed Programs list and click Change/Remove. After you confirm that you want to remove the program, the Uninstall program removes the program. Follow any other prompts to complete the uninstall process.

FIGURE 35.42

The Add or Remove Programs window in Windows XP displaying the Currently Installed Programs list

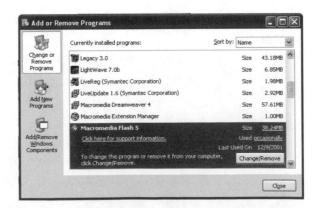

INSTALLING A PROGRAM

Insert the CD or disk containing the program. If the CD does not use AutoStart, click the Add New Programs icon in the Add or Remove Programs window. Then, click the CD or Floppy button. Follow the prompts in the wizard to search for the installation program, and then click Finish to start setup.

ADDING AND REMOVING WINDOWS COMPONENTS

Windows XP's Add/Remove Windows Components window lets you install or remove Windows components from your Windows installation. The component list that you see is similar to that shown in Figure 35.22, and the steps to install or remove components are relatively the same as in previous Windows versions.

STARTUP DISK

Windows XP does not provide an option to create a startup disk. Instead, you can boot into your computer with the Windows setup CD-ROM and run the Recovery Console. This is a DOS-based command utility that allows you to perform several different disk functions. You can also optionally install the Recovery Console onto your hard drive (*before* you crash!). Then, it will appear as a startup option when your system boots up. The steps to install the Recovery Console are outlined in the Windows XP Help and Support Center topic titled "Install the Recovery Console as a Startup Option."

Setting the Date/Time

To open the Date/Time Properties window in Windows XP, open Control Panel and click the Date, Time, Language, and Regional Options icon. In the resulting window, you can either pick the Change the Date and Time task or click the Date and Time icon.

TIP You can also open the Date/Time Properties window by double-clicking the time display in the Windows system tray.

As you'd expect, you set the date and time on the Date & Time tab. To set the date, choose the month and year you want from the selection lists and choose the day you want from the calendar. To change the time, click the item you want to change (hours, minutes, or seconds) in the list box and either type in a new time or click the up/down arrows to scroll to the correct time.

If you really dislike setting your clock all the time, Windows XP provides an option to keep your system clock ticking at the right time. Click the Internet Time tab to synchronize your PC clock with an Internet Time Server. Choose a server from the drop-down list, and click Update Now to update the time immediately. To keep your clock in perfect sync from then on, check the Automatically Synchronize with an Internet Time Server option (it's checked by default).

NOTE Automatic time synchronization can only occur when you're connected to the Internet.

To change your time zone, choose the Time Zone tab and select the appropriate time zone from the drop-down list. This tab also features an option that automatically adjusts your clock for daylight saving changes.

Changing Display Options

In Control Panel, click the Appearance and Themes category, then click the Display icon to open the Display Properties window. (You can also right-click the desktop and choose Properties).

Click the Desktop tab to display a set of options that are similar to those shown in Figure 35.25, and choose the Settings tab to display options that are similar to those shown in Figure 35.26. The steps for changing your screen resolution and color display are similar to those discussed previously.

To set properties for your adapter, monitor, and color management (among other things), click the Advanced button. The tabs that appear in the resulting window vary depending on your video card's driver, but they all have at least these four tabs: General, Adapter, Monitor, and Troubleshoot.

GENERAL

The General tab (similar to Figure 35.27) lets you change the system font size and specify whether the system restarts after you change display parameters:

Display (Font Size)   You can choose small, large, or custom font sizes. Large fonts are 125 percent the size of the Small (normal) fonts. If you select the Custom Setting option, you'll see the Custom DPI Setting window, which displays settings similar to those shown in Figure 35.28.

Compatibility   When you change the color depth of the display (from the Color palette list on the Settings tab, as shown in Figure 35.26), Windows will prompt you to restart, or not, depending on what you choose here. If you choose not to restart after changing the color depth, it may affect the quality or colors in your display.

ADAPTER

The Adapter tab helps you control the settings for your video card. Click the Properties button to open a Properties window for your video adapter. You'll see three tabs: General, Driver, and Resources.

General   Use the General tab to view the properties for your video adapter. If you're having problems with your video card, click the Troubleshoot button to open the Video Display Troubleshooter in the Windows XP Help and Support Center. You'll be prompted to step through a series of steps to help determine how to resolve the problem.

Driver   To choose a different driver, click the Update Driver and work through the Hardware Update Wizard. If the new driver gives you a new headache, you can click the Roll Back Driver button to revert to a driver that worked previously.

Resources   Use the Resources tab to view the resources used by your video adapter. The Resource Settings list displays the memory ranges, IRQs, and I/O ranges that are used by your video adapter. It also informs you if your video adapter conflicts with any other devices in your system.

MONITOR

On the Monitor tab, click the Properties button to change the monitor. You'll see a Troubleshooter button here, which opens the Video Display Troubleshooter. Click the Driver tab to update, roll back, or uninstall the drivers for your monitor, using steps similar to those discussed for the Adapter tab.

The Monitor tab in Windows XP also displays a drop-down list that allows you to choose a screen refresh rate. You have the option to hide modes that your monitor cannot display. If you don't have your owner's manual on hand to verify what is supported, it might be a good idea to enable this option. Why? Choosing improper refresh rates can lead to partial or total damage of your monitor! Be careful when selecting those refresh rates.

TROUBLESHOOT

The Troubleshoot tab provides a hardware acceleration slider that is similar to the Performance tab shown in Figure 35.32. Again, leave this set to Full unless you are having problems with video compatibility with a specific program.

Check the Enable Write Combining option if you need to speed up the display of information to your screen. Note, however, that the increased speed can sometimes corrupt your screen display, and you should clear the check box if you experience problems.

Modems

If you have a modem, choose Network and Internet Connections from Control Panel. Then, choose Phone and Modem Options from the See Also section in the left pane. The Phone and Modem Options window has three tabs: Dialing Rules, Modems, and Advanced, as shown in Figure 35.43.

FIGURE 35.43

The Phone and Modem Options window in Windows XP

CONNECTED MODEMS

In Windows XP, the Modems tab shows you the modems that are connected to your computer. You can also add or remove modems. Click the Properties button to view additional properties for the selected modem.

Dialing Rules

Use the Dialing Rules tab (shown in Figure 35.44) to configure your location. Click the Edit button to configure your location, including the area code, the number to dial for an outside line, and so on.

FIGURE 35.44

The Dialing Rules
tab in Windows XP

Adding or Removing Modems

On the Modems tab in the Phone and Modem Options window, click the Add button to add a new modem. This runs the Add New Modem Wizard, which is a specialized version of the Add New Hardware Wizard you saw earlier in the chapter.

The Remove button removes a modem's driver from the system. After you remove a modem's driver, you also need to physically remove the modem from the PC (if it's internal) or disconnect it (if it's an external model). Otherwise, Windows may redetect it and reinstall its driver the next time you start the PC.

Modem Properties

On the Modems tab in the Phone and Modem Options window, choose a modem from the Modem list and then click the Properties button to open the modem's Properties box. In Windows XP, this has five tabs: General, Modem, Diagnostics, Advanced, and Driver.

Use the General tab to view the status of your modem, as well as the make and manufacturer of the device. Click the Troubleshoot button to run the Modem Troubleshooter when you are having problems.

On the Modem tab in the Modem Properties window, you can choose or view the modem's COM port, adjust its speaker volume (if it has one), and set its maximum speed.

Use the Diagnostics tab to query your modem for commands and responses, and to view modem logging information.

In Windows XP, you can control connection and call preferences in the Default Preferences window. To open this window, click the Change Default Preferences button on the Advanced tab. This opens the Modem Default Preferences dialog box, which consists of two tabs: the General tab lets you configure call and data connection preferences, and the Advanced tab lets you choose hardware settings.

And finally, the last tab in the Phone and Modem Options dialog box is the Driver tab, which allows you to view driver details, or update, roll back, or uninstall your modem driver.

DIAGNOSTICS

In Windows XP, the Diagnostics tab of the Modems Properties window is somewhat similar to the Diagnostics tab for previous versions of Windows (see Figure 35.35). Choose the modem and then click the Query Modem button (in Windows XP). After a few seconds, a report appears. If at least some of the lines report "OK," then the modem is installed and working correctly.

System

To view the System Properties window in Windows XP, choose Start ➢ Control Panel ➢ Printers and Other Hardware, and then click the System icon in the See Also section. This window features seven tabs: General, Computer Name, Hardware, Advanced, System Restore, Automatic Updates, and Remote.

In Windows XP, the General tab displays general system information similar to that for classic Windows versions. The Computer Name tab allows you to view or change the network name for your computer. The Hardware tab enables you to add hardware, open Device Manager (described in the next section), or configure hardware profiles. The Advanced tab allows administrators to adjust settings for performance, user profiles, and startup and recovery. The System Restore tab enables you to turn System Restore features on or off, and to select the drives that are used to store and monitor restore settings. The Automatic Updates tab lets you configure or disable automatic updates of Windows XP. Finally, the Remote tab enables or disables the Remote Assistance feature on your computer.

NOTE   Windows XP's Remote Assistance feature is an alternative for those who have trouble diagnosing and managing hardware problems on their own. It allows a trusted friend or associate to connect to your computer from a remote location, over the Internet or a network, to view and manage your system remotely, by invitation. It's important to mention that you can decide whether or not to use this feature, and enable it through the Remote tab in the System Properties window. You can also set a limit on the number of days that your computer allows connections to be made.

DEVICE MANAGER

If you're familiar with previous versions of Windows, you'll find Windows XP's Device Manager to be quite similar. It's getting there that is a little bit different. Choose Start ➢ Control Panel ➢ Performance and Maintenance. Then click the System icon to open the System Properties window. On the Hardware tab, click the Device Manager button.

As with Device Manager in previous versions of Windows (see Figure 35.36), you'll see a list of all the devices installed on your system. The steps that you use to view, organize, and check problems for your hardware are very similar to those discussed for the previous Windows versions.

To view performance information in Windows XP, choose the Advanced tab in the System Properties window. Click the Settings button in the Performance section to open the Performance Options window. Here, you can configure options for visual effects, processor scheduling, memory usage, and virtual memory.

Using Windows' *Other* Utilities

There are more utilities available in Windows than are displayed in Control Panel. Some of these utilities are a bit technical in terms of what they monitor or do, and Microsoft does a pretty good job of keeping them hidden from casual users. However, if you're having problems with some new piece of hardware you've installed, you'll probably find at least some of these utilities essential to your ability to troubleshoot the problem.

System Monitor

The System Monitor utility is useful for checking your computer's current performance. Use System Monitor when your system is slowing down or locking up; it can tell you which device is using your system's resources when the problem occurs.

You launch System Monitor by selecting Start ➤ Programs ➤ Accessories ➤ System Tools ➤ System Monitor. The System Monitor window automatically displays your processor usage, as shown in Figure 35.45. If you want to monitor other system items, select Edit ➤ Add Item and then select the category you want to monitor.

NOTE   *In Windows XP, choose Start ➤ Control Panel ➤ Performance and Maintenance ➤ Administrative Tools ➤ Performance to view a similar graph.*

FIGURE 35.45

System Monitor

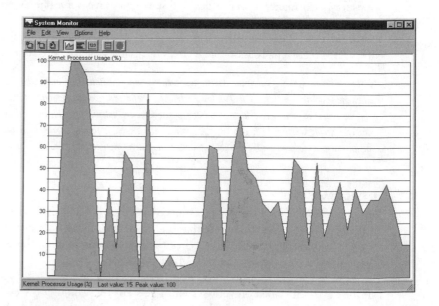

Microsoft System Information

Microsoft System Information (MSI) is a utility, new with Windows 98, that organizes a lot of system information and maintenance tools all in one place. You launch MSI by selecting Start ➤ Programs ➤ Accessories ➤ System Tools ➤ System Information. In Windows XP, choose Start ➤ Run. Enter **msinfo32.exe** in the Open box, and then click OK to run the utility.

As you can see in Figure 35.46, the left pane of the MSI window displays information about the four key parts of your system: Hardware Resources, Components, Software Environment, and Applications. (Some systems will also list an Internet Explorer item in the left pane.) Click the plus sign (+) next to one of the categories to display additional subcategories. When you highlight a specific subcategory, information about that topic appears in the right-hand pane.

FIGURE 35.46

Microsoft System Information

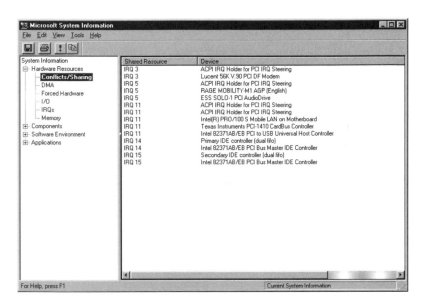

MSI is particularly useful for finding device conflicts. Open the Hardware Resources category and then select Conflicts/Sharing. The right-hand pane will now display a list of all shared IRQs—one of which is probably causing your current problem. Identify the problem IRQ, and then use Device Manager to either reconfigure or reinstall the device to use a different IRQ.

NOTE   Windows uses Microsoft System Information not only as a utility unto itself, but also as a kind of gateway to a number of other system utilities. Many of the so-called "hidden" tools discussed next are accessible from the Tools menu in the MSI utility—including the Windows Report Tool, Update Wizard Uninstall, System File Checker, the Signature Verification Tool, Registry Checker, the Automatic Skip Driver Agent, Dr. Watson, the System Configuration Utility, Scan-Disk, and Version Conflict Manager.

DirectX Diagnostic Tool

The DirectX Diagnostic Tool provides information about any DirectX components and drivers installed on your system, and gives you a way to test their sound and graphics output. You can also use this tool to disable or adjust particularly problematic hardware acceleration features. Like many of Windows' so-called hidden tools, this one is probably more useful to tech support personnel than it is to the typical user; the information gathered by this utility can provide useful technical information about any problems you encounter when running DirectX applications.

NOTE *This tool is available only if you have DirectX controls installed on your system. In Windows XP, choose Start ➤ Run, enter* **dxdiag** *in the Run window, and click OK.*

Information about DirectX components and drivers is displayed on separate tabs in the DirectX Diagnostic Tool window. For example, the System tab displays basic system information, and the DirectX Files tab, shown in Figure 35.47, displays the properties for each DirectX file installed on your system.

FIGURE 35.47

The DirectX Diagnostic Tool displaying the DirectX Files tab

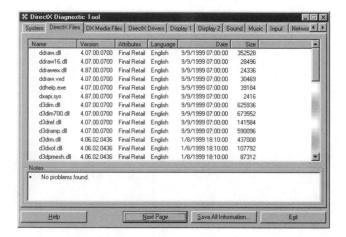

If you're having trouble running DirectX applications on your system, examine the file listings on these tabs for any obvious discrepancies. For example, if an input device (such as a joystick) isn't working, go to the Input tab and make sure that particular device is listed. (If it isn't, use Control Panel's Add/Remove Hardware applet to add the device to your system.) If your system is running erratically, go to the DirectX Drivers tab and look in the Certified column for any drivers labeled *No* (for uncertified). (Uncertified drivers have not been tested by Microsoft for full compatibility with the latest version of DirectX and could be interfering with your system performance.) You might also want to go to the DirectX Files tab and look in the Attributes column for any file that is not labeled *Final Retail*. (It's possible that a specific application has gotten out the door without all the final files in place, which can cause the application to run slower than normal, erratically, or not at all.) In other words, examine the listings on each tab and look for any items that aren't like the others—chances are that's the file causing your problem.

TESTING YOUR SYSTEM

The DirectX Diagnostic Tool also includes built-in tests for DirectDraw, Direct3D, DirectSound, DirectMusic, and DirectPlay. Each test is run at the click of a button, as follows:

DirectDraw   Select the Display tab and click the Test DirectDraw button. A series of windowed and full-screen tests will be executed.

NOTE *If you have more than one video card installed in your system, you'll have multiple Display pages.*

Direct3D   Select the Display tab and click the Test Direct3D button. A spinning cube should appear.

DirectSound   Select the Sound tab and click the Test DirectSound button. A series of sounds in different formats should play.

DirectMusic   Select the Music tab and click the Test DirectMusic button. A sample MIDI song should play. (You run this test on all MIDI devices activated on your system; make your selection from the Test Using This Port list.)

DirectPlay   This tests your system's capability for connecting to and communicating with other systems, which is necessary for playing multiplayer games. Go to the Network tab and click the Test DirectPlay button. When the DirectPlay Test window appears, make a selection from the Service Provider list and click OK to execute the test.

FIXING DIRECTX-RELATED PROBLEMS

Some DirectX problems are relatively easy to fix. (Some aren't.)

Sometimes you can fix a DirectX problem by restoring previous versions of the audio or video drivers. To do this, go to the More Help tab and click the Restore button, if it's visible. (If you don't have any older drivers installed on your system, this option won't be available.) This runs the DirectX Setup program; click the Restore Audio Drivers or Restore Display Drivers button to restore your audio or video drivers.

If you're experiencing audio-related problems, you may need to adjust the audio acceleration of your hardware. Go to the Sound tab and adjust the Hardware Sound Acceleration Level slider.

If necessary, you can disable the video acceleration on your system. Select the Display tab and click the Disable button next to DirectDraw Acceleration, Direct3D Acceleration, or AGP Support.

Windows Report Tool

You use the Windows Report Tool, shown in Figure 35.48, to create a report that can be sent to Microsoft Technical Support, detailing the specifics of a given problem.

FIGURE 35.48

Windows
Report Tool

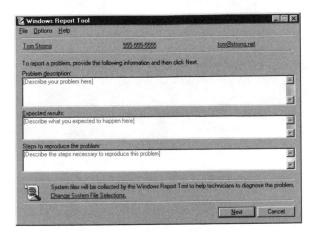

The Windows Report Tool window looks more or less like a "fill-in-the-blanks" type of e-mail response form—and, in essence, that's what it is. Enter a description of your problem, the expected results (like, "I want my system to run normally!"), and how to reproduce the current problem. When you click the Next button, the Windows Report Tool automatically copies pertinent information about your system and files, and attaches this information to a message that is sent to Microsoft Technical Support. The tech support folks will find this information useful and (you hope) suggest an effective course of action for getting your computer up and running again.

NOTE *In Windows XP, the Windows Error Reporting feature serves a similar purpose. From Control Panel, choose Performance and Maintenance, then select System. On the Advanced tab, click the Error Reporting button. The Error Reporting window allows you to enable or disable error reporting, and to choose programs for reporting to Microsoft Technical Support.*

Update Wizard Uninstall

When you run Windows Update (discussed later in this chapter), Windows is automatically updated with new or updated files or patches designed to improve the operation of the operating system. Unfortunately, updates sometimes cause problems that didn't exist before—which is where Update Wizard Uninstall comes in.

When you launch this utility, it displays a list of all the updates that have been installed on your system. Choose the specific update that you want to uninstall, and Update Wizard Uninstall reinstalls the older version of the driver or system file—thus "unupdating" that particular component.

System File Checker

System File Checker, shown in Figure 35.49, is a small but versatile utility that you can use to verify the integrity of key system files and then restore any files that have been corrupted. You also use System File Checker to extract any compressed files (such as drivers) from your Windows installation CD. It is not included with Windows XP.

To look for and then restore any altered or corrupted files, select the Scan for Altered Files option. System File Checker will scan your system, looking for key system files that have somehow been altered from their original states. (System File Checker compares each file with information stored in a *verification data file;* any discrepancy is counted as an alteration.) If a corrupted file is found, you will be prompted to restore the original file, normally from your Windows installation CD.

FIGURE 35.49

System File Checker

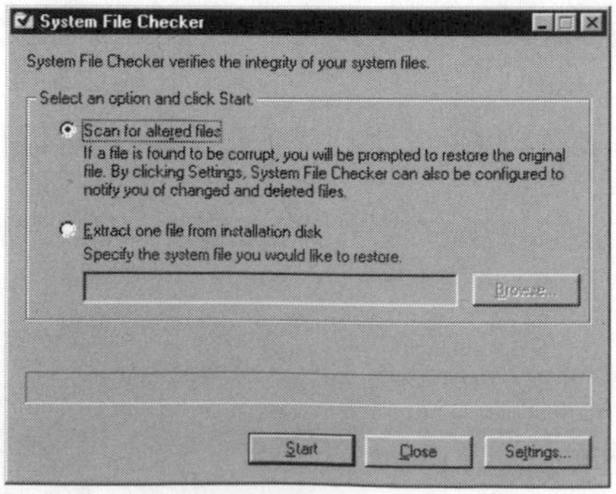

You can change the type of file that System File Checker checks—as well as where it looks for those files—by clicking the Settings button to display the System File Checker Settings window. When you select the Search Criteria tab, you can add or remove folders to check, as well as add or remove file types to check.

To restore a specific system file without scanning your hard disk first—or to install a new driver from your installation CD—select the Extract One File from Installation Disk option, then click the Browse button and select the file you want to restore. This extracts the selected file from its CAB file on your Windows installation CD, without you having to go through the entire Windows installation procedure just to get to that single file.

Signature Verification Tool

The Signature Verification Tool locates *certified* and *uncertified* files on your system. Certified, or signed, files have been granted a Microsoft digital signature that states that the file is an unaltered copy of the original file; uncertified, or unsigned, files are less trustworthy.

To be honest, there's not a lot of applicability for the Signature Verification Tool, outside the occasional hunt for files altered by computer viruses. Since antivirus programs do a much better job of hunting down these files, I don't know when you'd actually use this utility.

Registry Checker

Registry Checker is a utility that serves two functions. First, you can use it to find and fix errors in the Windows Registry. Second, you can use it to restore backup copies of the Registry—which is useful if you've ever damaged or corrupted the Registry. I'll discuss this utility in more detail toward the end of this chapter, in the "Fixing a Corrupted Registry" section.

Automatic Skip Driver Agent

The Automatic Skip Driver Agent (ASD) can be a very valuable tool—especially if you're having problems that occur during the Windows startup procedure. ASD identifies specific drivers that caused the operating system to stop responding on previous startups and then marks those drivers so that they're bypassed on subsequent startups.

If ASD identifies and disables a problem driver, you can reenable that driver by using the ASD utility. If the startup then proceeds as normal, great. If not, ASD will once again disable the driver when you restart your computer and display a suggested course of action. This utility is not included in Windows XP.

Dr. Watson

Dr. Watson is a familiar tool to experienced Windows users. It takes a snapshot of your system whenever a system fault occurs, which aids in the diagnosis of tricky problems.

By intercepting software faults, Dr. Watson identifies the software that failed and offers a general description of the cause. In some cases, Dr. Watson will diagnose the problem and offer a suggested course of action. You can also feed the information that Dr. Watson collects to tech support personnel; it will often provide the detailed technical information they need to find and fix tricky system problems.

System Configuration Utility

The System Configuration Utility, shown in Figure 35.50, is the tool you turn to when none of the other tools included with Windows helps you solve your problem. It automates major system troubleshooting, duplicating the procedures used by Microsoft's tech support staff when they try to diagnose system configuration problems. This utility leads you through a series of steps that, one by one, disable various components of your system on startup, until you're able to isolate the item that's causing your specific problem.

NOTE   *Heavy-duty tech-type folks sometimes refer to the System Configuration Utility by its filename:* MSCONFIG.EXE.

FIGURE 35.50

The System Configuration Utility (Windows 98 SE version)

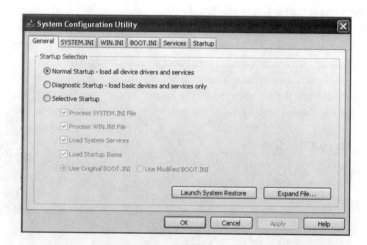

If your computer now starts normally, you know the problem was somewhere in those two files. If your computer still acts up, restart your system, select Step-by-Step Confirmation again, and this time choose to process all the files except AUTOEXEC.BAT.

If your computer now starts normally, you know the problem was with something that was loaded in the CONFIG.SYS file. You can turn off any or all commands in this file by returning to the System Configuration Utility and selecting the Config.sys tab. Working one line at a time, select an item in this file, click OK, and then reboot your computer. If your system works okay, the item you selected is okay; if your system fouls up, the item you selected is the cause of the problem. Working methodically, you can isolate the line (typically a device being loaded) that is causing your problem.

If, after working through these steps, your computer still acts up, select the Startup tab. Here you see a list of all the programs that are launched every time you start Windows. Work through this list, line by line (rebooting your computer after each change, of course), to determine whether one of these programs is causing your system problem.

If you work through the entire Startup list and still can't isolate your problem, return to the General tab and click the Advanced button to display the Advanced Troubleshooting Settings window.

From this window, you can disable specific devices on startup. Again, work through each device methodically, rebooting each time you deselect a device, to try to isolate the problem device.

Even though this process is time-consuming, more often than not it *will* help you isolate your problem. Of course, once the problem is isolated, you still have to fix it—usually by reinstalling a missing or corrupted driver file.

THE OTHER TABS

Moving to the right of the General tab, the next four tabs in the System Configuration Window display the contents of your system's key configuration files—`CONFIG.SYS`, `AUTOEXEC.BAT`, `SYSTEM.INI`, and `WIN.INI`. In Windows XP, you won't see these four tabs, but you will see one named for `BOOT.INI`. When you check a specific line on one of these tabs, you will cause that command to be executed during the diagnostic startup process. Deselecting a line will cause that command *not* to be executed.

The final tab, Startup, lists those files that launch automatically whenever you start your computer. You'd be surprised how many little files start up on startup—and these puppies are often the cause of conflict-related problems. As with the other tabs, checking a line will cause that program to run; deselecting a line will cause the program *not* to launch.

NOTE *The tabs in the Windows Me version of the System Configuration Utility are a little different from those in the Windows 98 version. In particular, you'll see a tab labeled Environment in Windows Me. The settings on this tab allow you to enable or disable particular environment variables, such as the TEMP and PATH variables. In previous versions of Windows, these variables were managed by the* `AUTOEXEC.BAT` *and* `CONFIG.SYS` *files. Since Windows Me does away with Real Mode DOS and therefore doesn't run those files on startup, these environment variables must be managed from the System Configuration Utility.*

The System Configuration Utility is an extremely powerful and useful diagnostic tool. Using it, however, can be very time-consuming; it's sometimes helpful to have a general idea what you're looking for, so you don't have to work through the entire list of potential problem causes. The utility, especially with its more advanced options, can also be a little intimidating to casual users. If you're baffled by what's going on here, you're better off leaving this level of troubleshooting to the pros.

ScanDisk

ScanDisk is the Windows-based version of the utility that finds and fixes errors on your hard disk drive(s). I won't go into more detail here, since ScanDisk is discussed in-depth in Chapter 16, "Care and Feeding of Hard Drives."

Version Conflict Manager

The Version Conflict Manager utility is used to restore old drivers that have been replaced by newer versions. If you install a new piece of software or hardware and then immediately notice problems with your system, there's a good chance that the problems are caused by the software copying a new version of the driver over the version previously installed on your hard drive. (This can be especially problematic if the new program actually copies an older version of a driver over the newer version previously installed on your system.)

Since previous versions of most drivers are automatically backed up and saved on your hard disk, you can use Version Conflict Manager to restore those drivers. When you launch this utility, you'll see a list of all files that have been backed up, along with the dates they were backed up and the version numbers of both backup and current files. If you notice that a backed-up file has a newer version number than the current file, chances are that's your problem. When you restore a backup file with Version Conflict Manager, the backup version is made current, and the current version is backed up—which returns that driver to the state it was in prior to the last installation.

NOTE *In Windows XP, the System Restore feature is used to restore old drivers. To turn System Restore on or off, choose Start ➤ Control Panel ➤ Performance and Maintenance ➤ System. Click the System Restore tab in the System Properties window.*

Updating Your System with Windows Update and AutoUpdate

Just because you have an older version of Windows doesn't mean that it can't be improved. Microsoft has a habit of releasing updated versions of critical system files to improve performance or—more often—to fix specific bugs.

In the old days, you would be aware of these updates only if you called technical support with a specific problem, and then the tech support folks sent you the update on disk. Starting with Windows 98, however, Microsoft has included a Windows Update utility (as well as a more automatic AutoUpdate utility in Windows Me) that enables any system to be automatically updated as soon as updated system files become available. When you run Windows Update or AutoUpdate, the utility compares the files on your computer system with a database of files on Microsoft's Web site, and then automatically downloads and installs any new or updated files your system needs for optimal operation.

Running Windows Update

If you're running Windows 98 (first or second editions) or Windows 2000/XP, you'll find Windows Update as an option off the Start menu.

You run Windows Update by selecting Start ➤ Windows Update (or Start ➤ All Programs ➤ Windows Update in Windows XP). Windows will then launch Internet Explorer and automatically navigate to the Windows Update Web page. Once there, you should click the Product Updates link to scan the files on your hard disk and update those drivers that have been updated since your last visit.

As you can see, Windows Update is, more or less, a manually operated utility. If you want to more completely automate the update process, you have to upgrade to Windows Me and its AutoUpdate utility.

Using AutoUpdate

AutoUpdate is a more automatic update utility, found in Windows Me and XP. Like Windows Update, it uses the Internet to check for updated system files, and then downloads and installs those files on your PC. Unlike Windows Update, AutoUpdate will check for and download updates automatically, without your manual intervention.

NOTE   The files that AutoUpdate checks for and downloads essentially comprise a subset of the files tracked with Windows Update. For this reason, Windows Me and XP still include the Windows Update utility, for when you need a more complete system file check.

Within a day or two of your first installing Windows Me or XP, the AutoUpdate program will launch itself and ask whether you'd like to enable the AutoUpdate feature. (No telling when this initial program will run; it seems to be on some sort of timer related to the installation of the operating system.) When you're presented with the Update Settings window, you have three options:

Automatically Download Updates and Notify Me when They Are Ready to Be Installed
This option runs AutoUpdate automatically, in the background. If you don't want to be bothered with system updates, choose this option.

Notify Me before Downloading Any Updates and Notify Me Again when They Are Ready to Be Installed   This option runs AutoUpdate automatically, but prompts you before any files are downloaded or installed. If you want to be informed before any changes are made to your system, choose this option.

Turn Off Automatic Updating. I Will Update My Computer Manually   As it says, this option turns off AutoUpdate. Your system will *not* be automatically updated.

Once AutoUpdate is activated, it will activate a small executable file (noticeable in the list of running tasks) once a day and poll the Microsoft Web site for updates. If you chose the first option, you will not be prompted during this process; it happens automatically. If you chose the second option, you'll be notified before any files are downloaded; you can choose to download the files now or remember them for a later download.

NOTE   Interestingly, AutoUpdate not only checks for updated system files, but it also takes the opportunity to update itself, if a newer version of the program is available.

You can change your AutoUpdate settings post-installation by opening Control Panel and launching the Automatic Updates applet. This will display the Update Settings window, where you can change your settings—or restore any previous updates that you declined to install at the time.

Recovering Your System with Windows Me's System Restore

If you've been using computers for any length of time, you may have had the misfortune to come across the sort of catastrophic problem that requires you to completely reinstall your operating system. (Some troubles are so complex that they can't be fixed, only replaced.) If this has ever happened to you, you'll appreciate a new feature of Windows Me and XP, called *System Restore*. With System Restore, reinstallations are a thing of the past—because it can automatically restore your system to the state it was in before the problem cropped up.

Think of System Restore as a safety net for your essential system files. It isn't a backup program per se; it simply notes system-level changes that have been made at various points in time and (when activated) reverses those changes.

TIP   If you're running an older (pre-Windows Me/XP) version of Windows, you can obtain the same automatic restore functionality with third-party utilities such as Roxio's GoBack (`www.roxio.com/en/products/goback/`).

Setting System Restore Points

System Restore actively monitors your system and notes changes made when you install new applications. Each time it notes a change, it automatically creates what it calls a *restore point*—essentially a "snapshot" of your system at that point in time. (Actually, it's a snapshot of the Windows Registry, along with selected dynamic system files.)

When activated, System Restore also creates a new restore point after every 10 hours of system use—and you can choose to manually create a new restore point at any other time. For example, you probably should create a restore point any time you add a new piece of hardware or peripheral to your system.

To set a restore point manually, select Start ➢ Programs (All Programs in XP) ➢ Accessories ➢ System Tools ➢ System Restore. When the System Restore window opens, select Create a Restore Point and click Next. You'll be prompted to provide a name and description to this new restore point; do so and click Next, and the restore point will be created.

If an installation goes bad, you can run System Restore and pick a restore point before the problem installation. System Restore will then undo any changes made to monitored files, capturing the file state at the time of the restore point. It also replaces the current Registry with the one captured at the restore point. This will restore your system to the pre-installation (that is, *working*) state.

WARNING   Since System Restore monitors only system files, you cannot use it to restore changed or damaged data files. So if you use System Restore, you'll still need to back up your important data files on a regular basis.

RESTORING YOUR SYSTEM

Restoring your system from a restore point is as simple as picking the point and letting System Restore do the rest of the work.

You start by selecting Start ➢ Programs (All Programs in XP) ➢ Accessories ➢ System Tools ➢ System Restore. When the System Restore window opens, select Restore My Computer to an Earlier Time; then click Next. The next window displays a calendar showing the current month (you can also move back and forward through the months), with some dates highlighted in bold; each highlighted date contains at least one restore point. Select a restore point and then click Next to continue the restoration procedure. When the process is complete, System Restore reboots your system, and you should be up and ready to go (in about 30–45 minutes, that is—it takes that long to complete a restore).

Let's look at an example of System Restore at work. Assume you've just installed a new piece of software, a game that promises state-of-the-art 3D graphics and animation. The game plays okay, but when you exit to Windows you notice that something has screwed up your system's video, which is stuck in 640 × 480 VGA mode. Now, in the past you may have spent half the afternoon resetting settings and reinstalling drivers—or, in the most extreme cases, reinstalling Windows. With System Restore, you simply pick a restore point prior to the installation of your new game, and your system is restored to its previous working condition. (In this case, not only will your video be restored, but the new game will be uninstalled.) It's that simple.

NOTE *System Restore doesn't perform an actual restore/backup operation, so it will not return your entire system to a pristine state. Some changes made between restore points will remain—such as new icons on your desktop or nonessential files left in otherwise deleted directories—which means that you might have a little cleanup work to do after you avail yourself of the utility.*

Reconfiguring and Disabling System Restore

System Restore, while extremely useful, doesn't come without a cost—in disk space. Each restore point includes copies of your key system files, in compressed format, which are then stored on your hard disk. Make too many restore points, and your hard disk space starts getting eaten up. (System Restore needs a *minimum* of 200MB disk space—and can use a lot more!)

By default, System Restore appropriates 12 percent of the total space on the system partition (usually drive C). You can change this number by right-clicking My Computer, selecting Properties, and then selecting the Performance tab. Click the File System button to display the File System Properties window, select the Hard Disk tab, and you'll see a System Restore Disk Space Use option. Adjust this number lower if you don't want to give up the disk space (this will also limit the number of restore points you can store); adjust this number higher to store more restore points. (System Restore operates on a first-in, first-out basis, so your most recent restore points will always be available.)

SYSTEM FILE PROTECTION

System Restore incorporates a feature called *System File Protection (SFP)*. SFP works in the background to ensure that when you install a new application, that application doesn't overwrite key system files (such as DLLs). This issue of new programs overwriting files used by other programs has been a long-standing problem in the Windows world, and SFP was designed to prevent installation programs from misbehaving in this manner. In all, it's a terrific idea and helps to improve the stability of the Windows Me platform.

SFP contains a database of system files to monitor, almost 900 files in all, called the SFP Monitor. In addition, a copy of each file in the database is kept in a hidden location on your hard disk. When one of the monitored files is overwritten or deleted, SFP Monitor automatically restores the original version of the file—unless the new version is a more recent version. If the new version of the file is more recent, then SFP stores a copy of that version in its hidden folder. This process occurs automatically, totally without user intervention.

The list of protected files can be found in the Windows Me Restore directory (C:\Windows\System\Restore\Filelist.xml). As you can see by examining this list, SFP protects core system files—*not* data files or program files installed by other programs.

Of course, you can choose to turn off System Restore completely. You also do this in the File System Properties window. Select the Troubleshooting tab and then select the Disable System Restore option. You can reenable System Restore by deselecting this option.

I recommend that if you're running Windows Me or XP, you use System Restore. In fact, this life-saving utility might be the only significant reason to upgrade from Windows 98/2000 to Windows Me/XP. It's the sort of system insurance that Windows should have had from the start.

Using Other Software Tools

In addition to the utilities built into the Windows operating system, there are other software tools that often prove useful for tracking down hardware-related problems. This section looks at a few of those tools.

Windows Resource Kit

Microsoft's Windows Resource Kits provide a wide variety of tools and utilities that add more functionality to the operating system—particularly for network administrators. There are separate Resource Kits for all but one version of Windows.

NOTE   *No Windows Resource Kit is available for Windows Me.*

Here's a brief list of some of the more useful tools found in the Windows 98 Resource Kit. (See `http://support.microsoft.com/support/kb/articles/Q247/0/24.ASP` for a complete list of tools in the Windows 98 Resource Kit; see `http://mspress.microsoft.com/Books/1340.htm` for ordering information.)

Animated Cursor Editor   Enables you to create cursors with animated effects.

Batch98   Creates files for an automated Windows installation—useful for network-based installations.

Checklinks   Finds and eliminates dead links and shortcuts on your system—a good utility to run after you've deleted an application from your hard drive.

ClipTray   Enables advanced management of the Windows Clipboard.

Code Page Changer   Changes the code pages in MS-DOS programs to match Windows' regional settings.

Default Printer   Places an icon on the Taskbar that lets you switch printers with a single click.

Dependency Walker   Determines the minimum number of files necessary to launch an application. Also can determine if a file is shared but no longer in use by another application.

FAT32 Conversion Information Tool   Estimates the amount of disk space gained by converting a hard disk to the FAT32 file system.

FileWise   Enables network administrators to compare the differences between two files or between two PCs on the network.

Lfnback   Lets you use long filenames with older disk utilities.

Microsoft File Information   A very useful utility that provides detailed information about Windows system files—including the date the file was created, in which CAB file the file was originally stored on the Windows installation CD, where the file resides on your hard disk, and the file size.

Minitel TTF Files   Configures HyperTerminal to emulate French Minitel terminals.

Network Monitor Service   Enables remote monitoring of network performance.

Password List Editor   Removes entries from a Windows password list.

Quiktray   Lets you add items to or remove items from the Taskbar. You can use Quiktray to create shortcuts to your favorite programs or files, directly in the Taskbar.

Remote Registry Service   Enables remote viewing and editing of Registry entries; for network administrators.

RPC Print Provider   Lets Windows 98 PCs administer print queues on Windows NT networks.

SNMP Agent   Lets Windows 98 PCs communicate on SNMP networks.

Text File Viewer   Displays the contents of text files.

Time Zone Editor   Creates and edits time zone entries for the Date/Time function.

TimeThis   A script that times how long it takes for a PC to execute a specific command.

TweakUI   A separate utility that enables you to "tweak" various aspects of the operating system, including menu speed, animation effects, shortcut names, desktop and Control Panel icons, and boot behavior.

USB Viewer   Displays configuration information about any USB devices installed on your system; a very useful utility for tracking down problems with USB peripherals.

UUCode   Enables you to encode and decode information in the popular UUEncoding encryption format.

Waitfor   A script that makes a PC wait for a signal sent over a network.

Where   Finds files on your hard disk.

WinDiff   Compares and contrasts the contents of files and directories.

Windows 98 INF Installer   Enables the addition of new drivers and INF files to the Windows setup.

Windows Boot Editor   Manages all aspects of your PC's bootup process—you can change the startup screen, automatically boot to the startup menu, disable ScanDisk, and make other changes.

Winset   A script that sets global Windows environment variables.

It's hard to say that any specific utility in the Windows 98 Resource Kit is a necessity—especially when the entire kit costs about $70. However, if you're managing a large number of Windows-based computers over a network, the Resource Kit might be worth the expense; many of its utilities are specifically targeted toward network administrators, and do ease the task of installing and managing Windows on multiple PCs.

NOTE *Different Resource Kits are available for each of the two versions of Windows 2000. The Windows 2000 Server Resource Kit contains nearly 300 software tools—including tools for group policy management, user migration, drive share configuration, application security, and automated application installation. The Windows 2000 Professional Resource Kit contains more than 200 software tools. See* `www.microsoft.com/windows2000/library/resources/reskit/rktour/default.asp` *for more information.*

Third-Party Tools

In addition to Microsoft-supplied tools, a number of system utilities are available from third-party vendors, such as Symantec and McAfee. These tools typically supplement the utilities included with your operating system, and can be quite useful in helping to prevent and repair major system problems.

NORTON UTILITIES

The granddaddy of system utility programs is the venerable Norton Utilities, published by Symantec. The latest version of this program, Norton Utilities 2002, works with all recent versions of Windows—including Windows 98/Me/NT/2000/XP.

Norton Utilities is actually a collection of utilities, each designed to monitor or repair a specific area of system performance. Included in this latest version are Norton WinDoctor (diagnoses and fixes Windows-related problems), Norton Speed Disk (defragments and reorganizes your hard disk), Norton Disk Doctor (detects and repairs various hard drive problems), Norton System Doctor (looks for and fixes potential disk and system problems), and several more useful utilities.

A copy of Norton Utilities will set you back about $50 ($30 for the upgrade). See the Symantec Web site (`www.symantec.com/nu/nu_9x/`) for more information.

NOTE *If you like Norton Utilities, you may also want to check out Norton SystemWorks, which combines Norton Utilities with Norton AntiVirus, Norton CleanSweep, and Norton Web Services in a single $70 package.*

McAFEE UTILITIES

Symantec's biggest competitor is McAfee, and their McAfee Utilities product competes head-to-head with Norton Utilities. The various tools included in McAfee Utilities are designed to prevent system crashes, diagnose and repair hard drive problems, defragment your hard drive, repair the Windows Registry, personalize the Windows environment, back up your essential documents, and undo system configuration changes.

At about $50, McAfee Utilities is priced comparably to Norton Utilities, for similar (but not identical) functionality. (McAfee Utilities is also Windows 95/98/Me-specific; as I write this, the product won't work with Windows NT/2000/XP.) See the McAfee Web site (`www.mcafee.com`) for more information.

SHAREWARE UTILITIES

In addition to these commercial utilities, there are many freeware and shareware utilities that can help you manage and troubleshoot your system hardware. In fact, so many software tools are available that I can't mention them all here. I recommend you go to the Tucows download site (`www.tucows.com`) and check out the utilities available for your operating system—you'll probably find something you want to download right away!

Managing the Windows Registry

The majority of your system's configuration is stored in a huge database of information called the Windows Registry. The Registry contains all the properties you set via Control Panel, settings for each of the applications installed on your system, and configuration information for all your system's hardware and peripherals.

The Registry is updated automatically whenever you change a configuration through normal means. You can also make changes directly to the Registry, using a utility called the Registry Editor that is discussed later in this section. Know, however, that editing the Registry directly is a tricky proposition—if you do something wrong, you could make your system totally inoperable. For that reason, you should edit the Registry only if it's necessary to correct an otherwise hard-to-fix problem—and you should back up the Registry before attempting any edits.

Understanding the Registry

Why have a Registry? Well, in the old days of computing, when you wanted to install a new software program, you just copied the files for the program onto your hard disk and ran them. Some programs were a little large, so they might be broken into task-specific modules that made it easier to maintain them. Later, some programmers found that they could maintain a library of modules that did certain tasks that they could use over and over in different programs.

Eventually, this led to the concept of object-oriented programming, whereby each object in a program has a set of qualities or capabilities that define it. An object can have an image or an icon that is connected to it. It can use special kinds of windows, and so on. These resources are maintained in different places. The Registry keeps track of all the pieces of your programs so it can find them when it needs them.

Prior to Windows 95, that information was stored in the WIN.INI and SYSTEM.INI files—as well as in separate INI files for individual applications. Windows 95 (and all subsequent versions of Windows) replaced all these different configuration files with the Windows Registry. All settings for new devices and new software programs are now written directly to the Registry, bypassing the old WIN.INI and SYSTEM.INI files.

In the name of compatibility, however, the WIN.INI and SYSTEM.INI files still exist—and may still be used by any older (pre-Windows 95) software and hardware still installed on your system. For that reason, Windows still has to maintain all those older configuration files, even though they're used only for older programs and devices that may (or may not) be installed on your system. Unfortunately, Windows loads *all* these files on startup—and you may still have to check the WIN.INI and SYSTEM.INI files if you experience a problem with any legacy program or peripheral.

The thing to remember is that all new hardware and software use the Registry, while older hardware and software use the older configuration files.

Backing Up and Restoring the Registry

Because editing the Registry is risky—even for experienced computer users—you should back up the Registry files before you commence making any changes. This will give you the option of restoring the pre-edited Registry, just in case anything goes wrong.

NOTE   If you're running Windows Me or XP, the System Restore feature automatically backs up your Registry whenever a restore point is created. If you're going to edit your Registry, make sure you create a new restore point immediately prior to making any changes.

The Registry is composed of two hidden files, SYSTEM.DAT and USER.DAT, located in the \Windows folder. Before you can back up these files, you first have to "unhide" them. You do this by selecting Start ➢ Settings ➢ Folder Options (or Start ➢ Control Panel ➢ Appearance and Themes ➢ Folder Options in Windows XP) to display the Folder Options window. Select the View tab and then select the Show All Files option.

Once the Registry files are unhidden, use either My Computer or Windows Explorer to create a new subfolder in the \Windows folder; name this new subfolder Registry. Now copy the SYSTEM.DAT and USER.DAT files from the \Windows folder to the \Windows\Registry folder.

TIP   To be extra safe, you can also copy the Registry files to another medium, such as a CD-RW, Zip disk, or floppy disk (in compressed format). This enables you to keep a copy of your Registry away from your PC—and allows a faster restore if something catastrophic happens to your computer system.

After you've backed up the Registry, if you encounter any Registry-related problems (after the installation of new software or hardware, for example), all you have to do is restore the backup files to return your system to the state it was in prior to encountering these problems. Note, however, that you can't restore these files from regular Windows mode; you have to perform the Registry restore from either Safe mode or MS-DOS mode.

To perform a Registry restore, begin by rebooting your system and pressing F8 during the boot process; select Safe Mode from the Windows Startup menu to start up in Safe mode. While in Safe mode, use My Computer or Windows Explorer to copy the SYSTEM.DAT and USER.DAT files from the \Windows\Registry folder back into the \Windows folder. (This will overwrite the existing—and problematic—Registry files.) Now you can reboot your computer in normal mode, and your system will be restored to its previous condition.

Even though you should still make manual backups of your Registry files before attempting major Registry changes, Windows 98/Me/2000/XP (but not Windows 95) automatically makes backup copies of the Registry files every time you start your computer. When Windows starts, a hidden program called Registry Checker automatically scans your Registry for errors; if it notices a problem, it replaces the current version of the Registry with the "clean" backup copy. (Read ahead for more information about using Registry Checker to fix a corrupted Registry.)

You can also use Registry Checker to manually restore the backup copy Windows made the last time you started your computer. Note, however, that you have to use Windows' MS-DOS mode to restore this Registry backup.

To enter MS-DOS mode, select Start ➤ Shut Down, and then select Restart in MS-DOS Mode. When your computer reboots, you'll see the now-antiquated C:\> prompt at the top of your screen. At the prompt, type **CD C:\WINDOWS\COMMAND** and press Enter. At the prompt, type **SCANREG/RESTORE** and press Enter. This launches Registry Checker, which will automatically restore the backup copy of your Registry. When the restore is complete, press Ctrl+Alt+Del to restart your computer (back into regular Windows mode).

WARNING   Although using Registry Checker to restore a backup is easier than manually restoring a backup, it may not be able to restore your most recent backup of the Registry. Remember, any backup you make after starting the current session of Windows will be more up-to-date than the backup made at startup. Plus, Registry Checker is relatively dumb; if the prior version of the Registry was corrupted, Registry Checker will blindly restore the corrupted version.

Fixing a Corrupted Registry

You can also use Registry Checker to fix a corrupted Registry. It's a good idea to run Registry Checker before you try to restore a backup copy of the Registry—if the problems in the Registry are minor, Registry Checker can fix them for you and save you the hassle of a full restore process.

You can run Registry Checker from the Microsoft System Information utility (select Tools ➤ Registry Checker), or directly from Windows (select Start ➤ Run to display the Run window; type **SCANREG** in the Open box, and click OK). Registry Checker will launch and start scanning your Registry for errors. Any errors it finds, it will automatically fix. When it's done scanning, Registry Checker makes another backup of the Registry, for safekeeping.

Editing the Registry

Most of the time you won't need to bother with the Registry—it operates in the background, automatically updated whenever you change a Windows setting or install a new piece of software or hardware. However, there will come a time when you experience a particularly vexing system problem that can be fixed only by editing a particular value in the Registry—typically on the instructions of one of your vendors' tech support people. (Trust me, it happens.) When worse comes to worst, you need to know how to edit the Registry—which you do via the Registry Editor utility.

USING THE REGISTRY EDITOR

The Registry Editor is a powerful utility that lets you edit individual values in the Registry. You start the Registry Editor by selecting Start ➤ Run to display the Run window; type **REGEDIT** in the Open box and then click OK.

The Registry Editor window has two panes, as shown in Figure 35.51. The left-hand pane displays the different parameters or settings, called *keys*; all keys have numerous *subkeys*. The right-hand pane displays the values, or configuration information, for each key.

FIGURE 35.51

Windows Registry

You display the different levels of subkeys the same way you open folders and subfolders in Windows Explorer: by clicking the plus sign (+) next to a specific item. You edit a particular value by highlighting the subkey in the left-hand pane and then double-clicking the value in the right-hand pane. This displays the Edit Value (or Edit String) window. Enter a new value in the Value Data box and then click OK.

Registry settings are changed *as you make the changes*—there is no Save command in the Registry Editor. There is also no Undo command, so be careful about the changes you make—they're final!

To add a new value to a subkey, right-click the subkey and select one of the New ➤ Value options from the pop-up menu. (You can choose from String Value, Binary Value, or DWORD Value; the instructions for whatever you're adding should indicate the type of value to add.) Type a name for the new value, then double-click the value to display the Edit Value (or Edit String) window. Enter the new value in the Value Data box, then click OK.

You can also add new subkeys to the Registry. Just right-click the key where you want to add the subkey, then select New ➤ Key from the pop-up menu. A new subkey (with a temporary name) appears; type a name for the new subkey, and then press Enter.

To delete a subkey or value, right-click the item and select Delete. Remember, however, that all changes are final—once a subkey is deleted, it's gone!

UNDERSTANDING REGISTRY KEYS

When you edit the Registry, there are literally thousands of separate keys that contain configuration information. These keys are organized into a handful of *root* keys, as follows:

HKEY_CLASSES_ROOT   Contains all file associations.

HKEY_CURRENT_USER   Contains profile settings for each user on this PC.

HKEY_LOCAL_MACHINE   Contains settings for this specific PC—this is where the majority of the settings reside and is the section you're most likely to edit.

HKEY_USERS   Contains settings used by all users.

HKEY_CURRENT_CONFIG   Contains universal system preferences.

HKEY_DYN_DATA   Contains hardware status and driver settings.

TIP   You can search for specific keys or settings by selecting Edit ➤ Find.

You'll find most hardware-related settings under the HKEY_LOCAL_MACHINE key, under the Driver, Hardware, and HwDiag subkeys. Most software-related settings are also under the HKEY_LOCAL_MACHINE key, under the vendor's dedicated subkey. Key Windows system settings are found under the HKEY_LOCAL_MACHINE\Microsoft\Windows\CurrentVersion\ subkey.

TIP   Look in the HKEY_LOCAL_MACHINE\SOFTWARE\Microsoft\Windows\CurrentVersion\Run subkey for programs and drivers that are launched whenever Windows starts—these easily overlooked devices are often the cause of particularly nasty driver conflicts.

Troubleshooting Tips

If you're having problems with the software side of your computer—that is, with Windows—try some of these ideas for fixing it up:

◆ If you don't have an Accessibility icon in your Control Panel, add the Accessibility tools with Add/Remove Programs. Choose Accessibility from the list of categories on the Windows Setup tab.

◆ If Windows doesn't automatically detect your new hardware, use the Add New Hardware icon in Control Panel to detect it.

◆ Use the Microsoft System Information and System Configuration Utility tools to track down pesky device conflicts and driver problems.

◆ If a device conflict prevents Windows from seeing the device, try removing devices that are possibly competing with the new device and adding them back in after the new device is working.

◆ If you're running Windows Me or XP, use System Restore to restore previous system parameters if a new installation messes up your system.

◆ Older devices may not be Plug and Play compatible; check older circuit boards for jumpers or switches that set a particular I/O address or IRQ.

◆ Sometimes removing a device from Device Manager and allowing the system to redetect it will assign a different IRQ to the device and avert a conflict.

◆ Use the Have Disk option to install an updated driver from a disk or from a download.

◆ After removing a program from Windows, its folder may be left on the hard disk, along with a few stray files. You can manually delete these.

◆ If the settings choices on the Settings tab of the Display Properties window are less than what you know your video card will support (for example, if it shows only 16 colors and only 640 × 480 standard VGA resolution when you have a better-than-VGA video card—that is, any video card made in the last eight years or so), perhaps the video driver being used is wrong. Windows may have incorrectly detected it as Standard VGA. In that case, choose Advanced. On the Adapter tab, choose Change to install a different video driver.

◆ If your modem isn't working but you don't know whether it is a problem with the modem itself or with the phone line, run a diagnostic check. Choose Modems from Control Panel. On the Diagnostics tab, choose the modem and click More Info. If at least some of the lines in the resulting report say "OK," the modem itself is working.

USING WINDOWS TROUBLESHOOTERS

Windows 98/Me/XP (but *not* Windows 95!) include several *Troubleshooters* that walk you through device conflicts on your system. Using one of these Troubleshooters is an easy way to find and fix hardware problems.

The Troubleshooters are found in the Windows Help system. To see a list of Troubleshooters, select Start ➤ Help to display the Help window, then select the Contents tab and click Troubleshooting. When you select a specific Troubleshooter, it will display in the right-hand pane of the Help window.

Each Troubleshooter leads you step by step through a series of questions designed to track down the solution to your specific problem. All you have to do is answer the interactive questions in the Troubleshooter, and you'll be led to the probable solution to your problem.

Windows Troubleshooters can help you diagnose and fix many (but not all) common system problems. It's a good idea to try the appropriate Troubleshooter before attempting to track down a problem on your own—hey, you never know, it might be an easy problem to fix!

Well, I hope you learned much and enjoyed reading this edition of *The Complete PC Upgrade & Maintenance Guide*. My goal with this book has been to instruct not only how to remove and install new hardware and maintain your system, but to provide background information, in a layperson's terms, of how computers and software actually work. It's this foundation that will help you understand the technologies of decades to come—how they work, how they fit into the big picture, and how they will affect older technologies. PC technology will continue to evolve, and as it does we'll find ourselves increasingly reliant on our PCs, both in the home and the office. Knowing how to fix or diagnose a PC or make it perform better is, and will continue to be, a highly prized talent.

And so I thank you for choosing the 2003 edition of this book as your guide through the vast amounts of information, gotchas, real-world stories, and asides. Also, I'd like to add a hearty thanks to those of you who have been loyal readers throughout the years.

Good luck in your computing endeavors!

Appendix A

A Short Overview on Reading Hexadecimal

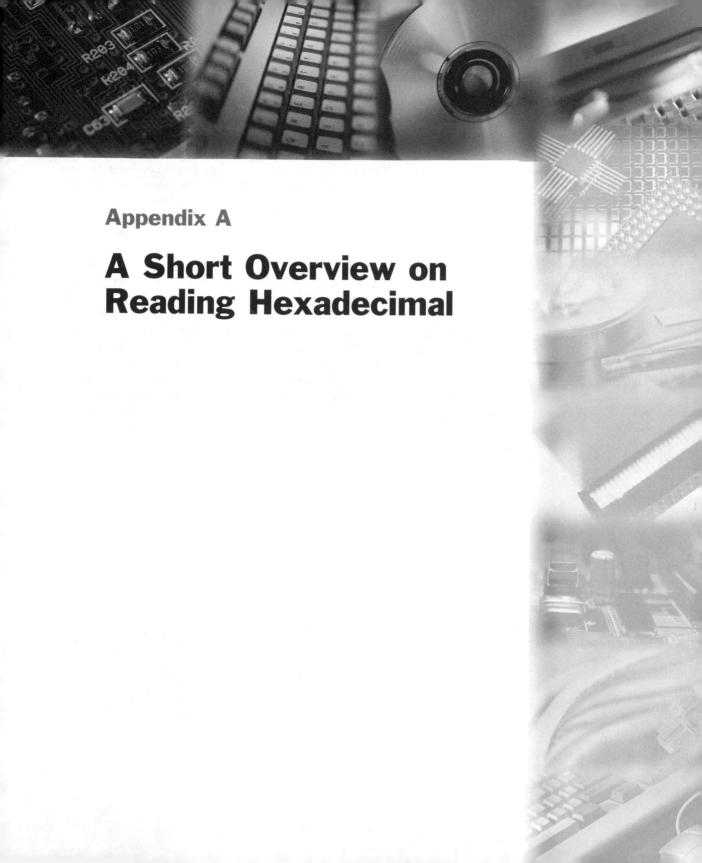

Introduction

THROUGHOUT THIS BOOK, and in other technical publications, you see numbers expressed not in *decimal*, the numeric system that we're all accustomed to, but rather in *hexadecimal*, a somewhat different system. This appendix is a quick guide to what you need to know about hexadecimal.

The decimal system is based on the number 10 as we know it—the number of fingers on most people's hands. *Dec-*, a word root, permeates the language: *decathlon* refers to a contest with 10 sporting events, *decimate* literally means to kill every 10th man, and *December* is the name of what once was the 10th month. We write "ten" as "10," but that's really only correct if we base the numbering system on 10. Strictly speaking, the number that I wrote is "one zero," and it means different things in different number systems.

Look at the sequence of how we write the first 11 numbers: 0, 1, 2, 3, 4, 5, 6, 7, 8, 9, 10. Why is "ten" written with two digits, not with one digit, as all the numbers before are? Because the system is based on 10. So ten is written 10, pretty much by definition once you decide that you're using 10 as your number base. Next, look at 10 times 10, or 100: it is written 100—the first number with three digits. Ditto for the first number with four digits—1000, which is 10 times 10 times 10. Why'd we pick 10 as a basis for a number system? No one knows, but the obvious guess is that 10 is, again, the number of fingers that most people have.

For reasons that aren't really worth pursuing here, it's easiest to talk about numbers in a computer system (memory or I/O addresses, for example) not in a number system based on 10, but rather on 8 or 16. A base-8 system is called *octal*, and a base-16 system is called *hexadecimal*, or *hex* for short. PCs tend to use hex, so I'll discuss that here. You don't even have to know hex in its entirety, just a few salient points.

Counting in Hex

Recall that a base-10 system uses 10 single-digit numbers up to, but not including, the number 10 (0–9). A base-16 system, similarly, has 16 single-digit numbers up to, but not including, 16 (0–9 and A–F). You can see a base-16 system in Table A.1.

TABLE A.1: HEX DIGITS AND DECIMAL EQUIVALENTS

HEX DIGIT	DECIMAL VALUE
0	0
1	1
2	2
3	3
4	4
5	5
6	6
7	7
8	8
9	9
A	10
B	11
C	12
D	13
E	14
F	15
10	16

As you can see, the next number after F is 10 (which is 16 in decimal). Next would come 11 (which is 17 in decimal). With any numbering system, you count from 0 to the highest number in the system and then go to 10. In decimal, the two-digit numbers increase up to 99, the last two-digit number. Hex goes up to FF. One hundred in hex is not 10 times 10, but 16 times 16—which is 100 in hex, 256 in decimal.

Reading Memory Hex Addresses

You will recall that the typical PC, when running DOS, can address 1MB of memory—640KB for user data and programs and 384KB of reserved area for video memory, ROMs, and buffers. Let's look at how to read memory addresses in hex.

First, understand that to a computer, 1MB is a binary number equivalent to decimal 1,048,576. It's composed of 16 64KB (65,536 decimal) *segments*. Conveniently, 10,000 in hex is equal to 64KB.

And 640KB is 10 64KB segments, so the low 640KB is the address range from 00000 to one short of A0000, or 9FFFF. All of the addresses in 64KB increments are shown in Table A.2.

TABLE A.2: MEMORY ADDRESSES IN DECIMAL AND HEX

DECIMAL ADDRESS	HEXADECIMAL ADDRESS	PRECEDING HEX ADDRESS
0KB	00000	N/A
64KB	10000	0FFFF
128KB	20000	1FFFF
192KB	30000	2FFFF
256KB	40000	3FFFF
320KB	50000	4FFFF
384KB	60000	5FFFF
448KB	70000	6FFFF
512KB	80000	7FFFF
576KB	90000	8FFFF
640KB	A0000	9FFFF
704KB	B0000	AFFFF
768KB	C0000	BFFFF
832KB	D0000	CFFFF
896KB	E0000	DFFFF
960KB	F0000	EFFFF
1024KB	100000	FFFFF

So when you see that a VGA display adapter puts memory in addresses A0000–BFFFF, you know that the board is using the addresses starting just above 640KB and going up to just short of 768KB. And when you see that the BIOS ROM is addressed from FC000 to FFFFF, you know that it's using addresses right up to the top of the first megabyte.

You've endured enough theory for the moment. Right now, let's put it to good use. Here are a couple of examples.

Example 1: Counting in Hex—Determining the Size of a Range

If COM1 uses I/O addresses 3F8 to 3FF, how many I/O addresses does that mean that it uses?

Count 'em up: 3F8, 3F9, 3FA (remember that A comes after 9), 3FB, 3FC, 3FD, 3FE, 3FF—eight addresses.

Example 2: Comparing Overlapping ROM Address Ranges

Let's look at a hypothetical example concerning the installation of a ScanJet interface card. When installing this card, you should be concerned that the address of the ROM on the ScanJet card doesn't conflict with the addresses of any other ROM in the system.

Now let's say that the only thing in the system with ROM is a VGA, but what is its ROM address? C0000–C5FFF. The scanner interface has a factory default of C4000–C7FFF. That would be okay for an EGA, as the EGA's ROM ends at C3FFF, just short of C4000. But the VGA's ROM goes all the way up to C5FFF, which tromps all over the range C4000–C7FFF.

You may have had some trouble following that, so let's review exactly what the quandary is.

1. The factory default address for the scanner is C4000–C7FFF. Note that this is a range of values: C4001, C4002… C7FFF, and there are lots of them—16KB of addresses, in fact.

2. The address range of the EGA ROM (if there were an EGA in the system) is C0000–C3FFF, and that range does not conflict with the ScanJet's range. The last value in the EGA range is C3FFF. C4000 comes after C3FFF in hex. You compare numbers in hex just as you do in decimal. If they've got the same number of digits, just compare the leftmost one. In this case, they've both got hex digits "C" in the leftmost position, so there's no difference. If the leftmost digits are the same, look immediately to the right. The number 4 comes after 3, so C4000 is after C3FFF.

3. The address range of the VGA ROM is C0000–C5FFF, and that conflicts with the ScanJet ROM range of C4000–C7FFF. The top of the VGA ROM range is C5FFF. The bottom of the ScanJet ROM range is C4000, which is below C5FFF. Again, how do you know? Compare them: the C in the leftmost position is the same; the 4 and 5 are different. The C5FFF, then, is above C4000—the starting point for the ScanJet ROM—and so the VGA range overlaps the ScanJet ROM range.

So we've briefly looked at how to use hex when looking at I/O address ranges and memory address ranges. If you'd like to get into the nitty-gritty details, like actually converting hex to decimal and back, read on. But you don't need to know any more.

Converting Hex to Decimal

This isn't tough, but you may live your whole life without having to know how to do it, if you prefer. This is especially true because the Windows calculator can do the conversions for you if you're in a hurry. But for those of you pioneers who want to know how it's done, here's what you do.

First, look back at Table A.1. Use it to convert each of the hex digits to decimal. For example, F in hex is 15 decimal, 8 in hex is 8 decimal, and so on. For this example we'll use the hex number C801F—how do you convert it to decimal?

1. **Write the hex number on a piece of paper. Create a column labeled "Subtotal" on your paper. Put a zero in it.** Work from left to right, crossing out hex digits as you convert them. Subtotal is where you'll accumulate the decimal value. So write down C801F, and put a zero under Subtotal.

2. **Examine the hex number.** If there are no digits left, stop. Subtotal contains your converted decimal value. Otherwise, remove the leftmost digit from what remains of the hex number, convert it to decimal, and add it to the subtotal. So remove the C and convert it to decimal—12, in this case—and add it to the subtotal. The subtotal becomes 12 for the moment. Cross out the C in the hex number, and you've got 801F left.

3. **Go back to step 2.** Step 2 says to first see if there are any hex digits left. There are, so continue: Multiply the subtotal (12) by 16 so it becomes 192. Take the leftmost digit—8—from the hex number, convert it to decimal (8 hex is equal to 8 decimal), and add it to the subtotal (192 + 8 = 200). Cross out the 8 in the hex number, leaving 01F.

4. Hex digits remain, so it's back to step 2 again. Subtotal times 16 makes the subtotal equal to 3200 (200 × 16). The next hex digit is 0; subtotal plus zero leaves it unchanged. Cross out the 0 in the hex number, leaving 1F.

5. The subtotal times 16 is 51,200 (3200 × 16). The next hex digit is 1, which is equal to 1 decimal. Add it to the subtotal, making the subtotal 51,201. Cross 1 from the hex number, leaving F.

6. Subtotal (51,201) times 16 is 819,216. The next hex digit is F, which is equal to 15 decimal. Add it to the subtotal (819,216 + 15), and you get 819,231. Cross out F from the hex number, leaving nothing.

7. There's nothing left in the hex number, so the subtotal is the desired result. C801F hex is equal to 819,231.

For those of you who prefer a simpler approach, open the Windows Calculator (choose Start ➢ Programs ➢ Accessories ➢ Calculator). Then choose Scientific from the View menu. Make sure the Hex (hexadecimal) button is selected and enter the number you want to convert. Then click the Dec (decimal) button, and the calculator will display the converted number.

Converting Decimal to Hex

This involves just about the reverse process. Let's convert 75,000 from decimal to hex.

1. **Divide the decimal number by 16. Convert the remainder to a hex digit and make that the *rightmost hex digit*.** That's the first digit in the subtotal. The number 75,000 divided by 16 yields a quotient of 4687 and a remainder of 8. Because 8 decimal is just 8 hex, the rightmost hex digit is 8.

2. **Divide the quotient by 16. Make the remainder the next hex digit—put it to the left of the subtotal.** Dividing 4687 by 16 yields a new quotient of 292 and a remainder of 15. As 15 decimal is F hex, the next hex digit is F, so the subtotal is now F8.

3. **If the new quotient is zero, stop.** Otherwise, just keep dividing the quotient by 16 and putting the hex remainder to the left of the subtotal. Dividing 292 by 16 yields a new quotient of 18 and a remainder of 4, so 4 goes in the subtotal. It's now 4F8.

4. **Divide 18 by 16** and you get a quotient of 1 with remainder 2, so the subtotal becomes 24F8.

5. **Finally, divide 1 by 16** and you get quotient 0, remainder 1, so the subtotal is now the final total—124F8. 124F8 hex equals 75,000 decimal.

To convert decimal to hex using the Windows Calculator, open the Scientific Calculator again. This time, make sure the Dec (decimal) button is selected and enter the number you want to convert. Then click the Hex (hexadecimal) button, and the calculator will display the converted new number.

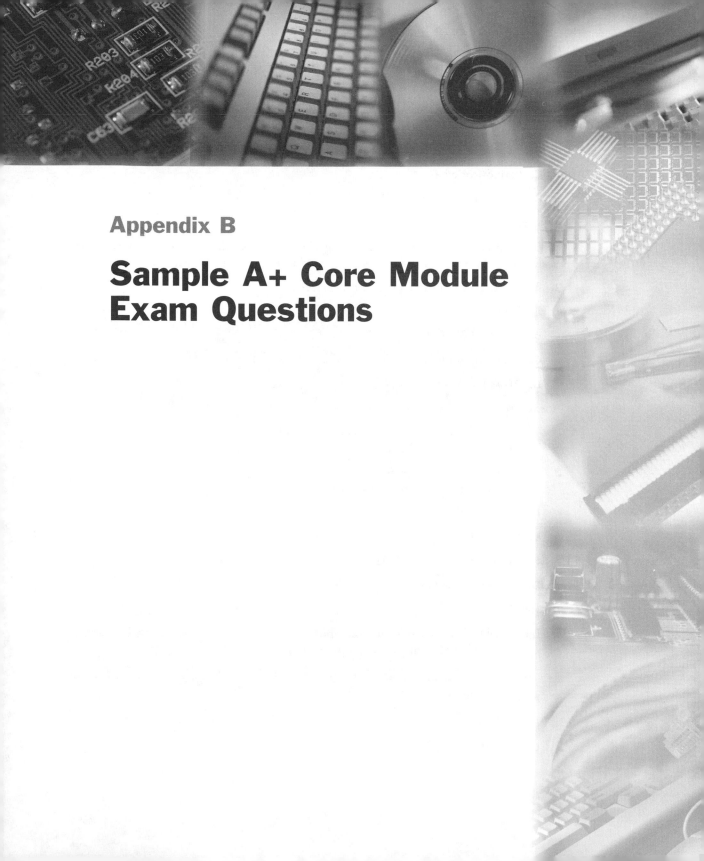

Appendix B

Sample A+ Core Module Exam Questions

1. Which of the following operate as repeaters?

   A. Hub

   B. Switch

   C. Both of the above

   D. Neither of the above

Answer: C

Both hubs and switches retransmit the signal in at least one direction, so they are repeaters. In fact, most bridges, routers, and gateways could be considered repeaters, too.

2. Block 9 refers to which hex range of memory?

   A. 70000 to 7FFFF

   B. 80000 to 8FFFF

   C. 90000 to 9FFFF

   D. A0000 to AFFFF

Answer: B

The hex ranges start with 00000 to 0FFFF, so 80000 to 8FFFF would be the ninth block. This corresponds to 512 to 575KB.

3. After being sent in for repairs, a co-worker's computer gives occasional "out of memory" errors. What might you try to solve this?

   A. Add more RAM.

   B. Reboot the computer.

   C. Remove and reseat the RAM.

   D. Format the hard drive.

Answer: B

It is possible that a reboot might solve things, but as the machine has recently been serviced, reseating the RAM would be the best thing to try.

4. The _____ is the parameter storage for the _____.

   A. CMOS, BIOS

   B. RAM, CMOS

   C. Hard drive, BIOS

D. BIOS, CMOS

Answer: A

The CMOS is the memory chip that stores the parameters that are used during bootup by the BIOS. The CMOS is volatile memory, so it maintains power with the use of a CMOS battery. This explains why there are CMOS checksum errors when a CMOS battery needs to be replaced.

5. A processor that has a 133MHz bus speed and a clock multiplier of 7 is rated at what speed?

   A. 466MHz

   B. 667MHz

   C. 1.0GHz

   D. 933MHz

Answer: D

To get a processor's clock speed, multiply the multiplier by the bus speed.

6. Which of the following can use flat ribbon cables to connect to the motherboard or controller? (Select all that apply.)

   A. IDE hard drive

   B. Power supply

   C. Floppy drive

   D. DVD drive

   E. SCSI hard drive

Answer: A, C, D, E

IDE hard drives and DVD drives (plus regular CD drives) all use 40-wire ribbon cables. Newer IDE hard drives use 80-wire ribbon cables. SCSI hard drives use either a 50-wire or 68-wire ribbon cable. Newer SCSI drives can use SCSI 160-wire ribbon cables. A floppy drive uses a 34-wire ribbon cable. Power supplies do not use ribbon cables of any type.

7. When using an Uninterruptible Power Supply (UPS), the computer (or equipment) is

_____.

   A. never powered by the UPS battery only

   B. powered by the UPS battery only in the event of a voltage drop

   C. always powered by both the UPS battery and the wall plug, except in the event of a voltage drop

   D. always powered by the UPS battery

Answer: D

A UPS always runs the equipment from the battery. It does this to prevent a momentary complete absence of power that would occur when switching from the power supplied from the wall to the power supplied by the battery. This means that the battery is constantly being charged and drained at the same time.

8. Which connector used for adding peripherals to a computer has the fastest data rate?

   A. Serial

   B. SCSI

   C. FireWire

   D. Parallel

   E. USB

Answer: C

In order from slowest to fastest: Serial, Parallel, USB, SCSI, and FireWire. FireWire allows speeds of up to 400Mbps.

9. IEEE 1284 defines what?

   A. Ultra3 SCSI

   B. FireWire

   C. USB

   D. Enhanced Parallel Port

Answer: D

Enhanced parallel ports were defined by IEEE 1284 (not to be confused with IEEE 1394, which defines FireWire). The two implementations of IEEE 1284 are called EPP and ECP. Both increase the speed of the parallel port connection and remain compatible with older parallel ports.

10. When you are going to dispose of a computer, which are the acceptable methods of disposal? (Select all that apply.)

   A. Put it in the municipal garbage or dump.

   B. Recycle it.

   C. Use it for spare parts.

   D. Bury it in the ground.

Answer: B, C

Because computers contain several valuable or hazardous materials, recycling or reusing the parts are the best answers. Disposing of it in the garbage is not acceptable because computers contain hazardous materials such as lead and battery acid.

11. Which type of memory offers the best performance?

   A. DDR SDRAM

   B. SDRAM

   C. RIMM

   D. DRAM

Answer: C

The RIMM is the newest and fastest type of RAM used in computers. It runs at up to 800MHz and has memory bandwidth of up to 1.6GBps.

12. SDRAM is an acronym for _____.

   A. Special Digital Random Access Memory

   B. Synchronous Digital Random Access Memory

   C. Synchronous Dynamic Random Access Memory

   D. Special Digital Random Access Memory

Answer: C

SDRAM is synchronized with the processor bus speed. This prevents waits when the processor is accessing memory.

13. DIMMs have how many pins? (Select all that apply.)

   A. 184

   B. 168

   C. 72

   D. 30

Answer: B, C

DIMMs have 72 pins if they are single-sided or 168 pins if double-sided. SIMMs also have 72 pins but are shorter than DIMMs.

14. The Intel 8088 processor could address how much memory?

   A. 640KB

   B. 16MB

   C. 4GB

D. 1024KB

Answer: D

The 8088 could address 1MB, or 1024KB of memory. Programs could actually use only 640KB of this memory.

15. An Intel 286 processor can address how much RAM?

A. 1024KB

B. 1024MB

C. 16MB

D. 4GB

Answer: C

The Intel 286 was the first processor that could address 16MB of memory. Current processors can address up to 4GB. Processors prior to the 286 could only address 1MB.

16. A _____ is made of the same track from each platter on a hard drive.

A. Sector

B. Full track

C. Cylinder

D. Head

Answer: C

A cylinder consists of the same track on each platter (top and bottom). If a hard drive had four platters, all eight surfaces' track 2 would make up cylinder 2. For this reason, a hard drive will always have the same number of tracks as it does cylinders.

17. After installing a second hard drive in a computer, you find that the computer no longer works and that neither hard drive is recognized. What should be the first thing you do?

A. Remove the new hard drive and replace it with a different one.

B. Make sure that the original hard drive is set to Master and the new hard drive is set to Slave.

C. Remove the original hard drive and see if the computer boots.

D. Use a different cable to connect the hard drives to the computer.

Answer: B

Although any of these answers might solve the problem, the best place to start would be checking that one drive is set as the Master and the other is set as the Slave. After verifying that, the next best step would be to disconnect the new hard drive to make sure the original hard drive was still working without the new drive installed.

18. Which of the following are magnetic storage? (Select all that apply.)

   A. Tape drive

   B. Floppy drive

   C. CD-ROM drive

   D. CD-RW drive

Answer: A, B

Tape drives and floppy drives both store data magnetically. CD drives are optical because they use a laser to read (and write) data.

19. Which of the following can be cleaned? (Select all that apply.)

   A. Hard drive

   B. CD-ROM drive

   C. Floppy drive

   D. Tape drive

Answer: B, C, D

Because hard drives are sealed at the factory, it is impossible to clean them. The other devices listed can and should be cleaned from time to time. They have moving parts, which can get dirty over time. In the case of a CD-ROM drive, the lens needs to be cleaned so the laser light is not obstructed. For tape and floppy drives, the heads can accumulate dirt over time and can lead to unreliable reading or writing.

20. Which of the following commands will make a floppy disk bootable?

   A. SYS A:

   B. FORMAT A:

   C. FORMAT A: /S

   D. SYS A: /S

Answer: A, C

Both SYS A: and FORMAT A: /S will make a floppy bootable. However, the FORMAT command will format the disk as well, erasing everything that was on it.

21. When installing a floppy drive, which steps are required? (Select all that apply.)

   A. Mounting the drive in the case

  B. Selecting either Master or Slave

  C. Configuring the drive's number of heads, cylinders, and sectors in the BIOS

  D. Attaching the power cable to the drive

  E. Attaching the ribbon cable to the drive and the controller

Answer: A, D, E

Installing a floppy drive is fairly simple. You do not need to configure the drive in the BIOS (except maybe selecting the type of drive). There is also no Master or Slave setting. A single floppy drive should be connected after the twist in the cable. A dual floppy drive setup should have the A drive after the twist in the cable and the B drive before the twist.

22. ATA-2 allows a maximum of how many drives?

  A. 1

  B. 2

  C. 3

  D. 4

Answer: D

ATA-2 and newer standards can support up to four drives. However, you can only install two drives per controller bus. In order to install all four drives, you must configure a primary Master and Slave and a secondary Master and Slave.

23. SCSI stands for _____.

  A. Small Computer Standard Interface

  B. Simple Computer Standard Interface

  C. Small Computer Systems Interface

  D. Simple Computer Systems Interface

Answer: C

The acronym SCSI stands for Small Computer Systems Interface.

24. Wide Ultra SCSI has a bus width of _____ bits, a maximum data speed of _____ MBps and uses a _____ pin connector.

  A. 8, 10, 50

  B. 16, 40, 68

  C. 16, 20, 50

  D. 8, 20, 50

Answer: B

Wide SCSI transfers data 16 bits at a time (twice as "wide" as 8 bit). Ultra SCSI uses a 68-pin connector and can transfer up to 40Mbps per second.

25. By default, which IRQs are available with an ISA bus? (Select all that apply.)

    A. IRQ10

    B. IRQ11

    C. IRQ12

    D. IRQ13

Answer: A, B

IRQs 10 and 11 are available (so is 15). IRQ12 is the bus mouse port, and IRQ13 is the math coprocessor.

26. PCI cards can run at a bus speed of up to _____ MHz and at _____ bits.

    A. 33, 32

    B. 33, 64

    C. 66, 32

    D. 66, 64

Answer: D

Although many of today's PCI cards run at 133MHz with a 32-bit data bus, PCI can run at up to 166MHz and 64-bit. Many new 1000MB NICs run at this speed. However, you should note that slightly older PCIs can run at 133MHz and 64-bit. The newer ones can run at 200 and 400MHz.

27. ISA slots operate at what speed? (Select all that apply.)

    A. 8MHz

    B. 10MHz

    C. 33MHz

    D. 66MHz

Answer: A, B

The ISA bus operates at 8MHz, or 10MHz in turbo mode. PCI bus operates at both 33 and 66MHz.

28. What does PCMCIA stand for?

    A. Portable Computer Memory Card Interchange Association

    B. Personal Computer Modem Card Interchange Association

   C. Portable Computer Modem Card International Association

   D. Personal Computer Memory Card International Association

Answer: D

PCMCIA was originally designed to expand the amount of memory in portable computers, but is now more commonly used to add peripheral devices, such as a modem, NIC, or removable hard drive.

29. After installing a new serial mouse, you notice that your modem is no longer functioning. What is the most likely cause of the problem?

   A. The modem and the serial mouse are both using the same IRQ.

   B. The modem was ruined by ESD.

   C. The serial mouse is bad.

   D. The modem and serial mouse are both using the same bus speed.

Answer: A

They are probably both using the same IRQ. The first step would be to verify that they are on different COM ports and using different IRQs.

30. What are the three most common types of printers? (Select all that apply.)

   A. Impact

   B. Sprayed ink

   C. Photographic

   D. Laser

Answer: A, B, D

Impact (dot-matrix), sprayed ink (inkjet), and laser (electrophotographic) printers are the three types of printers. The "photographic" type is purely fictitious.

31. A parallel port printer generally uses what kind of cable?

   A. DB-25M to BNC male

   B. Centronics 50 male to DB-25M

   C. DB-25M to male Centronics 36

   D. Centronics 36 male to Centronics 36 male

Answer: C

The parallel port on the back of the computer is a DB-25F, so it matches to a DB-25M connector. The printer side of the cable has a Centronics 36 male connector to match up with the

Centronics 36 female on the back of the printer. Centronics 50 cables are generally used for external SCSI.

32. If you are trying to install a parallel port printer with a 12-foot printer cable and you experience problems during and after installation, what is the likely cause of the problem?

   A. A bad printer

   B. A bad cable

   C. The parallel port is malfunctioning

   D. The printer cable is too long

Answer: D

The first thing to test would be the cable. Parallel port cables should be no longer than 10 feet. Most computer stores sell 6- and 12-foot cables. Try a 6-footer; it will probably work.

33. When using an inkjet printer, what can cause streaking or poor printing quality? (Select all that apply.)

   A. Excessive use

   B. Using recycled inkjet cartridges

   C. Dirt build-up on the nozzles

   D. Bad fuser

Answer: B, C

Using a recycled inkjet cartridge is not recommended. Dirt can build up on the inkjet nozzles, and this is a common cause of poor print quality. It is virtually impossible to damage an inkjet printer by excessive use. Inkjet printers do not use a fuser; only laser printers use those.

34. Which type of printer uses a cartridge of liquid ink?

   A. Laser

   B. Dot-matrix

   C. Bubble jet

   D. Daisy-wheel

Answer: C

Daisy-wheel and dot-matrix printers use an ink ribbon. Laser printers use toner. Only the bubble jet printers use liquid ink in a cartridge.

35. Some laser printers produce _____ from the high voltage they use.

   A. Ozone

   B. Carbon dioxide

    C. Carbon monoxide

    D. Hydrogen dioxide

Answer: A

Ozone is produced by the high-voltage coronas inside some laser printers. For this reason, some printers have a filter to remove the ozone and prevent it from damaging the printer.

36. Which of the following is *not* a step in the EP printing process?

    A. Cleaning

    B. Writing

    C. Transferring

    D. Finishing

Answer: D

Finishing is not a part of the process. Cleaning is the final step in the process.

37. The _____ step of the EP printing process transfers the toner to the areas that were exposed during the writing step.

    A. Cleaning

    B. Transferring

    C. Developing

    D. Fusing

Answer: C

The developing step transfers the toner from the developing cylinder to the EP drum. The next step, transferring, actually puts the image on the paper.

38. In an office with 10 or more computers sharing one printer, which is the best option?

    A. A printer shared from one desktop computer

    B. A USB printer that is moved from one computer to another

    C. A printer connected to the network with a NIC

    D. A printer/fax accessed by dial-up

Answer: C

Although any of these options are usable (some more than others), the best option is to have a network printer. With a shared printer, the user whose computer was attached to the printer would experience poor performance when other people were printing. Using a fax machine as a printer would tie up two phone lines and be very slow.

39. When inspecting a computer, you notice that it spontaneously reboots or shuts down after about 5 minutes. You also notice that the computer is almost completely silent. What is the most likely cause of the problem?

    A. Hard drive failure

    B. Sound card failure

    C. Power supply failure

    D. Fan failure

Answer: D

    A fan may have failed. Generally, you can hear the computer fans from outside the computer. Hard drives do have moving parts and make noise, but they are usually very quiet. Most likely a system fan has failed and the computer is overheating. It may take a few minutes for the computer to overheat; that's why it doesn't fail immediately.

40. A _____ network is one in which all of the computers take the role of both server and workstation. This type of network makes administration difficult.

    A. Server-based

    B. Node

    C. Wide-area

    D. Peer-to-peer

Answer: D

    Peer-to-peer networks are most common in a home or small office setting. Since there is no centralized control, administration is difficult. These types of networks are useful for sharing resources such as printers and scanners.

41. A _____ topology is one that has a single cable that attaches to every computer on the network. This type of network topology does not require every computer to be connected to two other computers. Ethernet is an example.

    A. Mesh

    B. Ring

    C. Bus

    D. Star

Answer: C

A bus topology uses one cable. It is similar to a ring topology, but it doesn't require that every computer be connected to two other computers to form a logical ring.

42. When cleaning components inside a computer, which is the best for removing dust?

   A. Damp cloth

   B. Compressed air

   C. Dry, lint-free cloth

   D. Soap and water

Answer: B

Compressed air is great for cleaning out dust from moving parts such as fans. Dry cloths may cause ESD, water can short out components, and wiping components may damage them.

43. A _____ network is one where every computer on the network is directly cabled to every other computer on the network. This type of network is only used on very small LANs.

   A. Mesh

   B. Ring

   C. Bus

   D. Star

Answer: A

In a mesh network, every computer is directly connected to every other computer. This is very inefficient for large networks because so many cables would be necessary.

44. The _____ layer of the OSI model is the layer that allows access to network services such as printing and file access.

   A. Presentation

   B. Transport

   C. Data Link

   D. Application

Answer: D

The Application layer is the "final" layer of the OSI model. It is the layer that workstations interact with.

45. Which layer of the OSI model arranges data into chunks called "frames"?

    A. Physical

    B. Data Link

    C. Session

    D. Presentation

Answer: B

The Data Link layer creates frames and adds data marking the beginning and the end of the data stream. This layer allows for error checking and correction.

46. What is the correct order of the seven layers in the OSI model?

    A. Application, Data Link, Physical, Transport, Network, Presentation, Session,

    B. Presentation, Session, Transport, Application, Network, Data Link, Physical

    C. Application, Presentation, Session, Transport, Network, Data Link, Physical

    D. Presentation, Session, Data Link, Physical, Transport, Application, Network

Answer: C

The OSI model works both in the direction shown above and in the opposite direction. If it didn't, sending and receiving wouldn't be possible.

47. What Ethernet designation transmits at 10Mbps, with baseband communication, and can cover 500 meters?

    A. 10Base-T

    B. 10Base-2

    C. 10Base-TX

    D. 10Base-5

Answer: D

10 stands for 10Mbps, Base stands for baseband, and the 5 for 500 meters. Similarly, 10Base-2 is 10Mbps, with baseband, and 185 meters. Not so obviously, 10Base-T is 10Mbps, baseband, and 100 meters.

48. Which of the following are motherboard form factors? (Select all that apply.)

    A. AT

    B. NTX

    C. ATX

    D. PCI

Answer: A, C

Both the AT and ATX are actual motherboard form factors. PCI is an expansion slot type. NTX does not exist; however, NLX is a form factor used in "low profile" computer cases.

49. Which type of cable is capable of transmitting at 10Mbps and contains four twisted pairs of wires with three twists per foot?

   A. Category 1

   B. Category 2

   C. Category 3

   D. Category 4

Answer: C

Category 3 wire was very popular when 10Mbps networks were standard. More and more companies are replacing their Category 3 wires with new Category 5 or Category 5e wire to upgrade to a 100Mbps network.

50. Which type of transmission medium generally allows the longest distance and most security?

   A. Twisted-pair

   B. Coaxial

   C. Infrared

   D. Fiber-optic

Answer: D

Fiber-optic can transmit over 10 miles and has a very limited chance of data being intercepted without the sending or receiving party knowing. More specifically, single-mode fiber allows distances of 5 to 93 miles and multimode fiber allows 5 to 6 miles.

51. Which of the following does a multimeter measure?

   A. Velocity

   B. Static electricity

   C. Voltage

   D. Processor speed

Answer: C

Multimeters commonly measure such electrical properties as voltage, current, and resistance.

52. Which of the following can be reprogrammed more than once? (Select all that apply.)

   A. EEPROM

   B. ROM

   C. EPROM

D. PROM

Answer: A, C

ROM can only be written to once when it is manufactured, and it can never be changed. PROM can be programmed, but only once. EPROM can be erased and reprogrammed by using ultraviolet light. EEPROM can be electronically erased and then reprogrammed more than once.

53. What media access method uses a centralized intelligent device to ask each workstation if they have anything to send?

   A. Polling

   B. Bus

   C. Mesh

   D. Token passing

Answer: A

A network with polling has a server that goes from computer to computer asking if the computer wants to send anything. If it does, it allows it to send the data. These types of networks are fairly rare now because of the special equipment that is required.

54. When installing a new expansion board such as an AGP video card, which of the following are advisable?

   A. Leave the computer plugged in so there is less risk of ESD.

   B. Wear an antistatic wrist strap.

   C. Use a rubber mat under your feet.

   D. Do not wear shoes.

Answer: B, C

Using antistatic devices such as antistatic wrist straps and mats is a great idea. A rubber mat underfoot is also a good idea. If you do not wear shoes, you still may have static that builds up on your socks. Leaving the computer plugged in is a bad idea. It could cause you to get electrocuted, even if the computer is off.

55. Which of the following are input devices? (Select all that apply.)

   A. Mouse

   B. Touch screen monitor

   C. Speakers

   D. Printer

Answer: A, B

The mouse and touch screen monitor are both input devices (although the touch screen is also an output device). Printers and speakers are output devices.

56. A parallel port uses which kind of connector?

    A. DB-9

    B. RJ-45

    C. PS/2

    D. DB-25

Answer: D

The DB-25 connector is the parallel port connector (most often used with printers, scanners, and external zip drives). DB-9 is a serial cable connector. RJ-45 is a network cable connector. PS/2 is most commonly used for mice and keyboards.

57. IRQ1 is reserved for the _____ .

    A. Sound card

    B. Keyboard

    C. PS/2 mouse

    D. COM1

Answer: B

The keyboard is the only device that should ever be assigned to IRQ1.

58. Which of the following are used to prevent electrostatic discharge? (Select all that apply.)

    A. Antistatic bags

    B. ESD mats

    C. Maintaining low relative humidity

    D. Maintaining low temperatures

Answer: A, B

Antistatic bags prevent additional static from getting to computer components, and ESD mats remove excess static. Both low relative humidity and low temperature can increase the chance of ESD occurring.

59. Which DMA channels are available on AT computers?

    A. 2

    B. 3

    C. 4

    D. 5

E. 6

Answer: B, C, D, E

DMA channels 3–7 are generally available. Any channel lower than 3 is assigned to RAM refresh, the hard disk controller, or the floppy disk controller.

60. Put the following steps of installing a hard drive in order.

1. Attach the hard drive to the computer case, usually with four screws.

2. Power up the computer and set the drive settings in the BIOS.

3. Attach the power connector and the ribbon cable.

A. 1, 2, 3

B. 2, 1, 3

C. 1, 3, 2

D. 3, 2, 1

Answer: C

It is very important to attach the hard drive to the case before powering it up. It has moving parts, so starting it without having it mounted securely in place could damage it.

61. A computer has been in use for several years and has never had a problem; then one day it starts showing an error 161 on bootup. What is the most likely cause?

A. Video card failure

B. Power supply failure

C. Dead CMOS battery

D. Hard drive motor failure

Answer: C

This probably means the CMOS battery is dead. They usually last three years or so before they need to be replaced. After replacing the battery, you will most likely need to go into the BIOS and reset the parameters.

62. What are the most common causes of crinkled paper coming out of a laser printer? (Select all that apply.)

A. The printer is out of toner.

B. The printer's gears are stripped.

C. The printer has an obstructed paper path.

D. The printer overheated.

Answer: B, C

The printer is probably obstructed by something or its gears have been stripped by paper feeding incorrectly. Obstructions are usually caused by paper from a previous jam. When cleaning out a paper jam, make sure you get all the paper.

63. You get a call about a computer not working. What are the first questions you should ask? (Select all that apply.)

   A. What did you do that made it stop working?

   B. Has any new software been added?

   C. Has any new hardware been added?

   D. Can the problem be reproduced?

Answer: B, C, D

Do not imply that the person you are talking to "broke" the computer. Anything could have happened to make the computer malfunction. If the user can't reproduce the problem, you can consider the case closed. After all, if they can't make it malfunction again, what are you supposed to do? The most common causes of computer problems are recently installed software or hardware.

64. What does PCI stand for?

   A. Personal Computer Interconnect

   B. Peripheral Computer Interconnect

   C. Personal Computer Interchange

   D. Peripheral Component Interconnect

Answer: D

The PCI bus was developed to keep pace with the newer Pentium-class processors.

65. If you find that a computer's power supply is no longer able to power up a computer, which is the best alternative?

   A. Purchase a new power supply to replace the bad one.

   B. Take it to a service center for repairs.

   C. Open it to see if any of the components have failed.

   D. Replace the fan inside the power supply.

Answer: A

Since power supplies are generally cheap, replacement is the best option. Power supplies can hold a deadly charge for a very long time, even if they are not plugged in, so you should never open one.

Glossary

Numbers and Symbols

*
See asterisk.

/
See slash.

//
See double slash.

:
See colon.

?
See question mark.

@
See at symbol.

****
See backslash.

¼-inch cartridge
See quarter-inch cartridge.

10/100
A term used to indicate that a device can support both Ethernet (at a data transfer rate of 10Mbps) and Fast Ethernet (at a data transfer rate of 100Mbps).

10Base-T
A version of the Ethernet networking standard that uses unshielded twisted-pair cable and RJ-45 connectors.

10Base-T cable
A popular Ethernet cable that uses unshielded twisted-pair wiring and RJ-45 connectors at each end. You should use Category 3 10Base-T cable with 10Mbps Ethernet networks.

10Base-TX cable
A popular Ethernet cable that uses unshielded twisted-pair wiring and RJ-45 connectors at each end. You should use Category 5 10Base-TX cable with 100Mbps Ethernet networks.

10Mbps
An abbreviation for 10 megabits per second, the standard Ethernet network data rate.

100Mbps
An abbreviation for 100 megabits per second, the standard Fast Ethernet network data rate.

1394
See IEEE 1394.

23B+D
A common abbreviation for Primary Rate ISDN, which has 23 B or bearer channels, and one D or data channel.

24/7
An abbreviation for round-the-clock availability, implying that the service is available 24 hours a day for seven days per week.

24-bit color
A color display in which the level of each of the primary colors is represented by 8 bits of information. A 24-bit color image can contain over 16 million separate colors.

2B+D
A common abbreviation for Basic Rate ISDN, which has 2 B or bearer channels, and one D or data channel.

A

a-b box

A switching box that allows a peripheral device such as a printer to be shared between two or more computers. It can be switched manually or through software.

AC adapter

A small external power supply that converts main electrical power to the low-voltage DC required for a laptop or notebook computer or other device needing its own power supply.

Accelerated Graphics Port

Abbreviated AGP. A specification developed by Intel to support high-speed, high-resolution 3D graphics and video images.

AGP uses a dedicated point-to-point connection between main memory and the graphics controller so that images can be displayed faster and more smoothly than when they have to travel across the main system bus. AGP runs at 66MHz and supports data transfer rates of up to 533Mbps.

accelerator board

An add-in, printed circuit board that replaces or augments the main processor with a higher-performance processor. Using an accelerator board can reduce upgrading costs substantially because you won't need to replace the monitor, case, keyboard, and so on. However, the main processor is not the only component that affects the overall performance of your system. Other factors, such as disk-access time and video speed, contribute to a system's performance.

access

To use, write to, or read from a file, or to log in to a computer system or network.

access time

The period of time that elapses between a request for information from disk or memory and the arrival of that information at the requesting device.

Memory-access time refers to the time it takes to transfer a character between memory and the processor. Disk-access time refers to the time it takes to place the read/write heads over the requested data. RAM (random access memory) may have an access time of 80ns or less, while hard disk access time would be less than 10ms.

ACPI

See Advanced Configuration and Power Interface.

active hub

A device that amplifies transmission signals in a network, allowing signals to be sent over a much greater distance than is possible with a passive hub.

An active hub may have ports for coaxial, twisted-pair, or fiber-optic cable connections, as well as LEDs to show that each port is operating correctly.

active-matrix display

A high-quality, liquid-crystal display used in laptop and notebook computers with a wide viewing angle and very narrow depth. Also known as a thin-film transistor (TFT) display.

active termination

A technique used to terminate a Small Computer System Interface (SCSI). Active termination reduces electrical interference in a long string of SCSI devices.

adapter

A printed circuit board that plugs into a computer's expansion bus to provide added capabilities.

Common adapters include video adapters, joystick controllers, and input/output (I/O) adapters, as well as other devices, such as internal modems, CD-ROMs, and network interface cards (NICs). One adapter can often support several different devices. Some modern PC designs incorporate many of the functions previously performed by these individual adapters on the motherboard.

address

1. The precise location in memory or on disk where a piece of information is stored. Each byte in memory and each sector on a disk has its own unique address.

2. The unique identifier for a specific node on a network. An address may be a physical address specified by switches or jumpers on the network interface card hardware or a logical address established by the network operating system.

3. To reference or manage a storage location.

4. Information used by a network or the Internet to specify a specific location in the form `username@hostname`, where `username` is your username, logon name, or account name or number, and `hostname` is the name of the Internet Service Provider (ISP) or computer system you use. The hostname may consist of several different parts, each separated from the next by a period.

address bus

The electronic channel, usually from 20 to 64 lines wide, used to transmit the signals that specify locations in memory.

The number of lines in the address bus determines the number of memory locations that the processor can access because each line carries one bit of the address. A 20-line address bus (used in early Intel 8086/8088 processors) can access 1MB of memory, a 24-line address bus can access 16MB, and a 32-line address bus can access more than 4GB. A 64-line address bus can access 16EB.

ADSL

See asymmetric digital subscriber line.

Advanced Configuration and Power Interface

Abbreviated ACPI. An interface specification developed by Intel, Microsoft, and Toshiba for controlling power use on the PC and all other devices attached to the system. A BIOS-level hardware specification, ACPI is dependent on specific hardware that allows the operating system to direct power management and system configuration.

Advanced Power Management

Abbreviated APM. An API specification from Microsoft and Intel intended to monitor and extend battery life on a laptop computer by shutting down

certain system components after a period of inactivity.

Advanced SCSI Programming Interface

Abbreviated ASPI. A programming standard that defines how Small Computer System Interface (SCSI) devices work together and with the other components that make up the PC.

Advanced Technology Attachment

Abbreviated ATA. The ANSI X3T10 term for the disk drive interface standard known as Integrated Drive Electronics (IDE).

Advanced Technology Attachment Packet Interface

Abbreviated ATAPI. An interface standard used to connect a CD-ROM drive to an Enhanced IDE adapter.

aftermarket

The market for related hardware, software, and peripheral devices created by the sale of a large number of computers of a specific type.

alphanumeric

Consisting of letters, numbers, and sometimes special control characters, spaces, and other punctuation characters.

AGP

See Accelerated Graphics Port.

American Standard Code for Information Interchange

Abbreviated ASCII, pronounced "as-kee." A standard coding scheme that assigns numeric values to letters, numbers, punctuation characters, and control characters to achieve compatibility among different computers and peripheral devices. In ASCII, each character is represented by a unique integer value, from 0 to 255.

analog

Describes any device that represents changing values by a continuously variable physical property, such as a voltage in a circuit. Analog often refers to transmission methods developed to transmit voice signals rather than high-speed digital signals.

anonymous FTP

A method used to access an Internet computer with FTP that does not require you to have an account on the target computer system. Simply log on to the Internet computer with the username *anonymous* and use your e-mail address as your password. This access method was originally provided as a courtesy so that system administrators could see who had logged on to their system, but now it is often required to gain access to an Internet computer that has FTP service.

You cannot use anonymous FTP with every computer on the Internet; only with those systems set up to offer the service. The system administrator decides which files and directories will be open to public access, and the rest of the system is considered to be off limits and cannot be accessed by anonymous FTP users. Some sites only allow you to download from them; as a security precaution, you are not allowed to upload files to them.

antistatic device

Any device designed to minimize electrical shocks caused by a build-up of static electricity, including special floor mats, wrist bands, even sprays and lotions.

antivirus program

A program that detects or eliminates a computer virus. Some antivirus programs can detect suspicious activity on your computer as it happens; others must be run periodically as part of your normal housekeeping activities.

An antivirus program locates and identifies a virus by looking for characteristic patterns or suspicious activity in the system, such as unexpected disk access or EXE files changing in some unusual way. It recognizes the virus by comparing information from the system against a database of known viruses, which is kept on disk.

API

See Application Programming Interface.

APM

See Advanced Power Management.

Application Programming Interface

Abbreviated API. The complete set of all operating system functions that an application can use to perform such tasks as managing files and displaying information.

An API provides a standard way to write an application, and it also describes how the application should use the functions it provides. Using an API is quicker and easier than developing functions from scratch and helps to ensure some level of consistency among all the applications developed for a specific operating system.

In operating systems that support a graphical user interface, the API also defines functions to support windows, icons, pull-down menus, and other components of the interface. In network operating systems, an API defines a standard method that applications can use to take advantage of all the network features.

application-specific integrated circuit

Abbreviated ASIC. A computer chip developed for a specific purpose, designed by incorporating standard cells from a library rather than created from scratch. Also known as a gate array, ASICs are found in all sorts of appliances, including modems, security systems, digital cameras, even microwave ovens and automobiles.

architecture

1. The overall design and construction of all or part of a computer, particularly the processor hardware and the size and ordering sequence of its bytes.

2. The overall design of software, including interfaces to other software, the operating system, and the network.

archive

1. To transfer files to some form of long-term storage, such as magnetic tape or large-capacity disk, when the files are no longer needed on a regular basis but must be maintained for periodic reference.

2. On the Internet, a site containing a collection of files available via anonymous FTP.

3. A compressed file.

archive file

A single file that contains one or more files or directories that may have been compressed to save space. Archives are often used as a way to transport large numbers of related files across the Internet.

arrow keys

Any of the four keys labeled with arrows pointing down, up, left, and right, which are used to move the on-screen cursor.

ASCII

See American Standard Code for Information Interchange.

ASCII extended character set

The second group of characters, from 128 to 255, in the ASCII character set. The extended ASCII character set used in the PC includes mathematical symbols and characters from the PC line-drawing set.

ASCII file

A file that contains only text characters from the ASCII character set. An ASCII file can include letters, numbers, and punctuation symbols but does not contain any hidden text-formatting codes. Also known as a text file or an ASCII text file.

ASCII standard character set

A character set that consists of the first 128 (from 0 to 127) ASCII characters. The values 0 to 31 are used for nonprinting control codes, and the range from 32 to 127 is used to represent the letters of the alphabet and common punctuation symbols. The entire set from 0 to 127 is referred to as the standard ASCII character set. All computers that use ASCII can understand the standard ASCII character set.

ASIC

See application-specific integrated circuit.

ASPI

See Advanced SCSI Programming Interface.

assembly language

A low-level programming language in which each program statement must correspond to a single machine language instruction that the processor can execute.

Assembly languages are specific to a given microprocessor or microprocessor family and, as such, are not portable; programs written for one type of processor must be rewritten before they can be used on another type of processor.

asterisk

You can use the asterisk (*) as a wildcard character to represent one or more unknown characters in a filename or filename extension.

asymmetric digital subscriber line

Abbreviated ADSL. A high-speed data transmission technology originally developed by Bellcore and now standardized by ANSI as T1.413 that delivers high bandwidth over existing twisted-pair copper telephone lines. Also called asymmetric digital subscriber loop.

ADSL supports speeds in the range of 1.5 to 9Mbps in the downstream direction (from the network to the customer), and upstream speeds in the range of 16 to 640Kbps, hence the term asymmetric.

Asynchronous Transfer Mode

Abbreviated ATM. A method used for transmitting voice, video, and data over high-speed LANs and WANs. ATM uses continuous bursts of fixed-length packets called cells to transmit data. The basic packet consists of 53 bytes, 5 of which are used for control functions and 48 for data.

ATM is a connection-oriented protocol, and two kinds of connection are possible: permanent virtual circuits (PVCs), in which connections are created manually, and switched virtual circuits (SVCs), in which connections are made automatically. Speeds of up to 2.488Gbps have been achieved in testing.

ATM will find wide acceptance in the LAN and WAN arenas as a solution to integrating disparate networks over large geographical distances. Also known as cell relay.

asynchronous transmission

A method of data transmission that uses start bits and stop bits to coordinate the flow of data so the time intervals between individual characters do not need to be equal. Parity may also be used to check the accuracy of the data received.

ATA

See Advanced Technology Attachment.

ATAPI

See Advanced Technology Attachment Packet Interface.

at symbol

The separating character (@) between account name and domain name in an Internet e-mail address.

Athlon

A family of microprocessors introduced by AMD in 1999. The Athlon, also known as the K7 processor, represents the successor of the K6 family of microprocessors and adds several notable features, including much improved FPU power. The original Athlon had 22 million transistors, a 200MHz bus, and a 512K half speed L2 cache. An addition to the Athlon family was the faster Thunderbird. The Thunderbird has 37 million transistors on a smaller die as well as a full speed 256K L2 cache.

attenuation

The decrease in power of a signal with increasing distance. Attenuation is measured in decibels, and it increases as the power of the signal decreases. The best cables (those exhibiting the least attenuation) are fiber-optic lines, and the worst cables are unshielded, untwisted-pair lines, such as the silver, flat-satin cables used in short-run telephone and modem lines.

In a LAN, attenuation can become a problem when cable lengths exceed the stated network specification; however, the useful length of a cable may be extended by the use of a repeater.

ATM

See Asynchronous Transfer Mode.

attribute

1. A file attribute is a technique for describing access to and properties of files and directories within a file system. You may see the term attribute used interchangeably with the term property.

2. A screen attribute controls a character's background and foreground colors, as well as other characteristics, such as underlining, reverse video, and blinking.

3. In operating systems, a characteristic that indicates whether a file is a read-only file, a hidden file, or a system file, or if the file has changed in some way since it was last backed up.

auto-answer

A feature of a modem that allows it to answer incoming calls automatically.

auto-dial

A feature of a modem that allows it to open a telephone line and start a call. To auto-dial, the modem sends a series of pulses or tones that represents a stored telephone number.

B

backslash

1. Used to separate directory or subdirectory names in a path statement or when changing to another directory from a command prompt.

2. A shorthand name for the root directory. Sometimes called the reverse slash or backslant. It goes from the upper left to the lower right (\ ).

backup

An up-to-date copy of all your files. There are several reasons to make a backup:

◆ Insurance against possible hard disk or file-server failure. Hard disks often fail completely, taking all your work with them. If this failure occurs, you can reload your files and directories from the backup copy. A backup is your insurance against disk failure affecting the thousands or possibly tens of thousands of files you might have on your file server.

◆ Protection against accidental deletion of files or directories. Again, if you mistakenly delete a file or directory, you can retrieve a copy from your last backup.

◆ Protection against the new version of software you are about to install not working to your expectations; make a backup before installing new software.

◆ As an archive at the end of a project, when a person leaves your company, or at the end of a financial period such as year-end close.

Your decision when or how often to make a backup depends on how frequently important data on your system changes. If you rely on certain files always being available on your system, it is crucial that you make regular, consistent backups.

backward compatibility

Full compatibility with earlier versions of the same application or computer system.

bad sector

An area on a hard disk or floppy disk that cannot be used to store data because of a manufacturing defect or accidental damage.

Some operating systems will find, mark, and isolate bad sectors. Almost all hard disks have some bad sectors, often listed in the bad track table. Usually, bad sectors are a result of the manufacturing process and not a concern; the operating system will mark them as bad, and you will never even know they are there.

bad track table

A list of the defective areas on a hard disk, usually determined during final testing of the disk at the factory. Some disk-preparation programs ask you to enter information from this list to reduce the time that a low-level format takes to prepare the disk for use by the operating system.

bandwidth

1. In communications, the difference between the highest and lowest frequencies available for transmission in any given range.

2. In networking, the transmission capacity of a computer or a communications channel, stated in megabits per second (Mbps).

Basic Rate ISDN

Abbreviated BRI. An ISDN (Integrated Services Digital Network) service that offers two 64Kbps B channels used for data transfer and one 16Kbps D channel used for signaling and control information.

Each B channel can carry a single digital voice call or can be used as a data channel; the B channels can also be combined into a single 128Kbps data channel.

baud rate

In communications equipment, a measurement of the number of state changes (from 0 to 1 or vice versa) per second on an asynchronous communications channel.

Baud rate is often assumed to correspond to the number of bits transmitted per second, but baud rate and bits per second (bps) are not always the same. In modern high-speed digital communications systems, one state change can be made to represent more than one data bit.

BEDO DRAM

See Burst Extended Data Out DRAM.

binary

Any scheme that uses two different states, components, conditions, or conclusions.

In mathematics, the binary or base-2 numbering system uses combinations of the digits 0 and 1 to represent all values. The more familiar decimal system has a base of 10 (0–9).

Unlike computers, people find binary numbers that consist of long strings of 0s and 1s difficult to read, so most programmers use hexadecimal (base-16) or octal (base-8) numbers instead.

Binary also refers to an executable file containing a program.

BIOS

Acronym for basic input/output system, pronounced "bye-ose." In the PC, the BIOS is a set of instructions that tests the hardware when the computer is first turned on, starts to load the operating system, and lets the computer's hardware and operating system communicate with applications and peripheral devices, such as hard disks, printers, and video adapters. These instructions are stored in ROM (read-only memory) as a permanent part of the computer.

As new hardware is developed, new BIOS routines must be created to service those devices. For example, BIOS support has been added for power management and for ever-larger hard disks.

If you are experiencing problems accessing such devices after adding them to an existing system, your computer's BIOS may be out-of-date. Contact your computer supplier for information about BIOS updates.

bit

Contraction of binary digit. A bit is the basic unit of information in the binary numbering system, representing either 0 (off) or 1 (on). Bits can be grouped to form larger storage units; the most common grouping is the 8 bits, called a byte.

bit rate

The rate at which bits are transmitted over a communications channel, described in terms of bits per second (bps).

bits per inch

Abbreviated bpi. The number of bits that a tape or tape cartridge can store per inch of length.

bits per second

Abbreviated bps. The number of binary digits, or bits, transmitted every second during a data transfer procedure. Bits per second is a measurement of the speed of operation of equipment, such as a computer's data bus or a modem that connects a computer to a communications circuit.

BNC connector

A small connector with a half-turn locking shell for coaxial cable, used with thin Ethernet and RG-62 cabling.

boot

To load an operating system into memory, usually from a hard disk, although occasionally from a floppy disk. Booting is generally an automatic procedure that begins when you turn on or reset your computer.

A set of instructions contained in ROM (read-only memory) begins executing. The instructions run a series of Power-On Self Tests (POSTs) to check that devices such as hard disks are in working order, then locate and load the operating system, and finally pass control over to that operating system.

boot sector virus

A virus that infects the master boot record of a computer by overwriting the original boot code with infected boot code. This kind of virus is usually spread to a hard disk by using an infected floppy disk as a boot disk.

bootable disk

Any disk capable of loading and starting the operating system. Bootable floppy disks are becoming less common because operating systems are growing larger. In some cases, all the files needed to start the operating system will not fit on even the largest-capacity floppy disk, which makes it impossible to boot from a floppy disk.

bpi

See bits per inch.

bps

See bits per second.

brain damaged

An expression used to describe any poorly designed program or piece of hardware that does not include those features most users would consider essential. The implication is that the designer should have known better than to leave those features out of the product.

breakout box

A small device that can be connected into a multicore cable for testing the signals in a transmission. Small LEDs in the breakout box indicate when a signal is transmitted over one of the lines. Switches or short jumper cables can be used to reroute these signals to other pins as required for troubleshooting.

BRI

See Basic Rate ISDN.

brownout

A short period of low voltage, often the result of an unusually heavy demand for power, that may cause your computer to crash. If your area experiences frequent brownouts, consider using a UPS (uninterruptible power supply) as a battery backup system.

buffer

An area of memory set aside for temporary storage of data. Often, the data remains in the buffer until some external event finishes. A buffer can compensate for the differences in transmission or processing speed between two devices or between a computer and a peripheral device, such as a printer or modem.

Buffers are implemented in a variety of different ways, including first-in-first-out (FIFO) used for pipes and last-in-last-out used for stacks and circular buffers such as event logs.

bug

A logical or programming error in hardware or software that causes a malfunction of some sort. If the problem is in software, it can be fixed by changes to the program. If the fault is in hardware, new circuits must be designed and constructed. Some bugs are fatal and may cause a program to stop responding or cause data loss; others are just annoying, and many are not even noticeable.

burned-in address

The hardware address on a network interface card. This address is assigned by the manufacturer of the interface card, which ensures that every card has a unique address.

Burst Extended Data Out DRAM

Abbreviated BEDO DRAM. A type of EDO dynamic RAM that manages data in bursts of four items at a time to increase speed. This approach takes advantage of the fact that memory requests usually refer to a series of sequential addresses.

bus

An electronic pathway along which signals are sent from one part of a computer to another. A PC contains several buses, each used for a different purpose:

- The address bus allocates memory addresses.

- The data bus carries data between the processor and memory.

- The control bus carries signals from the control unit.

bus mastering

A technique that allows certain advanced bus architectures to delegate control of data transfers between the central processing unit (CPU) and associated peripheral devices to an add-in board. This technique gives greater system bus access and higher data transfer speeds.

In the PC, bus mastering is supported by all of the common architectures except for the older Industry Standard Architecture (ISA).

byte

Contraction of binary digit eight. A group of bits. In computer storage terms, a byte usually holds a single character, such as a number, letter, or symbol. A byte usually contains 8 bits, but on some older computer systems, a byte may only have 7 bits or may have as many as 11.

Because bytes represent a very small amount of storage, they are usually grouped into kilobytes (1024 bytes), megabytes (1,048,576 bytes), and gigabytes (1,073,741,824 bytes) for convenience when describing hard disk capacity or computer memory size.

C

cable modem

A modem that sends and receives signals through a coaxial cable connected to a cable television system, rather than through conventional telephone lines.

Cable modems, with speeds of up to 500Kbps, are faster than current conventional modems but are subject to performance changes as system load increases. Theoretical data rates are much higher than those achieved with conventional modems; downstream rates of up to 36Mbps are possible, with 3Mbps to 10Mbps likely, and upstream rates up to 10Mbps.

cache

Pronounced "cash." A special area of memory, managed by a cache controller, which improves performance by storing the contents of frequently accessed memory locations and their addresses.

A memory cache and a disk cache are not the same. This entry describes a memory cache, which is implemented in hardware and speeds up access to memory. A disk cache is software that improves hard disk performance.

When the processor references a memory address, the cache checks to see if it holds that address. If it does, the information is passed directly to the processor, so random access memory (RAM) access is not necessary. A cache can speed up operations in a computer whose RAM access is slow compared with its processor speed, because cache memory is always faster than normal RAM.

There are several different types of cache:

> **direct-mapped cache** A location in the cache corresponds to several specific locations in memory, so when the processor calls for certain data, the cache can locate it quickly. However, since

several blocks in RAM correspond to that same location in the cache, the cache may spend its time refreshing itself and calling main memory.

> **fully associative cache** Information from RAM may be placed in any free blocks in the cache, so that the most recently accessed data is usually present; however, the search to find that information may be slow because the cache has to index the data in order to find it.

> **set-associative cache** Information from RAM is kept in sets, and these sets may have multiple locations, each holding a block of data; each block may be in any of the sets, but it will only be in one location within that set. Search time is shortened, and it is less likely that frequently used data will be overwritten. A set-associative cache may use two, four, or eight sets.

cache memory

Pronounced "cash memory." A relatively small section of very fast memory (often static RAM) reserved for the temporary storage of the data or instructions likely to be needed next by the processor.

Cache memory integrated directly onto the microprocessor is called primary cache or L1 cache, while cache memory located in an external circuit is known as secondary cache or L2 cache.

carrier signal

A signal of chosen frequency generated to carry data, often used for long-distance transmissions. A carrier signal does not convey any information until the data is added to the signal by modulation and then decoded on the receiving end by demodulation.

cascading

A technique used to connect two Ethernet hubs together when expanding the network; sometimes called daisy chaining. Cascading usually requires a special cable.

Category 1–5

The Telecommunications Industry Association and Electronics Industry Association (TIA/EIA) 586 cabling standards, sometimes abbreviated Cat 1–5, as follows:

Category 1 For unshielded twisted-pair (UTP) telephone cable. This cable may be used for voice but is not suitable for data transmissions.

Category 2 For UTP cable for use at speeds up to 4Mbps. Category 2 cable is similar to IBM Cabling System Type 3 cable.

Category 3 For UTP cable for use at speeds up to 10Mbps. Category 3 cable is the minimum requirement for 10Base-T and is required for token ring. This cable has four pairs of conductors and three twists per foot.

Category 4 For the lowest acceptable grade of UTP cable for use with 16Mbps token ring.

Category 5 For 100-ohm, four-wire twisted-pair copper cable for use at speeds up to 100Mbps with Ethernet or ATM. This cable is low-capacitance and shows low crosstalk when installed according to specifications.

CAV

See constant angular velocity.

CCD

See charge-coupled device.

CD-R

See CD-recordable.

CD-recordable

Abbreviated CD-R. Using CD-R, you can write to the disc just once; after that, the disc can only be read from and not written to.

From a functional point of view, a CD-R and a CD-ROM are identical; you can read CD-R discs using almost any CD-ROM drive, although the processes that create the discs are slightly different. Low-cost CD-R drives are available from several manufacturers, including Kao, Kodak, Mitsui, Phillips, Ricoh, Sony, TDK, 3M, and Verbatim.

CD-rewritable

Abbreviated CD-RW. A CD format that can be written to and erased up to 1,000 times.

From a functional point of view, a CD-RW and a CD-ROM are identical, but not all CD-ROM drives can read CD-RW discs. Low-cost CD-RW drives are available from several manufacturers, including Kodak, Mitsui, Phillips, and Sony.

CD-ROM

Acronym for Compact Disc Read-Only Memory. A high-capacity, optical storage device that uses the same technology used to make ordinary music discs to store large amounts of information. A single 4.72-inch disc can hold up to 650 megabytes.

CD-ROMs are important components of multimedia applications. They are also used to store encyclopedias, dictionaries, and other large reference works, as well as libraries of fonts and clip art for desktop publishing. CD-ROMs have replaced floppy disks as the distribution mechanism for software packages, including network operating systems and large applications, so you can load the whole package from a single compact disc and an operating system from a set of discs.

A CD-ROM uses the constant linear velocity data-encoding scheme to store information in a single, spiral track, divided into many equal-length segments. To read data, the CD-ROM disk drive must increase the rotational speed as the read head gets closer to the center of the disk and decrease as the head moves back out.

CD-ROM disk drive

A disk device that uses compact disc technology for information storage. Many CD-ROM disk drives also have headphone jacks, external speaker jacks, and a volume control.

CD-ROM disk drives designed for computer use are more expensive than audio CD players are, because CD-ROM disk drives are manufactured to much higher tolerances. If a CD player misreads a small amount of data, the human ear probably will not detect the difference; if a CD-ROM disk drive misreads a few bytes of a program, the program will not run.

The two most popular CD-ROM drive interface cards are SCSI (Small Computer System Interface) and ATAPI (Advanced Technology Attachment Packet Interface). ATAPI is part of the Enhanced IDE specification introduced by Western Digital in 1994.

CD-ROM Extended Architecture

Abbreviated CD-ROM/XA. An extension to the CD-ROM format developed by Microsoft, Phillips, and Sony that allows for the storage of audio and visual information on compact disc, so you can play the audio at the same time you view the visual data.

CD-ROM/XA is compatible with the High Sierra specification, also known as ISO standard 9660.

CD-ROM/XA

See CD-ROM Extended Architecture.

CD-RW

See CD-rewritable.

Celeron

A low-cost version of Intel's Pentium II microprocessor. The Celeron includes an integrated 128KB L2 cache, supports Intel's MMX technology, and is available in a wide range of speeds.

charge-coupled device

Abbreviated CCD. A device in which the semiconductor elements are connected so that the electrical output from one provides the input to the next. CCDs are used in the light-detection circuitry in digital and video cameras.

chassis

The metal frame into which the PC's components, including power supply, printed circuit boards, and fan, are mounted.

checksum

A method of providing information for error detection, usually calculated by summing a set of values.

The checksum is usually appended to the end of the data that it is calculated from, so that they can be compared. A checksum cannot detect all possible errors and cannot be used to correct an error in the data.

chip

A slang expression for integrated circuit.

chipset

A group of integrated circuits designed to perform as a unit.

CISC

See complex instruction set computing.

Class A certification

An FCC certification for computer equipment, including mainframe computers and minicomputers destined for industrial, commercial, or office use, rather than for personal use at home. The Class A commercial certification is less restrictive than the Class B certification for residential use because it assumes that most residential areas are more than 30 feet away from any commercial computer equipment.

Class B certification

An FCC certification for computer equipment, including PCs, laptops, and portables destined for use in the home rather than in a commercial setting. Class B levels of radio frequency interference (RFI) must be low enough so that they do not interfere with radio or television reception when there is more than one wall and 30 feet separating the computer from the receiver. Class B certification is more restrictive than the commercial Class A certification.

Clear To Send

Abbreviated CTS. A hardware signal defined by the RS-232-C standard that indicates that the transmission can proceed.

clock

An electronic circuit that generates regularly spaced timing pulses at speeds up to millions of cycles per second. These pulses are used to synchronize the flow of information through the computer's internal communications channels.

clock speed

The internal speed of a computer or processor, normally expressed in megahertz (MHz) or gigahertz (GHz). Also known as clock rate.

The faster the clock speed, the faster the computer will perform a specific operation (assuming the other components in the system, such as disk drives, can keep up with the increased speed).

The Intel 8088 processor used in the original IBM PC had a clock speed of 4.77MHz—painfully slow when compared with speeds used by modern processors, which can run at clock speeds of a gigahertz or more.

clone

A computer that contains all the same hardware elements as a name-brand system but which is usually cheaper.

cluster

The basic unit of data storage recorded onto a hard or floppy disk during a low-level format. Usually contains two or more sectors.

clustering

In networking, the grouping of several servers in a way that allows them to appear to be one server from the point of view of network clients. Clustering improves data security, increases network capacity, and provides live backup in the event a server fails.

CLV

See constant linear velocity.

CMOS

See Complementary Metal-Oxide Semiconductor.

coaxial cable

A high-capacity cable used in networking that contains a solid inner copper core surrounded by plastic insulation and an outer braided copper or foil sheath. Depending on the diameter of the cable, it may be known as thinnet (thin Ethernet, used for office installations) or thicknet (thick Ethernet, used for facility-wide applications).

codec

1. Acronym for coder/decoder. A device that converts analog signals (such as voice or video) into a digital bit stream suitable for transmission, and then converts those digital signals back into analog signals at the receiving end.

2. Acronym for compression/decompression. An overall term to describe the hardware and software used in processing animation, digital video, and stereo-quality audio.

cold boot

The computer startup process that begins when you turn on power to the computer. You are doing a cold boot when you first turn on your computer. A cold boot might also be necessary if a program or the operating system crashes and freezes entirely. If your keyboard is operational, a warm boot may suffice.

collision

An attempt by two computers on the network to send a message at exactly the same instant; Ethernet automatically resends both messages, but with altered timing so they do not collide and are received properly.

colon

The symbol used after the protocol name in a Universal Resource Locator (URL).

command line

An interface between the user and the command processor that allows you to enter commands from the keyboard for execution by the operating system.

command processor

The part of the operating system that displays the command prompt on the screen, interprets and executes all the commands and filenames that you enter, and displays error messages when appropriate. Also called the command interpreter. The command processor also contains the system environment.

command prompt

A symbol (character or group of characters) on the screen that lets you know that the operating system is available and ready to receive input.

command-line argument

A parameter that alters the default mode of a command. In many operating systems, a command-line argument is one or more letters or numbers preceded by the slash (/) character. With some commands, you can group several arguments together. Sometimes called a command-line switch.

communications parameters

Any of several settings required to allow computers to communicate successfully. In asynchronous transmissions, commonly used in modem communications, the settings for baud rate, number of data bits, number of stop bits, and parity parameters must all be correct.

communications protocol

1. A standard way of communicating between computers or between computers and terminals. Communications protocols vary in complexity, ranging from Xmodem, a simple file-transfer protocol used to transfer files from one PC to another, to the seven-layer OSI reference model used as the theoretical basis for many large, complex computer networks.

2. A hardware interface standard, such as RS-232-C.

compact disc

Abbreviated CD. A nonmagnetic, polished, optical disk used to store large amounts of digital information. A CD can store approximately 650MB of information, equivalent to more than 450 floppy disks. This storage capacity translates into approximately 300,000 pages of text or 72 minutes of music, all on a single 4.72-inch disc.

Digital information is stored on the compact disc as a series of microscopic pits and smooth areas that have different reflective properties. A beam of laser light shines on the disc so that the reflections can be detected and converted into digital data.

compatibility

The extent to which a given piece of hardware or software conforms to an accepted standard, regardless of the original manufacturer.

In hardware, compatibility is often expressed in terms of widely accepted models—this designation implies that the device will perform in the same way as the standard device.

In software, compatibility is usually described as the ability to read data file formats created by another vendor's software, or the ability to work together and share data.

Complementary Metal Oxide Semiconductor

Abbreviated CMOS, pronounced "see-moss." A type of integrated circuit used in processors and for memory.

CMOS devices operate at very high speeds and use little power, so they generate little heat. In the PC, battery-backed CMOS memory is used to store operating parameters, such as the hard disk type and the date and time, when the computer is switched off.

CMOS is easily damaged by static electricity, so take appropriate precautions.

complex instruction set computing

Abbreviated CISC, pronounced "sisk." A processor that can recognize and execute more than 100 different assembly-language, or low-level, instructions. CISC processors can be powerful, but the instructions take a high number of clock cycles to execute.

This complexity is in contrast to the simplicity of reduced instruction set computing (RISC) processors, in which the number of available instructions has been cut to a minimum. RISC processors are common in workstations and can be designed to run up to 70 percent faster than CISC processors.

COM port

The device name used for a serial communications port.

compressed file

A file that has been processed by a special utility so that it occupies as little hard disk space as possible.

When the file is needed, the same program decompresses the file back into its original form so that it can be read by the computer.

Popular compression techniques include schemes that replace commonly occurring sequences of characters by tokens that take up less space. Some utilities use Huffman coding to shrink a file, while others use adaptive Lempel-Ziv coding.

connection speed

The speed of a data communications circuit. Some circuits are symmetrical and can maintain the same speed in both directions, while others are asymmetrical and use a faster speed in one direction, usually the downstream side.

constant angular velocity

Abbreviated CAV. An unchanging speed of rotation. Hard disks use a CAV encoding scheme. The constant rate of rotation means that sectors on the disk are at the maximum density along the inside track of the disk. As the read/write heads move outward, the sectors must spread out to cover the increased track circumference, and therefore the data transfer rate falls off.

constant linear velocity

Abbreviated CLV. A changing speed of rotation. CD-ROM disk drives use a CLV encoding scheme to make sure that the data density remains constant. Information on a compact disc is stored in a single, spiral track, divided into many equal-length segments. To read the data, the CD-ROM disk drive must increase the rotational speed as the read head gets closer to the center of the disc and decrease as the head moves back out.

control character

A nonprinting character with a special meaning.

Control characters, such as Carriage Return, Line Feed, Bell, or Escape, perform a specific operation on a terminal, printer, or communications line. They are grouped together as the first 32 characters in the ASCII character set.

You can type a control character from the keyboard by pressing and holding the Ctrl key while you simultaneously press another key. For example, if you press and hold the Ctrl key and then press C, you generate Ctrl+C.

corona wire

In a laser printer, the wire that applies an electrostatic charge to the paper.

crash

1. An unexpected program halt, sometimes due to a hardware failure but most often due to a software error, from which there is no recovery. You usually need to reboot the computer to recover after a crash.

2. A disk drive failure, sometimes called a head crash, which leaves the hard disk unusable.

CRC

See cyclical redundancy check.

cross-linked clusters

Clusters on a hard or floppy disk allocated to more than one file due to a storage error.

crosstalk

In computer communications, any interference from a physically adjacent channel that corrupts the signal and causes transmission errors.

Ctrl+Alt+Del

A three-key combination used to reset the machine and reload the operating system. By pressing Ctrl+Alt+Del, you initiate a warm boot, which restarts the computer without going through the Power-On Self Tests (POSTs) normally run when the computer goes through a cold boot.

In Windows 98/2000/XP, the sequence opens a dialog box from which you can either end a task or shut down the computer. Sometimes called the three-finger salute.

Ctrl key

A key on the keyboard that, when pressed at the same time as another key, generates a nonprinting control character.

CTS

See Clear To Send.

cursor

A special character displayed on a monitor to indicate where the next character will appear when it is typed. In text or character mode, the cursor is usually a blinking rectangle or underline. In a graphical user interface, the mouse cursor can take many shapes, depending
on the current operation and its screen location.

cursor-movement keys

The keys on the keyboard that move the cursor, also called cursor-control keys. These keys include the four arrow keys and the Home, Page Up, End, and Page Down keys.

On full-sized keyboards, cursor-movement keys are often found on the numeric keypad; laptops and notebooks often have separate cursor-movement keys.

cut through

A technique used by some Ethernet hardware to speed up packet forwarding. Only the first few bytes of the packet are examined before it is forwarded or filtered. This process is much faster than looking at the whole packet, but it does allow some bad packets to be forwarded.

cyclical redundancy check

Abbreviated CRC. A complex calculation method used to check the accuracy of a digital transmission over a communications link or to ensure the integrity of a file stored on a hard disk.

The sending computer uses one of several formulas to calculate a value from the information contained in the data, and this value is appended to the message block before it is sent. The receiving computer performs the same calculation on the same data and compares this number with the received CRC. If the two CRCs do not match, indicating a transmission error occurred, the receiving computer asks the sending computer to retransmit the data.

This procedure is known as a redundancy check because each transmission includes extra or redundant error-checking values as well as the data itself.

As a security check, a CRC may be used to compare the current size of an executable file against the original size to determine if the file has been tampered with or changed in some way.

D

D channel

The data channel in ISDN (Integrated Services Digital Network), used for control signals and customer data. In the Base Rate ISDN (BRI), the D channel operates at 16Kbps; in the Primary Rate ISDN (PRI), it operates at 64Kbps.

daisy chaining

See cascading.

DAT

See Digital Audio Tape.

data bits

In asynchronous transmissions, the bits that actually make up the data. Usually, 7 or 8 data bits are grouped together. Each group of data bits in a transmission is preceded by a start bit and followed by an optional parity bit as well as one or more stop bits.

Data Carrier Detected

Abbreviated DCD. A hardware signal defined by the RS-232-C standard that indicates the modem is ready to transmit.

data compression

Any method of encoding data so that it occupies less space than it did in its original form, thus allowing that data to be stored, backed up, retrieved, or transmitted more efficiently.

Data compression is used in fax and many other forms of data transmission, CD-ROM publishing, and in still- and video-image manipulation.

Data Set Ready

Abbreviated DSR. A hardware signal defined by the RS-232-C standard that indicates the device is ready to operate.

DB connector

Any of several types of cable connectors used for parallel or serial cables. The number following the letters DB (for data bus) indicates the number of pins that the connector usually has; a DB25 connector can have up to 25 pins, and a DB9 connector can have up to 9. In practice, not all the pins (and not all the lines in the cable) may be present in the larger connectors. If your situation demands that all the lines be present, make sure you buy the right cable. Common DB connectors include the following:

DB9 Defined by the RS-449 standard as well as the ISO (International Organization for Standardization).

DB25 A standard connector used with RS-232-C wiring, with 25 pins (13 on the top row and 12 on the bottom).

DB37 Defined as the RS-449 primary channel connector.

DB15, DB19, and DB50 connectors are also available.

DCD

See Data Carrier Detected.

DDR SDRAM

See Double Data Rate syncDRAM

decibel

Abbreviated dB. One-tenth of a bel, a unit of measurement common in electronics that quantifies the loudness or strength of a signal. A decibel is a relative measurement derived by comparing a measured level against a known reference.

decimal

The base-10 numbering system that uses the familiar numbers 0–9; also known as the base-10 radix, or the decimal radix.

defragmentation

The process of reorganizing and rewriting files so that they occupy one large area on a hard disk rather than several smaller areas.

When a file on a hard disk is updated, it may be written into different areas all over the disk. This outcome is particularly likely when the hard disk is continuously updated over a long period of time. This file fragmentation can lead to significant delays in loading files, but its effect can easily be reversed by reorganizing and rewriting the file.

defragmenter

Any utility that rewrites all the parts of a fragmented file into contiguous areas on a hard disk. A defragmenter (such as the Microsoft Windows utility Disk Defragmenter) can restore performance lost because of file fragmentation.

demand paging

A common form of virtual memory management, in which pages of information are read into memory from disk only when required by the program.

demodulation

In communications, the process of retrieving the data from a modulated carrier signal; the reverse of modulation.

Desktop Management Interface

Abbreviated DMI. A standard API for identifying desktop workstation hardware components automatically, without intervention from the user.

At a minimum, DMI identifies the manufacturer, component name, version, serial number (if appropriate), and installation time and date of any component installed in a networked workstation. This information is designed to help network administrators resolve configuration problems quickly and easily and to indicate when and where system upgrades should be applied. PCs, Macintosh computers, and Unix systems are all covered by DMI.

DMI is backed by Digital Equipment Corporation (DEC), IBM, Intel, Microsoft, Novell, Sun, and more than 300 other vendors.

desktop video

The combination of video capture hardware and application software that controls the display of video or television pictures on a desktop PC.

Desktop video is becoming increasingly important with the sharp increase in video-conferencing applications now available.

device

A general term used to describe any computer peripheral or hardware element that can send or receive data.

Some examples are modems, printers, serial ports, disk drives, cameras, and game ports. Some devices require special software, or device drivers, to control or manage them; others have built-in intelligence.

device dependence

The requirement that a specific hardware component be present for a program to work. Device-dependent software is often difficult to move or port to another computer because of its reliance on specific hardware.

device driver

A small program that allows a computer to communicate with and control a device. Each operating system contains a standard set of device drivers for the keyboard, the monitor, and so on. When you add specialized peripheral devices, such as a network interface card, you must install the appropriate device driver so that the operating system knows how to manage the device.

device independence

The ability to produce similar results in a wide variety of environments without requiring the presence of specific hardware.

The Java programming language and the PostScript page-description language are examples of device independence. Java runs on a wide range of computers,

from the PC to a Cray; PostScript is used by many different printer manufacturers.

diagnostic program

A program that tests computer hardware and peripheral devices for correct operation. Some faults, known as hard faults, are relatively easy to find, and the diagnostic program will diagnose them correctly every time. Other faults, called soft faults, can be difficult to find, because they occur under specific circumstances rather than every time the memory location is tested.

Most computers run a simple set of system checks when the computer is first turned on. The PC tests are stored in read-only memory (ROM) and are known as Power-On Self Tests (POSTs). If a POST detects an error condition, the computer will stop and display an error message on the screen.

differential backup

A backup of a hard disk that includes only the information that has changed since the last complete backup was made.

A differential backup assumes that a full backup already exists, and in the event of an accident, this complete backup will be restored before the differential backup is reloaded.

differential SCSI

A Small Computer System Interface (SCSI) bus wiring scheme that uses two wires for each signal on the bus. One wire carries the signal, while the other carries its inverse. Differential SCSI minimizes the effects of external interference and so allows longer SCSI cable lengths to be used.

digital

Describes any device that represents values in the form of binary digits or bits.

Digital Audio Tape

Abbreviated DAT. A method of recording information in digital form on a small audio tape cassette, originally developed by Sony and Hewlett-Packard. The most common format is a 4-millimeter, helical-scan drive, which can hold more than 3 gigabytes of information. DATs can be used as backup media; however, like all tape devices, they are relatively slow.

digital signal processing

Abbreviated DSP. An integrated circuit used in high-speed data manipulation. You will find DSP chips integrated into sound cards, modems, and video conferencing hardware where they are used in communications, image manipulation, and other data-acquisition applications.

digital subscriber line

Abbreviated DSL. A high-speed data transmission technology originally developed by Bellcore that delivers high bandwidth over existing twisted-pair copper telephone lines.

There are several different DSL services, providing data rates from 16Kbps to 52Mbps. The services can be symmetrical, with the same data rate in both upstream and downstream directions, or asymmetrical, with the downstream capacity greater than the upstream capacity. Asymmetric services are particularly suitable for Internet users, because more information is downloaded than is uploaded.

As DSL data rates increase, the distance over which the service is provided decreases; certain users who are located too far from the telephone company's central office may not be able to obtain the higher speeds, or in some cases, may not be able to receive the service at all.

digital versatile disc

See digital video disc.

digital video disc

Abbreviated DVD; sometimes called digital versatile disc. A compact disc format. A standard single-layer single-sided disc can currently store 4.7GB of information; a two-layer standard increases this to 8.5GB, and eventually double-sided discs are expected to store 17GB per disc. DVD drives can also read conventional compact discs.

digital video disc-erasable

Abbreviated DVD-E. An extension to the digital video disc format to allow multiple rerecordings.

digital video disc-recordable

Abbreviated DVD-R. An extension to the digital video disc format to allow one-time recording.

digital video disc-ROM

Abbreviated DVD-ROM. A computer-readable form of digital video disc with either 4.7 or 8.5GB of storage per side.

DIMM

See Dual Inline Memory Module.

DIP

See Dual Inline Package.

DIP switch

A small switch used to select the operating mode of a device, mounted as a Dual Inline Package. DIP switches can be either sliding or rocker switches, and they are often grouped together for convenience. They are used in printed circuit boards, printers, modems, and many other peripheral devices.

direct memory access

Abbreviated DMA. A method of transferring information directly from a mass-storage device, such as a hard disk, into memory without the information passing through the processor. Because the processor is not involved in the transfer, DMA is fast. An alternative data transfer method known as programmed input/output moves data between a hard disk and memory via the processor, and so is much slower.

direct-mapped cache

See cache.

directory

In a hierarchical file system, a convenient way of organizing and grouping files and other directories on a disk. Sometimes called a folder.

The beginning directory is known as the root directory, from which all other directories must branch.

Directories inside another directory are called subdirectories.

You can list the files in a directory in a variety of different ways: by name, by creation date and time, by file size, or by icon.

disk cache

Pronounced "disk cash." An area of computer memory where data is temporarily stored on its way to or from a disk.

When an application asks for information from the hard disk, the cache program first checks to see if that data is already in the cache memory. If it is, the disk cache program loads the information from the cache memory rather than from the hard disk. If the information is not in memory, the cache program reads the data from the disk, copies it into the cache memory for future reference, and then passes the data to the requesting application.

disk controller

The electronic circuitry that controls and manages the operation of floppy and hard disks.

A single disk controller may manage more than one hard disk. Many disk controllers also manage floppy disks and compatible tape drives. In the PC, the disk controller may be a printed circuit board inserted into the expansion bus, or it may be part of the hard disk drive itself.

disk drive

A peripheral storage device that reads and writes magnetic or optical disks. When more than one disk drive is installed on a computer, the operating system assigns each drive (or logical drive) a unique name.

Several types of disk drive are in common use: floppy disk drives, hard disk drives, compact disc drives, digital video disc drives, Zip drives, and magneto-optical disk drives.

disk optimizer

A utility that rearranges files and directories on a disk for optimum performance. By reducing or eliminating file fragmentation (storage in pieces in different locations on the hard disk), a disk optimizer can restore the original level of performance of your disk system. Also, it is usually easier to undelete, or recover, an unfragmented file than a fragmented one.

Many disk optimizers will not only rewrite files as contiguous files, but will also place specific unchanging files in particular locations on the disk, optimize directories, even place specific applications on the disk so they load more quickly.

DLL

See dynamic-link library.

DMA

See direct memory access.

DMI

See Desktop Management Interface.

docking station

A hardware system into which a portable computer fits so that it can be used as a full-fledged desktop computer.

Docking stations vary from simple port replicators that allow you access to parallel and serial ports and a mouse to complete systems that give you access to network connections, CD-ROMs, and even a tape backup system. The portable computer and docking station are designed as two parts of the same system; you cannot swap computers and docking stations from different manufacturers or even from different models from the same manufacturer.

Double Data Rate syncDRAM

Abbreviated DDR SDRAM. A variation of SDRAM that maximizes output by using both the leading and following edge of the clock tick to perform operations.

double slash

Notation used with a colon to separate the communications protocol from the host computer name in a Universal Resource Locator (URL) as in `http://www.sybex.com`.

download

1. In communications, to transfer a file or files from one computer to another over a network or using a modem.

2. To send information, such as font information or a PostScript file, from a computer to a printer.

DRAM

See dynamic RAM.

drive letter

A designation used to specify a PC disk drive. For example, the first floppy disk drive is usually referred to as drive A, and the first hard disk drive is usually referred to as drive C.

DSL

See digital subscriber line.

DSP

See digital signal processing.

DSR

See Data Set Ready.

Dual Inline Memory Module

Abbreviated DIMM. A group of memory chips mounted on a small circuit board. DIMMs have two sets of connectors that connect to different circuits, and they have a 64-bit data path.

Dual Inline Package

Abbreviated DIP. A standard housing constructed of hard plastic commonly used to hold an integrated circuit. The circuit's leads are connected to two parallel rows of pins designed to fit snugly into a socket; these pins may also be soldered directly to a printed circuit board.

duplex

In asynchronous transmissions, the ability to transmit and receive on the same channel at the same time; also referred to as full duplex. Half-duplex channels can transmit only or receive only.

DVD

See digital video disc.

DVD-E

See digital video disc-erasable.

DVD-R

See digital video disc-recordable.

DVD-ROM

See digital video disc-ROM.

dynamic-link library

Abbreviated DLL. A program module that contains executable code and data that can be used by applications, or even by other DLLs in performing a specific task.

DLLs are used extensively throughout the family of Microsoft Windows products. DLLs may have filename extensions of DLL, DRV, or FON.

The DLL is linked into the application only when the program runs, and it is unloaded again when no longer needed. If two DLL applications are running at the same time and both perform a particular function, only one copy of the code for that function is loaded, for more efficient use of limited memory.

Another benefit of using dynamic linking is that the EXE files are not as large as they would be without DLLs, because frequently used routines can be put into a DLL rather than repeated in each EXE file that uses them. A smaller EXE file means saved disk space and faster program loading.

dynamic RAM

Abbreviated DRAM, pronounced "dee-ram." A common type of computer memory that uses capacitors and transistors storing electrical charges to represent memory states. These capacitors lose their electrical charge, so they need to be refreshed every millisecond, during which time they cannot be read by the processor.

DRAM chips are small, simple, cheap, easy to make, and hold approximately four times as much information as a static RAM (SRAM) chip of similar complexity. However, they are slower than SRAM.

E

E

See exa-.

EB

See exabyte.

ECP

See extended capabilities port.

EDO RAM

Abbreviation for Extended Data Out RAM. A type of random access memory (RAM) that keeps data available to the processor while the next memory access is being initialized, thus speeding up overall access times. EDO RAM is significantly faster than conventional dynamic RAM.

EIDE

See Enhanced IDE.

EISA

See Extended Industry Standard Architecture.

electromagnetic interference

Abbreviated EMI. Any electromagnetic radiation released by an electronic device that disrupts the operation or performance of another device.

EMI is produced by many sources commonly found in an office environment, including fluorescent lights, photocopiers, and motors such as those used in elevators. EMI is also produced by natural atmospheric or solar activity.

electrostatic

A term used to describe an electrical charge that is not flowing along a conductor. Electrostatic charges are used in laser printers and in copiers to attach particles of toner to a photoconducting drum as a part of the printing process.

electrostatic discharge

Abbreviated ESD. A discharge of static electricity, often from human hands, onto an integrated circuit, which usually results in severe damage to the integrated circuit.

ELF

See extremely low-frequency emission.

EMI

See electromagnetic interference.

encode

1. To compress a video file using a codec so that the file can be transmitted in the shortest possible time.

2. To convert a binary file into a form suitable for data transmission.

Enhanced IDE

Abbreviated EIDE, contraction of enhanced and Integrated Drive Electronics (IDE). An extension to the IDE standard, EIDE supports larger hard disks, allows you to connect four drives to your PC rather than just two, allows data transfer rates of up to 13.3MBps, and also supports the ATAPI interface, which connects CD-ROM drives, optical disks, and tape drives.

enhanced parallel port

Abbreviated EPP. A parallel port specification, developed by Microsoft and Hewlett-Packard, that allows for high-speed, two-way communication between the computer and a peripheral other than a printer or scanner. EPP is used with external drives, is a part of the IEEE 1284 standard for advanced parallel ports, and can provide data rates in excess of 1Mbps.

EPP

See enhanced parallel port.

error

The difference between the expected and the actual.

In computing, the way that the operating system reports unexpected, unusual, impossible, or illegal events is by displaying an error number or error message. Errors range from trivial, such as an attempt to write a file to a disk drive that does not contain a disk, to fatal, such as when a serious operating system bug renders the system useless.

In communications, errors are often caused by line noise and signal distortion. Parity or cyclical redundancy check (CRC) information is often added as overhead to the data stream, and techniques such as error detection and correction are employed to detect and correct as many errors as possible.

error detection and correction

A mechanism used to determine whether transmission errors have occurred and, if so, to correct those errors.

Some programs or transmission protocols simply request a retransmission of the affected block of data if an error is detected. More complex protocols attempt to both detect and determine at the receiving end what the correct transmission should have been.

error handling

The way that a program copes with errors or exceptions that occur as the program is running.

Good error handling manages unexpected events or wrongly entered data gracefully, usually by opening a dialog box to prompt the user to take the appropriate action or enter the correct information. Badly written programs may simply stop running when the wrong data is entered or when an unanticipated disk error occurs.

error message

A message from the program or the operating system that contains information about a condition that requires some human intervention to solve.

Error messages can indicate relatively trivial problems, such as a disk drive that does not contain a disk, as well as fatal problems, such as when a serious operating system bug renders the system useless and requires a system reboot.

error rate

In communications, the ratio between the number of bits received incorrectly and the total number of bits in the transmission, also known as bit error rate (BER).

Some methods for determining error rate use larger or logical units, such as blocks, packets, or frames. In these cases, the measurement of error rate is expressed in terms of the number of units found to be in error out of the total number of units transmitted.

ESD

See electrostatic discharge.

Ethernet

A popular network protocol and cabling scheme with a transfer rate of 10Mbps, originally developed by Xerox in 1970 by Dr. Robert Metcalf. Ethernet uses a bus topology, and network nodes are connected by either thick or thin coaxial cable, fiber-optic cable, or twisted-pair cable.

Ethernet uses CSMA/CD (Carrier Sense Multiple Access/Collision Detection) to prevent network failures or collisions when two devices try to access the network at exactly the same time.

The original DIX (Digital Equipment, Intel, Xerox), or Blue Book, standard has evolved into the slightly more complex IEEE 802.3 standard, and the ISO's 8802.3 specification.

The advantages of Ethernet include:

- It's easy to install at a moderate cost.

- Technology is available from many sources and is very well known.

- It offers a variety of cabling options.

- It works very well in networks with only occasional heavy traffic.

And the disadvantages include:

- Heavy traffic can slow down the network.

- A break in the main cable can bring down large parts of the network.

- Troubleshooting a bus topology can prove difficult.

Ethernet address

The address assigned to a network interface card by the original manufacturer, or by the network administrator if the card is configurable.

This address identifies the local device address to the rest of the network, and allows messages to reach the correct destination. Also known as the Media Access Control (MAC) or hardware address.

Ethernet packet

A variable-length unit in which information is transmitted on an Ethernet network.

An Ethernet packet consists of a synchronization preamble, a destination address, a source address, a type code indicator, a data field that can vary from 46 to 1500 bytes, and a cyclical redundancy check (CRC) that provides a statistically derived value used to confirm the accuracy of the data.

exa-

Abbreviated E. A prefix meaning one quintillion or 1018. In computing, the prefix means 1,152,921,504,606,846,976, or the power of 2 closest to one quintillion (260).

exabyte

Abbreviated EB. One quintillion bytes, or 1,152,921,504,606,846,976 bytes.

extended capabilities port

Abbreviated ECP. A parallel port specification, developed by Microsoft and Hewlett-Packard, that allows for high-speed, two-way communication between the computer and the peripheral attached to the port, usually a printer or scanner. ECP is a part of the IEEE 1284 standard for advanced parallel ports.

Extended Industry Standard Architecture

Abbreviated EISA. A 32-bit bus standard introduced in 1988, now mostly eclipsed by the PCI bus.

extremely low-frequency emission

Abbreviated ELF. Radiation emitted by a computer monitor and other common electrical appliances.

ELF emissions fall into the range of 5 to 2000Hz and decline with the square of the distance from the source. Emissions are not constant around a monitor; they are higher from the sides and rear and weakest from the front of the screen. Low-emission models are available, and laptop computers with an LCD display do not emit any ELF fields.

F

fading

In both electrical and wireless systems, a decrease in a signal's strength.

Fading may be due to physical obstructions of the transmitter or receiver, distance from the source of the transmission, or some form of external interference from other signals or from atmospheric conditions.

fall back

A technique used by modems to adjust their data rate in response to changing line conditions.

far-end crosstalk

Abbreviated FEXT. Interference that occurs when signals on one twisted-pair are coupled with another pair as they arrive at the far end of a multipair cable system.

FEXT becomes a problem on short loops supporting high-bandwidth services such as very high-bit-rate digital subscriber line (VDSL) because of the high carrier frequencies used.

Fast Ethernet

A term applied to the IEEE 802.3 Higher Speed Ethernet Study Group proposals, which were originally developed by Grand Junction Networks, 3Com, SynOptics, Intel, and others. Also known as 100Base-T.

Fast Ethernet modifies the existing Ethernet standard to allow speeds of 10 or 100Mbps, or both, and uses CSMA/CD access method.

The official standard defines three specifications for different cabling types:

◆ 100Base-TX for two-pair Category 5 unshielded twisted-pair.

◆ 100Base-T4 for four-pair Category 3, 4, or 5 unshielded twisted-pair.

◆ 100Base-FX for fiber-optic cable.

Fast IR

A 4Mbps extension to the Serial Infrared Data Link Standard that provides wireless data transmission between IrDA-compliant devices.

fast page-mode RAM

See page-mode RAM.

Fast SCSI

A version of the SCSI-2 interface that can transfer data 8 bits at a time at data rates of up to 10MBps. The Fast SCSI connector has 50 pins.

Fast/Wide SCSI

A version of the SCSI-2 interface that can transfer data 16 bits at a time at data rates of up to 20MBps. The Fast/Wide SCSI connector has 68 pins.

FAT

See file allocation table.

FAT16

In Microsoft Windows, a file allocation table that uses a 16-bit cluster addressing scheme which restricts the maximum hard disk size to 2.6GB. Also, FAT16 is inefficient in disk-space utilization as the default cluster size can be as large as 32KB.

FAT32

In Microsoft Windows 95 (release 2) and later versions of Windows, a file allocation table that uses a 32-bit cluster addressing scheme to support hard disks larger than 2.6GB, as well as a default cluster size of as small as 4KB. FAT32 can support hard disks of up to 2 terabytes in size.

fax modem

An adapter that fits into a PC expansion slot providing many of the capabilities of a full-sized fax machine but at a fraction of the cost.

The advantages of a fax modem include ease of use and convenience; the main disadvantage is that the material you want to fax must be present in digital form in the computer. Unless you have access to a scanner, you cannot fax handwritten notes, line art, or certain kinds of graphics. Most faxes sent directly from a PC using a fax modem are text files.

FCC certification

Approval by the FCC (Federal Communications Commission) that a specific computer model meets its standards for radio frequency interference (RFI) emissions.

There are two levels of certification:

◆ Class A certification, which is for computers used in commercial settings, such as mainframes and minicomputers.

◆ The more stringent Class B certification, for computers used in the home and in home offices, such as PCs, laptops, and portables.

FDDI

See Fiber Distributed Data Interface.

female connector

Any cable connector with receptacles designed to receive the pins on the male connector.

Fiber Distributed Data Interface

Abbreviated FDDI. The ANSI X3T9.5 specification for fiber-optic networks transmitting at a speed of up to 100Mbps over a dual, counter-rotating, token ring topology.

FDDI's 100Mbps speed is close to the internal speed of most computers, which makes it a good choice to serve as a super backbone linking two or more LANs, or as a fiber-optic bus connecting high-performance engineering workstations. FDDI is suited to systems that require the transfer of large amounts of information, such as medical imaging, three-dimensional seismic processing, and oil reservoir simulation.

The FDDI-II version of the standard is designed for networks transmitting real-time full-motion video (or other information that cannot tolerate any delays) and requires that all nodes on the network use FDDI-II; otherwise the network automatically reverts to FDDI.

An FDDI network using multimode fiber-optic cable can include as many as 500 stations up to 2 kilometers (1.25 miles) apart; with single-mode fiber, run length increases up to 60 kilometers (37.2 miles) between stations. This type of network can also run over shielded and unshielded twisted-pair cabling (when it is known as CDDI, or Copper Distributed Data Interface) for shorter distances.

fiber-optic cable

A transmission technology that sends pulses of light along specially manufactured optical fibers.

Each fiber consists of a core, thinner than a human hair, surrounded by a sheath with a much lower refractive index. Light signals introduced at one end of the cable are conducted along the cable as the signals are reflected from the sheath.

Fiber-optic cable is lighter and smaller than traditional copper cable, is immune to electrical interference, offers better security, and has better signal-transmitting qualities. However, it is more expensive than traditional cables and is more difficult to repair.

file

A named collection of information that appears to the user as a single entity and is stored on disk.

A file can contain a program or part of a program, just data, or a user-created document. Files may actually be fragmented or stored in many different places across the disk. The operating system manages the task of locating all the pieces when a request is made to read the file.

file allocation table

Abbreviated FAT, pronounced "fat." A table, maintained by the operating systems, that lists all the blocks of disk space available on a disk.

The FAT includes the location of each block, as well as whether it is in use, available for use, or damaged in some way and therefore unavailable. Because files are not necessarily stored in consecutive blocks on a disk, the FAT also keeps track of which pieces belong to which file.

file compression

A technique that shrinks program or data files so that they occupy less disk space. The file must then be extracted or decompressed before use. Some types of files, such as word processor documents, can be com-

pressed by 50 percent or more. Recompressing an already compressed file usually makes the file slightly larger because of the compression overhead.

File compression can be automatic and performed by the operating system, or it can be manual and be performed by a file-compression program.

file format

A file structure that defines the way information is stored in the file and how the file appears on the screen or on the printer.

The simplest file format is a plain ASCII file. Some of the more complex formats are DCA (Document Content Architecture) and RTF (Rich Text Format), which include control information for use by a printer; TIFF (Tagged Image File Format) and EPS (Encapsulated PostScript), which hold graphics information; and DBF (Xbase database file) and DB (Paradox file), which are database formats. Word processing programs, such as Microsoft Word, also create files in special formats.

file fragmentation

Storage of files in pieces scattered on a disk. As files grow on a hard disk, they can be divided into several small pieces. By fragmenting files, the operating system makes reasonable use of the disk space available.

The problem with file fragmentation is that the disk heads must move to different locations on the disk to read or write to a fragmented file. This process takes more time than reading the file as a single piece. To speed up file operations, you can use a disk optimizer or defragmenter.

file transfer protocol

Abbreviated FTP. The TCP/IP Internet protocol used when transferring single or multiple files from one computer system to another.

FTP uses a client/server model, in which a small client program runs on your computer and accesses a larger FTP server running on an Internet host. FTP provides all the tools needed to look at directories and files, change to other directories, and transfer text and binary files from one system to another.

file-infecting virus

Any virus that infects files on disk, usually executable files with filename extensions of COM, EXE, and OVL. An unexpected change in the file size may indicate an infection. In certain cases, the original program is replaced with a new file containing an infected program.

filename

The name of a file on a disk used so that both you and the operating system can find the file again. Every file in a directory must have a unique name, but files in different directories can share the same name.

FireWire

See IEEE 1394.

firmware

Any software stored in a form of read-only memory (ROM), erasable programmable read-only memory (EPROM), or electrically erasable programmable read-only memory (EEPROM) that maintains its contents when power is removed.

flash memory

A special form of read-only memory (ROM) that can be erased at signal levels commonly found inside the PC.

This ability allows the contents to be reprogrammed without removing the chips from the computer. Also, once flash memory has been programmed, you can remove the expansion board it is mounted on and plug it into another computer without loss of the new information.

flat panel display

A thin video display that does not use CRT technology. Flat panel displays were originally used in laptop and other portable computers, but now they are available as desktop units.

flow control

1. In communications, control of the rate at which information is exchanged between two computers over a transmission channel. Flow control is needed when one of the devices cannot receive the information at the same rate as it can be sent, usually because some processing is required on the receiving end before the next transmission unit can be accepted. Flow control can be implemented either in hardware or in software.

2. In networking, control of the flow of data throughout the network, ensuring that network segments are not congested. A router controls data flow by routing around any trouble spots.

FM synthesis

Abbreviation for frequency modulation synthesis. A method used by a sound board to simulate musical instruments. FM synthesis is cheaper than wavetable synthesis but is also of lower quality.

footprint

The amount of desktop space or floor space occupied by a computer, printer, or monitor.

forced perfect termination

A technique used to terminate a Small Computer System Interface (SCSI). Forced perfect termination actively monitors the bus to ensure that no signal reflection occurs.

formatting

The process of initializing a new, blank floppy disk or hard disk so that it can be used to store information.

forward error correction

A technique used to control errors that insert extra or redundant bits into the data stream. The receiving device uses the redundant bits to detect and, if possible, correct the errors in the data.

four-wire circuit

A transmission system in which two half-duplex circuits, consisting of two wires each, are combined to create one full-duplex circuit.

fps

See frames per second.

frame

1. A block of data suitable for transmission as a single unit, also referred to as a packet or block. Some media can support multiple frame formats.

2. In digital video, one screen of information, including both text and graphics.

frames per second

Abbreviated fps. The number of video frames displayed each second. While 24fps is considered the slowest frame rate that provides convincing motion to the human eye, most Internet video runs at between 5 and 15fps.

free memory

Any area of memory not currently in use. Often refers to the memory space remaining for applications to use after the operating system and the system device drivers have been loaded.

fried

A slang expression for burned-out hardware, especially hardware that has suffered from a power surge. Also applied to people, as in "My brain is fried; I haven't slept since last weekend."

FTP

See file transfer protocol.

ftp

A command used to transfer files to and from remote computers using the file transfer protocol. You can use ftp to log in to an Internet computer and transfer text and binary files.

When you use ftp, you start a client program on your computer that connects to a server program on the Internet computer. The commands that you give to ftp are translated into instructions that the server program executes for you.

The original ftp program started life as a Unix utility, but versions are now available for all popular operating systems; ftp is also built into all the major Web browsers.

full backup

A backup that includes all files on a hard disk or set of hard disks. A network administrator must decide how often to perform a full backup, balancing the need for security against the time taken for the backup.

full-duplex

Abbreviated FDX. The capability for simultaneous transmission in two directions, so that devices can be sending and receiving data at the same time.

full-page display

Any monitor capable of displaying a whole page of text. Full-page displays are useful for graphical art and desktop publishing applications, as well as medical applications.

fully associative cache

See cache.

function keys

The set of programmable keys on the keyboard that can perform special tasks assigned by the current application.

Most keyboards have 10 or 12 function keys (F1 to F10 or F1 to F12), some of which are used by an application as shortcut keys. For example, many programs use F1 to gain access to the Help system. In some programs, the use of function keys is so complex that special plastic key overlays are provided as guides for users.

G

G

See giga-.

gauge

A measurement of the physical size of a cable. Under the American Wire Gauge (AWG) standards, higher numbers indicate thinner cable.

GB

See gigabyte.

gender changer

A special intermediary connector for use with two cables that each have only male connectors or only female connectors.

giga-

A prefix meaning 1 billion, or 109.

gigabit

Abbreviated Gb or Gbit. Usually 1,073, 741,824 binary digits or bits of data. Sometimes used as equivalent to one billion bits.

Gigabit Ethernet

A 1Gbps (1000Mbps) extension of the IEEE 802.3 Ethernet standard, also known as 1000Base-X.

This standard has been developed by the IEEE 802.3z Task Group and a number of interested companies collectively known as the Gigabit Ethernet Alliance. Gigabit Ethernet runs over multimode fiber-optic cable and is intended for use as a backbone and a way to connect high-speed routers, switches, and hubs.

gigabyte

Abbreviated GB. Strictly speaking, one billion bytes; however, in computing, in which bytes are most often counted in powers of 2, a gigabyte becomes 230, or 1,073,741,824 bytes.

H

H.323

A videoconferencing standard defined by the International Telecommunication Union (ITU) that defines videoconferencing from the desktop over LANs, intranets, and the Internet.

H.323 specifies techniques for compressing and transmitting real-time voice, video, and data between a pair of videoconferencing workstations. It also describes signaling protocols for managing audio and video streams, as well as procedures for breaking data into packets and synchronizing transmissions across communications channels.

half-duplex

Abbreviated HDX. In asynchronous transmissions, the ability to transmit on the same channel in two directions, but only in one direction at a time.

handshaking

The exchange of control codes or particular characters to maintain and coordinate data flow between two devices, so that data is only transmitted when the receiving device is ready to accept the data.

Handshaking can be implemented in either hardware or software, and it occurs between a variety of devices. For example, the data flow might be from one computer to another computer, or from a computer to a peripheral device, such as a modem or printer.

hang

1. When a program waits for an event that never occurs, as in, "The program hangs waiting for a character from the keyboard."

2. A slang expression used when attaching a new piece of hardware to a system, usually an external device attached by one or more cables, as in, "I'm going to hang a new tape drive on the server this afternoon."

hard disk

That part of a hard disk drive that stores data, rather than the mechanism for reading and writing to it. Sometimes called a platter.

hard disk controller

The circuitry used to control and coordinate a hard disk drive.

Many hard disk controllers are capable of managing more than one hard disk, as well as floppy disks and tape drives. On some PCs, the hard disk controller is built into the motherboard, and in others, the controlling circuitry is mounted on the drive itself, eliminating the need for a separate controller.

hard disk drive

A storage device that uses a set of rotating, magnetically coated disks called platters to store data or programs. In everyday use, the terms hard disk, hard disk drive, and hard drive are used interchangeably, because the disk and the drive mechanism are a single unit.

A typical hard disk platter rotates at several thousand revolutions per minute, and the read/write heads float on a cushion of air from 10 to 25 millionths of an inch thick, so that the heads never come into contact with the recording surface. The whole unit is hermetically sealed to prevent airborne contaminants from entering and interfering with these close tolerances.

Hard disks range in storage capacity from a few tens of megabytes to several terabytes. The more storage space on the disk, the more important your backup strategy becomes. Hard disks are reliable, but they do fail, and usually at the most inconvenient moment.

hard disk interface

A standard way of accessing the data stored on a hard disk. Several different hard disk interface standards have evolved over time, including the ST506 Interface, Enhanced Small Device Interface (ESDI), Integrated Drive Electronics Interface (IDE), and Small Computer System Interface (SCSI).

hard disk type

A number stored in a PC's CMOS RAM memory area that defines certain hard disk characteristics, such as the number of read/write heads and the number of cylinders on the disk. This number is not accessible directly from the operating system. Some PCs require a special configuration program to access the hard disk type; others permit access via the computer's built-in ROM BIOS setup program.

hard reset

A system reset made by pressing the computer's reset button, or by turning the power off and then on again. A hard reset is used only when the system has crashed so badly that pressing Ctrl+Alt+Del to reboot does not work.

hardware

All the physical electronic components of a computer system, including peripheral devices, printed-circuit boards, displays, and printers. If you can stub your toe on it, it must be hardware.

hardware address

The address assigned to a network interface card by the original manufacturer, or if the interface card is configurable, by the network administrator.

This address identifies the local device address to the rest of the network and allows messages to find the correct destination. Also known as the physical address, Media Access Control (MAC) address, or Ethernet address.

hardware compatibility list

A list of all the hardware devices supported by Microsoft Windows NT and Windows 2000/XP. Items on this list have actually been tested and verified to work properly with Windows.

hardware dependent

The requirement that a specific hardware component be present for a program to work. Hardware-dependent software is often difficult to move or port to another computer.

hardware independent

The ability to produce similar results in a wide variety of environments, without requiring the presence of specific hardware. The Java programming language and the Post-Script page-description language are both examples of hardware independence. Java runs on a wide range of computers, from the PC to a mainframe; PostScript is used by many printer manufacturers.

hardware interrupt

An interrupt or request for service generated by a hardware device, such as a keystroke from the keyboard or a tick from the clock. Because the processor may receive several such signals simultaneously, hardware interrupts are usually assigned a priority level and processed according to that priority.

HDSL

See high-bit-rate digital subscriber line.

hertz

Abbreviated Hz. A unit of frequency measurement; 1Hz equals one cycle per second.

hexadecimal

Abbreviated hex. The base-16 numbering system that uses the digits 0 to 9, followed by the letters A to F, which are equivalent to the decimal numbers 10 through 15.

Hex is a convenient way to represent the binary numbers computers use internally, because it fits neatly into the 8-bit byte. All the 16 hex digits 0 to F can be represented in 4 bits, and two hex digits (one digit for each set of 4 bits) can be stored in a single byte. This means that 1 byte can contain any one of 256 different hex numbers, from 0 through FF.

hidden file

Any file that has the hidden attribute set, which indicates to the operating system that information about the file should not appear in normal directory listings. There may also be further restrictions on a hidden file, and you may not be able to delete, copy, or display the contents of such a file.

High Sierra specification

A specification for CD-ROM data that served as the basis for the ISO (International Organization for Standardization) 9660 standard. It is called High Sierra because it was defined at a meeting held near Lake Tahoe in November 1985.

high-bit-rate digital subscriber line

Abbreviated HDSL. A high-speed data transmission technology originally developed by Bellcore that delivers high bandwidth over existing twisted-pair copper telephone lines.

HDSL is the most common digital subscriber line (DSL) service and provides T1 data rates of 1.544Mbps

over lines of up to 3.6 kilometers (12,000 feet) in length. HDSL is symmetric, providing the same data rate in each direction.

The service is not intended for residential purposes but is used in the telephone company's own private data networks, Internet servers, and interexchange connections.

hooked vector

An intercepted interrupt vector that now points to a replacement interrupt service routine (ISR) rather than to the original service routine.

hub

A device used to extend a network so that additional workstations can be attached. There are two main types of hub:

♦ Active hubs amplify transmission signals to extend cable length and ports.

♦ Passive hubs split the transmission signal, allowing additional workstations to be added, usually at a loss of distance.

In some star networks, a hub is the central controlling device.

Huffman coding

In data compression, a method of encoding data on the basis of the relative frequency of the individual elements. Huffman coding is often used with text files, where the coding is based on the frequency of occurrence of each letter, because it is a lossless compression method. Huffman coding is used in fax transmissions.

Hz

See hertz.

I

IC

See integrated circuit.

IDE

See Integrated Drive Electronics.

IEEE 1394

An IEEE standard for a digital Plug and Play bus, originally conceived by Apple Computer in 1986. IEEE 1394 supports up to 63 nodes per bus and up to 1023 buses.

Three speeds for device connections are available:

- ◆ 100Mbps

- ◆ 200Mbps

- ◆ 400Mbps

All devices are hot pluggable, and both self-powered and bus-powered devices can be attached to the same bus. Also known as FireWire, IEEE 1394 uses six-pair shielded twisted-pair cable and is intended for high-end applications such as digitized video.

impedance

An electrical property of a cable that combines capacitance (the ability to store an electrical charge), inductance (the ability to store energy in the form of a magnetic field), and resistance (the ability to impede or resist the flow of electric current), measured in ohms.

Impedance can be described as the apparent resistance to the flow of alternating current at a given frequency. Mismatches in impedance along a cable cause distortions and reflections. Each transmission protocol and network topology specifies its own standards for impedance.

incremental backup

A backup of a hard disk that consists of only those files created or modified since the last backup was performed.

infection

The presence of a virus or Trojan Horse, which may be active in memory or which may be present on the hard disk.

An infection may remain hidden from the user for a considerable time. Some viruses are triggered by specific dates or by particular events on the system. Many macro viruses act immediately when you open the e-mail attachment containing the virus.

Infrared Data Association

Abbreviated IrDA. A trade association of over 150 computer and telecommunications hardware and software suppliers, including Hewlett-Packard, Apple Computer, AST, Compaq, Dell, IBM, Intel, Motorola, Novell, and others.

IrDA is concerned with standards definitions for products that use wireless communications.

infrared transmission

A method of wireless transmission that uses part of the infrared spectrum to transmit and receive signals.

Infrared transmissions take advantage of a frequency range just below that of visible light, and they usually require a line of sight connection between transmitter and receiver.

Infrared transmission can be used to send documents from portable computers to printers, to transmit data between portable computers, to exchange information between computers and cellular telephones and faxes, and to connect to home entertainment systems. Almost every manufacturer of portable devices is implementing infrared communications at some level.

inkjet printer

A nonimpact printer that sprays a mist of liquid ink through tiny jets in the print head to form characters or graphics on the page.

inoculate

To protect a file against attack from a virus by recording characteristic information about it and then monitoring any changes.

input/output

Abbreviated I/O. The transfer of data between the computer and its peripheral devices, disk drives, terminals, and printers.

input/output bound

Abbreviated I/O bound. A condition in which the speed of operation of the input/output port limits the speed of program execution. Getting the data into and out of the computer is more time-consuming than actually processing that same data.

install

To configure and prepare hardware or software for operation.

Many application packages have their own installation programs, which copy all the required files from the original distribution disks into appropriate directories on your hard disk and then help to configure the program to your own operating requirements. Microsoft Windows programs are installed by a program called Setup.

instruction set

The set of machine-language instructions that a processor recognizes and can execute.

An instruction set for reduced instruction set computing (RISC) may only contain a few instructions; a computer that uses complex instruction set computing (CISC) may be able to recognize several hundred instructions.

integrated circuit

Abbreviated IC, also known as a chip. A small semiconductor circuit that contains many electronic components.

Integrated Drive Electronics

Abbreviated IDE. A hard disk interface that removes the need for a separate disk controller card by integrating the required circuitry onto the drive itself or onto the motherboard; no expansion slot is needed.

Integrated Services Digital Network

Abbreviated ISDN. A standard for a worldwide digital communications network originally designed to replace all current systems with a completely digital, synchronous, full-duplex transmission system.

Computers and other devices connect to ISDN via simple, standardized interfaces. They can transmit voice, video, and data, all on the same line.

interface

The point at which a connection is made between two hardware devices, between a user and a program or operating system, or between two applications.

In hardware, an interface describes the logical and physical connections used, as in RS-232-C, and is often considered to be synonymous with the term port.

A user interface consists of the means by which a program communicates with the user, including a command line, menus, dialog boxes, online help systems, and so on.

Software interfaces are Application Program Interfaces (APIs) and consist of the codes and messages used by programs to communicate behind the scenes.

interleaved memory

A method of speeding up access by dividing dynamic RAM (DRAM) into two (or more) separate banks.

DRAM requires that its contents be updated at least every thousandth of a second, and while this update is taking place, it cannot be read by the processor. Interleaved memory divides available memory into banks so that the processor can read from one bank while the other is cycling, and so does not have to wait.

internal modem

A modem that plugs into the expansion bus of a personal computer, or into the PC Card connector of a laptop computer.

Internet

The world's largest computer network, consisting of millions of computers supporting tens of millions of users in hundreds of different countries. The Internet is growing at such a phenomenal rate that any size estimates are quickly out-of-date.

The Internet was originally established to meet the research needs of the U.S. Defense industry, but it has grown into a huge global network serving universities, academic researchers, commercial interests, government agencies, and private individuals in the U.S. and the rest of the world.

The Internet uses TCP/IP protocols, and Internet computers run many different operating systems, including many variations of Unix, VMS, and Microsoft Windows.

No government agency, single person, or corporate entity controls the Internet; there is no Internet Corporation working behind the scenes. All decisions on methods and standards are made by committees based on input from users.

Internet use falls into several major areas, including:

e-mail   Well over 80 percent of the people who use the Internet on a regular basis use it for e-mail. You can send e-mail to recipients in over 150 countries on the Internet, as well as to subscribers of commercial online services such as America Online.

IRC chat   A service that connects large numbers of users in real-time group discussions.

mailing lists   Private discussion groups accessed by e-mail.

Usenet newsgroups   Larger public discussion groups that focus on a specific subject. Posts and threads in newsgroups are accessed using a newsreader.

World Wide Web   A hypertext-based system for finding and accessing Internet resources; the World Wide Web is one of the fastest growing and most exciting of all Internet applications.

Other Internet applications such as Gopher, ftp and anonymous ftp, and Telnet have either been overshadowed by the growth of the World Wide Web, or have seen their function absorbed into the popular Web browsers.

The sheer volume of information available through the Internet is staggering; however, due to the fact that the Internet is a casual grouping of many networks, there is often no easy way to determine the location of specific information. This has led to the emergence of several prominent portal sites and a number of popular search engines.

Internet access can be via a permanent network connection or by dial-up through one of the many Internet Service Providers (ISPs).

internet
Abbreviation for internetwork. Two or more networks using different networking protocols, connected by means of a router. Users on an

internetwork can access the resources of all connected networks.

Internet address
An address on the Internet. An Internet address usually takes the form *someone@abc.def.xyz*, where *someone* is a user's name or part of a user's name, *@abc* is the network computer of the user, and *def* is the name of the host organization. The last three letters denote the kind of institution the user belongs to: edu for educational, com for commercial, gov for government, mil for the military, org for nonprofit organizations, and net for Internet administrative organizations.

Internet Protocol
Abbreviated IP, IP version 4, and IPv4. The protocol that regulates packet forwarding by tracking addresses, routing outgoing messages, and recognizing incoming messages in TCP/IP networks and the Internet.

Internet Service Provider
Abbreviated ISP. A company that provides commercial or residential customers access to the Internet via dedicated or dial-up connections. An ISP will normally have several servers and a high-speed connection to an Internet backbone. Some ISPs also offer Web site hosting services and free e-mail to their subscribers.

Internetwork Packet Exchange
Abbreviated IPX. Part of Novell NetWare's native protocol stack, used to transfer data between the server and workstations on the network. IPX packets are encapsulated and carried by the packets used in Ethernet and the frames used in Token Ring networks.

interprocess communication
Abbreviated IPC. A term that describes all the methods used to pass information between two programs running on the same computer in a multitasking operating system, or between two programs running on a network, including pipes, shared memory, mes-

sage queues, sockets, semaphores, and Object Linking and Embedding (OLE).

interrupt

A signal to the processor generated by a device under its control, such as the system clock, that interrupts normal processing.

An interrupt indicates that an event requiring the processor's attention has occurred, causing the processor to suspend and save its current activity and then branch to an interrupt service routine (ISR).

In the PC, interrupts are often divided into three classes:

◆ Internal hardware

◆ External hardware

◆ Software

The Intel family of processors supports 256 prioritized interrupts, of which the first 64 are reserved for use by the system hardware or by the operating system.

interrupt handler

Special software located in the operating system kernel that manages and processes system interrupts. Also known as an interrupt service routine.

When an interrupt occurs, the processor suspends and saves its current activity and then branches to the interrupt handler. This routine processes the interrupt, whether it was generated by the system clock, a keystroke, or a mouse click. When the ISR is complete, it returns control to the suspended process.

Each type of interrupt is processed by its own specific interrupt handler. A table, called the interrupt vector table, maintains a list of addresses for these specific interrupt handlers.

interrupt request

Abbreviated IRQ. Hardware lines that carry a signal from a device to the processor.

A hardware interrupt signals that an event has taken place that requires the processor's attention. The interrupt may come from the keyboard, the network interface card, or the system's disk drives.

interrupt vector table

A list of addresses, maintained by the operating system kernel, for specific software routines known as interrupt handlers.

intranet

A private corporate network that uses Internet software and TCP/IP networking protocol standards.

Many companies use intranets for tasks as simple as distributing a company newsletter and as complex as posting and updating technical support bulletins to service personnel worldwide. An intranet does not always include a permanent connection to the Internet.

I/O

See input/output.

I/O bound

See input/output bound.

IP

See Internet Protocol.

IP address

The unique 32-bit number that identifies a computer on the Internet or other Internet Protocol network.

An IP address is usually written (in decimal) as four numbers separated by dots or periods, and can be divided into two parts. The network address is made up from the high-order bits in the address, and the host address comprises the rest. In addition, the host part of the address can be further subdivided to allow for a subnet address.

These numbers are very difficult for most people to remember, so humans tend to refer to computers by their domain names instead.

IPX

See Internetwork Packet Exchange.

IrDA

See Infrared Data Association.

IRQ

See interrupt request.

ISDN
See Integrated Services Digital Network.

J

Joint Photographic Experts Group
Abbreviated JPEG. An image-compression standard and file format that defines a set of compression methods for high-quality images such as photographs, single video frames, or scanned pictures; JPEG does not work very well when compressing text, line art, or vector graphics.

JPEG uses lossy compression methods that result in some loss of the original data; when you decompress the original image, you don't get exactly the same image that you started with, although JPEG was specifically designed to discard information not easily detected by the human eye.

JPEG can store 24-bit color images in as many as 16 million colors; files in Graphics Interchange Format (GIF) form can only store 256 colors.

JPEG
See Joint Photographic Experts Group.

jumper
A small plastic and metal connector that completes a circuit, usually to select one option from a set of several user-definable options. Jumpers are often used to select one particular hardware configuration from a choice of configurations.

K

K
See kilo-.

Kb
See kilobit.

KB
See kilobyte.

Kbit
See kilobit.

Kbps
See kilobits per second.

Kbyte
See kilobyte.

kernel
The most fundamental part of an operating system. The kernel stays resident in memory at all times, often hidden from the user, and manages system memory, the file system, and disk operations.

The kernel also runs processes and provides inter-process communications between those processes, including synchronization of events, scheduling, message passing, management of input and output routines, and memory management.

keystroke
The action of pressing and then releasing a key on the keyboard to initiate some action or enter a character.

kilo-
A prefix indicating 1000 in the metric system. Because computing is based on powers of 2, kilo usually means 210, or 1024. To differentiate between these two uses, a lowercase k is used to indicate 1000 (as in kHz), and an uppercase K is used to indicate 1024 (as in KB).

kilobit
Abbreviated Kb or Kbit. 1024 bits (binary digits).

kilobits per second
Abbreviated Kbps. The number of bits, or binary digits, transmitted every second, measured in multiples of 1024bps. Used as an indicator of communications transmission rates.

kilobyte
Abbreviated K, KB, or Kbyte. 1024 bytes.

L

L1 cache
See level 1 cache.

L2 cache
See level 2 cache.

LAN
See local area network.

laptop computer
See notebook computer.

laser printer
A printer that is based on the same technology as that used by photocopiers.

A laser and a rotating mirror create an image of the page on a rotating photosensitive drum. This image is converted into an electrostatic charge that attracts and holds the toner. Electrostatically charged paper is rolled against the drum, and the toner is transferred to the paper and fused to the paper using heat. The last step is to remove the electrostatic charge from the drum and collect any excess toner.

latency
The time it takes for the area of a hard disk containing the required information to rotate to a position under the read/write head. The faster the hard disk platter rotates, the lower the latency.

LBA
See logical block addressing.

LCC
See leadless chip carrier.

leadless chip carrier
Abbreviated LCC. A method used to mount integrated circuits onto a board. Although similar in appearance to the cheaper plastic leadless chip carrier (PLCC), LCCs are made from a ceramic material, and the two chip carriers are incompatible.

level 1 cache
Abbreviated L1 cache. A primary cache built into microprocessors to increase speed. The L1 cache can be read in a single clock cycle, so it is always tried first. The Intel Pentium contains two separate 512 KB L1 caches, one each for data and instructions. Also called a primary cache.

level 2 cache
Abbreviated L2 cache. A secondary cache located between the L1 or primary cache and the rest of the system. A level 2 cache is often larger than the primary cache, and it is usually slower. Also called a secondary cache.

line analyzer
Any device that monitors and displays information about a transmission on a communications channel. A line analyzer is used for troubleshooting and load monitoring.

local area network
Abbreviated LAN. A group of computers and associated peripheral devices connected by a communications channel, capable of sharing files and other resources between several users.

logic bomb
A sabotage attack on a system timed to go off some time in the future; essentially a Trojan Horse with a fuse.

A logic bomb goes off at a certain time or when triggered by a certain event, and then performs some operation. It might release a virus, delete files, or send comments to a terminal. An unhappy programmer may plant a logic bomb on a system timed to go off long after they have left the company so as to avoid suspicion.

logical block addressing
Abbreviated LBA. An element of the Enhanced IDE standard that allows a hard disk to store more than 8.4GB of information.

logical drive
The internal division of a large hard disk into smaller units. One single physical drive may be organized

into several logical drives for convenience, with each one appearing to the user to be a separate drive.

logical unit number

Abbreviated LUN. The logical address of a Small Computer System Interface (SCSI) device when several devices are attached to a single SCSI device ID. The LUN is usually set to zero, unless the SCSI adapter supports multiple LUNs on a single SCSI device ID.

loopback

A troubleshooting test in which a signal is transmitted from a source to a destination and then back to the source again so that the signal can be measured and evaluated or the data contained in the signal can be examined for accuracy and completeness.

lossless compression

Any data compression method that compresses a file by rearranging or recoding the data that it contains in a more compact fashion.

With lossless compression, there is no loss of original data when the file is decompressed. Lossless compression methods are used on program files and on images such as medical X-rays, when data loss cannot be tolerated, and can typically reduce a file to 40 percent of its original size.

Many lossless compression programs use a method known as the Lempel-Ziv-Welch (LZW) algorithm, which searches a file for redundant strings of data and converts them to smaller tokens. When the compressed file is decompressed, this process is reversed.

lossy compression

Any data compression method that compresses a file by discarding any data that the compression mechanism decides is not needed.

Original data is lost when the file is decompressed. Lossy compression methods may be used for shrinking audio or image files when absolute accuracy is not required and the loss of data will not be noticed; however, this technique is unsuitable for more critical applications in which data loss cannot be tolerated, such as with medical images or program files. Lossy compression can typically reduce a file to as little as 5 percent of its original size.

LPT ports

The device name used to denote a parallel communications port, often used with a printer.

LUN

See logical unit number.

M

M

See mega-.

m

See milli-.

machine language

The native binary language used internally by the computer; also known as machine code.

Machine language is difficult for humans to read and understand. Programmers create applications using high-level languages, which are translated into a form that the computer can understand by an assembler, a compiler, or an interpreter. Whichever method is used, the result is machine language.

macro virus

An executable program that attaches itself to a document created in Microsoft Word or Excel, or to an e-mail created in Outlook. When you open the attachment and execute the macro, the virus runs and does whatever damage it was programmed to do. Both the Melissa and ILOVEYOU viruses were Visual Basic programs distributed as an e-mail attachment.

male connector

Any cable connector with pins designed to engage the sockets on the female connector.

map

1. To direct a request for a file or service to an alternative resource. For example, in a virtual memory system, an operating system can translate or map a virtual memory address into a physical address; in a network, drive letters are assigned to specific volumes and directories.

2. An expression of the structure of an object. For example, a memory map describes the use and layout of physical memory.

mask

A binary number that is used to remove bits from another binary number by use of one of the logical operators (AND, OR, NOT, XOR) to combine the binary number and the mask. Masks are used in IP addresses and file permissions.

MB

See megabyte.

Mb

See megabit.

Mbps

See megabits per second.

mean time between failures

Abbreviated MTBF. The statistically derived average length of time for which a system component operates before failing. MTBF is expressed in thousands or tens of thousands of hours, also called power-on hours or POH.

mean time to repair

Abbreviated MTTR. The statistically derived average length of time that it takes to repair a component.

meg

A common abbreviation for megabyte.

mega-

Abbreviated M. A prefix meaning one million in the metric system. Because computing is based on powers of 2, mega usually means 220 or 1,048,576; the power of 2 closest to one million.

megabit

Abbreviated Mb or Mbit. Usually 1,048,576 binary digits or bits of data. Often used as equivalent to 1 million bits.

megabits per second

Abbreviated Mbps. A measurement of the amount of information moving across a network or communications link in one second, measured in multiples of 1,048,576 bits.

megabyte

Abbreviated MB. Usually 1,048,576 bytes. Megabytes are a common unit of measurement for computer memory or hard disk capacity.

megahertz

Abbreviated MHz. One million cycles per second. A processor's clock speed is often expressed in megahertz.

The original IBM PC operated an Intel 8088 processor running at 4.77MHz; a Pentium processor runs at 800MHz; and modern systems are capable of running at more than 1000MHz or 1GHz.

memory

The primary physical RAM (random access memory) installed in the computer. The operating system copies applications from disk into memory, where all program execution and data processing takes place, and then writes the results back to disk. The amount of memory installed in the computer can determine the size and number of programs that it can run, as well as the size of the largest data file.

memory address

The exact location in memory that stores a particular data item or program instruction.

memory board

A printed circuit board containing memory chips. When all the sockets on a memory board are filled and the board contains the maximum amount of memory that it can manage, it is said to be "fully populated."

memory cache

An area of high-speed memory on the processor that stores commonly used code or data obtained from slower memory, eliminating the need to access the system's main memory to fetch instructions.

The Intel Pentium contains two separate 512KB L1 or primary caches, one each for data and instructions.

memory chip

A chip that holds data or program instructions. A memory chip may hold its contents temporarily, as in the case of RAM (random access memory), or permanently, as in the case of ROM (read-only memory).

memory leak

A programming error that causes a program to request new areas of computer memory rather than reusing the memory already assigned to it. This causes the amount of memory in use by the program to increase as time goes on. In a worst case, the application may consume all available memory and stop the computer.

memory management

The way in which the operating system handles the use of memory, usually as a combination of physical memory and virtual memory.

When applications are loaded, they are assigned space in which to run and store data. As they are removed, the memory space they occupied is released for use by the next program to run.

memory management unit

Abbreviated MMU. The part of the processor that manages the mapping of virtual memory addresses to actual physical addresses.

In some systems, such as those based on early Intel or Motorola processors, the MMU was a separate chip; however, in most modern systems, the MMU is integrated into the processor itself.

memory map

The organization and allocation of memory in a computer. A memory map will give an indication of the amount of memory used by the operating system, as well as the amount remaining for use by applications.

memory-resident

Always located in the computer's memory and available for use; not swapped out.

MHz

See megahertz.

microcode

Low-level instructions that define how a particular microprocessor works by specifying what the processor does when it executes a machine-language instruction.

micron

A unit of measurement. One millionth of a meter, corresponding to approximately 1/25,000 of an inch. The core diameter of fiber-optic cable for networks is often specified in terms of microns; 62.5 microns is a common size.

microprocessor

A central processor unit on a single chip, often referred to as the processor. The first microprocessor was developed by Intel in 1969.

MIDI

See Musical Instrument Digital Interface.

milli-

Abbreviated m. A prefix meaning one thousandth in the metric system, often expressed as 10^{-3}.

millisecond

Abbreviated ms or msec. A unit of measurement equal to one thousandth of a second. In computing, hard disk and CD-ROM drive access times are often described in terms of milliseconds; the higher the number, the slower the disk system.

millivolt

Abbreviated mv. A unit of measurement equal to one thousandth of a volt.

mirroring

The process of duplicating stored information in real time to protect vital data from unexpected hardware failures.

MJ

See modular jack.

MMU

See memory management unit.

mobile computing

1. The everyday use of a portable computer as a normal part of the workday.

2. Techniques used to establish links to a network by employees who move from one remote location to another, such as members of a sales staff or telecommuters who work from home. Once the connection is made, users log in and access network resources as easily as if they were working from a computer in the corporate office.

modem

Contraction of modulator/demodulator, a device that allows a computer to transmit information over a telephone line.

The modem translates between the digital signals that the computer uses and analog signals suitable for transmission over telephone lines. When transmitting, the modem modulates the digital data onto a carrier signal on the telephone line. When receiving, the modem performs the reverse process to demodulate the data from the carrier signal.

modular jack

Abbreviated MJ. The jack used to connect telephone cables to a wall-mounted face plate.

modulation

In communications, the process used by a modem to add the digital signal onto the carrier signal, so that the signal can be transmitted over a telephone line. The frequency, amplitude, or phase of a signal may be modulated to represent a digital or analog signal.

Moore's Law

Moore's Law states that the number of transistors on a chip of a given size doubles approximately every 18 months. Named for Intel's Gordon Moore, who first made this statement in 1965.

motherboard

The main printed circuit board in a computer, containing the central processing unit, appropriate coprocessor and support chips, device controllers, and memory. It may also include expansion slots to give access to the computer's internal bus.

Motion Picture Experts Group

Abbreviated MPEG. A set of image-compression standards and file formats that defines a compression method for desktop audio, animation, and video.

MPEG is a lossy compression method that results in some data loss when a video clip is compressed. The following standards are available:

MPEG-1 The original MPEG standard, designed for CD-ROM use, with a bandwidth of 1.5Mbps, two audio channels, and noninterlaced video.

MPEG-2 An extension to MPEG-1 designed for broadcast television, including HDTV (High-Definition Television), with a bandwidth of up to 40Mbps, five audio channels, interlaced video, and a wider range of frame sizes.

MPEG-3 A standard designed for HDTV until it was discovered that MPEG-2 covered HDTV. This standard is no longer used.

MPEG-4 A standard designed for video phones and multimedia applications, with a bandwidth of up to 64Kbps.

mouse

A small input device with one or more buttons used with graphical user interfaces. As the mouse moves, an on-screen mouse cursor follows; all movements are relative. Once the pointer is in the correct position on the screen, you press one of the mouse buttons to initiate an action or operation.

MPEG

See Motion Picture Experts Group.

ms

See millisecond.

MTBF

See mean time between failures.

MTTR

See mean time to repair.

multimedia

A computer technology that displays information using a combination of full-motion video, animation, sound, graphics, and text, with a high degree of user interaction.

multimode fiber

A fiber-optic cable with a wide core that provides multiple routes for light waves to travel.

Its wider diameter of between 25 to 200 microns prevents multimode fiber from carrying signals as far as single-mode fiber due to modal dispersion.

multipart virus

A form of virus that infects both the boot sector of a hard disk and executable files. Multipart viruses are difficult to detect as they use stealth and polymorphic techniques to avoid detection.

multiple zone recording

Abbreviated MZR. A method of increasing the storage capacity of a hard disk by using constant angular velocity (CAV) techniques. CAV allows for the storage of additional data on the disk's outer edges, which would otherwise not be filled to their full capacity.

Musical Instrument Digital Interface

Abbreviated MIDI. A serial interface standard and communications protocol that defines the connections between a computer and a synthesizer. MIDI devices can be used to create, record, and play back music.

mv

See millivolt.

MZR

See multiple zone recording.

N

n

See nano-.

name resolution

The process of translating the appropriate numerical IP address, which is required by a computer, into a name that is more easily understood and remembered by a person.

In the TCP/IP environment, names such as `www.sybex.com` are translated into their IP equivalents by the Domain Name Service (DNS). In a Microsoft Windows NT/2000 Server environment, NetBIOS names are resolved into IP addresses by Windows Internet Naming Service (WINS).

nano-

Abbreviated n. A prefix meaning one billionth in the American numbering scheme, and one thousand millionth in the British system.

nanosecond

Abbreviated ns. One billionth of a second. The speed of computer memory and logic chips is measured in nanoseconds.

narrow SCSI

A Small Computer System Interface (SCSI) or SCSI-2 interface capable of transferring only 8 bits of data at a time.

NAT

See Network Address Translation.

National Television Standards Committee

Abbreviated NTSC. The standards-setting body for television and video in the United States. Most European and Asian countries use a different standard known as PAL (phase alteration line). The two standards are incompatible.

near-end crosstalk

Abbreviated NEXT. Any interference that occurs close to a connector at either end of a cable. NEXT is usually measured near the source of the test signal.

NetBEUI

Abbreviation for NetBIOS Extended User Interface, pronounced "net-boo-ee." A network device driver supplied with Microsoft's LAN Manager, Windows for Workgroups, Windows NT, Windows 98, and Windows 2000. NetBEUI will work with Windows XP, but you must manually install it from the installation CD. NetBEUI communicates with the network interface card via the NDIS (Network Driver Interface Specification).

NetBEUI is a small protocol with no networking layer and therefore no routing capability. It is suitable only for small networks; you cannot build internetworks using NetBEUI, and so it is often replaced with TCP/IP.

Microsoft has added extensions to NetBEUI in Windows NT to remove the limitation of 254 sessions per node, and calls this extended NetBEUI the NetBIOS Frame (NBF).

NetBIOS

Acronym for network basic input/output system, pronounced "net-bye-ose." A session-layer network protocol, originally developed in 1984 by IBM and Sytek, to manage data exchange and network access.

NetBIOS provides an API with a consistent set of commands for requesting lower-level network services to transmit information from node to node, thus separating applications from the underlying network operating system. Many vendors provide either their own version of NetBIOS or an emulation of its communications services in their own products.

netiquette

A contraction of network etiquette. The set of unwritten rules governing the use of e-mail and other computer and network services.

Like any culture, the online world has its own rules and conventions, and if you understand and observe these conventions, you can take your place in the online community without problems. Here are a few tips:

- Remember that the people reading your post are human; if you wouldn't say it to their face, don't post it in your e-mail.

- Lurk before you leap. Spend a few days reading the posts in a newsgroup or mailing list before you post anything of your own.

- If you use a signature file to close your e-mail, remember to keep it short; people don't want to read lots of cute stuff every time you post.

- Don't post messages in uppercase as it is the e-mail equivalent of YELLING; to add emphasis, place an asterisk before and after a word.

- Don't flame or mount personal attacks on other users.

- Check your grammar and spelling before you post.

- Don't be shy; if you are an expert, share your knowledge with others.

network

A group of computers and associated peripheral devices connected by a communications channel capable of sharing files and other resources between several users.

A network can range from a peer-to-peer network connecting a small number of users in an office or department, to a LAN connecting many users over permanently installed cables and dial-up lines, to a metropolitan area network (MAN) or WAN connecting users on several different networks spread over a wide geographic area.

network adapter
See network interface card.

Network Address Translation
Abbreviated NAT. A term used to describe the process of converting between IP addresses on an intranet or other private network and Internet IP addresses.

network device driver
Software that controls the physical function of a network interface card, coordinating between the card and the other workstation hardware and software.

Network Driver Interface Specification
Abbreviated NDIS. A device-driver specification, originally developed by Microsoft and 3Com in 1990, that is independent of both the underlying network interface card hardware and the protocol being used. NDIS also allows multiple protocol stacks to be used at the same time in the same computer.

network interface card
Abbreviated NIC. In networking, the PC expansion board that plugs into a personal computer or server and works with the network operating system and the appropriate device drivers to control the flow of information over the network. Novell NetWare documentation uses the term network board, and some Microsoft documentation uses network adapter.

The network interface card is connected to the network media (twisted-pair, coaxial, or fiber-optic cable) and is designed for a specific type of network such as Ethernet, token ring, FDDI, or ARCnet.

network operating system
Abbreviated NOS. In typical client/server architecture LANs, the NOS consists of two parts. The largest and most complex part is the system software running on the file server. This system software coordinates many functions, including user accounts and network access information, security, resource sharing, administrative functions, UPS and power monitoring, data protection, and error detection and control. A much smaller component of the NOS runs on each of the networked PCs or workstations attached to the network.

In peer-to-peer networks, a part of the NOS is installed on each PC or workstation attached to the network and runs on top of or as a part of the PC operating system. In some cases, the NOS may be installed on one PC designated as a file server, but this PC is not dedicated to the file server function; it is also available to run applications.

network printer
A printer attached to and accessible from the network. A network printer may be attached to a file server, a printer server, or may have its own direct connection to the network.

network protocol
A formal specification that defines the procedures to follow when transmitting and receiving data over the network. Protocols define the format, timing, sequence, and error checking used on the network. TCP/IP, NetBEUI, and IPX/SPX are three of the most common protocols in use.

newsgroup
A Usenet e-mail discussion group devoted to a single topic. Subscribers to a newsgroup post articles that can be read by all the other subscribers.

Newsgroup names fit into a formal structure in which each component of the name is separated from the next by a period. The leftmost portion of the name represents the category of the newsgroup, and the name gets more specific from left to right.

The major top-level newsgroup categories are listed below:

alt Newsgroups that fall outside the main categories outlined below.

comp Computer science and related topics, including information about operating systems and hardware, as well as more advanced topics such as graphics and robotics.

misc Anything that does not fit into any of the other categories.

news Information on Usenet and newsgroups.

rec Recreational activities, such as hobbies, the arts, movies, and books.

sci Discussion groups on scientific topics, including math, physics, and biology.

soc Groups that address social and cultural issues.

talk Groups that concentrate on controversial subjects.

Private newsgroups are often available on corporate intranets, where organization, structure, and subject matter are decided by the system administrator.

newsreader

An application used to read articles posted to Usenet newsgroups. Newsreaders are of two kinds: *threaded* newsreaders group the posts into threads of related articles; *unthreaded* newsreaders present articles in their original order of posting without regard for the subject. Of the two, threaded newsreaders are much easier to use and are available in most popular Web browsers.

NEXT

See near-end crosstalk.

NIC

See network interface card.

noise

In communications, extraneous signals on a transmission channel that degrade the quality or performance of the channel. Noise is often caused by interference from nearby power lines, electrical equipment, or spikes in the AC line voltage.

nominal velocity of propagation

The speed at which a signal moves through a cable, expressed as a percentage or fraction of the speed of light in a vacuum. Some cable testers use this speed, along with the time it takes for a signal to return to the testing device, to calculate cable lengths.

notebook computer

A small, portable computer that is light enough to carry comfortably, with a flat screen and keyboard that fold together.

Advances in battery technology allow notebook computers to run for many hours between charges. Some models can mate with a docking station to perform as a full-sized desktop system back at the office, and many portable computers allow direct connection to the network via a network interface card (NIC).

ns

See nanosecond.

NTSC

See National Television Standards Committee.

null

A character that has all the binary digits set to zero (ASCII 0), and therefore has no value.

In programming, a null character is used for several special purposes, including padding fields or serving as delimiter characters. In the C programming language, for example, a null character indicates the end of a character string.

null modem

A short serial cable that connects two personal computers so that they can communicate without the use of modems.

The cable connects the two computers' serial ports, and certain lines in the cable are crossed over so that the wires used for sending by one computer are used for receiving data by the other computer.

O

OCR

See optical character recognition.

octet

The Internet's own term for a unit of data containing exactly 8 bits. Some of the computer systems attached to the Internet have bytes with more than 8 bits, hence the need for this term.

OEM

See original equipment manufacturer.

offline

Describes a printer or other peripheral device that is not in ready mode and is therefore unavailable for use.

online

1. Most broadly, any work done on a computer instead of by more traditional manual means.

2. Any function available directly on a computer, such as an application's help system.

3. Describes a peripheral device, such as a printer or modem, when it is directly connected to a computer and ready to operate.

4. In communications, describes a computer connected to a remote computer over a network or a modem link.

online service

A service that provides an online connection via modem for access to various services. Online services fall into these main groups:

> **commercial services**   Services such as America Online charge a monthly membership fee for

access to online forums, e-mail services, software libraries, and online conferences.

> **Internet**   The Internet is a worldwide network of computer systems and is not always easy to use, but the wealth of information available is staggering. The main problem for casual users is that there is no central listing of everything that is available.

> **specialist databases**   Specific databases aimed at researchers can be accessed through online services such as Dow Jones News/Retrieval for business news and Lexis and Nexis for the legal information and news archives.

operating system

Abbreviated OS. That software responsible for allocating system resources, including memory, processor time, disk space, and peripheral devices such as printers, modems, and monitors. All applications use the operating system to gain access to these resources as necessary. The operating system is loaded into the computer as it boots, and it remains in memory until the computer is turned off.

optical character recognition

Abbreviated OCR. The computer recognition of printed or typed characters. OCR is usually performed using a standard optical scanner and special software, although some systems use special readers. The text is reproduced just as though it had been typed. Certain advanced systems can even resolve neatly handwritten characters.

optical mouse

A mouse that must be used on a mouse pad containing a special grid. The mouse shines a small beam of light on the grid that conveys mouse movements back to the computer.

original equipment manufacturer

Abbreviated OEM. The original manufacturer of a hardware subsystem or component. For example, Canon makes the print engine used in many laser printers, including those from Hewlett-Packard (HP); in this case, Canon is the OEM and HP is a value-added reseller (VAR).

output

Computer-generated information that is displayed on the screen, printed, written to disk or tape, or sent over a communications link to another computer.

P

P

See peta-.

paged memory management unit

Abbreviated PMMU. A specialized chip designed to manage virtual memory. High-end processors, such as the Motorola 68040 and the Intel Pentium, have all the functions of a PMMU built into the chip itself.

page-mode RAM

A memory-management technique used to speed up the performance of dynamic RAM (DRAM).

In a page-mode memory system, the memory is divided into pages by specialized DRAM chips. Consecutive accesses to memory addresses in the same page result in a page-mode cycle that takes about half the time of a regular DRAM cycle.

Palm

The hand-held computer from 3Com Corporation, which has proved to be extremely popular.

parallel communications

The transmission of information from computer to computer, or from computer to peripheral device, in which all the bits that make up the character are transmitted at the same time over a multiline cable.

parallel port

An input/output (I/O) port that manages information 8 bits at a time, often used to connect a parallel printer.

parity

In communications, a simple form of error checking that uses an extra or redundant bit after the data bits but before the stop bit or bits. Parity may be set as follows:

odd parity   Indicates that the sum of all the 1 bits in the byte plus the parity bit must be odd. If the total is already odd, the parity bit is set to 0; if it is even, the parity bit is set to 1.

even parity   If the sum of all the 1 bits is even, the parity bit must be set to 0; if it is odd, the parity bit must be set to 1.

mark parity   The parity bit is always set to 1 and is used as the eighth bit.

space parity   The parity bit is set to 0 and is used as the eighth bit.

none   If parity is set to none, there is no parity bit, and no parity checking is performed.

The parity settings used by both communicating computers must match. Most online services, such as America Online, use no parity and an 8-bit data word.

parity bit

An extra or redundant bit used to detect data transmission errors.

parity checking

A check mechanism applied to a character or series of characters that uses the addition of extra or redundant parity bits.

Parity checking is useful for a variety of purposes, including asynchronous communications and computer memory coordination.

parity error

A mismatch in parity bits that indicates an error in transmitted data.

partition

A portion of a hard disk that the operating system treats as if it were a separate drive. In Windows, a hard disk can be divided into several partitions. A primary partition, generally assigned the drive letter C, might contain files that start the computer running. You could also set up a non-Windows partition to be used by a different operating system.

partition table

An area of storage on a hard disk that contains information about the partitions the disk contains. This information is usually recorded during the initial preparation of the hard disk before it is formatted.

passive termination

A method used to terminate a Small Computer System Interface (SCSI) chain of devices. Passive termination is a simple termination method that works best with four or fewer devices on a SCSI daisy chain.

password

A security method that identifies a specific authorized user of a computer system or network by a unique string of characters.

In general, passwords should be a mixture of upper- and lowercase letters and numbers and should be longer than six characters.

Passwords should be kept secret and changed frequently. The worst passwords are the obvious ones: people's names or initials, place names, phone numbers, birth dates, and anything to do with computers or *Star Trek*. There are a limited number of words in the English language, and it is easy for a computer to try them all relatively quickly.

PB

See petabyte.

PC Card

A term that describes plug-in cards that conform to the PCMCIA (Personal Computer Memory Card International Association) standard. A PC Card is about the size of a credit card and uses a 68-pin connector with longer power and ground pins that will always engage before the signal pins engage.

Several versions of the standard have been approved by PCMCIA:

Type I The thinnest PC Card, only 3.3 millimeters (0.13 inch) thick, used for memory enhancements, including dynamic RAM, static RAM, and flash memory.

Type II A card used for modems or network interface cards, 5 millimeters (0.2 inch) thick; may also hold a Type I card.

Type III A 10.5-millimeter (0.4 inch) card, used for mini-hard disks and other devices that need more space, including wireless network interface cards; may also hold two Type I or Type II cards.

In theory, each PC Card adapter can support 16 PC Card sockets (if there is enough space), and up to 255 adapters can be installed in a PC that follows the PCMCIA standard; in other words, PCMCIA allows up to 4080 PC Cards on one computer.

The majority of PC Card devices are modems, Ethernet and Token Ring network adapters, dynamic RAM, and flash memory cards, although mini-hard disks, wireless LAN adapters, and SCSI adapters are also available.

PC Card slot

An opening in the case of a portable computer, intended to receive a PC Card; also known as a PCMCIA slot.

PC Memory Card International Association

Abbreviated PCMCIA. A nonprofit association, formed in 1989, with more than 320 members in the computer and electronics industries, that developed a standard for credit card–sized plug-in adapters designed for portable computers.

PCI local bus

Abbreviation for Peripheral Component Interconnect local bus. A specification introduced by Intel in 1992 for a local bus that allows up to 10 PCI-compliant expansion cards to be plugged into the computer. One of these expansion cards must be the PCI controller card, but the others can include a video card, network interface card, SCSI interface, or any other basic function.

The PCI controller exchanges information with the computer's processor, either 32 or 64 bits at a time, and allows intelligent PCI adapters to perform certain tasks concurrently with the main processor by using bus-mastering techniques.

PCI is compatible with ISA, EISA, and MCA expansion buses for backward compatibility with older technologies. PCI can operate at a bus speed of 32MHz and can manage a maximum throughput of 132MBps with a 32-bit data path, or a rate of 264MBps with a 64-bit data path. PCI also supports Plug and Play.

PCI-X

A revision to the PCI standard proposed by IBM, Hewlett-Packard, and Compaq, that increases the bus width to 64 bits, the bus speed to 133MHz, and the maximum throughput to 1GBps. Several vendors also offer hot-plug PCI slots that allow you to replace a failed component without a system reboot.

PCMCIA

See PC Memory Card International Association.

PCMCIA slot

See PC Card slot.

PDA

See personal digital assistant.

peer-to-peer

A network architecture in which two or more PCs can communicate with each other directly without the need for any intermediary devices. In a peer-to-peer system, a PC can be both a client and a server.

peer-to-peer network

A LAN in which drives, files, and printers on each PC can be available to every other PC on the network, eliminating the need for a dedicated file server. Each PC can still run local applications.

Peer-to-peer networks introduce their own system management problems, including administration and responsibility for system backup, reliability, and security. Peer-to-peer systems are often used in relatively small networks, with two to ten users.

Pentium

A family of microprocessors introduced by Intel in 1993. The Pentium represents the continuing evolution of the 80486 family of microprocessors and adds several notable features, including instruction code and data caches and a built-in floating-point processor and memory management unit. It also has a superscalar design and dual pipelining (which allows the Pentium to execute more than one instruction per clock cycle), a 32-bit address bus, and a 64-bit data bus. The Pentium is equivalent to 3.1 million transistors, more than twice that of the 80486.

Pentium II

A family of microprocessors from Intel. The Pentium II includes several notable features, including integrated L1/L2 caches of up to 2MB, which can be accessed at the full clock speed, and a built-in floating-point processor and memory management unit. It also has a superscalar design and dual pipelining, which allows the Pentium II to execute more than one instruction per clock cycle.

Available in a whole range of clock speeds, the Pentium II can use a 100MHz system bus and is equivalent to 7.5 million transistors, more than twice that of the Pentium.

Pentium III

A family of microprocessors introduced by Intel in 1999. The Pentium III includes 50 new floating-point instructions and 8 new registers to speed up floating-point calculations in scientific and engineering calculation, along with 12 new multimedia instructions to increase MPEG-2 performance and speech recognition. The most controversial feature is the processor serial number, designed to increase network and online shopping security but feared by many as a threat to privacy.

Available in a whole range of clock speeds, the Pentium III can use the Pentium II 100MHz system bus and is equivalent to 9.5 million transistors.

Pentium 4

A family of microprocessors introduced by Intel in 2000. The Pentium 4 is based on the all-new Net-

Burst micro-architecture. It features Hyper-pipelined technology, a rapid execution engine, an execution trace cache, enhanced floating point/multimedia instructions, and the second generation of Internet Streaming Single Instruction Multiple Data (SIMD) Extensions.

Available in a range of clock speeds starting at 1.3GHz, the Pentium 4 uses a 400MHz system bus and is equivalent to 42 million transistors.

Pentium Pro

A family of microprocessors introduced by Intel in 1995. The Pentium Pro is optimized for the execution of 32-bit software and is available with clock speeds from 150 to 200MHz. With a 32-bit data bus running at 60 or 66MHz, it supports superscalar architecture and pipelines and contains the equivalent of 5.5 million transistors.

Dynamic execution (a combination of branch prediction and speculative execution) allows the processor to anticipate and schedule the next instructions for execution. Pentium Pro offers up to 1MB of level 2 cache that runs at the same speed as the processor.

period

The . character; pronounced "dot." Used to indicate the name of the current directory in a pathname and used to separate the different elements in a domain name, as in www.sybex.com.

Peripheral Component Interconnect

See PCI local bus.

permanent swap file

A swap file that, once created, is used over and over again. This file is used in virtual memory operations, where hard disk space is used in place of RAM.

personal digital assistant

Abbreviated PDA. A tiny, pen-based, battery-powered computer that combines personal organization software with fax and e-mail facilities into a unit that fits into your pocket. PDAs are available from several manufacturers.

peta-

Abbreviated P. A metric system prefix for one quadrillion, or 1015. In computing, based on the binary system, peta has the value of 1,125,899,906,842,624, or the power of 2 (250) closest to 1 quadrillion.

petabyte

Abbreviated PB. Usually 1,125,899,906,842,624 bytes (250), but may also refer to 1 quadrillion bytes (1015).

PGA

See pin grid array.

PhotoCD

A standard for storing 35mm photographs taken with an ordinary (nondigital) camera onto CD-ROM.

physical device

An item of hardware, such as a disk drive or a tape drive, which is physically separate from other devices.

physical drive

A real device in the computer that you can see or touch, as opposed to a conceptual or logical drive. One physical drive may be divided into several logical drives, which are parts of the hard disk that function as if they were separate disk drives.

pin grid array

Abbreviated PGA. A method of mounting integrated circuits onto boards. PGA is often used with integrated circuits that have a very large number of pins.

pinouts

The configuration and purpose of each pin in a multipin connector.

PIO

See programmed input/output.

pipeline burst cache

A secondary or L2 cache associated with a microprocessor that allows fast data transfer rates. Pipeline burst cache requires RAM chips that can synchronize with the microprocessor's clock.

pipeline stall

A microprocessor design error that leads to delays in the processing of an instruction.

pipelining

In processor architecture, a method of fetching and decoding instructions that ensures that the processor never needs to wait; as soon as one instruction is executed, the next one is ready.

plastic leadless chip carrier

Abbreviated PLCC. A method used to mount integrated circuits onto a board. Although similar in appearance to the more expensive leadless chip carrier (LCC), which is made from a ceramic material, the two chip carriers are incompatible.

PLCC

See plastic leadless chip carrier.

Plug and Play

Abbreviated PnP. A standard from Compaq, Microsoft, Intel, and Phoenix that defines techniques designed to make PC configuration simple and automatic. A user can plug in a new device and the operating system will recognize it and configure it automatically when the system is next started.

PnP adapters contain configuration information stored in nonvolatile memory, which includes vendor information, serial number, and checksum information. The PnP chipset allows each adapter to be isolated, one at a time, until all cards have been properly identified by the operating system.

The PnP-compatible BIOS isolates and identifies PnP cards at boot time, and when you insert a new card, the BIOS performs an autoconfiguration sequence enabling the new card with appropriate settings.

PMMU

See paged memory management unit.

PnP

See Plug and Play.

Point-to-Point Protocol

Abbreviated PPP. A TCP/IP protocol used to transmit data over serial lines and dial-up telephone point-to-point connections.

PPP allows a PC to establish a temporary direct connection to the Internet via modem and appear to the host system as if it were an Ethernet port on the host's network.

PPP provides an automatic method of assigning an IP (Internet Protocol) address so that mobile users can connect to the network at any point.

polymorphic virus

A form of virus that can change its appearance to avoid detection. The virus encrypts itself using a special formula each time an infection occurs. Virus-detecting software uses special scanning techniques to find and remove polymorphic viruses.

POP

See Post Office Protocol.

port

1. The point at which a communications circuit terminates at a network, serial, or parallel interface card, usually identified by a specific port number or name.

2. A number used to identify a connection point to a specific Internet protocol.

port number

The default identifier for a TCP/IP or Internet process.

For example, ftp, HTML, and Telnet are all available at preassigned unique port numbers so that the computer knows how to respond when it is contacted on a specific port; Web servers use port 80, and SMTP e-mail is always delivered to port 25. You can override these defaults by specifying different values in a URL, but whether they will work or not depends on the configuration on the target system.

port replicator

A device containing standard computer ports used to avoid constantly connecting and disconnecting peripherals from a portable computer.

A port replicator duplicates your computer's ports and may even add a Small Computer System Interface (SCSI) port or a second Universal Serial Bus port. The external monitor, full-sized keyboard, and mouse you use in the office are connected to the port replicator; when it is time to take the portable computer on the road, you just unplug the port replicator, leaving everything attached to the replicator for your return.

portal

A large Web site that acts as a gateway to the Internet and may also offer search facilities, free e-mail, online chat, and instant messaging, as well as other services including hard news, sports, and personal finance. Many portals make money by selling advertising space.

POST

See Power-On Self Test.

post

An individual article or e-mail message sent to a Usenet newsgroup or mailing list, rather than a message sent to an individual.

Post Office Protocol

Abbreviated POP. An Internet mail server protocol that also provides an incoming mail storage mechanism.

POP works with Simple Mail Transfer Protocol (SMTP), which actually moves the e-mail from one system to another, and the latest version of the standard is POP3.

When a client connects to a POP3 server, all the messages addressed to that client are downloaded; there is no ability to download messages selectively. Once the messages are downloaded, the user can delete or modify messages without further interaction with the server.

In some locations, POP3 is being replaced by another standard, Internet Mail Access Protocol (IMAP) version 4.

PostScript

A page-description language from Adobe Systems that offers flexible fonts and high-quality graphics. PostScript uses Englishlike commands for page layout and to scale fonts and is used with high-quality printers.

power conditioning

The use of protective and conditioning devices to filter out power surges and spikes and to ensure clean power. There are three main types of power conditioning devices:

suppression device   Protects against sudden destructive transient voltages.

regulation device   Modifies the power waveform back to a clean sine wave. A UPS (uninterruptible power supply) is a common form of voltage regulator. It may be online, actively modifying the power, or offline, available only after the line voltage drops below a certain level.

isolation device   Protects against noise. These types of devices are often expensive.

Because power conditioning is expensive, usually just the servers or hosts in a network are protected.

power supply

A part of the computer that converts the power from a wall outlet into the lower voltages, typically 5 to 12 volts DC (direct current), required internally in the computer. PC power supplies are usually rated in watts, ranging from 90 to 300 watts. If the power supply in a computer fails, nothing works—not even the fan.

power surge

A sudden, brief, and often destructive increase in line voltage. A power surge may be caused by an electrical appliance, such as a photocopier or elevator, or by power being reapplied after an outage.

Power-On Self Test

Abbreviated POST. A set of diagnostic programs loaded from ROM (read-only memory) before any attempt is made to load the operating system, designed to ensure that the major system components are present and operating. If a problem is found, the POST firmware writes an error message in the screen, sometimes with a diagnostic code number indicating the type of fault located.

PPP

See Point-to-Point Protocol.

primary cache

See level 1 cache.

Primary Rate ISDN

Abbreviated PRI. An ISDN (Integrated Services Digital Network) service that provides 23 B (bearer channels), capable of speeds of 64Kbps, and one D (data channel), also capable of 64Kbps. The combined capacity of 1.544Mbps is equivalent to one T1 channel.

printer emulation

The ability of a printer to change modes so that it behaves like a printer from another manufacturer. For example, many dot matrix printers offer an Epson printer emulation in addition to their own native mode. Most laser printers offer a Hewlett-Packard LaserJet emulation.

programmed input/output

Abbreviated PIO. A method of moving data between a hard disk and memory via the processor. An alternative data transfer method known as direct memory access (DMA) bypasses the processor and moves data directly between the hard disk and memory.

protocol stack

The several layers of software that define the computer-to-computer or computer-to-network protocol.

Several companies have developed important proprietary protocol stacks, including Novell NetWare's IPX/SPX, but the trend these days is moving toward more open systems such as TCP/IP.

Q

QIC

See quarter-inch cartridge.

quarter-inch cartridge

Abbreviated QIC. A set of tape standards defined by the Quarter-Inch Cartridge Drive Standards Association, a trade association established in 1987. Several standards are in use today.

question mark

A wildcard character (?) used in many operating systems to represent a single character in a filename or filename extension.

R

radio frequency interference

Abbreviated RFI. Many electronic devices, including radios, televisions, computers, and peripherals, can interfere with other signals in the radio frequency range by producing electromagnetic radiation. The use of radio frequencies is generally regulated by government agencies.

RAID

See Redundant Array of Inexpensive Disks.

RAM

See random access memory.

RAM chip

A semiconductor storage device, either dynamic RAM or static RAM.

random access

Describes the ability of a storage device to go directly to the required memory address without needing to read from the beginning every time data is requested.

In a random-access device, the information can be read directly by accessing the appropriate memory address. There is nothing random or haphazard about random access; a more precise term is direct access.

random access memory

Abbreviated RAM. The main system memory in a computer, used for the operating system, applications, and data.

rate-adaptive digital subscriber line

Abbreviated RADSL. An asymmetric digital subscriber line (ADSL) service with a provision for testing the line length and quality before starting the service and adjusting the line speed accordingly.

read-after-write verification

A method of checking that data is written to a hard disk correctly. Data is written to the disk and then read back and compared with the original data still held in memory. If the data read from the disk matches, the data in memory is released. If the data does not match, that block on the disk is marked as bad, and another attempt is made to write the data elsewhere on the disk.

README file

A plain text file containing information about the software, placed on the distribution disks by the manufacturer.

The filename may vary slightly; it might be READ.ME, README.1ST, README.TXT, or README.DOC, for example. README files may contain last minute, important information that is not in the program manuals or online help system.

You should always look for a README file when installing a new program on your system; it may contain information pertinent to your specific configuration. You can open a README file in any word processor or text editor because the file does not contain embedded formatting commands or program-specific characters.

read-only

Describes a file or other collection of information that may only be read; it may not be updated in any way or deleted.

Certain important operating system files are designated as read-only files to prevent accidental deletion. Also, certain types of ROM and some devices such as archive backup tapes and CD-ROMs can be read from but not changed.

read-only memory

Abbreviated ROM. A semiconductor-based memory system that stores information permanently, retaining its contents when power is switched off. ROMs are used for firmware, such as the BIOS used in the PC. In some portable computers, applications and even the operating system are stored in ROM.

reboot

To restart the computer and reload the operating system, usually after a crash.

In some cases, you may be able to restart the computer from the keyboard; in more severe crashes, you may have to turn the computer off and then back on again.

reduced instruction set computing

Abbreviated RISC, pronounced "risk." A processor that recognizes only a limited number of assembly-language instructions.

RISC chips are relatively cheap to produce and debug, because they usually contain fewer than 128 different instructions. RISC processors are commonly used in workstations, and they can be designed to run up to 70 percent faster than processors that use complex instruction set computing (CISC).

Redundant Array of Inexpensive Disks

Abbreviated RAID. Also seen as Redundant Array of Independent Disks. In networking and mission-critical applications, a method of using several hard disk drives (often SCSI or Integrated Drive Electronics, or

IDE, drives) in an array to provide fault tolerance in the event that one or more than one drive fails.

Each of the different levels of RAID is designed for a specific use:

RAID 0   Data is striped over one or more drives, but there is no redundant drive. RAID 0 provides no fault tolerance because the loss of a hard disk means a complete loss of data. Some classification schemes omit RAID 0 for this reason.

RAID 1   Two hard disks of equal capacity duplicate or mirror each other's contents. One disk continuously and automatically backs up the other disk. This method is also known as disk mirroring or disk duplexing, depending on whether one or two independent hard disk controllers are used.

RAID 2   Bit-interleaved data is written across several drives and then parity and error-correction information is written to additional separate drives. The specific number of error-correction drives depends on the allocation algorithm in use.

RAID 3   Bit-interleaved data is written across several drives, but only one parity drive is used. If an error is detected, the data is reread to resolve the problem. The fact that data is reread in the event of an error may add a small performance penalty.

RAID 4   Data is written across drives by sectors rather than at the bit level, and a separate drive is used as a parity drive for error detection. Reads and writes occur independently.

RAID 5   Data is written across drives in sectors, and parity information is added as another sector, just as if it were ordinary data. This level of RAID can provide faster performance as the parity information is written across all the drives, rather than to a single parity drive.

There is not much difference in speed or quality among these levels. The appropriate level of RAID for any particular installation depends on network usage. RAID levels 1, 3, and 5 are available commercially, and levels 3 and 5 are proving popular for networks.

Registry
In the Microsoft Windows family of operating systems, a system database containing configuration information.

The operating system continually references the Registry database for information on users and groups, the applications installed on the system and the types of document each can create, what hardware is available and which ports are in use, and property sheets for folders and application icons.

Changes to the Registry are usually made automatically as configuration information is changed using Control Panel applications or the Administrative Tools; however, knowledgeable users can make changes directly using the Windows Registry Editor.

restore
To copy files from a backup or archival storage to their normal location, especially when the files are being copied to replace files lost by accident.

retensioning
A maintenance operation required by certain tape drives to ensure correct tape tension; retensioning fast forwards and then rewinds the entire tape or tape cartridge.

RFI
See *radio frequency interference.*

RISC
See *reduced instruction set computing.*

RJ-11
A commonly used modular telephone connector. RJ-11 is a four-wire (two-pair) connector most often used for voice communications.

RJ-45

A commonly used modular telephone connector. RJ-45 is an eight-wire (four-pair) connector used for data transmission over unshielded twisted-pair cable (UTP) and leased telephone line connections.

ROM

See read-only memory.

RS-232-C

A recommended standard interface established by the Telecommunications Industry Association and the Electronic Industries Association (TIA/EIA). Also known as TIA/EIA-232.

The standard defines the specific electrical, functional, and mechanical characteristics used in asynchronous transmissions between a computer (data terminal equipment, or DTE) and a peripheral device (data communications equipment, or DCE). RS is the abbreviation for recommended standard, and the C denotes the third revision of that standard. RS-232-C is compatible with the CCITT V.24 and V.28 standards, as well as ISO IS2110.

RS-232-C uses a 25-pin or 9-pin DB connector and is used for serial communications between a computer and a peripheral device, such as a printer, modem, or mouse. The maximum cable limit of 15.25 meters (50 feet) can be extended by using high-quality cable, line drivers to boost the signal, or short-haul modems.

S

sag

A short-term drop in line voltage to between 70 and 90 percent of the nominal voltage.

SAN

See Storage Area Network.

SCSI

Acronym for Small Computer System Interface, pronounced "scuzzy."

A high-speed parallel interface defined by the ANSI X3T9.2 committee. SCSI is used to connect a computer to peripheral devices using just one port. Devices connected in this way are said to be "daisy-chained" together, and each device must have a unique identifier or priority number.

SCSI is often used to connect hard disks, tape drives, CD-ROM drives, and other mass storage media, as well as scanners and printers.

Features of the SCSI definition include:

◆ The bus can manage simultaneous reads and writes.

◆ The original standard supports up to seven devices on a single host adapter; new standards support up to 16 devices and a bus length of up to 25 meters (80 feet).

◆ SCSI devices have their own control circuitry and can disconnect from the host adapter to process tasks on their own, freeing up the bus for other purposes.

SCSI-1

A commonly used name for the first Small Computer System Interface (SCSI) definition, published in 1986 with an 8-bit parallel interface and a maximum data transfer rate of 5MBps.

SCSI-2

A 1994 extension to the Small Computer System Interface (SCSI) definition.

This standard broadened the 8-bit data bus to 16 or 32 bits (also known as Wide SCSI), doubling the data transfer rate to 10 or 20MBps (also known as Fast SCSI). Wide SCSI and Fast SCSI can be combined to give Fast-Wide SCSI, with a 16-bit data bus and a maximum data transfer rate of 20MBps. SCSI-2 is backward compatible with SCSI-1, but for maximum benefit, you should use SCSI-2 devices with a SCSI-2 controller.

SCSI-2 also adds new commands, and although the connector is physically smaller, it uses 68 pins rather than the 50 in SCSI-1. Higher data transfer rates are achieved by using synchronous rather than asynchronous transfers.

SCSI-3

An extension to the Small Computer System Interface (SCSI) standard.

This definition increased the number of connected peripherals from 7 to 16, increased cable lengths, added support for a variety of interfaces including a serial interface, a Fibre Channel interface, an IEEE 1394 interface, and support for Serial Storage Architecture and several packet interfaces.

Data transfer rates depend on the hardware implementation, but data rates in excess of 160MBps are possible.

SCSI bus

Another name for the Small Computer System Interface (SCSI) interface and communications protocol.

SCSI terminator

The Small Computer System Interface (SCSI) interface must be correctly terminated to prevent signals echoing on the bus.

Many SCSI devices have built-in terminators that engage when they are needed. With some older SCSI devices, you must add an external SCSI terminator that plugs into the device's SCSI connector.

SDRAM

See synchronous DRAM.

SDSL

See single-line digital subscriber line.

search engine

A special Web site that lets you perform keyword searches to locate interesting Web pages.

To use a search engine, you enter one or more keywords or, in some cases, a more complex search string such as a Boolean expression. The search engine returns a list of matching Web pages, newsgroups, and FTP archives taken from its database, usually ranked in some way, containing the expression you are looking for, along with a brief text description of the material.

Searching this database is much faster than actually searching the Internet, but the accuracy and relevance of the information it contains depends on how often the data is updated and what proportion of the Web is actually searched for new content.

secondary cache

See level 2 cache.

sector

A portion of one of the concentric tracks recorded on a hard or floppy disk during a low-level format, usually capable of storing 512 bytes of information.

seek time

The time it takes to move a disk drive's read/write head to a specific location on the disk.

Sequenced Packet Exchange

Abbreviated SPX. A set of Novell NetWare protocols implemented on top of IPX to form a transport-layer interface.

SPX provides additional capabilities over IPX. For example, it guarantees packet delivery by having the destination node verify that the data was received correctly. If no response is received within a specified time, SPX retransmits the packet. If several retransmissions fail to return an acknowledgment, SPX assumes that the connection has failed and informs the operator. All packets in the transmission are sent in sequence, and they all take the same path to their destination node.

sequential access

An access method used by some storage devices, such as tapes, that requires them to start at the beginning to find a specific storage location. If the information you are looking for is toward the end of the tape, access can take a long time.

serial communications

The transmission of information from computer to computer, or from computer to peripheral device, one bit at a time.

Serial communications can be synchronous and controlled by a clock, or asynchronous and coordinated by start and stop bits embedded in the data stream. The sending and receiving devices must both use the same baud rate, parity setting, and other communication parameters.

Serial Line Internet Protocol

Abbreviated SLIP. A protocol used to run Internet Protocol over serial lines or telephone connections using modems.

SLIP allows a computer to establish a temporary direct connection to the Internet via modem and appear to the host system as if it were a port on the host's network.

SLIP is being replaced by PPP (Point-to-Point Protocol).

serial port

A port on the computer that supports serial communications, in which information is processed one bit at a time.

RS-232-C is a common protocol used on serial ports when communicating with modems, printers, mice, and other peripherals; USB (Universal Serial Bus) is replacing RS-232-C.

set-associative cache

See cache.

SGRAM

See Synchronous Graphics RAM.

shielded cable

Cable protected against electromagnetic and radio frequency interference (RFI) by metal-backed Mylar foil and plastic or PVC.

shielded twisted-pair cable

Abbreviated STP. Cable with a foil shield and copper braid surrounding the pairs of wires.

The wires have a minimum number of twists per foot of cable length; the greater the number of twists, the lower the cross talk. STP offers high-speed transmission for useful distances, and it is often associated with Token Ring networks, but its bulk quickly fills up wiring conduits.

short circuit

Often abbreviated to short. A circuit that is accidentally completed at a point too close to its origin to allow normal or complete operation. In cabling, a short circuit often occurs when two stripped wires touch.

SIMM

See Single Inline Memory Module.

Simple Mail Transfer Protocol

Abbreviated SMTP. The TCP/IP protocol that provides a simple e-mail service and is responsible for moving e-mail messages from one e-mail server to another. SMTP provides a direct end-to-end mail delivery, which is rather unusual; most mail systems use store-and-forward protocols.

The e-mail servers run either Post Office Protocol (POP) or Internet Mail Access Protocol (IMAP) to distribute e-mail messages to users.

Single Inline Memory Module

Abbreviated SIMM. A group of memory chips mounted on a small circuit board. SIMMs have one set of connectors, and they have a 32-bit data path.

Single Large Expensive Disk

Abbreviated SLED. The traditional alternative to RAID (Redundant Array of Inexpensive Disks), used by most networks.

single-line digital subscriber line

Abbreviated SDSL; sometimes called symmetrical digital subscriber line. A symmetrical, bidirectional digital subscriber line service that operates on one twisted-pair wire.

SDSL can provide data rates of up to the T1 rate of 1.544Mbps over a cable length of up to 1,000 feet, and because it operates above the voice frequency, voice and data can be carried on the same connection at the same time.

single-mode fiber

Narrow diameter fiber-optic cable in which lasers rather than LEDs are used to transmit signals through the cable.

Single-mode fiber allows only one route for a light wave to pass through, and it can transmit signals over considerable distances. For this reason, it is often used in telephone networks rather than in LANs.

slash

The / character. Used to separate command-line switches that alter the default settings for an operating system command.

SLED

See Single Large Expensive Disk.

SLIP

See Serial Line Internet Protocol.

Small Computer System Interface

See SCSI.

SMTP

See Simple Mail Transfer Protocol.

spike

A short, transient electrical signal, often of very high amplitude.

SPX

See Sequenced Packet Exchange.

SRAM

See static RAM.

start bit

In asynchronous transmissions, a start bit is transmitted to indicate the beginning of a new data word.

static RAM

Abbreviated SRAM, pronounced "ess-ram." A type of computer memory that retains its contents as long as power is applied; it does not need constant refreshment, as required by dynamic RAM (DRAM) chips.

An SRAM chip can store only about one-fourth of the information that a DRAM chip of the same complexity can hold. However, SRAM is much faster than DRAM and is often used in caches.

stealth virus

A form of virus that attempts to hide from antivirus software and from the operating system by remaining in memory.

stop bit

In asynchronous transmissions, a stop bit is transmitted to indicate the end of the current data word. Depending on the convention in use, one or two stop bits are used.

Storage Area Network

Abbreviated SAN. A method used to physically separate the storage function of the network from the data processing function.

SAN provides a separate network devoted to storage, and so helps to reduce network traffic by isolating large data transfers such as backups. Most of the SAN vendors, including StorageTek and Compaq, use a Fibre Channel–based SAN system, although IBM has proposed a proprietary architecture.

store-and-forward

A method that temporarily stores messages at intermediate nodes before forwarding them to the next destination. This technique allows routing over networks that are not available at all times and lets users take advantage of off-peak rates when traffic and costs might be lower.

STP

See shielded twisted-pair cable.

straight-tip connector

Abbreviated ST. A fiber-optic cable connector that maintains the perfect alignment of the ends of the connected fibers, required for efficient light transmission.

streaming tape

A high-speed tape backup system designed to optimize throughput; the tape is not stopped during a backup. To use streaming tape, the computer and backup software must be fast enough to keep up with the tape drive.

stripe set

A single volume created across multiple hard disk drives and accessed in parallel to optimize disk-access time.

subdirectory

A directory contained within another directory. The root directory is the top-level directory, from which all other directories must branch. In common use, subdirectory is synonymous with directory or folder.

subnet

A logical network created from a single IP address. A mask is used to identify bits from the host portion of the address to be used for subnet addresses.

subnet address

The subnet portion of an IP address. In a subnetted network, the host part of the IP address is divided into a subnet portion and a host portion by a subnet mask.

subnet mask

A number, or more correctly, a bit pattern, that identifies which parts of an IP address correspond to the network, subnet, and host portions of the address. Also referred to as an address mask.

superpipelining

A preprocessing technique used by some microprocessors in which two or more execution stages (such as fetch, decode, execute, or write back) are divided into two or more pipelined stages, giving considerably higher performance.

superscalar

A microprocessor architecture that contains more than one execution unit, or pipeline, allowing the processor to execute more than one instruction per clock cycle.

For example, the Pentium processor is superscalar, with two side-by-side pipelines for integer instructions. The processor determines whether an instruction can be executed in parallel with the next instruction in line. If it does not detect any dependencies, the two instructions are executed.

surge

A short, sudden, and often destructive increase in line voltage. A voltage-regulating device, known as a surge

suppressor, can protect computer equipment against surges.

surge suppressor

A voltage-regulating device placed between the computer and the AC line connection that protects the computer system from power surges; also known as a surge protector.

swap

To temporarily move a process from memory to disk, so that another process can use that memory space. When space becomes available again, the process is swapped back into memory. This allows more processes to be loaded than there is physical memory space to run them simultaneously.

swap file

On a hard disk, a file used to store parts of running programs that have been swapped out of memory temporarily to make room for other running programs.

A swap file may be permanent, always occupying the same amount of hard disk space even though the application that created it may not be running, or temporary, created as and when needed.

In Windows 2000 documentation, the swap file is called the paging file.

swapping

The process of exchanging one item for another. In a virtual memory system, swapping occurs when a program requests a virtual memory location that is not currently in memory. Swapping may also refer to changing floppy or compact disks as needed when using a single disk drive.

symmetrical digital subscriber line

See single-line digital subscriber line.

synchronous DRAM

Abbreviated SDRAM or syncDRAM. A high-speed memory technology, faster than EDO RAM, used in high-end systems and servers. SDRAM runs at higher speeds than conventional DRAM by using a technique that attempts to predict the location of the next memory address to be accessed.

Synchronous Graphics RAM

Abbreviated SGRAM. A type of high-speed dynamic RAM used in video adapters.

T

T

See tera-.

T.120

A group of communications and applications protocols that support real-time, multipoint data communications over LANs, ISDN, dial-up, and Internet connections. T.120 became well known after Microsoft incorporated it into the NetMeeting package.

tape cartridge

A self-contained tape storage module, containing tape much like that in a video cassette. Tape cartridges are primarily used to back up hard disk systems.

tape drive

A computer peripheral device that reads from and writes to magnetic tape.

The drive may use tape on an open reel or from an enclosed tape cartridge. Because tape management software must search from the beginning of the tape every time it wants to find a file (a process called sequential access), tape is too slow to use as a primary storage system; however, tapes are frequently used to back up hard disks.

TB

See terabyte.

TCP

See Transmission Control Protocol.

TCP ports

In a TCP/IP network when a computer connects with another computer to access a specific service, an end-to-end connection is established and a socket is

set up at each end of the connection. This socket is created at a particular port number, depending on the application in use.

TCP/IP

See Transmission Control Protocol/Internet Protocol.

Telnet

A terminal emulation protocol, part of the TCP/IP suite of protocols, that provides remote terminal-connection services.

The most common terminal emulations are for Digital Equipment Corporation (DEC) VT-52, VT-100, and VT-220 terminals, although many companies offer additional add-in emulations.

temporary swap file

A swap space that is created every time it is needed. A temporary swap file can consist of several discontinuous pieces of hard disk space. A temporary swap file does not occupy hard disk space if the application that created it is not running.

tera-

Abbreviated T. A prefix meaning 1012 in the metric system, or 1,000,000,000,000; commonly referred to as one trillion in the American numbering system, and one million million in the British numbering system.

terabyte

Abbreviated TB. In computing, usually 240, or 1,099,511,627,776 bytes. Terabytes are used to represent extremely large hard disk capacities.

terminal emulation

A method of operation or software that makes a PC act like a terminal attached to a mainframe, usually for the purpose of telecommunications. Communications programs often include popular emulations, such as ANSI, VT-52, VT-100, VT-200, and TTY.

terminator

A device attached to the last peripheral device in a series, or the last node on a network.

For example, the last device on a SCSI bus must terminate the bus; otherwise, the bus will not perform properly. A 50-ohm resistor is placed at both ends of an Ethernet cable to prevent signals reflecting and interfering with the transmission.

text mode

A mode in which the computer displays characters on the screen using the built-in character set but does not show any graphics characters or a mouse pointer. Also known as character mode.

TFT display

See active-matrix display.

thick Ethernet

Connecting coaxial cable used on an Ethernet network; also known as thicknet.

The cable is one centimeter (0.4 inch) thick, almost as thick as your thumb, and can be used to connect network nodes up to a distance of approximately 1006 meters (3300 feet). Thick Ethernet is primarily used for facility-wide installations.

thicknet

See thick Ethernet.

thin Ethernet

Connecting coaxial cable used on an Ethernet network; also known as thinnet.

The cable is five millimeters (0.2 inch) thick, about as thick as your little finger, and can be used to connect network nodes up to a distance of approximately 165 meters (500 feet). Thin Ethernet is primarily used for office installations.

thin film transistor display

See active-matrix display.

thinnet

See thin Ethernet.

thrashing

An excessive amount of disk activity that causes a virtual memory system to spend all its time swapping pages in and out of memory and no time executing the application.

Thrashing can be caused when poor system configuration creates a swap file that is too small or when insufficient memory is installed in the computer. Increasing the size of the swap file or adding memory are often the best ways to reduce thrashing.

thread

1. A concurrent process that is part of a larger process or program. In a multitasking operating system, a single program may contain several threads, all running at the same time. For example, one part of a program can be making a calculation while another part is drawing a graph or chart.

2. A connected set of postings to a Usenet newsgroup. Many newsreaders present postings as threads rather than in strict chronological order.

throughput

A measure of the data transfer rate through a complex communications or networking scheme.

Throughput is considered to be an indication of the overall performance of the system. For example, the throughput of a server depends on the processor type, operating system in use, hard disk capacity, network interface card in use, and the size of the data transfer buffer.

In communications, throughput is usually measured as the number of bits or packets processed each second.

TIA/EIA 586

A standard, jointly defined by the Telecommunications Industry Association and the Electronic Industries Association (TIA/EIA), for telecommunications wiring used in commercial buildings.

The standard is designed to:

◆ Specify a generic wiring system for all commercial buildings.

◆ Define media types, as well as connections and terminations.

◆ Provide a basis for interoperation between competing products and services in wiring, design, installation, and management.

◆ Allow for the wiring of a building before the definition of the products that will use that wiring, and allow for elegant future expansion.

TIA/EIA 586 applies to all unshielded twisted-pair wiring that works with Ethernet, Token Ring, ISDN, and other networking systems.

TIA/EIA structured cabling standards

Standards specified by the Telecommunications Industries Association and the Electronics Industry Association (TIA/EIA), including:

◆ ANSI/TIA/EIA-568-1991 Commercial Building Telecommunications Wiring.

◆ TIA/EIA TSB-36 Additional Cable Specifications for UTP Cables. 1991.

◆ TIA/EIA TSB-40 Telecommunications Systems Bulletin—Additional Transmission Specifications for UTP Connecting Hardware. 1992.

◆ ANSI/TIA/EIA-568A 1995. Revises the original 568 document and adds material from TSB-36 and TSB-40.

◆ ANSI/TIA/EIA-569-1990 Commercial Building Standard for Telecommunications Pathways and Spaces.

◆ ANSI/TIA/EIA-570-1991 Residential and Light Commercial Telecommunications Wiring Standard.

◆ ANSI/TIA/EIA-606-1993 Administration Standard for the Telecommunications Infrastructure of Commercial Buildings.

◆ ANSI/TIA/EIA-607-1994 Commercial Building Grounding and Bonding Requirements for Telecommunications.

Local codes and standards may impose additional requirements.

Token Ring network

IBM's implementation of the token ring network architecture, which uses a token-passing protocol transmitting at 4 or 16Mbps.

Using standard telephone wiring, a Token Ring network can connect up to 72 devices; with shielded twisted-pair (STP) wiring, each ring can support up to 256 nodes. Although it is based on a closed-loop ring structure, a Token Ring network uses a star-shaped cluster of up to eight nodes, all attached to the same wiring concentrator or multistation access unit (MAU). The MAUs are then connected to the main ring circuit.

A Token Ring network can include personal computers, minicomputers, and mainframes. The IEEE 802.5 standard defines token ring networks.

token ring network

A LAN with a ring structure that uses token passing to regulate traffic on the network and avoid collisions.

On a token ring network, the controlling network interface card generates a token that controls the right to transmit. This token is continuously passed from one node to the next around the network.

When a node has information to transmit, it captures the token, sets its status to busy, and adds the message and the destination address. All other nodes continuously read the token to determine if they are the recipient of a message. If they are, they collect the token, extract the message, and return the token to the sender. The sender then removes the message and sets the token status to free, indicating that it can be used by the next node in sequence.

top-level domains

On the Internet, the highest category of host name, which either signifies the type of institution or the country of its origin.

In the United States, the most common top-level domains include:

> **com**   A commercial organization. Most companies end up in this category.

edu An educational establishment such as a university.

gov A branch of the United States government.

int An international organization such as NATO or the United Nations.

mil A branch of the United States military.

net A network organization.

org A nonprofit organization.

Most countries also have unique domains named after their international abbreviations; for example, ca represents Canada, uk represents Great Britain, and jp represents Japan.

topology

The map of a network. Physical topology describes where the cables are run and where the workstations, nodes, routers, and gateways are located. Networks are usually configured in bus, ring, star, or mesh topologies. Logical topology refers to the paths that messages take to get from one user on the network to another.

TP

See twisted-pair cable.

track

One of the concentric data areas recorded onto a hard or floppy disk during a low-level format.

trackball

A device used for pointing, designed as a space-saving alternative to the mouse.

A trackball contains a movable ball that you rotate with your fingers to move the cursor on the screen. Because it does not need the area of flat space that a mouse needs, trackballs are popular with users of portable computers; Microsoft has released a small trackball that clips onto the side of a laptop computer, and IBM has developed a dual-button, touch-sensitive pointing stick called the TrackPoint.

Transmission Control Protocol

Abbreviated TCP. The transport-level protocol used in the TCP/IP suite of protocols. It works above IP in the protocol stack, and provides reliable data delivery over connection-oriented links.

TCP adds a header to the datagram that contains the information needed to get the datagram to its destination. The source port number and the destination port number allow data to be sent back and forth to the correct processes running on each computer. A sequence number allows the datagrams to be rebuilt in the correct order in the receiving computer, and a checksum verifies that the data received is the same as the data sent.

Transmission Control Protocol/Internet Protocol

Abbreviated TCP/IP. A set of communications protocols first developed by the Defense Advanced Research Projects Agency (DARPA) in the late 1970s. The set of TCP/IP protocols encompasses media access, packet transport, session communications, file transfer, e-mail, and terminal emulation.

TCP/IP is a widely published open standard and, while completely independent of any specific hardware or software company, it is supported by a huge number of vendors and is available on many different computers, from PCs to mainframes, running many different operating systems. Many corporations, universities, and government agencies use TCP/IP, and it is also the basis of the Internet.

TCP/IP is separated from the network hardware and will run over Ethernet, token ring, X.25 networks, and dial-up connections. It is a routable protocol, so datagrams can be sent over specific routes, and it has reliable and efficient data-delivery mechanisms. TCP/IP uses a common expandable addressing scheme, so any system can address any other system, even in a network as large as the Internet, and new networks can be added without service disruptions.

The popularity that the TCP/IP family of protocols enjoys today did not arise just because the protocols were available or even because the United States government mandated their use. They are popular because they are robust, solid protocols that solve many of the most difficult networking problems and do so in an elegant and efficient way.

transmission medium

The physical cabling used to carry network information, such as fiber-optic, coaxial, shielded twisted-pair (STP), or unshielded twisted-pair (UTP) cabling.

Trojan Horse

A type of computer virus that pretends to be a useful program, such as a game or a utility program, to entice you to use it, when in reality it contains special code that will intentionally damage any system onto which it is loaded.

twisted-pair cable

Abbreviated TP. Cable that comprises two or more pairs of insulated wires twisted together, at six twists per inch.

In twisted-pair cable, one wire carries the signal and the other is grounded. The cable may be shielded or unshielded. Telephone wire installed in modern buildings is often twisted-pair wiring.

Type 1–9 cable

IBM Cabling System specifications, as follows:

Type 1 cable   Shielded, twisted, dual-pair cable with 22-gauge solid conductors and a braided shield. Used with Token Ring networks.

Type 2 cable   Two-pair, shielded cable with solid conductors and a braided shield. Type 2 also includes four pairs of unshielded voice-grade lines, giving a total of six pairs in the same sheath.

Type 3 cable   Four unshielded, solid, twisted pairs, used for voice or data. IBM's variant of twisted-pair telephone wire.

Type 4 cable   No published specification.

Type 5 cable   Dual 100/140-micron fiber-optic cable; IBM now recommends 125-micron

fiber-optic cable, which is the current industry standard for fiber-optic cable.

Type 6 cable   Shielded, two-pair, braided cable used for patch cables. Type 6 is more flexible than Type 1 cable.

Type 7 cable   No published specification.

Type 8 cable   Shielded, dual-pair cable with no twists, housed in a flat jacket; commonly used under carpets.

Type 9 cable   Shielded, dual-pair, plenum cable with solid or braided conductors and a fire-resistant outer coating, for use between floors in a building.

U

UART

See Universal Asynchronous Receiver/Transmitter.

UDP

See User Datagram Protocol.

Ultra SCSI

An extension of the SCSI-2 standard that increases the data transfer rate to 20Mbps independent of the bus width. Ultra SCSI supports four to eight devices depending on cable type and length.

Ultra Wide SCSI

An extension of the SCSI-2 standard that increases the data transfer rate to 80Mbps over a 16-bit bus. Ultra2 SCSI supports up to 16 devices.

Ultra2 SCSI

An extension of the SCSI-2 standard that increases the data transfer rate to 40Mbps over an 8-bit bus. Ultra2 SCSI supports up to eight devices.

uncompress

The process of restoring a compressed file to its original form.

Uniform Resource Locator

Abbreviated URL. An address for a resource on the Internet.

URLs are used as a linking mechanism between Web pages and as an access method for Web browsers to access Web pages.

A URL specifies the protocol to be used to access the resource (such as HTTP or FTP), the name of the server where the resource is located (as in `www.sybex.com`), the path to that resource (as in `/catalog`), and the name of the document to open (`/index.html`).

uninterruptible power supply

Abbreviated UPS, pronounced "you-pea-ess." An alternative power source, usually consisting of a set of batteries, used to power a computer system if the normal power service is interrupted or falls below acceptable levels.

A UPS system is usually applied only to the most critical devices on the network, such as servers, routers, gateways, and independent hard disks. They are of two main types:

◆ An online UPS continuously monitors and modifies the power flowing through the unit. If an outage occurs, the UPS continues to provide regulated power.

◆ A standby UPS monitors the AC level, but only switches in when the power drops below a preset level; it contains circuitry capable of switching to backup power in 5ms or less.

Universal Asynchronous Receiver/Transmitter

Abbreviated UART; pronounced "you-art." An electronic module that combines the transmitting and receiving circuitry needed for asynchronous communications over a serial line.

Universal Serial Bus

Abbreviated USB. A standard from Intel and Microsoft for a high-speed peripheral bus designed to remove the need for almost all the connectors on the back of a personal computer.

USB defines the ports and bus characteristics with data transfer rates of up to 12Mbps over a single cable of up to 5 meters (16 feet) long. USB is capable of supporting up to 63 devices, such as external CD-ROM drives, printers, external modems, mice, and the keyboard, without rebooting the system, and also supplies power to some devices so there is no need for separate power cords or batteries. Most personal computers will have two USB ports.

unshielded cable

Any cable not protected from electromagnetic interference or radio frequency interference (RFI) by an outer foil shield.

unshielded twisted-pair cable

Abbreviated UTP. Cable that contains two or more pairs of twisted copper wires.

The greater the number of twists, the lower the crosstalk. UTP is offered in both voice grade and data grade. The advantages of UTP include ease of installation and low cost of materials. Its drawbacks are limited signaling speeds and shorter maximum cable-segment lengths.

UPS

See uninterruptible power supply.

UPS monitoring

The process that a server uses to make sure that an attached UPS (uninterruptible power supply) system is functioning properly.

URL

See Uniform Resource Locator.

USB

See Universal Serial Bus.

Usenet newsgroups

The individual discussion groups within Usenet.

Usenet newsgroups contain articles posted by Internet and Usenet subscribers; very few of them actually contain hard news.

Most newsgroups are concerned with a single subject, and the range of subjects throughout Usenet is simply phenomenal; if people are interested in a topic, you will find a newsgroup for that topic.

User Datagram Protocol

Abbreviated UDP. The connectionless, transport-level protocol used in the TCP/IP suite of protocols, usually bundled with IP-layer software. Because UDP does not add overhead, as does connection-oriented TCP, UDP is often used with SNMP (Simple Network Management Protocol) applications.

Multicast applications such as Mbone and the Real-time Transport Protocol that deliver audio and video streams use UDP as their delivery mechanism because the acknowledgment and retransmission services offered by TCP are not needed and add too much overhead. If a packet of audio data is lost, retransmission is neither practical nor desirable.

UTP

See unshielded twisted-pair cable.

V

V.90

A modem standard; also known as the 56K modem standard. V.90 describes an asymmetric connection, with theoretical speeds of up to 56Kbps downstream and an upstream connection rate of up to 33.6Kbps.

V.90 modems attain their high speed by assuming the circuit is a digital circuit and reducing the number of analog-to-digital conversions they perform, except for the conversion that takes place for outbound traffic at your modem.

Whether you actually achieve these rates depends on the quality of the phone line and the distance to the local telephone company central office. If the other end of the connection is not digital, the modem switches into full analog mode at 28.8 or 33.6Kbps.

In order to reduce crosstalk between adjacent lines, the FCC has placed restrictions on maximum signal strength levels and so 54Kbps is the theoretical maximum data rate.

vaccine

A utility program designed to protect files from viruses. By adding a small amount of code to an existing file, the vaccine program causes an alert to be generated if a virus does attack.

VBScript

A version of Microsoft Visual Basic used as a scripting language in the Microsoft Internet Explorer Web browser.

very high-bit-rate digital subscriber line

Abbreviated VDSL. A higher-speed version of asymmetrical digital subscriber line (ADSL).

VDSL is asymmetrical with a higher downstream data transfer rate than its upstream rate. Upstream rates can be from 1.6Mbps to 2.3Mbps, while downstream rates range from 12.96Mbps to 51.84Mbps, depending on the distance involved.

very low-frequency emission

Abbreviated VLF. Radiation emitted by a computer monitor and other common household electrical appliances, such as televisions, hair dryers, electric blankets, and food processors.

VLF emissions range from 2 to 400kHz and decline with the square of the distance from the source. Emissions are not constant around a computer monitor; they are higher from the sides and rear and weakest from the front of the screen.

Sweden is the only country to have defined a set of standards for monitor emissions. In 1990, Mat Oct Provadet (MPR), the Swedish National Board for Meterology and Testing, revised its guidelines for acceptable VLF emissions as less than or equal to 25 nanoTesla (nT). A nanoTesla is a unit of measurement for small magnetic fields.

video adapter

An adapter that provides the text and graphics output to the monitor. Some video adapters, such as the SVGA, are included in the circuitry on the motherboard rather than as separate plug-in boards.

video conferencing

A method used to allow people at remote locations to join in a conference and share information. Originally done with analog video and expensive satellite links, video conferencing is now performed with compressed digital video transmitted over a LAN or the Internet.

From an application standpoint, video conferencing has gone way beyond looking at a picture of a person; users can look at and update charts, make drawings or sketches on a chalkboard, update spreadsheets, and so on, all online.

video RAM

Abbreviated VRAM, pronounced "vee-ram." Special-purpose RAM with two data paths for access (conventional RAM has just one). These two paths let a VRAM board manage two functions at once: refreshing the display and communicating with the processor. VRAM does not require the system to complete one function before starting the other, so it allows faster operation for the whole video system.

virtual memory

A memory-management technique that allows information in physical memory to be swapped out to a hard disk if necessary.

This technique provides applications with more memory space than is actually available in the computer. True virtual-memory management requires specialized hardware in the processor for the operating system to use; it is not just a matter of writing information out to a swap area on the hard disk at the application level.

In a virtual memory system, programs and their data are divided into smaller pieces called *pages*. When more memory is needed, the operating system decides which pages are least likely to be needed soon (using an algorithm based on frequency of use, most recent use, and program priority), and it writes these pages out to disk. The memory space that they used is now available to the rest of the system for other applications. When these pages are needed again, they are loaded back into real memory, displacing other pages.

virus

A program intended to damage a computer system without the user's knowledge or permission.

A virus clones itself from disk to disk, or from system to system over a network. Numbers are hard to come by, but certain authorities claim that there are approximately 30,000 known viruses, with 400 new ones appearing each month.

A virus may attach itself to another program or to the partition table or boot track on a hard disk. When a certain event occurs, a date passes, or a specific program executes, the virus is triggered into action. Others, including the ILOVEYOU virus, take advantage of the trusting relationship that exists between Microsoft Office applications and run as scripts as soon as an e-mail attachment is opened.

VLF

See very low-frequency emission.

VRAM

See video RAM.

W

wait state

A clock cycle during which no instructions are executed because the processor is waiting for data from memory.

Static RAM chips and paged-mode RAM chips can store information without being constantly refreshed by the processor, thus eliminating the wait state. A computer that can process information without wait states is known as a zero-wait-state computer.

WAN

See wide area network.

warm boot

A reboot performed after the operating system has been running for some period of time, by pressing Ctrl+Alt+Del rather than cycling the power to the computer.

wavetable synthesis

A method used by a sound board to simulate musical instruments. Wavetable synthesis uses digitized samples of real orchestral instruments, which are edited and mixed to produce music. FM synthesis is cheaper than wavetable synthesis but is also of much lower quality.

Web browser

A client application that lets you look at hypertext documents, follow links to other HTML documents, and download files on the Internet or on a corporate intranet.

When you find something that interests you as you browse through a hypertext document, you can click on that object, and the system automatically takes care of accessing the Internet host that holds the document you requested; you don't need to know the IP address, the name of the host system, or any other details. A Web browser will also display the graphics in a Web page, play audio and video clips, and execute small Java or ActiveX programs called applets.

Netscape Navigator and Microsoft Internet Explorer are examples of popular Web browsers.

Web page

Information placed on a Web server for viewing with a Web browser. A Web page may contain text, graphics, audio or video clips, and links to other Web pages.

Web server

A hardware and software package that provides services to client computers running Web browsers.

Clients make requests in the form of HTTP messages; the server responds to these messages, returning Web pages or other requested documents to the client. Most Web servers run one of the versions of Unix, or Microsoft Windows 2000 Server.

Web site

A group of HTML documents and associated scripts supported by a Web server on the World Wide Web.

Most Web sites have a home page used as a starting point or index into the site, with other Web pages or even other Web sites connected by links. To connect to a Web site, you need an Internet connection and a Web browser.

Webcam

A low-cost video camera used to capture live images for display on a Web site. Webcams are used to display traffic information, activity inside a person's apartment, fish tanks, scenic views, and street scenes.

wide area network

Abbreviated WAN. A network that connects users across large distances, often crossing the geographical boundaries of cities or states.

Wide SCSI

A version of the SCSI-2 standard that provides data transfer rates of up to 20MBps over a 16-bit data bus.

Wide Ultra SCSI

A version of the SCSI-2 standard that provides data transfer rates of up to 40MBps over a 16-bit data bus.

Wide Ultra2 SCSI

A version of the SCSI-2 standard that provides data transfer rates of up to 80MBps over a 16-bit data bus.

wildcard character

A character that represents one or more unknown characters. In many operating systems, a question mark (?) represents a single unknown character in a filename or filename extension, and an asterisk (*) represents any number of unknown characters.

Windows Internet Naming Service

Abbreviated WINS. A Microsoft Windows NT Server and Windows 2000 Server service that maps NetBIOS computer names used in Windows networks to IP addresses used in TCP/IP-based networks. WINS is almost completely automated; it builds its own database and manages updates to the database.

WINS

See Windows Internet Naming Service.

Wintel

A contraction of Windows and Intel. Referring to an Intel-based computer that runs Microsoft Windows.

wireless communications

A method of connecting a node or a group of nodes into the main network using a technology other than conventional cabling.

The following methods are in use:

infrared line of sight   High-frequency light waves are used to transmit data between nodes up to 24.4 meters (80 feet) apart using an unobstructed path; infrared beams cannot pass through masonry walls. Data rates are relatively high, in the tens of megabits per second range.

high-frequency radio   High-frequency radio signals transmit data to nodes from 12.2 to 39.6 meters (40 to 130 feet) apart, depending on the nature of obstructions separating them; the signal can penetrate thin walls but not supporting masonry. Data rates are usually less than 1Mbps.

spread-spectrum radio   A small set of frequencies is available for wireless LANs without FCC approval. The 902 to 928MHz band is known as the Industrial, Scientific, Medical (ISM) band and is not regulated. The 2.4 to 2.483GHz band is regulated and requires an FCC license for use. Spread-spectrum nodes can be up to 243.8 meters (800 feet) apart in an open environment, and these radio waves can pass through masonry walls. However, in an environment with fully enclosed offices, distances are limited to 33.5 meters (110 feet). Data rates are usually less than 1Mbps.

Wireless LANs are not always completely wireless. They may be used to replace the cabling on certain network segments or to connect groups of networks that use conventional cabling.

World Wide Web

Abbreviated WWW, W3, or simply the Web. A huge collection of hypertext pages on the Internet.

World Wide Web concepts were developed in Switzerland by the European Laboratory for Particle Physics (known as CERN), but the Web is not just a tool for scientists; it is one of the most flexible and exciting tools in existence.

Hypertext links connect pieces of information (text, graphics, animation, audio, and video) in separate HTML pages located at the same or at different Internet sites, and you explore these pages and links using a Web browser such as Netscape Navigator or Microsoft Internet Explorer.

You can also access a Web resource directly if you specify the appropriate URL (Uniform Resource Locator).

World Wide Web traffic is growing faster than most other Internet services, and the reason for this becomes obvious once you try a capable Web browser; it is very easy and a lot of fun to access World Wide Web information.

write-back cache

A technique used in cache design for writing information back into main memory.

In a write-back cache, the cache stores the changed block of data but only updates main memory under certain conditions, such as when the whole block must be overwritten because a newer block must be loaded into the cache, or when the controlling algorithm determines that too much time has elapsed since the last update. This method is rather complex to implement, but is much faster than other designs.

write-through cache

A technique used in cache design for writing information back into main memory.

In a write-through cache, each time the processor returns a changed bit of data to the cache, the cache updates that information in both the cache and in main memory. This method is simple to implement but is not as fast as other designs; delays can be introduced when the processor must wait to complete write operations to slower main memory.

WWW

See World Wide Web.

X

XON/XOFF

In asynchronous transmissions between two PCs, a simple method of flow control.

The receiving PC sends an XOFF control character (ASCII 19, Ctrl+S) to pause the transmission of data when the receive buffer is full, and then sends an XON character (ASCII 17, Ctrl+Q) when it is ready to continue the transmission.

Z

ZBR

See Zone Bit Recording.

zero insertion force socket

Abbreviated ZIF socket. A specially designed chip socket that makes replacing a chip easier and safer.

To change a chip in a ZIF socket, you raise a lever beside the socket to free the original chip's pins from the socket. Then slide the old chip out and slide in the replacement chip, taking care to align the pins and holes. Finally, lower the lever again. A ZIF socket minimizes damage to the delicate pins that connect the chip to the rest of the system.

ZIF socket

See zero insertion force socket.

Zip drive

A popular removable storage device from Iomega Corporation, capable of 100MB or 250MB of storage on relatively cheap, portable, 3½-inch disks.

Zip drives have emerged as the de facto standard personal computer backup device.

ZIP file

A file whose contents have been compressed by one of the popular file-compression utilities, such as PKZIP, WinZip, or other comparable program; the filename extension is ZIP.

A ZIP file can contain a single compressed file, or a whole collection of archives. A file compressed in this way is said to have been zipped.

To uncompress a ZIP file, use the same utility that compressed it originally. Some ZIP files are self-extracting and can uncompress themselves when you click their icon.

Zone Bit Recording

Abbreviated ZBR. A Seagate Technologies term for multiple zone recording.

Index

Note to the Reader: Throughout this index **boldfaced** page numbers indicate primary discussions of a topic. *Italicized* page numbers indicate illustrations.

Numbers

"0 hard disk(s) found" message, 511
1PCBuilder mailing list, 920
2.1GB barrier, **379**
2B+D abbreviation, 1075
3D audio, **702–703**
3D video boards, **673–674**
3Dfx chip sets, 674
3DNow! Technology instructions, 116
4.2GB barrier, **379**
5-bit error correction, 374
6x86 CPU, **115**
8-bit boards
    vs. 16-bit, **279–280**
    conflicts with, **279–280**
    slots for, 143–144, *145–146*
    sound cards, 692–693
8 mm format, 717–719
8.4GB barrier, **379**
10/100 devices, 1075
10Base-2 networks, 180
10Base-5 networks, 182
10Base-T cable, 1075
10Base-T networks, 180, 182, *183*, 1075
10Base-TX cable, 1075
10Mbps, 1075
11-bit error correction, 374
16-bit applications, system file backups for, **483**
16-bit boards
    conflicts with, **279–280**
    slots for, **144–147**, *145–146*
    sound cards, 692–693
23B+D abbreviation, 1075
24/7 availability, 1075
24-bit color, 1075
30-pin memory chips, 119, *120*, 313
32-bit boards
    slots for, **147–148**
    sound cards, 692–693
32GB barrier, **379**
50-ohm cable terminators, 801
"55" error message, **579–580**
64-bit bus, **151–154**, *152*
64-bit sound cards, 692–693
70-bit error correction, 374

72-Hz video, 673
72-pin memory chips, 119, *120*, 313
75-ohm cable terminators, 801
80-Hz video, 673
96-bit sound cards, 692–693
100Mbps, 1075
101-key keyboard, 648
110 Alert product, 192, *193*
120-Hz video, 673
168-pin memory chips, 313
386 extension, 127
528MB barrier, **379**
"1701" message, 511
"1780" message, 511–512
"1781" message, 511–512
"1790" message, 511–512
"1791" message, 511–512
3270 PC communications controller
    connectors for, 180
    emulating, 173
4004 microprocessor, **929–930**, *929*
5250 PC communications controller, 173
8008 microprocessor, **930**
8041 microprocessor, 161
8042 microprocessor, 161
8048 microprocessor, 161
8086 CPU and computers
    characteristics of, **106**
    data path for, **91**
    specifications for, 102
8087 coprocessor, 96
8088 CPU and computers, 89
    characteristics of, **106**
    data path for, **91**
    memory addresses in, 126
    specifications for, 102
8250 UARTs, 615–616
8259 interrupt controller, **262–266**
8284A chip, 160
8514 adapters
    characteristics of, **669–670**, 680
    interlacing in, **672–673**
16450 UARTs, 616
16550 UARTs, 616
80186 CPU, 103, **106**
80188 CPU, 89, **106**

80286 CPU and computers
    characteristics of, **106–107**
    data path for, 92
    protected mode in, 133–137
    specifications for, 103
80386 CPU and computers
    characteristics of, **107–108**
    data path for, **92**
    efficiency of, 89
    specifications for, 103
80486 CPU and computers
    cache memory on, **93**
    characteristics of, **108–109**
    data path for, 92
    efficiency of, 89
    specifications for, 103
82284 chip, 160

A

A/B switches
    defined, 1076
    for printers, 543
A value in hexadecimal numbering system, 1049
A3D API, 702
A97M prefix, 469
Aark24 MIDI cards, 705
AboveBoard memory board, 138
abrasive head cleaners, 524–525
absolute sectors, **450–452**
AC adapters, 1076
AC Monitor product, 340
AC power
    cables and connectors for, **64–66**
    checking, **338–341**
    for notebooks, 887
Accelerated Graphics Processing (AGP)
    bus, 27, **154–155**, *154*
    benefits of, 664
    defined, 1076
    description, 29
    for ultimate computer, 952
    in upgrading, 940, *941*
accelerators, 165, **667–668**
    connectors for, *181*
    defined, 1076

in PC selection, 855
settings for, **1010**, *1011*
access, 1076
access times
    of CD-ROM drives, **759–760**
    defined, 1076
    of disk drives, 352, **365–367**, 955
accessibility options, **991**
    display, **995–996**, *995–996*, **1019**, *1019*
    general, **997**, **998**, **1019**
    keyboard, **992–994**, *992–994*, **1017–1018**, *1018*
    mouse, **996**, **997**, **1019**
    quick steps for, **987**
    sound, **994–995**, *995*
    in Windows XP, **1017–1019**, *1018–1019*
acetate, triboelectric value of, 205
acknowledgments with SCSI, 406
ACPI (Advanced Configuration and Power Interface), 1077
Active-Hardware site, 909
active hubs, **831**, 1076
active-matrix displays, 1076
active partitions, 441
active SCSI termination
    and built-in termination, 404–405
    defined, 1076
    vs. passive, **420–421**, *421*
    for SCSI-3, **408**, 412
ActiveX scripts, 469, 472
actuator arms, *356*, 357–358
    stepper motors for, **365**
    voice coils for, **364–365**, *364*
Adaptec AHA1542 SCSI adapter, 413
adapter boards. *See also* controllers; network interface cards (NICs)
    identifying, **178–184**
    need for, 161
Adapter Unit Interface (AUI)
    for hubs, 834
    for network interface cards, 792, *792*
    for thicknet, 182
adapters
    defined, 1076
    drivers for, *1008*, **1009**, **1022**
    refresh rates for, **1009**
adaptive differential pulse code modulation (ADPCM) standard, 756–757
Add New Hardware Wizard, 823, **998–1002**, *998*, *1001*, 1019
Add New Modem Wizard, 1012, 1024

Add or Remove Programs window, 1020–1021, *1020*
Add/Remove Programs feature, **1003–1005**, *1003*
    for installing programs, **1004**, *1004*
    for removing programs, **1003–1004**
    for Startup Disk, 1005, *1005*
    for Windows programs, **1004–1005**, *1004*
address bus, 1077
address lines, error beeps for, 291
Address Resolution Protocol (ARP), 813
addresses
    burned-in, 1083
    defined, 1076–1077
    in EISA bus, 150
    hardware, 1104
    in hexadecimal numbering system, **1049–1051**
    with hubs, 833–834, *834*
    I/O. *See* I/O addresses
    Internet, 1108
    IP, 1109
    in IPX/SPX, **810**, *810*
    for memory, **136–137**
        CPU limits, **100–101**
        defined, 1113
        vs. I/O addresses, **143**
        planning for, 126
    for parallel ports, 539
    with PC Card bus, 157
    ROM, **267–269**
    in TCP/IP, **812–813**
adjustable bus and memory speeds, **276–277**
ADPCM (adaptive differential pulse code modulation) standard, 756–757
ADSL (asymmetric digital subscriber line)
    characteristics of, 629–630
    defined, 1079
ADSL Lite, 630
Advanced Configuration and Power Interface (ACPI), 1077
Advanced Micro Devices (AMD) CPUs and microprocessors, 22, 82
    Athlon, **116–117**
    Duron, **117**
    K5/K6, **115–116**
    operating frequencies of, 962
    pipelines in, 90
    slots for, 101
    specifications for, 105
    for upgrades, 938

advanced power management (APM)
    systems, 63
    defined, 1077
    handling, **64**
Advanced SCSI Programming Interface (ASPI), 427
    defined, 1077
    as standard, **428**
Advanced Settings for FilterKeys dialog box, 993, *993*
Advanced Technology Attachment (ATA) protocol
    Fast ATA-2, **383–384**
    specifications for, **382–383**
Advanced Technology Attachment Packet Interface (ATAPI), 1077
Advanced Troubleshooting Settings window, 1032–1033
advice, online sources of, **902**
aftermarket, 1077
AGP (Accelerated Graphics Processing)
    bus, 27, **154–155**, *154*
    benefits of, 664
    defined, 1076
    description, 29
    for ultimate computer, 952
    in upgrading, 940, *941*
AHA1542 SCSI host adapter, 413
air, triboelectric value of, 205
air cleaners, 196
AirPort wireless networks, 816
aligning print heads, 560
all-in-one combo devices, **536**
allocation errors, FAT, **494–495**, **503**, *503*
alphanumeric characters, 1077
alt newsgroups, 915
Altair bus, **142**
AltaVista search engine, **908**
alternating current (AC)
    cables and connectors for, **64–66**
    checking, **338–341**
    for notebooks, 887
aluminum
    for CD-ROM disks, 753
    triboelectric value of, 205
AM radios for RFI monitoring, 200–201
AMD (Advanced Micro Devices) CPUs and microprocessors, 22, 82
    Athlon, **116–117**
    K5/K6, **115–116**
    operating frequencies of, 962
    pipelines in, 90
    slots for, 101

specifications for, 105
    for upgrades, 938
America Online (AOL), 922
American Standard Code for Information
    Interchange (ASCII), 1077
AMI (American Megatrends)
    BIOS from, 50, 131
    error beeps for, **290**
    in upgrading, 854
ammonia and laser printers, 583
AmpCast site, 699
amplification
    controllers for, 162
    of signals, 687
amplitude
    in QAM, 726
    of sound waves, **687**, *687*
amps in power calculations, 336
analog camcorders, 719
analog capture systems, **731–733**
analog channel test units, 641
analog devices, 1077
Analog Protection System (APS), 720
AnandTech site, 909
AND logic gates, 930
Animated Cursor Editor tool, 1038
anonymous FTP
    defined, 1078
    support for, 912
ANSI/TIA/EIA structured cabling
    standards, 1136–1137
antistatic devices
    defined, 1078
    spray, 206
    wrist straps, **44**
AntiVirus program, 474
antivirus programs, 474, 1078. *See also*
    viruses
any key kits, 220
AnyPoint Home Network kit, 816, 944
AOL (America Online), 922
AOL prefix, 469
APIs (Application Programming Interfaces)
    for 3D video, 674
    defined, 1078
    and redirectors, **805–806**
APM (advanced power management)
    systems, 63
    defined, 1077
    handling, **64**
Apple bus, 142
Apple II computers, clock rate for, 83
applet viruses, **469**

Application Programming Interfaces (APIs)
    for 3D video, 674
    defined, 1078
    and redirectors, **805–806**
application servers, 790
application-specific integrated circuits
    (ASICs), 1078
applications, system information for, 1027
APS (Analog Protection System), 720
architecture, 1078
archive bits, 455
archive files, 1079
archiving, 1078
ARCNet network boards, 132, 180
areal density, 368
ARP (Address Resolution Protocol), 813
arrow keys, 1079
Ars Technica site, 909
articles, newsgroup, 914
ARTISTdirect Network site, 699
asbestos, triboelectric value of, 205
ASCII (American Standard Code for
    Information Interchange), 1077
ASCII extended character set, 1079
ASCII files, 1079
ASCII standard character set, 1079
ASD (Automatic Skip Drive Agent), **1031**
ash particles, dust from, 196
ASICs (application-specific integrated
    circuits), 1078
ASPI (Advanced SCSI Programming
    Interface), 427
    defined, 1077
    as standard, **428**
assembly, **68–69**
    of cables and edge connectors, **69–70**,
        70
    mistakes in, **70–72**
assembly language, 1079
assumptions in troubleshooting, 217
AST Research, 149
asterisks (*), 1079
asymmetric digital subscriber line (ADSL)
    characteristics of, 629–630
    defined, 1079
asynchronous ports, **168–169**, **615**, *615*,
    618
asynchronous SCSI, **406**
Asynchronous Transfer Mode (ATM)
    defined, 1079
    in DSL, 629
asynchronous transfers with USB, 170
asynchronous transmissions, 1080

AT Attachment Packet Interface (ATAPI)
    for CD-ROM drives, 761
    defined, 1077
    purpose of, 383
AT bus, **144–147**, *145–146*. *See also* ISA
    (Industry Standard Architecture) bus
AT computers
    change-line support in, 529
    clock rate for, 83
    configuring, 275–276
    form factor for, **330**
    hard disk drive recognition in, **398**
    keyboard for, 648
at symbols (@), 1080
ATA (Advanced Technology Attachment)
    protocol
    Fast ATA-2, **383–384**
    specifications for, **382–383**
ATAPI (AT Attachment Packet Interface)
    for CD-ROM drives, 761
    defined, 1077
    purpose of, 383
Athlon CPU
    characteristics of, **116–117**
    defined, 1080
    internal cache memory on, 96
    operating frequencies of, 962
    as Pentium competitor, 114
    for upgrading, 852
ATM (Asynchronous Transfer Mode)
    defined, 1079
    in DSL, 629
attachments, viruses in, 472
attack in sound waves, *691*, 692
attenuation, 687
    defined, 1080
    vs. interference, **794**
ATTRIB command, 456
attributes
    defined, 1080
    in directory entries, 455–456
ATX cases, **849–850**
ATX motherboards
    power supplies for, **331–333**
    for ultimate computer, 951
audio. *See* sound and sound cards
audio/video enthusiasts, PC features for,
    860, **863**
Audiogalaxy site, 699
AUI (Adapter Unit Interface)
    for hubs, 834
    for network interface cards, 792, *792*
    for thicknet, 182

auto-answer feature, 1080
auto-dial feature, 1080
AutoCAD program, DOS extenders for, 135
autoconfiguring controllers, 379
AutoDetect function, 397
autodetection, disk drive, **514**
AUTOEXEC.BAT file
    in boot process, **301–302**
    checking, **1032–1033**
    TSRs in, **127**
Automatic Reset option, 997, 1019
Automatic Skip Drive Agent (ASD), **1031**
Automatically Download Updates option, 1035
Automatically Synchronize with an Internet Time Server option, 1021
AutoOpen macro, 467
autosizing monitors, 677
autotranslating for hard disk drives, 380
AutoUpdate utility, **1034–1035**
availability in digital broadband communications, 626
average latency period, 367
average seek time, **365–367**
Award BIOS in PC selection, 854
Award Software International, BIOS by, 50, 131
AWE32 sound cards, 692
AWE64 sound cards, 692

B

B value in hexadecimal numbering system, 1049
Baby AT computers, form factor for, **330–331**
baby food driver tester method, 224
backbones, fiber optic cable for, 799
background information, online sources of, **901**
Background tab, *1006*
backplane design, 79
backslashes (\), 1080
backup power supplies, **343–345**, *343*
Backup Wizard, 933
backups, **479–480**
    of configuration, **50–52**
    defined, **1080–1081**
    hard disk drives for, **487**
    hardware-based, 173
    of MBR, **462**, **480–482**

for old computer data, **933–934**, *933–934*
online, **487**
options for, **485–489**
partition information, 443
Registry, **484–485**, **1042–1043**
removable drives for, **486–487**
for security, 842
software for, **487–488**
strategies for, **488**
of system files, **483–485**
tape drives for, **486**
before upgrades, 875, **880–881**
for viruses, 472–473
backward compatibility, 1081
bad areas in hard disk drives, **444**
"Bad or missing XXXX.DRV" message, 301
bad sectors, 456
    defined, 1081
    report on, 494–495
    testing for, **490–492**
bad track tables, 1081
balanced SCSI, 404
banding with inkjet printers, 557
bandwidth
    in cable broadband, **636–637**
    defined, 1081
    of DRAM, 316
    in sampling, 690
    with switches, 836
banks, memory, 119
bar code readers, 654
barium coating on floppy diskettes, 522
Basic Input/Output System. *See* BIOS (Basic Input/Output System)
BASIC language, 520
Basic Rate ISDN (BRI), 1081
Batch98 tool, 1038
batteries
    in backup power supplies, **343–345**, *343*
    for CMOS configuration, 171–172, 275
        connecting, 72
        holders for, 277
        identifying, 177, *177*
        in motherboard removal, 67
        replacing, **277–278**
    for notebooks, **874**, **887**
        buying, **889–890**
        caring for, **887–888**

        charging, **888–889**
        conserving power in, **890**, *890*
        replacing, 889
baud rate, 1081
BEDO DRAM (Burst Extended Data Out DRAM)
    defined, 1083
    development of, 120
beep codes
    for AMI BIOS, **290**
    for Phoenix BIOS, **290–292**
belts for printers, 534
bent pins on keyboard connectors, **652**
Berg connectors
    for power supplies, 334, *334*
    removing, 62, *62*
    for sound cards, 693, *693*
Bernoulli boxes, 485
bezels, 884
bidirectional cables, 555
bidirectional parallel ports, 169, 538–539
BIN files, viruses in, 466
binary numbering system, 1081
binding interfaces, **807–808**
BIOS (Basic Input/Output System)
    in boot process, **296–299**, *296*
    for CD-ROM drives, **763–764**
    chips for, **776**
    CMOS information read by, **299–300**
    compatibility of, 131
    DBR loading by, **301–302**
    defined, 1082
    diagnostic program for, 228
    disk drive size limitations in, **376–380**
    in flash RAM, **131–132**
    for hard disk drives
        autodetection by, **514**
        and CMOS configuration, **396–398**
        for DMA support, 353
        for physical geometry, **361–362**
        SCSI, 51
    inventory and testing by, **299**
    for keyboards, **652**
    manufacturers of, 29
    MBR loading by, **300**
    memory for, 131
    memory tests by, **297**
    in notebooks, **880**
    in PC selection, **854**
    for Plug and Play, 273–274

scans for, 297–298
  for SCSI, **428**
  setting up, **970–972**, *971*
  setup program in, 276
  timeouts with, **299**
BIOS extenders for notebooks, 880
bit blitting, 165, 667
bit depth of scanner images, 605
bit rate, 1082
bit width of SCSI systems, 408–409
bitlines in flash memory, *774, 775*
bitmaps
  with accelerators, 667
  for scanner images, 606
bits
  defined, 1082
  for sound cards, 953
bits per inch (bpi)
  defined, 1082
  in floppy diskettes, 522
bits per second (bps), 1082
BitShift translation algorithm, 379
biz newsgroups, 915
black and white TV video, **722–726**, *723*
Black Box parallel port extender, 543
black wires
  in AC supplies, 65–66
  in DC supplies, 332
  in phone lines, 641
blank partition tables, **513–514**
bleeder fuses, 342
block-addressable memory, **665**
block PIO (BPIO) transfer, 382
block transfers for bitmaps, 667
blocks in flash memory, 775
blue color
  in CCD chips, pixels for, 715–716,
    716
  in TV video, **722–726**, *723–727*
  in VGA, pages for, 130
  in video capture board, 736–737
blue wires in AC supplies, 65–66
Bluetooth specification, 800
Bluetooth wireless networks, 816, 887
BNC connectors
  defined, 1082
  identifying, **179–180**, *179, 183*
  for LANs, 800–801, *801*
boards. *See* expansion boards
Boh Tech site, 909
bombs, **471**
boot floppies, preparing, **489–490**, 974
BOOT.INI file, checking, 1033

boot process, **295**
  AUTOEXEC.BAT file in, **301–302**
  CMOS information read in, **299–300**
  COMMAND.COM loading,
    301–302
  CONFIG.SYS file in, **301**
  DBR loading, **301–302**
  from floppy disks, 509
  hardware in, **296**
  initialization in, **297–299**
  inventory and testing by, 299
  lockups in, **299**
  MBR loading, **300**
  on Plug and Play systems, **273–274**
  power in, **295**
  ROM in, **296–299**, *296*
  system file execution, 301
  timeouts in, **299**
boot records
  backing up, **480–482**
  loading, **300**
  for logical drives, 458–459, *459*
  program in, 300
  reading, **509–513**
boot sector viruses, 301
  characteristics of, **466**
  defined, 1082
bootable disks
  defined, 1082
  floppy, **489–490**, 509
  hard, SCSI software for, **427–428**
bootable partitions, **300–301**
booting, 1082
bpi (bits per inch)
  defined, 1082
  in floppy diskettes, 522
BPIO (block PIO) transfer, 382
bps (bits per second), 1082
braces and brackets for RFI suppression,
  200
brain damaged products, 1082–1083
branch prediction technique, 94
brand name PCs, **849–852**
brass, triboelectric value of, 205
breakout boxes, 586, **642**, 1083
BRI (Basic Rate ISDN), 1081
bridge circuits for PCI bus, 151
brightness with video capture boards, 736
broadband communications systems. *See*
  digital broadband communications
broadband wireless access (BWA),
  639–640
Broadcast.com site, 703

broadcast video for video capture, **721**
brown wires in AC supplies, 65–66
brownouts
  backup power supplies for, 343
  defined, 1083
  problems from, **204**
browsers
  defined, 1143
  for World Wide Web, 905–906
buffer overruns, firewalls for, 844
buffer underruns in CD-ROM recording,
  764–765
buffers. *See also* caches
  for CD-ROM drives, **760–761**
  conflicts in, **267–269**
  defined, 1083
  in flow control, 620
  memory for, **132–133**
  for SDRAM, 318
  in UARTs, 616
BUFFERS statements, executing, 301
bugs
  defined, 1083
  in video capture, **744–745**
building code requirements, 821
building computers. *See* ultimate computer
bulk floppy erasers, 198
bulk transfers with USB, 170
burn-in, **227**
burned-in addresses, 1083
burning MP3 files to CDs, **698–699**
burst counters, 318
Burst Extended Data Out DRAM (BEDO
  DRAM)
  defined, 1083
  development of, 120
bus mastering
  with CardBus, 158
  defined, 1083
  in EISA bus, 150
  in MCA bus, **149**
  with network interface cards, 829
  operation of, **259**, *259*
  with PC Card, 157
  in PCI bus, **153**
  in SCSI, **413**
bus mouse, I/O addresses for, 251
bus width of DRAM, 316
buses, 25–29, *25*, 141–142
  address, 1077
  AGP, **154–155**, *154*
  Altair, **142**

AT, **144–147**, *145–146*
CardBus, **158–159**
data paths for, **142–143**
defined, 1083
DMA controllers on, 257–258
EISA, **149–150**
FireWire, **159–160**
for hard disk drives, 354
improving, **147**
for interrupts and Direct Memory
    Access, **143**
MCA, **148–149**
and memory size, **143**
Mini PCI, **157–158**
for network interface cards, **792**
PC Card, **155–157**, *156*
in PC selection, **853–854**
PCI, **151–154**, *152*
speed of, **146–148**, 276–277
summary, **158–159**
Universal Serial Bus, **169–171**, *170*
VESA local bus, 148, 151
for video boards, **663–664**
in video capture, **733–734**
buttons for mouse, **655**
BWA (broadband wireless access),
    639–640
bytes
    defined, 1083
    on disks, 356

C

C value in hexadecimal numbering system,
    1049
C3 CPUs, **116**
cable broadband, 626, **635**
    bandwidth sharing in, **636–637**
    installing and configuring, **636**
    operation of, **635**
    satellite communications, **637–639**
cable modems, 954, 1084
cable ripper cases, 54
cables. *See also* connectors
    for breakout boxes, 642
    for CD-ROM drives, 763, 769, 980
    for communications systems,
        643–644
    connecting, **69–70**, *70*
    in cover removal, 54
    diagrams for, **55–56**
    disconnecting, **62–63**, *62*
    for DVD decoder cards, 976

for floppy disk drives, 63, **523–524**,
    524, 526–527, 968, *969*
for hard disk drives
    IDE, **394–396**, *395*
    in troubleshooting, 512
for home networks, 943
for hubs, 832–833
for IDE adapters, 937–938
for keyboards, 650–651, **653**
for laser printers, **582–583**
for MIDI, 695
for modems, 624
for network interface cards, 792
for networks, **793–795**
    coaxial, 797, *797*
    connectors for, **800–803**,
        801–803
    fiber optic, **798–799**, *798–799*
    installing, **818–821**
    interference vs. attenuation in,
        794
    summary, **803**
    twisted-pair, **795–797**, *795*
noise from, 199
for parallel ports, 539
for power supplies, 337
for printers, 538, **543**
removing, **62–63**
routing, **71–72**
in satellite communications, 639
screws for, 222
for SCSI
    data path in, 407
    issues in, **411–412**
    length of, 408
    noise in, 403
    size of, 429
    types of, **416–420**, *417–420*
for serial communications, 616,
    621–622
for serial ports, 168
for sound cards, 693–694, *693*
for speaker, 67
in video capture, **728–729**, *729*, 734
cache memory
    defined, 1084
    in upgrading, 940, *941*
caches, 32. *See also* buffers
    for CD-ROM drives, **760–761**
    on CPUs, **92–96**
    defined, 1084
    error beeps for, 290

for hard disk drives, 353, **375–376**
for instructions, 90
for memory
    matching, **320**
        for SCSI devices, 413
        and system speed, **121–122**
    in multiprocessor systems, **320**
    in PC selection, 854
    in Pentium Pro, 110–111
    for SCSI, 413
    for SDRAM, 318
caddies for CD-ROM, **757–758**
Cakewalk Pro Audio sequencing program,
    705–706
calculator for hexadecimal numbers, 828
calendars, system, 32, **160**, **171–172**
call preferences for modems, 1013, 1024
call waiting, problems with, 911
CAM (Common Access Method) SCSI
    standard, 426
camcorders for video capture, **714–719**,
    717
Camera Pro Max product, 719
cameras
    flash memory for, 775
    modems for, 954
    serial ports for, 169
    Universal Serial Bus for, 170
    for video capture, **715–716**
"Cannot reload COMMAND.COM,
    system halted" message, 302
capacitive keyboards, **649–650**
capacitors
    in power supplies, 330
    replacing, 305
capacity of flash memory, **784**
Caps Lock key, sound with, 994
capture boards for video capture, **730**
    analog, **731–733**
    digital, **731**
    installing, **734–735**
    off-line compression in, **741–744**
    overlays and previews with, **732–733**
    real-time compression in, **732**,
        738–741, *740*
carbonic acid, 209
card services manager, **269–270**
Card Services standard, 157
CardBus, **158–159**
CardDeluxe MIDI cards, 705
cards. *See* expansion boards
carpets, static from, 206
Carrier Detect lines in RS-232 sessions, 619

carrier signals
    defined, 1084
    in QAM, 726
carrying cases for notebooks, **891**
cartridges for inkjet printers, **550–551,**
    560–561
    carriers for, **551**
    recharged, 536
cascading techniques, 1084
cases
    for generic computers, **849–850**
    for inkjet printers, **549–550**
    for notebooks, **891**
    preparing, **958–959,** *958*
    for ultimate computer, **949–951,** *949*
cassettes, **520**
categories of network cable, **795–797,**
    1085
Cathode-Ray Tubes (CRTs). *See also*
  monitors
    dust on, 196
    magnetism from, 197
CAV (constant angular velocity), 1089
CCDs (charge-coupled devices)
    defined, 1086
    operation of, **715–716**
    in scanners, 604
CCFLs (cold cathode fluorescent lamps),
    604
CD modem light, 643
CD Read/Write (CD-RW) drives,
    750–751
    for backups, **487**
    defined, 1085
    disk composition for, **754**
    for MP3 files, **699**
    software for, **487–488**
CD-recordable (CD-R) drives, 30,
    750–751
    defined, 1085
    disc composition for, **754**
CD-ROM discs
    burning MP3 files to, **699**
    composition of, **753–754**
    defined, 1085, 1088
    loading, **757–758**
    reading, **753**
    recording, **764–765**
    viruses in, 473
CD-ROM drives, 30, **748**
    BIOS configuration for, **763–764**
    buffers for, **760–761**
    cables for, 62–63, 763, 769

compatibility of, **751**
connectors for, 180, *184*
controllers for, **166**
data modes for, 756–757
defined, 1085–1086
drivers for, **764,** 769
frame padding for, **744**
heat from, 191
identifying, 174
installing, **749,** **763–764,** **972–973,**
    973, **980,** *981*
interface types for, **761–763**
internal and external, **758**
maintaining, **768**
multimedia kits for, **762–763**
multisession capability of, **757**
in PC selection, **855**
    audio/video enthusiast, 863
    home, 862
    road warriors, 865
    small business, 864
    student, 862
performance characteristics of,
    758–761
physical characteristics of, **758**
reading CDs with, **753**
and sound cards, 694
speed of, **758–760**
standards for, **755–757**
troubleshooting, **768–769**
types of, **750–751**
for ultimate computer, **956**
Zone Bit Recording with, 360–361
CD-ROM I/O port, 251
CD-ROM/XA standard, **756–757,** 1086
CDFS (Compact Disc File System), 756
CDs. *See* CD-ROM discs
Celeron CPU
    data path for, 92
    defined, 1086
    heat in, 110–111, 191
    internal cache memory on, 96
    introduction of, **112**
    operating frequencies of, 961
    pipelines in, 90, 100
    slots for, 101–102
    specifications for, 104
    for upgrading, 852
    word size for, 91
central office (CO) for DSL, 629
central processing units. *See* CPUs (central
    processing units)

Centronics cables and connectors, **179,**
    179, 184, 416–420, *417*
Centronics interface, **538–539**
Centronics port, **167–168**
certified files, 1031
CF (CompactFlash) cards, 774, **776–777,**
    776
CGA (Color/Graphics Adapter)
    characteristics of, 679
    connectors for, 180
    horizontal scan frequency for, 674
    resolution and colors with, 669
CGMS (Copy General Management
    System), 720
chaining SCSI devices, **416–420,** *417–419*
change-support lines, **528–529**
channel test units, 641
channels
    in IRC, 920–921
    in ISDN, 627
character recognition with scanners, **607**
character scanners, 173
charge-coupled devices (CCDs)
    defined, 1086
    operation of, **715–716**
    in scanners, 604
charging batteries, **888–889**
chassis, 1086
chat
    defined, 1108
    finding channels in, **921**
    operation of, **920–921**
    for technical information, **921–922**
cheater lines, 279
checkerboard memory tests, **322**
Checkit diagnostic program
    evaluation of, **228**
    for memory tests, 322
Checklinks tool, 1038
checksums
    defined, 1086
    error beeps for, 290
    for ROM, 303
chip creep, 231, 292, 306
chip inserters, 47–48, *48*
chip removers
    for keyboard keys, 651
    problems with, **48,** *48*
chip sets
    for 3D video boards, 674
    defined, 1086
    and DIMM slots, **315**

chips, 302–303
　defined, 1086
　families of, **206**
　identifying, **304**
　memory. *See* memory chips
　noise damage in, 340
　pins on, **306**, *306*
　recalls of, 303
　size of, 313
　sockets for, 131, **306–307**
　soldering and desoldering, **305**
　temperature of, 191, **303–304**
　testing, **303**
CHK files, 501
CHKDSK program
　for cross-linked clusters, **504–506**, *505*
　for FAT allocation errors, **503**, *503*
　for invalid clusters, **503**
　for invalid subdirectories, **502–503**
　for lost clusters, **499–502**
　operation of, **494–495**
　with subdirectories, 457
chloride, triboelectric value of, 205
chrominance signals, 726
circuit design, microprocessor development for, 929
CISC (complex instruction set computing)
　in Cyrix 6x86, 116
　defined, 1088
CISs (contact image sensors) in scanners, 604
cladding in fiber optic cable, 798, *798*
clarity of signals, 687
Class A certification, 1086
Class B certification, 200, 1086
clean command for laser printers, **594**
clean up piece in pipelines, 99
cleaning
　CD-ROM discs, 768
　connectors, 231
　floppy disk drive heads, **524–525**
　inkjet printers, 553–554, 557, **560**
　keyboards, 650–651
　laser printer blades, 570
　laser printer drums, **570**
　mice, **656**
　printers, 534, **594–595**
cleaning fluids, 209
cleaning pads in laser printers, 575
Clear To Send (CTS) lines
　defined, 1086
　in flow control, 620
　in RS-232 sessions, 619

CLECs (competitive local exchange carriers), 629
Click & Learn site, 909
clicks in speakers, 289
client/server networks, 789
clients
　in IRC, 921
　on networks, 790
　redirectors as, 805
ClipTray tool, 1038
clock/calendar boards, 275
clock doublers, **84–85**
clock triplers, **85–86**
clocks
　and bus speed, **146–147**
　for CPUs, **960–963**
　defined, **1086–1087**
　error beeps for, 292
　IRQ for, 263
　speed of
　　for CPUs, 83–84, **960–963**
　　defined, 1087
　　for DRAM, 316
　　in EISA bus, 150
　system, 32, **160**, **171–172**
clones, 1087
closed control systems, 364
cloudy laser printer output, **578–579**
clustering, 1087
clusters, 450, **452–454**
　bad, **490–492**
　cross-linked, **504–506**, *505*
　defined, 1087
　in directory entries, 456–458
　FAT entries for, 455–457
　in FCSI, **410**
　invalid, **503**
　lost, **499–502**, *500*, *502*
　in partitioning, **436–438**
　size of, **436–438**, 453–454
　in unerasing files, **495–498**
CLV (constant linear velocity), 1089
CM (Configuration Manager), **273–274**
CMOS battery, 171–172, 275
　connecting, 72
　holders for, 277
　identifying, 177, *177*
　in motherboard removal, 67
　replacing, **277–278**
CMOS (Complementary Metal Oxide Semiconductor) chips
　defined, 1088
　ESD damage to, **206**

setting up, **970–972**
CMOS memory
　backing up, **50–52**
　on clock/calendar chip, **171–172**
　configuring, **275–277**
　error beeps for, 290
　evolution of drive tables for, **397**
　hard disk drive problems from, **512**
　for hard drive disk type, **480**
　purpose of, **396–397**
　reading information in, **299–300**
　in XT computers, 397
CMPnet site, 909
CNET site, 909
CO (central office) for DSL, 629
coating on floppy diskettes, 522
coaxial arresters, 342
coaxial cable
　connectors for, **800–801**, *801*
　defined, 1087
　for networks, 797, *797*, 943
cobalt coating on floppy diskettes, 522
Code Page Changer tool, 1038
code requirements for network cable, 821
codecs
　in capture boards
　　for off-line compression, **742**, *743*
　　for real-time compression, **738–741**, *740*
　defined, 1087
　for fiber optic cable, 798
　security of, 698
coffee, board damage from, 209
cold boots, 1087
cold cathode fluorescent lamps (CCFLs), 604
"COLD RESET" message, 588
collisions
　defined, 1087
　repeaters for, **839–840**
colons (:), 1087
color depth
　compatibility of, **1008**, 1022
　setting, 1006, 1022
　of video cards, **952–953**
Color Display monitor, 679
Color/Graphics Adapter (CGA)
　characteristics of, 679
　connectors for, 180
　horizontal scan frequency for, 674
　resolution and colors with, 669
color monitors, 678–681

color printers
    inkjet. *See* inkjet printers
    laser, **572**
color sub-sampling compression, 740, *740*
colorkey overlay technique, 720
colors
    with CCD chips, **715–716**, *716*
    connectors for, 182
    in inkjet printers, **554–555**
    with scanner images, 605
    in TV video, **722–726**, *723–727*
    and video boards, 165, **668–672**
    in video capture, **736–737**
COM files, viruses in, 466
COM ports, 1088. *See also* serial ports
combo scanners, 602
Command AntiVirus program, 474
COMMAND.COM program, 127,
    301–302
command line, 1087
command-line arguments, 1088
command processors, 1087
command prompt, 1088
command shell, **127**
COMMDLG.DLL file, 225
commercial online services, 1120
Common Access Method (CAM) SCSI
    standard, 426
common grounds, **339–341**
common outlet line, 338–339
communication options in upgrading,
    942–944
communications parameters, 1088
communications protocols, 1088
communications systems, **614**
    cables for, **643–644**
    controllers for, **168–169**, *169*
    digital broadband, **625**
        cable broadband, **635–637**
        DSL, **629–635**
        ISDN, **627–628**
        selecting type, **625–627**
    ports for, **642**
    serial. *See* serial communications
comp newsgroups, 915
Compact Disc File System (CDFS), 756
compact discs. *See also* CD-ROM drives
    composition of, **753–754**
    defined, 1085, 1088
    loading, **757–758**
    reading, **753**
    recording, **764–765**
    viruses in, 473

CompactFlash (CF) cards, 774, **776–777**,
    776
Compaq Computer in Watchzone group,
    149
Compaq computers
    and bus speed, **147**
    setup with, 50
    static column RAM in, 120
compatibility. *See also* standards
    of BIOS, 131
    of buses, 144–146
    of CD-ROM drives, **751**, **755–757**,
        769
    of color depth, **1008**, 1022
    controllers for, **161–163**
    of Cyrix CPUs, 115
    defined, 1081, 1088
    of DVD drives, 956
    of DVD formats, 766
    of FireWire bus, 159
    of floppy disk drives, 166
    of hard disk drive hardware, **392–393**
    of hardware, **26–27**
    of integrated motherboards, **163**
    of IRQ levels, 265
    of keyboards, 648, 650
    of local buses, 150
    of MCA bus, 148
    of microprocessors, 938
    of MMX processors, 97–98
    modularity for, 76, 79
    with multiple displays, 678
    of Nx586 CPU, 116
    of PCI bus, **153**
    of proprietary PCs, **851**
    in protected mode, 134–135
    of SCSI devices, **411**, **426–427**
    in software, **27–28**
    of sound card interfaces, 694
    of sound cards, 953
    of television signals, 726
Compatibility Warning dialog box, 678
competitive local exchange carriers
    (CLECs), 629
Complementary Metal Oxide
    Semiconductor (CMOS) chips. *See also*
    CMOS memory
    defined, 1088
    ESD damage to, **206**
    setting up, **970–972**
complex instruction set computing (CISC)
    in Cyrix 6x86, 116
    defined, 1088

component video interface, 722, **727–728**,
    727
components, system information for, 1027
composite monitors, 679
composite video interface, 722, *726–727*,
    727–728
composite video signals, 182
compressed air
    for expansion boards, 196
    for flooded computers, 208
    for keyboard cleaning, 651
compression
    defined, 1088–1089
    MMX processors for, 97
    for MP3 audio files, 696
    status of, 1017
    in video capture, **738–741**
        in capture boards, **732**
        lossy and lossless, **738–741**, *740*
        off-line, **741–744**
compuhelp mailing list, 920
CompuServe online service, 922
Computer Hope site, 909
computer viruses. *See* viruses
computers
    building. *See* ultimate computer
    evolution of, **928–930**, *929*
    old. *See* old computers
computertalkshop mailing list, 920
Computing.Net site, 909
Concept virus, 467
conditioning laser printers drums, **570**
conductors in coaxial cable, 797, *797*
conduits
    for network cable, 819–820
    for Palm devices, 894
"CONFIG LANGUAGE" message, 591
CONFIG.SYS file
    CD-ROM drivers in, 764
    checking, **1032–1033**
    device drivers in, 127
    loading and executing, **301**
configuration
    backing up, **50–52**
    of cable broadband, **636**
    of DSL, **632–633**
    of expansion boards, **243**
        addresses and buffers in,
            267–269
        bus mastering in, **259**
        conflicts in, **243–248**, **270–272**
        DMA channels in, **256–259**,
            256

IRQ levels in, **260–267**
MCA, **148–149**
network interface cards,
    824–829, *826–827*
PC Cards, **269–270**
with Plug and Play, **272–280**
of LPT ports, **278–280**
method of, 33
of satellite communications, **638–639**
of SCSI devices, **410–412**
software setup for, **275–277**
of System Restore, **1037–1038**
Configuration Manager (CM), **273–274**
conflicts
8-bit vs. 16-bit boards, **279–280**
and Add New Hardware Wizard,
    998–999
with buffers, **267–269**
with CD-ROM drives, 769
DIP switches in, **247–248**
with I/O addresses, **252–254**, *253*
from integrated motherboards, 280
with IRQ levels, **264–267**
and LPT ports, 279
MSI for, 1027
with PC Card boards, **269–270**
resolving, **246–248**, **270–272**
scenarios for, **243–246**
with versions, **1033–1034**
with video capture cards, 734
connecting to modems, **1012–1013**, 1,024
connections
for scanners, **608**
speed of, 1089
connectors, 28, 35. *See also* cables
BNC, **179–180**, *179*
for CD-ROM drives, 980
Centronics, **179**, *179*
checking, **221–222**
cleaning, 231
corrosion on, 209
D, **178–179**, *178*
DIN, 180, *180*
for DSL, 632
for DVD decoder cards, 976
FireWire, 181
for home recording studios, 706
HP, **178–179**, *178*
identifying, **178–184**
for keyboards, **650–651**, *650*, 973
for LAN adapters, 885
for MIDI, 705
miniature D shell, *178*

miniature DIN, 180, *180*
miniplug, 180
for mouse, 973
for network interface cards, 792, *792*
for networks, **800–803**, *801–803*
for PC Card slots, 155–156
for ports, **983**
for power supplies, **57–58**, *58*,
    63–66, *64*, **331–335**, *332–334*
RCA jacks and plugs, 180
RJ-13 and RJ-45, **180**
for SCSI, 414, *414*
for serial communications, 615, *615*
standards for, 142
USB, 181, *181*
constant angular velocity (CAV), 1089
constant linear velocity (CLV), 1089
contact image sensors (CISs) in scanners,
    604
contacts for keyboard, **649–650**
contaminants in laser printers, **585**
Content Scrambling System (CSS), 720
contiguous memory blocks, 128
continuous diagnostic modes, 227
contrast
    accessibility options for, *995–996*,
        996, 1018, *1019*
    with video capture boards, 736
control characters, 1089
control gates in flash memory, 774–775,
    774
CONTROL.INI files, backing up, 483
control lines for printers, 168
Control Panel, **991**, *991*
    for accessibility options, **991**
    accessibility options for
        display, **995–996**, *996*
        general, **997**, *998*
        keyboard, **992–994**, *992–994*
        mouse, **996**, *997*
        sound, **994–995**, *995*
    for boot floppies, 489
    for COM ports, 267
    for date and time, **1005**, *1006*
    for display, **1006–1010**, *1006–1010*
    for hardware, **998–999**
        not found by system,
            1001–1003, *1001–1002*
        wizard for, **998–1002**, *998*
    for modems, **1010–1013**,
        1011–1013
    for programs, **1003–1005**, *1003*

installing, **1004**, *1004*
    removing, **1003–1004**
    Windows, **1004–1005**, *1004*
quick steps for, **987–990**
for sound cards, 975
for System settings, **1014–1017**
in Windows XP. *See* Windows XP
    Control Panel
control transfers with USB, 170
controllers, 22, **161**, **173**
    autoconfigure, 379
    caches for, 376
    for CD-ROM drives, **166**
    for communications, **168–169**, *169*
    for floppy disk drives, **165–166**, 523
    for hard disk drives, 29, **166–167**
        buffer addresses for, 268–269
        defined, **1103–1104**
        I/O addresses for, 251
        identifying, 177, *177*
    for isolation, **161–163**
    for laser printers, **565**
    for memory, **122**
    memory for, 132
    on motherboards, **163**
    for networks, **172**
    for printers, **167–168**, 538
    SCSI interface, 165
    for sound, **172–173**
    for tape drives, 167
    for USB ports, **540–541**
    video adapters, **163–165**, *164*
conventional memory
    and GP faults, 745
    location of, **125**
conversions
    controllers for, 162
    digital-to-analog, *164*, 165, **668**
    hexadecimal numbers, **828**,
        1051–1052
"Convert directory to file (Y/N)?" message,
    502
"Convert lost chains to files" message, 501
converters for ISDN, 628
coolant for chip testing, 304
copiers
    in all-in-one combos, 536
    noise from, 339
copper wire for networks, **793**
Coppermine chip set, 112
coprocessors, **96**
    for displays, **667–668**

error beeps for, 292
for Intel 80486, 108
IRQ for, 264
MMX, **96–98**
for Pentium 4, 114
COPY command, 507
Copy General Management System
(CGMS), 720
copy protection
and DVDs, **720–721**
and floppy disk drive speed, 528
problems with, 138
copy stands, magnetism from, 197
copying
files, 507
hard disk drives, **489**, **934**
copyright laws, 911
copyright notice, 974
copyrighted material, music files, 698
cords and lightning protection, 346–347
core voltages for CPUs, 960
corona in laser printers, 570, *571*, 572
cleaning, 578–579, **594–595**
defined, 1089
in image transfer, 574
and vertical white streaks, **577–578**
corporate PCs, features for, **861**, **864**
corrosion
from heat, 194
from liquids, **208–209**
corruption
in Registry, repairing, **1043**
with repeaters, 840
costs in computer evolution, 928
cotton, triboelectric value of, 205
counting in hexadecimal, **1049**
counts, repeater, 840
covers
keyboard, 208, 651
removing, **52–55**, *53–54*
CP/M (Control Program for
Microcomputers) operating system, 529
CPS (cycles per second), 688
CPUReview.com site, 909
CPUs (central processing units), 22,
25–27, *25*, **82–83**. *See also specific CPUs
by name*
for accelerators, 667
caches on, **92–96**
clock speed for, 83–84, **960–963**
compatibility of, 938
Cyrix, **115**

data paths for, **91–92**
development of, **929–930**, *929*
error beeps for, 290
fans on, 336
heat from, 191
for home recording studios, 706
identifying, **174–175**, *175*
installing, 2–3, *2–3*, **78**, **959**,
959–960
Intel 8088, **106**
Intel 80286, **106–107**
Intel 80386, **107–108**
Intel 80486, **108–109**
Itanium, **117–118**
in keyboards, 648
in laser printers, **566**
memory addressing by, **100–101**
microcode efficiency in, **89**
MMX, **96–98**
multipliers for, **963**, *963*
numeric coprocessors for, **96–98**
in PC selection, **852–853**
audio/video enthusiast, 863
corporate, 864
gamer, 862–863
home, 862
small business, 863
student, 862
with PCI bus, 151
Pentium challengers, **115–118**
pipelines in, **89–90**, **98–100**, 115
plugging in, **963–965**, *964–965*
removing, 66
size of, 931, *931*
slots for, **101–102**
sockets for, **101–102**, **942**, *942*
specifications for, **102–106**
speed of, 28, **83–88**, **98–100**,
108–112
type of, 28
for ultimate computer, 951
upgrading, **938**
value of, 931
and video boards, **663**
in video capture, **733–734**, 738
voltages for, **960**, *960*
word size for, **90–91**, **102–105**
crackers, 634
crash-prevention tools, limitations of, 229
crashes
defined, 1089
troubleshooting, **234–235**
CrashGuard tool, 229

CRCs (cyclical redundancy checks), 1090
Create a Restore Point option, 1036
credit card hard drives, **884**
credit card purchases, 866
cross-linked clusters
causes of, **504–506**, *505*
defined, 1089
cross-posts on newsgroups, 914
crossover cables, 802
crosstalk, **198–199**, 1089
CRTs (Cathode-Ray Tubes). *See also*
monitors
dust on, 196
magnetism from, 197
crystals, 340
CSS (Content Scrambling System), 720
Ctrl key, 1089
Ctrl+Alt+Del key combination, 1089
CTS (Clear To Send) lines
defined, 1086
in flow control, 620
in RS-232 sessions, 619
Cubase VST sequencing program,
705–706
curling of laser printer paper, 585
current in power calculations, 336
cursor, 1090
cursor-movement keys, 1090
Custom DPI Setting window, 1022
Custom Font Size window, 1007–1008,
1008
cut-through switching
defined, 1090
vs. store-and-forward, 836–837, *837*
CuteFTP client, 912
CyberNOT filtering service, 634
cycles per second (CPS), 688
cyclical redundancy checks (CRCs), 1090
cylinders in hard disk drives, 352,
355–360, *358–359*
for absolute sectors, 450–452, *450*
in disk drive geometry, 361
documenting, 51
and head skew, **373**
with IDE addressing, 378–379
INT 13 BIOS interface for, 377
in sector translation, 362
Cyrix CPUs, 22, 82, **115**
386DRU2, **109**
internal cache memory on, 96
pipelines in, 90
specifications for, 104

D

D/A (digital-to-analog) conversions, *164*, *165*, **668**

D channels, 1090

D shell connectors
identifying, **178–179**, *178*, 182
for monitors, 679
for SCSI, 418, *418*
for twisted-pair cable, 802, *802*

D value in hexadecimal numbering system, 1049

DAC (digital-to-analog) conversions, *164*, *165*, **668**

DACK line, 256

daisy chaining
with FireWire bus, 159
with SCSI, **416–420**, *417–419*
with Universal Serial Bus, 170

daisywheel printers, 534

DALnet IRC channel, 921

data areas on disks, 444, 454, *455*

data bits
defined, 1090
for serial ports, 545

data buses for hard disk drives, 354

data cables and connectors
diagrams for, **55–56**
for floppy disk drives, 63

Data Carrier Detect (DCD) lines
defined, 1090
in flow control, 620
in RS-232 sessions, 619

Data Circuit-terminating Equipment (DCE), 618–619

data compression
defined, 1090
MMX processors for, 97
for MP3 audio files, 696
in video capture, **738–741**
in capture boards, **732**
lossy and lossless, **738–741**, *740*
off-line, **741–744**

data conversions
controllers for, 162
digital-to-analog, *164*, 165, **668**
hexadecimal numbers, **828**, **1051–1052**

data dependency in 6x86, 115

"Data error reading drive" message, **506–508**, **526–527**

data input for laser printers, **569**

Data Link Control (DLC) protocol, 542

Data-Link layer devices, 838

data modes for CD-ROM, 756–757

Data Over Cable Service Interface Specification (DOCSIS), 635–637

data paths, **91–92**
for buses, **142–143**
for CardBus, 158
for EISA bus, 150
in Intel 80386, 107
for MCA bus, 148
for PC Card bus, 157
for PCI bus, 152
for RDRAM, 317

data protection. *See also* viruses
backups for, **479–480**, **485–489**
boot floppies for, **489–490**
firewalls for, 844
media tests for, **490–492**

data rate in off-line video compression, **743–744**

data recovery. *See* recovering

Data Set Ready (DSR) lines
defined, 1091
in flow control, 620
in RS-232 sessions, 619

Data Terminal Equipment (DTE), 618–619

Data Terminal Ready (DTR) lines
in laser printers, 569
in RS-232 sessions, 619

data transfer methods with USB, 170

data transfer rates
for CD-ROM drives, **758–759**
for hard disk drives, 365
caches for, **375–376**
defined, 352
external transfer rate dependencies in, **375**
internal, **368**
optimizing, **374–376**
in ultimate computer, 955
and interleave factor, **368–373**
for network interface cards, **792–793**
of SCSI systems, 408–409

date codes on chips, 304

Date/Time Properties window, 1005, *1006*, 1021

dates
in BIOS, 970–971
in chip codes, 304
quick steps for, **989**
setting, **1005**, *1006*, **1021**

system clock/calendar for, **171–172**
time zones in, 1005, 1021

DATs (Digital Audio Tapes)
defined, **1092–1093**
with SCSI, 407, 694

daughterboards, 101

Dazzle Digital Video Creator, 731

DB connectors, 1091

DB9 connectors, *35*, 178
defined, 1091
diagrams for, 620, *621–622*
for RS-232, 618
for video adapters, *181*, 182

DB15 connectors, 182

DB25 connectors, *35*
defined, 1091
diagrams for, 620, *621*
for ports, *181*, 182, 615, *615*
for RS-232, 618

DB37 connectors, 1091

DBRs (DOS Boot Records)
loading, **301–302**
for logical drives, 458–459, *459*
purpose of, **454**

DBS (direct broadcast satellite) systems, 721

DC bias in laser printers, 573

DC power supplies for laser printers, **586**

DCD (Data Carrier Detect) lines
defined, 1090
in flow control, 620
in RS-232 sessions, 619

DCE (Data Circuit-terminating Equipment), 618–619

DDR (double data rate) SDRAM, 319
defined, 1094
development of, 123
for video, 665

dead fans, 192

dead hard disk drives, resurrecting, **508**
booting from floppy disks for, 509
checking cables, 512
checking CMOS, **512**
data recovery services for, **514–515**
modern drives, **513**
priorities in, **509**
reading MBR in, **509–513**
recovering partition table in, **513–514**
temperature problems, 512
tracing failures in, **509**, *510*

dead machines, troubleshooting, **288**
boot process in, **295–302**, *296*

expansion boards, **292–293**
power supplies, **288–289**
DEBUG program, **480–482**
decay in sound waves, *691*, 692
decibels, 1091
decimal numbering system, 250, 1048,
  1051–1052, 1091
decode instructions, 90
decode piece in pipelines, 99
decoders for DVD drives, 956
dedicated servo positioning, 365
Default Printer tool, 1038
Defrag utility
  lost data from, **507**
  for video capture, 737
defragmentation, 1091
defragmenters, 1091
Deja.com site, 918
delayed writes, 376
delays with repeaters, 840
Dell Computer setup, 50
Dell Inspiron 7500 computer, 79
delta encoding technique, **739**
demagnetizing floppy drive heads, 525
demand paging, 1091
demodulation, 1091
denial-of-service (DoS) attacks, **843**
density, hard disk drive, 368
dependencies
  in 6x86, 115
  in pipelines, 98–99
Dependency Walker tool, 1038
Deschutes chip, 87
Deskpro 286/12, **147**
desktop case style
  description, 950
  disassembling, **52–54**, *53–54*
Desktop Manager Interface (DMI),
  1091–1092
desktop video, 1092
desoldering chips, **305**
developing cylinders in laser printers, 573,
  574
device conflicts. *See* conflicts
device dependence, 1092
device drivers. *See* drivers
device independence, 1092
Device Manager, **999–1000**, *999*,
  1019–1020
  for COM ports, 267
  for I/O addresses, 252
  for keyboards, 652
  for mice, 657

for network interface cards, 825–827,
  826–827
organization of, **1014–1016**, *1014*
for removing devices, 247
in Windows XP, 1025
devices, 1092
DHCP (Dynamic Host Configuration
  Protocol), 813
diagnostic programs, **226**
  defined, 1092
  for expansion boards, 272
  features in, **226–228**
  for laser printers, **587**
  for modems, **1013**, *1013*, 1025
  third-party, **228–229**
  Windows, **229–230**. *See also* Windows
    utilities
diagnostic startups, 1032, *1032*
Diagnostics tab, **1013**, *1013*, 1025
diagonal cutters, 46, *46*
diagrams
  for DIP switches, 57, *57*
  using documentation with, **72–73**
  for expansion boards, **56–57**
  for floppy disk drives, 63
  for jumpers, 57
  for motherboards, **57–58**, 66, *67*
  for notebooks, 876
  for power connectors, 64
  for power switches, 66
  for ribbon cables, **55–56**
  in troubleshooting, **216–217**
Dialing Properties dialog box, **1012**, *1012*
Dialing Rules tab, 1023, *1024*
dialing with modems, **1012**, *1012*, 1023,
  1024
Diamond Multimedia MP3 players, 701
dictionaries in VCE, 739
dielectrics in coaxial cable, 797, *797*
differential backups, 488, 1092
differential SCSI, 404, 1092
digests in mailing lists, 919
DigiDrive product, 784
Digital Audio Tapes (DATs)
  defined, 1092–1093
  with SCSI, 407, 694
digital broadband communications, 625
  cable broadband, **635–637**
  DSL, **629–635**
  ISDN, **627–628**
  selecting type, **625–627**
  wireless, **639–640**
digital camcorders, 719

digital cameras
  flash memory for, 775
  serial ports for, 169
  still cameras, **721**
  Universal Serial Bus for, 170
  for video capture, **715–716**
digital devices, 1092
digital interface for capture boards, **731**
digital monitors, **675–676**
Digital Signal Processing (DSP), 1093
digital sound, **701–702**
Digital Subscriber Line (DSL), 626,
  628–629
  configuring, **632 633**
  defined, 1093
  installing, **631–633**
  operation of, **629**
  security for, **634–635**
  speed and distance in, **631**
  types of, **629–630**
digital temperature probes, 194, 304
digital thermometers, 194
digital-to-analog (D/A) conversions, *164*,
  165, **668**
digital video capture and transfer, **735–736**
Digital Video Disk drives. *See* DVD (Digital
    Video Disk) drives
digital video disk-eraseable (DVD-E), 1093
digital video disk-recordable (DVD-R),
  1093
digital video disk-ROM (DVD-ROM)
  defined, 1093
  vs. DVD-video, 752
  recordable, **752**
Digital8 format, 717–719
digitizing in audio, 688
DIMMs (Dual In-line Memory Modules),
  119, *120*, **313–314**
  and chip sets, **315**
  defined, 1095
  installing, **966**
  for notebooks, 877
  for SDRAM, 317–318
  in upgrading, 940, *941*
DIN plugs and connectors
  identifying, 180
  for keyboards, *650*, 651, 940
  for mouse, 940
  for parallel ports, 182
diodes, replacing, 305
DIP (Dual In-line Packages)
  for CPUs, 106, *107*
  defined, 1095

extractors for, **48**, *48*
for memory, 119
DIP memory chips, **313**
DIP switches. *See also* jumpers
    defined, 1093
    diagrams for, 57, *57*
    for I/O addresses, 254
    labeling of, **247–248**
    on motherboards, 275
    for printers, 544
    for resource conflicts, **244**, *245*, *247*
    for ROM addresses, 268
DirecDuo system, 637
direct broadcast satellite (DBS) systems, 721
Direct Cable Connection utility, 892
direct-drive TTL monitors, 679
direct-mapped caches, 1084
Direct Memory Access. *See* DMA (Direct Memory Access) channels
Direct-to-Drum laser printing method, 572
Direct3D test, 1028
DirectDraw test, 1027
DirectMusic test, 1029
directories
    defined, 1093–1094
    entries in, 449
    FAT for, **454–457**, *455–456*
    Internet, **907–908**
    invalid, **502–503**
    phantom, **528–529**
directory bits, 455
DirectPlay test, 1029
DirectSound test, 1029
DirectSound3D API, 702
DirectX API, 674
DirectX Diagnostics Tool, **1027–1029**, *1028*
DirectX drivers, 1010
DIRECWAY system, **637–638**
Disable System Restore option, 1037
disabling
    BIOS for SCSI, **428**
    motherboard circuitry, 952
    System Restore, **1037–1038**
disassembly, **38**
    computer cover removal, **52–55**, *53–54*
    configuration backups in, **50–52**
    diagrams for, **55–58**
    disk drive removal, **60–63**
    expansion board removal, **59–60**, *59–60*

keyboards, **653–654**
laser printers, 576, *577*
monitor removal in, 52
motherboard removal, **66–68**, *67–68*
necessity of, **49**
notebooks, **881–882**
parts storage in, **49–50**
power supply removal, **63–66**, *64–65*
quick steps for, **39–41**
workspace for, 49
disconnects in SCSI-2, 406
disk caches, 1094
disk controllers
    defined, 1094
    for hard disk drives. *See* hard disk drives
Disk Doctor utility, 1040
disk drives. *See also* CD-ROM drives; floppy disk drives; hard disk drives
    cables for, **62–63**, *62*
    defined, 1094
    geometry in, **361**
    power supplies and connectors for, 62–63, *62*
    removing, **60–63**, *61–62*, **526**
    screws for, **61**
    Zone Bit Recording in, **360–361**, 363
Disk Manager program, 398, 443, 445
disk optimizers, 1094
disk quotas, 461
DISKCOPY command, 507
DiskEdit program, 510
DiskOnKey product, 781
disks. *See also* CD-ROM drives; disk drives; floppy disk drives; floppy diskettes; hard disk drives
    absolute and DOS sectors on, **450–452**
    CD-ROM. *See* compact discs
    clusters on, **452–454**
    DBR on, **454**
    FAT on, **454–457**, *455–456*
    hardware structure of, **355–360**, *356–359*
    logical drive structure of, **458–459**, *458–459*
    subdirectories on, **457–458**
DISKTOOL utility, 51
display chips, **667–668**
Display Properties window, 1006–1007, *1006*, **1022–1023**
Display tab, 995, *995*, 1018

DisplayMate diagnostic program, **229**
displays. *See* monitors; video and video boards
distance
    in DSL, **631**
    in ESD, 206
distorted laser printer images, 593
dithering
    with capture boards, 732
    with scanner images, 611
DIV operator, 451
DIX (DEC-Intel-Xerox) connectors, 182
DLC (Data Link Control) protocol, 542
DLLs (dynamic link libraries)
    defined, 1095
    operation of, **223–225**
    viruses in, 466
DM manufacturer code, 304
DMA (Direct Memory Access) channels, **34**
    bus lines for, **143–144**
    and bus mastering, **149**
    for CD-ROM drives, 769
    defined, 1093
    in diagnostic programs, **227**
    in EISA bus, 150
    error beeps for, 290–291
    for hard disk drives, 353
    for network interface cards, 824, **828–829**
    operation of, **256–258**, *256*
    with PC Card bus, 157
    vs. PIO, **382**
    with Plug and Play, 273
    for SCSI adapters, 413
    for sound cards, 693
    using, **258–259**
DMA controllers, I/O addresses for, 251
DMI (Desktop Manager Interface), 1091–1092
DMV virus, 467
DNS (Domain Name Service) servers, 812
DNS IP numbers, 633
docking stations, 1094
DOCSIS (Data Over Cable Service Interface Specification), 635–637
documentation
    using diagrams with, **72–73**
    for network cable, 821
    online sources of, **901**
    for SETUP program access, 50
    for switch settings, 247–248
    in troubleshooting, **215**, **217**

Dolby Digital processors, 702
Domain Name Service (DNS) servers, 812
DoS (denial-of-service) attacks, **843**
DOS (Disk Operating System) and disks,
 448–450
   absolute and DOS sectors, **450–452**
   clusters, **452–454**
   DBR, **454**
   disk errors, **490–492**, *491*
   FAT, **454–457**, *455–456*
   FAT32, **460**
   logical drive structure, **458–459**, *459*
   NTFS, **461–462**
   subdirectories, **457–458**
DOS Boot Records (DBRs)
   loading, **301–302**
   for logical drives, 458–459, *459*
   purpose of, **454**
DOS extenders, 135
DOS partitions, **438–443**, *439–441*
DOS sectors, **450–452**
dot-matrix printers, **534–535**
dot pitch
   for LCD displays, 676
   for monitors, **675**
dotted quad format, 813
double data rate (DDR) SDRAM, **319**
   defined, 1094
   development of, 123
   for video, 665
double-density floppy diskettes, 522
double-sided printing, 581
double slashes (//), 1094
doubler chips, **84–85**
downloading files
   defined, 1095
   FTP sites for, **912–913**
   patches, drivers, and utilities, **911**
downstream rates
   in cable broadband, 635
   in DSL, 630
   in satellite communications, 637
DPTs (Drive Parameter Tables), 379
Dr. Watson tool, *229*, **1031**
draft mode with inkjet printers, 556
DRAM (Dynamic RAM), **120–121**,
 315–317
   defined, 1095
   ECC, **318**
   FPM and EDO, **317**
   interleaving, 315, **319**
   refreshing, 257

SDRAM, **317–319**
   vs. SRAM, **93**
drawer-type cases, **67**
DREQ line, 256
drive cards, **884**
Drive Copy program, 881
"Drive failure, Hard disk failure" message,
   511
drive letters
   defined, 1095
   for networks, 804
   for partitions, **442**
drive motors, heat from, 191
Drive Parameter Tables (DPTs), 379
drive tables, CMOS, **397**
Drive Up program, 443, 445
DriveCopy program, 934
DriveImage software, **489**
DriverGuide.com site, 907, 909
drivers
   for adapters, *1008*, **1009**, 1022
   for CD-ROM drives, **764**, 769
   for compatibility, **27–28**
   defined, 1092
   for FireWire bus, 159
   for flash memory, **782–783**
   for hard disk drives, 398
   for inkjet printers, 556, 558
   on Internet and online services, **902**,
    911, **1002–1003**
   manufacturer Web sites for, 907
   memory for, **127**
   for network cards, **807–808**,
    823–824, *823*
   for partitioning hard disk drives,
    442–443
   for Plug and Play, 274
   problems with, **223–225**
   for scanners, **605**, 609
   for SCSI, **412**, **426–427**, *426*
   for super VGA boards, 164
   version conflicts for, **1033–1034**
   for video, 681
Drivers.com site, 907, 909
drives. *See* CD-ROM drives; disk drives;
   floppy disk drives; hard disk drives
dropped frames in video capture, 738
drum scanners, 603
drums in laser printers, 569, *569*
   cleaning, **570**
   conditioning, **570**, *571*
   writing on, **570–572**, *571*
DRV files, viruses in, 466

DSL (Digital Subscriber Line), 626,
 628–629
   configuring, **632–633**
   defined, 1093
   installing, **631–633**
   operation of, **629**
   security for, **634–635**
   speed and distance in, **631**
   types of, **629–630**
DSL access multiplexers (DSLAMs), 629
DSP (Digital Signal Processing), 1093
DSR (Data Set Ready) lines
   defined, 1091
   in flow control, 620
   in RS-232 sessions, 619
DTE (Data Terminal Equipment),
 618–619
DTR (Data Terminal Ready) lines
   in laser printers, 569
   in RS-232 sessions, 619
dual-booting, 435
dual displays, **677–678**
Dual In-line Memory Modules (DIMMs),
   119, *120*, **313–314**
   and chip sets, **315**
   defined, 1095
   installing, **966**
   for notebooks, 877
   for SDRAM, 317–318
   in upgrading, 940, *941*
Dual In-line Packages (DIP). *See also* DIP
   switches
   for CPUs, 106, *107*
   defined, 1095
   extractors for, **48**, *48*
   for memory, 119
dual-layer DVD discs, 754
dual-ported memory chips, **664–665**
dumb terminals, 173
duplex
   defined, 1095
   for MIDI, 705
Duron CPU, 852
   characteristics of, **117**
   internal cache memory on, 96
dust
   covers for, 196
   floppy disk drive damage from, 525
   handling, **196**
duty cycles, **195**
DVD (Digital Video Disk) drives, 30, **166**
   for backups, 487
   decoder cards for, **976**, *977*

defined, 1093
for digital audio, 702
identifying, 174
installing, 18–19, *18–19*, **749**,
    972–973, *973*, **980**
for MP3 files, 699
for notebook/laptop computers, **885**
in PC selection, **855**
    audio/video enthusiast, 863
    gamer, 863
    home, 862
    road warriors, 865
troubleshooting, **769–770**
types of, **751–752**
for ultimate computer, **956**
for video capture, **720–721**
DVD discs
    composition of, **754**
    formats for, **766–767**
    producing, **767–768**
    recording, **765–768**
DVD-E (digital video disk-eraseable), 1093
DVD-R (digital video disk-recordable),
    766, 1093
DVD-RAM format, **766**
DVD recorders, 30
DVD-ROM (digital video disk-ROM), 1093
    defined, 1093
    vs. DVD-video, 752
    recordable, **752**
DVD-RW format, **766–767**
DVD+RW format, **767**
DVD-video, 752
Dvorak keyboard, 654
dynamic execution, 110–111
Dynamic Host Configuration Protocol
    (DHCP), 813
dynamic IP addresses, 812–813
dynamic link libraries (DLLs)
    defined, 1095
    operation of, **223–225**
    viruses in, 466
dynamic linking, 224–225
Dynamic RAM (DRAM), **120–121**,
    315–317
    defined, 1095
    ECC, **318**
    FPM and EDO, **317**
    interleaving, 315, **319**
    refreshing, 257
    SDRAM, **317–319**
    vs. SRAM, **93**

E

e-business, 118
e-mail
    defined, 1108
    firewalls for, 843
    LANs for, **791**
    mailing lists, **919–920**
    viruses in, **468**, 472
E (exa-) prefix, 1098
E value in hexadecimal numbering system,
    1049
E70 monitors, 676–677
EarthWeb site, 910
EasyDisk product, 781
EAX extensions for 3D audio, 702
EB (exabytes), 1098
"EC LOAD" message, 591
ECC (Error Correcting Codes)
    for CD-ROM, 756
    and disk errors, 491–492
    in hard disk drives, 353
    operation of, 370, *370–371*,
        373–374
ECC (Error Correction Code) memory,
    124
    evaluating, **318**
    setting up, 972
ECHS (Extended CHS) mode, 362–363
eClassical site, 699
ECP ports (enhanced capabilities ports),
    168
    characteristics of, 538–539
    defined, 1098
EDC (Error Detection Code), 756
edge connectors
    cleaning, 231
    connecting, **69–70**, *70*
Edit Input/Output Range dialog box,
    1015, *1016*
Edit Value window, 1044
editing
    Registry, **1043–1044**, *1044*
    scanner images, **611**
EDO (Extended Data Out) memory
    defined, 1096
    development of, 120
    vs. FPM, **317**
EDPTs (Enhanced Drive Parameter Tables),
    380
eDualHead feature, 677
EEPROM (electrically erasable
    programmable read only memory). *See*
    flash memory

efficiency
    in microcode, **89**
    pipelines for, **89–90**
efficient partitions, **436–438**
EFnet IRC channel, 921
EGA (Enhanced Graphics Adapter), 164
    buffer addresses for, 269, 665
    characteristics of, 680
    connectors for, *181*
    horizontal scan frequency for, 674
    monitors for, 679
    resolution and colors with, 669
EIA (Electronics Industry Association),
    cable grading by, **795–796**
EIDE (Enhanced Integrated Drive
    Electronics) disk interface, 166–167
    data transfer rates in, 374–375
    defined, 1096
    and Fast ATA-2, **383–384**
    popularity of, 27
    ROM on, 268
EISA (Extended Industry Standard
    Architecture) bus, **149–150**
    bus mastering on, 259
    defined, 1098
    description of, 354
    DMA controllers on, 257
    setting up, 276
eJay MP3 Station Plus MP3 players, 700
electric screwdrivers, 43
electrically erasable programmable read only
    memory (EEPROM). *See* flash memory
electro magnetic pulses (EMPs), 206
electromagnetic interference (EMI)
    crosstalk, **198–199**
    defined, 1096
    RFI, **199–201**
electromagnetism, **197–198**
    EMI, **198–201**
    ESD, **204–207**
    power noise, **201–204**
electronic mail (e-mail)
    defined, 1108
    firewalls for, 843
    LANs for, **791**
    mailing lists, **919–920**
    viruses in, **468**, 472
Electronics Industry Association (EIA),
    cable grading by, **795–796**
electrostatic charges, 1096
electrostatic discharge (ESD)
    anti-static wrist straps for, **44**
    causes of, **204–206**

damage from, **206**
defined, 1096
from desoldering, 305
with memory chips, 321, 323
preventing, **206–207**
in workspace, 49
ELF (extremely low-frequency) emissions, 1098
Elvis in laser printers, 596–597
embedded servo positioning, 364–365
emergency boot floppies, **489–490**
EMI (electromagnetic interference)
crosstalk, **198–199**
defined, 1096
RFI, **199–201**
EMPs (electro magnetic pulses), 206
EMS (Expanded Memory Standard)
development of, **138**
operation of, **138–140**
emulation
printer, **543–544**, 1127
terminal, 1135
emulation boards and programs, **173**
EMusic site, 699
encoding, 1096
encryption in NTFS, 461
End Of File (EOF) FAT entries, 456
energy, 340
"ENGINE TEST" message, 588
engineers, 929
enhanced capabilities ports (ECP ports), 168
characteristics of, 538–539
defined, 1098
Enhanced Color Display monitor, 679
Enhanced Drive Parameter Tables (EDPTs), 380
Enhanced Graphics Adapter (EGA), 164
buffer addresses for, 269, 665
characteristics of, 680
connectors for, *181*
horizontal scan frequency for, 674
monitors for, 679
resolution and colors with, 669
Enhanced Integrated Drive Electronics (EIDE) disk interface, 166–167
data transfer rates in, 374–375
defined, 1096
and Fast ATA-2, **383–384**
popularity of, *27*
ROM on, 268
enhanced keyboard, 648

enhanced parallel ports (EPP ports), 168
characteristics of, 538
defined, 1096
ENQ/ACK flow control, 620
envelopes with laser printers, 576
environmental considerations
for laser printers, **583–584**
for satellite communications, 638
EOF (End Of File) FAT entries, 456
EPP ports (enhanced parallel ports), 168
characteristics of, 538
defined, 1096
EPROM (erasable programmable read-only memory)
for 4004 microprocessor, 930
programmers for, 130
Epson America, 149
EPTs (extended partition tables), 459, *459*
erasable programmable read-only memory (EPROM)
for 4004 microprocessor, 930
programmers for, 130
erase lamps in laser printers, 570
erased files, recovering, **495–498**, *496*
error-checking in TCP/IP, 811
Error Correcting Codes (ECC)
for CD-ROM, 756
and disk errors, 491–492
in hard disk drives, 353
operation of, 370, *370–371*, **373–374**
Error Correction Code (ECC) memory, **124**
evaluating, **318**
setting up, 972
error detection and correction, 1097
Error Detection Code (EDC), 756
error handling, 1097
error messages
defined, 1097
for inkjet printers, **559–560**
for laser printers, **587–592**
list of. *See* messages
"ERROR" messages, 589–590
error rate, 1097
errors, 1096–1097
false messages, **321–322**
on hard disk drives, **444**
with SCSI, **416**
"Errors found. F parameter not specified" message, 501
"ERRORUNIT" message, 590

ESD (electrostatic discharge)
anti-static wrist straps for, **44**
causes of, **204–206**
damage from, **206**
defined, 1096
from desoldering, 305
with memory chips, 321, 323
preventing, **206–207**
in workspace, 49
Ethernet addresses, 1097–1098
Ethernet cards and networks, 172
conflicts with, **252–254**, *253*, **270–272**
connectors for, 180, 182, *183*
defined, 1097
in Dell Inspiron 7500 computers, 79
for homes, **815–816**, **943**
I/O addresses for, 251
memory for, 132
network interface cards for, 792
for offices, **814**
PC Cards, 270
for ultimate computer, 956
UTP cable in, 795
Ethernet connections for DSL, 633
Ethernet packets, 1098
EtherTalk protocol, 542
etiquette
defined, 1117
in newsgroups, **916**
even parity
defined, 1121
for serial ports, 545
event logging
setting up, 972
in SNMP, 831
events, sounds for, 975
exa- (E) prefix, 1098
exabytes (EB), 1098
Excel8_Extras virus, 470
EXE files, viruses in, 466
execute piece in pipelines, 99
execution
dynamic, 110–111
of instructions, 90
execution trace caches, 114
exit trays in inkjet printers, **551**
expanded memory, 126, **138–140**, *139*
Expanded Memory Standard (EMS)
development of, **138**
operation of, **138–140**
expansion boards
8-bit vs. 16-bit, **279–280**

Add New Hardware Wizard for,
   998–1002, *998*, **1019–1020**
addresses for, **248–255**, **267–269**
attaching, **979–980**, *979*
buffers for, **267–269**
configuring. *See* configuration
conflicts with, **243–248**, **270–272**
connecting, **69–70**, *70*
for controllers, **163**
diagrams for, **56–57**
DMA channels for, **256–259**, *256*
drivers for, **1002–1003**
failures in, **292–293**
fixing vs. repairing, **294–295**
handling, 71
identifying, **59–60**, *60*, **178–184**
installing, **240–242**
IRQ levels for, **260–267**
for MCA, **148–149**
memory, 147, 150
not found by system, **1001–1003**,
   1001–1002, **1020**
PC Card board setup, **269–270**
with Plug and Play, **272–280**
quick steps for, **987–988**
removing, **59–60**, *59–60*
repairing, **307**
      chip insertion and removal,
         306–307
      chip testing, **303–304**
      soldering and desoldering, **305**
ROM on, **298**
slots for. *See* expansion slots
speed of, 146
swapping, 288
testing, **272**
troubleshooting, **230–231**, **280–281**,
   284–288, **292–293**
video. *See* video and video boards
expansion buses, 354
expansion chassis, 251
expansion I/O ports in laser printers, 566
expansion slots, **25–26**
      buses for, **141–142**, *145–146*
      for CPUs, **101–102**
      for generic computers, 850
      identifying, 176, *176*
      number of, 33
      for PC Card bus, 157
      RFI from, 200
      speed of, 148
      for ultimate computer, 951
      in upgrading, **940–942**, *941*

ExpertCity.com site, 910
Experts Exchange site, 910
Extend My Windows Desktop Onto This
   Monitor option, 678
extended capabilities ports (ECPs)
      characteristics of, **538–539**
      defined, **1098**
Extended CHS (ECHS) mode, **362–363**
Extended Data Out (EDO) memory
      defined, **1096**
      development of, 120
      vs. FPM, **317**
extended DOS partitions, **438–441**
Extended Graphics Array (XGA)
      characteristics of, **670–672**, 680
      video RAM for, **666**
Extended Industry Standard Architecture
   (EISA) bus, **149–150**
      bus mastering on, 259
      defined, **1098**
      description of, 354
      DMA controllers on, 257
      setting up, 276
extended memory, 126
      operation of, **133–138**, *136*
      for video, 666
extended partition tables (EPTs), 459, *459*
extenders
      BIOS, 880
      DOS, 135
      parallel port, 543
      vs. repeaters, **840**
extensions in directory entries, **455–457**
external cache, 93
external CD-ROM drives, **758**
external data transfer rates for NICs,
   792–793
external hard disks, 880
external modems, **622**, 943, 954, *955*
external network numbers, 810, *810*
external SCSI devices, sample setup with,
   424–425, *424–425*
external SCSI terminators, **421–423**, *422*
external tape drives, 173, 486
external transfer rate dependencies, **375**
Extra Hands Work Station, 305
extra high density floppy diskettes, 522
Extract One File From Installation Disk
   option, 1031
extractors, **46–48**, *47–48*, 66
extremely low-frequency (ELF) emissions,
   1098

EZ Drive program, 443, 445
EZ-SCSI system, 427

F

/F option for CHKDSK, 501
F-Secure Anti-Virus, 474
F-Secure site, **474–475**
F value in hexadecimal numbering system,
   1049
fabrics in FCSI, 410
fading, **1098**
fall back technique, **1098**
fans, *35*
      on CPUs, 336
      dead, **192**
      failures in, 335
      importance of, **190–191**
      for Pentium II CPU, 111, *111*
      for power supplies, 336
      startup problems in, **289**
FAQs (Frequently Asked Questions), **901**,
   914
far-end crosstalk (FEXT), **1098**
Fast ATA-2, **383–384**
Fast Ethernet, **1098**
Fast IR extension, **1098**
Fast Page Mode memory, 120
Fast SCSI interface, 407, 413, **1099**
Fast-Wide SCSI interface, 407, 413, **1099**
FASTDISK driver, 380
FAT (File Allocation Table), **436–438**,
   449–450, **454–457**, *455–456*
      allocation errors in, **503**, *503*
      cross-linked clusters in, **504–506**, *505*
      damaged, **494–495**
      defined, **1100**
      entries in, **495–496**, *495–496*
      erased files in, **495–498**, *496*
      in formatting, **444**
      invalid clusters in, **503**
      lost clusters in, **500–501**, *500*, *502*
      recovering, 499
      for subdirectories, **457–458**
FAT16 file system
      cluster size in, **436–438**
      defined, **1099**
FAT32 Conversion Information tool, 1038
FAT32 file system, **460**
      cluster size in, **436–438**
      defined, **1099**
fault tolerance in Pentium, **110**
fax modems, **1099**

faxback services, **898**
faxes in all-in-one combos, 536
FC-AL (Fibre Channel Arbitrated Loop), 410
"FC" message, 592
FCBS statements, executing, 301
FCC (Federal Communications Commission) certification, **199–200**
    Class A, 1086
    Class B, 200, 1086
    defined, 1099
FCSI (Fibre Channel System Initiative), **410**
FDDI (Fiber Distributed Data Interface), 1099–1100
FDISK program
    for MBR, 300, 510
    for partitioning drives, 434, **438–441**, *439–441*
FDM (Frequency Division Multiplexing), 800
FDX (full-duplex)
    defined, 1102
    for MIDI, 705
"FE CARTRIDGE" message, 592
feature connectors
    with capture boards, 732
    for coprocessors, 667
Federal Communications Commission (FCC) certification, **199–200**
    Class A, 1086
    Class B, 200, 1086
    defined, 1099
feed guide assemblies in laser printers, **584–585**, 595
feed rollers in laser printers, 584–585
female connectors, 1099
fetch instructions, 90
FEXT (far-end crosstalk), 1098
Fiber Distributed Data Interface (FDDI), 1099–1100
fiber optic cable
    benefits of, 199
    connectors for, **802–803**, *803*
    defined, 1100
    for networks, 793, **798–799**, *798*
        multimode, **798–799**, *799*
        single-mode, **798–799**
Fibre Channel Arbitrated Loop (FC-AL), 410
Fibre Channel networks, 799
Fibre Channel System Initiative (FCSI), **410**

File Allocation Table (FAT), 436–438, 449–450, **454–457**, *455–456*
    allocation errors in, **503**, *503*
    cross-linked clusters in, **504–506**, *505*
    damaged, **494–495**
    defined, 1100
    entries in, **495–496**, *495–496*
    erased files in, **495–498**, *496*
    in formatting, **444**
    invalid clusters in, **503**
    lost clusters in, **500–501**, *500, 502*
    recovering, 499
    for subdirectories, **457–458**
file compression, 1100. *See also* data compression
"File creation error" message, 501
file format, 1100
file fragmentation, 1100
file infectors
    characteristics of, **465–466**
    defined, 1101
file sharing with DSL, **634**
file systems, status of, 1017
file transfer protocol (FTP)
    defined, 1100–1101
    sites, **912–913**
FILE0000.CHK files, 501
FileCopy program, 881, 934
filenames
    defined, 1101
    in directory entries, 455–457
files
    defined, 1100
    fragmented, **492–494**, *492–493*
    read-only, 1128
    recovering, **495–498**, *496*
    saving, **498**
    sharing, **634**
    size of, 456, 503
    synchronizing, **892–894**
FILES statements, executing, 301
FileWise tool, 1038
FilterKeys option, **992–994**, *993*, 1017
filters, packet, **845**
finding
    IRC channels, **921**
    mailing lists, **919–920**
    newsgroups, **916–918**
    text on disks, 498
    Web sites, **906–908**
fire code requirements for network cable, 821
fire hazards, 66

firewalls, 204, **843–845**
FireWire bus
    for capture boards, **731**
    for CD-ROMs, **762**
    connectors for, 181
    defined, 31
    description of, 355
    development of, **159–160**
    installing hard disk drives for, **384–385**
    for ultimate computer, 957
    for video capture, 722, **728–729**
firmware, 1101
First Aid tool, 229
fixed disk drives. *See* hard disk drives
fixed wireless technology, 639
flash memory, **772**
    benefits of, **131–132**
    capacity of, **784**
    CompactFlash cards, **776–777**, *776*
    connecting, **773**
    cost of, **776**
    defined, 1101
    drivers for, **782–783**
    formatting, **783–784**
    memory sticks, **778**, *778*
    MultiMediaCards, **778–779**, *779*
    multiple devices, **784**
    non-computer uses, **782**
    operation of, **774–775**, *774*
    on PC Cards, 155, **781**
    with Plug and Play, 273
    recognizing, **783**
    Secure Digital Cards, **779**, *780*
    selecting, **781**
    for setup information, 278
    SmartMedia cards, **777–778**, *777*
    storing data in, **774–775**, *774*
    USB drives, **780–781**, *780*
Flash USBDrive, 781
flashable ROM, 303
FlashDio product, 781
flashlights, 47
flat-panel displays
    benefits of, **675–676**
    defined, 1101
flat-screen displays, **855–856**
flatbed scanners, **601–602**, *602*
flexible flashlights, 47
flicker, **672–673**
floating gates, **774–775**, *774*
floating-point coprocessors, **96**
    error beeps for, 292

I/O addresses for, 251
for Intel 80486, 108
IRQ for, 264
MMX, **96–98**
for Pentium 4, 114
flooding, 208
floppy disk drives, 33, **518**, **523**
cables for, 63, **523–524**, *524*,
526–527, 968, *969*
change line support in, **528–529**
cleaning heads on, **524–525**
controllers for, **165–166**, 251–252,
523, **938–939**, *939*
dust in, 196
environmental factors with, **525**
future of, **521**
in generic computers, 850
heat from, 191
history of, **520–521**
I/O addresses for, 251–252
identifying, 174
installing, 12–13, *12–13*, **526**,
968–969, *969*, 981
interleave factor for, **369**, *369*
IRQs for, 263
maintaining, **524–525**
motors in, 195
in notebooks, 892
in PC selection, **855**
in Pentium computers, 932
power supplies and connectors for,
334
removing, **526**
replacing, **519**
rotation speed of, **528**
troubleshooting, 294, **526–530**
for ultimate computer, 955
in XT computers, 523
floppy diskettes, **522–523**, *522*
backing up hard drives to, 485
boot floppies, **489–490**
booting from, 509
cluster sizes on, 453–454
hardware structure of, **355–360**,
356–359
and magnetism, **197–198**
protecting, **525**
reading, **526–527**
flow control, **618–620**, 1101
fluorescent lights, crosstalk from, 199
FM (frequency modulation) synthesis
defined, 1101
process of, **691–692**, *691*

FM synthesis interface, I/O addresses for,
251
"FONT PRINTOUT" message, 588
fonts
for laser printers, **580**
setting, **1007–1008**, *1007–1008*,
1022
footprints, 1101
forced perfect termination, 1101
forceps, 46
form factors for power supplies, **330–335**,
332–334
format conversions, controllers for, 162
format problems with inkjet printers, **558**
FORMAT program
for formatting, **444**
recovering from, **499**
formatting
CD-RW disks, 754
defined, 1101
flash memory cards, **783–784**
hard disk drives, **432**
bad areas in, **444**
low-level, **434**, **490–492**
process for, **444**
quick steps in, **433**
third-party tools for, **445**
troubleshooting, **445**
recovering data from, **499**
forward error correction, 1101
four-layer boards, 294, 305
four-wire circuits, 1102
Fourier decompositions, 686
Fowler-Nordheim tunneling process, 775
FPM DRAM, **317**
fps (frames per second)
defined, 1102
for display, 132
fragmented files, **492–494**, *492–493*
fragmented memory, 128
frame buffer chips, **667**
frame captures, **737–738**
frame rates of video cards, 953
frames
defined, 1102
in delta encoding, 739
memory for, **132–133**
in off-line compression, **743**, *743*
removable, 949, *949*
in video capture, **737**, *737*
frames per second (fps)
defined, 1102
for display, 132

framing with switches, 836
free memory, 1102
freeware, 911
frequencies
monitor, **676–677**
and network interference, **793–794**,
794
in QAM, 726
sound waves, 686, **688**, *688*
of wireless devices, 541, 658
frequency bands in DSL, 629
Frequency Division Multiplexing (FDM),
800
frequency modulation (FM) synthesis
defined, 1101
process of, **691–692**, *691*
Frequency Shift Keying (FSK), 800
Frequently Asked Questions (FAQs), **901**,
914
fried hardware, 1102
friends for technical support, **899–900**
front panel lights, installing, **983–984**
FSK (Frequency Shift Keying), 800
FTP (file transfer protocol), **1100–1101**
ftp command, 1102
FTP sites, **912–913**
FTPFind site, 913
full backups
in backup strategies, 488
defined, 1102
full-duplex (FDX)
defined, 1102
for MIDI, 705
full height hard disk drives, 879
full-page displays, 1102
full tower case style, 950
fully-associative caches, 1084
function keys
in 101-key keyboard, 648
defined, 1102
fur, triboelectric value of, 205
fuser rollers in laser printers, 575, *576*, 595
fuses for surge suppressors, 342
fusing assemblies in laser printers, 595

G

G (giga-) prefix, 1103
games
3D audio for, **702–703**
optical mice for, 656
PC features for, **859**, **862–863**
upgrading for, **944**
viruses in, 473

garbled output with inkjet printers, **558**
gas discharge tubes, 342
gate A20, error beeps for, 292
gateway IP numbers, 632
gateways for LANs, 173
gauges, 1103
gauss, 197
Gb (gigabits), 1103
GB (gigabytes), 101, 1103
gears in inkjet printers, 550
GeForce chip set, 674
gender changers, 1103
"General failure reading drive" message,
   526–527
General Protection (GP) faults
   causes of, 135
   with video capture, **744–745**
General tab
   for accessibility options, **997**, *997*,
     1019
   for display settings, **1007–1008**,
     1007, 1022
   for modems, **1011–1013**, *1011*
   for System Configuration Utility,
     1032–1033, *1032*
   for System Properties, 999, *999*
generic PCs, **849–852**
geometry in disk drives, **361**
GetMusic site, 699
Ghost program, **489**, 881, 934
giga- (G) prefix, 1103
Gigabit Ethernet, 1103
gigabits (Gb), 1103
gigabytes (GB), 101, 1103
glass
   for camera lenses, 715
   triboelectric value of, 205
glass plate in scanners, 604
Glide API, 674
GoBack utility, 1036
gold, triboelectric value of, 205
Google Groups site, **918**
Google search engine, **908**
GP (General Protection) faults
   causes of, 135
   with video capture, **744–745**
graded index fiber optic cable, **798–799**,
   799
gradients in encoding, 741
graphics
   3D video boards for, **673–674**
   AGP bus for, **154–155**, *154*
   MMX processors for, 97

graphics accelerator boards. *See* accelerators
graphics coprocessors, **667–668**
grayscale video images, 722–723, *723*
green color
   in CCD chips, pixels for, 715–716,
     716
   in TV video, **722–726**, *723–727*
   in VGA, pages for, 130
   in video capture board, 736–737
green wires in phone lines, 641
groaning sounds in laser printers, **593**
ground straps, 207
grounds
   for notebook upgrades, 876
   for power supplies, **339–341**
   in RS-232 communications, 618
   for serial communications, 641
group scheduling, **791**
guarantees for network cable installation,
   821
gummed media with laser printers, 575

H

H.323 standard, 1103
hackers, 634
hair, triboelectric value of, 205
hair dryers for chip testing, 304
half-duplex (HDX)
   defined, 1103
   for MIDI, 705
hand-held computers, serial ports for, 169
handheld scanners, 602
handshaking
   defined, 1103
   with SCSI, 406
handwriting recognition, 88
hangs, 1103
hard disk drives, 25, **350**
   access time of, **365–367**
   activity lights for, 983
   ATA for, **382–383**
   for backups, 487
   backups for, **479–480**, **485–489**
   bad areas on, **444**
   boot records on. *See* boot records
   cables for
     disconnecting, **62–63**
     IDE, **394–396**, *395*
     in troubleshooting, 512
   caches for, 353, **375–376**
   in CD-ROM recording, 765

CMOS configuration for, 51,
   396–398
compatibility of, **392–393**
controllers for, 29, **166–167**
   buffer addresses for, 268–269
   defined, 1103–1104
   I/O addresses for, 251
   identifying, 177, *177*
copying, **489**
crashes, troubleshooting, **234–235**
data transfer rates of, 365
   caches for, **375–376**
   defined, 352
   external transfer rate
     dependencies in, **375**
   internal, **368**
   optimizing, **374–376**
   in ultimate computer, 955
dead. *See* resurrecting hard disk drives
defined, **1104**
ECC codes for, **373–374**
with FAT damaged, **494–495**
formatting, **432**
   bad areas in, **444**
   low-level, **434**, **490–492**
   process for, **444**
   quick steps in, **433**
   third-party tools for, **445**
   troubleshooting, **445**
future of, **351**
in generic computers, 850
hardware structure of, **355–360**,
   356–359
heat from, 191
for home recording studios, 706
identifying, 174
installing. *See* installing
interfaces for, **352–355**, 1104
interleave factor for, **368–373**,
   369–373
IRQs for, 264
logical, 435
   cluster size in, **436–438**
   partitioning, 440–441
   structure of, **458–459**, *458–459*
logical block addressing for, **362–364**,
   380
with lost clusters, **499–502**, *500*, *502*
master/slave jumpers in, **393–396**
media errors on, **506–508**
media tests for, **490–492**
motors in, 195
mounting, **880**

in notebooks, **873**, 879–884
for old computer data, **934**, *934*
operating system limitations for,
    380–381
parking heads in, 365
partitioning. *See* partitioning hard disk
    drives
for PC Card bus, 156, **884**
in PC selection, **854**
    audio/video enthusiast, 863
    corporate, 864
    gamer, 863
    road warriors, 865
    small business, 863
    student, 862
in Pentium computers, 932
PIO transfer in, **381–382**
and power surges, 203
protecting data. *See* data protection;
    viruses
recovering data. *See* recovering
rotational latency period of, **367**
searching for text on, **497–498**
sector translation in, **362–364**
seek time of, **365–367**
size limitations in, **376–380**
stepper motors for, **365**
for System Restore, 1037
terms for, **352–355**
testing, **883**
timeouts with, **299**
tracing failures in, **509**, *510*
type information for, **480**, 1104
for ultimate computer, **955**
unfragmenting files on, **492–494**,
    492–493
in video capture, **733–734**
viruses on. *See* viruses
voice coils for, **364–365**, *364*
Hard Disk tab, 1037
hard errors on hard drives, **444**
hard resets, 1104
hard rubber, triboelectric value of, 205
hardware
    in boot process, **296**
    compatibility in, **26–27**
    Control Panel for, **998–999**,
        1019–1020
        not found by system,
            1001–1003, *1001*, **1020**
        quick steps for, **987–988**
        wizard for, **998–1002**, *998*

controllers for, **161–163**
defined, 1104
in diagnostic programs, 227
installation problems, **234**
in reading MBR, **509–513**
software faults from, **225**
system information for, 1027
hardware addresses, 1104
hardware compatibility list, 1104
hardware decoders for DVD drives, 956
hardware-dependence, 1104
hardware-independence, 1104
hardware interrupts, **1104–1105**
Hardware Update Wizard, 1022
HardwareCentral site, 910
Hare virus, 470
Hawking, Stephen, 997
Hayes modems, 617
HD manufacturer code, 304
"HDD Configuration Error" message, 883
HDD label, 983
HDSL (high-bit-rate digital subscriber line)
    characteristics of, 630
    defined, 1105
HDTV (High Definition Television), 719
HDX (half-duplex)
    defined, 1103
    for MIDI, 705
heads
    disk, 355–356, *356*
        for absolute sectors, 450–452,
            450
        cleaning, **524–525**
        and cylinder skew, **373**
        in disk drive geometry, 361
        documenting, 51
        with IDE addressing, 378–379
        INT 13 BIOS interface for, 377
        number of, 352
        parking, 365
        positioning, 352
        in sector translation, 362
    inkjet printer
        aligning, 560
        cleaning, 553–554, **560**
    scanner, 604
hearing problems, accessibility options for,
    994–995, *995*, **1018**
heartbeat function, 345
heat, **190**
    and box design, **191–192**
    from brownouts, 204
    and CD-ROM discs, 768

for chip testing, **303–304**
and CPU speed, **86–88**
and duty cycles, **195**
fans for, **190–191**
with floppy disk drives, 525
heat sinks for, 107, **191**
hot spots, 336
for inkjet printers, 552
in Intel 80286, 107
in linear power supplies, 328
and modems, 624
in Pentium CPUs, **110–111**
and printers, 535–537, 575, **583**
sensor devices for, **192–193**, *193*
from sunbeams, **195**
and temperature ranges, **194**
thermal shock, **195**
heat sinks
    for CPUs, 107, 174
    installing, 965, *965*
    purpose of, **191**
    for RIMMs, 966
hemostats, **46**
Hercules Graphics Controller (HGC), 680
hertz (Hz), 688, 1105
Hewlett-Packard in Watchzone group, 149
Hewlett-Packard ScanJet interface card,
    1050–1051
hexadecimal (hex) numbering system, **1048**
    addresses in, **250**, **1049–1051**
    converting in, **828**, **1051–1052**
    counting in, **1049**
    defined, 1105
HFS (Hierarchical File System) format,
    756
HGC (Hercules Graphics Controller), 680
Hi8 camcorders, 717–719
hidden bits, 455
hidden files
    defined, 1105
    executing, 301
Hierarchical File System (HFS) format,
    756
hierarchies in newsgroups, **915–916**
high-bit-rate digital subscriber line (HDSL)
    characteristics of, 630
    defined, 1105
High Definition Television (HDTV), 719
high-density floppy diskettes, 522
high-frequency radio, 1144
high-level formatting, **444**
high-resolution mode with inkjet printers,
    556

High Sierra format, **756**, 1105
Hitachi America, prefix for, 304
hive files, backing up, 484
HKEY_ keys, **1044–1045**
hoaxes, virus, **471–472**, **474–475**
holographic storage, 351
home networks, **815–817**, 943
home PCs, features for, **858–859**, **861–862**
home recording studios, **706–707**
home theater systems, **695**
HomeConnect digital camera, 719
HomePNA networks, 800, 816
HomeRF wireless networks, 816, **886–887**
hooked vectors, 1105
horizontal resolution in video capture, **718**
horizontal scan frequency of monitors, **674**
horizontal streaks on laser printer pages, **578**, *579*
horizontal synchronization in video, 728
host adapters for SCSI, 403
    choosing, **412–413**
    controllers in, 167
    installing, **413–414**, *414*
    issues in, **411**
    ROM on, 268
hot spots, 336
hot-swapping
    on PC Card bus, 156
    with USB ports, 539
hot wires
    in AC supplies, 65–66
    in outlets, 338–339
HotBot search engine, **908**
HotHardware site, 910
HotKeys, 649
HP connectors, 178–179, *178*, 418, *418*
HP ScanJet interface card, **1050–1051**
hubs, **829**
    architecture of, **832–834**, *832–834*
    categories of, **831–832**
    defined, 1105
    in Ethernet networks, 816
    switching, **835–837**, *835–837*
    types of, **829–831**, *830*
    for ultimate computer, 957
    for USB bus, 170, 540
hue of color, **736–737**
Huffman technique
    for compression, 739
    defined, 1105
humanities newsgroups, 915

humidity
    and CD-ROM discs, 768
    and printer paper, 581, 584
    and static, 204–206
hyper-pipelined technology, **100**
hyperlinks in World Wide Web, **905–906**
Hz (hertz), 688, 1105

I

I/O (input/output), 1106
I/O addresses, **143**, **249–250**, *249*
    for CD-ROM drives, 769
    conflicts in, **252–254**, *253*
    in diagnostic programs, **227**
    in EISA bus, 150
    hexadecimal numbers for, **250**
    for network interface cards, 824, **828**
    for parallel ports, 539
    for PC Cards, 269–270
    with Plug and Play, 273
    for SCSI adapters, 413
    uses of, **250–252**
I/O boards in generic computers, **850**
I/O bound condition, 1106
"I/O CONFIG ERR" message, 589
I/O voltages for CPUs, 960
I signals, **726–727**
IBM
    MCA bus by, **148–149**
    site for, 434
IBM Data Connectors, 802, *802*
IBM PC computers. *See* PC computers
IBM PC/AT computers. *See* AT computers
IBM PC/XT computers. *See* XT computers
IBM PS/2 computers, **148–149**
IBM twisted-pair cable, **796–797**
icons in system tray, 1008
ICs (integrated circuits), 1107
ICS (Internet Connection Sharing), **817**
ICSA site, 474
IDE (Integrated Drive Electronics) disk
    interface
    addressing in, **378–379**
    cables for, **394–396**, *395*
    for CD-ROM drives, **761–762**
    data transfer rates in, 375
    defined, 1107
    installing drives, 8–9, *8–9*
    low-level formatting for, **434**
    master/slave jumpers in, **393–396**
    sector translation with, 362

terminology for, **391–392**
    upgrading, **937–938**, *938*
identifying parts, **174**
    chips, **304**
    circuits boards and connectors, **178–184**
    expansion boards, 59–60, *60*
    on motherboard, **174–177**, *175–177*
IDs
    for chips, 304
    for SCSI devices, 404, **414–415**, *429*
    for sectors, 369
IDSL (ISDN digital subscriber line), 630
IEEE 1284 ports, 168
IEEE 1394 bus
    for capture boards, **731**
    for CD-ROMs, **762**
    connectors for, 181
    defined, 31, 1106
    description of, 355
    development of, **159–160**
    installing hard disk drives for, **384–385**
    for ultimate computer, 957
    for video capture, 722, **728–729**
iFeel mice, 656
IM (instant messaging), viruses from, **468–469**
images
    in laser printers
        development of, **573–574**, *574*, **596**
        fusion process for, **574–576**, *576*
        problems with, **593**
        transferring, **574**, *574*
    for scanners
        editing, **611**
        quality of, **604–605**
        size of, **606–607**
        viewing and printing, **611–612**
imaging chips, **667–668**
impact printers, **534–535**
impedance, 1106
in-line bar code readers, 654
incremental backups
    in backup strategies, 488
    defined, 1106
Indeo codec, **740–741**
indicator lights, 226
Industry Standard Architecture (ISA) bus, **144–147**, *145–146*
    bus mastering on, 259, 413

description of, 354
DMA controllers on, 257
for network interface cards, 792
support for, 26
in upgrading, 940, *941*
infections, 1106. *See also* viruses
Infrared Data Association (IrDA), 1106
infrared (IR) devices
input, 657–658
printers, 541–542
infrared line of sight communications, 1144
infrared (IR) signals
defined, 1106
for wireless networks, 800, 821
.INI files, backing up, **483**
initialization
in boot process, **297–299**
of CD-ROM drives, **769**
initiators in SCSI, 415
ink
in inkjet printers, 557
removing from fabric, 534
"Ink Low" message, 559
inkjet printers, **548–549**
cartridge carriers for, **551**
cartridges for, **550–551**, **560–561**
cases for, **549–550**
cleaning, **560**
color problems in, **554–555**
dead, **555**
defined, 1106
error messages for, **559–560**
exit trays in, **551**
garbled output with, **558**
maintaining, **535–536**, **560**
operation of, **551–552**
paper for, **559–560**
paper-feed mechanisms for, **550**
poor quality with, **556–558**, *557*
printing problems in, **552–554**, *553–554*
slow and intermittent printing with, **555–556**
troubleshooting, **552–559**, **561**
inner conductors in coaxial cable, 797, *797*
inoculating, 1106
input interface for laser printers, **565–566**
input jacks for sound cards, 953–954, *954*
input/output, 1106. *See also* I/O addresses
input/output bound condition, 1106
inrush current, 202
inserters, chip, 47–48

Install/Uninstall tab, 1003, *1003*
installing
cable broadband, **636**
capture boards, **734–735**
CD-ROM drives, 749, **763–764**, 972–973, *973*, **980**, *981*
CPUs, 2–3, *2–3*, **78**, **959**, *959–960*
defined, 1107
in digital broadband communications, 626
DSL, **631–633**
DVD decoder cards, **976**, *977*
DVD drives, 18–19, *18–19*, **749**, 972–973, *973*
expansion boards, **240–242**
floppy disk drives, 12–13, *12–13*, 526, **968–969**, *969*, 981
front panel lights, **983–984**
hard disk drives, **388**, 969, *969*
cables for, **394–396**, *395*
configuration information for, **396–398**
formatting in, **444**
hardware compatibility in, **392–393**
IDE, 8–9, *8–9*
IEEE 1394, **384–385**
master/slave jumpers in, **393–396**
in notebooks, **881–884**
steps in, **389–392**
in ultimate computer, **981–982**, *982*
hardware, problems from, **234**
heat sinks, 965, *965*
keyboards, mice, and trackballs, **647**
memory, **311–312**, **323–324**
modems, 976
motherboards, 275
network cables, **818–821**
network card drivers, **823–824**, *823*
network interface cards, **787–788**, **822–823**
operating system, **973–974**
PC cams, **712**
power supplies, 6–7, *6–7*
programs, **1004**, *1004*, 1021
satellite communications, **638–639**
SCSI cards, 10–11, *10–11*, **401–402**
SCSI hardware, **412**
SDRAM, 4–5, *4–5*
sound cards, 16–17, *16–17*, **685**, **696**, 974–976, *975*

video boards, 14–15, *14–15*, 661–662, **966–968**
video capture boards, 711
Windows programs, **1004–1005**, *1004*
wireless communications, 639
Zip drives, **980**, *981*
instant messaging (IM), viruses from, **468–469**
instruction sets, 1107
instructions
cache memory for, 320
CPU, **89–90**
INT 13 BIOS interface
and disk errors, 491
extensions to, **377–378**
operation of, **377**
with SCSI, 427
integrated circuits (ICs), 1107
Integrated Drive Electronics (IDE) disk interface
addressing in, **378–379**
cables for, **394–396**, *395*
for CD-ROM drives, **761–762**
data transfer rates in, 375
defined, 1107
installing drives, 8–9, *8–9*
low-level formatting for, **434**
master/slave jumpers in, **393–396**
sector translation with, 362
terminology for, **391–392**
upgrading, **937–938**, *938*
integrated motherboards
compatibility of, **163**
conflicts from, **280**
maintenance of, **294–295**
Integrated Services Digital Network (ISDN)
defined, 1107
operation of, **627–628**
requirements for, **628**
Intel 4004 microprocessor, **929–930**, *929*
Intel 8008 microprocessor, **930**
Intel 8041 microprocessor, 161
Intel 8042 microprocessor, 161
Intel 8048 microprocessor, 161
Intel 8086 CPU and computers
characteristics of, **106**
data path for, **91**
specifications for, 102
Intel 8087 coprocessor, 96
Intel 8088 CPU and computers, 89
characteristics of, **106**

data path for, **91**
memory addresses in, 126
specifications for, 102
Intel 8259 interrupt controller, **262–266**
Intel 80186 CPU, 103, **106**
Intel 80188 CPU, 89, **106**
Intel 80286 CPU and computers
  characteristics of, **106–107**
  data path for, 92
  protected mode in, 133–137
  specifications for, 103
Intel 80386 CPU and computers
  characteristics of, **107–108**
  data path for, **92**
  efficiency of, 89
  specifications for, 103
Intel 80486 CPU and computers
  cache memory on, **93**
  characteristics of, **108–109**
  data path for, 92
  efficiency of, 89
  specifications for, 103
Intel OverDrive microprocessor, **86–87**
  data path for, 92
  introduction of, **108–109**
Intel Pentium. *See* Pentium CPU and
  computers
intelligent hubs, **831–834**, *834*
intelligent power supplies, 289
IntelliMouse Explorer, 655, *655*
interface controllers for laser printers, **565**
interface to system bus in hard disk drives,
  353
interfaces, **27**, 177, *177. See also* controllers
  for CD-ROM, **761–763**
  defined, 1107
  for hard disk drives, **352–355**
  for keyboard, 288, *650*
  for mouse, **656**
  for printers, **167–168**, **537**,
    565–566
  RS-232. *See* RS-232 ports
  for scanners, **604–605**
  SCSI. *See* SCSI (Small Computer
    Systems Interface)
  for sound cards, **693–694**
  for ultimate computer, 957, *957*
  for video capture, **722–729**
interference
  vs. attenuation, **794**
  EMI
    crosstalk, **198–199**

defined, 1096
RFI, **199–201**
  with fiber optic cable, 798
  with laser printers, 581
  in networks, **793–794**
  power noise, **201–204**
  from wireless input devices, 657
interlaced displays, **672–673**
interleaved memory, 1107
interleaving
  DRAM, 315, **319**
  hard disk drives, **368–373**, *369–373*
intermittent problems
  chips, **304**
  inkjet printers, **555–556**
internal cache memory
  on Athlon CPUs, 117
  on Intel 80486 CPU and
    computers, 93
  on Itanium CPU, **96**
  in laptops, 93
  on Pentium CPU, **94**
  on Pentium III, **95**, *95*
  on Pentium 4, 114
  on Pentium Pro, **110–111**
  SRAM for, 93
internal CD-ROM drives, **758**
internal data transfer rate, **368**
internal modems, 622, 943, 954, 1107
internal network numbers, 810, *810*
internal SCSI cables, 419–420, *420*
internal SCSI devices, sample setup with,
  423–425, *423–425*
internal SCSI terminators, **421–423**
internal tape backups, 173
international capability of printers, 544
Internet and online services, **896**
  addresses on, 1108
  advantages in, **902–905**
  cautions in using, 923
  chat, **920–922**
  for computer purchases, 865–866
  convenience of, **903–904**
  costs of, **902–903**
  defined, 1107–1108
  for drivers, **1002–1003**
  followups on, **904–905**
  FTP sites, **912–913**
  information on, 901
  mailing lists, **919–920**
  misinformation on, 923
  newsgroups, **913–919**

patches, drivers, and utilities on, **911**
personal information on, **923**
proprietary, **922**
quick steps in, **897**
streaming media on, **703–704**
vs. traditional support methods,
  898–900
troubleshooting, **924–925**
viruses on, **923**
World Wide Web. *See* World Wide
  Web (WWW)
Internet commerce, 118
Internet Connection Sharing (ICS), **817**
Internet Gateway product, 634
Internet Guard Dog program, 474
Internet-over-cable. *See* cable broadband
Internet Packet Exchange (IPX) protocol
  defined, 1108
  operation of, **810**
Internet Protocol (IP), 810–811, 1108
Internet Relay Chat (IRC)
  defined, 1108
  finding channels in, **921**
  operation of, **920–921**
  for technical information, **921–922**
Internet Service Providers (ISPs), 1108
Internet streaming, **744**
Internet Time tab, 1021
internets, 1108
Internetwork Packet Exchange (IPX), 1108
InterNIC organization, 812–813
interpolation with scanners, 605
interprocess communication (IPC),
  1108–1109
interrupt handlers, 1109
interrupt masks, error beeps for, 291
interrupt service routines, 262
interrupt vector tables, 1109
interrupt vectors, memory for, **126–127**
interrupts and IRQ levels, **34**
  bus lines for, **143–144**
  for CD-ROM drives, 769
  choosing, **262–264**
  for COM ports, **243–248**, **266–267**
  conflicts with, **264–267**
  defined, 1109
  Device Manager for, 1015
  in diagnostic programs, **227**
  for disk access, **261**, *261*
  in EISA bus, 150
  in MCA bus, **149**
  for mice, 656

for network interface cards, **824–828**, *826–827*
operation of, **261–262**
for PC Cards, 269–270
with Plug and Play, 273
vs. polling, **260**
for SCSI adapters, 413
sharing, **267**
software, 131
for sound cards, 693
with UARTs, 616
with Universal Serial Bus, 170
for video capture cards, 734
in XT computers, **262–263**
intranets, 1109
invalid clusters, **503**
"Invalid CMOS information-run SETUP" message, 50
"Invalid configuration" message, 511
invalid subdirectories, **502–503**
inventory functions
in boot process, **299**
in diagnostic programs, **226–227**
IO.SYS file
executing, 301
loading, 301
ionizers, 196
IP (Internet Protocol), 810–811, 1108
IP addresses, 812–813, 817, 1109
IP numbers for DSL, **633–635**
IP session hijacking, 844
IP spoofing, 843
IPC (interprocess communication), 1108–1109
IPX (Internet Packet Exchange) protocol
defined, 1108
operation of, **810**
IPX/SPX protocol
for network printers, 542
operation of, **810**, *810*
IR (infrared) devices
input, **657–658**
printers, **541–542**
IR (infrared) signals
defined, 1106
for wireless networks, 800, 821
IRC (Internet Relay Chat)
defined, 1108
finding channels in, **921**
operation of, **920–921**
for technical information, **921–922**
IrDA (Infrared Data Association), 1106

iron oxide
on floppy diskettes, 522
in toner, 597
IRQ (interrupt request) levels. *See* interrupts and IRQ levels
ISA (Industry Standard Architecture) bus, **144–147**, *145–146*
bus mastering on, 259, 413
description of, 354
DMA controllers on, 257
for network interface cards, 792
support for, 26
in upgrading, 940, *941*
ISDN (Integrated Services Digital Network)
defined, 1107
operation of, **627–628**
requirements for, **628**
ISDN digital subscriber line (IDSL), 630
ISO 9660 standard, **756**
ISO 10149 standard, **755–756**
isolation
controllers for, **161–163**
of power supplies, **340–341**
of printer problems, **542–543**
segment, **839**
isolation devices, 1126
isolation transformers, 339, 343
ISPs (Internet Service Providers), 1108
Itanium CPU, **117–118**
internal cache memory on, **96**
slots for, 101–102
specifications for, 104
IUMA site, 699

J

jackets in coaxial cable, 797, *797*
jacks
for network interface cards, 792, *792*
for sound cards, 953–954, *954*
jam sensors in laser printers, 585
jams in inkjet printers, 558–560
Java prefix, 469
Java scripts, viruses in, 469, 472
JavaScript scripts, viruses in, 469, 472
Jaz drives
for backups, 486
benefits of, 167
for old computer data, 933, *933*
JenniCam, 719
JetDirect card, 542
jeweler's screwdrivers, 871

Joint Photographic Experts Group (JPEG), 1110
journaling in NTFS, **462**
joystick ports on sound cards, 954, *954*
joysticks
connectors for, *35*, 178, *178*, 183
for gamer computers, 863
I/O addresses for, 251
with Universal Serial Bus, 170
JPEG (Joint Photographic Experts Group), 1110
JPEG compression technique, 606, 739
jumpers
for CD-ROM drives, 763
defined, 1110
diagrams for, 57
for I/O addresses, 254
for master/slave controllers, **393–396**
for resource conflicts, **244**, *245*
for ROM addresses, 268
for ZIF sockets, 942

K

K (kilobytes), 1110
K5/K6 CPU
characteristics of, **115–116**
operating frequencies of, 962
pipelines in, 90
k12 newsgroups, 915
k56 flex modem standard, 624
Kbps (kilobits per second)
defined, 1110
for MP3 audio files, 697
Kbs (kilobits), 1110
kernels, 223, 1110
key frames
in delta encoding, 739
in off-line compression, **743**, *743*
"Keyboard failure" message, 652
"Keyboard not present" message, 652
keyboards, 33, **161**, 646
accessibility options for, **992**, *992*, **1017–1018**, *1018*
FilterKeys, **992–994**
StickyKeys, **992**, *993*, 1017
ToggleKeys, **994**
cables for, 650–651, **653**
connectors for, *35*, 180, *180*, **650–651**, *650*
covers for, 208, 651
disassembling, **653–654**
Dvorak, 654

enhanced, 648
error beeps for, 291
I/O addresses for, 251
installing, **647**
interfaces for, 288, *650*
IRQ for, **262–263**
maintaining, **651**
for mouse actions, **996**, *997*
in PC selection, **856**
   small business, 864
   student, 862
problems with, **293**
replacing, 650, **654**
setup for, 276
spills on, **208**, 651
switch design for, **649–650**
troubleshooting, **651–654, 658**
types of, **648–649**, *648–649*
in ultimate computer, **973**
with Universal Serial Bus, 170
upgrading, 940
wireless, 657–658
keyed cables, 69
keylock connection, 58, 67, 72
KEYLOCK label, 983
keypads, numeric, 648
keys in Registry, **1043–1045**, *1044*
keystrokes, 1110
kHz (kilohertz)
   for horizontal scan frequency, 674
   for MP3 audio files, 697
kilo- prefix, 1110
kilobits (Kbs), 1110
kilobits per second (Kbps)
   defined, 1110
   for MP3 audio files, 697
kilobytes (K), 1110
kilohertz (kHz)
   for horizontal scan frequency, 674
   for MP3 audio files, 697
kits for hard disk drives, 955
Kmp3 MP3 players, 701
knots in cords for lightning protection, 346–347

L

L1 (level 1) cache memory, **93**
   defined, 1111
   in Pentium 4, 114
   in Pentium Pro, 110–111
L2 (level 2) cache memory, 32, **93**
   defined, 1111

   in Pentium 4, 114
   in Pentium Pro, 110–111
   setting up, 972
L2F (Layer 2 Forwarding), 815
L2TP (Layer 2 Tunneling Protocol), 815
label bits, 455
labels
   for DIP switches, **247–248**
   for expansion boards, 60
   for network cable, **820**
   for parts in disassembly, 50
LADDR (Layered Device Driver
   Architecture) SCSI standard, 427
lamps in scanners, 604
LAN (local area network) boards. *See*
   network interface cards (NICs)
landing zones, 51
lands on CD-ROM disks, 753
languages in printers, 544
LANs (local area networks), **789**, 1111. *See*
   also networks
LapLink program, 881
LapLinkFTP client, 912
laptop computers. *See* notebook/laptop
   computers
Large fonts setting, 1007, 1022
laser diodes in laser printers, 571
laser printers, **564**
   blank line down side of page, 579
   cable and ports for, **582–583**
   charting problems in, **586**
   cleaning, **594–595**
   cloudy, faded output from, **578–579**
   color, **572**
   contaminants in, **585**
   CPUs in, **566**
   data input for, **569**
   defined, 1111
   diagnostics for, **587**
   disassembling, 576, *577*
   drum preparation in, **569–572**, *569,*
   571
   environmental considerations for,
   583–584
   errant toner in, **594**
   error messages for, **587–592**
   fonts for, **580**
   horizontal streaks on page, **578**, *579*
   host interface testing, 586
   images in
      development of, **573–574**, *574,*
      596
      fusion process for, **574–576**, *576*

   problems with, **593**
      transferring, **574**, *574*
   input interface for, **565–566**
   interface controllers for, **565**
   maintaining, **537**
   memory in, **566–568, 579**
   multiple sheets picked up by, **580**
   operation of, **568–569**, *568–569*
   paper feed in, **572–573**, *573*
   paper issues with, **584–585**, 596
   paper jams in, **581, 585**
   power for, 339, **581**
   print quality in, **596**
   printer control languages for, **567**
   resetting, **581–582**
   rumors about, **596**
   smearing on page, **578**
   squeaking and groaning sounds in, **593**
   startup problems in, **579–580**
   testing, **581**
   toner cartridges for, **592–593**
   vertical white streaks on page,
      577–578, 593
   voltage test for, **586**
lasers for reading CD-ROM disks, 753
Last Mile in DSL, 629
LASTDRIVE statements, executing, 301
latches for memory chips, 878
latency
   defined, 1111
   in satellite communications, 638
latency period, **367**
Layer 2 Forwarding (L2F), 815
Layer 2 Tunneling Protocol (L2TP), 815
Layered Device Driver Architecture
   (LADDR) SCSI standard, 427
laziness, well-planned, 215
LBA (logical block addressing), 353,
   362–364
   with CHS, **380**
   defined, 1111
LC1800 power conditioners, 343
LCCs (leadless chip carriers), 1111
LCD monitors, **675–676**
LCNs (Logical Cluster Numbers), 461
lead, triboelectric value of, 205
leadless chip carriers (LCCs), 1111
LEDs (light-emitting diodes)
   for fiber optic cable, 798
   in optical mice, 655
   for panel lights, **983–984**
legacy devices, 242
lenses for camcorders, 715

level 1 (L1) cache memory, **93**
  defined, 1111
  in Pentium 4, 114
  in Pentium Pro, 110–111
level 2 (L2) cache memory, 32, **93**
  defined, 1111
  in Pentium 4, 114
  in Pentium Pro, 110–111
  setting up, 972
Lfnback tool, 1039
LHARC program, 739
libraries, DLL
  defined, 1095
  operation of, **223–225**
  viruses in, 466
licenses for network applications, 790
LIF (low insertion force) sockets, 66
light
  and infrared printers, **541–542**
  and laser printers, 583
light-emitting diodes (LEDs)
  for fiber optic cable, 798
  in optical mice, 655
  for panel lights, **983–984**
lightning
  and phone lines, 625
  protection from, **201–202, 345–347**
lights, 47
LIM (Lotus Intel Microsoft) standard, 126, **138–140**, *139*
line analyzers, 1111
line art with scanners, 610
line noise, **641**
linear power supplies, **328**
linear sector addresses, 361, 452
lines vs. pixels, **718**
LineStein digital adapter, 640
link editors, 224
linked lists in FAT entries, 456
linking
  DLLs, 224
  in World Wide Web, **905–906**
Linux, MP3 players for, 701
Liquid Audio format, 698
Liquid Audio site, 699
liquids, **208–209**
Listen.com site, 699
Listz
  for IRC channels, 921
  for mailing lists, 919
lithium batteries
  for CMOS, 275
  replacing, 278

LLC (Logical Link Control) layer, 838
loading
  CD-ROM discs, **757–758**
  COMMAND.COM file, **301–302**
  CONFIG.SYS file, **301**
  DBR, **301–302**
  MBR, **300**
local area network (LAN) boards. *See*
  network interface cards (NICs)
local area networks (LANs), **789**, 1111. *See also* networks
local buses, 148, **150**
  for hard disk drives, 354
  VESA, **151**
  for video, 664
local computer stores, 865
locking latches for memory chips, 878
locking resources, 274
lockups, **233–234**
logarithms, 688
logging
  setting up, 972
  in SNMP, 831
logging modes in diagnostic programs, 227
Logic Audio sequencing program, 705
logic bombs, **471**
logic gates, 930
logical block addressing (LBA), 353, **362–364**
  with CHS, **380**
  defined, 1111
Logical Cluster Numbers (LCNs), 461
logical drives, 435
  cluster size in, **436–438**
  defined, **1111–1112**
  partitioning, 440–441
  structure of, **458–459**, *458–459*
logical geometry in disk drives, **361**
Logical Link Control (LLC) layer, 838
logical sub-unit numbers (LSUNs) in SCSI, 416
logical unit numbers (LUNs)
  defined, 1112
  in SCSI, **415–416**
loopbacks
  defined, 1112
  for diagnostic programs, 228
  for LAN boards, 272
  for serial communications, **642–643**
lossless compression, **738–741**, 1112
lossy compression, **738–741**, 1112
lost clusters, **499–502**, *500, 502*

Lotus 1–2–3
  copy protection for, 138
  DOS extenders for, 135
  expanded memory for, 138
loudness in sound waves, **687**, *687*
Love Bug virus, **468**
low insertion force (LIF) sockets, 66
low-level formatting
  need for, **434**
  with SpinRite, **490–492**
LPT ports, 1112. *See also* parallel ports
LPX computers, form factor for, **330–331**
LSI-11 CPUs, data paths for, 91
LSL program, 807
LSUNs (logical sub-unit numbers) in SCSI, 416
LT 1086 chip, 421, *421*
lumens, 724
luminance signals, **724–726**
LUNs (logical unit numbers)
  defined, 1112
  in SCSI, **415–416**
Lycos MP3 Search site, 699

M

M (mega-) prefix, 1113
m (milli-) prefix, 1114
M1 CPUs, 90
MAC (Media Access Control) layer, 838
machine language, 1112
Macintosh computers, expansion slots in, 141–142
Macintosh SCSI cabling, 418
macro viruses
  defined, 1112
  operation of, **466–467**
magazines, **900**
MagicMover tool, **489**
MAGIX MP3 players, 700
magnetic disks, 351
magnetic tip screwdrivers, 45
magnetism
  with floppy diskettes, **525**
  problems from, **197–198**
  from speakers, 695
mail, electronic
  defined, 1108
  firewalls for, 843
  LANs for, **791**
  viruses in, **468**, 472
mail order companies, 865

mailing lists, 1108
  finding, **919–920**
  operation of, **919**
  for technical information, **920**
mainboards. *See* motherboards
mainframe computers, emulating, 173
maintaining. *See also* preventive maintenance
    concerns
    CD-ROM drives, **768**
    floppy disk drives, **524–525**
    inkjet printers, **535–536**, 560
    keyboards, **651**
    mice, **656**
    modems, **624–625**
    notebooks, **891–892**
    power supplies, **335–337**
    printers, **534–537**
male connectors, 1112
managed hubs, **831–834**, *834*
manners
    defined, 1117
    in newsgroups, **916**
manufacturer codes on chips, 304
manufacturers
    chip recalls by, 303
    Web sites for, **906–907**
maps
    defined, 1113
    in notebook upgrades, 876
    in SNMP, 831
mark parity, 1121
mask registers, I/O addresses for, 251
masks, 1113
Master Boot Records (MBRs)
    backing up, **462, 480–482**
    loading, **300**
    for logical drives, 459, *459*
    program in, 300
    reading, **509–513**
master controllers in IDE drives, **393–396**
master DMA register, error beeps for, 291
master drives, **937–938**
Master File Table (MFT), 461
math coprocessors, **96**
    error beeps for, 292
    I/O addresses for, 251
    for Intel 80486, 108
    IRQ for, 264
    MMX, **96–98**
    for Pentium 4, 114
Matrix Math (MMX) CPUs and
    technology
    implementation of, 110

numeric coprocessors for, **96–98**
specifications for, 103
Matrox Millennium G550 graphics cards,
    677
maximum correctable error burst length,
    353
Maxtor site, 434
Mb (megabits), 1113
MB (megabytes), 101, 1113
Mbps (megabits per second), 1113
MBRs (Master Boot Records)
    backing up, **462, 480–482**
    loading, **300**
    for logical drives, 459, *459*
    program in, 300
    reading, **509–513**
MCA (Micro Channel Architecture) bus,
    148–149
    bus mastering on, 259
    description of, 354
    DMA controllers on, 257
    setting up, 276
McAfee AVERT Virus Information Library
    site, 474
McAfee Internet Guard Dog program, 474
McAfee Utilities, **1040**
McAfee VirusScan program, 474
MCGA (Multi Color Graphics Array), 680
MDA (Monochrome Display Adapter)
    characteristics of, 679
    memory for, 129
MDRAM (Multibank DRAM) for video,
    665
mean time between failures (MTBF), 1113
mean time to repair (MTTR), 1113
Media Access Control (MAC) layer, 838
media errors, **506–508**
media tests
    operation of, **490–492**
    pattern testing in, **492**
Media Type settings, 556
meg, 1113
mega- (M) prefix, 1113
megabits (Mb), 1113
megabits per second (Mbps), 1113
megabytes (MB), 101, 1113
megahertz (MHz), **83–88**, 1113
Melissa virus, 467
memory, 25, *25*, 32, **118, 310**. *See also*
    buffers; caches
    addresses for, **136–137**
        CPU limits, **100–101**
        defined, 1114

vs. I/O addresses, **143**
    planning for, 126
boards for. *See* memory boards
in boot process, **297**
and buses, **143**
chips for. *See* memory chips
CMOS. *See* CMOS memory
on current systems, **140–141**
defined, 1113
for device drivers, **127**
ECC, **124**, 318
errors in
    beeps for, 290–292
    false messages, 321–322
expanded, **138–140**, *139*
extended, **133–138**, *136*, 666
first megabyte, **126**
flash. *See* flash memory
for frame captures, **737–738**
for frames, **132–133**
for games, 944
and GP faults, **744–745**
for hard disk drive caches, **375–376**
for home recording studios, 706
identifying, **175–176**, *176*
for inkjet printers, **559**
installing, **311–312**
interleaving, **319**
internal cache, **92–96**
for interrupt vectors, **126–127**
in laser printers, **566–568**, 579
lockups from, **233–234**
managing, **125–126**
for motherboards, 966
in notebooks, 155–157, **872,**
    875–879
with PC Card, 157
in PC selection, **854**
    audio/video enthusiast, 863
    corporate, 864
    gamer, 862
    home, 862
    road warriors, 865
    small business, 863
PIO with, **254–255**, *255*
quantity vs. speed, **121–122**
RDRAM, **122–123**, *123*
reserved memory area, **130–133**, *133*
ROM. *See* BIOS (Basic Input/Output
    System); ROM (Read Only
    Memory)
for scanners, 610

SDRAM, 317–319
in setup, 276
speed of, **119–124**, 276, **316–317**
static vs. dynamic, 257, **316**
status of, 1017
for Super VGA boards, 129
testing, 272, **297**
troubleshooting, **324–325**
for TSRs, **127**
for ultimate computer, 951
in upgrading, 940, *941*
for user programs, **127–128**
for video, **128–130**, *129*, *164*, *165*,
664–666, 669–672, 952–953
in video capture, 734
virtual, 1142
memory boards
defined, 1113
local buses for, 150
speed of, 147, 150
memory chips
caches for, **320**
defined, 1114
heat from, 191
installing, **323–324**
packages for, **118–119**, *120*,
313–314
size of, **315**
speed of, **313–314**, 319, **321**
testing, 303, **322–324**, *323*
"MEMORY CONFIG" message, 589
memory leaks, 1114
memory management, 1114
memory management units (MMUs), 1114
memory managers, 268
memory maps, 1114
memory-resident programs
in AUTOEXEC.BAT file, **127**
defined, 1114
viruses in, 470
memory sticks, **778**, *778*
"MENU RESET" message, 588
"MENUS LOCKED" message, 592
Merced CPU, **117–118**
messages
"0 hard disk(s) found", 511
"1701", 511
"1780", 511–512
"1781", 511–512
"1790", 511–512
"1791", 511–512
"Bad or missing XXXX.DRV", 301

"Cannot reload COMMAND.COM,
system halted", 302
"COLD RESET", 588
"CONFIG LANGUAGE", 591
"Convert directory to file (Y/N)?",
502
"Convert lost chains to files", 501
"Data error reading drive", **506–508**,
526–527
"Drive failure, Hard disk failure", 511
"EC LOAD", 591
"ENGINE TEST", 588
"ERROR", 589–590
"Errors found. F parameter not
specified", 501
"ERRORUNIT", 590
"FC", 592
"FE CARTRIDGE", 592
"File creation error", 501
"FONT PRINTOUT", 588
"General failure reading drive",
526–527
"HDD Configuration Error", 883
"I/O CONFIG ERR", 589
"Ink Low", 559
"Invalid CMOS information-run
SETUP", 50
"Invalid configuration", 511
"Keyboard failure", 652
"Keyboard not present", 652
"MEMORY CONFIG", 589
"MENU RESET", 588
"MENUS LOCKED", 592
"MF FEED", 592
"MIO NOT READY", 589
"Missing operating system", 300
"NO EP CART", 588
"NO FONT", 592
"Non-system disk or disk error", 301
"Out of Memory", **559**
"Out of Paper", **559**
"PAPER JAM", 560, 588
"PAPER OUT", 588
"PC LOAD", 592
"PE FEED", 592
"PE TRAY", 592
"Print Head Failure", 560
"PRINT OVERRUN", 589
"PRINTER OPEN", 588
"PRINTING TEST", 588
"READY", 588
"recording inhibited", 720
"REMOVE PAGE", 590

"RESET", 588
"RESET TO SAVE", 588
"Run SETUP - configuration lost",
511
"Sector not found", 526–527
"SELF TEST", 588
"SERVICE", 590–591
"SKIP SELF TEST", 589
"TONER LOW", 589
"USER MAINTENANCE", 592
"WARMING UP", 588
metal detectors, 197
Metal Oxide Varistors (MOVs), 340–343
metal standoffs for motherboards, 68
meters
for laser printer testing, 586
for power, 336
"MF FEED" message, 592
MFT (Master File Table), 461
MHz (megahertz), 1113
mice, **161**, **646**
accessibility options for, **996**, *997*,
1019
buttons and wheels for, **655**, *655*
cleaning, **656**
connectors for, 180, *180*, *183*
defined, 1116
I/O addresses for, 251
installing, **647**
interfaces for, **656**
IRQ for, 263
in PC selection, **856**
ports for, 169
positioning methods for, **655–656**
troubleshooting, **657**
types of, **654**
in ultimate computer, **973**
upgrading, 940
Micro Channel Architecture (MCA) bus,
148–149
bus mastering on, 259
description of, 354
DMA controllers on, 257
setting up, 276
microcode, 1114
microcode efficiency in CPUs, **89**
microns, 1114
microphones, connectors for, 180
microprocessors, 1114. *See also* CPUs
(central processing units)
Microsoft bus mouse, 656
Microsoft File Information tool, 1039
Microsoft Network (MSN), 922

Microsoft Personal Support Center site, 910

Microsoft System Information (MSI), **1026–1027**, *1027*

microswitches in keyboards, 649–650

microwave wireless communications, **639–640**

mid-sized tower case style, 950

MIDI (Music Instrument Digital Interface)
  boards for, 693
  cables for, 695
  defined, 1116
  for FM synthesis, 691
  for games, 702
  for musicians, **704–705**
  sound cards for, 953

Midi files, sound cards for, 953

MIDI ports, I/O addresses for, 251

military specification, chip prefix for, 304

milli- (m) prefix, 1114

milliseconds (ms), 118, 1114

millivolts (mv), 1115

min/max troubleshooting technique, 288

Mini PCI bus, **157–158**

mini-tower case style, 950

miniature D shell connectors, **178–179**, *178*

miniature DIN connectors, 180, *180*
  for keyboards, *650*, 651, 940
  for mouse, 940

MiniDV format, 717, 719

Minimalist computers, 693

miniplug connectors, 180

Minitel TTF Files tool, 1039

"MIO NOT READY" message, 589

mIRC client, 921

mirroring and mirror sets
  defined, 1115
  in MFT, 461
  software for, 487

mirrors
  in laser printers, 593
  in scanners, 604
  as tools, 47

misc newsgroups, 915

misinformation on Internet, **923**

"Missing operating system" message, 300

mixing for musicians, **706–707**

Mixman Studio sequencing program, 705

MJ (modular jacks), 1115

MMCs (MultiMediaCards), **778–779**, *779*

MMUs (memory management units), 1114

MMX CPUs and technology
  implementation of, 110
  numeric coprocessors for, **96–98**
  specifications for, 103

mobile computing, 1115

MOD operator, 451

modal dispersion, 799

MODE command, **545**

Modem Default Preferences dialog box, 1024

modem isolators, 625

Modem on Hold feature, 624

Modem Ready (MR) light, 643

Modem Saver tester, 641

modems, 614. *See also* serial communications
  cable, 1084. *See also* cable broadband
  connectors for, *35*, 182, *183*
  Control Panel for, **1010–1013**, *1011–1013*
  defined, 1115
  external, **622**
  indicator lights for, 226
  installing, 976
  ISDN, 628
  lightning damage to, **202**
  maintaining, **624–625**
  operation of, **616–617**
  on PC Card bus, 156
  in PC selection, **857**
  ports for, **168–169**
  problems with, **640**, **642–643**
  quick steps for, **990**
  settings for, **1012–1013**, **1024**
  speed of, **622–623**
  standards for, **623–624**
  testing, **1013**, *1013*, 1025
  troubleshooting, **236**
  for ultimate computer, **954**, *955*
  for upgrading, **943**
  Windows XP Control Panel for, **1023–1025**, *1023–1024*

Modems tab, *1023*, 1024

modes for CD-ROM, 756–757

modular hubs, 829–831, *830*

modular jacks (MJ), 1115

modularity for compatibility, 76, 79

modulation
  defined, 1115
  frequency of, **691–692**, *691*

modules, NetWare, 807

Molex connectors, 62, *62*, 334, *334*

Monitor tab, **1009–1010**, *1010*, 1022–1023

monitors, 674. *See also* video and video boards
  descriptions of, 1006
  in disassembly, 52
  dot pitch for, **675**
  flat-panel, **675–676**
  for games, 944
  horizontal-scan frequency of, **674**
  multi-frequency, **676–677**
  multiple displays, **677–678**
  noninterlaced, **672–673**
  for notebooks, 892
  old type, **678–681**
  in PC selection, **855–856**
    audio/video enthusiast, 863
    corporate, 864
    home, 862
    small business, 864
  settings for, **1009–1010**, *1010*, **1022–1023**
  size of, **675**
  troubleshooting, **235–236**
  vertical-scan frequencies of, **672–673**

monochrome adapters, I/O addresses for, 252

Monochrome Display Adapter (MDA)
  characteristics of, 679
  memory for, 129

Monochrome Display monitors, 679

monochrome monitors, 679

monochrome video, **722–726**, *723*

Monster cables, 729

Monterey sound cards, 707

Moore's Law, 1115

motherboards
  components on, **79–80**, *80–81*
  controllers on, **163**
  CPUs for, **959–966**, *959–960*, *963–965*
  defined, 1115
  diagnostic program for, 228
  diagrams for, **57–58**
  in generic computers, **850**
  identifying parts on, **174–177**, *175–177*
  installing, 275
  integrated
    compatibility of, **163**
    conflicts from, **280**
    maintenance of, **294–295**
  IRQ for, 263
  memory on, **966**

in PC selection, **854**
in Pentium computers, 932–933
in proprietary computers, 850
removing, **66–68**, *67–68*
seating, **71**
for ultimate computer, **951–952**
upgrading, **936**
in XT computers, 275
motion detection by mice, 655–656
Motion Picture Experts Group (MPEG),
1115
motors
and brownouts, 204
duty cycles in, 195
heat from, 191
magnetism from, 197
noise from, 199, 339
power for, 328
stepper, **365**
turning off, 203
mountain/valley memory tests, *322*, *323*
mounting hard disk drives, **880**
mouse, **161**, **646**
accessibility options for, **996**, *997*,
1019
buttons and wheels for, **655**, *655*
cleaning, **656**
connectors for, 180, *180*, *183*
defined, 1116
I/O addresses for, 251
installing, **647**
interfaces for, **656**
IRQ for, 263
in PC selection, **856**
ports for, 169
positioning methods for, **655–656**
troubleshooting, **657**
types of, **654**
in ultimate computer, **973**
upgrading, **940**
Mouse tab, 996, *997*, 1019
Moving Picture Experts Group (MPEG)
compression, **976**
MOVs (Metal Oxide Varistors), 340–343
MP3 audio files, **696–697**
benefits of, **697–698**
burning to CDs, **698–699**
hardware for, **701**
software for, **700–701**
MP3.com site, 699
mp3blaster MP3 players, 701
MPEG (Motion Picture Experts Group),
1115

MPEG (Moving Picture Experts Group)
compression technique, **976**
mpg123 MP3 players, 701
MPU-401 interface, 705
MR (Modem Ready) light, 643
ms (milliseconds), 118, 1114
MS-DOS and disks, **448–450**
absolute and DOS sectors, **450–452**
clusters, **452–454**
DBR, **454**
disk errors, **490–492**, *491*
FAT, **454–457**, *455–456*
logical drive structure, **458–459**, *459*
subdirectories, **457–458**
MSCONFIG tool, 230
MSDOS.SYS file, 301
MSI (Microsoft System Information),
1026–1027, *1027*
MSN (Microsoft Network), 922
MTBF (mean time between failures), 1113
MTTR (mean time to repair), 1113
Multi Color Graphics Array (MCGA), 680
multi-frequency monitors, **676–677**
Multi-Function printers, 536
Multibank DRAM (MDRAM) for video,
665
multibranch prediction in 6x86, 115
multichannel SCSI host adapters,
407–408, 413
multifinger tools, 45, *45*
multimedia. *See also* CD-ROM drives; sound
and sound cards; video capture
defined, 1116
MMX technology for, **96–98**
MP3 audio files, **696–701**
multimedia keys, 649
multimedia kits, **762–763**
MultiMediaCards (MMCs), **778–779**, *779*
multimeters
for laser printer testing, 586
for power, 336
multimode fiber optic cable
defined, 1116
operation of, **798–799**, *799*
multipartite viruses
defined, 1116
operation of, **470**
MultiPass printers, 536
multiple-channel information, digital audio
for, 702
multiple displays, **677–678**
multiple transport stacks, **813**, *814*
multiple zone recording (MZR), 1116

multipliers for CPUs, **963**, *963*
multiprocessor systems, **320**
multiscan monitors, 679
multisession CD-ROM drives, **757**
Multisync monitor, 676
multitasking, 107
cross-linked clusters from, 506
memory protection for, 134–135
UARTs for, 616
music
four-part cycle, 691–692, *691*
MIDI for, 693
MP3 audio files, **696–701**
music CDs, standard for, 755
Music Instrument Digital Interface (MIDI)
boards for, 693
cables for, 695
defined, 1116
for FM synthesis, 691
for games, 702
for musicians, **704–705**
sound cards for, 953
musicians
MIDI for, **704–705**
recording and mixing for, **706–707**
sound for, **704**
MUSICMATCH Jukebox MP3 players,
700
MUSICMATCH site, 699
mv (millivolts), 1115
My Briefcase feature, **892–893**
My Computer for removing devices, 247
MZR (multiple zone recording), 1116

N

n (nano-) prefix, 1116
N chip prefix, 304
N-ports in FCSI, 410
name resolution, 1116
names
of 6x86 registers, 115
for partitions, **442**
for viruses, **469**
NAND flash memory, 775
nano- (n) prefix, 1116
nanoseconds (ns), 118, 1116
Napster site, 699
narrow SCSI, 1117
NAT (Network Address Translation)
defined, 1118
for IP addresses, 634

National Electrical Manufacturers
    Association (NEMA), cable grading by,
    795–796
National Semiconductor, prefix for, 304
National Television Standards Committee
    (NTSC), 1117
National Television Standards Committee
    (NTSC) interface, **723**
Native Macintosh CD format, 756
Natural Keyboards, 649–650, *649*, 654
NCPs (NetWare Control Protocols), 805
NDIS (Network Driver Interface
    Specification)
        defined, 1118
        vs. ODI, 808
near-end crosstalk (NEXT), 1117
neatness in network cable installation,
    819–820
NEC
        CPU specifications, 104
        in Watchzone group, 149
NEMA (National Electrical Manufacturers
    Association), cable grading by, 795–796
NetBEUI (NetBIOS Extended User
    Interface)
        benefits and limitations of, **809–810**
        defined, 1117
NetBIOS (Network Basic Input/Output
    System)
        defined, 1117
        development of, 809
NetBurst microarchitecture, 99, **113–114**
netiquette
        defined, 1117
        in newsgroups, **916**
NetWare Control Protocols (NCPs), 805
NetWare modules, 807
Network Address Translation (NAT)
        defined, 1118
        for IP addresses, 634
Network Basic Input/Output System
    (NetBIOS)
        defined, 1117
        development of, 809
network binding interfaces, **807–808**
network device drivers, 1118
Network Driver Interface Specification
    (NDIS)
        defined, 1118
        vs. ODI, 808
network file system drivers, 803–804,
    806–807

network interface cards (NICs), 35, **172**
    for cable broadband, 636
    categories of, **791–793**
    configuring, **824–829**, *826–827*
    conflicts in, **270–272**
    connectors on, 178, *178*
    defined, 1118
    DMA channels for, **828–829**
    drivers for, **807–808**, **823–824**, *823*
    for DSL, 632
    grounding problems with, 339
    I/O addresses for, **828**
    installing, **787–788**, **822–823**
    interrupts requests for, **824–828**,
        826–827
    for notebooks, **886**, *886*
    in PC selection, **857**
    ROM on, 268
    testing, 272
    for ultimate computer, 957
network interface in laser printers, **566**
Network layer devices, 838
Network Monitor Service tool, 1039
network numbers in IPX/SPX, 810, *810*
network operating system (NOS), 1118
network printers
    defined, 1118
    operation of, **542**
network transport protocols, **808–809**
    defined, 1118
    IPX/SPX, **810**, *810*
    multiple transport stacks, 813, *814*
    NetBEUI, **809–810**
    TCP/IP, **810–813**
networks, **786**
    backups on, 880
    cables for, **793–795**
        coaxial, **797**, *797*
        connectors for, **800–803**,
            801–803
        fiber optic, **798–799**, *798–799*
        installing, **818–821**
        interference vs. attenuation in,
            794
        summary, **803**
        twisted-pair, **795–797**, *795*
    choosing, **814–817**
    connectors for, 179–180, 182, *183*
    crosstalk in, 199
    defined, **1117–1118**
    in FCSI, **410**
    hubs in, **829**

    architecture of, **832–834**,
        832–834
    categories of, **831–832**
    defined, 1105
    switches, **835–837**, *835–837*
    types of, **829–831**, *830*
    for ultimate computer, 957
    in IRC, 921
    LANs, **789**, 1111
    memory frames for, 132
    models of, **838**
    NICs for. *See* network interface cards
        (NICs)
    for office interaction, **791**
    PC Cards for, 270
    protocols for. *See* protocols
    repeaters in, **838–839**
        benefits of, **839**
        for coaxial cable, 797
        for collisions, **839–840**
        vs. extenders, **840**
        operation of, **839**
        for segment isolation, **839**
    routers in, **841**
    security for, **842**
        firewalls for, **843–845**
        passwords for, **842–843**
        tips for, **842**
    sharing on
        applications, **789–790**
        peripheral devices, **790**
    in ultimate computer, **956–957**
    in upgrading, **943**
    wireless, **800**, **821–822**
neutral outlet line, 338–339
new product information, online sources of,
    900–901
news newsgroups, 915
newsgroups, **913**
    defined, 1108, **1118–1119**,
        1140–1141
    finding, **916–918**
    hierarchies in, **915–916**
    netiquette in, **916**
    operation of, **914–915**
    for technical information, **918–919**
newsreaders, 1119
NexGen CPUs
    characteristics of, **116**
    pipelines in, 90
NEXT (near-end crosstalk), 1117
NiCad batteries for CMOS, 275
nicknames in IRC, 921

NICs. *See* network interface cards (NICs)

NNTP newsgroups, **913**
    defined, 1108
    finding, 916–918
    hierarchies in, 915–916
    netiquette in, 916
    operation of, 914–915
    for technical information, 918–919

"NO EP CART" message, 588

"NO FONT" message, 592

node numbers in IPX/SPX, 810

Node ports in FCSI, 410

nodes in cable broadband, **636**

noise
    in buses, 148
    defined, 1119
    with fiber optic cable, 798
    with laser printers, 581
    memory errors from, 321
    in modem connections, 943
    power conditioners for, 342
    in power line, **201–204**
    and power supplies, **340**
    RFI, **199–201**
    with SCSI, 403
    in serial communications, **641**
    from serial ports, 168
    and signals, 687

nominal velocity of propagation, 1119

"Non-system disk or disk error" message, 301

noncontiguous files, unfragmenting, **492–494**, *492–493*

none parity setting
    defined, 1121
    for serial ports, 545

noninterlaced monitors, **672–673**

nonvolatile memory (NVRAM), 131. *See also* flash memory
    for Plug and Play, 273
    for setup information, 278

NOR flash memory, 775

normal mode with inkjet printers, 556

Northern Light search engine, **908**

Norton AntiVirus program, 474

Norton Utilities, **1040**
    for bad areas, 444
    for CMOS information, 51
    for file size, 503
    for reading MBR, 510
    for restoring files, **496–498**
    for searching for text on disks, 498

NOS (network operating system), 1118

NOT logic gates, 930

notches on chips, 306, *306*, 878

notebook/laptop computers, **870–871**
    access to, 877
    batteries for, **278**, **874**, **887**
        buying, **889–890**
        caring for, **887–888**
        charging, **888–889**
        conserving power in, **890**, *890*
        replacing, **889**
    cases for, **891**
    defined, 1119
    DVD drives for, **885**
    hard disk drive upgrades in, **873**, **879–884**
    internal cache memory in, **93**
    keyboards in, 649
    LAN adapters for, **885–886**, *886*
    maintaining, **891–892**
    memory modules in, 313–314
    memory upgrades in, **872**, **875–879**
    PC Card bus for, **155–157**, *156*
    synchronizing files for, **892–894**
    troubleshooting, **894**
    Universal Serial Bus for, 170

Notification option, 997, 1019

Notify Me Before Downloading Any Updates option, 1035

nozzles in inkjet printers, 551, 553–554, 557

NRAM, 278

ns (nanoseconds), 118, 1116

NT File System (NTFS), cluster size in, 437–438

NT1 devices, 628

NTFS file system, **461–462**

NTSC (National Television Standards Committee), 1117

NTSC (National Television Standards Committee) interface, **723**

Nuclear virus, 467

null characters, 1119

null modems, *620–621*, 1119–1120

numbering systems, hexadecimal, **1048**
    addresses in, **250**, **1049–1051**
    converting in, **828**, **1051–1052**
    counting in, **1049**

numeric coprocessors, **96**
    error beeps for, 292
    I/O addresses for, 251
    in Intel 80486 CPU, 108
    IRQ for, 264
    MMX, **96–98**
    in Pentium 4, 114

numeric keypads, 648

NumLock key, sound with, 994

nut drivers, 42, *43*

nVidia, chip sets from, 674

NVRAM (nonvolatile memory), 131. *See also* flash memory
    for Plug and Play, 273
    for setup information, 278

Nx586 CPU
    characteristics of, **116**
    pipelines in, 90

nylon, triboelectric value of, 205

Nyquist's Theorem, 690

O

observations in troubleshooting, **217–218**

obsolete drivers, **1002–1003**

OCR (optical character recognition)
    defined, 1120
    with scanners, **607**

octal numbering system, 1048

octets, 1120

odd parity
    defined, 1121
    for serial ports, 545

ODI (Open Datalink Interface), 808

OEMs (original equipment manufacturers), 1120–1121

off-line compression in video capture, **741–742**
    codecs for, **742**, *743*
    data rate and compression quality in, **743–744**
    key frames in, **743**, *743*
    padding for CD-ROM with, **744**
    for RealVideo files, **744**

office interaction, networks for, **791**

OfficeJet printers, 536

offline devices, 1120

offline UPSs, 345

OHCI (Open Host Controller Interface), 159

ohmmeters, 653

OKICOLOR 8 printers, 572

old computers
    components in, **932–933**
    determining, **931**
    saving data from, **933–934**, *933–934*
    upgrading
        EIDE adapters, **937–938**, *938*
        floppy controllers, **938–939**, *939*
        games in, **944**
        home networks in, **943**

keyboards and mice, **940**
microprocessors, **938**
modems, **943**
motherboards, **936–937**
options in, **942–944**
paths for, **935**
planning, **936**
ports, **939–940**, *939*
slots, **940–942**, *941*
video and sound, **940**
Olivetti, 149
omnibus connectors, 142
onboard caches, 353, 376
one and a half clock speeds, **86**
one-way linked lists in FAT entries, 456
online backups, **487**
online devices, 1120
online services, 1120. *See also* Internet and
online services
open control systems, 365
Open Datalink Interface (ODI), 808
Open Host Controller Interface (OHCI),
159
OpenGL API, 674
operands, instruction, 90
operating systems
defined, 1120
and disks, **448–450**
absolute and DOS sectors,
450–452
clusters, **452–454**
DBR, **454**
FAT, **454–457**, *455–456*
logical drive structure, **458–459**
subdirectories, **457–458**
functions of, 223
and hard disk drives, **380–381**
for home recording studios, 706
installing, **973–974**
partitions for, 435
rebuilding, **485**
operator errors, **219–221**
optical character recognition (OCR)
defined, 1120
with scanners, **607**
optical disks, 351
optical drives. *See* CD-ROM drives; DVD
(Digital Video Disk) drives
optical fiber standard, **410**
optical mice
defined, 1120
operation of, **655–656**
optical RS-232 isolators, 625

optional I/O interface in laser printers,
566
OR logic gates, 930
Orange Book CD-ROM standard, 755
original equipment manufacturers (OEMs),
1120–1121
oscilloscopes, 641
out of band management, 834
"Out of Memory" message, **559**
out-of-order completion
in 6x86, 115
in Pentium Pro, 110
"Out of Paper" message, **559**
outlets
checking, **338–339**
for laser printers, 581
output, 1121
output jacks for sound cards, 953–954, *954*
OverDrive chip, **86–87**
data path for, 92
introduction of, **108–109**
overflow, flow control for, 620
overlays with capture boards, **732–733**
overscan lines, 674
overvoltage conditions, **204**, 340
OVL files, viruses in, 466
oxidation, 208
ozone from laser printers, **583–584**

P

P (peta-) prefix, 1124
P-Tags, 782
packages
for CPUs, 106–107, *107*
for memory chips, 118–119, *120*,
313–314
packet filtering, **845**
padding for CD-ROM, **744**
page frames and paging, **129–130**,
132–133
for expanded memory, **138–140**, *139*
for video memory, **666**
page-mode RAM, 1121
page registers, I/O addresses for, 251
paged memory management units
(PMMUs), 1121
PAL (Programmable Array Logic)
components, 929
Palm Desktop software, 894
Palm devices
defined, 1121
syncing data with, **893–894**, *893*

panel lights, installing, **983–984**
panic
damage from, 72
in troubleshooting, **214**
paper
for inkjet printers, **559–560**
for laser printers, **584–585**
curled and wrinkled, 585
feeds for, **550**, **572–573**, *573*
fusing image to, **574–576**, *576*
jammed, **581**, 585
quality of, 596
triboelectric value of, 205
paper guides in inkjet printers, 559
"PAPER JAM" messages, 560, 588
"PAPER OUT" message, 588
Paper Type settings, 556
parallel communication, 1121
parallel instruction processing, 87
parallel interfaces for scanners, **605**
parallel ports, 31, *35*, **167–168**
for CD-ROM drives, 755
configuring, **278–280**
conflicts with, **246**
connectors on, 178, *178*, *181*, 182,
983
defined, 1121
Device Manager for, 1014
error beeps for, 292
extenders for, 543
for generic computers, 850
I/O addresses for, 251–252
IRQ for, 263
for laser printers, **582–583**
loopback plugs for, 228
LPT2, 279
in PC selection, 856
polling, **260**, *261*
for printers, **537–539**, **544–545**, 565
for scanners, **609–610**
vs. serial, 614
support for, 539
for upgrading, **939**, *939*
parallel-processing CPUs, **98–100**
parasitic viruses, 465
parent subdirectories, 457
parity
defined, 1121
error beeps for, **290–291**
for serial ports, 545
parity bits
defined, 1121
for SCSI, **416**

parity checking, 1121
parity errors
    defined, 1121
    lockups from, 124
    from power supplies, 321
parking heads, 365
partially erased files, recovering, 497–498
partitioning hard disk drives, **432**, **434–435**
    backing up information for, **443**
    clusters in, **436–438**
    with device drivers, **442–443**
    and logical drive structure, **458–459**, *458–459*
    names in, **442**
    options in, **435**
    steps in, **433**, **438–443**, *439–441*
    third-party tools for, **445**
    troubleshooting, **445**
PartitionMagic utility, 437, 445
partitions and partition tables
    active, 441
    blank, **513–514**
    bootable, **300–301**
    defined, **1121–1122**
    reading, **509–513**
    size limitations on, **380–381**
partners in DSL, 632
parts, identifying, **174**
    chips, **304**
    circuit boards and connectors, **178–184**
    expansion boards, **59–60**, *60*
    on motherboard, **174–177**, *175–177*
pass-through interfaces, 694
passes for scanners, 604
passive hubs, **831**
passive SCSI termination, 404–405
    vs. active, **420–421**, *421*
    defined, 1122
    for SCSI 1 and SCSI-2, 412
Password List Editor tool, 1039
passwords
    defined, 1122
    for network security, **842–843**
    setup for, **277**
patches, downloading, 911
patience in troubleshooting, **214**
pattern testing methods, **492**
pausing printers, 555
PB (petabytes), 1124
PC Camera product, 719

PC cams
    installing, **712**
    for video capture, **719**
PC Card bus, **155–157**, *156*
    DMA controllers on, 257
    for notebook hard drives, 879, **884**
    socket and card services for, **156–157**
PC Card slots, 1122
PC Cards
    configuring, **269–270**
    defined, 1122
    flash memory, **781**
    Plug and Play for, **269**
    status of, 1017
PC-cillin 2000 program, 474
PC computers
    configuring, 275
    form factor for, **330**
    memory on, 126
    UARTs in, 615
PC Guide site, 910
"PC LOAD" message, 592
PC Mechanic site, 910
PC Memory Card International Association (PCMCIA), 1122
PC Parrot program, 684
PC-Technician program, **228–229**, 322
PCA (Printed Circuit Assembly), **580**
PCDJ Phat MP3 players, 700
pchelp mailing list, 920
pchelp4u mailing list, 920
PCI (Peripheral Component Interconnect) bus, 25–27, **151–154**, *152*
    bus mastering in, **153**, 259
    compatibility of, **153**
    data paths for, 152
    defined, **1122–1123**
    description of, 354
    DMA controllers on, 257
    I/O addresses for, 252
    IRQ sharing on, **267**
    for network interface cards, 792, 824
    in PC selection, 853–854
    setting up, **153–154**, **276–277**
    speed of, **152–153**
    for upgrading, 940, *941*
PCI-X standard, 1123
PCL (Printer Control Languages), 35, **567**
PCM (Pulse Code Modulation), **688–690**, *689–691*
PCM Upstream feature, 624
PCMCIA (PC Memory Card International Association), 1122

PCMCIA cards. *See* PC Card bus; PC Cards
PCs (personal computers)
    development of, 930
    purchasing. *See* purchasing PCs
PCsupport.com site, 910
PCTIPS.com site, 910
pctoolbin mailing list, 920
PDAs (personal digital assistants), 1124
"PE FEED" message, 592
"PE TRAY" message, 592
peer-to-peer architecture, 1123
peer-to-peer networks, 789, 1123
pellet arresters, 342
pencil erasers, 209
Pentium CPU and computers, 22, 25
    cache memory on, **94**
    challengers to, **115–118**
    components in, **932–933**
    data path for, 92
    defined, 1123
    fault tolerance in, **110**
    introduction of, **109–110**
    motherboards in, *80–81*
    in multiprocessor systems, 320
    operating frequencies of, 961–962
    pipelines in, **98–100**
    specifications for, 103
    speed of, **86–87**, **98–100**
Pentium II CPU and computers
    data path for, 92
    defined, 1123
    heat in, 111, *111*, 191
    internal cache memory on, **95**
    introduction of, **112**
    MMX technology in, 98
    motherboards in, *81*
    pipelines in, **99–100**
    slots for, **101–102**
    specifications for, 103
    speed of, 87
    word size for, 91
Pentium III CPU and computers
    data path for, 92
    defined, 1123
    heat sensors in, 193
    internal cache memory on, **95**, *95*
    introduction of, **113**
    motherboards in, *81*
    slots for, **101–102**
    specifications for, 103
    for video capture, 734
Pentium 4 CPU and computers, *81*
    data path for, 92

defined, 1123–1124
internal cache memory on, 96
introduction of, **113–114**
pipelines in, **99–100**
specifications for, 104
for video capture, 734
Pentium OverDrive chip
data path for, 92
introduction of, **86–87**
Pentium Pro CPU and computers
data path for, 92
defined, 1124
internal cache memory on, 94–95, 110–111
operation of, **110–111**, *111*
pipelines in, 90, **99–100**, 110–111
word size in, 91
Perase setting, 754
performance
of disk drives
caches for, **375–376**
CD-ROM drives, **758–761**
data transfer rates in, **374–376**
ECC codes for, **373–374**
interleave factor in, **368–373**
rotational latency period, **367**
seek time, **365–367**
System Monitor for, **1026**, *1026*
of video, **1010**, *1011*
Performance tab, **1010**, *1011*, **1016–1017**, *1016*
periodic waves, 686
periods (.)
defined, 1124
in subdirectory entries, 457, 499, 503
Peripheral Component Interconnect bus. *See* PCI (Peripheral Component Interconnect) bus
peripheral controllers, I/O addresses for, 251
peripheral IDs with SCSI, **414–415**, 429
peripheral vision, 672–673
peripherals
bus mastering for, **259**, *259*
DMA channels for, **256–259**, *256*
on networks, **790**
programmed input/output with, **254–255**, *255*
SCSI, **411**
permanent swap files, 1124
persistent connections, 633
personal area networks, 800

personal computers (PCs)
development of, 930
purchasing. *See* purchasing PCs
personal digital assistants (PDAs), 1124
Personal Tags, 782
peta- (P) prefix, 1124
petabytes (PB), 1124
PGA (Pin Grid Array) chips, 46
defined, 1124
for Intel 80286, 107, *107*
for Intel 80486, 108
PGA (Professional Graphics Adapter), 680
phantom directories, **528–529**
phantom disks with SCSI, 429
phase
in power calculations, 336
in QAM, 726
phase outlet line, 338–339
Phillips screwdrivers, 42, *43*
Phoenix BIOS
compatibility with, 131
error beeps for, **290–292**
in PC selection, 854
setup with, 50
Phone and Modem Options dialog box, 1023–1025, *1023–1024*
phone lines
isolators for, 624
for modems, 623
for networks, **800**, **816**, **944**
noise in, **641**
in satellite communications, 638
phones, magnetism from, 197
PhotoCD standard
defined, 1124
multisession drives for, 757
photodetectors for CD-ROM, 753
photomultiplier tubes (PMTs), 603
photosites in scanners, 604
physical devices, 1124
physical drives, 1124
physical geometry in disk drives, **361**
physical interface in communications systems, 617–618
Physical layer devices, 838
physical security, 842
pickup tools, 45, *45*
piconets, 800
piezo inkjet printers, 552
pin 1 rule, **69–70**, *70*
pin counts in SCSI systems, 408–409
Pin Grid Array (PGA) chips, 46
defined, 1124

for Intel 80286, 107, *107*
for Intel 80486, 108
pincushioning, 229
pinouts, 1124
PIO (programmed input/output)
BIOS support for, 375
defined, 1127
vs. DMA, **382**
importance of, 353
modes in, **381–382**
operation of, **254–255**, *255*
pipeline burst cache, 1124–1125
pipeline stalls, 1125
pipelines
in CPUs, **89–90**
6x86, 115
K5, 116
Nx586, 116
Pentium, **98–100**
Pentium 4, **99–100**
Pentium Pro, **99–100**, 110–111
defined, 1125
in SDRAM, 318
pirated software
MP3 audio files, **698**
network applications, 790
viruses in, 473
pits
on CD-ROM disks, 753–754
on DVD discs, 754
pixels, 667
in CCD chips, **715–716**, *716*
in compression, 739
in LCD monitors, 676
vs. lines, **718**
in video capture, **724**, *724*
PKZIP program, 739
plain old telephone service (POTS) for DSL, 629
planar boards, 80
planning
network cable installation, **818**
upgrades, **936**
plastic coated media with laser printers, 575
Plastic Leadless Chip Carriers (PLCCs), 46
defined, 1125
for Intel 80286, 106–107, *107*
for Intel 80386, 107
plastic lenses for cameras, 715
plastic spacers for motherboards, 67–68, *68*
platinum, triboelectric value of, 205
platters in hard disk drives, **356–358**, *356*, *358*

PLCCs (Plastic Leadless Chip Carriers), 46
  defined, 1125
  for Intel 80286, 106–107, *107*
  for Intel 80386, 107
pliers, **46**, *46*
Plug and Play (PnP) standard, 29, **242**
  boot process on, 273–274
  defined, 1125
  ideal operation of, 272–273
  in operating system installation, 974
  for PC Cards, 157, **269**
  in PC selection, 853
  with PCI bus, 153
  resource conflicts with, 246–247
  setting up, 972
  with Universal Serial Bus, 170
plugging in CPUs, **963–965**, *964–965*
plugs
  on anti-static wrist straps, 44
  BNC, 179
  for keyboards, *650*, 651
PMMUs (paged memory management
  units), 1121
PMTs (photomultiplier tubes), 603
PnP standard. *See* Plug and Play (PnP)
  standard
Pocket DigiDrive product, 784
Point-to-Point Protocol (PPP), 1125
Point-to-Point Protocol over Ethernet
  (PPPoE), **633**
Point-to-Point Tunneling Protocol (PPTP),
  815
polling, **260**, *261*
polyester, triboelectric value of, 205
polygon measurement for video cards, 953
polymorphic viruses, **470**, 1125
polyurethane, triboelectric value of, 205
polyvinyl, triboelectric value of, 205
POP (Post Office Protocol), 1126
POP3 IP numbers for DSL, 633
port numbers, 1125
port replicators, 1126
portals, 1126
ports, 31, 161. *See also* parallel ports; serial
  ports
  asynchronous, **615**, *615*
  conflicts with, **243–248**, 264
  connectors for, **983**
  defined, 1125
  Device Manager for, 1014
  extra, **266–267**
  FireWire bus for, **159–160**
  for generic computers, 850

in hubs, **832–834**, *832–834*
I/O addresses for, 251–252
infrared, **541–542**
for laser printers, **582–583**
loopback plugs for, 228
polling, **260**, *261*
for scanners, **609–610**
serial vs. parallel, 614
Universal Serial Bus for, **169–171**,
  170
upgrading, **939–940**, *939*
Ports dialog box, 267
POS (Programmable Option Select)
  feature, 149
positioning methods for mice, **655–656**
POST (Power On Self Test)
  defined, **1127**
  for drive information, 513
  for MBR problems, 511
Post Office Protocol (POP), 1126
posts, 1126
PostScript language, 567, 1126
POTS (plain old telephone service) for
  DSL, 629
power
  in boot process, **295**
  for CPUs, 86
  formula for, 205
  for hard disk drives, 394, *394*
  for laser printers, **581**
  in transmissions, 687
Power applet, 890, *890*
power conditioners, 204, 341
  benefits of, **342–343**
  defined, 1126
power connection, identifying, 174, *175*
Power Good line, 336–337
power line networks, **800**, **816**
power management, **277**
  identifying, 63
  for notebooks, **890**, *890*
  switches for, **64**
Power Meter product, 336
power meters, 336
power noise, **201–204**
Power On Self Test (POST)
  defined, **1127**
  for drive information, 513
  for MBR problems, 511
power plugs, *35*
power strips, 340

power supplies, **160–161**, *160*, **328**
  backup, **343–345**, *343*
  on buses, 143
  cables and connectors for, **57–58**, *58*,
    63–64, *64*
      for disk drives, 62–63, *62*, 334,
        526
      from outlet, **64–66**, *65*
  common grounds for, **339–341**
  components of, **330**
  cool, 193
  damage caused by, **288**
  defined, 1126
  for disk drives, 528
  dust in, 196
  for FireWire bus, 159
  fluctuations in, 215
  form factors for, **330–335**, *332–334*
  identifying, 174
  installing, **6–7**, *6–7*
  isolating, **340–341**
  for laser printers, **586**
  and lightning, **345–347**
  load problems for, **339**
  location of, 950
  maintaining and upgrading, **335–337**
  memory errors from, **321**
  and noise, **340**
  opening, **330**
  outlet wiring problems, **338–339**
  in Pentium computers, 932
  power conditioners for, 204,
    341–343
  protecting, **337–347**
  removing, **63–66**, *64–65*
  replacing, **329**, **337**
  screws for, 54, *54*
  for speakers, 695
  surge suppressors for, **342**
  testing, **967**
  troubleshooting, **288–289**, **337**, **347**
power surges
  defined, **1126–1127**
  protection from, **202–204**
power switches
  rear, 63
  soft, 58
PPP (Point-to-Point Protocol), 1125
PPPoE (Point-to-Point Protocol over
  Ethernet), **633**
PPTP (Point-to-Point Tunneling Protocol),
  815

precompensation, disk write, 353
prefixes in chip identification, 304
preformatted tapes, 486
pressure rollers in laser printers, 575, *576*
preventive maintenance concerns, **186**
    dust, **196**
    electrostatic discharge, **204–207**
    EMI, **198–201**
    for hard disk drives
        backups, **479–480**, **485–489**
        boot floppies for, **489–490**
        media tests for, **490–492**
        unfragmenting files, **492–494**,
            492–493
        for viruses. *See* viruses
    heat and thermal shock, **190–195**
    magnetism, **197–198**
    power noise, **201–204**
    quick steps in, **187–189**
    troubleshooting tips, **209–210**
    water and liquids, **208–209**
previews with capture boards, **732–733**
PRI (Primary Rate ISDN), 1127
price/performance ratios of proprietary
    computers, **852**
primary colors in color video, 723–724,
    724
primary corona in laser printers, 570, 595
primary DOS partitions
    creating, 438–441, *441*
    names for, 442
primary memory, 100. *See also* memory
Primary Rate ISDN (PRI), 1127
Princeton Graphics HX12 monitor, 679
PRINT.DLL file, 225
"Print Head Failure" message, 560
print heads, 534–535
"PRINT OVERRUN" message, 589
print quality in laser printers, **596**
Printed Circuit Assembly (PCA), **580**
Printer Control Languages (PCLs), 35, **567**
"PRINTER OPEN" message, 588
Printer Properties dialog box, 552–553, *553*
printers, **532**
    in all-in-one combos, **536**
    cables for, 538, **543**
    cleaning, 534
    connecting and testing, **533**
    connectors for, 179, *179*, 181
    dust in, 196
    emulation of, **543–544**, 1127
    indicator lights for, 226
    inkjet. *See* inkjet printers

interfaces for, **167–168**, **537**
isolating problems in, **542–543**
laser. *See* laser printers
magnetism from, 197
maintaining, **534–537**
network, **542**, 1118
in PC selection, **857**
ports for, **537–542**, **544–545**
power for, 339
print heads in, **534–535**
troubleshooting, **236–237**, **542–546**,
    597–598
Printers list, 555
printing
    dynamic linking for, 224–225
    polling for, **260**, *261*
    scanner images, **612**
"PRINTING TEST" message, 588
priority of interrupts, 262, **265–266**
private buses, 148
privilege rings, 134–135, *134*
Pro Audio sequencing program, 705
Pro Tools, 706
processor core frequency, 85
processors. *See* CPUs (central processing
    units)
product code, 974
product documentation and information,
    online sources of, **901**
Professional Graphics Adapter (PGA), 680
PROGMAN.INI files, backing up, 483
program infectors, 465
Programmable Array Logic (PAL)
    components, 929
Programmable Interrupt Controllers, I/O
    addresses for, 251
programmable keyboards, 654
Programmable Option Select (POS)
    feature, 149
programmed input/output (PIO)
    BIOS support for, 375
    defined, 1127
    importance of, 353
    modes in, **381–382**
    operation of, **254–255**, *255*
programs
    cache memory considerations in, **320**
    Control Panel for, **988**, **1003–1005**,
        1003, **1020–1021**
    installing, **1004**, *1004*, 1021
    memory for, **127–128**
    removing, **1003–1004**, 1020, *1020*
PROM blasters, 130

Properties dialog box, 554, *554*
proprietary items
    bus slots, 148, 151
    computers, **851–852**
    vs. generic, **849–852**
    memory, 155
    online services, **922**
protected mode, **134–137**
protecting
    data. *See also* viruses
        backups for, **479–480**,
            485–489
        boot floppies for, **489–490**
        media tests for, **490–492**
    hard disk drives, 51
    power supplies, **337–347**
protection violations, 135
PROTMAN.SYS program, 807
protocol-based technology, 319
PROTOCOL.INI file, 274
protocol stacks, 1127
protocols, **803–804**
    communications, 1088
    network card drivers for, **807–808**
    network file system drivers for,
        806–807
    for network printers, 542
    network transport, **808–809**
        defined, 1118
        IPX/SPX, **810**, *810*
        multiple transport stacks, **813**,
            814
        NetBEUI, **809–810**
        TCP/IP, **810–813**
    redirectors in, **804–806**
Protonic.com site, 910
proxy services, **844–845**
PS/2 computers, **148–149**
PS/2 keyboard, 648, *648*, 650
PS/2 style connectors, *35*
Pulse Code Modulation (PCM), **688–690**,
    689–691
punch-ins in recordings, 706
purchasing PCs, **848**
    name brand vs. generic, **849–852**
    parts selection for, **852**
        BIOS, **854**
        buses, **853–854**
        CD-ROM and DVD drives, **855**
        CPUs, **852–853**
        floppy disks drives, **855**
        hard disk drives, **854**
        keyboards, **856**

memory, **854**
modems and network adapters, **857**
monitors, **855–856**
motherboards, **854**
mouse, **856**
parallel ports, 856
printers, **857**
serial ports, 856
sound cards, **856**
speakers, **856**
USB ports, **857**
video boards, **855**
system comparisons for
audio/video enthusiast, **863**
categories in, **857–861**
corporate, **864**
gamer, **862–863**
home, **861**
road warriors, **864–865**
small business, **863–864**
student, **862**
tips for, **866–867**
vendors for, **865**
PWR label, 983
Pwrite setting, 754

Q

Q Drive, 781
Q signals, **726–727**
QAM (Quadrature Amplitude Modulation), 726
QIC (quarter-inch cartridge) standard, 1127
quality
with inkjet printers, **556–558**
of laser printer printing, **596**
of off-line video compression, **743–744**
of scanner images, **604–605**
Quantum site, 434
quarter-inch cartridge (QIC) standard, 1127
question marks (?), 1127
Quick Connect feature, 624
Quick UnDelete program, **496–498**
QuickCam product, 719
QuickTime technology, 703
QuikTray tool, 1039

R

R manufacturer code, 304
radio-controlled wireless keyboards, **657–658**

Radio Frequency Interference (RFI), **199–201**
defined, 1127
with fiber optic cable, 798
memory errors from, 321
in networks, **793–794**
shielding, 341
radio frequency (RF) output
for video capture, 722, 727
for wireless networks, 800, 821
radios for RFI monitoring, 200–201
RADSL (rate-adaptive digital subscriber line)
characteristics of, 630
defined, 1128
RAID (Redundant Array of Inexpensive Disks), 1128–1129
raised image media with laser printers, 575
RAM (random access memory). *See* memory
RAM chips, 1127
Rambus DRAM (RDRAM), **122–123**, *123*
cost of, 317
data path of, 317
Rambus Inline Memory Modules (RIMMs), 122–123, *123*, 966
RAMPage memory board, 138
random access, 118
random-access memory, 1128
random access storage, 1128
Ranish Partition Manager (RPM), 462
rate-adaptive digital subscriber line (RADSL)
characteristics of, 630
defined, 1128
rayon, triboelectric value of, 205
RCA jacks and plugs, **180**, *181*
for sound cards, 694
for video boards, 182
RCDDIAG program, 272
RD modem light, 643
RDRAM (Rambus DRAM), **122–123**, *123*
cost of, 317
data path of, 317
read-after-write verification, 1128
read-only bits, 455
read-only files, 1128
Read Only Memory (ROM). *See* BIOS (Basic Input/Output System); ROM (Read Only Memory)
read/write heads, 355–356, *356*
for absolute sectors, 450–452, *450*

cleaning, **524–525**
and cylinder skew, 373
in disk drive geometry, 361
documenting, 51
with IDE addressing, 378–379
INT 13 BIOS interface for, 377
number of, 352
parking, 365
positioning, 352
in sector translation, 362
reading
from CD-ROM, **753**
floppy diskettes, **526–527**
MBR, **509–513**
sectors, 358, **365–367**, *366*
README files, 1128
"READY" message, 588
real mode, 135
real-time compression, **732**, **738–741**, *740*
real-time messaging viruses, **468–469**
RealAudio technology, 703
RealJukebox MP3 players, 700
RealVideo files, **744**
reassembly, **68–69**
cables and edge connectors, **69–70**, *70*
mistakes in, **70–72**
rebooting
defined, 1128
in troubleshooting, **215**
rec newsgroups, 915
recalls, chip, 303
receivers, wireless, 657
recharged printer cartridges, 536
recharging batteries, **888–889**
reconfiguring System Restore, **1037–1038**
recordable CD drives. *See* CD Read/Write (CD-RW) drives; CD-recordable (CD-R) drives
recordable DVD drives, **752**
recorders for video capture, **716–719**, *717*
recording
CD-ROM discs, **764–765**
DVD discs, **765–768**
for musicians, **706–707**
"recording inhibited" message, 720
recording polarity of floppy diskettes, 522
recovering
hard disk data, **494**
cross-linked clusters, **504–506**, *505*
from dead drives. *See* resurrecting hard disk drives
erased files, **495–498**, *496*

and FAT, **494–495**, **503**, *503*
from formatted hard disks, **499**
invalid clusters, **503**
invalid subdirectories, **502–503**
lost clusters, **500–501**, *500*, *502*
media errors, **506–508**
system data, **1035–1036**
configuring and disabling System
Restore for, **1037–1038**
restore points in, **1036**
restoring system, **1036–1037**
Recycle Bin, 495
recycled toner cartridges, 537
Red, Green, Blue (RGB) monitors, 679
Red Book CD-ROM standard, 755
red color
in CCD chips, pixels for, 715–716,
716
in TV video, **722–726**, *723–727*
in VGA, pages for, 130
in video capture board, 736–737
red wires in phone lines, 641
redirect bombs, 843
redirectors, **804–806**
reduced instruction set computing (RISC)
defined, 1128
in K5 CPU, 116
Redundant Array of Inexpensive Disks
(RAID), **1128–1129**
Reed-Solomon algorithm, 374
reference points for power supplies,
339–340
refilling inkjet printer cartridges, **560–561**
refresh rates for adapters, **1009**
refreshing
dynamic memory, 257, 316
error beeps for, 290
regional newsgroups, 915
register-to-register transfers, 89
registered SDRAM, 318
registers
in 6x86, 115
I/O addresses for, 251
in MMX processors, 97
and word size, 90–91
registration assemblies in laser printers, 595
registration rollers in laser printers, 572,
574
Registry, **1041**
backing up, **484–485**, **1042–1043**
checking, **1031**
corrupted, **1043**

defined, 1129
editing, **1043–1044**, *1044*
keys in, **1043–1045**
purpose of, **1003**, **1041–1042**
restore points for, 1036
restoring, **1042–1043**
Registry Checker, **1031**, 1042–1043
Registry Editor, 1041, **1043–1044**, *1044*
regulation devices, 1126
relative sector numbers, **450–452**
release in sound waves, *691*, 692
reliability of video editing systems, 730
remainder operator, 451
Remote Registry Service tool, 1039
removable drives
for backups, **486–487**
software for, 488
removable frames, 949, *949*
removable media for old computer data,
933–934, *933*
"REMOVE PAGE" message, 590
removing
cables, **62–63**
computer cover, **52–55**, *53–54*
CPUs, 66
disk drives, **60–63**, *61–62*, **526**
expansion boards, **59–60**, *59–60*
motherboards, **66–68**, *67–68*
power supplies, **63–66**, *64–65*
programs, **1003–1004**, 1020, *1020*
renaming registers in 6x86, 115
repair policy for network cable, 821
repairing expansion boards, 307
chip insertion and removal, **306–307**
chip testing, **303–304**
soldering and desoldering, **305**
reparse points in NTFS, 462
repeat rate, keyboard, 993
repeaters, **838–839**
benefits of, **839**
for coaxial cable, 797
for collisions, **839–840**
vs. extenders, **840**
operation of, **839–840**
for segment isolation, **839**
replacing
configuration batteries, **277–278**
expansion boards, vs. repairing,
294–295
keyboards, 650, 654
notebook batteries, **889**
power supplies, **329**, **337**
rescue tools, limitations of, 229

reserved memory area
buffers and frames in, **132–133**, *133*
flash memory in, **131–132**
ROM in, **130–131**
Reset lines, 143
"RESET" message, 588
"RESET TO SAVE" message, 588
resetting laser printers, **581–582**
resistance in DC supplies, 333
resistors
in ground straps, 207
replacing, 305
for SCSI termination, **420–421**
resolution
of CCD chips, 715–716
with inkjet printers, 556
lines vs. pixels in, **718**
of monitors, 674
of recorders, 717–719, *717*
of scanner images, **604–605**
setting, 1006, 1022
of video, 165
of video boards, **668–672**, **952–953**
in video capture, 715, 736
resource conflicts, **243–246**
8-bit vs. 16-bit boards, **279–280**
with buffers, **267–269**
DIP switches in, **247–248**
with I/O addresses, **252–254**
with IRQ levels, **264–267**
and LPT ports, **279**
with PC Card boards, **269–270**
resolving, **246–248**, **270–272**
Resource Kit, **1038–1040**
resources, locking, 274
Resources tab
for COM ports, 267
for network interface cards, 825,
826–827
Restore My Computer to an Earlier Time
option, 1036
restore points in System Restore, **1036**
restoring
defined, 1129
files, **495–498**
formatted hard disks, **499**
Registry, **1042–1043**
system, **1036–1037**
resurrecting hard disk drives, **508**
booting from floppy disks for, 509
checking cables, 512
checking CMOS, **512**

data recovery services for, **514–515**

modern drives, **513**

priorities in, **509**

reading MBR in, **509–513**

recovering partition table in, **513–514**

temperature problems, 512

tracing failures in, **509**, *510*

retensioning, 1129

retrieving tools, **45**, *45*

return wires, 65–66, 338–339

reviews, online sources of, **901**

reviving hard disk drives. *See* resurrecting hard disk drives

RF (radio frequency) output

for video capture, 722, 727

for wireless networks, 800, 821

RFI (Radio Frequency Interference), **199–201**

defined, 1127

with fiber optic cable, 798

memory errors from, 321

in networks, **793–794**

shielding, 341

RGB connectors, 182

RGB (Red, Green, Blue) monitors, 679

ribbon cables

connecting, **69–70**, *70*

diagrams for, **55–56**

for floppy disk drives, **523–524**, *524*, 968, *969*

for SCSI, 419–420, *420*

ribbons for printers, 534–535

RIMMs (Rambus Inline Memory Modules), 122–123, *123*, 966

Ring Indicator signal, 619

RIO MP3 player, 701

RISC (reduced instruction set computing)

defined, 1128

in K5 CPU, 116

RJ-11 connectors

defined, 1129

identifying, 182, *183*

RJ-13 connectors, **180**

RJ-45 connectors

defined, 1130

for DSL, 632

identifying, **180**, 182, *183*

for network interface cards, 792, *792*

for twisted-pair cable, 800, *802*

RMS power, 336

road warrior PCs, features for, **861**, **864–865**

rocker switches, 247–248, *247*

Rockwell Telecommunications, prefix for, 304

Roll Back Driver option, 1022

ROM (Read Only Memory), 118. *See also* BIOS (Basic Input/Output System)

for 4004 microprocessor, 930

for BASIC language, 520

in boot process, **296–299**, *296*

conflicts in, **267–269**

defined, 1128

diagnostic programs for, **227**

on expansion boards, **298**

flashable, 303

hexadecimal addresses with, **1049–1051**

identifying, 176

with Plug and Play, 273

in reserved memory area, **130–131**

for SCSI adapters, 413

testing, 303

root directories

entries in, 454

number of files in, 501

root keys, **1044–1045**

rotation speed of floppy disk drives, 528

rotational latency period, **367**

routers, 841

routing cables, **71–72**

routing tables, 841

RPC Print Provider tool, 1039

RPM (Ranish Partition Manager), 462

RS-232 isolators, 625

RS-232 ports, **168–169**, *169*, 615, **642**

cables for, 538, *621–622*, **643–644**

flow control with, **620**

operation of, **618–619**

RS-232 standard

defined, **1130**

reasons for, **617–620**

rubber, triboelectric value of, 205

run length compression, 739

"Run SETUP - configuration lost" message, 511

runlists in NTFS, 461

runs in NTFS, 461

S

S-100 bus, **142**

S chip prefix, 304

S/PDIF (Sony/Philips Digital Interface Format), 694, **701–702**, 706

S-video interface, **727–729**

S-video output, 722

Safe Mode

booting in, 216

for restoring Registry, 1042

sags, 1130

salicylic acid chromium chelate in toner, 597

salt, board damage from, 208

sampling by sound cards, **688–690**, *689–691*

SANs (Storage Area Networks)

defined, 1133

in FCSI, **410**

SASI (Shugart Associates System Interface), 403, 405

satellite communications, 626, **637**

installing and configuring, **638–639**

operation of, **638**

two-way, 637

for video capture, 721

satellite speakers, 695

saturation of color, 736

saving data

in old computers, **933–934**, *933–934*

process of, **498**

SCAM (SCSI Configure AutoMagically), 415

scan codes, keyboard, 650

Scan for Altered Files option, 1030

ScanDisk program, 1033

for bad areas, 444

for invalid subdirectories, 502

for lost clusters, 501

operation of, **494–495**

reporting errors by, 379

ScanJet, ROM for, **1050–1051**

scanners, **600**

connecting, **601**

connections for, **608**

images from

editing, **611**

quality of, **604–605**

size of, **606–607**

viewing and printing, **611–612**

interface cards for, 132, 173

interfaces for, **604–605**

maintaining, 607

optical character recognition with, **607**

ports for, **609–611**

resources for, 610

scanning by, **603–604**, *603*

settings for, **610–611**
troubleshooting, **612**
TWAIN drivers for, **605**, 609
types of, **602–603**, *602*
Universal Serial Bus for, 170
scatter/gather DMA transfer, 382
scheduling
    backups, 488
    LANs for, **791**
sci newsgroups, 915
Scour site, 699
screen
    expansion boards for. *See* video and
        video boards
    monitors. *See* monitors
screw-mounted adapters (SMAs), 803
screwdrivers, **42–43**, *43*
    magnetic tip, 45
    for notebooks, 871, 875
screws
    for cables, 222
    for disk drives, **61**
    for expansion boards, 59
    for inkjet printers, 549
    for keyboards, 653
    for motherboards, 67
    for network interface cards, 822–823
    for notebooks, 881
    for power supplies, 64
    removing, 52–55
    retrieving, 45
    storing, 49–50
scripting in SCSI-2, 406
Scroll Lock key, sound with, 994
SCSI (Small Computer Systems Interface),
    400, **403**
    asynchronous and synchronous, **406**
    benefits of, **403–404**
    BIOS for, **428**
    bus mastering with, **413**
    cables for, 403, 407, **411–412**,
        416–420, *417–420*, 429
    CD-ROMs with, **762**
    compatibility in, **411**
    configurations for, **410–412**
    connectors for, *178*, 179, 182, *184*
    daisy chaining with, **416–420**,
        417–419
    data transfer rates in, 374–375
    defined, **1130–1131**
    fast and wide, 407
    and Fibre Channel, **410**
    FireWire bus for, 159

for hard disk drives, 167
hardware installation with, **412**
host adapters for, 165, 403
    choosing, **412–413**
    controllers in, 167
    installing, **413–414**, *414*
    issues in, **411**
    ROM on, 268
installing cards for, 10–11, *10–11*,
    401–402
low-level formatting for, **434**
parity with, **416**
peripheral IDs with, **414–415**, 429
sample setup, **423–425**
for scanners, 173, **605**
SCSI-1, **405–406**, **416–420**, *418*
SCSI-2, **406–407**, 413, 419, *419*
SCSI-3, **407–409**, **426**
sector translation with, 362
single-ended vs. differential, 404
software for, **426–427**
for sound, 694
standards for, **426–427**
summary, **408–409**
for tape drives, 167, 173
terminating, **404–405**, **408**, **412**,
    420–426, *422*
terms for, 404–405
troubleshooting, **429**
with video capture, 733
SCSI bus, 1131
SCSI Configure AutoMagically (SCAM),
    415
SCSI devices
    availability of, 27
    BIOS for, 51
SCSI terminators, 1131
SD (Secure Digital) Cards, **779**, *780*
SD modem light, 643
SDRAM (Synchronous Dynamic Random
    Access Memory), **317–319**
    benefits of, **121**, *121*
    DDR, 123, **319**
    defined, **1134–1135**
    installing, 4–5, *4–5*
    introduction of, 119
    SLDRAM, **319**
SDSL (single-line digital subscriber line)
    characteristics of, 630
    defined, 1132
Seagate
    hard disk drives by, servos in, 365
    site for, 434

search engines
    defined, 1131
    popular, **907–908**
searching
    for IRC channels, **921**
    for mailing lists, **919–920**
    for newsgroups, **916–918**
    for text on disks, 498
    for Web sites, **906–908**
seating motherboards, **71**
SECCs (Single Edge Contact Cartridges),
    101
secondary memory, 100, 118. *See also* disk
    drives; floppy disk drives; floppy
    diskettes; hard disk drives
SECs (Single Edge Cartridges), 95, *95*
"Sector not found" errors, 526–527
sector translation, 353, **362–364**
sectors, 355–356, **359–360**, *359*
    absolute and DOS, **450–452**
    bad, 456
        defined, 1081
        report on, 494–495
        testing for, 490–492
    on CD-ROM disks, 753
    defined, 1131
    in disk drive geometry, 361
    documenting, 51
    in formatting, **444**
    on hard disk drives, 352
    with IDE addressing, 378–379
    IDs for, 369
    INT 13 BIOS interface for, 377
    logical block addressing for, **362–364**,
        380
    reading, 358, **365–367**, *366*
    in sector translation, 362
    in Zone Bit Recording, **360–361**,
        363
Secure Digital (SD) Cards, **779**, *780*
Secure Digital Music Initiative, 698
security
    in cable broadband, **637**
    for DSL, **634–635**
    for MP3 audio files, 698
    for networks, **842**
        firewalls for, 204, **843–845**
        passwords for, **842–843**
        tips for, **842**
    protected mode for, 134–137
seek time
    defined, 1131
    of hard disk drives, **365–367**

segments
    address, table of, 1049–1050
    network
        with NetBEUI, 809
        repeaters for, **839**
Select Device dialog box, 1001–1002, *1002*
self-test for scanners, 608
"SELF TEST" message, 588
self-tests
    for capture boards, 734
    for printers, 543, 587
SelfHelpDesk site, 910
sensors
    for heat, **192–193**, *193*
    in laser printers, 576
separation pads in laser printers, 584–585
separation pawls in laser printers, 595
Sequenced Package Exchange (SPX), 1131
sequencing, MIDI, **704–705**
sequential access, 118, 1131
serial communications, **614**, 1131
    asynchronous ports for, **615**, *615*
    cables for, **616**, *621–622*
    flow control in, **618–620**
    line noise in, **641**
    modems, 616–617, **622–625**
    RS-232 standard for, **617–620**
    troubleshooting, **640–644**
    UARTs for, **615–616**
Serial Line Internet Protocol (SLIP), 1132
serial numbers on chips, 304
serial ports, 31, **168–169**, *169*
    conflicts with, **243–248**, **264**
    connectors on, 178, *178*, **983**
    defined, 1132
    Device Manager for, 1014
    extra, **266–267**
    for generic computers, 850
    I/O addresses for, 251–252
    IRQ for, 263
    loopback plugs for, 228
    vs. parallel, 614
    in PC selection, 856
    on power supplies, 345
    for printers, **541**, **544–545**,
        565–566
    for serial communications, **642**
    Universal Serial Bus for, **169–171**,
        170
    for upgrading, **939–940**, *939*
serial SCSI, **408**
SerialKey option, 997, 1019
Server Message Blocks (SMBs), 805

servers
    in client/server networks, 789
    in IRC, 921
"SERVICE" messages, 590–591
serviceability of proprietary PCs, **851–852**
servo systems, 357, 364–365
session hijacking, 844
Set as Default option, 555
set-associative caches, 1084
SET COMSPEC statements, 302
Settings for High Contrast dialog box, 996,
    996, 1018, *1019*
Settings for MouseKeys dialog box, 996,
    997
Settings for SoundSentry dialog box, 995,
    995
Settings tab, 1006, *1006*
setup
    diagnostic programs for, 227
    information for, **275–277**
setup disks, storing, 248
SETUP programs
    for CD-ROM drives, **764**
    for CMOS information, **50–51**, **276**
SFP (System File Protection) feature, **1037**
SFX motherboards, power supplies for, **331**
SGRAM (Synchronous Graphics RAM)
    defined, **1135**
    for video, 665
shadow packets, terminators for, 801
ShareFun virus, **467**
shareware programs, 911
    third-party tools, **1041**
    viruses in, 473
sharing
    interrupts, **149**, **267**
    on networks
        applications, **789–790**
        bandwidth, **627**
        peripheral devices, **790**
sharpness of scanner images, 605
sheet-fed scanners, 602
SHELL statements, executing, 301–302
shells, 127
shielded cable, 1132
shielded speakers, 695
shielded twisted-pair (STP) cable
    defined, 1132
    for networks, 795, *795*
shielding
    in coaxial cable, 797, *797*
    for crosstalk reduction, 199
    for power supplies, 341

shipping laser printers, 594
short circuits, 289, 1132
Show All Folders option, 1042
Show Settings Icon on Taskbar option,
    1008
ShowSounds feature, 995, 1018
Shugart Associates System Interface (SASI),
    403, 405
sign-on messages for SCSI devices, 429
signal-to-noise ratios, 687
signature bytes, 298
Signature Verification Tool, **1031**
SIIA (Software and Information Industry
    Association), 790
silicon, triboelectric value of, 205
silk, triboelectric value of, 205
silver, triboelectric value of, 205
SIMD (Single Instruction, Multiple Data)
    technique, 97
SIMM (Single Inline Memory Module)
    memory, 119, *120*, **313–314**
    defined, 1132
    identifying, 175
    in laser printers, 568
    removing, **324**, *324*
    for SDRAM, 317
    in upgrading, 940
Simple Mail Transfer Protocol (SMTP)
    defined, 1132
    with DSL, 633
    session hijacking, 844
Simple Network Management Protocol
    (SNMP), 831
simplification for troubleshooting, **216**
sine-wave power supplies, 343–345, *343*
sine waves, *686–688*, **687–688**
Single Edge Cartridges (SECs), 95, *95*
Single Edge Contact Cartridges (SECCs),
    101
single-ended SCSI, 404
Single Inline Memory Module (SIMM)
    memory, 119, *120*, **313–314**
    defined, 1132
    identifying, 175
    in laser printers, 568
    removing, **324**, *324*
    for SDRAM, 317
    in upgrading, 940
Single Inline Pin Packages (SIPP) memory
    chips
    size of, 313
    for terminators, 422–423, *422*

Single Instruction, Multiple Data (SIMD) technique, 97
Single Large Expensive Disk (SLED), 1132
single-layer DVD discs, 754
single-line digital subscriber line (SDSL)
   characteristics of, 630
   defined, 1132
single-mode fiber optic cable
   defined, 1132
   operation of, **798–799**
SIPP (Single Inline Pin Packages) memory chips
   size of, 313
   for terminators, 422–423, *422*
size
   CD-ROM disks, 753
   chips, 313, **315**
   clusters, **436–438**, 453–454
   in computer evolution, 928
   in directory entries, 456
   DVD discs, 766–767
   files, 456, 503
   fonts, **1007–1008**, *1007–1008*, 1022
   frames in video capture, **737**
   hard disk drives, **376–380**
   microprocessors, 931, *931*
   monitors, **675**
   partitions and partition tables, **380–381**
   scanner images, **606–607**
   screen, 676
   screws, 42
skew, cylinder, **373**
skin, triboelectric value of, 205
skin resistance and ESD, 205
"SKIP SELF TEST" message, 589
skirts on expansion boards, 146, *146*
slashes (/), 1133
slave controllers, **393–396**
slave DMA register, error beeps for, 292
slave drives, 937–938
SLDRAM (synchronous link DRAM), **319**
SLED (Single Large Expensive Disk), 1132
slide switches, 247–248, *247*
slim-line case style, 52–53
slim-line hard drives, 879
SLIP (Serial Line Internet Protocol), 1132
slots, 25–26
   buses for, **141–142**, *145–146*
   for CPUs, **101–102**
   for generic computers, 850

identifying, 176, *176*
number of, 33
for PC Card bus, 157
RFI from, 200
speed of, 148
for ultimate computer, 951
in upgrading, **940–942**, *941*
slow printing with inkjet printers, **555–556**
small business PCs, **860**, **863–864**
Small Computer Systems Interface. *See* SCSI (Small Computer Systems Interface)
Small fonts setting, 1007, 1022
Small Outline DIMMs (SODIMMs), 313–314
smart cards, 782
Smart-UPS 420 product, 345
Smart Video Recorder, 739–740
SmartMedia cards, 774, **777–778**, *777*
Smartmodems, 617
SMAs (screw-mounted adapters), 803
SMBs (Server Message Blocks), 805
smearing on laser printer pages, **578**
smoking
   dust from, 196
   floppy disk drive damage from, 525
SMP (symmetric multiprocessing), 110
SMPTE (Society of Motion Picture and Television Engineers), 705
SMTP (Simple Mail Transfer Protocol)
   defined, 1132
   with DSL, 633
   session hijacking, 844
SNA (Systems Network Architecture), 173
SNMP (Simple Network Management Protocol), 831
SNMP Agent tool, 1039
soc newsgroups, 915
Society of Motion Picture and Television Engineers (SMPTE), 705
Socket Services standard, **156**
sockets
   on circuit boards, 230, 292
   for CPUs, **101–102**, **942**, *942*
   for memory chips, **306–307**, 324
   for ROM, 131
SODIMMs (Small Outline DIMMs), 313–314
soft errors on hard drives, **444**
soft power switches, 58, 64
software. *See also* drivers
   for backups, **487–488**
   for CD-ROM recording, 764

for chip testing, **303**
compatibility in, **27–28**
DLLs and VxDs, **223–225**
faulty, **225–226**
for flow control, 620
for I/O addresses, 254
lockups from, **233**
for MP3 audio files, **700–701**
for SCSI, **426–427**
system information for, 1027
troubleshooting, 216, **222–226**, **1045–1046**
for video capture, **735–741**, **744–745**
Software and Information Industry Association (SIIA), 790
software decoders for DVD drives, 956
software interrupts, 131
software setup in EISA bus, 150
solder jigs, 305
solder pads, 69
soldering, 230, 293, **305**
solid copper wire for networks, 793
Sonicnet site, 699
Sonique MP3 player, 700
sonograms, 685, *685*
Sony/Philips Digital Interface Format (S/PDIF), 694, **701–702**, 706
sound and sound cards, 22, *24*, 34, **172–173**, 684
   3D audio, **702–703**
   accessibility options for, **994–995**, *995*, **1018**
   address conflicts with, **253–254**, *253*
   characteristics of, **692–694**, *693*
   connectors for, *184*
   digital and surround, **701–702**
   with DVD drives, 770
   FM synthesis by, **691–692**, *691*
   for games, **944**
   inputs and outputs for, **694–695**
   installing, 16–17, *16–17*, **685**, 696, **974–976**, *975*
   MP3, **696–701**
   for musicians, **704–706**
   in PC selection, **856**
   ROM on, 268
   sampling for, **688–690**, *689–691*
   sound characteristics, **685–688**, **686–688**
   speaker systems for, **695–696**
   streaming media, **703–704**
   with ToggleKeys function, 994

troubleshooting, **707**
for ultimate computer, **952–954**, *954*
upgrading, **940**
in video capture, **729**
wavetable synthesis for, **692**
Sound Blaster sound cards, 172
address conflicts with, **253–254**, *253*
installing, **974–976**, *975*
introduction of, 953
sampling with, 692–693
Sound Blaster Live!, 692–693
Sound tab, 994, *995*, 1018
sounds in laser printers, **593**
Sounds Properties window, 975, *975*
SoundSentry feature, **994–995**, *995*, 1018
space parity, 1121
spacers for motherboards, 67–68, *68*
spade lugs, 66
spamming, 914
sparse files in NTFS, **462**
speakers
clicks in, 289
connections for, 22, *24, 35*, 58, 67,
72
for games, 944
installing, 983
magnetism from, 198
in PC selection, **856**
for sound boards, **695–696**
Universal Serial Bus for, 171
specialist databases, 1120
specifications for CPUs, **102–106**
speculative execution in 6x86, 115
speech recognition, 88, 97
speed
AGP bus, 154
buses, **146–148**, 276–277
cable broadband, 635
CD-ROM drives, 30, **758–760**
communications systems, 643
in computer evolution, 928
CPU, 28, **83–88**, 102–105,
108–112, **960–963**
in digital broadband communications,
627
disk drive access, **365–367**
DSL, **628–629**, **631**
EISA bus, 150
FireWire bus, 159
floppy disk drive rotation, **528**
hard disk drives, **955**
ISDN, 627

memory, 119–124, 276, **316–317**
memory boards, 148, 150
memory chips, **313–314**, **319**, **321**.
See also caches
modems, **622–623**, 954
parallel ports, 538
PC Card bus, 157
PCI bus, **152–153**
Pentium, **98–100**
satellite communications, 637
serial ports, 168, 545
UARTs, 616
USB bus, 170
video, 664, **667–668**
video capture boards, 732
video cards, **952–953**
video editing systems, 730
speed codes on chips, 304
Speed Disk utility, 1040
speed matching, controllers for, **161–163**
SpeedDisk program, **507**
SpeedStor program, 398
spikes, 340
defined, 1133
surge suppressors for, **342**
spills, **208**, 651
spinning speed of CD-ROM drives, 758
SPKR label, 983
spread-spectrum radio, 1144
spreadsheets for memory tests, 272
spring-loaded twist (ST) connectors, 803,
803
springs in keyboards, 650
SPS (Standby Power Supplies), **343–345**,
343
SPX (Sequenced Package Exchange), 1131
square solder pads, 69
square wave power supplies, 343–345, *343*
squeaking sounds in laser printers, **593**
SRAM (Static RAM)
cost of, 119
on CPU, **93**
defined, 1133
vs. DRAM, 257, **316**
ST (spring-loaded twist) connectors,
803, *803*
ST (straight-tip connector), 1133
stabilizer bars in scanners, 604
stacked hubs, 829
STACKS statements, executing, 301
stand-alone hubs, **829–831**, *830*
Standard CMOS Setup screen, 970–971,
971

standards. *See also* compatibility
for CD-ROM, **755–757**
for connectors, 142
for modems, **623–624**
for SCSI, **426–427**
standby batteries, 278
Standby Power Supplies (SPS), **343–345**,
343
standoffs for motherboards, 68, **977–978**,
977
Stang, Dave, 226
start bits, 1133
starting clusters in directory entries,
456–458
Startup Disk tab, 489, 1005, *1005*
startup disks, **52**
startup problems
in laser printers, **579–580**
troubleshooting, **232–233**
Startup tab, 1033
stateful inspection, **845**
static charge eliminators in laser printers,
574
static column RAM, 120
static electricity
anti-static wrist straps for, **44**
causes of, **204–206**
damage from, **206**
from desoldering, 305
with memory chips, 321, 323
preventing, **206–207**
in workspace, 49
static IP numbers for DSL, **633–635**
static linking, 224
Static RAM (SRAM)
cost of, 119
on CPU, **93**
defined, 1133
vs. DRAM, 257, **316**
status information for printers, 168
status lights for hubs, 831
stealth viruses
defined, 1133
operation of, **470**
steel wool, triboelectric value of, 205
Step-By-Step Confirmation option, 1032
step-index fiber optic cable, **798–799**, *799*
stepper motors, **365**
stereo speakers, 695
StickyKeys option, 992, *993*, 1017
still cameras for video capture, **721**
still capture boards, 730

stop bits
defined, 1133
for serial ports, 545
Storage Area Networks (SANs)
defined, 1133
in FCSI, **410**
store-and-forward switching
vs. cut-through, 836–837, *837*
defined, 1133
STP (shielded twisted-pair) cable
defined, **1132**
for networks, 795, *795*
straight-slot screwdrivers, 42
straight-through cables, 523
straight-tip connector (ST), 1133
stranded copper wire for networks, 793
streaks
with inkjet printers, 557
with laser printers, **577–578**, *579*,
593
streaming tape, 1133
streaming technology, **703–704**, **744**
stripe masks in CCD chips, 715
stripe sets, 1133
stripes with inkjet printers, 557
stripping screws, 42
student PCs, features for, **859**, **862**
Sturgeon's Law, 228
styrene acrylate copolymer in toner, 597
subdirectories
defined, 1134
in FAT, **457–458**
invalid, **502–503**
subkeys in Registry, **1043–1045**, *1044*
subnet addresses, 1134
subnet masks, 812–813, 1134
subnets, 1134
subscribing to mailing lists, 919
subwoofers, 695, 702
suffixes in chip identification, 304
sunbeams, **195**
sunlight and CD-ROM discs, 768
Super VGA adapters, 680
Super VGA boards, 164
dot pitch for, 675
memory for, 128
refresh rates with, 673
resolution and colors with, 669–670
super VHS recorders, **717–719**
SuperDisk, 521
superpipelining
in 6x86, 115
defined, 1134

superscalar CPUs
defined, 1134
pipelines in, **98–100**
support
Internet and online services for,
898–900
newsgroups for, **913–919**
proprietary online services, **922**
surfaces, disk, 356
SurfDoubler product, 634
surge protectors
defined, 1134
for hard disk drives, 478
for notebooks, 888
for phone lines, 625
for power supplies, **342**
UPS as, 345
surges, 340
defined, 1134
power-up, **202–204**
transient, **204**
surround sound, **695**, **701–702**
survpc mailing list, 920
sustain in sound waves, *691*, *692*
SVGA (Super VGA) adapters, 680
SVGA (Super VGA) boards, 164
dot pitch for, 675
memory for, 128
refresh rates with, 673
resolution and colors with, 669–670
swap files, 1134
swapping
defined, 1134
expansion boards, 288
switchboxes, 580
switches, **835–837**, *835–837*. *See also* DIP
switches; jumpers
for keyboard, **649–650**
power, **63–66**
switching power supplies, **328**
switching times for SPS, 343
Symantec site, 474
symmetric multiprocessing (SMP), 110
synchronization
of notebook files, **892–894**
in video, 726–727, 728
Synchronous Dynamic Random Access
Memory (SDRAM), **317–319**
benefits of, **121**, *121*
DDR, 123, **319**
defined, **1134–1135**
introduction of, 119
SLDRAM, **319**

Synchronous Graphics RAM (SGRAM)
defined, 1135
for video, 665
synchronous link DRAM (SLDRAM),
319
synchronous SCSI, **406**
SYS files, viruses in, 466
SysReq key, 648
System applet, 267
system bits, 455
system boards. *See* motherboards
system boot disks
creating, **52**
preparing, **489–490**, 974
system bus
frequency of, 85
for video and video boards, **663–664**
system bus interfaces for hard disk drives,
354
system clock/calendar, 32, **160**, **171–172**
System Commander utility, 445
system comparisons, categories in,
857–861
audio/video enthusiast, **863**
corporate, **864**
gamer, **862–863**
home, **861–862**
road warrior, **864–865**
small business, **863–864**
student, **862**
System Configuration Utility, **1032–1033**,
1032
SYSTEM.DAT file
backing up, 484
in Registry, 1042
System Doctor utility, 1040
System File Checker, 229–230,
1030–1031, *1030*
System File Protection (SFP) feature, **1037**
system files
backing up, **483–485**
checking, **1030–1031**, *1030*
executing, 301
system information, MSI for, **1026–1027**,
1027
System Information tool, 229–230
SYSTEM.INI file
backing up, 483
checking, 1033
for compatibility, 1041
system inventory functions in diagnostic
programs, **226–227**
System Monitor utility, **1026**, *1026*

System Properties window
for Device Manager, 999, *999*,
1014–1017, *1014*
for performance, **1016–1017**, *1016*
for removing devices, 247
in Windows XP, **1025**
system resources, status of, 1017
System Restore, **1035–1036**
reconfiguring and disabling,
1037–1038
restore points in, **1036**
restoring system with, **1036–1037**
System tab, 1028, *1028*
system tests, **967–968**, **982**
System Tools, 229–230
system tray, icons in, 1008
Systems Network Architecture (SNA), 173

T

T (tera-) prefix, 1135
T.120 protocols, 1135
T-connectors
identifying, 179, *179*
for network interface cards, 800–801,
801
Tahiti sound cards, 707
talk newsgroups, 915
talking heads, 739
Tandy, 149
tannic acids, 209
tape cartridges, 1135
tape drives, **173**
for backups, **486**
cables for, 63
controllers for, **167**
defined, 1135
for old computer data, **934**
software for, 488
Tarbell interface, 520
target IDs in SCSI, **415–416**
TB (terabytes), 1135
TBLD label, 983
TCP (Transmission Control Protocol)
defined, 1138
functions of, 810–811
TCP/IP (Transmission Control
Protocol/Internet Protocol), **810–813**,
811
defined, **1138–1139**
for network printers, 542
TCP ports, 1135
tea, board damage from, 209

TEAC America, floppy disk drives by, 855
technical information and support
Internet and online services for,
898–900
IRC for, **921–922**
mailing lists for, **920**
newsgroups for, **913–919**
proprietary online services for, **922**
World Wide Web for, **908–912**
technology, improvements in, **928–930**,
929
TechTutorials.com, 911
TechWeb site, 911
teflon, triboelectric value of, 205
telcos for DSL, 632
Telecommunications Industry Association
(TIA), cable grading by, **795–796**
telephone lines
isolators for, 625
for modems, 623
for networks, **800**, **816**, **944**
noise in, **641**
in satellite communications, 638
telephones, magnetism from, 197
television signals, **722–726**, *723–726*
Telnet protocol, 1135
temperature. *See also* heat
with diskettes, 525
hard disk drive problems from, 512
probes for, 194, 304
safe ranges, **194**
thermal shock, **195**
temperature chip testing, **303–304**
temporary swap files, 1135
tera- (T) prefix, 1135
terabytes (TB), 1135
terminal adapters for ISDN, 628
terminal emulation, 1135
Terminate and Stay Resident (TSR)
programs
in AUTOEXEC.BAT file, **127**
viruses in, 470
terminators and termination
active vs. passive, **420–421**, *421*
built-in, 404–405
for CD-ROM drives, 769
for coaxial cable, 800–801
defined, **1135–1136**
SCSI, **404–405**, **408**, **412**,
420–426, *422*
testing
by BIOS, **299**
capture boards, 734

chips, **303**
DirectX Diagnostics Tool for,
1028–1029
expansion boards, **272**
hard disk drive media, **490–492**
hard disk drives, **883**
laser printers, **581**
memory, **297**
memory chips, **322–324**, *323*
modems, **1013**, *1013*, 1025
network cable, 820
outlet wiring, 338–339
power supplies, **967**
scanners, 608
system tests, **967–968**, **982**
Text File Viewer tool, 1039
text mode, 1136
text on disks, searching for, 498
Text Search program, 498
Texwipe product, 209
thermal inkjet printers, 552
thermal shock
with computers, **195**
with diskettes, 525
thermal-transfer printers, **536–537**
thermistors, 535, 575
thermometers
CPU, 87
PC, 194
thick Ethernet, 1136
thickness of floppy diskettes, 522
thicknet cable, 797
thicknet networks, 180, 182
thin Ethernet, 1136
thinnet networks, 180, 182
third hands, 305
third-party tools, **1040**
diagnostic, **228–229**
for formatting and partitioning, **445**
McAfee Utilities, **1040**
Norton Utilities, **1040**
shareware, **1041**
thrashing, 1136
threads, 1136
throughput, 1136
ThumbDrive product, 781
TIA (Telecommunications Industry
Association), cable grading by, **795–796**
TIA/EIA 232D ports, **168–169**, *169*,
615, **642**
cables for, 538, *621–622*, **643–644**
flow control with, **620**
operation of, **618–619**

TIA/EIA 586 standard, 1136–1137
TIA/EIA structured cabling standards, 1137
TIF format for scanner images, 606
tightening screws, 42
time
    in BIOS, 970–971
    clock/calendar for, **171–172**
    quick steps for, **989**
    setting, **1005**, *1006*, **1021**
time bombs, **471**
Time Zone Editor tool, 1039
time zones, setting, 1005, 1021
timeouts, hard disk drive, **299**
timers
    connections for, 58
    error beeps for, 290, 292
    I/O addresses for, 251
    IRQ for, 263
TimeThis tool, 1039
tint of color, **736–737**
TNT chip set, 674
TNT2 chip set, 674
ToggleKeys function, **994**, **1017–1018**
Token Ring network cards
    memory for, 132
    ROM on, 268
Token Ring networks, 410, 1137
    cable in, 795
    defined, 1137
    network interface cards for, 792
tolerances in SNMP, 832
Tom's Hardware Guide site, 911
toner cartridges
    problems with, **592–593**
    recycled, 537
toner in laser printers, 570, 573, *574*
    ammonia effect on, 583
    cleaning, **594**
    composition of, 577–578
    light effect on, 583
    "TONER LOW" message, 589
tools, **42**
    anti-static wrist straps, **44**
    chip inserters, 47–48
    chip removers, **46–48**, *47–48*
    hemostats, **46**
    lights, 47
    mirrors, 47
    for notebooks, 875, 881
    pliers, **46**, *46*
    retrieving, **45**, *45*
    screwdrivers, **42–43**, *43*

top-level domains, 1137–1138
topologies, 1138
Torx screwdrivers, 43
Toshiba, floppy disk drives by, **521**
tower cases
    in building computers, 950
    removing, **54–55**, *54*
TP (twisted-pair) cable
    connectors for, **802**, *802*
    for crosstalk reduction, 199
    defined, 1139
    for DSL, 629
    for networks, 182, **795–797**, *795*, *943*
TR modem light, 643
trace caches, 114
Traceroute utility, 841
traces, 141
track density, 368
trackballs, **656**
    defined, 1138
    installing, **647**
tracks, **355–360**, *357–358*
    on CD-ROM disks, 753
    defined, 1138
    on floppy diskettes, 522
transceivers in wireless technology, 639
transfer corona wires, 574, *574*, 578–579, 595–596
transfer rates, 368
    for CD-ROM drives, **758–759**
    for hard disk drives, 365
        caches for, **375–376**
        defined, 352
        external transfer rate
            dependencies in, **375**
        internal, **368**
        optimizing, **374–376**
        in ultimate computer, 955
    and interleave factor, **368–373**
    for network interface cards, **792–793**
    of SCSI systems, 408–409
transformers
    isolation, 339, 342
    in power supplies, 328
transients, **204**
transistors
    in flash memory, 774
    replacing, 305
Transmission Control Protocol (TCP)
    defined, 1138
    functions of, 810–811

Transmission Control Protocol/Internet
    Protocol (TCP/IP), **810–813**, *811*
    defined, 1138–1139
    for network printers, 542
transmission media, 1139
transport protocols, **808–809**
    IPX/SPX, **810**, *810*
    multiple transport stacks, **813**, *814*
    NetBEUI, **809–810**
    TCP/IP, **810–813**
transport stacks
    binding interfaces for, 807–808
    multiple, **813**, *814*
Trend Micro site, 474–475
triboelectric value, 205
tripler chips, **85–86**
Trojan horses, **470**
    defined, 1139
    firewalls for, **843**
Trojan prefix, 469
Troubleshooters, **1046**
troubleshooting, 212, **293–294**
    assumptions in, 217
    boot process in, **295–302**, *296*
    CD-ROM drives, **768–769**
    connectors, **221–222**
    dead machines, **288**
        boot process in, **295–302**, *296*
        expansion boards, **292–293**
        power supplies, **288–289**
    diagnostic programs for, **226**
        for expansion boards, **272**
        features in, **226–228**
        third-party, **228–229**
    diagrams in, **216–217**
    documentation in, **215**, 217
    DVD drives, **769–770**
    emergencies, **237–238**
    expansion boards, **230–231**,
        280–281, **284–288**, **292–293**,
        307
        chip insertion and removal,
            306–307
        chip testing, **303–304**
        soldering and desoldering, **305**
    external indicators in, **226**
    floppy disk drives, **526–530**
    formatting, **445**
    hard disk crashes, **234–235**
    after hardware installation, **234**
    inkjet printers, **552–559**, 561
    Internet and online services, **924–925**
    keyboards, **651–654**, 658

lockups, 233–234
memory, 324–325
mice, **657**
modem connections, 236
monitors, 235–236
notebook computers, 894
observations in, 217–218
operator errors, 219–221
order of steps in, 215
panicking in, **214**
patience in, **214**
power supplies, 288–289, 337, 347
printers, 236–237, 542–546,
    597–598
rebooting in, **215**
rules of, **214**
scanners, **612**
SCSI, **429**
serial communications, 640–644
simplification for, **216**
software, 216, **222–226**, **1045–1046**
sound, **707**
startup problems, 232–233
steps in, 213–214, 218–219
support for, 231–232
ultimate computer installation, **984**
USB ports, 540–541
video, **681**
video capture, 745–746
viruses, 475–476
Windows diagnostic programs for,
    229–230
Windows Report Tool for,
    1029–1030, *1029*
TSR (Terminate and Stay Resident)
    programs
    in AUTOEXEC.BAT file, **127**
    viruses in, 470
TTL (Transistor-Transistor Logic) chips,
    206
TTL monitors, 679
Tucows site, 1041
tuner cards for video capture, 721
Tunes site, 699
tunneling protocols, 815
tunnels for cable broadband, 635
Turbo-Cool power supplies, 193
Turbo LED, 983
Turn Off Automatic Updates option, 1035
turning off computers, **202–204**
TV tuner cards, 721
TWAIN drivers for scanners, **605**, 609
TweakUI tool, 1039

twisted-pair (TP) cable
    connectors for, **802**, *802*
    for crosstalk reduction, 199
    defined, 1139
    for DSL, 629
    for networks, 182, **795–797**, *795*, 943
twists in cable, 523–524, *524*, 968, *969*
two and a half clock speeds, **86–87**
two-way satellite communications, 637
two-way set-associative caches, 94
Type 1–9 cable, 796–797, 1139
Type 1 PC Card slots, 155–156
Type 2 PC Card slots, 155–156
Type 3 PC Card slots, 155–156, 884
types, CPU, 28

U

U pipelines in Pentium, **98–99**
UARTs (Universal Asynchronous
    Receivers/Transmitters), 31
    defined, 1140
    for modems, 623
    for serial communications, **615–616**
UDP (User Datagram Protocol), 1141
ultimate computer, **946**
    BIOS for, **970–972**, *971*
    cases for, **949–951**, *949*, **958–959**,
        958
    CD-ROM drives for, **956**, **972–973**,
        973, **980**, *981*
    DVD decoder cards for, **976**, *977*
    DVD drives for, **956**, **972–973**, *973*
    expansion boards for, **979–980**, *979*
    floppy disk drives for, **968–969**, *969*,
        981
    front panel lights and speaker for,
        983–984
    hard disk drives for, **955**, **969**, *969*,
        981–982, *982*
    interfaces for, **957**, *957*
    keyboards and mouse in, **973**
    modems for, **954**, *955*, 976
    motherboards for, **951–952**,
        959–966, **977–978**, *977*
    networking in, **956–957**
    operating system for, **973–974**
    port connectors for, **983**
    power supplies for, **978**, *978*
    quick steps for, **947–948**
    sound cards for, **952–954**, *954*,
        974–976, *975*
    troubleshooting, **984**

video boards for, **952–953**, **966–968**
    Zip drives for, **955**, **980**, *981*
Ultra HiNote 2000 computer, 93
Ultra SCSI, **407–409**
Ultra Wide SCSI, 1139
Ultra2 SCSI, 1139
UltraPlayer MP3 player, 700
unbalanced SCSI, 404
unbuffered SDRAM, 318
uncertified files, 1031
uncompressing, 1139
undelete program, 495
Undernet IRC channel, 921
underscanning, 675
undervoltage conditions, **204**, 340
unerasing files, **495–498**, *496*
unformatters, **499**
unfragmenting files, **492–494**, *492–493*,
    507
unidirectional ports, 169
Uniform Resource Locators (URLs), 1140
uninstalling programs, **1003–1004**, 1020,
    1020
Uninterruptible Power Supplies (UPSs)
    defined, 1140
    operation of, **343–345**, *343*
Universal Asynchronous
    Receivers/Transmitters (UARTs), 31
    defined, 1140
    for modems, 623
    for serial communications, **615–616**
universal SCSI drivers, 426, *426*
Universal Serial Bus. *See* USB (Universal
    Serial Bus)
Unix, MP3 players for, 701
unmoderated newsgroups, 914
unshielded cable, 1140
unshielded speakers, 695
unshielded twisted-pair (UTP) cable
    defined, 1140
    for network interface cards, 792
    for networks, 795–796, *795*
unused slots, RFI from, 200
Update Device Driver Wizard, *1008*, 1009
update sequence numbering (USN)
    journaling, **462**
Update Settings window, 1035
Update Wizard Uninstall, **1030**
updating
    with AutoUpdate, **1034–1035**
    Update Wizard Uninstall for, **1030**
    virus protection software, 472
    with Windows Update, **1034**

upgradability of proprietary PCs, **851**
upgradable PCs, modularity of, 79
upgrading
  communication options in, **942–944**
  DVDs in notebooks, **885**
  floppy controllers, **938–939**, *939*
  games in, **944**
  hard disk drives in notebooks,
    879–884
  home networks in, **943**
  IDE adapters, **937–938**, *938*
  keyboards and mice, **940**
  LAN adapters, **885–886**, *886*
  memory in notebooks, **875–879**
  microprocessors, **938**
  modems in, **943**
  motherboards, **936–937**
  paths for, **935**
  planning, **936**
  ports, **939–940**, *939*
  power supplies, **335–337**
  slots in, **940–942**, *941*
  video and sound, **940**
UPS monitoring, 1140
UPSs (uninterruptible power supplies)
  defined, 1140
  operation of, **343–345**, *343*
upstream rates in broadband
  communications, **627**
  cable broadband, 635
  DSL, 630
  satellite communications, 637
URLs (Uniform Resource Locators), 1140
USB (Universal Serial Bus), 32, **169–170**,
  170
  benefits of, **170–171**
  for CD-ROMs, **762**
  connectors for, 181, *181*
  defined, 1140
  description of, 355
  for keyboards, **650–651**
  for mice, **656**
  for modems, 616
  in PC selection, **857**
  ports for, *35*
  for printers, **539–541**
  for satellite communications, 639
  for scanners, **604–605**
  troubleshooting, **540–541**
  for ultimate computer, 951, 957, *957*
  for upgrading, **940**
  USB 2, **171**
USB drives, **773**, **780–781**, *780*

USB Viewer tool, 1039
Use Automatic Settings option, 1015
Use High Contrast option, **996**, *996*, 1018
Use Shortcut option, 996
Use SoundSentry option, 995
Usenet newsgroups, **913**
  defined, 1108, **1140–1141**
  finding, **916–918**
  hierarchies in, **915–916**
  netiquette in, 916
  operation of, **914–915**
  for technical information, **918–919**
USER.DAT file
  backing up, 484
  in Registry, 1042
User Datagram Protocol (UDP), 1141
user-definable hard disk drive types, 51,
  397
user-induced power surges, **202–204**
"USER MAINTENANCE" message, 592
user programs, memory for, **127–128**
USN (update sequence numbering)
  journaling, **462**
utilities, online sources for, **902**, **911**
UTP (unshielded twisted-pair) cable
  defined, 1140
  for network interface cards, 792
  for networks, **795–796**, *795*
UUCode tool, 1039

V

V.90 protocol
  characteristics of, 630
  defined, 1141
V-dot modem standards, 624
V pipelines in Pentium, **98–99**
V20 CPUs, 104
V30 CPUs, 104
vaccines, 1141
Variable Content Encoding (VCE), 739
variable frequency monitors (VFM), 676
varistors
  in laser printers, 570, *571*
  in MOVs, **340–342**
VBS prefix, 469
VBScript language, 1141
VCE (Variable Content Encoding), 739
VCRs (videocassette recorders), **720**, 735
VDSL (very high-bit-rate digital subscriber
  line)
  characteristics of, 630
  defined, 1141

vector quantization compression technique,
  741
vendors for purchasing PCs, **865**
ventilation
  in box design, **191–192**
  for laser printers, 537
  for modems, 624
  for power supplies, 335
  for printers, 583
verification data files, 1030
Version Conflict Manager, **1033–1034**
vertical-scan frequencies of monitors,
  672–673
vertical synchronization, 728
vertical white streaks on laser printer pages,
  577–578, *593*
very high-bit-rate digital subscriber line
  (VDSL)
  characteristics of, 630
  defined, 1141
very low-frequency (VLF) emission, 1141
VESA Local Bus (VLB), 148, **151**
  description of, 355
  DMA controllers on, 257
VFM (variable frequency monitors), 676
VGA (Video Graphics Array) boards, 164,
  164
  buffer addresses for, 269, **665–666**
  connectors for, *181*
  defined, 680
  dot pitch for, 675
  horizontal scan frequency for, 674
  memory for, 129, 132
  refresh rates with, 673
  resolution and colors with, **668–670**
VHS recorders for video capture, **717–719**
VHS-C recorders for video capture, 717
VIA Technology, CPUs and
  microprocessors by, **116**
video and video boards, 22, **30–31**,
  163–165, *164*, **660**
  3D, **673–674**
  accessibility options for, **995–996**,
    995–996, **1019**, *1019*
  AGP bus for, **154–155**, *154*
  buffer addresses for, 268
  and buses, 148, **151**, **663–664**
  buying, **661**
  connectors for, *35*, 178, *178*, *181*,
    182
  Control Panel for, **1006–1010**,
    1006–1010
  and CPU, **663**

defined, 1141
diagnosing problems in, 272
diagnostic program for, **229**
error beeps for, 290–291
for games, 944
for generic computers, 850
installing, 14–15, *14–15*, 661–662,
   966–968
memory for, **128–130**, *129*, *164*,
   165, **664–666**, 669–672,
   952–953
monitors for, **674–678**
operation of, **663**, *663*
in PC selection, **855**
in Pentium computers, 932
problems with, **293–294**
quick steps for, **989**
resolution and colors with, **668–672**
speeding up, **667–668**
troubleshooting, **287**, **681**
for ultimate computer, **952–953**
for upgrading, **940**
vertical scan frequencies in, 672–673
video imaging chips on, **667–668**
Windows XP Control Panel for,
   1022–1023
video cable in laser printers, 570
video capture, **710**, **713**, *713*
adjustments in, **736–737**
audio interface for, **729**
broadcast video for, **721**
bugs in, **744–745**
cables for, **729**, *729*
camcorders for, **714–719**, *717*
capture boards for, **730**
components for, 713–714, *714*
composite, S-video, and component
   interface in, **727–728**, *727*
connectors for, 182
CPU, bus, and disk systems in,
   733–734
digital, **735–736**
DVDs for, **720–721**
frame captures in, **737–738**
frame size and rate in, **737**, *737*
installing boards for, **711**
interface for, **722–729**
MMX processors for, 97
off-line compression in, **741–744**
PC cams for, **719**
real-time compression in, **738–741**,
   740

software for, **735–741**, **744–745**
still cameras for, **721**
troubleshooting, **745–746**
VCRs for, **720**
video modes for, **736**
video sources for, **735**
video conferencing, 1142
video coprocessors, **667–668**
Video Graphics Array (VGA) boards, 164,
   164
buffer addresses for, 269, **665–666**
connectors for, *181*
defined, 680
dot pitch for, 675
horizontal scan frequency for, 674
memory for, 129, 132
refresh rates with, 673
resolution and colors with, **668–670**
video imaging chips, **667–668**
video memory aperture, **665–666**
video modes for video capture, **736**
video RAM (VRAM)
characteristics of, **664–665**
defined, 1142
video sources for video capture, **735**
Video Spigot product, 740
videocassette recorders (VCRs), **717–720**,
   735
viewing scanner images, **611–612**
ViewSonic monitors, 676–677
virtual device drivers (VxDs), **223–225**
virtual machine emulators, 462
virtual memory, 140
defined, 1142
status of, 1017
virtual private networking (VPN), **815**
VirtualDr site, 911
Virus Bulletin site, 474
Virus Hoax Listings site, 475
viruses, **464–465**
antivirus software for, **474**
attack methods of, **470–471**
boot sector, 301, **466**
defined, 1142
downloading, 911
example, **471**
file infectors, **465–466**
firewalls for, **843**
hoaxes, **471–472**, **474–475**
on Internet and online services, **923**
lockups from, 234
in macros, **466–467**

protection against, **472–473**
real-time messaging, **468–469**
Signature Verification Tool for, 1031
symptoms of, **475**
troubleshooting, **475–476**
types of, **465–466**
Web applet, **469**
Web sites for information on, **474**
worms, **468**
VirusScan program, 474
VisiCalc program, 930
VLB (VESA Local Bus), 148, **151**
description of, 355
DMA controllers on, 257
VLF (very low-frequency) emission, 1141
VMS format, CD standard for, 756
VMWare, 462
voice capabilities in modems, 954
voice coils, **364–365**, *364*
voice recognition, 88, 97
volatile memory, 100, 171
voltages
on buses, 143, 158
for CPUs, 86, **960**, *960*
for DRAM, 316
for keyboards, **653**
for laser printers, **586**
for phone line, **641**
in power calculations, 336
for ZIF sockets, 942
volume in sound waves, **687**, *687*
Voodoo chip sets, 674
VPN (virtual private networking), **815**
VRAM (Video RAM)
characteristics of, **664–665**
defined, 1142
VXD files, viruses in, 466
VxDs (virtual device drivers), **223–225**

W

W32/Hello worm, 468
W32 prefix, 469
W95 prefix, 469
W97M prefix, 469
wait states, 1142
Waitfor tool, 1039
walking bit errors, **322**
WANs (wide-area networks)
defined, 1143
vs. LANs, 789
warm boots, 1142

WARM (Write And Read Many times)
    optical drives, 427
"WARMING UP" message, 588
warranties for modems, 624
Watchzone group, 149
water and liquids, **208–209**
wattage ratings for power supplies, 336
wavetable synthesis, **692**, 953, 1143
WD manufacturer code, 304
WD-40 lubricant, 535
Web applet viruses, **469**
Web browsers, 905–906, 1143
Web cams
    defined, 1143
    for video capture, **719**
Web pages, 1143
Web servers, 1143
Web sites, 1143
WebTechGeek site, 911
Western Digital
    prefix for, 304
    site for, 434
wet disk technology, 351
wheels for mouse, **654**
Where tool, 1039
white noise, 943
white papers, **901**
white streaks on laser printer pages,
    577–578, 593
white wires in AC supplies, 65–66
wide-area networks (WANs)
    defined, 1143
    vs. LANs, 789
Wide SCSI, 407, 413
Wide Ultra SCSI, 1143
Wide Ultra2 SCSI, 1143
widescreen format, 769
WiFi networks, 817, 886
wildcard characters, 1080, 1127, 1143
WildList Organization International site,
    474
WIN.INI file
    checking, 1033
    for compatibility, 1041
    purpose of, 483
Winamp MP3 player, 700
WinDif tool, 1039
WinDoctor utility, 1040
Window RAM (WRAM), **665**
Windows 3.x operating system
    drivers for, 127
    multitasking in, 134–135

Windows 95/98 operating systems
    for IEEE 1394 support, 384
    Troubleshooters in, **1046**
Windows 98 INF Installer tool, 1039
Windows Boot Editor tool, 1039
Windows directory, 974
Windows Internet Naming Service
    (WINS) servers, 812, 1143
Windows Media Player, 700, 703
Windows programs
    diagnostic, **229–230**
    installing, **1004–1005**, *1004*, 1021
Windows Report Tool, **1029–1030**, *1029*
Windows Resource Kit, **1038–1040**
Windows Setup tab, 1004–1005, *1004*
Windows Update utility, **1034**
Windows utilities
    Automatic Skip Drive Agent, **1031**
    DirectX Diagnostics Tool,
        1027–1029, *1028*
    Dr. Watson, **1031**
    MSI, **1026–1027**, *1027*
    Registry Checker, **1031**
    ScanDisk, 1033
    Signature Verification Tool, **1031**
    System Configuration Utility,
        1032–1033, *1032*
    System File Checker, **1030–1031**,
        1030
    System Monitor, **1026**, *1026*
    Update Wizard Uninstall, **1030**
    Version Conflict Manager,
        1033–1034
    Windows Report Tool, **1029–1030**,
        1029
Windows XP Control Panel
    for accessibility options, **1017–1019**,
        1018–1019
    for date and time, **1021**
    for display, **1022–1023**
    for hardware, **1019–1020**
    for modems, **1023–1025**,
        1023–1024
    for programs, **1020–1021**, *1020*
    for System settings, **1025**
WinDrivers.com site, 911
WINFILE.INI files, backing up, 483
Winmodems, **622**
WINS (Windows Internet Naming
    Service) servers, 812, 1143
Winset tool, 1039
Wintel systems, 82, 1144

wireless communications
    defined, 1144
    LAN cards, **886–887**
    microwave, **639–640**
    networks, **800**, **821–822**
        for homes, **816–817**
        for offices, **815**
wireless devices
    input, **657–658**
    printers, **541–542**
wiring
    checking, **338–339**
    in phone lines, 641
    with serial communications, **641**
WNT prefix, 469
wool, triboelectric value of, 205
Word, viruses from, **466–467**
Word Macro Virus Protection Tool, 467
word size
    for CPU, **90–91**, **102–105**
    in MMX processors, 97
wordlines in flash memory, 774, *774*
workspace
    for disassembly, 49
    for notebook upgrades, **875**
World Wide Web (WWW), **905**
    clicking and linking on, **905–906**
    defined, 1108, 1144
    searching for sites on, **906–908**
    for technical information, **908–912**
WORM (Write Once, Read Many times)
    disks, 427
worms, operation of, **468**
WRAM (Window RAM), **665**
wrinkling of laser printer paper, 585
Write And Read Many times (WARM)
    optical drives, 427
write-back algorithms, 94
write-back caches, 1144
write back instructions, 90
write caching, 376
Write Once, Read Many times (WORM)
    disks, 427
write precompensation, 353
write precompensation cylinders,
    documenting, 51
write-protection for viruses, 473
write-through algorithms, 94
write-through caches, 1144
writing on laser printer drums, **570–572**,
    571

WWW (World Wide Web), **905**
    clicking and linking on, **905–906**
    defined, 1108, 1144
    searching for sites on, **906–908**
    for technical information, **908–912**
Wyse Technology, 149

X

X axis motion in mice, 655
X-ray machines, 197
X2 modem standard, 624
X97M prefix, 469
XA standard, **756–757**
XCOPY command, 488
Xenix operating system, 435
Xeon CPU, 87
    data path for, 92
    heat in, 111, 191
    internal cache memory on, 96
    introduction of, **112**
    pipelines in, 90, 100
    specifications for, 104
    word size for, 91
XGA (Extended Graphics Array)
    characteristics of, **670–672**, 680
    video RAM for, **666**

XGA-2, characteristics of, **670**
Xircom PC Cards, 156
XMMS MP3 players, 701
XON/XOFF flow control, 620, 1145
XT computers
    change-line support in, 529
    clock rate for, 83
    CMOS in, 397
    configuring, 275
    floppy disk drive controllers in, 523
    form factor for, **330**
    interrupts in, **262–263**
    keyboards for, 648
    UARTs in, 615

Y

Y axis motion in mice, 655
Y/C interface, **727–729**
Y signals, **724–726**
Yahoo! directory, **908**
Yahoo! Groups list, 920
Yellow Book CD-ROM standard, **755–756**
yellow wires in phone lines, 641
YUV9 compression technique, 732, 740

Z

ZBR (Zone Bit Recording)
    defined, 352
    in logical block addressing, 363
    sectors in, **360–361**
ZDNet site, 911
Zenith in Watchzone group, 149
Zero-Surge Protector, 342
ZIF (Zero Insertion Force) sockets
    defined, 1145
    operation of, 66, 942, *942*, 964–965, *964–965*
    for PGAs, 46
Zip drives, 486
    defined, 1145
    installing, **980**, *981*
    for old computer data, 933, *933*
    for ultimate computer, **955**
Zip files, 1145
Zone Bit Recording (ZBR)
    defined, 352, 1145
    in logical block addressing, 363
    sectors in, **360–361**

TELL US WHAT YOU THINK!

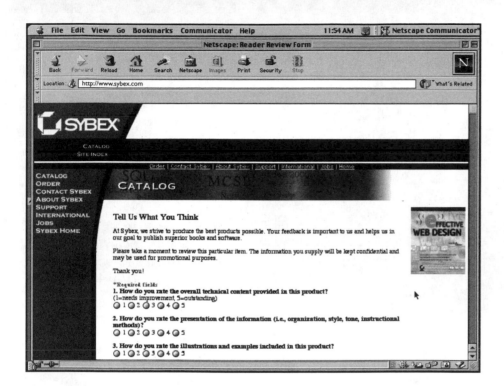

Your feedback is critical to our efforts to provide you with the best books and software on the market. Tell us what you think about the products you've purchased. It's simple:

1. Visit the Sybex website
2. Go to the product page
3. Click on **Submit a Review**
4. Fill out the questionnaire and comments
5. Click **Submit**

With your feedback, we can continue to publish the highest quality computer books and software products that today's busy IT professionals deserve.

www.sybex.com

SYBEX Inc. • 1151 Marina Village Parkway, Alameda, CA 94501 • 510-523-8233

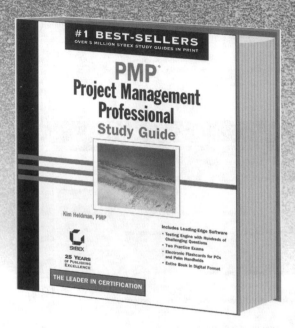

The Mark Minasi
Windows® Administrator Series

First Three Titles of an Expanding Series

By Jeremy Moskowitz
0-7821-2881-5 • $49.99

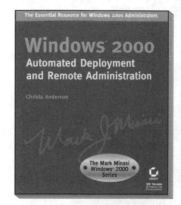

By Christa Anderson
0-7821-2885-8 • $49.99

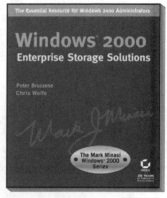

By J. Peter Bruzzese
and Chris Wolfe
0-7821-2883-1 • $49.99

- **Mark Minasi** serves as the series editor, chooses topics and authors, and reviews each book

- Concise, focused material based upon real-world implementation of Windows 2000 Server

- Designed to provide Windows 2000 Systems Administrators with specific in-depth technical solutions

Mark Minasi, MCSE, is recognized as one of the world's best teachers of NT/2000. He teaches NT/2000 classes in 15 countries. His best-selling *Mastering Windows 2000 Server* books have more than 500,000 copies in print.

25 YEARS
OF PUBLISHING
EXCELLENCE

SYBEX® WWW.SYBEX.COM

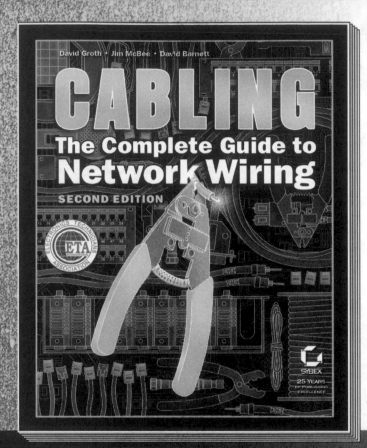

CABLING:
The Complete Guide to Network Wiring

Cabling: The Complete Guide to Network Wiring
David Groth, Jim McBee, and David Barne.
ISBN 0-7821-2958-7
808pp • $49.99

The most comprehensive guide to network cabling available!

- Coverage spans cabling system design and installation, electrical and security issues, cabling components, and documenting and troubleshooting your system.

- Provides all the information you need to know to work safely and effectively with cables in the workplace.

- Includes a full-color section for quick identification of connectors and cables, as well as vendor information and recommendations.

SYBEX®

www.sybex.com

From self-study guides to advanced computer-based training, simulated testing programs to last-minute review guides, Sybex has the most complete CompTIA training solution on the market.

Sybex Covers
CompTIA
CERTIFICATION PROGRAMS

Study Guides

Designed for optimal learning, Sybex Study Guides provide you with comprehensive coverage of all exam objectives. Hands-on exercises and review questions help reinforce your knowledge.

STUDY
- In-depth coverage of exam objectives
- Hands-on exercises
- CD includes: test engine, flashcards for PCs and Palm devices, PDF version of entire book

Virtual Trainers™
software

Based on the content of the Study Guides, Sybex Virtual Trainers offer you advanced computer-based training, complete with animations and customization features.

- Customizable study planning tools
- Narrated instructional animations
- Preliminary assessment tests
- Results reporting

Virtual Test Centers™
software

Powered by an advanced testing engine, Sybex's new line of Virtual Test Centers give you the opportunity to test your knowledge before sitting for the real exam.

PRACTICE
- Hundreds of challenging questions
- Computer adaptive testing
- Support for drag-and-drop and hot-spot formats
- Detailed explanations and cross-references

Exam Notes™

Organized according to the official exam objectives, Sybex Exam Notes help reinforce your knowledge of key exam topics and identify potential weak areas requiring further study.

REVIEW
- Excellent quick review before the exam
- Concise summaries of key exam topics
- Tips and insights from experienced instructors
- Definitions of key terms and concepts

*Look to Sybex for exam prep materials on major CompTIA certifications, including A+®, Network+™, I-Net+™, Server+™, and Linux+™. For more information about CompTIA and Sybex products, visit **www.sybex.com**.*

CompTIA.
One Industry. One Voice.

SYBEX®
www.sybex.com

Sybex—The Leader in Certification

→ CD #1
Mark Minasi PC Upgrading Videos

The CD in the front of the book contains approximately 60 minutes of video created exclusively by Sybex and Mark Minasi. These videos explore the essential upgrades that users generally make to their PCs and follow the format used in Mark Minasi's $800 Upgrading and Maintenance seminars.

No other PC book contains this much, or such up-to-date videos.

The contents include:

→ **The Central Processing Unit** Examine the new Pentium cartridges and learn how to install them.

→ **Motherboards** Take a tour of all of the components on today's typical motherboard.

→ **Power Supply** Learn how to replace a power supply in a matter of minutes.

→ **Computer Memory** Learn about types of memory and memory boards, and see how to install and uninstall SDRAM cards.

→ **Installing a DVD drive** Watch Mark install a DVD decoder card and the DVD drive itself; learn how to make all the right connections—without making any mistakes.

→ **Installing a Hard Drive** See how to install a drive, set the master/slave switches, connect all of the data and power cables—whether this is your first hard drive in your PC or your second or third.

→ **Circuit Boards** Learn tips and tricks about installing most circuit boards in your PC—from video cards to modems.

→ **Installing Sound Cards** Watch Mark install a sound card and connect it to a CD player.

The CD also provides Apple QuickTime, which you can use to view the files. QuickTime and the QuickTime logo are trademarks used under license. QuickTime is registered in the U.S. and other countries.

NOTE *To view the files you'll need a Pentium 120 and a 4x CD-ROM drive although a Pentium 166 or better is recommended.*